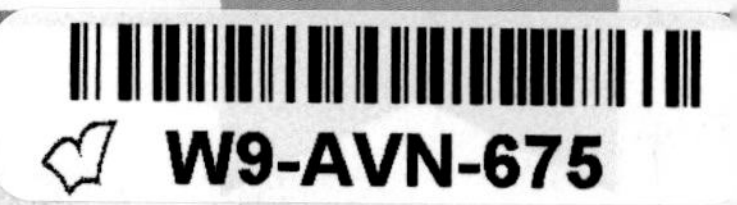

THE ESSENTIAL WORLD HISTORY

WILLIAM J. DUIKER
The Pennsylvania State University

JACKSON J. SPIELVOGEL
The Pennsylvania State University

Australia • Brazil • Japan • Korea • Mexico • Singapore • Spain • United Kingdom • United States

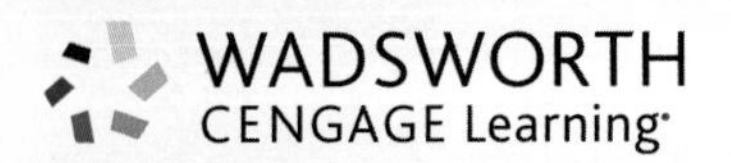

The Essential World History, Seventh Edition
William J. Duiker, Jackson J. Spielvogel

Senior Publisher: Suzanne Jeans

Acquiring Sponsoring Editor: Brooke Barbier

Senior Development Editor: Margaret McAndrew Beasley

Assistant Editor: Jamie Bushell

Editorial Assistant: Katie Coaster

Senior Media Editor: Lisa Ciccolo

Market Development Manager: Melissa Larmon

Senior Content Project Manager: Jane Lee

Senior Art Director: Cate Rickard Barr

Production Technology Analyst: Jeff Joubert

Manufacturing Planner: Sandra Milewski

Rights Acquisition Specialist, Image: Jennifer Meyer Dare

Rights Acquisition Specialist, Text: Jennifer Meyer Dare

Production Service: Orr Book Services

Text Designer: Shawn Girsberger

Cover Designer: Emily Chionchio, Roycroft Design

Cover Image: *Musicians with Their Instruments*, miniature, Persian, 19th century, detail. Credit: The Art Archive/Kharbine-Tapabor/Stephane Marant.

Compositor: Cenveo

© 2014, 2011, 2007 Wadsworth, Cengage Learning

ALL RIGHTS RESERVED. No part of this work covered by the copyright herein may be reproduced, transmitted, stored, or used in any form or by any means graphic, electronic, or mechanical, including but not limited to photocopying, recording, scanning, digitizing, taping, Web distribution, information networks, or information storage and retrieval systems, except as permitted under Section 107 or 108 of the 1976 United States Copyright Act, without the prior written permission of the publisher.

For product information and technology assistance, contact us at
Cengage Learning Customer & Sales Support, 1-800-354-9706

For permission to use material from this text or product,
submit all requests online at **www.cengage.com/permissions**.
Further permissions questions can be emailed to
permissionrequest@cengage.com.

Library of Congress Control Number: 2012921058

ISBN-13: 978-1-133-60658-1
ISBN-10: 1-133-60658-X

Wadsworth
20 Channel Center Street
Boston, MA 02210
USA

Cengage Learning is a leading provider of customized learning solutions with office locations around the globe, including Singapore, the United Kingdom, Australia, Mexico, Brazil and Japan. Locate your local office at **international.cengage.com/region**.

Cengage Learning products are represented in Canada by Nelson Education, Ltd.

For your course and learning solutions, visit **www.cengage.com**. Purchase any of our products at your local college store or at our preferred online store **www.cengagebrain.com**.
Instructors: Please visit **login.cengage.com** and log in to access instructor-specific resources.

Printed in Canada
2 3 4 5 16 15 14 13

CTIC OCEAN
NORWAY
FINLAND
SWEDEN
ESTONIA
LATVIA
LITHUANIA
DEN.
BELARUS
NETH.
POLAND
GERMANY
CZ.
UKRAINE
SLK.
LUX.
AUS.
HUNG.
MOLDOVA
ANCE
SLN.
CR.
ROMANIA
WITZ.
B. H.
SE.
ITALY
K.
BULGARIA
MO.
MAC.
ALBANIA
GREECE
GEORGIA
TURKEY
ARMENIA
CYPRUS
AZERBAIJAN
MALTA
TUNISIA
SYRIA
LEBANON
ISRAEL
IRAQ
IRAN
JORDAN
KUWAIT
BAHRAIN
QATAR
GERIA
LIBYA
EGYPT
SAUDI ARABIA
UNITED ARAB EMIRATES
OMAN
NIGER
CHAD
ERITREA
YEMEN
SUDAN
DJIBOUTI
A
BENIN
NIGERIA
ETHIOPIA
CENTRAL AFRICAN REP.
TOGO
CAMEROON
SOMALIA
GUINEA
UGANDA
KENYA
RWANDA
NCIPE
GABON
DEM. REP. OF CONGO
EP. OF CONGO
BURUNDI
TANZANIA
SEYCHELLES
COMOROS
ANGOLA
ZAMBIA
MALAWI
ZIMBABWE
MADAGASCAR
NAMIBIA
MAURITIUS
BOTSWANA
MOZAMBIQUE
SWAZILAND
SOUTH AFRICA
LESOTHO
RUSSIA
KAZAKHSTAN
MONGOLIA
UZBEKISTAN
KYRGYZSTAN
TURKMENISTAN
TAJIKISTAN
N. KOREA
S. KOREA
JAPAN
PACIFIC OCEAN
AFGHANISTAN
PEOPLE'S REPUBLIC OF CHINA
PAKISTAN
BHUTAN
NEPAL
BANGLADESH
TAIWAN
INDIA
MYANMAR (BURMA)
LAOS
Mariana Islands (U.S.)
Wake I. (U.S.)
VIETNAM
THAILAND
MARSHALL ISLANDS
Guam (U.S.)
PHILIPPINES
CAMBODIA (KAMPUCHEA)
SRI LANKA
BRUNEI DARUSSALAM
PALAU
FEDERATED STATES OF MICRONESIA
MALDIVES
MALAYSIA
KIRIBATI
SINGAPORE
NAURU
INDIAN OCEAN
INDONESIA
PAPUA NEW GUINEA
SOLOMON IS.
TUVALU
TIMOR LESTE
VANUATU
FIJI
New Caledonia (France)
AUSTRALIA
NEW ZEALAND
ABBREVIATIONS
AUS. AUSTRIA
BEL. BELGIUM
B. H. BOSNIA AND HERZEGOVINA
CR. CROATIA
CZ. CZECH REPUBLIC
DEN. DENMARK
HUNG. HUNGARY
K. KOSOVO
LUX. LUXEMBOURG
MAC. MACEDONIA
MO. MONTENEGRO
NETH. NETHERLANDS
SE. SERBIA
SLK. SLOVAKIA
SLN. SLOVENIA
SWITZ. SWITZERLAND
0°
20°E
40°E
60°E
80°E
100°E
120°E
140°E
160°E

ABOUT THE AUTHORS

WILLIAM J. DUIKER is liberal arts professor emeritus of East Asian studies at The Pennsylvania State University. A former U.S. diplomat with service in Taiwan, South Vietnam, and Washington, D.C., he received his doctorate in Far Eastern history from Georgetown University in 1968, where his dissertation dealt with the Chinese educator and reformer Cai Yuanpei. At Penn State, he has written widely on the history of Vietnam and modern China, including the widely acclaimed *The Communist Road to Power in Vietnam* (revised edition, Westview Press, 1996), which was selected for a Choice Outstanding Academic Book Award in 1982–1983 and 1996–1997. Other recent books are *China and Vietnam: The Roots of Conflict* (Berkeley, 1987); *Sacred War: Nationalism and Revolution in a Divided Vietnam* (McGraw-Hill, 1995); and *Ho Chi Minh: A Life* (Hyperion, 2000), which was nominated for a Pulitzer Prize in 2001. While his research specialization is in the field of nationalism and Asian revolutions, his intellectual interests are considerably more diverse. He has traveled widely and has taught courses on the history of communism and non-Western civilizations at Penn State, where he was awarded a Faculty Scholar Medal for Outstanding Achievement in the spring of 1996.

TO YVONNE,
FOR ADDING SPARKLE TO THIS BOOK, AND TO MY LIFE
W.J.D.

JACKSON J. SPIELVOGEL is associate professor emeritus of history at The Pennsylvania State University. He received his Ph.D. from The Ohio State University, where he specialized in Reformation history under Harold J. Grimm. His articles and reviews have appeared in such journals as *Moreana*, *Journal of General Education*, *Catholic Historical Review*, *Archiv für Reformationsgeschichte*, and *American Historical Review*. He has also contributed chapters or articles to *The Social History of the Reformation*, *The Holy Roman Empire: A Dictionary Handbook*, *Simon Wiesenthal Center Annual of Holocaust Studies*, and *Utopian Studies*. His work has been supported by fellowships from the Fulbright Foundation and the Foundation for Reformation Research. At Penn State, he helped inaugurate the Western civilization courses as well as a popular course on Nazi Germany. His book *Hitler and Nazi Germany* was published in 1987 (sixth edition, 2010). He is the author of *Western Civilization* published in 1991 (eighth edition, 2012). Professor Spielvogel has won five major university-wide teaching awards. During the year 1988–1989, he held the Penn State Teaching Fellowship, the university's most prestigious teaching award. In 1996, he won the Dean Arthur Ray Warnock Award for Outstanding Faculty Member and in 2000 received the Schreyer Honors College Excellence in Teaching Award.

TO DIANE,
WHOSE LOVE AND SUPPORT MADE IT ALL POSSIBLE
J.J.S.

BRIEF CONTENTS

DETAILED CONTENTS

PART II New Patterns of Civilization (500–1500 C.E.) 142

6 THE AMERICAS 144

7 FERMENT IN THE MIDDLE EAST: THE RISE OF ISLAM 168

8 EARLY CIVILIZATIONS IN AFRICA 196

DOCUMENTS

CHAPTER 1

CHAPTER 2

CHAPTER 3

CHAPTER 4

CHAPTER 5

CHAPTER 6

CHAPTER 7

CHAPTER 8

CHAPTER 9

CHAPTER 10

CHAPTER 11

CHAPTER 12

CHAPTER 13

CHAPTER 14

CHAPTER 15

CHAPTER 16

CHAPTER 17

CHAPTER 18

CHAPTER 19

CHAPTER 20

CHAPTER 21

CHAPTER 22

(Continued on page 836)

MAPS

FEATURES

OPPOSING VIEWPOINTS

COMPARATIVE ESSAY

FILM & HISTORY

PREFACE

FOR SEVERAL MILLION YEARS after primates first appeared on the surface of the earth, human beings lived in small communities, seeking to survive by hunting, fishing, and foraging in a frequently hostile environment. Then suddenly, in the space of a few thousand years, there was an abrupt change of direction as human beings in a few widely scattered areas of the globe began to master the art of cultivating food crops. As food production increased, the population in those areas rose correspondingly, and people began to congregate in larger communities. Governments were formed to provide protection and other needed services to the local population. Cities appeared and became the focal point of cultural and religious development. Historians refer to this process as the beginnings of civilization.

For generations, historians in Europe and the United States pointed to the rise of such civilizations as marking the origins of the modern world. Courses on Western civilization conventionally began with a chapter or two on the emergence of advanced societies in Egypt and Mesopotamia and then proceeded to ancient Greece and the Roman Empire. From Greece and Rome, the road led directly to the rise of modern civilization in the West.

There is nothing inherently wrong with this approach. Important aspects of our world today can indeed be traced back to these early civilizations, and all human beings the world over owe a considerable debt to their achievements. But all too often this interpretation has been used to imply that the course of civilization has been linear in nature, leading directly from the emergence of agricultural societies in ancient Mesopotamia to the rise of advanced industrial societies in Europe and North America. Until recently, most courses on world history taught in the United States routinely focused almost exclusively on the rise of the West, with only a passing glance at other parts of the world, such as Africa, India, and East Asia. The contributions made by those societies to the culture and technology of our own time were often passed over in silence.

Two major reasons have been advanced to justify this approach. Some have argued that it is more important that young minds understand the roots of their own heritage than that of peoples elsewhere in the world. In many cases, however, the motivation for this Eurocentric approach has been the belief that since the time of Socrates and Aristotle Western civilization has been the sole driving force in the evolution of human society.

Such an interpretation, however, represents a serious distortion of the process. During most of the course of human history, the most advanced civilizations have been not in the West, but in East Asia or the Middle East. A relatively brief period of European dominance culminated with the era of imperialism in the late nineteenth century, when the political, military, and economic power of the advanced nations of the West spanned the globe. During recent generations, however, that dominance has gradually eroded, partly as a result of changes taking place within Western societies and partly because new centers of development are emerging elsewhere on the globe—notably in Asia, with the growing economic strength of China and India and many of their neighbors.

World history, then, has been a complex process in which many branches of the human community have taken an active part, and the dominance of any one area of the world has been a temporary rather than a permanent phenomenon. It will be our purpose in this book to present a balanced picture of this story, with all respect for the richness and diversity of the tapestry of the human experience. Due attention must be paid to the rise of the West, of course, since that has been the most dominant aspect of world history in recent centuries. But the contributions made by other peoples must be given adequate consideration as well, not only in the period prior to 1500 when the major centers of civilization were located in Asia, but also in our own day, when a multipolar picture of development is clearly beginning to emerge.

Anyone who wishes to teach or write about world history must decide whether to present the topic as an integrated whole or as a collection of different cultures. The world that we live in today, of course, is in many respects an interdependent one in terms of economics as well as culture and communications, a reality that is often expressed by the phrase "global village." The convergence of peoples across the surface of the earth into an integrated world system began in early times and intensified after the rise of capitalism in the early modern era. In growing recognition of this trend, historians trained in global history, as well as instructors in the growing number of world history courses, have now begun to speak and write of a "global approach" that turns attention away from the study of individual civilizations and focuses instead on the "big picture" or, as the world historian Fernand Braudel termed it, interpreting world history as a river with no banks.

On the whole, this development is to be welcomed as a means of bringing the common elements of the evolution of human society to our attention. But this approach also involves two problems. For the vast majority of their time on earth, human beings have lived in partial or virtually total isolation from each other. Differences in climate, location, and geographic features have created human societies very different from each other in culture and historical experience. Only in relatively recent times (the commonly accepted date has long been the beginning of the age of European exploration at the end of the fifteenth century, but some would now push it back to the era of the Mongol Empire or even further) have cultural interchanges begun to create a common "world system," in which events taking place in one part of the world are rapidly transmitted throughout the globe, often with momentous consequences. In recent generations, of course, the process of global interdependence has been proceeding even more rapidly. Nevertheless, even now the process is by no means complete, as ethnic and regional differences continue to exist and to shape the course of world history. The tenacity of these differences and sensitivities is reflected not only in the rise of internecine conflicts in such divergent areas as Africa, India, and Eastern Europe, but also in the emergence in recent years of such regional organizations as the African Union, the Association for the Southeast Asian Nations, and the European Union.

The second problem is a practical one. College students today are all too often not well informed about the distinctive character of civilizations such as China and India and, without sufficient exposure to the historical evolution of such societies, will assume all too readily that the peoples in these countries have had historical experiences similar to ours and will respond to various stimuli in a similar fashion to those living in western Europe or the United States. If it is a mistake to ignore those forces that link us together, it is equally a mistake to underestimate those factors that continue to divide us and to differentiate us into a world of diverse peoples.

Our response to this challenge has been to adopt a global approach to world history while at the same time attempting to do justice to the distinctive character and development of individual civilizations and regions of the world. The presentation of individual cultures is especially important in Parts I and II, which cover a time when it is generally agreed that the process of global integration was not yet far advanced. Later chapters begin to adopt a more comparative and thematic approach, in deference to the greater number of connections that have been established among the world's peoples since the fifteenth and sixteenth centuries. Part V consists of a series of chapters that center on individual regions of the world while at the same time focusing on common problems related to the Cold War and the rise of global problems such as overproduction and environmental pollution.

We have sought balance in another way as well. Many textbooks tend to simplify the content of history courses by emphasizing an intellectual or political perspective or, most recently, a social perspective, often at the expense of sufficient details in a chronological framework. This approach is confusing to students whose high school social studies programs have often neglected a systematic study of world history. We have attempted to write a well-balanced work in which political, economic, social, religious, intellectual, cultural, and military history have been integrated into a chronologically ordered synthesis.

Features of the Text

To enliven the past and let readers see for themselves the materials that historians use to create their pictures of the past, we have included several **primary sources** (boxed documents) in each chapter that are keyed to the discussion in the text. The documents include examples of the religious, artistic, intellectual, social, economic, and political aspects of life in different societies and reveal in a vivid fashion what civilization meant to the individual men and women who shaped it by their actions. Questions at the end of each source aid students in analyzing the documents.

Each chapter has a **lengthy introduction** to help maintain the continuity of the narrative and to provide a synthesis of important themes. Anecdotes in the chapter introductions dramatically convey the major theme or themes of each chapter. A **timeline** at the end of each chapter enables students to see the major developments of an era at a glance and within cross-cultural categories, while the more **detailed chronologies** reinforce the events discussed in the text. An **annotated bibliography** at the end of each chapter reviews the most recent literature on each period and also gives references to some of the older, "classic" works in each field.

Maps and extensive illustrations serve to deepen the reader's understanding of the text. **Map captions** are designed to enrich students' awareness of the importance of geography to history, and numerous **spot maps** enable students to see at a glance the region or subject being discussed in the text. Map captions also include a question to guide students' reading of the map. To facilitate understanding of cultural movements, illustrations of artistic works discussed in the text are placed near the discussions. **Chapter outlines and focus questions, including critical thinking questions**, at the beginning of each chapter give students a useful overview and guide them to the main subjects of each chapter. The focus questions are then repeated at the beginning of each major section in the chapter to reinforce the main themes. A **glossary of important terms** (boldfaced in the text when they are introduced and defined) is provided at the back of the book to maximize reader comprehension. A **guide to pronunciation** is now provided in parentheses in the text, following the first mention of a complex name or term.

Comparative essays, keyed to the seven major themes of world history (see p. xxxx), enable us to more concretely draw comparisons and contrasts across geographic, cultural, and chronological lines. Some new essays have been added to the seventh edition. **Comparative illustrations**, also keyed to the seven major themes of world history, continue to be a feature in each chapter. Both the comparative essays and the comparative illustrations conclude with focus questions to help students develop their analytical skills. We hope that the comparative essays and the comparative illustrations will assist instructors who wish to encourage their students to adopt a comparative approach to their understanding of the human experience.

The **Film & History** feature, now appearing in many chapters, presents a brief analysis of the plot as well as the historical significance, value, and accuracy of popular films. New features have been added on films such as *Gladiator*, *Marie Antoinette*, and *Letters from Iwo Jima*.

The **Opposing Viewpoints** feature presents a comparison of two or three primary sources to facilitate student analysis of historical documents. This feature has been expanded and now appears in almost every chapter. Focus questions are included to help students evaluate the documents.

New to This Edition

After reexamining the entire book and analyzing the comments and reviews of many colleagues who have found the book to be a useful instrument for introducing their students to world history, we have also made a number of other changes for the seventh edition.

We have continued to strengthen the global framework of the book, but not at the expense of reducing the attention assigned to individual regions of the world. New material, including new comparative sections, has been added to most chapters to help students be aware of similar developments globally.

The enthusiastic response to the primary sources (boxed documents) led us to evaluate the content of each document carefully and add new documents throughout the text, including new comparative documents in the Opposing Viewpoints features.

The **Suggested Reading** sections at the end of each chapter have been thoroughly updated and are organized under subheadings to make them more useful. New illustrations were added to every chapter. **Chapter Notes** appear at the end of the book.

A new format has been added to the end of each chapter. The **Chapter Summary** is illustrated with thumbnail images of chapter illustrations and combined with a **Chapter Timeline**. A **Chapter Review** has been added to assist students in studying the chapter. This review includes **Upon Reflection** essay questions and a list of **Key Terms** from the chapter.

Also new to the seventh edition are **historiographical subsections**, which examine how and why historians differ in their interpretation of specific topics. To keep up with the ever-growing body of historical scholarship, new or revised material has been added throughout the book on many topics (see the specific notes below).

Chapter-by-Chapter Content Revisions

Chapter 1 New and revised material on early humans; new historiographical subsection: "The Spread of Humans: Out of Africa or Multiregional?"; new material on gender roles in the Neolithic Age; new material on the role of Kushite monarchs in Egypt; new material on the early history of Israel; new historiographical subsection: "Was There a United Kingdom of Israel?"; new material on Zoroastrianism.

Chapter 2 New Opposing Viewpoints feature: "The Search for Truth"; new historiographical subsection: "Who Were the Aryans?"; revised sections on Vedic religion and class and caste in India.

Chapter 3 Revised opening vignette and Map 3.1; new Opposing Viewpoints feature: "A Debate over Good and Evil"; new material on the following: Shang religion, Qin politics, and cities in ancient China; new historiographical subsections: "The Shang Dynasty: China's Mother Culture?" and "Are All Hydraulic Societies Despotic?"

Chapter 4 New material on Greek religion, with special emphasis on the Olympic games; new Opposing Viewpoints feature: "Women in Athens and Sparta"; new material on the Greek impact on Roman civilization; new historiographical subsection: "The Legacy: Was Alexander Great?"

Chapter 5 New Film & History feature on *Gladiator*; new historiographical subsection: "What Caused the Fall of the Western Roman Empire?"; new material on Han political, economic, and social policies; new section on "A Comparison of Rome and China."

Chapter 6 New material on the following: the Olmecs, including their use of chocolate, and Wari culture in South America; revised chapter summary to include more comparisons with other ancient cultures; new historiographical subsections: "The Olmecs: Mother Culture or First Among Equals?" and "The Mystery of Mayan Decline."

Chapter 7 New document: "Winning Hearts and Minds in Murcia"; new paragraph on the meaning of *jihad*; expanded discussion of Arab scholarship; revised opening vignette; new historiographical subsection: "Moorish Spain: An Era of 'Cultural Tolerance'?"; new comparative illustration on medieval mapmaking.

Chapter 8 New document: "The Nyanga Meet the Pygmies of Gabon"; new historiographical subsection: "Africa: A Continent Without History?"; new "Critical Thinking" question; revised content on Axum, Kush, Bantu migrations, and Swahili culture; new information on the origins of agriculture in Africa.

Chapter 9 Revised chapter title and Map 9.1; new historiographical subsection: "When Did the Indians Become Hindus?"; new material on early migrations to Southeast Asia and rice culture.

Chapter 10 Shortened opening section; new material on the following: civil service examinations, Tang land reforms, and the decline of noble families; expanded discussions of women's roles and the role of the emperor and popular religion; new Opposing Viewpoints feature: "A Meeting of Two Worlds" (exchange of letters between Pope Innocent IV and the Mongols); two new historiographical subsections: "The Mongols: A Reputation Undeserved?" and "Why Were Zhenghe's Voyages Abandoned?"; new document: "Beautiful Women: The Scapegoats of Legend"; new comparative illustration on "The Two Worlds of Tang China."

Chapter 11 New historiographical subsection: "Was Japan a Feudal Society?"; new document: "How the Earth Was Formed."

Chapter 12 New Opposing Viewpoints feature: "Lords and Vassals in Europe and Japan"; new material on England and France; new section on the Iberian kingdoms; new historiographical subsection: "What Were the Effects of the Crusades?"

Chapter 13 Clarified use of terms Later Roman Empire, Eastern Roman Empire, and Byzantine Empire; new material on the Byzantine capital of Constantinople as a "God-guarded city"; new Opposing Viewpoints feature: "Causes of the Black Death: Contemporary Views"; new document: "Christian Crusaders Capture Constantinople"; new historiographical subsection: "Was There a Renaissance for Women?"

Chapter 14 Added material on Latin America from Chapter 18; new historiographical subsection: "Christopher Columbus: Hero or Villain?"; revised comparative essay on "The Columbian Exchange"; new material on Africa.

Chapter 15 New material on religious piety on the eve of the Reformation; new material on the impact of the Reformation on common people as seen in the Peasants' War; new material on the Catholic Reformation; new historiographical subsection: "Catholic Reformation or Counter-Reformation?"; new material in comparative illustration of Louis XIV and Kangzi.

Chapter 16 Reorganized section on the Mughals; new document: "Designing the Perfect Society" (on *Jalali's Ethics*); new historiographical subsection: "The Mughal Dynasty: A 'Gunpowder Empire'?"

Chapter 17 New material on seizure of Taiwan; new document: "Be My Brother, or I'll Bash Your Head In!" (on Japanese-Korean war); new historiographical subsection: "The Qing Economy: Ready for Takeoff?"; revised section on Korea.

Chapter 18 Moved discussion of Latin American society to Chapter 14; new material on French colonization; new document: "British Victory in India"; new Film & History feature on *Marie Antoinette*; new material on the French monarchy on the eve of the Revolution.

Chapter 19 New material on the Industrial Revolution in Great Britain and the United States; new material on working laws; new material on the emergence of a world economy; new historiographical subsection: "Did Industrialization Bring an Improved Standard of Living?"

Chapter 20 New material on Zapata; new material on positive aspects of American society; new material on education and the Catholic Church.

Chapter 21 New comparative essay on "Imperialisms Old and New"; new historiographical subsection: "Imperialism: The Balance Sheet"; revised material on Africa and traditional resistance.

Chapter 22 Revised sections on the Chinese economy, Japan's "closed country" policy, and Meiji reforms; revised comparative essay on "Imperialism and the Global Environment"; new Opposing Viewpoints feature: "The Wonders of Western Civilization: Two Views"; new historiographical subsection: "What Explains Japanese Uniqueness?"

Chapter 23 New historiographical subsection: "The Assassination of Francis Ferdinand: A Blank Check?"; new material on the global nature of World War I; new material on the impact of Woodrow Wilson's rhetoric on self-determination for the colonial world; new Opposing Viewpoints feature: "Three Voices of Peacemaking."

Chapter 24 Expanded section on Palestine between the wars; new section on the rise of nationalism in Egypt; new Opposing Viewpoints feature: "Islam in the Modern World: Two Views" (Atatürk and Iqbal); added comparison of Latin America and Asian countries; new historiographical subsection: "Taisho Democracy: An Aberration?"

Chapter 25 New material on the war in Asia; new material and new illustration on the Battle of Stalingrad; new material on the Holocaust; new section entitled "World War II and the European Colonies: Decolonization"; new Film & History feature, *Letters from Iwo Jima*.

Chapter 26 Reorganized material on Dien Bien Phu and Taiwan; revised and reduced material on denazification.

Chapter 27 New historiographical subsection: "Why Did the Soviet Union Collapse?"; new document: "The Rights and Duties of Soviet Citizens"; new Opposing Viewpoints feature: "Students Appeal for Democracy" (on Tiananmen Square demonstrations); revised and updated section on China.

Chapter 28 New material on France, Germany, Great Britain, Eastern Europe, Russia, and the United States; new material on the European Union and the euro; new material on the West and Islam; new discussion of green urban planning, including new comparative illustration on "Green Urbanism"; new material on popular culture; new Opposing Viewpoints feature: "Islam and the West: Secularism in France."

Chapter 29 New comparative illustration on "Wealth and Poverty in the Middle East"; new Film & History feature on *Persepolis*; new historiographical subsection: "The Destiny of Africa: Unity or Diversity?"; updated material on the Middle East.

Chapter 30 Expanded section on Pakistan; new material on the following: Hindu-Muslim relations, caste and sexual relations, and Indian literature; new historiographical subsection: "What Is the Future of India?"; updated material on Indonesia; revised sections on Japanese politics and society.

Epilogue New material on global communications and global financial markets.

Because courses in world history at American and Canadian colleges and universities follow different chronological divisions, a one-volume comprehensive edition, a two-volume edition of this text, and a volume covering events to 1500 are being made available to fit the needs of instructors. Teaching and learning ancillaries include the following.

Instructor Resources

PowerLecture DVD with ExamView® and JoinIn®
ISBN-10: 113394406X | ISBN-13: 9781133944065
This dual platform, all-in-one multimedia resource includes the Instructor's Resource Manual; Test Bank including essay questions, key term identifications, multiple choice, and true/false questions; Microsoft® PowerPoint® slides of both lecture outlines and images and maps from the text that can be used as offered, or customized by importing personal lecture slides or other material; and JoinIn® PowerPoint® slides with clicker content. Also included is ExamView, an easy-to-use assessment and tutorial system that allows instructors to create, deliver, and customize tests in minutes. Instructors can build tests with as many as 250 questions using up to twelve question types, and using ExamView's complete word-processing capabilities, they can enter an unlimited number of new questions or edit existing ones.

eInstructor's Resource Manual Prepared by Dave Pretty of Winthrop University. This manual has many features, including instructional objectives, chapter outlines, thought/discussion questions for the primary sources, possible class lecture topics, student research and project topics, relevant worldwide websites/resources, and relevant video collections. Available on the instructor's companion website.

WebTutor™ on Blackboard
ISBN-10: 1285083245 | ISBN-13: 9781285083247 PAC
ISBN-10: 1285083199 | ISBN-13: 9781285083193 IAC
With WebTutor's text-specific, preformatted content and total flexibility, instructors can easily create and manage their own custom course website. WebTutor's course management tool gives instructors the ability to provide virtual office hours, post syllabi, set up threaded discussions, track student progress with the quizzing material, and much more. For students, WebTutor offers real-time access to a full array of study tools, including animations and videos that bring the book's topics to life, plus chapter outlines, summaries, learning objectives, glossary flashcards (with audio), practice quizzes, and weblinks.

WebTutor™ on WebCT®
ISBN-10: 1285083237 | ISBN-13: 9781285083230 PAC
ISBN-10: 1285083202 | ISBN-13: 9781285083209 IAC
With WebTutor's text-specific, preformatted content and total flexibility, instructors can easily create and manage their own custom course website. WebTutor's course management tool gives instructors the ability to provide virtual office hours, post syllabi, set up threaded discussions, track student progress with the quizzing material, and much more. For students, WebTutor offers real-time access to a full array of study tools, including animations and videos that bring the book's topics to life, plus chapter outlines, summaries, learning objectives, glossary flashcards (with audio), practice quizzes, and web links.

CourseMate
ISBN-10: 1285083482 | ISBN-13: 9781285083483 PAC
ISBN-10: 128508344X | ISBN-13: 9781285083445 IAC
ISBN-10:1285083318 | ISBN-13: 9781285083315 SSO
Cengage Learning's History CourseMate brings course concepts to life with interactive learning, study, and exam preparation tools that support the printed textbook. History CourseMate includes an integrated eBook; interactive teaching and learning tools including quizzes, flashcards, videos, and more; and EngagementTracker, a first-of-its-kind tool that monitors student engagement in the course. Learn more at www.cengagebrain.com.

Aplia
ISBN-10: 1285083032 | ISBN-13: 9781285083032 1-term PAC
ISBN-10: 1285083075 | ISBN-13: 9781285083070 1-term IAC
ISBN-10: 1285083024 | ISBN-13: 9781285083025 2-term PAC
ISBN-10: 1285083067 | ISBN-13: 9781285083063 2-term IAC
Aplia™ is an online interactive learning solution that improves comprehension and outcomes by increasing student effort and engagement. Founded by a professor to enhance his own courses, Aplia provides automatically graded assignments with detailed, immediate explanations on every question. The interactive assignments have been developed to address the major concepts covered in *The Essential World History*, seventh edition, and are designed to promote critical thinking and engage students more fully in their learning. Question types include questions built around animated maps, primary sources such as newspaper extracts, and imagined scenarios, such as engaging in a conversation with Benjamin Franklin or finding a diary and having to fill in some blank words; more in-depth primary source question sets that address a major topic with a number of related primary sources; and questions that promote deeper analysis of historical evidence. Images, video clips, and audio clips are incorporated into many of the questions. Students get immediate feedback on their work (not only what they got right or wrong, but why), and they can choose to see another set of related questions if they want to practice further. A searchable eBook is available inside the course as well so that students can easily reference it as they are working. Map-reading and writing tutorials are available as well to get students off to a good start.

Aplia's simple-to-use course management interface allows instructors to post announcements, upload course materials, host student discussions, e-mail students, and manage the gradebook; personalized support from a knowledgeable and friendly support team also offers assistance in customizing assignments to the instructor's course schedule. To learn more and view a demo for this book, visit www.aplia.com.

CourseReader
CourseReader is an online collection of primary and secondary sources that lets you create a customized electronic reader in minutes. With an easy-to-use interface and assessment tool, you can choose exactly what your students will be assigned—simply search or browse Cengage Learning's extensive document database to preview and select your customized collection of readings. In addition to print sources of all types (letters, diary entries, speeches, newspaper accounts, and more), the collection includes a growing number of images and video and audio clips.

Each primary source document includes a descriptive headnote that puts the reading into context and is further supported by both critical thinking and multiple-choice questions designed to reinforce key points. For more information, visit www.cengage.com/coursereader.

Cengagebrain.com
Save your students time and money. Direct them to www.cengagebrain.com for a choice of formats and savings and a better chance to succeed in your class. *Cengagebrain.com*, Cengage Learning's online store, is a single destination for more than 10,000 new textbooks, eTextbooks, eChapters, study tools, and audio supplements. Students have the freedom to purchase à la carte exactly what they need when they need it. Students can save 50 percent on the electronic textbook and can pay as little as $1.99 for an individual eChapter.

Student Resources

Book Companion Site
ISBN-10: 1133939007 | ISBN-13: 9781133939009
A website for students features a wide assortment of resources to help students master the subject matter. The website, prepared by Alan Hester of Greenville Technical College, includes a glossary, flashcards, focus questions, sample quizzes, suggested readings, and primary source links.

CL eBook
This interactive multimedia eBook links out to rich media assets such as video and MP3 chapter summaries. Through this eBook, students can also access primary sources, audio chapter summaries, zoomable and animated maps, web field trips, and more than 25 videos. Available at www.cengagebrain.com.

Doing History: Research and Writing in the Digital Age, 2e
ISBN-10: 1133587887 | ISBN-13: 9781133587880
Prepared by Michael J. Galgano, J. Chris Arndt, and Raymond M. Hyser of James Madison University.

Whether you're starting down the path as a history major or simply looking for a straightforward and systematic guide to writing a successful paper, you'll find this text to be an indispensable handbook to historical research. This text's "soup to nuts" approach to researching and writing about history addresses every step of the process, from locating your sources and gathering information, to writing clearly and making proper use of various citation styles to avoid plagiarism. You'll also learn how to make the most of every tool available to you—especially the technology that helps you conduct the process efficiently and effectively. The second edition includes a special appendix linked to CourseReader (see above), where you can examine and interpret primary sources online.

The History Handbook, 2e
ISBN-10: 049590676X | ISBN-13: 9780495906766
Prepared by Carol Berkin of Baruch College, City University of New York, and Betty Anderson of Boston University. This book teaches students both basic and history-specific study skills such as how to take notes, get the most out of lectures and readings, read primary sources, research historical topics, and correctly cite sources. Substantially less expensive than comparable skill-building texts, *The History Handbook* also offers tips for conducting Internet research and evaluating online sources. Additionally, students can purchase and download the eAudio version of *The History Handbook* or any of its eighteen individual units at www.cengagebrain.com to listen to on the go.

Writing for College History, 1e
ISBN-10: 061830603X | ISBN-13: 9780618306039
Prepared by Robert M. Frakes of Clarion University. This brief handbook for survey courses in American history, Western civilization/European history, and world civilization guides students through the various types of writing assignments they encounter in a history class. Providing examples of student writing and candid assessments of student work, this text focuses on the rules and conventions of writing for the college history course.

The Modern Researcher, 6e
ISBN-10: 0495318701 | ISBN-13: 9780495318705
Prepared by Jacques Barzun and Henry F. Graff of Columbia University. This classic introduction to the techniques of research and the art of expression is widely used in history courses, but is also appropriate for writing and research methods courses in other departments. Barzun and Graff thoroughly cover every aspect of research, from the selection of a topic through the gathering of material, analysis, writing, revision, and publication of findings. They present the process not as a set of rules but through actual cases that put the subtleties of research in a useful context. Part One covers the principles and methods of research; Part Two covers writing, speaking, and getting one's work published.

Reader Program
Cengage Learning publishes a number of readers; some contain exclusively primary sources, others are devoted to essays and secondary sources, and still others provide a combination of primary and secondary sources. All of these readers are designed to guide students through the process of historical inquiry. Visit Cengage.com/history for a complete list of readers.

Rand McNally Historical Atlas of the World
ISBN-10: 0618841911 | ISBN-13: 9780618841912
This valuable resource features more than seventy maps that portray the rich panoply of the world's history from preliterate times to the present. They show how cultures and civilizations were linked and how they interacted. The maps make it clear that history is not static. Rather, it is about change and movement across time. The maps show change by presenting the dynamics of expansion, cooperation, and conflict. This atlas includes maps that display the world from the beginnings of civilization; the political development of all major areas of the world; expanded coverage of Africa, Latin America, and the Middle East; the current Islamic world; and world population change in 1900 and 2000.

Document Exercise Workbook
Volume 1: ISBN-10: 0534560830 | ISBN-13: 9780534560836
Volume 2: ISBN-10: 0534560849 | ISBN-13: 9780534560843
Prepared by Donna Van Raaphorst of Cuyahoga Community College. This collection of exercises is based around primary sources. Available in two volumes.

Custom Options

Nobody knows your students like you, so why not give them a text that is tailored to their needs? Cengage Learning offers custom solutions for your course—whether that involves making a small modification to *The Essential World History* to match your syllabus or combining multiple sources to create something truly unique. You can pick and choose chapters, include your own material, and add additional map exercises along with the *Rand McNally Atlas* to create a text that fits the way you teach. Ensure that your students get the most out of their textbook dollar by giving them exactly what they need. Contact your Cengage Learning representative to explore custom solutions for your course.

ACKNOWLEDGMENTS

BOTH AUTHORS GRATEFULLY acknowledge that without the generosity of many others, this project could not have been completed.

William Duiker would like to thank Kumkum Chatterjee and On-cho Ng for their helpful comments about issues related to the history of India and premodern China. His longtime colleague Cyril Griffith, now deceased, was a cherished friend and a constant source of information about modern Africa. Art Goldschmidt has been of invaluable assistance in reading several chapters of the manuscript, as well as in unraveling many of the mysteries of Middle Eastern civilization. Finally, he remains profoundly grateful to his wife, Yvonne V. Duiker, Ph.D. She has not only given her usual measure of love and support when this appeared to be an insuperable task, but she has also contributed her own time and expertise to enrich the sections on art and literature, thereby adding life and sparkle to this, as well as the earlier editions of the book. To her, and to his daughters Laura and Claire, he will be forever thankful for bringing joy to his life.

Jackson Spielvogel would like to thank Art Goldschmidt, David Redles, and Christine Colin for their time and ideas. Daniel Haxall of Kutztown University provided valuable assistance with materials on postwar art, popular culture, Postmodern art and thought, and the digital age. He is especially grateful to Kathryn Spielvogel for her work as research associate. Above all, he thanks his family for their support. The gifts of love, laughter, and patience from his daughters, Jennifer and Kathryn, his sons, Eric and Christian, and his daughters-in-law, Liz and Laurie, and his sons-in-law, Daniel and Eddie, were especially valuable. He also wishes to acknowledge his grandchildren, Devyn, Bryn, Drew, Elena, Sean, Emma, and Jackson, who bring great joy to his life. Diane, his wife and best friend, provided him with editorial assistance, wise counsel, and the loving support that made a project of this magnitude possible.

Thanks to Wadsworth's comprehensive review process, many historians were asked to evaluate our manuscript. We are grateful to the following for the innumerable suggestions that have greatly improved our work:

Henry Abramson
Florida Atlantic University

Eric H. Ash
Wayne State University

William Bakken
Rochester Community College

Suzanne Balch-Lindsay
Eastern New Mexico University

Michael E. Birdwell
Tennessee Technological University

Eric Bobo
Hinds Community College

Michael Bonislawski
Cambridge College

Connie Brand
Meridien Community College

Eileen Brown
Norwalk Community College

Paul Buckingham
Morrisville State College

Thomas Cardoza
University of California, San Diego

Alistair Chapman
Westmont College

Nupur Chaudhuri
Texas Southern University

Richard Crane
Greensboro College

Wade Dudley
East Carolina University

E. J. Fabyan
Vincennes University

Kenneth Faunce
Washington State University

Jamie Garcia
Hawaii Pacific University

Steven Gosch
University of Wisconsin—Eau Claire

Donald Harreld
Brigham Young University

Janine C. Hartman
University of Connecticut

Greg Havrilcsak
University of Michigan—Flint

Thomas Hegerty
University of Tampa

Sanders Huguenin
University of Science and Arts of Oklahoma

Ahmed Ibrahim
Southwest Missouri State University

C. Barden Keeler
Gulf Coast High School

Marilynn Fox Kokoszka
Orchard Ridge Campus, Oakland Community College

James Krippner-Martinez
Haverford College

Oscar Lansen
University of North Carolina—Charlotte

David Leinweber
Oxford College, Emory University

Susie Ling
Pasadena City College

Moira Maguire
University of Arkansas at Little Rock

Andrew McGreevy
Ohio University

Daniel Miller
Calvin College

Michael Murdock
Brigham Young University

Mark Norris
Grace College

Elsa A. Nystrom
Kennesaw State University

S. Mike Pavelec
Hawaii Pacific University

Matthew Phillips
Kent State University

Randall L. Pouwels
University of Central Arkansas

Margaret Power
Illinois Institute of Technology

Pamela Sayre
Henry Ford Community College

Philip Curtis Skaggs
Grand Valley State University

Laura Smoller
University of Arkansas at Little Rock

Beatrice Spade
University of Southern Colorado

Jeremy Stahl
Middle Tennessee State University

Clif Stratton
Washington State University

Kate Transchel
California State University, Chico

Justin Vance
Hawaii Pacific University

Lorna VanMeter
Ball State University

Michelle White
University of Tennessee at Chattanooga

Edna Yahil
Washington State University—Swiss Center

The authors are truly grateful to the people who have helped us to produce this book. We especially want to thank Clark Baxter, whose faith in our ability to do this project was inspiring. Margaret McAndrew Beasley thoughtfully, wisely, efficiently, and pleasantly guided the overall development of this edition. We also thank Brooke Barbier for her valuable editorial insights. We want to express our gratitude to John Orr, whose good humor, well-advised suggestions, and generous verbal support made the production process easier. Pat Lewis was, as usual, a truly outstanding copyeditor. Abigail Baxter provided valuable assistance in obtaining illustrations and permissions for the illustrations.

THEMES FOR UNDERSTANDING WORLD HISTORY

AS THEY PURSUE their craft, historians often organize their material on the basis of themes that enable them to ask and try to answer basic questions about the past. Such is our intention here. In preparing the seventh edition of this book, we have selected several major themes that we believe are especially important in understanding the course of world history. Thinking about these themes will help students to perceive the similarities and differences among cultures since the beginning of the human experience.

In the chapters that follow, we will refer to these themes frequently as we advance from the prehistoric era to the present. Where appropriate, we shall make comparisons across cultural boundaries or across different time periods. To facilitate this process, we have included a comparative essay in each chapter that focuses on a particular theme within the specific time period covered by that chapter. For example, the comparative essay in Chapter 6 deals with the human impact on the natural environment during the premodern era, while the essay in Chapter 30 discusses the same issue in the contemporary world. Each comparative essay is identified with a particular theme, although many essays touch on multiple themes.

We have sought to illustrate these themes through the use of comparative illustrations in each chapter. These illustrations are comparative in nature and seek to encourage the reader to think about thematic issues in cross-cultural terms, while not losing sight of the unique characteristics of individual societies. Our seven themes, each divided into two subtopics, are listed below.

1. *Politics and Government* The study of politics seeks to answer certain basic questions that historians have about the structure of a society: How were people governed? What was the relationship between the ruler and the ruled? What people or groups of people (the political elites) held political power? What actions did people take to guarantee their security or change their form of government?

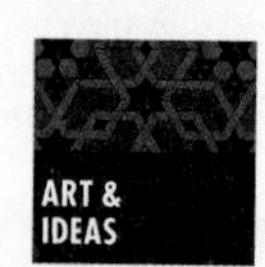

2. *Art and Ideas* We cannot understand a society without looking at its culture, or the common ideas, beliefs, and patterns of behavior that are passed on from one generation to the next. Culture includes both high culture and popular culture. High culture consists of the writings of a society's thinkers and the works of its artists. A society's popular culture encompasses the ideas and experiences of ordinary people. Today, the media have embraced the term *popular culture* to describe the current trends and fashionable styles.

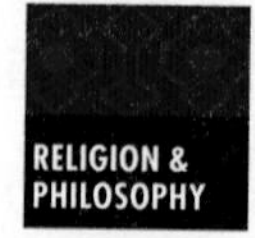

3. *Religion and Philosophy* Throughout history, people have sought to find a deeper meaning to human life. How have the world's great religions, such as Hinduism, Buddhism, Judaism, Christianity, and Islam, influenced people's lives? How have they spread to create new patterns of culture in other parts of the world?

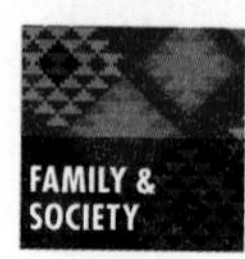

4. *Family and Society* The most basic social unit in human society has always been the family. From a study of family and social patterns, we learn about the different social classes that make up a society and their relationships with one another. We also learn about the role of gender in individual societies. What different roles did men and women play in their societies? How and why were those roles different?

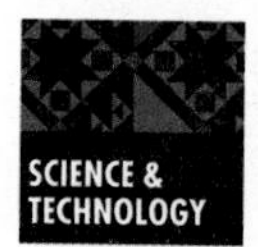

5. *Science and Technology* For thousands of years, people around the world have made scientific discoveries and technological innovations that have changed our world. From the creation of stone tools that made farming easier to advanced computers that guide our airplanes, science and technology have altered how humans have related to their world.

6. *Earth and the Environment* Throughout history, peoples and societies have been affected by the physical world in which they live. Climatic changes alone have been an important factor in human history. Through their economic activities, peoples and societies, in turn, have also made an impact on their world. Human activities have affected the physical environment and even endangered the very existence of entire societies and species.

7. *Interaction and Exchange* Many world historians believe that the exchange of ideas and innovations is the driving force behind the evolution of human societies. Knowledge of agriculture, writing and printing, metalworking, and navigational techniques, for example, spread gradually from one part of the world to other regions and eventually changed the face of the entire globe. The process of cultural and technological exchange took place in various ways, including trade, conquest, and the migration of peoples.

A NOTE TO STUDENTS ABOUT LANGUAGES AND THE DATING OF TIME

ONE OF THE MOST difficult challenges in studying world history is coming to grips with the multitude of names, words, and phrases in unfamiliar languages. Unfortunately, this problem has no easy solution. We have tried to alleviate the difficulty, where possible, by providing an English-language translation of foreign words or phrases, a glossary, and a pronunciation guide in parentheses in the text. The issue is especially complicated in the case of Chinese because two separate systems are commonly used to transliterate the spoken Chinese language into the Roman alphabet. The Wade-Giles system, invented in the nineteenth century, was the most frequently used until recent years, when the pinyin system was adopted by the People's Republic of China as its own official form of transliteration. We have opted to use the latter, as it appears to be gaining acceptance in the United States, but the initial use of a Chinese word is accompanied by its Wade-Giles equivalent in parentheses for the benefit of those who may encounter the term in their outside reading.

In our examination of world history, we also need to be aware of the dating of time. In recording the past, historians try to determine the exact time when events occurred. World War II in Europe, for example, began on September 1, 1939, when Adolf Hitler sent German troops into Poland, and ended on May 7, 1945, when Germany surrendered. By using dates, historians can place events in order and try to determine the development of patterns over periods of time.

If someone asked you when you were born, you would reply with a number, such as 1994. In the United States, we would all accept that number without question, because it is part of the dating system followed in the Western world (Europe and the Western Hemisphere). In this system, events are dated by counting backward or forward from the birth of Christ (assumed to be the year 1). An event that took place 400 years before the birth of Christ would commonly be dated 400 B.C. (before Christ). Dates after the birth of Christ are labeled as A.D. These letters stand for the Latin words *anno domini*, which mean "in the year of the Lord" (or the year of the birth of Christ). Thus, an event that took place 250 years after the birth of Christ is written A.D. 250, or in the year of the Lord 250. It can also be written as 250, just as you would not give your birth year as A.D. 1994, but simply as 1994.

Some historians now prefer to use the abbreviations B.C.E. ("before the common era") and C.E. ("common era") instead of B.C. and A.D. This is especially true of world historians who prefer to use symbols that are not so Western or Christian oriented. The dates, of course, remain the same. Thus, 1950 B.C.E. and 1950 B.C. are the same year, as are A.D. 40 and 40 C.E. In keeping with the current usage by many world historians, this book will use the terms B.C.E. and C.E.

Historians also make use of other terms to refer to time. A decade is 10 years; a century is 100 years; and a millennium is 1,000 years. The phrase "fourth century B.C.E." refers to the fourth period of 100 years counting backward from 1, the assumed date of the birth of Christ. Since the first century B.C.E. would be the years 100 B.C.E. to 1 B.C.E., the fourth century B.C.E. would be the years 400 B.C.E. to 301 B.C.E. We could say, then, that an event in 350 B.C.E. took place in the fourth century B.C.E.

The phrase "fourth century C.E." refers to the fourth period of 100 years after the birth of Christ. Since the first period of 100 years would be the years 1 to 100, the fourth period or fourth century would be the years 301 to 400. We could say, then, for example, that an event in 350 took place in the fourth century. Likewise, the first millennium B.C.E. refers to the years 1000 B.C.E. to 1 B.C.E.; the second millennium C.E. refers to the years 1001 to 2000.

The dating of events can also vary from people to people. Most people in the Western world use the Western calendar, also known as the Gregorian calendar after Pope Gregory XIII who refined it in 1582. The Hebrew calendar, on the other hand, uses a different system in which the year 1 is the equivalent of the Western year 3760 B.C.E., considered by Jews to be the date of the creation of the world. Thus, the Western year 2013 is the year 5773 on the Jewish calendar. The Islamic calendar begins year 1 on the day Muhammad fled from Mecca, which is the year 622 on the Western calendar.

PART I

The First Civilizations and the Rise of Empires (Prehistory to 500 C.E.)

FOR HUNDREDS OF THOUSANDS of years, human beings lived in small groups or villages, seeking to survive by hunting, fishing, and foraging in an often hostile environment. Then, in the space of a few thousand years, an abrupt change occurred as people in a few areas of the globe began to master the art of cultivating food crops. As food production increased, the population in these areas grew, and people began to live in larger communities. Cities appeared and became centers of cultural and religious development. Historians refer to these changes as the beginnings of civilization.

How and why did the first civilizations arise? What role did cross-cultural contacts play in their development? What was the nature of the relationship between these permanent settlements and nonagricultural peoples living elsewhere in the world? Finally, what brought about the demise of these early civilizations, and what legacy did they leave for their successors in the region? The first civilizations that emerged in Mesopotamia, Egypt, India, and China in the fourth and third millennia B.C.E. all shared a number of basic characteristics. Perhaps most important was that each developed in a river valley that was able to provide the agricultural resources needed to maintain a large population.

The emergence of these sedentary societies had a major impact on the social organizations, religious beliefs, and ways of life of the peoples living in them. As the population increased and cities sprang up, centralized authority became a necessity. And in the cities, new forms of livelihood arose to satisfy the growing demand for social services and consumer goods. Some people became artisans or merchants, while others became warriors, scholars, or priests. In some cases, the early cities reflected the hierarchical character of the society as a whole, with a central royal palace surrounded by an imposing wall to separate the rulers from the remainder of the urban population.

Although the emergence of the first civilizations led to the formation of cities governed by elites, the vast majority of the population consisted of peasants or slaves working on the lands of the wealthy. In general, rural peoples were less affected by the changes than their urban counterparts. Farmers continued to live in simple mud-and-thatch huts, and many continued to face legal restrictions on their freedom of action and movement. Slavery was common in virtually all ancient societies.

Within these civilizations, the nature of social organization and relationships also began to change. As the concept of private property spread, people were less likely to live in large kinship groups, and the nuclear family became increasingly prevalent. Gender roles came to be differentiated, with men working in the fields or at various specialized occupations and women remaining in the home. Wives were less likely to be viewed as partners than as possessions under the control of their husbands.

These new civilizations were also the sites of significant religious and cultural developments. All of them

Bibliothèque, Louvre, Paris//© Erich Lessing/Art Resource, NY

gave birth to new religions that sought to explain and even influence the forces of nature. Winning the approval of the gods was deemed crucial to a community's success, and a professional class of priests emerged to handle relations with the divine world.

Writing was an important development in the evolution of these new civilizations. Eventually, all of them used writing as both a means of communication and an avenue of creative expression.

From the beginnings of the first civilizations around 3000 B.C.E., the trend was toward the creation of larger territorial states with more sophisticated systems of control. This process reached a high point in the first millennium B.C.E. Between 1000 and 500 B.C.E., the Assyrians and Persians amassed empires that encompassed large areas of the Middle East. The conquests of Alexander the Great in the fourth century B.C.E. created an even larger, if short-lived, empire that soon divided into four kingdoms. Later, the western portion of these kingdoms, along with the Mediterranean world and much of western Europe fell subject to the mighty empire of the Romans. At the same time, much of India became part of the Mauryan Empire. Finally, in the last few centuries B.C.E., the Qin and Han dynasties of China created a unified Chinese empire.

At first, these new civilizations had relatively little contact with peoples in the surrounding regions. But evidence is growing that a regional trade had started to take hold in the Middle East, and probably in southern and eastern Asia as well, at a very early date. As the population increased, the volume of trade rose with it, and the new civilizations moved outward to acquire new lands and access needed resources. As they expanded, they began to encounter peoples along the periphery of their empires.

Not much evidence has survived to chronicle the nature of these first encounters, but it is likely that the results varied widely according to time and place. In some cases, the growing civilizations found it relatively easy to absorb isolated communities of agricultural or food-gathering peoples that they encountered. Such was the case in southern China and southern India. But in other instances, notably among the nomadic or seminomadic peoples in the central and northeastern parts of Asia, the problem was more complicated and often resulted in bitter and extended conflict.

Contacts between these nomadic or seminomadic peoples and settled civilizations probably developed gradually over a long period of time. Often the relationship, at least at the outset, was mutually beneficial, as each needed goods produced by the other. Nomadic peoples in Central Asia also served as an important link for goods and ideas transported over distances between sedentary civilizations as early as 3000 B.C.E. Overland trade throughout southwestern Asia was already well established by the third millennium B.C.E.

Eventually, the relationship between the settled peoples and the nomadic peoples became increasingly characterized by conflict. Where conflict occurred, the governments of the sedentary civilizations used a variety of techniques to resolve the problem, including negotiations, conquest, or alliance with other pastoral peoples to isolate their primary tormentors.

In the end, these early civilizations collapsed not only as a result of nomadic invasions but also because of their own weaknesses, which made them increasingly vulnerable to attacks along the frontier. Some of their problems were political, and others were related to climatic change or environmental problems.

The fall of the ancient empires did not mark the end of civilization, of course, but rather served as a transition to a new stage of increasing complexity in the evolution of human society. ◆

CHAPTER 1

Early Humans and the First Civilizations

© Nik Wheeler/CORBIS

Excavation of Warka showing the ruins of Uruk

CHAPTER OUTLINE AND FOCUS QUESTIONS

The First Humans

Q How did the Paleolithic and Neolithic Ages differ, and how did the Neolithic Revolution affect the lives of men and women?

The Emergence of Civilization

Q What are the characteristics of civilization, and where did the first civilizations emerge?

Civilization in Mesopotamia

Q How are the chief characteristics of civilization evident in ancient Mesopotamia?

Egyptian Civilization: "The Gift of the Nile"

Q What are the basic features of the three major periods of Egyptian history? What elements of continuity are evident in the three periods? What are their major differences?

New Centers of Civilization

Q What was the significance of the Indo-Europeans? How did Judaism differ from the religions of Mesopotamia and Egypt?

The Rise of New Empires

Q What methods and institutions did the Assyrians and Persians use to amass and maintain their respective empires?

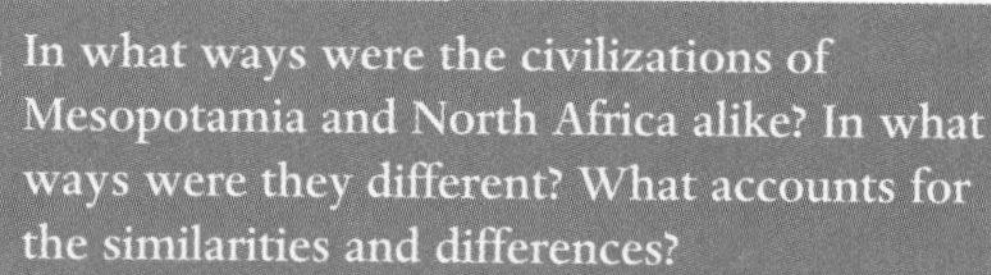

CRITICAL THINKING

Q In what ways were the civilizations of Mesopotamia and North Africa alike? In what ways were they different? What accounts for the similarities and differences?

IN 1849, A DARING YOUNG ENGLISHMAN made a hazardous journey into the deserts and swamps of southern Iraq. Braving high winds and temperatures that reached 120 degrees Fahrenheit, William Loftus led a small expedition southward along the banks of the Euphrates River in search of the roots of civilization. As he said, "From our childhood we have been led to regard this place as the cradle of the human race."

Guided by native Arabs into the southernmost reaches of Iraq, Loftus and his small band of explorers were soon overwhelmed by what they saw. He wrote, "I know of nothing more exciting or impressive than the first sight of one of these great piles, looming in solitary grandeur from the surrounding plains and marshes." One of these piles, known to the natives as the mound of Warka, contained the ruins of Uruk, one of the first cities in the world and part of the world's first civilizations.

Southern Iraq, known to the ancient Greeks as Mesopotamia, was one of the areas in the world where civilization began. In the fertile valleys of large rivers—the Tigris and Euphrates in Mesopotamia, the Nile in Egypt, the Indus in India, and the Yellow River in

China—intensive agriculture became capable of supporting large groups of people. In these regions, civilization was born. The first civilizations emerged in western Asia (now known as the Middle East) and Egypt, where people developed organized societies and created the ideas and institutions that we associate with civilization.

Before considering the early civilizations of western Asia and Egypt, however, we must briefly examine our prehistory and observe how human beings made the shift from hunting and gathering to agricultural communities and ultimately to cities and civilization.

The First Humans

FOCUS QUESTION: How did the Paleolithic and Neolithic Ages differ, and how did the Neolithic Revolution affect the lives of men and women?

The earliest humanlike creatures—known as **hominids**—lived in Africa some 3 to 4 million years ago. Called Australopithecines (aw-stray-loh-PITH-uh-synz), or "southern ape-men," by their discoverers, they flourished in eastern and southern Africa and were the first hominids to make simple stone tools. Australopithecines may also have been bipedal—that is, they may have walked upright on two legs, a trait that would have enabled them to move over long distances and make use of their arms and legs for different purposes.

In 1959, Louis and Mary Leakey discovered a new form of hominid in Africa that they labeled *Homo habilis* ("skilled human"). The Leakeys believed that *Homo habilis*, which had a brain almost 50 percent larger than that of the Australopithecines, was the earliest toolmaking hominid. Their larger brains and ability to walk upright allowed these hominids to become more sophisticated in searching for meat, seeds, and nuts for nourishment.

A new phase in early human development occurred around 1.5 million years ago with the emergence of *Homo erectus* ("upright human"). A more advanced human form, *Homo erectus* made use of larger and more varied tools and was the first hominid to leave Africa and move into Europe and Asia.

The Emergence of *Homo sapiens*

Around 250,000 years ago, a crucial stage in human development began with the emergence of *Homo sapiens* (HOH-moh SAY-pee-unz) ("wise human being"). The first anatomically modern humans, known as *Homo sapiens sapiens* ("wise, wise human being"), appeared in Africa between 200,000 and 150,000 years ago. Recent evidence indicates that they began to spread outside Africa around 70,000 years ago. Map 1.1 shows probable dates for different movements, although many of these are still controversial.

These modern humans, who were our direct ancestors, soon encountered other hominids, such as the Neanderthals, whose remains were first found in the Neander valley in Germany. Neanderthal remains have since been found in both Europe and western Asia and have been dated to between 200,000 and 30,000 B.C.E. Neanderthals relied on a variety of stone tools and were the first early people to bury their dead. By 30,000 B.C.E., *Homo sapiens sapiens* had replaced the Neanderthals, who had largely become extinct.

THE SPREAD OF HUMANS: OUT OF AFRICA OR MULTIREGIONAL? The movements of the first modern humans were rarely sudden or rapid. Groups of people advanced beyond their old hunting grounds at a rate of only 2 to 3 miles per generation. This was enough, however, to populate the world in some tens of thousands of years. Some scholars, who advocate a multiregional theory, have suggested that advanced human creatures may have emerged independently in different parts of world, rather than in Africa alone. But the latest genetic, archaeological, and climatic evidence strongly supports the out-of-Africa theory as the most likely explanation of human origin. In any case, by 10,000 B.C.E., members of the *Homo sapiens sapiens* species could be found throughout the world. By that time, it was the only human species left. All humans today, whether Europeans, Australian Aborigines, or Africans, belong to the same subspecies of human being.

The Hunter-Gatherers of the Paleolithic Age

One of the basic distinguishing features of the human species is the ability to make tools. The earliest tools were made of stone, and so this early period of human history (c. 2,500,000–10,000 B.C.E.) has been designated the **Paleolithic Age** (*paleolithic* is Greek for "old stone").

For hundreds of thousands of years, humans relied on hunting and gathering for their daily food. Paleolithic peoples had a close relationship with the world around them, and over a period of time, they came to know which animals to hunt and which plants to eat. They did not know how to grow crops or raise animals, however. They gathered wild nuts, berries, fruits, and a variety of wild grains and green plants. Around the world, they captured and consumed various animals, including buffalo, reindeer, and fish.

The hunting of animals and the gathering of wild plants no doubt led to certain patterns of living. Paleolithic

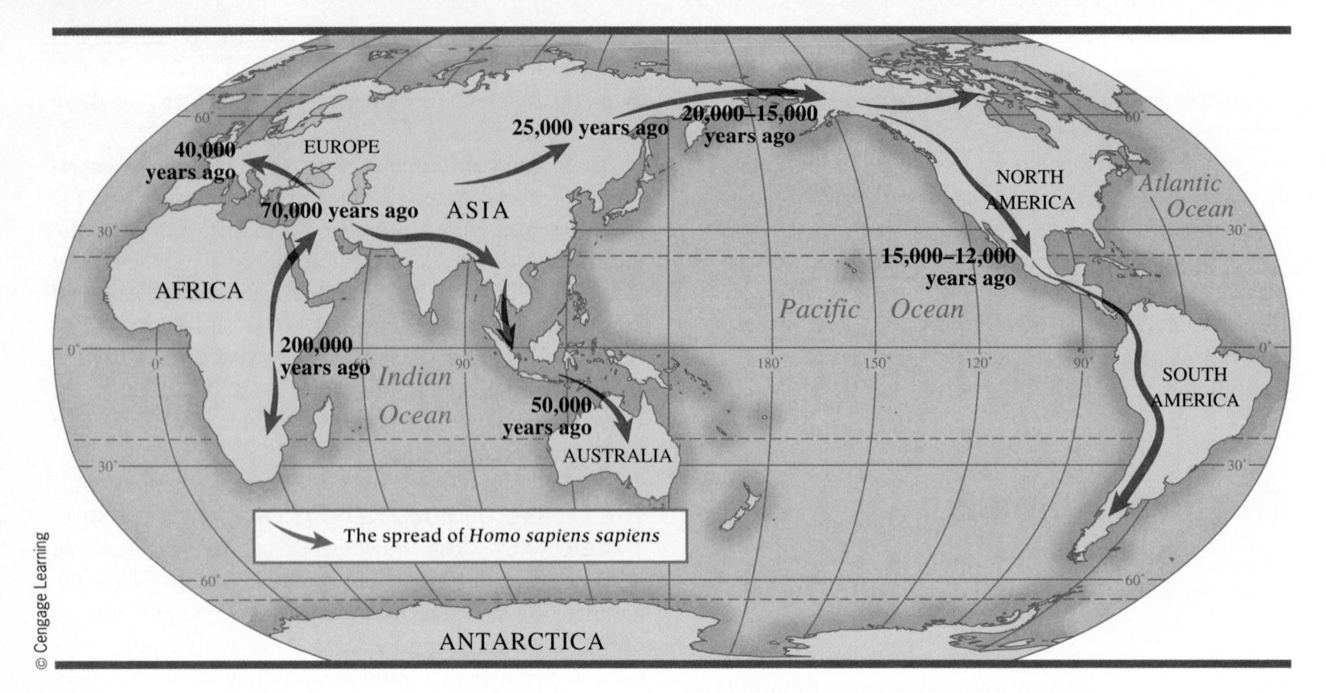

© Cengage Learning

MAP 1.1 The Spread of *Homo sapiens sapiens*. *Homo sapiens sapiens* spread from Africa beginning about 70,000 years ago. Living and traveling in small groups, these anatomically modern humans were hunter-gatherers.

Given that some diffusion of humans occurred during ice ages, how would such climate change affect humans and their movements, especially from Asia to Australia and Asia to North America?

people probably lived in small bands of twenty or thirty. They were nomadic, moving from place to place to follow animal migrations and vegetation cycles. Over the years, their tools became more refined and more useful. The invention of the spear and later the bow and arrow made hunting considerably easier. Harpoons and fishhooks made of bone increased the catch of fish.

Both men and women were responsible for finding food—the chief work of Paleolithic people. Since women bore and raised the children, they generally stayed close to the camps, but they played an important role in acquiring food by gathering berries, nuts, and grains. Men hunted for wild animals, an activity that often took them far from camp. Because both men and women played important roles in providing for the band's survival, scientists have argued that a rough equality existed between men and women.

Some groups of Paleolithic people, especially those who lived in cold climates, found shelter in caves. Over time, they created new types of shelter as well. Perhaps the most common was a simple structure of wood poles or sticks covered with animal hides. The systematic use of fire, which archaeologists believe began around 500,000 years ago, made it possible for the caves and human-made structures to have light and heat. Fire also enabled early humans to cook their food, which made it taste better, last longer, and, in the case of some plants such as wild grain, easier to chew and digest.

The making of tools and the use of fire—two important technological innovations of Paleolithic peoples—remind us how crucial the ability to adapt was to human survival. But Paleolithic peoples did more than just survive. The cave paintings of large animals found in southwestern France and northern Spain bear witness to the cultural activity of Paleolithic peoples. A cave discovered in southern France in 1994 contains more than three hundred paintings of lions, oxen, owls, bears, and other animals. Most of these are animals that Paleolithic people did not hunt, which suggests that the paintings were made for religious or even decorative purposes.

The Neolithic Revolution, c. 10,000–4000 B.C.E.

The end of the last ice age around 10,000 B.C.E. was followed by what is called the **Neolithic Revolution**, a significant change in living patterns that occurred in the New Stone Age (*neolithic* is Greek for "new stone"). The name "New Stone Age" is misleading, however. Although Neolithic peoples made a new type of polished stone axes, this was not the most significant change they introduced.

COMPARATIVE ESSAY

From Hunter-Gatherers and Herders to Farmers

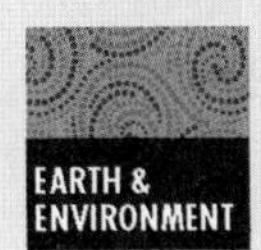

About ten thousand years ago, human beings began to practice the cultivation of crops and the domestication of animals. The first farmers undoubtedly used simple techniques and still relied primarily on other forms of food production, such as hunting, foraging, and pastoralism (herding). The real breakthrough came when farmers began to cultivate crops along the floodplains of river systems. The advantage was that crops grown in such areas were not as dependent on rainfall and therefore produced a more reliable harvest. An additional benefit was that the sediment carried by the river waters deposited nutrients in the soil, enabling a farmer to cultivate a single plot of ground for many years without moving to a new location. Thus, the first truly sedentary (nonmigratory) societies were born.

The spread of river valley agriculture in various parts of Asia and Africa was the decisive factor in the rise of the first civilizations. The increase in food production in these regions made possible a significant growth in population, while efforts to control the flow of water to maximize the irrigation of cultivated areas and to protect the local inhabitants from hostile forces outside the community led to the first steps toward cooperative activities on a large scale. The need to oversee the entire process brought about the emergence of an elite that was eventually transformed into a government.

We shall investigate this process in the next several chapters as we explore the rise of civilizations in the Mediterranean, the Middle East, South Asia, China, and the Americas. We shall also raise a number of important questions: Why did human communities in some areas that had the capacity to support agriculture not take the leap to farming? Why did other groups that had managed to master the cultivation of crops not take the next step and create large and advanced societies? Finally, what happened to the existing communities of hunter-gatherers who were overrun or driven out as the agricultural revolution spread throughout the world?

Over the years, a number of possible explanations, some of them biological, others cultural or environmental in nature, have been advanced to answer such questions. According to Jared Diamond, in *Guns, Germs, and Steel: The Fates of Human Societies*, the ultimate causes of such differences lie not within the character or cultural values of the resident population but in the nature of the local climate and topography. These influence the degree to which local crops and animals can be put to human use and then be transmitted to adjoining regions. In Mesopotamia, for example, the widespread availability of edible crops, such as wheat and barley, helped promote the transition to agriculture in the region. At the same time, the absence of land barriers between Mesopotamia and its neighbors to the east and west facilitated the rapid spread of agricultural techniques and crops to climatically similar regions in the Indus River valley and Egypt.

What role did agriculture play in the emergence of civilization?

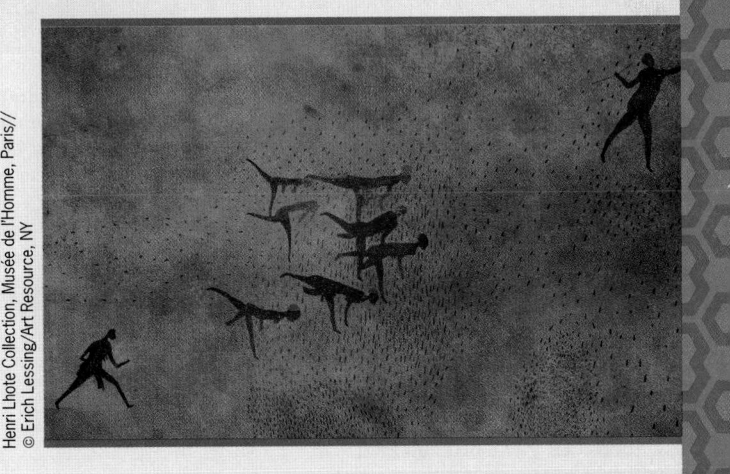

Henri Lhote Collection, Musée de l'Homme, Paris// © Erich Lessing/Art Resource, NY

Women's Work. This rock painting from a cave in modern-day Algeria, dating from around the fourth millennium B.C.E., shows women harvesting grain.

A REVOLUTION IN AGRICULTURE The biggest change was the shift from hunting animals and gathering plants for sustenance (food gathering) to producing food by systematic agriculture (food production). The planting of grains and vegetables provided a regular supply of food, while the domestication of animals, such as sheep, goats, cattle, and pigs, added a steady source of meat, milk, and fibers such as wool for clothing. The growing of crops and the taming of food-producing animals created a new relationship between humans and nature, which historians like to speak of as an agricultural revolution (see the comparative essay "From Hunter-Gatherers and Herders to Farmers" above).

Revolutionary change is dramatic and requires great effort, but the ability to acquire food on a regular basis gave humans greater control over their environment and enabled them to give up their nomadic ways of life and live in settled communities. The increase in food supplies also led to a noticeable expansion of the population.

Systematic agriculture developed independently in different areas of the world between 8000 and 5000 B.C.E. Inhabitants of the Middle East began cultivating wheat and barley and domesticating pigs, cattle, goats, and sheep by 8000 B.C.E. From the Middle East, farming spread into southeastern Europe and by 4000 B.C.E. was well established in central Europe and the coastal regions of the Mediterranean. The cultivation of wheat and barley also spread from western Asia into the Nile valley of Egypt by 6000 B.C.E. and soon spread up the Nile to other areas of Africa. In the woodlands and tropical forests of Central Africa, a separate farming system emerged, based on the cultivation of tubers or root crops such as yams. The cultivation of wheat and barley also moved eastward into the highlands of northwestern and central India between 7000 and 5000 B.C.E. By 5000 B.C.E., rice was being cultivated in Southeast Asia, and from there it spread into southern China. In northern China, the cultivation of millet and the domestication of pigs and dogs seem well established by 6000 B.C.E. In the Western Hemisphere, Mesoamericans (inhabitants of present-day Mexico and Central America) domesticated beans, squash, and maize (corn) as well as dogs and fowl between 7000 and 5000 B.C.E.

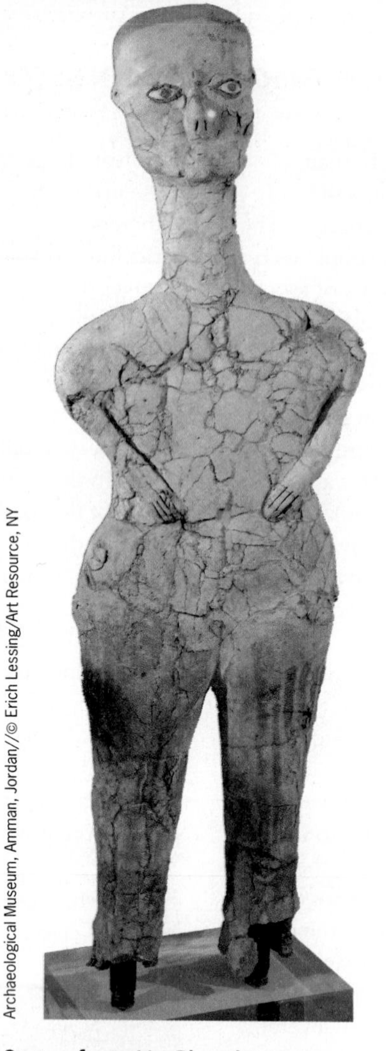

Archaeological Museum, Amman, Jordan//© Erich Lessing/Art Resource, NY

Statue from Ain Ghazal. This life-size statue made of plaster and bitumen was discovered in 1984 in Ain Ghazal, an archaeological site near Amman, Jordan. Dating from 6500 B.C.E., it is among the oldest known statues of the human figure. Although it appears lifelike, the features are too generic to be a portrait of a particular individual. The purpose and meaning of this sculpture may never be known.

CONSEQUENCES OF THE NEOLITHIC REVOLUTION The growing of crops on a regular basis gave rise to relatively permanent settlements, which historians refer to as Neolithic farming villages or towns. Although Neolithic villages appeared in Europe, India, Egypt, China, and Mesoamerica, the oldest and most extensive ones were located in the Middle East. Çatal Hüyük (chaht-ul hoo-YOOK), located in modern Turkey, had walls that enclosed 32 acres, and its population probably reached six thousand inhabitants during its high point from 6700 to 5700 B.C.E. People lived in simple mudbrick houses that were built so close to one another that there were few streets. To get to their homes, people had to walk along the rooftops and enter the house through a hole in the roof.

The Neolithic agricultural revolution had far-reaching consequences. Once people settled in villages or towns, they built houses for protection and other structures for the storage of goods. As organized communities stored food and accumulated material goods, they began to engage in trade. People also began to specialize in certain crafts, and a division of labor developed. Pottery was made from clay and baked in a fire to make it hard. The pots were used for cooking and to store grains. Woven baskets were also used for storage. Stone tools became more refined as flint blades were used to make sickles and hoes for use in the fields. Vegetable fibers from such plants as flax and cotton were used to make thread that was woven into cloth. In the course of the Neolithic Age, many of the food plants consumed today came to be cultivated.

The change to systematic agriculture in the Neolithic Age also had consequences for the relationship between men and women. Men assumed the primary responsibility for working in the fields and herding animals, jobs that kept them away from the home. Women remained behind, grinding grain into flour, caring for the children, weaving clothes, and performing other household tasks that required considerable labor. In time, as work outside the home was increasingly perceived as more important than work done at home, men came to play the more dominant role in society, which gave rise to the practice of **patriarchy** (PAY-tree-ark-ee), or a society dominated by men, a basic pattern that has persisted to our own times.

Other patterns set in the Neolithic Age also proved to be enduring elements of human history. Fixed dwellings, domesticated animals, regular farming, a division of labor, men holding power—all of these are part of the human story For all of our scientific and technological progress, human survival still depends on the growing and storing of food, an accomplishment of people in the Neolithic Age. The Neolithic Revolution was truly a turning point in human history.

Between 4000 and 3000 B.C.E., significant technical developments began to transform the Neolithic towns. The invention of writing enabled records to be kept, and the use of metals marked a new level of human control over the environment and its resources. Already before 4000 B.C.E., artisans had discovered that metal-bearing rocks could be heated to liquefy metals, which could then be cast in molds to produce tools and weapons that were more useful than stone instruments. Although copper was the first metal to be used for producing tools, after 4000 B.C.E., metalworkers in western Asia discovered that combining copper and tin formed bronze, a much harder and more durable metal than copper alone. Its widespread use has led historians to speak of the Bronze Age from around 3000 to 1200 B.C.E.; thereafter, bronze was increasingly replaced by iron.

At first, Neolithic settlements were hardly more than villages. But as their inhabitants mastered the art of farming, more complex human societies gradually emerged. As wealth increased, these societies began to develop armies and to wall off their cities for protection. By the beginning of the Bronze Age, the concentration of larger numbers of people in river valleys was leading to a whole new pattern for human life.

The Emergence of Civilization

FOCUS QUESTION: What are the characteristics of civilization, and where did the first civilizations emerge?

As we have seen, early human beings formed small groups and developed a simple culture that enabled them to survive. As human societies grew and developed greater complexity, civilization came into being. A **civilization** is a complex culture in which large numbers of people share a variety of common elements. Historians have identified a number of basic characteristics of civilization, including the following:

1. *An urban focus.* Cities became the centers for political, economic, social, cultural, and religious development.
2. *New political and military structures.* An organized government bureaucracy arose to meet the administrative demands of the growing population, and armies were organized to gain land and power and for defense.
3. *A new social structure based on economic power.* While kings and an upper class of priests, political leaders, and warriors dominated, there also existed large groups of free common people (farmers, artisans, craftspeople) and, at the very bottom of the social hierarchy, a class of slaves.
4. *The development of more complexity in a material sense.* Surpluses of agricultural crops freed some people to work in occupations other than farming. Demand among ruling elites for luxury items encouraged the creation of new products. And as urban populations exported finished goods in exchange for raw materials from neighboring populations, organized trade grew substantially.
5. *A distinct religious structure.* The gods were deemed crucial to the community's success, and a professional priestly class, serving as stewards of the gods' property, regulated relations with the gods.
6. *The development of writing.* Kings, priests, merchants, and artisans began to use writing to keep records.
7. *New and significant artistic and intellectual activity.* For example, monumental architectural structures, usually religious, occupied a prominent place in urban environments.

The first civilizations that developed in Mesopotamia and Egypt will be examined in detail in this chapter. But civilizations also developed independently in other parts of the world. Between 3000 and 1500 B.C.E., the valleys of the Indus River in India supported a flourishing civilization that extended hundreds of miles from the Himalayas to the coast of the Arabian Sea (see Chapter 2). Another river valley civilization emerged along the Yellow River in northern China about four thousand years ago (see Chapter 3). Under the Shang dynasty of kings, which ruled from c. 1570 to c. 1045 B.C.E., this civilization contained impressive cities with huge city walls and royal palaces.

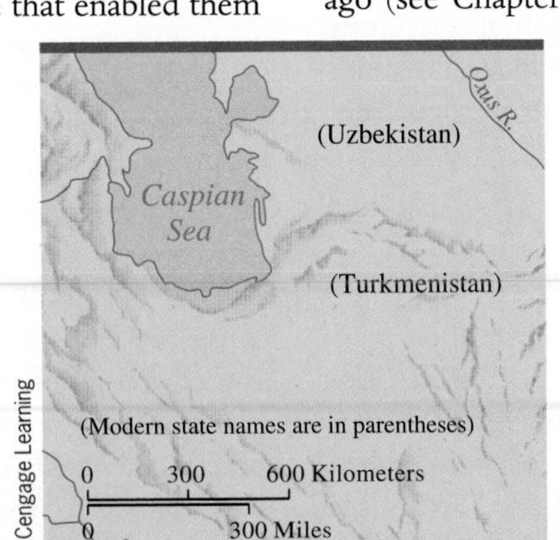

Central Asian Civilization

Scholars have believed for a long time that civilization emerged only in these four areas—in the fertile river valleys of the Tigris and Euphrates, the Nile, the Indus, and the Yellow River. Recently, however, archaeologists have discovered other early civilizations. One of these flourished in Central Asia (in what are now the republics of Turkmenistan and

Uzbekistan) around four thousand years ago. People in this civilization built mudbrick buildings, raised sheep and goats, had bronze tools, used a system of irrigation to grow wheat and barley, and developed a writing system.

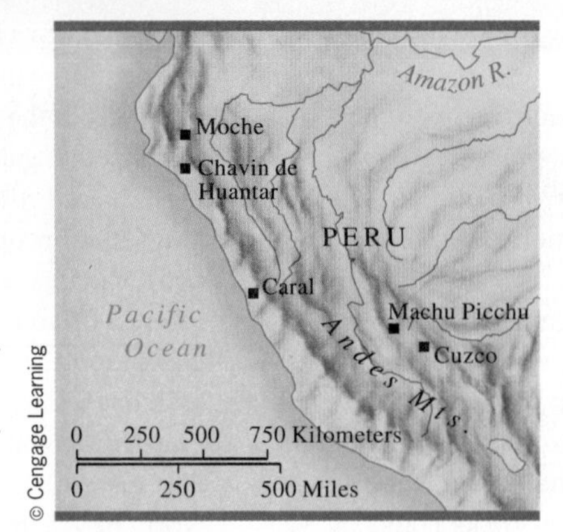

Caral, Peru

Another early civilization was discovered in the Supe River valley of Peru, in South America. At the center of this civilization was the city of Caral, which flourished around 2600 B.C.E. It contained buildings for officials, apartment buildings, and grand residences, all built of stone. The inhabitants of Caral also developed a system of irrigation by diverting a river more than a mile upstream into their fields.

Civilization in Mesopotamia

FOCUS QUESTION: How are the chief characteristics of civilization evident in ancient Mesopotamia?

The Greeks called the valley between the Tigris and Euphrates Rivers Mesopotamia (mess-uh-puh-TAY-mee-uh), the "land between the rivers." The region receives little rain, but the soil of the plain of southern Mesopotamia was enlarged and enriched over the years by layers of silt deposited by the two rivers. In late spring, the Tigris and Euphrates overflow their banks and deposit their fertile silt, but since this flooding depends on the melting of snows in the upland mountains where the rivers begin, it is irregular and sometimes catastrophic. In such circumstances, farming could be accomplished only with human intervention in the form of irrigation and drainage ditches. A complex system was required to control the flow of the rivers and produce the crops. Large-scale irrigation made possible the expansion of agriculture in this region, and the abundant food provided the material base for the emergence of civilization in Mesopotamia.

The City-States of Ancient Mesopotamia

The creators of the first Mesopotamian civilization were the Sumerians (soo-MER-ee-unz *or* soo-MEER-ee-unz), a people whose origins remain unclear. By 3000 B.C.E., they had established a number of independent cities, including Eridu, Ur, Uruk, Umma, and Lagash (see Map 1.2). As the cities expanded, they came to exercise political and economic control over the surrounding countryside, forming city-states, which were the basic units of Sumerian civilization.

SUMERIAN CITIES Sumerian cities were surrounded by walls. Uruk, for example, was encircled by a wall 6 miles long with defense towers located every 30 to 35 feet along it. City dwellings, built of sun-dried bricks, included both the small flats of peasants and the larger dwellings of the civic and priestly officials. Although Mesopotamia had little stone or wood for building purposes, it did have plenty of mud. Mudbricks, easily shaped by hand, were left to bake in the hot sun until they were hard enough to use for building. People in Mesopotamia were remarkably creative with mudbricks, inventing the arch and the dome and constructing some of the largest brick buildings in the world.

The most prominent building in a Sumerian city was the temple, which was dedicated to the chief god or goddess of the city and often built atop a massive stepped tower called a **ziggurat** (ZIG-uh-rat). The Sumerians believed that gods and goddesses owned the cities, and much wealth was used to build temples as well as elaborate houses for the priests and priestesses who served the deities. Priests and priestesses, who supervised the temples and their property, had great power. Ruling power in Sumerian city-states, however, was primarily in the hands of kings.

Sumerians viewed kingship as divine in origin—kings, they believed, derived their power from the gods and were the agents of the gods. As one person said in a petition to his king: "You in your judgment, you are the son of Anu [god of the sky]; your commands, like the work of a god, cannot be reversed. Your words, like rain pouring down from heaven, are without number."[1] Regardless of their origins, kings had power—they led armies and organized workers for the irrigation projects on which Mesopotamian farming depended. The army, the government bureaucracy, and the priests and priestesses all aided the kings in their rule.

ECONOMY AND SOCIETY The economy of the Sumerian city-states was primarily agricultural, but commerce and industry became important as well. The people of Mesopotamia produced woolen textiles, pottery, and metalwork. The Sumerians imported copper, tin, and timber in exchange for dried fish, wool, barley, wheat, and metal goods. Traders traveled by land to the eastern Mediterranean in the west and by sea to India in

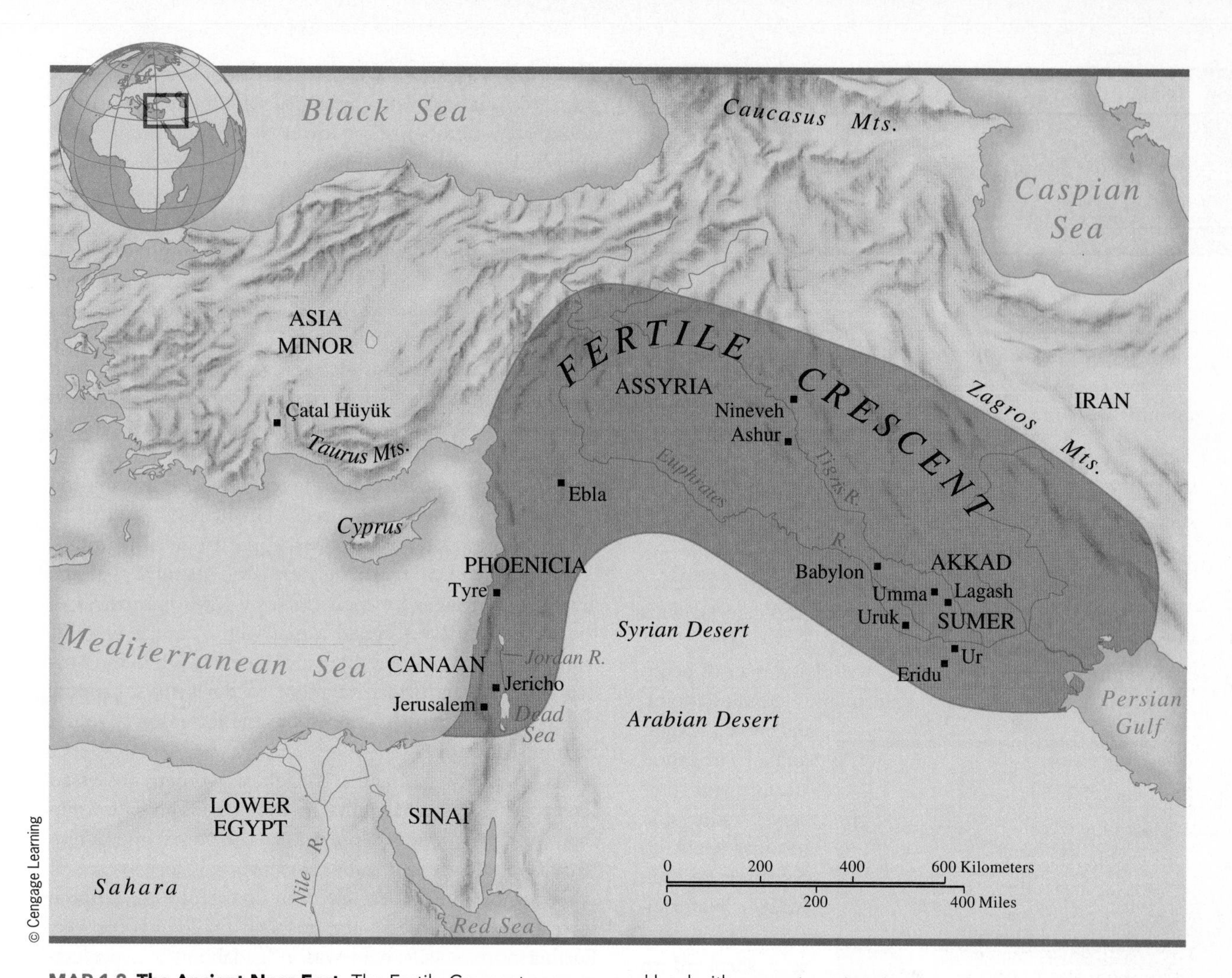

© Cengage Learning

MAP 1.2 The Ancient Near East. The Fertile Crescent encompassed land with access to water at the Persian Gulf, the Mediterranean Sea, and the Tigris and Euphrates Rivers. Employing flood management and irrigation systems, the peoples of the region established civilizations based on agriculture. These civilizations developed writing, law codes, and economic specialization.

Q *What geographic aspects of the Mesopotamian city-states made conflict between them likely?*

the east. The introduction of the wheel, which had been invented around 3000 B.C.E. by nomadic people living in the region north of the Black Sea, led to carts with wheels that made the transport of goods easier.

Sumerian city-states probably contained four major social groups: elites, dependent commoners, free commoners, and slaves. Elites included royal and priestly officials and their families. Dependent commoners included the elites' clients who worked for the palace and temple estates. Free commoners worked as farmers, merchants, fishers, scribes, and craftspeople. Probably 90 percent or more of the population were farmers. Slaves belonged to palace officials, who used them in building projects; to temple officials, who used mostly female slaves to weave cloth and grind grain; and to rich landowners, who used them for farming and domestic work.

Empires in Ancient Mesopotamia

As the number of Sumerian city-states grew and the states expanded, new conflicts arose as city-state fought city-state for control of land and water. Located in the flat land of Mesopotamia, the Sumerian city-states were also open to invasion. To the north of the Sumerian city-states were the Akkadians (uh-KAY-dee-unz). We call them a Semitic people because of the type of language they spoke (see Table 1.1). Around 2340 B.C.E., Sargon, leader of the Akkadians, overran the Sumerian city-states and established an empire that included most of Mesopotamia as well as lands westward to the Mediterranean. Attacks from neighboring hill peoples eventually caused the Akkadian empire to fall, and its end by 2100 B.C.E. brought a return to independent city-states and the

TABLE 1.1 Some Semitic Languages

Akkadian	*Assyrian*	Hebrew
Arabic	*Babylonian*	*Phoenician*
Aramaic	*Canaanitic*	*Syriac*

NOTE: Languages in italic type are no longer spoken.

conflicts between them. It was not until 1792 B.C.E. that a new empire came to control much of Mesopotamia under Hammurabi (ham-uh-RAH-bee), who ruled over the Amorites or Old Babylonians, a large group of Semitic-speaking seminomads.

HAMMURABI'S EMPIRE Hammurabi (1792–1750 B.C.E.) employed a well-disciplined army of foot soldiers who carried axes, spears, and copper or bronze daggers. He learned to divide his opponents and subdue them one by one. Using such methods, he gained control of Sumer and Akkad, creating a new Mesopotamian kingdom with its capital at Babylon.

Hammurabi, the man of war, was also a man of peace who took a strong interest in state affairs. He built temples, defensive walls, and irrigation canals; encouraged trade; and brought about an economic revival. Indeed, Hammurabi saw himself as a shepherd to his people: "I am indeed the shepherd who brings peace, whose scepter is just. My benevolent shade was spread over my city. I held the people of the lands of Sumer and Akkad safely on my lap."[2] After his death, however, a series of weak kings were unable to keep Hammurabi's empire united, and it finally fell to new invaders.

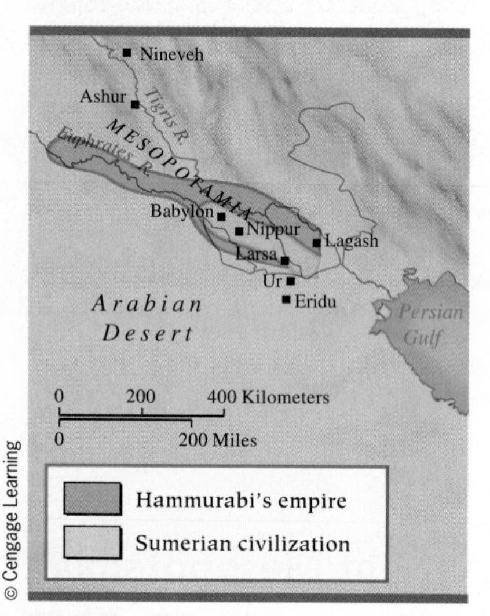

Hammurabi's Empire

THE CODE OF HAMMURABI Hammurabi is best remembered for his law code, a collection of 282 laws. Although many scholars today view Hammurabi's collection less as a code of laws and more as an attempt by Hammurabi to portray himself as the source of justice to his people, the code still gives us a glimpse of the values of the Mesopotamian society of his time (see the box on p. 11).

The Code of Hammurabi reveals a society with a system of strict justice. Penalties for criminal offenses were severe and varied according to the social class of the victim. A crime against a member of the upper class (a noble) by a member of the lower class (a commoner) was punished more severely than the same offense against a member of the lower class. Moreover, the principle of "an eye for an eye, a tooth for a tooth" was fundamental to this system of justice. This meant that punishments should fit the crime: "If a free man has destroyed the eye of a member of the aristocracy, they shall destroy his eye" (Code of Hammurabi, No. 196). Hammurabi's code reflected legal and social ideas prevailing in southwestern Asia at the time, as the following verse from the Hebrew Bible demonstrates: "If anyone injures his neighbor, whatever he has done must be done to him: fracture for fracture, eye for eye, tooth for tooth. As he has injured the other, so he is to be injured" (Leviticus 24:19–20).

The largest category of laws in the Code of Hammurabi focused on marriage and the family. Parents arranged marriages for their children. After the marriage, the parties involved signed a marriage contract; without it, no one was considered legally married. While the husband provided a bridal payment to the bride's parents, the woman's parents were responsible for a dowry to the new husband.

As in many patriarchal societies, women possessed fewer privileges and rights in the married relationship than men. A woman's place was in the home, and failure to fulfill her expected duties was grounds for divorce. If she was not able to bear children or tried to leave home to engage in business, her husband could divorce her. Furthermore, a wife who was a "gadabout, . . . neglecting her house [and] humiliating her husband, shall be prosecuted" (Code of Hammurabi, No. 143).

Sexual relations were strictly regulated as well. Husbands, but not wives, were permitted sexual activity outside marriage. A wife and her lover caught committing adultery were pitched into the river, although if the husband pardoned his wife, the king could pardon the guilty man. Incest was strictly forbidden. If a father had incestuous relations with his daughter, he would be banished. Incest between a son and his mother resulted in both being burned.

Fathers ruled their children as well as their wives. Obedience was duly expected: "If a son has struck his father, he shall cut off his hand" (Code of Hammurabi, No. 195). If a son committed a serious enough offense, his father could disinherit him, although fathers were not permitted to disinherit their sons arbitrarily.

The Culture of Mesopotamia

A spiritual worldview was of fundamental importance to Mesopotamian culture. To the peoples of Mesopotamia,

The Code of Hammurabi

Although it is not the earliest Mesopotamian law code, Hammurabi's is the most complete. The law code emphasizes the principle of retribution ("an eye for an eye") and punishments that vary according to social status. Punishments could be severe. The following examples illustrate these concerns.

The Code of Hammurabi

25. If fire broke out in a free man's house and a free man, who went to extinguish it, cast his eye on the goods of the owner of the house and has appropriated the goods of the owner of the house, that free man shall be thrown into that fire.
129. If the wife of a free man has been caught while lying with another man, they shall bind them and throw them into the water. If the husband of the woman wishes to spare his wife, then the king in turn may spare his subject.
131. If a free man's wife was accused by her husband, but she was not caught while lying with another man, she shall make affirmation by god and return to her house.
196. If a free man has destroyed the eye of a member of the aristocracy, they shall destroy his eye.
198. If he has destroyed the eye of a commoner or broken the bone of a commoner, he shall pay one mina of silver.
199. If he has destroyed the eye of a free man's slave or broken the bone of a free man's slave, he shall pay one-half his value.
209. If a free man struck another free man's daughter and has caused her to have a miscarriage, he shall pay ten shekels of silver for her fetus.
210. If that woman has died, they shall put his daughter to death.
211. If by a blow he has caused a commoner's daughter to have a miscarriage, he shall pay five shekels of silver.
212. If that woman has died, he shall pay one-half mina of silver.
213. If he struck a free man's female slave and has caused her to have a miscarriage, he shall pay two shekels of silver.
214. If that female slave has died, he shall pay one-third mina of silver.

What do these points of law from the Code of Hammurabi reveal to you about Mesopotamian society?

Source: Pritchard, James B., ed., *Ancient Near Eastern Texts Relating to the Old Testament,* 3rd Edition with Supplement. Copyright © 1950, 1955, 1969, renewed 1978 by Princeton University Press. Reprinted by permission of Princeton University Press.

the gods were living realities who affected all aspects of life. It was crucial, therefore, that the correct hierarchies be observed. Leaders could prepare armies for war, but success really depended on a favorable relationship with the gods. This helps explain the importance of the priestly class and the reason why even the kings took great care to dedicate offerings and monuments to the gods.

THE IMPORTANCE OF RELIGION The physical environment had an obvious impact on the Mesopotamian view of the universe. Ferocious floods, heavy downpours, scorching winds, and oppressive humidity were all part of the Mesopotamian climate. These conditions and the resulting famines easily convinced Mesopotamians that this world was controlled by supernatural forces, which often were not kind or reliable. In the presence of nature, people in Mesopotamia could easily feel helpless, as this poem relates:

> *The rampant flood which no man can oppose,*
> *Which shakes the heavens and causes earth to tremble,*
> *In an appalling blanket folds mother and child,*
> *Beats down the canebrake's full luxuriant greenery,*
> *And drowns the harvest in its time of ripeness.*[3]

The Mesopotamians discerned cosmic rhythms in the universe and accepted its order but perceived that it was not completely safe because of the presence of willful, powerful cosmic powers that they identified with gods and goddesses.

With its numerous gods and goddesses animating all aspects of the universe, Mesopotamian religion was a form of **polytheism**. The four most important deities were An, god of the sky and hence the most important force in the universe; Enlil (EN-lil), god of wind; Enki (EN-kee), god of the earth, rivers, wells, and canals, as well as inventions and crafts; and Ninhursaga (nin-HUR-sah-guh), a goddess associated with soil, mountains, and vegetation, who came to be worshiped as a mother goddess, the "mother of all children," who manifested her power by giving birth to kings and conferring the royal insignia on them.

THE CULTIVATION OF NEW ARTS AND SCIENCES The realization of writing's great potential was another aspect of Mesopotamian culture. Around 3000 B.C.E., the Sumerians invented a **cuneiform** (kyoo-NEE-uh-form) ("wedge-shaped") system of writing. Using a reed stylus, they made wedge-shaped impressions on clay tablets, which were then baked or dried in the sun. Once dried, these tablets were virtually indestructible, and the several hundred thousand that have been found so far have been a valuable source of information for modern scholars. Sumerian writing evolved from pictures of concrete objects to simplified and stylized signs, leading eventually to a phonetic system that made possible the written expression of abstract ideas.

Writing was important because it enabled a society to keep records and maintain knowledge of previous practices and events (see the comparative illustration on p. 13). Writing also made it possible for people to communicate ideas in new ways, which is especially evident in the most famous piece of Mesopotamian literature, the *Epic of Gilgamesh*, an epic poem that records the exploits of a legendary king, Gilgamesh (GILL-guh-mesh), who embarks on a search for the secret of immortality. But his efforts fail; Gilgamesh remains mortal. The desire for immortality, one of humankind's great searches, ends in complete frustration. "Everlasting life," as this Mesopotamian epic makes clear, is only for the gods.

People in Mesopotamia also made outstanding achievements in mathematics and astronomy. In math, the Sumerians devised a number system based on 60, using combinations of 6 and 10 for practical solutions. Geometry was used to measure fields and erect buildings. In astronomy, the Sumerians made use of units of 60 and charted the heavenly constellations. Their calendar was based on twelve lunar months and was brought into harmony with the solar year by adding an extra month from time to time.

Egyptian Civilization: "The Gift of the Nile"

FOCUS QUESTIONS: What are the basic features of the three major periods of Egyptian history? What elements of continuity are evident in the three periods? What are their major differences?

"The Egyptian Nile," wrote one Arab traveler, "surpasses all the rivers of the world in sweetness of taste, in length of course and usefulness. No other river in the world can show such a continuous series of towns and villages along its banks." The Nile River was crucial to the development

Pictographic sign, c. 3100 B.C.E.									
Interpretation	star	?sun over horizon	?stream	ear of barley	bull's head	bowl	head + bowl	lower leg	?shrouded body
Cuneiform sign, c. 2400 B.C.E.									
Cuneiform sign c. 700 B.C.E. (turned through 90°)									
Phonetic value*	dingir, an	u$_4$, ud	a	še	gu$_4$	nig$_2$, ninda	ku$_2$	du, gin, gub	lu$_2$
Meaning	god, sky	day, sun	water, seed, son	barley	ox	food, bread	to eat	to walk, to stand	man

*Some signs have more than one phonetic value and some sounds are represented by more than one sign; for example, u$_4$ means the fourth sign with the phonetic value *u*.

From *Cultural Atlas of Mesopotamia & the Ancient Near East* by Michael Roaf/ Courtesy Andromeda Oxford Limited, Oxford, England

The Development of Cuneiform Writing. This chart shows the evolution of writing from pictographic signs around 3100 B.C.E. to cuneiform signs by about 700 B.C.E. Note that the sign for star came to mean "god" or "sky." Pictographic signs for head and bowl came eventually to mean "to eat" in their simplified cuneiform version.

Louvre, Paris//© Réunion des Musées Nationaux/Art Resource, NY

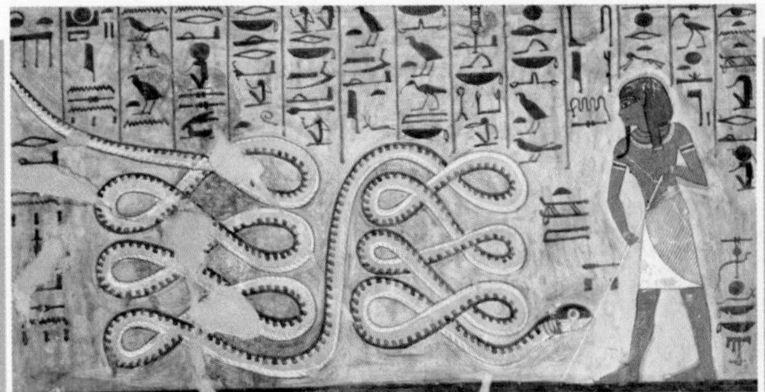

© Sandro Vannini/CORBIS

Kabah, Yucatan//© Erich Lessing/Art Resource, NY

COMPARATIVE ILLUSTRATION

Early Writing. Pictured at the left is the upper part of the cone of Uruinimgina, covered in cuneiform script from an early Sumerian dynasty. The first Egyptian writing was also pictographic, as shown in the hieroglyphs in th detail from the mural in the tomb of Ramesses I at the top right. In Central America, the Mayan civilization had a well-developed writing system, also based on hieroglyphs, as seen at the right in the text carved on a stone platform in front of the Palace of the Large Masks in Kabah, Mexico.

What common feature is evident in these early writing systems? How might you explain that?

of Egyptian civilization (see the box on p. 14). Egypt, like Mesopotamia, was a river valley civilization.

The Importance of Geography

The Nile is a unique river, beginning in the heart of Africa and coursing northward for thousands of miles. It is the longest river in the world. The Nile was responsible for creating an area several miles wide on both banks of the river that was fertile and capable of producing abundant harvests. The "miracle" of the Nile was its annual flooding. The river rose in the summer from rains in Central Africa, crested in Egypt in September and October, and left a deposit of silt that enriched the soil. The Egyptians called this fertile land the "Black Land" because it was dark in color from the silt and the crops that grew on it so densely. Beyond these narrow strips of fertile fields lay the deserts (the "Red Land"). About 100 miles before it empties into the Mediterranean, the river splits into two major branches, forming the delta, a triangular-shaped territory called Lower Egypt to distinguish it from Upper Egypt, the land upstream to the south (see Map 1.3). Egypt's important cities developed at the apex of the delta.

Unlike Mesopotamia's rivers, the flooding of the Nile was gradual and usually predictable, and the river itself was seen as life-enhancing, not life-threatening. Although a system of organized irrigation was still necessary, the small villages along the Nile could create such systems without the massive state intervention that was required in Mesopotamia. Egyptian civilization consequently tended to remain more rural, with many small population centers congregated along a narrow band on both sides of the Nile.

The surpluses of food that Egyptian farmers grew in the fertile Nile valley made Egypt prosperous. But the Nile also served as a unifying factor in Egyptian history. In ancient times, the Nile was the fastest way to travel through the land, making both transportation and communication easier. Winds from the north pushed sailboats south, and the current of the Nile carried them north.

The Significance of the Nile River and the Pharaoh

Two of the most important sources of life for the ancient Egyptians were the Nile River and the pharaoh. Egyptians perceived that the Nile made possible the abundant food that was a major source of their well-being. This *Hymn to the Nile*, probably from the nineteenth and twentieth dynasties in the New Kingdom, expresses the gratitude Egyptians felt for the Nile.

Hymn to the Nile

Hail to you, O Nile, that issues from the earth and comes to keep Egypt alive! . . .
He that waters the meadows which Re created, in order to keep every kid alive.
He that makes to drink the desert and the place distant from water: that is his dew coming down from heaven. . . .
The lord of fishes, he who makes the marsh-birds to go upstream. . . .
He who makes barley and brings emmer [wheat] into being, that he may make the temples festive.
If he is sluggish, then nostrils are stopped up, and everybody is poor. . . .
When he rises, then the land is in jubilation, then every belly is in joy, every backbone takes on laughter, and every tooth is exposed.
The bringer of good, rich in provisions, creator of all good, lord of majesty, sweet of fragrance. . . .
He who makes every beloved tree to grow, without lack of them.

The Egyptian king, or pharaoh, was viewed as a god and the absolute ruler of Egypt. His significance and the gratitude of the Egyptian people for his existence are evident in this hymn from the reign of Sesotris III (c. 1880–1840 B.C.E.).

Hymn to the Pharaoh

He has come unto us that he may carry away Upper Egypt; the double diadem [crown of Upper and and Lower Egypt] has rested on his head.
He has come unto us and has united the Two Lands; he has mingled the reed with the bee [symbols of Lower and Upper Egypt].
He has come unto us and has brought the Black Land under his sway; he has apportioned to himself the Red Land.
He has come unto us and has taken the Two Lands under his protection; he has given peace to the Two Riverbanks.
He has come unto us and has made Egypt to live; he has banished its suffering.
He has come unto us and has made the people to live; he has caused the throat of the subjects to breathe. . . .
He has come unto us and has done battle for his boundaries; he has delivered them that were robbed.

How do these two hymns underscore the importance of the Nile River and the institution of the pharaoh to Egyptian civilization?

Sources: Hymn to the Nile: Pritchard, James B., ed., *Ancient Near Eastern Texts Relating to the Old Testament*, 3rd Edition with Supplement. Copyright © 1950, 1955, 1969, renewed 1978 by Princeton University Press. Reprinted by permission of Princeton University Press. Hymn to the Pharaoh: Reprinted from *The Literature of the Ancient Egyptians*, Adolf Ermann. Copyright © 1927 by E. P. Dutton.

Unlike Mesopotamia, which was subject to constant invasion, Egypt had natural barriers that gave it some protection from invasion. These barriers included deserts to the west and east; cataracts (rapids) on the southern part of the Nile, which made defense relatively easy; and the Mediterranean Sea to the north. These barriers, however, were only effective when they were combined with Egyptian fortifications at strategic locations. Nor did barriers prevent the development of trade.

The regularity of the Nile floods and the relative isolation of the Egyptians created a sense of security and a feeling of changelessness. To the ancient Egyptians, when the Nile flooded each year, "the fields laugh and people's faces light up." Unlike people in Mesopotamia, Egyptians faced life with a spirit of confidence in the stability of things. Ancient Egyptian civilization was characterized by a remarkable degree of continuity for thousands of years.

The Importance of Religion

Religion, too, provided a sense of security and timelessness for the Egyptians. Actually, they had no word for religion because it was an inseparable element of the world order to which Egyptian society belonged. The Egyptians

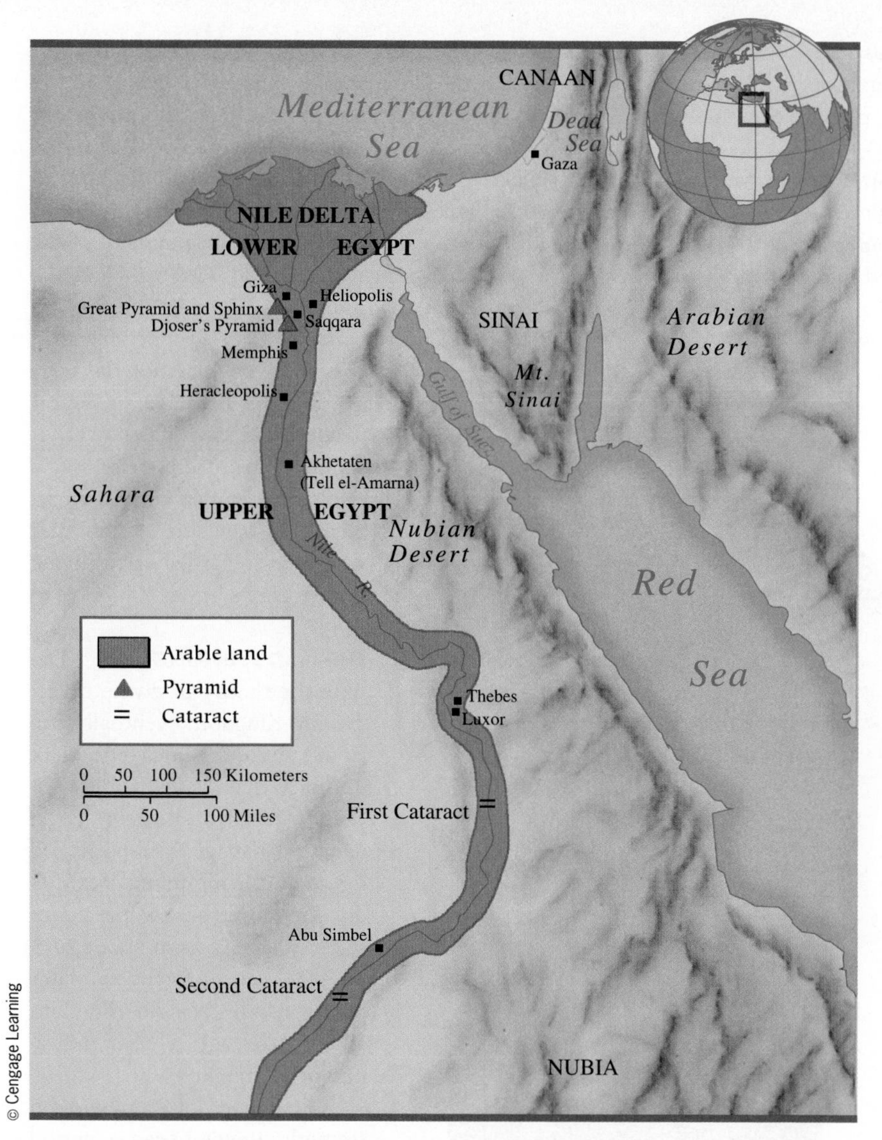

© Cengage Learning

MAP 1.3 Ancient Egypt. Egyptian civilization centered on the life-giving water and flood silts of the Nile River, with most of the population living in Lower Egypt, where the river splits to form the Nile delta. Most of the pyramids, built during the Old Kingdom, are clustered south and west of Cairo.

Q *How did the lands to the east and west of the river help to protect Egypt from invasion?*

were polytheistic and had a remarkable number of gods associated with heavenly bodies and natural forces, hardly surprising in view of the importance to Egypt's well-being of the sun, the river, and the fertile land along its banks. The sun was the source of life and hence worthy of worship. The sun god took on different forms and names, depending on his specific role. He was worshiped as Atum in human form and as Re (RAY), who had a human body but the head of a falcon. The Egyptian ruler took the title of "Son of Re," since he was seen as an earthly form of Re. River and land deities included Osiris (oh-SY-russ) and Isis (Y-sis) with their child Horus, who was related to the Nile and to the sun as well. Osiris became especially important as a symbol of resurrection or rebirth.

The Course of Egyptian History: The Old, Middle, and New Kingdoms

Modern historians have divided Egyptian history into three major periods known as the Old Kingdom, the Middle Kingdom, and the New Kingdom. They were periods of long-term stability characterized by strong monarchical authority, competent bureaucracy, freedom from invasion, much construction of temples and pyramids, and considerable intellectual and cultural activity. But between the periods of stability were eras of instability known as the Intermediate Periods.

THE OLD KINGDOM The history of Egypt begins around 3100 B.C.E. when King Menes united the villages of both Upper and Lower Egypt into a single kingdom and created the first Egyptian royal dynasty. Henceforth, the ruler would be called "king of Upper and Lower Egypt," and one of the royal crowns would be the Double Crown, combining the White Crown of Upper Egypt and the Red Crown of Lower Egypt. Just as the Nile served to unite Upper and Lower Egypt physically, the king served to unite the two areas politically (see the box on p. 14).

The Old Kingdom encompassed the third through sixth dynasties of Egyptian kings, lasting from around 2686 to 2180 B.C.E. It was an age of prosperity and splendor, made visible in the construction of the greatest and largest pyramids in Egypt's history. Kingship was a divine institution in ancient Egypt and formed part of a universal scheme: "What is the king of Upper and Lower Egypt? He is a god by whose dealings one lives, the father and mother of all men, alone by himself, without an equal."[4] In obeying their king, subjects helped maintain the cosmic order. A breakdown in royal power meant that citizens were offending divinity and weakening the universal structure. Among the various titles of Egyptian kings, that of **pharaoh** (originally meaning "great house" or "palace," referring to the royal palace) eventually came to be the most common.

Although theoretically absolute in their power, in practice Egyptian kings did not rule alone. By the fourth dynasty, a bureaucracy with regular procedures had developed. In time, Egypt was divided into provinces or *nomes*, as they were later called by the Greeks—twenty-two in Upper Egypt and twenty in Lower Egypt. A governor, called a *nomarch* by the Greeks, was head of each nome and was responsible to the king.

THE PYRAMIDS One of the great achievements of Egyptian civilization, the building of pyramids, occurred in the time of the Old Kingdom. Pyramids were built as part of a larger complex of buildings dedicated to the dead—in effect, a city of the dead. The area included a large pyramid for the king's burial, smaller pyramids for his family, and several mastabas (MAS-tuh-buhs), rectangular structures with flat roofs used as tombs for the pharaoh's noble officials.

The tombs were well prepared for their residents, their rooms furnished and stocked with numerous supplies, including chairs, boats, chests, weapons, games, dishes, and a variety of food. The Egyptians believed that human beings had two bodies—a physical one and a spiritual one, which they called the *ka*. If the physical body was properly preserved (by mummification) and the tomb was furnished with all the objects of regular life, the *ka* could return, surrounded by earthly comforts, and continue its life despite the death of the physical body.

The largest and most magnificent of all the pyramids was built under King Khufu (KOO-foo). Constructed at Giza around 2540 B.C.E., this famous Great Pyramid covers 13 acres, measures 756 feet at each side of its base, and stands 481 feet high (see the comparative illustration on p. 147 in Chapter 6). Its four sides are almost precisely oriented to the four points of the compass. The interior included a grand gallery to the burial chamber, which was built of granite with a lidless sarcophagus for the pharaoh's body. The Great Pyramid still stands as a visible symbol of the power of Egyptian kings of the Old Kingdom and the spiritual conviction that underlay Egyptian society. No pyramid built later ever matched its size or splendor. The pyramid was not only the king's tomb but also an important symbol of royal power. It could be seen from miles away, reminding people of the glory, might, and wealth of the ruler who was regarded as a living god on earth.

Museum of Fine Arts, Boston/© Erich Lessing/Art Resource, NY

Statue of King Menkaure and His Queen. During the Old Kingdom, kings (eventually called pharaohs) were regarded as gods, divine instruments who maintained the fundamental order and harmony of the universe and wielded absolute power. Seated and standing statues of kings were commonly placed in Egyptian royal tombs. Seen here are the standing portraits of King Menkaure and his queen, Khamerernebty, from the fourth dynasty. By artistic convention, rulers were shown in rigid poses, reflecting their timeless nature. Husband and wife show no emotion but are seen looking out into space.

THE MIDDLE KINGDOM Despite the theory of divine order, the Old Kingdom eventually collapsed, ushering in a period of disorder that lasted about 125 years. Finally, a new royal dynasty managed to pacify all Egypt and inaugurated the Middle Kingdom, a new period of stability lasting from about 2055 to 1650 B.C.E. Egyptians later portrayed the Middle Kingdom as a golden age, a clear indication of its stability.

As evidence of its newfound strength, Egypt began a period of expansion. Lower Nubia was conquered, and fortresses were built to protect the new southern frontier. The government also sent armies into Canaan and Syria, although they did not remain there. Pharaohs also sent traders to Kush, Syria, Mesopotamia, and Crete.

The Middle Kingdom was characterized by a new concern of the pharaohs for the people. In the Old Kingdom, the pharaoh had been viewed as an inaccessible god-king. Now he was portrayed as the shepherd of his people with the responsibility to build public works and provide for the public welfare. Pharaohs of the Middle Kingdom undertook a number of helpful projects. The draining of swampland in the Nile delta provided thousands of acres of new farmland.

DISORDER AND A NEW ORDER: THE NEW KINGDOM The Middle Kingdom came to an end around 1650 B.C.E. with the invasion of Egypt by a people from western Asia known to the Egyptians as the Hyksos (HIK-sohs). The Hyksos used horse-drawn war chariots and overwhelmed the Egyptian soldiers, who fought from donkey carts. For almost a hundred years, the Hyksos ruled much of Egypt, but the conquered took much from their conquerors. From the Hyksos, the Egyptians learned to use bronze in making new farming tools and weapons. They also mastered the military skills of the Hyksos, especially the use of horse-drawn war chariots.

Eventually, a new line of pharaohs—the eighteenth dynasty—made use of the new weapons to throw off Hyksos domination, reunite Egypt, establish the New Kingdom (c. 1550–1070 B.C.E.), and launch the Egyptians along a new militaristic path. During the period of the New Kingdom, Egypt created an empire and became the most powerful state in the Middle East.

Massive wealth aided the power of the New Kingdom pharaohs. The Egyptian rulers showed their wealth by building new temples. Queen Hatshepsut (hat-SHEP-soot) (c. 1503–1480 B.C.E.), one of the first women to become pharaoh in her own right, built a great temple at Deir el Bahri (dayr ahl BAH-ree) near Thebes. Hatshepsut was succeeded by her nephew, Thutmosis (thoot-MOH-suss) III (c. 1480–1450 B.C.E.), who led seventeen military campaigns into Syria and Canaan and even reached the Euphrates River. Egyptian forces occupied Canaan and Syria and also moved westward into Libya.

The eighteenth dynasty was not without its troubles, however. Amenhotep (ah-mun-HOH-tep) IV (c. 1364–1347 B.C.E.) introduced the worship of Aten, god of the sun disk, as the sole god (see the box on p. 18) and pursued his worship with great enthusiasm. Changing his own name to Akhenaten (ah-kuh-NAH-tun) ("Servant of Aten"), the pharaoh closed the temples of other gods. Nevertheless, his attempt at religious change failed. Egyptians were unwilling to abandon their traditional ways and beliefs, especially since they saw the destruction of the old gods as subversive of the very cosmic order on which Egypt's survival and continuing prosperity depended. At the same time, Akhenaten's preoccupation with his religious revolution caused him to ignore foreign affairs and led to the loss of both Syria and Canaan. Akhenaten's changes were soon undone after his death by the boy-pharaoh Tutankhamun (too-tang-KAH-mun), who restored the old gods. The eighteenth dynasty itself came to an end in 1333.

CHRONOLOGY The Egyptians	
Early Dynastic Period (Dynasties 1–2)	c. 3100–2686 B.C.E.
Old Kingdom (Dynasties 3–6)	c. 2686–2180 B.C.E.
First Intermediate Period (Dynasties 7–10)	c. 2180–2055 B.C.E.
Middle Kingdom (Dynasties 11–12)	c. 2055–1650 B.C.E.
Second Intermediate Period (Dynasties 13–17)	c. 1650–1550 B.C.E.
New Kingdom (Dynasties 18–20)	c. 1550–1070 B.C.E.
Postempire (Dynasties 21–31)	c. 1070–30 B.C.E.

The nineteenth dynasty managed to restore Egyptian power one more time. Under Ramesses (RAM-uh-seez) II (c. 1279–1213 B.C.E.), the Egyptians regained control of Canaan, but new invasions in the thirteenth century by the "Sea Peoples," as the Egyptians called them, destroyed Egyptian power in Canaan and drove the Egyptians back within their old frontiers. The days of Egyptian empire were ended, and the New Kingdom itself expired with the end of the twentieth dynasty in 1070. For the next thousand years, despite periodic revivals of strength, Egypt was dominated by Libyans, Nubians, Persians, and finally Macedonians after the conquest of Alexander the Great (see Chapter 4). In the first century B.C.E., Egypt became a province in Rome's mighty empire.

Society and Daily Life in Ancient Egypt

For thousands of years, Egyptian society managed to maintain a simple structure, organized along hierarchical lines with the god-king at the top. The king was surrounded by an upper class of nobles and priests who participated in the elaborate rituals of life that surrounded the pharaoh. This ruling class ran the government and managed its own landed estates, which provided much of its wealth.

Below the upper classes were merchants and artisans. Merchants engaged in an active trade up and down the Nile as well as in town and village markets. Some merchants also engaged in international trade; they were sent by the king to Crete and Syria, where they obtained wood and other products. Expeditions traveled into Nubia for ivory and down the Red Sea to Punt for incense and spices. Eventually, trade links were established between ports on the Red Sea and lands as far away as the Indonesian archipelago. Egyptian artisans made an incredible variety of well-built and beautiful goods: stone dishes; painted boxes made of clay; wooden

OPPOSING VIEWPOINTS

Akhenaten's *Hymn to Aten* and Psalm 104 of the Hebrew Bible

Amenhotep IV, more commonly known as Akhenaten, created a religious upheaval in Egypt by introducing the worship of Aten, god of the sun disk, as the chief god. Akhenaten's reverence for Aten is evident in this hymn. Some authorities have noted a similarity in spirit and wording to Psalm 104 of the Old Testament. In fact, some scholars have argued that there might be a connection between the two.

Hymn to Aten

Your rays suckle every meadow.
When you rise, they live, they grow for you.
You make the seasons in order to rear all that you have made,
The winter to cool them,
And the heat that they may taste you.
You have made the distant sky in order to rise therein,
In order to see all that you do make.
While you were alone,
Rising in your form as the living Aten,
Appearing, shining, withdrawing or approaching,
You made millions of forms of yourself alone.

Cities, towns, fields, road, and river—
Every eye beholds you over against them,
For you are the Aten of the day over the earth. . . .
The world came into being by your hand,
According as you have made them.
When you have risen they live,
When you set they die.
You are lifetime your own self,
For one lives only through you.
Eyes are fixed on beauty until you set.
All work is laid aside when you set in the west.
But when you rise again,
Everything is made to flourish for the king. . . .
Since you did found the earth
And raise them up for your son,
Who came forth from your body: the King of Upper and Lower Egypt, . . . Akh-en-Aten, . . . and the
Chief Wife of the King . . . Nefert-iti, living and youthful forever and ever.

Psalm 104:19–25, 27–30

The moon marks off the seasons,
and the sun knows when to go down.
You bring darkness, it becomes night,
and all the beasts of the forest prowl.

The lions roar for their prey
and seek their food from God.

The sun rises, and they steal away;
they return and lie down in their dens.

Then man goes out to his work,
to his labor until evening.

How many are your works, O Lord!
In wisdom you made them all;
the earth is full of your creatures.

There is the sea, vast and spacious,
teeming with creatures beyond number—
living things both large and small. . . .

These all look to you
to give them their food at the proper time.

When you give it to them,
they gather it up;
when you open your hand,
they are satisfied with good things.

When you hide your face,
they are terrified;
when you take away their breath,
they die and return to the dust.

When you send your Spirit,
they are created,
and you renew the face of the earth.

What are the similarities between Akhenaten's Hymn to Aten and Psalm 104 of the Hebrew Bible? How do you explain the similarities? What are the significant differences between the two, and what do they tell you about the differences between the religion of the Egyptians and the religion of ancient Israel?

Sources: Hymn to Aten: Pritchard, James B., ed., *Ancient Near Eastern Texts Relating to the Old Testament*, 3rd Edition with Supplement. Copyright © 1950, 1955, 1969, renewed 1978 by Princeton University Press. Reprinted by permission of Princeton University Press. Psalm 104:19–25, 27–30: Reprinted from the Holy Bible, New International Version.

furniture; gold, silver, and copper tools and containers; paper and rope made of papyrus; and linen clothing.

By far, the largest number of people in Egypt simply worked the land. In theory, the king owned all the land but granted portions of it to his subjects. Large sections were in the possession of nobles and the temple complexes. Most of the lower classes were serfs or common people, bound to the land, who cultivated the estates. They paid taxes in the form of crops to the king, nobles, and priests; lived in small villages or towns; and provided military service and forced labor for building projects.

Ancient Egyptians had a very positive attitude toward daily life on earth. They married young (girls at twelve, boys at fourteen) and established a home and family. The husband was master in the house, but wives were respected and in charge of the household and education of the children. From a book of wise sayings (which the Egyptians called "instructions") came this advice: "If you are a man of standing, you should found your household and love your wife at home as is fitting. Fill her belly; clothe her back. . . . Make her heart glad as long as you live."[5] Women's property and inheritance remained in their hands, even in marriage. Although most careers and public offices were closed to women, some did operate businesses. Peasant women worked long hours in the fields and at numerous domestic tasks. Upper-class women could function as priestesses, and four queens even became pharaohs in their own right.

The Culture of Egypt: Art and Writing

Commissioned by kings or nobles for use in temples or tombs, Egyptian art was largely functional. Wall paintings and statues of gods and kings in temples served a spiritual purpose. They were an integral part of the performance of ritual, which was thought necessary to preserve the cosmic order and hence the well-being of Egypt. Likewise, the mural scenes and sculptured figures found in the tombs had a specific function: they were supposed to assist the journey of the deceased into the afterworld.

Egyptian art was also formulaic. Artists and sculptors were expected to observe a strict canon of proportions that determined both form and presentation. This canon gave Egyptian art a distinctive appearance for thousands of years. Especially characteristic was the convention of combining the profile, semiprofile, and frontal views of the human body in relief work and painting in order to represent each part of the body accurately. This fashion created an art that was highly stylized yet still allowed distinctive features to be displayed.

Writing emerged in Egypt during the first two dynasties. The Greeks later labeled Egyptian writing **hieroglyphics** (HY-uh-roh-glif-iks), meaning "priest carvings" or "sacred writings." Hieroglyphs were sacred characters used as picture signs that depicted objects and had a sacred value at the same time. Although hieroglyphs were later simplified for writing purposes into two scripts, they never developed into an alphabet. Egyptian hieroglyphs were initially carved in stone, but later the two simplified scripts were written on papyrus, paper made from the reeds that grew along the Nile.

The Spread of Egyptian Influence: Nubia

The civilization of Egypt had an impact on other peoples in the lands of the eastern Mediterranean. Egyptian products have been found in Crete and Cretan products in Egypt (see Chapter 4). Egyptian influence is also evident in early Greek statues. The Egyptians also had an impact to the south in sub-Saharan Africa in Nubia (the northern part of modern Sudan). In fact, some archaeologists have

Bibliothèque, Louvre, Paris//© Erich Lessing/Art Resource, NY

Nubians in Egypt. During the New Kingdom, Egypt expanded to include Canaan and Syria to the north and the kingdom of Nubia to the south. Nubia had emerged as an African kingdom around 2300 B.C.E. Shown here is a fourteenth-century B.C.E. painting from an Egyptian official's tomb. Nubians are arriving in Egypt with bags and rings of gold. Nubia was a major source of gold for the Egyptians.

recently suggested that the African kingdom of Nubia may have arisen even before the kingdoms of Egypt.

It is clear that contacts between the upper and lower Nile had been established by the late third millennium B.C.E., when Egyptian merchants traveled to Nubia to obtain ivory, ebony, frankincense, and leopard skins. A few centuries later, Nubia had become an Egyptian tributary. At the end of the second millennium B.C.E., Nubia profited from the disintegration of the Egyptian New Kingdom to become the independent state of Kush. Egyptian influence continued, however, as Kushite culture borrowed extensively from Egypt, including religious beliefs, the practice of interring kings in pyramids, and hieroglyphs.

But in the first millennium B.C.E., Kush also had a direct impact on Egypt. During the second half of the eighth century B.C.E., Kushite monarchs took control of Egypt and founded the twenty-fifth dynasty of Egyptian rulers. It was not until 663 B.C.E. that the last Kushite ruler was expelled from Egypt. During this period, the Kushite rulers of Egypt even aided the Israelites in their struggle with the Assyrians (see "The Children of Israel" later in this chapter).

Although its economy was probably founded primarily on agriculture and animal husbandry, Kush developed into a major trading state in Africa that endured for hundreds of years. Its commercial activities were stimulated by the discovery of iron ore in a floodplain near the river at Meroë (MER-oh-ee *or* MER-uh-wee). Strategically located at the point where a land route across the desert to the south intersected the Nile River, Meroë eventually became the capital of the state. In addition to iron products, Kush and Meroë supplied goods from Central and East Africa, notably ivory, gold, ebony, and slaves, to the Roman Empire, Arabia, and India.

New Centers of Civilization

FOCUS QUESTIONS: What was the significance of the Indo-Europeans? How did Judaism differ from the religions of Mesopotamia and Egypt?

Our story of civilization so far has been dominated by Mesopotamia and North Africa. But significant developments were also taking place on the fringes of these civilizations. Agriculture had spread into the Balkan peninsula of Europe by 6500 B.C.E., and by 4000 B.C.E., Neolithic peoples in southern France, central Europe, and the coastal regions of the Mediterranean had domesticated animals and begun to farm largely on their own.

One outstanding feature of late Neolithic Europe was the erection of **megaliths** (*megalith* is Greek for "large stone"). The first megalithic structures were built around 4000 B.C.E., more than a thousand years before the great pyramids were built in Egypt. Between 3200 and 1500 B.C.E., standing stones, placed in circles or lined up in rows, were erected throughout the British

© Steve Vidler/SuperStock

Stonehenge. By far the most famous megalithic construction, Stonehenge in England consists of a series of concentric rings of standing stones. Its construction sometime between 2100 and 1900 B.C.E. was no small accomplishment. The eighty bluestones used at Stonehenge weighed 4 tons each and were transported to the site from 135 miles away. Like other megalithic structures, Stonehenge indicates a remarkable awareness of astronomy on the part of its builders, as well as an elaborate coordination of workers.

Isles and northwestern France. Other megalithic constructions have been found as far north as Scandinavia and as far south as the islands of Corsica, Sardinia, and Malta. Archaeologists have demonstrated that the stone circles were used as observatories not only to detect such simple astronomical phenomena as the midwinter and midsummer sunrises but also to make such sophisticated observations as the major and minor standstills of the moon.

Nomadic Peoples: Impact of the Indo-Europeans

On the fringes of civilization lived nomadic peoples who depended on hunting and gathering, herding, and sometimes a bit of farming for their survival. Most important were the pastoral nomads who on occasion overran civilized communities and forged their own empires. Pastoral nomads domesticated animals for both food and clothing and moved along regular migratory routes to provide steady sources of nourishment for their animals.

The Indo-Europeans were among the most important nomadic peoples. These groups spoke languages derived from a single parent tongue. Indo-European languages include Greek, Latin, Persian, Sanskrit, and the Germanic languages (see Table 1.2). The original Indo-European-speaking peoples were probably based somewhere in the steppe region north of the Black Sea or in southwestern Asia, in modern Iran or Afghanistan, but around 2000 B.C.E., they began to move into Europe, India, and western Asia. The domestication of horses and the importation of the wheel and wagon from Mesopotamia facilitated the Indo-European migrations to other lands.

One group of Indo-Europeans who moved into Asia Minor and Anatolia (modern Turkey) around 1750 B.C.E. coalesced with the native peoples to form the Hittite kingdom, with its capital at Hattusha (Bogazköy in modern Turkey). Between 1600 and 1200 B.C.E., the Hittites created their own empire in western Asia and even threatened the power of the Egyptians. The Hittites were the first of the Indo-European peoples to use iron, enabling them to construct weapons that were stronger and cheaper to make because of the widespread availability of iron ore.

Territorial States in Western Asia: The Phoenicians

During its heyday, the Hittite Empire was one of the great powers in western Asia. But around 1200 B.C.E., new waves of invading Indo-European peoples destroyed the Hittite empire. The destruction of the Hittite kingdom and the weakening of Egypt around 1200 B.C.E. left no dominant powers in western Asia, allowing a patchwork of petty kingdoms and city-states to emerge, especially in the area of Syria and Canaan. The Phoenicians (fuh-NEE-shunz) were one of these peoples.

TABLE 1.2 Some Indo-European Languages

SUBFAMILY	LANGUAGES
Indo-Iranian	*Sanskrit*, Persian
Balto-Slavic	Russian, Serbo-Croatian, Czech, Polish, Lithuanian
Hellenic	Greek
Italic	*Latin*, Romance languages (French, Italian, Spanish, Portuguese, Romanian)
Celtic	Irish, Gaelic
Germanic	Swedish, Danish, Norwegian, German, Dutch, English

NOTE: Languages in italic type are no longer spoken.

A Semitic-speaking people (see Table 1.1 on p. 10), the Phoenicians lived in the area of Canaan along the Mediterranean coast on a narrow band of land 120 miles long. Their newfound political independence after the demise of Hittite and Egyptian power helped the Phoenicians expand the trade that was already the foundation of their prosperity. The Phoenicians improved their ships and became great international sea traders. They charted new routes, not only in the Mediterranean but also in the Atlantic Ocean, where they sailed north to Britain and south along the west coast of Africa. The Phoenicians established a number of colonies in the western Mediterranean; Carthage, the Phoencians' most famous colony, was located on the north coast of Africa.

Culturally, the Phoenicians are best known as transmitters. Instead of using pictographs or signs to represent whole words and syllables as the Mesopotamians and Egyptians did, the Phoenicians simplified their writing by using twenty-two different signs to represent the sounds of their speech. These twenty-two characters or letters could be used to spell out all the words in the Phoenician language. Although the Phoenicians were not the only people to invent an alphabet, theirs would have special significance because it was eventually passed on to the Greeks. From the ancient Greek alphabet came the modern Greek, Roman, and Cyrillic alphabets in use today.

The "Children of Israel"

To the south of the Phoenicians lived another group of Semitic-speaking people known as the Israelites. Although they were a minor factor in the politics of the region, their **monotheism**—belief in one God—later influenced both Christianity and Islam and flourished as a world religion in its own right. The Israelites had a tradition concerning their origins and history that was eventually written down as part of the Hebrew Bible, known to

Christians as the Old Testament. Many scholars today doubt that the biblical account reflects the true history of the early Israelites. They argue that the early books of the Bible, written centuries after the events described, preserve only what the Israelites came to believe about themselves and that recent archaeological evidence often contradicts the details of the biblical account. What is generally agreed, however, is that between 1200 and 1000 B.C.E., the Israelites emerged as a distinct group of people, possibly organized in tribes or a league of tribes.

WAS THERE A UNITED KINGDOM OF ISRAEL? According to the Hebrew Bible, the Israelites established a united kingdom of Israel beginning with Saul and David. By the time of Solomon (c. 970–930 B.C.E.), the son of David, the Israelites had supposedly established control over all of Canaan and made Jerusalem the capital of a united kingdom. According to the biblical account, Solomon did even more to strengthen royal power. He expanded the government and army and extended the trading activities of the Israelites. Solomon is portrayed as a great builder, who was responsible for the Temple in the city of Jerusalem. The Israelites viewed the Temple as the symbolic center of their religion and hence of the kingdom of Israel itself. Under Solomon, ancient Israel supposedly reached the height of its power

The accuracy of this biblical account of the united kingdom of Israel under Saul, David, and Solomon has recently been challenged by a new generation of archaeologists and historians. Although they mostly accept Saul, David, and Solomon as historical figures, they view them more as chief warlords than as kings. If a kingdom of Israel did exist during these years, it was not as powerful or as well organized as the Hebrew Bible says. Furthermore, they argue, there is no definitive archaeological evidence that Solomon built the Temple in Jerusalem.

THE KINGDOMS OF ISRAEL AND JUDAH There may or not have been a united kingdom of Israel, but after the death of Solomon, tensions between northern and southern tribes in Israel led to the establishment of two separate kingdoms—the kingdom of Israel, composed of the ten northern tribes, with its capital eventually at Samaria, and the kingdom of Judah, consisting of two southern tribes, with its capital at Jerusalem (see Map 1.4). In 722 or 721 B.C.E., the Assyrians (uh-SEER-ee-unz) overran the kingdom of Israel and deported many Israelites to other parts of the Assyrian Empire. These dispersed Israelites (the "ten lost tribes") merged with neighboring peoples and gradually lost their identity.

The southern kingdom of Judah managed to retain its independence for a while as Assyrian power declined, but a new enemy soon appeared on the horizon. The Chaldeans (kal-DEE-unz) defeated Assyria, conquered

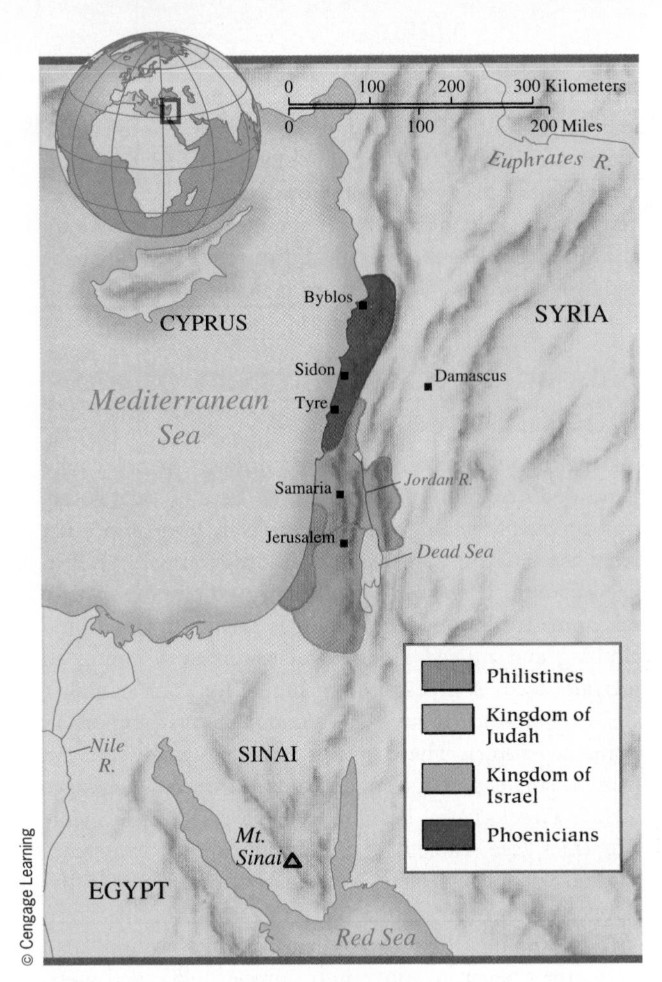

© Cengage Learning

MAP 1.4 The Israelites and Their Neighbors in the First Millennium B.C.E. After the death of Solomon, tensions between the tribes in Israel led to the creation of two kingdoms—a northern kingdom of Israel and a southern kingdom of Judah. With power divided, the Israelites could not resist invasions that dispersed many of them from Canaan. Some, such as the "ten lost tribes," never returned. Others were sent to Babylon but were later allowed to return under the rule of the Persians.

Q *Why was Israel more vulnerable to the Assyrian Empire than Judah was?*

the kingdom of Judah, and completely destroyed Jerusalem in 586 B.C.E. Many upper-class people from Judah were deported to Babylon; the memory of their exile is still evoked in the stirring words of Psalm 137:

> *By the rivers of Babylon, we sat and wept when we remembered Zion. . . .*
> *How can we sing the songs of the Lord while in a foreign land?*
> *If I forget you, O Jerusalem, may my right hand forget its skill.*
> *May my tongue cling to the roof of my mouth if I do not remember you,*
> *If I do not consider Jerusalem my highest joy.*[6]

But the Babylonian captivity of the people of Judah did not last. A new set of conquerors, the Persians, destroyed the Chaldean kingdom and allowed the people of Judah to return to Jerusalem and rebuild their city and Temple. The revived kingdom of Judah remained under Persian control until the conquests of Alexander the Great in the fourth century B.C.E. The people of Judah survived, eventually becoming known as the Jews and giving their name to Judaism, the religion of Yahweh (YAH-way), the Israelite God.

THE SPIRITUAL DIMENSIONS OF ISRAEL According to the Hebrew conception, there is but one God called Yahweh, who created the world and everything in it. This omnipotent creator was not removed from the life he had created, but was a just and good God who expected goodness from his people. If they did not obey his will, they would be punished. But he was primarily a God of mercy and love: "The Lord is gracious and compassionate, slow to anger and rich in love. The Lord is good to all; he has compassion on all he has made."[7] Each individual could have a personal relationship with this being.

Three aspects of the Hebrew religious tradition had special significance: the covenant, the law, and the prophets. The Israelites believed that during the exodus from Egypt, when Moses, according to biblical tradition, led his people out of bondage and into the promised land, God made a covenant or contract with the tribes of Israel, who believed that Yahweh had spoken to them through Moses. The Israelites promised to obey Yahweh and follow his law. In return, Yahweh promised to take special care of his chosen people, "a peculiar treasure unto me above all people."

This covenant between Yahweh and his chosen people could be fulfilled, however, only by obedience to the law of God. Most important were the ethical concerns that stood at the center of the law. These commandments spelled out God's ideals of behavior: "You shall not murder. You shall not commit adultery. You shall not steal."[8] True freedom consisted of following God's moral standards voluntarily. If people chose to ignore the good, then suffering and evil would follow.

The Israelites believed that certain religious teachers, called prophets, were sent by God to serve as his voice to his people. The golden age of prophecy began in the mid-eighth century B.C.E. and continued during the time when the people of Israel and Judah were threatened by Assyrian and Chaldean conquerors. These "men of God" went through the land warning the Israelites that they had failed to keep God's commandments and would be punished for breaking the covenant: "I will punish you for all your iniquities."

Out of the words of the prophets came new concepts that enriched the Jewish tradition. The prophets embraced a concern for all humanity. All nations would someday come to the God of Israel: "All the earth shall worship you." This vision encompassed the establishment of peace for all the nations of the world. In the words of the prophet Isaiah: "He will judge between the nations and will settle disputes for many people. They will beat their swords into plowshares and their spears into pruning hooks. Nation will not take up sword against nation, nor will they train for war anymore."[9]

Although the prophets developed a sense of universalism, the demands of the Jewish religion (the need to obey God) eventually encouraged a separation between the Jews and their non-Jewish neighbors. Unlike most other peoples of the Middle East, the Jews could not simply be amalgamated into a community by accepting the gods of their conquerors and their neighbors. To remain faithful to the demands of their God, they might even have to refuse loyalty to political leaders.

The Rise of New Empires

FOCUS QUESTION: What methods and institutions did the Assyrians and Persians use to amass and maintain their respective empires?

Small and independent states could exist only as long as no larger state dominated western Asia. New empires soon arose, however, and conquered vast stretches of the ancient world.

The Assyrian Empire

The first of these empires was formed in Assyria, located on the upper Tigris River. The Assyrians were a Semitic-speaking people who exploited the use of iron weapons to establish an empire that by 700 B.C.E. included Mesopotamia, parts of the Iranian plateau, sections of Asia Minor, Syria, Canaan, and Egypt down to Thebes (see Map 1.5). But in less than a hundred years, internal strife and resentment of Assyrian rule led subject peoples to rebel against it. The capital city of Nineveh fell to a coalition of Chaldeans and Medes in 612 B.C.E., and in 605 B.C.E., the rest of the empire was finally divided between the two powers.

At its height, the Assyrian Empire was ruled by kings whose power was considered absolute. The Assyrians developed an efficient system of communication to administer their empire more effectively. They established a network of staging posts throughout the empire and used relays of horses (mules or donkeys in the mountains) to carry messages.

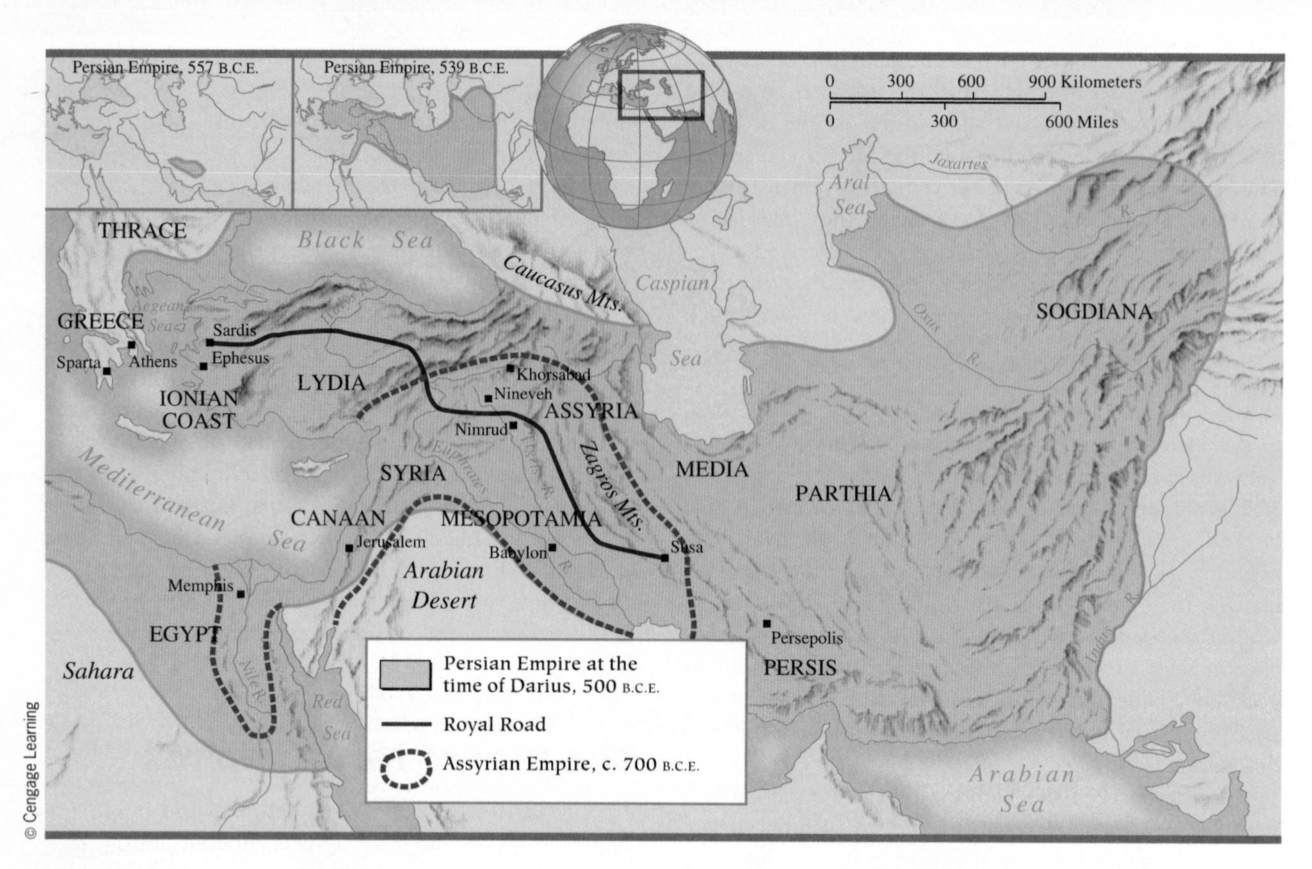

© Cengage Learning

MAP 1.5 The Assyrian and Persian Empires. Cyrus the Great united the Persians and led them in a successful conquest of much of the Near East, including most of the lands of the Assyrian Empire. By the time of Darius, the Persian Empire was the largest the world had yet seen.

Q *How did Persian policies attempt to overcome the difficulties of governing far-flung provinces?*

The Assyrians were outstanding conquerors. Over many years of practice, they developed effective military leaders and fighters. The Assyrian army was large, well organized, and disciplined. It included a standing army of infantry as its core, accompanied by cavalry and horse-drawn war chariots that were used as mobile platforms for shooting arrows. Moreover, the Assyrians had the first large armies equipped with iron weapons.

Another factor in the effectiveness of the Assyrian military machine was its use of terror as an instrument of warfare (see the box on p. 25). As a matter of regular policy, the Assyrians laid waste to the land in which they were fighting, smashing dams, looting and destroying towns, setting crops on fire, and cutting down trees, particularly fruit trees. They were especially known for committing atrocities on their captives. King Ashurnasirpal (ah-shur-NAH-zur-pahl) recorded this account of his treatment of prisoners:

> 3,000 of their combat troops I felled with weapons. . . . Many of the captives taken from them I burned in a fire. Many I took alive; from some of these I cut off their hands to the wrist, from others I cut off their noses, ears and fingers; I put out the eyes of many of the soldiers. . . . I burned their young men and women to death.[10]

The Persian Empire

After the collapse of the Assyrian Empire, the Chaldeans, under their king Nebuchadnezzar (neb-uh-kud-NEZZ-ur) II (605–562 B.C.E.), made Babylonia the leading state in western Asia. Nebuchadnezzar rebuilt Babylon as the center of his empire, giving it a reputation as one of the great cities of the ancient world. But the splendor of Chaldean Babylonia proved to be short-lived when Babylon fell to the Persians in 539 B.C.E.

The Persians were an Indo-European-speaking people who lived in southwestern Iran. Primarily nomadic, the Persians were organized in tribes until the Achaemenid (ah-KEE-muh-nud) dynasty managed to unify them. One of the dynasty's members, Cyrus (559–530 B.C.E.), created a powerful Persian state that stretched from Asia Minor in the west to western India in the east. In 539, Cyrus entered Meospotamia and captured Babylon. His

The Assyrian Military Machine

The Assyrians achieved a reputation for possessing a mighty military machine. They were able to use a variety of military tactics and were successful whether they were waging guerrilla warfare, fighting set battles, or laying siege to cities. In these three selections, Assyrian kings boast of their military conquests.

King Sennacherib (704–681 B.C.E.) Describes a Battle with the Elamites in 691

At the command of the god Ashur, the great Lord, I rushed upon the enemy like the approach of a hurricane. . . . I put them to rout and turned them back. I transfixed the troops of the enemy with javelins and arrows. . . . I cut their throats like sheep. . . . My prancing steeds, trained to harness, plunged into their welling blood as into a river; the wheels of my battle chariot were bespattered with blood and filth. I filled the plain with the corpses of their warriors like herbage. . . . As to the sheikhs of the Chaldeans, panic from my onslaught overwhelmed them like a demon. They abandoned their tents and fled for their lives, crushing the corpses of their troops as they went. . . . In their terror they passed scalding urine and voided their excrement into their chariots.

King Sennacherib Describes His Siege of Jerusalem in 701

As to Hezekiah, the Jew, he did not submit to my yoke, I laid siege to 46 of his strong cities, walled forts, and the countless small villages in their vicinity, and conquered them by means of well-stamped earth-ramps, and battering-rams brought thus near to the walls combined with the attack by foot soldiers, using mines, breaches, as well as sapper work. I drove out of them 200,150 people, young and old, male and female, horses, mules, donkeys, camels, big and small cattle beyond counting, and considered them booty. Himself I made a prisoner in Jerusalem, his royal residence, like a bird in a cage. I surrounded him with earthwork in order to molest those who were leaving his city's gate.

King Ashurbanipal (669–627 B.C.E.) Describes His Treatment of Conquered Babylon

I tore out the tongues of those whose slanderous mouths had uttered blasphemies against my god Ashur and had plotted against me, his god-fearing prince; I defeated them completely. The others, I smashed alive with the very same statues of protective deities with which they had smashed my own grandfather Sennacherib—now finally as a belated burial sacrifice for his soul. I fed their corpses, cut into small pieces, to dogs, pigs, . . . vultures, the birds of the sky, and also to the fish of the ocean. After I had performed this and thus made quiet again the hearts of the great gods, my lords, I removed the corpses of those whom the pestilence had felled, whose leftovers after the dogs and pigs had fed on them were obstructing the streets, filling the places of Babylon, and of those who had lost their lives through the terrible famine.

Based on their own descriptions, what did Assyrian kings believe was important for military success? Do you think their accounts may be exaggerated? Why?

Sources: King Sennacherib (704–681 B.C.E.) Describes a Battle with the Elamites in 691: Reprinted with permission from Pan Macmillan, London, from *The Might That Was Assyria* by H. W. Saggs. Copyright © 1984 by Sidgwick & Jackson Limited. King Sennacherib Describes His Siege of Jerusalem in 701 and King Ashurbanipal (669–627 B.C.E.) Describes His Treatment of Conquered Babylon: Pritchard, James B., ed., *Ancient Near Eastern Texts Relating to the Old Testament*, 3rd Edition with Supplement. Copyright © 1950, 1955, 1969, renewed 1978 by Princeton University Press. Reprinted by permission of Princeton University Press.

treatment of Babylonia showed remarkable restraint and wisdom. Babylonia was made into a Persian province, but many government officials were kept in their positions. Cyrus also issued an edict permitting the Jews, who had been brought to Babylon in the sixth century B.C.E., to return to Jerusalem with their sacred temple objects and to rebuild their Temple as well.

To his contemporaries, Cyrus the Great deserved to be called the Great. He must have been an unusual ruler for his time, a man who demonstrated considerable wisdom and compassion in the conquest and organization of his empire. Unlike the Assyrian rulers of an earlier empire, he had a reputation for mercy. Medes, Jews, and Babylonians all accepted him as their legitimate ruler.

Cyrus's successors extended the territory of the Persian Empire. His son Cambyses (kam-BY-seez) (530–522 B.C.E.) undertook a successful invasion of Egypt. Darius (duh-RY-uss) (521–486 B.C.E.) added a new Persian province in western India that extended to the Indus River and then moved into Europe, conquering Thrace and

Apadana, Persepolis, Iran/© Gianni Dagli Orti/The Art Archive at Art Resource, NY

Darius, the Great King. Darius ruled the Persian Empire from 521 to 486 B.C.E. He is shown here on his throne in Persepolis, a new capital city that he built. In his right hand, Darius holds the royal staff. In his left hand, he grasps a lotus blossom with two buds, a symbol of royalty.

creating the largest empire the world had yet seen. His contact with the Greeks led him to undertake an invasion of the Greek mainland (see Chapter 4).

CIVIL ADMINISTRATION AND THE MILITARY Darius strengthened the basic structure of the Persian government by creating a more rational division of the empire into twenty provinces called satrapies. Each **satrapy** (SAY-truh-pee) was ruled by a governor or satrap (SAY-trap), literally a "protector of the kingdom." Satraps collected tributes, were responsible for justice and security, raised military levies for the royal army, and normally commanded the military forces within their satrapies. In terms of real power, the satraps were miniature kings who created courts imitative of the Great King's.

An efficient system of communication was crucial to sustaining the Persian Empire. Well-maintained roads facilitated the rapid transit of military and government personnel. One in particular, the so-called Royal Road (see Map 1.5), stretched from Sardis, the center of Lydia in Asia Minor, to Susa, the chief capital of the Persian Empire. Like the Assyrians, the Persians established way stations equipped with fresh horses for the king's messengers.

In this vast administrative system, the Persian king occupied an exalted position. All subjects were the king's servants, and he, the Great King, was the source of all justice, possessing the power of life and death over everyone. At its height, much of the power of the Persian Empire depended on the military. By the time of Darius, the Persian monarchs had created a standing army of professional soldiers. This army was truly international in character, composed of contingents from the various peoples who made up the empire. At its core were a cavalry force of ten thousand and an elite infantry force of the same size known as the Immortals because they were never allowed to fall below ten thousand in number. When one was killed, he was immediately replaced.

After Darius, Persian kings became more and more isolated at their courts, surrounded by luxuries paid for by the immense quantities of gold and silver that flowed into their treasuries, located in the capital cities. Both their hoarding of wealth and their later overtaxation of their subjects are seen as crucial factors in the ultimate weakening of the Persian Empire.

PERSIAN RELIGION: ZOROASTRIANISM Of all the Persians' cultural contributions, the most original was their religion, **Zoroastrianism**. According to Persian tradition, Zoroaster (ZOR-oh-ass-tur) was born in 660 B.C.E. After a period of wandering and solitude, he experienced revelations that caused him to be revered as a prophet of the "true religion." His teachings were eventually written down in the third century B.C.E. in the Zend Avesta, the sacred book of Zoroastrianism.

CHRONOLOGY Early Empires	
The Assyrians	
Height of power	700 B.C.E.
Fall of Nineveh	612 B.C.E.
Empire destroyed	605 B.C.E.
The Persians	
Unification under Achaemenid dynasty	600s B.C.E.
Conquests of Cyrus the Great	559–530 B.C.E.
Cambyses and conquest of Egypt	530–522 B.C.E.
Reign of Darius	521–486 B.C.E.

Zoroaster's spiritual message was basically monotheistic. To Zoroaster, the religion he preached was the only perfect one, and Ahuramazda (uh-HOOR-uh-MAHZ-duh) (the "Wise Lord") was the only god. Ahuramazda was the supreme deity, "creator of all things." According to Zoroaster, Ahuramazda also possessed qualities that all humans should aspire to, such as good thought, right action, and piety. Although Ahuramazda was supreme, he was not unopposed; this gave a dualistic element to Zoroastrianism. At the beginning of the world, the good spirit of Ahuramazda was opposed by the evil spirit, later identified as Ahriman.

Humans also played a role in this cosmic struggle between good and evil. Ahuramazda gave all humans free will and the power to choose between right and wrong. The good person chooses the right way of Ahuramazda. Zoroaster taught that there would be an end to the struggle between good and evil. Ahuramazda would eventually triumph, and at the last judgment at the end of the world, the final separation of good and evil would occur. Individuals, too, would be judged. Each soul faced a final evaluation of its actions. If a person had performed good deeds, he or she would achieve paradise; if evil deeds, the soul would be thrown into an abyss of torment. Some historians believe that Zoroastrianism, with its emphasis on good and evil, heaven and hell, and a last judgment, had an impact on Christianity, a religion that eventually surpassed it in significance.

CHAPTER SUMMARY

Humanlike creatures first emerged in Africa around 3 to 4 million years ago. Over a period of time, Paleolithic people learned to create sophisticated tools, to use fire, and to adapt to and even change their physical world. They were primarily nomads, who hunted animals and gathered wild plants for survival. The agricultural revolution of the Neolithic Age, which began around 10,000 B.C.E., dramatically changed human patterns of living. The growing of food on a regular basis and the taming of animals enabled humans to stop their nomadic ways and settle in permanent settlements, which gave rise to more complex human societies.

These more complex human societies, which we call the first civilizations, emerged around 3000 B.C.E. in the river valleys of Mesopotamia, Egypt, India, and China. An increase in food production in these regions led to a significant growth in human population and the rise of cities. The peoples of Southwest Asia and Egypt developed cities and struggled with the problems of organized states as they moved from individual communities to larger territorial units and eventually to empires. They invented writing to keep records and created literature. They constructed monumental buildings to please their gods, give witness to their power, and preserve their culture. They developed new political, military, social, and religious structures to deal with the basic problems of human existence and organization. These first civilizations left detailed records that allow us to view how they grappled with three of the fundamental problems that humans have pondered: the nature of human relationships, the nature of the universe, and the role of divine forces in that cosmos.

By the middle of the second millennium B.C.E., much of the creative impulse of the Mesopotamian and Egyptian civilizations was beginning to wane. Around 1200 B.C.E., a number of small states emerged, but all of them were eventually overshadowed by the rise of the great empires of the Assyrians and Persians. The Assyrian Empire was the first to unite almost all of the ancient Middle East. Even larger, however, was the empire of the Great Kings of Persia. The many years of peace that the Persian Empire brought to the Middle East facilitated trade and the general well-being of its peoples. It is no wonder that many peoples expressed their gratitude for being subjects of the Great Kings of Persia. Among these peoples were the Hebrews, who created no empire but nevertheless left an important spiritual legacy. The embrace of monotheism created in Judaism one of the world's greatest religions, one that went on to influence the development of both Christianity and Islam.

CHAPTER TIMELINE

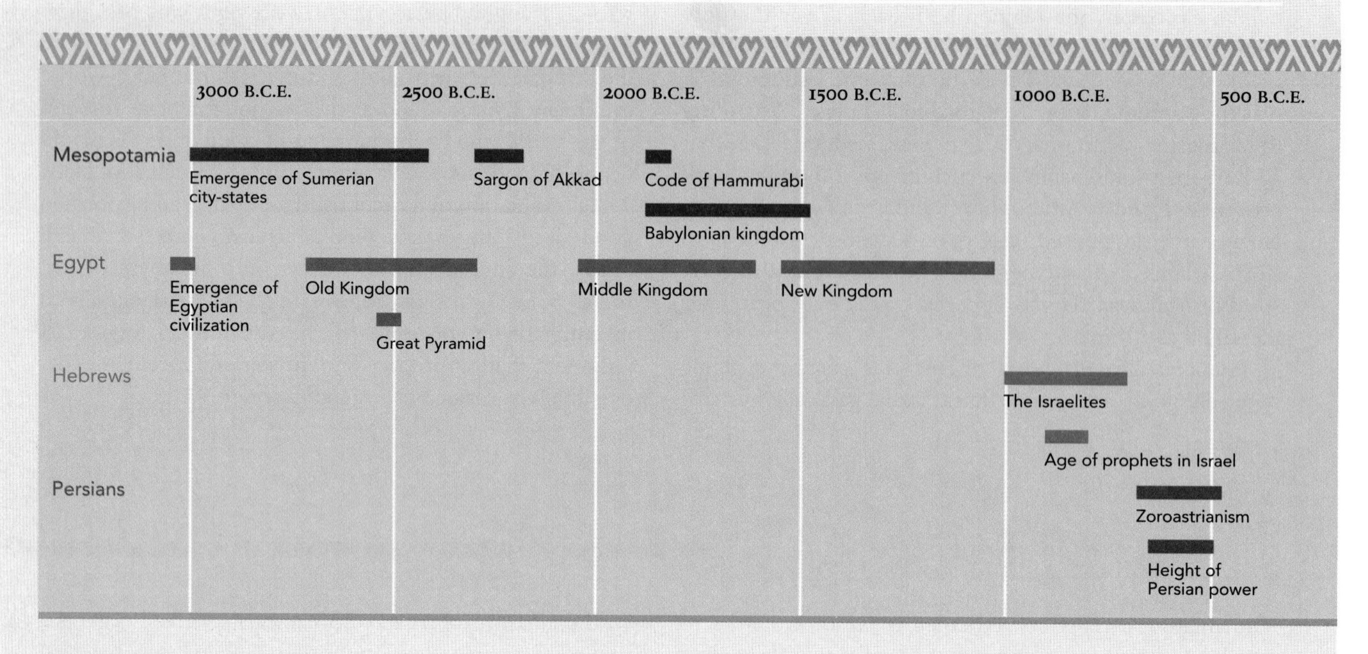

CHAPTER REVIEW

Upon Reflection

Q What achievements did early humans make during the Paleolithic and Neolithic Ages, and how did those achievements eventually make possible the emergence of civilization?

Q What roles did geography, environmental conditions, religion, politics, economics, and women and families play in the civilizations of Southwest Asia and Egypt?

Q Compare and contrast the administrative and military structure and attitudes toward subject peoples of the Assyrian and Persian Empires.

Key Terms

hominids (p. 3)
Paleolithic Age (p. 3)
Neolithic Revolution (p. 4)
patriarchy (p. 6)
civilization (p. 7)
ziggurat (p. 8)
polytheism (p. 11)
cuneiform (p. 12)
pharaoh (p. 16)
hieroglyphics (p. 19)
megaliths (p. 20)
monotheism (p. 21)
satrapy (p. 26)
Zoroastrianism (p. 26)

Suggested Reading

THE PREHISTORIC WORLD For a brief but sound survey, see **I. Tattersall, *The World from Beginnings to 4000 B.C.E.*** (Oxford, 2008). Also of considerable value in examining the prehistory of humankind is **S. Mithen, *After the Ice: A Global Human History, 20,000–5000 B.C.*** (Cambridge, Mass., 2006). On the role of women in prehistory, see **J. M. Adovasio, O. Soffer,** and **J. Page, *The Invisible Sex: Uncovering the True Roles of Women in Prehistory*** (New York, 2007).

ANCIENT NEAR EAST A very competent general survey of the ancient Near East is **M. Van de Mieroop, *A History of the Ancient Near East, ca. 3000–323 B.C.*,** 2nd ed. (Oxford, 2006). For a detailed survey, see **A. Kuhrt, *The Ancient Near East, c. 3000–330 B.C.*,** 2 vols. (London, 1996). On the economic and social history of the ancient Near East, see **D. C. Snell, *Life in the Ancient Near East*** (New Haven, Conn., 1997).

ANCIENT MESOPOTAMIA A beautifully illustrated survey of ancient Mesopotamia can be found in **M. Roaf, *Cultural Atlas of Mesopotamia and the Ancient Near East*** (New York, 1996). For a summary of the historical and archaeological evidence on the Sumerians, see **H. Crawford, *Sumer and the Sumerians,*** 2nd ed. (Cambridge, 2004). For a reference work on daily life, see **S. Bertman, *Handbook to Life in Ancient Mesopotamia*** (New York, 2003).

ANCIENT EGYPT For a good introduction to ancient Egypt, see **T. G. H. James, *Ancient Egypt*** (Ann Arbor, Mich., 2005), and **I. Shaw, ed., *The Oxford History of Ancient Egypt*** (New York, 2000). Daily life in ancient Egypt can be examined in **R. David, *Handbook to Life in Ancient Egypt*** (Cambridge, Mass., 1993). On the interaction of the Egyptians with the Nubians and other peoples in Africa south of Egypt, see **D. B. Redford, *From Slave to Pharaoh: The Black Experience of Ancient Egypt*** (Baltimore, 2004).

ANCIENT ISRAEL There is an enormous literature on ancient Israel. For an important revisionist view on the archaeological aspects, see **I. Finkelstein** and **N. Silberman, *The Bible Unearthed: Archaeology's New Vision of Ancient Israel*** (New York, 2002). For a historical narrative, see **H. Shanks, *Ancient Israel: A Short History from Abraham to the Roman Destruction of the Temple,*** rev. ed. (Englewood Cliffs, N.J., 1998). On the controversies surrounding the history of the Israelites, see **J. M. Golden, *Ancient Canaan and Israel*** (Oxford, 2004)).

THE ASSYRIAN AND PERSIAN EMPIRES A detailed account of Assyrian political, economic, social, military, and cultural history is **H. W. F. Saggs, *The Might That Was Assyria*** (London, 1984). On the Persian Empire, see **L. Allen, *The Persian Empire*** (Chicago, 2005). On the history of Zoroastrianism, see **S. A. Nigosian, *The Zoroastrian Faith: Tradition and Modern Research*** (New York, 1993).

Visit the CourseMate website at **www.cengagebrain.com** for additional study tools and review materials for this chapter.

Krishna and Arjuna preparing for battle

© The Trustees of the Chester Beatty Library (InE 1479), Dublin/The Bridgeman Art Library

CHAPTER 2

Ancient India

CHAPTER OUTLINE AND FOCUS QUESTIONS

The Emergence of Civilization in India: Harappan Society

Q What were the chief features of Harappan civilization, and in what ways was it similar to the civilizations that arose in Egypt and Mesopotamia?

The Aryans in India

Q What were some of the distinctive features of the class system introduced by the Aryan peoples, and what effects did it have on Indian civilization?

Escaping the Wheel of Life: The Religious World of Ancient India

Q What are the main tenets of Brahmanism and Buddhism? How did they differ, and how did each religion influence Indian civilization?

The Rule of the Fishes: India After the Mauryas

Q Why was India unable to maintain a unified empire in the first millennium B.C.E., and how was the Mauryan Empire temporarily able to overcome the tendencies toward disunity?

The Exuberant World of Indian Culture

Q In what ways did the culture of ancient India resemble and differ from the cultural experience of ancient Mesopotamia and Egypt?

CRITICAL THINKING

Q What are some of the key factors that explain why India became one of the first regions to create an advanced society in the ancient world? To what degree does it merit comparison with Mesopotamia and Egypt as the site of one of the first civilizations?

ARJUNA WAS DESPONDENT as he prepared for battle. In the opposing army were many of his friends and colleagues, some of whom he had known since childhood. In despair, he turned for advice to Krishna (KHRISH-nuh), his chariot driver, who, unknown to Arjuna (ahr-JOO-nuh), was in actuality an incarnation of the Indian deity Vishnu (VISH-noo). "Do not despair of your duty," Krishna advised his friend.

To be born is certain death,
to the dead, birth is certain.
It is not right that you should sorrow
for what cannot be avoided. . . .
If you do not fight this just battle
you will fail in your own law
and in your honor,
and you will incur sin.

Krishna's advice to Arjuna is contained in the Bhagavad Gita (bah-guh-vahd GEE-tuh), one of India's most sacred classical writings, and reflects one of the key tenets in Indian philosophy—the belief in reincarnation, or rebirth of the soul. It also points up the importance of doing one's duty without regard for the consequences. Arjuna was a warrior, and according to Aryan (AR-ee-un) tribal tradition, he was obliged to follow the code of his class. "There is more joy in doing one's own duty badly," advised Krishna, "than in doing another man's duty well."

In advising Arjuna to fulfill his obligation as a warrior, the author of the Bhagavad Gita, writing around the second century B.C.E. about a battle that took place almost a thousand years earlier, was by implication urging all readers to adhere to their own responsibility as members of one of India's major classes. Henceforth, this hierarchical vision of a society divided into groups, each with clearly distinct roles, would become a defining characteristic of Indian history.

The Bhagavad Gita is part of a larger work, called the Mahabharata (muh-hahb-huh-RAH-tuh), that deals with the early history of the Aryan peoples who entered India from beyond the mountains north of the Khyber Pass between 1500 and 1000 B.C.E. When the Aryans, a pastoral people speaking a branch of the Indo-European family of languages, arrived in India, the subcontinent had already had a thriving civilization for almost two thousand years. The Indus valley civilization, although not as well known in the West as the civilizations of Mesopotamia and Egypt, was just as old, and its political, social, and cultural achievements were also impressive. That civilization, known to historians by the names of its two major cities, Harappa (huh-RAP-uh) and Mohenjo-Daro (moh-HEN-joh-DAH-roh), emerged in the late fourth millennium B.C.E., flourished for more than a thousand years, and then came to an abrupt end about 1500 B.C.E. It was soon replaced by a new society dominated by the Aryan peoples. The new civilization that emerged represented a rich mixture of the two cultures—Harappan and Aryan—and evolved over the next three thousand years into what we know today as India.

The Emergence of Civilization in India: Harappan Society

FOCUS QUESTION: What were the chief features of Harappan civilization, and in what ways was it similar to the civilizations that arose in Egypt and Mesopotamia?

The vast region of the Indian subcontinent is home to a rich mixture of peoples: people speaking one of the languages in the Dravidian family, who probably descended from the Indus River culture that flourished at the dawn of Indian civilization, more than four thousand years ago; Aryans, descended from the pastoral peoples who flooded southward from Central Asia in the second millennium B.C.E.; and hill peoples, who may have lived in the region prior to the rise of organized societies and thus may have been the earliest inhabitants of all.

Although today this beautiful mosaic of peoples and cultures has been broken up into a number of separate independent states, the region still possesses a coherent history that despite its internal diversity is recognizably Indian.

A Land of Diversity

India was and still is a land of diversity. This is evident in its languages and cultures as well as in its physical characteristics. India possesses an incredible array of languages. It has a deserved reputation, along with the Middle East, as a cradle of religion. Two of the world's major religions, Hinduism and Buddhism, originated in India.

In its size and diversity, India seems more like a continent than a single country. That diversity begins with the geographic environment. The Indian subcontinent, shaped like a spade hanging from the southern ridge of Asia, is composed of a number of core regions. In the far north are the Himalayan and Karakoram mountain ranges, home to the highest mountains in the world. Directly south of the Himalayas and the Karakoram range is the rich valley of the Ganges (GAN-jeez), India's "holy river" and one of the core regions of Indian culture. To the west is the Indus River valley. Today, the latter is a relatively arid plateau that forms the backbone of the modern state of Pakistan, but in ancient times, it enjoyed a more balanced climate and served as the cradle of Indian civilization.

South of India's two major river valleys lies the Deccan (DEK-uhn), a region of hills and an upland plateau that extends from the Ganges valley to the southern tip of the Indian subcontinent. The interior of the plateau is relatively hilly and dry, but the eastern and western coasts are occupied by lush plains, which are historically among the most densely populated regions of India. Off the southeastern coast is the island known today as Sri Lanka. Although Sri Lanka is now a separate country quite distinct politically and culturally from India, the island's history is intimately linked with that of its larger neighbor.

Harappan Civilization: A Fascinating Enigma

In the 1920s, archaeologists discovered agricultural settlements dating back well over six thousand years in the lower reaches of the Indus River valley in what is now modern Pakistan. Those small mudbrick villages eventually gave rise to the sophisticated human communities that historians call Harappan civilization. Although today the area is relatively arid, during the third and fourth millennia B.C.E., it evidently received much more abundant rainfall, and the valleys of the Indus River and its tributaries supported a thriving civilization that may have covered a total area of more than 600,000 square miles, from the Himalayas to the coast of the Indian Ocean. More than seventy sites have been unearthed since the area was first discovered in the 1850s, but the main sites are at the two major cities, Harappa, in the Punjab (pun-JAHB), and Mohenjo-Daro, nearly 400 miles to the south near the mouth of the Indus River (see Map 2.1).

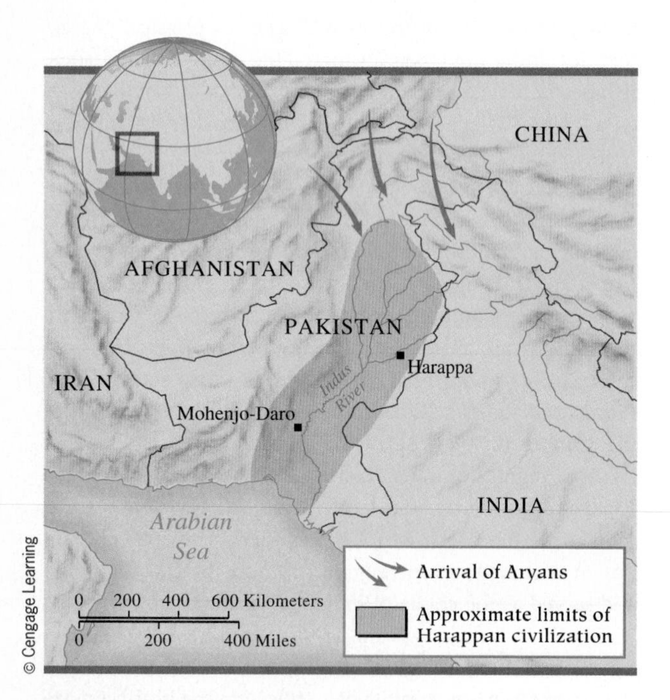

© Cengage Learning

MAP 2.1 Ancient Harappan Civilization. This map shows the location of the first civilization that arose in the Indus River valley, which today is located in Pakistan.

Based on this map, why do you think Harappan civilization resembled the civilizations of Mesopotamia and Egypt?

POLITICAL AND SOCIAL STRUCTURES In several respects, Harappan civilization closely resembled the cultures of Mesopotamia and the Nile valley. Like them, it probably began in tiny farming villages scattered throughout the river valley, some dating back to as early as 6500 or 7000 B.C.E. These villages thrived and grew until, by the middle of the third millennium B.C.E., they could support a privileged ruling elite living in walled cities of considerable magnitude and affluence. The center of power was the city of Harappa, which was surrounded by a brick wall more than 40 feet thick at its base and more than 3.5 miles in circumference. The city was laid out on an essentially rectangular grid, with some streets as wide as 30 feet. Most buildings were constructed of kiln-dried mudbricks and were square in shape, reflecting the grid pattern. At its height, the city may have had as many as 80,000 inhabitants, making it as large as some of the most populous Sumerian urban centers.

Both Harappa and Mohenjo-Daro were divided into large walled neighborhoods, with narrow lanes separating the rows of houses. Houses varied in size, with some as high as three stories, but all followed the same general plan based on a square courtyard surrounded by rooms. Bathrooms featured an advanced drainage system, which carried wastewater out to drains located under the streets and thence to sewage pits beyond the city walls.

Unfortunately, Harappan writing has not yet been deciphered, so historians know relatively little about the organization of the Harappan state. Recent archaeological evidence, however, suggests that unlike its contemporaries in Egypt and Sumer, Harappa was not a centralized monarchy claiming divine origins but a collection of more than 1,500 towns and cities loosely connected by ties of trade and alliance and ruled by a coalition of landlords and rich merchants. There were no royal precincts or imposing burial monuments, and there are few surviving stone or terra-cotta images that might represent kings, priests, or military commanders. It is possible however, that religion had advanced beyond the stage of spirit worship to belief in a single god or goddess of fertility. Presumably, priests at court prayed to this deity to maintain the fertility of the soil and guarantee the annual harvest.

As in Mesopotamia and Egypt, the Harappan economy was based primarily on agriculture. Wheat, barley, rice, and peas were apparently the primary crops. The presence of cotton seeds at various sites suggests that the Harappan peoples may have been the first to master the cultivation of this useful crop and possibly introduced it, along with rice, to other societies in the region. But Harappa also developed an extensive trading network that extended to Sumer and other civilizations to the west.

The City of the Dead. One of the two major cities of the ancient Indus River civilization was Mohenjo-Daro (below). In addition to rows of residential housing, it had a ceremonial center, with a palatial residence and a sacred bath that was probably used by the priests to achieve ritual purity. The bath is reminiscent of water tanks in modern Hindu temples, such as the Minakshi Temple in Madurai (right), where the faithful wash their feet prior to religious devotion. Water is an integral part of Hindu temple complexes, as symbolically it represents Vishnu's cosmic ocean and Shiva's reception of the holy Ganges on his head. Water is also a vital necessity in India's arid climate.

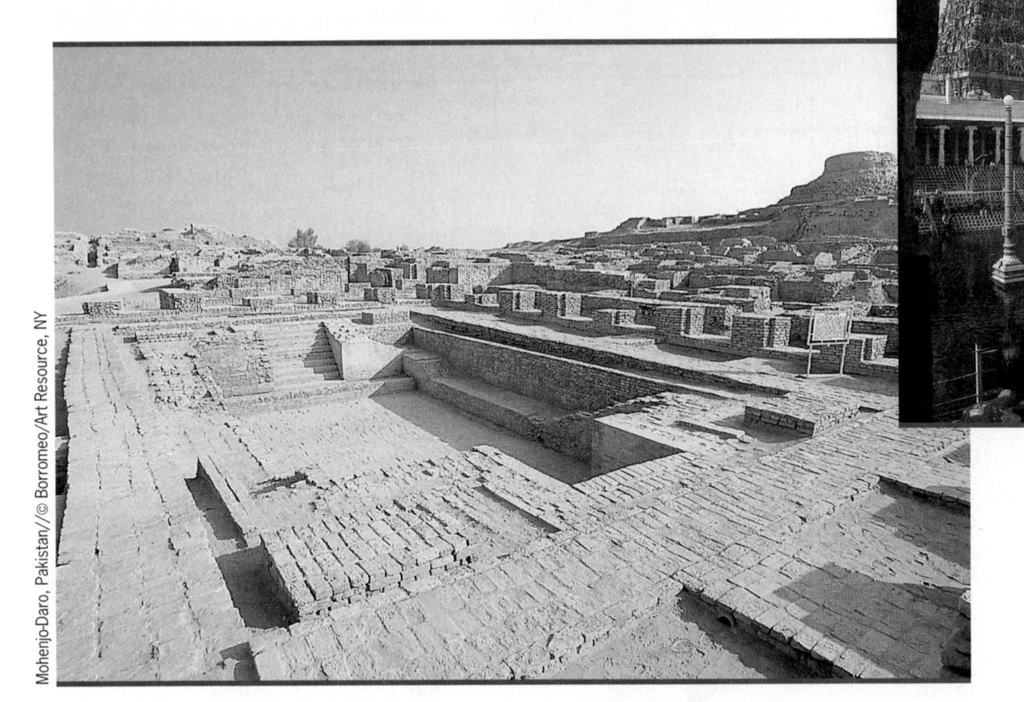

Mohenjo-Daro, Pakistan//© Borromeo/Art Resource, NY

© William J. Duiker

Textiles and foodstuffs were apparently imported from Sumer in exchange for metals such as copper, lumber, precious stones, and various types of luxury goods. Much of this trade was conducted by ship via the Persian Gulf, although some undoubtedly went by land.

HARAPPAN CULTURE Archaeological remains indicate that the Indus valley peoples possessed a culture as sophisticated in some ways as that of the Sumerians to the west. The aesthetic quality of some Harappan pottery and sculpture is superb, rivaling equivalent work produced elsewhere. Sculpture was the Harappans' highest artistic achievement. Some artifacts possess a wonderful vitality of expression. Fired clay seals show a deft touch in carving animals such as elephants, tigers, rhinoceroses, and antelope, and figures made of copper or terra-cotta show a lively sensitivity and a sense of grace and movement.

Writing was another achievement of Harappan society and dates back at least to the beginning of the third millennium B.C.E. (see the comparative essay "Writing and Civilization" on p. 35). Unfortunately, the only surviving examples of Harappan writing are the pictographic symbols inscribed on the clay seals. The script contained more than four hundred characters, but most are too stylized to be identified by their shape, and scholars have thus far been unable to decipher them. There are no apparent links with Mesopotamian scripts, although, like the latter, Harappan writing may have been used primarily to record commercial transactions. Until the script is deciphered, much about the Harappan civilization must remain, as one historian termed it, a fascinating enigma.

THE COLLAPSE OF HARAPPAN CIVILIZATION One of the great mysteries of Harappan civilization is how it came to an end. Archaeologists working at Mohenjo-Daro have discovered signs of first a gradual decay and then a sudden destruction of the city and its inhabitants around 1500 B.C.E. Many of the surviving skeletons have been found in postures of running or hiding, reminiscent of the ruins of the Roman city of Pompeii, destroyed by the eruption of Mount Vesuvius in 79 C.E.

These tantalizing signs of flight before a sudden catastrophe once led scholars to surmise that the city of Mohenjo-Daro (the name was applied by archaeologists and means "city of the dead") and perhaps the remnants of Harappan civilization were destroyed by the Aryans, pastoral peoples from the north who arrived in the subcontinent around the middle of the second millennium B.C.E. Although the Aryans were considered to be less sophisticated culturally than the Harappans, like many nomadic peoples they excelled at the art of war. As in Mesopotamia and the Nile valley, contacts between pastoral and agricultural peoples proved unstable and often ended in armed conflict. Today, however, historians are doubtful that the Aryan peoples were directly responsible for the final destruction of Mohenjo-Daro. More likely, Harappan civilization had already fallen on hard times, perhaps as a result of climatic change in the Indus valley. Archaeologists have found clear signs of social decay, including evidence of trash in the streets, neglect of public services, and overcrowding in urban neighborhoods. Mohenjo-Daro itself may have been destroyed by an epidemic or by natural phenomena such as floods, an earthquake, or a shift in the course of the Indus River. If that was the case, any migrating peoples arrived in the area after the greatness of Harappan civilization had already passed.

National Museum, New Delhi/© DeA Picture Library/Art Resource, NY

A Mother Goddess. Between 2600 and 1900 B.C.E., Harappan craftsmen created a variety of terra-cotta objects, including whimsical toy animals, whistles, and tops, as well as dice, for children. Most remarkable, perhaps, are the numerous female figurines, such as the one shown here, with wide hips, bejeweled breasts, fan-shaped headdresses, and numerous strands of necklaces. Sharing their physical attributes with fertility deities in other early civilizations, these mother goddesses represent an idealized form of feminine beauty, which became a recurring feature of Indian art through the ages.

WHO WERE THE ARYANS? Historians know relatively little about the origins and culture of the Aryans. The traditional view is that they were Indo-European-speaking peoples who inhabited vast areas in the steppes north and east of the Black and Caspian Seas. The Indo-Europeans were pastoral peoples who migrated from season to season in search of fodder for their herds. Historians have credited them with a number of technological achievements, including the invention of horse-drawn chariots and the stirrup, both of which were eventually introduced throughout much of the Eurasian supercontinent.

Whereas many other Indo-European-speaking peoples moved westward and eventually settled throughout Europe, the Aryans moved south across the Hindu Kush into the plains of northern India. Between 1500 and 1000 B.C.E., they gradually advanced eastward from the Indus valley, across the fertile plain of the Ganges, and later southward into the Deccan Plateau. Eventually, they extended their political mastery over the entire subcontinent and its Dravidian-speaking inhabitants, although the indigenous culture survived to remain a prominent element in the evolution of traditional Indian civilization.

In recent years, a new theory has been proposed by some Indian historians, who contend that the Aryan peoples did not migrate into the Indian subcontinent from Central Asia, but were in fact the indigenous population that had originally created the Indus River civilization. Most scholars, however, continue to support the migration hypothesis, although the evidence is not conclusive. They point out that the spoken language of the Aryan people, known as Sanskrit, is widely recognized as a branch of the Indo-European family of languages. Moreover, the earliest account produced by the Aryan people themselves, known as the Rig Veda (RIK VAY-duh) (see the next section), describes a culture based primarily on pastoralism, a pursuit not particularly suited to the Indus River valley. A definitive solution to the debate will have to await further evidence.

COMPARATIVE ESSAY

Writing and Civilization

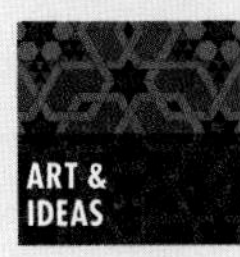

In the year 3250 B.C.E., King Scorpion of Egypt issued an edict announcing a major victory for his army over rival forces in the region. Inscribed in limestone on a cliff face in the Nile River valley, that edict is perhaps the oldest surviving historical document in the world today.

According to prehistorians, human beings began to create the first spoken language about 50,000 years ago. As human beings spread from Africa to other continents, that first system gradually fragmented into innumerable separate languages. By the time the agricultural revolution began about 10,000 years ago, there may have been nearly twenty distinct language families in existence around the world (see Map 2.2 on p. 36).

During the later stages of the agricultural revolution, the first writing systems also began to be created in various regions around the world. The first successful efforts were apparently achieved in Mesopotamia and Egypt, but knowledge of writing soon spread to peoples along the shores of the Mediterranean and in the Indus River valley in South Asia. Wholly independent systems were also invented in China and Mesoamerica. Writing was used for a variety of purposes. King Scorpion's edict suggests that one reason was to enable a ruler to communicate with his subjects on matters of official concern. In other cases, the purpose was to enable human beings to communicate with supernatural forces. In China and Egypt, for example, priests used writing to communicate with the gods. In Mesopotamia and in the Indus River valley, merchants used writing to record commercial and other legal transactions. Finally, writing was also used to present ideas in new ways, giving rise to such early Mesopotamian literature as *The Epic of Gilgamesh*.

How did such early written languages evolve into the complex systems in use today? In almost all cases, the first systems consisted of pictographs, pictorial images of various concrete objects such as trees, water, cattle, body parts, and the heavenly bodies. Eventually, such signs became more stylized to facilitate transcription—much as we often use a cursive script instead of block printing today. Finally, and most important for their future development, these pictorial images began to take on specific phonetic meaning so that they could represent sounds in the written language. Most sophisticated written systems eventually evolved to a phonetic script, based on an alphabet of symbols that represented all sounds in the spoken language, but others went only part way by adding phonetic signs to the individual character to suggest pronunciation while keeping part of the original pictograph to indicate meaning. Most of the latter systems, such as hieroglyphics in Egypt and cuneiform in Mesopotamia, eventually became extinct, but the ancient Chinese writing system survives today, although in changed form.

For what purposes were writing systems developed in the ancient world? What appears to have been the initial purpose of the Harappan script?

Archaeological Museum, New Delhi/© Scala/Art Resource, NY

Harappan Seals. The Harappan peoples, like their contemporaries in Mesopotamia, developed a writing system to record their spoken language. Unfortunately, it has not yet been deciphered. Most extant examples of Harappan writing are found on fired clay seals depicting human figures and animals. These seals have been found in houses and were probably used to identify the owners of goods for sale. Other seals may have been used as amulets or have had other religious significance. Several depict religious figures or ritualistic scenes of sacrifice.

The Aryans in India

FOCUS QUESTION: What were some of the distinctive features of the class system introduced by the Aryan peoples, and what effects did it have on Indian civilization?

After they settled in India, the Aryans gradually adapted to the geographic realities of their new homeland and abandoned the pastoral life for agricultural pursuits. They were assisted by the introduction of iron, which probably came from the Middle East, where it had been introduced by the Hittites (see Chapter 1) about 1500 B.C.E. The invention of the iron plow, along with the development of irrigation, allowed the Aryans and their indigenous subjects to clear the dense jungle growth along the Ganges River and transform the Ganges valley into one of the richest agricultural regions in South Asia. The Aryans also developed their first writing system, based on the Aramaic (ar-uh-MAY-ik) script of the Middle East, and were thus able to transcribe the legends that previously had been passed down from generation to generation by memory (see Map 2.2). Most of what is known about the early Aryans is based on oral traditions passed on in the Rig Veda, an ancient work that was written down after the Aryans arrived in India (it is one of several Vedas, or collections of sacred instructions and rituals).

From Chieftains to Kings

As in other Indo-European societies, each of the various Aryan groups was led by a chieftain, called a **raja** (RAH-juh) ("prince"), who was assisted by a council of elders composed of other leading members of the community; like them, he was normally a member of the warrior class, called the ***kshatriya*** (kshuh-TREE-yuh). The chief derived his power from his ability to protect his people from rival groups, an ability that was crucial in the warring kingdoms and shifting alliances that were typical of early Aryan society. Though the rajas claimed to be representatives of the gods, they were not viewed as gods themselves (see the box on p. 37).

As Indian society grew in size and complexity, the chieftains began to be transformed into kings, usually called **maharajas** (mah-huh-RAH-juhs) ("great princes"). Nevertheless, the tradition that the ruler did not possess absolute authority remained strong. Like all human beings, the ruler was required to follow the ***dharma*** (DAR-muh), a set of laws that set behavioral standards for all individuals and classes in Indian society.

THE IMPACT OF THE GREEKS While competing groups squabbled for precedence in India, powerful new empires were rising to the west. First came the Persian Empire of Cyrus and Darius. Then came the Greeks. After two centuries of sporadic rivalry and warfare, the

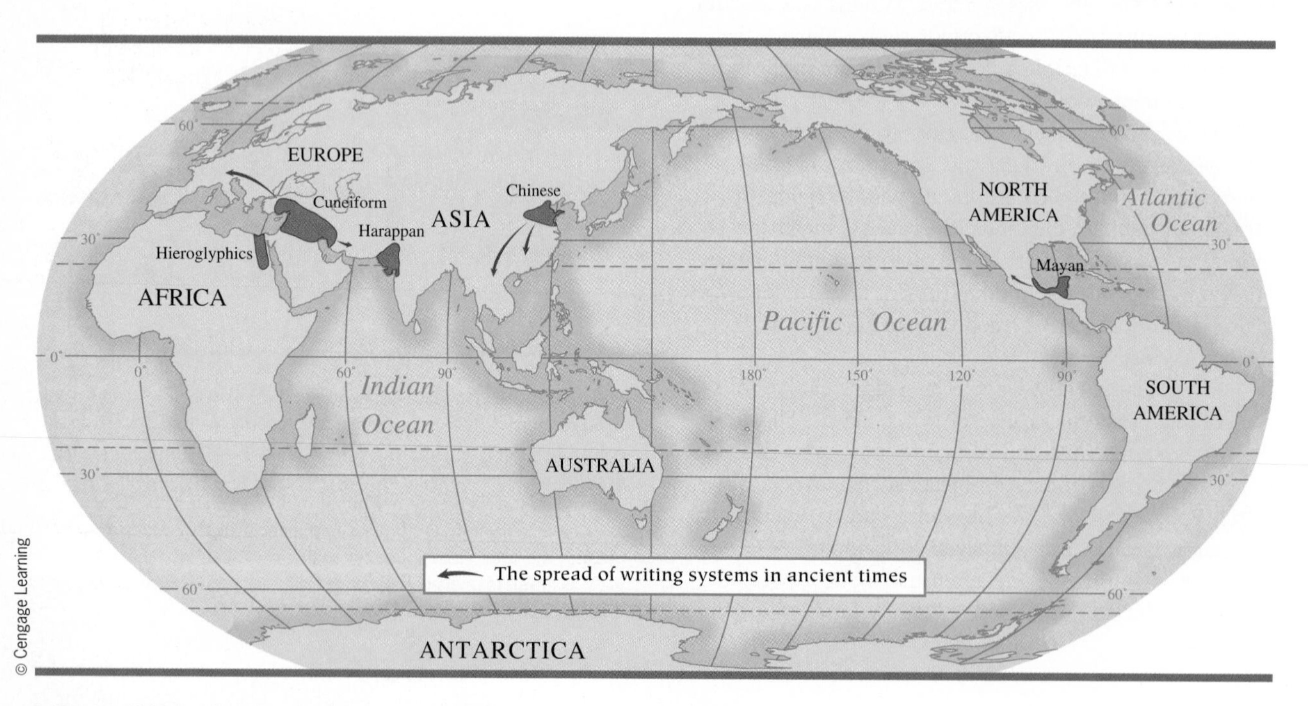

© Cengage Learning

MAP 2.2 Writing Systems in the Ancient World. One of the chief characteristics of the first civilizations was the development of a system of written communication.

Based on the comparative essay on p. 35, in what ways were these first writing systems similar, and how were they different?

The Origins of Kingship

POLITICS & GOVERNMENT

Both India and China had a concept of a golden age in the remote past that provided a model for later governments and peoples to emulate. This passage from the famous Indian epic known as the Mahabharata describes a three-stage process in the evolution of government in human society. Yudhisthira (yoo-dis-THY-ruh) and Bhishma (BIHSH-muh) are two of the main characters in the story.

The Mahabharata

Yudhisthira said: "This word 'king' [*raja*] is so very current in this world, O Bharata; how has it originated? Tell me that, O grandfather."

Bhishma said: "Currently, O best among men, do you listen to everything in its entirety—how kingship originated first during the golden age [*krtayuga*]. Neither kingship nor king was there in the beginning, neither scepter [*danda*] nor the bearer of a scepter. All people protected one another by means of righteous conduct, O Bharata, men eventually fell into a state of spiritual lassitude. Then delusion overcame them. Men were thus overpowered by infatuation, O leader of men, on account of the delusion of understanding; their sense of righteous conduct was lost. When understanding was lost, all men, O best of the Bharatas, overpowered by infatuation, became victims of greed. Then they sought to acquire what should not be acquired. Thereby, indeed, O lord, another vice, namely, desire, overcame them. Attachment then attacked them, who had become victims of desire. Attached to objects of sense, they did not discriminate between what should be said and what should not be said, between the edible and inedible and between right and wrong. When this world of men had been submerged in dissipation, all spiritual knowledge [*brahman*] perished; and when spiritual knowledge perished, O king, righteous conduct also perished."

When spiritual knowledge and righteous conduct perished, the gods were overcome with fear, and fearfully sought refuge with Brahma, the creator. Going to the great lord, the ancestor of the worlds, all the gods, afflicted with sorrow, misery, and fear, with folded hands said: "O Lord, the eternal spiritual knowledge, which had existed in the world of men, has perished because of greed, infatuation, and the like, therefore we have become fearful. Through the loss of spiritual knowledge, righteous conduct also has perished, O God. Therefore, O Lord of the three worlds, mortals have reached a state of indifference. Verily, we showered rain on earth, but mortals showered rain [religious offerings] up to heaven. As a result of the cessation of ritual activity on their part, we faced a serious peril. O grandfather, decide what is most beneficial to use under these circumstances."

Then, the self-born lord said to all those gods: "I will consider what is most beneficial; let your fear depart, O leaders of the gods."

Thereupon he composed a work consisting of a hundred thousand chapters out of his own mind, wherein righteous conduct [*dharma*], as well as material gain [*artha*] and enjoyment of sensual pleasures [*kama*] were described. This group, known as the threefold classification of human objectives, was expounded by the self-born lord; so, too, a fourth objective, spiritual emancipation [*moksha*], which aims at a different goal, and which constitutes a separate group by itself.

Then the gods approached Vishnu, the lord of creatures, and said: "Indicate to us that one person among mortals who alone is worthy of the highest eminence." Then the blessed lord god Narayana reflected, and brought forth an illustrious mind-born son, called Virajas [who, in this version of the origins of the Indian state, became the first king].

What is the author's purpose here? How does this vision compare with other views in the ancient world on the reasons for the emergence of political leadership? What differences and similarities do you see between this description and the portrayal of kingship in Egypt in Hymn to the Pharaoh *in Chapter 1?*

Source: From *Sources of Indian Tradition*, Vol. 1, 2e, by Ainslee Embree. Copyright © 1988 by Columbia University Press. Reprinted with the permission of the publisher.

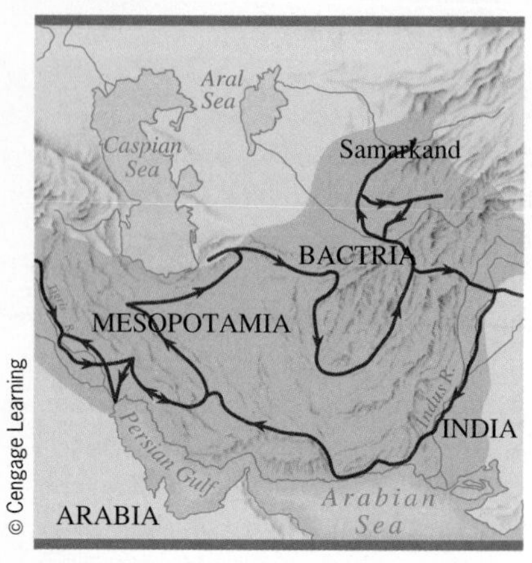

Alexander the Great's Movements in Asia

Greeks achieved a brief period of regional dominance in the late fourth century B.C.E. with the rise of Macedonia under Alexander the Great. Alexander had heard of the riches of India, and in 330 B.C.E., after conquering Persia, he launched an invasion of the east (see Chapter 4). In 326 B.C.E., his armies arrived in the plains of northwestern India. They departed almost as suddenly as they had come, leaving in their wake Greek administrators and a veneer of cultural influence that would affect the area for generations to come.

The Mauryan Empire

The Alexandrian conquest was only a brief interlude in the history of the Indian subcontinent, but it played a formative role, for on the heels of Alexander's departure came the rise of the first dynasty to control much of the region. The founder of the new state, who took the royal title Chandragupta Maurya (chun-druh-GOOP-tuh MOWR-yuh) (324–301 B.C.E.), drove out the Greek administrators who had remained after the departure of Alexander and solidified his control over the northern Indian plain. He established the capital of his new Mauryan Empire at Pataliputra (pah-tah-lee-POO-truh) (modern Patna) in the Ganges valley (see Map 2.3 on p. 50).

Little is known of Chandragupta Maurya's empire. Most accounts of his reign rely on the scattered remnants of a lost work written by Megasthenes (muh-GAS-thuh-neez), a Greek ambassador to the Mauryan court, in about 302 B.C.E. Chandragupta Maurya was apparently advised by a brilliant court official named Kautilya (kow-TIL-yuh), whose name has been attached to a treatise on politics called the *Arthasastra* (ar-thuh-SAS-truh). The work actually dates from a later time, but it may well reflect Kautilya's ideas.

Although the author of the *Arthasastra* follows Aryan tradition in stating that the happiness of the king lies in the happiness of his subjects, the treatise also asserts that when the sacred law of the *dharma* and practical politics collide, the latter must take precedence: "Whenever there is disagreement between history and sacred law or between evidence and sacred law, then the matter should be settled in accordance with sacred law. But whenever sacred law is in conflict with rational law, then reason shall be held authoritative."[1] The *Arthasastra* also emphasizes ends rather than means, achieved results rather than the methods employed. For this reason, it has often been compared to Machiavelli's famous political treatise, *The Prince*, written more than a thousand years later during the Italian Renaissance (see Chapter 15).

As described in the *Arthasastra*, Chandragupta Maurya's government was highly centralized and even despotic: "It is power and power alone which, only when exercised by the king with impartiality, and in proportion to guilt, over his son or his enemy, maintains both this world and the next."[2] The king possessed a large army and a secret police responsible to his orders (according to the Greek ambassador Megasthenes, Chandragupta Maurya was chronically fearful of assassination, a not unrealistic concern for someone who had allegedly come to power by violence). Reportedly, all food was tasted in his presence, and he made a practice of never sleeping twice in the same bed in his sumptuous palace. To guard against corruption, a board of censors was empowered to investigate cases of possible malfeasance and incompetence within the bureaucracy.

The ruler's authority beyond the confines of the capital may often have been limited, however. The empire was divided into provinces that were ruled by governors. At first, most of these governors were appointed by and reported to the ruler, but later the position became hereditary. The provinces themselves were divided into districts, each under a chief magistrate appointed by the governor. At the base of the government pyramid was the village, where the vast majority of the Indian people lived. The village was governed by a council of elders; membership in the council was normally hereditary and was shared by the wealthiest families in the village.

Caste and Class: Social Structures in Ancient India

When the Aryans arrived in India, they already possessed a strong class system based on a ruling warrior class and other social groupings characteristic of a pastoral society. In the subcontinent, they encountered peoples living by farming or, in some cases, by other pursuits such as fishing, hunting, or food gathering. The ultimate result was a set of social institutions and class divisions that have continued to have relevance down to the present day.

THE CLASS SYSTEM At the crux of the social system that emerged from the clash of cultures was the concept of a hierarchical division of society that placed each individual within a ritual framework that defined the person's occupation and status within the broader community. In part, this division may have been an outgrowth of attitudes held by the Aryan peoples with regard to the indigenous population. The Aryans, who followed primarily pastoral pursuits, tended to look askance at their new neighbors, who lived by tilling the soil. Further, the Aryans, a mostly light-skinned people, were contemptuous of the indigenous peoples, who were darker. Light skin came to imply high status, whereas dark skin suggested the opposite.

The concept of color, however, was only the physical manifestation of a division that took place in Indian society on the basis of economic functions. Indian classes (called ***varna***, literally, "color," and commonly but mistakenly translated as "castes" in English) did not simply reflect an informal division of labor. Instead, at least in theory, they were a set of rigid social classifications that determined not only one's occupation but also one's status in society and one's hope for ultimate salvation (see "Escaping the Wheel of Life" later in this chapter). There were five major *varna* in Indian society in ancient times. At the top were two classes, collectively viewed as the aristocracy, which clearly represented the ruling elites in Aryan society prior to their arrival in India: the priests and the warriors.

The priestly class, known as the ***brahmins***, was usually considered to be at the top of the social scale. Descended from seers who had advised the ruler on religious matters in Aryan tribal society—*brahmin* meant "one possessed of ***Brahman*** (BRAH-mun)," a term for the supreme god in the Hindu religion—they were eventually transformed into an official class after their religious role declined in importance. Megasthenes described this class as follows:

> From the time of their conception in the womb they are under the care and guardianship of learned men who go to the mother and . . . give her prudent hints and counsels, and the women who listen to them most willingly are thought to be the most fortunate in their offspring. After their birth the children are in the care of one person after another, and as they advance in years their masters are men of superior accomplishments. The philosophers reside in a grove in front of the city within a moderate-sized enclosure. They live in a simple style and lie on pallets of straw and [deer] skins. They abstain from animal food and sexual pleasures, and occupy their time in listening to serious discourse and in imparting knowledge to willing ears.[3]

The second class was the *kshatriya*, the warriors. Although often listed below the *brahmins* in social status, many *kshatriyas* were probably descended from the ruling warrior class in Aryan society prior to the conquest of India and thus may have originally ranked socially above the *brahmins*, although they were ranked lower in religious terms. Like the *brahmins*, the *kshatriyas* were originally identified with a single occupation—fighting—but as the character of Aryan society changed, they often switched to other forms of employment.

CHRONOLOGY Ancient India	
Harappan civilization	c. 2600–1900 B.C.E.
Arrival of the Aryans	c. 1500 B.C.E.
Life of Gautama Buddha	c. 560–480 B.C.E.
Invasion of India by Alexander the Great	326 B.C.E.
Mauryan dynasty founded	324 B.C.E.
Reign of Chandragupta Maurya	324–301 B.C.E.
Reign of Ashoka	269–232 B.C.E.
Collapse of Mauryan dynasty	183 B.C.E.
Rise of Kushan kingdom	c. first century C.E.

The third-ranked class in Indian society was the ***vaisya*** (VISH-yuh) (literally, "commoner"). The *vaisyas* were usually viewed in economic terms as the merchant class. Some historians have speculated that the *vaisyas* were originally guardians of the tribal herds but that after settling in India, many moved into commercial pursuits. Megasthenes noted that members of this class "alone are permitted to hunt and keep cattle and to sell beasts of burden or to let them out on hire. In return for clearing the land of wild beasts and birds which infest sown fields, they receive an allowance of corn from the king. They lead a wandering life and dwell in tents."[4] Although this class ranked below the first two in social status, it shared with them the privilege of being considered "**twice-born**," a term used to refer to males who had undergone a ceremony at puberty whereby they were initiated into adulthood and introduced into Indian society.

Below the three "twice-born" classes were the ***sudras*** (SOO-druhs *or* SHOO-druhs), who represented the great bulk of the Indian population. The *sudras* were not considered fully Aryan, and the term probably originally referred to the indigenous population. Most *sudras* were peasants or artisans or worked at other forms of manual labor. They had only limited rights in society.

At the lowest level of Indian society, and in fact not even considered a legitimate part of the class system itself, were the untouchables (also known as outcastes, or **pariahs**). The untouchables probably originated as a slave class consisting of prisoners of war, criminals, ethnic minorities, and other groups considered outside Indian society. Even after slavery was outlawed, the untouchables were given menial and degrading tasks that other Indians would not accept, such as collecting trash, handling dead bodies, or serving as butchers or tanners. One historian estimates that they may have accounted for a little more than 5 percent of the total population of India in antiquity.

The life of the untouchables was extremely demeaning. They were not considered fully human, and their very presence was considered polluting to members of the other *varna*. No Indian would touch or eat food handled or prepared by an untouchable. Untouchables lived in special ghettos and were required to tap two sticks together to announce their presence when they traveled outside their quarters so that others could avoid them.

Technically, the class divisions were absolute. Individuals supposedly were born, lived, and died in the same class. In practice, some upward or downward mobility probably took place, and there was undoubtedly some flexibility in economic functions. But throughout most of Indian history, class taboos remained strict. Members were generally not permitted to marry outside their class (although in practice, men were occasionally allowed to marry below their class but not above it).

THE *JATI* The people of ancient India did not belong to a particular class as individuals but as part of a larger kinship group commonly referred to as the ***jati*** (JAH-tee) (in Portuguese, *casta*, which evolved into the English term *caste*), a system of extended families that originated in ancient India and still exists in somewhat changed form today. Although the origins of the *jati* system are unknown (there are no indications of strict class distinctions in Harappan society), the *jati* eventually became identified with a specific kinship group living in a specific area and carrying out a specific function in society. Each *jati* was identified with a particular *varna*, and each had, at least in theory, its own separate economic function.

The *jatis* were thus the basic social organization into which traditional Indian society was divided. Each *jati* was itself composed of hundreds or thousands of individual nuclear families and was governed by its own council of elders. Membership in this ruling council was usually hereditary and was based on the wealth or social status of particular families within the community.

In theory, each *jati* was assigned a particular form of economic activity. Obviously, though, not all families in a given *jati* could take part in the same vocation, and as time went on, members of a single *jati* commonly engaged in several different lines of work. Sometimes an entire *jati* would have to move its location in order to continue a particular form of activity. In other cases, a *jati* would adopt an entirely new occupation in order to remain in a certain area. Such changes in habitat or occupation introduced the possibility of movement up or down the social scale. In this way, an entire *jati* could sometimes engage in upward mobility, even though that normally was not possible for individuals, who were tied to their class identity for life.

The class system in ancient India may sound highly constricting, but there were persuasive social and economic reasons why it survived for so many centuries. In the first place, it provided an identity for individuals in a highly hierarchical society. Although an individual might rank lower on the social scale than members of other classes, it was always possible to find others ranked even lower. Perhaps equally important, the *jati* was a primitive form of welfare system. Each *jati* was obliged to provide for any of its members who were poor or destitute. The *jati* also provided an element of stability in a society that all too often was in a state of political instability.

Daily Life in Ancient India

Beyond these rigid social stratifications was the Indian family. Not only was life centered around the family, but the family, not the individual, was the most basic unit in society.

THE FAMILY The ideal social unit was an extended family with three generations living under the same roof. It was essentially patriarchal, except along the Malabar coast, near the southwestern tip of the subcontinent, where a matriarchal form of social organization prevailed down to modern times. In the rest of India, the oldest male traditionally possessed legal authority over the entire family unit.

The family was linked together in a religious sense by a series of commemorative rites to ancestral members. These rituals, which originated in the Vedic era, consisted of family ceremonies to honor the departed and to link the living and the dead. The male family head was responsible for leading the ceremonies. At his death, his eldest son had the duty of conducting the funeral rites.

The importance of the father and the son in family ritual underlined the importance of males in Indian society. Male superiority was expressed in a variety of ways. Women could not serve as priests (although in practice, some were accepted as seers), nor were they normally permitted to study the Vedas. In general, males had a monopoly on education, since the primary goal of learning to read was to carry on family rituals. In high-class families, young men began Vedic studies with a ***guru*** (teacher). Some then went on to higher studies in one of the major cities. The goal of such an education might be either professional or religious.

MARRIAGE In general, only males could inherit property, except in a few cases when there were no sons. According to law, a woman was always considered a minor. Divorce was prohibited, although it sometimes took place. According to the *Arthasastra*, a wife who had been deserted by her husband could seek a divorce. Polygamy was fairly rare and apparently occurred mainly among the higher classes, but husbands were permitted to take a second wife if the first was barren. Producing children was an important aspect of marriage, both because children provided security for their parents in old age and because they were a physical proof of male potency. Child marriage was common for young girls, whether because of the desire for children or because daughters represented an economic liability to their parents. But perhaps the most graphic symbol of women's subjection to men was the ritual of ***sati*** (suh-TEE) (often written *suttee),* which encouraged the wife to throw herself on her dead husband's funeral pyre. The Greek visitor Megasthenes reported "that he had heard from some persons of wives burning themselves along with their deceased husbands and doing so gladly; and that those women who refused to burn themselves were held in disgrace."[5] All in all, it was undoubtedly a difficult existence. According to the *Law of Manu*, an early treatise on social organization and behavior in ancient India, probably written in the first or second century B.C.E., a woman was subordinated to men throughout her life—first to her father, then to her husband, and finally to her sons:

She should do nothing independently
even in her own house.
In childhood subject to her father,
in youth to her husband,
and when her husband is dead to her sons,
she should never enjoy independence. . . .

She should always be cheerful,
and skillful in her domestic duties,
with her household vessels well cleansed,
and her hand tight on the purse strings. . . .

Though he be uncouth and prone to pleasure,
though he have no good points at all,
the virtuous wife should ever
worship her lord as a god.[6]

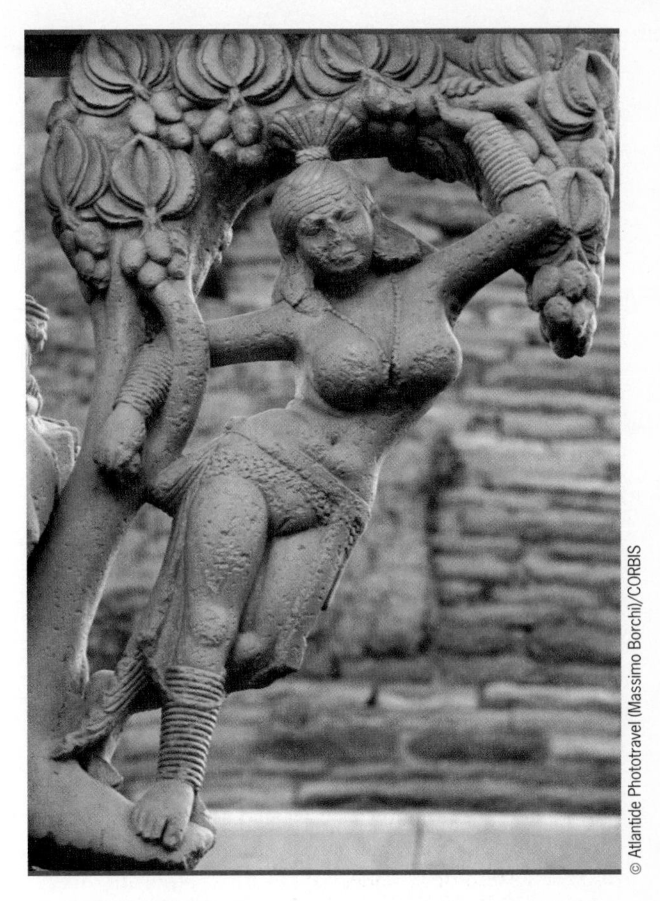

© Atlantide Phototravel (Massimo Borchi)/CORBIS

Female Earth Spirit. This earth spirit, carved on a gatepost of the Buddhist stupa at Sanchi (SAHN-chee) 2,200 years ago, illustrates how earlier Indian representations of the fertility goddess were incorporated into Buddhist art. Women were revered as powerful fertility symbols and considered dangerous when menstruating or immediately after giving birth. Voluptuous and idealized, this earth spirit was believed to be able to cause a tree to blossom by wrapping her leg around the trunk or even merely touching a branch with her arm.

THE ROLE OF WOMEN At the root of female subordination to the male was the practical fact that, as in most agricultural societies, men did most of the work in the fields. Females were viewed as having little utility outside the home and indeed were considered an economic burden, since parents were obliged to provide a dowry to acquire a husband for a daughter. Female children also appeared to offer little advantage in maintaining the family unit, since they joined the families of their husbands after the wedding ceremony.

Despite all of these indications of female subjection to the male, there are numerous signs that in some ways women often played an influential role in Indian society, and the code of behavior set out in the *Law of Manu* stressed that they should be treated with respect (see the box on p. 42). Indians appeared to be fascinated by female sexuality, and tradition held that women often used their sexual powers to achieve domination over men. The author of the Mahabharata, a vast epic of early Indian society, complained that "the fire has never too many logs, the ocean never too many rivers, death never too many living souls, and fair-eyed woman never too many men." Despite the legal and social constraints, women often played an important role within the family unit, and many were admired and honored for their talents. It is probably significant that paintings and sculpture from ancient and medieval India frequently show women in a role equal to that of men.

The Position of Women in Ancient India

FAMILY & SOCIETY

An indication of the ambivalent attitude toward women in ancient India is displayed in this passage from the *Law of Manu*, which states that respect for women is the responsibility of men. At the same time, it also makes clear that the place of women is in the home.

The *Law of Manu*

Women must be honored and adorned by their father, brothers, husbands, and brother-in-law who desire great good fortune.

Where women, verily, are honored, there the gods rejoice, where, however they are not honored, there all sacred rites prove fruitless.

Where the female relations live in grief—that family soon perishes completely; where, however, they do not suffer from any grievance—that family always prospers. . . .

The father who does not give away his daughter in marriage at the proper time is censurable; censurable is the husband who does not approach his wife in due season; and after the husband is dead, the son, verily is censurable, who does not protect his mother.

Even against the slightest provocations should women be particularly guarded; for unguarded they would bring grief to both the families.

Regarding this as the highest *dharma* of all four classes, husbands though weak, must strive to protect their wives.

His own offspring, character, family, self, and *dharma* does one protect when he protects his wife scrupulously. . . .

The husband should engage his wife in the collections and expenditure of his wealth, in cleanliness, in *dharma*, in cooking food for the family, and in looking after the necessities of the household. . . .

Women destined to bear children, enjoying great good fortune, deserving of worship, the resplendent lights of homes on the one hand and divinities of good luck who reside in the houses on the other—between these there is no difference whatsoever.

How do these attitudes toward women compare with those we have encountered in the Middle East and North Africa?

Source: From *Sources of Indian Tradition*, Vol. 1, 2e, by Ainslee Embree. Copyright © 1988 by Columbia University Press. Reprinted with the permission of the publisher.

Homosexuality was not unknown in India. It was condemned in the law books, however, and generally ignored by literature, which devoted its attention entirely to erotic heterosexuality. The *Kamasutra* (KAH-mah-soo-truh), a textbook on sexual practices and techniques dating from the second century C.E. or slightly thereafter, mentions homosexuality briefly and with no apparent enthusiasm.

The Economy

The arrival of the Aryans did not drastically change the economic character of Indian society. Not only did most Aryans eventually take up farming, but it is likely that agriculture expanded rapidly under Aryan rule with the invention of the iron plow and the spread of northern Indian culture into the Deccan Plateau. One consequence of this process was to shift the focus of Indian culture from the Indus valley farther eastward to the Ganges River valley, which even today is one of the most densely populated regions on earth. The flatter areas in the Deccan Plateau and in the coastal plains were also turned into cropland.

INDIAN FARMERS For most Indian farmers, life was harsh. Among the most fortunate were those who owned their own land, although they were required to pay taxes to the state. Many others were sharecroppers or landless laborers. They were subject to the vicissitudes of the market and often paid exorbitant rents to their landlord. Concentration of land in large holdings was limited by the tradition of dividing property among all the sons, but large estates worked by hired laborers or rented out to sharecroppers were not uncommon, particularly in areas where local rajas derived much of their wealth from their property.

Another problem for Indian farmers was the unpredictability of the climate. India is in the monsoon zone.

The monsoon is a seasonal wind pattern in southern Asia that blows from the southwest during the summer months and from the northeast during the winter. The southwest monsoon, originating in the Indian Ocean, is commonly marked by heavy rains. When the rains were late, thousands starved, particularly in the drier areas, which were especially dependent on rainfall. Strong governments attempted to deal with such problems by building state-operated granaries and maintaining the irrigation works; but strong governments were rare, and famine was probably all too common. The staple crops in the north were wheat, barley, and millet, with wet rice common in the fertile river valleys. In the south, grain and vegetables were supplemented by various tropical products, cotton, and spices such as pepper, ginger, cinnamon, and saffron.

TRADE AND MANUFACTURING By no means were all Indians farmers. As time passed, India became one of the most advanced trading and manufacturing civilizations in the ancient world. After the rise of the Mauryas, India's role in regional trade began to expand, and the subcontinent became a major transit point in a vast commercial network that extended from the rim of the Pacific to the Middle East and the Mediterranean Sea. This regional trade went both by sea and by camel caravan. Maritime trade based on the seasonal monsoon winds across the Indian Ocean may have begun as early as the fifth century B.C.E. It extended eastward as far as Southeast Asia and China and southward as far as the straits between Africa and the island of Madagascar. Westward went spices, teakwood, perfumes, jewels, textiles, precious stones and ivory, and wild animals. In return, India received gold, tin, lead, and wine. The subcontinent had, indeed, become a major crossroads of trade in the ancient world.

India's expanding role as a manufacturing and commercial hub of the ancient world was undoubtedly a spur to the growth of the state. Under Chandragupta Maurya, the central government became actively involved in commercial and manufacturing activities. It owned mines and vast crown lands and undoubtedly earned massive profits from its role in regional commerce. Separate government departments were established for trade, agriculture, mining, and the manufacture of weapons, and the movement of private goods was vigorously taxed. Nevertheless, a significant private sector also flourished; it was dominated by great caste guilds, which monopolized key sectors of the economy. A money economy probably came into operation during the second century B.C.E., when copper and gold coins were introduced from the Middle East. This in turn led to the development of banking.

Escaping the Wheel of Life: The Religious World of Ancient India

FOCUS QUESTIONS: What are the main tenets of Brahmanism and Buddhism? How did they differ, and how did each religion influence Indian civilization?

Like Indian politics and society, Indian religion is a blend of Aryan and Dravidian culture. The intermingling of those two civilizations gave rise to an extraordinarily complex set of religious beliefs and practices, filled with diversity and contrast. Out of this cultural mix came two of the world's great religions, Buddhism and Hinduism, and several smaller ones, including Jainism and Sikhism. Early Aryan religious beliefs, however, are known to historians as **Brahmanism**.

Brahmanism

Evidence about the earliest religious beliefs of the Aryan peoples comes primarily from sacred texts such as the Vedas, a set of four collections of hymns and religious ceremonies transmitted by memory through the centuries by Aryan priests. Many of these religious ideas were probably common to all of the Indo-European peoples before their separation into different groups at least four thousand years ago. Early Aryan beliefs were based on the common concept of a pantheon of gods and goddesses representing great forces of nature similar to the immortals of Greek mythology. The Aryan ancestor of the Greek father-god Zeus, for example, may have been the deity known in early Aryan tradition as Dyaus (DYOWS) (see Chapter 4).

The parent god Dyaus was a somewhat distant figure, however, and was eventually overshadowed by other, more functional gods possessing more familiar human traits. For a while, the primary Aryan god was the great warrior god Indra. Indra summoned the Aryan tribal peoples to war and was represented in nature by thunder. Later, Indra declined in importance and was replaced by Varuna (vuh-ROO-nuh), lord of justice. Other gods and goddesses represented various forces of nature or the needs of human beings, such as fire, fertility, and wealth.

The concept of sacrifice was a key element in Aryan religious belief in Vedic times. As in many other ancient cultures, the practice may have begun as human sacrifice, but later animals were used as substitutes. The priestly class, the *brahmins*, played a key role in these ceremonies. Another element of Indian religious belief in ancient times was the ideal of asceticism.

Although there is no reference to such practices in the Vedas, by the sixth century B.C.E., self-discipline, which involved subjecting oneself to painful stimuli or even self-mutilation, had begun to replace sacrifice as a means of placating or communicating with the gods. Apparently, the original motive for asceticism was to achieve magical powers, but later, in the Upanishads (oo-PAHN-ih-shahds)—a set of commentaries on the Vedas compiled in the sixth century B.C.E.—it was seen as a means of spiritual meditation that would enable the practitioner to reach beyond material reality to a world of truth and bliss beyond earthly joy and sorrow (see the box on p. 45). It is possible that another motive was to permit those with strong religious convictions to communicate directly with metaphysical reality without having to rely on the priestly class at court.

Asceticism, of course, has been practiced in other religions, including Christianity and Islam, but it seems particularly identified with **Hinduism**, the religion that emerged from early Indian religious tradition. Eventually, asceticism evolved into the modern practice of body training that we know as ***yoga*** ("union"), which is accepted today as a meaningful element of Hindu religious practice.

REINCARNATION Another new concept also probably began to appear around the time the Upanishads were written—the idea of **reincarnation**. This is the idea that the individual soul is reborn in a different form after death and progresses through several existences on the wheel of life until it reaches its final destination in a union with the Great World Soul, *Brahman*. Because life is harsh, this final release is the objective of all living souls. From this concept comes the term *Brahmanism*, referring to the early form of Aryan religious tradition.

A key element in this process is the idea of ***karma***—that one's rebirth in a next life is determined by one's *karma* (actions) in this life. Hinduism, as it emerged from Brahmanism in the first century C.E., placed all living species on a vast scale of existence, including the four classes and the untouchables in human society. The current status of an individual soul, then, is not simply a cosmic accident but the inevitable result of actions that that soul has committed in a past existence.

At the top of the scale are the *brahmins*, who by definition are closest to ultimate release from the law of reincarnation. The *brahmins* are followed in descending order by the other classes in human society and the world of the beasts. Within the animal kingdom, an especially high position is reserved for the cow, which even today is revered by Hindus as a sacred beast. Some have speculated that the cow's sacred position may have descended from the concept of the sacred bull in Harappan culture.

The concept of *karma* is governed by the *dharma*, a law regulating human behavior. The *dharma* imposes different requirements on different individuals depending on their status in society. Those high on the social scale, such as *brahmins* and *kshatriyas*, are held to a more strict form of behavior than are *sudras*. The *brahmin*, for example, is expected to abstain from eating meat, because that would entail the killing of another living being, thus interrupting its *karma*.

How the concept of reincarnation originated is not known, although it was apparently not unusual for early peoples to believe that the individual soul would be reborn in a different form in a later life. In any case, in India the concept may have had practical causes as well as consequences. In the first place, it tended to provide religious sanction for the rigid class divisions that had begun to emerge in Indian society after the arrival of the Aryans, and it provided moral and political justification for the privileges of those on the higher end of the scale.

At the same time, the concept of reincarnation provided certain compensations for those lower on the ladder of life. For example, it gave hope to the poor that if they behaved properly in this life, they might improve their condition in the next. It also provided a means for unassimilated groups such as ethnic minorities to find a place in Indian society while at the same time permitting them to maintain their distinctive way of life.

The ultimate goal of achieving "good" *karma,* as we have seen, was to escape the cycle of existence. To the sophisticated, the nature of that release was a spiritual union of the individual soul with the Great World Soul, *Brahman*, described in the Upanishads as a form of dreamless sleep, free from earthly desires. Such a concept, however, was undoubtedly too ethereal for the average Indian, who needed a more concrete form of heavenly salvation, a place of beauty and bliss after a life of disease and privation.

Popular Religion

Little is known about the religious beliefs of the vast majority of the Indian people during this formative stage in South Asian society. In all likelihood, popular religion during the first millennium B.C.E. was a distant reflection of its counterpart in India today, which is peopled with a multitude of very human gods and goddesses. It has been estimated that the Hindu pantheon contains more than 33,000 deities. Only a small number are primary ones, however, notably the so-called trinity of gods: Brahman the Creator, Vishnu the Preserver, and Shiva (SHIV-uh) (originally the Vedic god Rudra) the Destroyer. Although Brahman (sometimes in his concrete form called Brahma) is considered to be the highest god, Vishnu and Shiva take precedence in the devotional exercises of many Hindus, who can be roughly divided into Vishnuites and Shaivites. In addition to the trinity of gods, all of whom have wives with readily identifiable roles and personalities,

OPPOSING ≮ VIEWPOINTS

The Search for Truth

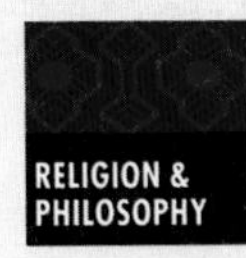

At the time the Rig Veda was originally composed in the second millennium B.C.E., *brahmins* at court believed that the best way to communicate with the gods was through sacrifice, a procedure that was carried out through the intermediation of the fire god Agni. The first selection is an incantation uttered by priests at the sacrificial ceremony.

By the middle of the first millennium B.C.E., however, the tradition of offering sacrifices had come under attack by opponents, who argued that the best way to seek truth and tranquillity was by renouncing material existence and adopting the life of a wandering mendicant. In the second selection, from the Mundaka Upanishad, an advocate of this position forcefully presents his views. The similarity with the fervent believers of early Christianity, who renounced the corrupting forces of everyday life by seeking refuge in isolated monasteries in the desert, is striking.

The Rig Veda

I extol Agni, the household priest, the divine minister of the sacrifice, the chief priest, the bestower of blessings.

May that Agni, who is to be extolled by ancient and modern seers, conduct the gods here.

Through Agni may one gain day by day wealth and welfare which is glorious and replete with heroic sons.

O Agni, the sacrifice and ritual which you encompass on every side, that indeed goes to the gods.

May Agni, the chief priest, who possesses the insight of a sage, who is truthful, widely renowned, and divine, come here with the gods.

O Agni, O Angiras ["messenger"], whatever prosperity you bring to the pious is indeed in accordance with your true function.

O Agni, illuminator of darkness, day by day we approach you with holy thought bringing homage to you.

*Presiding at ritual functions, the brightly shining custodian of the cosmic order [*rta*], thriving in your own realm.*

O Agni, be easy of access to us as a father to his son. Join us for our well-being.

The Mundaka Upanishad

Unsteady, indeed, are those boats in the form of sacrifices, eighteen in number, in which is prescribed only the inferior work. The fools who delight in this sacrificial ritual as the highest spiritual good go again and again through the cycle of old age and death.

Abiding in the midst of ignorance, wise only according to their own estimate, thinking themselves to be learned, but really obtuse, these fools go round in a circle like blind men led by one who is himself blind.

Abiding manifoldly in ignorance they, all the same, like immature children think to themselves: "We have accomplished our aim." Since the performers of sacrificial ritual do not realize the truth because of passion, therefore, they, the wretched ones, sink down from heaven when the merit that qualified them for the higher world becomes exhausted.

Regarding sacrifice and merit as most important, the deluded ones do not know of any other higher spiritual good. Having enjoyed themselves only for a time on top of the heaven won by good deeds [sacrifice, etc.] they reenter this world or a still lower one.

Those who practice penance [*tapas*] and faith in the forest, the tranquil ones, the knowers of truth, living the life of wandering mendicancy—they depart, freed from passion, through the door of the sun, to where dwells verily . . . the imperishable Soul [*atman*].

Having scrutinized the worlds won by sacrificial rites, a *brahmin* should arrive at nothing but disgust. The world that was not made is not won by what is done [i.e., by sacrifice]. For the sake of that knowledge he should go with sacrificial fuel in hand as a student, in all humility to a preceptor [*guru*] who is well versed in the [Vedic] scriptures and also firm in the realization of Brahman.

Unto him who has approached him in proper form, whose mind is tranquil, who has attained peace, does the knowing teacher teach, in its very truth, that knowledge about Brahman by means of which one knows . . . the only Reality.

In which passages in these two documents do you find a reference to the idea of karma *(see the discussion under "Reincarnation" in the text)? Which document makes use of the concept, and how? What role does ascetism play in these documents?*

Source: From *Sources of Indian Tradition*, Vol. 1, 2e, by Ainslee Embree. Copyright © 1988 by Columbia University Press. Reprinted with the permission of the publisher.

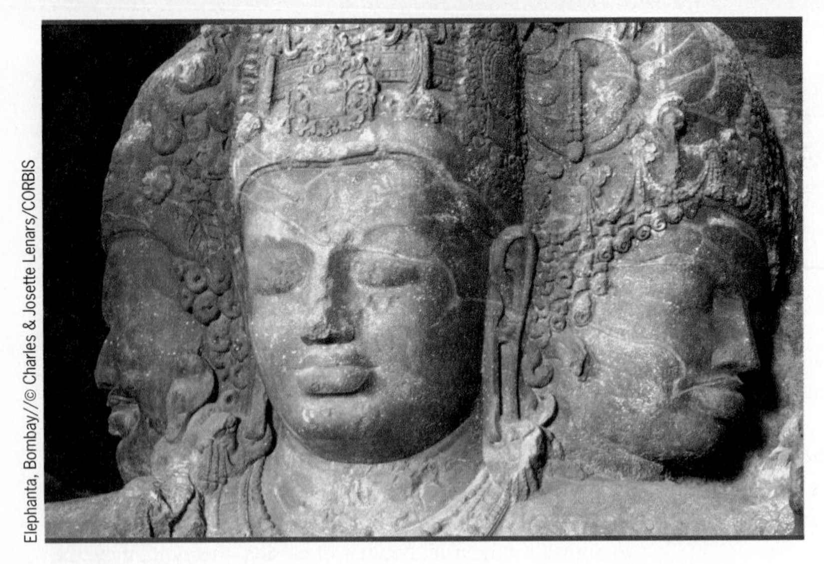

Elephanta, Bombay//© Charles & Josette Lenars/CORBIS

The Three Faces of Shiva. In the first centuries C.E., Hindus began to adopt Buddhist rock art. One outstanding example is at the Elephanta Caves, near the modern city of Mumbai (Bombay). Dominating the cave is this 18-foot-high triple-headed statue of Shiva, representing the Hindu deity in all his various aspects. The central figure shows him in total serenity, enveloped in absolute knowledge. The angry profile on the left portrays him as the destroyer, struggling against time, death, and other negative forces. The right-hand profile shows his loving and feminine side in the guise of his beautiful wife, Parvati.

there are countless minor deities, each again with his or her own specific function. A notable example is Ganesha, described in Indian literature as a son of Shiva who was accidentally beheaded by his father in a fit of anger. When Shiva repented of his action, he provided his son with the head of an elephant. Even today the widely revered Ganesha is often viewed as the god of good fortune.

The rich variety and the earthy character of many of these deities are somewhat misleading, however, for Hindus regard the multitude of gods simply as different manifestations of one ultimate reality. The various deities also provide a way for ordinary Indians to personify their religious feelings. Even though some individuals among the early Aryans attempted to communicate with the gods through animal sacrifice or asceticism, most Indians undoubtedly sought to satisfy their own individual religious needs through devotion, which they expressed through ritual ceremonies and offerings at a temple. Such offerings were not only a way of seeking salvation but also a means of satisfying all the aspirations of daily life.

Over the centuries, Indian religious belief changed radically from its origins in Aryan pastoral society. An early belief in deities representing forces of nature gradually gave way to a more elitist system, with a priestly class at court performing sacrifices in order to obtain heavenly favors. During the first millennium B.C.E., religious belief began to evolve into a more personal experience, with an emphasis on ethics as a means of obtaining a union between ***Atman*** (AHT-mun), the individual soul, and *Brahman*, the ultimate reality.[7]

The average Indian, however, would probably have thought of heavenly salvation in more concrete terms, as a place where the hardships of earthly life would give way to pleasure and delight. In later centuries, the Brahmanical beliefs and practices of early Aryan society would gradually be replaced by a more popular faith that would henceforth become known as Hinduism. We will discuss that transformation in Chapter 9.

Buddhism: The Middle Path

In the sixth century B.C.E., a new doctrine appeared in northern India that soon began to rival the popularity of Brahmanical beliefs throughout the subcontinent. This new doctrine was called **Buddhism**.

THE LIFE OF SIDDHARTHA GAUTAMA The historical founder of Buddhism, Siddhartha Gautama (si-DAR-tuh GAW-tuh-muh), was a native of a small principality in the foothills of the Himalaya Mountains in what is today southern Nepal. He was born in the mid-sixth century B.C.E., the son of a ruling *kshatriya* family (see the comparative illustration on p. 47). According to tradition, the young Siddhartha was raised in affluent surroundings and trained, like many other members of his class, in the martial arts. On reaching maturity, he married and began to raise a family. At the age of twenty-nine, however, he suddenly discovered the pain of illness, the sorrow of death, and the degradation caused by old age in the lives of ordinary people and exclaimed, "Would that sickness, age, and death might be forever bound!" From that time on, he decided to dedicate his life to determining the cause and seeking the cure for human suffering.

To find the answers to these questions, Siddhartha abandoned his home and family and traveled widely. At first, he tried to follow the model of the ascetics, but he eventually decided that self-mortification did not lead to a greater understanding of life and abandoned the practice. Then one day, after a lengthy period of meditation under a tree, he finally achieved enlightenment as to the meaning of life and spent the remainder of his life preaching it. His conclusions, as embodied in his teachings, became the philosophy (or, as some would have it, the religion) of Buddhism. According to legend, the Devil (the Indian term is *Mara*) attempted desperately to tempt

COMPARATIVE ILLUSTRATION

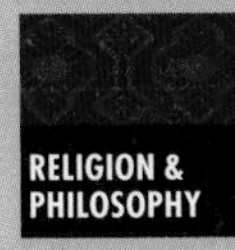

The Buddha and Jesus. As Buddhism evolved, transforming Siddhartha Gautama, known as the Buddha, from mortal to god, Buddhist art changed as well. Statuary and relief panels began to illustrate the story of his life. At the left, in a frieze from the second century C.E., the infant Siddhartha is seen emerging from the hip of his mother, Queen Maya. Although dressed in draperies that reflect Greek influences from Alexander the Great's brief incursion into northwestern India, her sensuous stance and the touching of the tree evoke the female earth spirit of traditional Indian art. On the right is a Byzantine painting depicting the infant Jesus with his mother, the Virgin Mary, dating from the sixth century C.E. Notice that a halo surrounds the head of both the Buddha and Jesus. The halo—a circle of light—is an ancient symbol of divinity. In Hindu, Greek, and Roman art, the heads of gods were depicted emitting sunlike divine radiances. Early kings adopted crowns made of gold and precious gems to symbolize their own divine authority.

What similarities and differences do you see in these depictions of the mothers of key religious figures?

him with political power and the company of beautiful girls. But Siddhartha Gautama resisted:

> *Pleasure is brief as a flash of lightning*
> *Or like an autumn shower, only for a moment. . . .*
> *Why should I then covet the pleasures you speak of?*
> *I see your bodies are full of all impurity:*
> *Birth and death, sickness and age are yours.*
> *I seek the highest prize, hard to attain by men—*
> *The true and constant wisdom of the wise.*[8]

BUDDHISM AND BRAHMANISM How much the modern doctrine of Buddhism resembles the original teachings of Siddhartha Gautama is open to debate, since much time has elapsed since his death and original texts relating his ideas are lacking. Nor is it certain that Siddhartha even intended to found a new religion or doctrine. In some respects, his ideas could be viewed as a reformist form of Brahmanism, designed to transfer responsibility from the priests to the individual, much as the sixteenth-century German monk Martin Luther saw his ideas as a reformation of Christianity. Siddhartha accepted much of the belief system of Brahmanism, if not all of its practices. For example, he accepted the concept of reincarnation and the role of *karma* as a means of influencing the movement of individual souls up and down in the scale of life. He praised nonviolence and borrowed the idea of living a life of simplicity and chastity from the ascetics. Moreover, his vision of metaphysical reality—commonly known as **Nirvana**—is closer to the Aryan concept of *Brahman* than it is to the Christian concept of heavenly salvation. Nirvana, which involves an extinction of selfhood and a final reunion with the Great World Soul, is sometimes likened to a dreamless sleep or to a kind of "blowing out" (as of a candle). Buddhists occasionally remark that someone who asks for a description does not understand the concept.

At the same time, the new doctrine differed from existing practices in a number of key ways. In the first place, Siddhartha denied the existence of an individual soul. To him, the concept of *Atman*—the individual soul—meant that the soul was subject to rebirth and thus did not achieve a complete liberation from the cares of this world. In fact, Siddhartha denied the ultimate reality of the material world in its entirety and taught that it was an illusion to be transcended. Siddhartha's idea of achieving Nirvana was based on his conviction that the pain, poverty, and sorrow that afflict human beings are caused essentially by their attachment to the things of this world. Once worldly cares are abandoned, pain and sorrow can be overcome. With this knowledge comes ***bodhi*** (BOH-dee), or wisdom (source of the term *Buddhism* and the familiar name for Gautama the Wise: Gautama Buddha).

Achieving this understanding is a key step on the road to Nirvana, which, as in Brahmanism, is a form of release from the wheel of life. According to tradition, Siddhartha transmitted this message in a sermon to his disciples in a deer park at Sarnath (see the box on p. 49), not far from the modern city of Benares—also known as Varanasi (vah-RAH-nah-see). Like so many messages, it is deceptively simple and is enclosed in four noble truths: life is suffering; suffering is caused by desire; the way to end suffering is to end desire; and the way to end desire is to avoid the extremes of a life of vulgar materialism and a life of self-torture and to follow the **Middle Path**. Also known as the Eightfold Way, the Middle Path calls for right knowledge, right purpose, right speech, right conduct, right occupation, right effort, right awareness, and right meditation.

Buddhism also differed in its relative egalitarianism. Although Siddhartha accepted the idea of reincarnation (and hence the idea that human beings differ as a result of *karma* accumulated in a previous existence), he rejected the division of humanity into rigidly defined classes based on previous reincarnations and taught that all human beings could aspire to Nirvana as a result of their behavior in this life—a message that likely helped Buddhism win support among people at the lower end of the social scale.

In addition, Buddhism was much simpler than existing beliefs. Siddhartha rejected the panoply of gods that had become identified with Brahmanism and forbade his followers to worship his person or his image after his death. In fact, many Buddhists view Buddhism as a philosophy rather than a religion.

After Siddhartha Gautama's death in 480 B.C.E., dedicated disciples carried his message the length and breadth of India. Buddhist monasteries were established throughout the subcontinent, and temples and **stupas** (STOO-puhs) (stone towers housing relics of the Buddha) sprang up throughout the countryside.

Women were permitted to join the monastic order but only in an inferior position. As Siddhartha had explained, women are "soon angered," "full of passion," and "stupid": "that is the reason . . . why women have no place in public assemblies . . . and do not earn their living by any profession." Still, the position of women tended to be better in Buddhist societies than it was elsewhere in ancient India.

JAINISM During the next centuries, Buddhism began to compete actively with the existing Aryan beliefs, as well as with another new faith known as **Jainism** (JY-ni-zuhm). Jainism was founded by Mahavira (mah-hah-VEE-ruh), a contemporary of Siddhartha Gautama. Resembling Buddhism in its rejection of the reality of the material world, Jainism was more extreme in practice. Whereas Siddhartha Gautama called for the "middle way" between passion and luxury and pain and self-torture, Mahavira preached a doctrine of extreme simplicity to his followers, who kept no possessions and relied on begging for a living. Some even rejected clothing and wandered through the world naked. Perhaps because of its insistence on a life of poverty, Jainism failed to attract enough adherents to become a major doctrine and never received official support. According to tradition, however, Chandragupta Maurya accepted Mahavira's doctrine after abdicating the throne and fasted to death in a Jain monastery.

ASHOKA, A BUDDHIST MONARCH Buddhism received an important boost when Ashoka (uh-SHOH-kuh), the grandson of Chandragupta Maurya, converted to Buddhism in the third century B.C.E. Ashoka (269–232 B.C.E.) is widely considered the greatest ruler in the history of India. By his own admission, as noted in rock edicts placed around his kingdom, Ashoka began his reign conquering, pillaging, and killing, but after his conversion to Buddhism, he began to regret his bloodthirsty past and attempted to rule benevolently.

Ashoka directed that banyan trees and shelters be placed along the road to provide shade and rest for weary

How to Achieve Enlightenment

One of the most famous passages in Buddhist literature is the sermon at Sarnath, which Siddhartha Gautama delivered to his followers in a deer park outside the holy city of Varanasi (Benares), in the Ganges River valley. Here he set forth the key ideas that would define Buddhist beliefs for centuries to come. During an official visit to Sarnath nearly three centuries later, Emperor Ashoka ordered the construction of a stupa (reliquary) in honor of the Buddha's message.

The Sermon at Benares

Thus have I heard: at one time the Lord dwelt at Benares at Isipatana in the Deer Park. There the Lord addressed the five monks:

"These two extremes, monks, are not to be practiced by one who has gone forth from the world. What are the two? That conjoined with the passions and luxury, low, vulgar, common, ignoble, and useless; and that conjoined with self-torture, painful, ignoble, and useless. Avoiding these two extremes the Tathagata has gained the enlightenment of the Middle Path, which produces insight and knowledge and tends to calm, to higher knowledge, enlightenment, Nirvana.

"And what, monks, is the Middle Path, of which the Tathagata has gained enlightenment, which produces insight and knowledge, and tends to calm, to higher knowledge, enlightenment, Nirvana? This is the noble Eightfold Way: namely, right view, right intention, right speech, right action, right livelihood, right effort, right mindfulness, right concentration. This, monks, is the Middle Path, of which the Tathagata has gained enlightenment, which produces insight and knowledge, and tends to calm, to higher knowledge, enlightenment, Nirvana.

"1. Now this, monks, is the noble truth of pain: birth is painful, old age is painful, sickness is painful, death is painful, sorrow, lamentation, dejection, and despair are painful. Contact with unpleasant things is painful, not getting what one wishes is painful. In short the five groups of graspings are painful.

"2. Now this, monks, is the noble truth of the cause of pain: the craving, which tends to rebirth, combined with pleasure and lust, finding pleasure here and there; namely, the craving for passion, the craving for existence, the craving for nonexistence.

"3. Now this, monks, is the noble truth of the cessation of pain, the cessation without a remainder of craving, the abandonment, forsaking, release, nonattachment.

"4. Now this, monks, is the noble truth of the way that leads to the cessation of pain: this is the noble Eightfold Way; namely, right view, right intention, right speech, right action, right livelihood, right effort, right mindfulness, right concentration.

"And when, monks, in these four noble truths my due knowledge and insight with its three sections and twelve divisions was well purified, then, monks, . . . I had attained the highest complete enlightenment. This I recognized. Knowledge arose in me, insight arose that the release of my mind is unshakable; this is my last existence; now there is no rebirth."

How did Siddhartha Gautama reach the conclusion that following the "four noble truths" was the proper course for living a moral life? How do his ideas compare with the commandments that God gave to the Israelites (see Chapter 1)?

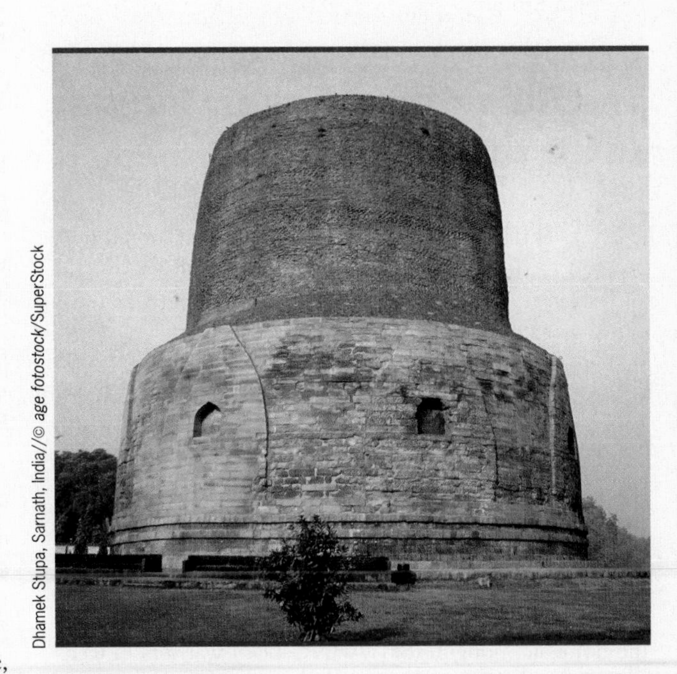

Dhamek Stupa, Sarnath, India//© *age fotostock*/SuperStock

The stupa at Sarnath.

Source: From *The Teachings of the Compassionate Buddha*, E. A. Burtt, ed. Copyright 1955 by Mentor. Used by permission of the E. A. Burtt Estate.

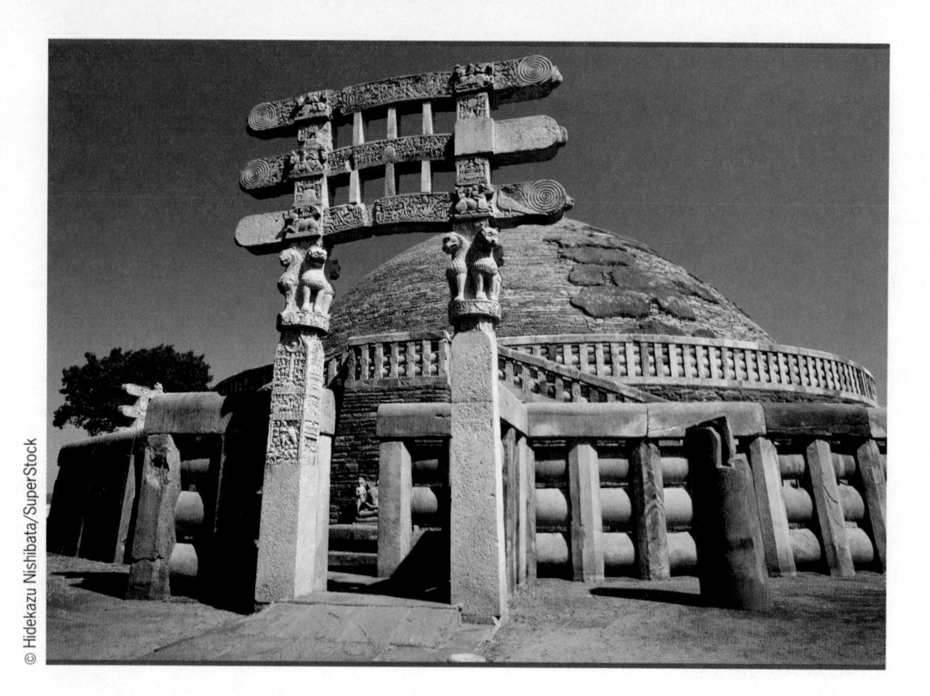

© Hidekazu Nishibata/SuperStock

Sanchi Gate and Stupa. Constructed during the reign of Emperor Ashoka in the third century B.C.E., the stupa at Sanchi was enlarged over time, eventually becoming the greatest Buddhist monument in the Indian subcontinent. Originally intended to house a relic of the Buddha, the stupa became a holy place for devotion and a familiar form of Buddhist architecture. Sanchi's four elaborately carved stone gates, each over 40 feet high, tell stories of the Buddha set in joyful scenes of everyday life. Christian churches would later portray events in the life of Jesus to instruct the faithful.

travelers. He sent Buddhist missionaries throughout India and ordered the erection of stone pillars with official edicts and Buddhist inscriptions to instruct people in the proper way (see Map 2.3). According to tradition, his son converted the island of Sri Lanka to Buddhism, and the peoples there accepted a tributary relationship with the Mauryan Empire.

The Rule of the Fishes: India After the Mauryas

FOCUS QUESTION: Why was India unable to maintain a unified empire in the first millennium B.C.E., and how was the Mauryan Empire temporarily able to overcome the tendencies toward disunity?

After Ashoka's death in 232 B.C.E., the Mauryan Empire began to decline. In 183 B.C.E., the last Mauryan ruler was overthrown by one of his military commanders, and India reverted to disunity. A number of new kingdoms, some of them perhaps influenced by the memory of the Alexandrian conquests, arose along the fringes of the subcontinent in Bactria, known today as Afghanistan. In the first century C.E., Indo-European-speaking peoples fleeing from the nomadic Xiongnu (SHYAHNG-noo) warriors in Central Asia seized power in the area and proclaimed the new Kushan (koo-SHAHN) kingdom (see Chapter 9). For the next two centuries, the Kushanas extended their political sway over northern India as far as the central Ganges valley, while other kingdoms scuffled for predominance elsewhere on the subcontinent. India would not see unity again for another five hundred years.

Several reasons for India's failure to maintain a unified empire have been proposed. Some historians suggest that a decline in regional trade during the first millennium C.E. may have contributed to the growth of small land-based kingdoms, which drew their primary income from agriculture. The tenacity of the Aryan tradition with its emphasis on tribal rivalries may also have contributed. Although the Mauryan rulers tried to impose a more centralized organization, clan loyalties once again came to the fore after the collapse of the Mauryan dynasty. Furthermore, the behavior of the ruling class was characterized by what Indians call the "rule of the fishes," which glorified warfare as the natural activity of the king and the aristocracy. The *Arthasastra*, which set forth a model of a centralized Indian state, assumed that war was the "sport of kings." Still, this was not an uneventful period in the history of India, as Indo-Aryan ideas continued to spread toward the south and both Brahmanism and Buddhism evolved in new directions.

The Exuberant World of Indian Culture

FOCUS QUESTION: In what ways did the culture of ancient India resemble and differ from the cultural experience of ancient Mesopotamia and Egypt?

Few cultures in the world are as rich and varied as that of India. Most societies excel in some forms of artistic and literary achievement and not in others, but India has produced

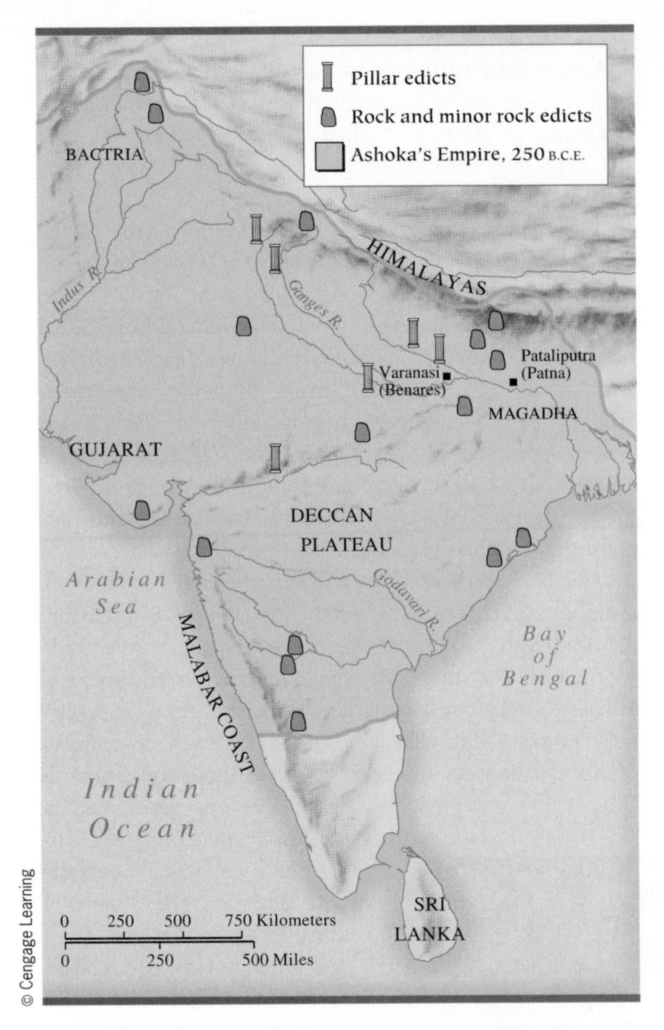

© Cengage Learning

MAP 2.3 The Empire of Ashoka. Ashoka, the greatest Indian monarch, reigned over the Mauryan Empire in the third century B.C.E. This map shows the extent of his empire, and the location of the pillar edicts that were erected along major trade routes.

Q *Why do you think the pillars and rocks were placed where they were?*

great works in almost all fields of cultural endeavor—art and sculpture, science, architecture, and literature.

Literature

The earliest known Indian literature consists of the four Vedas, which were passed down orally from generation to generation until they were finally written down after the Aryans arrived in India. The Rig Veda dates from the second millennium B.C.E. and consists of more than a thousand hymns that were used at religious ceremonies. The other three Vedas were written considerably later and contain instructions for performing ritual sacrifices and other ceremonies.

The language of the Vedas was **Sanskrit** (SAN-skrit), part of the Indo-European family of languages. After the Aryans entered India, Sanskrit gradually declined as a spoken language and was replaced in northern India by a simpler tongue known as **Prakrit** (PRAH-krit). Nevertheless, Sanskrit continued to be used as the language of the bureaucracy and literary expression for many centuries after that and, like Latin in medieval Europe, served as a common language of communication between various regions of India. In the south, a variety of Dravidian languages continued to be spoken.

After the development of a new writing system sometime in the first millennium B.C.E., India's holy literature was probably inscribed on palm leaves stitched together into a book somewhat similar to the first books produced on papyrus or parchment in the Mediterranean region. Also written for the first time were India's great historical epics, the Mahabharata and the Ramayana (rah-mah-YAH-nah). Both of these epics may have originally been recited at religious ceremonies, but they are essentially historical writings that recount the martial exploits of great Aryan rulers and warriors.

The Mahabharata, consisting of more than 90,000 stanzas, was probably written about 100 B.C.E. and describes in great detail a war between cousins for control of the kingdom about 1000 B.C.E. Interwoven in the narrative are many fantastic legends of the Hindu gods. Above all, the Mahabharata is a tale of moral confrontations. The most famous section of the book is the Bhagavad Gita, a sermon by the legendary Indian figure Krishna on the eve of a major battle. In this sermon, Krishna sets forth one of the key ethical maxims of Indian society: in taking action, one must be indifferent to success or failure and consider only the moral rightness of the act itself.

The Ramayana, written at about the same time, is much shorter than the Mahabharata. It is an account of a semilegendary ruler named Rama (RAH-mah) who, as the result of a palace intrigue, is banished from the kingdom and forced to live as a hermit in the forest. Later, he fights the demon-king of Sri Lanka (Ceylon), who has kidnapped his beloved wife, Sita (SEE-tuh). Like the Mahabharata, the Ramayana is strongly imbued with religious and moral significance. Rama himself is portrayed as the ideal Aryan hero, a perfect ruler and an ideal son, while Sita projects the supreme duty of female chastity and wifely loyalty to her husband. The Ramayana is a story of the triumph of good over evil, duty over self-indulgence, and generosity over selfishness. It combines filial and erotic love, conflicts of human passion, character analysis, and poetic descriptions of nature.

The Ramayana also has all the ingredients of an enthralling adventure: giants, wondrous flying chariots, invincible arrows and swords, and magic potions and mantras. One of the real heroes of the story is the monkey-king Hanuman, who flies from India to Sri Lanka to set the great battle in motion. It is no wonder that for millennia the Ramayana has remained a favorite among Indians of all age groups and in recent years inspired a hugely popular TV version.

Architecture and Sculpture

After literature, the greatest achievements of early Indian civilization were in architecture and sculpture. Some of the earliest examples of Indian architecture stem from the time of Emperor Ashoka, when Buddhism became the religion of the state. Until the time of the Mauryas, Aryan buildings had been constructed of wood. With the rise of the empire, stone began to be used as artisans arrived in India seeking employment after the destruction of the Persian Empire by Alexander. Many of these stone carvers accepted the patronage of Emperor Ashoka, who used them to spread Buddhist ideas throughout the subcontinent.

There were three main types of religious structures: the pillar, the stupa, and the rock chamber. During Ashoka's reign, many stone columns were erected alongside roads to commemorate the events in the Buddha's life and mark pilgrim routes to holy places. Weighing up to 50 tons each and rising as high as 32 feet, these polished sandstone pillars were topped with a carved capital, usually depicting lions uttering the Buddha's message. Ten remain standing today.

A stupa was originally meant to house a relic of the Buddha, such as a lock of his hair or a branch of the famous Bodhi tree, and was constructed in the form of a burial mound (the pyramids in Egypt also derived from burial mounds). Eventually, the stupa became a place for devotion and the most familiar form of Buddhist architecture. Stupas rose to considerable heights and were surmounted with a spire, possibly representing the stages of existence en route to Nirvana. According to legend, Ashoka ordered the construction of 84,000 stupas throughout India to promote the Buddha's message. A few survive today.

The final form of early Indian architecture is the rock chamber carved out of a cliff on the side of a mountain. Ashoka began the construction of these chambers to provide rooms to house monks or wandering ascetics and to serve as halls for religious ceremonies. The chambers were rectangular in form, with pillars, an altar, and a vault, reminiscent of Roman basilicas in the West. The three most famous chambers of this period are at Bhaja, Karli, and Ellora (el-LOR-uh); this last one contains twenty-nine rooms (see the comparative illustration on p. 237).

All three forms of architecture were embellished with decorations. Consisting of detailed reliefs and freestanding statues of deities, other human figures, and animals, these decorations are permeated with a sense of nature and the vitality of life. Many reflect an amalgamation of popular and sacred themes, of Buddhist, Vedic, and pre-Aryan religious motifs, such as male and female earth spirits. Until the second century C.E., Siddhartha Gautama was represented only through symbols, such as the wheel of life, the Bodhi tree, and the footprint, perhaps because artists deemed it improper to portray him in human form, since he had escaped his corporal confines into enlightenment. After the spread of Mahayana

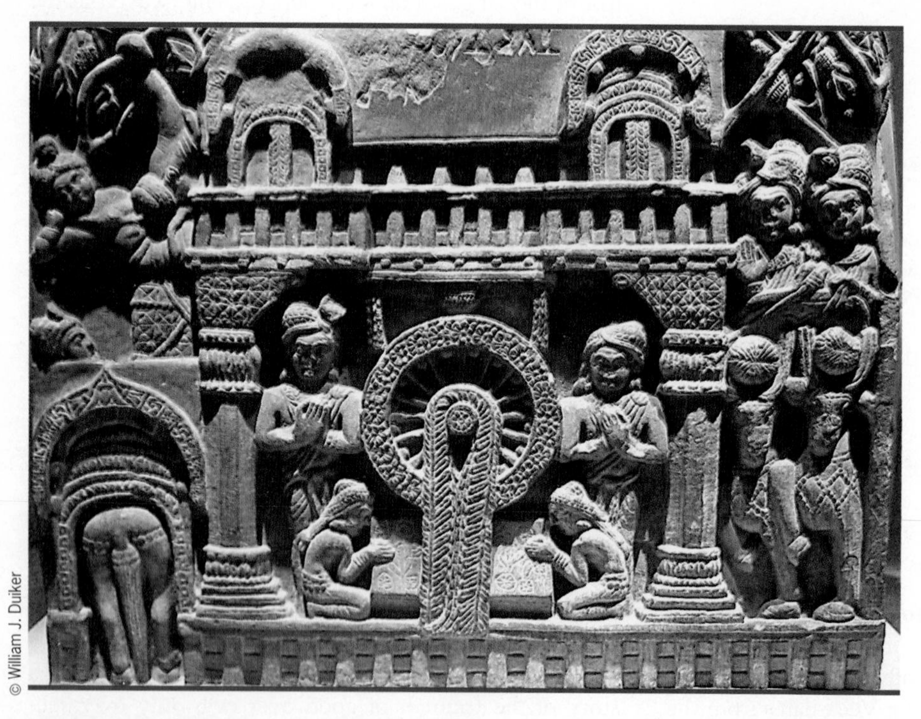

© William J. Duiker

Symbols of the Buddha. Early Buddhist sculptures depicted the Buddha only through visual symbols that represented his life on the path to enlightenment. In this relief from the stupa at Bharhut, carved in the second century B.C.E., we see four devotees paying homage to the Buddha, who is portrayed as a giant wheel dispensing his "wheel of the law." The riderless horse on the left represents Siddhartha Gautama's departure from his father's home as he set out on his search for the meaning of life.

Buddhism in the second century, when the Buddha began to be portrayed as a god, his image began to appear in stone as an object for divine worship.

By this time, India had established its own unique religious art. The art is permeated by sensuousness and exuberance and is often overtly sexual. These scenes are meant to express otherworldly delights, not the pleasures of this world. The sensuous paradise that adorned the religious art of ancient India represented salvation and fulfillment for the ordinary Indian.

Science

Our knowledge of Indian science is limited by the paucity of written sources, but it is evident that ancient Indians had amassed an impressive amount of scientific knowledge in a number of areas. Especially notable was their work in mathematics, where they devised the numerical system that we know as "Arabic numerals" and use today, and in astronomy, where they charted the movements of the heavenly bodies and recognized the spherical nature of the earth at an early date. Their ideas of physics were similar to those of the Greeks; matter was divided into the five elements of earth, air, fire, water, and ether. Many of their technological achievements are impressive, notably the quality of their textiles and the massive stone pillars erected during the reign of Ashoka. The pillars weighed up to 50 tons each and were transported many miles to their final destination.

CHAPTER SUMMARY

While the peoples of North Africa and the Middle East were actively building the first civilizations, a similar process was getting under way in the Indus River valley. Much has been learned about the nature of the Indus valley civilization in recent years, but the lack of written records limits our understanding. How did the Harappan people deal with the fundamental human problems mentioned at the close of Chapter 1? The answers remain tantalizingly elusive.

As often happened elsewhere, however, the collapse of Harappan civilization did not lead to the total disappearance of its culture. The new society that eventually emerged throughout the subcontinent after the coming of the Aryans was an amalgam of two highly distinctive cultures, each of which made a significant contribution to the politics, social institutions, and creative impulse of ancient Indian civilization.

With the rise of the Mauryan dynasty in the fourth century B.C.E., the distinctive features of a great civilization begin to be clearly visible. It was extensive in its scope, embracing the entire Indian subcontinent and eventually, in the form of Buddhism and Hinduism, spreading to China and Southeast Asia. But the underlying ethnic, linguistic, and cultural diversity of the Indian people posed a constant challenge to the unity of the state. After the collapse of the Mauryas, the subcontinent would not come under a single authority again for several hundred years.

In the meantime, another great experiment was taking place far to the northeast, across the Himalaya Mountains. Like many other civilizations of antiquity, the first Chinese state was concentrated on a major river system. And like them, too, its political and cultural achievements eventually spread far beyond their original habitat. In the next chapter, we turn to the civilization of ancient China.

CHAPTER TIMELINE

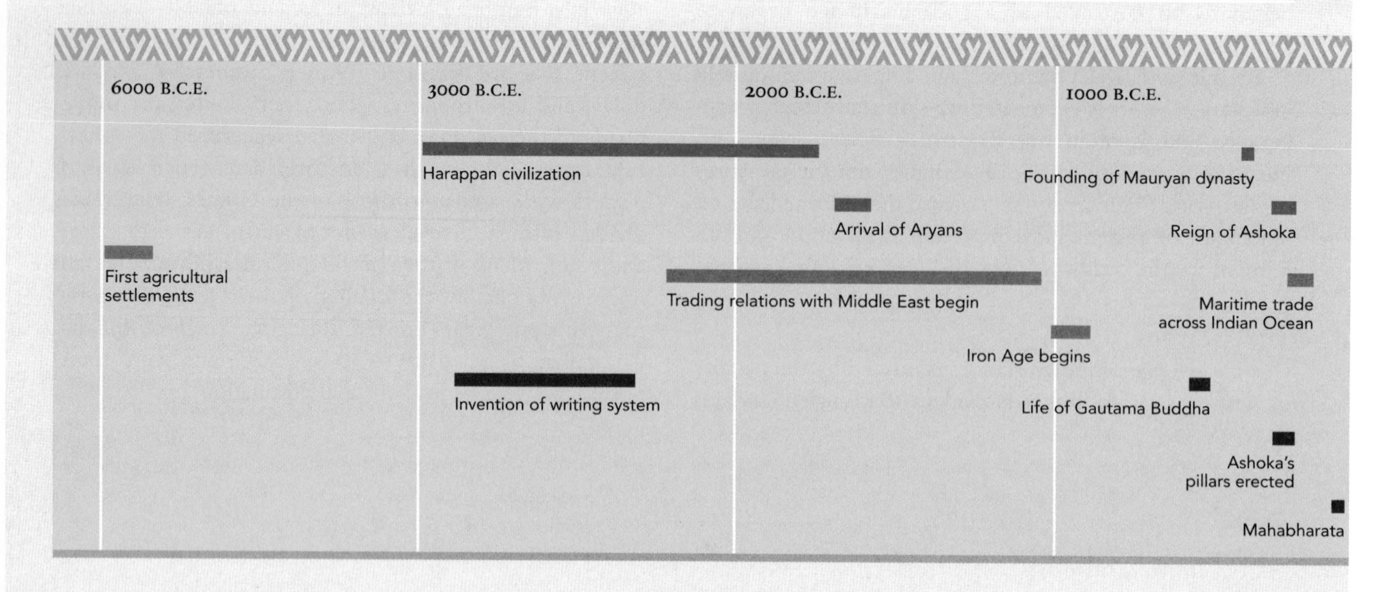

CHAPTER REVIEW

Upon Reflection

Q What is the debate over the origins of the Aryan peoples, and why do many historians of India consider it to be such an important question?

Q Why was Buddhism able to make such inroads among the Indian people at a time when Brahmanical beliefs had long been dominant in the subcontinent?

Q What were some of the main characteristics of Indian politics and government during the first millennium B.C.E., and how can they be compared and contrasted with those of ancient Egypt and Mesopotamia?

Key Terms

raja (p. 36)
kshatriya (p. 36)
maharajas (p. 36)
dharma (p. 36)
varna (p. 39)
brahmins (p. 39)
Brahman (p. 39)
vaisya (p. 39)
twice-born (p. 39)
sudras (p. 39)
pariahs (p. 39)
jati (p. 40)
guru (p. 40)
sati (p. 41)
Brahmanism (p. 43)
Hinduism (p. 44)
yoga (p. 44)
reincarnation (p. 44)
karma (p. 44)
Atman (p. 46)
Buddhism (p. 46)
Nirvana (p. 48)
bodhi (p. 48)
Middle Path (p. 48)
stupas (p. 48)
Jainism (p. 48)
Sanskrit (p. 51)
Prakrit (p. 51)

Suggested Reading

THE EMERGENCE OF CIVILIZATION IN INDIA: GENERAL WORKS Several standard histories of India provide a good overview of the ancient period. One of the most readable and reliable is **S. Wolpert, *New History of India,*** 7th ed. (New York, 2003). Also see **B. Metcalf** and **T. Metcalf, *A Concise History of India*** (Cambridge, 2001). **R. Thapar, *Early India: From the Origins to AD 1300*** (London, 2002), provides an excellent review of recent scholarship by an Indian historian.

HARAPPAN SOCIETY Because of the relative paucity of archaeological exploration in South Asia, evidence for the Harappan period is not as voluminous as for areas such as Mesopotamia and the Nile valley. Some of the best work has been written by scholars who actually worked at the sites. One fine account is **J. M. Kenoyer,** ***Ancient Cities of the Indus Valley Civilization*** (Karachi, 1998). Commercial relations between Harappa and its neighbors are treated in **S. Ratnagar,** ***Encounters: The Westerly Trade of the Harappan Civilization*** (Oxford, 1981). For information on the invention of the first writing systems, see **J. T. Hooker, ed.,** ***Reading the Past: Ancient Writing from Cuneiform to the Alphabet*** (London, 1990), and **A. Hurley,** ***The Alphabet: The History, Evolution, and Design of the Letters We Use Today*** (New York, 1995).

ESCAPING THE WHEEL OF LIFE: THE RELIGIOUS WORLD OF ANCIENT INDIA There are a number of good books on the introduction of Buddhism into Indian society. The Buddha's ideals are presented in **P. Williams** (with **A. Tribe**), ***Buddhist Thought: A Complete Introduction to the Indian Tradition*** (London, 2000). Also see **J. Strong,** ***The Buddha: A Short Biography*** (Oxford, 2004). On the early development of Hinduism, see **E. Bryant,** ***The Quest for the Origins of Vedic Culture*** (Oxford, 2001), and **V. Narayan,** ***Hinduism*** (Oxford, 2004). For a comparative treatment, see **K. Armstrong,** ***The Great Transformation: The Beginning of Our Religious Traditions*** (New York, 2006).

THE EXUBERANT WORLD OF INDIAN CULTURE There are a number of excellent surveys of Indian art, including the concise ***Indian Art,*** rev. ed. (London, 1997), by **R. Craven**. See also **V. Dehejia,** ***Devi: The Great Goddess*** (Washington, D.C., 1999) and ***Indian Art*** (London, 1997). Numerous editions of Sanskrit literature are available in English translation. Many are available in the multivolume Harvard Oriental Series. For a shorter annotated anthology of selections from the Indian classics, consult **S. N. Hay, ed.,** ***Sources of Indian Tradition,*** 2 vols. (New York, 1988). On the role played by women writers in ancient India, see **S. Tharu** and **K. Lalita, eds.,** ***Women Writing in India: 600 B.C. to the Present,*** vol. 1 (New York, 1991).

Visit the CourseMate website at **www.cengagebrain.com** for additional study tools and review materials for this chapter.

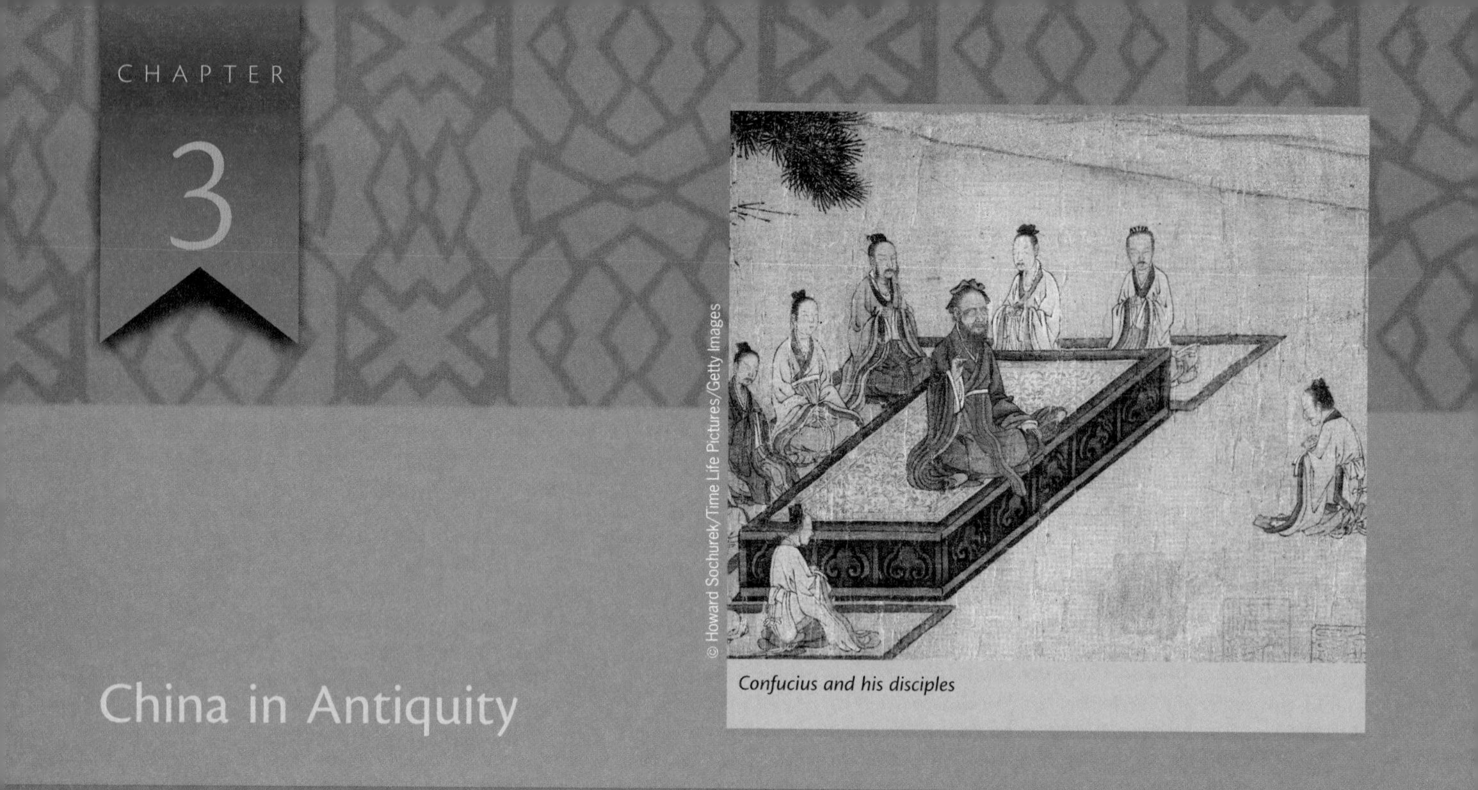

© Howard Sochurek/Time Life Pictures/Getty Images

Confucius and his disciples

China in Antiquity

CHAPTER OUTLINE AND FOCUS QUESTIONS

The Dawn of Chinese Civilization

Q How did geography influence the civilization that arose in China?

The Zhou Dynasty

Q What were the major tenets of Confucianism, Legalism, and Daoism, and what role did each play in early Chinese history?

The First Chinese Empire: The Qin Dynasty (221–206 B.C.E.)

Q What role did nomadic peoples play in early Chinese history? How did that role compare with the role played by nomadic peoples in other parts of Asia?

Daily Life in Ancient China

Q What were the key aspects of social and economic life in early China?

Chinese Culture

Q What were the chief characteristics of the Chinese writing system? How did it differ from the scripts used in Egypt and Mesopotamia?

CRITICAL THINKING

Q The civilization of ancient China resembled those of its contemporaries in Mesopotamia and Egypt in several respects, but the contrasts were equally significant. What were some of these differences, and how might geography and the environment have helped to account for them?

TOWARD THE END of the sixth century B.C.E., Chinese society was in a state of increasing disarray. The political principles that had governed society since the founding of the Zhou (JOE) dynasty six centuries earlier were widely ignored, and squabbling principalities scuffled for primacy as the power of the Zhou court steadily declined. The common people groaned under the weight of an oppressive manorial system that left them at the mercy of their aristocratic lords.

In the midst of this turmoil, a wandering scholar who went by the name of Kung fuci, or K'ung Fu-tzu, meaning Master Kung, traveled the length of the kingdom observing events and seeking employment as a political counselor. In the process, he attracted a number of disciples, to whom he expounded a set of ideas that in later years served as the guiding principles for the Chinese Empire. Some of his ideas are strikingly modern in their thrust. Among them is the revolutionary proposition that government depends on the will of the people.

But Master Kung, or Confucius (kun-FOO-shuss), the Latin term by which he is known to much of the world today, saw himself not as a revolutionary, but as a true conservative, seeking to preserve elements in Chinese history that had been neglected by his contemporaries. In his view, the principles that he sought to instill into his society had all been previously established many centuries in the past, during a "golden age" at the dawn of Chinese history when governments supposedly ruled on the basis of high moral principle: "If the government seeks to rule by decrees and the threat of punishment, the people will have no sense of shame; but if they are governed by virtue and a sense of propriety, they will feel shame and seek to behave correctly.'"

That statement is from the *Analects*, a collection of remarks attributed to Confucius that were gathered together by his disciples and published after his death in the fifth century B.C.E. The dichotomy between tradition and change was a key component in Confucian philosophy that would be reflected in many ways over the course of the next 2,500 years.

The civilization that produced Confucius had originated more than 1,500 years earlier along the two great river systems of East Asia, the Yellow and the Yangtze (YANG-tsee). This vibrant new civilization, which we know today as ancient China, expanded gradually over its neighboring areas. By the third century B.C.E., it had emerged as a great empire, as well as the dominant cultural and political force in the entire region.

Like Sumer, Harappa, and Egypt, the civilization of ancient China began as a collection of autonomous villages cultivating food crops along a major river system. Improvements in agricultural techniques led to a food surplus and the growth of an urban civilization characterized by more complex political and social institutions, as well as new forms of artistic and intellectual creativity.

Like its counterparts elsewhere, ancient China faced the challenge posed by the appearance of pastoral peoples on its borders. Unlike Harappa, Sumer, and Egypt, however, ancient China was able to surmount that challenge, and many of its institutions and cultural values survived intact down to the beginning of the twentieth century. For that reason, Chinese civilization is sometimes described as the oldest continuous civilization on earth.

The Dawn of Chinese Civilization

FOCUS QUESTION: How did geography influence the civilization that arose in China?

According to Chinese legend, Chinese society was founded by a series of rulers who brought the first rudiments of civilization to the region nearly five thousand years ago. The first was Fu Xi (foo SHEE) (Fu Hsi), the ox-tamer, who "knotted cords for hunting and fishing," domesticated animals, and introduced the beginnings of family life. The second was Shen Nong (shun NOONG) (Shen Nung), the divine farmer, who "bent wood for plows and hewed wood for plowshares." He taught the people the techniques of agriculture. Last came Huang Di (hwahng DEE) (Huang Ti), the Yellow Emperor, who "strung a piece of wood for the bow, and whittled little sticks of wood for the arrows." Legend credits Huang Di with creating the Chinese system of writing, as well as with inventing the bow and arrow.[1] Modern historians, of course, do not accept the literal accuracy of such legends but view them instead as part of the process whereby early peoples attempted to make sense of the world and their role in it. Nevertheless, such re-creations of a mythical past often contain an element of truth. Although there is no clear evidence that the "three sovereigns" actually existed, their achievements do symbolize some of the defining characteristics of Chinese civilization: the interaction between nomadic and agricultural peoples, the importance of the family as the basic unit of Chinese life, and the development of a unique system of writing.

The Land and People of China

Although human communities have existed in China for several hundred thousand years, the first *Homo sapiens* arrived in the area sometime after 40,000 B.C.E. as part of the great migration out of Africa. Around the eighth millennium B.C.E., the early peoples living along the riverbanks of northern and central China began to master the cultivation of crops. A number of these early agricultural settlements were in the neighborhood of the Yellow River, where they gave birth to two Neolithic societies known to archaeologists as the **Yangshao** (yahng-SHOW ["ow" as in "how"]) and the **Longshan** (loong-SHAHN) cultures (sometimes identified in terms of their pottery as the painted and black pottery cultures, respectively). Similar communities began to appear in the Yangtze valley in central China and along the coast to the south. The southern settlements were based on the cultivation of rice rather than dry crops such as millet, barley, and wheat (the last was an import from the Middle East in the second millennium B.C.E.), but they were as old as those in the north. Thus, agriculture, and perhaps other elements of early civilization, may have developed spontaneously in several areas of China rather than radiating outward from one central region.

At first, these simple Neolithic communities were hardly more than villages, but as the inhabitants mastered the rudiments of agriculture, they gradually gave rise to more sophisticated and complex societies. In a pattern that we have seen elsewhere, civilization gradually spread from these nuclear settlements in the valleys of the Yellow and Yangtze Rivers to other lowland areas of eastern and central China. The two great river valleys, then, can be considered the core regions in the development of Chinese civilization (see Map 3.1).

Although these densely cultivated valleys eventually became two of the great food-producing areas of the ancient world, China is more than a land of fertile fields. In fact, only 12 percent of the total land area is arable, compared with 23 percent in the United States. Much of the remainder consists of mountains and deserts that ring the country on its northern and western frontiers.

This often arid and forbidding landscape is a dominant feature of Chinese life and has played a significant role in Chinese history. The geographic barriers served to isolate the Chinese people from advanced agrarian societies in other parts of Asia. The frontier regions in the Gobi (GOH-bee) Desert, Central Asia, and the Tibetan plateau were sparsely inhabited by peoples of Mongolian, Indo-European, or Turkish extraction. Most were pastoral societies, and as in the other river valley civilizations, their contacts with the Chinese were often characterized by mutual distrust and conflict. Although less numerous than the Chinese, many of these peoples possessed impressive skills in war and were sometimes aggressive in seeking wealth or territory in the settled regions south of the Gobi Desert. Over the next two thousand years, the northern frontier became one of the great fault lines of conflict in Asia as Chinese armies attempted to protect precious farmlands from marauding peoples operating beyond the frontier. When China was unified and blessed with capable rulers, it could usually keep the nomadic intruders at bay and even bring them under a loose form of Chinese administration. But in times of internal weakness, China was vulnerable to attack from the north, and on several occasions, nomadic peoples succeeded in overthrowing native Chinese rulers and setting up their own dynastic regimes.

From other directions, China normally had little to fear. To the east lay the China Sea, a lair for pirates and the source of powerful typhoons that occasionally ravaged the Chinese coast but otherwise rarely a source of concern. South of the Yangtze River was a hilly region inhabited by a mixture of peoples of varied language and ethnic stock who lived by farming, fishing, or food gathering. They were gradually absorbed in the inexorable expansion of Chinese civilization.

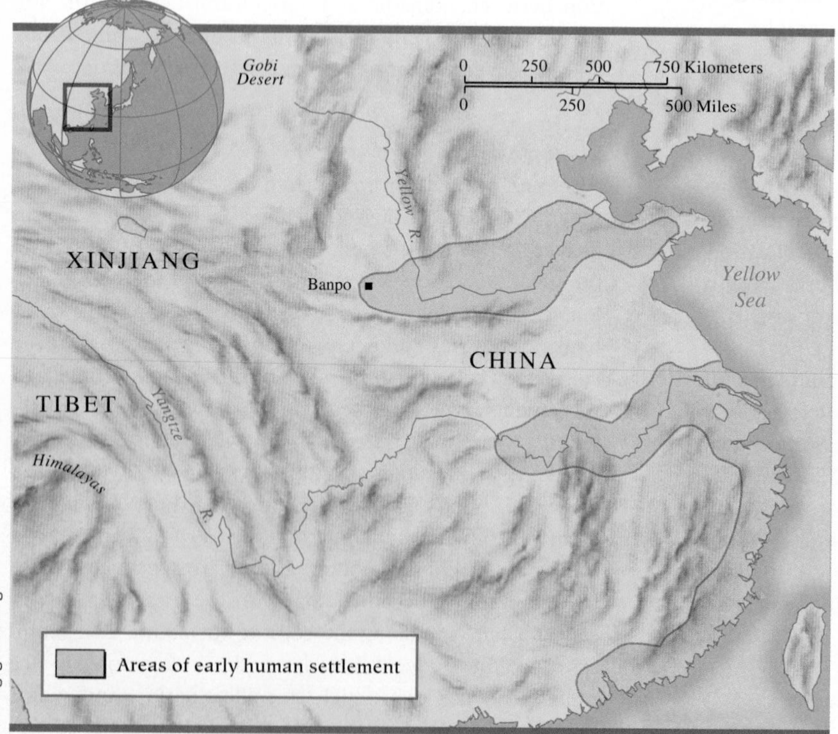

© Cengage Learning

MAP 3.1 Neolithic China. Like the ancient civilizations that arose in North Africa and western Asia, early Chinese society emerged along the banks of two major river systems, the Yellow and the Yangtze. China was separated from the other civilizations by snow-capped mountains and forbidding deserts, however, and thus was compelled to develop essentially on its own, without contacts from other societies going through a similar process.

Based on the discussions in the preceding chapters, what are the advantages and disadvantages of close contact with other human societies?

The Shang Dynasty

Historians of China have traditionally dated the beginning of Chinese civilization to the founding of the Xia (shee-AH) (Hsia) dynasty more than four thousand years ago. Although the precise date for the rise of the Xia is in dispute, recent archaeological evidence confirms its existence. Legend maintains that the founder was a ruler named Yu, who is also credited with introducing irrigation and draining the floodwaters that periodically threatened to inundate the northern China plain. The Xia dynasty was replaced by a second dynasty, the Shang (SHAHNG), around the sixteenth century B.C.E. The late Shang capital at Anyang (ahn-YAHNG), just north of the Yellow River in north-central China, has been excavated by archaeologists. Among the finds were thousands of so-called oracle bones, ox and chicken bones or turtle shells that were used by Shang rulers for divination (seeking to foretell future events by interpreting divine signs) and to communicate with the gods. The inscriptions on these oracle bones are the earliest known form of Chinese writing and provide much of our information about the beginnings of civilization in China. They describe a culture gradually emerging from the Neolithic to the early Bronze Age.

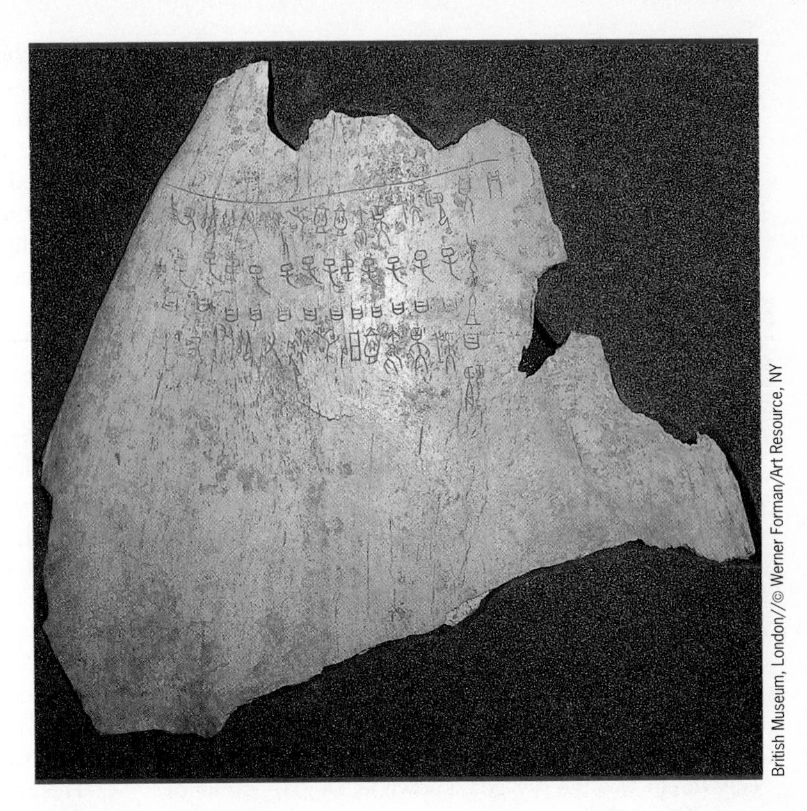

British Museum, London//© Werner Forman/Art Resource, NY

Shell and Bone Writing. The earliest known form of true writing in China dates back to the Shang dynasty and was inscribed on shells or animal bones. Questions for the gods were scratched on bones, which cracked after being exposed to fire. The cracks were then interpreted by sorcerers. The questions often expressed practical concerns: Will it rain? Will the king be victorious in battle? Will he recover from his illness? Originally composed of pictographs and ideographs four thousand years ago, Chinese writing has evolved into an elaborate set of symbols that combine meaning and pronunciation in a single character.

POLITICAL ORGANIZATION China under the Shang dynasty was a predominantly agricultural society ruled by an aristocratic class whose major concerns were war and maintaining control over key resources such as metal and salt. One ancient chronicler complained that "the big affairs of state consist of sacrifice and soldiery."[2] Combat was carried on by means of two-horse chariots. The appearance of chariots in China in the mid-second millennium B.C.E. coincides roughly with similar developments elsewhere, leading some historians to suggest that the Shang ruling class may originally have invaded China from elsewhere in Asia. But items found in Shang burial mounds are similar to Longshan pottery, implying that the Shang ruling elites were linear descendants of the indigenous Neolithic peoples in the area. If that was the case, the Shang may have acquired their knowledge of horse-drawn chariots through contact with the peoples of neighboring regions.

Some recent support for that assumption has come from evidence unearthed in the sandy wastes of Xinjiang (SHIN-jyahng), China's far-northwestern province. There archaeologists have discovered corpses dating back as early as the second millennium B.C.E. with physical characteristics that resemble those of Europeans. They are also clothed in textiles similar to those worn at the time in Europe, suggesting that they may have been members of an Indo-European migration from areas much farther to the west. If that is the case, they were probably familiar with advances in chariot making that occurred a few hundred years earlier in what today are southern Russia and Kazakhstan (ka-zak-STAN *or* kuh-zahk-STAHN). By about 2000 B.C.E., spoked wheels were being deposited at grave sites in Ukraine and also in the Gobi Desert, just north of the great bend of the Yellow River. It is thus likely that the new technology became available to the founders of the Shang dynasty and may have aided their rise to power in northern China.

The Shang king ruled with the assistance of a central bureaucracy in the capital city. His realm was divided into a number of territories governed by aristocratic

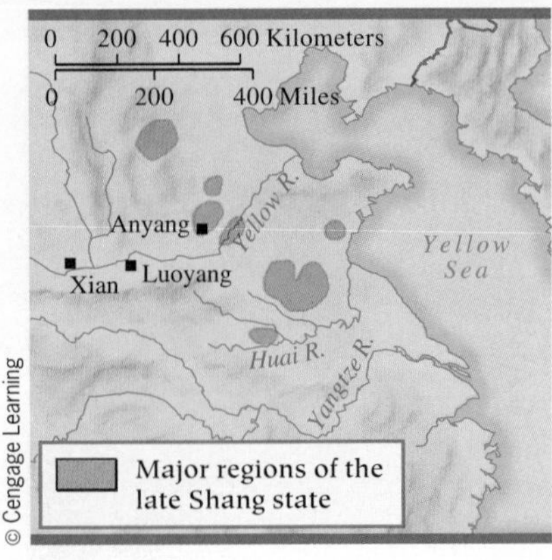

Shang China

chieftains, but the king appointed these chieftains and could apparently depose them at will. He was also responsible for the defense of the realm and controlled large armies that often fought on the fringes of the kingdom. The transcendent importance of the ruler was graphically displayed in the ritual sacrifices undertaken at his death, when hundreds of his retainers were buried with him in the royal tomb.

As the inscriptions on the oracle bones make clear, the Shang ruling elite believed in the existence of supernatural forces and thought that they could communicate with those forces to obtain divine intervention on matters of this world. In fact, the purpose of the oracle bones was to communicate with the gods. Supreme among the heavenly forces was the sky god, known as Di (Ti). Evidence from the oracle bones suggests that the king was already being viewed as an intermediary between heaven and earth. In fact, an early Chinese character for king (王) consists of three horizontal lines connected by a single vertical line; the middle horizontal line represents the king's place between human society and the divine forces in nature.

The early Chinese also had a clear sense of life in the hereafter. Though some of the human sacrifices discovered in the royal tombs were presumably intended to propitiate the gods, others were meant to accompany the king or members of his family on the journey to the next world (see the comparative illustration on p. 61). From this conviction would come the concept of the **veneration of ancestors** (mistakenly known in the West as "ancestor worship") and the practice, which continues to the present day in many Chinese communities, of burning replicas of physical objects to accompany the departed on their journey to the next world.

SOCIAL STRUCTURES In the Neolithic period, the farm village was apparently the basic social unit of China, at least in the core region of the Yellow River valley. Villages were organized by clans rather than by nuclear family units, and all residents probably took the common clan name of the entire village. In some cases, a village may have included more than one clan. At Banpo (Pan P'o), an archaeological site near modern Xian (shee-AHN) that dates back at least eight thousand years, the houses in the village are separated by a ditch, which some scholars think may have served as a divider between two clans. The individual dwellings at Banpo housed nuclear families, but a larger building in the village was apparently used as a clan meeting hall. The clan-based origins of Chinese society may help explain the continued importance of the joint family in traditional China, as well as the relatively small number of family names in Chinese society. Even today there are only about four hundred commonly used family names in a society of more than one billion people, and the colloquial name for the common people in China today is "the old hundred names."

By Shang times, the classes were becoming increasingly differentiated. It is likely that some poorer peasants did not own their farms but were obliged to work the land of the chieftain and other elite families in the village. The aristocrats not only made war and served as officials (indeed, the first Chinese character for *official* originally meant "warrior"), but they were also the primary landowners. In addition to the aristocratic elite and the peasants, there were a small number of merchants and artisans, as well as slaves, probably consisting primarily of criminals or prisoners taken in battle.

The Shang are perhaps best known for their mastery of the art of bronze casting. Utensils, weapons, and ritual objects made of bronze (see the comparative essay "The Use of Metals" on p. 62) have been found in royal tombs in urban centers throughout the area known to be under Shang influence. It is also clear that the Shang had achieved a fairly sophisticated writing system that would eventually spread throughout East Asia and evolve into the written language that is still used in China today.

THE SHANG DYNASTY: CHINA'S "MOTHER CULTURE"? Until recently, the prevailing wisdom among historians—both Chinese and non-Chinese—was that the Yellow River valley was the ancient heartland of Chinese civilization and that technological and cultural achievements gradually radiated from there to other areas in East Asia. Here, it was thought, occurred the first technological breakthroughs, including the development of a writing system, advanced farming techniques, and the ability to make bronze ritual vessels. Supporting this idea was the fact that the first significant archaeological finds in China, including the last Shang capital at Anyang, were made in that region.

Today, this **diffusion hypothesis**, as it is sometimes called, is no longer so widely accepted. The remains of early agricultural communities have now been unearthed in the Yangtze River valley and along the southern coast, and a rich trove of bronze vessels has been discovered in grave sites in central Sichuan (suh–CHWAHN) province. Such finds suggest that although the Yellow River

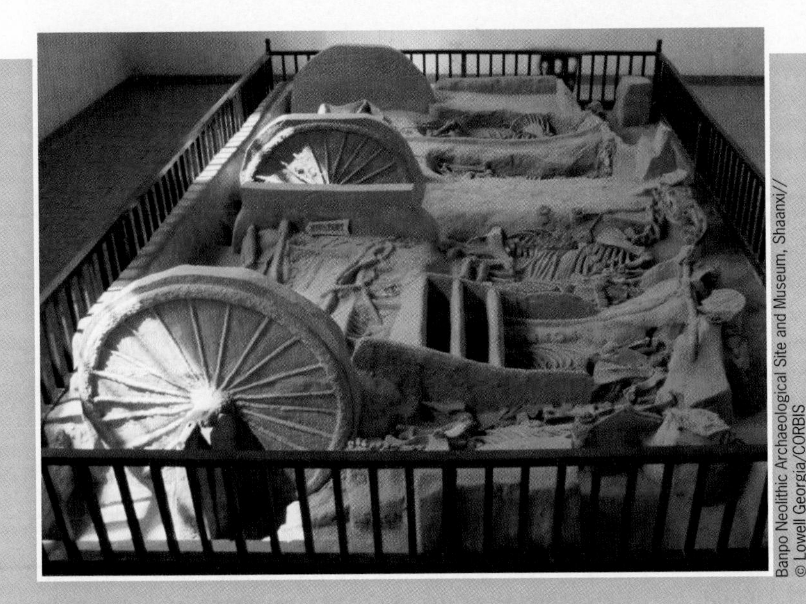

Banpo Neolithic Archaeological Site and Museum, Shaanxi// © Lowell Georgia/CORBIS

© William J. Duiker

© Egyptian National Museum, Cairo/ The Bridgeman Art Library

COMPARATIVE ILLUSTRATION

RELIGION & PHILOSOPHY

The Afterlife and Prized Possessions Like the pharaohs in Egypt, Chinese rulers filled their tombs with prized possessions from daily life. It was believed that if the tombs were furnished and stocked with supplies, including chairs, boats, chests, weapons, games, and dishes, the spiritual body could continue its life despite the death of the physical body. In the photo on the left, we see the remains of a chariot and horses in a burial pit in China's Hebei province that dates from the early Zhou dynasty. The lower photo on the right shows a small boat from the tomb of Tutankhamun in the Valley of the Kings in Egypt. The tradition of providing items of daily use for the departed continues today in Chinese communities throughout Asia. The papier-mâché vehicle in the photo at the upper right will be burned so that it will ascend in smoke to the world of the spirits.

How did Chinese tombs compare with the tombs of Egyptian pharaohs? What do the differences tell you about these two societies? What do all of the items shown here have in common?

civilization may have taken the lead in some areas, such as complex political organization and the development of writing, similar advances were already under way in other parts of China.

The Zhou Dynasty

FOCUS QUESTION: What were the major tenets of Confucianism, Legalism, and Daoism, and what role did each play in early Chinese history?

In the eleventh century B.C.E., the Shang dynasty was overthrown by an aggressive young state located somewhat to the west of Anyang, the Shang capital, near the great bend of the Yellow River as it begins to flow directly eastward to the sea. The new dynasty, which called itself the Zhou (Chou), survived for about eight hundred years and was thus the longest-lived dynasty in the history of China. According to tradition, the last Shang ruler was a tyrant who oppressed the people (Chinese sources assert that he was a degenerate who built "ponds of wine" and ordered the composing of lustful music that "ruined the morale of the nation"),[3] leading the ruler of the principality of Zhou to revolt and establish a new dynasty.

The Zhou located their capital in their home territory, near the present-day city of Xian. Later they established a second capital city at modern Luoyang (LWOH-yahng), farther to the east, to administer new territories captured from the Shang. This practice of having eastern and western capitals would endure off and on in China for nearly two thousand years.

Political Structures

The Zhou dynasty (c. 1045–221 B.C.E.) adopted the political system of its predecessors, with some changes. The Shang practice of dividing the kingdom into a number of

COMPARATIVE ESSAY

The Use of Metals

Around 6000 B.C.E., people in western Asia discovered how to use metals. They soon realized the advantage in using metal rather than stone to make both tools and weapons. Metal could be shaped more precisely, allowing artisans to make more refined tools and weapons with sharp edges and more regular shapes. Copper, silver, and gold, which were commonly found in their elemental form, were the first metals to be used. These were relatively soft and could be easily pounded into different shapes. But an important step was taken when people discovered that a rock that contained metal could be heated to liquefy the metal (a process called smelting). The liquid metal could then be poured into molds of clay or stone to make precisely shaped tools and weapons.

Copper was the first metal to be used in making tools. The first known copper smelting furnace, dated to 3800 B.C.E., was found in the Sinai. At about the same time, however, artisans in Southeast Asia discovered that tin could be added to copper to make bronze. By 3000 B.C.E., artisans in West Asia were also making bronze. Bronze has a lower melting point than copper, making it easier to cast, and it is also harder and corrodes less. By 1400 B.C.E., the Chinese were making bronze decorative objects as well as battle-axes and helmets. The widespread use of bronze has led historians to speak of the period from around 3000 to 1200 B.C.E. as the Bronze Age, although this is somewhat misleading in that many peoples continued to use stone tools and weapons even after bronze became available.

But there were limitations to the use of bronze. Tin was not as available as copper, so bronze tools and weapons were expensive. After 1200 B.C.E., bronze was increasingly replaced by iron, which was probably first used around 1500 B.C.E. in western Asia, where the Hittites made new weapons from it. Between 1500 and 600 B.C.E., iron making spread across Europe, North Africa, and Asia. Bronze continued to be used, but mostly for jewelry and other domestic purposes. Iron was used to make tools and weapons with sharper edges. Because iron weapons were cheaper than bronze ones, larger numbers of warriors could be armed, and wars could be fought on a larger scale.

Iron was handled differently from bronze: it was heated until it could be beaten into a desired shape. Each hammering increased the strength of the metal. This wrought iron, as it was called, was typical of iron manufacturing in the West until the late Middle Ages. In China, however, the use of heat-resistant clay in the walls of blast furnaces raised temperatures to 1,537 degrees Celsius, enabling artisans in the fourth century B.C.E. to liquefy iron so that it too could be cast in a mold. Europeans would not develop such blast furnaces until the fifteenth century C.E.

What were the advantages and disadvantages of making objects out of bronze in early human societies? Why was it eventually replaced by iron as the metal of choice?

© Ashmolean Museum, University of Oxford, UK/The Bridgeman Art Library

Bronze Axhead. This axhead, manufactured during the second millennium B.C.E., was made by pouring liquid metal into an ax-shaped mold of clay or stone. When the metal had cooled, artisans polished the surface to produce a sharp cutting edge.

territories governed by officials appointed by the king was continued under the Zhou. At the apex of the government hierarchy was the Zhou king, who was served by a bureaucracy of growing size and complexity. It now included several ministries responsible for rites, education, law, and public works. Beyond the capital, the Zhou kingdom was divided into a number of principalities, governed by members of the hereditary aristocracy, who were appointed by the king and were at least theoretically subordinated to his authority.

THE MANDATE OF HEAVEN But the Zhou kings also introduced some innovations. According to the *Rites of Zhou*, one of the oldest surviving documents on statecraft,[4] the Zhou dynasty ruled China because it possessed the **mandate of Heaven**. According to this concept, Heaven (now viewed as an impersonal law of nature rather than as an anthropomorphic deity) maintained order in the universe through the Zhou king, who thus ruled as a representative of Heaven but not as a divine being. The king, who was selected to rule because of his talent and virtue, was responsible for governing the people with compassion and efficiency. It was his duty to appease the gods in order to protect the people from natural calamities or bad harvests. But if the king failed to rule effectively, he could, theoretically at least, be overthrown and replaced by a new ruler. As noted earlier, this idea was used to justify the Zhou conquest of the Shang. Eventually, the concept of the heavenly mandate would become a cardinal principle of Chinese statecraft. Each founder of a new dynasty would routinely assert that he had earned the mandate of Heaven, and who could disprove it except by overthrowing the king? As a pragmatic Chinese proverb put it, "He who wins is the king; he who loses is the rebel."

In asserting that the ruler had a direct connection with the divine forces presiding over the universe, Chinese tradition reflected a belief that was prevalent in all ancient civilizations. But whereas in some societies, notably in Mesopotamia and Greece (see Chapter 4), the gods were seen as capricious and not subject to human understanding, in China, Heaven was viewed as an essentially benevolent force devoted to universal harmony and order that could be influenced by positive human action. Was this attitude a consequence of the fact that China, though subject to some of the same climatic vicissitudes that plagued other parts of the world, experienced a somewhat more predictable and beneficial environment than regions like the Middle East?

By the sixth century B.C.E., the Zhou dynasty began to decline. As the power of the central government disintegrated, bitter internal rivalries arose among the various principalities, where the governing officials had succeeded in making their positions hereditary at the expense of the king. As the power of these officials grew, they began to regulate the local economy and seek reliable sources of revenue for their expanding armies, such as a uniform tax system and government monopolies on key commodities such as salt and iron.

Later Chinese would regard the period of the early Zhou dynasty, as portrayed in the *Rites of Zhou* (which, of course, is no more an unbiased source than any modern government document), as a golden age when there was harmony in the world and all was right under Heaven. Whether the system functioned in such an ideal manner, of course, is open to question. In any case, the golden age did not last, whether because it never existed in practice or because of the increasing complexity of Chinese civilization. Perhaps, too, its disappearance was a consequence of the intellectual and moral weakness of the later rulers of the Zhou royal house.

Economy and Society

During the Zhou dynasty, the essential characteristics of Chinese economic and social institutions began to take shape. The Zhou continued the pattern of land ownership that had existed under the Shang: the peasants worked on lands owned by their lord but also had land of their own that they cultivated for their own use. The practice was called the **well-field system** because the Chinese character for well (井) resembles a simplified picture of the division of the farmland into nine separate segments. Each peasant family tilled an outer plot for its own use and then joined with other families to work the inner one for the hereditary lord. How widely this system was used is unclear, but it represented an ideal described by Confucian scholars of a later day. As the following passage from the *Book of Songs* indicates, life for the average farmer was not easy. The "big rat" is probably the government or a lord who has imposed high taxes on the peasants.

Big rat, big rat
Do not eat my millet!
Three years I have served you,
But you will not care for me.
I am going to leave you
And go to that happy land;
Happy land, happy land,
Where I will find my place.[5]

Trade and manufacturing were carried out by merchants and artisans, who lived in walled towns under the direct control of the local lord. Merchants did not operate independently but were considered the property of the local lord and on occasion could even be bought and sold like chattels. A class of slaves performed a variety of menial tasks and perhaps worked on local irrigation projects. Most of them were probably prisoners of war captured during conflicts with the neighboring principalities. Scholars do not know how extensive slavery was in ancient times, but slaves probably did not constitute a large portion of the total population.

The period of the later Zhou, from the sixth to the third century B.C.E., was an era of significant economic growth and technological innovation, especially in agriculture. During that time, large-scale water control projects were undertaken to regulate the flow of rivers and distribute water evenly to the fields, as well as to construct canals to facilitate the transport of goods from one region to another (see the comparative illustration on p. 64). Perhaps the most impressive technological achievement of the period was the construction of the massive water control project on the Min River, a tributary of the Yangtze. This system of canals and spillways, which was put into operation by the state of Qin a few years before the end of the Zhou dynasty, diverted excess water from the river into the local irrigation network and watered an area populated by as many as 5 million people. The system is still in use today, more than two thousand years later.

© William J. Duiker

© William J. Duiker

COMPARATIVE ILLUSTRATION

SCIENCE & TECHNOLOGY

Early Agricultural Technology. For centuries, farmers across the globe have adopted various techniques to guarantee the flow of adequate amounts of water for their crops. One of the most effective ways to irrigate fields in hilly regions is to construct terraces to channel the flow of water from higher elevations. Shown on the right is a hillside terrace in northern China, an area where dry crops such as oats and millet have been cultivated since the sixth millennium B.C.E. The illustration on the left shows a terraced hillside in the southwestern corner of the Arabian peninsula. Excavations show that despite dry conditions through much of the peninsula, terraced agriculture has been practiced in mountainous parts of the region for as long as five thousand years.

Q *In what other areas of the Middle East is irrigated agriculture practiced?*

Food production was also stimulated by a number of advances in farm technology. By the mid-sixth century B.C.E., the introduction of iron had led to the development of iron plowshares, which permitted deep plowing for the first time. Other innovations dating from the later Zhou were the use of natural fertilizer, the collar harness, and the technique of leaving land fallow to preserve or replenish nutrients in the soil. By the late Zhou dynasty, the cultivation of wet rice had become one of the prime sources of food in China. Although rice was difficult and time-consuming to produce, it replaced other grain crops in areas with a warm climate because of its good taste, relative ease of preparation, and high nutritional value.

The advances in agriculture, which enabled the population of China to rise as high as 20 million people during the late Zhou era, were also undoubtedly a major factor in the growth of commerce and manufacturing. During the late Zhou, economic wealth began to replace noble birth as the prime source of power and influence. Utensils made of iron became more common, and trade developed in a variety of useful commodities, including cloth, salt, and various manufactured goods.

One of the most important items of trade in ancient China was silk. There is evidence of silkworm raising as early as the Neolithic period. Remains of silk material have been found on Shang bronzes, and a large number of fragments have been recovered in tombs dating from the mid-Zhou era. Silk cloth was used not only for clothing and quilts but also to wrap the bodies of the dead prior to burial. Fragments have been found throughout Central Asia and as far away as Athens, suggesting that the famous Silk Road stretching from central China westward to the Middle East and the Mediterranean Sea was in operation as early as the fifth century B.C.E. (see Chapters 5 and 10).

In fact, however, a more important item of trade that initially propelled merchants along the Silk Road was probably jade. Blocks of the precious stone were mined in the mountains of northern Tibet as early as the sixth millennium B.C.E. and began to appear in China during the Shang dynasty. Praised by Confucius as a symbol of purity and virtue, it assumed an almost sacred quality among Chinese during the Zhou dynasty.

With the development of trade and manufacturing, China began to move toward a money economy. The first form of money, as in much of the rest of the world, may have been seashells (the Chinese character for goods or property contains the ideographic symbol for "shell": 貝), but by the Zhou dynasty, pieces of iron shaped like a knife or round coins with a hole in the middle so that they could be carried in strings of a thousand were being used. Most ordinary Chinese, however, simply used a system of barter. Taxes, rents, and even the salaries of government officials were normally paid in grain.

The Hundred Schools of Ancient Philosophy

In China, as in other great river valley societies, the birth of civilization was accompanied by the emergence of an organized effort to comprehend the nature of the cosmos and the role of human beings within it. Speculation over such questions began in the very early stages of civilization and culminated at the end of the Zhou era in the "hundred schools" of ancient philosophy, a wide-ranging debate over the nature of human beings, society, and the universe.

EARLY BELIEFS The first hint of religious belief in ancient China comes from relics found in royal tombs of Neolithic times. By then, the Chinese had already developed a religious sense beyond the primitive belief in the existence of spirits in nature. The Shang had begun to believe in the existence of one transcendent god, known now as Shang Di, who presided over all the forces of nature. As time went on, the Chinese concept of religion evolved from a vaguely anthropomorphic god to a somewhat more impersonal symbol of universal order known as Heaven (*Tian*, or *T'ien*). There was also much speculation among Chinese intellectuals about the nature of the cosmic order. One of the earliest ideas was that the universe was divided into two primary forces of good and evil, light and dark, male and female, called the *yang* and the *yin*, represented symbolically by the sun (*yang*) and the moon (*yin*). According to this theory, life was a dynamic process of interaction between the forces of *yang* and *yin*. Early Chinese could only attempt to understand the process and perhaps to have some minimal effect on its operation. They could not hope to reverse it. It is sometimes asserted that this belief has contributed to the heavy element of fatalism in Chinese popular wisdom. The Chinese have traditionally believed that bad times will be followed by good times, and vice versa.

The belief that there was some mysterious "law of nature" that could be interpreted by human beings led to various attempts to predict the future, such as the Shang oracle bones and other methods of divination. Philosophers invented ways to interpret the will of nature, while shamans, playing a role similar to the *brahmins* in India, were employed at court to assist the emperor in his policy deliberations until at least the fifth century C.E. One of the most famous manuals used for this purpose was the *Yi Jing* (*I Ching*), known in English as the *Book of Changes*.

CONFUCIANISM Such efforts to divine the mysterious purposes of Heaven notwithstanding, Chinese thinking about metaphysical reality also contained a strain of pragmatism, which is readily apparent in the ideas of the great philosopher Confucius. Confucius was born in the state of Lu, in the modern province of Shandong (SHAHN-doong), in 551 B.C.E. After reaching maturity, he apparently hoped to find employment as a political adviser in one of the principalities into which China was divided at that time, but he had little success in finding a patron. Nevertheless, he made an indelible mark on history as an independent (and somewhat disgruntled) political and social philosopher.

In conversations with his disciples contained in the *Analects*, Confucius often adopted a detached and almost skeptical view of Heaven. "If you are unable to serve men," he commented on one occasion, "how can you serve the spirits? If you do not understand life, how can you understand death?" In many instances, he appeared to advise his followers to revere the deities and the ancestral spirits but to keep them at a distance. Confucius believed it was useless to speculate too much about metaphysical questions. Better by far to assume that there was a rational order to the universe and then concentrate one's attention on ordering the affairs of this world (see the box on p. 66).[6]

Confucius's interest in philosophy, then, was essentially political and ethical. The universe was constructed in such a way that if human beings could act harmoniously in accordance with its purposes, their own affairs would prosper. Much of his concern was with human behavior. The key to proper behavior was to behave in accordance with the ***Dao*** (DOW) (Way). Confucius assumed that all human beings had their own *Dao*, depending on their individual role in life, and it was their duty to follow it. Even the ruler had his own *Dao*, and he ignored it at his peril, for to do so could mean the loss of the mandate of Heaven. The idea of the *Dao* is reminiscent of the concept of *dharma* in ancient India and played a similar role in governing the affairs of society.

Two elements in the Confucian interpretation of the *Dao* are particularly worthy of mention. The first is the concept of duty. It was the responsibility of all individuals to subordinate their own interests and aspirations to the broader needs of the family and the community. Confucius assumed that if each individual worked hard to fulfill his or her assigned destiny, the affairs of society as a whole would prosper as well. In this respect, it was important for the ruler to set a good example. If he followed his "kingly way," the beneficial effects would radiate throughout society.

The second key element is the idea of humanity, sometimes translated as "human-heartedness." This concept involves a sense of compassion and empathy for others. It is similar in some ways to Christian concepts, but with a subtle twist. Where Christian teachings call on human beings to "behave toward others as you would have them behave toward you," the Confucian maxim is put in a different way: "Do not do unto others what you

The Wit and Wisdom of Confucius

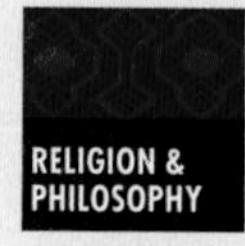

RELIGION & PHILOSOPHY

The *Analects* (*Lun Yu*), a collection of sayings supposedly uttered by the ancient Chinese philosopher Confucius and drawn up after his death by his disciples, is considered to be a primary source for the Master's ideas and thought. The degree to which the collection provides an accurate account of his remarks on various subjects has long been a matter of debate among specialists. Some scholars argue that the sayings in the *Analects* reflect the views of Confucius's followers two centuries after his death in the fifth century B.C.E. more than they do those of the Master himself.

Whatever the truth of this contention, the sayings in the *Analects* are generally accepted to be representative of Confucius's own views and have provided moral and philosophical guidance to countless generations of Chinese over the centuries. As such, they have played a major role in shaping the lives and culture of the Chinese people. Presented here are a number of familiar passages from the *Analects* on a variety of subjects.

The Confucian *Analects*

On Human Nature

17.2. By their nature, men are quite similar; in practice, they become far apart.

17.3. Only the wisest and the most ignorant of men cannot be changed.

16.9. Confucius said: Those born with innate knowledge are the highest of men; those who become learned are next in line; those who study but fail to learn follow; those who are ignorant yet do not study are the lowest of men.

On Morality

4.5. All men desire wealth and honor. But unless they can be achieved by virtuous means, they should not be sought after.

4.16. The moral man seeks righteousness; the immoral man seeks profit.

6.28. The virtuous man thinks of the needs of others before those of his own; he seeks to benefit others before himself.

15.23. Tzu Kung [one of the Master's disciples] asked if there was one word that could be applied as a standard for virtuous behavior. Confucius replied: It is reciprocity; do not do unto others what you would not wish done to yourself.

On Filial Piety

2.6. What is filial piety? Confucius said: Parents are concerned when their children become ill.

2.5. [Asked about filial piety] Confucius replied: It consists in not being disobedient; when they are alive, parents should be served according to the rules of propriety; after their death, they should be buried correctly and sacrifices should be carried out in a proper manner.

4.18. Confucius said: When serving one's parents, it is permissible to remonstrate with them, but in a respectful manner; if they do not agree, one should not oppose their wishes and even accept punishment without complaint.

On Education

2.15. Study without thought is a waste of time; thought without study is dangerous.

8.12. It is rare to find a man who has studied for three years without making progress.

On Government

2.3. If the government seeks to rule by decrees and the threat of punishment, the people will have no sense of shame; but if they are governed by virtue and a sense of propriety, they will feel shame and seek to behave correctly.

13.6. If its conduct is correct, a government can succeed without issuing directives; if not, directives will not be obeyed.

12.7. Confucius said: Without the confidence of the people, government cannot succeed.

On Religion

13.3. With regard to what he does not know, the superior man reserves judgment.

7.20. The Master did not comment on the supernatural, on feats of strength, on disorder, and on the spirits.

6.20. To meet one's human obligations, to respect the spirits but maintain distance from them, such indeed may be called wisdom.

11.11. [Asked about serving the spirits of the departed], Confucius replied: If you are unable to serve men, how can you serve the spirits? If you do not understand life, how can you understand death?

Confucius is viewed by some observers as a reformer, and by others as a conservative. Based on the information available to you in this chapter, how would you classify his ideas, as expressed in the Analects?

Source: *The Four Books: Confucian Analects*, by James Legge (Hong Kong: The International Publication Society, n.d.). Translation by William J. Duiker and © 2011 William J. Duiker.

would not wish done to yourself." To many Chinese, this attitude symbolizes an element of tolerance in the Chinese character that has not always been practiced in other societies.[7]

Confucius may have considered himself a failure because he never attained the position he wanted, but many of his contemporaries found his ideas appealing, and in the generations after his death, his message spread widely throughout China. Confucius was an outspoken critic of his times and lamented the disappearance of what he regarded as the golden age of the early Zhou.

In fact, however, Confucius was not just another disgruntled Chinese conservative mourning the passing of the good old days; rather, he was a revolutionary thinker, many of whose key ideas looked forward rather than backward. Perhaps his most striking political idea was that the government should be open to all men of superior quality, and not limited to those of noble birth. As one of his disciples reports in the *Analects*: "The Master said, by their nature, men are quite similar; in practice, they become far apart."[8] Confucius undoubtedly had himself in mind as one of those "superior" men, but the rapacity of the hereditary lords must have added strength to his convictions.

The concept of rule by merit was, of course, not an unfamiliar idea in the China of his day; the *Rites of Zhou* had clearly stated that the king himself deserved to rule because of his talent and virtue, rather than as the result of noble birth. In practice, however, aristocratic privilege must often have opened the doors to political influence, and many of Confucius's contemporaries must have regarded his appeal for government by talent as both exciting and dangerous. Confucius did not explicitly question the right of the hereditary aristocracy to play a leading role in the political process, nor did his ideas have much effect in his lifetime. Still, they introduced a new concept that was later implemented in the form of a bureaucracy selected through a civil service examination.

Confucius's ideas, passed on to later generations through the *Analects* as well as through writings attributed to him, had a strong impact on Chinese political thinkers of the late Zhou period, a time when the existing system was in disarray and open to serious question. But as with most great thinkers, Confucius's ideas were sufficiently ambiguous to be interpreted in contradictory ways. Some, like the philosopher Mencius (370–290 B.C.E.), stressed the humanistic side of Confucian ideas, arguing that human beings were by nature good and hence could be taught their civic responsibilities by example. He also stressed that the ruler had a duty to govern with compassion:

> It was because Chieh and Chou lost the people that they lost the empire, and it was because they lost the hearts of the people that they lost the people. Here is the way to win the empire: win the people and you win the empire. Here is the way to win the people: win their hearts and you win the people. Here is the way to win their hearts: give them and share with them what they like, and do not do to them what they do not like. The people turn to a human ruler as water flows downward or beasts take to wilderness.[9]

Here is a prescription for political behavior that could win wide support in our own day. Other thinkers, however, rejected Mencius's rosy view of human nature and argued for a different approach (see the box on p. 68).

LEGALISM A school of thought that became quite popular during the "hundred schools" era in ancient China was the philosophy of **Legalism**. Taking issue with the view of Mencius and other disciples of Confucius that human nature was essentially good, the Legalists argued that human beings were by nature evil and would follow the correct path only if coerced by harsh laws and stiff punishments. These thinkers were referred to as the School of Law because they rejected the Confucian view that government by "superior men" could solve society's problems and argued instead for a system of impersonal laws.

The Legalists also disagreed with the Confucian belief that the universe has a moral core. They therefore believed that only firm action by the state could bring about social order. Fear of harsh punishment, more than the promise of material reward, could best motivate the common people to serve the interests of the ruler. Because human nature was essentially corrupt, officials could not be trusted to carry out their duties in a fair and evenhanded manner, and only a strong ruler could create an orderly society. All human actions should be subordinated to the effort to create a strong and prosperous state subject to his will.

DAOISM One of the most popular alternatives to **Confucianism** was the philosophy of **Daoism** (DOW-iz-uhm) (frequently spelled Taoism). According to Chinese tradition, the Daoist school was founded by a contemporary of Confucius popularly known as Lao Tzu (LOW ["ow" as in "how"] dzuh) (Lao Zi), or the Old Master. Many modern scholars, however, are skeptical that Lao Tzu actually existed.

Obtaining a clear understanding of the original concepts of Daoism is difficult because its primary document, a short treatise known as the *Dao De Jing* (DOW deh JING) (sometimes translated as *The Way of the Tao*), is an enigmatic book whose interpretation has baffled scholars for centuries. The opening line, for example, explains less what the *Dao* is than what it is not: "The Tao [Way] that can be told of is not the eternal Tao. The name that can be named is not the eternal name."[10]

OPPOSING ≺ VIEWPOINTS

A Debate over Good and Evil

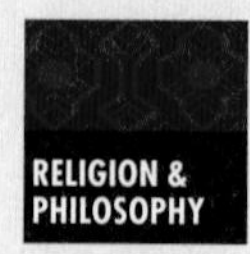

RELIGION & PHILOSOPHY

During the latter part of the Zhou dynasty, one of the major preoccupations of Chinese philosophers was to determine the essential qualities of human nature. In the *Analects*, Confucius was cited as asserting that humans' moral instincts were essentially neutral at birth; their minds must be cultivated to bring out the potential goodness therein. In later years, the Master's disciples elaborated on this issue. The great humanitarian philosopher Mencius maintained that human nature was essentially good. But his rival Xunzi (SHYOON-zuh) (Hsün Tzu) took the opposite tack, arguing that evil was inherent in human nature and could be eradicated only by rigorous training at the hands of an instructor. Later, Xunzi's views would be adopted by the Legalist philosophers of the Qin dynasty, although his belief in the efficacy of education earned him a place in the community of Confucian scholars.

The Book of Mencius

Mencius said, . . . "The goodness of human nature is like the downward course of water. There is no human being lacking in the tendency to do good, just as there is no water lacking in the tendency to flow downward. Now by striking water and splashing it, you may cause it to go over your head, and by damming and channeling it, you can force it to flow uphill. But is this the nature of water? It is the force that makes this happen. While people can be made to do what is not good, what happens to their nature is like this. . . .

"All human beings have a mind that cannot bear to see the sufferings of others. . . .

"Here is why. . . . Now, if anyone were suddenly to see a child about to fall into a well, his mind would always be filled with alarm, distress, pity, and compassion. That he would react accordingly is not because he would use the opportunity to ingratiate himself with the child's parents, nor because he would seek commendation from neighbors and friends, nor because he would hate the adverse reputation. From this it may be seen that one who lacks a mind that feels pity and compassion would not be human; one who lacks a mind that feels shame and aversion would not be human; one who lacks a mind that feels modesty and compliance would not be human; and one who lacks a mind that knows right and wrong would not be human.

"The mind's feeling of pity and compassion is the beginning of humaneness; the mind's feeling of shame and aversion is the beginning of lightness; the mind's feeling of modesty and compliance is the beginning of propriety; and the mind's sense of right and wrong is the beginning of wisdom."

The Book of Xunzi

Human nature is evil; its goodness derives from conscious activity. Now it is human nature to be born with a fondness for profit. Indulging this leads to contention and strife, and the sense of modesty and yielding with which one was born disappears. One is born with feelings of envy and hate, and, by indulging these, one is led into banditry and theft, so that the sense of loyalty and good faith with which he was born disappears. One is born with the desires of the ears and eyes and with a fondness for beautiful sights and sounds, and by indulging these, one is led to licentiousness and chaos, so that the sense of ritual, rightness, refinement, and principle with which one was born is lost. Hence, following human nature and indulging human emotions will inevitably lead to contention and strife, causing one to rebel against one's proper duty, reduce principle to chaos, and revert to violence. Therefore one must be transformed by the example of a teacher and guided by the way of ritual and right before one will attain modesty and yielding, accord with refinement and ritual and return to order. From this perspective it is apparent that human nature is evil and that its goodness is the result of conscious activity.

Mencius said, "Now human nature is good, and [when it is not] this is always a result of having lost or destroyed one's nature." I say that he was mistaken to take such a view. Now, it is human nature that, as soon as a person is born, he departs from his original substance and from his rational disposition so that he must inevitably lose and destroy them. Seen in this way, it is apparent that human nature is evil.

What arguments does each of these Confucian thinkers advance to support his point of view about the essential elements of human nature? In your view, which argument is more persuasive?

Source: Excerpt from William Theodore de Bary and Irene Bloom, *Sources of Chinese Tradition*, Vol. I, 2nd ed (New York, 1999). Copyright © 1999 by Columbia University Press.

The Daoist Answer to Confucianism

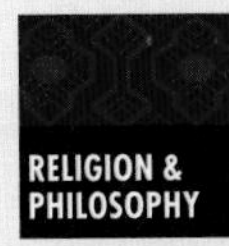

The *Dao De Jing* (*The Way of the Tao*) is the great classic of philosophical Daoism (Taoism). Traditionally attributed to the legendary Chinese philosopher Lao Tzu (Old Master), it was probably written sometime during the era of Confucius. This opening passage illustrates two of the key ideas that characterize Daoist belief: it is impossible to define the nature of the universe, and "inaction" (not Confucian "action") is the key to ordering the affairs of human beings.

The Way of the Tao

The Tao that can be told of is not the eternal Tao;
The name that can be named is not the eternal name.
The Nameless is the origin of Heaven and Earth;
The Named is the mother of all things.

Therefore let there always be nonbeing, so we may see their subtlety.
And let there always be being, so we may see their outcome.
The two are the same,
But after they are produced, they have different names.
They both may be called deep and profound.
Deeper and more profound,
The door of all subtleties!
When the people of the world all know beauty as beauty,
There arises the recognition of ugliness.
When they all know the good as good,
There arises the recognition of evil.
Therefore:
Being and nonbeing produce each other;
Difficult and easy complete each other;
Long and short contrast each other;
High and low distinguish each other;
Sound and voice harmonize each other;
Front and behind accompany each other.

Therefore the sage manages affairs without action
And spreads doctrines without words.
All things arise, and he does not turn away from them.
He produces them but does not take possession of them.
He acts but does not rely on his own ability.
He accomplishes his task but does not claim credit for it.
It is precisely because he does not claim credit that his accomplishment remains with him.

What was Lao Tzu, the presumed author of this document, trying to express about the basic nature of the universe? Is there a moral order that can be comprehended by human thought? What would Lao Tzu have to say about Confucian moral teachings?

Source: From *The Way of Lao Tzu* (Tao-te Ching), by Wing-Tsit Chan, trans. Copyright © 1963 by Macmillan College Publishing Company, Inc.

Nevertheless, the basic concepts of Daoism are not especially difficult to understand. Like Confucianism, Daoism does not anguish over the underlying meaning of the cosmos. Rather, it attempts to set forth proper forms of behavior for human beings here on earth. In most other respects, however, Daoism presents a view of life and its ultimate meaning that is almost diametrically opposed to that of Confucianism. Where Confucian doctrine asserts that it is the duty of human beings to work hard to improve life here on earth, Daoists contend that the true way to interpret the will of Heaven is not action but inaction (*wu wei*). The best way to act in harmony with the universal order is to act spontaneously and let nature take its course (see the box above).

Such a message could be very appealing to people who were uncomfortable with the somewhat rigid flavor of the Confucian work ethic and preferred a more individualistic approach. This image would eventually find graphic expression in Chinese landscape painting, which in its classical form would depict naturalistic scenes of mountains, water, and clouds and underscore the fragility and smallness of individual human beings.

Daoism achieved considerable popularity in the waning years of the Zhou dynasty. It was especially popular among intellectuals, who may have found it appealing as an escapist antidote in a world characterized by growing disorder.

POPULAR BELIEFS Daoism also played a second role as a loose framework for popular spiritualistic and animistic beliefs among the common people. Popular Daoism was less a philosophy than a religion; it comprised a variety of rituals and forms of behavior that were regarded as a means of achieving heavenly salvation or even a state of immortality on earth. Daoist sorcerers practiced various types of exercises for training the mind and body in the hope of achieving power, sexual prowess, and long life. It was primarily this form of Daoism that survived into a later age.

The philosophical forms of Confucianism and Daoism did not provide much meaning to the mass of the population, for whom philosophical debate over the ultimate meaning of life was less important than the daily struggle for survival. Even among the elites, interest in the occult and in astrology was high, and magico-religious ideas coexisted with interest in natural science and humanistic philosophy throughout the ancient period.

For most Chinese, Heaven was not a vague, impersonal law of nature, as it was for many Confucian and Daoist intellectuals. Instead, it was a terrain peopled with innumerable gods and spirits of nature, both good and evil, who existed in trees, mountains, and streams as well as in heavenly bodies. As human beings mastered the techniques of farming, they called on divine intervention to guarantee a good harvest. Other gods were responsible for the safety of fishers, transportation workers, or prospective mothers.

Another aspect of popular religion was the belief that the spirits of deceased human beings lived in the atmosphere for a time before ascending to Heaven or descending to hell. During that period, surviving family members had to care for the spirits through proper ritual, or they would become evil spirits and haunt the survivors.

Thus, in ancient China, human beings were offered a variety of interpretations of the nature of the universe. Confucianism satisfied the need for a rational doctrine of nation building and social organization at a time when the existing political and social structure was beginning to disintegrate. Philosophical Daoism provided a more sensitive approach to the vicissitudes of fate and nature, as well as a framework for a set of diverse animistic beliefs at the popular level. But neither could satisfy the deeper emotional needs that sometimes inspire the human spirit. Neither could effectively provide solace in a time of sorrow or the hope of a better life in the hereafter. Something else would be needed to fill the gap.

The First Chinese Empire: The Qin Dynasty (221–206 B.C.E.)

FOCUS QUESTIONS: What role did nomadic peoples play in early Chinese history? How did that role compare with the role played by nomadic peoples in other parts of Asia?

During the last two centuries of the Zhou dynasty (the fourth and third centuries B.C.E.), the authority of the king became increasingly nominal, and several of the small principalities into which the Zhou kingdom had been divided began to evolve into powerful states that presented a potential challenge to the Zhou ruler himself. Chief among these were Qu (CHOO) (Ch'u) in the central Yangtze valley, Wu (WOO) in the Yangtze delta, and Yue (yoo-EH) (Yueh) along the southeastern coast. At first, their mutual rivalries were in check, but by the late fifth century B.C.E., competition intensified into civil war, giving birth to the so-called Period of the Warring States (see the box on p. 72). Powerful principalities vied with each other for preeminence and largely ignored the now purely titular authority of the Zhou court (see Map 3.2). New forms of warfare emerged with the invention of iron weapons and the introduction of foot soldiers and cavalry armed with powerful crossbows. Cities that erected high walls as protection found that their opponents countered by developing new techniques for siege warfare.

By the mid-fourth century B.C.E., the relatively young state of Qin (CHIN), located in the original homeland of the Zhou, had emerged as a key player in these conflicts by adopting a number of reforms in agriculture, government administration, military organization, and fiscal policy. As a result of policies put into effect by the adviser Shang Yang (SHAHNG yahng) in the mid-fourth century B.C.E., Qin society was ruled with ruthless efficiency. In the words of Sima Qian (SUH-mah chee-AHN), a famous historian of the Han (HAHN) dynasty:

> He commanded that the people . . . supervise each other and be mutually liable. Anyone who failed to report criminal activity would be chopped in two at the waist. . . . Those who had achievements in the army would in proportion receive an increase in rank. . . . Those who . . . through their farming and weaving contributed much grain and cloth would be remitted [from tax and forced labor], while those who worked for peripheral profits [in trade and crafts] and those who were idle or poor would be confiscated as slaves. . . . He equalized the military levies and land tax and standardized the measures of capacity, weight, and length.[11]

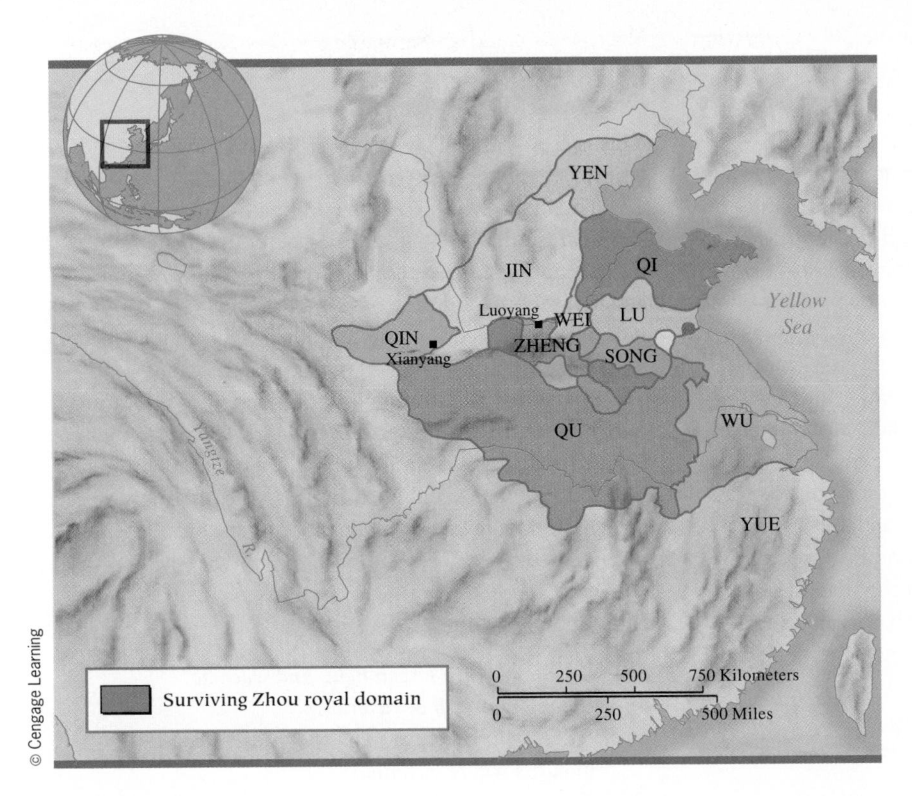

© Cengage Learning

MAP 3.2 China During the Period of the Warring States. From the fifth to the third centuries B.C.E., China was locked in an era of civil strife known as the Period of the Warring States. This map shows the Zhou dynasty capital at Luoyang, along with the major states that were squabbling for precedence in the region.

Why did most of the early states emerge in areas adjacent to China's two major river systems, the Yellow and the Yangtze?

Benefiting from a strong defensive position in the mountains to the west of the great bend of the Yellow River, as well as from their control of the rich Sichuan plains, the Qin gradually subdued their main rivals through conquest or diplomatic maneuvering. In 221 B.C.E., the Qin ruler declared the establishment of a new dynasty, the first truly unified government in Chinese history.

One of the primary reasons for the triumph of the Qin was probably the character of the first Qin ruler, known to history as Qin Shi Huangdi (chin shee hwang-DEE) (Ch'in Shih Huang Ti), or the First Emperor of Qin. A man of forceful personality and immense ambition, Qin Shi Huangdi had ascended to the throne of Qin in 246 B.C.E. at the age of thirteen. Described as having "the chest of a bird of prey, the voice of a jackal, and the heart of a tiger," the new king found the Legalist views of his adviser Li Su (lee SUH) (Li Ssu) all too appealing. In 221 B.C.E., Qin Shi Huangdi defeated the last of his rivals and founded a new dynasty with himself as emperor (see Map 3.3).

Political Structures

The Qin dynasty transformed Chinese politics. Philosophical doctrines that had proliferated during the late Zhou period were prohibited, and Legalism was adopted as the official ideology. Those who opposed the policies of the new regime were punished and sometimes executed, while books presenting ideas contrary to the official orthodoxy were publicly put to the torch, perhaps the first example of book burning in history (see the box on p. 74).

Legalistic theory gave birth to a number of fundamental administrative and political developments, some of which would survive the Qin and serve as a model for future dynasties. In the first place, unlike the Zhou, the Qin was a highly centralized state. The central bureaucracy was divided into three primary ministries: a civil authority, a military authority, and a censorate, whose inspectors surveyed the efficiency of officials throughout the system. This would later become standard administrative procedure for future Chinese dynasties.

Below the central government were two levels of administration: provinces and counties. Unlike the Zhou system, officials at these levels did not inherit their positions but were appointed by the court and were subject to dismissal at the emperor's whim. Apparently, some form of merit system was used, although there is no evidence that selection was based on performance in an examination. The civil servants may have been chosen on the recommendation of other government officials. A penal code provided for harsh punishments for all wrongdoers. Officials were watched by the censors, who reported directly to the throne. Those guilty of malfeasance in office were executed.

Society and the Economy

Qin Shi Huangdi, who had a passion for centralization, unified the system of weights and measures, standardized the monetary system and the written forms of Chinese

The Art of War

POLITICS & GOVERNMENT

With the possible exception of the nineteenth-century German military strategist Carl von Clausewitz, probably no writer on the art of war is more famous or respected than the ancient Chinese thinker Sun Tzu (SOON dzuh). Yet surprisingly little is known about him. Recently discovered evidence suggests that he lived sometime in the fifth century B.C.E., during the chronic conflict of the Period of the Warring States, and that he was an early member of an illustrious family of military strategists who advised Zhou rulers for more than two hundred years. But despite the mystery surrounding his life, there is no doubt of his influence on later generations of military planners. Among his most avid followers in modern times have been the revolutionary leaders Mao Zedong and Ho Chi Minh, as well as the Japanese military strategists who planned the attacks on Port Arthur and Pearl Harbor.

The following brief excerpt from his classic, *The Art of War*, provides a glimmer into the nature of his advice, still so timely today.

Selections from Sun Tzu

Sun Tzu said:

"In general, the method for employing the military is this: Attaining one hundred victories in one hundred battles is not the pinnacle of excellence. Subjugating the enemy's army without fighting is the true pinnacle of excellence. . . .

"Thus the highest realization of warfare is to attack the enemy's plans; next is to attack their alliances; next to attack their army; and the lowest is to attack their fortified cities.

"This tactic of attacking fortified cities is adopted only when unavoidable. Preparing large movable protective shields, armored assault wagons, and other equipment and devices will require three months. Building earthworks will require another three months to complete. If the general cannot overcome his impatience but instead launches an assault wherein his men swarm over the walls like ants, he will kill one-third of his officers and troops, and the city will still not be taken. This is the disaster that results from attacking [fortified cities].

"Thus, one who excels at employing the military subjugates other people's armies without engaging in battle, captures other people's fortified cities without attacking them, and destroys other people's states without prolonged fighting. He must fight under Heaven with the paramount aim of 'preservation.' . . .

"In general, the strategy of employing the military is this: If your strength is ten times theirs, surround them; if five, then attack them; if double, then divide your forces. If you are equal in strength to the enemy, you can engage him. If fewer, you can circumvent him. If outmatched, you can avoid him. . . .

"Thus there are five factors from which victory can be known:

One who knows when he can fight, and when he cannot fight, will be victorious.
One who recognizes how to employ large and small numbers will be victorious.
One whose upper and lower ranks have the same desires will be victorious.
One who, fully prepared, awaits the unprepared will be victorious.
One whose general is capable and not interfered with by the ruler will be victorious.

These five are the Way (Tao) to know victory. . . .

"Thus, it is said that one who knows the enemy and knows himself will not be endangered in a hundred engagements. One who does not know the enemy but knows himself will sometimes be victorious, sometimes meet with defeat. One who knows neither the enemy nor himself will invariably be defeated in every engagement."

Why are the ideas of Sun Tzu about the art of war still so popular among military strategists after 2,500 years? What advice might he give leaders of the United States and other nations on dealing with the problem of international terrorism today?

Source: From *Sun Tzu: The Art of War*, Ralph D. Sawyer (Boulder: Westview Press, 1994), pp. 177–179.

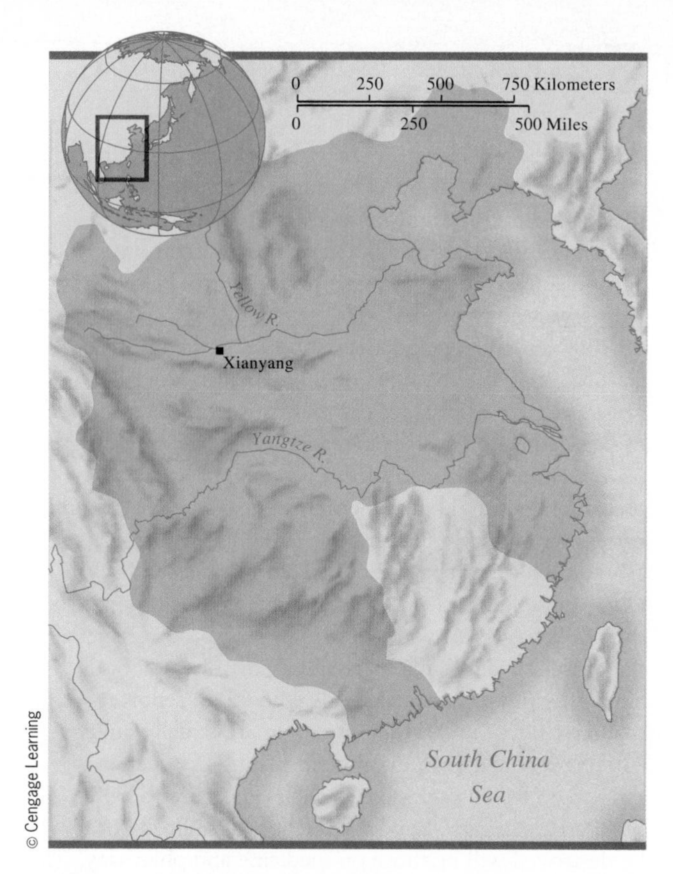

© Cengage Learning

MAP 3.3 The Qin Empire, 221–206 B.C.E. After a struggle of several decades, the state of Qin was finally able to subdue its rivals and create the first united empire in the history of China. The capital was located at Xianyang, near the modern city of Xian.

Q *What factors may have aided Qin in its effort to dominate the region?*

characters, and ordered the construction of a system of roads extending throughout the empire. He also attempted to eliminate the remaining powers of the landed aristocrats and divided their estates among the peasants, who were now taxed directly by the state. He thus eliminated potential rivals and secured tax revenues for the central government. Members of the aristocratic clans were required to live in the capital city at Xianyang (shi-AHN-yahng) (Hsien-yang), just north of modern Xian, so that the court could monitor their activities. Such a system may not have been advantageous to the peasants in all respects, however, since the central government could now collect taxes more effectively and mobilize the peasants for military service and for various public works projects. The Qin dynasty was equally unsympathetic to the merchants, whom it viewed as parasites. Private commercial activities were severely restricted and heavily taxed, and many vital forms of commerce and manufacturing, including mining, wine making, and the distribution of salt, became government monopolies.

Qin Shi Huangdi was equally aggressive in foreign affairs. His armies continued the gradual advance to the south that had taken place during the final years of the Zhou dynasty, extending the border of China to the edge of the Red River in modern Vietnam. To supply the Qin armies operating in the area, a Canal was dug in order to provide direct inland navigation from the Yangtze River in central China to what is now the modern city of Guangzhou (gwahng-JOE) (Canton) in the south.

Beyond the Frontier: The Nomadic Peoples and the Great Wall

The main area of concern for the Qin emperor, however, was in the north, where a nomadic people, known to the Chinese as the Xiongnu (SHYAHNG-noo) (Hsiung-nu) and possibly related to the Huns (see Chapter 5), had become increasingly active in the area of the Gobi Desert. The area north of the Yellow River had been sparsely inhabited since prehistoric times. During the Qin period, the climate of northern China was somewhat milder and moister than it is today, and parts of the region were heavily forested. The local population probably lived by hunting and fishing, practicing limited forms of agriculture, or herding animals such as cattle or sheep.

As the climate gradually became drier, people were forced to rely increasingly on animal husbandry as a means of livelihood. Their response was to master the art of riding on horseback and to adopt the nomadic life. Organized loosely into communities consisting of a number of kinship groups, they ranged far and wide in search of pasture for their herds of cattle, goats, or sheep. As they moved seasonally from one pasture to another, they often traveled several hundred miles carrying their goods and their circular felt tents, called *yurts*.

But the new way of life presented its own challenges. Increased food production led to a growing population, which in times of drought outstripped the available resources. Rival groups then competed for the best pastures. After they mastered the art of fighting on horseback sometime during the middle of the first millennium B.C.E., territorial warfare became commonplace throughout the entire frontier region from the Pacific Ocean to Central Asia.

By the end of the Zhou dynasty in the third century B.C.E., the nomadic Xiongnu posed a serious threat to the security of China's northern frontier, and a number of

Memorandum on the Burning of Books

Li Su, the author of the following passage, was a chief minister of the First Emperor of Qin. An exponent of Legalism, Li Su hoped to eliminate all rival theories on government. His recommendation to the emperor on the subject was recorded by the Han dynasty historian Sima Qian. The emperor approved the proposal and ordered that all books contrary to the spirit of Legalist ideology be destroyed on pain of death. Fortunately, some texts were preserved by being hidden or even memorized by their owners and were thus available to later generations. For centuries afterward, the First Emperor of Qin and his minister were singled out for criticism because of their intolerance and their effort to control the minds of their subjects. Totalitarianism, it seems, is not a modern concept.

Sima Qian, *Historical Records*

In earlier times the empire disintegrated and fell into disorder, and no one was capable of unifying it. Thereupon the various feudal lords rose to power. In their discourses they all praised the past in order to disparage the present and embellished empty words to confuse the truth. Everyone cherished his own favorite school of learning and criticized what had been instituted by the authorities. But at present Your Majesty possesses a unified empire, has regulated the distinctions of black and white, and has firmly established for yourself a position of sole supremacy. And yet these independent schools, joining with each other, criticize the codes of laws and instructions. Hearing of the promulgation of a decree, they criticize it, each from the standpoint of his own school. At home they disapprove of it in their hearts; going out they criticize it in the thoroughfare. They seek a reputation by discrediting their sovereign; they appear superior by expressing contrary views, and they lead the lowly multitude in the spreading of slander. If such license is not prohibited, the sovereign power will decline above and partisan factions will form below. It would be well to prohibit this.

Your servant suggests that all books in the imperial archives, save the memoirs of Ch'in, be burned. All persons in the empire, except members of the Academy of Learned Scholars, in possession of the *Book of Odes*, the *Book of History*, and discourses of the hundred philosophers should take them to the local governors and have them indiscriminately burned. Those who dare to talk to each other about the *Book of Odes* and the *Book of History* should be executed and their bodies exposed in the marketplace. Anyone referring to the past to criticize the present should, together with all members of his family, be put to death. Officials who fail to report cases that have come under their attention are equally guilty. After thirty days from the time of issuing the decree, those who have not destroyed their books are to be branded and sent to build the Great Wall. Books not to be destroyed will be those on medicine and pharmacy, divination by the tortoise and milfoil, and agriculture and arboriculture. People wishing to pursue learning should take the officials as their teachers.

Why did the Legalist thinker Li Su believe that his proposal to destroy dangerous ideas was justified? Are there examples of similar thinking in our own time? Are there occasions when it might be permissible to outlaw unpopular ideas?

Source: Excerpt from *Sources of Chinese Tradition*, by William Theodore de Bary. Copyright © 1960 by Columbia University Press. Reprinted with the permission of the publisher.

Chinese principalities in the area began to build walls and fortifications to keep them out. But warriors on horseback possessed significant advantages over the infantry of the Chinese.

Qin Shi Huangdi's answer to the problem was to strengthen the walls to keep the marauders out. In Sima Qian's words:

> [The] First Emperor of the Ch'in dispatched Meng T'ien to lead a force of a hundred thousand men north to attack the barbarians. He seized control of all the lands south of the Yellow River and established border defenses along the river, constructing forty-four walled district cities overlooking the river and manning them with convict laborers transported to the border for garrison duty. Thus, he utilized the

natural mountain barriers to establish the border defenses, scooping out the valleys and constructing ramparts and building installations at other points where they were needed. The whole line of defenses stretched over ten thousand *li* [a *li* is one-third of a mile] from Lin-t'ao to Liao-tung and even extended across the Yellow River and through Yang-shan and Pei-chia.[12]

Today, of course, we know Qin Shi Huangdi's project as the Great Wall, which extends nearly 4,000 miles from the sandy wastes of Central Asia to the sea. Parts of it are constructed of granite blocks, and its top is wide enough to serve as a roadway for horse-drawn chariots. Although the wall that appears in most photographs today was built 1,500 years after the Qin, during the Ming dynasty (see Chapter 10), some of the walls built by the Qin are still standing. Their construction was a massive project that required the efforts of thousands of laborers, many of whom met their deaths there and, according to legend, are now buried within the wall.

The Fall of the Qin

The Legalist system put in place by the First Emperor of Qin was designed to achieve maximum efficiency as well as total security for the state. It did neither. Qin Shi Huangdi was apparently aware of the dangers of factions within the imperial family and established a class of **eunuchs** (males whose testicles have been removed) who served as personal attendants for himself and female members of the royal family. The original idea may have been to restrict the influence of male courtiers, and the eunuch system later became a standard feature of the Chinese imperial system. But as confidential advisers to the royal family, eunuchs were in a position of influence. The rivalry between the "inner" imperial court and the "outer" court of bureaucratic officials led to tensions that persisted until the end of the imperial system.

By ruthlessly gathering control over the empire into his own hands, Qin Shi Huangdi had hoped to establish a rule that, in the words of Sima Qian, "would be enjoyed by his sons for ten thousand generations." In fact, his centralizing zeal alienated many key groups. Landed aristocrats and Confucian intellectuals, as well as the common people, groaned under the censorship of thought and speech, harsh taxes, and forced labor projects. "He killed men," recounted the historian, "as though he thought he could never finish, he punished men as though he were afraid he would never get around to them all, and the whole world revolted against him."[13] Shortly after the emperor died in 210 B.C.E., the dynasty quickly descended into factional rivalry, and four years later it was overthrown.

The disappearance of the Qin brought an end to an experiment in absolute rule that later Chinese historians would view as a betrayal of humanistic Confucian principles. But in another sense, the Qin system was a response—though somewhat extreme—to the problems of administering a large and increasingly complex society. Although later rulers would denounce Legalism and enthrone Confucianism as the new state orthodoxy, in practice they would make use of a number of the key tenets of Legalism to administer the empire and control the behavior of their subjects (see Chapters 5 and 10).

CHRONOLOGY Ancient China

Xia (Hsia) dynasty	?–c. 1570 B.C.E.
Shang dynasty	c. 1570–c. 1045 B.C.E.
Zhou (Chou) dynasty	c. 1045–221 B.C.E.
Life of Confucius	551–479 B.C.E.
Period of the Warring States	403–221 B.C.E.
Life of Mencius	370–290 B.C.E.
Qin (Ch'in) dynasty	221–206 B.C.E.
Life of the First Emperor of Qin	259–210 B.C.E.
Formation of Han dynasty	202 B.C.E.

ARE ALL HYDRAULIC SOCIETIES DESPOTIC? Thus, the Qin dynasty's single-minded effort to bring about the total regimentation of Chinese society left a mixed legacy for later generations. Some observers, notably the China scholar Karl Wittfogel, have speculated that the need to establish and regulate a vast public irrigation network, as had been created in China under the Zhou dynasty, led naturally to the emergence of a form of **Oriental despotism** that would henceforth be applied in all such **hydraulic societies**. Recent evidence, however, disputes this view, suggesting that the emergence of strong central government followed, rather than preceded, the establishment of a large irrigation system, which often began as a result of local initiatives rather than as a product of central planning. The preference for autocratic rule is probably better explained by the desire to limit the emergence of powerful regional landed interests and maintain control over a vast empire.

Daily Life in Ancient China

FOCUS QUESTION: What were the key aspects of social and economic life in early China?

Few social institutions have been as closely identified with China as the family. As in most agricultural civilizations, the family served as the basic economic and social unit in society. In traditional China, however, it took on an almost sacred quality as a microcosm of the entire social order.

The Role of the Family

In Neolithic times, the farm village, organized around the clan, was the basic social unit in China, at least in the core region of the Yellow River valley. Even then, however, the smaller family unit was becoming more important, at least among the nobility, who attached considerable significance to the ritual veneration of their immediate ancestors.

During the Zhou dynasty, the family took on increasing importance, in part because of the need for cooperation in agriculture. The cultivation of rice, which had become the primary crop along the Yangtze River and in the provinces to the south, is highly labor-intensive. The seedlings must be planted in several inches of water in a nursery bed and then transferred individually to the paddy beds, which must be irrigated constantly. During the harvest, the stalks must be cut and the kernels carefully separated from the stalks and husks. As a result, children—and the labor they supplied—were considered essential to the survival of the family, not only during their youthful years but also later, when sons were expected to provide for their parents. Loyalty to family members came to be considered even more important than loyalty to the broader community or the state. Confucius commented that it is the mark of a civilized society that a son should protect his father even if the latter has committed a crime against the community.

At the crux of the concept of family was the idea of **filial piety**, which called on all members of the family to subordinate their personal needs and desires to the patriarchal head of the family. More broadly, it created a hierarchical system in which every family member had his or her place. All Chinese learned the **five relationships** that were the key to a proper social order. The son was subordinate to the father, the wife to her husband, the younger brother to the older brother, and all were subject to their king. The final relationship was the proper one between friend and friend. Only if all members of the family and the community as a whole behaved in a properly filial manner would society function effectively.

A stable family system based on obedient and hardworking members can serve as a bulwark for an efficient government, but putting loyalty to the family and the clan over loyalty to the state can also present a threat to a centralizing monarch. For that reason, the Qin dynasty attempted to destroy the clan system in China and assert the primacy of the state. Legalists even imposed heavy taxes on any family with more than two adult sons in order to break down the family concept. The Qin reportedly also originated the practice of organizing several family units into larger groups of five and ten families that would exercise mutual control and surveillance. Later dynasties continued the practice under the name of the ***Bao-jia*** (BOW-jah ["ow" as in "how"]) (*Pao-chia*) **system**.

But the efforts of the Qin to eradicate or at least reduce the importance of the family system ran against tradition and the dynamics of the Chinese economy, and under the Han dynasty, which succeeded the Qin in 202 B.C.E., the family revived and increased in importance. With official encouragement, the family system began to take on the character that it would possess until our own day. Not only was the family the basic economic unit, but it was also the basic social unit for education, religious observances, and training in ethical principles.

Lifestyles

We know much more about the lifestyle of the elites than that of the common people in ancient China. The first houses were probably constructed of wooden planks, but later Chinese mastered the art of building in tile and brick. By the first millennium B.C.E., most public buildings and the houses of the wealthy were probably constructed in this manner. By Han times, most Chinese probably lived in simple houses of mud, wooden planks, or brick with thatch or occasionally tile roofs. But in some areas, especially the loess (LESS) (a type of soil common in North China) regions of northern China, cave dwelling remained common down to modern times. The most famous cave dweller of modern times was Mao Zedong, who lived in a cave in Yan'an (yuh-NAHN) during his long struggle against Chiang Kai-shek.

Chinese houses usually had little furniture; most people squatted or sat with their legs spread out on the packed mud floor. Chairs were apparently not introduced until the sixth or seventh century C.E. Clothing was simple, consisting of cotton trousers and shirts in the summer and wool or burlap in the winter.

The staple foods were millet in the north and rice in the south. Other common foods were wheat, barley, soybeans, mustard greens, and bamboo shoots. In early times, such foods were often consumed in the form of porridge, but by the Zhou dynasty, stir-frying in a wok was becoming common. When possible, the Chinese family would vary its diet of grain foods with vegetables, fruit (including pears, peaches, apricots, and plums), and fish or meat; but for most, such additions to the daily plate of rice, millet, or soybeans were a rare luxury.

Chinese legend hints that tea—a plant originally found in upland regions in southern China and Southeast Asia—was introduced by the mythical emperor Shen Nong. In fact, however, tea drinking did not become widespread in China until around 500 C.E. By then it was lauded for its medicinal qualities and its capacity to soothe the spirit. Alcohol in the form of ale was drunk at least by the higher classes and by the early Zhou era had already begun to inspire official concern. According to the *Book of History*, "King Wen admonished . . . the young nobles . . . that they should not ordinarily use spirits; and throughout all the states he required that they should be drunk only on occasion of sacrifices, and that then virtue should preside so that there might be no drunkenness."[14] For the poorer classes, alcohol in any form was probably a rare luxury.

Cities

Under the Qin, cities began to take on the importance they would hold through later Chinese history. Urban centers were divided into neighborhoods—perhaps a forerunner of the grid pattern used in later imperial cities—as a means of facilitating control over the population. As mentioned earlier, landed aristocrats, many of them former opponents of the Qin, were forcibly resettled in the new capital of Xianyang—a practice that would also be followed in France and Japan in later centuries. Their villas and gardens aped the splendor of the imperial palace.

Cities became the cultural hubs of Chinese society, although their residents made up only a tiny proportion of the total population. In the crowded streets, nobles sought to avoid rubbing shoulders with commoners, while merchants, workers, wandering gangs, and prostitutes imitated the mannerisms of the elite. As a poem of the time satirically noted:

In the city, if they love to have their hair dressed up high,
Then everywhere else they dress their hair an inch higher.
In the city, if they love to enlarge their eyebrows,
Then everywhere else they will make their eyebrows
cover half their foreheads.
In the city, if they love large sleeves,
Then everywhere else they will use up whole bolts of silk.[15]

The Humble Estate: Women in Ancient China

Male dominance was a key element in the social system of ancient China. As in many traditional societies, the male was considered of transcendent importance because of his role as food procurer or, in the case of farming communities, food producer. In ancient China, men worked in the fields, and women raised children and took care of the home. These different roles based on gender go back to prehistoric times and are embedded in Chinese creation myths. According to legend, Fu Xi's wife Nu Wa (noo WAH) assisted her husband in organizing society by establishing the institution of marriage and the family. Yet Nu Wa was not just a household drudge. After Fu Xi's death, she became China's first female sovereign.

During ancient times, apparently women normally did not occupy formal positions of authority, but they often became a force in politics, especially at court where wives of the ruler or other female members of the royal family were often influential in palace intrigues. Such activities were frowned on, however, as the following passage from the *Book of Songs* attests:

A clever man builds a city,
A clever woman lays one low;
With all her qualifications, that clever woman
Is but an ill-omened bird.
A woman with a long tongue
Is a flight of steps leading to calamity;
For disorder does not come from heaven,
But is brought about by women.
Among those who cannot be trained or taught
Are women and eunuchs.[16]

The nature of gender relationships was also graphically demonstrated in the Chinese written language. The character for man (男) combines the symbols for strength and rice field, while the character for woman (女) represents a person in a posture of deference and respect. The character for peace (安) is a woman under a roof. A wife is symbolized by a woman with a broom. Male chauvinism has deep linguistic roots in China.

Confucian thought, while not denigrating the importance of women as mothers and homemakers, accepted the dual roles of men and women in Chinese society. Men governed society. They carried on family ritual through the veneration of ancestors. They were the warriors, scholars, and ministers. Their dominant role was firmly enshrined in the legal system. Men were permitted to have more than one wife and to divorce a spouse who did not produce a male child. Women were denied the right to own property, and there was no dowry system in ancient China that would have provided the wife with a degree of financial security from her husband and his family. As the third-century C.E. poet Fu Xuan (foo SHWAHN), a woman, lamented:

How sad it is to be a woman
Nothing on earth is held so cheap.
No one is glad when a girl is born.
By her the family sets no store.
No one cries when she leaves her home
Sudden as clouds when the rain stops.[17]

Chinese Culture

FOCUS QUESTIONS: What were the chief characteristics of the Chinese writing system? How did it differ from the scripts used in Egypt and Mesopotamia?

Modern knowledge about artistic achievements in ancient civilizations is limited because often little has survived the ravages of time. Fortunately, many ancient civilizations, such as Egypt and Mesopotamia, were located in relatively arid areas where many artifacts were preserved, even over thousands of years. In more humid regions, such as China and South Asia, the cultural residue left by the civilizations of antiquity has been adversely affected by climate.

As a result, relatively little remains of the cultural achievements of the prehistoric Chinese aside from Neolithic pottery and the relics found at the site of the Shang dynasty capital at Anyang. In recent years, a rich trove from the time of the Qin Empire has been unearthed near the tomb of Qin Shi Huangdi near Xian in central China and at Han tombs nearby. But little remains of the literature of ancient China and almost none of the painting, architecture, and music.

Metalwork and Sculpture

Discoveries at archaeological sites indicate that ancient China was a society rich in cultural achievement. The pottery found at Neolithic sites such as Longshan and Yangshao exhibits a freshness and vitality of form and design, and the ornaments, such as rings and beads, show a strong aesthetic sense.

BRONZE CASTING The pace of Chinese cultural development began to quicken during the Shang dynasty, which ruled in northern China from the sixteenth to the eleventh century B.C.E. At that time, objects cast in bronze began to appear. Various bronze vessels were produced for use in preparing and serving food and drink in the ancestral rites. Later vessels were used for decoration or for dining at court.

The method of casting used was one reason for the extraordinary quality of Shang bronze work. Bronze workers in most ancient civilizations used the lost-wax method, in which a model was first made in wax. After a clay mold had been formed around it, the model was heated so that the wax would melt away, and the empty space was filled with molten metal. In China, clay molds composed of several sections were tightly fitted together prior to the introduction of the liquid bronze. This technique, which had evolved from ceramic techniques used during the Neolithic period, enabled the artisans to apply the design directly to the mold and thus contributed to the clarity of line and rich surface decoration of the Shang bronzes.

Bronze casting became a large-scale business, and more than ten thousand vessels of an incredible variety of form and design survive today. Factories were located not only in the Yellow River valley but also in Sichuan province, in southern China. The art of bronze working continued into the Zhou dynasty, but the quality and originality declined. The Shang bronzes remain the pinnacle of creative art in ancient China.

© William J. Duiker

A Shang Wine Vessel. Used initially as food containers in royal ceremonial rites during the Shang dynasty, Chinese bronzes were the product of an advanced technology unmatched by any contemporary civilization. This wine vessel displays a deep green patina as well as a monster motif, complete with large globular eyes, nostrils, and fangs, typical of many Shang bronzes. Known as the *taotie* (TOW-tee-YUH ["ow" as in "how"]), this fanciful beast is normally presented in silhouette as two dragons face to face so that each side forms half of the mask. Although the *taotie* presumably served as a guardian force against evil spirits, scholars are still not aware of its exact significance for early Chinese peoples.

One reason for the decline of bronze casting in China was the rise in popularity of iron. Iron making developed in China around the ninth or eighth century B.C.E., much later than in the Middle East, where it had been mastered almost a millennium earlier. Once familiar with the process, however, the Chinese quickly moved to the forefront. Ironworkers in Europe and the Middle East, lacking the technology to achieve the high temperatures necessary to melt iron ore for casting, were forced to work with wrought iron, a cumbersome and expensive process. By the fourth century B.C.E., the Chinese had invented the blast furnace, powered by a worker operating a bellows. They were therefore able to manufacture

© William J. Duiker
© Martin Puddy/Getty Images

The Tomb of Qin Shi Huangdi. The First Emperor of Qin ordered the construction of an elaborate mausoleum, an underground palace complex protected by an army of terra-cotta soldiers and horses to accompany him on his journey to the afterlife. This massive formation of six thousand life-size armed soldiers, discovered accidentally by farmers in 1974, reflects Qin Shi Huangdi's grandeur and power.

cast-iron ritual vessels and agricultural tools centuries before an equivalent technology appeared in the West.

Another reason for the deterioration of the bronze-casting tradition was the development of cheaper materials such as lacquerware and ceramics. Lacquer, made from resins obtained from the juice of sumac trees native to the region, had been produced since Neolithic times, and by the second century B.C.E., it had become a popular method of applying a hard coating to objects made of wood or fabric. Pottery, too, had existed since early times, but technological advances led to the production of a high-quality form of pottery covered with a brown or gray-green glaze, the latter known popularly as celadon. By the end of the first millennium B.C.E., both lacquerware and pottery had replaced bronze in popularity, much as plastic goods have replaced more expensive materials in our own time.

THE FIRST EMPEROR'S TOMB In 1974, in a remarkable discovery, farmers digging a well about 35 miles east of Xian unearthed a number of terra-cotta figures in an underground pit about one mile east of the burial mound of the First Emperor of Qin. Chinese archaeologists sent to work at the site discovered a vast terra-cotta army that they believed was a re-creation of Qin Shi Huangdi's imperial guard, which was to accompany the emperor on his journey to the next world.

One of the astounding features of the terra-cotta army is its size. The army is enclosed in four pits that were originally encased in a wooden framework, which has since disintegrated. More than a thousand figures have been unearthed in the first pit, along with horses, wooden chariots, and seven thousand bronze weapons. Archaeologists estimate that there are more than six thousand figures in that pit alone.

Equally impressive is the quality of the work. Slightly larger than life-size, the figures were molded of finely textured clay and then fired and painted. The detail on the uniforms is realistic and sophisticated, but the most striking feature is the individuality of the facial features of the soldiers. Apparently, ten different head shapes were used and were then modeled further by hand to reflect the variety of ethnic groups and personality types in the army.

The discovery of the terra-cotta army also shows that the Chinese had come a long way from the human sacrifices that had taken place at the death of Shang sovereigns more than a thousand years earlier. But the project must have been ruinously expensive and is additional evidence of the burden the Qin ruler imposed on his subjects. One historian has estimated that one-third of the national income in Qin and Han times may have been spent on preparations for the ruler's afterlife. The emperor's mausoleum has not yet been unearthed, but it is enclosed in a mound nearly 250 feet high and is surrounded by a rectangular wall nearly 4 miles around. According to the Han historian Sima Qian, the ceiling is a replica of the heavens, while the floor contains a relief model of the entire Qin kingdom, with rivers flowing in mercury. According to tradition, traps were set within the mausoleum to prevent intruders, and the workers applying the final touches were buried alive in the tomb with its secrets.

Language and Literature

Precisely when writing developed in China cannot be determined, but certainly by Shang times, as the oracle bones demonstrate, the Chinese had developed a simple but functional script. Like many other languages of antiquity, it was primarily ideographic and pictographic in form. Symbols, usually called "characters," were created to represent an idea or to form a picture of the object to be represented. For example, the Chinese characters for mountain (山), the sun (日), and the moon (月) were meant to represent the objects themselves. Other characters, such as "big" (大) (a man with his arms outstretched), represent an idea. The character "east" (東) symbolizes the sun coming up behind the trees.

Each character, of course, would be given a sound by the speaker when pronounced. In other cultures, this process led to the abandonment of the system of ideographs and the adoption of a written language based on phonetic symbols. The Chinese language, however, has never entirely abandoned its original ideographic format, although the phonetic element has developed into a significant part of the individual character. In that sense, the Chinese written language is virtually unique in the world today.

One reason the language retained its ideographic quality may have been the aesthetics of the written characters. By the time of the Han dynasty, if not earlier, the written language came to be seen as an art form as well as a means of communication, and calligraphy became one of the most prized forms of painting in China.

Even more important, if the written language had developed in the direction of a phonetic alphabet, it could no longer have served as the written system for all the peoples of an expanding civilization. Although the vast majority spoke a tongue derived from a parent Sinitic language (a system distinguished by its variations in pitch, a characteristic that gives Chinese its lilting quality even today), the languages spoken in various regions of the country differed from each other in pronunciation and to a lesser degree in vocabulary and syntax; for the most part, they were (and are today) mutually unintelligible.

The Chinese answer to this problem was to give all the spoken languages the same writing system. Although any character might be pronounced differently in different regions of China, that character would be written the same way (after the standardization undertaken under the Qin) no matter where it was written. This system of written characters could be read by educated Chinese from one end of the country to the other. It became the language of the bureaucracy and the vehicle for the transmission of Chinese culture to all Chinese from the Great Wall to the southern border and even beyond. The written language, however, was not identical with the spoken. Written Chinese evolved a totally separate vocabulary and grammatical structure from the spoken tongues. As a result, those who used it required special training.

The earliest extant form of Chinese literature dates from the Zhou dynasty. It was written on silk or strips of bamboo and consisted primarily of historical records such as the *Rites of Zhou*, philosophical treatises such as the *Analects* and *The Way of the Tao*, and poetry, as recorded in the

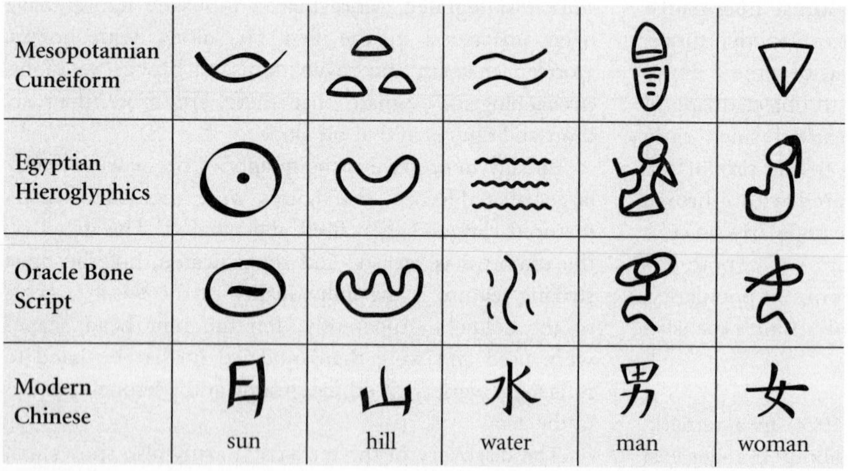

Mesopotamian Cuneiform					
Egyptian Hieroglyphics					
Oracle Bone Script					
Modern Chinese	日 sun	山 hill	水 water	男 man	女 woman

Ripley Center, Smithsonian Institution, Washington, DC// Photo © William J. Duiker

Pictographs in Ancient Cultures. Virtually all written languages evolved from pictographs—representations of physical objects that were eventually stylized and tied to sounds in the spoken language. This chart shows pictographs that originated independently in three ancient cultures and the stylized modern characters into which the Chinese oracle pictographs evolved.

Book of Songs and the *Song of the South*. In later years, when Confucian principles had been elevated to a state ideology, the key works identified with the Confucian school were integrated into a set of so-called Confucian Classics. These works became required reading for generations of Chinese schoolchildren and introduced them to the forms of behavior that would be required of them as adults.

Music

From early times in China, music was viewed not just as an aesthetic pleasure but also as a means of achieving political order and refining the human character. In fact, music may have originated as an accompaniment to sacred rituals at the royal court. According to the *Historical Records*, a history written during the Han dynasty: "When our sage-kings of the past instituted rites and music, their objective was far from making people indulge in the . . . amusements of singing and dancing. . . . Music is produced to purify the heart, and rites introduced to rectify the behavior."[18] Eventually, however, music began to be appreciated for its own sake as well as to accompany singing and dancing.

A wide variety of musical instruments were used, including flutes, various stringed instruments, bells and chimes, drums, and gourds. Bells cast in bronze were first used as musical instruments in the Shang period; they were hung in rows and struck with a wooden mallet. The finest were produced during the mid-Zhou era and are considered among the best examples of early bronze work in China.

By the late Zhou era, bells had begun to give way as the instrument of choice to strings and wind instruments, and the purpose of music shifted from ceremony to entertainment. This led conservative critics to rail against the onset of an age of debauchery.

Ancient historians stressed the relationship between music and court life, but it is highly probable that music, singing, and dancing were equally popular among the common people. The *Book of History*, purporting to describe conditions in the late third millennium B.C.E., suggests that ballads emanating from the popular culture were welcomed at court. Nevertheless, court music and popular music differed in several respects. Among other things, popular music was more likely to be motivated by the desire for pleasure than for the purpose of law and order and moral uplift. Those differences continued to be reflected in the evolution of music in China down to modern times.

CHAPTER SUMMARY

Of the great classical civilizations discussed in Part I of this book, China was the last to come into full flower. By the time the Shang began to emerge as an organized state, the societies in Mesopotamia and the Nile valley had already reached an advanced level of civilization. Unfortunately, not enough is known about the early stages of these civilizations to allow us to determine why some developed earlier than others, but one likely reason for China's comparatively late arrival was that it was virtually isolated from other emerging centers of culture elsewhere in the world and thus was compelled to develop essentially on its own. Only at the end of the first millennium B.C.E. did China come into regular contact with other civilizations in South Asia, the Middle East, and the Mediterranean.

Once embarked on its own path toward the creation of a complex society, however, China achieved results that were in all respects the equal of its counterparts elsewhere. By the rise of the first unified empire in the late third century B.C.E., the state extended from the edge of the Gobi Desert in the north to the subtropical regions near the borders of modern Vietnam in the south. Chinese philosophers had engaged in debate over intricate questions relating to human nature and the state of the universe, and China's artistic and technological achievements—especially in terms of bronze casting and the terra-cotta figures entombed in Qin Shi Huangdi's mausoleum—were unsurpassed throughout the world.

Meanwhile, another great civilization was beginning to take form on the northern shores of the Mediterranean Sea. Unlike China and the other ancient societies discussed thus far, this new civilization in Europe was based as much on trade as on agriculture. Yet the political and cultural achievements of ancient Greece were the equal of any of the great human experiments that had preceded it and soon began to exert a significant impact on the rest of the ancient world.

CHAPTER TIMELINE

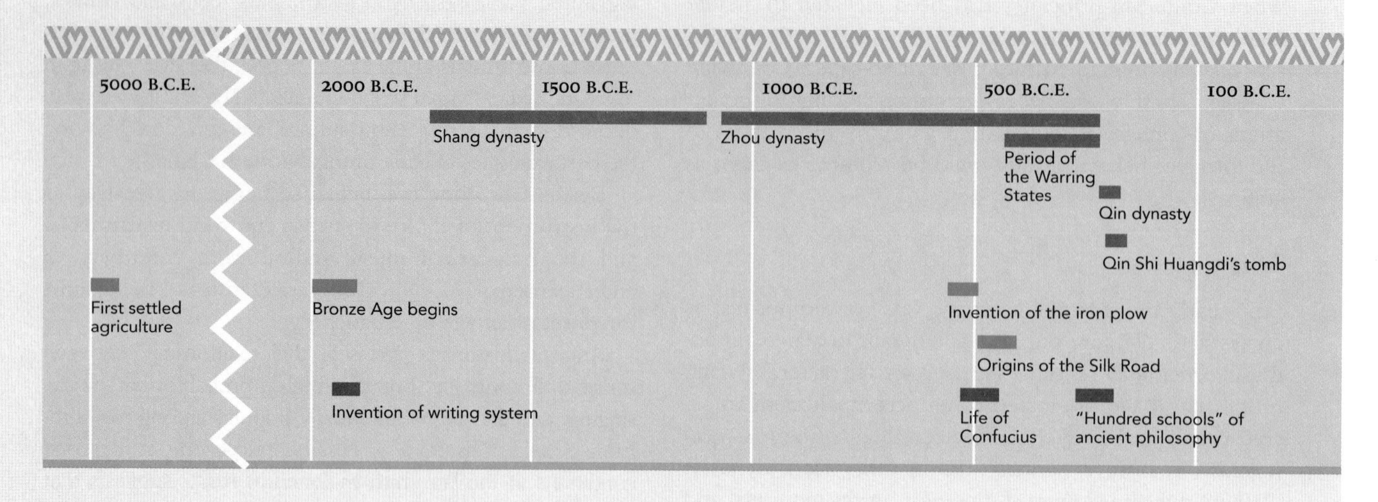

CHAPTER REVIEW

Upon Reflection

Q What were some of the key contributions in political structures, social organization, and culture that the Shang dynasty bequeathed to its successor, the Zhou dynasty? Does the Shang deserve to be called the "mother culture" of China?

Q How did the first emperor of the Qin dynasty transform the political, social, and economic institutions of early China?

Q What contributions did the ancient Chinese people make in the field of metallurgy? How do their achievements compare with developments in ancient Egypt and the Middle East?

Key Terms

Yangshao (p. 57)
Longshan (p. 57)
veneration of ancestors (p. 60)
diffusion hypothesis (p. 60)
mandate of Heaven (p. 62)
well-field system (p. 63)
Dao (p. 65)
Legalism (p. 67)
Confucianism (p. 67)
Daoism (p. 67)
eunuchs (p. 75)
Oriental despotism (p. 75)
hydraulic societies (p. 75)
filial piety (p. 76)
five relationships (p. 76)
***Bao-jia* system** (p. 76)

Suggested Reading

THE DAWN OF CHINESE CIVILIZATION For an authoritative overview of the ancient period, see **M. Loewe** and **E. L. Shaughnessy, *The Cambridge History of Ancient China from the Origins of Civilization to 221 B.C.*** (Cambridge, 1999).

The period of the Neolithic era and the Shang dynasty has received increasing attention in recent years. For an impressively documented and annotated overview, see **K. C. Chang et al., *The Formation of Chinese Civilization: An Archaeological Perspective*** (New Haven, Conn., 2005), and **R. Thorp, *China in the Early Bronze Age*** (Philadelphia, 2005). Also see **D. Keightley, *The Ancestral Landscape: Time, Space, and Continuity in Late Shang China*** (Berkeley, Calif., 2005).

THE ZHOU AND QIN DYNASTIES The Zhou and Qin dynasties have also received considerable attention. The former is exhaustively analyzed in **Cho-yun Hsu** and **J. M. Linduff, *Western Zhou Civilization*** (New Haven, Conn., 1988). **N. Di Cosmo, *Ancient China and Its Enemies: The Rise of Nomadic Power in East Asian History*** (Cambridge, 2002) traces China's relations with some of its neighbors. On bronze casting, see **E. L. Shaughnessy, *Sources of Eastern Zhou History*** (Berkeley, Calif., 1991). For recent treatments of the tumultuous Qin dynasty, see **M. Lewis, *The Early Chinese Empires: Qin and Han*** (Cambridge, Mass., 2007), and **C. Holcombe, *The***

Genesis of East Asia, 221 B.C.–A.D. 907 (Honolulu, 2001).

The philosophy of ancient China has attracted considerable attention from Western scholars. For excerpts from all the major works of the "hundred schools," consult **W. T. de Bary** and **I. Bloom, eds.,** ***Sources of Chinese Tradition,*** vol. 1 (New York, 1999). On Confucius, see **B. W. Van Norden, ed.,** ***Confucius and the Analects: New Essays*** (Oxford, 2002).

Environmental issues are explored in **M. Elvin,** ***The Retreat of the Elephants: An Environmental History of China*** (New Haven, Conn., 2004).

CHINESE CULTURE For an introduction to classical Chinese literature, consult **V. H. Mair, ed.,** ***The Columbia Anthology of Traditional Chinese Literature*** (New York, 1994), and **S. Owen, ed.,** ***An Anthology of Chinese Literature: Beginnings to 1911*** (New York, 1996). For a comprehensive introduction to Chinese art, consult **M. Sullivan,** ***The Arts of China,*** 4th ed. (Berkeley, Calif., 1999), with good illustrations in color. Also of interest is **P. B. Ebrey,** ***The Cambridge Illustrated History of China*** (Cambridge, 1999). On some recent finds, consult **J. Rowson,** ***Mysteries of Ancient China: New Discoveries from the Early Dynasties*** (New York, 1996). On Chinese music, see **J. F. So, ed.,** ***Music in the Age of Confucius*** (Washington, D.C., 2000).

Visit the CourseMate website at **www.cengagebrain.com** for additional study tools and review materials for this chapter.

The Civilization of the Greeks

© British Museum, London/The Bridgeman Art Library

A bust of Pericles

CHAPTER OUTLINE AND FOCUS QUESTIONS

Early Greece

Q How did the geography of Greece affect Greek history? Who was Homer, and why was his work used as the basis for Greek education?

The Greek City-States (c. 750–c. 500 B.C.E.)

Q What were the chief features of the *polis*, or city-state, and how did the city-states of Athens and Sparta differ?

The High Point of Greek Civilization: Classical Greece

Q What did the Greeks mean by *democracy*, and in what ways was the Athenian political system a democracy? What effect did the two great conflicts of the fifth century—the Persian Wars and the Peloponnesian War—have on Greek civilization?

The Rise of Macedonia and the Conquests of Alexander

Q How was Alexander the Great able to amass his empire, and what was his legacy?

The World of the Hellenistic Kingdoms

Q How did the political and social institutions of the Hellenistic world differ from those of Classical Greece?

CRITICAL THINKING

Q In what ways did the culture of the Hellenistic period differ from that of the Classical period, and what do those differences suggest about society in the two periods?

DURING THE ERA of civil war in China known as the Period of the Warring States, a civil war also erupted on the northern shores of the Mediterranean Sea. In 431 B.C.E., two very different Greek city-states—Athens and Sparta—fought for domination of the Greek world. The people of Athens felt secure behind their walls, and in the first winter of the war, they held a public funeral to honor those who had died in battle. On the day of the ceremony, the citizens of Athens joined in a procession, with the relatives of the dead wailing for their loved ones. As was the custom in Athens, one leading citizen was asked to address the crowd, and on this day it was Pericles who spoke to the people. He talked about the greatness of Athens and reminded the Athenians of the strength of their political system: "Our constitution," he said, "is called a democracy because power is in the hands not of a minority but of the whole people. When it is a question of settling private disputes, everyone is equal before the law. Just as our political life is free and open, so is our day-to-day life in our relations with each other. . . . Here each individual is interested not only in his own affairs but in the affairs of the state as well."

In this famous funeral oration, Pericles gave voice to the ideal of democracy and the importance of the individual, ideals that were quite different from those of some other ancient societies, in which the individual was subordinated to a larger order based on obedience to an exalted ruler. The Greeks asked some basic questions about human life: What is the nature of the universe? What is the purpose of human existence? What is our relationship to divine forces? What constitutes a community? What constitutes a state? What is truth, and how do we realize it? Not only did the Greeks provide answers to these questions, but they also created a system of logical, analytical thought to examine them. Their answers and their system of rational thought laid the intellectual foundation of Western civilization's understanding of the human condition.

The remarkable story of ancient Greek civilization begins with the arrival of the Greeks around 1900 B.C.E. By the eighth century B.C.E., the characteristic institution of ancient Greek life, the *polis*, or city-state, had emerged. Greek civilization flourished and reached its height in the Classical era of the fifth century B.C.E., but the inability of the Greek states to end their fratricidal warfare eventually left them vulnerable to the Macedonian king Philip II and helped bring an end to the era of independent Greek city-states.

Although the city-states were never the same after their defeat by the Macedonian monarch, this defeat did not end the influence of the Greeks. Philip's son Alexander led the Macedonians and Greeks on a spectacular conquest of the Persian Empire and opened the door to the spread of Greek culture throughout the Middle East.

Early Greece

FOCUS QUESTIONS: How did the geography of Greece affect Greek history? Who was Homer, and why was his work used as the basis for Greek education?

Geography played an important role in Greek history. Compared to Mesopotamia and Egypt, Greece occupied a small area, a mountainous peninsula that encompassed only 45,000 square miles of territory, about the size of the state of Louisiana. The mountains and the sea were especially significant. Much of Greece consists of small plains and river valleys surrounded by mountain ranges 8,000 to 10,000 feet high. The mountains isolated Greeks from one another, causing Greek communities to follow their own separate paths and develop their own ways of life. Over a period of time, these communities became so fiercely attached to their independence that they were only too willing to fight one another to gain advantage. No doubt the small size of these independent Greek communities fostered participation in political affairs and unique cultural expressions, but the rivalry among them also led to the internecine warfare that ultimately devastated Greek society.

The sea also influenced Greek society. Greece had a long seacoast, dotted by bays and inlets that provided numerous harbors. The Greeks also inhabited a number of islands to the west, south, and particularly the east of the Greek mainland. It is no accident that the Greeks became seafarers who sailed out into the Aegean and Mediterranean Seas to make contact with the outside world and later to establish colonies that would spread Greek civilization throughout the Mediterranean region.

Greek topography helped determine the major territories into which Greece was ultimately divided (see Map 4.1). South of the Gulf of Corinth was the Peloponnesus (pell-uh-puh-NEE-suss), virtually an island connected to the mainland by a narrow isthmus. Consisting mostly of hills, mountains, and small valleys, the Peloponnesus was the location of Sparta. Northeast of the Peloponnesus was the Attic peninsula (or Attica), the site of Athens, hemmed in by mountains to the north and west and surrounded by the sea to the south and east. Northwest of Attica was Boeotia (bee-OH-shuh) in central Greece, with its chief city of Thebes (THEEBZ). To the north of Boeotia was Thessaly, which contained the largest plains and became a great producer of grain and horses. To the north of Thessaly lay Macedonia, which was not of much importance in Greek history until 338 B.C.E., when the Macedonian king conquered the Greeks.

Minoan Crete

The earliest civilization in the Aegean region emerged on the large island of Crete, southeast of the Greek mainland. A Bronze Age civilization that used metals, especially bronze, in making weapons had been established there by 2800 B.C.E. This civilization was discovered at the turn of the twentieth century by the English archaeologist Arthur Evans, who named it "Minoan" (mih-NOH-uhn) after Minos (MY-nuss), a legendary king of Crete. In language and religion, the Minoans were not Greek, although they did have some influence on the peoples of the Greek mainland.

Evans's excavations on Crete at the beginning of the twentieth century unearthed an enormous palace complex at Knossus (NOSS-suss), near modern Iráklion

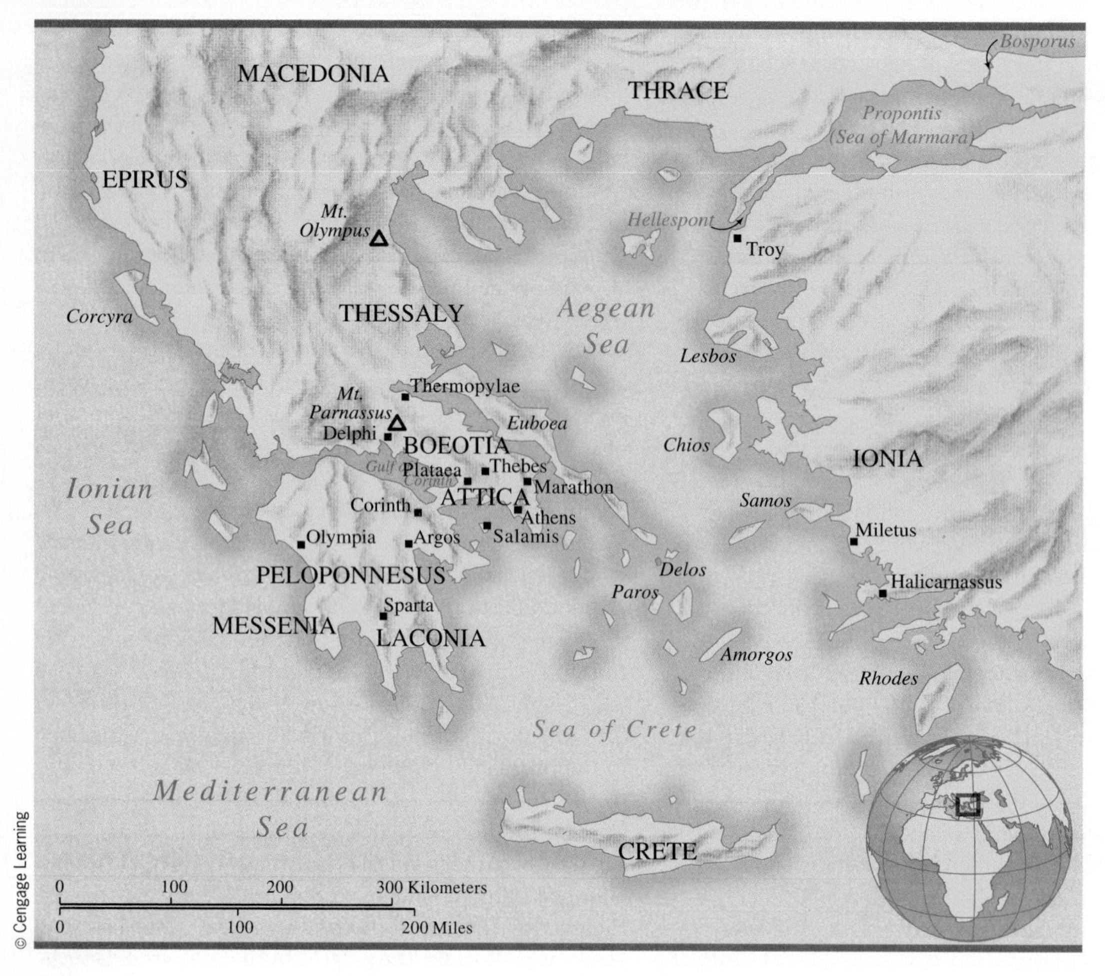

© Cengage Learning

MAP 4.1 Ancient Greece (c. 750–338 B.C.E.). Between 750 and 500 B.C.E., Greek civilization witnessed the emergence of the city-state as the central institution in Greek life and the Greeks' colonization of the Mediterranean and Black Seas. Classical Greece lasted from about 500 to 338 B.C.E. and encompassed the high points of Greek civilization in the arts, science, philosophy, and politics, as well as the Persian Wars and the Peloponnesian War.

How does the geography of Greece help explain the rise and development of the Greek city-state?

(Heracleion). The remains revealed a prosperous culture, with Knossus as the apparent center of a far-ranging "sea empire" based on trade.

The Minoan civilization reached its height between 2000 and 1450 B.C.E. The palace at Knossus, the royal seat of the kings, was an elaborate structure that included numerous private living rooms for the royal family and workshops for making decorated vases, ivory figurines, and jewelry. The complex even had bathrooms with elaborate drains, like those found at Mohenjo-Daro in India. The rooms were decorated with brightly colored frescoes showing sporting events and nature scenes.

Around 1450 B.C.E., the centers of Minoan civilization on Crete suffered a sudden and catastrophic collapse. Some historians believe that a tsunami triggered by a powerful volcanic eruption on the island of Thera was responsible for the devastation, but most historians maintain that the destruction was the result of invasion and pillage of a weakened Cretan society by mainland Greeks known as the Mycenaeans.

The First Greek State: Mycenae

The term *Mycenaean* (my-suh-NEE-uhn) is derived from Mycenae (my-SEE-nee), a remarkable fortified site excavated by the amateur German archaeologist Heinrich Schliemann (HYN-rikh SHLEE-mahn) starting in 1870. Mycenae was one center in a civilization that flourished between 1600 and 1100 B.C.E. The Mycenaean Greeks were part of the Indo-European family of peoples (see

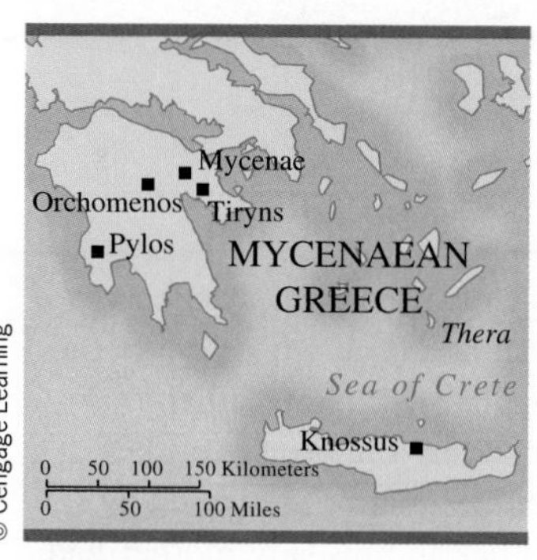

© Cengage Learning

Minoan Crete and Mycenaean Greece

Chapter 1) who spread from their original location into southern and western Europe, India, and Persia. One group entered the territory of Greece from the north around 1900 B.C.E. and eventually managed to gain control of the Greek mainland and develop a civilization.

Mycenaean civilization, which reached its high point between 1400 and 1200 B.C.E., consisted of a number of powerful monarchies based in fortified palace complexes, which were built on hills and surrounded by gigantic stone walls, such as those found at Mycenae. These various centers of power probably formed a loose confederacy of independent states, with Mycenae being the strongest.

The Mycenaeans were above all a warrior people who prided themselves on their heroic deeds in battle. Some scholars believe that the Mycenaeans spread outward and conquered Crete. The most famous of all their supposed military adventures has come down to us in the epic poetry of Homer (see "Homer" later in this chapter). Did the Mycenaean Greeks, led by Agamemnon, king of Mycenae, sack the city of Troy on the northwestern coast of Asia Minor around 1250 B.C.E.? Scholars have been debating this question since Schliemann's excavations began. Many believe in the Homeric legend even if the details have become shrouded in mystery.

By the late thirteenth century B.C.E., Mycenaean Greece was showing signs of serious trouble. Mycenae itself was burned around 1190 B.C.E., and other Mycenaean centers show a similar pattern of destruction as new waves of Greek-speaking invaders moved into Greece from the north. By 1100 B.C.E., Mycenaean culture was coming to an end, and the Greek world was entering a new period of considerable insecurity.

The Greeks in a Dark Age (c. 1100–c. 750 B.C.E.)

After the collapse of Mycenaean civilization, Greece entered a difficult era of declining population and falling food production; not until 850 B.C.E. did farming—and Greece itself—revive. Because of both the difficult conditions and the fact that we have few records to help us reconstruct what happened in this period, historians refer to it as the Dark Age.

During the Dark Age, large numbers of Greeks left the mainland and migrated across the Aegean Sea to various islands and especially to the southwestern shore of Asia Minor, a strip of territory that came to be called Ionia (y-OH-nee-uh). Two other major groups of Greeks settled in established parts of Greece. The Aeolian (ee-OH-lee-uhn) Greeks of northern and central Greece colonized the large island of Lesbos and the adjacent territory of the mainland. The Dorians (DOR-ee-unz) established themselves in southwestern Greece, especially in the Peloponnesus, as well as on some of the south Aegean islands, including Crete.

As trade and economic activity began to recover, iron replaced bronze in the construction of weapons, making them affordable for more people. At some point in the eighth century B.C.E., the Greeks adopted the Phoenician alphabet to give themselves a new system of writing. And near the very end of the Dark Age appeared the work of Homer, who has come to be viewed as one of the greatest poets of all time.

HOMER The first great epics of early Greece, the *Iliad* and the *Odyssey*, were based on stories that had been passed down from generation to generation. It is generally assumed that early in the eighth century B.C.E., Homer made use of these oral traditions to compose the *Iliad*, his epic poem of the Trojan War. The war was sparked by Paris, a prince of Troy, who kidnapped Helen, wife of the king of the Greek state of Sparta, outraging all the Greeks. Under the leadership of the Spartan king's brother, Agamemnon of Mycenae, the Greeks attacked Troy. After ten years of combat, the Greeks finally sacked the city. The *Iliad* is not so much the story of the war itself, however, as it is the tale of the Greek hero Achilles (uh-KIL-eez) and how the "wrath of Achilles" led to disaster. The *Odyssey*, Homer's other masterpiece, is an epic romance that recounts the journeys of another Greek hero, Odysseus (oh-DISS-ee-uss), from the fall of Troy until his eventual return to his wife, Penelope, twenty years later.

The Greeks regarded the *Iliad* and the *Odyssey* as authentic history as recorded by one poet, Homer. They gave the Greeks an idealized past, somewhat like the concept of the golden age in ancient China, with a legendary age of heroes, and came to be used as standard texts for the education of generations of Greek males. As one Athenian stated, "My father was anxious to see me develop into a good man . . . and as a means to this end he compelled me to memorize all of Homer."[1] The values Homer inculcated were essentially the aristocratic values of courage and honor (see the box on p. 88). It was important to strive for the excellence befitting a hero, which the Greeks called *arete*. In the warrior-aristocratic world of Homer, *arete* is won in a struggle or contest. Through his willingness to fight, the hero protects his family and friends, preserves his own honor and his family's, and earns his reputation. In the

Homer's Ideal of Excellence

ART & IDEAS

The *Iliad* and the *Odyssey*, which the Greeks believed were written by Homer, were used as basic texts for the education of Greeks for hundreds of years during antiquity. This passage from the *Iliad*, describing the encounter between Hector, prince of Troy, and his wife, Andromache (an-DRAH-muh-kee), illustrates the Greek ideal of gaining honor through combat. At the end of the passage, Homer also reveals what became the Greek attitude toward women: they are supposed to spin and weave and take care of their households and children.

Homer, *Iliad*

Hector looked at his son and smiled, but said nothing. Andromache, bursting into tears, went up to him and put her hand in his. "Hector," she said, "you are possessed. This bravery of yours will be your end. You do not think of your little boy or your unhappy wife, whom you will make a widow soon. Some day the Achaeans [Greeks] are bound to kill you in a massed attack. And when I lose you I might as well be dead. . . . I have no father, no mother, now. . . . I had seven brothers too at home. In one day all of them went down to Hades' House. The great Achilles of the swift feet killed them all. . . .

"So you, Hector, are father and mother and brother to me, as well as my beloved husband. Have pity on me now; stay here on the tower; and do not make your boy an orphan and your wife a widow. . . ."

"All that, my dear," said the great Hector of the glittering helmet, "is surely my concern. But if I hid myself like a coward and refused to fight, I could never face the Trojans and the Trojan ladies in their trailing gowns. Besides, it would go against the grain, for I have trained myself always, like a good soldier, to take my place in the front line and win glory for my father and myself. . . ."

As he finished, glorious Hector held out his arms to take his boy. But the child shrank back with a cry to the bosom of his girdled nurse, alarmed by his father's appearance. He was frightened by the bronze of the helmet and the horsehair plume that he saw nodding grimly down at him. His father and his lady mother had to laugh. But noble Hector quickly took his helmet off and put the dazzling thing on the ground. Then he kissed his son, dandled him in his arms, and prayed to Zeus and the other gods: "Zeus, and you other gods, grant that this boy of mine may be, like me, preeminent in Troy; as strong and brave as I; a mighty king of Ilium. May people say, when he comes back from battle, 'Here is a better man than his father.' Let him bring home the bloodstained armor of the enemy he has killed, and make his mother happy."

Hector handed the boy to his wife, who took him to her fragrant breast. She was smiling through her tears, and when her husband saw this he was moved. He stroked her with his hand and said, "My dear, I beg you not to be too much distressed. No one is going to send me down to Hades before my proper time. But Fate is a thing that no man born of woman, coward or hero, can escape. Go home now, and attend to your own work, the loom and the spindle, and see that the maidservants get on with theirs. War is men's business; and this war is the business of every man in Ilium, myself above all."

What important ideals for Greek men and women are revealed in this passage from the Iliad? How do the women's ideals compare with those for ancient Indian and Chinese women?

Source: From *The Iliad* by Homer, translated by E. V. Rieu (Penguin Classics 1950). Copyright © 1950 the Estate of E. V. Rieu. Reproduced by permission of Penguin Books Ltd.

Homeric world, aristocratic women, too, were expected to pursue excellence. Penelope, for example, the wife of Odysseus, remains faithful to her husband and displays great courage and intelligence in preserving their household during her husband's long absence.

To later generations of Greeks, these heroic values formed the core of aristocratic virtue, a fact that explains the tremendous popularity of Homer as an educational tool. Homer gave to the Greeks a universally accepted model of heroism, honor, and nobility. But in time, as a new world of city-states emerged in Greece, new values of cooperation and community also transformed what the Greeks learned from Homer.

The Greek City-States (c. 750–c. 500 B.C.E.)

FOCUS QUESTION: What were the chief features of the *polis*, or city-state, and how did the city-states of Athens and Sparta differ?

During the Dark Age, Greek villages gradually expanded and evolved into independent city-states. In the eighth century B.C.E., Greek civilization burst forth with new energies, beginning the period that historians have called the Archaic Age of Greece. Two major developments stand out in this era: the evolution of the city-state, or what the Greeks called a ***polis*** (plural, *poleis*), as the central institution in Greek life and the Greeks' colonization of the Mediterranean and Black Seas.

The *Polis*

In the most basic sense, a *polis* (POH-liss) could be defined as a small but autonomous political unit in which all major political, social, and religious activities were carried out at one central location. The *polis* consisted of a city, town, or village and its surrounding countryside. The city, town, or village was the focus, a central point where the citizens of the *polis* could assemble for political, social, and religious activities. In some *poleis*, this central meeting point was a hill, like the Acropolis (uh-KRAH-puh-liss) at Athens, which could serve as a place of refuge during an attack and later, at some sites, came to be the religious center on which temples and public monuments were erected. Below the acropolis would be an *agora* (AG-er-ah), an open space or plaza that served both as a market and as a place where citizens could assemble.

Poleis varied greatly in size, from a few square miles to a few hundred square miles. They also varied in population. Athens had a population of about 250,000 by the fifth century B.C.E. But most *poleis* were much smaller, consisting of only a few hundred to several thousand people.

Although our word *politics* is derived from the Greek term *polis*, the *polis* itself was much more than just a political institution. It was a community of citizens in which all political, economic, social, cultural, and religious activities were focused. As a community, the *polis* consisted of citizens with political rights (adult males), citizens with no political rights (women and children), and noncitizens (slaves and resident aliens). All citizens of a *polis* possessed fundamental rights, but these rights were coupled with responsibilities. The loyalty that citizens felt for their city-states also had a negative side, however. City-states distrusted one another, and the division of Greece into fiercely patriotic sovereign units helped bring about its ruin.

A NEW MILITARY SYSTEM: THE HOPLITES The development of the *polis* was paralleled by the emergence of a new military system. Greek fighting had previously been dominated by aristocratic cavalrymen, who reveled in individual duels with enemy soldiers. By 700 B.C.E., however, a new military order came into being that was based on **hoplites** (HAHP-lyts), heavily armed infantrymen who wore bronze or leather helmets, breastplates, and greaves (shin guards). Each carried a round shield, a short sword, and a thrusting spear about 9 feet long. Hoplites advanced into battle as a unit, forming a **phalanx** (a rectangular formation) in tight order, usually eight ranks deep. As long as the hoplites kept their order, were not outflanked, and did not break, they either secured victory or at the very least suffered no harm. The phalanx was easily routed, however, if it broke its order. Thus, the safety of the phalanx depended on the solidarity and discipline of its members. As one seventh century B.C.E. poet observed, a good hoplite was a "short man firmly placed upon his legs, with a courageous heart, not to be uprooted from the spot where he plants his legs."[2]

The hoplite force had political as well as military repercussions. The aristocratic cavalry was now outdated. Since each hoplite provided his own armor, men of property, both aristocrats and small farmers, made up the new phalanx. Those who could become hoplites and fight for the state could also challenge aristocratic control.

Colonization and the Growth of Trade

Between 750 and 550 B.C.E., large numbers of Greeks left their homeland to settle in distant lands. The growing gulf between rich and poor, overpopulation, and the development of trade were all factors that led to the establishment of colonies. Invariably, each colony saw itself as an independent *polis* whose links to the mother *polis* (the *metropolis*) were not political but were based on sharing common social, economic, and especially religious practices.

In the western Mediterranean, new Greek settlements were established along the coastline of southern Italy, southern France, eastern Spain, and northern Africa west of Egypt. To the north, the Greeks set up colonies in Thrace, where they sought good farmland to grow grains. Greeks also settled along the shores of the Black Sea and secured the approaches to it with cities on the Hellespont and Bosporus, most notably Byzantium, site of the later Constantinople (Istanbul). In establishing these settlements, the Greeks spread their culture throughout the Mediterranean basin. Moreover, colonization helped the Greeks foster a greater sense of Greek identity. Before the eighth century, Greek communities were mostly isolated from one another, leaving many neighboring states on unfriendly terms. Once Greeks from different communities went abroad and found

Museo Nazionale di Villa Giulia, Rome/© Scala/Art Resource, NY

The Hoplite Forces. The Greek hoplites were infantrymen equipped with large round shields and long thrusting spears. In battle, they advanced in tight phalanx formation and were dangerous opponents as long as this formation remained unbroken. This vase painting of the seventh century B.C.E. shows two groups of hoplite warriors engaged in battle. The piper on the left is leading another line of soldiers preparing to enter the fray.

peoples with different languages and customs, they became more aware of their own linguistic and cultural similarities.

Colonization also led to increased trade and industry. The Greeks on the mainland sent their pottery, wine, and olive oil to the colonized areas; in return, they received grains and metals from the west and fish, timber, wheat, metals, and slaves from the Black Sea region. In many *poleis*, the expansion of trade and industry created a new group of rich men who desired political privileges commensurate with their wealth but found such privileges impossible to gain because of the power of the ruling aristocrats.

Tyranny in the Greek *Polis*

The aspirations of the new industrial and commercial groups laid the groundwork for the rise of **tyrants** in the seventh and sixth centuries B.C.E. They were not necessarily oppressive or wicked, as the modern English word *tyrant* connotes. Greek tyrants were rulers who came to power in an unconstitutional way; a tyrant was not subject to the law. Many tyrants were actually aristocrats who opposed the control of the ruling aristocratic faction in their cities. The support for the tyrants, however, came from the new rich, who had made their money in trade and industry, as well as from poor peasants who were becoming increasingly indebted to landholding aristocrats. Both groups were opposed to the domination of political power by aristocratic **oligarchies** (*oligarchy* means "rule by the few").

Once in power, the tyrants built new marketplaces, temples, and walls that not only glorified the city but also enhanced their own popularity. Tyrants also favored the interests of merchants and traders. Despite these achievements, however, **tyranny** was largely extinguished by the end of the sixth century B.C.E. Greeks believed in the rule of law, and tyranny made a mockery of that ideal.

Although tyranny did not last, it played a significant role in the evolution of Greek history by ending the rule of narrow aristocratic oligarchies. Once the tyrants were eliminated, the door was open to the participation of new and more people in governing the affairs of the community. Although this trend culminated in the development of democracy in some communities, in other states expanded oligarchies of one kind or another managed to remain in power. Greek states exhibited considerable variety in their governmental structures; this can perhaps best be seen by examining the two most famous and most powerful Greek city-states, Sparta and Athens.

Sparta

Located in the southeastern Peloponnesus, Sparta, like other Greek states, faced the need for more land. Instead of sending its people out to found new colonies, the Spartans conquered the neighboring Laconians and later, beginning around 730 B.C.E., undertook the conquest of neighboring Messenia despite its larger size and population. Messenia possessed a large, fertile plain ideal for growing grain. After its conquest in the seventh century B.C.E., many Messenians, like some of the Laconians earlier, were reduced to serfom—they were known as ***helots*** (HEL-uts), a name derived from a Greek word for "capture"—and made to work for the Spartans. To ensure control over their conquered Laconian and Messenian *helots*, the Spartans made a conscious decision to create a military state.

THE NEW SPARTA Between 800 and 600 B.C.E., the Spartans instituted a series of reforms that are associated with the name of the lawgiver Lycurgus (ly-KUR-guss) (see the box on p. 92). Although historians are not sure that Lycurgus ever existed, there is no doubt about the result of the reforms that were made: the lives of Spartans were now rigidly organized and tightly controlled (to this day, the word *spartan* means "highly self-disciplined"). Boys were taken from their mothers at the age of seven and put under the control of the state. They lived in military-style barracks, where they were subjected to harsh discipline to make them tough and given an education that stressed military training and obedience to authority. At twenty, Spartan males were enrolled in the army for regular military service. Although allowed to marry, they continued to live in the barracks and ate all their meals in public dining halls with fellow soldiers. Meals were simple; the famous Spartan black broth consisted of a piece of pork boiled in blood, salt, and vinegar, causing a visitor who ate in a public mess to remark that he now understood why Spartans were not afraid to die. At thirty, Spartan males were allowed to vote in the assembly and live at home, but they remained in military service until the age of sixty.

While their husbands remained in military barracks, Spartan women lived at home. Because of this separation, Spartan women had greater freedom of movement and greater power in the household than was common elsewhere in Greece. Spartan women were expected to exercise and remain fit to bear and raise healthy children. Like the men, Spartan women engaged in athletic exercises in the nude. Many Spartan women upheld the strict Spartan values, expecting their husbands and sons to be brave in war. The story is told that as a Spartan mother was burying her son, an old woman came up to her and said, "You poor woman, what a misfortune." "No," replied the mother, "because I bore him so that he might die for Sparta and that is what has happened, as I wished."[3]

THE SPARTAN STATE The so-called Lycurgan reforms also reorganized the Spartan government, creating an oligarchy. Two kings were primarily responsible for military affairs and served as the leaders of the Spartan army on its campaigns. A group of five men, known as the *ephors* (EFF-urz), were elected each year and were responsible for the education of youth and the conduct of all citizens. A council of elders, composed of the two kings and twenty-eight citizens over the age of sixty, decided on the issues that would be presented to an assembly. This assembly of all male citizens did not debate but only voted on the issues put before it by the council of elders.

To make their new military state secure, the Spartans deliberately turned their backs on the outside world. Foreigners, who might bring in new ideas, were discouraged from visiting Sparta. Nor were Spartans, except for military reasons, allowed to travel abroad, where they might pick up new ideas dangerous to the stability of the state. Likewise, Spartan citizens were discouraged from studying philosophy, literature, the arts, or any other subject that might encourage new thoughts. The art of war was the Spartan ideal, and all other arts were frowned on.

Athens

By 700 B.C.E., Athens had established a unified *polis* on the peninsula of Attica. Although early Athens had been ruled by a monarchy, by the seventh century B.C.E., it had fallen under the control of its aristocrats. They possessed the best land and controlled political life by means of a council of nobles, assisted by a board of nine officials called archons. Although there was an assembly of full citizens, it possessed few powers.

Near the end of the seventh century B.C.E., Athens faced political turmoil because of serious economic problems. Increasing numbers of Athenian farmers found themselves sold into slavery when they were unable to repay loans they had obtained from their aristocratic neighbors, pledging themselves as collateral. Repeatedly, there were cries to cancel the debts and give land to the poor.

In 594 B.C.E., the ruling Athenian aristocrats responded to this crisis by giving full power to make changes to Solon (SOH-lun), a reform-minded aristocrat. Solon canceled all land debts, outlawed new loans based on humans as collateral, and freed people who had fallen into slavery for debts. He refused, however, to carry out land redistribution. Thus, Solon's reforms, though popular, did not truly solve Athens's problems. Aristocratic factions continued to vie for power, and poor peasants could not get land. Internal strife finally led to the very institution Solon had hoped to avoid—tyranny. Pisistratus (puh-SIS-truh-tuss), an aristocrat, seized power in 560 B.C.E. Pursuing a foreign policy that aided Athenian trade, Pisistratus remained popular with the mercantile and

The Lycurgan Reforms

To maintain their control over the conquered Messenians, the Spartans instituted the reforms that created their military state. In this account of the lawgiver Lycurgus, who may or may not have been a real person, the Greek historian Plutarch discusses the effect of these reforms on the treatment and education of boys.

Plutarch, *Lycurgus*

Lycurgus was of another mind; he would not have masters bought out of the market for his young Spartans, . . . nor was it lawful, indeed, for the father himself to breed up the children after his own fancy; but as soon as they were seven years old they were to be enrolled in certain companies and classes, where they all lived under the same order and discipline, doing their exercises and taking their play together. Of these, he who showed the most conduct and courage was made captain; they had their eyes always upon him, obeyed his orders, and underwent patiently whatsoever punishment he inflicted; so that the whole course of their education was one continued exercise of a ready and perfect obedience. The old men, too, were spectators of their performances, and often raised quarrels and disputes among them, to have a good opportunity of finding out their different characters, and of seeing which would be valiant, which a coward, when they should come to more dangerous encounters. Reading and writing they gave them, just enough to serve their turn; their chief care was to make them good subjects, and to teach them to endure pain and conquer in battle. To this end, as they grew in years, their discipline was proportionately increased; their heads were close-clipped, they were accustomed to go barefoot, and for the most part to play naked.

After they were twelve years old, they were no longer allowed to wear any undergarments; they had one coat to serve them a year; their bodies were hard and dry, with but little acquaintance of baths and unguents; these human indulgences they were allowed only on some few particular days in the year. They lodged together in little bands upon beds made of the rushes which grew by the banks of the river Eurotas, which they were to break off with their hands with a knife; if it were winter, they mingled some thistle down with their rushes, which it was thought had the property of giving warmth. By the time they were come to this age there was not any of the more hopeful boys who had not a lover to bear him company. The old men, too, had an eye upon them, coming often to the grounds to hear and see them contend either in wit or strength with one another, and this as seriously . . . as if they were their fathers, their tutors, or their magistrates; so that there scarcely was any time or place without someone present to put them in mind of their duty, and punish them if they had neglected it.

[Spartan boys were also encouraged to steal their food.] They stole, too, all other meat they could lay their hands on, looking out and watching all opportunities, when people were asleep or more careless than usual. If they were caught, they were not only punished with whipping, but hunger, too, being reduced to their ordinary allowance, which was but very slender, and so contrived on purpose, that they might set about to help themselves, and be forced to exercise their energy and address. This was the principal design of their hard fare.

What does this passage from Plutarch's account of Lycurgus reveal about the nature of the Spartan state? Why would the entire program have been distasteful to the Athenians?

Source: From Plutarch, *The Lives of the Noble Grecians and Romans*, translated by John Dryden, and revised by Arthur Hugh Clough. (New York: Modern Library).

industrial classes. But the Athenians rebelled against his son and ended the tyranny in 510 B.C.E. When the aristocrats attempted to reestablish an aristocratic oligarchy, Cleisthenes (KLYSS-thuh-neez), another aristocratic reformer, opposed their plan and, with the backing of the Athenian people, gained the upper hand in 508 B.C.E.

Cleisthenes created the Council of Five Hundred to supervise foreign affairs and the treasury and propose laws that would be voted on by the assembly. The Athenian assembly, composed of all male citizens, was given final authority on the passing of laws after free and open debate. Since the assembly of citizens now had the central role in the Athenian political system, the reforms of Cleisthenes had created the foundations for Athenian democracy.

The High Point of Greek Civilization: Classical Greece

FOCUS QUESTIONS: What did the Greeks mean by *democracy*, and in what ways was the Athenian political system a democracy? What effect did the two great conflicts of the fifth century—the Persian Wars and the Peloponnesian War—have on Greek civilization?

Classical Greece is the name given to the period of Greek history from around 500 B.C.E. to the conquest of Greece by the Macedonian king Philip II in 338 B.C.E. Many of the cultural contributions of the Greeks occurred during this period. The age began with a mighty confrontation between the Greek states and the mammoth Persian Empire.

The Challenge of Persia

As the Greeks spread throughout the Mediterranean, they came into contact with the Persian Empire to the east. The Ionian Greek cities in western Asia Minor had already fallen subject to the Persian Empire by the mid-sixth century B.C.E. An unsuccessful revolt by the Ionian cities in 499 B.C.E., assisted by the Athenians, led the Persian ruler Darius (duh-RY-uss) to seek revenge by attacking the mainland Greeks. In 490 B.C.E., the Persians landed an army on the plain of Marathon, only 26 miles from Athens. The Athenians and their allies were clearly outnumbered, but the Greek hoplites charged across the plain of Marathon and crushed the Persian forces.

Xerxes (ZURK-seez), the new Persian monarch after the death of Darius in 486 B.C.E., vowed revenge and planned to invade Greece. In preparation for the attack, some of the Greek states formed a defensive league under Spartan leadership. The Athenians, in the meantime, had acquired a new leader, Themistocles (thuh-MISS-tuh-kleez), who persuaded his fellow citizens to pursue a new military policy by developing a navy. By the time of the Persian invasion in 480 B.C.E., the Athenians had produced a fleet of about two hundred vessels.

Xerxes led a massive invasion force into Greece: close to 150,000 troops, almost seven hundred naval ships, and hundreds of supply ships to keep the large army fed. The Greeks tried to delay the Persians at the pass of Thermopylae (thur-MAHP-uh-lee), along the main road into central Greece. A Greek force numbering close to nine thousand men, under the leadership of a Spartan king and his contingent of three hundred Spartans, held off the Persian army for several days. The Spartan troops were especially brave. When told that Persian arrows would darken the sky in battle, one Spartan warrior supposedly responded: "That is good news. We will fight in the shade!" Unfortunately for the Greeks, a traitor told the Persians how to use a mountain path that would allow them to outflank the Greek force. The Spartans fought to the last man.

The Athenians, now threatened by the onslaught of the Persian forces, abandoned their city. While the Persians sacked and burned Athens, the Greek fleet remained offshore near the island of Salamis (SAH-luh-miss) and challenged the Persian navy. Although the Greeks were outnumbered, they managed to outmaneuver the Persian fleet and utterly defeated it. A few months later, early in 479 B.C.E., the Greeks formed the largest Greek army seen up to that time and decisively defeated the Persian army at Plataea (pluh-TEE-uh), northwest of Attica. The Greeks had won the war and were now free to pursue their own destiny.

The Growth of an Athenian Empire in the Age of Pericles

After the defeat of the Persians, Athens took over the leadership of the Greek world by forming a defensive alliance against the Persians called the Delian League in the winter of 478–477 B.C.E. The league had its main headquarters on the island of Delos, but its chief officials, including the treasurers and commanders of the fleet, were Athenian. Under the leadership of the Athenians, the Delian League pursued the attack against the Persian Empire. Virtually all of the Greek states in the Aegean were liberated from Persian control. In 454 B.C.E., the Athenians moved the treasury of the league from Delos to Athens. By controlling the Delian League, Athens had created an empire.

At home, Athenians favored the new imperial policy, especially after 461 B.C.E., when politics came to be dominated by a political faction led by a young aristocrat named Pericles (PER-i-kleez). Under Pericles, who remained a leading figure in Athenian politics for more than three decades, Athens embarked on a policy of expanding democracy at home and its new empire abroad. This period of Athenian and Greek history, which historians have subsequently labeled the Age of Pericles, witnessed the height of Athenian power and the culmination of its brilliance as a civilization.

During the Age of Pericles, the Athenians became deeply attached to their democratic system. The sovereignty of the people was embodied in the assembly, which consisted of all male citizens over eighteen years of age. In the 440s, that was probably a group of about 43,000. Not all attended, however, and the number present at the meetings, which were held every ten days on a hillside east of the Acropolis, seldom reached 6,000. The assembly passed all laws and made final decisions on war and foreign policy.

Routine administration of public affairs was handled by a large body of city magistrates, usually chosen by lot without regard to class and typically serving only one-year terms. This meant that many male citizens held public office at some time in their lives. A board of ten officials known as generals—*strategoi* (strah-tay-GOH-ee)—was elected by public vote to guide affairs of state, although their power depended on the respect they had attained. Generals were usually wealthy aristocrats, even though the people were free to select otherwise. The generals could be reelected, enabling individual leaders to play an important political role. Pericles's frequent reelection (fifteen times) as one of the ten generals made him one of the leading politicians between 461 and 429 B.C.E.

Pericles expanded the Athenians' involvement in democracy, which is what by now the Athenians had come to call their form of government. Power was in the hands of the people; male citizens voted in the assemblies and served as jurors in the courts. Lower-class citizens were now eligible for public offices formerly closed to them. Pericles also introduced state pay for officeholders, including the widely held jury duty. This meant that even poor citizens could afford to participate in public affairs and hold public office. Nevertheless, although the Athenians developed a system of government that was unique in its time in which citizens had equal rights and the people were the government, aristocrats continued to hold the most important offices, and many people, including women, slaves, and foreigners residing in Athens, were not given the same political rights.

Under Pericles, Athens became the leading center of Greek culture. The Persians had destroyed much of the city during the Persian Wars, but Pericles used the money from the treasury of the Delian League to set in motion a massive rebuilding program. New temples and statues soon made the greatness of Athens more visible. Art, architecture, and philosophy flourished, and Pericles proudly boasted that Athens had become the "school of Greece." But the achievements of Athens alarmed the other Greek states, especially Sparta, and soon all Greece was confronting a new war.

The Great Peloponnesian War and the Decline of the Greek States

During the forty years after the defeat of the Persians, the Greek world came to be divided into two major camps: Sparta and its supporters and the Athenian maritime empire. Sparta and its allies feared the growing Athenian empire. Then, too, Athens and Sparta had created two very different kinds of societies, and neither state was able to tolerate the other's system. A series of disputes finally led to the outbreak of war in 431 B.C.E.

At the beginning of the war, both sides believed they had winning strategies. The Athenians planned to remain behind the protective walls of Athens while the overseas empire and the navy would keep them supplied. Pericles knew that the Spartans and their allies could beat the Athenians in open battles, which was the chief aim of the Spartan strategy. The Spartans and their allies attacked Athens, hoping that the Athenians would send out their army to fight beyond the walls. But Pericles was convinced that Athens was secure behind its walls and stayed put.

In the second year of the war, however, plague devastated the crowded city of Athens and wiped out possibly one-third of the population. Pericles himself died the following year (429 B.C.E.), a severe loss to Athens. Despite the losses from the plague, the Athenians fought on in a

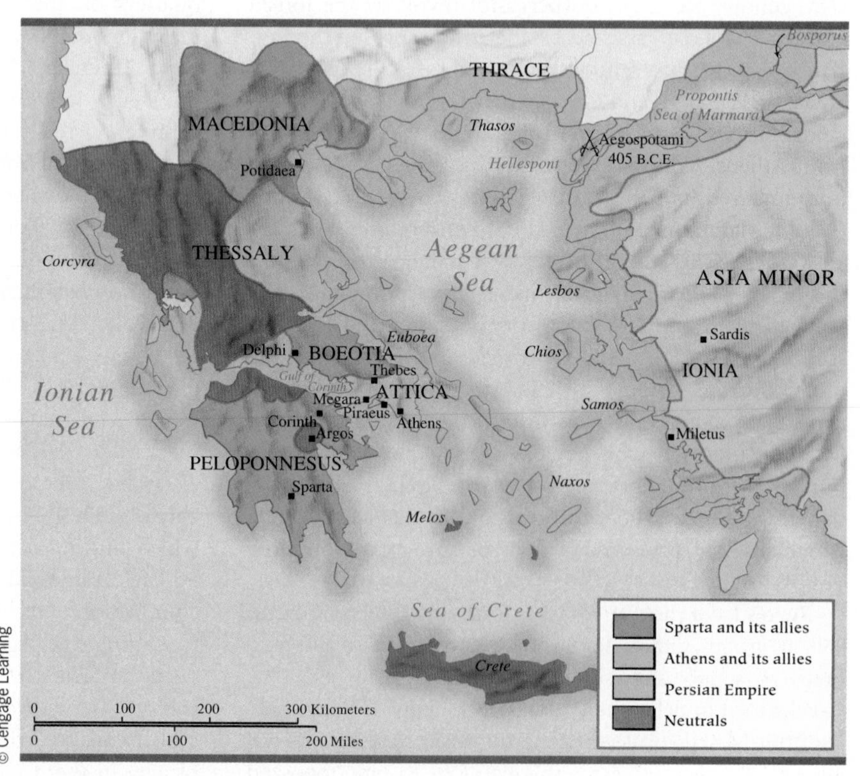

© Cengage Learning

The Great Peloponnesian War (431–404 B.C.E.)

struggle that dragged on for twenty-seven years. A final crushing blow came in 405 B.C.E., when the Athenian fleet was destroyed at Aegospotami (ee-guh-SPOT-uh-my) on the Hellespont. Athens was besieged and surrendered in 404 B.C.E. Its walls were torn down, the navy was disbanded, and the Athenian empire was no more. The great war was finally over.

The Great Peloponnesian War weakened the major Greek states and led to new alliances among them. The next seventy years of Greek history are a sorry tale of efforts by Sparta, Athens, and Thebes, a new Greek power, to dominate Greek affairs. In continuing their petty wars, the Greeks remained oblivious to the growing power of Macedonia to their north.

The Culture of Classical Greece

Classical Greece was a period of remarkable intellectual and cultural growth throughout the Greek world, and Periclean Athens was the most important center of Classical Greek culture.

THE WRITING OF HISTORY History as we know it, as the systematic analysis of past events, was introduced to the Western world by the Greeks. Herodotus (huh-ROD-uh-tuss) (c. 484–c. 425 B.C.E.) wrote *History of the Persian Wars*, which is commonly regarded as the first real history in Western civilization. The central theme of Herodotus's work was the conflict between the Greeks and the Persians, which he viewed as a struggle between freedom and despotism. Herodotus traveled extensively and questioned many people to obtain his information. He was a master storyteller and sometimes included considerable fanciful material, but he was also capable of exhibiting a critical attitude toward the materials he used.

Thucydides (thoo-SID-uh-deez) (c. 460–c. 400 B.C.E.) was a better historian by far; indeed, he is considered the greatest historian of the ancient world. Thucydides was an Athenian and a participant in the Peloponnesian War. He had been elected a general, but a defeat in battle led the fickle Athenian assembly to send him into exile, which gave him the opportunity to write his *History of the Peloponnesian War*.

Unlike Herodotus, Thucydides was not concerned with underlying divine forces or gods as explanatory causal factors in history. He saw war and politics in purely rational terms, as the activities of human beings. He examined the causes of the Peloponnesian War in a clear and objective fashion, placing much emphasis on accuracy and the precision of his facts. Thucydides also provided remarkable insight into the human condition. He believed that political situations recur in similar fashion and that the study of history is therefore of great value in understanding the present.

GREEK DRAMA Drama as we know it in Western culture originated with the Greeks. Plays were presented in outdoor theaters as part of religious festivals. The plays followed a fairly stable form. Three male actors who wore masks acted all the parts. A chorus, also male, spoke lines that explained and commented on the action.

The first Greek dramas were tragedies, plays based on the suffering of a hero and usually ending in disaster. Aeschylus (ESS-kuh-luss) (525–456 B.C.E.) is the first tragedian whose plays are known to us. As was customary in Greek tragedy, his plots are simple, and the entire drama focuses on a single tragic event and its meaning. Greek tragedies were sometimes presented in a trilogy (a set of three plays) built around a common theme. The only complete trilogy we possess, called the *Oresteia* (uh-res-TY-uh), was composed by Aeschylus. The theme of this trilogy is derived from Homer. Agamemnon, the king of Mycenae, returns a hero from the defeat of Troy. His wife, Clytemnestra, avenges the sacrificial death of her daughter Iphigenia by murdering Agamemnon, who had been responsible for Iphigenia's death. In the second play of the trilogy, Agamemnon's son Orestes avenges his father by killing his mother. Orestes is then pursued by the avenging Furies, who torment him for killing his mother. Evil acts breed evil acts, and suffering is the human lot, suggests Aeschylus. In the end, however, reason triumphs over the forces of evil.

Another great Athenian playwright was Sophocles (SAHF-uh-kleez) (c. 496–406 B.C.E.), whose most famous work was *Oedipus the King*. In this play, the oracle of Apollo foretells that a man (Oedipus) will kill his own father and marry his mother. Despite all attempts at prevention, the tragic events occur. Although it appears that Oedipus suffered the fate determined by the gods, Oedipus also accepts that he himself as a free man must bear responsibility for his actions: "It was Apollo, friends, Apollo, that brought this bitter bitterness, my sorrows, to completion. But the hand that struck me was none but my own."[4]

The third outstanding Athenian tragedian, Euripides (yoo-RIP-uh-deez) (c. 485–406 B.C.E.), moved beyond his predecessors by creating more realistic characters. His plots also became more complex, with a greater interest in real-life situations. Euripides was controversial because he questioned traditional moral and religious values. For example, he was critical of the traditional view that war was glorious. Instead, he portrayed war as brutal and barbaric.

Greek tragedies dealt with universal themes still relevant to our day. They probed such issues as the nature of good and evil, the rights of the individual, the nature of divine forces, and the essence of human beings. Over and over, the tragic lesson was repeated: humans were free and yet could operate only within limitations imposed by the gods. Striving to do one's best may not always lead to success in human terms but is nevertheless always a worthy endeavor. Greek pride in human accomplishment and independence was real. As the chorus chanted in Sophocles's *Antigone* (an-TIG-uh-nee): "Is there anything more wonderful on earth, our marvelous planet, than the miracle of man?"[5]

THE ARTS: THE CLASSICAL IDEAL The artistic standards established by the Greeks of the Classical period have largely dominated the arts of the Western world. Greek art was concerned with expressing eternally true ideals. Its subject matter was basically the human being, expressed harmoniously as an object of great beauty. The Classical style, based on the ideals of reason, moderation, symmetry, balance, and harmony in all things, was meant to civilize the emotions.

In architecture, the most important form was the temple dedicated to a god or goddess. At the center of Greek temples were walled rooms that housed the statues of deities and treasuries where gifts to the gods and goddesses were safeguarded. These central rooms were surrounded by a screen of columns that made Greek temples open structures rather than closed ones. The columns were originally made of wood but were changed to marble in the fifth century B.C.E.

Some of the finest examples of Greek Classical architecture were built in fifth-century Athens. The most famous building, regarded as the greatest example of the Classical Greek temple, was the Parthenon, built between 447 and 432 B.C.E. Consecrated to Athena, the patron goddess of Athens, the Parthenon was also dedicated to the glory of the city-state and its inhabitants. The structure typifies the principles of Classical architecture: calmness, clarity, and the avoidance of superfluous detail.

Greek sculpture also developed a Classical style. Statues of the male nude, the favorite subject of Greek sculptors, exhibited relaxed attitudes; their faces were self-assured, their bodies flexible and smoothly muscled. Although the figures possessed natural features that made them lifelike, Greek sculptors sought to achieve not realism but a standard of ideal beauty. Polyclitus (pahl-ee-KLY-tuss), a fifth-century sculptor, wrote a treatise (now lost) on proportion that he illustrated in a work known as the *Doryphoros* (doh-RIF-uh-rohss). His theory maintained that the use of ideal proportions, based on mathematical ratios found in nature, could produce an ideal human form, beautiful in its perfected and refined features. This search for ideal beauty was the dominant feature of the Classical standard in sculpture.

THE GREEK LOVE OF WISDOM Athens became the foremost intellectual and artistic center in Classical Greece. Its reputation was perhaps strongest of all in philosophy, a Greek term that originally meant "love of wisdom." Socrates, Plato, and Aristotle raised basic

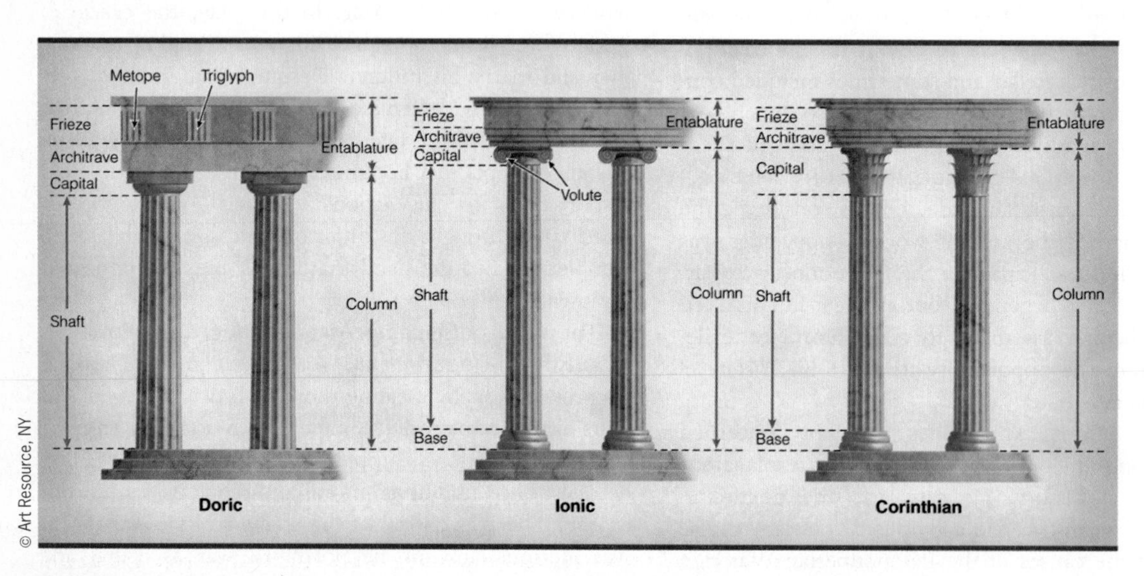

© Art Resource, NY

Doric, Ionic, and Corinthian Orders. The Greeks used columns of different shapes and sizes in their temples. The Doric order, which had thick, fluted columns with simple capitals (the decorated tops of the columns), evolved first in the Dorian Peloponnesus. The Greeks considered the Doric order grave, dignified, and masculine. The Ionic style was first developed in western Asia Minor and consisted of slender columns with spiral-shaped capitals. The Greeks characterized the Ionic order as slender, elegant, and feminine. Corinthian columns, with their more detailed capitals modeled after acanthus leaves, came later, near the end of the fifth century B.C.E.

© Adam Crowley/Photodisc/Getty Images

The Parthenon. The arts in Classical Greece were designed to express the eternal ideals of reason, moderation, symmetry, balance, and harmony. In architecture, the most important form was the temple, and the greatest example is the Parthenon, built in Athens between 447 and 432 B.C.E. Located on the Acropolis, the Parthenon was dedicated to Athena, the patron goddess of Athens, but it also served as a shining example of the power and wealth of the Athenian empire.

questions that have been debated for more than two thousand years; they are, for the most part, the very same philosophical questions we wrestle with today (see the comparative essay "The Axial Age" on p. 99).

Socrates (SAHK-ruh-teez) (469–399 B.C.E.) left no writings, but we know about him from his pupils. Socrates was a stonemason whose true love was philosophy. He taught a number of pupils, although not for pay, because he believed that the goal of education was solely to improve the individual. His approach, still known as the **Socratic method**, employs a question-and-answer technique to lead pupils to see things for themselves using their own reason. Socrates believed that all knowledge is within each person; only critical examination was needed to call it forth. This was the real task of philosophy, since "the unexamined life is not worth living."

Socrates questioned authority, and this soon led him into trouble. Athens had had a tradition of free thought and inquiry, but its defeat in the Peloponnesian War had created an environment intolerant of open debate and soul-searching. Socrates was accused of corrupting the youth of Athens by his teaching. An Athenian jury convicted him and sentenced him to death.

One of Socrates's disciples was Plato (PLAY-toh) (c. 429–347 B.C.E.), considered by many the greatest philosopher of Western civilization. Unlike his master Socrates, who wrote nothing, Plato wrote a great deal. He was fascinated with the question of reality: How do we know what is real? According to Plato, a higher world of eternal, unchanging Ideas or Forms has always existed. To know these Forms is to know truth. These ideal Forms constitute reality and can be apprehended only by a trained mind, which, of course, is the goal of philosophy. The objects that we perceive with our senses are simply reflections of the ideal Forms. They are shadows; reality is in the Forms themselves.

Plato's ideas of government were set out in a dialogue titled *The Republic*. Based on his experience in Athens, Plato had come to distrust the workings of democracy. It was obvious to him that individuals could not attain an ethical life unless they lived in a just and rational state. Plato's search for the just state led him to construct an ideal state in which the population was divided into three basic groups. At the top was an upper class of philosopher-kings: "Unless . . . political power and philosophy meet together . . . there can be no rest from troubles . . . for states, nor yet, as I believe, for all mankind."[6] The second group consisted of the courageous; they would be the warriors who protected the society. All the rest made up the masses, essentially people driven not by wisdom or courage but by desire. They would be the producers of society—the artisans, tradespeople, and farmers. Contrary to common Greek custom, Plato also believed that men and women should have the same education and equal access to all positions.

Plato established a school at Athens known as the Academy. One of his pupils, who studied there for twenty years, was Aristotle (AR-iss-tot-ul) (384–322 B.C.E.). Aristotle did not accept Plato's theory of ideal Forms. Instead, he believed that by examining individual objects, we can perceive their form and arrive at universal principles, but these principles do not exist as a separate higher world of reality beyond material things; rather they are a part of things themselves. Aristotle's interests, then, lay in analyzing and classifying things based on thorough research and investigation. His interests were wide-ranging, and he wrote treatises on an enormous number of subjects: ethics, logic, politics, poetry, astronomy, geology, biology, and physics.

Like Plato, Aristotle wished for an effective form of government that would rationally direct human affairs. Unlike Plato, he did not seek an ideal state but tried to find the best form of government by a rational examination

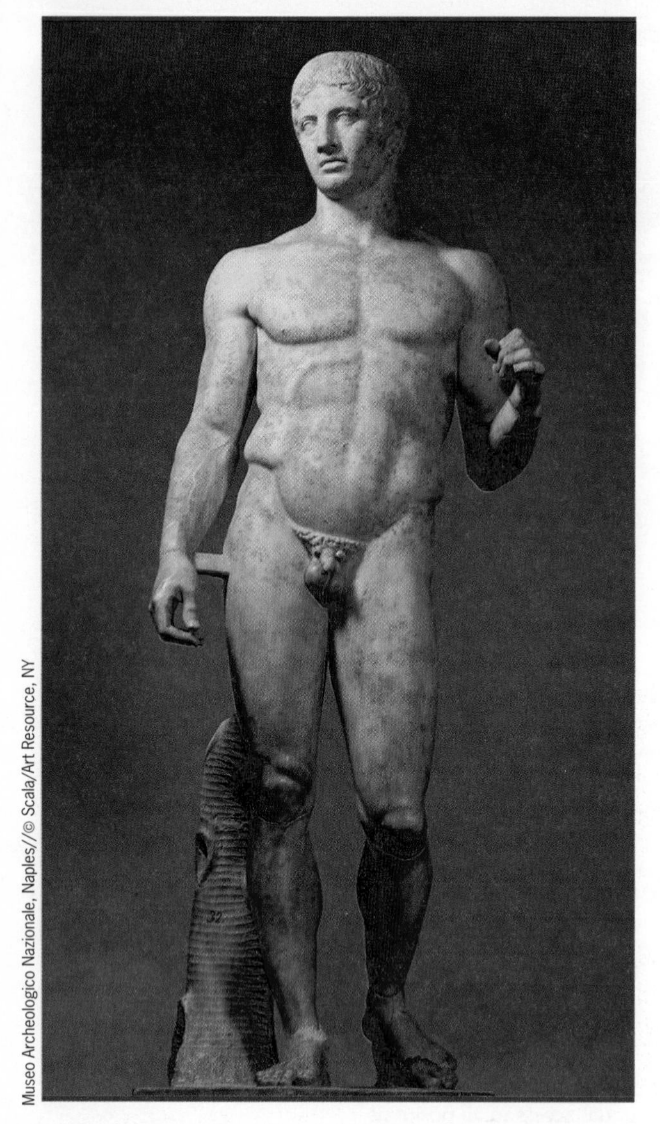
Museo Archeologico Nazionale, Naples//© Scala/Art Resource, NY

Doryphoros. This statue, known as the *Doryphoros*, or spear carrier, is by the fifth-century B.C.E. sculptor Polyclitus, who believed it illustrated the ideal proportions of the human figure. Classical Greek sculpture moved away from the stiffness of earlier figures but retained the young male nude as the favorite subject. The statues became more lifelike, with relaxed poses and flexible, smooth-muscled bodies. The aim of sculpture, however, was not simply realism but rather the expression of ideal beauty.

of existing governments. For his *Politics*, Aristotle examined the constitutions of 158 states and identified three good forms of government: monarchy, aristocracy, and constitutional government. He favored constitutional government as the best form for most people.

Aristotle's philosophical and political ideas played an enormous role in the development of Western thought during the Middle Ages (see Chapter 12). So did his ideas on women. Aristotle maintained that women were biologically inferior to men: "A woman is, as it were, an infertile male. She is female in fact on account of a kind of inadequacy." Therefore, according to Aristotle, women must be subordinated to men, not only in the community but also in marriage: "The association between husband and wife is clearly an aristocracy. The man rules by virtue of merit, and in the sphere that is his by right; but he hands over to his wife such matters as are suitable for her."[7]

Greek Religion

As was the case throughout the ancient world, Greek religion played an important role in Greek society and was intricately connected to every aspect of daily life; it was both social and practical. Public festivals, which originated from religious practices, served specific functions: boys were prepared to be warriors, girls to be mothers. Because religion was related to every aspect of life, citizens had to have a proper attitude toward the gods. Religion was a civic cult necessary for the well-being of the state. Temples dedicated to a god or goddess were the major buildings of Greek society.

The poetry of Homer gave an account of the gods that provided Greek religion with a definite structure. Over a period of time, most Greeks came to accept a basic polytheistic religion with twelve chief gods and goddesses who supposedly lived on Mount Olympus, the highest mountain in Greece. Among the twelve were Zeus (ZOOSS), the chief deity and father of the gods; Athena, goddess of wisdom and crafts; Apollo, god of the sun and poetry; Aphrodite, goddess of love; and Poseidon, brother of Zeus and god of the seas and earthquakes.

Because the Greeks wanted the gods to look favorably on their activities, ritual assumed enormous proportions in Greek religion. Prayers were often combined with gifts to the gods based on the principle "I give so that you, the gods, will give in return." Ritual meant sacrifices, whether of animals or agricultural products. Animal sacrifices were burned on an altar in front of a temple or on a small altar in front of a home.

Festivals also developed as a way to honor the gods and goddesses. Some of these (the Panhellenic celebrations) came to have significance for all Greeks and were held at special locations, such as those dedicated to the worship of Zeus at Olympia or to Apollo at Delphi. The great festivals featured numerous events in honor of the gods, including athletic competitions to which all Greeks were invited.

According to tradition, such games were first conducted at the Olympic festival in 776 B.C.E. and then held every four years thereafter to honor Zeus. Initially, the

COMPARATIVE ESSAY

The Axial Age

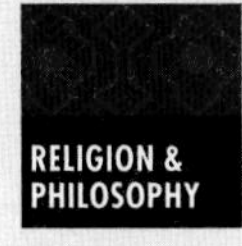

RELIGION & PHILOSOPHY

By the fourth century B.C.E., important regional civilizations existed in China, India, Southwest Asia, and the Mediterranean basin. During their formative periods between 700 and 300 B.C.E., all were characterized by the emergence of religious and philosophical thinkers who established ideas—or "axes"—that remained the basis for religions and philosophical thought in those societies for hundreds of years. Consequently, some historians have referred to the period when these ideas developed as the "Axial Age."

By the seventh century B.C.E., concepts of monotheism had developed in Persia through the teachings of Zoroaster and in Canaan through the Hebrew prophets. In Judaism, the Hebrews developed a world religion that influenced the later religions of Christianity and Islam. During the fifth and fourth centuries B.C.E. in Greece, the philosophers Socrates, Plato, and Aristotle not only proposed philosophical and political ideas crucial to the Greek world and later Western civilization but also conceived of a rational method of inquiry that became important to modern science.

During the sixth century B.C.E., two major schools of thought—Confucianism and Daoism—emerged in China. Both sought to spell out the principles that would create a stable order in society. And although their views of reality were diametrically opposed, both came to have an impact on Chinese civilization that lasted into the twentieth century.

Two of the world's greatest religions, Hinduism and Buddhism, began in India during the Axial Age. Hinduism was an outgrowth of the religious beliefs of the Aryan peoples who settled in India. These ideas were expressed in the sacred texts known as the Vedas and in the Upanishads, which were commentaries on the Vedas compiled in the sixth century B.C.E. With its belief in reincarnation, Hinduism provided justification for India's rigid class system. Buddhism was the product of one man, Siddhartha Gautama, known as the Buddha, who lived in the sixth century B.C.E. The Buddha's simple message of achieving wisdom created a new spiritual philosophy that would rival Hinduism. Although a product of India, Buddhism also spread to other parts of the world.

Museo Archeologico Nazionale, Naples//© Erich Lessing/Art Resource, NY

Philosophers in the Axial Age. This mosaic from the Roman city of Pompeii depicts a gathering of Greek philosophers at the school of Plato.

Although these philosophies and religions developed in different areas of the world, they had some features in common. Like the Chinese philosophers Confucius and Lao Tzu, the Greek philosophers Plato and Aristotle had different points of view about the nature of reality. Thinkers in India and China also developed rational methods of inquiry similar to those of Plato and Aristotle. And regardless of their origins, when we speak of Judaism, Hinduism, Buddhism, Confucianism, Daoism, or Greek philosophical thought, we realize that the ideas of the Axial Age not only spread around the world at different times but are also still an integral part of our world today.

What do historians mean when they speak of the Axial Age? What do you think could explain the emergence of similar ideas in different parts of the world during this period?

Olympic contests consisted of foot races and wrestling, but later boxing, javelin throwing, and various other contests were added. Competitions were always between individuals, not groups, and were not without danger to the participants. Athletes competed in the nude, and rules were rather relaxed. Wrestlers, for example, were allowed to gouge eyes and even pick up their opponents and bring them down head first onto a hard surface. The Greek Olympic games came to an end in 393 C.E., when a Christian Roman emperor banned them as pagan exercises. Fifteen hundred years later, the games were revived through the efforts of a French baron, Pierre de Coubertin (PYAYR duh koo-ber-TANH). In 1896, the first modern Olympic games were held in Athens, Greece.

As another practical side of Greek religion, Greeks wanted to know the will of the gods. To do so, they made use of the oracle, a sacred shrine dedicated to a god or goddess who revealed the future. The most famous was the oracle of Apollo at Delphi (DEL-fy), located on the side of Mount Parnassus (par-NASS-suss), overlooking the Gulf of Corinth. At Delphi, a priestess listened to questions while in a state of ecstasy that was believed to be induced by Apollo. Her responses were interpreted by the priests and given in verse form to the person asking questions. Representatives of states and individuals traveled to Delphi to consult the oracle of Apollo. Responses were often enigmatic and at times even politically motivated. Croesus (KREE-suss), the king of Lydia in Asia Minor who was known for his incredible wealth, sent messengers to the oracle at Delphi, asking whether he should go to war with the Persians. The oracle replied that if Croesus attacked the Persians, he would destroy a mighty empire. Overjoyed to hear these words, Croesus made war on the Persians but was crushed. A mighty empire was indeed destroyed—his own.

Daily Life in Classical Athens

The *polis* was, above all, a male community: only adult male citizens took part in public life. In Athens, this meant the exclusion of women, slaves, and foreign residents, or roughly 85 percent of the population of Attica. There were probably 150,000 citizens in Athens, of whom about 43,000 were adult males who exercised political power. Resident foreigners, who numbered about 35,000, received the protection of the laws but were also subject to some of the responsibilities of citizens, including military service and the funding of festivals. The remaining social group, the slaves, numbered around 100,000. Most slaves in Athens worked in the home as cooks and maids or worked in the fields. Some were owned by the state and worked on public construction projects.

The Athenian economy was largely based on agriculture and trade. Athenians grew grains, vegetables, and fruit for local consumption. Grapes and olives were cultivated for wine and olive oil, which were used locally and also exported. The Athenians raised sheep and goats for wool and dairy products. Because of the size of the population and the lack of abundant fertile land, Athens had to import 50 to 80 percent of its grain, a staple in the Athenian diet. Trade was thus very important to the Athenian economy.

FAMILY AND RELATIONSHIPS The family was a central institution in ancient Athens. It was composed of husband, wife, and children (a nuclear family), although other dependent relatives and slaves were regarded as part of the family economic unit. The family's primary social function was to produce new citizens.

Adult female citizens could participate in most religious cults and festivals but were otherwise excluded from public life. They could not own property beyond personal items and always had a male guardian. An Athenian woman was expected to be a good wife. Her foremost obligation was to bear children, especially male children who would preserve the family line. A wife was also to take care of her family and her house, either doing the household work herself or supervising the slaves who did the actual work (see the box on p. 101).

Male homosexuality was also a prominent feature of Athenian life. The Greek homosexual ideal was a relationship between a mature man and a young male. While the relationship was frequently physical, the Greeks also viewed it as educational. The older male (the "lover") won the love of his "beloved" through his value as a teacher and the devotion he demonstrated in training his charge. In a sense, this love relationship was seen as a way of initiating young males into the male world of political and military dominance. The Greeks did not feel that the coexistence of homosexual and heterosexual predilections created any special problems for individuals or their society.

The Rise of Macedonia and the Conquests of Alexander

FOCUS QUESTION: How was Alexander the Great able to amass his empire, and what was his legacy?

While the Greek city-states were continuing to fight each other, to their north a new and ultimately powerful kingdom was emerging in its own right. To the Greeks, the Macedonians were little more than barbarians, a mostly rural folk organized into tribes rather than city-states.

OPPOSING VIEWPOINTS

Women in Athens and Sparta

In Classical Athens, a woman's place was in the home. She had two major responsibilities as a wife—bearing and raising children and managing the household. In the first selection, from a dialogue on estate management, Xenophon (ZEN-uh-fuhn) relates the instructions of an Athenian to his new wife. Although women in Sparta had the same responsibilities as women in Athens, they assumed somewhat different roles as a result of the Spartan lifestyle. The second, third, and fourth selections, taken from accounts by three ancient Greek writers, demonstrate these differences.

Xenophon, *Oeconomicus*

[Ischomachus addresses his new wife:] For it seems to me, dear, that the gods with great discernment have coupled together male and female, as they are called, chiefly in order that they may form a perfect partnership in mutual service. For, in the first place that the various species of living creatures may not fail, they are joined in wedlock for the production of children. Secondly, offspring to support them in old age is provided by this union, to human beings, at any rate. Thirdly, human beings live not in the open air, like beasts, but obviously need shelter. Nevertheless, those who mean to win stores to fill the covered place, have need of someone to work at the open-air occupations; since plowing, sowing, planting and grazing are all such open-air employments; and these supply the needful food. . . . For he made the man's body and mind more capable of enduring cold and heat, and journeys and campaigns; and therefore imposed on him the outdoor tasks. To the woman, since he had made her body less capable of such endurance, I take it that God has assigned the indoor tasks. And knowing that he had created in the woman and had imposed on her the nourishment of the infants, he meted out to her a larger portion of affection for newborn babes than to the man. . . .

Your duty will be to remain indoors and send out those servants whose work is outside, and superintend those who are to work indoors, and to receive the incomings, and distribute so much of them as must be spent, and watch over so much as is to be kept in store, and take care that the sum laid by for a year be not spent in a month. And when wool is brought to you, you must see that cloaks are made for those that want them. You must see too that the dry corn [grain] is in good condition for making food. One of the duties that fall to you, however, will perhaps seem rather thankless: you will have to see that any servant who is ill is cared for.

Xenophon, *Constitution of the Spartans*

First, to begin at the beginning, I will start with the begetting of children. Elsewhere those girls who are going to have children and are considered to have been well brought up are nourished with the plainest diet which is practicable and the smallest amount of luxury good possible; wine is certainly not allowed them at all, or only if well diluted. Just as the majority of craftsmen are sedentary, the other Greeks expect their girls to sit quietly and work wool. But how can one expect girls brought up like this to give birth to healthy babies? Lycurgus (see p. 92) considered slave girls quite adequate to produce clothing, and thought that for free women the most important job was to bear children. In the first place, therefore, he prescribed physical training for the female sex no less than for the male; and next, just as for men, he arranged competitions of racing and strength for women also, thinking that if both parents were strong their children would be more robust.

Aristotle, *Politics*

Now, this license of the [Spartan] women, from the earliest times, was to be expected. For the men were absent from home for long periods of time on military expeditions, fighting the war against the Argives and again against the Arkadians and Messenians . . . And nearly two-fifths of the whole country is in the hands of women, both because there have been numerous heiresses, and because large dowries are customary. And yet it would have been better to have regulated them, and given none at all or small or even moderate ones. But at present it is possible for a man to give an inheritance to whomever he chooses.

Plutarch, *Lycurgus*

Since Lycurgus regarded education as the most important and finest duty of the legislator, he began at the earliest stage by looking at matters relating to

(Continued)

marriages and births. . . . For he exercised the girls' bodies with races and wrestling and discus and javelin throwing, so that the embryos formed in them would have a strong start in strong bodies and develop better, and they would undergo their pregnancies with vigor and would cope well and easily with childbirth. He got rid of daintiness and sheltered upbringing and effeminacy of all kinds, by accustoming the girls no less than the young men to walking naked in processions and dancing and singing at certain festivals, when young men were present and watching. . . . The nudity of the girls had nothing disgraceful in it for modesty was present and immorality absent, but rather it made them accustomed to simplicity and enthusiastic as to physical fitness, and gave the female sex a taste of noble spirit, inasmuch as they too had a share in valor and ambition.

In what ways were the lifestyles of Athenian and Spartan women the same? In what ways were they different? How did the Athenian and Spartan views of the world shape their conceptions of gender and gender roles, and why were those conceptions different?

Sources: Xenophon, *Oeconomicus*. From *Xenophon: Memoribilia and Oeconomicus*, Volume IV, Loeb Classical Library 168, translated by E. C. Marchant, Cambridge, Mass.: Harvard University Press, 1923. The Loeb Classical Library ® is a registered trademark of the President and Fellows of Harvard College. Xenophon, *Constitution of the Spartans*, Aristotle, *Politics*, and Plutarch, *Lycurgus*. Xenophon, Constitution of the Spartans, Aristotle, Politics, and Plutarch, Lycurgus. From *Ancient Greece: Social and Historical Documents from Archaic Times to the Death of Socrates*. Edited by Matthew Dillon and Lynda Garland. London: Routledge, 1994, pp. 393–95. Copyright © 1994 Matthew and Lynda Garland.

Not until the end of the fifth century B.C.E. did Macedonia emerge as an important kingdom. But when Philip II (359–336 B.C.E.) came to the throne, he built an efficient army and turned Macedonia into the strongest power in the Greek world—one that was soon drawn into the conflicts among the Greeks.

The Athenians at last took notice of the new contender. Fear of Philip led them to ally with a number of other Greek states and confront the Macedonians at the Battle of Chaeronea (ker-uh-NEE-uh), near Thebes, in 338 B.C.E. The Macedonian army crushed the Greeks, and Philip quickly gained control of all Greece, bringing an end to the freedom of the Greek city-states. He insisted that the Greek states form a league and then cooperate with him in a war against Persia. Before Philip could undertake his invasion of Asia, however, he was assassinated, leaving the task to his son Alexander.

Alexander the Great

Alexander was only twenty when he became king of Macedonia. In many ways, he had been prepared to rule by his father, who had taken Alexander along on military campaigns and had given him control of the cavalry at the important battle of Chaeronea. After his father's assassination, Alexander moved quickly to assert his authority, securing the Macedonian frontiers and quashing a rebellion in Greece. He then turned to his father's dream, the invasion of the Persian Empire.

ALEXANDER'S CONQUESTS There is no doubt that Alexander was taking a chance in attacking Persia, which was still a strong state. In the spring of 334 B.C.E.,

British Museum, London//© The Trustees of The British Museum/Art Resource, NY

Alexander the Great. This marble head of Alexander the Great was made in the second or first century B.C.E. The long hair and tilt of his head reflect the description of Alexander in the literary sources of the time. Alexander claimed to be descended from Heracles, a Greek hero worshiped as a god, and when he proclaimed himself pharaoh of Egypt, he gained recognition as a living deity. It is reported that one statue, now lost, showed Alexander gazing at Zeus. At the base of the statue were the words "I place the earth under my sway; you, O Zeus, keep Olympus."

Alexander entered Asia Minor with an army of some 37,000 men. About half were Macedonians, the rest Greeks and other allies. The cavalry, which would play an important role as a strike force, numbered about 5,000. By the following spring, the entire western half of Asia Minor was in Alexander's hands (see Map 4.2). Meanwhile, the Persian king, Darius III, mobilized his forces to stop Alexander's army, but the subsequent Battle of Issus (ISS-uss) in 333 B.C.E. resulted in yet another Macedonian success. Alexander then turned south, and by the winter of 332, Syria, Palestine, and Egypt were under his control.

In 331 B.C.E., Alexander turned east and fought a decisive battle with the Persians at Gaugamela (gaw-guh-MEE-luh), northwest of Babylon. After his victory, Alexander entered Babylon and then proceeded to the Persian capitals at Susa and Persepolis, where he acquired the Persian treasuries and took possession of vast quantities of gold and silver. By 330, Alexander was again on the march, pursuing Darius. After Darius was killed by one of his own men, Alexander took the title and office of the Great King of the Persians. Over the next three years, he traveled east and northeast, as far as modern Pakistan. By the summer of 327 B.C.E., he had entered India, which at that time was divided into a number of warring states. In 326 B.C.E., Alexander and his armies arrived in the plains of northwestern India. At the Battle of the Hydaspes River, Alexander won a brutally fought battle (see the box on p. 104). When Alexander made clear his determination to march east to conquer more of India, his soldiers, weary of campaigning year after year, mutinied and refused to go further. Alexander returned to Babylon, where he planned more campaigns. But in June 323 B.C.E., weakened by wounds, fever, and probably excessive alcohol consumption, he died at the age of thirty-two (see the Film & History feature on p. 105).

THE LEGACY: WAS ALEXANDER GREAT? Alexander is one of the most puzzling significant figures in history.

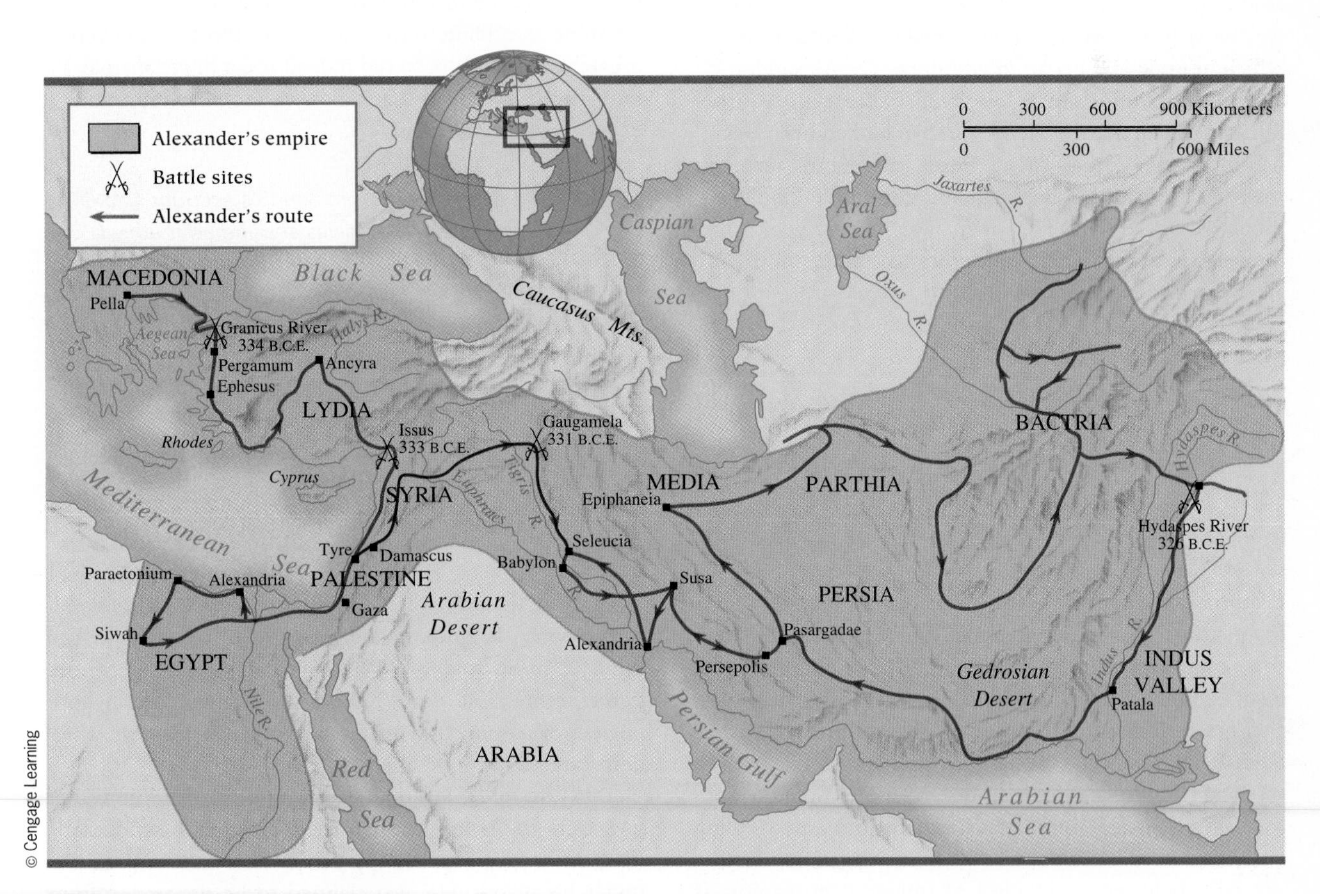

© Cengage Learning

MAP 4.2 The Conquests of Alexander the Great. In just twelve years, Alexander the Great conquered vast territories. Dominating lands from west of the Nile to east of the Indus, he brought the Persian Empire, Egypt, and much of the Middle East under his control and laid the foundations for the Hellenistic world.

Q *Approximately how far did Alexander and his troops travel during those twelve years, and what kinds of terrain did they encounter on their journey?*

Alexander Meets an Indian King

In his campaigns in India, Alexander fought a number of difficult battles. At the Battle of the Hydaspes River, he faced a strong opponent in the Indian king Porus. After defeating Porus, Alexander treated him with respect, according to Arrian, Alexander's ancient biographer.

Arrian, *The Campaigns of Alexander*

Throughout the action Porus had proved himself a man indeed, not only as a commander but as a soldier of the truest courage. When he saw his cavalry cut to pieces, most of his infantry dead, and his elephants killed or roaming riderless and bewildered about the field, his behavior was very different from that of the Persian King Darius: unlike Darius, he did not lead the scramble to save his own skin, but so long as a single unit of his men held together, fought bravely on. It was only when he was himself wounded that he turned the elephant on which he rode and began to withdraw. . . . Alexander, anxious to save the life of this great soldier, sent . . . [to him] an Indian named Meroes, a man he had been told had long been Porus's friend. Porus listened to Meroes's message, stopped his elephant, and dismounted; he was much distressed by thirst, so when he had revived himself by drinking, he told Meroes to conduct him with all speed to Alexander.

Alexander, informed of his approach, rode out to meet him. . . . When they met, he reined in his horse, and looked at his adversary with admiration: he was a magnificent figure of a man, over seven feet high and of great personal beauty; his bearing had lost none of its pride; his air was of one brave man meeting another, of a king in the presence of a king, with whom he had fought honorably for his kingdom.

Alexander was the first to speak. "What," he said, "do you wish that I should do with you?" "Treat me as a king ought," Porus is said to have replied. "For my part," said Alexander, pleased by his answer, "your request shall be granted. But is there not something you would wish for yourself? Ask it." "Everything," said Porus, "is contained in this one request."

The dignity of these words gave Alexander even more pleasure, and he restored to Porus his sovereignty over his subjects, adding to his realm other territory of even greater extent. Thus he did indeed use a brave man as a king ought, and from that time forward found him in every way a loyal friend.

What do we learn from Arrian's account about Alexander's military skills and Indian methods of fighting?

Source: From *The Campaigns of Alexander* by Arrian, translated by Aubrey de Selincourt. Viking Press, 1976.

Historians relying on the same sources draw vastly different pictures of him. For some, his military abilities, extensive conquests, and creation of a new empire alone justify calling him Alexander the Great. Other historians also praise Alexander's love of Greek culture and his intellectual brilliance, especially in matters of warfare. In the lands that he conquered, Alexander attempted to fuse the Macedonians, Greeks, and Persians into a new ruling class. Did he do this because he was an idealistic visionary who believed in an ideal of universal humanity, as some suggest? Or was he merely trying to bolster his power and create an autocratic monarchy?

Those historians who see Alexander as aspiring to autocratic monarchy present a very different portrait of him as a ruthless Machiavellian. One has titled his biography *Alexander the Great Failure*. These critics ask if a man who slaughtered indigenous peoples, who risked the lives of his solders for his own selfish reasons, whose fierce temper led him to kill his friends, and whose neglect of administrative duties weakened his own kingdom can really be called great.

But how did Alexander view himself? We know that he sought to imitate Achilles, the warrior-hero of Homer's *Iliad*. Alexander kept a copy of the *Iliad*—and a dagger—under his pillow. He also claimed to be descended from Heracles, the Greek hero who came to be worshiped as a god.

Regardless of his ideals, motives, or views about himself, one fact stands out: Alexander ushered in a new age, the Hellenistic era. The word *Hellenistic* is derived from a

FILM & HISTORY

Alexander (2004)

Warner Bros./The Kobal Collection/Jaap Buitendijk/Art Resource, NY

Alexander (Colin Farrell) reviews his troops before the Battle of Gaugamela.

Alexander is a product of director Oliver Stone's lifelong fascination with Alexander, the king of Macedonia who conquered the Persian Empire in the fourth century B.C.E. and launched the Hellenistic era. Stone's epic film cost $150 million, which resulted in an elaborate and in places visually beautiful film. Narrated by the aging Ptolemy (Anthony Hopkins), Alexander's Macedonian general who took control of Egypt after his death, the film tells the story of Alexander (Colin Farrell) through an intermix of battle scenes, scenes showing the progress of Alexander and his army through the Middle East and India, and flashbacks to his early years. Stone portrays Alexander's relationship with his mother, Olympias (Angelina Jolie), as instrumental in his early development while also focusing on his rocky relationship with his father, King Philip II (Val Kilmer). The movie focuses on the major battle at Gaugamela in 331 B.C.E. where the Persian leader Darius was forced to flee, and then follows Alexander as he conquers the rest of the Persian Empire and continues east into India. After his troops threaten to mutiny, Alexander returns to Babylon, where he dies on June 10, 323 B.C.E.

The enormous amount of money spent on the film enabled Stone to achieve a stunning visual spectacle, but as history, the film leaves much to be desired. The character of Alexander is never developed in depth. He is shown at times as a weak character who is plagued by doubts over his decisions and often seems obsessed with his desire for glory. Alexander is also portrayed as an idealistic leader who believed that the people he conquered wanted change, that he was "freeing the people of the world," and that Asia and Europe would grow together into a single entity. But was Alexander an idealistic dreamer, as Stone apparently believes, or was he a military leader who, following the dictum that "fortune favors the bold," ran roughshod over the wishes of his soldiers in order to follow his dream and was responsible for mass slaughter in the process? The latter is a perspective that Stone glosses over, but Ptolemy probably expresses the more realistic notion that "none of us believed in his dream." The movie also does not elaborate on Alexander's wish to be a god. Certainly, Alexander aspired to divine honors; at one point he sent instructions to the Greek cities to "vote him a god." Stone's portrayal of Alexander is perhaps most realistic in presenting his drinking binges and his bisexuality, which was common in the Greco-Roman world. The movie shows not only his marriage to Roxane (Rosario Dawson), daughter of a Bactrian noble, but also his love for his lifelong companion, Hephaestion (Jared Leto), and his sexual relationship with the Persian male slave Bagoas (Francisco Bosch).

The film contains a number of inaccurate historical details. Alexander's first encounters with the Persian royal princesses and Bagoas did not occur when he entered Babylon for the first time. Alexander did not kill Cleitas in India, and he was not wounded in India at the Battle of Hydaspes but at the siege of Malli. Specialists in Persian history have also argued that the Persian military forces were much more disciplined than they are depicted in the film.

Greek word meaning "to imitate Greeks." It is an appropriate way, then, to describe an age that saw the extension of the Greek language and ideas to the non-Greek world of the Middle East. Alexander's destruction of the Persian monarchy opened up opportunities for Greek engineers, intellectuals, merchants, administrators, and soldiers. Those who followed Alexander and his successors participated in a new political unity based on the principle of monarchy. His vision of empire no doubt inspired the Romans, who were, of course, Alexander's real heirs.

But Alexander also left a cultural legacy. As a result of his conquests, Greek language, art, architecture, and

CHRONOLOGY The Rise of Macedonia and the Conquests of Alexander	
Reign of Philip II	359–336 B.C.E.
Battle of Chaeronea; conquest of Greece	338 B.C.E.
Reign of Alexander the Great	336–323 B.C.E.
Alexander's invasion of Asia	334 B.C.E.
Battle of Gaugamela	331 B.C.E.
Fall of Persepolis	330 B.C.E.
Alexander's entry into India	327 B.C.E.
Death of Alexander	323 B.C.E.

literature spread throughout the Middle East. The urban centers of the Hellenistic Age, many founded by Alexander and his successors, became springboards for the diffusion of Greek culture. While the Greeks spread their culture in the east, they were also inevitably influenced by eastern ways. Thus, Alexander's legacy included one of the basic characteristics of the Hellenistic world: the clash and fusion of different cultures.

The World of the Hellenistic Kingdoms

FOCUS QUESTION: How did the political and social institutions of the Hellenistic world differ from those of Classical Greece?

The united empire that Alexander created by his conquests crumbled after his death. All too soon, Macedonian military leaders were engaged in a struggle for power, and by 300 B.C.E., four Hellenistic kingdoms had emerged as the successors to Alexander (see Map 4.3): Macedonia under the Antigonid (an-TIG-uh-nid) dynasty, Syria and the east under the Seleucids (suh-LOO-sids), the Attalid (AT-uh-lid) kingdom of Pergamum (PURR-guh-mum) in western Asia Minor, and

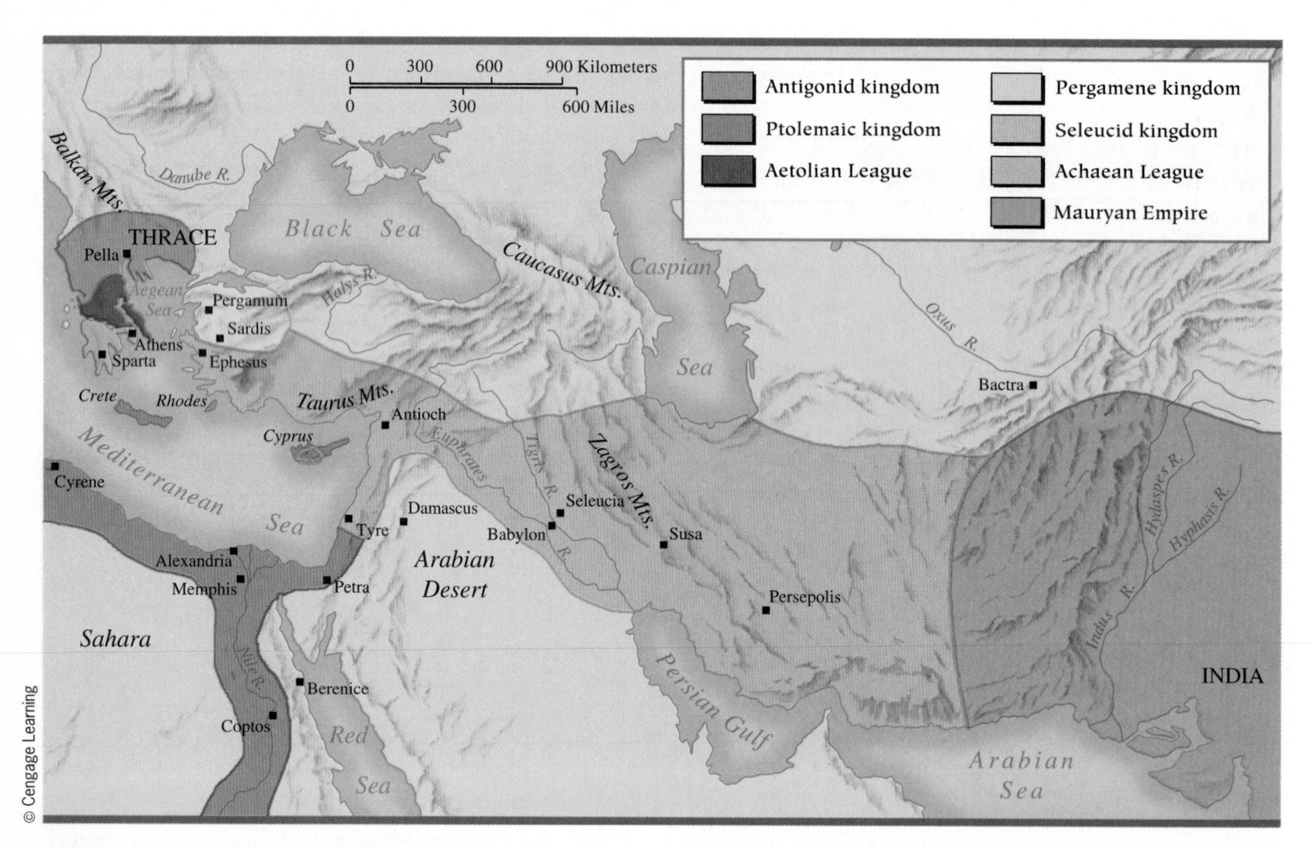

© Cengage Learning

MAP 4.3 The World of the Hellenistic Kingdoms. Alexander died unexpectedly at the age of thirty-two and did not designate a successor. After his death, his generals struggled for power, eventually establishing four monarchies that spread Hellenistic culture and fostered trade and economic development.

Which kingdom encompassed most of the old Persian Empire?

Egypt under the Ptolemies (TAHL-uh-meez). All were eventually conquered by the Romans.

Political Institutions and the Role of Cities

Although Alexander had apparently planned to fuse Greeks and easterners—he used Persians as administrators, encouraged his soldiers to marry easterners, and did so himself—Hellenistic monarchs who succeeded him relied primarily on Greeks and Macedonians to form the new ruling class. Even those easterners who did advance to important adminstrative posts had learned Greek (all government business was transacted in Greek) and had become Hellenized in a cultural sense. The Greek ruling class was determined to maintain its privileged position.

Alexander had founded new cities and military settlements, and Hellenistic kings did likewise. The new population centers varied considerably in size and importance. Military settlements were meant to maintain order and might consist of only a few hundred men strongly dependent on the king. But there were also new independent cities with thousands of people. Alexandria in Egypt was the largest city in the Mediterranean region by the first century B.C.E.

Hellenistic rulers encouraged a massive spread of Greek colonists to the Middle East. Greeks and Macedonians provided not only recruits for the army but also a pool of civilian administrators and workers who contributed to economic development. Even architects, engineers, dramatists, and actors were in demand in the new Greek cities. Many Greeks and Macedonians were quick to see the advantages of moving to the new urban centers and gladly sought their fortunes in the Middle East. The Greek cities of the Hellenistic era were the chief agents in the spread of Greek culture in the Middle East—as far, in fact, as modern Afghanistan and India.

Culture in the Hellenistic World

Although the Hellenistic kingdoms encompassed vast territories and many diverse peoples, the diffusion of Greek culture throughout the Hellenistic world provided a sense of unity. The Hellenistic era was a period of considerable accomplishment in many areas, especially science and philosophy. Although these achievements occurred throughout the Hellenistic world, certain centers, especially the great city of Alexandria, stood out. Alexandria became home to poets, writers, philosophers, and scientists—scholars of all kinds. The library there became the largest in ancient times, with more than 500,000 scrolls.

The founding of new cities and the rebuilding of old ones provided numerous opportunities for Greek architects and sculptors. The Hellenistic monarchs were particularly eager to spend their money to beautify and adorn the cities within their states. The buildings of the Greek homeland—gymnasiums, baths, theaters, and temples—lined the streets of these cities.

Both Hellenistic monarchs and rich citizens patronized sculptors. Hellenistic sculptors traveled throughout this world, attracted by the material rewards offered by wealthy patrons. These sculptors maintained the technical skill of the Classical period, but they moved away from the idealism of fifth-century Classicism to a more emotional and realistic art, which is evident in numerous statues of old women, drunks, and little children at play. Hellenistic artistic styles even affected artists in India (see the comparative illustration on p. 108).

A GOLDEN AGE OF SCIENCE The Hellenistic era witnessed a more conscious separation of science from philosophy. In Classical Greece, what we would call the physical and life sciences had been divisions of philosophical inquiry. Nevertheless, by the time of Aristotle, the Greeks had already established an important principle of scientific investigation: empirical research or systematic observation as the basis for generalization. In the Hellenistic Age, the sciences tended to be studied in their own right.

By far the most famous scientist of the Hellenistic period was Archimedes (ahr-kuh-MEE-deez) (287–212 B.C.E.). Archimedes was especially important for his work on the geometry of spheres and cylinders and for establishing the value of the mathematical constant pi. Archimedes was also a practical inventor. He may have devised the so-called Archimedean screw used to pump water out of mines and to lift irrigation water. During the Roman siege of his native city of Syracuse, he constructed a number of devices to thwart the attackers. Archimedes's accomplishments inspired a wealth of semi-legendary stories. Supposedly, he discovered specific gravity by observing the water he displaced in his bath and became so excited by his realization that he jumped out of the water and ran home naked, shouting, "Eureka!" ("I have found it"). He is said to have emphasized the importance of levers by proclaiming to the king of Syracuse: "Give me a lever and a place to stand on, and I will move the earth." The king was so impressed that he encouraged Archimedes to lower his sights and build defensive weapons instead.

PHILOSOPHY While Alexandria became the renowned cultural center of the Hellenistic world, Athens remained the prime center for philosophy. After Alexander the Great, the home of Socrates, Plato, and Aristotle continued to attract the most illustrious philosophers from the

Kanellopoulos Museum, Athens//© Gianni Dagli Orti/The Art Archive at Art Resource, NY

National Museum of Pakistan, Karachi//© Borromeo/Art Resource, NY

COMPARATIVE ILLUSTRATION

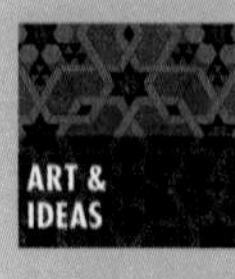

Hellenistic Sculpture and a Greek-Style Buddha. Shown on the left is a Greek terra-cotta statuette of a draped young woman, made as a tomb offering near Thebes, probably around 300 B.C.E. The incursion of Alexander into western India resulted in some Greek cultural influences there. During the first century B.C.E., Indian sculptors in Gandhara, which today is part of Pakistan, began to make statues of the Buddha in a style that combined Indian and Hellenistic artistic traditions, as in the stone sculpture of the Buddha on the right. Note the wavy hair topped by a bun tied with a ribbon, also a feature of earlier statues of Greek deities. This Buddha is also wearing a Greek-style toga.

Q *How do you explain the influence of Hellenistic styles in India? What can you conclude from this example about the impact of conquerors on conquered people?*

Greek world, who chose to establish their schools there. New schools of philosophical thought reinforced Athens's reputation as a philosophical center.

Epicurus (ep-i-KYOOR-uss) (341–270 B.C.E.), the founder of **Epicureanism** (ep-i-kyoo-REE-uh-niz-uhm), established a school in Athens near the end of the fourth century B.C.E. Epicurus believed that human beings were free to follow self-interest as a basic motivating force. Happiness was the goal of life, and the means to achieve it was the pursuit of pleasure, the only true good. But the pursuit of pleasure was not meant in a physical, hedonistic sense (as our word *epicurean* has come to mean) but rather referred to freedom from emotional turmoil and worry. To achieve this kind of pleasure, one had to free oneself from public affairs and politics. But this was not a renunciation of all social life, for to Epicurus, a life could be complete only when it was based on friendship. His own life in Athens was an embodiment of his teachings. Epicurus and his friends created their own private community where they could pursue their ideal of true happiness.

Another school of thought was **Stoicism** (STOH-i-siz-uhm), which became the most popular philosophy of the Hellenistic world and later flourished in the Roman Empire as well. It was the product of a teacher named Zeno (ZEE-noh) (335–263 B.C.E.), who came to Athens and began to teach in a public colonnade known as the Painted Portico (the *Stoa Poikile*—hence the name Stoicism). Like Epicureanism, Stoicism was concerned with how individuals find happiness. But Stoics took a radically different approach to the problem. To them, happiness, the supreme good, could be found only by living in harmony with the divine will, by which people gained inner peace. Life's problems could not disturb these people, and they could bear whatever life offered (hence our word *stoic*). Unlike Epicureans, Stoics did not believe in the need to separate oneself from the world and politics. Public service was regarded as noble, and the real Stoic was a good citizen and could even be a good government official.

Both Epicureanism and Stoicism focused primarily on human happiness, and their popularity would suggest a fundamental change in the Greek lifestyle. In the Classical Greek world, the happiness of individuals and the meaning of life were closely associated with the life of the *polis*. A person found fulfillment in the community. In the Hellenistic kingdoms, the sense that one could find fulfillment through life in the *polis* had weakened. People sought new philosophies that offered personal happiness, and in the cosmopolitan world of the Hellenistic states, with their mixtures of peoples, a new openness to thoughts of universality could also emerge. For some people, Stoicism embodied this larger sense of community.

CHAPTER SUMMARY

Unlike the great centralized empires of the Persians and the Chinese, ancient Greece consisted of a large number of small, independent city-states, of which the most famous were Sparta, a militaristic *polis* ruled by an oligarchy, and Athens, which became known for its democratic institutions although slaves and women had no political rights. Despite the small size of their city-states, the ancient Greeks created a civilization that was the fountainhead of Western culture. Socrates, Plato, and Aristotle established the foundations of Western philosophy. Western literary forms are largely derived from Greek poetry and drama. Greek notions of harmony, proportion, and beauty have remained the touchstones for all subsequent Western art. A rational method of inquiry, so important to modern science, was conceived in ancient Greece. Many political terms are Greek in origin, and so too are concepts of the rights and duties of citizenship, especially as they were conceived in Athens, the first great democracy the world had seen. Especially during the Classical era of the fifth century B.C.E., a century that began with the Persian Wars, the Greeks raised and debated the fundamental questions about the purpose of human existence, the structure of human society, and the nature of the universe that have concerned thinkers ever since.

But the growth of an Athenian empire in that same century led to a mighty conflict with Sparta—the Great Peloponnesian War—that resulted in the weakening of the Greek city-states and opened the door to an invasion by Philip II of Macedonia that put an end to their freedom in 338 B.C.E. But Greek culture did not die, and a new age, known as the Hellenistic era, eventually came into being.

That era began with the conquest of the Persian Empire by Alexander the Great, the young successor to his father, Philip II. Though a great military leader, Alexander was not a good political administrator. He failed to establish any definite structure for the empire he had conquered, and four Hellenistic kingdoms eventually emerged as his successors. The society that developed within those kingdoms is known as *Hellenistic*, meaning Greek-like or in imitation of the Greeks. The Greek language became the dominant one as Greek ideas became influential. Greek merchants, artists, philosophers, and soldiers found opportunities and rewards throughout the Near East, now a world of kingdoms rather than independent city-states.

The Hellenistic period was, in its own way, a vibrant one. New cities arose and flourished. New philosophical doctrines—such as Epicureanism and Stoicism—captured the minds of many. Significant achievements occurred in science, and Greek culture spread throughout the Near East and made an impact wherever it was carried. Although the Hellenistic era achieved a degree of political stability, by the late third century B.C.E., signs of decline were beginning to multiply, and the growing power of Rome eventually endangered the Hellenistic world.

CHAPTER TIMELINE

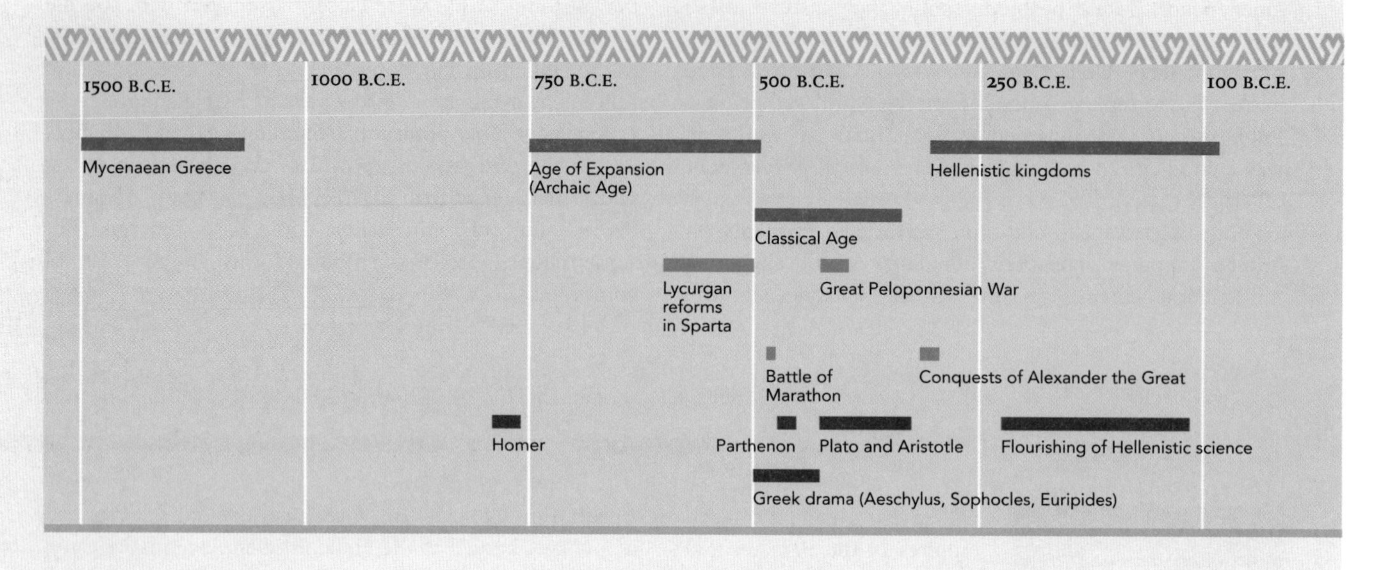

CHAPTER REVIEW

Upon Reflection

Q What was the *polis*, and why do many historians consider it an important development in the political history of Western civilization?

Q The Classical Age in Greece is known for its literary, artistic, and intellectual achievements. What basic characteristics of Greek culture are reflected in the major achievements of the Greeks in the writing of history, drama, the arts, and philosophy? What universal human concerns did these same achievements reflect?

Q What were the main achievements of the Hellenistic kingdoms, and why did they fail to bring any lasting order to the lands of the Near East?

Key Terms

polis (p. 89)
hoplites (p. 89)
phalanx (p. 89)
tyrants (p. 90)
oligarchies (p. 90)
tyranny (p. 90)
helots (p. 91)
Socratic method (p. 97)
Epicureanism (p. 108)
Stoicism (p. 108)

Suggested Reading

GENERAL WORKS A good general introduction to Greek history is **S. B. Pomeroy et al., *Ancient Greece: A Political, Social, and Cultural History*** (New York, 1998). On the Greek way of war, see **V. D. Hanson, *The Wars of the Ancient Greeks,*** rev. ed. (London, 2006).

EARLY GREEK HISTORY Early Greek history is examined in **J. Hall, *History of the Archaic Greek World, c. 1200–479 B.C.*** (London, 2006). On Sparta, see **P. Cartledge, *The Spartans*** (New York, 2003). On early Athens, see **R. Osborne, *Demos*** (Oxford, 1985). The Persian Wars are examined in **P. Green, *The Greco-Persian Wars*** (Berkeley, Calif., 1996).

CLASSICAL GREECE A general history of Classical Greece can be found in **P. J. Rhodes, *A History of the Greek Classical World, 478–323 B.C.*** (London, 2006). For a recent account of the Great Peloponnesian War, see **D. Kagan, *The Peloponnesian War*** (New York, 2003).

GREEK CULTURE AND SOCIETY For a history of Greek art, see **M. Fullerton, *Greek Art*** (Cambridge, 2000). On philosophy, a detailed study is available in **W. K. C. Guthrie, *A History of Greek Philosophy,*** 6 vols. (Cambridge, 1962–1981). On the family and women, see **S. Blundell, *Women in Ancient Greece*** (Cambridge, Mass., 1995).

THE HELLENISTIC ERA For a general introduction, see **P. Green, *The Hellenistic Age: A Short History*** (New York, 2007). The best general survey of the Hellenistic era is **G. Shipley, *The Greek World After Alexander, 323–30 B.C.*** (New York, 2000). There are considerable differences of opinion on Alexander the Great. Good biographies include **P. Cartledge, *Alexander the Great*** (New York, 2004); **G. M. Rogers, *Alexander*** (New York, 2004); and **P. Green, *Alexander of Macedon*** (Berkeley, Calif., 1991). On the various Hellenistic monarchies, see the collection of essays in **C. Habicht, *Hellenistic Monarchies*** (Ann Arbor, Mich., 2006).

HELLENISTIC CULTURE For a general introduction to Hellenistic culture, see **J. Onians, *Art and Thought in the Hellenistic Age*** (London, 1979).

Visit the CourseMate website at **www.cengagebrain.com** for additional study tools and review materials for this chapter.

CHAPTER

5

The First World Civilizations: Rome, China, and the Emergence of the Silk Road

© Dulwich Picture Gallery, London/The Bridgeman Art Library

Horatius defending the bridge as envisioned by Charles Le Brun, a seventeenth-century French painter

CHAPTER OUTLINE AND FOCUS QUESTIONS

Early Rome and the Republic

Q What policies and institutions help explain the Romans' success in conquering Italy? How did Rome achieve its empire from 264 to 133 B.C.E., and what problems did Rome face as a result of its growing empire?

The Roman Empire at Its Height

Q What were the chief features of the Roman Empire at its height in the second century C.E.?

Crisis and the Late Empire

Q What reforms did Diocletian and Constantine institute, and to what extent were the reforms successful? What characteristics of Christianity enabled it to grow and ultimately to triumph?

The Glorious Han Empire (202 B.C.E.–221 C.E.)

Q What were the chief features of the Han Empire?

CRITICAL THINKING

Q In what ways were the Roman Empire and the Han Chinese Empire similar, and in what ways were they different?

ALTHOUGH THE ASSYRIANS, PERSIANS, AND INDIANS under the Mauryan dynasty had created empires, they were neither as large nor as well controlled as the Han and Roman Empires that flourished at the beginning of the first millennium C.E. They were the largest political entities the world had yet seen. The Han Empire extended from Central Asia to the Pacific Ocean; the Roman Empire encompassed the lands around the Mediterranean, parts of the Middle East, and western and central Europe. Although there were no diplomatic contacts between the two civilizations, the Silk Road linked the two great empires together commercially.

Roman history is the remarkable story of how a group of Latin-speaking people, who established a small community on a plain called Latium in central Italy, went on to conquer all of Italy and then the entire Mediterranean world. Why were the Romans able to do this? Scholars do not really know all the answers, but the Romans had their own explanation. Early Roman history is filled with legendary tales of the heroes who made Rome great. One of the best known is the story of Horatius at the bridge.

Threatened by attack from the neighboring Etruscans, Roman farmers abandoned their fields and moved into the city, where they would be protected by the walls. One weak point in the Roman defenses, however, was a wooden bridge over the Tiber River. Horatius was on guard at the bridge when a sudden assault by the

Etruscans caused many Roman troops to throw down their weapons and flee. Horatius urged them to make a stand at the bridge; when they hesitated, he told them to destroy the bridge behind him while he held the Etruscans back. Astonished at the sight of a single defender, the confused Etruscans threw their spears at Horatius, who caught them on his shield and barred the way. By the time the Etruscans were about to overwhelm the lone defender, the Roman soldiers had brought down the bridge. Horatius then dived fully armed into the water and swam safely to the other side through a hail of arrows. Rome had been saved by the courageous act of a Roman who knew his duty and was determined to carry it out. Courage, duty, determination—these qualities would serve the many Romans who believed that it was their divine mission to rule nations and peoples. As one writer proclaimed: "By heaven's will, my Rome shall be capital of the world."

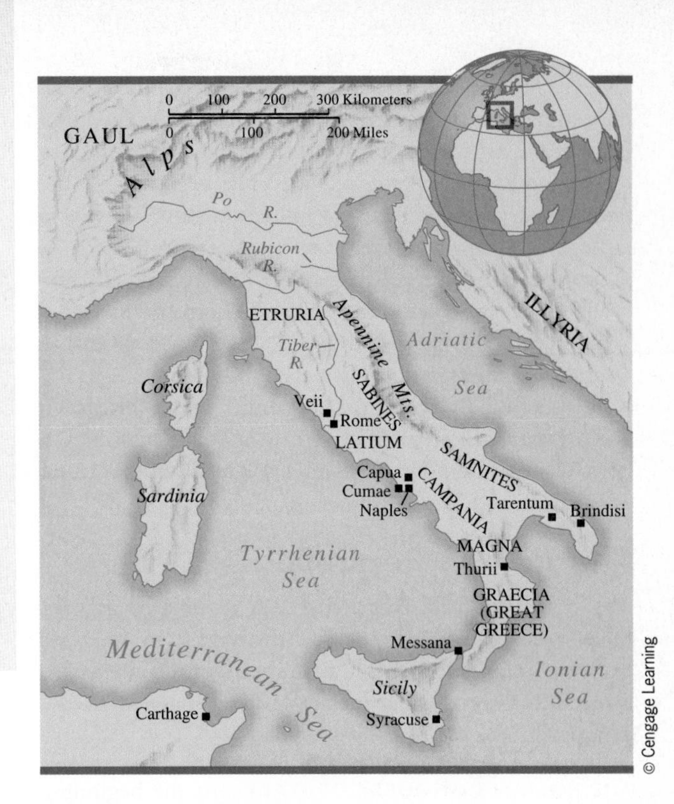

MAP 5.1 Ancient Italy. Ancient Italy was home to several groups of people. Both the Etruscans in the north and the Greeks in the south had a major influence on the development of Rome.

Once Rome conquered the Etruscans, the hill peoples, and other local groups, what aspects of the Italian peninsula helped make it defensible against outside enemies?

Early Rome and the Republic

FOCUS QUESTIONS: What policies and institutions help explain the Romans' success in conquering Italy? How did Rome achieve its empire from 264 to 133 B.C.E., and what problems did Rome face as a result of its growing empire?

Italy is a peninsula extending about 750 miles from north to south (see Map 5.1). It is not very wide, however, averaging about 120 miles across. The Apennines form a ridge down the middle of Italy that divides west from east. Nevertheless, Italy has some fairly large fertile plains that are ideal for farming. Most important are the Po River valley in the north; the plain of Latium (LAY-shee-um), on which Rome was located; and Campania (kahm-PAH-nyuh *or* kam-PAY-nyuh) to the south of Latium. To the east of the Italian peninsula is the Adriatic Sea and to the west the Tyrrhenian Sea, bounded by the large islands of Corsica and Sardinia. Sicily lies just west of the "toe" of the boot-shaped Italian peninsula.

Geography had an impact on Roman history. Although the Apennines bisected Italy, they were less rugged than the mountain ranges of Greece and did not divide the peninsula into many small isolated communities. Italy also possessed considerably more productive agricultural land than Greece, enabling it to support a large population. Rome's location was favorable from a geographic point of view. Located 18 miles inland on the Tiber River, Rome had access to the sea and yet was far enough inland to be safe from pirates. Built on seven hills, it was easily defended.

Moreover, the Italian peninsula juts into the Mediterranean, making Italy an important crossroads between the western and eastern ends of the sea. Once Rome had unified Italy, involvement in Mediterranean affairs was natural. And after the Romans had conquered their Mediterranean empire, governing it was made easier by Italy's central location.

Early Rome

According to Roman legend, Rome was founded by twin brothers, Romulus and Remus, in 753 B.C.E., and archaeologists have found that by around that time, a village of huts had been built on the tops of Rome's hills. The early Romans, basically a pastoral people, spoke Latin, which, like Greek, belongs to the Indo-European family of languages (see Table 1.2 in Chapter 1). The Roman historical tradition also maintained that early Rome (753–509 B.C.E.) had been under the control of seven kings and that two of the last three had been Etruscans (i-TRUSS-kunz), people who lived north of Rome in Etruria. Historians believe that the king list may have some historical accuracy. What is certain is that Rome did fall under the influence of the Etruscans for about a hundred years during the period of the kings and that by the beginning of the sixth century, under Etruscan influence, Rome began to emerge as a city. The Etruscans were responsible for an outstanding building program. They constructed the first roadbed of the chief street through Rome, the Sacred Way, before 575 B.C.E. and oversaw the development of temples, markets, shops, streets, and houses. By 509 B.C.E., supposedly when the monarchy was overthrown and a republican form of government was established, a new Rome had emerged, essentially a result of the fusion of Etruscan and native Roman elements.

The Roman Republic

The transition from monarchy to a republican government was not easy. Rome felt threatened by enemies from every direction and, in the process of meeting these threats, embarked on a military course that led to the conquest of the entire Italian peninsula.

THE ROMAN CONQUEST OF ITALY At the beginning of the Republic, Rome was surrounded by enemies, including the Latin communities on the plain of Latium. If we are to believe Livy (LIV-ee), one of the chief ancient sources for the history of the early Roman Republic, Rome was engaged in almost continuous warfare with these enemies for the next hundred years. In his account, Livy provided a detailed narrative of Roman efforts. Many of his stories were legendary in character; writing in the first century B.C.E., he used his stories to teach Romans the moral values and virtues that had made Rome great. These included tenacity, duty, courage, and especially discipline (see the box on p. 115).

By 340 B.C.E., Rome had crushed the Latin states in Latium. During the next fifty years, the Romans waged a successful struggle with hill peoples from central Italy and then came into direct contact with the Greek communities. The Greeks had arrived on the Italian peninsula in large numbers during the age of Greek colonization (750–550 B.C.E.; see Chapter 4). Initially, the Greeks settled in southern Italy and then crept around the coast and up the peninsula. The Greeks had much influence on Rome. They cultivated olives and grapes, passed on their alphabet, and provided artistic and cultural models through their sculpture, architecture, and literature. By 267 B.C.E., the Romans had completed the conquest of southern Italy by defeating the Greek cities. After crushing the remaining Etruscan states to the north in 264 B.C.E., Rome had conquered most of Italy.

To rule Italy, the Romans had created the Roman Confederation in 338 B.C.E. Under this system, Rome allowed some peoples—especially the Latins—to have full Roman citizenship. Most of the remaining communities were made allies. They remained free to run their own local affairs but were required to provide soldiers for Rome. Moreover, the Romans made it clear that loyal allies could improve their status and even have hope of becoming Roman citizens. The Romans had found a way to give conquered peoples a stake in Rome's success.

In the course of their expansion throughout Italy, the Romans had pursued consistent policies that help explain their success. The Romans were superb diplomats who excelled in making the correct diplomatic decisions. In addition, the Romans were not only good soldiers but also persistent ones. The loss of an army or a fleet did not cause them to quit but spurred them on to build new armies and new fleets. Finally, the Romans had a practical sense of strategy. As they conquered, the Romans established colonies—fortified towns—at strategic locations throughout Italy. By building roads to these settlements and connecting them, the Romans created an impressive communications and military network that enabled them to rule effectively and efficiently (see the comparative illustration on p. 116). By insisting on military service from the allies in the Roman Confederation, Rome essentially mobilized the entire military manpower of all Italy for its wars.

THE ROMAN STATE After the overthrow of the monarchy, Roman nobles, eager to maintain their position of power, established a republican form of government. The chief executive officers of the Roman Republic were the **consuls** (KAHN-sulls) and **praetors** (PREE-turs). Two consuls, chosen annually, administered the government and led the Roman army into battle. The office of praetor was created in 366 B.C.E. The praetor was in charge of civil law (law as it applied to Roman citizens), but he could also lead armies and govern Rome when the consuls were away from the city. As the Romans' territory expanded, they added another praetor to judge cases in which one or both people were noncitizens. The Roman state also had a number of administrative officials who handled specialized duties, such as the administration of financial affairs and the supervision of the public games of Rome.

The Roman **senate** came to hold an especially important position in the Roman Republic. The senate or council of elders was a select group of about three hundred men who served for life. The senate could only advise the magistrates, but this advice was not taken lightly and by the third century B.C.E. had virtually the force of law.

The Roman Republic also had a number of popular assemblies. By far the most important was the **centuriate assembly**. Organized by classes based on wealth, it was

Cincinnatus Saves Rome: A Roman Morality Tale

There is perhaps no better account of how the virtues of duty and simplicity enabled good Roman citizens to prevail during the travails of the fifth century B.C.E. than Livy's account of Cincinnatus (sin-suh-NAT-uss). He was chosen dictator, supposedly in 457 B.C.E., to defend Rome against the attacks of the Aequi (EE-kwy). The position of dictator was a temporary expedient used only in emergencies; the consuls would resign, and a leader with unlimited power would be appointed for a limited period (usually six months). In this account, Cincinnatus did his duty, defeated the Aequi, and returned to his simple farm in just fifteen days.

Livy, *The Early History of Rome*

The city was thrown into a state of turmoil, and the general alarm was as great as if Rome herself were surrounded. Nautius was sent for, but it was quickly decided that he was not the man to inspire full confidence; the situation evidently called for a dictator, and, with no dissentient voice, Lucius Quinctius Cincinnatus was named for the post.

Now I would solicit the particular attention of those numerous people who imagine that money is everything in this world, and that rank and ability are inseparable from wealth: let them observe that Cincinnatus, the one man in whom Rome reposed all her hope of survival, was at that moment working a little three-acre farm . . . west of the Tiber, just opposite the spot where the shipyards are today. A mission from the city found him at work on his land—digging a ditch, maybe, or plowing. Greetings were exchanged, and he was asked—with a prayer for divine blessing on himself and his country—to put on his toga and hear the Senate's instructions. This naturally surprised him, and, asking if all were well, he told his wife Racilia to run to their cottage and fetch his toga. The toga was brought, and wiping the grimy sweat from his hands and face he put it on; at once the envoys from the city saluted him, with congratulations, as Dictator, invited him to enter Rome, and informed him of the terrible danger of Municius's army. A state vessel was waiting for him on the river, and on the city bank he was welcomed by his three sons who had come to meet him, then by other kinsmen and friends, and finally by nearly the whole body of senators. Closely attended by all these people and preceded by his lictors he was then escorted to his residence through streets lined with great crowds of common folk who, be it said, were by no means so pleased to see the new Dictator, as they thought his power excessive and dreaded the way in which he was likely to use it.

[Cincinnatus proceeds to raise an army, march out, and defeat the Aequi.]

In Rome the Senate was convened by Quintus Fabius the City Prefect, and a decree was passed inviting Cincinnatus to enter in triumph with his troops. The chariot he rode in was preceded by the enemy commanders and the military standards, and followed by his army loaded with its spoils. . . . Cincinnatus finally resigned after holding office for fifteen days, having originally accepted it for a period of six months.

What values did Livy emphasize in his account of Cincinnatus? How important were those values to Rome's success? Why did Livy say he wrote his history? As a writer in the Augustan Age, would he have pleased or displeased Augustus by writing a history with such a purpose?

Source: From *The Early History of Rome: Books I–V of the History of Rome From Its Foundation* by Livy, translated by Aubrey de Sélincourt with an introduction by R. M. Ogilvie (Penguin Classics 1960, Reprinted with a new Introduction 1971). Copyright © the Estate of Aubrey de Sélincourt, 1960. Introduction copyright © R. M. Ogilvie, 1971. Reproduced by permission of Penguin Books Ltd.

structured in such a way that the wealthiest citizens always had a majority. This assembly elected the chief magistrates and passed laws. Another assembly, the **council of the plebs**, came into being as a result of the struggle of the orders.

This struggle arose as a result of the division of early Rome into two groups, the **patricians** and the **plebeians**. The patricians were great landowners, who constituted the aristocratic governing class. Only they could be consuls, magistrates, and senators. The plebeians constituted the considerably larger group of nonpatrician large landowners, less wealthy landholders, artisans, merchants, and small farmers. Although they, too, were citizens, they did not have the same rights as the patricians. Both

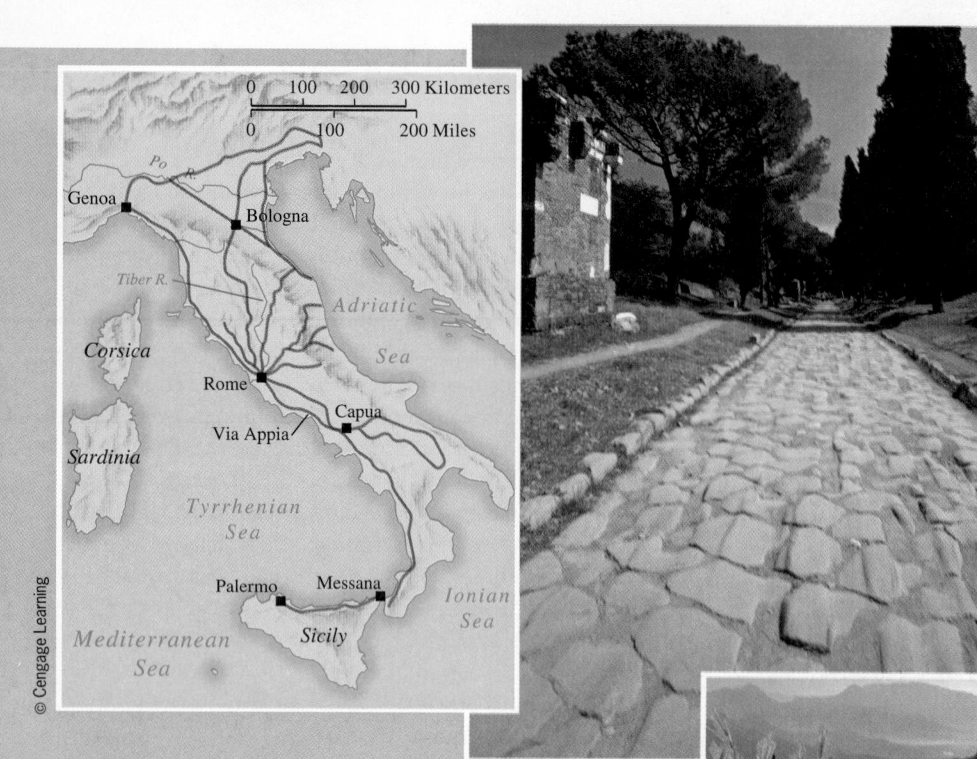

© Cengage Learning

© Jon Arnold Images Ltd (Walter Bibikow)/Alamy

© China Tourism Press/Getty Images

COMPARATIVE ILLUSTRATION

INTERACTION & EXCHANGE

Roman and Chinese Roads. The Romans built a remarkable system of roads. After laying a foundation of gravel, which allowed for drainage, the Roman builders topped it with flagstones, closely fitted together. Unlike other peoples who built similar kinds of roads, the Romans did not follow the contours of the land but made their roads as straight as possible to facilitate communications and transportation, especially for military purposes. Seen here in the top photo is a view of the Via Appia (Appian Way), built in 312 B.C.E. to make it easy for Roman armies to march from Rome to the newly conquered city of Capua, a distance of 152 miles. By the beginning of the fourth century C.E., the Roman Empire contained 372 major roads covering 50,000 miles.

Like the Roman Empire, the Han Empire relied on roads constructed with stone slabs, as seen in the lower photo, for the movement of military forces. The First Emperor of Qin was responsible for the construction of 4,350 miles of roads, and by the end of the second century C.E., China had almost 22,000 miles of roads. Although roads in both the Roman and Chinese Empires were originally constructed for military purposes, they came to be used for communications and commercial traffic as well.

Q *What was the importance of roads to the Roman and Han Empires?*

patricians and plebeians could vote, but only the patricians could be elected to governmental offices. Both had the right to make legal contracts and marriages, but intermarriage between patricians and plebeians was forbidden. At the beginning of the fifth century B.C.E., the plebeians began a struggle to obtain both political and social equality with the patricians.

The struggle between the patricians and plebeians dragged on for hundreds of years, but the plebeians ultimately were successful. The council of the plebs, a popular assembly for plebeians only, was created in 471 B.C.E., and new officials, known as **tribunes of the plebs**, were given the power to protect plebeians against arrest by patrician magistrates. A new law allowed marriages between patricians and plebeians, and in the fourth century B.C.E., plebeians were permitted to become consuls. Finally, in 287 B.C.E., the council of the plebs received the right to pass laws for all Romans.

The struggle between the patricians and plebeians had a significant impact on the development of the Roman state.

Theoretically, by 287 B.C.E., all Roman citizens were equal under the law, and all could strive for political office. But in reality, as a result of the right of intermarriage, a select number of patrician and plebeian families formed a new senatorial aristocracy that came to dominate the political offices. The Roman Republic had not become a democracy.

The Roman Conquest of the Mediterranean (264–133 B.C.E.)

After their conquest of the Italian peninsula, the Romans found themselves face to face with a formidable Mediterranean power—Carthage (KAHR-thij). Founded around 800 B.C.E. on the coast of North Africa by Phoenicians, Carthage had flourished and assembled an enormous empire in the western Mediterranean. By the third century B.C.E., the Carthaginian Empire included the coast of northern Africa, southern Spain, Sardinia, Corsica, and western Sicily. The presence of Carthaginians in Sicily, so close to the Italian coast, made the Romans apprehensive. In 264 B.C.E., the two powers began a lengthy struggle for control of the western Mediterranean (see Map 5.2).

In the First Punic (PYOO-nik) War (the Latin word for Phoenician was *Punicus*), the Romans resolved to conquer Sicily. The Romans—a land power—realized that they could not win the war without a navy and promptly developed a substantial naval fleet. After a long struggle, a Roman fleet defeated the Carthaginian navy off Sicily, and the war quickly came to an end. In 241 B.C.E., Carthage gave up all rights to Sicily and had to pay an indemnity. Sicily became the first Roman province.

Carthage vowed revenge and extended its domains in Spain to compensate for the territory lost to Rome. When the Romans encouraged one of Carthage's Spanish allies to revolt against Carthage, Hannibal (HAN-uh-bul), the greatest of the Carthaginian generals, struck back, beginning the Second Punic War (218–201 B.C.E.).

This time, the Carthaginian strategy aimed at bringing the war home to the Romans and defeating them in their own backyard. Hannibal crossed the Alps with an army

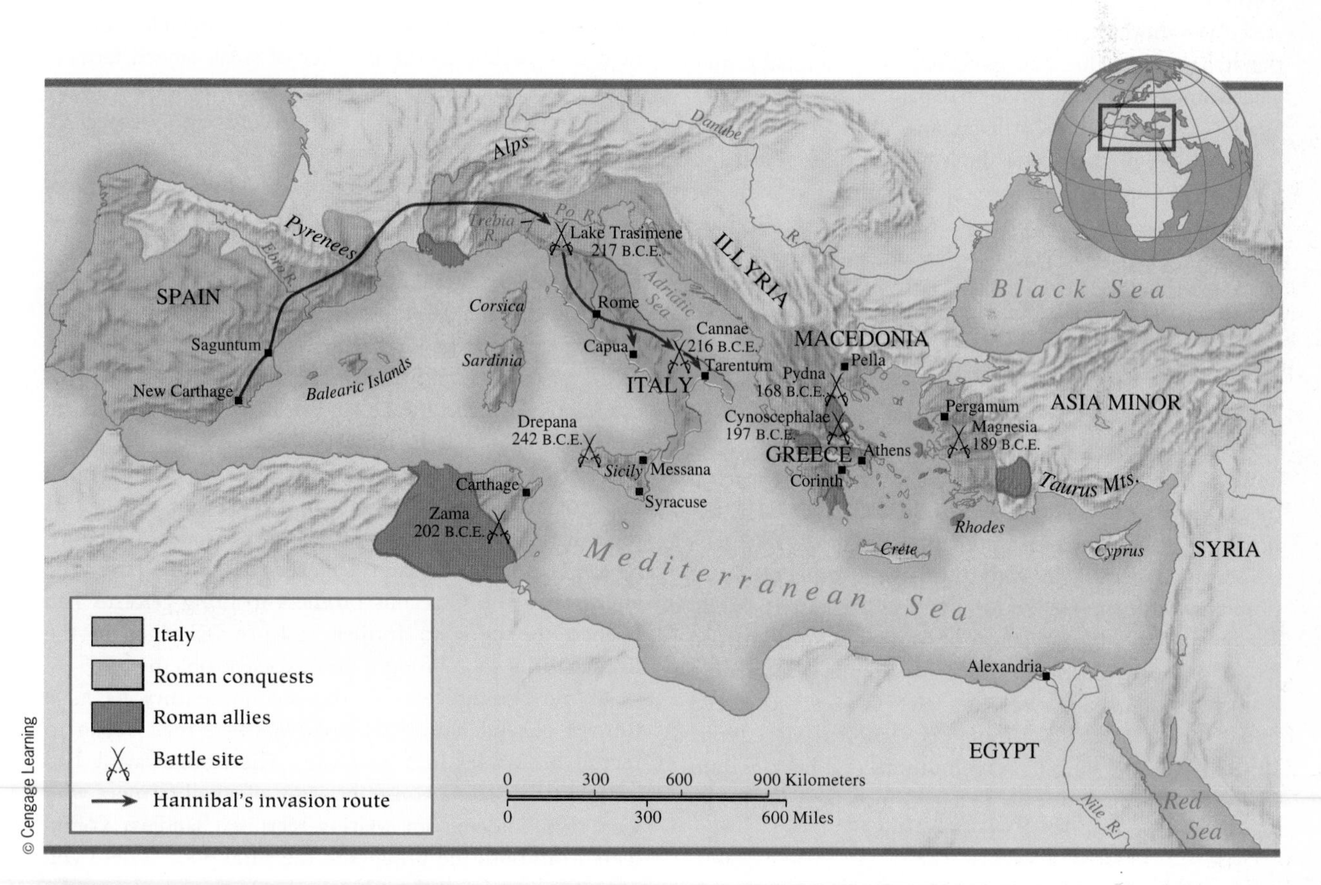

© Cengage Learning

MAP 5.2 Roman Conquests in the Mediterranean, 264–133 B.C.E. Beginning with the Punic Wars, Rome expanded its holdings, first in the western Mediterranean at the expense of Carthage and later in Greece and western Asia Minor.

Q *What aspects of Mediterranean geography, combined with the territorial holdings and aspirations of Rome and the Carthaginians, made the Punic Wars more likely?*

CHRONOLOGY The Roman Conquest of Italy and the Mediterranean

Conquest of Latium completed	340 B.C.E.
Creation of the Roman Confederation	338 B.C.E.
First Punic War	264–241 B.C.E.
Second Punic War	218–201 B.C.E.
Battle of Cannae	216 B.C.E.
Roman seizure of Spain	206 B.C.E.
Battle of Zama	202 B.C.E.
Third Punic War	149–146 B.C.E.
Macedonia made a Roman province	148 B.C.E.
Destruction of Carthage	146 B.C.E.
Kingdom of Pergamum to Rome	133 B.C.E.

of 30,000 to 40,000 men and inflicted a series of defeats on the Romans. At Cannae (KAH-nee) in 216 B.C.E., the Romans lost an army of almost 40,000 men. Rome seemed on the brink of disaster but refused to give up, raised yet another army, and began to reconquer some of the Italian cities that had gone over to Hannibal's side. The Romans also sent troops to Spain, and by 206 B.C.E., Spain was freed of the Carthaginians.

The Romans then took the war directly to Carthage, forcing the Carthaginians to recall Hannibal from Italy. At the Battle of Zama (ZAH-muh) in 202 B.C.E., the Romans crushed Hannibal's forces, and the war was over. By the peace treaty signed in 201 B.C.E., Carthage lost Spain, which became another Roman province. Rome had become the dominant power in the western Mediterranean.

Fifty years later, the Romans fought their third and final struggle with Carthage. In 146 B.C.E., Carthage was destroyed. For ten days, Roman soldiers burned and pulled down all of the city's buildings. The inhabitants—50,000 men, women, and children—were sold into slavery. The territory of Carthage became a Roman province called Africa.

During its struggle with Carthage, Rome also had problems with the Hellenistic states in the eastern Mediterranean, and after the defeat of Carthage, Rome turned its attention there. In 148 B.C.E., Macedonia was made a Roman province, and two years later, Greece was placed under the control of the Roman governor of Macedonia. In 133 B.C.E., the king of Pergamum deeded his kingdom to Rome, giving Rome its first province in Asia. Rome was now master of the Mediterranean Sea.

The Decline and Fall of the Roman Republic (133–31 B.C.E.)

By the middle of the second century B.C.E., Roman domination of the Mediterranean Sea was complete. Yet the process of creating an empire had weakened the internal stability of Rome, leading to a series of crises that plagued the empire for the next hundred years.

GROWING UNREST AND A NEW ROLE FOR THE ROMAN ARMY By the second century B.C.E., the senate had become the effective governing body of the Roman state. It comprised three hundred men, drawn primarily from the landed aristocracy; they remained senators for life and held the chief magistracies of the Republic. The senate directed the wars of the third and second centuries and took control of both foreign and domestic policy, including financial affairs.

Of course, these aristocrats formed only a tiny minority of the Roman people. The backbone of the Roman state had traditionally been the small farmers. But over time, many small farmers had found themselves unable to compete with large, wealthy landowners and had lost their lands. By taking over state-owned land and by buying out small peasant owners, these landed aristocrats had amassed large estates, called ***latifundia*** (lat-i-FOON-dee-uh), that used slave labor. Thus, the rise of the *latifundia* contributed to a decline in the number of small citizen farmers who were available for military service. Moreover, many of these small farmers drifted to the cities, especially Rome, forming a large class of landless poor.

Some aristocrats tried to remedy this growing economic and social crisis. Two brothers, Tiberius and Gaius Gracchus (ty-BEER-ee-uss and GY-uss GRAK-us), came to believe that the underlying cause of Rome's problems was the decline of the small farmer. To help the landless poor, they bypassed the senate by having the council of the plebs pass land reform bills that called for the government to reclaim public land held by large landowners and to distribute it to landless Romans. Many senators, themselves large landowners whose estates included large areas of public land, were furious. A group of senators took the law into their own hands and murdered Tiberius in 133 B.C.E. Gaius later suffered the same fate. The attempts of the Gracchus brothers to bring reforms had opened the door to further violence. Changes in the Roman army soon brought even worse problems.

In the closing years of the second century B.C.E., a Roman general named Marius (MAR-ee-uss) began to recruit his armies in a new way. The Roman army had traditionally been a conscript army of small farmers who were landholders, but Marius recruited landless volunteers from both the urban and the rural poor. These volunteers swore an oath of loyalty to their general, not the senate, and thus formed a professional-type army no longer subject to the state. Moreover, to recruit these men, generals would promise them land, but then the generals would have to play politics to get laws passed that would provide the land promised to their veterans. Marius had created a new system of military recruitment that placed much power in the hands of the individual generals.

THE COLLAPSE OF THE REPUBLIC The first century B.C.E. was characterized by two important features: the jostling for dominance of a number of powerful individuals and the civil wars generated by their conflicts. Three individuals came to hold enormous military and political power—Crassus (KRASS-uss), Pompey (PAHM-pee), and Julius Caesar. Crassus was known as the richest man in Rome and led a successful military command against a major slave rebellion. Pompey had returned from a successful military command in Spain in 71 B.C.E. and had been hailed as a military hero. Julius Caesar also had a military command in Spain. In 60 B.C.E., Caesar joined with Crassus and Pompey to form a coalition that historians call the First Triumvirate (*triumvirate* means "three-man rule").

The combined wealth and influence of these three men was enormous, enabling them to dominate the political scene and achieve their basic aims: Pompey received a command in Spain, Crassus a command in Syria, and Caesar a special military command in Gaul (modern France). When Crassus was killed in battle in 53 B.C.E., his death left two powerful men with armies in direct competition. Caesar had conquered all of Gaul and gained fame, wealth, and military experience as well as an army of seasoned veterans who were loyal to him. When leading senators endorsed Pompey as the less harmful to their cause and voted for Caesar to lay down his command and return as a private citizen to Rome, Caesar refused. He chose to keep his army and moved into Italy illegally by crossing the Rubicon, the river that formed the southern boundary of his province. Caesar marched on Rome and defeated the forces of Pompey and his allies. Caesar was now in complete control of the Roman government.

Caesar was officially made **dictator** in 47 B.C.E. and three years later was named dictator for life. Realizing the need for reforms, he gave land to the poor and increased the senate to nine hundred members. He also reformed the calendar by introducing the Egyptian solar year of 365 days (with later changes in 1582, it became the basis of our own calendar). Caesar planned much more in the way of building projects and military adventures in the east, but in 44 B.C.E., a group of leading senators assassinated him.

Within a few years after Caesar's death, two men had divided the Roman world between them—Octavian (ahk-TAY-vee-un), Caesar's grandnephew and adopted son, took the western portion, and Antony, Caesar's ally and assistant, the eastern half. But the empire of the Romans, large as it was, was still too small for two masters, and Octavian and Antony eventually came into conflict. Antony allied himself closely with the Egyptian queen Cleopatra VII. At the Battle of Actium in Greece in 31 B.C.E., Octavian's forces smashed the army and navy of Antony and Cleopatra, who both fled to Egypt, where they committed suicide a year later. Octavian, at the age of thirty-two, stood supreme over the Roman world. The civil wars had ended. And so had the Republic.

The Roman Empire at Its Height

FOCUS QUESTION: What were the chief features of the Roman Empire at its height in the second century C.E.?

With the victories of Octavian, peace finally settled on the Roman world. Although civil conflict still erupted occasionally, the new imperial state constructed by Octavian experienced remarkable stability for the next two hundred years. The Romans imposed their peace on the largest empire established in antiquity.

The Age of Augustus (31 B.C.E.–14 C.E.)

In 27 B.C.E., Octavian proclaimed the "restoration of the Republic." He understood that only traditional republican forms would satisfy the senatorial aristocracy. At the same time, Octavian was aware that the Republic could not be fully restored. Although he gave some power to the senate, Octavian in reality became the first Roman emperor. The senate awarded him the title of Augustus, "the revered one"—a fitting title in view of his power and one that had previously been reserved for gods. Augustus proved highly popular, but the chief source of his power was his continuing control of the army. The senate gave Augustus the title of *imperator* (im-puh-RAH-tur) (our word *emperor*), or commander in chief.

Augustus maintained a standing army of twenty-eight legions, or about 150,000 men (a legion was a military unit of about 5,000 troops). Only Roman citizens could be legionaries, but subject peoples could serve as auxiliary forces, which numbered around 130,000 under Augustus. Augustus was also responsible for setting up a **praetorian guard** of roughly 9,000 men who had the important task of guarding the emperor.

While claiming to have restored the Republic, Augustus inaugurated a new system for governing the provinces. Under the Republic, the senate had appointed the governors of the provinces. Now certain provinces were given to the emperor, who assigned deputies known as

Braccio Nuovo, Museo Chiaramonti, Vatican Museums, Vatican State//© Scala/Art Resource, NY

Augustus. Octavian, Caesar's adopted son, emerged victorious from the civil conflict that rocked the Republic after Caesar's assassination. The senate awarded him the title of Augustus. This marble statue from Prima Porta, an idealized portrait, is based on Greek rather Roman models. The statue was meant to be a propaganda piece, depicting a youthful general addressing his troops. At the bottom stands Cupid, the son of Venus, goddess of love, meant to be a reminder that the Julians, Caesar's family, claimed descent from Venus and thus that the ruler had a divine background.

legates to govern them. The senate continued to name the governors of the remaining provinces, but the authority of Augustus enabled him to overrule the senatorial governors and establish a uniform imperial policy.

Augustus also stabilized the frontiers of the Roman Empire. He conquered the central and maritime Alps and then expanded Roman control of the Balkan peninsula up to the Danube River. His attempt to conquer Germany failed when three Roman legions led by a general named Varus were massacred in 9 C.E. by a coalition of German tribes. His defeats in Germany taught Augustus that Rome's power was not unlimited and also devastated him; for months, he would beat his head on a door, shouting "Varus, give me back my legions!"

Augustus died in 14 C.E. after dominating the Roman world for forty-five years. He had created a new order while placating the old by restoring traditional values. By the time of his death, his new order was so well established that few agitated for an alternative. Indeed, as the Roman historian Tacitus (TASS-i-tuss) pointed out, "Practically no one had ever seen truly Republican government. . . . Political equality was a thing of the past; all eyes watched for imperial commands."[1]

The Early Empire (14–180)

There was no serious opposition to Augustus's choice of his stepson Tiberius (ty-BEER-ee-uss) as his successor. By his actions, Augustus established the Julio-Claudian dynasty; the next four successors of Augustus were related to his family or that of his wife, Livia.

Several major tendencies emerged during the reigns of the Julio-Claudians (14–68 C.E.). In general, more and more of the responsibilities that Augustus had given to the senate tended to be taken over by the emperors, who also instituted an imperial bureaucracy, staffed by talented freedmen, to run the government on a daily basis. As the Julio-Claudian successors of Augustus acted more openly as real rulers rather than "first citizens of the state," the opportunity for arbitrary and corrupt acts also increased. Nero (NEE-roh) (54–68), for example, freely eliminated people he wanted out of the way, including his own mother, whose murder he arranged. Without troops, the senators proved unable to oppose these excesses, but the Roman legions finally revolted. Abandoned by his guards, Nero chose to commit suicide by stabbing himself in the throat after uttering his final words, "What an artist the world is losing in me!"

THE FIVE GOOD EMPERORS (96–180) Many historians see the ***Pax Romana*** (PAKS *or* PAHKS ro-MAH-nuh) (the Roman peace) and the prosperity it engendered as the chief benefits of Roman rule during the first and second centuries C.E. These benefits were especially noticeable during the reigns of the five so-called **good emperors**. These rulers treated the ruling classes with respect, maintained peace in the empire, and supported generally beneficial domestic policies. Though absolute monarchs, they were known for their tolerance and diplomacy. By adopting capable men as their sons and successors, the first four of these emperors reduced the chances of succession problems.

Under the five good emperors, the powers of the emperor continued to expand at the expense of the senate. Increasingly, imperial officials appointed and directed by the emperor took over the running of the government.

The good emperors also extended the scope of imperial administration to areas previously untouched by the imperial government. Trajan (TRAY-jun) (98–117) implemented an alimentary program that provided state funds to assist poor parents in raising and educating their children. The good emperors were widely praised for their extensive building programs. Trajan and Hadrian (HAY-dree-un) (117–138) were especially active in constructing public works—aqueducts, bridges, roads, and harbor facilities—throughout the empire.

FRONTIERS AND THE PROVINCES Although Trajan extended Roman rule into Dacia (modern Romania), Mesopotamia, and the Sinai peninsula (see Map 5.3), his successors recognized that the empire was overextended and returned to Augustus's policy of defensive imperialism. Hadrian withdrew Roman forces from much of Mesopotamia. Although he retained Dacia and Arabia, he went on the defensive in his frontier policy by reinforcing the fortifications along a line connecting the Rhine and Danube Rivers and building a defensive wall 80 miles long across northern Britain to keep the Scots out of Roman Britain. By the end of the second century, the Roman forces were established in permanent bases behind the frontiers.

At its height in the second century C.E., the Roman Empire was one of the greatest states the world had seen. It covered about 3.5 million square miles and had a population, like that of Han China, estimated at more than 50 million. While the emperors and the imperial administration provided a degree of unity, considerable leeway was given to local customs, and the privileges of Roman

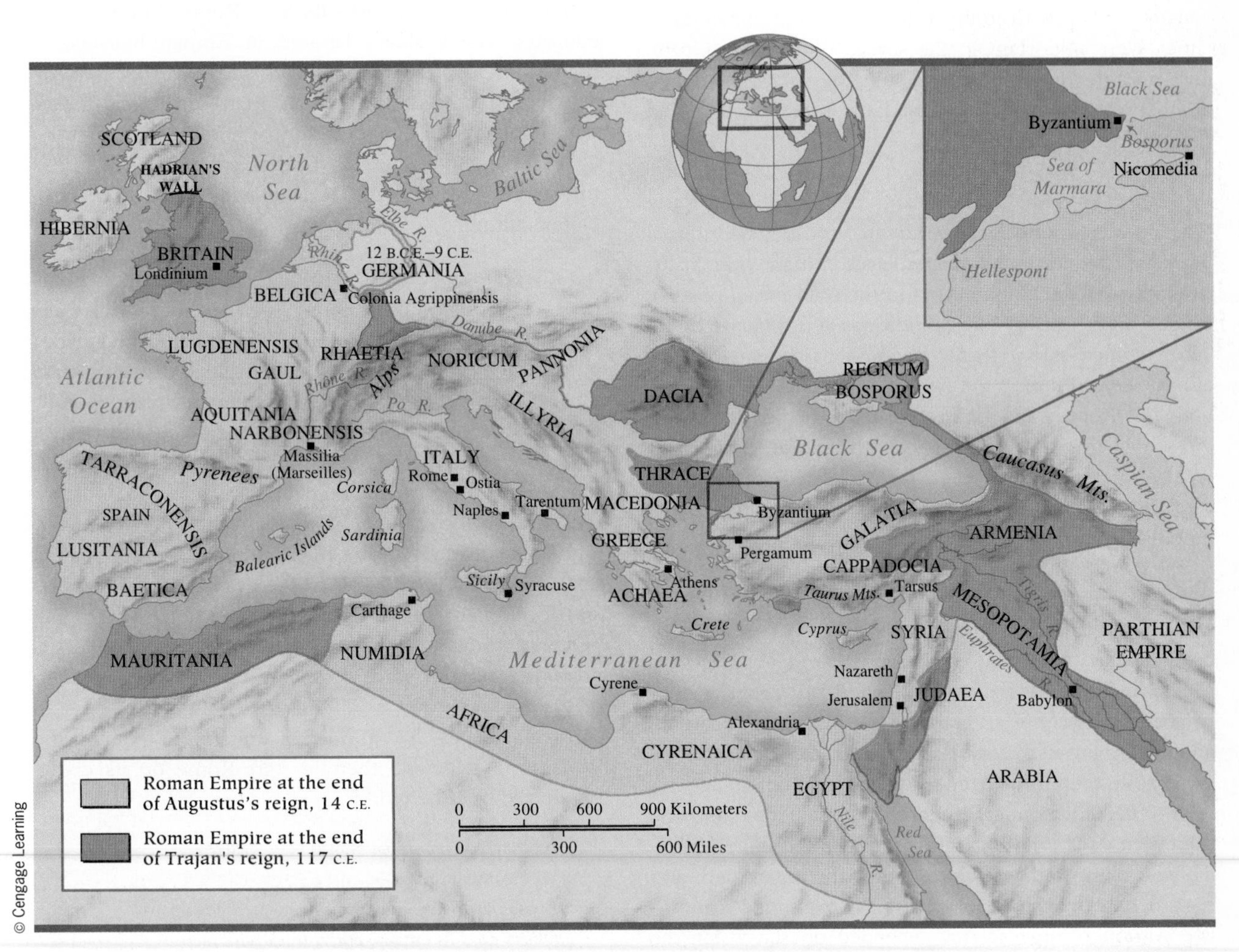

© Cengage Learning

MAP 5.3 The Roman Empire from Augustus Through Trajan (14–117). Augustus and later emperors continued the expansion of the Roman Empire, adding more resources but also increasing the tasks of administration and keeping the peace. Compare this map with Map 5.2.

Q *Which of Trajan's acquisitions were relinquished during Hadrian's reign? Why?*

citizenship were extended to many people throughout the empire. In 212, the emperor Caracalla (kar-uh-KAL-uh) completed the process by giving Roman citizenship to every free inhabitant of the empire. Latin was the language of the western part of the empire, while Greek was used in the east. Roman culture spread to all parts of the empire and freely mixed with Greek culture, creating what has been called Greco-Roman civilization.

The administration and cultural life of the Roman Empire depended greatly on cities and towns. A provincial governor's staff was not large, so it was left to local city officials to act as Roman agents in carrying out many government functions, especially those related to taxes. Most towns and cities were not large by modern standards. The largest was Rome, but there were also some large cities in the east: Alexandria in Egypt numbered more than 300,000 inhabitants. In the west, cities were usually small, with only a few thousand inhabitants. Cities were important in the spread of Roman culture, law, and the Latin language, and they resembled one another with their temples, markets, amphitheaters, and other public buildings.

PROSPERITY IN THE EARLY EMPIRE The Early Empire was a period of considerable prosperity. Internal peace resulted in unprecedented levels of trade. Merchants from all over the empire came to the chief Italian ports of Puteoli on the Bay of Naples and Ostia at the mouth of the Tiber. Long-distance trade beyond the Roman frontiers also developed during the Early Empire. Developments in both the Roman and Chinese Empires helped foster the growth of this trade. Although both empires built roads chiefly for military purposes, the roads also came to be used to facilitate trade. Moreover, by creating large empires, the Romans and Chinese not only established internal stability but also pacified bordering territories, thus reducing the threat that bandits posed to traders. As a result, merchants developed a network of trade routes that brought these two great empires into commercial contact. Most important was the overland Silk Road, a regular caravan route between West and East (see "Imperial Expansion and the Origins of the Silk Road" later in this chapter).

Despite the profits from trade and commerce, agriculture remained the chief pursuit of most people and the underlying basis of Roman prosperity. The large *latifundia* still dominated agriculture, especially in southern and central Italy, but small peasant farms continued to flourish. Although large estates depended on slaves for the raising of sheep and cattle, the lands of some *latifundia* were also worked by free tenant farmers who paid rent in labor, produce, or sometimes cash.

Despite the prosperity of the Roman world, an enormous gulf existed between rich and poor. The development of towns and cities, so important to the creation of any civilization, is based largely on the agricultural surpluses of the countryside. In ancient times, the margin of surplus produced by each farmer was relatively small. Therefore, the upper classes and urban populations had to be supported by the labor of a large number of agricultural producers, who never found it easy to produce much more than they needed for themselves.

Culture and Society in the Roman World

One of the notable characteristics of Roman culture and society is the impact of the Greeks. Greek ambassadors, merchants, and artists traveled to Rome and spread Greek thought and practices. After their conquest of the Hellenistic kingdoms, Roman generals shipped Greek manuscripts and artworks back to Rome. Multitudes of educated Greek slaves labored in Roman households. Rich Romans hired Greek tutors and sent their sons to Athens to study. As the Roman poet Horace (HOR-uss) said, "Captive Greece took captive her rude conqueror." Greek thought captivated the less sophisticated Roman minds, and the Romans became willing transmitters of Greek culture.

ROMAN LITERATURE The high point of Latin literature was reached in the age of Augustus, often called the golden age of Latin literature. The most distinguished poet of the Augustan Age was Virgil (VUR-jul) (70–19 B.C.E.). The son of a small landholder in northern Italy, he welcomed the rule of Augustus and wrote his greatest work in the emperor's honor. Virgil's masterpiece was the *Aeneid* (ih-NEE-id), an epic poem clearly intended to rival the work of Homer. The connection between Troy and Rome is made in the poem when Aeneas (ih-NEE-uss), a hero of Troy, survives the destruction of that city and eventually settles in Latium—establishing a link between Roman civilization and Greek history. Aeneas is portrayed as the ideal Roman—his virtues are duty, piety, and faithfulness. Virgil's overall purpose was to show that Aeneas had fulfilled his mission to establish the Romans in Italy and thereby start Rome on its divine mission to rule the world.

> *Let others fashion from bronze more lifelike,*
> *breathing images—*
> *For so they shall—and evoke living faces from marble;*
> *Others excel as orators, others track with their*
> *instruments*
> *The planets circling in heaven and predict when*
> *stars will appear.*
> *But, Romans, never forget that government is your*
> *medium!*

Be this your art—to practice men in the habit of peace,
Generosity to the conquered, and firmness against
aggressors.[2]

As Virgil expressed it, ruling was Rome's gift.

ROMAN ART The Romans were also dependent on the Greeks for artistic inspiration. The Romans developed a taste for Greek statues, which they placed not only in public buildings but also in their private houses. The Romans' own portrait sculpture was characterized by an intense realism that included even unpleasant physical details. Wall paintings and frescoes in the homes of the rich realistically depicted landscapes, portraits, and scenes from mythological stories.

The Romans excelled in architecture, a highly practical art. Although they continued to adapt Greek styles and made use of colonnades and rectangular structures, the Romans were also innovative. They made considerable use of curvilinear forms: the arch, vault, and dome. The Romans were also the first people in antiquity to use concrete on a massive scale. They constructed huge buildings—public baths, such as those of Caracalla, and amphitheaters capable of seating 50,000 spectators. These large buildings were made possible by Roman engineering skills. These same skills were put to use in constructing roads, aqueducts, and bridges: a network of 50,000 miles of roads linked all parts of the empire, and in Rome, almost a dozen aqueducts kept the population of one million supplied with water.

ROMAN LAW One of Rome's chief gifts to the Mediterranean world of its day and to later generations was its system of law. Rome's first code of laws was the Twelve Tables of 450 B.C.E., but that was designed for a simple farming society and proved inadequate for later needs. So, from the Twelve Tables, the Romans developed a system of civil law that applied to all Roman citizens. As Rome expanded, problems arose between citizens and noncitizens and also among noncitizen residents of the empire. Although some of the rules of civil law could be used in these cases, special rules were often needed. These rules gave rise to what was known as the *law of nations*, defined as the part of the law that applied to both Romans and foreigners. Under the influence of Stoicism, the Romans came to identify their law of nations with **natural law**, a set of universal laws based on reason. This enabled them to establish standards of justice that applied to all people.

These standards of justice included principles that we would immediately recognize. A person was regarded as innocent until proved otherwise. People accused of wrongdoing were allowed to defend themselves before a judge. A judge, in turn, was expected to weigh evidence carefully before arriving at a decision. These principles lived on long after the fall of the Roman Empire.

THE ROMAN FAMILY At the heart of the Roman social structure stood the family, headed by the ***paterfamilias*** (pay-tur-fuh-MEE-lee-uss)—the dominant male. The household also included the wife, sons with their wives and children, unmarried daughters, and slaves. Like the Greeks, Roman males believed that females needed male guardians. The *paterfamilias* exercised that authority; upon his death, sons or nearest male relatives assumed the role of guardians.

Fathers arranged the marriages of their daughters. In the Republic, women married "with legal control" passing from father to husband. By the mid-first century B.C.E., the dominant practice had changed to "without legal control," which meant that married daughters officially remained within the father's legal power. Since the fathers of most married women died sooner or later, not being in the "legal control" of a husband made possible independent property rights that forceful women could translate into considerable power within the household and outside it.

Some parents in upper-class families provided education for their daughters by hiring private tutors or sending them to primary schools. At the age when boys were entering secondary schools, however, girls were pushed into marriage. The legal minimum age for marriage was twelve, although fourteen was a more common age in practice (for males, the legal minimum age was fourteen, and most men married later). Although some Roman doctors warned that early pregnancies could be dangerous for young girls, early marriages persisted because women died at a relatively young age. A good example is Tullia, Cicero's beloved daughter. She was married at sixteen, widowed at twenty-two, remarried one year later, divorced at twenty-eight, remarried at twenty-nine, and divorced at thirty-three. She died at thirty-four, which was not unusually young for women in Roman society.

By the second century C.E., significant changes were occurring in the Roman family. The *paterfamilias* no longer had absolute authority over his children; he could no longer sell his children into slavery or have them put to death. Moreover, the husband's absolute authority over his wife also disappeared, and by the late second century, upper-class Roman women had considerable freedom and independence.

SLAVES AND THEIR MASTERS Although slavery was a common institution throughout the ancient world, no people possessed more slaves or relied so much on slave labor as the Romans eventually did. Slaves were used in

Museo Archeologico Nazionale, Naples//© Erich Lessing/Art Resource, NY

Roman Women. Roman women, especially those of the upper class, had more freedom than women in Classical Athens despite the persistent male belief that women required guardianship. This mural decoration, found in the remains of a villa destroyed by the eruption of Mount Vesuvius, shows a group of Pompeian ladies with their slave hairdresser.

many ways in Roman society. The rich owned the most and the best. In the late Roman Republic, it became a badge of prestige to be attended by many slaves. Greek slaves were in much demand as tutors, musicians, doctors, and artists. Roman businessmen would employ them as shop assistants or craftspeople. Slaves were also used as farm laborers; huge gangs of slaves worked the large landed estates under pitiful conditions. Many slaves of all nationalities were used as menial household workers, such as cooks, waiters, cleaners, and gardeners. Contractors used slave labor to build roads, aqueducts, and other public structures.

The treatment of Roman slaves varied. There are numerous instances of humane treatment by masters and even reports of slaves protecting their owners from danger out of gratitude and esteem. But slaves were also subject to severe punishments, torture, abuse, and hard labor that drove some to run away, despite stringent laws against aiding a runaway slave. Some slaves revolted against their owners and even murdered them, causing some Romans to live in unspoken fear of their slaves (see the box on p. 125).

Near the end of the second century B.C.E., large-scale slave revolts occurred in Sicily, where enormous gangs of slaves were subjected to horrible working conditions on large landed estates. The most famous uprising on the Italian peninsula occurred in 73 B.C.E. Led by a gladiator named Spartacus (SPAR-tuh-kuss), the revolt broke out in southern Italy and involved 70,000 slaves. Spartacus managed to defeat several Roman armies before being trapped and killed in southern Italy in 71 B.C.E. Six thousand of his followers were crucified, the traditional form of execution for slaves.

IMPERIAL ROME At the center of the colossal Roman Empire was the ancient city of Rome. Truly a capital city, Rome had the largest population of any city in the empire, close to one million by the time of Augustus. Only Chang'an, the imperial capital of the Han Empire in China, had a comparable population during this time.

Both food and entertainment were provided on a grand scale for the inhabitants of Rome. The poet Juvenal (JOO-vuh-nul) said of the Roman masses: "But nowadays, with no vote to sell, their motto is 'Couldn't care less.' Time was when their plebiscite elected generals, heads of state, commanders of legions: but now they've pulled in their horns, there's only two things that concern them: Bread and Circuses."[3] Public spectacles were provided by the emperor as part of the great religious festivals celebrated by the state. Most famous were the gladiatorial shows, which took place in amphitheaters. Perhaps the most famous was the amphitheater known as the Colosseum, constructed in Rome to seat 50,000 spectators. In most cities and towns, amphitheaters were the biggest buildings, rivaled only by the circuses (arenas) for races and the public baths.

Gladiatorial games were held from dawn to dusk (see the Film & History feature on p. 126). Contests to the death between trained fighters formed the central focus of these games, but the games included other forms of entertainment as well. Criminals of all ages and both genders were sent into the arena without weapons to face certain death from wild animals who would tear them to pieces. Numerous types of animal contests were also held: wild beasts against each other, such as bears against buffaloes; staged hunts with men shooting safely from behind iron bars; and gladiators in the arena with bulls, tigers, and lions. It is recorded that five thousand beasts were killed in one day of games when Emperor Titus inaugurated the Colosseum in 80 C.E.

The Roman Fear of Slaves

The lowest stratum of the Roman population consisted of slaves. They were used extensively in households, at the court, as artisans in industrial enterprises, as business managers, and in numerous other ways. Although some historians have argued that slaves were treated more humanely during the Early Empire, these selections by the Roman historian Tacitus and the Roman statesman Pliny (PLIN-ee) indicate that slaves still rebelled against their masters because of mistreatment. Many masters continued to live in fear of their slaves, as witnessed by the saying "As many enemies as you have slaves."

Tacitus, *The Annals of Imperial Rome*

Soon afterwards the City Prefect, Lucius Pedanius Secundus, was murdered by one of his slaves [61 C.E.]. Either Pedanius had refused to free the murderer after agreeing to a price, or the slave, in a homosexual infatuation, found competition from his master intolerable. After the murder, ancient custom required that every slave residing under the same roof must be executed. But a crowd gathered, eager to save so many innocent lives; and rioting began. The senatehouse was besieged. Inside, there was feeling against excessive severity, but the majority opposed any change. Among the latter was Gaius Cassius Longinus, who when his turn came spoke as follows. . . .

"An ex-consul has been deliberately murdered by a slave in his own home. None of his fellow-slaves prevented or betrayed the murderer, though the senatorial decree threatening the whole household with execution still stands. Exempt them from the penalty if you like. But then, if the City Prefect was not important enough to be immune; who will be? Who will have enough slaves to protect him if Pedanius's four hundred were too few? Who can rely on his household's help if even fear for their own lives does not make them shield us?"

[The sentence of death was carried out.]

Pliny the Younger to Acilius

This horrible affair demands more publicity than a letter—Larcius Macedo, a senator and ex-praetor, has fallen a victim to his own slaves. Admittedly he was a cruel and overbearing master, too ready to forget that his father had been a slave, or perhaps too keenly conscious of it. He was taking a bath in his house at Formiae when suddenly he found himself surrounded; one slave seized him by the throat while the others struck his face and hit him in the chest and stomach and—shocking to say—in his private parts. When they thought he was dead they threw him onto the hot pavement, to make sure he was not still alive. Whether unconscious or feigning to be so, he lay there motionless, thus making them believe that he was quite dead. Only then was he carried out, as if he had fainted with the heat, and received by his slaves who had remained faithful, while his concubines ran up, screaming frantically. Roused by their cries and revived by the cooler air he opened his eyes and made some movement to show that he was alive, it being now safe to do so. The guilty slaves fled, but most of them have been arrested and a search is being made for the others. Macedo was brought back to life with difficulty, but only for a few days; at least he died with the satisfaction of having revenged himself, for he lived to see the same punishment meted out as for murder. There you see the dangers, outrages, and insults to which we are exposed. No master can feel safe because he is kind and considerate; for it is their brutality, not their reasoning capacity, which leads slaves to murder masters.

What do these texts reveal about the practice of slavery in the Roman Empire? What were Roman attitudes toward the events described in these selections?

Sources: Tacitus, *The Annals of Imperial Rome*. From *The Annals of Imperial Rome* by Tacitus, translated by Michael Grant (Penguin Classics, 1956, Sixth revised edition 1989). Copyright © Michael Grant Publications Ltd, 1956, 1959, 1971, 1989. Reproduced by permission of Penguin Books Ltd. Pliny the Younger to Acilius. From THE LETTERS OF THE YOUNGER PLINY, translated with an introduction by Betty Radice (Penguin Classics 1963, Reprinted 1969). Copyright © Betty Radice, 1963, 1969. Reproduced by permission of Penguin Books Ltd.

FILM & HISTORY

Gladiator (2000)

The film *Gladiator*, directed by Ridley Scott, is a fictional story set in the Roman Empire near the end of the second century C.E. In the movie, Emperor Marcus Aurelius (Richard Harris) informs his son Commodus (Joaquin Phoenix) that he intends to turn over imperial power to his successful and respected general, Maximus (Russell Crowe), in the hope that this decent and honest man can restore the Roman Senate and revive the Republic. Commodus reacts by killing his father, assuming the position of emperor, and ordering the deaths of Maximus, his wife, and son. Maximus escapes but returns too late to Spain to save his wife and child. He is captured and then sold into slavery to Proximo (Oliver Reed), who trains him to be a gladiator. Maximus is eventually sent to Rome, where he becomes a superhero in the gladiatorial games in the Roman Colosseum, all the time awaiting an opportunity to avenge the death of his wife and son by killing Commodus. Maximus becomes involved in a plot with Lucilla (Connie Nielsen), the emperor's sister, and Gracchus (Derek Jacobi), a Roman senator, to rejoin his army, march on Rome, and overthrow the emperor. When Commodus discovers the plot, he challenges the captured Maximus to a duel in the Colosseum but stabs him first to ensure his own success. Despite his injury, Maximus kills the emperor in combat.

Gladiator is a relatively exciting story, but how much of it is based on historical facts? With the exception of Marcus Aurelius, Commodus, and Lucilla, all the characters are fictional. Marcus Aurelius was a kind emperor with a love of philosophy and died in 180, probably from plague, and certainly not by his son's hands, as depicted in the film. Commodus ruled from 180 to 192, although he was only eighteen when he became emperor, not in his late twenties as in the movie; and he had blond hair, not dark hair. Commodus was an unstable and cruel young man who was strongly attracted to gladiatorial contests. He was, in fact, obsessed with performing in the arena, especially with slaughtering animals. He was not killed in the Colosseum, however, but strangled by his wrestling partner on the last day of 192.

Contrary to the movie, Marcus Aurelius had no intention of restoring the Republic; by 180, most Romans had become well accustomed to the empire. Marcus Aurelius had in fact already made his son Commodus a joint ruler in 177. Nor had Marcus Aurelius banned gladiatorial games, as the movie claims. And although Commodus's sister Lucilla did enter into a plot with some senators to assassinate her brother, the plot of 182 failed, and the conspirators, including Lucilla, were executed.

© DreamWorks/Courtesy The Everett Collection, Inc.

Maximus (Russell Crowe) triumphs in the Roman Colosseum.

Although *Gladiator* shows little concern for historical facts, the movie did demonstrate that many people are still interested in ancient history. It became one of the highest earning films of 2000 and won numerous awards including Academy Award for Best Picture and Best Actor for Russell Crowe. Moreover, the film helped to renew interest in Roman history—sales of biographies of historical Roman figures and Marcus Aurelius's *Meditations* increased noticeably in the years after the movie was released.

Crisis and the Late Empire

FOCUS QUESTIONS: What reforms did Diocletian and Constantine institute, and to what extent were the reforms successful? What characteristics of Christianity enabled it to grow and ultimately to triumph?

During the reign of Marcus Aurelius, the last of the five good emperors, a number of natural catastrophes struck Rome. To many Romans, these natural disasters seemed to portend an ominous future for Rome. New problems arose soon after the death of Marcus Aurelius in 180. This same era also saw the growth of Christianity and its eventual adoption as the official religion of Rome.

Crises in the Third Century

In the course of the third century, the Roman Empire came near to collapse. Military monarchy under the Severan rulers (193–235), which restored order after a series of civil wars, was followed by military anarchy. For the next forty-nine years, the Roman imperial throne was occupied by anyone who had the military strength to seize it—a total of twenty-two emperors, only two of whom did not meet a violent death. At the same time, the empire was beset by a series of invasions, no doubt exacerbated by the civil wars. In the east, the Sassanid (suh-SAN-id) Persians made inroads into Roman territory. Germanic tribes also poured into the empire. Not until the end of the third century were most of the boundaries restored.

Invasions, civil wars, and plague came close to causing an economic collapse of the Roman Empire in the third century. There was a noticeable decline in trade and small industry, and the labor shortage caused by the plague affected both military recruiting and the economy. Farm production deteriorated significantly as fields were ravaged by invaders or, even more often, by the defending Roman armies. The monetary system began to collapse as a result of debased coinage and inflation. Armies were needed more than ever, but financial strains made it difficult to pay and enlist more soldiers. By the mid-third century, the state had to hire Germans to fight under Roman commanders.

The Late Roman Empire

At the end of the third and the beginning of the fourth century, the Roman Empire gained a new lease on life through the efforts of two strong emperors, Diocletian (dy-uh-KLEE-shun) and Constantine (KAHN-stun-teen). Under their rule, the empire was transformed into a new state, the so-called Late Empire, distinguished bv a new governmental structure, a rigid economic and social system, and a new state religion—Christianity (see "Transformation of the Roman World: The Development of Christianity" later in this chapter).

THE REFORMS OF DIOCLETIAN AND CONSTANTINE Both Diocletian (284–305) and Constantine (306–337) extended imperial control by strengthening and expanding the administrative bureaucracies of the Roman Empire. A hierarchy of officials exercised control at the various levels of government. The army was enlarged, and mobile units were set up that could be quickly moved to support frontier troops when the borders were threatened.

Constantine's biggest project was the construction of a new capital city in the east, on the site of the Greek city of Byzantium on the shores of the Bosporus. Eventually renamed Constantinople (modern Istanbul), the city was developed for defensive reasons and had an excellent strategic location. Calling it his "New Rome," Constantine endowed the city with a forum, large palaces, and a vast amphitheater.

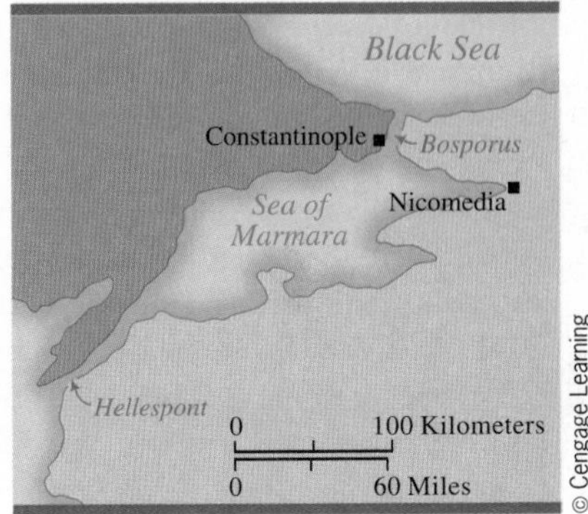

Location of Constantinople, the "New Rome"

The political and military reforms of Diocletian and Constantine also greatly enlarged two institutions—the army and the civil service—that drained most of the public funds. Though more revenues were needed to pay for the army and bureaucracy, the population was not growing, so the tax base could not be expanded. To ensure the tax base and keep the empire going despite the shortage of labor, the emperors issued edicts that forced people to remain in their designated vocations. Basic jobs, such as bakers and shippers, became hereditary. The fortunes of free tenant farmers also declined. Soon they found themselves bound to the land by large landowners who took advantage of depressed agricultural conditions to enlarge their landed estates.

THE END OF THE WESTERN EMPIRE Constantine had reunited the Roman Empire and restored a semblance of order. After his death, however, the empire continued to divide into western and eastern parts, which had virtually become two independent states by 395. In the course of the fifth century, while the empire in the east remained intact under the Roman emperor in Constantinople, the empire in the west disintegrated as more and more Germans moved in and challenged Roman authority.

Although the Romans had established a series of political frontiers along the Rhine and Danube Rivers, Romans and Germans often came into contact across these boundaries. Until the fourth century, the empire had proved capable of absorbing these people without harm to its political structure. In the late fourth century, however, the Germanic tribes came under new pressure when the Huns, a fierce tribe of nomads from the steppes of Asia who may have been related to the Xiongnu (SHYAHNG-noo), the invaders of the Han Empire in China, moved into the Black Sea region, possibly attracted by the riches of the empire to the south. Among the groups displaced by the Huns were the Visigoths (VIZ-uh-gahthz), who moved south and west, crossed the Danube into Roman territory, and settled down as Roman allies. But the Visigoths soon revolted, and the Roman attempt to stop them at Adrianople in 378 led to a crushing defeat for Rome.

Increasing numbers of Germans now crossed the frontiers. In 410, the Visigoths sacked Rome. Vandals poured into southern Spain and Africa, Visigoths into Spain and Gaul. The Vandals crossed into Italy from North Africa and ravaged Rome again in 455. By the middle of the fifth century, the western provinces of the Roman Empire had been taken over by Germanic peoples who were in the process of setting up independent kingdoms. At the same time, a semblance of imperial authority remained in Rome, although the real power behind the throne tended to rest in the hands of important military officials known as masters of the soldiers. These military commanders controlled the government and dominated the imperial court. In 476, Odoacer (oh-doh-AY-sur), a new master of the soldiers, himself of German origin, deposed the Roman emperor, the boy Romulus Augustulus (RAHM-yuh-lus ow-GOOS-chuh-luss). To many historians, the deposition of Romulus signaled the end of the Roman Empire in the west. Of course, this is only a symbolic date, as much of direct imperial rule had already been lost in the course of the fifth century.

WHAT CAUSED THE FALL OF THE WESTERN ROMAN EMPIRE? The end of the Roman Empire in the west has given rise to numerous theories that attempt to provide a single, all-encompassing reason for the "decline and fall of the Roman Empire." These include the following: Christianity's emphasis on a spiritual kingdom undermined Roman military virtues and patriotism; traditional Roman values declined as non-Italians gained prominence in the empire; lead poisoning caused by water pipes and cups made of lead resulted in a mental decline; plague decimated the population; Rome failed to advance technologically because of slavery; and Rome was unable to achieve a workable political system. There may be an element of truth in each of these theories, but all of them have also been challenged. History is an intricate web of relationships, causes, and effects. No single explanation will ever suffice to explain historical events. One thing is clear, however. Weakened by a shortage of manpower, the Roman army in the west was simply not able to fend off the hordes of people moving into Italy and Gaul. In contrast, the Eastern Roman Empire, which would survive for another thousand years, remained largely free from invasion.

Transformation of the Roman World: The Development of Christianity

The rise of Christianity marked a fundamental break with the dominant values of the Greco-Roman world. To understand the rise of Christianity, we must first examine both the religious environment of the Roman world and the Jewish background from which Christianity emerged.

The Roman state religion focused on the worship of a pantheon of Greco-Roman gods and goddesses, including Juno, the patron goddess of women; Minerva, the goddess of craftspeople; Mars, the god of war; and Jupiter Optimus Maximus (JOO-puh-tur AHP-tuh-muss MAK-suh-muss) ("best and greatest"), who became the patron deity of Rome and assumed a central place in the religious life of the city. The Romans believed that the observance of proper ritual by state priests brought them into a right relationship with the gods, thereby guaranteeing security, peace, and prosperity, and that their success in creating an empire confirmed that they enjoyed the favor of the gods. As the first-century B.C.E. politician Cicero claimed, "We have overcome all the nations of the world because we have realized that the world is directed and governed by the gods."[4]

The polytheistic Romans were extremely tolerant of other religions. They allowed the worship of native gods and goddesses throughout their provinces and even adopted some of the local deities. In addition, beginning with Augustus, emperors were often officially made gods by the Roman senate, thus bolstering support for the emperors (see the comparative essay "Rulers and Gods" on p. 129).

As the Romans expanded into the eastern Mediterranean, they came into contact with the various peoples of the east, including the Jews. Roman involvement with the Jews began in 63 B.C.E., and by 6 C.E., Judaea (which embraced the old Israelite kingdom of Judah) had been made a province and placed under the direction of a Roman procurator. But unrest continued, augmented by

COMPARATIVE ESSAY

Rulers and Gods

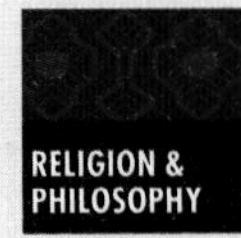

All of the world's earliest civilizations believed that there was a close relationship between rulers and gods. In Egypt, pharaohs were considered gods whose role was to maintain the order and harmony of the universe in their own kingdom. In the words of an Egyptian hymn, "What is the king of Upper and Lower Egypt? He is a god by whose dealings one lives, the father and mother of all men, alone by himself, without an equal." In Mesopotamia, India, and China, rulers were thought to rule with divine assistance. Kings were often believed to derive their power from the gods and to be the agents or representatives of the gods. In ancient India, rulers claimed to be representatives of the gods because they were descended from Manu, the first man who had been made a king by Brahman, the supreme god. Many Romans certainly believed that their success in creating an empire was a visible sign of divine favor.

This supposed connection to the gods also caused rulers to seek divine aid in the affairs of this world. This led to the art of divination, or an organized method of discovering the intentions of the gods. In Mesopotamian and Roman society, one form of divination involved the examination of the livers of sacrificed animals; features seen in the livers were interpreted to foretell events to come. The Chinese used oracle bones to receive advice from supernatural forces that were beyond the power of human beings. Questions to the gods were scratched on turtle shells or animal bones, which were then exposed to fire. Shamans then interpreted the meaning of the resulting cracks on the surface of the shells or bones as messages from supernatural forces. The Greeks divined the will of the gods by use of the oracle, a sacred shrine dedicated to a god or goddess who revealed the future in response to a question.

Underlying all of these divinatory practices was a belief in a supernatural universe—a world inhabited by divine forces on which humans depended for their well-being. It was not until the Scientific Revolution of the modern world that many people began to believe in a natural world that was not governed by spiritual forces.

What role did spiritual forces play in early civilizations?

© Fitzwilliam Museum, University of Cambridge, UK/ The Bridgeman Art Library

Vishnu. Brahman the Creator, Shiva the Destroyer, and Vishnu the Preserver are the three chief Hindu gods of India. Vishnu is known as the Preserver because he mediates between Brahman and Shiva and is thus responsible for maintaining the stability of the universe.

divisions among the Jews themselves. One group, the Essenes, awaited a Messiah who would save Israel from oppression, usher in the kingdom of God, and establish paradise on earth. Another group, the Zealots, were militant extremists who advocated the violent overthrow of Roman rule. A Jewish revolt in 66 C.E. was crushed by the Romans four years later. The Jewish Temple in Jerusalem was destroyed, and Roman power once more stood supreme in Judaea.

THE ORIGINS OF CHRISTIANITY Jesus of Nazareth (c. 6 B.C.E.– c. 29 C.E.) was a Palestinian Jew who grew up in Galilee, an important center of the militant Zealots. Jesus's message was simple. He reassured his fellow Jews that he did not plan to undermine their traditional religion. What was important was not strict adherence to the letter of the law but the transformation of the inner person: "So in everything, do to others what you would have them do to you, for this sums up the Law and the Prophets."[5] God's command was simply to love God and one another: "Love the Lord your God with all your heart and with all your soul and with all your mind and with all your strength. The second is this: Love your neighbor as yourself."[6] In the Sermon on the Mount, Jesus presented the ethical concepts—humility, charity, and brotherly love—that would form the basis of the value system of medieval Western civilization.

To the Roman authorities of Palestine, however, Jesus was a potential revolutionary who might transform Jewish expectations of a messianic kingdom into a revolt against Rome. Therefore, Jesus found himself denounced on many sides, and the procurator Pontius Pilate ordered his crucifixion. But that did not solve the problem. A few loyal followers of Jesus spread the story that Jesus had overcome death, had been resurrected, and had then ascended into heaven. The belief in Jesus's resurrection became an important tenet of Christian doctrine. Jesus was now hailed as "the anointed one" (*Christus* in Greek), the Messiah who would return and usher in the kingdom of God on earth.

Christianity began, then, as a religious movement within Judaism and was viewed that way by Roman authorities for many decades. One of the prominent figures in early Christianity, however, Paul of Tarsus (c. 5–c. 67), believed that the message of Jesus should be preached not only to Jews but to Gentiles (non-Jews) as well. Paul taught that Jesus was the savior, the son of God, who had come to earth to save all humans, who were all sinners as a result of Adam's sin of disobedience against God. By his death, Jesus had atoned for the sins of all humans and made possible their reconciliation with God and hence their salvation. By accepting Jesus as their savior, they too could be saved.

THE SPREAD OF CHRISTIANITY Christianity spread slowly at first. Although the teachings of early Christianity were mostly disseminated by the preaching of convinced Christians, written materials also appeared. Among them were a series of epistles (letters) written by Paul outlining Christian beliefs for different Christian communities. Some of Jesus's disciples may also have preserved some of the sayings of the master in writing and would have passed on personal memories that became the basis of the written *gospels*—the "good news" concerning Jesus—which by the end of the first century C.E. had become the authoritative record of Jesus's life and teachings and formed the core of the New Testament.

Although Jerusalem was the first center of Christianity, its destruction by the Romans in 70 C.E. dispersed the Christians and left individual Christian churches with considerable independence. By 100, Christian churches had been established in most of the major cities of the east and in some places in the western part of the empire. Many early Christians came from the ranks of Hellenized Jews and the Greek-speaking populations of the east. But in the second and third centuries, an increasing number of followers came from Latin-speaking peoples.

Initially, the Romans did not pay much attention to the Christians, whom they regarded as simply another Jewish sect. As time passed, however, the Roman attitude toward Christianity began to change. The Romans tolerated other religions as long as they did not threaten public order or public morals. But because Christians refused to worship the state gods and emperors, many Romans came to view them as harmful to the Roman state. Nevertheless, Roman persecution of Christians in the first and second centuries was only sporadic and local, never systematic. In the second century, Christians were largely ignored as harmless (see the box on p. 131). By the end of the reigns of the five good emperors, Christians still represented a small minority, but one of considerable strength.

THE TRIUMPH OF CHRISTIANITY Christianity grew slowly in the first century, took root in the second, and by the third had spread widely. Why was Christianity able to attract so many followers? First, the Christian

Catacomb of S. Domitilla, Rome/© Scala/Art Resource, NY

Jesus and His Apostles. Pictured is a fourth-century C.E. fresco from a Roman catacomb depicting Jesus and his apostles. Catacombs were underground cemeteries where early Christians buried their dead. Christian tradition holds that in times of imperial repression, Christians withdrew to the catacombs to pray and hide.

OPPOSING ✂ VIEWPOINTS

Roman Authorities and a Christian on Christianity

At first, Roman authorities were uncertain how to deal with the Christians. In the second century, Christians were often viewed as harmless and yet were subject to persecution if they persisted in their beliefs. The first selection—an exchange between Pliny the Younger and the emperor Trajan—illustrates this approach. Pliny, the governor of the province of Bithynia in northwestern Asia Minor, wrote to the emperor for advice about how to handle people accused of being Christians. Trajan's response reflects the general attitude toward Christians taken by emperors in the second century. The final selection is from *Against Celsus*, written about 246 by Origen of Alexandria. In it, Origen defended the value of Christianity against Celsus, a philosopher who had launched an attack on Christians and their teachings.

An Exchange Between Pliny and Trajan

Pliny to Trajan

It is my custom to refer all my difficulties to you, Sir, for no one is better able to resolve my doubts and to inform my ignorance.

I have never been present at an examination of Christians. Consequently, I do not know the nature of the extent of the punishments usually meted out to them, nor the grounds for starting an investigation and how far it should be pressed. . . .

For the moment this is the line I have taken with all persons brought before me on the charge of being Christians. I have asked them in person if they are Christians, and if they admit it, I repeat the question a second and third time, with a warning of the punishment awaiting them. If they persist, I order them to be led away for execution. . . .

Now that I have begun to deal with this problem, as so often happens, the charges are becoming more widespread and increasing in variety. An anonymous pamphlet has been circulated which contains the names of a number of accused persons. . . .

I have therefore postponed any further examination and hastened to consult you. The question seems to me to be worthy of your consideration, especially in view of the number of persons endangered; for a great many individuals of every age and class, both men and women, are being brought to trial, and this is likely to continue. It is not only the towns, but villages and rural districts too which are infected through contact with this wretched cult. I think though that it is still possible for it to be checked and directed to better ends, for there is no doubt that people have begun to throng the temples which had been almost entirely deserted for a long time.

Trajan to Pliny

You have followed the right course of procedure, my dear Pliny, in your examination of the cases of persons charged with being Christians, for it is impossible to lay down a general rule to a fixed formula. These people must not be hunted out; if they are brought before you and the charge against them is proved, they must be punished, but in the case of anyone who denies that he is a Christian, and makes it clear that he is not by offering prayers to our gods, he is to be pardoned as a result of his repentance however suspect his past conduct may be. But pamphlets circulated anonymously must play no part in any accusation. They create the worst sort of precedent and are quite out of keeping with the spirit of our age.

Origen, *Against Celsus*

[Celsus] says that Christians perform their rites and teach their doctrines in secret, and they do this with good reason to escape the death penalty that hangs over them. He compares the danger to the risks encountered for the sake of philosophy as by Socrates. . . . I reply to this that in Socrates's cases the Athenians at once regretted what they had done, and cherished no grievance against him. . . . But in the case of the Christians the Roman Senate, the contemporary emperors, the army, . . . and the relatives of believers fought against the gospel and would have hindered it; and it would have been defeated by the combined force of so many unless it had overcome and risen above the opposition by divine power, so that it has conquered the whole world that was conspiring against it. . . .

He [also] ridicules our teachers of the gospel who try to elevate the soul in every way to the Creator of the universe. . . . He compares them [Christians] to wool-workers in houses, cobblers, laundry-workers, and the most obtuse yokels, as if they called children quite in infancy and women to evil practices, telling them to leave their father and teachers and to follow them. But

(Continued)

let Celsus . . . tell us how we make women and children leave noble and sound teaching, and call them to wicked practices. But he will not be able to prove anything of any kind against us. On the contrary, we deliver women from licentiousness and from perversion caused by their associates, and from all mania for theaters and dancing, and from superstition.

What were Pliny's personal opinions of Christians? Why was he willing to execute them? What was Trajan's response, and what were its consequences for the Christians? What major points did Origen make about the benefits of the Christian religion? Why did the Roman authorities consider these ideas dangerous to the Roman state?

Sources: An Exchange Between Pliny and Trajan. From THE LETTERS OF THE YOUNGER PLINY, translated with an introduction by Betty Radice (Penguin Classics 1963, Reprinted 1969). Copyright © Betty Radice, 1963, 1969. Reproduced by permission of Penguin Books Ltd. Origin, *Against Celsius.* From Origen, *Contra Celsum.* Trans. Henry Chadwick. Copyright © 1953. Reprinted with the permission of Cambridge University Press.

message had much to offer the Roman world. The promise of salvation, made possible by Jesus's death and resurrection, made a resounding impact on a world full of suffering and injustice. Christianity seemed to imbue life with a meaning and purpose beyond the simple material things of everyday reality. Second, Christianity seemed familiar. It was regarded as simply another of the mystery religions, common in the Hellenistic east, that offered immortality as the result of the sacrificial death of a savior-god. At the same time, it offered more than the other mystery religions did. Jesus had been a human figure, not a mythological one, and people found it easier to relate to him.

Moreover, the sporadic persecution of Christians by the Romans in the first and second centuries not only did little to stop the growth of Christianity, but in fact served to strengthen it as an institution in the second and third centuries by causing it to become more organized. Crucial to this change was the emerging role of the bishops, who began to assume more control over church communities. The Christian church was creating a well-defined hierarchical structure in which the bishops and clergy were salaried officers separate from the laity or regular church members.

As the Christian church became more organized, some emperors in the third century responded with more systematic persecutions, but their efforts failed. The last great persecution occurred at the beginning of the fourth century, but by that time, Christianity had become too strong to be eradicated by force. After Constantine became the first Christian emperor, Christianity flourished. Although Constantine was not baptized until the end of his life, in 313 he issued the Edict of Milan officially tolerating Christianity. Under Theodosius (thee-uh-DOH-shuss) the Great (378–395), it was made the official religion of the Roman Empire. In less than four centuries, Christianity had triumphed.

The Glorious Han Empire (202 B.C.E.–221 C.E.)

FOCUS QUESTION: What were the chief features of the Han Empire?

During the same centuries that Roman civilization was flourishing in the West, China was the home of its own great empire. The fall of the Qin dynasty in 206 B.C.E. was followed by a brief period of civil strife as aspiring successors competed for hegemony. Out of this strife emerged one of the greatest and most durable dynasties in Chinese history—the Han (HAHN). The Han dynasty would later become so closely identified with the advance of Chinese civilization that even today the Chinese sometimes refer to themselves as "people of Han" and to their language as the "language of Han."

The founder of the Han dynasty was Liu Bang (lyoo BAHNG) (Liu Pang), a commoner of peasant origin who would be known historically by his title of Han Gaozu (HAHN gow-DZOO) (Han Kao Tsu, or Exalted Emperor of Han; 202–195 B.C.E.). Under his strong rule and that of his successors, the new dynasty quickly moved to consolidate its control over the empire and promote the welfare of its subjects. Efficient and benevolent, at least by the standards of the time, Gaozu maintained the centralized political institutions of the Qin but abandoned its harsh Legalistic approach to law enforcement. Han rulers discovered in Confucian principles a useful foundation for the creation of a new state philosophy. Under the Han, Confucianism began to take on the character of an official ideology.

Confucianism and the State

The integration of Confucian doctrine with Legalist institutions, creating a system generally known as **State Confucianism**, took a while to accomplish. In doing this, the Han rulers retained many of the Qin institutions. For example, they borrowed the tripartite division of the central government into civilian and military authorities and a censorate. The government was headed by a "grand council" including representatives from all three segments of government. The Han also retained the system of local government, dividing the empire into provinces and districts.

Finally, the Han sought to apply the Qin system of selecting government officials on the basis of merit rather than birth. Shortly after founding the new dynasty, Emperor Gaozu decreed that local officials would be asked to recommend promising candidates for public service. Thirty years later, in 165 B.C.E., the first known **civil service examination** was administered to candidates for positions in the bureaucracy. Shortly after that, an academy was established to train candidates. The first candidates were almost all from aristocratic or other wealthy families, and the Han bureaucracy itself was still dominated by the traditional hereditary elite. Still, the principle of selecting officials on the basis of talent had been established and would eventually become standard practice. By the end of the first century B.C.E., as many as 30,000 students were enrolled at the academy.

Under the Han dynasty, the population increased rapidly—by some estimates rising from about 20 million to more than 60 million at the height of the dynasty—creating a growing need for a large and efficient bureaucracy to maintain the state in proper working order. Unfortunately, the Han were unable to resolve all of the problems left over from the past. Factionalism at court remained a serious problem and undermined the efficiency of the central government. Equally important, despite their efforts, the Han rulers were never able to restrain the great aristocratic families, who continued to play a dominant role in political and economic affairs.

The Economy

Han rulers unwittingly contributed to their own problems by adopting fiscal policies that led eventually to greater concentration of land in the hands of the wealthy. They were aware that a free peasantry paying taxes directly to the state would both limit the wealth and power of the great noble families and increase the state's revenues. The Han had difficulty, however, in preventing the recurrence of the economic inequities that had characterized the last years of the Zhou (see the box on p. 134). The land taxes were relatively light, but the peasants also faced a number of other exactions, including military service and forced labor of up to one month annually. Although the use of iron tools brought new lands under the plow and food production increased steadily, the trebling of the population under the Han eventually reduced the average size of the individual farm plot to about one acre per capita, barely enough for survival. As time went on, many poor peasants were forced to sell their land and become tenant farmers, paying rents ranging up to half of the annual harvest. Thus, land once again came to be concentrated in the hands of the powerful landed clans, which often owned thousands of acres worked by tenants.

Although such economic problems contributed to the eventual downfall of the dynasty, in general the period of the early Han was one of unparalleled productivity and prosperity, marked by a major expansion of trade, both domestic and foreign. This was not necessarily due to official encouragement. In fact, the Han were as suspicious of private merchants as their predecessors had been and levied stiff taxes on trade in an effort to limit commercial activities. Merchants were also subject to severe social constraints. They were disqualified from seeking office, restricted in their place of residence, and generally viewed as parasites providing little true value to Chinese society.

The state itself directed much trade and manufacturing; it manufactured weapons, for example, and operated shipyards, granaries, and mines. The system of roads was expanded and modernized. Unlike the Romans, however, the Han rulers relied on waterways for the bulk of their transportation needs. To supplement the numerous major rivers crisscrossing the densely populated heartland of China, new canals were dug to facilitate the moving of goods from one end of the vast empire to the other.

The Han dynasty also began to move cautiously into foreign trade, mostly with neighboring regions in Central and Southeast Asia, although trade relations were established with areas as far away as India and the Mediterranean, where active contacts were maintained with the Roman Empire (see Map 5.4). Some of this long-distance trade was carried by sea through southern ports like Guangzhou (gwahng-JOE), but more was transported by overland caravans on the Silk Road (see the next section and Chapter 10) and other routes that led westward into Central Asia.

New technology contributed to the economic prosperity of the Han era. The Chinese made significant progress in such areas as textile manufacturing, water mills, and iron casting; skill at ironworking led to the production of steel a few centuries later. Paper was invented under the Han, and the development of the rudder and fore-and-aft rigging permitted ships to sail into the wind for the first time. Thus equipped, Chinese merchant ships carrying heavy cargoes could sail throughout the islands of Southeast Asia and into the Indian Ocean.

Imperial Expansion and the Origins of the Silk Road

The Han emperors continued the process of territorial expansion and consolidation that had begun under the Zhou and the Qin. Han rulers, notably Han Wudi (HAHN woo-DEE)

An Edict from the Emperor

EARTH & ENVIRONMENT

According to Confucian doctrine, Chinese monarchs ruled with the mandate of Heaven as long as they properly looked after the welfare of their subjects. One of their most important responsibilities was to maintain food production at a level sufficient to feed their people. Natural calamities such as floods, droughts, and earthquakes were interpreted as demonstrations of displeasure with the "Son of Heaven" on earth. In this edict, Emperor Wendi (180–157 B.C.E.) wonders whether he has failed in his duty to carry out his imperial *Dao* (Way), thus incurring the wrath of Heaven. After the edict was issued in 163 B.C.E., the government took steps to increase the grain harvest, bringing an end to the food shortages.

Han Shu (History of the Han Dynasty)

For the past years there have been no good harvests, and our people have suffered the calamities of flood, drought, and pestilence. We are deeply grieved by this, but being ignorant and unenlightened, we have been unable to discover where the blame lies. We have considered whether our administration has been guilty of some error or our actions of some fault. Have we failed to follow the Way of Heaven or to obtain the benefits of Earth? Have we caused disharmony in human affairs or neglected the gods that they do not accept our offerings? What has brought on these things? Have the provisions for our officials been too lavish or have we indulged in too many unprofitable affairs? Why is the food of the people so scarce? When the fields are surveyed, they have not decreased, and when the people are counted they have not grown in number, so that the amount of land for each person is the same as before or even greater. And yet there is a drastic shortage of food. Where does the blame lie? Is it that too many people pursue secondary activities to the detriment of agriculture? Is it that too much grain is used to make wine or too many domestic animals are being raised? I have been unable to attain a proper balance between important and unimportant affairs. Let this matter be debated by the chancellor, the nobles, the high officials, and learned doctors. Let all exhaust their efforts and ponder deeply whether there is some way to aid the people. Let nothing be concealed from us!

What reasons does Emperor Wendi advance to explain the decline in grain production in China? What are the possible solutions that he proposes? Does his approach meet the requirements for official behavior set out by Chinese philosophers such as Mencius?

Source: Excerpt from Sources of Chinese Tradition, by William Theodore de Bary. Copyright © 1960 by Columbia University Press. Reprinted with the permission of the publisher.

(Han Wu Ti, or Martial Emperor of Han), who ruled from 141 to 87 B.C.E., successfully completed the assimilation into the empire of the regions south of the Yangtze River, including the Red River delta in what is today northern Vietnam. Han armies also marched westward as far as the Caspian Sea, pacifying nomadic tribal peoples and extending China's boundary far into Central Asia (see Map 5.5).

The westward expansion apparently was originally planned as a means to fend off pressure from the nomadic Xiongnu peoples, who periodically threatened Chinese lands from their base area north of the Great Wall. In 138 B.C.E., Emperor Wudi dispatched the courtier Zhang Qian (JANG chee-AHN) (Chang Ch'ien) on a mission westward into Central Asia to seek alliances with peoples living there against the common Xiongnu menace. Zhang Qian returned home with ample information about political and economic conditions in Central Asia. The new knowledge enabled the Han court to establish the first Chinese military presence in the area of the Taklimakan (tah-kluh-muh-KAHN) Desert and the Tian Shan (TEE-en SHAHN) (Heavenly Mountains).

Chinese commercial exchanges with peoples in Central Asia now began to expand dramatically. Eastward into China came grapes, precious metals, glass objects, and horses from Persia and Central Asia. Horses were of particular significance because Chinese military strategists had learned of the importance of cavalry in their battles against the Xiongnu and sought the sturdy Ferghana horses of Bactria to increase their own military effectiveness. In return, China exported goods, especially silk, to countries to the west.

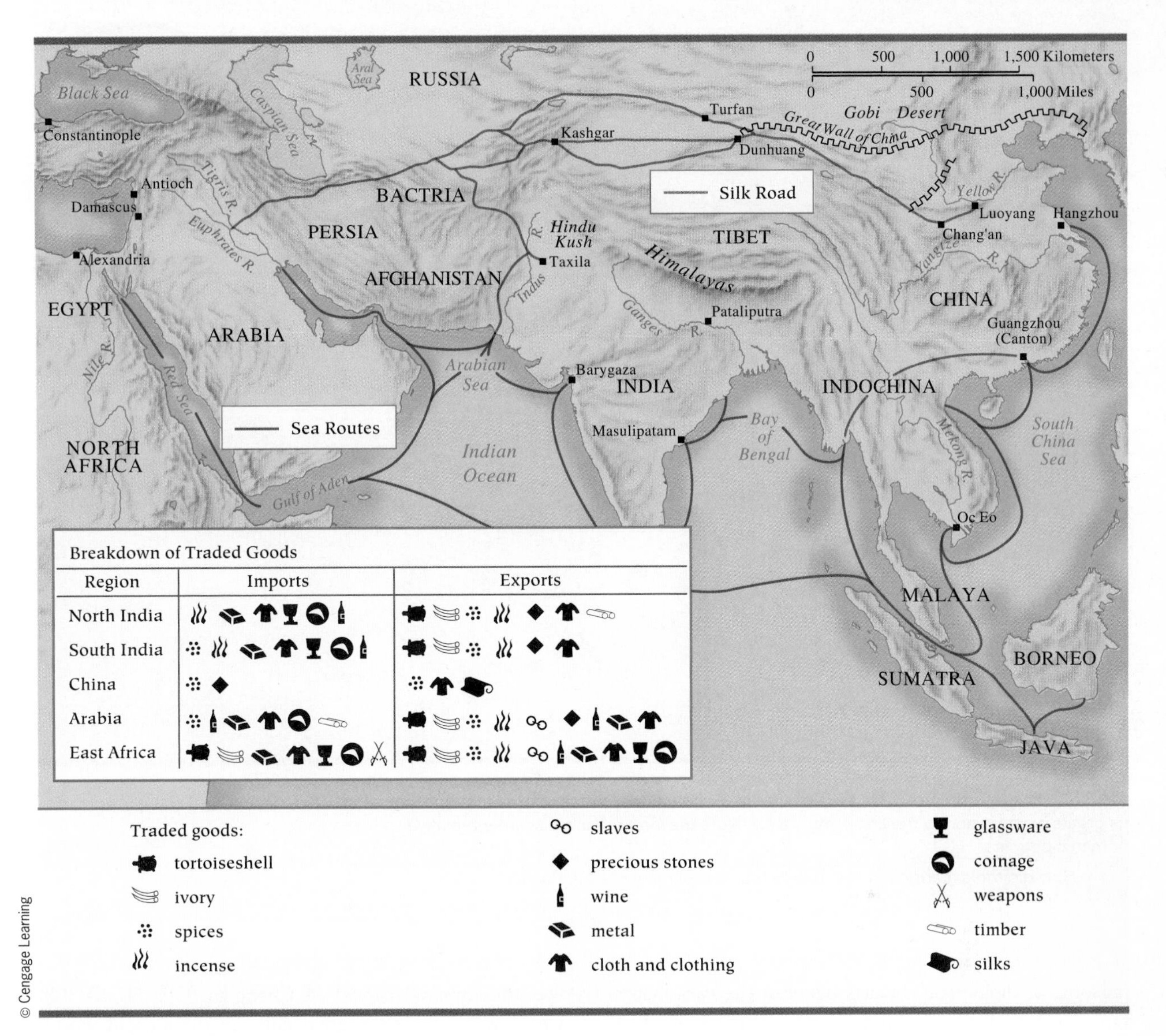

© Cengage Learning

MAP 5.4 Trade Routes of the Ancient World. This map shows the various land and maritime routes that extended from China toward other civilizations located to the south and west of the Han Empire. The various goods that were exchanged are identified at the bottom of the map.

Why do you think China had so few imports? What other patterns do you see?

Silk, a filament recovered from the cocoons of silkworms, had been produced in China since the fourth millennium B.C.E. Eventually, knowledge of the wonder product reached the outside world, and Chinese silk exports began to rise dramatically. By the second century B.C.E., the first items made from silk reached the Mediterranean region, stimulating the first significant contacts between China and Rome, its great counterpart in the west. The bulk of the trade went overland through Central Asia (thus earning this route its current name as the Silk Road), although significant exchanges also took place via the maritime route (see Chapter 9). Silk became a craze among Roman elites, leading to a vast outflow of silver from Rome to China and provoking the Roman emperor Tiberius to grumble that "the ladies and their baubles are transferring our money to foreigners."

The silk trade also stimulated a degree of mutual curiosity between the two great civilizations, but not much mutual knowledge or understanding. Roman authors such as Pliny and the geographer Strabo (who speculated that silk was produced from the leaves of a silk tree) wrote of a strange land called "Seres" far to the east, while Chinese sources mentioned the empire of "Great Qin" at the far end of the Silk Road to the west. So far as is known, no

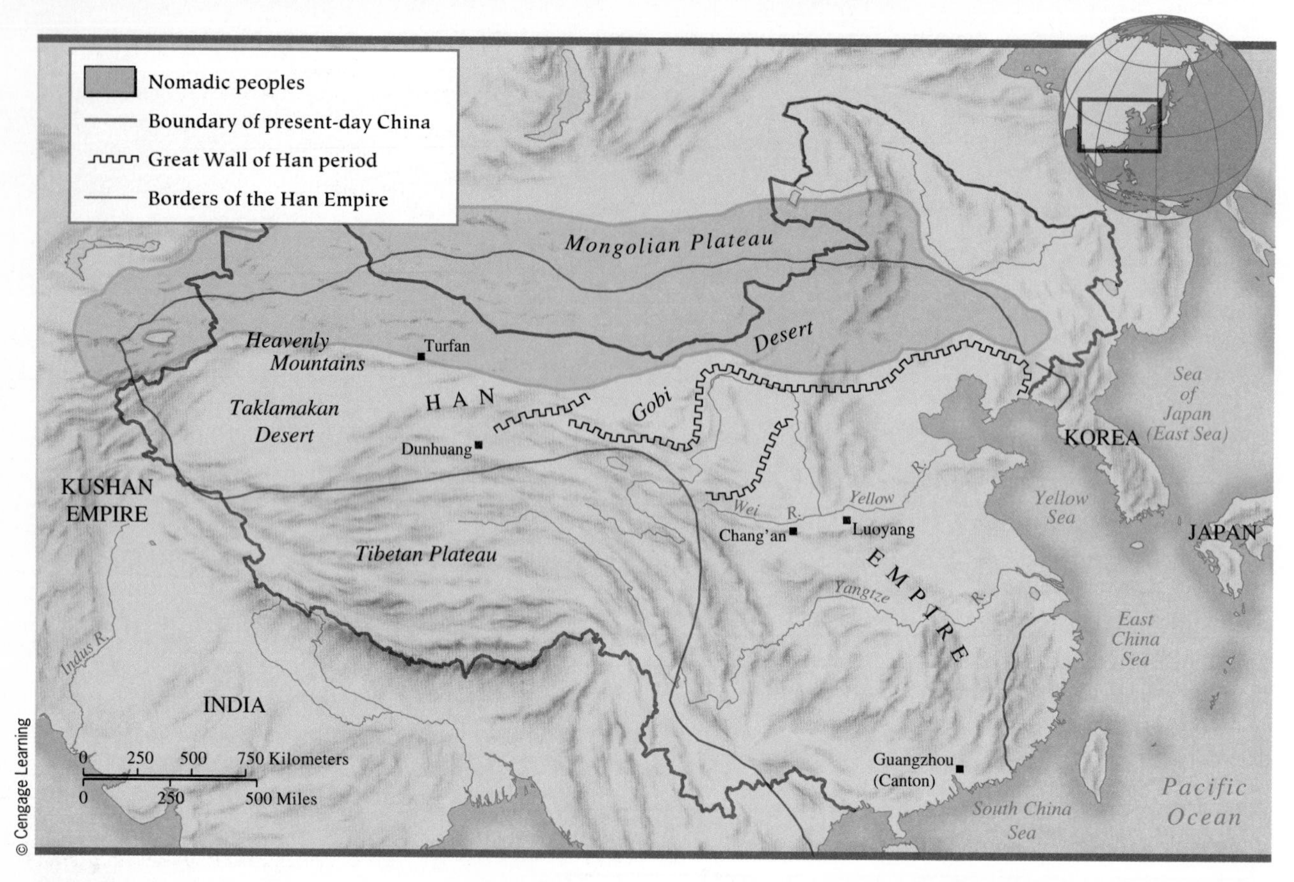

© Cengage Learning

MAP 5.5 The Han Empire. This map shows the territory under the control of the Han Empire at its greatest extent during the first century B.C.E. Note the Great Wall's placement relative to nomadic peoples.

How did the expansion of Han rule to the west parallel the Silk Road?

personal or diplomatic contacts between the two civilizations ever took place. But two great empires at either extreme of the Eurasian supercontinent had for the first time been linked together in a commercial relationship.

Social Changes

Under the Han dynasty, Chinese social institutions evolved into more complex forms than had been the case in past eras. The emergence of a free peasantry resulted in a strengthening of the nuclear family, which now became the prevailing social unit throughout the countryside, although the joint family—the linear descendant of the clan system in the Zhou dynasty—continued to hold sway in much of the countryside. Under the Han, women continued to play a secondary role in society, although they frequently exercised considerable influence within individual households.

The vast majority of Chinese continued to live in rural areas, but the number of cities, mainly at the junction of rivers and trade routes, was on the increase. The largest was the imperial capital of Chang'an (CHENG-AHN), which was one of the great cities of the ancient world, rivaling Rome in magnificence. The city covered a total area of nearly 16 square miles and was enclosed by a 12-foot earthen wall surrounded by a moat. Twelve gates provided entry into the city, and eight major avenues ran east-west or north-south. Each avenue was nearly 150 feet wide; a center strip in each avenue was reserved for the emperor, whose palace and gardens occupied nearly half of the southern and central parts of the city.

Religion and Culture

The Han dynasty's adoption of Confucianism as the official philosophy of the state did not have much direct impact on the religious beliefs of the Chinese people. The pantheon of popular religion was still peopled by local deities and nature spirits, some connected with popular Daoism. Sometime in the first century C.E., however, a new salvationist faith appeared on the horizon. Merchants from Central Asia carrying their wares over the Silk Road brought the Buddhist faith to China for the first time. At first, its influence was limited, as no Buddhist text was translated into Chinese from the original Sanskrit until the fifth century C.E. But the terrain was ripe for the introduction of a new religion into China, and the first Chinese monks departed for India shortly after the end of the Han dynasty.

Cultural attainments under the Han dynasty tended in general to reflect traditional forms, although there was considerable experimentation with new forms of expression. In literature, poetry and philosophical essays continued to be popular, but historical writing became the primary form of literary creativity. Historians such as Sima Qian (SUH-mah chee-AHN) and Ban Gu (bahn GOO) (the dynasty's official historian and the older brother of the female historian Ban Zhao) wrote works that became models for later dynastic histories. These historical works combined political and social history with biographies of key figures. Like so much literary work in China, their primary purpose was moral and political—to explain the underlying reasons for the rise and fall of individual human beings and dynasties.

Painting—often in the form of wall frescoes—became increasingly popular, although little has survived the ravages of time. In the plastic arts, bronze was steadily being replaced by iron as the medium of choice. More readily obtainable, it was better able to satisfy the growing popular demand during a time of increasing economic affluence.

Victoria and Albert Museum, London/© V&A Images, London/Art Resource, NY

Making Paper. One of China's most important contributions to the world was the invention of paper during the Han dynasty. Although the first known use of paper for writing dates back to the first century B.C.E., paper was also used for clothing, wrapping materials, military armor, and toilet tissue. It was even suggested to a prince in 93 B.C.E. that he use a paper handkerchief. Paper was made by pounding fibers of hemp and linen. Then the crushed fibers were placed on a flat mashed surface and soaked in a large vat. After the residue dried, it was peeled away as a sheet of paper, seen piled at the right in this eighteenth-century painting.

The Decline and Fall of the Han

In 9 C.E., the reformist official Wang Mang (wahng MAHNG), who was troubled by the plight of the peasants, seized power from the Han court and declared the foundation of the Xin (SHEEN) (New) dynasty. The empire had been crumbling for decades. As frivolous or depraved rulers amused themselves with the pleasures of court life, the power and influence of the central government began to wane, and the great noble families filled the vacuum, amassing vast landed estates and transforming free farmers into tenants. Wang Mang tried to confiscate the great estates and abolish slavery. In so doing, however, he alienated powerful interests, who conspired to overthrow him. In 23 C.E., beset by administrative chaos and a collapse of the frontier defenses, Wang Mang was killed in a coup d'état.

For a time, strong leadership revived some of the glory of the early Han. The court attempted to reduce land taxes and carry out land resettlement programs. The growing popularity of nutritious crops like rice, wheat, and soybeans, along with the introduction of new crops such as alfalfa and grapes, helped boost food production. But the monopoly of land and power by the great landed families continued. Weak rulers were isolated within their imperial chambers and dominated by powerful figures at court. Official corruption and the concentration of land in the hands of the wealthy led to widespread peasant unrest. The Han also continued to have problems with the Xiongnu beyond the Great Wall to the north. Nomadic raids on Chinese territory continued intermittently to the end of the dynasty, once reaching almost to the gates of the capital city.

Buffeted by insurmountable problems within and without, in the late second century C.E., the dynasty entered a period of inexorable decline. The population of the empire, which had been estimated at about 60 million in China's first census in the year 2 C.E., had shrunk to less than one-third that number two hundred years later. In the early third century C.E., the dynasty was finally brought to an end when power was seized by Cao Cao (TSOW tsow) (Ts'ao Ts'ao), a general known to later generations as one of the main characters in the famous Chinese epic *The Romance of the Three Kingdoms*. But Cao Cao was unable to consolidate his power, and China entered a period of almost constant anarchy and internal division, compounded by invasions by northern tribal peoples. The next great dynasty did not arise until the beginning of the seventh century, four hundred years later.

CHRONOLOGY **The Han Dynasty**	
Overthrow of Qin dynasty	206 B.C.E.
Formation of Han dynasty	202 B.C.E.
Reign of Emperor Wudi	141–87 B.C.E.
Zhang Qian's mission to Central Asia	138 B.C.E.
First silk goods arrive in Europe	Second century B.C.E.
Wang Mang interregnum	9–23 C.E.
First Buddhist merchants arrive in China	First century C.E.
Collapse of Han dynasty	221 C.E.

A Comparison of Rome and China

At the beginning of the first millennium C.E., two great empires—the Roman Empire in the West and the Han Empire in the East—dominated large areas of the world. Although there was little contact between them, the two empires exhibited some remarkable similarities. Both lasted for centuries, and both were extremely successful in establishing centralized control. Both built elaborate systems of roads in order to rule efficiently and relied on provincial officials, and especially on town and cities, for local administration. In both empires, settled conditions led to a high level of agricultural production that sustained large populations, estimated at between 50 and 60 million in each empire. Although both empires expanded into areas with different languages, ethnic groups, and ways of life, they managed to extend their legal and political institutions, their technical skills, and their languages throughout their empires.

The Roman and Han Empires also had similar social and economic structures. The family stood at the heart of the social structure, and the male head of the family was all-powerful. The family also inculcated the values that helped make the empires strong—duty, courage, obedience, and discipline. The wealth of both societies also depended on agriculture. Although a free peasantry provided a backbone of strength and stability in each empire, wealthy landowners were able to gradually convert the free peasants into tenant farmers and thereby ultimately to undermine the power of the imperial governments.

Of course, there were also significant differences. Merchants were more highly regarded and allowed more freedom in Rome than they were in China. One key reason for this difference is that whereas many inhabitants of the Roman Empire depended to a considerable degree on commerce to obtain such staples as wheat, olives, wine, cloth, and timber, the vast majority of Chinese were subsistence farmers whose needs—when they were supplied—could normally be met by the local environment. As a result, there was less social mobility in China than in Rome, and many Chinese peasants spent their entire lives without venturing far beyond their village gate.

Another difference is that over the four hundred years of the empires' existence, Chinese imperial authority was far more stable. With a more cohesive territory and a strong dynastic principle, Chinese rulers could easily pass on their authority to other family members. Although Roman emperors were accorded divine status by the Roman senate after death, accession to the Roman imperial throne depended less on solid dynastic principles and more on pure military force.

Both empires were periodically beset by invasions of nomadic peoples: the Han dynasty was weakened by the incursions of the Xiongnu, and the Western Roman Empire eventually collapsed in the face of incursions by the Germanic peoples. Yet, although the Han dynasty collapsed, the Chinese imperial tradition, along with the class structure and set of values that sustained that tradition, survived, and the Chinese Empire, under new dynasties, continued into the twentieth century as a single political entity. The Roman Empire, by contrast, collapsed and lived on only as an idea.

CHAPTER SUMMARY

Between 509 and 264 B.C.E., the Latin-speaking community of Rome expanded and brought about the union of almost all of Italy under its control. Even more dramatically, between 264 and 133 B.C.E., Rome expanded to the west and east and became master of the Mediterranean Sea and its surrounding territories, creating one of the largest empires in antiquity. Rome's republican institutions proved inadequate for the task of ruling an empire, however, and after a series of bloody civil wars, Augustus created a new order that established a Roman imperial state.

The Roman Empire experienced a lengthy period of peace and prosperity between 14 and 180. In the course of the third century, however, the empire came near to collapse due to invasions, civil wars, and economic decline. Although the emperors Diocletian and Constantine brought new life to the so-called Late Empire, their efforts only shored up the empire temporarily. Beginning in 395, the empire divided into western and eastern parts, and in 476, the Roman Empire in the west came to an end.

Although the Roman Empire in the west collapsed and lived on only as an idea, Roman achievements were bequeathed to the future. The Romance languages of today (French, Italian, Spanish, Portuguese, and Romanian) are based on Latin. Western practices of impartial justice and trial by jury owe much to Roman law. Aspects of Roman administrative practices survived in the Western world for centuries. The Romans also preserved the intellectual heritage of the Greco-Roman world of antiquity. But the heirs of Rome went on to create new civilizations—European, Islamic, and Byzantine—that led to a dramatically different phase in the development of human society.

The Han dynasty also created one of the greatest empires in antiquity. During the glory years of the Han dynasty, China extended the boundaries of its empire far into the sands of Central Asia and southward along the coast of the South China Sea into what is now Vietnam. The doctrine of State Confucianism provided an effective ideology for the state, and Chinese culture appeared unrivaled. In many respects, its scientific and technological achievements were unsurpassed.

One reason for China's striking success was that, unlike other civilizations of its time, it long was able to fend off the danger from nomadic peoples along the northern frontier. By the end of the second century B.C.E., however, the Xiongnu were becoming a threat, and tribal warriors began to nip at the borders of the empire. While the dynasty was strong, the problem was manageable, but when internal difficulties began to weaken the unity of the state, China became vulnerable to the threat from the north and entered its own time of troubles.

Like the Roman Empire, however, the Han Empire also left a rich legacy to its successors. The Confucian institutions and principles enshrined during the long years of Han rule survived several centuries of internal division and eventually reemerged as the governing doctrine of later Chinese empires down to the twentieth century.

CHAPTER TIMELINE

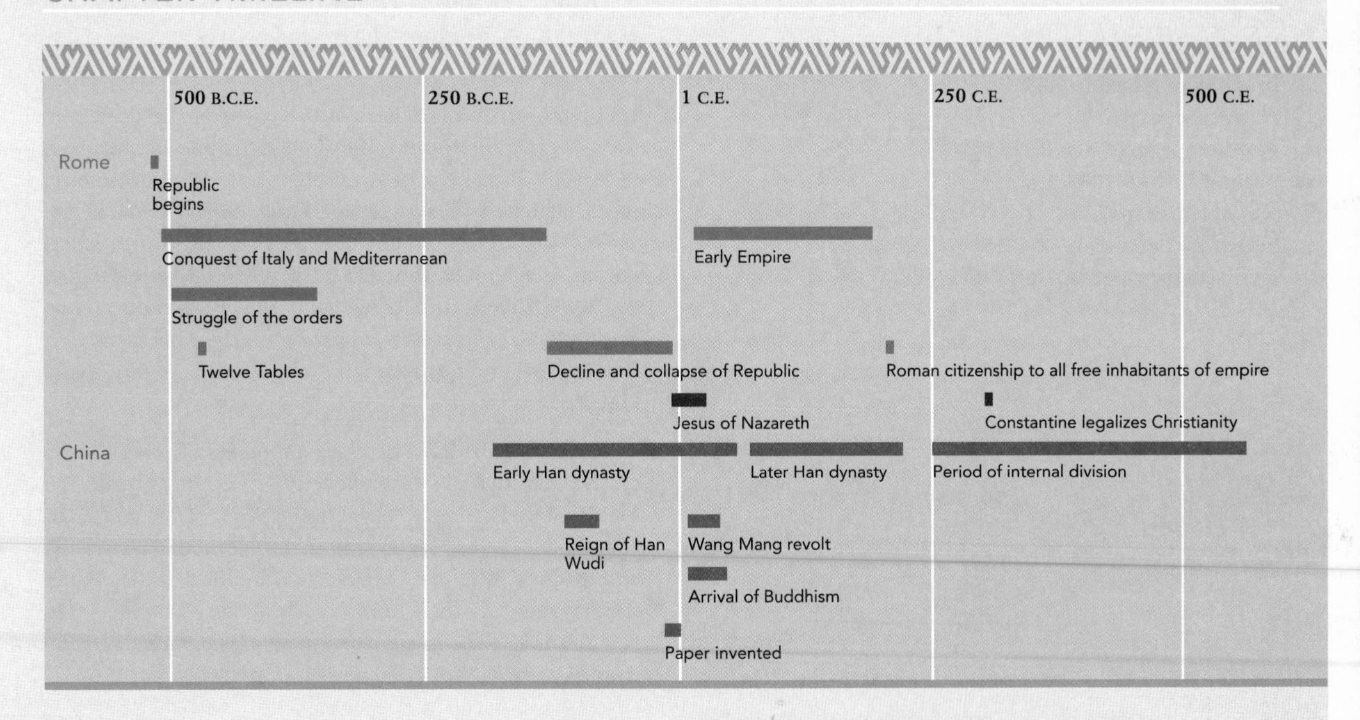

CHAPTER REVIEW

Upon Reflection

Q Was the fall of the Roman Republic due to systemic institutional weaknesses or the personal ambitions of generals and politicians? Explain your answer.

Q In what ways was the rule of the Roman emperors in the first and second centuries C.E., an improvement over the Republic of the first century B.C.E.? In what ways was their rule not an improvement over the last century of the Republic?

Q In what ways were the Roman and Han imperial systems of government alike? In what ways were they different?

Key Terms

consuls (p. 114)
praetors (p. 114)
senate (p. 114)
centuriate assembly (p. 114)
council of the plebs (p. 115)
patricians (p. 115)
plebeians (p. 115)
tribunes of the plebs (p. 116)
latifundia (p. 118)
dictator (p. 119)
praetorian guard (p. 119)
Pax Romana (p. 120)
good emperors (p. 120)
natural law (p. 123)
paterfamilias (p. 123)
State Confucianism (p. 132)
civil service examination (p. 133)

Visit the CourseMate website at **www.cengagebrain.com** for additional study tools and review materials for this chapter.

Suggested Reading

GENERAL SURVEYS OF ROMAN HISTORY For a general account of Roman history, see **M. T. Boatwright, D. J. Gargola,** and **R. J. A. Talbert,** ***The Romans: From Village to Empire*** (New York, 2004). A good survey of the Roman Republic is **M. H.Crawford,** ***The Roman Republic,*** 2nd ed. (Cambridge, Mass., 1993). The history of early Rome is well covered in **T. J. Cornell,** ***The Beginnings of Rome: Italy and Rome from the Bronze Age to the Punic Wars (c. 1000–264 B.C.)*** (London, 1995). An excellent account of basic problems in the late Republic can be found in **M. Beard** and **M. H. Crawford,** ***Rome in the Late Republic*** (London, 1984). On the role of Caesar, see **A. Goldsworthy,** ***Caesar: Life of a Colossus*** (New Haven, Conn., 2006).

EARLY ROMAN EMPIRE A good survey of the Early Roman Empire is **M. Goodman,** ***The Roman World, 44 B.C.–A.D. 180*** (London, 1997). See also **R. Mellor,** ***Augustus and the Creation of the Roman Empire*** (Boston, 2005), for a brief history with documents.

ROMAN SOCIETY AND CULTURE On Roman art and architecture, see **F. S. Kleiner,** ***A History of Roman Art*** (Belmont, Calif., 2006). On the Roman family, see **S. Dixon,** ***The Roman Family*** (Baltimore, 1992). On slavery, see **K. R. Bradley,** ***Slavery and Society at Rome*** (New York, 1994).

LATE ROMAN EMPIRE On the crises of the third century, see **D. S. Potter,** ***The Roman Empire at Bay, A.D. 180–395*** (New York, 2004). On the Late Roman Empire, see **S. Mitchell,** ***History of the Later Roman Empire, A.D. 284–641*** (Oxford, 2006). On the fall of the western empire, see **P. Heather,** ***The Fall of the Roman Empire: A New History of Rome and the Barbarians*** (New York, 2006). A useful work on early Christianity is **R. MacMullen,** ***Christianizing the Roman Empire*** (New Haven, Conn., 1984).

THE HAN EMPIRE There are a number of useful books on the Han dynasty. Two very good recent histories are **M. E. Lewis,** ***Early Chinese Empires: Qin and Han*** (Cambridge, Mass., 2007), and **C. Holcombe,** ***The Genesis of East Asia, 221 B.C.–A.D. 207*** (Honolulu, 2001). For a comparison of the Roman and Han Empires, see **W. Scheidel, ed.,** ***Rome and China: Comparative Perspectives on Ancient World Empires*** (Oxford, 2007).

PART II

New Patterns of Civilization (500–1500 C.E.)

BY THE BEGINNING of the first millennium C.E., the great states of the ancient world were in decline; some were even at the point of collapse. On the ruins of these ancient empires, new patterns of civilization began to take shape between 400 and 1500 C.E. In some cases, these new societies were built on the political and cultural foundations of their predecessors. The Tang dynasty in China and the Guptas in India both looked back to the ancient period to provide an ideological model for their own time. The Byzantine Empire carried on parts of the Classical Greek tradition while also adopting the powerful creed of Christianity from the Roman Empire. In other cases, new states incorporated some elements of the former Classical civilizations while heading in markedly different directions, as in the Arabic states in the Middle East and in the new European civilization of the Middle Ages. In Europe, the Renaissance of the fifteenth century brought an even greater revival of Greco-Roman culture.

During this period, a number of significant forces were at work in human society. The concept of civilization gradually spread from the heartland regions of the Middle East, the Mediterranean basin, the South Asian subcontinent, and China into new areas of the world—sub-Saharan Africa, central and western Europe, Southeast Asia, and even the islands of Japan, off the eastern edge of the Eurasian landmass. Across the oceans, unique but advanced civilizations began to take shape in isolation in the Americas. In the meantime, the vast migration of peoples continued, leading not only to bitter conflicts but also to increased interchanges of technology and ideas. The result was the transformation of separate and distinct cultures and civilizations into an increasingly complex and vast world system embracing not only technology and trade but also ideas and religious beliefs.

As had been the case during antiquity, the Middle East was at the heart of this activity. The Arab Empire, which took shape after the death of Muhammad in the early seventh century, provided the key link in the revived trade routes through the region. Muslim traders—both Arab and Berber—opened contacts with West African societies south of the Sahara, while their ships followed the monsoon winds eastward as far as the Spice Islands in Southeast Asia. Merchants from Central Asia carried goods back and forth along the Silk Road between the Middle East and China. For the next several hundred years, the great cities of the Middle East—Mecca, Damascus, and Baghdad—became among the wealthiest in the known world.

Islam's contributions to the human experience during this period were cultural and technological as well as economic. Muslim philosophers preserved the works of the ancient Greeks for posterity, Muslim scientists and

© Pierre Colombel/CORBIS

mathematicians made new discoveries about the nature of the universe and the human body, and Arab cartographers and historians mapped the known world and speculated about the fundamental forces in human society.

But the Middle East was not the only or necessarily even the primary contributor to the spread of civilization during this period. While the Arab Empire became the linchpin of trade between the Mediterranean and eastern and southern Asia, a new center of primary importance in world trade was emerging in East Asia, focused on China. China had been a major participant in regional trade during the Han dynasty, when its silks were already being transported to Rome via Central Asia, but its role had declined after the fall of the Han. Now, with the rise of the great Tang and Song dynasties, China reemerged as a major commercial power in East Asia, trading by sea with Southeast Asia and Japan and by land with the nomadic peoples of Central Asia. Like the Middle East, China was also a prime source of new technology. From China came paper, printing, the compass, and gunpowder. The double-hulled Chinese junks that entered the Indian Ocean during the Ming dynasty were slow and cumbersome but extremely seaworthy and capable of carrying substantial quantities of goods over long distances. Many inventions arrived in Europe by way of India or the Middle East, and their Chinese origins were therefore unknown in the West.

Increasing trade on a regional or global basis also led to the exchange of ideas. Buddhism was brought to China by merchants, and Islam first arrived in sub-Saharan Africa and the Indonesian archipelago in the same manner. Merchants were not the only means by which religious and cultural ideas spread, however. Sometimes migration, conquest, or relatively peaceful processes played a part. The case of the Bantu-speaking peoples in Central Africa is apparently an example of peaceful expansion; and although Islam sometimes followed the path of Arab warriors, they rarely imposed their religion by force on the local population. In some instances, as with the Mongols, the conquerors made no effort to convert others to their own religions. By contrast, Christian monks, motivated by missionary fervor, converted many of the peoples of central and eastern Europe. Roman Catholic monks brought Latin Christianity to the Germanic and western Slavic peoples, and monks from the Byzantine Empire largely converted the southern and eastern Slavic populations to Eastern Orthodox Christianity.

Another characteristic of the period between 500 and 1500 C.E. was the almost constant migration of nomadic and seminomadic peoples. Dynamic forces in the Gobi Desert, Central Asia, the Arabian peninsula, and Central Africa provoked vast numbers of peoples to abandon their homelands and seek their livelihood elsewhere. Sometimes the migration was peaceful. More often, however, migration produced violent conflict and sometimes invasion and subjugation. As had been the case during antiquity, the most active source of migrants was Central Asia. The region later gave birth to the fearsome Mongols, whose armies advanced to the gates of central Europe and conquered China in the thirteenth century. Wherever they went, they left a train of enormous destruction and loss of life. Inadvertently, the Mongols were also the source of a new wave of epidemics that swept through much of Europe and the Middle East in the fourteenth century. The spread of the plague—known at the time as the Black Death—took much of the population of Europe to an early grave.

But there was another side to the era of nomadic expansion. Even the invasions of the Mongols—the "scourge of God," as Europeans of the thirteenth and fourteenth centuries called them—had constructive as well as destructive consequences. After their initial conquests, for a brief period of three generations, the Mongols provided an avenue for trade throughout the most extensive empire (known as the *Pax Mongolica*) the world had yet seen. ◈

CHAPTER 6

The Americas

Museo Nacional de Antropologia e Historia, Mexico City//© SEF/Art Resource, NY

Warriors raiding a village to capture prisoners for the ritual of sacrifice

CHAPTER OUTLINE AND FOCUS QUESTIONS

The Peopling of the Americas

Q Who were the first Americans, and when and how did they come?

Early Civilizations in Central America

Q What were the main characteristics of religious belief in early Mesoamerica?

The First Civilizations in South America

Q What role did the environment play in the evolution of societies in South America?

Stateless Societies in the Americas

Q What were the main characteristics of stateless societies in the Americas, and how did they resemble and differ from the civilizations that arose there?

CRITICAL THINKING

Q In what ways were the early civilizations in the Americas similar to those discussed in Part I, and in what ways were they unique?

IN THE SUMMER OF 2001, a powerful hurricane swept through Central America, destroying houses and flooding villages all along the Caribbean coast of Belize and Guatemala. Farther inland, at the archaeological site of Dos Pilas (dohs PEE-las), it uncovered new evidence concerning a series of dramatic events that took place nearly 1,500 years earlier. Beneath a tree uprooted by the storm, archaeologists discovered a block of stones containing hieroglyphics that described a brutal war between two powerful city-states of the area, a conflict that ultimately contributed to the decline and fall of Mayan civilization, perhaps the most advanced society then in existence throughout Central America.

Mayan civilization, the origins of which can be traced back to about 500 B.C.E., was not as old as some of its counterparts that we have discussed in Part I of this book. But it was the most recent version of a whole series of human societies that had emerged throughout the Western Hemisphere as early as the third millennium B.C.E. Although these early societies are not yet as well known as those of ancient Egypt, Mesopotamia, and India, evidence is accumulating that advanced civilizations had existed in the Americas thousands of years before the arrival of the Spanish conquistadors led by Hernán Cortés in 1519.

The Peopling of the Americas

FOCUS QUESTION: Who were the first Americans, and when and how did they come?

The Maya (MY-uh) were only the latest in a series of sophisticated societies that had sprung up at various locations in North and South America since human beings first crossed the Bering Strait several millennia earlier. Most of these early peoples, today often referred to as **Amerindians**, lived by hunting and fishing or by food gathering. But eventually organized societies, based on the cultivation of agriculture, began to take root in Central and South America. One key area of development was on the plateau of central Mexico. Another was in the lowland regions along the Gulf of Mexico and extending into modern Guatemala. A third was in the central Andes Mountains, adjacent to the Pacific coast of South America. Others were just beginning to emerge in the river valleys and Great Plains of North America.

For the next two thousand years, these societies developed in isolation from their counterparts elsewhere in the world. This lack of contact with other human beings deprived them of access to technological and cultural developments taking place in Africa, Asia, and Europe. They did not know of the wheel, for example, and their written languages were rudimentary compared to equivalents in complex civilizations in other parts of the globe. But in other respects, their cultural achievements were the equal of those realized elsewhere. When the first European explorers arrived in the Americas at the turn of the sixteenth century, they described much that they observed in glowing terms.

The First Americans

When the first human beings arrived in the Western Hemisphere has long been a matter of dispute. In the centuries following the voyages of Christopher Columbus, speculation centered on the possibility that the first settlers to reach the American continents had crossed the Atlantic Ocean. Were they the lost tribes of Israel? Were they Phoenician seafarers from Carthage? Were they refugees from the legendary lost continent of Atlantis? In all cases, the assumption was that they were relatively recent arrivals.

By the mid-nineteenth century, under the influence of the new Darwinian concept of evolution, a new theory developed. It proposed that the peopling of America had taken place much earlier as a result of the migration of small communities across the Bering Strait at a time when the area was a land bridge uniting the continents of Asia and North America. Recent evidence, including numerous physical similarities between most early Americans and contemporary peoples living in northeastern Asia, has confirmed this hypothesis. The debate on when the migrations began continues, however. The archaeologist Louis Leakey (LEE-kee), one of the pioneers in the search for the origins of humankind in Africa, suggested that the first hominids may have arrived in America as long as 100,000 years ago. Most scholars today, however, suggest that the first Americans were members of *Homo sapiens sapiens* who crossed from Asia by foot between 10,000 and 15,000 years ago in pursuit of herds of bison and caribou that moved into the area in search of grazing land at the end of the last ice age. Some scholars think that early migrants from Asia may have followed a maritime route down the western coast of the Americas, supporting themselves by fishing and feeding on other organisms floating in the sea.

In recent years, a number of fascinating new possibilities have opened up. A recently discovered site at Cactus Hill, in central Virginia, shows signs of human habitation as early as 15,000 years ago. Other recent discoveries suggest that some early settlers may have originally come from Africa or from the South Pacific rather than from Asia. The question has not yet been definitively answered.

Nevertheless, it is now generally accepted that human beings were living in the Americas at least 15,000 years ago. They gradually spread throughout the North American continent and had penetrated almost to the southern tip of South America by about 11,000 B.C.E. These first Americans were hunters and food gatherers who lived in small nomadic communities close to the source of their food supply. Although it is not known when agriculture was first practiced, beans and squash seeds have been found at sites that date back at least 10,000 years. The cultivation of maize (corn), and perhaps other crops as well, appears to have been under way in the lowland regions near the modern city of Veracruz and in the Yucatán peninsula farther to the east. There, in the region that archaeologists call **Mesoamerica**, one of the first civilizations in the Western Hemisphere began to appear.

Early Civilizations in Central America

FOCUS QUESTION: What were the main characteristics of religious belief in early Mesoamerica?

The first signs of civilization in Mesoamerica appeared at the end of the second millennium B.C.E., with the emergence of what is called Olmec (AHL-mek *or* OHL-mek) culture in the hot, swampy lowlands along the coast of the Gulf of Mexico south of Veracruz (see Map 6.1).

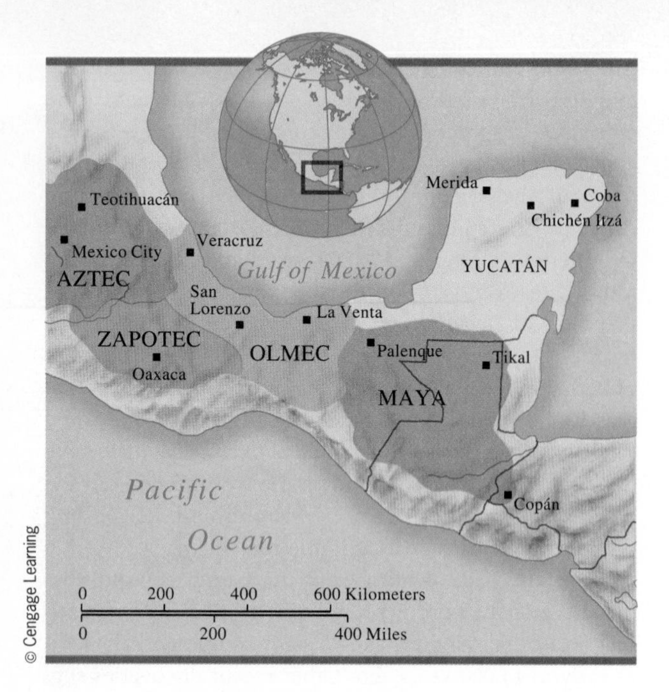

MAP 6.1 Early Mesoamerica. Mesoamerica was home to some of the first civilizations in the Western Hemisphere. This map shows the major urban settlements in the region.

Q *What types of ecological areas were most associated with Olmec, Mayan, and Aztec culture?*

The Olmecs: In the Land of Rubber

Olmec civilization was characterized by intensive agriculture along the muddy riverbanks in the area and by the carving of stone ornaments, tools, and monuments at sites such as San Lorenzo and La Venta. The site at La Venta contains a ceremonial precinct with a 30-foot-high earthen pyramid, the largest of its date in all Mesoamerica. The Olmec peoples organized a widespread trading network, carried on religious rituals, and devised an as yet undeciphered system of hieroglyphs that is similar in some respects to later Mayan writing (see "Mayan Hieroglyphs and Calendars" later in this chapter) and may be the ancestor of the first true writing systems in the Western Hemisphere.

Olmec society apparently consisted of several classes, including a class of skilled artisans who produced a series of massive stone heads, some of which are more than 10 feet high. The Olmec peoples supported themselves primarily by cultivating crops, such as corn and beans, but also engaged in fishing and hunting. The Olmecs apparently played a ceremonial game on a stone ball court, a ritual that would later be widely practiced throughout the region (see "The Maya" later in this chapter). The ball was made from the sap of a local rubber tree, thus providing the name *Olmec*: "people of the land of rubber."

Trade between the Olmecs and their neighbors was apparently quite extensive, and rubber was one of the products most desired by peoples in nearby regions. It was used not only for the manufacture of balls, but also for rubber bands and footwear, as the Olmec learned how to mix the raw latex (the sap of the rubber tree) with other ingredients to make it more supple.

Eventually, Olmec civilization began to decline, and it apparently collapsed around the fourth century B.C.E. During its heyday, however, it extended from Mexico City to El Salvador and perhaps to the shores of the Pacific Ocean.

The Zapotecs

Parallel developments were occurring at Monte Albán (MON-tee ahl-BAHN), on a hillside overlooking the modern city of Oaxaca (wah-HAH-kuh), in central Mexico. Around the middle of the first millennium B.C.E., the Zapotec (zah-puh-TEK) peoples created an extensive civilization that flourished for several hundred years in the highlands. Like the Olmec sites, Monte Albán contains a number of temples and pyramids, but they are located in much more awesome surroundings on a massive stone terrace atop a 1,200-foot-high mountain overlooking the Oaxaca valley. The majority of the population, estimated at about 20,000, dwelled on terraces cut into the sides of the mountain known to local residents as Danibaan, or "sacred mountain."

The government at Monte Albán was apparently theocratic, with an elite class of nobles and priests ruling over a population composed primarily of farmers and artisans. Like the Olmecs, the Zapotecs devised a written language that has not been deciphered. Zapotec society survived for several centuries following the collapse of the Olmecs, but Monte Albán was abandoned for unknown reasons in the late eighth century C.E.

Teotihuacán: America's First Metropolis

The first major metropolis in Mesoamerica was the city of Teotihuacán (tay-oh-tee-hwah-KAHN), capital of an early state about 30 miles northeast of Mexico City that arose around the third century B.C.E. and flourished for nearly a millennium until it collapsed under mysterious circumstances about 800 C.E. Along the main thoroughfare were temples and palaces, all dominated by the massive Pyramid of the Sun (see the comparative illustration on p. 147), under which archaeologists have discovered the remains of sacrificial victims, probably put to death during the dedication of the structure. In the vicinity are the remains of a large market where goods from distant

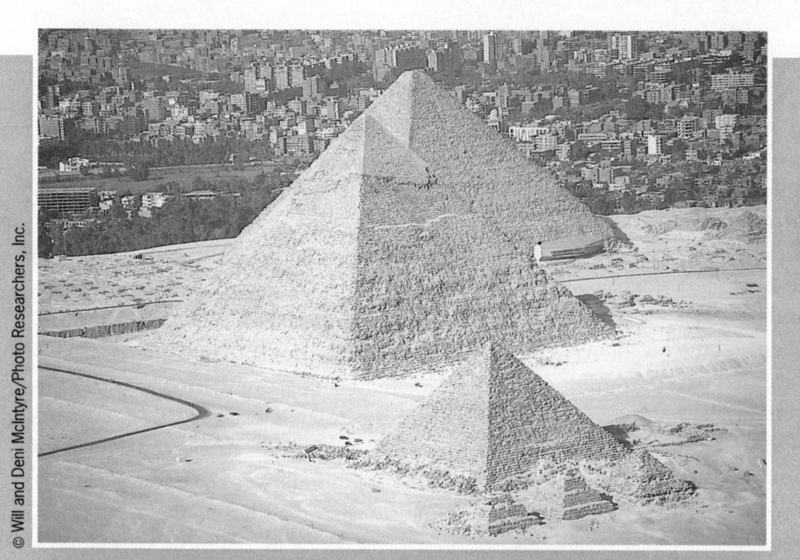

© Will and Deni McIntyre/Photo Researchers, Inc.

© SuperStock

COMPARATIVE ILLUSTRATION

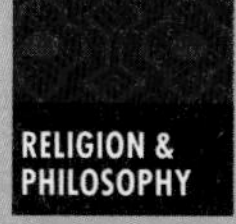

RELIGION & PHILOSOPHY

The Pyramid. The building of monumental structures known as pyramids was characteristic of a number of civilizations that arose in antiquity. The pyramid symbolized the link between the world of human beings and the realm of deities and was often used to house the tomb of a deceased ruler. Shown here are two prominent examples. The upper photo shows the pyramids of Giza, Egypt, built in the third millennium B.C.E. and located near the modern city of Cairo. Shown below is the Pyramid of the Sun at Teotihuacán, erected in central Mexico in the fifth century C.E. Similar structures of various sizes were built throughout the Western Hemisphere. The concept of the pyramid was also widely applied in parts of Asia. Scholars still debate the technical aspects of constructing such pyramids.

How do the pyramids erected in the Western Hemisphere compare with similar structures in other parts of the world? What were their symbolic meanings to the builders?

regions as well as agricultural produce grown by farmers in the vicinity were exchanged. The products traded included cacao, rubber, feathers, and various types of vegetables and meat. Pulque (POOL-kay), a liquor extracted from the agave (uh-GAH-vee) plant, was used in religious ceremonies. An obsidian mine nearby may explain the location of the city; obsidian is a volcanic glass that was prized in Mesoamerica for use in tools, mirrors, and the blades of sacrificial knives.

Most of the city consisted of one-story stucco apartment compounds; some were as large as 35,000 square feet, sufficient to house more than a hundred people. Each apartment was divided into several rooms, and the compounds were covered by flat roofs made of wooden beams, poles, and stucco. The compounds were separated by wide streets laid out on a rectangular grid and were entered through narrow alleys.

Living in the fertile Valley of Mexico, an upland plateau surrounded by magnificent snowcapped mountains, the inhabitants of Teotihuacán probably obtained the bulk of their wealth from agriculture. At that time, the valley floor was filled with swampy lakes containing the water runoff from the surrounding mountains. The combination of fertile soil and adequate water combined to make the valley one of the richest farming areas in Mesoamerica.

Sometime during the eighth century C.E., for unknown reasons, the wealth and power of the city began to decline. The next two centuries were a time of troubles throughout the region as principalities fought over limited farmland. The problem was later compounded when peoples from surrounding areas, attracted by the rich farmlands, migrated into the Valley of Mexico and began to compete for territory with the small city-states already established there. As the local population expanded, farmers began to engage in more intensive agriculture. They drained the lakes to build ***chinampas*** (chee-NAM-pahs), swampy islands crisscrossed by canals that provided water for their crops and easy transportation to local markets for their excess produce.

The Olmecs: Mother Culture or First Among Equals?

What were the relations among these early societies in Mesoamerica? Trade contacts were quite active, as the Olmecs exported rubber to their neighbors in exchange for salt and obsidian. During its heyday, Olmec influence extended throughout the region, leading some historians to surmise that it was a "mother culture," much as the Shang dynasty was once reputed to be in ancient China (see Chapter 3).

A seventh century B.C.E. pyramid recently unearthed in the southern Mexican state of Chiapas (chee-AH-pahs) contained tomb objects that bore some resemblance to counterparts in the Olmec site of La Venta, but also displayed characteristics unique to the Zoque (ZOH-kay) culture that was prevalent in that region at the time. Some scholars point to such indigenous elements to suggest that perhaps the Olmec were merely first among equals. This issue has not yet been resolved.

The Maya

Far to the east of the Valley of Mexico, another major civilization had arisen in what is now the state of Guatemala and the Yucatán peninsula. This was the civilization of the Maya, which was older than and just as sophisticated as the society at Teotihuacán.

ORIGINS It is not known when human beings first inhabited the Yucatán peninsula, but peoples contemporaneous with the Olmecs were already cultivating such crops as corn, yams, and manioc in the area during the first millennium B.C.E. As the population increased, an early civilization began to emerge along the Pacific coast directly to the south of the peninsula and in the highlands of modern Guatemala. Contacts were already established with the Olmecs to the west.

Since the area was a source for cacao trees and obsidian, the inhabitants soon developed relations with other early civilizations in the region. Cacao trees (whose name derives from the Mayan word *kakaw*) were the source of chocolate, which was drunk as a beverage by the upper classes, while cocoa beans, the fruit of the cacao tree, were used as currency in markets throughout the region.

As the population in the area increased, the inhabitants began to migrate into the central Yucatán peninsula and farther to the north. The overcrowding forced farmers in the lowland areas to shift from slash-and-burn cultivation to swamp agriculture of the type practiced in the lake region of the Valley of Mexico. By the middle of the first millennium C.E., the entire area was honeycombed with a patchwork of small city-states competing for land and resources. The largest urban centers such as Tikal (tee-KAHL) may have had 100,000 inhabitants at their height and displayed a level of technological and cultural achievement that was unsurpassed in the region. By the end of the third century C.E., Mayan civilization had begun to enter its classical phase.

POLITICAL STRUCTURES The power of Mayan rulers was impressive. One of the monarchs at Copán (koh-PAHN)—known to scholars as "18 Rabbit" from the hieroglyphs composing his name—ordered the construction of a grand palace requiring more than 30,000 person-days of labor. Around the ruler was a class of aristocrats whose wealth was probably based on the ownership of land farmed by their poorer relatives. Eventually, many of the nobles became priests or scribes at the royal court or adopted honored professions as sculptors or painters. As the society's wealth grew, so did the role of artisans and traders, who began to form a small middle class.

The majority of the population on the peninsula (estimated at roughly 3 million at the height of Mayan prosperity), however, were farmers. They lived on their *chinampa* plots or on terraced hills in the highlands. Houses were built of adobe and thatch and probably resembled the houses of the majority of the population in the area today. There was a fairly clear-cut division of labor along gender lines. The men were responsible for fighting and hunting, the women for homemaking and the preparation of cornmeal, the staple food of much of the population.

Some noblewomen, however, seem to have played important roles in both political and religious life. In the seventh century C.E., for example, Pacal (pa-KAL) became king of Palenque (pah-LEN-kay), one of the most powerful of the Mayan city-states, through the royal line of his mother and grandmother, thereby breaking the patrilineal descent twice. His mother ruled Palenque for three years and was the power behind the throne for her son's first twenty-five years of rule. Pacal legitimized his kingship by transforming his mother into a divine representation of the "first mother" goddess.

Scholars once believed that the Maya were a peaceful people who rarely engaged in violence. Now, however, it is thought that rivalry among Mayan city-states was endemic and often involved bloody clashes. Scenes from paintings and rock carvings depict a society preoccupied with war and the seizure of captives for sacrifice. The conflict mentioned at the beginning of this chapter is but one example. During the seventh century C.E., two powerful city-states, Tikal and Calakmul (kah-lahk-MOOL), competed for dominance throughout the region, setting up puppet regimes and waging bloody wars that wavered back and forth for years but ultimately resulted in the total destruction of Calakmul at the end of the century.

British Museum, London//© The Trustees of The British Museum/Art Resource, NY

A Mayan Bloodletting Ceremony. The Mayan elite drew blood at various ritual ceremonies. Here we see Lady Xok (SHOHK), the wife of a king of Yaxchilán (YAHS-chee-lahn)), passing a rope pierced with thorns along her tongue in a bloodletting ritual. Above her, the king holds a flaming torch. This vivid scene from an eighth-century C.E. palace lintel demonstrates the excellence of Mayan stone sculpture as well as the sophisticated weaving techniques shown in the queen's elegant gown.

MAYAN RELIGION Mayan religion was polytheistic. Although the names were different, Mayan gods shared many of the characteristics of deities of nearby cultures. The supreme god was named Itzámna (eet-SAHM-nuh) ("Lizard House"). Viewed as the creator of all things, he was credited with bringing maize, cacao, medicine, and writing to the Mayan people.

Deities were ranked in order of importance and had human characteristics, as in ancient Greece and India. Some, like the jaguar god of night, were evil rather than good. Some scholars believe that many of the nature deities may have been viewed as manifestations of one supreme godhead (see the box on p. 150). As at Teotihuacán, human sacrifice (normally by decapitation) was practiced to propitiate the heavenly forces.

Mayan cities were built around a ceremonial core dominated by a central pyramid surmounted by a shrine to the gods. Nearby were other temples, palaces, and a sacred ball court. Like many of their modern counterparts, Mayan cities suffered from urban sprawl, with separate suburbs for the poor and the middle class.

The ball court was a rectangular space surrounded by vertical walls with metal rings through which the contestants attempted to drive a hard rubber ball. Although the rules of the game are only imperfectly understood, it apparently had religious significance, and the vanquished players were sacrificed in ceremonies held after the close of the game. Most of the players were men, although there may have been some women's teams. Similar courts have been found at sites throughout Central and South America, with the earliest, located near Veracruz, dating back to around 1500 B.C.E.

MAYAN HIEROGLYPHS AND CALENDARS The Mayan writing system, developed during the mid-first millennium B.C.E., was based on hieroglyphs that remained undeciphered until scholars recognized that symbols appearing in many passages represented dates in the Mayan calendar (see the box on p. 151). This elaborate calendar, which measures time back to a particular date in August 3114 B.C.E., required a sophisticated understanding of astronomical events and mathematics to compile. Starting with these known symbols as a foundation, modern scholars have gradually deciphered the script. Like the scripts of the Sumerians and ancient Egyptians, the Mayan hieroglyphs were both ideographic and phonetic and were becoming more phonetic as time passed.

The responsibility for compiling official records in the Mayan city-states was given to a class of scribes, who wrote on deerskin or strips of tree bark. Unfortunately, virtually all such records have fallen victim to the ravages of a humid climate or were deliberately destroyed by Spanish missionaries after their arrival in the sixteenth century. As one Spanish bishop remarked at the time, "We found a large number of books in these characters and, as they contained nothing in which there were not to be seen superstition and lies of the devil, we burned

The Creation of the World: A Mayan View

RELIGION & PHILOSOPHY

Popul Vuh (puh-PUL VOO), a sacred work of the ancient Maya, is an account of Mayan history and religious beliefs. No written version in the original Mayan script is extant, but shortly after the Spanish conquest, it was written down, apparently from memory, in Quiché (kee-CHAY) (the spoken language of the Maya), using the Latin script. This version was later translated into Spanish. The following excerpt from the opening lines of Popul Vuh recounts the Mayan myth of the creation.

Popul Vuh: The Sacred Book of the Maya

This is the account of how all was in suspense, all calm, in silence; all motionless, still, and the expanse of the sky was empty.

This is the first account, the first narrative. There was neither man, nor animal, birds, fishes, crabs, trees, stones, caves, ravines, grasses, nor forests; there was only the sky.

The surface of the earth had not appeared. There was only the calm sea and the great expanse of the sky.

There was nothing brought together, nothing which could make a noise, nor anything which might move, or tremble, or could make noise in the sky.

There was nothing standing; only the calm water, the placid sea, alone and tranquil. Nothing existed.

There was only immobility and silence in the darkness, in the night. Only the Creator, the Maker, Tepeu, Gucumatz, the Forefathers, were in the water surrounded with light. They were hidden under green and blue feathers, and were therefore called Gucumatz. By nature they were great sages and great thinkers. In this manner the sky existed and also the Heart of Heaven, which is the name of God and thus He is called.

Then came the word. Tepeu and Gucumatz came together in the darkness, in the night, and Tepeu and Gucumatz talked together. They talked then, discussing and deliberating; they agreed, they united their words and their thoughts.

Then while they meditated, it became clear to them that when dawn would break, man must appear. Then they planned the creation, and the growth of the trees and the thickets and the birth of life and the creation of man. Thus it was arranged in the darkness and in the night by the Heart of Heaven who is called Huracan.

The first is called Caculha Huracan. The second is Chipi-Caculha. The third is Raxa-Caculha. And these three are the Heart of Heaven.

So it was that they made perfect the work, when they did it after thinking and meditating upon it.

What similarities and differences do you see between this account of the beginning of the world and those of other ancient civilizations?

Source: From Popul-Vuhl *The Sacred Book of the Ancient Quiche Maya*, translated by Adrian Recinos. Copyright © 1950 by the University of Oklahoma Press.

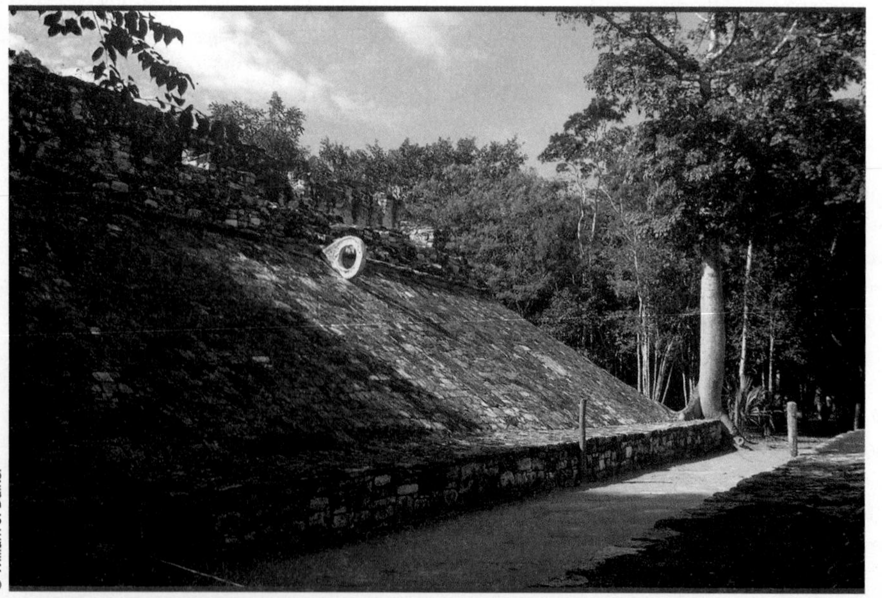

© William J. Duiker

A Ball Court. Throughout Mesoamerica, a dangerous game was played on ball courts such as this one. A large ball of solid rubber was propelled from the hip at such tremendous speed that players had to wear extensive padding. More than an athletic contest, the game had religious significance. The court is thought to have represented the cosmos and the ball the sun, and the losers were sacrificed to the gods in postgame ceremonies. The game is still played today in parts of Mexico (without the sacrifice, of course). Shown here is a well-preserved ball court at the Mayan site of Coba, in the Yucatán peninsula.

A Sample of Mayan Writing

The Maya were the only Mesoamerican people to devise a complete written language. Although the origins of the Mayan writing system are unknown, many specialists believe that it may have emerged from scripts invented earlier by the neighboring Zapotecs or Olmecs and that the Maya learned of these experiments through contacts with these peoples in the first millennium B.C.E.

Like the Sumerian and Egyptian scripts, the Mayan system was composed of a mixture of ideographs and phonetic symbols, which were written in double columns to be read from left to right and top to bottom. The language was rudimentary in many ways. It had few adjectives or adverbs, and the numbering system used only three symbols: a shell for zero, a dot for one, and a bar for five.

During the classical era from 300 to 900 C.E., the Maya used the script to record dynastic statistics with deliberate precision, listing the date of the ruler's birth, his accession to power, and his marriage and death while highlighting victories in battle, the capture of prisoners, and ritual ceremonies. The symbols were carved on stone panels, stelae, and funerary urns or were painted with a brush on folding-screen books made of bark paper; only four of these books from the late period remain extant today. A sample of Mayan hieroglyphs is shown below.

How do Mayan glyphs compare with the early forms of writing in Egypt, China, and Mesopotamia? Consider purpose, ease of writing, and potential for development into a purely phonetic system.

"birth of . . ."
"death of . . ."
warfare
bloodletting rite
"accession of . . ."
chucah "he captured . . ."
"captor of . . ."

From Atlas of Ancient America by Michael Coe, Dean Snow and Elizabeth Benson/Courtesy Andromeda Oxford Limited, Oxford, England

them all, which they regretted to an amazing degree, and which caused them much affliction."[1]

As a result, almost the only surviving written records dating from the classical Mayan era are those that were carved in stone. One of the most important repositories of Mayan hieroglyphs is at Palenque, an archaeological site deep in the jungles in the neck of the Mexican peninsula, considerably to the west of the Yucatán (see Map 6.2). In a chamber located under the Temple of Inscriptions, archaeologists discovered a royal tomb and a massive limestone slab covered with hieroglyphs. By deciphering the message on the slab, archaeologists for the first time identified a historical figure in Mayan history. He was the ruler named Pacal, known from his glyph as "The Shield"; Pacal ordered the construction of the Temple of Inscriptions in the mid-seventh century, and it was his body that was buried in the tomb at the foot of the staircase leading down into the crypt.

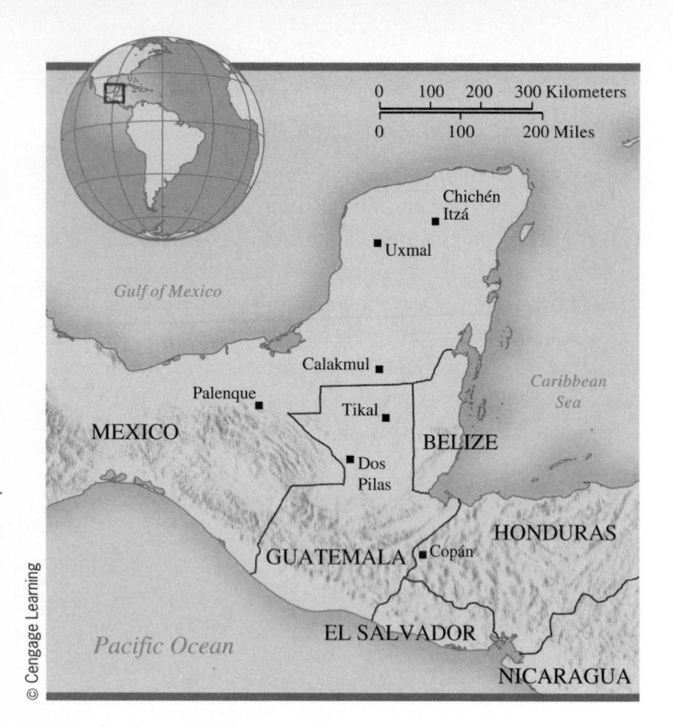

© Cengage Learning

MAP 6.2 The Maya Heartland. During the classical era, Mayan civilization was centered on modern-day Guatemala and the lower Yucatán peninsula. After the ninth century, new centers of power like Chichén Itzá and Uxmal began to emerge farther north.

Q *What factors appear to have brought an end to classical Mayan civilization?*

As befits their intense interest in the passage of time, the Maya also had a sophisticated knowledge of astronomy and kept voluminous records of the movements of the heavenly bodies. There were practical reasons for their concern. The arrival of the planet Venus in the evening sky, for example, was a traditional time to prepare for war. The Maya also devised the so-called Long Count, a system of calculating time based on a lunar calendar that calls for the end of the current cycle of 5,200 years in the year 2012 of the Western solar-based Gregorian calendar.

THE MYSTERY OF MAYAN DECLINE Sometime in the eighth or ninth century, the classical Mayan civilization in the central Yucatán peninsula began to decline. At Copán, for example, it ended abruptly in 822 C.E., when work on various stone sculptures ordered by the ruler suddenly ceased. The end of Palenque soon followed, and the city of Tikal was abandoned by 870 C.E. Whether the decline was caused by overuse of the land, incessant warfare, internal revolt, or a natural disaster such as a volcanic eruption is a question that has puzzled archaeologists for decades. Recent evidence supports the theory that overcultivation of the land due to a growing population gradually reduced crop yields. A long drought, which lasted throughout most of the ninth and tenth centuries C.E., may have played a major role, although the city-state of Tikal, blessed with fertile soil and the presence of nearby Lake Peten, did not appear to suffer from a lack of water. In general, though, as arable land and water became increasingly scarce, conflict among the various mini-states in the region may have intensified, accelerating the process leading to a final collapse.

Whatever the case, cities like Tikal and Palenque were abandoned to the jungles. In their place, newer urban

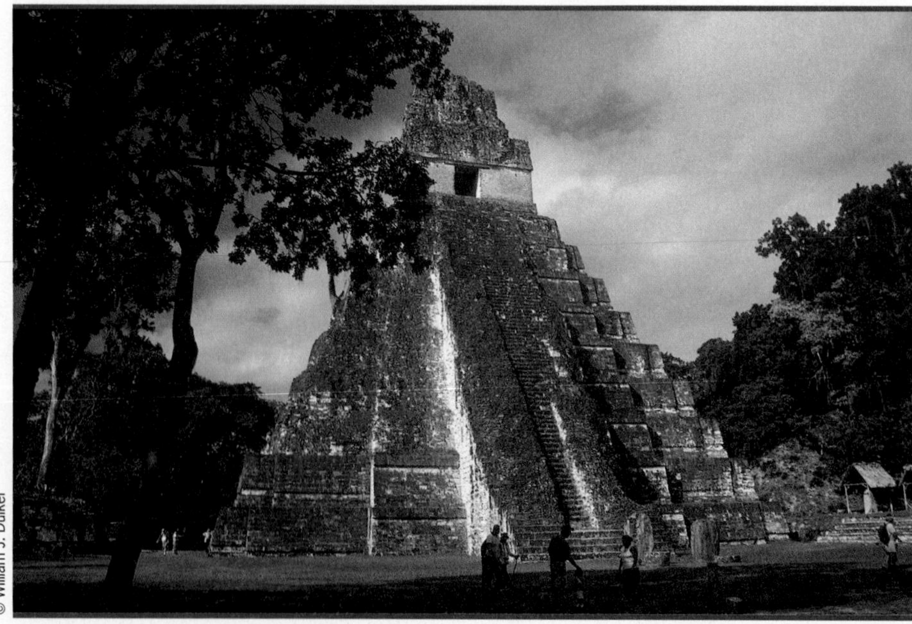

© William J. Duiker

Mayan Temple at Tikal. This eighth-century temple, peering over the treetops of a jungle at Tikal, represents the zenith of the engineering and artistry of the Mayan peoples. Erected to house the body of a ruler, such pyramidal tombs contained elaborate pieces of jade jewelry, polychrome ceramics, and intricate bone carvings depicting the ruler's life and various deities. This temple dominates a great plaza that is surrounded by a royal palace and various religious structures. With one of the steepest staircases in all of Mesoamerica, the ascent is not for the faint of heart.

centers in the northern part of the peninsula, like Uxmal (oosh-MAHL) and Chichén Itzá (chee-CHEN eet-SAH), continued to prosper, although the level of cultural achievement in this postclassical era did not match that of previous years. According to local history, this latter area was taken over by peoples known as the Toltecs (TOHL-teks), led by a man known as Kukulcan (koo-kul-KAHN)), who migrated to the peninsula from Teotihuacán in central Mexico sometime in the tenth century. Some scholars believe this flight was associated with the legend of the departure from that city of Quetzalcoatl (KWET-sul-koh-AHT-ul), a deity in the form of a feathered serpent who promised that he would someday return to reclaim his homeland.

The Toltecs apparently controlled the upper peninsula from their capital at Chichén Itzá for several centuries, but this area was less fertile and more susceptible to drought than the earlier regions of Mayan settlement, and eventually they too declined. By the early sixteenth century, the area was divided into a number of small principalities, and the cities, including Uxmal and Chichén Itzá, had been abandoned.

The Aztecs

Among the groups moving into the Valley of Mexico after the fall of Teotihuacán were the Mexica (meh-SHEE-kuh). No one knows their origins, although folk legend held that their original homeland was an island in a lake called Aztlán (az-TLAHN). From that legendary homeland comes the name *Aztec*, by which they are known to the modern world. Sometime during the early twelfth century, the Aztecs left their original habitat and, carrying an image of their patron deity, Huitzilopochtli (WEET-see-loh-POHSHT-lee), began a lengthy migration that climaxed with their arrival in the Valley of Mexico sometime late in the century.

Less sophisticated than many of their neighbors, the Aztecs were at first forced to seek alliances with stronger city-states. They were excellent warriors, however, and (like Sparta in ancient Greece and the state of Qin in Zhou dynasty China) soon used their prowess to become the leading city-state in the lake region. Establishing their capital at Tenochtitlán (teh-nahch-teet-LAHN), on an island in the middle of Lake Texcoco (tess-KOH-koh), they set out to bring the entire region under their domination (see Map 6.3).

For the remainder of the fifteenth century, the Aztecs consolidated their control over much of what is modern Mexico, from the Atlantic to the Pacific Ocean and as far south as the Guatemalan border. The new kingdom was not a centralized state but a collection of semiautonomous territories. To provide a unifying focus for the kingdom, the Aztecs promoted their patron god, Huitzilopochtli, as the guiding deity of the entire population, which now numbered several million.

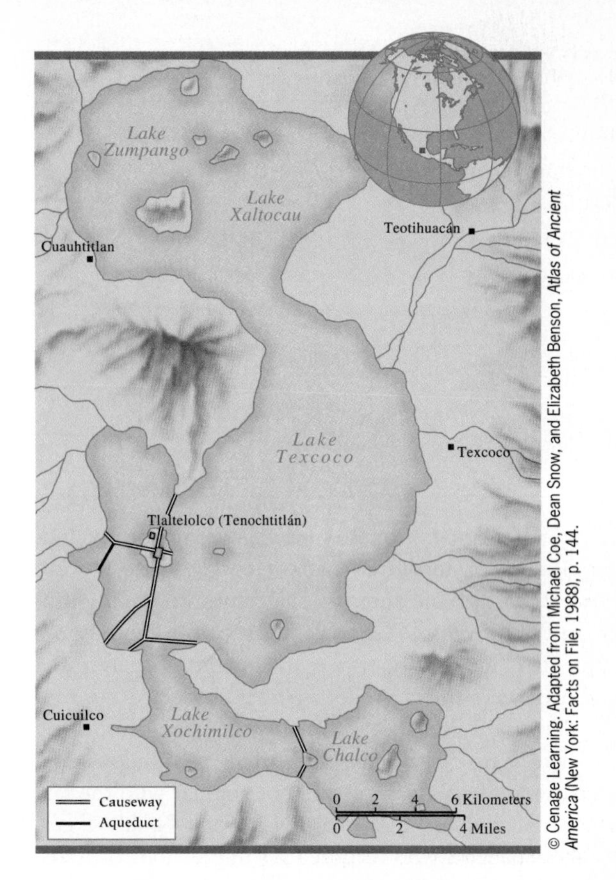

© Cengage Learning. Adapted from Michael Coe, Dean Snow, and Elizabeth Benson, *Atlas of Ancient America* (New York: Facts on File, 1988), p. 144.

MAP 6.3 The Valley of Mexico Under Aztec Rule. The Aztecs were one of the most advanced peoples in pre-Columbian Central America. The capital at Tenochtitlán—Tlaltelolco (tuh-lahl-teh-LOH-koh—was located at the site of modern-day Mexico City. Of the five lakes shown here, only Lake Texcoco remains today.

What was the significance of Tenochtitlán's location?

POLITICS Like all great empires in ancient times, the Aztec state was authoritarian. Power was vested in the monarch, whose authority had both a divine and a secular character. The Aztec ruler claimed descent from the gods and served as an intermediary between the material and the metaphysical worlds. Unlike many of his counterparts in other ancient civilizations, however, the monarch did not obtain his position by a rigid law of succession. On the death of the ruler, his successor was selected from within the royal family by a small group of senior officials, who were also members of the family and were therefore eligible for the position. Once placed on the throne, the Aztec ruler was advised by a small council of lords, headed by a prime minister who served as the chief executive of the government, and a bureaucracy. Beyond

CHRONOLOGY Early Mesoamerica	
Arrival of human beings in America	At least 15,000 years ago
Agriculture first practiced	c. 8000 B.C.E.
Rise of Olmec culture	c. 1200 B.C.E.
End of Olmec era	c. 400 B.C.E.
Teotihuacán civilization	c. 300 B.C.E.–800 C.E.
Origins of Mayan civilization	First millennium C.E.
Classical era of Mayan culture	300–900 C.E.
Tikal abandoned	870 C.E.
Migration of Mexica to Valley of Mexico	Late 1100s
Kingdom of the Aztecs	1300s–1400s

the capital, the power of the central government was limited. Rulers of territories subject to the Aztecs were allowed considerable autonomy in return for paying tribute, in the form of goods or captives, to the central government. The most important government officials in the provinces were the tax collectors, who collected the tribute. They used the threat of military action against those who failed to carry out their tribute obligations and therefore, understandably, were not popular with the taxpayers. According to Bernal Díaz (bair-NALL DEE-ahth), a Spaniard who recorded his impressions of Aztec society during a visit in the early sixteenth century:

> All these towns complained about Montezuma and his tax collectors, speaking in private so that the Mexican ambassadors should not hear them, however. They said these officials robbed them of all they possessed, and that if their wives and daughters were pretty they would violate them in front of their fathers and husbands and carry them away. They also said that the Mexicans [that is, the representatives from the capital] made the men work like slaves, compelling them to carry pine trunks and stone and firewood and maize overland and in canoes, and to perform other tasks, such as planting maize fields, and that they took away the people's lands as well for the service of their idols.[2]

SOCIAL STRUCTURES Positions in the government bureaucracy were the exclusive privilege of the hereditary nobility, all of whom traced their lineage to the founding family of the Aztec clan. Male children in noble families were sent to temple schools, where they were exposed to a harsh regimen of manual labor, military training, and memorization of information about Aztec society and religion. On reaching adulthood, they would select a career in the military service, the government bureaucracy, or the priesthood.

The remainder of the population consisted of commoners, indentured workers, and slaves. Most indentured workers were landless laborers who contracted to work on the nobles' estates, while slaves served in the households of the wealthy. Slavery was not an inherited status, and the children of slaves were considered free citizens.

The vast majority of the population were commoners. All commoners were members of large kinship groups called ***calpullis*** (kal-PUL-eez). Each *calpulli*, often consisting of as many as a thousand members, was headed by an elected chief, who ran its day-to-day affairs and served as an intermediary with the central government. Each *calpulli* was responsible for providing taxes (usually in the form of goods) and conscript labor to the state.

Each *calpulli* maintained its own temples and schools and administered the land held by the community. Farmland within the *calpulli* was held in common and could not be sold, although it could be inherited within the family. In the cities, each *calpulli* occupied a separate neighborhood, where its members often performed a particular function, such as metalworking, stonecutting, weaving, carpentry, or commerce. Apparently, a large proportion of the population engaged in some form of trade, at least in the densely populated Valley of Mexico, where an estimated half of the people lived in an urban environment. Many farmers brought their goods to the markets via the canals and sold them directly to retailers (see the box on p. 155).

Gender roles within the family were rigidly stratified. Male children were trained for war and were expected to serve in the army on reaching adulthood. Women were expected to work in the home, weave textiles, and raise children, although like their brothers they were permitted to enter the priesthood. As in most traditional societies, chastity and obedience were desirable female characteristics. Although women in Aztec society enjoyed more legal rights than women in some traditional Old World civilizations, they were still not equal to men. Women were permitted to own and inherit property and to enter into contracts. Marriage was usually monogamous, although noble families sometimes practiced **polygyny** (the state or practice of having more than one wife at a time). As in most societies at the time, parents usually selected their child's spouse, often for purposes of political or social advancement.

Classes in Aztec society were rigidly stratified. Commoners were not permitted to enter the nobility, although some occasionally rose to senior positions in the army or the priesthood as the result of exemplary service. As in medieval Europe, such occupations often provided a route of upward mobility for ambitious commoners. A woman of noble standing would sometimes marry a commoner because the children of such a union would inherit her higher status, and she could expect to be treated better by her husband's family, who would be proud of the marriage relationship.

Markets and Merchandise in Aztec Mexico

One of our most valuable descriptions of Aztec civilization is *The Conquest of New Spain*, written by Bernal Díaz, a Spaniard who visited Mexico in 1519. In the following passage, Díaz describes the great market at Tenochtitlán.

Bernal Díaz, *The Conquest of New Spain*

Let us begin with the dealers in gold, silver, and precious stones, feathers, cloaks, and embroidered goods, and male and female slaves who are also sold there. They bring as many slaves to be sold in that market as the Portuguese bring Negroes from Guinea. Some are brought there attached to long poles by means of collars round their necks to prevent them from escaping, but others are left loose. Next there were those who sold coarser cloth, and cotton goods and fabrics made of twisted thread, and there were chocolate merchants with their chocolate. In this way you could see every kind of merchandise to be found anywhere in New Spain, laid out in the same way as goods are laid out in my own district of Medina del Campo, a center for fairs, where each line of stalls has its own particular sort. So it was in this great market. There were those who sold sisal cloth and ropes and the sandals they wear on their feet, which are made from the same plant. All these were kept in one part of the market, in the place assigned to them, and in another part were skins of tigers and lions, otters, jackals, and deer, badgers, mountain cats, and other wild animals, some tanned and some untanned, and other classes of merchandise.

There were sellers of kidney beans and sage and other vegetables and herbs in another place, and in yet another they were selling fowls, and birds with great dewlaps, also rabbits, hares, deer, young ducks, little dogs, and other such creatures. Then there were the fruiterers; and the women who sold cooked food, flour and honey cake, and tripe, had their part of the market. Then came pottery of all kinds, from big water jars to little jugs, displayed in its own place, also honey, honey paste, and other sweets like nougat. Elsewhere they sold timber too, boards, cradles, beams, blocks, and benches, all in a quarter of their own.

Then there were the sellers of pitch pine for torches, and other things of that kind, and I must also mention, with all apologies, that they sold many canoe loads of human excrement, which they kept in the creeks near the market. This was for the manufacture of salt and the curing of skins, which they say cannot be done without it. I know that many gentlemen will laugh at this, but I assure them it is true. I may add that on all the roads they have shelters made of reeds or straw or grass so that they can retire when they wish to do so, and purge their bowels unseen by passersby, and also in order that their excrement shall not be lost.

Which of the items offered for sale in this account might also have been available in a market in Asia, Africa, or Europe? What types of goods mentioned here appear to be unique to the Americas?

Source: From *The Conquest of New Spain* by Bernal Diaz. Copyright © 1975. (Harmondsworth: Penguin), pp. 232–233.

LAND OF THE FEATHERED SERPENT: AZTEC RELIGION AND CULTURE The Aztecs, like their contemporaries throughout Mesoamerica, lived in an environment populated by a multitude of gods. Scholars have identified more than a hundred deities in the Aztec pantheon; some of them were nature spirits, like the rain god, Tlaloc (tuh-lah-LOHK), and some were patron deities, like the symbol of the Aztecs themselves, Huitzilopochtli. A supreme deity, called Ometeotl (oh-met-tee-AH-tul), represented the all-powerful and omnipresent forces of the heavens, but he was rather remote, and other gods, notably the feathered serpent Quetzalcoatl, had a more direct impact on the lives of the people. Representing the forces of creation, virtue, and learning and culture, Quetzalcoatl bears a distinct similarity to Shiva in Hindu belief. According to Aztec tradition, this godlike being had left his homeland in the Valley of Mexico in the tenth century, promising to return in triumph (see "The Mystery of Mayan Decline" earlier in this chapter).

Aztec cosmology was based on a belief in the existence of two worlds, the material and the divine. The earth was the material world and took the form of a flat

© William J. Duiker

Quetzalcoatl. Quetzalcoatl was one of the favorite deities of the Central American peoples. His visage of a plumed serpent, as shown here, was prominent in the royal capital of Teotihuacán. According to legend, Quetzalcoatl, the leader of the Toltecs, was tricked into drunkenness and humiliated by a rival god. In disgrace, he left his homeland but promised to return. In 1519, the Aztec monarch Moctezuma welcomed Hernán Cortés, the leader of the Spanish expedition, believing that he was a representative of Quetzalcoatl.

disk surrounded by water on all sides. The divine world, which consisted of both heaven and hell, was the abode of the gods. Human beings could aspire to a form of heavenly salvation but first had to pass through a transitional stage, somewhat like Christian purgatory, before reaching their final destination, where the soul was finally freed from the body. To prepare for the final day of judgment, as well as to help them engage in proper behavior through life, all citizens underwent religious training at temple schools during adolescence and took part in various rituals throughout their lives. The most devout were encouraged to study for the priesthood. Once accepted, they served at temples ranging from local branches at the *calpulli* level to the highest shrines in the ceremonial precinct at Tenochtitlán. In some respects, however, Aztec society may have been undergoing a process of secularization. By late Aztec times, athletic contests at the ball court had apparently lost some of their religious significance. Gambling was increasingly common, and wagering over the results of the matches was widespread. One province reportedly sent 16,000 rubber balls to the capital city of Tenochtitlán as its annual tribute to the royal court.

Aztec religion contained a distinct element of fatalism that was inherent in the creation myth, which described an unceasing struggle between the forces of good and evil throughout the universe. This struggle had led to the creation and destruction of four worlds, or suns. The world was now living in the time of the fifth sun. But that world, too, was destined to end with the destruction of this earth and all that is within it:

> *Even jade is shattered,*
> *Even gold is crushed,*
> *Even quetzal plumes are torn. . . .*
> *One does not live forever on this earth:*
> *We endure only for an instant!*[3]

In an effort to postpone the day of reckoning, the Aztecs practiced human sacrifice. The Aztecs believed that by appeasing the sun god, Huitzilopochtli, with sacrifices, they could delay the final destruction of their world. Victims were prepared for the ceremony through elaborate rituals and then brought to the holy shrine, where their hearts were ripped out of their chests and presented to the gods as a holy offering. It was an honor to be chosen for sacrifice, and captives were often used as sacrificial victims because they represented valor, the trait the Aztecs prized most.

Like the art of the Olmecs, most Aztec architecture, art, and sculpture had religious significance. At the center of the capital city of Tenochtitlán was the sacred precinct, dominated by the massive pyramid dedicated to Huitzilopochtli and the rain god, Tlaloc. According to Bernal Díaz, at its base the pyramid was equal to the plots of six large European town houses and tapered from there to the top, which was surmounted by a platform containing shrines to the gods and an altar for performing human sacrifices. The entire pyramid was covered with brightly colored paintings and sculptures.

Although little Aztec painting survives, it was evidently of high quality. Bernal Díaz compared the best work with that of Michelangelo. Artisans worked with stone and with soft metals such as gold and silver, which they cast using the lost-wax technique. They did not have the knowledge for making implements in bronze or iron, however. Stoneworking consisted primarily of representations of the gods and bas-reliefs depicting religious ceremonies. Among the most famous is the massive disk called the Stone of the Fifth Sun, carved for use at the central pyramid at Tenochtitlán.

The Aztecs had devised a form of writing based on hieroglyphs that represented an object or a concept. The symbols had no phonetic significance and did not constitute a writing system as such but could give the sense of a message and were probably used by civilian or religious officials as notes or memorandums for their orations. A trained class of scribes carefully painted the notes on paper made from the inner bark of fig trees. Unfortunately, many of these notes were destroyed by the Spaniards as part of their effort to eradicate all aspects of Aztec religion and culture.

The First Civilizations in South America

FOCUS QUESTION: What role did the environment play in the evolution of societies in South America?

South America is a vast continent, characterized by extremes in climate and geography. The north is dominated by the mighty Amazon River, which flows through dense tropical rain forests carrying the largest flow of water of any river system in the world (see Map 6.4). Farther to the south, the forests are replaced by prairies and steppes stretching westward to the Andes Mountains, which extend the entire length of the continent, from the Isthmus of Panama to the Strait of Magellan. Along the Pacific coast, on the western slopes of the mountains, are some of the driest desert regions in the world.

South America has been inhabited by human beings for more than 12,000 years. Wall paintings discovered at the "cavern of the painted rock" in the Amazon region suggest that Stone Age peoples were living in the area at least 11,000 years ago. Early peoples were hunters, fishers, and food gatherers, but there are indications that irrigated farming was practiced in the northern fringe of the Andes Mountains as early as 2000 B.C.E. Other farming communities of similar age have been discovered in the Amazon River valley and on the western slopes of the Andes, where evidence of terraced agriculture dates back about 5,000 years.

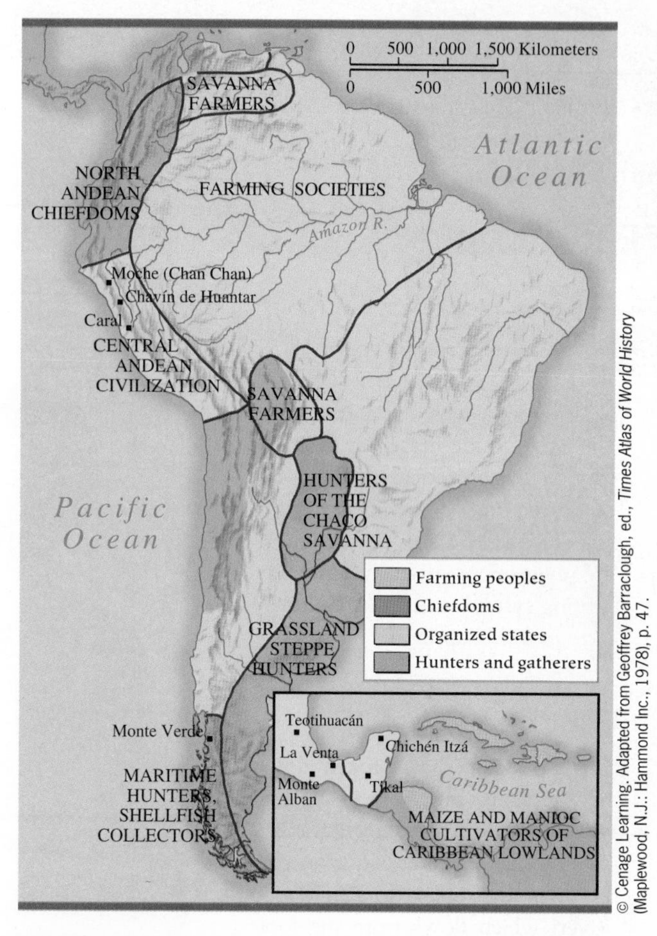

© Cenage Learning. Adapted from Geoffrey Barraclough, ed., Times Atlas of World History (Maplewood, N.J.: Hammond Inc., 1978), p. 47.

MAP 6.4 Early Peoples and Cultures of Central and South America. This map shows regions of early human settlements in Central and South America. Urban conglomerations appear in Mesoamerica (see inset) and along the western coast of South America.

Why do you think urban centers appeared in these areas?

Caral

By the third millennium B.C.E., complex societies had begun to emerge in the coastal regions of modern-day Peru and Ecuador. Some settlements were located along the coast, but the remnants of farming communities watered by canals have also been found in the valleys of the rivers flowing down from the Andes Mountains. Fish and agricultural products were traded to inland peoples for wool and salt.

By 3500 B.C.E.—a thousand years earlier than the earliest known cities in Mesoamerica—the first urban settlements appeared in the region. At Caral, a highly publicized site located 14 miles inland from the coast, the remnants of a 4,500-year-old city sit on the crest of a 60-foot-high pyramid. The inhabitants engaged in farming, growing squash, beans, and tomatoes, but also provided cotton to fishing communities along the coast, who used it to make fishnets. Land was divided in a manner similar to the well-field system in ancient China (see Chapter 3).

This culture reached its height during the first millennium B.C.E. with the emergence of the Chavín style, named for an inland site near the modern city of Chavín de Huantar (chah-VEEN day HWAHN-tahr). The ceremonial precinct at the site contained an impressive stone temple complete with interior galleries, a stone-block ceiling, and a system of underground canals that probably channeled water into the temple complex for ceremonial purposes. The structure was surrounded by stone figures depicting various deities and two pyramids. Evidence of metallurgy has also been found, with objects made of copper and gold. Another impressive technological

CHRONOLOGY **Early South America**	
First human settlements in South America	10,500 B.C.E.
Agriculture first practiced	c. 3200 B.C.E.
Founding of Caral	c. 2500 B.C.E.
Chavín style	First millennium B.C.E.
Moche civilization	c. 150–800 C.E.
Wari culture	c. 500–1000 C.E.
Civilization of Chimor	c. 1100–1450
Inka takeover in central Andes	1400s

achievement was the building in 300 B.C.E. of the first solar observatory in the Americas in the form of thirteen stone towers on a hillside north of Lima, Peru. There are even signs of a rudimentary writing system (see "Inka Culture" later in this chapter).

Moche

Chavín society had broken down by 200 B.C.E., but early in the first millennium C.E., another advanced civilization appeared in northern Peru, in the valley of the Moche River, which flows from the foothills of the Andes into the Pacific Ocean. It occupied an area of more than 2,500 square miles, and its capital city, large enough to contain more than 10,000 people, was dominated by two massive adobe pyramids standing as high as 100 feet. The smaller structure, known as the Pyramid of the Moon, covered a total of 15 acres and was adorned with painted murals depicting battles, ritual sacrifices, and various local deities.

Artifacts found at Moche (moh-CHAY), especially the metalwork and stone and ceramic figures, exhibit a high quality of artisanship. They were imitated at river valley sites throughout the surrounding area, which suggests that the authority of the Moche rulers may have extended as far as 400 miles along the coast. The artifacts also indicate that the people at Moche, like those in Central America, were preoccupied with warfare. Paintings and pottery as well as other artifacts in stone, metal, and ceramics frequently portray warriors, prisoners, and sacrificial victims. The Moche were also fascinated by the heavens, and much of their art consisted of celestial symbols and astronomical constellations.

© William J. Duiker

A Mind-Changing Experience. For thousands of years, peoples living in the Andes Mountains have chewed the leaf of the coca plant to relieve hunger, restore energy, and cure bodily ailments. At ceremonies held in local temples throughout the region, shamans often engaged in this practice to communicate with the spirits or with the ancestors of their constituents. This terra-cotta object, dating from the first millennium C.E. and unearthed in present-day Ecuador, shows a user entering a trance and having an "out-of-body" experience, as his alter ego emerges full-blown from the top of his head. The concentrated paste of the coca plant is used today in the manufacture of cocaine.

ENVIRONMENTAL PROBLEMS The Moche River valley is extremely arid, normally receiving less than an inch of rain annually. The peoples in the area compensated by building a sophisticated irrigation system to carry water from the river to the parched fields. At its zenith, Moche culture was spectacular. By the eighth century C.E., however, the civilization was in a state of collapse, the irrigation canals had been abandoned, and the remaining population had left the area and moved farther inland or suffered from severe malnutrition.

What had happened to bring Moche culture to this untimely end? Archaeologists speculate that environmental disruptions, perhaps brought on by changes in the temperature of the Pacific Ocean known as **El Niño**, led to alternating periods of drought and flooding of coastal regions, which caused the irrigated fields to silt up (see the comparative essay "History and the Environment" on p. 159). The warm water created by El Niño conditions also killed local marine life, severely damaging the local fishing industry.

Wari and Chimor

A few hundred miles to the south of Moche, a people known as the Wari (WAH-ree) culture began to expand from their former home in the Andes foothills and established communities along the coast in the vicinity of modern Lima, Peru. As the state of Moche declined, the Wari gradually spread northward in the eighth century and began to occupy many of the urban sites in the Moche valley. According to some scholars, they may even have made use of the Moche's sacred buildings

COMPARATIVE ESSAY

History and the Environment

In *The Decline and Fall of the Roman Empire,* published in 1788, the British historian Edward Gibbon raised a question that has fascinated historians ever since: What brought about the collapse of that once-powerful civilization that dominated the Mediterranean region for more than five centuries? Traditional explanations have centered on political or cultural factors, such as imperial overreach, moral decay, military weakness, or the impact of invasions. Recently, however, some historians have suggested that environmental factors, such as poisoning due to the use of lead water pipes and cups, the spread of malaria, or a lengthy drought in wheat-growing regions in North Africa, may have been at least contributory causes.

The current interest in the impact of the environment on the Roman Empire reflects a growing awareness among historians that environmental conditions may have been a key factor in the fate of several of the great societies in the ancient world. Climatic changes or natural disasters almost certainly led to the decline and collapse of civilization in the Indus River valley. In the Americas, massive flooding brought about by the El Niño effect (environmental conditions triggered by changes in water temperature in the Pacific Ocean) appears to be one possible cause for the collapse of the Moche civilization in what today is Peru, while drought and overcultivation of the land are often cited as reasons for the decline of the Maya in Mesoamerica.

Climatic changes continued to affect the fate of nations and peoples after the end of the ancient era. Drought and overuse of the land may have led to the gradual decline of Mesopotamia as a focal point of advanced civilization in the Middle East, while soil erosion and colder temperatures doomed an early attempt by the Vikings to establish a foothold in Greenland and North America. Sometimes the problems were self-inflicted, as on Easter Island, a remote outpost in the Pacific Ocean, where Polynesian settlers migrating from the west about 900 C.E. so denuded the landscape that by the fifteenth century, what had been a reasonably stable and peaceful society had descended into civil war and cannibalism.

Climatic changes, of course, have not always been detrimental to the health and prosperity of human beings. A warming trend that took place at the end of the last ice age eventually made much of the world more habitable for farming peoples about 10,000 years ago. The effects of El Niño may be beneficial to people living in some areas and disastrous for others. But human misuse of land and water resources is always dangerous to settled societies, especially those living in fragile environments.

Many ancient civilizations throughout the world were weakened or destroyed by changes taking place in the environment. Could some of these effects have been prevented by human action? If so, where and how?

© William J. Duiker

The Pyramid of the Sun at Moche

and appropriated their religious symbolism. In the process, the Wari created the most extensive land empire yet seen in South America. In the end, however, they too succumbed to the challenge posed by unstable environmental conditions.

Around 1100, a new power, the kingdom of Chimor (chee-MAWR), with its capital at Chan Chan (CHAHN CHAHN), at the mouth of the Moche River, emerged in the area. Built almost entirely of adobe, Chan Chan housed an estimated 30,000 residents in an area of more than 12 square miles that included a number of palace compounds surrounded by walls nearly 30 feet high. One compound contained an intricate labyrinth that wound its way progressively inward until it ended in a central chamber, probably occupied by the ruler. Like the Moche before them, the people of Chimor relied on irrigation to funnel the water from the river into their fields. An elaborate system of canals brought the water through hundreds of miles of hilly terrain to the fields near the coast. Nevertheless, by the fifteenth century, Chimor, too, had disappeared, a victim of floods and a series of earthquakes that destroyed the intricate irrigation system that had been the basis of its survival.

These early civilizations in the Andes were by no means isolated from other societies in the region. As early as 2000 B.C.E., local peoples had been venturing into the Pacific Ocean on wind-powered rafts constructed of balsa wood. By the late first millennium C.E., seafarers from the coast of Ecuador had established a vast trading network that extended southward to central Peru and as far north as western Mexico, more than 2,000 miles away. Items transported included jewelry, beads, and metal goods. In all likelihood, technological exchanges were an important by-product of the relationship.

Transportation by land, however, was more difficult. Although roads were constructed to facilitate communication between communities, the forbidding character of the terrain in the mountains was a serious obstacle, and the only draft animal on the entire continent was the llama, which is considerably less hardy than the cattle, horses, and water buffalo used in much of Asia. Such problems undoubtedly hampered the development of regular contacts with distant societies in the Americas, as well as the exchange of goods and ideas that had lubricated the rise of civilizations from China to the Mediterranean Sea.

The Inka

The Chimor kingdom was eventually succeeded in the late fifteenth century by an invading force from the mountains far to the south. In the late fourteenth century, the Inka were a small community in the area of Cuzco (KOOS-koh), a city located at an altitude of 10,000 feet in the mountains of southern Peru. In the 1440s, however, under the leadership of their powerful ruler Pachakuti (pah-chah-KOO-tee) (sometimes called Pachacutec, or "he who transforms the world"), the Inka peoples launched a campaign of conquest that eventually brought the entire region under their authority. Under Pachakuti and his immediate successors, Topa Inka (TOH-puh INK-uh) and Huayna Inka (WY-nuh INK-uh) (the word *Inka* means "ruler"), the boundaries of the empire were extended as far as Ecuador, central Chile, and the edge of the Amazon basin.

THE FOUR QUARTERS: INKA POLITICS AND SOCIETY Pachakuti created a highly centralized state (see Map 6.5). With a stunning concern for mathematical precision, he divided his empire, called Tahuantinsuyu (tuh-HWAHN-tin-SOO-yoo), or "the world of the four quarters," into provinces and districts. Each province contained about 10,000 residents (at least in theory) and was ruled by a governor related to the royal family. Excess inhabitants were transferred to other locations. The capital of Cuzco was divided into four quarters, or residential areas, and the social status and economic functions of the residents of each quarter were rigidly defined.

The state was built on forced labor. Often entire communities of workers were moved from one part of the country to another to open virgin lands or engage in massive construction projects. Under Pachakuti, the capital of Cuzco was transformed from a city of mud and

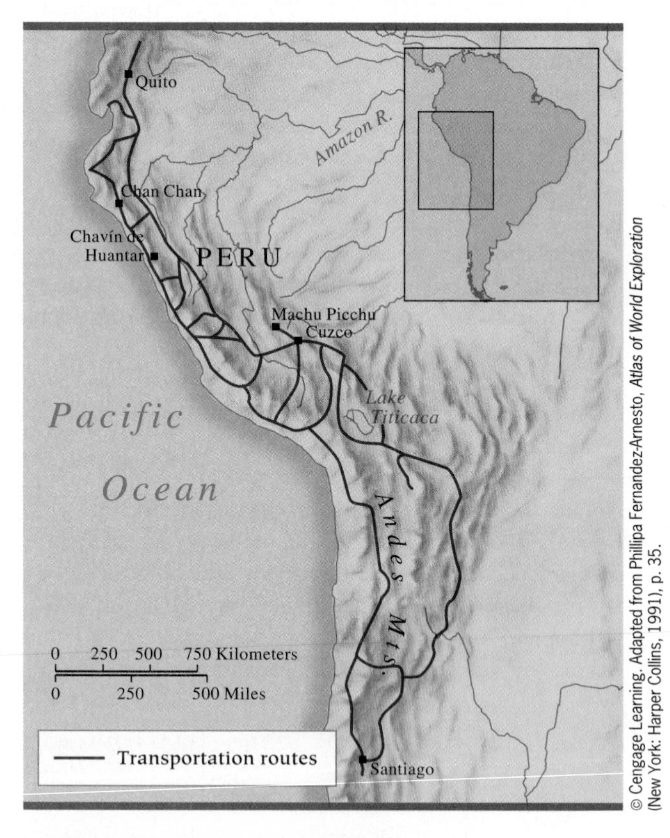

© Cengage Learning. Adapted from Phillipa Fernandez-Armesto, *Atlas of World Exploration* (New York: Harper Collins, 1991), p. 35.

MAP 6.5 The Inka Empire About 1500 C.E. The Inka were the last civilization to flourish in South America before the arrival of the Spanish. The impressive system of roads constructed to facilitate communication shows the extent of Inka control throughout the Andes Mountains.

Q *What made the extent of the Inka Empire such a remarkable achievement?*

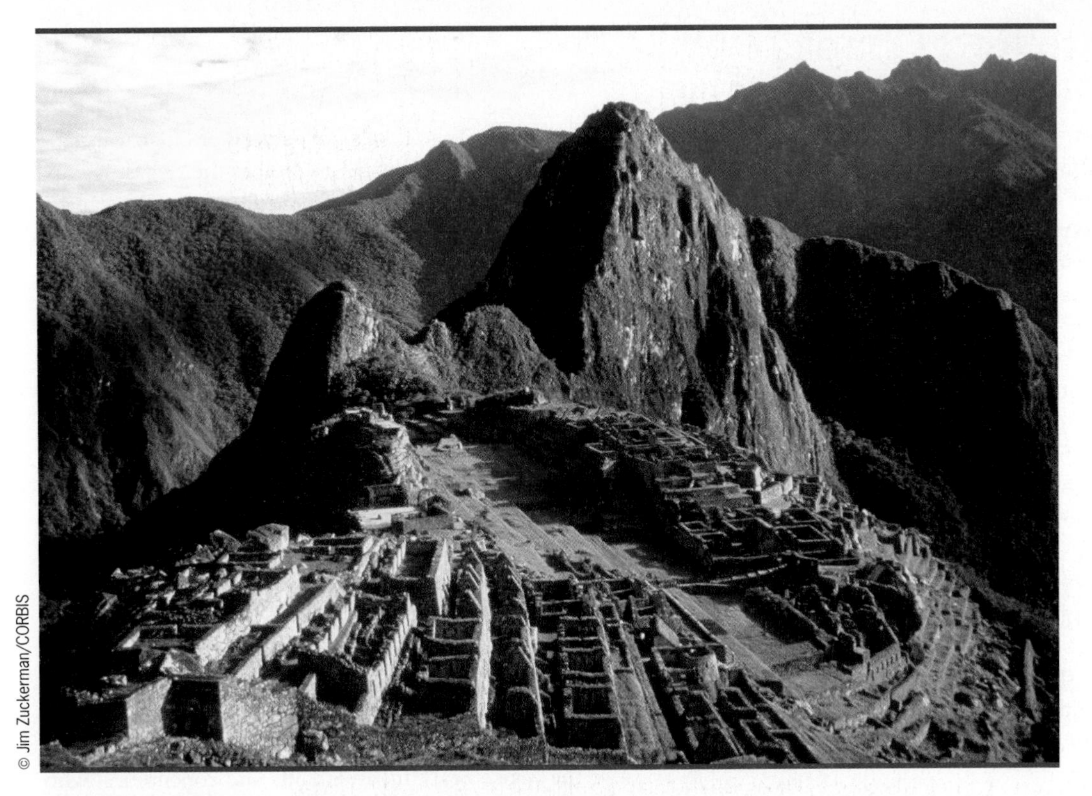

© Jim Zuckerman/CORBIS

Machu Picchu. Situated in the Andes in modern Peru, Machu Picchu reflects the glory of Inka civilization. To farm such rugged terrain, the Inka constructed terraces and stone aqueducts. To span vast ravines, they built suspension bridges made of braided fiber and fastened them to stone abutments on the opposite banks. The most revered of the many temples and stone altars at Machu Picchu was the thronelike "hitching post of the sun," so called because of its close proximity to the sun god.

thatch into an imposing metropolis of stone. The walls, built of close-fitting stones without the use of mortar, were a wonder to early European visitors. The most impressive structure in the city was a temple dedicated to the sun. According to a Spanish observer, "All four walls of the temple were covered from top to bottom with plates and slabs of gold."[4] Equally impressive are the ruins of the abandoned city of Machu Picchu (MAH-choo PEE-choo), built on a lofty hilltop far above the Urubamba River.

Another major construction project was a system of 24,800 miles of highways and roads that extended from the border of modern Colombia to a point south of modern Santiago, Chile. Two major roadways extended in a north-south direction, one through the Andes Mountains and the other along the coast, with connecting routes between them. Rest houses and storage depots were placed along the roads. Suspension bridges made of braided fiber and fastened to stone abutments on opposite banks were built over ravines and waterways. Use of the highways was restricted to official and military purposes. Trained runners carried messages rapidly from one way station to another, enabling information to travel up to 140 miles in a single day.

In rural areas, the population lived mainly by farming. In the mountains, the most common form was terraced agriculture, watered by irrigation systems that carried precise amounts of water into the fields, which were planted with maize, potatoes, and other crops. The plots were tilled by collective labor regulated by the state. Like other aspects of Inka society, marriage was strictly regulated, and men and women were required to select a marriage partner from within the immediate tribal group. For women, there was one escape from a life of domestic servitude. Fortunate maidens were selected to serve as "chosen virgins" in temples throughout the country (see the box on p. 162). Noblewomen were eligible to compete for service in the Temple of the Sun at Cuzco, while commoners might hope to serve in temples in the provincial capitals. Punishment for breaking the vow of chastity was harsh, and few evidently took the risk.

INKA CULTURE Like many other civilizations in pre-Columbian Latin America, the Inka state was built on war. Soldiers for the 200,000-man Inka army, the largest and best armed in the region, were raised by universal male conscription. Military units were moved rapidly

Virgins with Red Cheeks

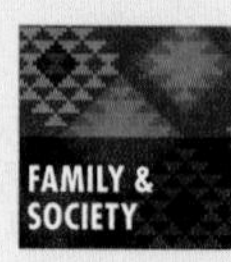

A letter from a Peruvian chief to King Philip III of Spain written four hundred years ago gives us a firsthand account of the nature of traditional Inkan society. The purpose of author Huaman Poma was both to justify the history and culture of the Inka peoples and to record their sufferings under Spanish domination. In his letter, Poma describes Inkan daily life from birth to death in minute detail. He explains the different tasks assigned to men and women, beginning with their early education. Whereas boys were taught to watch the flocks and trap animals, girls were taught to dye, spin, and weave cloth and perform other domestic chores. Most interesting, perhaps, was the emphasis that the Inka placed on virginity, as described in the selection presented here. The Inka's tradition of temple virgins is reminiscent of similar practices in ancient Rome, where young girls from noble families were chosen as priestesses to tend the sacred fire in the Temple of Vesta for thirty years. If one lost her virginity, she was condemned to be buried alive in an underground chamber.

Huaman Poma, *Letter to a King*

During the time of the Inkas certain women, who were called *accla* or "the chosen," were destined for lifelong virginity. Mostly they were confined in houses and they belonged to one of two main categories, namely sacred virgins and common virgins.

The so-called "virgins with red cheeks" entered upon their duties at the age of twenty and were dedicated to the service of the Sun, the Moon, and the Day-Star. In their whole life they were never allowed to speak to a man.

The virgins of the Inka's own shrine of Huanacauri were known for their beauty as well as their chastity. The other principal shrines had similar girls in attendance. At the less important shrines there were the older virgins who occupied themselves with spinning and weaving the silklike clothes worn by their idols. There was a still lower class of virgins, over forty years of age and no longer very beautiful, who performed unimportant religious duties and worked in the fields or as ordinary seamstresses.

Daughters of noble families who had grown into old maids were adept at making girdles, headbands, string bags, and similar articles in the intervals of their pious observances.

Girls who had musical talent were selected to sing or play the flute and drum at Court, weddings and other ceremonies, and all the innumerable festivals of the Inka year.

There was yet another class of *accla* or "chosen," only some of whom kept their virginity and others not. These were the Inka's beautiful attendants and concubines, who were drawn from noble families and lived in his palaces. They made clothing for him out of material finer than taffeta or silk. They also prepared a maize spirit of extraordinary richness, which was matured for an entire month, and they cooked delicious dishes for the Inka. They also lay with him, but never with any other man.

In this passage, one of the chief duties of a woman in Inkan society was to spin and weave. In what other traditional societies was textile making a woman's work? Why do you think this was the case?

Source: From *Letter to a King* by Guaman Poma de Ayala. Translated and edited by Christopher Dilke. Published by E. P. Dutton, New York, 1978.

along the highway system and were housed in the rest houses located along the roadside. Since the Inka had no wheeled vehicles, supplies were carried on the backs of llamas. Once an area was placed under Inka authority, the local inhabitants were instructed in the Quechua (KEH-chuh-wuh) language, which became the lingua franca of the state, and were introduced to the state religion. The Inka had no writing system but kept records using a system of knotted strings called ***quipu*** (KEE-poo), maintained by professionally trained officials, that were able to record all data of a numerical nature. What could not be recorded in such a manner was committed to memory and then recited when needed. The practice was apparently not invented by the Inka. Fragments of *quipu* have been found at Caral and dated at approximately 5,000 years ago. Nor apparently was the experiment limited to the Americas. A passage in the Chinese classic *The Way of the Tao* declares, "Let the people revert to communication by knotted cords."

As in the case of the Aztecs and the Maya, the lack of a fully developed writing system did not prevent the Inka from realizing a high level of cultural achievement. Most of what survives was recorded by the Spanish and consists of entertainment for the elites. The Inka had a highly developed tradition of court theater, including both tragic and comic works. There was also some poetry, composed in blank verse and often accompanied by music played on reed instruments. Inka architecture, as exemplified by massive stone structures at Cuzco and the breathtaking mountaintop palace at Machu Picchu, was stunning.

Stateless Societies in the Americas

FOCUS QUESTION: What were the main characteristics of stateless societies in the Americas, and how did they resemble and differ from the civilizations that arose there?

Beyond Central America and the high ridges of the Andes Mountains, on the Great Plains of North America, along the Amazon River in South America, and on the islands of the Caribbean Sea, other communities of Amerindians were also beginning to master the art of agriculture and to build organized societies.

Although human beings had occupied much of the continent of North America during the early phase of human settlement, the switch to farming as a means of survival did not occur until the third millennium B.C.E. at the earliest, and not until much later in most areas of the continent. Until that time, most Amerindian communities lived by hunting, fishing, or foraging.

The Eastern Woodlands

It was probably during the third millennium B.C.E. that peoples in the Eastern Woodlands (the land in eastern North America from the Great Lakes to the Gulf of Mexico) began to cultivate indigenous plants for food in a systematic way. As wild game and food became scarce, some communities began to place more emphasis on cultivating crops. This shift first occurred in the Mississippi River valley from Ohio, Indiana, and Illinois down to the Gulf of Mexico (see Map 6.6). Among the most commonly cultivated crops were maize, squash, beans, and various grasses.

As the population in the area increased, people began to congregate in villages, and sedentary communities began to develop in the alluvial lowlands, where the soil

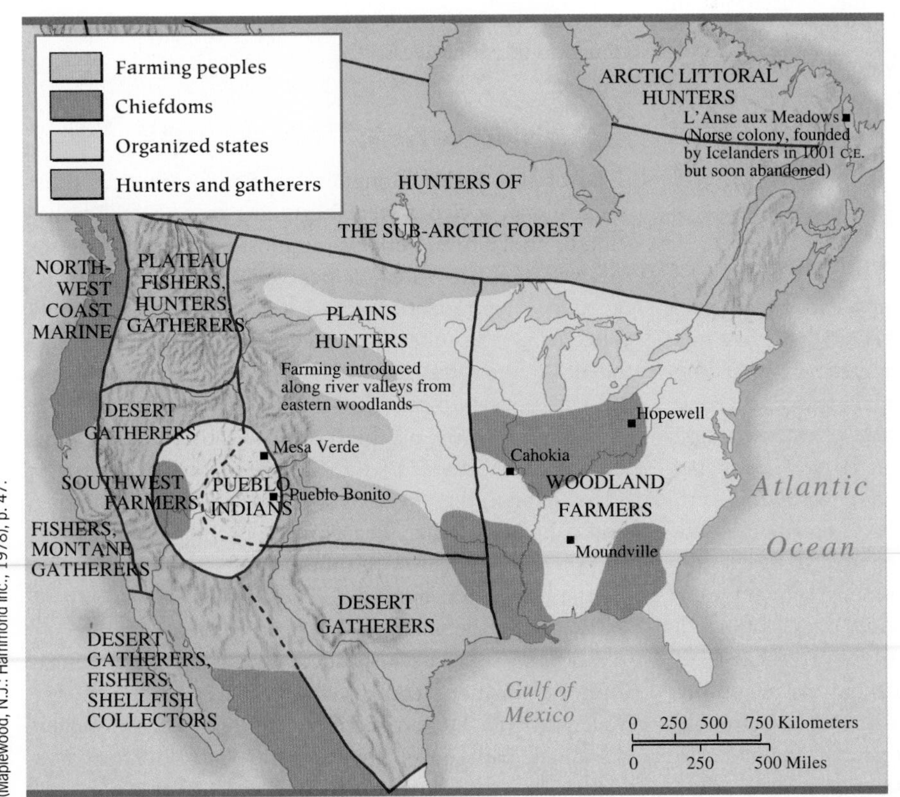

© Cengage Learning. Adapted from Geoffrey Barraclough, ed., *Times Atlas of World History* (Maplewood, N.J.: Hammond Inc., 1978), p. 47.

MAP 6.6 Early Peoples and Cultures of North America. This map shows regions of human settlement in pre-Columbian North America, including the short-lived Viking colony in Newfoundland.

How many varieties of economic activity are mentioned on this map?

could be cultivated for many years at a time because of the nutrients deposited by the river water. Village councils were established to adjudicate disputes, and in a few cases, several villages banded together under the authority of a local chieftain. Urban centers began to appear, some of them inhabited by 10,000 people or more. At the same time, regional trade increased. The people of the **Hopewell culture** in Ohio ranged from the shores of Lake Superior to the Appalachian Mountains and the Gulf of Mexico in search of metals, shells, obsidian, and manufactured items to support their economic needs and religious beliefs.

Cahokia

At the site of Cahokia, near the modern city of East Saint Louis, Illinois, archaeologists found a burial mound more than 98 feet high with a base larger than that of the Great Pyramid in Egypt. A hundred smaller mounds were also found in the vicinity. The town itself, which covered almost 300 acres and was surrounded by a wooden stockade, was apparently the administrative capital of much of the surrounding territory until its decline in the thirteenth century C.E. With a population of more than 20,000, it was once the largest city in North America until Philadelphia surpassed that number in the early nineteenth century. Cahokia carried on extensive trade with other communities throughout the region, and there are some signs of regular contacts with the civilizations in Mesoamerica, such as the presence of ball courts in the Central American style. But wars were not uncommon, leading the Iroquois, who inhabited much of the modern states of Pennsylvania and New York as well as parts of southern Canada, to create a tribal alliance called the League of Iroquois.

The Ancient Pueblo Peoples

West of the Mississippi River basin, most Amerindian peoples lived by hunting or food gathering. During the first millennium C.E., knowledge of agriculture gradually spread up the rivers to the Great Plains, and farming was practiced as far west as southwestern Colorado, where an extensive agricultural community was established in an area extending from northern New Mexico and Arizona to southwestern Colorado and parts of southern Utah. Although they apparently never discovered the wheel or used beasts of burden, these Ancient Pueblo peoples (formerly known by the Navajo name "Anasazi," or "alien ancient ones") created a system of roads that facilitated an extensive exchange of technology, products, and ideas throughout the region. By the ninth century, they had mastered the art of irrigation, which allowed them to expand their productive efforts to squash and beans, and had established an important urban center at Chaco Canyon, in southern New Mexico, where they built a walled city with dozens of three-story communal houses, called **pueblos**, with timbered roofs. Community religious functions were carried out in two large circular chambers called *kivas*. Clothing was made from hides or cotton cloth. At its height, **Pueblo Bonito** contained several hundred compounds housing several thousand residents. In the mid-twelfth century, the Ancient Pueblo peoples moved northward to Mesa Verde in southwestern Colorado. At first, they settled on top of the mesa, but eventually they retreated to the cliff face of the surrounding canyons.

Sometime during the late thirteenth century, however, Mesa Verde was also abandoned, and the inhabitants migrated southward. Their descendants, the Zuni and the Hopi, now occupy pueblos in central Arizona and New Mexico. For years, archaeologists surmised that a severe drought was the cause of the migration, but new evidence has raised doubts that decreasing rainfall, by itself, was a sufficient explanation. An increase in internecine warfare, perhaps brought about by climatic changes, may also have played a role in the decision to relocate. Some archaeologists point to evidence that cannibalism was practiced at Pueblo Bonito and suggest that migrants from the south may have arrived in the area, provoking bitter rivalries within Ancient Pueblo society. In any event, with increasing aridity and the importation of the horse by the Spanish in the sixteenth century, hunting revived, and mounted nomads like the Apache and the Navajo came to dominate much of the Southwest.

South America: The Arawak

East of the Andes Mountains in South America, other Amerindian societies were beginning to make the transition to agriculture. Perhaps the most prominent were the Arawak (AR-uh-wahk), a people living along the Orinoco River in modern Venezuela. Having begun to cultivate manioc (a tuber used today in the manufacture of tapioca) along the banks of the river, they gradually migrated down to the coast and then proceeded to move eastward along the northern coast of the continent. Some occupied the islands of the Caribbean Sea. In their new island habitat, they lived by a mixture of fishing, hunting, and cultivating maize, beans, manioc, and squash, as well as other crops such as peanuts, peppers, and pineapples. As the population increased, a pattern of political organization above the village level appeared, along with recognizable social classes headed by a chieftain whose authority included control over the economy. The Arawak practiced human sacrifice, and some urban centers contained ball courts, suggesting the possibility of contacts with Mesoamerica.

In most such societies, where clear-cut class stratifications had not as yet taken place, men and women were considered of equal status. Men were responsible for hunting, warfare, and dealing with outsiders, while women were accountable for the crops, the distribution of food, maintaining the household, and bearing and raising the children. Their roles were complementary and were often viewed as a divine division of labor. In such cases, women in the stateless societies of North America held positions of greater respect than their counterparts in the river valley civilizations of Africa and Asia.

Amazonia

Substantial human activity was also apparently taking place in the Amazon River valley. Scholars have been skeptical that advanced societies could take shape in the region because the soil lacked adequate nutrients to support a large population. Recent archaeological evidence, however, suggests that in some areas where decaying organic matter produces a rich soil suitable for farming—such as the region near the modern river port of Santarem—large agricultural societies may once have existed. More information about this previously unknown society must await further archaeological evidence.

CHAPTER SUMMARY

The first human beings did not arrive in the Americas until quite late in the prehistorical period. For the next several millennia, their descendants were forced to respond to the challenges of the environment in total isolation from other parts of the world. Nevertheless, around 5000 B.C.E., farming settlements began to appear in river valleys and upland areas in both Central and South America. Not long afterward—as measured in historical time—organized communities embarked on the long march toward creating advanced technological societies. Although the total number of people living in the Americas is a matter of debate, estimates range from 10 million to as many as 90 million people.

What is perhaps most striking about the developments in the Western Hemisphere is how closely the process paralleled those of other civilizations. Irrigated agriculture, long-distance trade, urbanization, and the development of a writing system were all hallmarks of the emergence of advanced societies of the classic type.

Some of the parallels, of course, were less appealing. States in the Western Hemisphere were every bit as addicted to warfare as their counterparts elsewhere. The widespread use of human sacrifice is reminiscent of similar practices in other ancient societies. Not much is yet known about relations between men and women in the Americas, but it appears that gender roles were as sharply delineated there as in much of Asia and the Mediterranean world.

In some respects, the societies that emerged in the Americas were not as advanced technologically as their counterparts elsewhere. They were not familiar with the process of smelting iron, for example, and they had not yet invented wheeled vehicles. Their writing systems were still in their infancy. Several possible reasons have been advanced to explain this technological gap. Geographic isolation—not only from people of other continents but also, in some cases, from each other—deprived them of the benefits of the diffusion of ideas that had enabled other societies to learn from their neighbors. Contacts among societies in the Americas were made much more difficult because of the topography and the diversity of the environment.

In some ways, too, they were not as blessed by nature. As the sociologist Jared Diamond has pointed out, the Americas did not possess many indigenous varieties of edible grasses that could encourage hunter-gatherers to take up farming. Nor were there abundant large mammals that could easily be domesticated for food and transport (horses had disappeared from the Western Hemisphere before the arrival of *Homo sapiens sapiens* at the end of the last ice age). It was not until the arrival of the Europeans that such familiar attributes of civilization became widely available for human use in the Americas.[5]

These disadvantages can help explain some of the problems that the early peoples of the Americas encountered in their efforts to master their environments. It is interesting to note that the spread of agriculture and increasing urbanization had already begun to produce a rising incidence of infectious diseases. It is also significant that in the Americas, as elsewhere, many of the first civilizations formed by the human species appear to have been brought to an end as much by environmental changes and disease as by war. In the next chapter, we shall return to Asia, where new civilizations were in the process of replacing the ancient empires.

CHAPTER TIMELINE

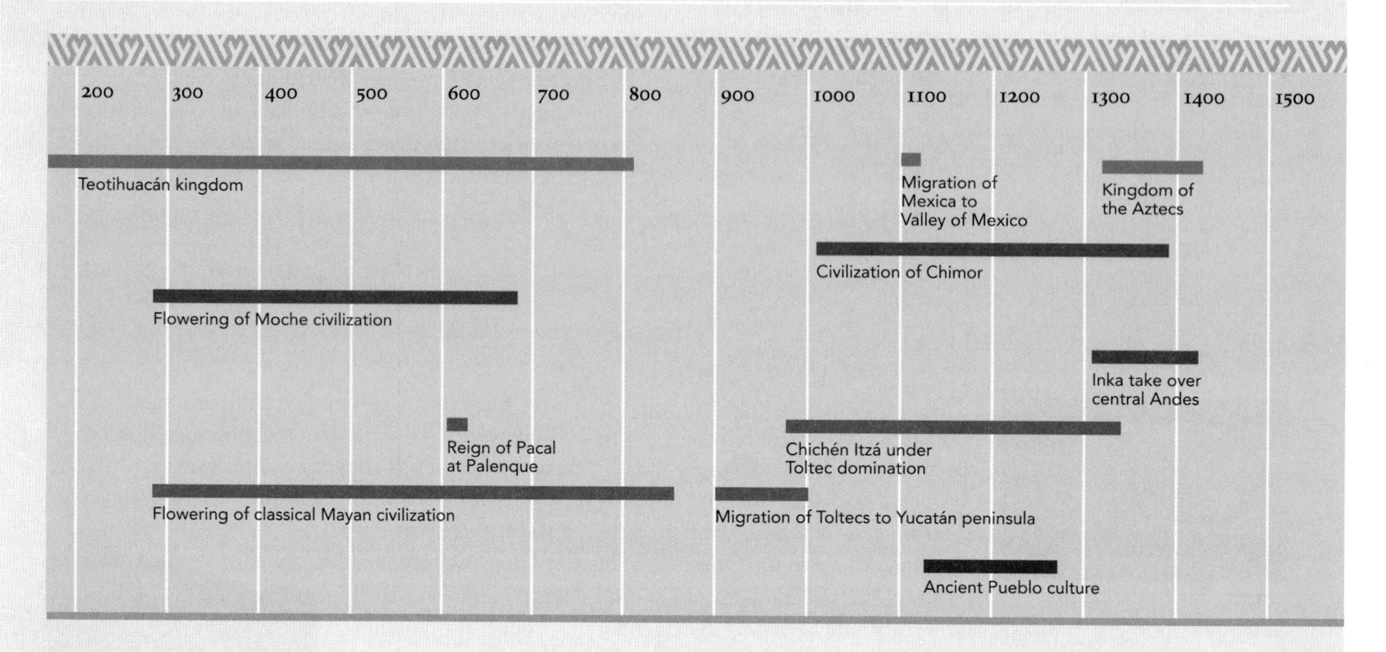

CHAPTER REVIEW

Upon Reflection

Q How did geographic and climatic factors affect the rise and fall of early societies in the Americas? Were similar factors at work among contemporary societies in other parts of the world?

Q What are some of the reasons advanced for the collapse of Mayan civilization in the late first millennium C.E.? Which do archaeologists find the most persuasive?

Q What common features linked the emerging societies in the Americas during the pre-Columbian period? Does it appear that technological and cultural achievements passed from one society to another as frequently as in other parts of the world?

Key Terms

Amerindians (p. 145)
Mesoamerica (p. 145)
chinampas (p. 147)
calpullis (p. 154)
polygyny (p. 154)
El Niño (p. 158)
quipu (p. 162)
Hopewell culture (p. 164)
pueblos (p. 164)
Pueblo Bonito (p. 164)

Suggested Reading

EARLY CIVILIZATIONS OF THE AMERICAS For a profusely illustrated and informative overview of the early civilizations of the Americas, see **M. D. Coe** and **R. Koontz, *Mexico: From the Olmecs to the Aztecs,*** 6th ed. (New York, 2008). A fascinating recent account that covers the entire pre-Columbian era is **C. Mann, *1491: New Revelations of the Americas Before Columbus*** (New York, 2006). Also see **W. Polk, *The Birth of America*** (New York, 2006).

MAYAN CIVILIZATION On Mayan civilization, see **D. Webster, *The Fall of the Ancient Maya: Solving the Mystery of the Maya Collapse*** (London, 2002), and **J. Sabloff, *The New Archeology and the Ancient Maya*** (New York, 1990). For a provocative study of religious traditions in a comparative context, see **B. Fagan, *From Black Land to Fifth Sun*** (Reading, Mass., 1998).

ANCIENT SOUTH AMERICA A worthy account of developments in South America is **G. Bawden, *The Moche*** (Oxford, 1996). On the Inka, see **N. Thomson, *A Sacred Landscape: The Search for Ancient Peru*** (Woodstock, N.Y., 2006).

ART, CULTURE, AND THE ENVIRONMENT OF THE ANCIENT AMERICAS On the art and culture of the ancient Americas, see **M. E. Miller, *Maya Art and Architecture*** (London, 1999); **E. Pasztory, *Pre-Columbian Art*** (Cambridge, 1998); and **M. Léon-Portilla** and **E. Shorris, *In the Language of Kings*** (New York, 2001). Writing systems are discussed in **M. Coe, *Breaking the Maya Code*** (New York, 1992), and **G. Upton, *Signs of the Inka Quipu*** (Austin, Tex., 2003). For a treatment of the role of the environment, see **B. Fagan, *Floods, Famine, and Emperors: El Niño and the Fate of Civilizations*** (New York, 1999), and **J. Diamond, *Collapse: How Societies Choose to Fail or Succeed*** (New York 2005).

Visit the CourseMate website at **www.cengagebrain.com** for additional study tools and review materials for this chapter.

CHAPTER 7

Ferment in the Middle East: The Rise of Islam

British Library, London//© British Library Board/The Bridgeman Art Library

Muhammad rises to heaven.

CHAPTER OUTLINE AND FOCUS QUESTIONS

The Rise of Islam

Q What were the main tenets of Islam, and how does the religion compare with Judaism and Christianity?

The Arab Empire and Its Successors

Q Why did the Arabs undergo such a rapid expansion in the seventh and eighth centuries, and why were they so successful in creating an empire?

Islamic Civilization

Q What were the main features of Islamic society and culture during its era of early growth?

CRITICAL THINKING

Q In what ways did the arrival of Islam change or maintain the political, social, and cultural conditions that had existed in the area before Muhammad?

IN THE YEAR 570, in the Arabian city of Mecca, there was born a child named Muhammad (moh-HAM-id *or* muh-HAHM-ud) whose life changed the course of world history. The son of a merchant, Muhammad grew to maturity in a time of transition. The Roman Empire, which had once been able to impose its hegemony over the Middle East, was only a distant memory. The region was now divided into many squabbling states, and the people adhered to many different faiths.

According to tradition, the young Muhammad became deeply concerned at the corrupt and decadent society of his day and took to wandering in the hills outside the city to meditate on the conditions of his time. On one of these occasions, he experienced visions that he was convinced had been inspired by Allah (AH-lah). Muslims believe that this message was conveyed to him by the angel Gabriel, who commanded Muhammad to preach the revelations that he would be given. Eventually, they would be transcribed into the Qur'an (kuh-RAN *or* kuh-RAHN)—the holy book of Islam—and provide inspiration to millions of people throughout the world. According to popular belief, Gabriel also took Muhammad, mounted on his faithful steed Buraq, on a mystical "night journey" to heaven, where Allah introduced him to paradise and hell so that on his return to earth he could instruct the faithful on their prospects in the next world (see the illustration above).

Within a few decades after Muhammad's death, the Middle East was united once again. The initial triumph may have been primarily political and military, based on the transformative power of a dynamic new religion that inspired thousands of devotees to extend their faith to neighboring regions. In any event, Islamic beliefs and culture exerted a powerful influence in all areas occupied by Arab armies. Initially, Arab beliefs and customs, as reflected through the prism of Muhammad's teachings, transformed the societies and cultures of the peoples living in the new empire. But eventually, the distinctive political and cultural forces that had long characterized the region began to reassert themselves. Factional struggles led to the decline and then the destruction of the empire.

Still, the Arab conquest left a powerful legacy that survived the decline of Arab political power. The ideological and emotional appeal of Islam remained strong throughout the Middle East and eventually extended into areas not occupied by Arab armies, such as the Indian subcontinent, Southeast Asia, and sub-Saharan Africa.

The Rise of Islam

FOCUS QUESTION: What were the main tenets of Islam, and how does the religion compare with Judaism and Christianity?

The Arabs were a Semitic-speaking people of southwestern Asia with a long history. They were mentioned in Greek sources of the fifth century B.C.E. and even earlier in the Old Testament. The Greek historian Herodotus had applied the name *Arab* to the entire peninsula, calling it Arabia. In 106 B.C.E., the Romans extended their authority to the Arabian peninsula, transforming it into a province of their growing empire.

During Roman times, the region was inhabited primarily by the **Bedouin** (BED-oo-un *or* BED-wuhn) Arabs, nomadic peoples who came originally from the northern part of the peninsula. Bedouin society was organized on a tribal basis. The ruling member of the tribe was called the ***sheikh*** (SHAYK *or* SHEEK) and was selected from one of the leading families by a council of elders called the ***majlis*** (MAHJ-liss). The *sheikh* ruled the tribe with the consent of the council. Each tribe was autonomous but felt a general sense of allegiance to the larger unity of all the clans in the region. In early times, the Bedouins had supported themselves primarily by sheepherding or by raiding passing caravans, but after the domestication of the camel during the second millennium B.C.E., the Bedouins began to participate in the caravan trade themselves and became major carriers of goods between the Persian Gulf and the Mediterranean Sea.

The Arabs of pre-Islamic times were polytheistic, with a supreme god known as Allah presiding over a community of spirits. It was a communal faith, involving all members of the tribe, and had no priesthood. Spirits were believed to inhabit natural objects, such as trees, rivers, and mountains, while the supreme deity was symbolized by a sacred stone. Each tribe possessed its own stone, but by the time of Muhammad, a massive black meteorite, housed in a central shrine called the Ka'aba (KAH-buh) in the commercial city of Mecca, had come to possess especially sacred qualities.

In the fifth and sixth centuries C.E., the economic importance of the Arabian peninsula began to increase. As a result of the political disorder in Mesopotamia—a consequence of the constant wars between the Eastern Roman (Byzantine) and Persian Empires—and in Egypt, the trade routes that ran directly across the peninsula or down the Red Sea became increasingly risky, and a third route, which passed from the Mediterranean through Mecca to Yemen and then by ship across the Indian Ocean, became more popular. The communities in that part of the peninsula benefited from the change and took a larger share of the caravan trade between the Mediterranean and the countries on the other side of the Indian Ocean. As a consequence, relations between the Bedouins of the desert and the increasingly wealthy merchant class of the towns began to become strained.

The Role of Muhammad

Into this world came Muhammad (also known as Mohammed), a man whose spiritual visions unified the Arab world (see Map 7.1) with a speed no one would have suspected possible. Born in Mecca to a merchant family and orphaned at the age of six, Muhammad (570–632) grew up to become a caravan manager and eventually married a rich widow, Khadija (kah-DEE-juh), who was also his employer. A member of the local Hashemite (HASH-uh-myt) clan of the Quraishi (koo-RY-shee) tribe, he lived in Mecca as a merchant for several years but, according to tradition, was apparently troubled by the growing gap between the Bedouin values of honesty and generosity and the acquisitive behavior of the affluent commercial elites in the city. Deeply concerned, he began to retreat to the nearby hills to meditate in isolation. There he encountered the angel Gabriel who commanded him to preach the revelations that he would be given.

It is said that Muhammad was acquainted with Jewish and Christian beliefs and came to believe that while Allah had already revealed himself in part through Moses and Jesus—and thus through the Hebraic and Christian traditions—the final revelations were now being given to him. Out of his revelations, which were eventually

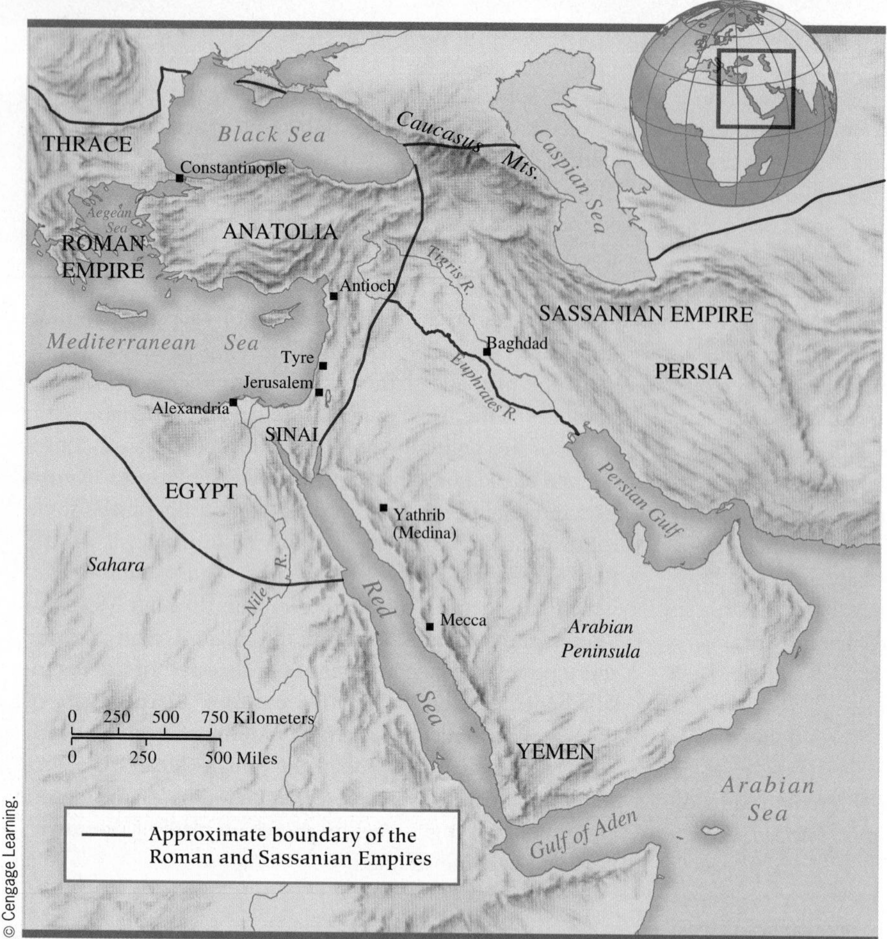

MAP 7.1 The Middle East in the Time of Muhammad. When Islam began to spread throughout the Middle East in the early seventh century, the dominant states in the region were the Eastern Roman Empire in the eastern Mediterranean and the Sassanian Empire in Persia.

What were the major territorial divisions existing at the time and the key sites connected to the rise of Islam?

dictated to scribes, came the Qur'an ("recitation," also spelled Koran), the holy scriptures of Islam (*Islam* means "submission," implying submission to the will of Allah). The Qur'an contained the guidelines by which followers of Allah, known as Muslims (practitioners of Islam), were to live. Like the Christians and the Jews, Muslims (also known as Moslems) were a "people of the Book," believers in a faith based on scripture.

Muslims believe that after returning home, Muhammad set out to comply with Gabriel's command by preaching to the residents of Mecca about his revelations. At first, many were convinced that he was a madman or a charlatan. Others were undoubtedly concerned that his vigorous attacks on traditional beliefs and the corrupt society around him could severely shake the social and political order. After three years of proselytizing, he had only thirty followers.

Discouraged, perhaps, by the systematic persecution of his followers, which was reportedly undertaken with a brutality reminiscent of the cruelties suffered by early Christians, as well as the failure of the Meccans to accept his message, in 622 Muhammad and some of his closest supporters (mostly from his own Hashemite clan) left the city and retreated north to the rival city of Yathrib, later renamed Medina (muh-DEE-nuh), or "city of the Prophet." That flight, known in history as the **Hegira** (huh-JY-ruh *or* HEH-juh-ruh) (*Hijrah*), marks the first date on the official calendar of Islam. At Medina, Muhammad failed in his original purpose—to convert the Jewish community in Medina to his beliefs. But he was successful in winning support from many residents of the city as well as from Bedouins in the surrounding countryside. From this mixture, he formed the first Muslim community—the ***umma*** (UM-mah). Returning to his birthplace at the head of a considerable military force, Muhammad conquered Mecca and converted the townspeople to the new faith. In 630, he made a symbolic visit to the Ka'aba, where he declared it a sacred shrine of Islam and ordered the destruction of the idols of the traditional faith. Two years later, Muhammad died, just as Islam was beginning to spread throughout the peninsula (see the Film & History feature on p. 171).

The Teachings of Muhammad

Like Christianity and Judaism, Islam is monotheistic. Allah is the all-powerful being who created the universe and everything in it. Islam is also concerned with salvation and offers the hope of an afterlife. Those who hope to achieve it must subject themselves to the will of Allah. Unlike Christianity, Islam makes no claim to the divinity of its founder. Muhammad, like Abraham, Moses, and other figures of the Old Testament, was a prophet, but

FILM & HISTORY

The Message (Muhammad: The Messenger of God) (1976)

© John Bryson//Time Life Pictures/Getty Images

Hamza, Muhammad's uncle (left, played by Anthony Quinn), is shown defending Muhammad's followers in the early years of Islam.

Over the years, countless commercial films depicting the early years of Christianity have been produced in Hollywood. In contrast, cinematic portrayals of the birth of other world religions such as Buddhism, Hinduism, and Islam have been rare. In the case of Islam, the reluctance has been based in part on the traditional prohibition against depicting the face and figure of the Prophet Muhammad. Reactions to depictions of the Prophet in European media in recent years have demonstrated that this issue remains highly sensitive in Muslim communities worldwide.

In the 1970s, a Syrian-American filmmaker, Moustapha Akkad, himself a Muslim, was dismayed at the widespread ignorance of the tenets of Islam in Western countries. He therefore decided to produce a full-length feature film on the life of Muhammad for presentation in Europe and the United States. When he failed to obtain financing from U.S. sources, he sought aid abroad and finally won the support of the Libyan leader Muammar Qaddafi. The resulting film was released in both English and Arabic versions in 1976.

The film seeks to present an accurate and sympathetic account of the life of the Prophet from his spiritual awakening in 610 to his return to Mecca in 630. To assuage Muslim concerns, neither the figure nor the voice of Muhammad appears in the film. None of his wives, daughters, or sons-in-law appear onscreen. The narrative is carried on through the comments and actions of his friends and disciples, notably the Prophet's uncle Hamza, ably played by the veteran American actor Anthony Quinn.

The film, shot on location in Libya and Morocco, is a sometimes moving account of the emergence of Islam in early-seventh-century Arabia. Although it does not dwell on the more esoteric aspects of Muslim beliefs, it stresses many of the humanistic elements of Islam, including respect for women and opposition to slavery, as well as the equality of all human beings in the eyes of God. Muhammad and his followers are shown as messengers of peace who are aroused to violence only in order to protect themselves from the acts of their enemies.

Though slow moving in spots and somewhat lengthy in the manner of the genre, *The Message* (also known as *Muhammad: The Messenger of God*) is beautifully filmed and contains a number of stirring battle scenes. Viewers come away with a fairly accurate and sympathetic portrait of the life of the Prophet and his message to the faithful.

he was also a man like other men. According to the Qur'an, because earlier prophets had corrupted his revelations, Allah sent his complete revelation through Muhammad.

At the heart of Islam is the Qur'an, with its basic message that there is no God but Allah and Muhammad is his Prophet. Consisting of 114 *suras* (SUR-uhz) (chapters) drawn together by a committee established after Muhammad's death, the Qur'an is not only the sacred book of Islam but also an ethical guidebook and a code of law and political theory combined.

As it evolved, Islam developed a number of fundamental tenets. At its heart was the need to obey the will of Allah. This meant following a basic ethical code consisting of what are popularly termed the **Five Pillars of Islam**: belief in Allah and Muhammad as his Prophet; standard prayer five times a day and public prayer on Friday at midday to worship Allah; observation of the holy month of **Ramadan** (RAH-muh-dan), including fasting from dawn to sunset; if possible, making a pilgrimage to Mecca at least once in one's lifetime; and giving alms, or *zakat* (zuh-KAHT), to the poor and unfortunate. The

© Mehmet Biber/Photo Researchers Inc.

The Ka'aba in Mecca. The Ka'aba, the shrine containing a black meteorite in the Arabian city of Mecca, is the most sacred site of the Islamic faith. Wherever Muslims pray, they are instructed to face Mecca; each thus becomes a spoke of the Ka'aba, the holy center of the wheel of Islam. If they are able to do so, all Muslims are encouraged to visit the Ka'aba at least once in their lifetime. Called the *hajj* (HAJ), this pilgrimage to Mecca represents the ultimate in spiritual fulfillment.

faithful who observed the law were guaranteed a place in an eternal paradise (a vision of a luxurious and cool garden shared by some versions of Eastern Christianity) with the sensuous delights so obviously lacking in the midst of the Arabian desert.

Islam was not just a set of religious beliefs but a way of life. After the death of Muhammad, Muslim scholars, known as the ***ulama*** (OO-luh-mah *or* oo-LAH-muh), drew up a law code, called the ***Shari'a*** (shah-REE-uh), to provide believers with a set of prescriptions to regulate their daily lives. Much of the *Shari'a* was drawn from existing legal regulations or from the ***Hadith*** (hah-DEETH), a collection of the sayings of the Prophet that was used to supplement the revelations contained in the holy scriptures.

Believers were subject to strict behavioral requirements. In addition to the Five Pillars, Muslims were forbidden to gamble, eat pork, drink alcoholic beverages, and engage in dishonest behavior. Sexual mores were also strict. Contacts between unmarried men and women were discouraged, and ideally marriages were to be arranged by the parents. In accordance with Bedouin custom, polygyny was permitted, but Muhammad attempted to limit the practice by restricting males to four wives (see the box on p. 173).

To what degree the traditional account of the exposition and inner meaning of the Qur'an can stand up to historical analysis is a matter of debate. Given the lack of verifiable evidence, the circumstances surrounding the life of Muhammad and his role in founding the religion of Islam remain highly speculative, and many Muslims are undoubtedly concerned that the consequences of rigorous examination might undercut key tenets of the Muslim faith. One of the problems connected with such an effort is that the earliest known versions of the Qur'an available today do not contain the diacritical marks that modern Arabic uses to clarify meaning, thus leaving much of the sacred text ambiguous and open to varying interpretations.

The Arab Empire and Its Successors

FOCUS QUESTION: Why did the Arabs undergo such a rapid expansion in the seventh and eighth centuries, and why were they so successful in creating an empire?

The death of Muhammad presented his followers with a dilemma. Although Muhammad had not claimed divine qualities, Muslims saw no separation between political and religious authority. Submission to the will of Allah meant submission to his Prophet Muhammad. According to the Qur'an, "Whoso obeyeth the messenger obeyeth Allah."[1] Muhammad's charismatic authority and political skills had been at the heart of his success. But Muslims have never agreed as to whether he named a successor, and although he had several daughters, he left no sons. In the male-oriented society of his day, who would lead the community of the faithful?

Shortly after Muhammad's death, a number of his closest followers selected Abu Bakr (ah-boo BAHK-ur), a wealthy merchant from Medina who was Muhammad's father-in-law and one of his first supporters, as **caliph** (KAY-liff) (*khalifa*, literally "successor"). The caliph was the temporal leader of the Islamic community and was also considered, in general terms, to be a religious leader, or ***imam*** (ih-MAHM). Under Abu Bakr's prudent leadership, the movement succeeded in suppressing factional

"Draw their Veils over Their Bosoms"

RELIGION & PHILOSOPHY

Before the Islamic era, many upper-class women greeted men on the street, entertained their husbands' friends at home, went on pilgrimages to Mecca, and even accompanied their husbands to battle. Such women were neither veiled nor secluded. Muhammad, however, specified that his own wives, who (according to the Qur'an) were "not like any other women," should be modestly attired and should be addressed by men from behind a curtain. Over the centuries, Muslim theologians, fearful that female sexuality could threaten the established order, interpreted Muhammad's "modest attire" and his reference to curtains to mean segregated seclusion and body concealment for all Muslim women. In fact, one strict scholar in fourteenth-century Cairo went so far as to prescribe that ideally a woman should be allowed to leave her home only three times in her life: when entering her husband's home after marriage, after the death of her parents, and after her own death.

In traditional Islamic societies, veiling and seclusion were more prevalent among urban women than among their rural counterparts. The latter, who worked in the fields and rarely saw people outside their extended family, were less restricted. In this excerpt from the Qur'an, women are instructed to "guard their modesty" and "draw veils over their bosoms." Nowhere in the Qur'an, however, does it stipulate that women should be sequestered or covered from head to toe.

Qur'an, Sura 24: "The Light"

And say to the believing women
That they should lower
Their gaze and guard
Their modesty: that they
Should not display their
Beauty and ornaments except
What [must ordinarily] appear
Thereof: that they should
Draw their veils over
Their bosoms and not display
Their beauty except
To their husbands, their fathers,
Their husbands' fathers, their sons,
Their husbands' sons,
Their brothers or their brothers' sons,
Or their sisters' sons,
Or their women, or the slaves
Whom their right hands
Possess, or male servants
Free of physical needs,
Or small children who
Have no sense of the shame
Of sex; and that they
Should not strike their feet
In order to draw attention
To their hidden ornaments.

How does the role of women in Islam compare with what we have seen in other traditional societies, such as India, China, and the Americas?

Source: Copyright © 1995 by M.E. Sharpe, Inc. From *Women in World History*. Volume 1. *Readings from Prehistory to 1500*, ed. Sarah Shaver Hughers and Brady Hughes (Armonk, NY: M.E. Sharpe, 1995), pp. 152–153. Used with permission of M.E. Sharpe, Inc. All Rights Reserved. Not for reproduction.

tendencies among some of the Bedouin tribes in the peninsula and began to direct its attention to wider fields. Muhammad had used the Arabic tribal custom of the *razzia* (RAZZ-ee-uh), or raid, in the struggle against his enemies. Now his successors turned to the same custom to expand the authority of the movement.

In recent discussions of the expansion of Islam after the death of Muhammad, the Arabic term ***jihad*** (jee-HAHD) has often been used to describe the process. The word appears in the Qur'an on several occasions, and it appears to have had multiple meanings, much as the word *crusade* does in English. Sometimes *jihad* is used in the sense of "striving in the way of the Lord," as a means of exhorting believers to struggle against the evil within themselves. In other cases, however, it has been translated as "holy war," justifying hostile action against the enemies of Islam. Many terrorist movements of the present day clearly view *jihad* in the latter sense. Because the word is so heavily laden with emotional connotations, it clearly should be used sparingly and with care.

Creation of an Empire

Once the Arabs had become unified under Muhammad's successor, they began directing outward against neighboring peoples the energy they had formerly directed against each other. The Byzantine and Sassanian (suh-SAY-nee-uhn) Empires were the first to feel the strength of the newly united Arabs, now aroused to a peak of zeal by their common faith. In 636, the Muslims defeated the Byzantine army at the Yarmuk (yahr-MOOK) River, north of the Dead Sea. Four years later, they took possession of the Byzantine province of Syria. To the east, the Arabs defeated a Persian force in 637 and then went on to conquer the entire empire of the Sassanids by 650. In the meantime, Egypt and other areas of North Africa were also brought under Arab authority (see Chapter 8).

What accounts for this rapid expansion of the Arabs after the rise of Islam in the early seventh century? Historians have proposed various explanations, ranging from a prolonged drought on the Arabian peninsula to the desire of Islam's leaders to channel the energies of their new converts. Another hypothesis is that the expansion was deliberately planned by the ruling elites in Mecca to extend their trade routes and bring surplus-producing regions under their control. Whatever the case, Islam's ability to unify the Bedouin peoples certainly played a role. Although the Arab triumph was made substantially easier by the ongoing conflict between the Byzantine and Persian Empires, which had weakened both powers, the strength and mobility of the Bedouin armies with their much vaunted cavalry should not be overlooked. Led by a series of brilliant generals, the Arabs assembled a large, highly motivated army, whose valor was enhanced by the belief that Muslim warriors who died in battle were guaranteed a place in paradise.

Once the armies had prevailed, Arab administration of the conquered areas was generally tolerant. Sometimes, due to a shortage of trained Arab administrators, government was left to local officials. Conversion to Islam was generally voluntary in accordance with the maxim in the Qur'an that "there shall be no compulsion in religion."[2] Those who chose not to convert were required only to submit to Muslim rule and pay a head tax in return for exemption from military service, which was required of all Muslim males. Under such conditions, the local populations often welcomed Arab rule as preferable to Byzantine rule or that of the Sassanid dynasty in Persia. Furthermore, the simple and direct character of the new religion, as well as its egalitarian qualities (all people were viewed as equal in the eyes of Allah), were undoubtedly attractive to peoples throughout the region.

The Rise of the Umayyads

The main challenge to the growing empire came from within. Some of Muhammad's followers had not agreed with the selection of Abu Bakr as the first caliph and promoted the candidacy of Ali, Muhammad's cousin and son-in-law, as an alternative. Ali's claim was ignored by other leaders, however, and after Abu Bakr's death, the office was passed to Umar (oo-MAR), another of Muhammad's followers. In 656, Umar's successor, Uthman (ooth-MAHN), was assassinated, and Ali, who fortuitously happened to be in Medina at that time, was finally selected for the position. But according to tradition, Ali's rivals were convinced that he had been implicated in the death of his predecessor, and a factional struggle broke out within the Muslim leadership. In 661, Ali himself was assassinated, and Mu'awiya (moo-AH-wee-yuh), the governor of Syria and one of Ali's chief rivals, replaced him in office. Mu'awiya thereupon made the caliphate hereditary in his own family, called the Umayyads (oo-MY-ads), who were a branch of the Quraishi clan. The new caliphate (KAY-luh-fayt), with its capital at Damascus, remained in power for nearly a century.

The factional struggle within Islam did not bring an end to Arab expansion. At the beginning of the eighth century, new attacks were launched at both the western and the eastern ends of the Mediterranean world (see Map 7.2). Arab armies advanced across North Africa and conquered the Berbers, a primarily pastoral people living along the Mediterranean coast and in the mountains in the interior. Muslim fleets seized several islands in the eastern Mediterranean. Then, around 710, Arab forces, supplemented by Berber allies under their commander, Tariq (tuh-REEK), crossed the Strait of Gibraltar and occupied southern Spain. The Visigothic kingdom, already weakened by internecine warfare, quickly collapsed, and by 725, most of the Iberian peninsula had become a Muslim state with its center in Andalusia (an-duh-LOO-zhuh). Seven years later, an Arab force, making a foray into southern France, was defeated by the army of Charles Martel between Tours (TOOR) and Poitiers (pwah-TYAY). For the first time Arab horsemen had met their match in the form of a disciplined force of Frankish infantry. Some historians think that internal exhaustion would have forced the invaders to retreat even without their defeat at the hands of the Franks. In any event, the Battle of Tours (or Poitiers) would be the high-water mark of Arab expansion in Europe.

In the meantime, in 717, another Muslim force had launched an attack on Constantinople with the hope of destroying the Byzantine Empire. But the Byzantines' use of Greek fire, a petroleum-based compound containing quicklime and sulfur, destroyed the Muslim fleet, thereby

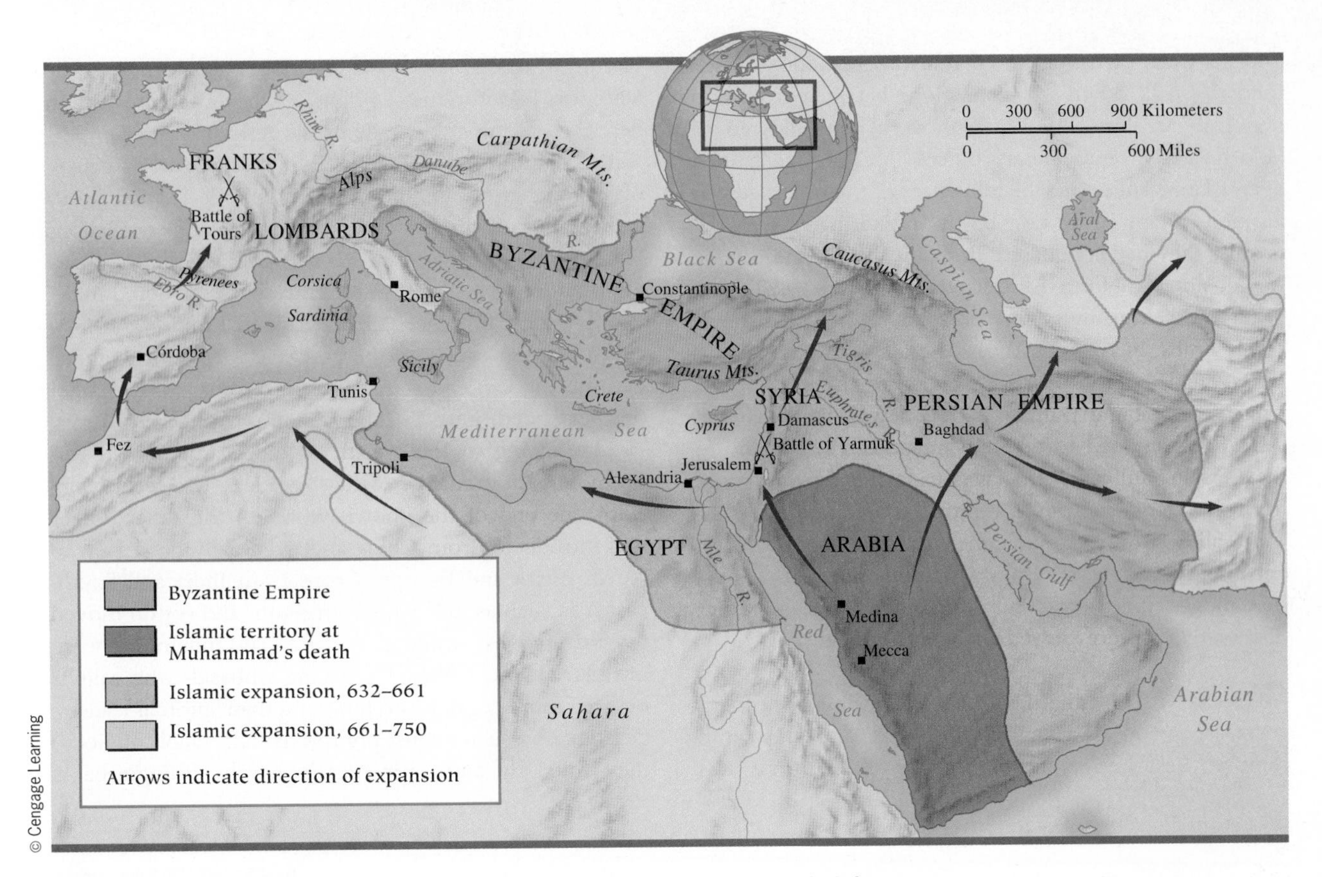

© Cengage Learning

MAP 7.2 The Expansion of Islam. This map shows the expansion of the Islamic faith from its origins in the Arabian peninsula. Muhammad's followers carried the religion as far west as Spain and southern France and eastward to India and Southeast Asia.

In which of these areas is the Muslim faith still the dominant religion?

saving the empire and indirectly Christian Europe, since the fall of Constantinople would have opened the door to an Arab invasion of eastern Europe. The Byzantine Empire and Islam now established an uneasy frontier in southern Asia Minor.

Succession Problems

Arab power also extended to the east, consolidating Islamic rule in Mesopotamia and Persia, and northward into Central Asia. But factional disputes continued to plague the empire. Many Muslims of non-Arab extraction resented the favoritism shown by local administrators to Arabs. In some cases, resentment led to revolt, as in Iraq, where Ali's second son, Hussein, disputed the legitimacy of the Umayyads and incited his supporters—to be known in the future as **Shi'ites** (SHEE-yts) (from the Arabic phrase *shi'at Ali*, "partisans of Ali")—to rise up against Umayyad rule in 680. Although Hussein's forces were defeated and Hussein himself died in the battle, a schism between Shi'ite and **Sunni** (SOON-nee) (usually translated as "orthodox") Muslims had been created that continues to this day.

Umayyad rule, always (in historian Arthur Goldschmidt's words) "more political than pious," created resentment, not only in Mesopotamia, but also in North Africa, where Berber resistance continued, especially in the mountainous areas south of the coastal plains. According to critics, the Umayyads may have contributed to their own demise by their decadent behavior. One caliph allegedly swam in a pool of wine and then imbibed enough of the contents to lower the level significantly. Finally, in 750, a revolt led by Abu al-Abbas (ah-boo al-ah-BUSS), a descendant of Muhammad's uncle, led to the overthrow of the Umayyads and the establishment of the Abbasid (uh-BAH-sid *or* AB-uh-sid) dynasty (750–1258) in what is now Iraq.

The Abbasids

The Abbasid caliphs brought political, economic, and cultural change to the world of Islam. While seeking to implant their own version of religious orthodoxy, they tried to break down the distinctions between Arab and non-Arab Muslims. All Muslims were now allowed to hold both civil and military offices. This change helped open Islamic culture to the influences of the occupied civilizations. Many Arabs now began to intermarry with the peoples they had conquered. In many parts of the Islamic world, notably North Africa and the eastern Mediterranean, most Muslim converts began to consider themselves Arabs. In 762, the Abbasids built a new capital city at Baghdad, on the Tigris River far to the east of the Umayyad capital at Damascus. The new capital was strategically positioned to take advantage of river traffic to the Persian Gulf and also lay astride the caravan route from the Mediterranean to Central Asia. The move eastward allowed Persian influence to come to the fore, encouraging a new cultural orientation. Under the Abbasids, judges, merchants, and government officials, rather than warriors, were viewed as the ideal citizens.

ABBASID RULE The new Abbasid caliphate experienced a period of splendid rule well into the ninth century. Best known of the caliphs of the time was Harun al-Rashid (hah-ROON al-rah-SHEED) (786–809), or Harun "the Upright," whose reign is often described as the golden age of the Abbasid caliphate. His son al-Ma'mun (al-muh-MOON) (813–833) was a patron of learning who founded an astronomical observatory and established a foundation for undertaking translations of Classical Greek works. This was also a period of growing economic prosperity. The Arabs had conquered many of the richest provinces of the Roman Empire and now controlled the routes to the east (see Map 7.3). Baghdad became the center of an enormous commercial market that extended into Europe, Central Asia, and Africa, greatly adding to the wealth of the Islamic world and promoting an exchange of culture, ideas, and technology from one end of the known world to the other. Paper was introduced from China and eventually passed on to North Africa and Europe. Crops from India and Southeast Asia such as rice, sugar, sorghum, and cotton moved toward the west, while glass, wine, and indigo dye were introduced into China. Under the Abbasids, the caliphs became more regal. More temporal than spiritual leaders, described by such august phrases as the "caliph of God," they ruled by autocratic means, hardly distinguishable

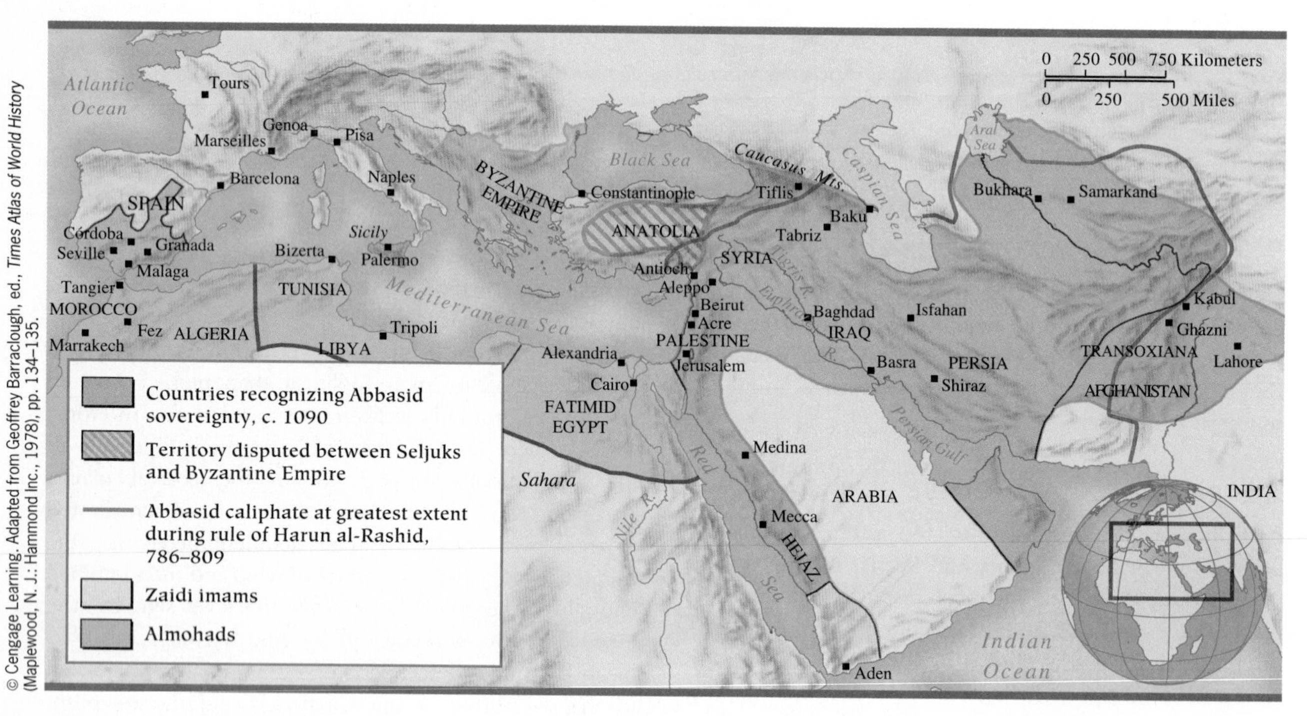

© Cengage Learning. Adapted from Geoffrey Barraclough, ed., *Times Atlas of World History* (Maplewood, N. J.: Hammond Inc., 1978), pp. 134–135.

MAP 7.3 The Abbasid Caliphate at the Height of Its Power. The Abbasids arose in the eighth century as the defenders of the Muslim faith and established their capital at Baghdad. With its prowess as a trading state, the caliphate was the most powerful and extensive state in the region for several centuries. The "Zaidi imams" indicated on the map were a group of dissident Shi'ites who established an independent kingdom on the southern tip of the Arabian peninsula.

Q *What were the major urban centers under the influence of Islam, as shown on this map?*

from the kings and emperors in neighboring states. A thirteenth-century Chinese author, who compiled a world geography based on accounts by Chinese travelers, left the following description of one of the later caliphs:

> The king wears a turban of silk brocade and foreign cotton stuff [buckram]. On each new moon and full moon he puts on an eight-sided flat-topped headdress of pure gold, set with the most precious jewels in the world. His robe is of silk brocade and is bound around him with a jade girdle. On his feet he wears golden shoes. . . . The king's throne is set with pearls and precious stones, and the steps of the throne are covered with pure gold.[3]

As the caliph took on more of the trappings of a hereditary autocrat, the bureaucracy assisting him in administering the expanding empire grew more complex as well. The caliph was advised by a council, called a *diwan* (di-WAHN), headed by a prime minister, known as a **vizier** (veh-ZEER) (*wazir*). The caliph did not attend meetings of the *diwan* in the normal manner but sat behind a screen and then communicated his divine will to the vizier. Some historians have ascribed the change in the caliphate to Persian influence, which permeated the empire after the capital was moved to Baghdad. Persian influence was indeed strong (the mother of the caliph al-Ma'mun, for example, was a Persian), but more likely, the increase in pomp and circumstance was a natural consequence of the growing power and prosperity of the empire.

INSTABILITY AND DIVISION Nevertheless, an element of instability lurked beneath the surface. The lack of spiritual authority may have weakened the caliphate in competition with its potential rivals, and disputes over the succession were common. At Harun's death, the rivalry between his two sons, Amin and al-Ma'mun, led to civil war and the destruction of Baghdad. As described by the tenth-century Muslim historian al-Mas'udi (al-muh-SOO-dee), "Mansions were destroyed, most remarkable monuments obliterated; prices soared. . . . Brother turned his sword against brother, son against father, as some fought for Amin, others for Ma'mun. Houses and palaces fueled the flames; property was put to the sack."[4]

Wealth contributed to financial corruption. By awarding important positions to court favorites, the Abbasid caliphs began to undermine the foundations of their own power and eventually became mere figureheads. Under Harun al-Rashid, members of his Hashemite clan received large pensions from the state treasury, and his wife, Zubaida (zoo-BY-duh), reportedly spent huge sums shopping while on a pilgrimage to Mecca. One powerful family, the Barmakids, amassed vast wealth and power until Harun al-Rashid eliminated the entire clan in a fit of jealousy.

The life of luxury enjoyed by the caliph and other political and economic elites in Baghdad seemingly undermined the stern fiber of Arab society as well as the strict moral code of Islam. Strictures against sexual promiscuity were widely ignored, and caliphs were rumored to maintain thousands of concubines in their harems. Divorce was common, homosexuality was widely practiced, and alcohol was consumed in public despite Islamic law's prohibition against imbibing spirits.

The process of disintegration was accelerated by changes that were taking place within the armed forces and the bureaucracy of the empire. Given the shortage of qualified Arabs for key positions in the army and the

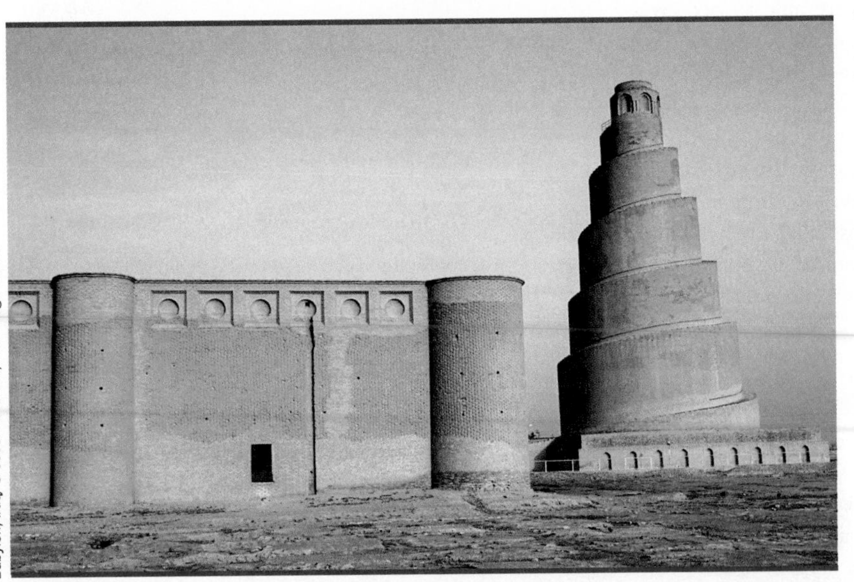

Babylon, Iraq/© Josef Polleross/The Image Works

The Great Mosque of Samarra. The ninth-century mosque of Samarra, located north of Baghdad in present-day Iraq, was for centuries the largest mosque in the Islamic world. Rising from the center of the city of Samarra, the capital of the Abbasids for over half a century and one of the largest medieval cities of its time, the imposing tower shown here is 156 feet in height. Its circular ramp may have inspired medieval artists in Europe as they imagined the ancient cultures of Mesopotamia. Although the mosque is in ruins today, its spiral tower still signals the presence of Islam to the faithful across the broad valley of the Tigris and Euphrates Rivers.

administration, the caliphate began to recruit officials from among the non-Arab peoples in the empire, such as Persians and Turks from Central Asia. These people gradually became a dominant force in the army and administration.

Provincial rulers also began to break away from central control and establish their own independent dynasties. Already in the eighth century, a separate caliphate had been established in Spain (see "Andalusia: A Muslim Outpost in Europe" later in the chapter). Environmental problems added to the regime's difficulties. The Tigris and Euphrates river system, lifeblood of Mesopotamia for three millennia, was beginning to silt up. Bureaucratic inertia now made things worse, as many of the country's canals became virtually unusable, leading to widespread food shortages.

The fragmentation of the Islamic empire accelerated in the tenth century. Morocco became independent, and in 973, a new Shi'ite dynasty under the Fatimids (FAT-uh-mids) was established in Egypt with its capital at Cairo. With increasing disarray in the empire, the Islamic world was held together only by the common commitment to the Qur'an and the use of the Arabic language as the prevailing means of communication.

The Seljuk Turks

In the eleventh century, the Abbasid caliphate faced yet another serious threat in the form of the Seljuk (SEL-jook) Turks. The Seljuk Turks were a nomadic people from Central Asia who had converted to Islam and flourished as military mercenaries for the Abbasid caliphate, where they were known for their ability as mounted archers. Moving gradually into Iran and Armenia as the Abbasids weakened, the Seljuk Turks grew in number until by the eleventh century, they were able to occupy the eastern provinces of the Abbasid empire. In 1055, a Turkish leader captured Baghdad and assumed command of the empire with the title of **sultan** (SUL-tun) ("holder of power"). While the Abbasid caliph remained the chief representative of Sunni religious authority, the real military and political power of the state was in the hands of the Seljuk Turks. The latter did not establish their headquarters in Baghdad, which now entered a period of decline. As the historian Khatib Baghdadi (kah-TEEB bag-DAD-ee) described:

> There is no city in the world equal to Baghdad in the abundance of its riches, the importance of its business, the number of its scholars and important people, the distinctions of its leaders and its common people, the extent of its palaces, inhabitants, streets, avenues, alleys, mosques, baths, docks and caravansaries, the purity of its air, the sweetness of its water, the freshness of its dew and its shade, the temperateness of its summer and winter, the healthfulness of its spring and fall, and its great swarming crowds. The buildings and the inhabitants were most numerous during the time of Harun al-Rashid, when the city and its surrounding areas were full of cooled rooms, thriving places, fertile pastures, rich watering-places for ships. Then the riots began, an uninterrupted series of misfortunes befell the inhabitants, its flourishing conditions came to ruin to such extent that, before our time and the century preceding ours, it found itself, because of the perturbation and the decadence it was experiencing, in complete opposition to all capitals and in contradiction to all inhabited countries.[5]

Baghdad would revive, but it would no longer be the "gift of God" of Harun al-Rashid.

By the last quarter of the eleventh century, the Seljuks were exerting military pressure on Egypt and the Byzantine Empire. In 1071, when the Byzantines foolishly challenged the Turks, their army was routed at Manzikert (MANZ-ih-kurt), near Lake Van in eastern Turkey, and the victors took over most of the Anatolian peninsula (see Map 7.4). In dire straits, the Byzantine Empire turned to the west for help, setting in motion the papal pleas that led to the **Crusades** (see the next section).

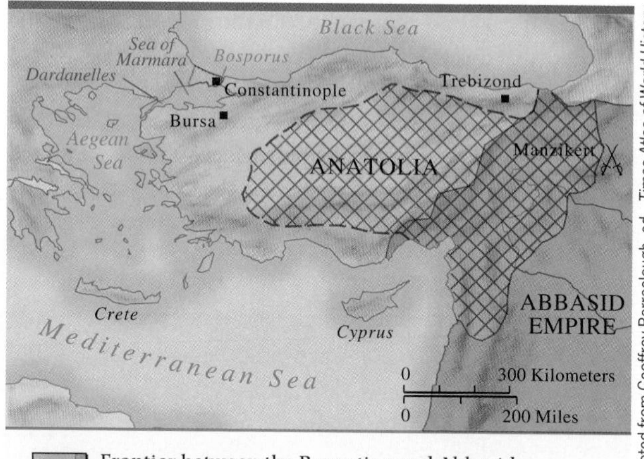

© Cengage Learning. Adapted from Geoffrey Barraclough, ed., *Times Atlas of World History* (Maplewood, N. J.: Hammond Inc., 1978), p. 135.

MAP 7.4 The Turkish Occupation of Anatolia. This map shows the expansion of the Seljuk Turks into the Anatolian peninsula in the eleventh and twelfth centuries. Later, another group of Turkic-speaking peoples, the Ottoman Turks, would move into the area, establishing their capital at Bursa in 1335 and eventually at Constantinople in 1453 (see Chapter 16).

Q *What role did the expansion of the Seljuk Turks play in the origin of the Crusades?*

In Europe, and undoubtedly within the Muslim world itself, the arrival of the Turks was regarded as a disaster. The Turks were viewed as barbarians who destroyed civilizations and oppressed populations. In fact, in many respects, Turkish rule in the Middle East was probably beneficial. Converted to Islam, the Turkish rulers temporarily brought an end to the fraternal squabbles between Sunni and Shi'ite Muslims while supporting the Sunnites. They put their energies into revitalizing Islamic law and institutions and provided much-needed political stability to the empire, which helped restore its former prosperity. Under Seljuk rule, Muslims began to organize themselves into autonomous brotherhoods, whose relatively tolerant practices characterized Islamic religious attitudes until the end of the nineteenth century, when increased competition with Europe led to confrontation with the West.

Seljuk political domination over the old Abbasid Empire, however, provoked resentment on the part of many Persian Shi'ites, who viewed the Turks as usurping foreigners who had betrayed the true faith of Islam. Among the regime's most feared enemies was Hasan al-Sabahh (hah-SAHN al-SAH-bah), a Cairo-trained Persian who formed a rebel group, popularly known as "assassins" (guardians), who for several decades terrorized government officials and other leading political and religious figures from their base in the mountains south of the Caspian Sea. Like their modern-day equivalents in the terrorist organization known as al-Qaeda, Sabahh's followers were highly motivated and were adept at infiltrating the enemy's camp in order to carry out their clandestine activities. The organization was finally eliminated by the invading Mongols in the thirteenth century.

The Crusades

Just before the end of the eleventh century, the Byzantine emperor Alexius I desperately asked for assistance from other Christian states in Europe to protect his empire against the invading Seljuk Turks. As part of his appeal, he said that the Muslims were desecrating Christian shrines in the Holy Land and molesting Christian pilgrims en route to the shrines. In actuality, the Muslims had never threatened the shrines or cut off Christian access to them. But tension between Christendom and Islam was on the rise, and the Byzantine emperor's appeal received a ready response in Europe. Beginning in 1096 and continuing into the thirteenth century, a series of Christian incursions on Islamic territories known as the Crusades brought the Holy Land and adjacent areas on the Mediterranean coast from Antioch to the Sinai peninsula under Christian rule (see Chapter 12). In 1099, the armies of the First Crusade succeeded in capturing Jerusalem after a long siege.

At first, Muslim rulers in the area were taken aback by the invading crusaders, whose armored cavalry presented a new challenge to local warriors, and their response was ineffectual. The Seljuk Turks by that time were preoccupied with events taking place farther to the east and took no action themselves. But in 1169, Sunni Muslims under the leadership of Saladin (SAL-uh-din) (Salah al-Din), vizier to the last Fatimid caliph, brought an end to the Fatimid dynasty. Proclaiming himself sultan, Saladin succeeded in establishing his control over both Egypt and Syria, thereby confronting the Christian states in the area with united Muslim power on two fronts. In 1187, Saladin's army invaded the kingdom of Jerusalem and destroyed the Christian forces concentrated there. Further operations reduced Christian occupation in the area to a handful of fortresses along the northern coast (see the comparative illustration on p. 180). Unlike the Christians of the First Crusade, who had slaughtered much of the population of Jerusalem when they captured the city, Saladin did not permit a massacre of the civilian population and even tolerated the continuation of Christian religious services in conquered territories. For a time, Christian occupation forces even carried on a lively trade relationship with Muslim communities in the region.

The Christians returned for another try a few years after the fall of Jerusalem, but the campaign succeeded only in securing some of the coastal cities. Although the Christians would retain a toehold on the coast for much of the thirteenth century (Acre, their last stronghold, fell to the Muslims in 1291), they were no longer a significant force in Middle Eastern affairs. In retrospect, the Crusades had only minimal importance in the history of the Middle East, although they may have served to unite the forces of Islam against the foreign invaders, thus creating a residue of distrust toward Christians that continues to resonate through the Islamic world today (see the box on p. 181). Far more important in their impact were the Mongols, a pastoral people who swept out of the Gobi Desert in the early thirteenth century to seize control over much of the known world (see Chapter 10). Beginning with the advances of Genghis Khan (JING-uss *or* GENG-uss KAHN) in northern China, Mongol armies later spread across Central Asia, and in 1258, under the leadership of Hu-legu (HOO-lay-goo), brother of the more famous Khubilai Khan (KOO-bluh KAHN), they seized Persia and Mesopotamia, bringing an end to the caliphate at Baghdad.

The Mongols

Unlike the Seljuk Turks, the Mongols were not Muslims, and they found it difficult to adapt to the settled conditions that they found in the major cities in the Middle East. Their treatment of the local population in conquered territories was brutal (according to one historian,

Syria//© Michael Nicholson/CORBIS

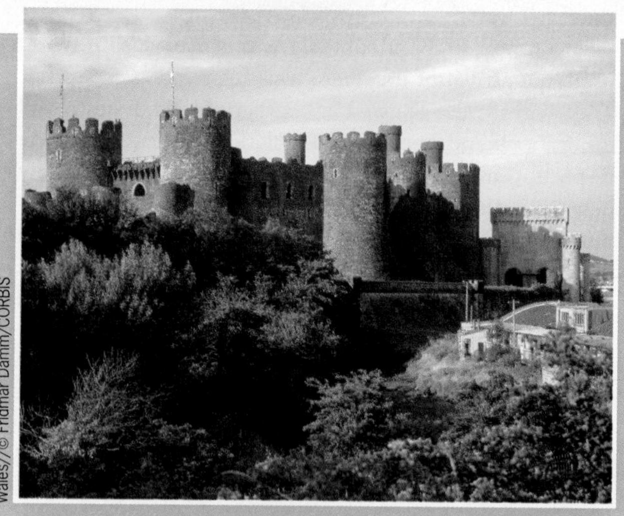

Wales//© Fridmar Damm/CORBIS

COMPARATIVE ILLUSTRATION

The Medieval Castle. Beginning in the eighth century, Muslim rulers began to erect fortified stone castles in the desert. So impressed were the crusaders by the innovative defenses that they began to incorporate similar features in their own European castles, which had previously been made of wood. In twelfth-century Syria, the crusaders constructed the imposing citadel known as the Krak des Chevaliers (KRAK de shuh-VAL-yay) (Castle of the Knights) on the foundation of a Muslim fort (left photo). This new model of a massive fortress of solid masonry spread to western Europe, as is evident in the castle shown in the right photo, built in the late thirteenth century in Wales.

Q *What types of warfare were used to defend—and attack—castles such as these?*

after conquering a city, they wiped out not only entire families but also their household pets) and destructive to the economy. Cities were razed to the ground, and dams and other irrigation works were destroyed, reducing prosperous agricultural societies to the point of mass starvation. The Mongols advanced as far as the Red Sea, but their attempt to seize Egypt failed, in part because of the effective resistance posed by the Mamluks (MAM-looks) (or Mamelukes, a Turkish military class originally composed of slaves), who had recently overthrown the administration set up by Saladin and seized power for themselves. Eventually, the Mongol rulers in the Middle East began to take on the coloration of the peoples they had conquered. Mongol elites converted to Islam, Persian influence became predominant at court, and the cities began to be rebuilt. By the fourteenth century, the Mongol Empire began to split into separate kingdoms and then to disintegrate. In the meantime, however, the old Islamic empire originally established by the Arabs in the seventh and eighth centuries had come to an end. The new center of Islamic civilization was in Cairo, now about to promote a renaissance in Muslim culture under the sponsorship of the Mamluks.

To the north, another new force began to appear on the horizon with the rise of the Ottoman Turks on the Anatolian peninsula. In 1453, Sultan Mehmet II seized Constantinople and brought an end to the Byzantine Empire. Then the Ottomans began to turn their attention to the rest of the Middle East (see Chapter 16).

Andalusia: A Muslim Outpost in Europe

After the decline of Baghdad, perhaps the brightest star in the Muslim firmament was in Spain, where a member of the Umayyad dynasty had managed to establish himself after his family's rule in the Middle East had been overthrown in 750. Abd al-Rathman (AHB-d al-rahkh-MAHN) escaped the carnage in Damascus and made his way to Spain, where Muslim power had recently replaced that of the Visigoths. By 756, he had legitimized his authority in southern Spain—known to the Arabs as *al-Andaluz* and to Europeans as Andalusia—and took the title of ***emir*** (EH-meer) (commander), with his capital at Córdoba (KOR-duh-buh). There he and his successors sought to build a vibrant new center for Islamic culture in the region. With the primacy of Baghdad now at an end, Andalusian rulers established a new caliphate in 929.

Now that the seizure of Crete, Sardinia, Sicily, and the Balearic Islands had turned the Mediterranean Sea into a Muslim lake, Andalusia became part of a vast trade network that stretched all the way from the Strait of Gibraltar to the Red Sea and beyond. Valuable new products,

OPPOSING ✂ VIEWPOINTS

The Siege of Jerusalem: Christian and Muslim Perspectives

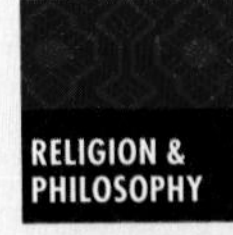

During the First Crusade, Christian knights laid siege to Jerusalem in June 1099. The first excerpt is taken from an account by Fulcher of Chartres, who accompanied the crusaders to the Holy Land. The second selection is by a Muslim writer, Ibn al-Athir, whose account of the First Crusade can be found in his history of the Muslim world.

Fulcher of Chartres, *Chronicle of the First Crusade*

Then the Franks [the crusaders] entered the city magnificently at the noonday hour on Friday, the day of the week when Christ redeemed the whole world on the cross. With trumpets sounding and with everything in an uproar, exclaiming: "Help, God!" they vigorously pushed into the city, and straightway raised the banner on the top of the wall. All the heathen, completely terrified, changed their boldness to swift flight through the narrow streets of the quarters. The more quickly they fled, the more quickly they put to flight.

Count Raymond and his men, who were bravely assailing the city in another section, did not perceive this until they saw the Saracens [Muslims] jumping from the top of the wall. Seeing this, they joyfully ran to the city as quickly as they could, and helped the others pursue and kill the wicked enemy.

Then some, both Arabs and Ethiopians, fled into the Tower of David; others shut themselves in the Temple of the Lord and of Solomon, where in the halls a very great attack was made on them. Nowhere was there a place where the Saracens could escape swordsmen.

On the top of Solomon's Temple, to which they had climbed in fleeing, many were shot to death with arrows and cast down headlong from the roof. Within this Temple, about ten thousand were beheaded. If you had been there, your feet would have been stained up to the ankles with the blood of the slain. What more shall I tell? Not one of them was allowed to live. They did not spare the women and children.

Account of Ibn al-Athir

In fact Jerusalem was taken from the north on the morning of Friday 22 Sha'ban 492/15 July 1099. The population was put to the sword by the Franks, who pillaged the area for a week. A band of Muslims barricaded themselves into the Oratory of David and fought on for several days. They were granted their lives in return for surrendering. The Franks honored their word, and the group left by night for Ascalon. In the Masjid al-Aqsa the Franks slaughtered more than 70,000 people, among them a large number of Imams and Muslim scholars, devout and ascetic men who had left their homelands to live lives of pious seclusion in the Holy Place. The Franks stripped the Dome of the Rock of more than forty silver candelabra, each of them weighing 3,600 drams, and a great silver lamp weighing forty-four Syrian pounds, as well as a hundred and fifty smaller candelabra and more than twenty gold ones, and a great deal more booty. Refugees from Syria reached Baghdad in Ramadan, among them the qadi Abu sa'd al-Harawi. They told the Caliph's ministers a story that wrung their hearts and brought tears to their eyes. On Friday they went to the Cathedral Mosque and begged for help, weeping so that their hearers wept with them as they described the sufferings of the Muslims in that Holy City: the men killed, the women and children taken prisoner, the homes pillaged. Because of the terrible hardships they had suffered, they were allowed to break the fast.

What happened to the inhabitants of Jerusalem when the Christian knights captured the city? How do you explain the extreme intolerance and brutality of the Christian knights? How do these two accounts differ, and how are they similar?

Sources: Fulcher of Chartres, *Chronicle of the First Crusade*. From *The First Crusade: The Chronicle of Fulcher of Chartres and Other Source Materials*, 2nd ed. Ed. Edward Peters (University of Pennsylvania Press, 1998), pp. 90–91. Account of Ibn al-Athir. From *Arab Historians of the Crusades*, ed. and trans. E. J. Costello. Berkeley: University of California Press, 1969.

Winning Hearts and Minds in Murcia

POLITICS & GOVERNMENT

Although the Muslim seizure of southern Spain in the eighth century was generally accomplished by force, the new rulers sometimes negotiated peace settlements with their enemies that protected the lives and property of their new subjects. This selection presents the text of a treaty established in 713 between the victorious Muslim ruler Abd al-Aziz (AHB-d al-ah-ZEEZ) and his defeated Christian rival from the city of Murcia (mur-SHEE-uh), the Visigothic noble Theodemir (thee-AHD-uh-meer). For Muslim conquerors like Aziz, it was sometimes more practical to "win the hearts and minds" of the local population than to seek to enslave them or to convert them to Islam by force.

A Treaty of Peace

In the name of God, the Merciful, the Compassionate. This text was written by Abd al-Azīz b. Mūsā b. Nusayr for Tudmīr b. Ghabdush, establishing a treaty of peace and the promise and protection of God and His Prophet (may God bless him and grant him His peace). We [Abd al-Azīz] will not set any special conditions for him or for any among his men, nor harass him, nor remove him from power. His followers will not be killed or taken prisoner, nor will they be separated from their women and children. They will not be coerced in matters of religion, their churches will not be burned, nor will sacred objects be taken from the realm as long as Theodemir remains sincere and fulfils the following conditions we have set for him:

He has reached a settlement concerning seven towns: Orihuela, Valentilla, Alicante, Mula, Bigastro, Ello, and Lorca.

He will not give shelter to fugitives, nor to our enemies, nor encourage any protected person to fear us, nor conceal news of our enemies.

He and each of his men shall also pay one dinar every year, together with four measures of wheat, four measures of barley, four liquid measures of concentrated fruit juice, four liquid measures of vinegar, four of honey and four of olive oil. Slaves must each pay half of this.

What kinds of restrictions were usually placed on non-Muslims in Andalusia?

Source: From O. R. Constable (ed.), *Medieval Iberia: Readings in Christian, Muslim, and Jewish Sources* (Philadelphia, 1997), pp. 37–38. Cited in H. Kennedy, *The Great Arab Conquests: How the Spread of Islam Changed the World We Live In* (Philadelphia, 2007), p. 315.

including cotton, sugar, olives, wheat, citrus, and the date palm, were introduced to the Iberian peninsula.

Andalusia also flourished as an artistic and intellectual center. The court gave active support to writers and artists, creating a brilliant culture focused on the emergence of three world-class cities—Córdoba, Seville, and Toledo. Intellectual leaders arrived in the area from all parts of the Islamic world, bringing their knowledge of medicine, astronomy, mathematics, and philosophy. With the establishment of a paper factory near Valencia, the means of disseminating such information dramatically improved, and the libraries of Andalusia became the wonder of their time (see "Philosophy and Science" later in this chapter).

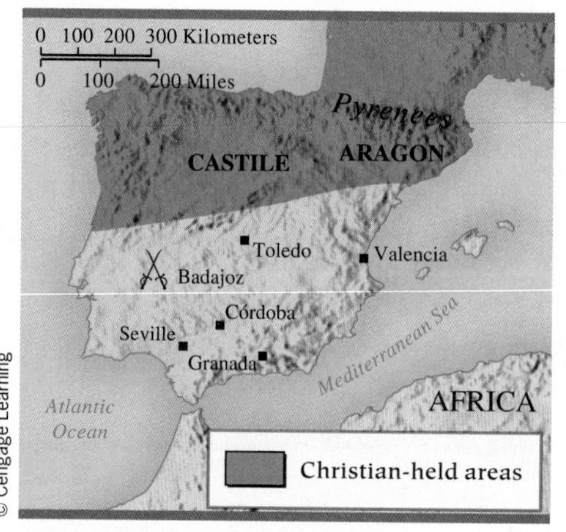

Spain in the Eleventh Century

A major reason for the rise of Andalusia as a hub of artistic and intellectual activity was the atmosphere of tolerance in social relations fostered by the state. Although Islam was firmly established as the official faith and non-Muslims were encouraged to convert as a means of furthering their careers, the policy of *convivéncia* (con-vee-VEN-cee-uh) (commingling) provided an environment for many Christians and Jews to maintain their religious beliefs and even obtain favors from the court (see the box above).

A TIME OF TROUBLES Unfortunately, the primacy of Andalusia as a cultural center was short-lived. By the end of the tenth century, factionalism was beginning to undermine the foundations of the emirate. In 1009, the royal palace at Córdoba was totally destroyed in a civil war. Twenty-two years later, the caliphate itself disappeared as the emirate dissolved into a patchwork of city-states.

In the meantime, the Christian kingdoms that had managed to establish themselves in the north of the Iberian peninsula were consolidating their position and beginning to expand southward. In 1085, Alfonso VI, the Christian king of Castile, seized Toledo, one of Andalusia's main intellectual centers. The new rulers continued to foster the artistic and intellectual activities of their predecessors. To recoup their recent losses, the Muslim rulers in Seville called on fellow Muslims, the Almoravids (al-MOR-uh-vids)—a Berber dynasty in Morocco—to assist in halting the Christian advance. Berber mercenaries defeated Castilian forces at Badajoz (bah-duh-HOHZ) in 1086 but then stayed in the area to establish their own rule over the remaining Muslim-held areas in southern Spain.

A warrior culture with no tolerance for heterodox ideas, the Almoravids quickly brought an end to the era of religious tolerance and intellectual achievement. But the presence of Andalusia's new warlike rulers was unable to stem the Christian advance. In 1215, Pope Innocent III called for a new crusade to destroy Muslim rule in southern Spain. Over the next two hundred years, Christian armies advanced relentlessly southward, seizing the cities of Seville and Córdoba. Only a single redoubt of Abd al-Rathman's glorious achievement remained: the remote mountain city of Granada (greh-NAH-duh), with its imposing hilltop fortress, the Alhambra (al-HAM-bruh).

MOORISH SPAIN: AN ERA OF "CULTURAL TOLERANCE"? In standard interpretations of European history, Western historians have usually described the *Reconquista* (ray-con-KEES-tuh) (reconquest) of southern Spain by the Christian kingdoms in the north as a positive development that freed the Spanish people from centuries of oppressive Muslim rule. In recent years, however, it has become fashionable to point to the Moorish era in Spain (the term *Moors* is often used to refer to the Muslims in Spain) as a period of "cultural tolerance," a time of diversity that was followed by the bloody era of the Spanish Inquisition, when the Catholic Church persecuted Muslims, Jews, and Christian heretics for their refusal to accept the true faith. This interpretation has been especially popular since the terrorist attacks in September 2001, as revisionist scholars seek to present a favorable image of Islam to counter the popular perception that all Muslims are sympathetic to terrorism against the West.

Some historians, however, argue that this portrayal of the Moorish era as a period of "cultural tolerance" overstates the case. They point out that even under the relatively benign rule of Abd al-Rathman, true religious tolerance was never achieved and that, in any event, any such era came to an end with the arrival of the Almoravids and the Almohads (AL-moh-hads), a Berber dynasty that supplanted the Almoravids in Andalusia in the twelfth century. For historian J. S. Elliot, the era was, at best, one of "cultural interaction," which was eventually followed by a hardening of attitudes on both sides of the cultural spectrum. If there was an era of religious diversity in Spain under Muslim rule, it was all too brief.

CHRONOLOGY Islam: The First Millennium

Life of Muhammad	570–632
Flight to Medina	622
Conquest of Mecca	630
Fall of Cairo	640
Defeat of Persians	650
Election of Ali to caliphate	656
Muslim entry into Spain	c. 710
Abbasid caliphate	750–1258
Construction of city of Baghdad	762
Reign of Harun al-Rashid	786–809
Umayyad caliphate in Spain	929–1031
Founding of Fatimid dynasty in Egypt	973
Capture of Baghdad by Seljuk Turks	1055
Seizure of Anatolia by Seljuk Turks	1071
First Crusade	1096
Saladin destroys Fatimid kingdom	1169
Mongols seize Baghdad	1258
Ottoman Turks capture Constantinople	1453

Islamic Civilization

FOCUS QUESTION: What were the main features of Islamic society and culture during its era of early growth?

To be a Muslim is not simply to worship Allah but also to live according to his law as revealed in the Qur'an, which is viewed as fundamental and immutable doctrine, not to be revised by human beings.

As Allah has decreed, so must humans behave. Therefore, Islamic doctrine must be consulted to determine questions of politics, economic behavior, civil and criminal law, and social ethics. In Islamic society, there is no demarcation between church and state, between the sacred and the secular.

Sage Advice from Father to Son

Tahir ibn Husayn (tah-HEER IB-un HOO-sayn) was born into an aristocratic family in Central Asia and became a key political adviser to al-Ma'mun, the Abbasid caliph of Baghdad in the early ninth century. Appointed in 821 to a senior position in Khurusan (kor-uh-SAHN), a district near the city of Herat in what is today Afghanistan, he wrote the following letter to his son, giving advice on how to wield authority most effectively. The letter so impressed al-Ma'mun that he had it widely distributed throughout his bureaucracy.

Letter of Tahir ibn Husayn

Look carefully into the matter of the land-tax which the subjects have an obligation to pay. . . . Divide it among the taxpayers with justice and fairness with equal treatment for all. Do not remove any part of the obligation to pay the tax from any noble person just because of his nobility or any rich person because of his richness or from any of your secretaries or personal retainers. Do not require from anyone more than he can bear, or exact more than the usual rate. . . .

[The ruler should also devote himself] to looking after the affairs of the poor and destitute, those who are unable to bring their complaints of ill-treatment to you personally and those of wretched estate who do not know how to set about claiming their rights. . . . Turn your attention to those who have suffered injuries and their orphans and widows and provide them with allowances from the state treasury, following the example of the Commander of the Faithful, may God exalt him, in showing compassion for them and giving them financial support, so that God may thereby bring some alleviation into their daily lives and by means of it bring you the spiritual food of His blessing and an increase of His favor. Give pensions from the state treasury to the blind, and give higher allowances to those who know of the Qur'an, or most of it by heart. Set up hospices where sick Muslims can find shelter, and appoint custodians for these places who will treat the patients with kindness and physicians who will cure their illnesses. . . .

Keep an eye on the officials at your court and on your secretaries. Give them each a fixed time each day when they can bring you their official correspondence and any documents requiring the ruler's signature. They can let you know about the needs of the various officials and about all the affairs of the provinces you rule over. Then devote all your faculties, ears, eyes, understanding and intellect, to the business they set before you: consider it and think about it repeatedly. Finally take those actions which seem to be in accordance with good judgment and justice.

How does Tahir's advice compare with that given in the political treatise Arthasastra, *discussed in Chapter 2? Would Tahir's letter provide an effective model for political leadership today?*

Source: H. Keller (ed.), *Ibn Abi Tahir Kitab Baghdad* (Leipzig, 1908), cited in H. Kennedy, *When Baghdad Ruled the Muslim World: The Rise and Fall of Islam's Greatest Dynasty* (Cambridge, MA, 2004), pp. 204–205.

Political Structures

For early converts, establishing political institutions and practices that conformed to Islamic doctrine was a daunting task. In the first place, the will of Allah, as revealed to his Prophet, was not precise about the relationship between religious and political authority, simply decreeing that human beings should "conduct their affairs by mutual consent." On a more practical plane, establishing political institutions for a large and multicultural empire presented a challenge for the Arabs, whose own political structures were relatively rudimentary and relevant only to small pastoral communities (see the box above).

During the life of Muhammad, the problem could be avoided, since he was generally accepted as both the religious and the political leader of the Islamic community—the *umma*. His death, however, raised the question of how a successor should be chosen and what authority that person should have. As we have seen, Muhammad's immediate successors were called caliphs. Their authority was purely temporal, although they were also considered in general terms to be religious leaders, with the title of *imam*. At first, each caliph was selected informally by leading members of the *umma*. Soon succession became hereditary in the Umayyad clan, but their authority was still limited, at least in theory, by the idea that they should consult with other leaders. Under the Abbasids, as we saw earlier, the caliphs took on more of the trappings of kingship and became more autocratic.

The Wealth of Araby: Trade and Cities in the Middle East

Overall, as we have noted, this era was probably one of the most prosperous periods in the history of the Middle East. Trade flourished, not only in the Islamic world but also with China (now in a period of efflorescence during the era of the Tang and the Song dynasties—see Chapter 10), with the Byzantine Empire, and with the trading societies in Southeast Asia (see Chapter 9). Trade goods were carried both by ship and by the "fleets of the desert," the camel caravans that traversed the arid land from Morocco in the far west to the countries beyond the Caspian Sea. From West Africa came gold and slaves; from China, silk and porcelain; from East Africa, gold, ivory, and rhinoceros horn; and from the lands of South Asia, sandalwood, cotton, wheat, sugar, and spices. Within the empire, Egypt contributed grain; Iraq, linens, dates, and precious stones; Spain, leather goods, olives, and wine; and western India, various textile goods. The exchange of goods was facilitated by the development of banking and the use of currency and letters of credit (see the comparative essay "Trade and Civilization" on p. 186).

Under these conditions, urban areas flourished. While the Abbasids were in power, Baghdad was probably the greatest city in the empire, but after the rise of the Fatimids in Egypt, the focus of trade shifted to Cairo, described by the traveler Leo Africanus as "one of the greatest and most famous cities in all the whole world, filled with stately and admirable palaces and colleges, and most sumptuous temples."[6] Other great commercial cities included Basra at the head of the Persian Gulf, Aden at the southern tip of the Arabian peninsula, Damascus in modern Syria, and Marrakech in Morocco. In the cities, the inhabitants were generally segregated by religion, with Muslims, Jews, and Christians living in separate neighborhoods. But all were equally subject to the most common threats to urban life—fire, flood, and disease.

The most impressive urban buildings were usually the palace for the caliph or the local governor and the great mosque. Houses were often constructed of stone or brick around a timber frame. The larger houses were often built around an interior courtyard, where the residents could retreat from the dust, noise, and heat of the city streets. Sometimes domestic animals such as goats or sheep would be stabled there. The houses of the wealthy were often multistoried, with balconies and windows covered with latticework to provide privacy for those inside. The poor in both urban and rural areas lived in simpler houses composed of clay or unfired bricks. The Bedouins lived in tents that could be dismantled and moved according to their needs.

The Arab Empire was clearly more urbanized than most other areas of the known world at the time. Yet the bulk of the population continued to live in the countryside, supported by farming or herding animals. During the early stages, most of the farmland was owned by independent peasants, but eventually some concentration of land in the hands of wealthy owners began to take place. Some lands were owned by the state or the court and were cultivated by slave labor, but plantation agriculture was not as common as it would be later in many areas of the world. In the valleys of rivers such as the Tigris, the Euphrates, and the Nile, the majority of the farmers were probably independent peasants.

Eating habits varied in accordance with economic standing and religious preference. Muslims did not eat pork, but those who could afford it often served other meats such as mutton, lamb, poultry, or fish. Fruit, spices, and various sweets were delicacies. The poor were generally forced to survive on boiled millet or peas with an occasional lump of meat or fat. Bread—white or whole meal—could be found on tables throughout the region except in the deserts, where boiled grain was the staple food.

Islamic Society

In some ways, Arab society was probably one of the most egalitarian of its time. Both the principles of Islam, which held that all were equal in the eyes of Allah, and the importance of trade to the prosperity of the state probably contributed to this egalitarianism. Although there was a fairly well defined upper class, consisting of the ruling families, senior officials, tribal elites, and the wealthiest merchants, there was no hereditary nobility as in many contemporary societies, and the merchants enjoyed a degree of respect that they did not receive in Europe, China, or India.

Not all benefited from the high degree of social mobility in the Islamic world, however. Slavery was widespread. Since a Muslim could not be enslaved, the supply came from sub-Saharan Africa or from non-Islamic populations elsewhere in Asia. Most slaves were employed in the army (which was sometimes a road to power, as in the case of the Mamluks) or as domestic servants, who were sometimes permitted to purchase their freedom. The slaves who worked the large estates experienced the worst living conditions and rose in revolt on several occasions.

The Islamic principle of human equality also fell short, as in most other societies of the day, in the treatment of women. Although the Qur'an instructed men to treat women with respect, and women did have the right to own and inherit property, in general the male was dominant in Muslim society. Polygyny was permitted, and the right of divorce was in practice restricted to the husband,

COMPARATIVE ESSAY

Trade and Civilization

In 2002, archaeologists unearthed the site of an ancient Egyptian port city on the shores of the Red Sea. Established sometime during the first millennium B.C.E., the city of Berenike (ber-eh-NEE-kay) linked the Nile River valley with ports as far away as the island of Java in Southeast Asia. The discovery of Berenike is only the latest piece of evidence confirming the importance of interregional trade since the beginning of the historical era. The exchange of goods between far-flung societies became a powerful engine behind the rise of advanced civilizations throughout the ancient world. Raw materials such as copper, tin, and obsidian; items of daily necessity including salt, fish, and other foodstuffs; and luxury goods such as gold, silk, and precious stones passed from one end of the Eurasian supercontinent to the other, across the desert from the Mediterranean Sea to sub-Saharan Africa, and throughout much of the Americas. Less well known but also important was the maritime trade that stretched from the Mediterranean across the Indian Ocean to port cities on the distant coasts of Southeast and East Asia.

During the first millennium C.E., the level of interdependence among human societies intensified as three major trade routes—across the Indian Ocean, along the Silk Road, and by caravan across the Sahara—created the framework for a single system of trade. The new global network was informational as well as commercial, transmitting technology and ideas, such as the emerging religions of Buddhism, Christianity, and Islam, to new destinations. There was a close relationship between missionary activities and trade. Buddhist merchants brought the teachings of Siddhartha Gautama to China, and Muslim traders carried Muhammad's words to Southeast Asia and sub-Saharan Africa. Indian traders carried Hindu beliefs and political institutions to Southeast Asia.

What caused the rapid expansion of trade during this period? One key factor was the introduction of technology that facilitated transportation. The development of the compass, improved techniques in mapmaking and shipbuilding, and greater knowledge of wind patterns all contributed to the expansion of maritime trade. Caravan trade, once carried by wheeled chariots or on the backs of oxen, now used the camel as the preferred beast of burden through the deserts of Africa, Central Asia, and the Middle East.

Another reason for the expansion of commerce during this period was the appearance of several multinational empires that created zones of stability and affluence in key areas of the Eurasian landmass. Most important were the emergence of the Abbasid Empire in the Middle East and the prosperity of China during the Tang and Song dynasties (see Chapter 10). The Mongol invasions in the thirteenth century temporarily disrupted the process but then established a new era of stability that fostered long-distance trade throughout the world.

Bibliothèque Nationale, Paris//© The Bridgeman Art Library

Arab traders in a caravan

The importance of interregional trade as a crucial factor in promoting the growth of human civilizations can be highlighted by comparing the social, cultural, and technological achievements of active trading states with those of communities that have traditionally been cut off from contacts with the outside world. We shall encounter many of these communities in later chapters. Even in the Western Hemisphere, where regional trade linked societies from the Great Plains of North America to the Andes Mountains in present-day Peru, geographic barriers limited the exchange of inventions and ideas, putting these societies at a distinct disadvantage when the first contacts with peoples across the oceans occurred at the beginning of the modern era.

What were the chief factors that led to the expansion of interregional trade during the first millennium C.E.? How did the growth of international trade contacts affect other aspects of society?

The Gift of the Robe

Ibn Battuta (IB-un ba-TOO-tuh) (1304–1377), a travel writer born in the Moroccan city of Tangier, is often described as the Muslim equivalent of his famous Italian counterpart Marco Polo. Over the course of a quarter of a century, he traveled widely throughout Africa and Asia, logging over 75,000 miles in the process. The fascinating personal account of his travels is a prime source of information about his times. In the excerpt presented here, he describes a visit to the city of Balkh (BAHLK), one of the fabled caravan stops on the Silk Road as it passed through Central Asia.

The Travels of Ibn Battuta

After a journey of a day and a half over a sandy desert in which there was no house, we arrived at the city of Balkh, which now lies in ruins. It has not been rebuilt since its destruction by the cursed Jengiz Khān. The situation of its buildings is not very discernible, although its extent may be traced. It is now in ruins, and without society.

Its mosque was one of the largest and handsomest in the world. Its pillars were incomparable: three of which were destroyed by Jengiz Khān, because it had been told him, that the wealth of the mosque lay concealed under them, provided as a fund for its repairs. When, however, he had destroyed them, nothing of the kind was to be found: the rest, therefore he left as they were.

The story about this treasure arose from the following circumstance. It is said, that one of the Califs of the house of Abbās was very much enraged at the inhabitants of Balkh, on account of some accident which had happened, and, on this account, sent a person to collect a heavy fine from them. Upon this occasion, the women and children of the city betook themselves to the wife of their then governor, who, out of her own money, built this mosque; and to her they made a grievous complaint. She accordingly sent to the officer, who had been commissioned to collect the fine, a robe very richly embroidered and adorned with jewels, much greater in value than the amount of the fine imposed. This, she requested might be sent to the Calif as a present from herself, to be accepted instead of the fine. The officer accordingly took the robe, and sent it to the Calif; who, when he saw it, was surprised at her liberality, and said: This woman must not be allowed to exceed myself in generosity. He then sent back the robe, and remitted the fine. When the robe was returned to her, she asked, whether a look of the Calif had fallen upon it; and being told that it had, she replied: No robe shall ever come upon me, upon which the look of any man, except my own husband, has fallen. She then ordered it to be cut up and sold; and with the price of it she built the mosque, with the cell and structure in the front of it. Still, from the price of the robe there remained a third, which she commanded to be buried under one of its pillars, in order to meet any future expenses which might be necessary for its repairs. Upon Jengiz Khān's hearing this story, he ordered these pillars to be destroyed; but, as already remarked, he found nothing.

Would a Muslim observer have considered the actions of the governor's wife described here to be meritorious? Why or why not?

Source: S. Lee (trans.), *The Travels of Ibn Battuta in the Near East, Asia, and Africa, 1325–1354* (Mineola, NY, 2004), pp. 93–94.

although some schools of legal thought permitted women to stipulate that their husband could have only one wife or to seek a separation in certain specific circumstances. Adultery and homosexuality were stringently forbidden (although such prohibitions were frequently ignored in practice), and custom required that women be cloistered in their homes and prohibited from social contacts with males outside their own family.

A prominent example of this custom was the harem, introduced at the Abbasid court during the reign of Harun al-Rashid. Members of the royal harem were drawn from non-Muslim female populations throughout the empire. The custom of requiring women to cover virtually all parts of their body when appearing in public was common in urban areas and continues to be practiced in many Islamic societies today. It should be noted, however, that these customs owed more to traditional Arab practice than to Qur'anic law (see the box above).

The Culture of Islam

The Arabs were heirs to many elements of the remaining Greco-Roman culture of the Roman Empire, and they assimilated Byzantine and Persian culture just as readily. In the eighth and ninth centuries, numerous Greek, Syrian, and Persian scientific and philosophical works were translated into Arabic and eventually found their way to Europe. As the chief language in the southern Mediterranean and the Middle East, Arabic became an international language. Later, Persian and Turkish also came to be important in administration and culture.

The spread of Islam led to the emergence of a new culture throughout the Arab Empire. This was true in all fields of endeavor, from literature to art and architecture. But pre-Islamic traditions were not extinguished and frequently combined with Muslim motifs, resulting in creative works of great imagination and originality.

PHILOSOPHY AND SCIENCE During the centuries following the rise of the Arab Empire, it was the Islamic world that was most responsible for preserving and spreading the scientific and philosophical achievements of ancient civilizations. At a time when ancient Greek philosophy was largely unknown in Europe, key works by Aristotle, Plato, and other Greek philosophers were translated into Arabic and stored in a "house of wisdom" in Baghdad, where they were read and studied by Muslim scholars. Eventually, many of these works were translated into Latin and were brought to Europe, where they exercised a profound influence on the later course of Christianity and Western philosophy.

The process began in the sixth century C.E., when the Byzantine ruler Justinian (see Chapter 13) shut down the Platonic Academy in Athens, declaring that it promoted heretical ideas. Many of the scholars at the Academy fled to Baghdad, where their ideas and the Classical texts they brought with them soon aroused local interest and were translated into Persian or Arabic. Later such works were supplemented by acquisitions in Constantinople and possibly also from the famous library at Alexandria.

The academies where the translations were carried out—often by families specializing in the task—were not true universities like those that would later appear in Europe. Instead, they were private operations working under the sponsorship of a great patron, many of whom were highly cultivated Persians living in Baghdad or other major cities. Dissemination of the translated works was stimulated by the arrival of paper in the Middle East, brought by Buddhist pilgrims from China passing along the Silk Road. Paper was much cheaper to manufacture than papyrus, and by the end of the eighth century, the first paper factories were up and running in Baghdad. Libraries and booksellers soon appeared.

What motives inspired this ambitious literary preservation project? At the outset, it may have simply been an effort to provide philosophical confirmation for existing religious beliefs as derived from the Qur'an. Eventually, however, more adventurous minds began to use the Classical texts not only to seek greater knowledge of the divine will but also to obtain a better understanding of the laws of nature.

Such was the case with the physician and intellectual Ibn Sina (IB-un SEE-nuh) (980–1037), known in the West as Avicenna (av-i-SENN-uh). In his own philosophical writings, he cited Aristotle to the effect that the world operated not only at the will of Allah but also by its own natural laws, laws that could be ascertained by

© Topkapi Palace Museum, Istanbul/The Bridgeman Art Library

Preserving the Wisdom of the Greeks. After the fall of the Roman Empire, the philosophical works of ancient Greece were virtually forgotten in Europe or were banned as heretical by the Byzantine Empire. It was thanks to Muslim scholars, who located copies at the magnificent library in Alexandria, Egypt, that many Classical Greek writings survived. Here young Muslim scholars are being trained in the Greek language so that they can translate Classical Greek writings into Arabic. Later the texts were translated back into Western languages and served as the catalyst for an intellectual revival in medieval and Renaissance Europe.

human reason. Such ideas eventually aroused the ire of traditional Muslim scholars, and although works by such ancient writers as Euclid, Ptolemy and Archimedes continued to be translated, the influence of Greek philosophy began to wane in Baghdad by the end of the eleventh century and did not recover.

By then, however, interest in Classical Greek ideas had spread to Spain. Philosophers such as Averroës (uh-VERR-oh-eez), whose Arabic name was Ibn Rushd (IB-un RUSH-ed *or* IB-un RUSHT), and Maimonides (my-MAH-nuh-deez) (Musa Ibn Maymun), a Jew who often wrote in Arabic, undertook their own translations and wrote in support of Avicenna's defense of the role of human reason. Both were born in Córdoba in the early twelfth century but were persecuted for their ideas by the Almohads, a Berber dynasty that had supplanted Almoravid authority in Andalusia, and both men ended their days in exile in North Africa.

By the thirteenth century, Christian rulers such as Alfonso X in Castile and Frederick II in Sicily were beginning to sponsor their own translations of Classical Greek works from Arabic into Latin. These translations soon made their way to the many new universities sprouting up all over Western Europe.

Although Islamic scholars are justly praised for preserving much of Classical Greek knowledge for the West, they also made considerable advances of their own. Nowhere is this more evident than in mathematics and the natural sciences. Islamic scholars adopted and passed on the numerical system of India, including the use of zero, and a ninth-century Persian mathematician founded the mathematical discipline of algebra (*al-jabr*, "the reduction"). Simplified "Arabic" numerals had begun to replace cumbersome Roman numerals in Italy by the thirteenth century.

In astronomy, Muslims set up an observatory at Baghdad to study the position of the stars. They were aware that the earth was round and in the ninth century produced a world map based on the tradition of the Greco-Roman astronomer Ptolemy (see the comparative illustration on p. 190). Aided by the astrolabe, an instrument designed to enable sailors to track their position by means of the stars, Muslim fleets and caravans opened up new trade routes connecting the Islamic world with other civilizations, and Muslim travelers such as al-Mas'udi and Ibn Battuta wrote accurate descriptions of political and social conditions throughout the Middle East.

Muslim scholars also made many new discoveries in optics and chemistry and, with the assistance of texts on anatomy by the ancient Greek physician Galen (GAY-lun) (c. 129–c. 200 C.E.), developed medicine as a distinct field of scientific inquiry. Avicenna compiled a medical encyclopedia that, among other things, emphasized the contagious nature of certain diseases and showed how they could be spread by contaminated water supplies. After its translation into Latin, Avicenna's work became a basic medical textbook for medieval European university students.

ISLAMIC LITERATURE Islam brought major changes to the literature of the Middle East. Muslims regarded the Qur'an as their greatest literary work, but pre-Islamic traditions continued to influence writers throughout the region.

The tradition of Arabic poetry was well established by the time of Muhammad. It extolled Bedouin tribal life, courage in battle, hunting, sports, and respect for the animals of the desert, especially the camel. Because the Arabic language did not possess a written script until the fourth century C.E., poetry was originally passed on by memory. Later, in the eighth and ninth centuries, it was compiled in anthologies.

Pre-Muslim Persia also boasted a long literary tradition, most of it oral and written down in later centuries in the Arabic alphabet. The Persian poetic tradition remained strong under Islam. Rabe'a of Qozdar (rah-BAY-uh of kuz-DAHR), Persia's first known woman poet, lived in the second half of the tenth century. Describing the suffering love brings, she wrote: "Beset with impatience I did not know / That the more one seeks to pull away, the tighter becomes the rope."[7]

In the West, the most famous works of Middle Eastern literature are undoubtedly the *Rubaiyat* (ROO-by-yaht) of Omar Khayyam (OH-mar ky-YAHM) and *Tales from 1001 Nights* (also called *The Arabian Nights*). Paradoxically, these two works are not as popular with Middle Eastern readers. Both, in fact, were freely translated into Western languages for nineteenth-century European readers, who developed a taste for stories set in exotic foreign places—a classic example of the tendency of Western observers to regard the customs and cultures of non-Western societies as strange or exotic.

Unfortunately, very little is known of the life or the poetry of the twelfth-century poet Omar Khayyam. Skeptical, reserved, and slightly contemptuous of his peers, he combined poetry with scientific works on mathematics and astronomy and a revision of the calendar that was more accurate than the Gregorian version devised in Europe hundreds of years later. Omar Khayyam did not write down his poems but composed them orally over wine with friends at a neighborhood tavern. They were recorded later by friends or scribes. Many poems attributed to him were actually written long after his death. Among them is the well-known couplet translated into English in the nineteenth century: "Here with a loaf of bread beneath the bough, / A flask of wine, a book of verse, and thou."

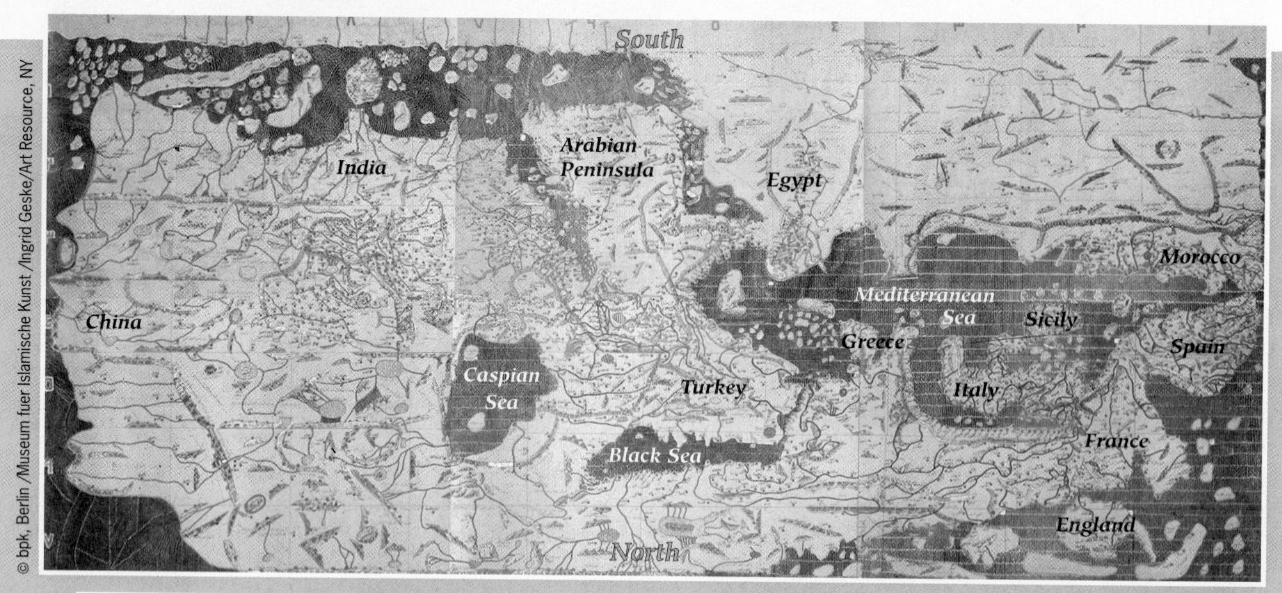

© bpk, Berlin /Museum fuer Islamische Kunst /Ingrid Geske/Art Resource, NY

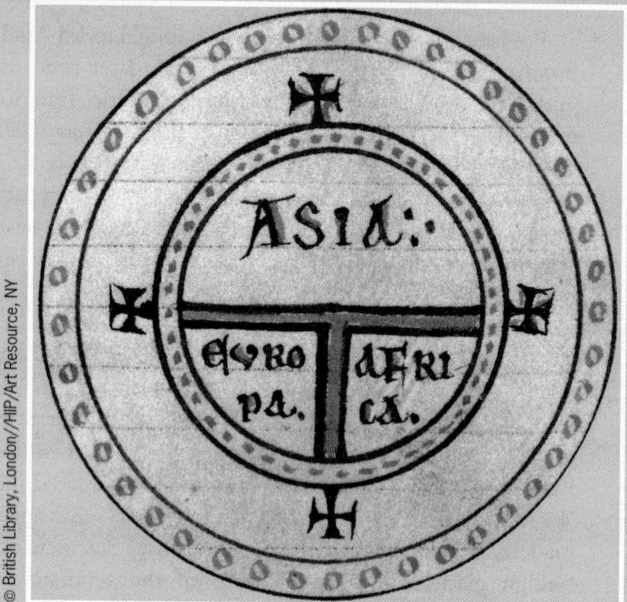

© British Library, London//HIP/Art Resource, NY

COMPARATIVE ILLUSTRATION

SCIENCE & TECHNOLOGY

A Twelfth-Century Map of the World. The twelfth-century Muslim geographer Al-Idrisi (al-ih-DREE-see) received his education in the Spanish city of Córdoba while it was under Islamic rule. Later he served at the court of the Norman king of Sicily, Roger II, where he created an atlas of the world based on Arab and European sources. In Muslim practice at the time, north and south were inverted from modern practice. Al-Idrisi's map, shown above, depicts the world as it was known at that time, stretching from the Spanish peninsula on the right to the civilization of China on the far left. It is also a testimonial to the vast extension of the power and influence of Islam in the five centuries since the death of Muhammad in 632. Maps drawn by Al-Idrisi's European contemporaries were still highly stylized, with the Christian holy city of Jerusalem placed at the center of the world, as in the map shown at the left.

How much of the world shown on al-Idrisi's map had been explored by Muslim fleets?

Omar Khayyam's poetry is simple and down to earth. Key themes are the impermanence of life, the impossibility of knowing God, and disbelief in an afterlife. Ironically, recent translations of his work appeal to modern attitudes of skepticism and minimalist simplicity that may make him even more popular in the West:

In youth I studied for a little while;
Later I boasted of my mastery.
Yet this was all the lesson that I learned:
We come from dust, and with the wind are gone.

Of all the travelers on this endless road
No one returns to tell us where it leads,
There's little in this world but greed and need;
Leave nothing here, for you will not return. . . .

Since no one can be certain of tomorrow,
It's better not to fill the heart with care.
Drink wine by moonlight, darling, for the moon
Will shine long after this, and find us not.[8]

Like Omar Khayyam's verse, *The Arabian Nights* was loosely translated into European languages and adapted to Western tastes. A composite of folktales, fables, and romances of Indian and indigenous origin, the stories interweave the natural with the supernatural. The earliest stories were told orally and were later transcribed, with many later additions, in Arabic and Persian versions. The famous story of Aladdin and the Magic Lamp, for example, was an eighteenth-century addition. Nevertheless, *The Arabian Nights* has entertained readers for centuries, allowing them to enter a land of wish fulfillment through extraordinary plots, sensuality, comic and tragic situations, and a cast of unforgettable characters.

Sadi (sah-DEE) (1210–1292), considered the Persian Shakespeare, remains to this day the favorite author in Iran. His *Rose Garden* is a collection of entertaining stories written in prose sprinkled with verse. He is also renowned for his sonnetlike love poems, which set a model for generations to come. Sadi was a master of the pithy maxim:

> *A cat is a lion in catching mice*
> *But a mouse in combat with a tiger.*
>
> *He has found eternal happiness who lived a good life,*
> *Because, after his end, good repute will keep his name alive.*
>
> *When thou fightest with anyone, consider*
> *Whether thou wilt have to flee from him or he from thee.*[9]

Some Arabic and Persian literature reflected the deep spiritual and ethical concerns of the Qur'an. Many writers, however, carried Islamic thought in novel directions. The thirteenth-century poet Rumi (ROO-mee), for example, embraced **Sufism** (SOO-fiz-uhm), a form of religious belief that called for a mystical relationship between Allah and human beings (the term *Sufism* stems from the Arabic word for "wool," referring to the rough wool garments that its adherents wore). Converted to Sufism by a wandering dervish (dervishes, from the word for "poor" in Persian, sought to achieve a mystical union with Allah through dancing and chanting in an ecstatic trance), Rumi abandoned orthodox Islam to embrace God directly through ecstatic love. Realizing that love transcends intellect, he sought to reach God through a trance attained by the whirling dance of the dervish, set to mesmerizing music. As he twirled, the poet extemporized some of the most passionate lyrical verse ever conceived. His faith and art remain an important force in Islamic society today.

The Islamic world also made a major contribution to historical writing, another discipline that was stimulated by the introduction of paper manufacturing. The first great Islamic historian was al-Mas'udi. Born in Baghdad in 896, he wrote about both the Muslim and the non-Muslim world, traveling widely in the process. His *Meadows of Gold* is the source of much of our knowledge about the golden age of the Abbasid caliphate. Translations of his work reveal a wide-ranging mind and a keen intellect, combined with a human touch that practitioners of the art in our century might find reason to emulate. Equaling al-Mas'udi in talent and reputation was the fourteenth-century historian Ibn Khaldun (IB-un kal-DOON). Combining scholarship with government service, Ibn Khaldun was one of the first historians to attempt a philosophy of history.

ISLAMIC ART AND ARCHITECTURE The art of Islam is a blend of Arab, Turkish, and Persian traditions. Although local influences can be discerned in Egypt, Anatolia, Spain, and other areas and the Mongols introduced an East Asian accent in the thirteenth century, for a long time Islamic art remained remarkably coherent over a wide area. First and foremost, the Arabs, with their new religion and their writing system, served as a unifying force. Fascinated by the mathematics and astronomy they inherited from the Romans or the Babylonians, they developed a sense of rhythm and abstraction that found expression in their use of repetitive geometric ornamentation. The Turks brought abstraction in figurative and nonfigurative designs, and the Persians added their lyrical poetical mysticism. Much Islamic painting, for example, consists of illustrations of Persian texts.

The ultimate expression of Islamic art is to be found in magnificent architectural monuments beginning in the late seventh century. The first great example is the Dome of the Rock, which was built in 691 to proclaim the spiritual and political legitimacy of the new religion to the ancient world. Set in the sacred heart of Jerusalem on Muhammad's holy rock and touching both the Western Wall of the Jews and the oldest Christian church, the Dome of the Rock remains one of the most revered Islamic monuments. Constructed on Byzantine lines with an octagonal shape and marble columns and ornamentation, the interior reflects Persian motifs with mosaics of precious stones. Although rebuilt several times and incorporating influences from both East and West, this first monument to Islam represents the birth of a new art.

At first, desert Arabs, whether nomads or conquering armies, prayed in an open court, shaded along the *qibla* (KIB-luh) (the wall facing the holy city of Mecca) by a thatched roof supported by rows of palm trunks. There was also a ditch where the faithful could wash off the dust of the desert prior to prayer. As Islam became better established, enormous mosques were constructed, but they were still modeled on the open court, which would be surrounded on all four sides with pillars supporting a wooden roof over the prayer area facing the *qibla* wall. At one time the largest mosque in the world, the Great Mosque of Samarra (SAM-er-uh *or* suh-MAR-uh) (constructed between 848 and 852) covered 10 acres and contained 464 pillars in aisles surrounding the court. Set in

Cordoba, Spain/© William J. Duiker

The Recycled Mosque. The site of the Great Mosque at Córdoba was originally dedicated to the Roman god Janus and later boasted a Christian church built by the Visigoths. In the eighth century, the Muslims incorporated parts of the old church into their new mosque, aggrandizing it over the centuries. After the Muslims were driven from Spain, the mosque reverted to Christianity, and in 1523, a soaring cathedral sprouted from its spine (shown below). Inside, the mosque and the cathedral seem to blend well aesthetically, a prototype for harmonious religious coexistence. Throughout history, societies have destroyed past architectural wonders, robbing older marble glories to erect new marvels. It is wonderful that the Great Mosque has survived with its glittering dome soaring above the *mihrab* chamber (shown in the upper photo).

© Nik Wheeler/CORBIS

the *qibla* wall was a niche, or ***mihrab*** (MEER-uhb), containing a decorated panel pointing to Mecca and representing Allah. Remains of the massive 30-foot-high outer wall still stand, but the most famous section of the Samarra mosque was its 90-foot-tall minaret, the tower accompanying a mosque from which the ***muezzin*** (myoo-EZ-in) (crier) calls the faithful to prayer five times a day.

No discussion of mosques would be complete without mentioning the famous ninth-century mosque at Córdoba in southern Spain, which is still in remarkable condition. Its 514 columns supporting double horseshoe arches transform this architectural wonder into a unique forest of trees pointing upward, contributing to a light and airy effect. The unparalleled sumptuousness and elegance make the Córdoba mosque one of the wonders of world art, let alone Islamic art.

Since the Muslim religion combines spiritual and political power in one, palaces also reflected the glory of Islam. Beginning in the eighth century with the spectacular castles of Syria, the rulers constructed large brick domiciles reminiscent of Roman design, with protective walls, gates, and baths. With a central courtyard surrounded by two-story arcades and massive gate-towers, they resembled fortresses as much as palaces. Characteristic of such "desert palaces" was the gallery over the entrance gate, with holes through which boiling oil could be poured down on the heads of attacking forces. Unfortunately, none of these structures has survived.

The ultimate remaining Islamic palace is the fourteenth-century Alhambra in Spain. The extensive succession of courtyards, rooms, gardens, and fountains created a fairy-tale castle perched high above the city of Granada. Every inch of surface is decorated in intricate floral and semiabstract patterns; much of the decoration is done in carved plasterwork so fine that it resembles lace. The Lion Court in the center of the harem is world renowned for its lion fountain and surrounding arcade with elegant columns and carvings.

Since antiquity, one of the primary occupations of women has been the spinning and weaving of cloth to

© William J. Duiker

The Qur'an as Sculptured Design. Muslim sculptors and artists, reflecting the official view that any visual representation of the Prophet Muhammad was blasphemous, turned to geometric patterns, as well as to flowers and animals, as a means of fulfilling their creative urge. The predominant motif, however, was the reproduction of Qur'anic verses in the Arabic script. Calligraphy, which was almost as important in the Middle East as it was in traditional China, used the Arabic script to decorate all of the Islamic arts, from painting to pottery, tile and ironwork, and wall decorations such as this carved plaster panel in a courtyard of the Alhambra palace in Spain. Since a recitation from the Qur'an was an important component of the daily devotional activities for all practicing Muslims, elaborate scriptural panels such as this one perfectly blended the spiritual and the artistic realms.

make clothing and other useful items for their families. In the Middle East, this skill reached an apogee in the art of the knotted woolen rug. Originating in the pre-Muslim era, rugs were initially used to insulate stone palaces against the cold as well as to warm shepherds' tents. Eventually, they were applied to religious purposes, since every practicing Muslim is required to pray five times a day on clean ground. Small rugs served as prayer mats for individual use, while larger and more elaborate ones were given by rulers as rewards for political favors. Bedouins in the Arabian desert covered their sandy floors with rugs to create a cozy environment in their tents.

In villages throughout the Middle East, the art of rug weaving has been passed down from mother to daughter over the centuries. Small girls as young as four years old took part in the process by helping to spin and prepare the wool shorn from the family sheep. By the age of six, girls would begin their first rug, and before adolescence, their slender fingers would be producing fine carpets. Skilled artisanship represented an extra enticement to prospective bridegrooms, and rugs often became an important part of a woman's dowry to her future husband. After the wedding, the wife would continue to make rugs for home use, as well as for sale to augment the family income. Eventually, rugs began to be manufactured in workshops by professional artisans, who reproduced the designs from detailed painted diagrams.

Most decorations on the rugs, as well as on all forms of Islamic art, consisted of Arabic script and natural plant and figurative motifs. Repeated continuously in naturalistic or semiabstract geometrical patterns called arabesques, these decorations completely covered the surface and left no area undecorated. This dense decor was also evident in brick, mosaic, and stucco ornamentation and culminated in the magnificent tile work of later centuries.

Representation of the Prophet Muhammad has traditionally been strongly discouraged in painting or in any other art form. Although no passage of the Qur'an forbids representational painting, the *Hadith* warned against any attempt to imitate God through artistic creation or idolatry, and this has been interpreted as an outright ban on such depictions.

Human beings and animals could still be represented in secular art, but relatively little survives from the early centuries aside from a very few wall paintings from the royal palaces. Although the Persians used calligraphy and art to decorate their books, the Arabs had no pictorial tradition of their own and only began to develop the art of book illustration in the late twelfth century to illustrate translations of Greek scientific works.

In the thirteenth century, a Mongol dynasty established at Tabriz (tah-BREEZ), west of the Caspian Sea, offered the Middle East its first direct contact with the art of East Asia. Mongol painting, done in the Chinese manner with a full brush and expressing animated movement and intensity (see Chapter 10), freed Islamic painters from traditional confines and enabled them to experiment with new techniques.

CHAPTER SUMMARY

After the collapse of Roman power in the west, the Eastern Roman Empire, centered on Constantinople, continued in the eastern Mediterranean and eventually emerged as the unique Christian civilization known as the Byzantine Empire, which flourished for hundreds of years. One of the greatest challenges to the Byzantine Empire, however, came from a new force—Islam—that blossomed in the Arabian peninsula and spread rapidly throughout the Middle East. In the eyes of some Europeans during the Middle Ages, the Arab Empire was a malevolent force that posed a serious threat to the security of Christianity. Their fears were not entirely misplaced, for within half a century after the death of Islam's founder, Muhammad, Arab armies overran Christian states in North Africa and the Iberian peninsula, and Turkish Muslims moved eastward onto the fringes of the Indian subcontinent.

But although the teachings of Muhammad brought war and conquest to much of the known world, they also brought hope and a sense of political and economic stability to peoples throughout the region. Thus, for many people in the medieval Mediterranean world, the arrival of Islam was a welcome event. Islam brought a code of law and a written language to societies that had previously lacked them. Finally, by creating a revitalized trade network stretching from West Africa to East Asia, it established a vehicle for the exchange of technology and ideas that brought untold wealth to thousands and a better life to millions.

Like other empires in the region, the Arab Empire did not last. It fell victim to a combination of internal and external pressures, and by the end of the thirteenth century, it was no more than a memory. But it left a powerful legacy in Islam, which remains one of the great religions of the world. In succeeding centuries, Islam began to penetrate into new areas beyond the edge of the Sahara and across the Indian Ocean into the islands of the Indonesian archipelago.

CHAPTER TIMELINE

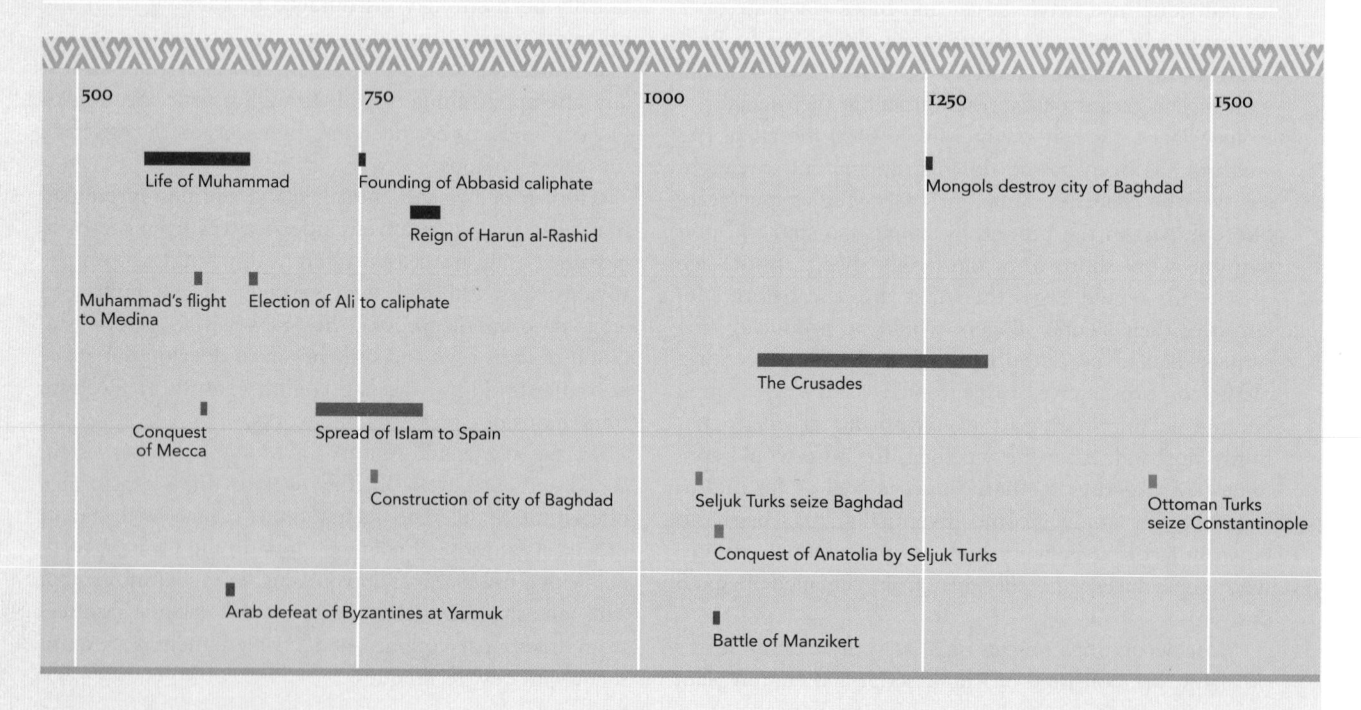

CHAPTER REVIEW

Upon Reflection

Q By what process was Arab power expanded throughout the Middle East and North Africa in the years following the death of Muhammad? What was the impact of that expansion on the subject peoples?

Q What role did the Abbasid Empire play in promoting the establishment of a trade network extending from East Asia to the Mediterranean Sea and beyond? Is it reasonable to say that the Muslim world was the linchpin of global trade during this period?

Q What circumstances do some historians refer to when they say that the Muslim governments in Spain provided an example of religious tolerance?

Key Terms

Bedouin (p. 169)
sheikh (p. 169)
majlis (p. 169)
Hegira (p. 170)
umma (p. 170)
Five Pillars of Islam (p. 171)
Ramadan (p. 171)
ulama (p. 172)
Shari'a (p. 172)
Hadith (p. 172)
caliph (p. 172)
imam (p. 172)
jihad (p. 173)
Shi'ites (p. 175)
Sunni (p. 175)
vizier (p. 177)
sultan (p. 178)
Crusades (p. 178)
emir (p. 180)
Sufism (p. 191)
mihrab (p. 192)
muezzin (p. 192)

Suggested Reading

THE RISE OF ISLAM Standard works on the rise of Islam include **J. Bloom** and **S. Blair,** ***Islam: A Thousand Years of Faith and Power*** (New Haven, Conn., 2002), and **J. L. Esposito, ed.,** ***The Oxford History of Islam*** (New York, 1999). Also see **K. Armstrong,** ***Islam: A Short History*** (New York, 2000). **F. Donner,** ***Muhammad and the Believers: At the Origins of Islam*** (Cambridge, Mass., 2010), and **K.-H. Ohlig** and **G.-R. Puin, eds.,** ***The Hidden Origins of Islam*** (Amherst, N.Y., 2008) adopt a revisionist stance in approaching the early years of Islam. For a standard and laudatory biography of the Prophet, see **K. Armstrong,** ***Muhammad: A Prophet for Our Time*** (New York, 2006).

Specialized works on various historical periods are numerous. For a view of the Crusades from an Arab perspective, see **C. Hillenbrand,** ***The Crusades: Islamic Perspectives*** (New York, 2001). In ***God of Battles: Christianity and Islam*** (Princeton, N.J., 1998), **P. Partner** compares the expansionist tendencies of the two great religions.

ABBASID EMPIRE On the Abbasid Empire, see **H. Kennedy's** highly readable ***When Baghdad Ruled the Muslim World: The Rise and Fall of Islam's Greatest Dynasty*** (Cambridge, Mass., 2004) and ***The Great Arab Conquests: How the Spread of Islam Changed the World We Live In*** (Philadelphia, 2007). Christian-Muslim contacts are discussed in **S. O'Shea,** ***Sea of Faith: Islam and Christianity in the Medieval Mediterranean World*** (New York, 2006).

SPAIN UNDER ISLAM On Spain during the Abbasid era, see **M. Menocal's** elegant study, ***Ornament of the World: How Muslims, Jews, and Christians Created a Culture of Tolerance in Medieval Spain*** (New York, 2002), and **R. Fletcher,** ***The Cross and the Crescent: Christianity and Islam from Muhammad to the Reformation*** (New York, 2005).

WOMEN On women, see **F. Hussain, ed.,** ***Muslim Women*** (New York, 1984), and **G. Nashat** and **J. E. Tucker,** ***Women in the Middle East and North Africa*** (Bloomington, Ind., 1998).

ISLAMIC ART For the best introduction to Islamic art, consult **J. Bloom** and **S. Blair,** ***Islamic Arts*** (London, 1997). For an excellent overview of world textiles, see **K. Wilson,** ***A History of Textiles*** (Boulder, Colo., 1982).

Visit the CourseMate website at **www.cengagebrain.com** for additional study tools and review materials for this chapter.

Early Civilizations in Africa

© Nick Greaves/Alamy

The Temple at Great Zimbabwe

CHAPTER OUTLINE AND FOCUS QUESTIONS

The Emergence of Civilization

Q How did the advent of farming and pastoralism affect the various peoples of Africa? How did the consequences of the agricultural revolution in Africa compare with its consequences in Eurasia and America?

The Coming of Islam

Q What effects did the coming of Islam have on African religion, society, political structures, trade, and culture?

States and Noncentralized Societies in Central and Southern Africa

Q What role did migrations play in the evolution of early African societies? How did the impact of these migrations compare with similar population movements elsewhere?

African Society

Q What role did lineage groups, women, and slavery play in African societies? In what ways did African societies in various parts of the continent differ? What accounted for these differences?

African Culture

Q What are some of the chief characteristics of African sculpture and carvings, music, and architecture, and what purpose did these forms of creative expression serve in African society?

CRITICAL THINKING

Q In what parts of Africa did the first states and city-states emerge? What conditions led to their appearance?

IN 1871, THE GERMAN EXPLORER Karl Mauch began to search southern Africa's central plateau for the colossal stone ruins of a legendary lost civilization. In late August, he found what he had been looking for. According to his diary: "Presently I stood before it and beheld a wall of a height of about 20 feet of granite bricks. Very close by there was a place where a kind of footpath led over rubble into the interior. Following this path I stumbled over masses of rubble and parts of walls and dense thickets. I stopped in front of a towerlike structure. Altogether it rose to a height of about 30 feet." Mauch was convinced that "a civilized nation must once have lived here." Like many other nineteenth-century Europeans, however, Mauch was equally convinced that the Africans who had lived there could never have built such splendid structures as the ones he had found at Great Zimbabwe (zim-BAHB-way). To Mauch and other archaeologists, Great Zimbabwe must have been the work of "a northern race closely akin to the Phoenician and Egyptian." It was not until the twentieth century that Europeans could overcome their prejudices and finally admit that Africans south of Egypt had also developed advanced civilizations with spectacular achievements.

The continent of Africa has played a central role in the long evolution of humankind. It was in Africa that the first hominids appeared more than 3 million years ago. It was probably in Africa that the immediate ancestors of modern human beings—*Homo sapiens*—emerged for the first time. The domestication of animals and perhaps the initial stages of the agricultural revolution may have occurred first in Africa. Certainly, one of the first states appeared in Africa, in the Nile valley in the northeastern corner of the continent, in the form of the kingdom of the pharaohs. Recent evidence suggests that Egyptian civilization was significantly influenced by cultural developments taking place to the south, in Nubia, in modern Sudan.

After the decline of the Egyptian empire during the first millennium B.C.E., the focus of social change began to shift from the lower Nile valley to other areas of the continent: to West Africa, where a series of major trading states began to take part in the caravan trade with the Mediterranean through the vast wastes of the Sahara; to the region of the upper Nile River, where the states of Kush and Axum dominated trade for several centuries; and to the eastern coast from the Horn of Africa, formally known as Cape Guardafui (GWAR-duh-fwee *or* GWAR-duh-foo-ee), to the straits between the continent and the island of Madagascar (ma-duh-GAS-kur), where African peoples began to play an active role in the commercial traffic of the Indian Ocean. In the meantime, a gradual movement of agricultural peoples brought Iron Age farming to the central portion of the continent, leading eventually to the creation of several states in the Congo River basin and the plateau south of the Zambezi (zam-BEE-zee) River.

The peoples of Africa, then, have played a significant role in the changing human experience since ancient times. Yet, in many respects, that role was a distinctive one, a fact that continues to affect the fate of the continent in our own day. The landmass of Africa is so vast, and its topography is so diverse, that communications within the continent, and between Africans and peoples living elsewhere in the world, have often been more difficult than in many neighboring regions. As a consequence, while some parts of the continent were directly exposed to the currents of change sweeping across Eurasia and were influenced by them to varying degrees, other regions were virtually isolated from the "great tradition" cultures discussed in Part I of this book and, like the cultures of the Americas, developed in their own directions, rendering generalizations about Africa difficult, if not impossible, to make.

The Emergence of Civilization

FOCUS QUESTIONS: How did the advent of farming and pastoralism affect the various peoples of Africa? How did the consequences of the agricultural revolution in Africa compare with its consequences in Eurasia and America?

After Asia, Africa is the largest of the continents (see Map 8.1). It stretches nearly 5,000 miles from the Cape of Good Hope in the south to the Mediterranean in the north and extends a similar distance from Cape Verde (VURD) on the west coast to the Horn of Africa on the Indian Ocean.

The Land

Africa is as physically diverse as it is vast. The northern coast, washed by the Mediterranean Sea, is mountainous for much of its length. South of the mountains lies the greatest desert on earth, the Sahara, which stretches from the Atlantic to the Indian Ocean. To the east is the Nile River, heart of the ancient Egyptian civilization. Beyond that lies the Red Sea, separating Africa from Asia.

The Sahara acts as a great divide separating the northern coast from the rest of the continent. Africa south of the Sahara contains a number of major regions. In the west is the so-called hump of Africa, which juts like a massive shoulder into the Atlantic Ocean. Here the Sahara gradually gives way to grasslands in the interior and then to tropical rain forests along the coast. This region, dominated by the Niger River, is rich in natural resources and was the home of many ancient civilizations.

Far to the east, bordering the Indian Ocean, is a very different terrain of snowcapped mountains, upland plateaus, grasslands, and lakes. Here, in the East African Rift valley in the lake district of modern Kenya, early hominids began their long trek toward civilization several million years ago.

Directly to the west lies the Congo basin, with its rain forests watered by the mighty Congo River. The forests of equatorial Africa then fade gradually into the hills, plateaus, and deserts of the south. This rich land contains some of the most valuable mineral resources known today.

The First Farmers

It is not certain when agriculture was first practiced on the continent of Africa. Until recently, historians assumed that crops were first cultivated in the lower Nile valley (the northern part near the Mediterranean) about seven or eight thousand years ago, when wheat and barley were introduced, possibly from the Middle East. Eventually, as explained in Chapter 1, this area gave rise to the civilization of ancient Egypt.

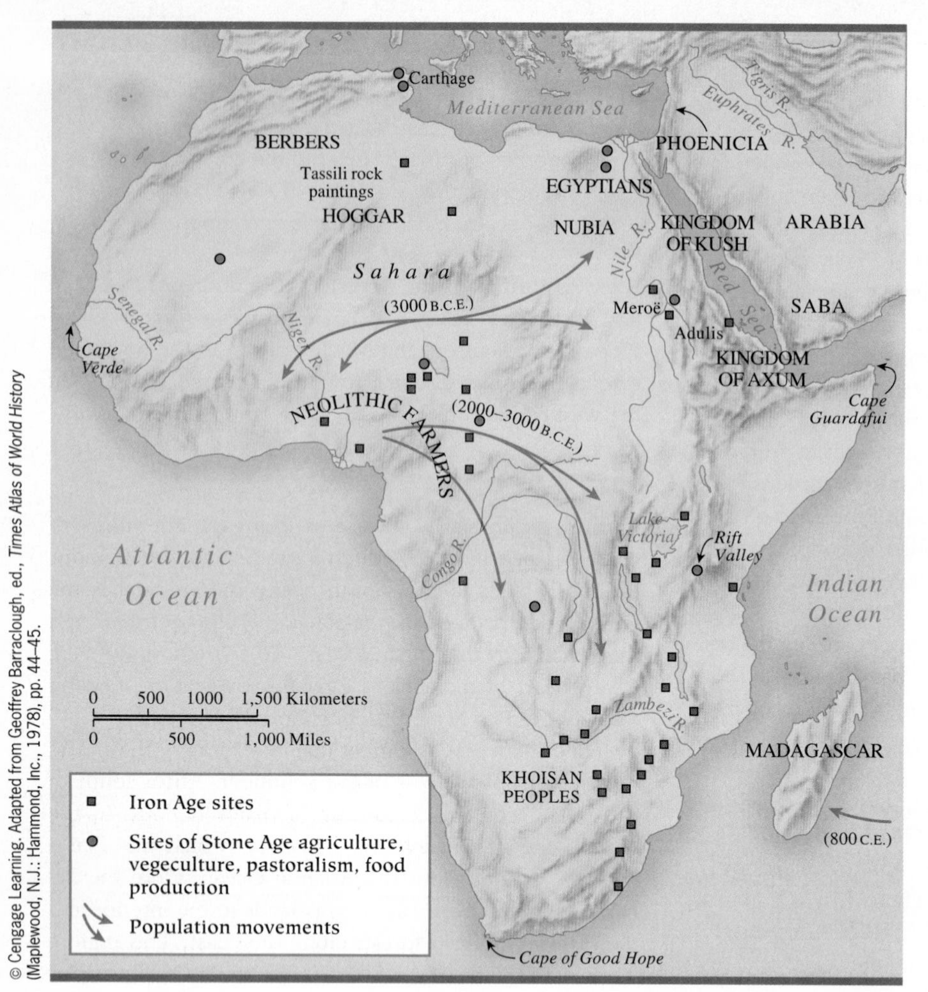

© Cengage Learning. Adapted from Geoffrey Barraclough, ed., *Times Atlas of World History* (Maplewood, N.J.: Hammond, Inc., 1978), pp. 44–45.

MAP 8.1 Ancient Africa. Modern human beings, the primate species known as *Homo sapiens*, first evolved on the continent of Africa. Some key sites of early human settlement are shown on this map.

Q *What are the main river systems on the continent of Africa?*

Recent evidence, however, suggests that this hypothesis may need some revision. South of Egypt, near the junction of the White Nile and the Blue Nile, is an area historically known as Nubia (see Chapter 1). By the ninth millennium B.C.E., peoples living in this area began to domesticate animals, first wild cattle and then sheep and goats, which had apparently originated in the Middle East. In areas where the climate permitted, they supplemented their diet by gathering wild grains and soon learned how to cultivate grains such as sorghum and millet, while also growing gourds and melons.

Eventually, the practice of agriculture began to spread westward across the Sahara. At that time, the world's climate was much cooler and wetter than it is today, but a warm, humid climate prevailed in parts of the Sahara, creating lakes and ponds, as well as vast grasslands (known as savannas) replete with game. Hence, indigenous peoples in the area were able to provide for themselves by hunting, food gathering, and fishing. By the seventh and sixth millennia B.C.E., however, conditions were becoming increasingly arid, forcing them to find new means of support. Rock paintings found in what are today some of the most inhabitable parts of the region (see the illustration that accompanies the comparative essay on p. 201) show that by the fourth millennium B.C.E. fishing and pastoralism in the heart of the Sahara were being supplemented by the limited cultivation of grain crops, including a drought-resistant form of dry rice.

Thus, the peoples of northern Africa, from Nubia westward into the heart of the Sahara, were among the earliest in the world to adopt settled agriculture as a means of subsistence. Shards of pottery found at archaeological sites in the area suggest that they were also among the first to manufacture clay pots. By 5000 B.C.E., they were cultivating cotton plants and manufacturing textiles.

After 4000 B.C.E., as the desiccation (drying up) of the Sahara intensified, many local inhabitants migrated eastward toward the Nile River and southward into the grasslands. As a result, farming began to spread into the savannas on the southern fringes of the desert and eventually into the tropical forest areas to the south. In the meantime, the foundation was being laid for the emergence of an advanced civilization in Egypt along the banks of the Nile River (see Chapter 1).

Axum and Meroë

To the south of Egypt in Nubia, the kingdom of Kush had emerged as a major trading state by the end of the second millennium B.C.E. (see Chapter 1). In the mid-first millennium B.C.E., however, Kush declined and was eventually replaced by a new state, which emerged farther to the south in the great bend of the Nile River near the

Fourth Cataract. The capital was at Meroë (MER-oh-ee *or* MER-uh-wee), which was located near extensive iron deposits. Once smelting techniques were developed, iron evidently provided the basis for much of the area's growing prosperity. Meroë eventually became a major trading hub for iron goods and other manufactures for the entire region.

In the meantime, a competitor to Meroë began to arise a few hundred miles to the southeast, in the mountainous highlands of present-day Ethiopia. The founders of Axum (AHK-soom) claimed descent from migrants to Africa from the kingdom of Saba (SAH-buh) (also known as Sheba), across the Red Sea on the southern tip of the Arabian peninsula. During antiquity, Saba was a major trading state, serving as a transit point for goods carried from South Asia to the Mediterranean basin. Biblical sources credited the "queen of Sheba" with vast wealth. In fact, much of that wealth had originated much farther to the east and passed through Saba en route to the Mediterranean. Whether migrants from Saba were responsible for founding Axum is sheer conjecture, but a similarity in architectural styles suggests that some form of relationship probably existed between the two states.

After Saba declined, perhaps because of the desiccation of the Arabian Desert, Axum survived for centuries. Like Saba, Axum owed much of its prosperity to its location on the trade route between India and the Mediterranean, and ships from Egypt stopped regularly at the port of Adulis (a-DOO-luss) on the Red Sea. Axum exported ivory, frankincense, myrrh, and slaves, while its primary imports were textiles, metal goods, wine, and olive oil. For a time, Axum competed for control of the ivory trade with the neighboring state of Meroë, and hunters from Axum armed with imported iron weapons scoured the entire region for elephants. Probably as a result of this competition, in the fourth century C.E., the Axumite ruler, claiming he had been provoked, launched an invasion of Meroë and conquered it, creating an empire that, in the view of some contemporaries, rivaled those of Rome and Persia (see Map 8.2).

Perhaps the most distinctive feature of Axumite civilization was its religion. Originally, the rulers of Axum (who claimed descent from King Solomon through the visit of the queen of Sheba to Israel in biblical times) followed the religion of Saba. But in the fourth century C.E., Axumite rulers adopted Christianity, possibly from Egypt. This commitment to the Egyptian form of Christianity—often called **Coptic** (KAHP-tik) from the local language of the day—was retained even after the collapse of Axum and the expansion of Islam through the area in later centuries. Later, Axum (now renamed Ethiopia) would be identified by some Europeans as the "hermit kingdom" and the home of Prester John, a legendary Christian king of East Africa.

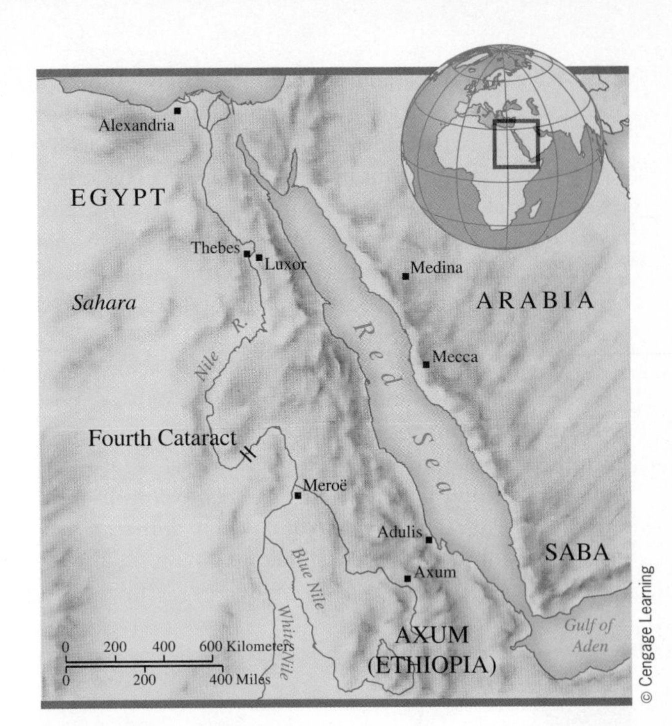

MAP 8.2 Ancient Ethiopia and Nubia. The first civilizations to appear on the African continent emerged in the Nile River valley. Early in the first century C.E., the state of Axum emerged in what today is the state of Ethiopia.

Q *Where were the major urban settlements in the region, as shown on this map?*

The Sahara and Its Environs

Meroë and Axum were part of the ancient trading network that extended from the Mediterranean into the Indian Ocean and were affected in various ways by the cross-cultural contacts that took place throughout that region. Elsewhere in Africa, somewhat different patterns prevailed; they varied from area to area depending on the geography and climate.

Historians do not know when goods first began to be exchanged across the Sahara in a north-south direction, but during the first millennium B.C.E., the commercial center of Carthage on the Mediterranean had become a focal point of the trans-Saharan trade. The **Berbers**, a pastoral people of North Africa, served as intermediaries, carrying food products and manufactured goods from Carthage across the desert and exchanging them for salt, gold and copper, skins, various agricultural products, and perhaps slaves.

This trade initiated a process of cultural exchange that would exert a significant impact on the peoples of tropical Africa. Among other things, it may have spread the knowledge of ironworking south of the desert. Although historians once believed that ironworking knowledge reached sub-Saharan Africa from Meroë in the upper Nile valley in the first centuries C.E., recent finds suggest that the peoples along the Niger River were smelting iron five or six hundred years earlier. Some scholars believe that the technique developed independently there, but others believe that it was introduced by the Berbers, who had learned it from the Carthaginians.

Whatever the case, the **Nok** (NAHK) **culture** in northern Nigeria eventually became one of the most active ironworking societies in Africa. Excavations have unearthed numerous terra-cotta and metal figures, as well as stone and iron farm implements, dating back as far as 500 B.C.E. The remains of smelting furnaces confirm that the iron was produced locally.

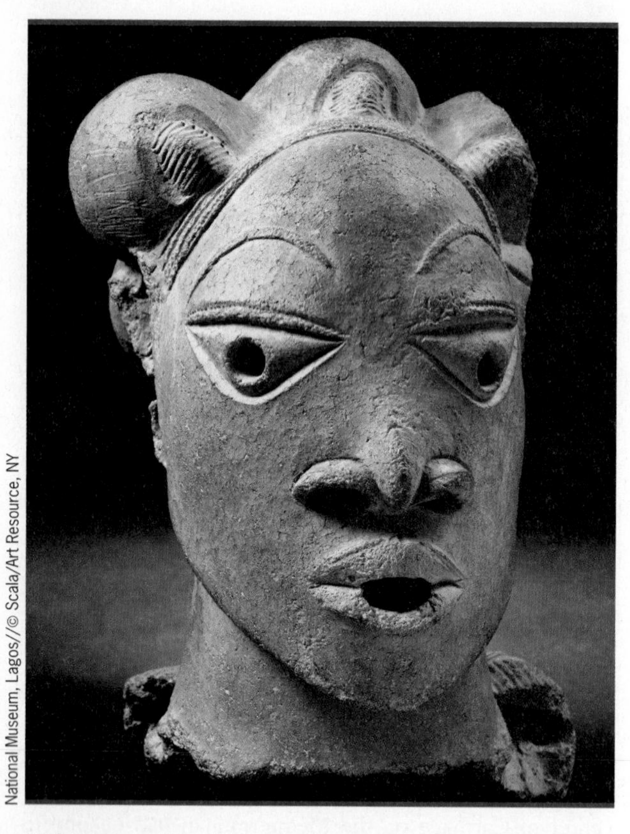
National Museum, Lagos//© Scala/Art Resource, NY

Nok Pottery Head. The Nok peoples of the Niger River are the oldest known culture in West Africa to have created sculptures. This terra-cotta head is typical of Nok culture sculptures produced between 500 B.C.E. and 200 C.E. Discovered by accident in the twentieth century by tin miners, these heads feature perforated eyes set in triangles or circles, stylized eyebrows, open thick lips, broad noses with wide nostrils, and large ears. Perhaps the large facial openings permitted the hot air to escape as the heads were fired. Although the function of these statues is not known for certain, they were likely connected with religious rituals or devotion to ancestors.

Early in the first millennium C.E., the introduction of the camel provided a major stimulus to the trans-Saharan trade. With its ability to store considerable amounts of food and water, the camel was far better equipped to handle the arduous conditions of the desert than the ox and donkey, which had been used previously. The camel caravans of the Berbers became known as the "fleets of the desert."

THE GARAMANTES Not all the peoples involved in the carrying trade across the Sahara were nomadic. Recent exploratory work in the Libyan Desert has revealed the existence of an ancient kingdom that for over a thousand years transported goods between societies along the Mediterranean Sea and sub-Saharan West Africa. The Garamantes (gar-uh-MAN-teez), as they were known to the Romans, carried salt, glass, metal, olive oil, and wine southward in return for gold, slaves, and various tropical products. To provide food for their communities in the heart of the desert, they constructed a complex irrigation system consisting of several thousand miles of underground channels. The technique is reminiscent of similar systems in Persia and Central Asia (see Chapter 9). Scholars believe that the kingdom declined as a result of the fall of the Roman Empire and the drying up of the desert.

East Africa

South of Axum, along the shores of the Indian Ocean and in the inland plateau that stretches from the mountains of Ethiopia through the lake district of Central Africa, lived a mixture of peoples, some living by hunting and food gathering and others following pastoral pursuits.

Beginning in the third millennium B.C.E., farming peoples speaking dialects of the Bantu (BAN-too) family of languages began to migrate from their original homeland in what today is Nigeria (see the comparative essay "The Migration of Peoples" on p. 201). By the early centuries C.E., they reached East Africa, where they may have been responsible for introducing the widespread cultivation of crops and knowledge of ironworking to much of East Africa, although there are signs of some limited iron smelting in the area before their arrival.

The Bantu settled in rural communities based on subsistence farming. The primary crops were millet and sorghum, along with yams, melons, and beans. The land was often tilled with both stone and iron tools—the latter were usually manufactured in a local smelter. Some people kept domestic animals such as cattle, sheep, goats, or chickens or supplemented their diets by hunting and food gathering. Because the population was minimal and an ample supply of cultivable land was available, most

COMPARATIVE ESSAY

The Migration of Peoples

About 50,000 years ago, a small band of *Homo sapiens sapiens* crossed the Sinai peninsula from Africa and began to spread out across the Eurasian supercontinent. Thus began a migration of peoples that continued with accelerating speed throughout the ancient era and beyond. By 40,000 B.C.E., their descendants had spread across Eurasia as far as China and eastern Siberia and had even settled the distant continent of Australia.

Who were these peoples, and what provoked their decision to change their habitat? Undoubtedly, the first migrants were foragers or hunters in search of wild game, but with the advent of agriculture and the domestication of animals about 12,000 years ago, other peoples began to migrate vast distances in search of fertile lands for farming and pasture.

The ever-changing climate was undoubtedly a major factor driving the process. In the fourth millennium B.C.E., the drying up of rich pasturelands in the Sahara forced the local inhabitants to migrate eastward toward the Nile River valley and the grasslands of East Africa. At about the same time, Indo-European-speaking farming peoples left the region of the Black Sea and moved gradually into central Europe in search of new farmlands. They were eventually followed by nomadic groups from Central Asia who began to occupy lands along the frontiers of the Roman Empire, while other bands of nomads threatened the plains of northern China from the Gobi Desert. In the meantime, Bantu-speaking farmers migrated from the Niger River southward into the rain forests of Central Africa and beyond. Similar movements took place in Southeast Asia and the Americas.

This steady flow of migrating peoples often had a destabilizing effect on sedentary societies in their path. Nomadic incursions were a constant menace to the security of China, Egypt, and the Roman Empire and ultimately brought them to an end. But this vast movement of peoples often had beneficial effects as well, spreading new technologies and means of livelihood. Although some migrants, like the Huns, came for plunder and left havoc in their wake, other groups, like the Celtic peoples and the Bantus, prospered in their new environment.

The most famous of all nomadic invasions represents a case in point. In the thirteenth century C.E., the Mongols left their homeand in the Gobi Desert and advanced westward into the Russian steppes and southward into China and Central Asia, leaving death and devastation in their wake. At the height of their empire, the Mongols controlled virtually all of Eurasia except its western and southern fringes, thus creating a zone of stability stretching from China to the shores of the Mediterranean in which a global trade and informational network could thrive.

Musée de l'Homme, Paris//© Erich Lessing/Art Resource, NY

Rock Paintings of the Sahara. Even before the Egyptians built their pyramids at Giza, other peoples far to the west in the vast wastes of the Sahara were creating their own art forms. These rock paintings, some of which date back to the fourth millennium B.C.E. and are reminiscent of similar examples from Europe, Asia, and Australia, provide a valuable record of a society that supported itself by a combination of farming, hunting, and herding animals. After the introduction of the horse around 1200 B.C.E., subsequent rock paintings depicted chariots and horseback riding. Eventually, camels began to appear in the paintings, a consequence of the increasing desiccation of the Sahara.

What have been some of the key reasons for the migration of large numbers of people throughout human history? Is the process still under way in our own day?

settlements were relatively small; each village formed a self-sufficient political and economic entity.

As early as the era of the New Kingdom in the second millennium B.C.E., Egyptian ships had plied the waters off the East African coast in search of gold, ivory, palm oil, and perhaps slaves. By the first century C.E., the region was an established part of a trading network that included the Mediterranean and the Red Sea. In that century, a Greek seafarer from Alexandria wrote an account of his travels down the coast from Cape Guardafui at the tip of the Horn of Africa to the Strait of Madagascar thousands of miles to the south. Called the *Periplus* (PER-ih-pluss), this work provides descriptions of the peoples and settlements along the African coast and the trade goods they supplied.

According to the *Periplus*, the port of Rhapta (RAHP-tuh) (possibly modern Dar es Salaam) was a commercial metropolis, exporting ivory, rhinoceros horn, and tortoiseshell and importing glass, wine, grain, and metal goods such as weapons and tools. The identity of the peoples taking part in this trade is not clear, but it seems likely that the area was inhabited primarily by various local peoples supplemented by a small number of immigrants from the Arabian peninsula. Out of this mixture would eventually emerge a cosmopolitan **Swahili** (swah-HEE-lee) culture (see "East Africa: The Land of the Zanj" later in this chapter) that continues to exist in coastal areas today. Beyond Rhapta was "unexplored ocean." Some contemporary observers believed that the Indian and Atlantic Oceans were connected. Others were convinced that the Indian Ocean was an enclosed sea and that the continent of Africa could not be circumnavigated.

Trade across the Indian Ocean and down the coast of East Africa, facilitated by the monsoon winds, would gradually become one of the most lucrative sources of commercial profit in the ancient and medieval worlds. Although the origins of the trade remain shrouded in mystery, traders eventually came by sea from as far away as the mainland of Southeast Asia. Early in the first millennium C.E., Malay (may-LAY) peoples bringing cinnamon to the Middle East began to cross the Indian Ocean directly and landed on the southeastern coast of Africa. Eventually, a Malay settlement was established on the island of Madagascar, where the population is still of mixed Malay-African origin. Although historians have proposed that Malay immigrants introduced such Southeast Asian foods as the banana and the yam to Africa, recent archaeological evidence suggests that these foods may have arrived in Africa as early as the third millennium B.C.E. With its high yield and ability to grow in uncultivated rain forest, the banana often became the preferred crop of the Bantu peoples.

The Coming of Islam

FOCUS QUESTION: What effects did the coming of Islam have on African religion, society, political structures, trade, and culture?

As described in Chapter 7, the rise of Islam during the first half of the seventh century C.E. had ramifications far beyond the Arabian peninsula. Arab armies swept across North Africa, incorporating it into the Arab Empire and isolating the Christian state of Axum to the south. Although East Africa and West Africa south of the Sahara were not occupied by the Arab forces, Islam eventually penetrated these areas as well.

African Religious Beliefs Before Islam

When Islam arrived, most African societies already had well-developed systems of religious beliefs. Like other aspects of African life, early African religious beliefs varied from place to place, but certain characteristics appear to have been shared by most African societies. One common feature was **pantheism**, belief in a single creator god from whom all things came. Sometimes the creator god was accompanied by a whole pantheon of lesser deities. The Ashanti (uh-SHAN-tee *or* uh-SHAHN-tee) people of Ghana (GAH-nuh) in West Africa believed in a supreme being called Nyame (NY-AH-may), whose sons were lesser gods. Each son served a different purpose: one was the rainmaker, another the compassionate, and a third was responsible for the sunshine. This heavenly hierarchy paralleled earthly arrangements: worship of Nyame was the exclusive preserve of the king through his priests; lesser officials and the common people worshiped Nyame's sons, who might intercede with their father on behalf of ordinary Africans.

Belief in an afterlife was closely connected to the importance of ancestors and the **lineage group**, or clan. Each lineage (LIN-nee-ij) group could trace itself back to a founding ancestor or group of ancestors. These ancestral souls would not be extinguished as long as the lineage group continued to perform rituals in their name. The rituals could also benefit the lineage group on earth, for the ancestral souls, being closer to the gods, had the power to influence, for good or evil, the lives of their descendants.

Such beliefs were challenged but not always replaced by the arrival of Islam. In some ways, the tenets of Islam were in conflict with traditional African beliefs and customs. Although the concept of a single transcendent deity presented no problems in many African societies, Islam's rejection of spirit worship and a priestly class ran counter to the beliefs of many Africans and was often ignored in practice. Similarly, as various Muslim travelers observed, Islam's insistence on the separation of men and women contrasted with the relatively informal relationships that prevailed in many African societies and was probably slow to take root. In the long run, imported ideas were synthesized with indigenous beliefs to create a unique brand of Africanized Islam.

The Arabs in North Africa

In 641, Arab forces advanced into Egypt, seized the delta of the Nile River, and brought two centuries of Byzantine rule to an end. To guard against attacks from the Byzantine fleet, they eventually built a new capital at Cairo, inland from the previous Byzantine capital of Alexandria, and began to consolidate their control over the entire region.

The Arab conquerors were probably welcomed by many, if not the majority, of the local inhabitants. Although Egypt had been a thriving commercial center under the Byzantines, the average Egyptian had not shared in this prosperity. Tax rates were generally high, and Christians were subjected to periodic persecution by the Byzantines, who viewed the local Coptic faith and other sects in the area as heresies. Although the new rulers continued to obtain much of their revenue from taxing the local farming population, tax rates were generally lower than they had been under the corrupt Byzantine government, and conversion to Islam brought exemption from taxation. During the next generations, many Egyptians converted to the Muslim faith, but Islam did not move into the upper Nile valley until several hundred years later. As Islam spread southward, it was adopted by many lowland peoples, but it had less success in the mountains of Ethiopia, where Coptic Christianity continued to win adherents (see the next section).

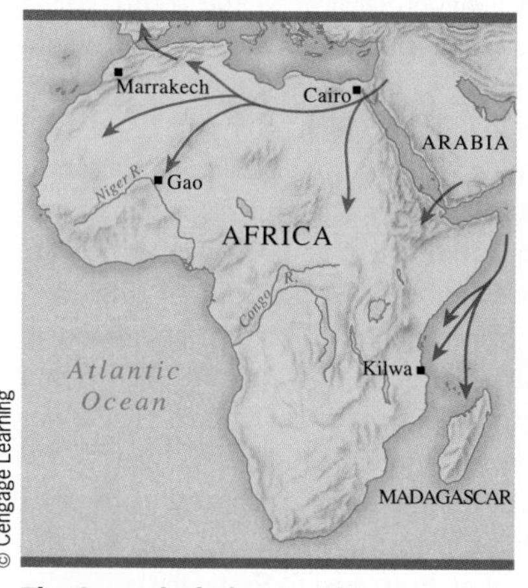

© Cengage Learning
The Spread of Islam in Africa

In the meantime, Arab rule was gradually being extended westward along the Mediterranean coast. When the Romans conquered Carthage in 146 B.C.E., they had called their new province Africa, thus introducing a name that would eventually be applied to the entire continent. After the fall of the Roman Empire, much of the area had reverted to the control of local Berber chieftains, but the Byzantines captured Carthage in the mid-sixth century C.E. In 690, the city was seized by the Arabs, who then began to extend their control over the entire area, which they called al-Maghrib (al-MAH-greb) ("the west").

At first, the local Berber peoples resisted their new conquerors, and for several generations, Arab rule was limited to the towns and lowland coastal areas. But Arab persistence eventually paid off, and by the early eighth century, the entire North African coast was under Arab rule. The Arabs were now poised to cross the Strait of Gibraltar and expand into southern Europe and to push south beyond the fringes of the Sahara.

CHRONOLOGY Early Africa

Origins of agriculture in Africa	c. 9000–5000 B.C.E.
Desiccation of the Sahara begins	c. 5000 B.C.E.
Kingdom of Kush in Nubia	c. 1070 B.C.E.–350 B.C.E.
Iron Age begins	c. Sixth century B.C.E.
Beginning of trans-Saharan trade	c. First millennium B.C.E.
Rise of Meroë	c. 300 B.C.E.
Rise of Axum.	First century C.E.
Arrival of Malays on Madagascar	Second century C.E.
Arrival of Bantu in East Africa	Early centuries C.E.
Conquest of Meroë by Axum	Fourth century C.E.
Origins of Ghana	Fifth century C.E.
Arab takeover of lower Nile valley	641 C.E.
Development of Swahili culture	c. First millennium C.E.
Spread of Islam across North Africa	Seventh century C.E.
Spread of Islam in Horn of Africa	Ninth century C.E.
Decline of Ghana	Twelfth century C.E.
Kingdom of Zimbabwe	c. 1100–c. 1450
Establishment of Zagwe dynasty in Ethiopia	c. 1150
Rise of Mali	c. 1250

The Kingdom of Ethiopia: A Christian Island in a Muslim Sea

By the end of the sixth century C.E., the kingdom of Axum, long a dominant force in the trade network through the Red Sea, was in a state of decline. Overexploitation of farmland had played a role in its decline, as had a shift in trade routes away from the Red Sea to the Arabian peninsula and Persian Gulf. By the beginning of the ninth century, the capital had been moved farther into the mountainous interior, and Axum was gradually transformed from a maritime power into an isolated agricultural society.

The rise of Islam on the Arabian peninsula hastened this process, as the Arab world increasingly began to serve as the focus of the regional trade passing through the area. By the eighth century, a number of Muslim trading states had been established on the African coast of the Red Sea, a development that contributed to the transformation of Axum into a landlocked, primarily agricultural society. At first, relations between Christian Axum and its Muslim neighbors were relatively peaceful, as the larger and more powerful Axumite kingdom attempted with some success to compel the coastal Islamic states to accept a tributary relationship. Axum's role in the local commercial network temporarily revived, and the area became a prime source for ivory, gold, resins like frankincense and myrrh, and slaves. Slaves came primarily from the south, where Axum had been attempting to subjugate restive tribal peoples living in the Amharic (am-HAR-ik) plateau beyond its southern border.

Beginning in the twelfth century, however, relations between Axum and its neighbors deteriorated as the Muslim states along the coast began to move inland to gain control over the growing trade in slaves and ivory. Axum responded with force and at first had some success in reasserting its hegemony over the area. But in the early fourteenth century, the Muslim state of Adal (a-DAHL), located at the juncture of the Indian Ocean and the Red Sea, launched a new attack on the Christian kingdom.

Axum also underwent significant internal change during this period. The Zagwe (ZAH-gweh) dynasty, which seized control of the country in the mid-twelfth century, centralized the government and extended the Christian faith throughout the kingdom, now known as Ethiopia. Military commanders or civilian officials who had personal or kinship ties with the royal court established vast landed estates to maintain security and facilitate the collection of taxes from the local population. In the meantime, Christian missionaries established monasteries and churches to propagate the faith in outlying areas. Close relations were reestablished with leaders of the Coptic church in Egypt and with Christian officials in the Holy Land. This process was continued by the Solomonids (sah-luh-MAHN-ids), who succeeded the Zagwe dynasty in 1270. But by the early fifteenth century, the state had become more deeply involved in an expanding conflict with Muslim Adal to the east, a conflict that lasted more than a century and gradually took on the characteristics of a holy war.

East Africa: The Land of the Zanj

The rise of Islam also had a lasting impact on the coast of East Africa, which the Greeks had called Azania and the Arabs called Zanj (ZANJ) referring to the "burnt skin" of the indigenous population. According to Swahili oral traditions, during the seventh and eighth centuries peoples from the Arabian peninsula and the Persian Gulf began to settle at ports along the coast and on the small islands offshore. Then, in the middle of the tenth century, a Persian from the city of Shiraz sailed to the area with his six sons. As his small fleet stopped along the coast, each son disembarked on one of the coastal islands and founded a small community; these settlements eventually grew into important commercial centers including Mombasa (mahm-BAH-suh), Pemba (PEM-buh), Zanzibar (ZAN-zi-bar) (literally, "the coast of the Zanj"), and Kilwa (KIL-wuh). Although this oral tradition may underestimate the indigenous population's growing involvement in local commerce, it also reflects the degree to which African merchants—who often served as middlemen between the peoples of the interior and the traders arriving from ports all around the Indian Ocean—saw themselves as part of an international commercial network.

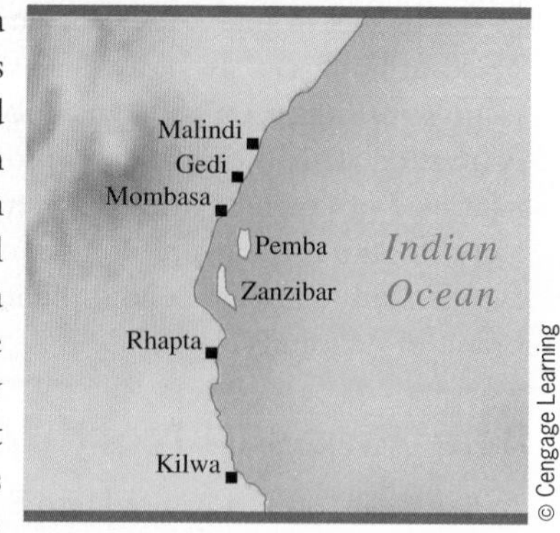

The Swahili Coast

In any case, by the ninth and tenth centuries, a string of trading ports stretched from Mogadishu (moh-guh-DEE-shoo) (today the capital of Somalia) in the north to Kilwa (south of present-day Dar es Salaam) in the south. Kilwa became especially important because it was near the southern limit for a ship hoping to complete the round-trip journey in a single season. Goods such as ivory, gold, and rhinoceros horn were exported across the Indian Ocean to countries as far away as China, while imports included iron goods, glassware, Indian textiles, and Chinese porcelain. Profits could be considerable, as evidenced by the merchants' lavish stone palaces, some of which still stand in Mombasa and Zanzibar. Though now in ruins, Kilwa was one of the most magnificent cities of its day. The fourteenth-century Arab traveler Ibn Battuta (IB-un ba-TOO-tuh) described it as "amongst the most beautiful of cities and most elegantly built. All of it is of wood, and the ceilings of its houses are of *al-dis* [reeds]."[1] Particularly impressive was the Husini Kubwa (hoo-SEE-nee KOOB-wuh), a massive palace with vaulted roofs capped with domes and elaborate stone carvings, surrounding an inner courtyard. Conditions for ordinary townspeople and the residents of smaller towns were not so luxurious, but nevertheless affluent urban residents lived in spacious stone buildings, with indoor plumbing and consumer goods imported from as far away as China and southern Europe.

Most of the coastal states were self-governing, although sometimes several towns were grouped together under a single dominant authority. Government revenue came primarily from taxes imposed on commerce. Some trade went on between these coastal city-states and the peoples of the interior, who provided gold and iron,

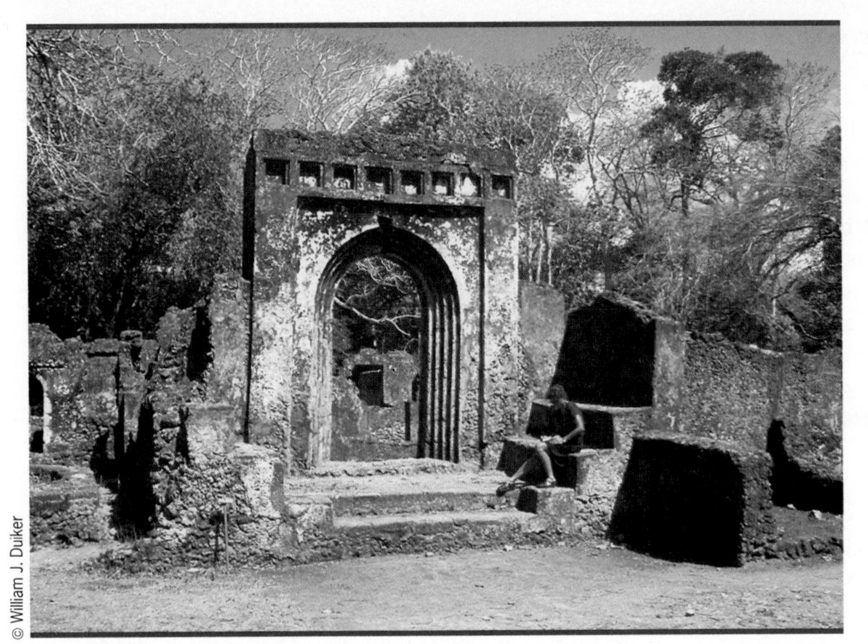
© William J. Duiker

A "Lost City" in Africa. Gedi (GEH-dee) was founded in the early thirteenth century and abandoned three hundred years later. Its romantic ruins suggest the grandeur of the Swahili civilization that once flourished along the eastern coast of Africa. Located 60 miles north of Mombasa, in present-day Kenya, Gedi once had several thousand residents but was eventually abandoned after it was attacked by nomadic peoples from the north. Today the ruins of the town, surrounded by a 9-foot wall, are dwarfed by towering baobab trees populated only by chattering monkeys. Shown here is the entrance to the palace, which probably served as the residence of the chief official in the town. Neighboring houses, constructed of coral stone, contained sumptuous rooms, with separate women's quarters and enclosed lavatories with urinal channels and double-sink washing benches. Artifacts found at the site came from as far away as Venice and China.

ivory, and various agricultural goods and animal products in return for textiles, manufactured articles, and weapons (see the box on p. 206). Relations apparently were not always friendly, and the coastal merchants sometimes resorted to force to obtain goods from the inland peoples. A Portuguese visitor recounted that "the men [of Mombasa] are oft-times at war and but seldom at peace with those of the mainland, and they carry on trade with them, bringing thence great store of honey, wax, and ivory."[2]

By the twelfth and thirteenth centuries, a cosmopolitan culture, eventually known as Swahili from the Arabic *sahel* (sah-HEL) meaning "coast" (thus, "peoples of the coast"), began to emerge throughout the coastal area. Intermarriage between the small number of immigrants and the local population was common, leading to the emergence of a ruling class, some of whom were of mixed heritage and could trace their genealogy to Arab or Persian ancestors. By this time, too, many members of the ruling class had converted to Islam. Middle Eastern urban architectural styles and other aspects of Arab culture were implanted within a society still predominantly African. Arabic words and phrases were combined with Bantu grammatical structures to form a distinct language, also known as Swahili; it is the national language of Kenya and Tanzania today.

The States of West Africa

During the eighth century, merchants from the Maghrib began to carry Muslim beliefs to the savannas south of the Sahara. At first, conversion took place on an individual basis rather than through official encouragement. The first rulers to convert to Islam were the royal family of Gao (GAH-oh) at the end of the tenth century. Five hundred years later, most of the population in the grasslands south of the Sahara had accepted Islam.

The expansion of Islam into West Africa had a major impact on the political system. By introducing Arabic as the first written language in the region and Muslim law codes and administrative practices from the Middle East, Islam provided local rulers with the tools to increase their authority and the efficiency of their governments. Moreover, as Islam gradually spread throughout the region, a common religion united previously diverse peoples into a more coherent community.

When Islam arrived in the grasslands south of the Sahara, the region was beginning to undergo significant political and social change. A number of major trading states were in the making, and they eventually transformed the Sahara into a leading avenue of world trade, crisscrossed by caravan routes leading to the Atlantic Ocean, the Mediterranean, and the Red Sea (see Map 8.3).

GHANA The first of these great commercial states was Ghana, which emerged in the fifth century C.E. in the upper Niger valley, a grassland region between the Sahara and the tropical forests along the West African coast. (The modern state of Ghana, which takes its name from this early trading society, is located in the forest region to the south.) The majority of the people in the area were farmers living in villages under a local chieftain. Gradually, these local communities were united to form the kingdom of Ghana. Although the people of the region had traditionally lived from agriculture, a primary reason for Ghana's growing importance was gold. The heartland of the state was located near one of the richest gold-producing areas in Africa. Ghanaian merchants transported the gold to Morocco, whence it was distributed

The Coast of the Zanj

From early times, the people living on the coast of East Africa took an active part in trade along the coast and across the Indian Ocean. The process began with the arrival of Arab traders early in the first millennium C.E. According to local legends, Arab merchants often married the daughters of the local chieftains and then received title to coastal territories as part of their wife's dowry. This description of the area was written by the Arab traveler al-Mas'udi (al-muh-SOO-dee), who visited the "land of the Zanj" in 916.

Al-Mas'udi in East Africa

The land of Zanj produces wild leopard skins. The people wear them as clothes, or export them to Muslim countries. They are the largest leopard skins and the most beautiful for making saddles. . . . They also export tortoiseshell for making combs, for which ivory is likewise used. . . . The Zanj are settled in that area, which stretches as far as Sofala, which is the furthest limit of the land and the end of the voyages made from Oman and Siraf on the sea of Zanj. . . . The Zanj use the ox as a beast of burden, for they have no horses, mules or camels in their land. . . . There are many wild elephants in this land but no tame ones. The Zanj do not use them for war or anything else, but only hunt and kill them for their ivory. It is from this country that come tusks weighing fifty pounds and more. They usually go to Oman, and from there are sent to China and India. This is the chief trade route. . . .

The Zanj have an elegant language and men who preach in it. One of their holy men will often gather a crowd and exhort his hearers to please God in their lives and to be obedient to him. He explains the punishments that follow upon disobedience, and reminds them of their ancestors and kings of old. These people have no religious law: their kings rule by custom and by political expediency.

The Zanj eat bananas, which are as common among them as they are in India; but their staple food is millet and a plant called kalari which is pulled out of the earth like truffles. They also eat honey and meat. They have many islands where the coconut grows: its nuts are used as fruit by all the Zanj peoples. One of these islands, which is one or two days' sail from the coast, has a Muslim population and a royal family. This is the island of Kanbulu [thought to be modern Pemba].

Why did Arab traders begin to settle along the coast of East Africa? What impact did the Arab presence have on the lives of the local population?

Source: From G. S. P. Freeman-Grenville, *The East African Coast: Select Documents*, copyright © 1962 by Oxford University Press. Used with permission of the author.

throughout the known world. This trade began in ancient times, as the Greek historian Herodotus relates:

> The Carthaginians also tell us that they trade with a race of men who live in a part of Libya beyond the Pillars of Heracles [the Strait of Gibraltar]. On reaching this country, they unload their goods, arrange them tidily along the beach, and then, returning to their boats, raise a smoke. Seeing the smoke, the natives come down to the beach, place on the ground a certain quantity of gold in exchange for the goods, and go off again to a distance. The Carthaginians then come ashore and take a look at the gold; and if they think it represents a fair price for their wares, they collect it and go away; if, on the other hand, it seems too little, they go back aboard and wait, and the natives come and add to the gold until they are satisfied. There is perfect honesty on both sides; the Carthaginians never touch the gold until it equals in value what they have offered for sale, and the natives never touch the goods until the gold has been taken away.[3]

Later, Ghana became known to Arab-speaking peoples in North Africa as "the land of gold." Actually, the name was misleading, for the gold did not come from Ghana, but from a neighboring people, who sold it to merchants from Ghana.

Eventually, other exports from Ghana found their way to the bazaars of the Mediterranean coast and beyond—ivory, ostrich feathers, hides, leather goods, and ultimately slaves. The origins of the slave trade in the area probably go back to the first millennium B.C.E., when Berber tribesmen seized African villagers in the regions south of the Sahara and sold them to buyers in Europe and the Middle East. In return, Ghana imported metal goods (especially weapons), textiles, horses, and salt.

Much of the trade across the desert was still conducted by the nomadic Berbers, but Ghanaian merchants

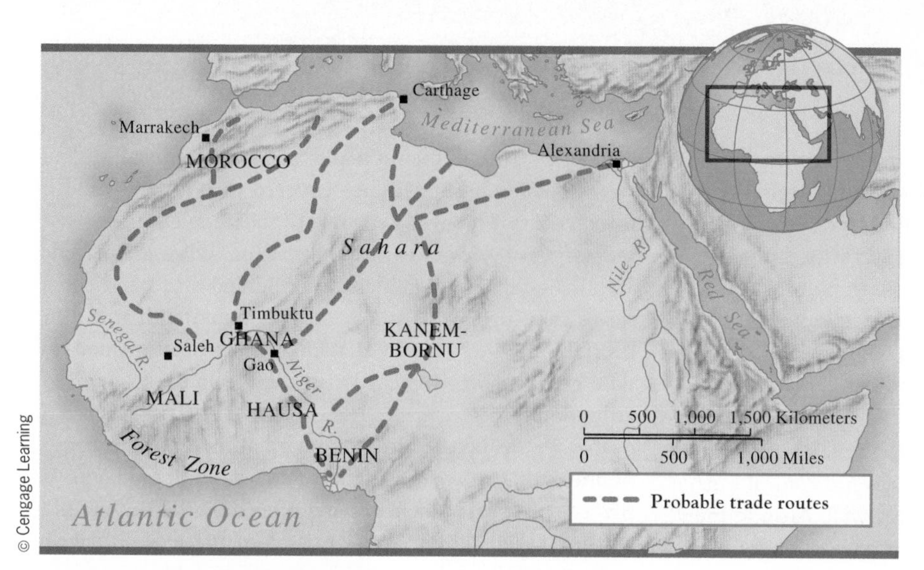

© Cengage Learning

MAP 8.3 Trans-Saharan Trade Routes. Trade across the Sahara began during the first millennium B.C.E. With the arrival of the camel from the Middle East, trade expanded dramatically.

What were the major cities involved in the trade, as shown on this map?

played an active role as intermediaries, trading tropical products such as bananas, kola nuts, and palm oil from the forest states of Guinea along the Atlantic coast to the south. By the eighth and ninth centuries, much of this trade was conducted by Muslim merchants, who purchased the goods from local traders (using iron and copper cash or cowrie shells from Southeast Asia as the primary means of exchange) and then sold them to Berbers, who carried them across the desert. The merchants who carried on this trade often became quite wealthy and lived in splendor in cities like Saleh (SAH-leh), the capital of Ghana. So did the king, of course, who taxed the merchants as well as the farmers and the producers.

Like other West African kings, the king of Ghana ruled by divine right and was assisted by a hereditary aristocracy composed of the leading members of the prominent clans, who also served as district chiefs responsible for maintaining law and order and collecting taxes. The king was responsible for maintaining the security of his kingdom, serving as an intermediary with local deities, and adjudicating disputes. The kings of Ghana did not convert to Islam themselves, although they welcomed Muslim merchants and apparently did not discourage their subjects from adopting the new faith (see the box on p. 208).

MALI The state of Ghana flourished for several hundred years, but by the twelfth century, weakened by ruinous wars with Berber tribesmen, it had begun to decline; it collapsed at the end of the century. In its place rose a number of new trading societies, including large territorial empires like Mali (MAHL-ee) in the

The Great Gate at Marrakech. The Moroccan city of Marrakech (mar-uh-KESH), founded in the ninth century C.E., was a major northern terminus of the trans-Saharan trade and one of the chief commercial centers in premodern Africa. Widely praised by such famous travelers as Ibn Battuta, the city was an architectural marvel in that all of its major public buildings were constructed of red sandstone. Shown here is the Great Gate to the city, through which camel caravans passed en route to and from the vast desert. In the Berber language, Marrakech means "pass without making a noise," a necessity for caravan traders who had to be alert to the danger of thieves in the vicinity.

© William J. Duiker

Royalty and Religion in Ghana

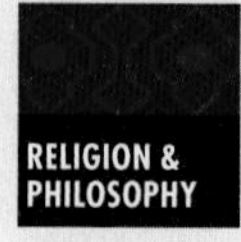

RELIGION & PHILOSOPHY

After its first appearance in West Africa in the decades following the death of Muhammad, Islam competed with native African religions for followers. Eventually, several local rulers converted to the Muslim faith. This passage by the Arab geographer al-Bakri (al-BAHK-ree) reflects religious tolerance in the state of Ghana during the eleventh century under a non-Muslim ruler with many Muslim subjects.

Al-Bakri's Description of Royalty in Ghana

The king's residence comprises a palace and conical huts, the whole surrounded by a fence like a wall. Around the royal town are huts and groves of thorn trees where live the magicians who control their religious rites. These groves, where they keep their idols and bury their kings, are protected by guards who permit no one to enter or find out what goes on in them.

None of those who belong to the imperial religion may wear tailored garments except the king himself and the heir-presumptive, his sister's son. The rest of the people wear wrappers of cotton, silk or brocade according to their means. Most of the men shave their beards and the women their heads. The king adorns himself with female ornaments around the neck and arms. On his head he wears gold-embroidered caps covered with turbans of finest cotton. He gives audience to the people for the redressing of grievances in a hut around which are placed 10 horses covered in golden cloth. Behind him stand 10 slaves carrying shields and swords mounted with gold. On his right are the sons of vassal kings, their heads plaited with gold and wearing costly garments. On the ground around him are seated his ministers, whilst the governor of the city sits before him. On guard at the door are dogs of fine pedigree, wearing collars adorned with gold and silver. The royal audience is announced by the beating of a drum, called *daba*, made out of a long piece of hollowed-out wood. When the people have gathered, his coreligionists draw near upon their knees sprinkling dust upon their heads as a sign of respect, whilst the Muslims clap hands as their form of greeting.

Why might an African ruler find it advantageous to adopt the Muslim faith? What kinds of changes would the adoption of Islam entail for the peoples living in West Africa?

Source: Adapted from translation quoted in J. S. Trimingham, *A History of Islam and West Africa*, copyright 1970 by Oxford University Press.

west, Songhai (song-GY) and Kanem-Bornu (KAH-nuhm-BOR-noo) toward the east, and small commercial city-states like the Hausa (HOW-suh) states, located in what is today northern Nigeria (see Map 8.4).

The greatest of the empires that emerged after the destruction of Ghana was Mali. Extending from the Atlantic coast inland as far as the trading cities of Timbuktu (tim-BUK-too) and Gao on the Niger River, Mali built its wealth and power on the gold trade. But the heartland of Mali was situated south of the Sahara in the savannas, where sufficient moisture enabled farmers to grow such crops as sorghum, millet, and rice. The farmers lived in villages ruled by a local chieftain, called a ***mansa*** (MAHN-suh), who served as both religious and administrative leader and was responsible for forwarding tax revenues from the village to higher levels of government.

The primary wealth of the country was accumulated in the cities. Here lived the merchants, who were mostly of local origin, although many were now practicing Muslims. Commercial activities were taxed but were apparently so lucrative that both the merchants and the kings prospered. One of the most powerful kings of Mali was Mansa Musa (MAHN-suh MOO-suh) (r. 1312–1337), whose primary contribution to his people was probably not economic prosperity but the Muslim faith. Mansa Musa strongly encouraged the building of mosques and the study of the Qur'an in his kingdom and imported scholars and books to introduce his subjects to the message of Allah. One visitor from Europe, writing in the late fifteenth century, reported that in Timbuktu "are a great store of doctors, judges, priests, and other learned men, that are bountifully maintained at the king's cost and charges. And hither are brought divers manuscripts of written books out of Barbary [North Africa] which are sold for more money than any other merchandise."[4]

The city of Timbuktu ("well of Bouctu," a Taureg woman who lived in the area) was founded in 1100 C.E. as a seasonal camp for caravan traders on the Niger River. Under Mansa Musa and his successors, the city gradually

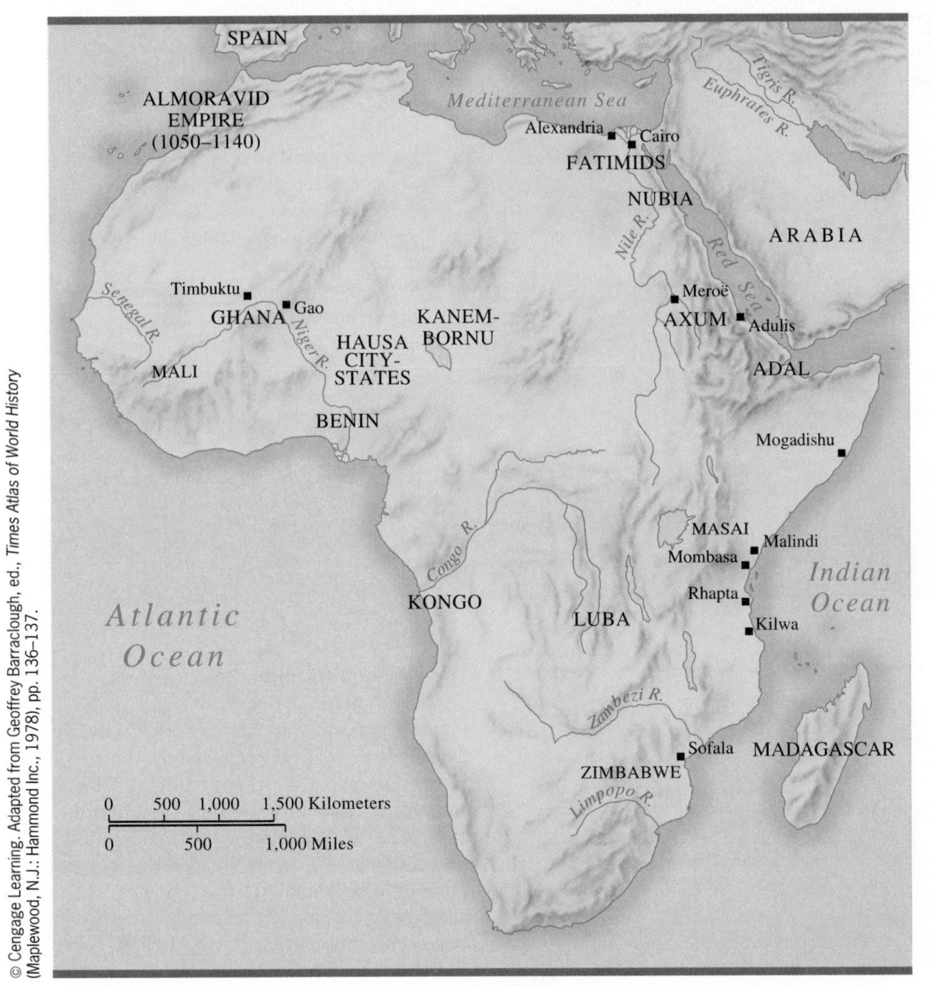

© Cengage Learning, Adapted from Geoffrey Barraclough, ed., *Times Atlas of World History* (Maplewood, N.J.: Hammond Inc., 1978), pp. 136–137.

MAP 8.4 The Emergence of States in Africa. By the end of the first millennium C.E., organized states had begun to appear in various parts of Africa.

Why did organized states appear in these particular areas and not in other places in Africa?

emerged as a major intellectual and cultural center in West Africa and the site of schools of law, literature, and the sciences.

States and Noncentralized Societies in Central and Southern Africa

FOCUS QUESTIONS: What role did migrations play in the evolution of early African societies? How did the impact of these migrations compare with similar population movements elsewhere?

In the southern half of the African continent, from the great basin of the Congo River to the Cape of Good Hope, states formed somewhat more slowly than in the north. Until the eleventh century C.E., most of the peoples in this region lived in what are sometimes called **noncentralized societies**, characterized by autonomous villages organized by clans and ruled by a local chieftain or clan head. Beginning in the eleventh century, in some parts of southern Africa, these independent villages gradually began to consolidate. Out of these groupings came the first states.

The Congo River Valley

One area where this process occurred was the Congo River valley, where the combination of fertile land and nearby deposits of copper and iron enabled the inhabitants to enjoy an agricultural surplus and engage in regional commerce. Two new states in particular underwent this transition. Sometime during the fourteenth century, the kingdom of Luba (LOOB-uh) was founded in the center of the continent, in a rich agricultural and fishing area near the shores of Lake Kisale. Luba had a relatively centralized government, in which the king appointed provincial governors, who were responsible for collecting tribute from the village chiefs. At about the same time, the kingdom of Kongo was formed just south of the mouth of the Congo River on the Atlantic coast (see the box on p. 211).

These new states were primarily agricultural, although both had a thriving manufacturing sector and took an active part in the growing exchange of goods throughout the region. As time passed, both began to expand southward to absorb the mixed farming and pastoral peoples in the area of modern Angola. In the drier grasslands to the south, other small communities continued to support themselves by herding, hunting, or food gathering. We know little about these peoples, however, since they possessed no writing system and had few visitors. A Portuguese sailor who encountered them in the late sixteenth century reported, "These people are herdsmen and cultivators. . . . Their main crop is millet, which

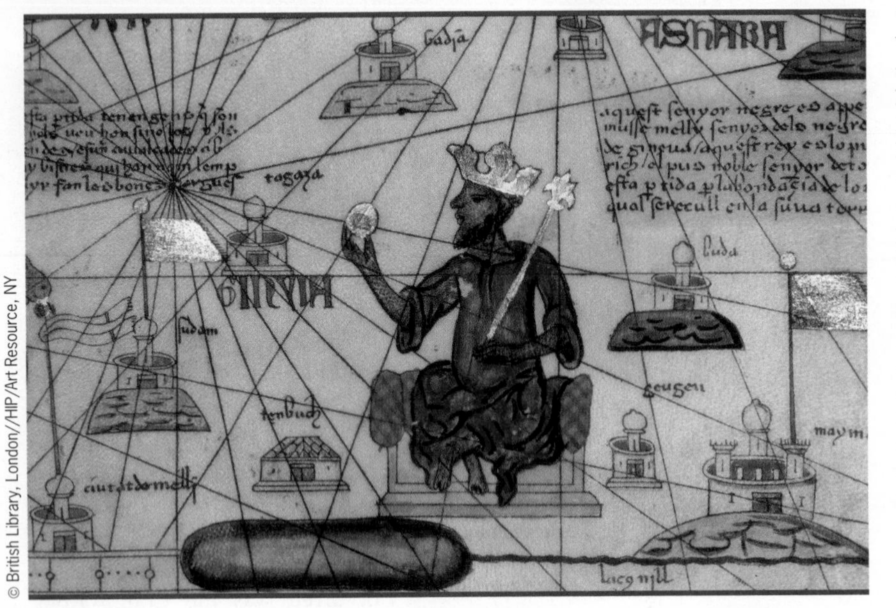

© British Library, London/HIP/Art Resource, NY

Mansa Musa. Mansa Musa, king of the West African state of Mali, was one of the richest and most powerful rulers of his day. During a famous pilgrimage to Mecca, he arrived in Cairo with a hundred camels laden with gold and gave away so much gold that its value depreciated there for several years. To promote the Islamic faith in his country, he bought homes in Cairo and Mecca to house pilgrims en route to the holy shrine, and he brought back to Mali a renowned Arab architect to build mosques in the trading centers of Gao and Timbuktu. His fame spread to Europe as well, evidenced by this Spanish map of 1375, which depicts Mansa Musa seated on his throne in Mali, holding an impressive gold nugget.

Musée des Arts Africains et Océanien /© Gianni Dagli Orti/The Art Archive at Art Resource, NY

The City of Timbuktu. The city of Timbuktu sat astride one of the major trade routes that passed through the Sahara between the kingdoms of West Africa and the Mediterranean Sea. Caravans transported food and various manufactured articles southward in exchange for salt, gold, copper, skins, agricultural goods, and slaves. Salt was at such a premium in Timbuktu that a young Moroccan wrote in 1513 that one camel's load brought 500 miles by caravan sold for 80 gold ducats, while a horse sold for only 40 ducats. Timbuktu became a prosperous city as well as a great center of Islamic scholarship. By 1550, it had three universities connected to its principal mosques and 180 Qur'anic schools. This pen-and-ink sketch was done by the French traveler René Caillie in 1828, when the city was long past its peak of prosperity and renown.

they grind between two stones or in wooden mortars to make flour. . . . Their wealth consists mainly in their huge number of dehorned cows. . . . They live together in small villages, in houses made of reed mats, which do not keep out the rain."[5]

Zimbabwe

Farther to the east, the situation was somewhat different. In the grasslands immediately to the south of the Zambezi River, a mixed economy involving farming, cattle herding, and commercial pursuits had begun to develop during the early centuries of the first millennium C.E. Characteristically, villages in this area were constructed inside walled enclosures to protect the animals at night. The most famous of these communities was Zimbabwe, located on the plateau of the same name between the Zambezi and Limpopo Rivers. From the twelfth century to the middle of the fifteenth, Zimbabwe was the most powerful and most prosperous state in the region and played a major role in the gold trade with the Swahili trading communities on the eastern coast.

The Nyanga Meet the Pygmies of Gabon

INTERACTION & EXCHANGE

Sometime in the distant past, the Nyanga peoples from the area that today comprises the Central African states of Rwanda and Uganda migrated into the Congo River valley, deep in the heart of the rain forests of equatorial Africa. There they encountered the Twa (indigenous peoples sometimes known today as pygmies), and soon began to adopt elements of their culture. In this selection, the Nyanga rulers have appropriated a local custom by calling on the indigenous bards to narrate the *Mwindo Epic*, which celebrates the arrival of their people into the area, led by their legendary chief Mwindo (MWEE-uh-doh).

The *Mwindo Epic*

After Mwindo had taken rest, he assembled all his people. They arrived. He told them: "I, Mwindo, the Little-one-just-born-he-walked, performer of many wonderful things. I tell you the news from the place from where I have come in the sky. When I arrived in the sky, I met with Rain and Moon and Sun and Kubikubi-Star and Lightning. These five personages forbade me to kill animals of the forest and of the village, and all the little animals of the forest, of the rivers, and the village, saying that the day I would dare to touch a thing in order to kill it, that day (the fire) would be extinguished; then Nkuba would come to take me without my saying farewell to my people, that then the return was lost forever." He also told them: "I have seen in the sky things unseen of which I could not divulge." When they had finished listening to Mwindo's words, those who were there dispersed. Shemwindo's and Nyamwindo's many hairs went say "high as that" as the long hairs of an *mpaca*-ghost; and in Tubondo the drums had not sounded anymore; the rooster had not crowed any more. On the day that Mwindo appeared there, his father's and his mother's long hairs were shaved, and the roosters crowed, and that day (all) the drums were being beaten all around.

When Mwindo was in his village, his fame grew and stretched widely. He passed laws to all his people, saying:

May you grow many foods and many crops.
May you live in good houses; may you moreover live in a beautiful village.
Don't quarrel with one another.
Don't pursue another's spouse.
Don't mock the invalid passing in the village.
And he who seduces another's wife will be killed!
Accept the chief; fear him; may he also fear you.
May you agree with one another, all together; no enmity in the land nor too much hate.
May you bring forth tall and short children; in so doing you will bring them forth for the chief.

After Mwindo has spoken like that, he went from then on to remain always in his village. He had much fame, and his father and his mother, and his wives and his people! His great fame went through his country; it spread into other countries, and other people from other countries came to pay allegiance to him.

How do Mwindo's laws compare with those of other ancient civilizations we have encountered?

Source: C. Hilliard (ed.), *Intellectual Traditions of Pre-Colonia Africa* (New York, McGraw-Hill, 1998), pp. 371–372.

The ruins of Zimbabwe's capital, known as Great Zimbabwe (the term *Zimbabwe* means "stone house" in the Bantu language), provide a vivid illustration of the kingdom's power and influence. Strategically situated between substantial gold reserves to the west and a small river leading to the coast, Great Zimbabwe was well placed to benefit from the expansion of trade between the coast and the interior. The town sits on a hill overlooking the river and is surrounded by stone walls, which enclosed an area large enough to hold more than 10,000 residents. The houses of the wealthy were built of cement on stone foundations, while those of the common people were of dried mud with thatched roofs. In the valley below is the royal palace, surrounded by a stone wall 30 feet high. Artifacts found at the site include household implements and ornaments made of gold and copper, as well as jewelry and even porcelain imported from China.

Most of the royal wealth probably came from two sources: the ownership of cattle and the king's ability to levy heavy taxes on the gold that passed through the kingdom en route to the coast. By the middle of the fifteenth century, however, the city was apparently abandoned, possibly because of environmental damage caused by overgrazing. With the decline of Zimbabwe, the focus of economic power began to shift northward to the valley of the Zambezi River.

Southern Africa

South of the East African plateau and the Congo basin is a vast land of hills, grasslands, and arid desert stretching almost to the Cape of Good Hope at the tip of the continent. As Bantu-speaking farmers spread southward during the final centuries of the first millennium B.C.E., they began to encounter Neolithic peoples in the area who still lived primarily by hunting and foraging.

Available evidence suggests that early relations between these two peoples were relatively harmonious. Intermarriage between members of the two groups was apparently not unusual, and many of the indigenous peoples were gradually absorbed into what became a dominantly Bantu-speaking pastoral and agricultural society that spread throughout much of southern Africa during the first millennium C.E.

THE KHOI AND THE SAN Two such peoples were the Khoi (KOI) and the San (SAHN), whose language, known as Khoisan (KOI-sahn), is distinguished by the use of "clicking" sounds. The Khoi were herders, whereas the San were hunter-gatherers who lived in small family communities of twenty to twenty-five members throughout southern Africa from Namibia in the west to the Drakensberg Mountains near the southeastern coast. Rock paintings found in caves throughout the area have helped archaeologists to learn more about the early life of the San. These multicolored paintings, which predate the coming of the Europeans, were drawn with a brush made of small feathers fastened to a reed. They depict various aspects of the San's lifestyle, including their hunting techniques and religious rituals.

Africa: A Continent Without History?

Until the second half of the twentieth century, the prevailing view among Western historians was that Africa was a continent without history, a land of scattered villages isolated from the main currents of world affairs. But in the decades after World War II, a new generation of historians trained in African studies, spurred on in part by the appearance in 1959 of Basil Davidson's path-breaking work, *Lost Cities of Africa*, began to contest that view. Their studies have demonstrated that throughout history not only were many African societies actively in contact with peoples beyond their shores, but also that they created a number of advanced civilizations of their own.

Although the paucity of written sources continues to present a challenge, historians are using other sources with increasing success to throw light on the African historical experience. African peoples were at the forefront of the agricultural revolution in the ninth and eighth millennia B.C.E., and although parts of the continent remained isolated from the main currents of world history, a number of African societies began as early as the first millennium C.E. to play an active role in the expanding global trade network, which stretched from the Mediterranean Sea deep into the Sahara. Another major commercial trade route ran from the Arabian peninsula down the coast of East Africa along the shores of the Indian Ocean. Thus, it is becoming increasingly clear that from the dawn of history the peoples of Africa have made a significant contribution to the human experience.

African Society

FOCUS QUESTIONS: What role did lineage groups, women, and slavery play in African societies? In what ways did African societies in various parts of the continent differ? What accounted for these differences?

Drawing generalizations about social organization, cultural development, and daily life in traditional Africa is difficult because of the extreme diversity of the continent and its inhabitants. One-quarter of all the languages in the world are spoken in Africa, and five of the major language families are found there. Ethnic divisions are equally pronounced. Because many of these languages did not have a system of writing until fairly recently, historians must rely on accounts of the occasional visitor, such as al-Mas'udi and the famous fourteenth-century chronicler Ibn Battuta. Such travelers, however, tended to come into contact mostly with the wealthy and the powerful, leaving us to speculate about what life was like for ordinary Africans during this early period.

Urban Life

African towns often began as fortified walled villages and gradually evolved into larger communities serving several purposes. Here, of course, were the center of government and the teeming markets filled with goods from distant regions. Here also were artisans skilled in metalworking or woodworking, pottery making, and other crafts. Unlike the rural areas, where a village was usually composed of a single lineage group or clan, the towns drew their residents from several clans, although individual clans usually lived in their own compounds and were governed by their own clan heads.

In the states of West Africa, the focal point of the major towns was the royal precinct. The relationship between the ruler and the merchant class differed from the situation in most Asian societies, where the royal family and the aristocracy were largely isolated from the remainder of the population. In Africa, the chasm between the king and the common people was not so great. Often the ruler would hold an audience to allow people to voice their complaints or to welcome visitors from foreign countries. In the city-states of the East African coast, the rulers were often wealthy merchants who, as in the town of Kilwa, "did not possess more country than the city itself."[6]

This is not to say that the king was not elevated above all others in status. In wealthier states, the walls of the audience chamber would be covered with sheets of beaten silver and gold, and the king would be surrounded by hundreds of armed soldiers and some of his trusted advisers. Nevertheless, the symbiotic relationship between the ruler and merchant class served to reduce the gap between the king and his subjects. The relationship was mutually beneficial, since the merchants received honors and favors from the palace while the king's coffers were filled with taxes paid by the merchants. Certainly, it was to the king's benefit to maintain law and order in his domain so that the merchants could ply their trade. As Ibn Battuta observed, among the good qualities of the states of West Africa was the prevalence of peace in the region. "The traveler is not afraid in it," he remarked, "nor is he who lives there in fear of the thief or of the robber by violence."[7]

Village Life

The vast majority of Africans lived in small rural villages. Their identities were established by their membership in a nuclear family and a lineage group. At the basic level was the nuclear family composed of parents and preadult children; sometimes it included an elderly grandparent and other family dependents as well. They lived in small round huts constructed of packed mud and topped with a conical thatch roof. In most African societies, these nuclear family units would in turn be combined into larger kinship communities known as households or lineage groups.

The lineage group was similar in many respects to the clan in China or the class system in India in that it was normally based on kinship ties, although sometimes outsiders such as friends or other dependents may have been admitted to membership. Throughout the precolonial era, lineages served, in the words of one historian, as the "basic building blocks" of African society. The authority of the leading members of the lineage group was substantial. As in China, the elders had considerable power over the economic functions of the other people in the group, which provided mutual support for all members.

A village would usually be composed of a single lineage group, although some communities may have consisted of several unrelated families. At the head of the village was the familiar "big man," who was often assisted by a council of representatives of the various households in the community. Often the "big man" was believed to possess supernatural powers, and as the village grew in size and power, he might eventually be transformed into a local chieftain or monarch.

The Role of Women

Although generalizations are risky, we can say that women were usually subordinate to men in Africa, as in most early societies. In some cases, they were valued for the work they could do or for their role in increasing the size of the lineage group. Polygyny was not uncommon, particularly in Muslim societies. Women often worked in the fields while the men of the village tended the cattle or went on hunting expeditions. In some communities, the women specialized in commercial activities. In one area in southern Africa, young girls were sent into the mines to extract gold because of their smaller physiques.

But there were some key differences between the role of women in Africa and elsewhere. In many African societies, lineage was **matrilinear** rather than **patrilinear**. As Ibn Battuta observed during his travels in West Africa, "A man does not pass on inheritance except to the sons of his sister to the exclusion of his own sons."[8] He said he had never encountered this custom before except among the unbelievers of the Malabar coast in India. Women were often permitted to inherit property, and the husband was often expected to move into his wife's house.

Relations between men and women were also sometimes more relaxed than in China or India, with none of the taboos characteristic of those societies. Again, in the words of Ibn Battuta, himself a Muslim:

> With regard to their women, they are not modest in the presence of men, they do not veil themselves in spite of their perseverance in the prayers. . . . The women there have friends and companions amongst men outside the prohibited degrees of marriage [i.e., other than brothers, fathers, etc.]. Likewise for the men, there are companions

Women and Islam in North Africa

FAMILY & SOCIETY

In Muslim societies in North Africa, as elsewhere, women were required to cover their bodies to avoid tempting men, but Islam's puritanical insistence on the separation of the sexes did not accord with the relatively informal relationships that prevailed in many African societies. In this excerpt from *The History and Description of Africa*, Leo Africanus describes the customs along the Mediterranean coast of Africa. A resident of Spain of Muslim parentage who was captured by Christian corsairs in 1518 and later served under Pope Leo X, Leo Africanus undertook many visits to Africa.

Leo Africanus, *The History and Description of Africa*

Their women (according to the guise of that country) go very gorgeously attired: they wear linen gowns dyed black, with exceeding wide sleeves, over which sometimes they cast a mantle of the same color or of blue, the corners of which mantle are very [attractively] fastened about their shoulders with a fine silver clasp. Likewise they have rings hanging at their ears, which for the most part are made of silver; they wear many rings also upon their fingers. Moreover they usually wear about their thighs and ankles certain scarfs and rings, after the fashion of the Africans. They cover their faces with certain masks having only two holes for the eyes to peep out at. If any man chance to meet with them, they presently hide their faces, passing by him with silence, except it be some of their allies or kinsfolks; for unto them they always [uncover] their faces, neither is there any use of the said mask so long as they be in presence. These Arabians when they travel any journey (as they oftentimes do) they set their women upon certain saddles made handsomely of wicker for the same purpose, and fastened to their camel backs, neither be they anything too wide, but fit only for a woman to sit in. When they go to the wars each man carries his wife with him, to the end that she may cheer up her good man, and give him encouragement. Their damsels which are unmarried do usually paint their faces, breasts, arms, hands, and fingers with a kind of counterfeit color: which is accounted a most decent custom among them.

Which of the practices described here are dictated by the social regulations of Islam? Does the author approve of the behavior of African women as described in this passage?

Source: From *The History and Description of Africa*, by Leo Africanus (New York: Burt Franklin), pp. 158–159.

> from amongst women outside the prohibited degrees. One of them would enter his house to find his wife with her companion and would not disapprove of that conduct.

When Ibn Battuta asked an African acquaintance about these customs, the latter responded: "Women's companionship with men in our country is honorable and takes place in a good way: there is no suspicion about it. They are not like the women in your country." Ibn Battuta noted his astonishment at such a "thoughtless" answer and did not accept further invitations to visit his friend's house.[9]

Such informal attitudes toward the relationship between the sexes were not found everywhere in Africa and were probably curtailed as many Africans converted to Islam (see the box above). But it is a testimony to the tenacity of traditional customs that the relatively puritanical views about the role of women in society brought by Muslims from the Middle East made little impression even among Muslim families in West Africa.

Slavery

African slavery is often associated with the period after 1500. Indeed, the slave trade did reach enormous proportions in the seventeenth and eighteenth centuries, when European slave ships transported millions of unfortunate victims abroad to Europe or the Americas (see Chapter 14).

Slavery did not originate with the coming of the Europeans, however. It had been practiced in Africa since ancient times and probably originated with prisoners of war who were forced into perpetual servitude. Slavery was common in ancient Egypt and became especially prevalent during the New Kingdom, when slaving expeditions brought back thousands of captives from the upper Nile to be used in labor gangs, for tribute, and even as human sacrifices.

Slavery persisted during the early period of state building, in the first and early second millennia C.E. Berber tribes may have regularly raided agricultural communities south of the Sahara for captives who were transported northward and eventually sold throughout the Mediterranean. Some were enrolled as soldiers, while others, often women, were used as domestic servants in the homes of the well-to-do. The use of captives for forced labor or exchange was apparently also common in African societies farther to the south and along the eastern coast.

Life was difficult for the average slave. The least fortunate were probably those who worked on plantations owned by the royal family or other wealthy landowners. Those pressed into service as soldiers were sometimes more fortunate, since in Muslim societies in the Middle East, they might at some point win their freedom. Many slaves were employed in the royal household or as domestic servants in private homes. In general, these slaves probably had the most tolerable existence. Although they ordinarily were not permitted to purchase their freedom, their living conditions were often decent and sometimes practically indistinguishable from those of the free individuals in the household. In some societies in North Africa, slaves reportedly made up as much as 75 percent of the entire population. Elsewhere the percentage was much lower, in some cases less than 10 percent.

African Culture

FOCUS QUESTION: What are some of the chief characteristics of African sculpture and carvings, music, and architecture, and what purpose did these forms of creative expression serve in African society?

In early Africa, as in much of the rest of the world at the time, creative expression, whether in the form of painting, literature, or music, was above all a means of serving religion and the social order. Though to the uninitiated a wooden mask or the bronze and iron statuary of southern Nigeria is simply a work of art, to the artist it was often a means of expressing religious convictions and common concerns. Some African historians reject the use of the term *art* to describe such artifacts because they were produced for spiritual or moral rather than aesthetic purposes.

Painting and Sculpture

The earliest extant art forms in Africa are rock paintings. The most famous examples are in the Tassili Mountains in the central Sahara, where the earliest paintings may date back as far as 5000 B.C.E., though the majority are a millennium or so younger. Some of the later paintings depict the two-horse chariots used to transport goods prior to the introduction of the camel. Rock paintings are also found elsewhere in the continent, including the Nile valley and in eastern and southern Africa. Those of the San peoples of southern Africa are especially interesting for their illustrations of ritual ceremonies in which village shamans induce rain, propitiate the spirits, or cure illnesses.

More familiar, perhaps, are African wood carvings and sculpture. The remarkable statues, masks, and headdresses were carved from living trees, after the artist had made a sacrifice to the tree's spirit. Costumed singers and dancers wore these masks and headdresses in performances in honor of the various spirits, revealing the identification and intimate connection of the African with the natural world. In Mali, for example, the 3-foot-tall Ci Wara (chee WAH-rah) headdresses, one female, the other male, were used to express meaning in performances that celebrated the mythical hero who had introduced agriculture. Terracotta and metal figurines served a similar purpose.

In the thirteenth and fourteenth centuries C.E., metalworkers at Ife (EE-fay) in what is now southern Nigeria produced handsome bronze and iron statues using the lost-wax method, in which melted wax is replaced in a mold by molten metal. The Ife sculptures may in turn have influenced artists in Benin (bay-NEEN), in West Africa, who produced equally impressive works in bronze during the same period. The Benin sculptures include bronze heads, relief plaques depicting life at court, ornaments, and figures of various animals.

Westerners once regarded African wood carvings and metal sculpture as a form of "primitive art," but the label is not appropriate. The metal sculpture of Benin, for example, is highly sophisticated, and some of the best works are considered masterpieces. Such artistic works were often created by artisans in the employ of the royal court.

Music

Like sculpture and wood carving, African music and dance often served a religious function. With their characteristic heavy rhythmic beat, dances were a means of communicating with the spirits, and the frenzied movements that are often identified with African dance were intended to represent the spirits acting through humans.

African music during the traditional period varied to some degree from one society to another. A wide variety of instruments were used, including drums and other percussion instruments, xylophones, bells, horns and flutes, and stringed instruments like the fiddle, harp, and zither. Still, the music throughout the continent had sufficient common characteristics to justify a few generalizations. In the first place, a strong rhythmic pattern was an important feature of most African music, although the desired effect was achieved through a wide variety of means, including gourds, pots, bells, sticks beaten together, and hand clapping as well as drums.

Another important feature was the integration of voice and instrument into a total musical experience. Musical instruments and the human voice were often woven together to tell a story, and instruments, such as the famous "talking drum," were frequently used to represent the voice. Choral music and individual voices were used in a pattern of repetition and variation, sometimes known as "call and response." Through this technique, the audience participated in the music by uttering a single phrase over and over as a choral response to the changing call sung by the soloist. Sometimes instrumental music achieved a similar result.

Much music was produced in the context of social rituals, such as weddings and funerals, religious ceremonies, and official inaugurations. It could also serve an educational purpose by passing on to the young people information about the history and social traditions of the community. In the absence of written languages in sub-Saharan Africa (except for the Arabic script, used in Muslim societies in East and West Africa), music served as the primary means of transmitting folk legends and religious traditions from generation to generation. Oral tradition, which was usually undertaken by a priestly class or a specialized class of storytellers, served a similar function.

Architecture

No aspect of African artistic creativity is more varied than architecture. From the pyramids along the Nile to the ruins of Great Zimbabwe south of the Zambezi River, from the Moorish palaces at Zanzibar to the turreted mud mosques of West Africa, African architecture shows a striking diversity of approach and technique that is unmatched in other areas of creative endeavor.

The earliest surviving architectural form found in Africa is the pyramid. The kingdom at Meroë apparently adopted the pyramidal form from Egypt during the last centuries of the first millennium B.C.E. Although used for the same purpose as their earlier counterparts at Giza, the pyramids at Meroë had a distinctive style; they were much smaller and were topped with a flat platform rather than rising to a point. Remains of temples with massive carved pillars at Meroë also reflect Egyptian influence.

Farther to the south, the kingdom of Axum was developing its own architectural traditions. Most distinctive were the carved stone pillars, known as stelae (STEE-lee), that were used to mark the tombs of dead kings. Some stood as high as 100 feet (see the comparative

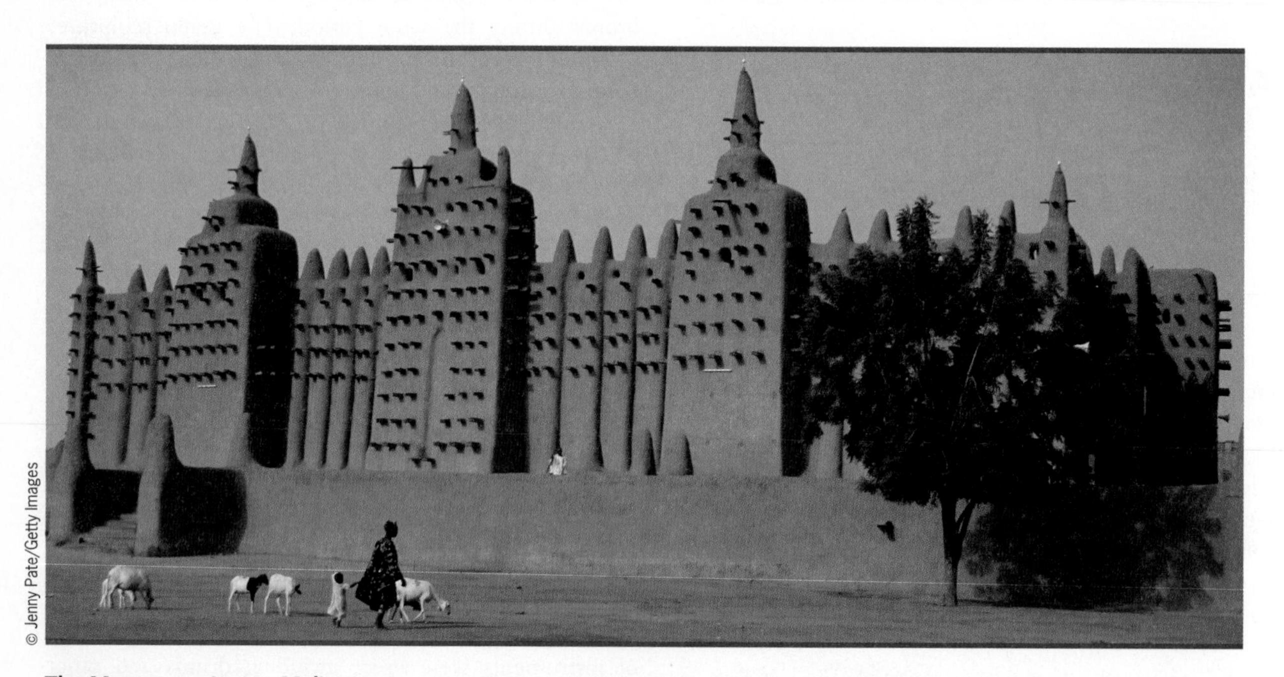
© Jenny Pate/Getty Images

The Mosque at Jenne, Mali. With the opening of the gold fields south of Mali, in present-day Ghana, Jenne (GEN-nay) became an important trading center for gold. Shown here is its distinctive mosque made of unbaked clay without reinforcements. The projecting timbers offered easy access for repairing the mud exterior, as was regularly required. The mosque was built in the fourteenth century and has since been reconstructed.

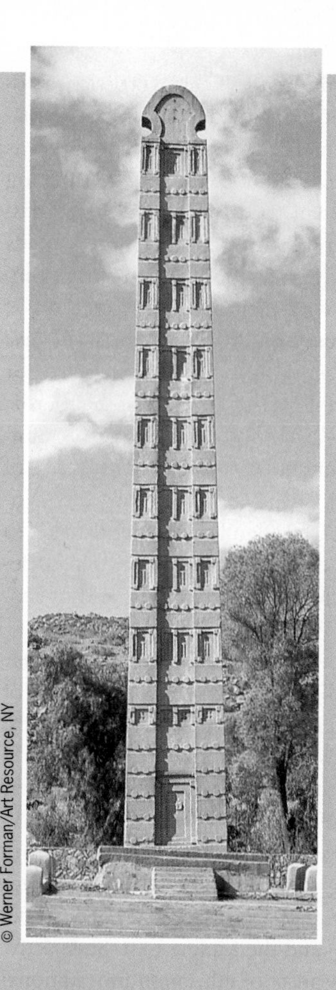

© Werner Forman/Art Resource, NY

© William J. Duiker

© Borromeo/Art Resource, NY

COMPARATIVE ILLUSTRATION

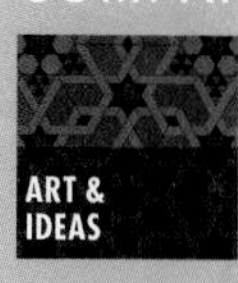

The Stele. A stele (STEE-luh) is a stone slab or pillar, usually decorated or inscribed and placed upright. Stelae were often used to commemorate the accomplishments of a ruler or significant figure. Shown at the left is the tallest of the Axum stelae still standing, in present-day Ethiopia. The stone stelae in Axum in the fourth century B.C.E. marked the location of royal tombs with inscriptions commemorating the glories of the kings. An earlier famous stele, seen in the center, is the obelisk at Luxor in southern Egypt. A similar kind of stone pillar, shown at the right, was erected in India during the reign of Ashoka in the third century B.C.E. (see Chapter 2) to commemorate events in the life of the Buddha. Archaeologists have also found stelae in ancient China, Greece, and Mexico.

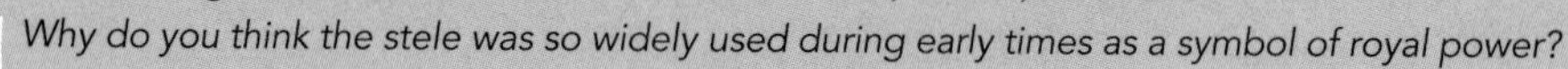

Q *Why do you think the stele was so widely used during early times as a symbol of royal power?*

illustration above). The advent of Christianity eventually had an impact on Axumite architecture. During the Zagwe dynasty in the twelfth and thirteenth centuries C.E., churches carved out of solid rock were constructed throughout the country (see the comparative illustration on p. 237 in Chapter 9). The earliest may have been built as early as the eighth century C.E. Stylistically, they combined indigenous techniques inherited from the pre-Christian period with elements borrowed from Christian churches in the Holy Land.

In West Africa, buildings constructed in stone were apparently a rarity until the emergence of states during the first millennium C.E. At that time, the royal palace, as well as other buildings of civic importance, was often built of stone or cement, while the houses of the majority of the population continued to be constructed of dried mud. On his visit to the state of Guinea on the West African coast, the sixteenth-century traveler Leo Africanus noted that the houses of the ruler and other elites were built of chalk with roofs of straw. Even then, however, well into the state-building period, mosques were often built of mud.

Along the east coast, the architecture of the elite tended to reflect Middle Eastern styles. In the coastal towns and islands from Mogadishu to Kilwa, the houses of the wealthy were built of stone and reflected Arabic influence. As elsewhere, the common people lived in huts of mud, thatch, or palm leaves. Mosques were built of stone.

The most famous stone buildings in sub-Saharan Africa are those at Great Zimbabwe. Constructed of carefully cut stones that were set in place without mortar, the great wall and the public buildings at Great Zimbabwe are an impressive monument to the architectural creativity of the peoples of the region.

Literature

Literature in the sense of written works did not exist in sub-Saharan Africa during the early traditional period, except in regions where Islam had brought the Arabic script from the Middle East. But African societies compensated for the absence of a written language with a rich tradition of oral lore. The **bard**, or professional storyteller, was an ancient African institution by which history was transmitted orally from generation to generation. In many West African societies, bards were highly esteemed and served as counselors to kings as well as protectors of local tradition. Bards were revered for their oratory and singing skills, phenomenal memory, and astute interpretation of history. As one African scholar wrote, the death of a bard was equivalent to the burning of a library.

Bards served several necessary functions in society. They were chroniclers of history, preservers of social customs and proper conduct, and entertainers who possessed a monopoly over the playing of several musical instruments, which accompanied their narratives. Because of their unique position above normal society, bards often played the role of mediator between hostile families or clans in a community. They were also credited with possessing occult powers and could read divinations and issue blessings and curses. Traditionally, bards also served as advisers to the king, sometimes inciting him to action (such as going to battle) through the passion of their poetry. When captured by the enemy, bards were often treated with respect and released or compelled to serve the victor with their art.

One of the most famous West African epics is *The Epic of Son-Jara*, which was passed down orally by bards for more than seven hundred years. It relates the heroic exploits of Son-Jara (sun-GAR-uh) (also known as Sunjata or Sundiata), the founder and ruler (1230–1255) of Mali's empire. Although Mansa Musa is famous throughout the world because of his flamboyant pilgrimage to Mecca in the fourteenth century, Son-Jara is more celebrated in West Africa because of the dynamic and unbroken oral traditions of the West African peoples.

Like the bards, women were appreciated for their storytelling talents, as well as for their role as purveyors of the moral values and religious beliefs of African societies. In societies that lacked a written tradition, women represented the glue that held the community together. Through the recitation of fables, proverbs, poems, and songs, mothers conditioned the communal bonding and moral fiber of succeeding generations in a way that was rarely encountered in the patriarchal societies of Europe, eastern and southern Asia, and the Middle East. Such activities were not only vital aspects of education in traditional Africa, but they also offered a welcome respite from the drudgery of everyday life and a spark to develop the imagination and artistic awareness of the young. Renowned for its many proverbs, Africa also offers the following: "A good story is like a garden carried in the pocket."

CHAPTER SUMMARY

Thanks to the dedicated work of a generation of archaeologists, anthropologists, and historians, we now have a much better understanding of the evolution of human societies in Africa than we did a few decades ago. Intensive efforts by archaeologists have demonstrated beyond reasonable doubt that the first hominids lived there. Recently discovered evidence suggests that farming may have been practiced in Africa more than 11,000 years ago.

Less is known about more recent African history, partly because of the paucity of written records. Still, historians have established that the first civilizations had begun to take shape in sub-Saharan Africa by the first millennium C.E., while the continent as a whole was an active participant in the emerging regional and global trade with the Mediterranean world and across the Indian Ocean.

Thus, the peoples of Africa were not as isolated from the main currents of human history as was once assumed. Although the state-building process in sub-Saharan Africa was still in its early stages compared with the ancient civilizations of India, China, and Mesopotamia, in many respects these new states were as impressive and sophisticated as their counterparts elsewhere in the world.

In the fifteenth century, a new factor was added to the equation. Urged on by the tireless efforts of Prince Henry the Navigator, Portuguese fleets began to probe southward along the coast of West Africa. At first, their sponsors were in search of gold and slaves, but at the end of the century, Vasco da Gama's voyage around the Cape of Good Hope signaled Portugal's determination to dominate the commerce of the Indian Ocean in the future. The new situation posed a challenge to the peoples of Africa, whose nascent states and technology would be severely tested by the rapacious demands of the Europeans.

CHAPTER TIMELINE

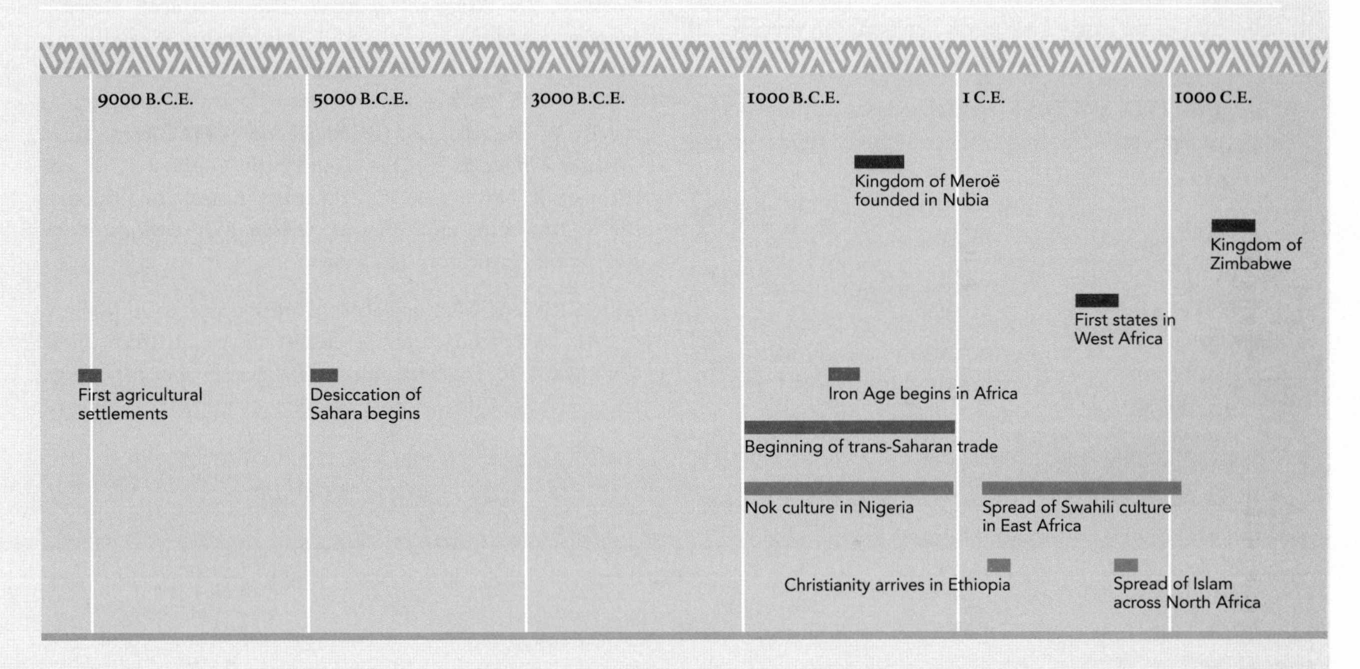

CHAPTER REVIEW

Upon Reflection

Q Where and under what conditions was agriculture first practiced on the continent of Africa? What effect did the advent of farming have on the formation of human communities there?

Q Although geographic barriers posed a challenge for African peoples in establishing communications with societies beyond their shores, by the end of the first millennium C.E. the continent had become an active player in the global trade network. What areas of Africa took part in this commercial expansion, and what products were exchanged?

Q The migration of the Bantu-speaking peoples was one of the most extensive population movements in world history. Trace the Bantu migration from its point of origin and discuss how it affected the later history of the continent.

Key Terms

Coptic (p. 199)
Berbers (p. 199)
Nok culture (p. 200)
Swahili (p. 202)
pantheism (p. 202)
lineage group (p. 202)
mansa (p. 208)
noncentralized societies (p. 209)
matrilinear (p. 213)
patrilinear (p. 213)
bard (p. 218)

Suggested Reading

GENERAL SURVEYS Several general surveys provide a useful overview of the early period of African history. The dean of African historians, and certainly one of the most readable, is **B. Davidson**. For a sympathetic portrayal of the African people, see his ***African History*** (New York, 1968) and ***Lost Cities in Africa,*** rev. ed. (Boston, 1970). A highly respected recent account is **C. Ehret, *The Civilizations of Africa: A History to 1800*** (Charlottesville, Va., 2002). Also see **V. B. Khapoya, *The African Experience: An Introduction*** (Englewood Cliffs, N.J., 1994). **R. O. Collins, ed., *Problems in African History: The Precolonial Centuries*** (New York, 1993), provides a useful collection of scholarly articles on key issues in precolonial Africa.

SPECIALIZED STUDIES Specialized studies are beginning to appear with frequency on many areas of the continent. For an account of archaeological finds, see **D. W. Phillipson, *African Archaeology*** (Cambridge, 2005). For a more detailed treatment of the early period, see the multivolume ***General History of Africa,*** sponsored by UNESCO (Berkeley, Calif., 1998). **R. O. Collins** has provided a useful service with his ***African History in Documents*** (Princeton, N.J., 1990). **C. Ehret, *An African Classical Age: Eastern and Southern Africa in World History, 1000 B.C. to A.D. 400*** (Charlottesville, Va., 1998), applies historical linguistics to make up for the lack of documentary evidence in the precolonial era. For African sources, see **C. Hilliard, ed., *Intellectual Traditions of Pre-Colonial Africa*** (Boston, 1998). Also see **D. A. Welsby, *The Kingdom of Kush: The Napataean Meroitic Empire*** (London, 1996), and **J. Middleton, *Swahili: An African Mercantile Civilization*** (New Haven, Conn., 1992). For a fascinating account of trans-Saharan trade, see **E. W. Bovill, *The Golden Trade of the Moors: West African Kingdoms in the Fourteenth Century,*** 2nd ed. (Princeton, N.J., 1995). On the early history of Ethiopia, see **S. Burstein, ed., *Ancient African Civilizations: Kush and Axum*** (Princeton, N.J., 1998).

AFRICAN ART For an excellent introduction to African art, see **M. B. Visond et al., *A History of Art in Africa*** (New York, 2001); **R. Hackett, *Art and Religion in Africa*** (London, 1996); and **F. Willet, *African Art,*** rev. ed. (New York, 1993).

CourseMate

Visit the CourseMate website at **www.cengagebrain.com** for additional study tools and review materials for this chapter.

CHAPTER

9

The Expansion of Civilization in South and Southeast Asia

© Thomas J. Abercrombie/National Geographic Images

One of the two massive carved statues of the Buddha formerly at Bamiyan

CHAPTER OUTLINE AND FOCUS QUESTIONS

The Silk Road

Q What were some of the chief destinations along the Silk Road, and what kinds of products and ideas traveled along the route?

India After the Mauryas

Q How did Buddhism change in the centuries after Siddhartha Gautama's death, and why did the religion ultimately decline in popularity in India?

The Arrival of Islam

Q How did Islam arrive in the Indian subcontinent, and why were Muslim peoples able to establish states there?

Society and Culture

Q What impact did Muslim rule have on Indian society? What are some of the most important cultural achievements of Indian civilization in the era between the Mauryas and the Mughals?

The Golden Region: Early Southeast Asia

Q What were the main characteristics of Southeast Asian social and economic life, culture, and religion before 1500 C.E.?

CRITICAL THINKING

Q New religions had a significant impact on the social and cultural life of peoples living in southern Asia during the period covered in this chapter. What factors caused the spread of these religions in the first place? What changes occurred as a result of the introduction of these new faiths? Were the religions themselves affected by their spread into new regions of Asia?

WHILE TRAVELING from his native China to India along the Silk Road in the early fifth century C.E., the Buddhist monk Fa Xian (fah SHEE-ahn) stopped en route at a town called Bamiyan (BAH-mee-ahn), a rest stop located deep in the mountains of what today is Afghanistan. At that time, Bamiyan was a major center of Buddhist studies, with dozens of temples and monasteries filled with students, all overlooked by two giant standing statues of the Buddha hewn directly out of the side of a massive cliff. Fa Xian was thrilled at the sight. "The law of Buddha," he remarked with satisfaction in his account of the experience, "is progressing and flourishing." He then continued southward to India, where he spent several years visiting Buddhists throughout the country. Because little of the literature from that period survives, Fa Xian's observations are a valuable resource for our knowledge of the daily lives of the Indian people.

The India that Fa Xian visited was no longer the unified land it had been under the Mauryan (MOWR-yun) dynasty. The overthrow of the Mauryas in the early second century B.C.E. had been followed by several hundred years of disunity, when the subcontinent was divided into a number of separate kingdoms and principalities. The dominant force in the north was the Kushan (KOO-shan) state, established by Indo-European-speaking peoples who had been driven out of what is now China's Xinjiang province by the Xiongnu (see Chapter 3). The Kushans penetrated into the mountains north of the Indus River, where they eventually formed a kingdom with its capital at Bactria, not far from modern Kabul (KAH-bul). Over the next two centuries, the Kushans expanded their supremacy along the Indus River and into the central Ganges valley.

Meanwhile, to the south, a number of kingdoms arose among the Dravidian-speaking peoples of the Deccan Plateau, which had been only partly under Mauryan rule. The most famous of these kingdoms was Chola (CHOH-luh) (sometimes spelled Cola) on the southeastern coast. Chola developed into a major trading power and sent merchant fleets eastward across the Bay of Bengal (ben-GAHL), where they introduced Indian culture as well as Indian goods to the peoples of Southeast Asia. In the fourth century C.E., Chola was overthrown by the Pallavas (puh-LAH-vuhz), who ruled from their capital at Kanchipuram (KAHN-chee-poo-rum), known today as Kanchi (KAHN-chee), just southwest of modern Chennai (CHEN-ny) (Madras), for the next four hundred years. 

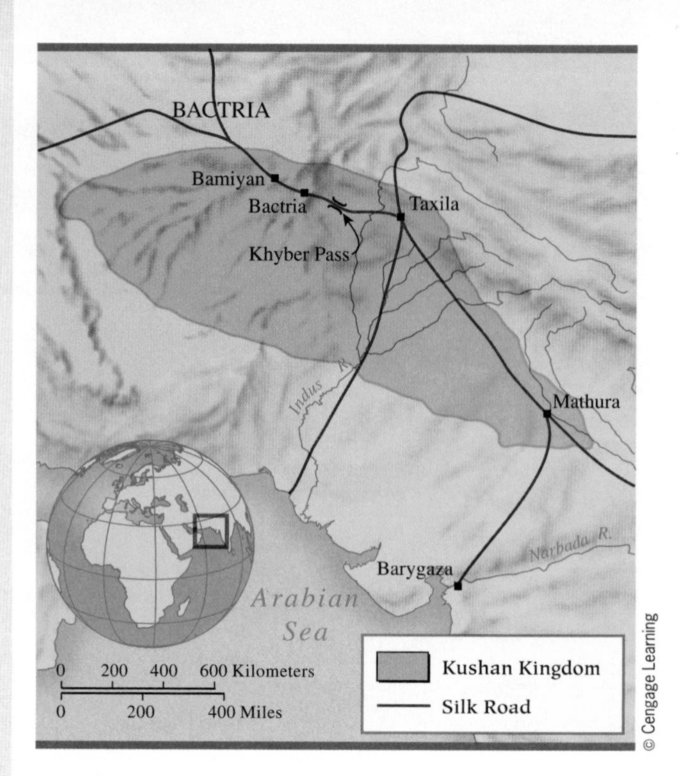

© Cengage Learning

MAP 9.1 The Kushan Kingdom and the Silk Road. After the collapse of the Mauryan Empire, a new state formed by recent migrants from the north arose north of the Indus River valley. For the next four centuries, the Kushan kingdom played a major role in regional trade via the Silk Road until it declined in the third century C.E.

What were the major products shipped along the Silk Road? Which countries beyond the borders of this map took an active part in trade along the Silk Road?

The Silk Road

FOCUS QUESTION: What were some of the chief destinations along the Silk Road, and what kinds of products and ideas traveled along the route?

The Kushan kingdom, with its power base beyond the Khyber Pass in modern Afghanistan, became the dominant political force in northern India in the centuries immediately after the fall of the Mauryas. Sitting astride the main trade routes across the northern half of the subcontinent, the Kushans thrived on the commerce that passed through the area (see Map 9.1). Much of that trade was between the Roman Empire and China and was transported along the route now known as the Silk Road, one segment of which passed through the mountains northwest of India (see Chapter 10). From there, goods were shipped to Rome through the Persian Gulf or the Red Sea.

Trade between India and Europe had begun even before the rise of the Roman Empire, but it expanded rapidly in the first century C.E., when sailors mastered the pattern of the monsoon winds in the Indian Ocean (from the southwest in the summer and the northeast in the winter). Commerce between the Mediterranean and the Indian Ocean, as described in the *Periplus* (PER-ih-pluss), a first-century C.E. account by a Greek participant, was extensive and often profitable, and it resulted in the establishment of several small trading settlements along the Indian coast. Rome imported ivory, indigo, textiles, precious stones, and pepper from India and silk from China. The Romans sometimes paid cash for these goods but also exported silver, wine, perfume, slaves, and glass and cloth from Egypt. Overall, Rome appears to have imported much more than it sold to the Far East.

The Silk Road was a conduit for technology and ideas as well as material goods. The first Indian monks to visit China may have traveled over the road during the second century C.E. By the time of Fa Xian, Buddhist monks from China were arriving in increasing numbers to visit holy sites in India. The exchange of visits not only enriched the study of Buddhism in the two countries but also led to a fruitful exchange of ideas and technological advances in astronomy, mathematics, and linguistics. According to one scholar, the importation of Buddhist writings from India encouraged the development of printing in China, and the Chinese also obtained lessons in health care from monks returned from the Asian subcontinent.

Indeed, the emergence of the Kushan kingdom as a major commercial power was due not only to its role as an intermediary in the Rome-China trade but also to the rising popularity of Buddhism. During the second century C.E., Kanishka (kuh-NISH-kuh), the greatest of the Kushan monarchs, began to patronize Buddhism. Under Kanishka and his successors, an intimate and mutually beneficial relationship was established between Buddhist monasteries and the local merchant community in thriving urban centers like Taxila (tak-SUH-luh) and Varanasi (vah-RAH-nah-see). Merchants were eager to build stupas and donate money to monasteries in return for social prestige and the implied promise of a better life in this world or the hereafter.

For their part, the wealthy monasteries ceased to be simple communities where monks could find a refuge from the material cares of the world; instead they became major consumers of luxury goods provided by their affluent patrons. Monasteries and their inhabitants became increasingly involved in the economic life of society, and Buddhist architecture began to be richly decorated with precious stones and glass purchased from local merchants or imported from abroad. The process was very similar to the changes that would later occur in the Christian church in medieval Europe.

It was from the Kushan kingdom that Buddhism began its long journey across the wastes of Central Asia to China and other societies in eastern Asia. As trade between the two regions increased, merchants and missionaries flowed from Bactria over the trade routes snaking through the mountains toward the northeast. At various stopping points on the trail, pilgrims erected statues and decorated mountain caves with magnificent frescoes depicting the life of the Buddha and his message to his followers. One of the most prominent of these centers was at Bamiyan, not far from modern-day Kabul, where believers carved two mammoth statues of the Buddha out of a sheer sandstone cliff. According to the Chinese pilgrim Fa Xian (see the box on p. 224), more than a thousand monks were attending a religious ceremony at the site when he visited the area in 400 C.E.

India After the Mauryas

FOCUS QUESTION: How did Buddhism change in the centuries after Siddhartha Gautama's death, and why did the religion ultimately decline in popularity in India?

The Kushan kingdom came to an end under uncertain conditions sometime in the third century C.E. In 320, a new state was established in the central Ganges valley by a local raja named Chandragupta (chun-druh-GOOP-tuh) (no relation to Chandragupta Maurya, the founder of the Mauryan dynasty). Chandragupta (r. 320–c. 335) located his capital at Pataliputra (pah-tah-lee-POO-truh), the site of the now decaying palace of the Mauryas. Under his successor Samudragupta (suh-moo-druh-GOOP-tuh) (r. c. 335–375), the territory under Gupta (GOOP-tuh) rule was extended into surrounding areas, and eventually the new kingdom became the dominant political force throughout northern India. It also established a loose suzerainty over the state of Pallava to the south, thus becoming the greatest state in the subcontinent since the decline of the Mauryan Empire. Under a succession of powerful, efficient, and highly cultured monarchs, notably Samudragupta and Chandragupta II (r. 375–415), India enjoyed a new "classical age" of civilization (see Map 9.2).

The Gupta Dynasty: A New Golden Age?

Historians of India have traditionally viewed the Gupta era as a time of prosperity and thriving commerce with China, Southeast Asia, and the Mediterranean. Great cities, notable for their temples and Buddhist monasteries as well as for their economic prosperity, rose along the main trade routes throughout the subcontinent. The religious trade also prospered, as pilgrims from across India and as far away as China came to visit the major religious centers.

As in the Mauryan Empire, much of the trade in the Gupta Empire was managed or regulated by the government. The Guptas owned mines and vast crown lands and earned massive profits from their commercial dealings. But there was also a large private sector, dominated by great *jati* (caste) guilds that monopolized key sectors of the economy. A money economy had probably been in operation since the second century B.C.E., when copper and gold coins had been introduced from the Middle East. This in turn led to the development of banking. Nevertheless, there are indications that the circulation of coins was limited. The Chinese missionary Xuan Zang (SHOO-wen ZAHNG), who visited India in the first half

A Portrait of Medieval India

Much of what we know about life in medieval India comes from the accounts of Chinese missionaries who visited the subcontinent in search of documents recording the teachings of the Buddha. Here the Buddhist monk Fa Xian, who spent several years there in the fifth century C.E., reports on conditions in the kingdom of Mathura (MAH-too-ruh) (Mo-tu-lo), a vassal state in western India that was part of the Gupta Empire. Although he could not have been pleased that the Gupta monarchs in India had adopted the Hindu faith, Fa Xian found that the people were contented and prosperous except for the untouchables, whom he called Chandalas.

Fa Xian, *The Travels of Fa Xian*

Going southeast from this somewhat less than 80 *joyanas*, we passed very many temples one after another, with some myriad of priests in them. Having passed these places, we arrived at a certain country. This country is called Mo-tu-lo. Once more we followed the Pu-na river. On the sides of the river, both right and left, are twenty *sangharamas*, with perhaps 3,000 priests. The law of Buddha is progressing and flourishing. Beyond the deserts are the countries of western India. The kings of these countries are all firm believers in the law of Buddha. They remove their caps of state when they make offerings to the priests. The members of the royal household and the chief ministers personally direct the food giving; when the distribution of food is over, they spread a carpet on the ground opposite the chief seat (the president's seat) and sit down before it. They dare not sit on couches in the presence of the priests. The rules relating to the almsgiving of kings have been handed down from the time of Buddha till now. Southward from this is the so-called middle country (Madhyadesa). The climate of this country is warm and equable, without frost or snow. The people are very well off, without poll tax or official restrictions. Only those who till the royal lands return a portion of profit of the land. If they desire to go, they go; if they like to stop, they stop. The kings govern without corporal punishment; criminals are fined, according to circumstances, lightly or heavily. Even in cases of repeated rebellion they only cut off the right hand. The king's personal attendants, who guard him on the right and left, have fixed salaries. Throughout the country the people kill no living thing nor drink wine, nor do they eat garlic or onions, with the exception of Chandalas only. The Chandalas are named "evil men" and dwell apart from others; if they enter a town or market, they sound a piece of wood in order to separate themselves; then men, knowing who they are, avoid coming in contact with them. In this country they do not keep swine nor fowls, and do not deal in cattle; they have no shambles [slaughterhouses] or wine shops in their marketplaces. In selling they use cowrie shells. The Chandalas only hunt and sell flesh.

To what degree do the practices described here appear to conform to the principles established by Siddhartha Gautama in his teachings? Would political advisers such as Kautilya and the Chinese philosopher Mencius have approved of the governmental policies?

Source: "Fu-kwo-ki," in Hiuen Tsang, Si-Yu Ki: *Buddhist Records of the Western World,* translated by Samuel Beal (London: Routledge and Kegan Paul). Used with permission.

of the seventh century, remarked that most commercial transactions were conducted by barter.[1]

But the good fortunes of the Guptas proved to be relatively short-lived. Beginning in the late fifth century C.E., incursions by nomadic warriors from the northwest gradually reduced the power of the empire. Soon northern India was once more divided into myriad small kingdoms engaged in seemingly constant conflict. In the south, however, emerging states like Chola and Pallava prospered from their advantageous position athwart the regional trade network stretching from the Red Sea eastward into Southeast Asia.

The Transformation of Buddhism

The Chinese pilgrims who traveled to India during the Gupta era encountered a Buddhism that had changed in a number of ways since the time of Siddhartha Gautama. They also found a doctrine that was beginning to decline in popularity in the face of the rise of Hinduism, as the Brahmanical religious beliefs of the Aryan people would eventually be called.

The transformation in Buddhism had come about in part because the earliest written sources were transcribed two centuries after Siddhartha's death and in part because his message was reinterpreted as it became part of

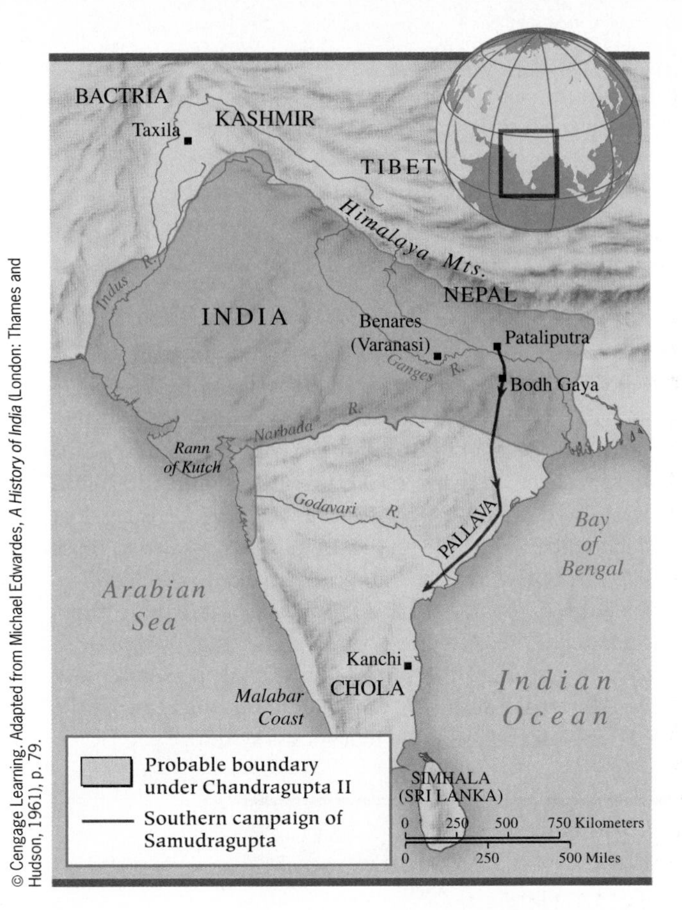

© Cengage Learning. Adapted from Michael Edwardes, *A History of India* (London: Thames and Hudson, 1961), p. 79.

MAP 9.2 The Gupta Empire. This map shows the extent of the Gupta Empire, the only major state to arise in the Indian subcontinent during the first millennium C.E. The arrow indicates the military campaign into southern India led by King Samudragupta.

Q *How did the Gupta Empire differ in territorial extent from its great predecessor, the Mauryan Empire?*

CHRONOLOGY Medieval India	
Kushan kingdom	c. 150 B.C.E.–c. 200 C.E.
Gupta dynasty	320–600s
Chandragupta I	320–c. 335
Samudragupta	c. 335–375
Chandragupta II	375–415
Arrival of Fa Xian in India	c. 406
Cave temples at Ajanta	Fifth century
Travels of Xuan Zang in India	630–643
Conquest of Sind by Arab armies	c. 711
Mahmud of Ghazni	997–1030
Delhi sultanate	1206–1527
Invasion of Tamerlane	1398

people's everyday lives. Abstract concepts of a Nirvana that cannot be described began to be replaced, at least in the popular mind, with more concrete visions of heavenly salvation, and Siddhartha was increasingly regarded as a divinity rather than as a sage. As a sign of that transformation, the face of the Buddha began to be displayed in sacred sculptures, along with clear suggestions that, like Jesus, he was of divine birth (see the comparative illustration on p. 47 in Chapter 2). The Buddha's teachings that all four classes were equal gave way to the familiar Brahmanical conviction that some people, by reason of previous reincarnations, were closer to Nirvana than others.

THERAVADA These developments led to a split in the movement. Purists emphasized what they insisted were the original teachings of the Buddha, describing themselves as the school of **Theravada** (thay-ruh-VAH-duh), or "the teachings of the elders." Followers of Theravada considered Buddhism a way of life, not a salvationist creed. Theravada stressed the importance of strict attention to personal behavior and the quest for understanding as a means of release from the wheel of life.

MAHAYANA In the meantime, another interpretation of Buddhist doctrine was emerging in the northwest. Here Buddhist believers, perhaps hoping to compete with other salvationist faiths circulating in the region, began to promote the view that Nirvana could be achieved through devotion and not just through painstaking attention to one's behavior. According to advocates of this school, eventually to be known as **Mahayana** (mah-huh-YAH-nuh) ("greater vehicle"), Theravada teachings were too demanding or too strict for ordinary people to follow and therefore favored the wealthy, who were more apt to have the time and resources to spend weeks or months away from their everyday occupations. Mahayana Buddhists referred to their rivals as **Hinayana** (hee-nuh-YAH-nuh), or "lesser vehicle," because in Theravada fewer would reach enlightenment. Mahayana thus attempted to provide hope for the masses in their efforts to reach Nirvana, but to the followers of Theravada, it did so at the expense of an insistence on proper behavior.

To advocates of the Mahayana school, salvation could also come from the intercession of a **bodhisattva** (boh-duh-SUT-vuh) ("he who possesses the essence of Buddhahood"). According to Mahayana beliefs, some individuals who had achieved *bodhi* and were thus eligible to enter the state of Nirvana after death chose instead, because of their great compassion, to remain on earth in spirit form to help all human beings achieve release from the life cycle. Followers of Theravada, who believed the concept of bodhisattva applied only to Siddhartha Gautama himself, denounced such ideas as "the teaching of demons." But to their proponents, such ideas extended the hope of salvation to the masses. Mahayana Buddhists revered the saintly individuals who, according to tradition, had become bodhisattvas at death and erected temples in their honor where the local population could pray and render offerings.

A final distinguishing characteristic of Mahayana Buddhism was its reinterpretation of Buddhism as a religion rather than a philosophy. Although Mahayana had philosophical aspects, its adherents increasingly regarded the Buddha as a divine figure, and an elaborate Buddhist cosmology developed. Nirvana was not a form of extinction but a true heaven.

Under Kushan rule, Mahayana achieved considerable popularity in northern India and for a while even made inroads in such Theravada strongholds as the island of Sri Lanka. But in the end, neither Mahayana nor Theravada was able to retain its popularity in Indian society. By the seventh century C.E., Theravada had declined rapidly on the subcontinent, although it retained its foothold in Sri Lanka and across the Bay of Bengal in Southeast Asia, where it remained an influential force to modern times (see Map 9.3). Mahayana prospered in the northwest for centuries, but eventually it was supplanted by a revived Hinduism and later by a new arrival, Islam. But Mahayana too would find better fortunes abroad, as it was carried over the Silk Road or by sea to China and then to Korea and Japan (see Chapters 10 and 11). In all three countries, Buddhism has coexisted with Confucian doctrine and indigenous beliefs to the present.

The Decline of Buddhism in India

Why was Buddhism unable to retain its popularity in its native India, although it became a major force elsewhere in Asia? Some have speculated that in denying the existence of the soul, Buddhism ran counter to traditional Indian belief. Perhaps, too, one of Buddhism's strengths was also a weakness. In rejecting the class divisions that defined the Indian way of life, Buddhism appealed to those very groups who lacked an accepted place in Indian society, such as the untouchables. But at the same time, it represented a threat to those with a higher status. Moreover, by emphasizing the responsibility of each person to seek an individual path to Nirvana, Buddhism undermined the strong social bonds of the Indian class system.

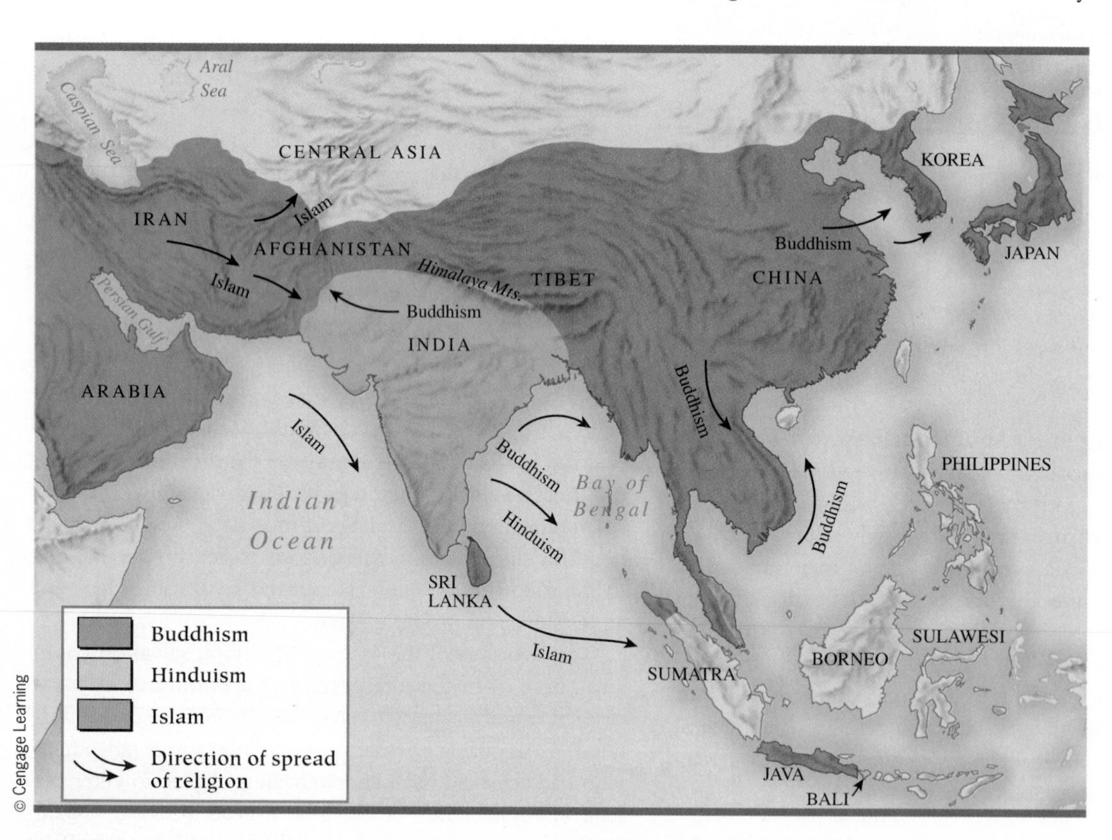

© Cengage Learning

MAP 9.3 The Spread of Religions in Southern and Eastern Asia, 600–1500 C.E. Between 600 and 1900 C.E., three of the world's great religions—Buddhism, Hinduism, and Islam—continued to spread from their original sources to different parts of southern and eastern Asia.

Q *Which religion had the greatest impact? How might the existence of major trade routes help explain the spread of these religions?*

Perhaps a final factor in the decline of Buddhism was the rise of **Hinduism**. In its early development, Brahminism had been highly elitist. Not only was observance of court ritual a monopoly of the *brahmin* class, but the major route to individual salvation, asceticism, was hardly realistic for the average Indian. In the centuries after the fall of the Mauryas, however, a growing emphasis on devotion—***bhakti*** (BAHK-tee)—as a means of religious observance brought the possibility of improving one's *karma* by means of ritual acts within the reach of Indians of all classes. It seems likely that Hindu devotionalism rose precisely to combat the inroads of Buddhism and reduce the latter's appeal among the Indian population. The Chinese Buddhist missionary Fa Xian, who visited India in the mid-Gupta era, reported that mutual hostility between the Buddhists and the *brahmins* was quite strong:

> Leaving the southern gate of the capital city, on the east side of the road is a place where Buddha once dwelt. Whilst here he bit [a piece from] the willow stick and fixed it in the earth; immediately it grew up seven feet high, neither more nor less. The unbelievers and Brahmans, filled with jealousy, cut it down and scattered the leaves far and wide, but yet it always sprang up again in the same place as before.[2]

For a while, Buddhism was probably able to stave off the Hindu challenge with its own salvationist creed of Mahayana, which also emphasized the role of devotion, but Buddhism's days as a dominant faith in the subcontinent were numbered. By the eighth century C.E., Hindu missionaries spread throughout southern India, where their presence was spearheaded by new temples honoring Shiva in Kanchipuram (Kanchi), the site of a famous Buddhist monastery, and at Mamallapuram (muh-MAH-luh-poor-um).

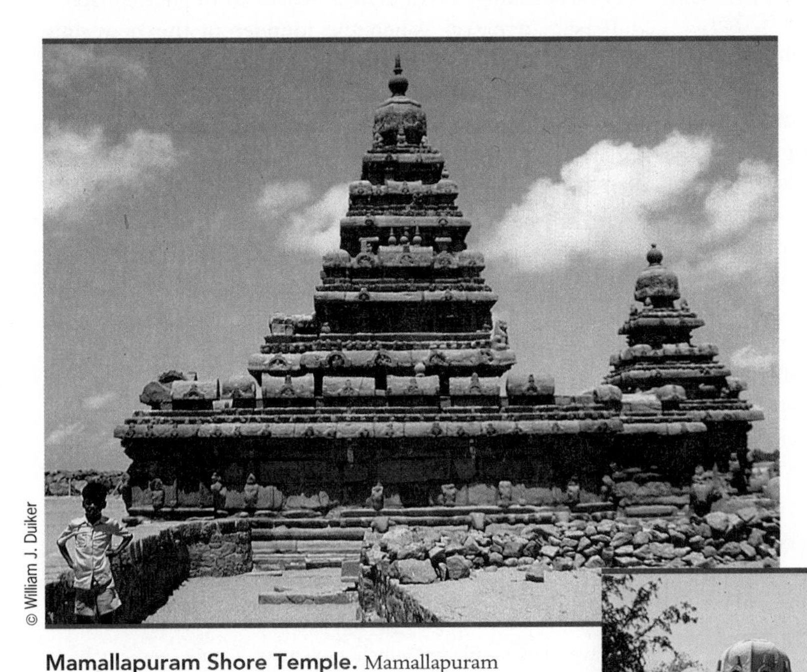

© William J. Duiker

Mamallapuram Shore Temple. Mamallapuram ("The City of the Great Warrior") was so named by one of the powerful kings of the Pallavan kingdom on the eastern coast of South India. From this port, ships embarked on naval expeditions to Sri Lanka and far-off destinations in Southeast Asia. Although the site was originally identified with the Hindu deity Vishnu, in the eighth century C.E. a Pallavan monarch built this shore temple in honor of Vishnu's rival deity, Shiva. It stands as a visual confirmation of the revival of the Hindu faith in southern India at the time. Centuries of wind and rain have eroded the ornate carvings that originally covered the large granite blocks. Nearby stands a group of five rock-cut monoliths (shown in the bottom photo) named after heroes in the Mahabharata. The seventh-century rock cutters carved these impressive shrines out of giant boulders.

© William J. Duiker

When Did the Indians Become Hindus?

When did Brahmanism—the faith brought to India by the Aryan peoples in the second millennium B.C.E.—evolve into Hinduism, the religion practiced by the majority of the Indian people today? That question has aroused considerable interest among historians of India in recent years. Of course, there is no single precise answer because the issue is partly a matter of definition and the transition was undoubtedly gradual.

Some observers point to the advent of Muslim rule in the northern parts of the subcontinent in the late first millennium C.E. (see "The Arrival of Islam" later in the chapter), when the indigenous people, labeled "Hindus" by the new arrivals, began to develop a greater sense of their distinct ethnic and cultural identity. Others point to the colonial era, when British policies reinforced an Indian sense of being "the Other," provoking the local peoples to defend their cultural and historical heritage.

Still other historians put the transition early in the first millennium C.E., when the Brahmanical emphasis on court sacrifice and asceticism was gradually replaced by a more populist tradition focused on personal worship, known as ***puja*** (POO-juh), and the achievement of individual goals. In that interpretation, the change to a faith more accessible to the masses may initially have been stimulated by the egalitarian tendencies of early Buddhism. In any event, by the end of the first millennium C.E., the religious faith originally known as Brahmanism had fought off the challenges of alternative belief systems while transforming itself into the religion of the majority of the Indian people.

The Arrival of Islam

FOCUS QUESTION: How did Islam arrive in the Indian subcontinent, and why were Muslim peoples able to establish states there?

While India was still undergoing a transition after the collapse of the Gupta Empire, the new and dynamic force of Islam was arising in the Arabian peninsula. As we have seen, during the seventh and eighth centuries, Arab armies carried the new faith westward to the Iberian peninsula and eastward across the arid wastelands of Persia and into the rugged mountains of the Hindu Kush. Islam first reached India through the Arabs in the eighth century, but a second onslaught in the tenth and eleventh centuries by Turkic-speaking converts had a more lasting effect.

Although Arab merchants had been active along the Indian coasts for centuries, Arab armies did not reach India until the early eighth century. When Indian pirates attacked Arab shipping near the delta of the Indus River, the Muslim ruler in Mesopotamia demanded an apology from the ruler of Sind (SINNED), a Hindu state in the Indus valley. When the latter refused, Muslim forces conquered lower Sind in 711 and then moved northward into the Punjab (pun-JAHB), bringing Arab rule into the frontier regions of the subcontinent for the first time.

The Empire of Mahmud of Ghazni

For the next three centuries, Islam made no further advances into India. But a second phase began at the end of the tenth century with the rise of the state of Ghazni (GAHZ-nee), located in the area of the old Kushan kingdom. The new kingdom was founded in 962 when Turkic-speaking slaves seized power from the Samanids, a Persian dynasty. When the founder of the new state died in 997, his brilliant and ambitious son, Mahmud (MAHKH-mood) of Ghazni (r. 997–1030), succeeded him. Through sporadic forays against neighboring Hindu kingdoms to the southeast, Mahmud was able to extend his rule throughout the upper Indus valley and as far south as the Indian Ocean (see Map 9.4). In wealth and cultural brilliance, his court at Ghazni rivaled that of the Abbasid dynasty in neighboring Baghdad. But he was not universally admired. Describing Mahmud's conquests in northwestern India, the contemporary historian al-Biruni (al-buh-ROO-nee) wrote:

> Mahmud utterly ruined the prosperity of the country, and performed wonderful exploits by which the Hindus became like atoms scattered in all directions, and like a tale of old in the mouth of the people. Their scattered remains cherish, of course, the most inveterate aversion towards all Muslims. This is the reason, too, why Hindu sciences have retired far away from those parts of the country conquered by us, and have fled to places which our hand cannot yet reach, to Kashmir, Benares, and other places.[3]

Resistance against the advances of Mahmud and his successors into northern India was led by the Rajputs (RAHJ-pootz), aristocratic Hindu clans who were probably descended from tribal groups that had penetrated into northwestern India from Central Asia in earlier centuries. The Rajputs possessed a strong military tradition and fought bravely, but their military tactics, based on infantry supported by elephants, were no match for the fearsome cavalry of the invaders, whose ability to strike with lightning speed contrasted sharply with the slow-footed forces of their adversaries. Although the power of Ghazni declined after Mahmud's death, a successor state in the area resumed the advance in the late twelfth

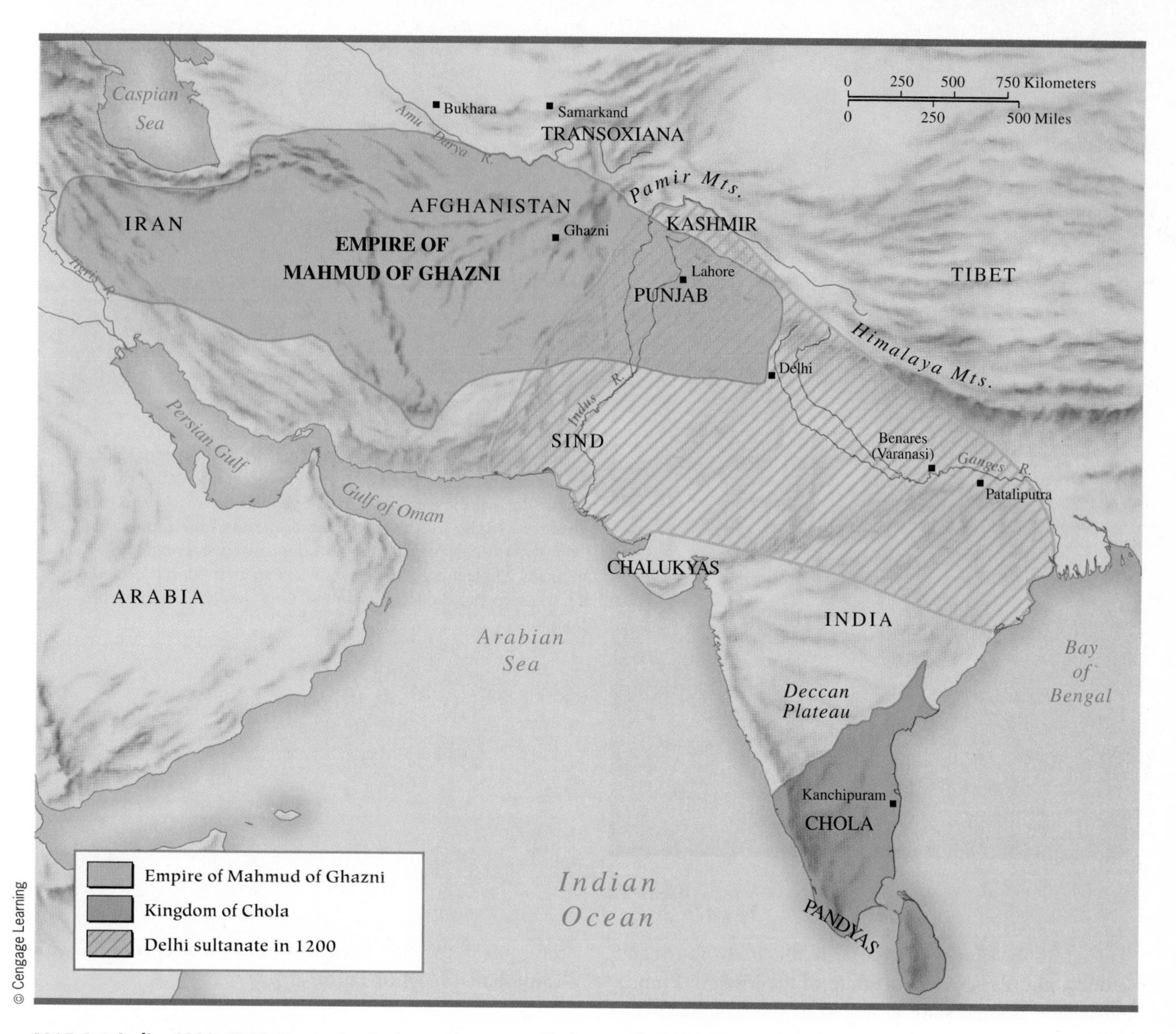

© Cengage Learning

MAP 9.4 India, 1000–1200. Beginning in the tenth century, Turkic-speaking peoples invaded northwestern India and introduced Islam to the peoples in the area. Most famous was the empire of Mahmud of Ghazni.

Locate the major trade routes passing through the area. What geographic features explain the location of those routes?

century, and by 1200, Muslim power, in the form of a new Delhi (DEL-ee) sultanate, had been extended over the entire plain of northern India.

The Delhi Sultanate

South of the Ganges River valley, Muslim influence spread more slowly and in fact had little immediate impact. Muslim armies launched occasional forays into the Deccan Plateau, but at first they had little success, even though the area was divided among a number of warring kingdoms, including the Cholas along the eastern coast and the Pandyas (PUHN-dee-ahz) far to the south.

One reason the Delhi sultanate failed to take advantage of the disarray of its rivals was the threat posed by the Mongols on the northwestern frontier (see Chapter 10). Mongol armies unleashed by the great tribal warrior Genghis Khan occupied Baghdad and destroyed the Abbasid caliphate in the 1250s, while other forces occupied the Punjab around Lahore (luh-HOR), from which they threatened Delhi on several occasions. For the next half-century, the attention of the sultanate was focused on the Mongols.

© William J. Duiker

© William J. Duiker

Kutub Minar. To commemorate their victory, in 1192 the Muslim conquerors of northern India constructed a magnificent mosque on the site of Delhi's largest Hindu temple. Much of the material for the mosque came from twenty-seven local Hindu and Jain shrines (right). Adjacent to the mosque soars the Kutub Minar (KUH-tub mee-NAHR), symbol of the new conquering faith. Originally 238 feet high, the tower bears an inscription proclaiming its mission to cast the long shadow of God over the realm of the Hindus.

That threat finally declined in the early fourteenth century with the gradual breakup of the Mongol Empire, and a new Islamic state emerged as the Tughluq (tug-LUK) dynasty (1320–1413) extended its power into the Deccan Plateau. In praise of his sovereign, the Tughluq monarch Ala-ud-din (uh-LAH-ud-DEEN), the poet Amir Khusrau (ah-MEER KOOS-roh) exclaimed:

Happy be Hindustan, with its splendor of religion,
Where Islamic law enjoys perfect honor and dignity;
In learning Delhi now rivals Bukhara;
Islam has been made manifest by the rulers.
From Ghazni to the very shore of the ocean
You see Islam in its glory.[4]

Such happiness was not destined to endure, however. During the latter half of the fourteenth century, the Tughluq dynasty gradually fell into decline. In 1398, a new military force crossed the Indus River from the northwest, raided the capital of Delhi, and then withdrew. According to some contemporary historians, as many as 100,000 Hindu prisoners were massacred before the gates of the city. Such was India's first encounter with Tamerlane (TAM-ur-layn).

Tamerlane

Tamerlane (c. 1330s–1405), also known as Timur-i-lang (Timur the Lame), was the ruler of a Mongol khanate based in Samarkand (SAM-ur-kand) to the north of the Pamir (pah-MEER) Mountains. His kingdom had been founded on the ruins of the Mongol Empire, which had begun to disintegrate as a result of succession struggles in the thirteenth century. Tamerlane, the son of a local aristocrat and of mixed Turko-Mongolian heritage, seized power in Samarkand in 1369 and immediately launched a program of conquest. During the 1380s, he brought the entire region east of the Caspian Sea under his authority and then conquered Baghdad and occupied Mesopotamia (see Map 9.5). After his brief foray into northern India, he turned to the west and raided the Anatolian peninsula. Defeating the army of the Ottoman Turks, he advanced almost as far as the Bosporus before withdrawing. "The

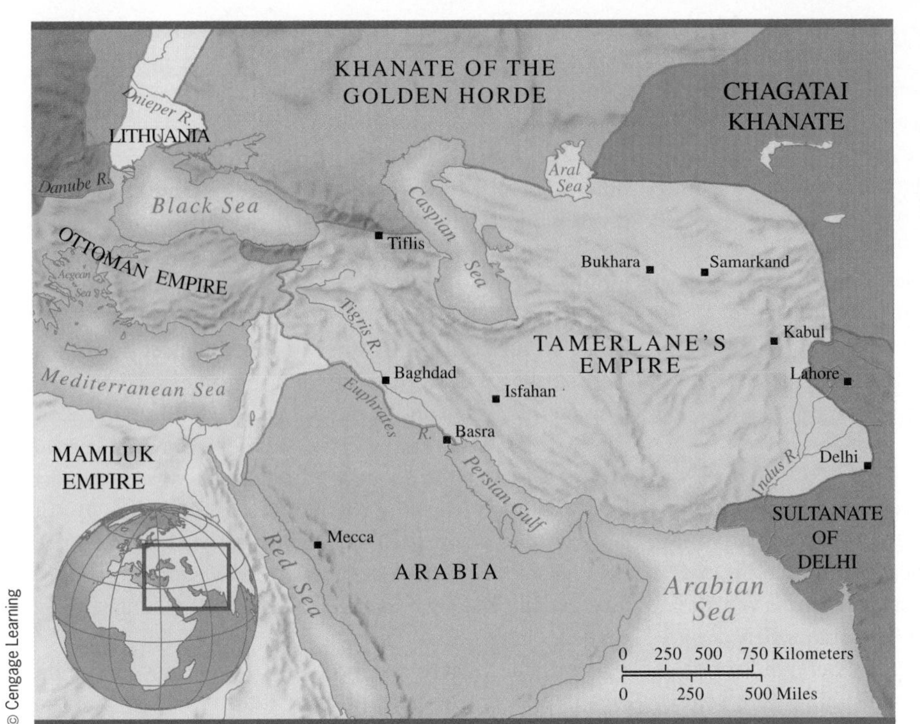

© Cengage Learning

MAP 9.5 The Empire of Tamerlane. In the fourteenth century, Tamerlane, a feared conqueror of Mongolian extraction, established a brief empire in Central Asia with his capital at Samarkand.

Q *Which of the states shown in this map were part of Muslim civilization?*

last of the great nomadic conquerors," as one recent historian described him, died in 1405 in the midst of a final military campaign.

The passing of Tamerlane removed a major menace from the diverse states of the Indian subcontinent. But the respite from external challenge was not a long one. By the end of the fifteenth century, two new challenges had appeared from beyond the horizon: the Mughals, a newly emerging nomadic power beyond the Khyber Pass in the north, and the Portuguese traders, who arrived by sea from the eastern coast of Africa in search of gold and spices. Both, in different ways, would exert a major impact on the later course of Indian civilization.

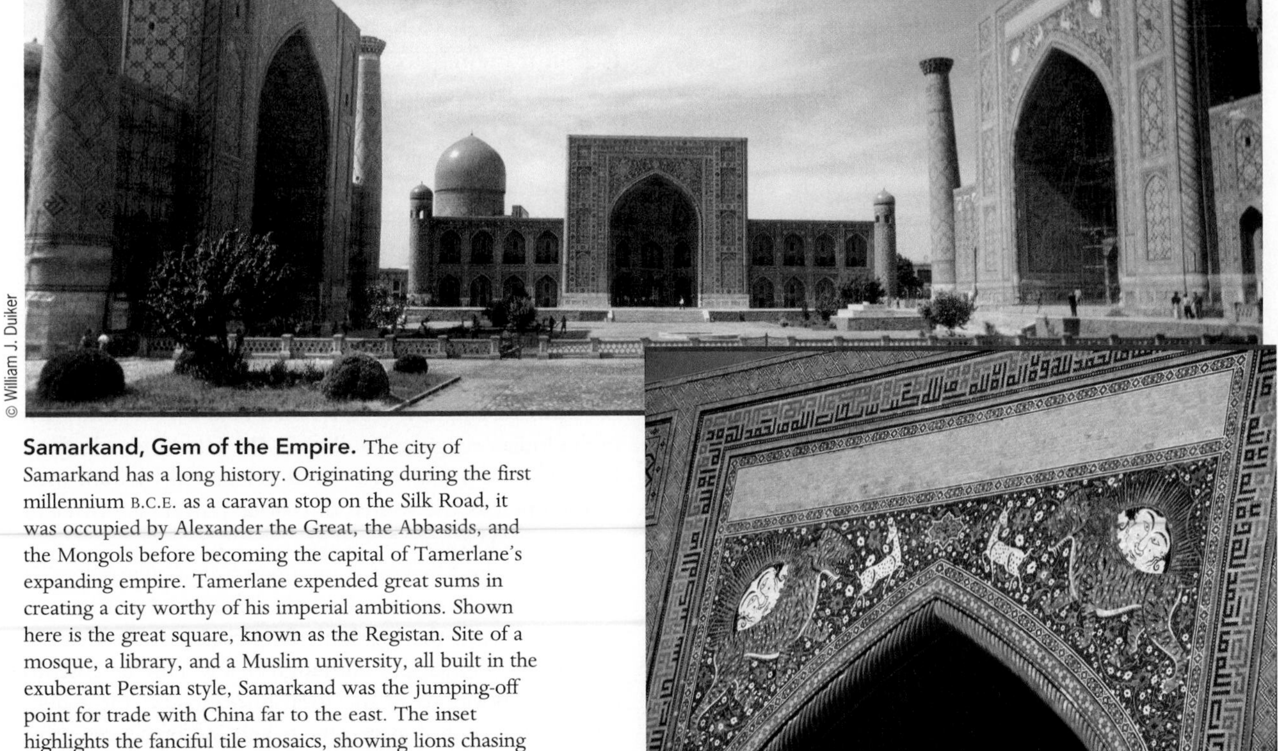

© William J. Duiker

© William J. Duiker

Samarkand, Gem of the Empire. The city of Samarkand has a long history. Originating during the first millennium B.C.E. as a caravan stop on the Silk Road, it was occupied by Alexander the Great, the Abbasids, and the Mongols before becoming the capital of Tamerlane's expanding empire. Tamerlane expended great sums in creating a city worthy of his imperial ambitions. Shown here is the great square, known as the Registan. Site of a mosque, a library, and a Muslim university, all built in the exuberant Persian style, Samarkand was the jumping-off point for trade with China far to the east. The inset highlights the fanciful tile mosaics, showing lions chasing deer while a rising sun smiles on the scene.

Society and Culture

FOCUS QUESTIONS: What impact did Muslim rule have on Indian society? What are some of the most important cultural achievements of Indian civilization in the era between the Mauryas and the Mughals?

The establishment of Muslim rule over the northern parts of the subcontinent had a significant impact on the society and culture of the Indian people.

Religion

Like their counterparts in other areas that came under Islamic rule, many Muslim rulers in India were relatively tolerant of other faiths and used peaceful means, if any, to encourage nonbelievers to convert to Islam. Even the more enlightened, however, could be fierce when their religious zeal was aroused. One ruler, on being informed that a Hindu fair had been held near Delhi, ordered the promoters of the event put to death. Hindu temples were razed, and mosques were erected in their place. Eventually, however, most Muslim rulers realized that not all Hindus could be converted and recognized the necessity of accepting what to them was an alien and repugnant religion. While Hindu religious practices were generally tolerated, non-Muslims were compelled to pay a tax to the state. Some Hindus likely converted to Islam to avoid the tax, but they were then expected to make the traditional charitable contribution required of Muslims in all Islamic societies.

Over time, millions of Hindus did turn to the Muslim faith. Some were individuals or groups in the employ of the Muslim ruling class, such as government officials, artisans, or merchants catering to the needs of the court. But many others were probably peasants from the *sudra* class or even untouchables who found in the egalitarian message of Islam a way of removing the stigma of low-class status in the Hindu social hierarchy.

Seldom have two major religions been so strikingly different. Whereas Hinduism tolerated a belief in the existence of several deities (although admittedly they were all considered by some to be manifestations of one supreme god), Islam was uncompromisingly monotheistic. Whereas Hinduism was hierarchical, Islam was egalitarian. Whereas Hinduism featured a priestly class to serve as an intermediary with the ultimate force of the universe, Islam permitted no one to come between believers and their god. Such differences contributed to the mutual hostility that developed between the adherents of the two faiths in the Indian subcontinent, but more mundane issues, such as the Muslim habit of eating beef and the idolatry and sexual frankness in Hindu art, were probably a greater source of antagonism at the popular level (see the box on p. 233).

In other cases, the two peoples borrowed from each other. Some Muslim rulers found the Indian idea of divine kingship appealing. In their turn, Hindu rajas learned by bitter experience the superiority of cavalry mounted on horses instead of elephants, the primary assault weapon in early India. Some upper-class Hindu males were attracted to the Muslim tradition of ***purdah*** (PUR-duh *or* POOR-duh) and began to keep their women in seclusion (termed locally "behind the curtain") from everyday society. Hindu sources claimed that one reason for adopting the custom was to protect Hindu women from the roving eyes of foreigners. But it is likely that many Indian families adopted the practice for reasons of prestige or because they were convinced that *purdah* was a practical means of protecting female virtue.

All in all, Muslim rule probably did not have a significant impact on the lives of most Indian women (see the comparative essay "Caste, Class, and Family" on p. 234). *Purdah* was more commonly practiced by the higher classes than by the lower classes. Though it was probably of little consolation, gender relations in poor and lower-class families were relatively egalitarian, as men and women worked together on press gangs or in the fields. Muslim customs apparently had little effect on the Hindu tradition of *sati* (suh-TEE) (see the box on p. 235). In fact, in many respects, Muslim women had more rights than their Hindu counterparts. They had more property rights than Hindu women and were legally permitted to divorce under certain conditions and to remarry after the death of their husband. The primary role for Indian women in general, however, was to produce children. Sons were preferred over daughters, not only because they alone could conduct ancestral rites but also because a daughter was a financial liability. A father had to provide a costly dowry for a daughter when she married, yet after the wedding, she would transfer her labor assets to her husband's family. Still, women held a place with men in the Indian religious pantheon. The Hindu female deity known as Devi (DAY-vee) was celebrated by both men and women as the source of cosmic power, bestower of wishes, and symbol of fertility.

Overall, the Muslims continued to view themselves as foreign conquerors and generally maintained a strict separation between the Muslim ruling class and the mass of the Hindu population. Although a few Hindus rose to important positions in the local bureaucracy, most high posts in the central government and the provinces were reserved for Muslims. Only with the founding of the

The Islamic Conquest of India

One consequence of the Muslim conquest of northern India was the imposition of many Islamic customs on Hindu society. In this excerpt, the fourteenth-century Muslim historian Zia-ud-din Barani (ZEE-ah-ud-DIN buh-RAH-nee) describes the attempt of one Muslim ruler, Ala-ud-din, to prevent the use of alcohol and gambling, both expressly forbidden in Muslim society. Ala-ud-din had seized power in Delhi from a rival in 1294.

A Muslim Ruler Suppresses Hindu Practices

He forbade wine, beer, and intoxicating drugs to be used or sold; dicing, too, was prohibited. Vintners and beer sellers were turned out of the city, and the heavy taxes which had been levied from them were abolished. All the china and glass vessels of the Sultan's banqueting room were broken and thrown outside the gate of Badaun, where they formed a mound. Jars and casks of wine were emptied out there till they made mire as if it were the season of the rains. The Sultan himself entirely gave up wine parties. Self-respecting people at once followed his example; but the ne'er-do-wells went on making wine and spirits and hid the leather bottles in loads of hay or firewood and by various such tricks smuggled it into the city. Inspectors and gatekeepers and spies diligently sought to seize the contraband and the smugglers; and when seized the wine was given to the elephants, and the importers and sellers and drinkers [were] flogged and given short terms of imprisonment. So many were they, however, that holes had to be dug for their incarceration outside the great thoroughfare of the Badaun gate, and many of the wine bibbers died from the rigor of their confinement and others were taken out half-dead and were long in recovering their health. The terror of these holes deterred many from drinking. Those who could not give it up had to journey ten or twelve leagues to get a drink, for at half that distance, four or five leagues from Delhi, wine could not be publicly sold or drunk. The prevention of drinking proving very difficult, the Sultan enacted that people might distill and drink privately in their own homes, if drinking parties were not held and the liquor not sold. After the prohibition of drinking, conspiracies diminished.

How does the approach of the ruler described here, a Muslim establishing regulations for moral behavior in a predominantly Hindu society, compare with the approaches adopted by Muslim rulers in African societies, as described in Chapter 8?

Source: Excerpt from *A History of India: From the Earliest Times to the Present Day* by Michael Edwardes (London: Thames & Hudson, 1961), p. 108.

Mughal dynasty was a serious effort undertaken to reconcile the differences.

One result of this effort was the religion of the Sikhs (SEEKS *or* see-ihks) ("disciples"). Founded by the guru Nanak (NAH-nuhk) in the early sixteenth century in the Punjab, **Sikhism** attempted to integrate the best of the two faiths in a single religion. Sikhism originated in the devotionalist movement in Hinduism, which taught that God was the single true reality. All else is illusion. But Nanak rejected the Hindu tradition of asceticism and mortification of the flesh and, like Muhammad, taught his disciples to participate in the world. Sikhism achieved considerable popularity in northwestern India, where Islam and Hinduism confronted each other directly, and eventually evolved into a militant faith that fiercely protected its adherents against its two larger rivals. In the end, Sikhism failed to reconcile Hinduism and Islam but instead provided an alternative to them.

One complication for both Muslims and Hindus as they tried to come to terms with their mixed society was the problem of class and caste. Could non-Hindus form castes, and if so, how were they related to the Hindu castes? Where did the Turkic-speaking elites who made up the ruling class in many of the Islamic states fit into the equation?

The problem was resolved in a pragmatic manner that probably followed an earlier tradition of assimilating non-Hindu tribal groups into the system. Members of the Turkic ruling groups formed social groups that were roughly equivalent to the Hindu *brahmin* or *kshatriya* class. Ordinary Indians who converted to Islam also formed Muslim castes, although at a lower level on the social scale. Many who did so were probably artisans

COMPARATIVE ESSAY

Caste, Class, and Family

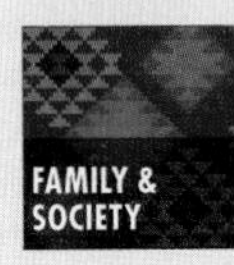
FAMILY & SOCIETY

Why have men and women played such different roles throughout human history? Why have some societies historically adopted the nuclear family, while others preferred the joint family or the clan? Such questions are controversial and often arouse vigorous debate, yet they are crucial to our understanding of the human experience.

As we know, the first human beings practiced hunting and foraging, living in small bands composed of one or more lineage groups and moving from place to place in search of sustenance. Individual members of the community were assigned different economic and social roles—usually with men as the hunters and women as the food gatherers—but such roles were not rigidly defined. The concept of private property did not exist, and all members shared the goods possessed by the community according to need.

© William J. Duiker

The Good Life. On the walls of the Buddhist temple of Borobudur are a series of bas-reliefs in stone depicting the path to enlightenment. The lower levels depict the pleasures of the material world. Shown here is a woman of leisure, assisted by her maidservants, at her toilette.

The agricultural revolution brought about dramatic changes in human social organizations. Although women, as food gatherers, may have been the first farmers, men—now increasingly deprived of their traditional role as hunters—began to replace them in the fields. As communities gradually adopted a sedentary lifestyle, women were increasingly assigned to domestic tasks in the home while raising the children. As farming communities grew in size and prosperity, vocational specialization and the concept of private property appeared, leading to the family as a legal entity and the emergence of a class system composed of elites, commoners, and slaves. Women were deemed inferior to men and placed in a subordinate status.

This trend toward job specialization and a rigid class system was less developed in pastoral societies, some of which still practiced a nomadic lifestyle and shared communal goods on a roughly equal basis within the community. Even within sedentary societies, there was considerable variety in the nature of social organizations. In some areas, the nuclear family consisted of parents and their dependent children. Other societies, however, adopted (either in theory or in practice) the idea of the joint family (ideally consisting of three generations of a family living under one roof) and sometimes even going a step further, linking several families under the larger grouping of the caste or the clan. Prominent examples of the latter tendency include India and China, although the degree to which reality conformed to these concepts is a matter of debate.

Such large social organizations, where they occurred, often established a rigid hierarchy of status within the community, including the subordination of women. At the same time, they sometimes played a useful role in society, providing a safety net or a ladder of upward mobility for disadvantaged members of the group, as well as a source of stability in societies where legitimate and effective authority at the central level was lacking.

What were some of the unique aspects of community and family life in traditional India? What do you think accounts for these unique characteristics?

who converted en masse to obtain the privileges that conversion could bring.

In most of India, then, Muslim rule did not substantially disrupt the class and caste system, although it may have become more fluid. One perceptive European visitor in the early sixteenth century reported that in Malabar (MAL-uh-bar), along the southwestern coast, there were separate castes for fishing, pottery making,

The Practice of *Sati*

FAMILY & SOCIETY

In the course of his extensive travels throughout Africa and Asia, the Muslim diarist Ibn Battuta—whom we first encountered in Chapters 7 and 8—spent several months in Muslim-held territories in India. In the following excerpt, he describes the Hindu practice of *sati*, in which a widow immolates herself on her deceased husband's funeral pyre as a means of expressing her fealty to her lord and master.

The Travels of Ibn Battuta

In this part, I also saw those women who burn themselves when their husbands die. The woman adorns herself, and is accompanied by a cavalcade of the infidel Hindus and Brahmans, with drums, trumpets, and men, following her, both Moslems and Infidels for mere pastime. The fire had been already kindled, and into it they threw the dead husband. The wife then threw herself upon him, and both were entirely burnt. A woman's burning herself, however, with her husband is not considered as absolutely necessary among them, but it is encouraged; and when a woman burns herself with her husband, her family is considered as being ennobled, and supposed to be worthy of trust. But when she does not burn herself, she is ever after clothed coarsely, and remains in constraint among her relations, on account of her want of fidelity to her husband.

The woman who burns herself with her husband is generally surrounded by women, who bid her farewell, and commission her with salutations for their former friends, while she laughs, plays, or dances to the very time in which she is to be burnt.

Some of the Hindus, moreover, drown themselves in the river Ganges to which they perform pilgrimages; and into which they pour the ashes of those who have been burnt. When any one intends to drown himself, he opens his mind on the subject to one of his companions, and says: You are not to suppose that I do this for the sake of any thing worldly; my only motive is to draw near to Kisāī, which is a name of God with them. And when he is drowned, they draw him out of the water, burn the body, and pour the ashes into the Ganges.

Why do historians evaluate documents such as this one with caution? Are there reasons to doubt the reliability of a Muslim's report on Hindu practices? What evidence do you find in this selection that Ibn Battuta was approaching Hindu society from the perspective of his own experience and applying the values of his own culture?

Source: S. Lee (trans.), *The Travels of Ibn Battuta in the Near East, Asia, and Africa, 1325–1354* (Mineola, NY, 2004), pp. 108–110.

weaving, carpentry and metalworking, salt mining, sorcery, and labor on the plantations. There were separate castes for doing the laundry, one for the elite and the other for the common people.

Economy and Daily Life

India's landed and commercial elites lived in the cities, often in conditions of considerable opulence. The rulers, of course, possessed the most wealth. One maharaja of a relatively small state in southern India, for example, had more than 100,000 soldiers in his pay along with 900 elephants and 20,000 horses. Another maintained a thousand high-class women to serve as sweepers of his palace. Each carried a broom and a brass basin containing a mixture of cow dung and water and followed him from one house to another, plastering the path where he was to tread. Most urban dwellers, of course, did not live in such style. Xuan Zang, the Chinese Buddhist missionary, left us a description of ordinary homes in a seventh-century urban area:

> Their houses are surrounded by low walls, and form the suburbs. The earth being soft and muddy, the walls of the towns are mostly built of brick or tiles. The towers on the walls are constructed of wood or bamboo; the houses have balconies and belvederes, which are made of wood, with a coating of lime or mortar, and covered with tiles. The different buildings have the same form as those in China; rushes, or dry branches, or tiles, or boards are used for covering

them. The walls are covered with lime and mud, mixed with cow's dung for purity. At different seasons they scatter flowers about. Such are some of their different customs.[5]

AGRICULTURE The majority of India's population (estimated at slightly more than 100 million in the first millennium C.E.), however, lived on the land. Most were peasants who tilled small plots with a wooden plow pulled by oxen and paid a percentage of the harvest to their landlord. The landlord in turn forwarded part of the payment to the local ruler. In effect, the landlord functioned as a tax collector for the king, who retained ultimate ownership of all farmland in his domain. At best, most peasants lived at the subsistence level. At worst, they were forced into debt and fell victim to moneylenders who charged exorbitant rates of interest.

In the north and in the upland regions of the Deccan Plateau, the primary grain crops were wheat and barley. In the Ganges valley and the southern coastal plains, the main crop was rice. Vegetables were grown everywhere, and southern India produced many spices, fruits, sugarcane, and cotton. The cotton plant apparently originated in the Indus River valley and spread from there. Although some cotton was cultivated in Spain and North Africa by the eighth and ninth centuries, India remained the primary producer of cotton goods. Spices such as cinnamon, pepper, ginger, sandalwood, cardamom, and cumin were also major export products.

FOREIGN TRADE Agriculture, of course, was not the only source of wealth in India. Since ancient times, the subcontinent had served as a major entrepôt for trade between the Middle East and the Pacific basin, as well as the source of other goods shipped throughout the known world. Although civil strife and piracy, heavy taxation of the business community by local rulers to finance their fratricidal wars, and increased customs duties between principalities may have contributed to a decline in internal trade, the level of foreign trade remained high, particularly in the kingdoms in the south and along the northwestern coast, which were located along the traditional trade routes to the Middle East and the Mediterranean Sea. Much of this foreign trade was carried on by wealthy Hindu castes with close ties to the royal courts. But there were other participants as well, including such non-Hindu minorities as the Muslims, the Parsis (PAR-seez), and the Jain community. The Parsis, expatriates from Persia who practiced the Zoroastrian religion, dominated banking and the textile industry in the cities bordering the Rann of Kutch (RUN of KUTCH). Later they would become a dominant economic force in the modern city of Mumbai (Bombay). The Jains became prominent in trade and manufacturing even though their faith emphasized simplicity and the rejection of materialism.

According to early European travelers, merchants often lived quite well. One Portuguese observer described the "Moorish" population in Bengal as follows:

> They have girdles of cloth, and over them silk scarves; they carry in their girdles daggers garnished with silver and gold, according to the rank of the person who carries them; on their fingers many rings set with rich jewels, and cotton turbans on their heads. They are luxurious, eat well and spend freely, and have many other extravagances as well. They bathe often in great tanks which they have in their houses. Everyone has three or four wives or as many as he can maintain. They keep them carefully shut up, and treat them very well, giving them great store of gold, silver and apparel of fine silk.[6]

Outside these relatively small, specialized trading communities, most manufacturing and commerce were in the hands of petty traders and artisans, who were generally limited to local markets. This failure to build on the promise of antiquity has led some historians to ask why India did not produce an expansion of commerce and growth of cities similar to the developments that began in Europe during the High Middle Ages or even in China during the Song dynasty (see Chapter 10). Some have pointed to the traditionally low status of artisans and merchants in Indian society, symbolized by the comment in the *Arthasastra* that merchants were "thieves that are not called by the name of thief."[7] Yet commercial activities were frowned on in many areas in Europe throughout the Middle Ages, a fact that did not prevent the emergence of capitalist societies in much of the West.

Another factor may have been the monopoly on foreign trade held by the government in many areas of India. More important, perhaps, was the impact of the class and caste system, which limited the ability of entrepreneurs to expand their activities and have dealings with other members of the commercial and manufacturing community. Successful artisans, for example, normally could not set up as merchants to market their products, nor could merchants compete for buyers outside their normal area of operations. The complex interlocking relationships among the various classes in a given region were a powerful factor inhibiting the development of a thriving commercial sector in medieval India.

SCIENCE AND TECHNOLOGY During this period, Indian thinkers played an important role in promoting knowledge of the sciences throughout the Eurasian world. The fifth-century astronomer Aryabhata (AHR-yuh-BAH-tuh), for example, accurately calculated the value of pi and measured the length of the solar year at

© William J. Duiker

© Werner Forman/Art Resource, NY

COMPARATIVE ILLUSTRATION

Rock Architecture. Along with the caves at Ajanta, one of the greatest examples of Indian rock architecture remains the eighth-century temple at Ellora (eh-LOR-uh), in central India, shown on the left. Named after Shiva's holy mountain in the Himalayas, the temple is approximately the size of the Parthenon in Athens but was literally carved out of a hillside. The builders dug nearly 100 feet straight down into the top of the mountain to isolate a single block of rock, removing more than 3 million cubic feet of stone in the process. Unlike earlier rock-cut shrines, which were constructed in the form of caves, the Ellora temple is open to the sky and filled with some of India's finest sculpture. The overall impression is one of massive grandeur.

This form of architecture also found expression in parts of Africa. In 1200 C.E., Christian monks in Ethiopia began to construct a remarkable series of eleven churches carved out of solid volcanic rock (right). After a 40-foot trench was formed by removing the bedrock, the central block of stone was hewed into the shape of a Greek cross; then it was hollowed out and decorated. These churches, which are still in use today, testify to the fervor of Ethiopian Christianity, which plays a major role in preserving the country's cultural and national identity.

Why do you think some early cultures made frequent use of rock architecture, while others did not? Why do you think the architectural form was discontinued?

slightly more than 365 days. Indian writings on astronomy, mathematics, and medicine were influential elsewhere in the region, while—as noted in Chapter 7—the Indian system of numbers, including the concept of zero, was introduced into the Middle East and ultimately replaced the Roman numerals then in use in medieval Europe.

The Wonder of Indian Culture

The era between the Mauryas and the Mughals in India was a period of cultural evolution as Indian writers and artists built on the literary and artistic achievements of their predecessors. This is not to say that Indian culture rested on its ancient laurels. To the contrary, this was an era of tremendous innovation in all fields of creative endeavor.

ART AND ARCHITECTURE At the end of antiquity, the primary forms of religious architecture were the Buddhist cave temples and monasteries. The first millennium C.E. witnessed the evolution of religious architecture from underground cavity to monumental structure (see the comparative illustration above).

The twenty-eight caves of Ajanta (uh-JUHN-tuh) in the Deccan Plateau are one of India's greatest artistic achievements. They are as impressive for their sculpture and painting as for their architecture. Except for a few examples from the second century B.C.E., most of the caves were carved out of solid rock over an incredibly short period of eighteen years, from 460 to 478 C.E. In contrast to the early unadorned temple halls, these temples were exuberantly decorated with ornate pillars, friezes, beamed ceilings, and statues of the Buddha and bodhisattvas. Several caves served as monasteries, which by then had been transformed from simple holes in the wall to large complexes with living apartments, halls, and shrines to the Buddha.

All of the inner surfaces of the caves, including the ceilings, sculptures, walls, door frames, and pillars, were painted in vivid colors. Perhaps best known are the wall paintings, which illustrate the various lives and incarnations of the Buddha. Similar rock paintings focusing on secular subjects can be found at Sigiriya (see-gee-REE-yuh), a fifth-century royal palace on the island of Sri Lanka.

Among the most impressive rock carvings in southern India are the cave temples at Mamallapuram (also known as Mahabalipuram), south of the modern city of Chennai (Madras). The sculpture, called *Descent of the Ganges River*, depicts the role played by Shiva in intercepting the heavenly waters of the Ganges and allowing them to fall gently on the earth. Mamallapuram also boasts an eighth-century shore temple (see the illustration on p. 227), which is one of the earliest surviving freestanding structures in the subcontinent.

From the eighth century until the time of the Mughals, Indian architects built a multitude of magnificent Hindu temples, now constructed exclusively above ground. Each temple consisted of a central shrine surmounted by a sizable tower, a hall for worshipers, a vestibule, and a porch, all set in a rectangular courtyard that might also contain other minor shrines. Temples became progressively more ornate until by the eleventh century, the sculpture began to dominate the structure itself. The towers became higher and the temple complexes more intricate, some becoming virtual walled compounds set one within the other and resembling a town in themselves.

The greatest example of medieval Hindu temple art is probably Khajuraho (khah-joo-RAH-hoh). Of the original eighty-five temples, dating from the tenth century, twenty-five remain standing today. All of the towers are buttressed at various levels on the sides, giving the whole a sense of unity and creating a vertical movement similar to Mount Kailasa (ky-LAH-suh) in the Himalayas, sacred to Hindus. Everywhere the viewer is entertained by voluptuous temple dancers bringing life to the massive structures. One is removing a thorn from her foot, another is applying eye makeup, and yet another is wringing out her hair.

LITERATURE During this period, Indian authors produced a prodigious number of written works, both religious and secular. Indian religious poetry was written in Sanskrit and also in the languages of southern India. As Hinduism was transformed from a contemplative to a more devotional religion, its poetry became more ardent and erotic and prompted a sense of divine ecstasy. Much of the religious verse extolled the lives and heroic acts of Shiva, Vishnu, Rama, and Krishna by repeating the same themes over and over, which is also a characteristic of Indian art. In the eighth century, a tradition of poet-saints inspired by intense mystical devotion to a deity emerged in southern India. Many were women who sought to escape the drudgery of domestic toil through an imagined sexual union with the god-lover, as in this poem by a twelfth-century mystic who expresses her sensuous joy in the physical-mystical union with her god:

> *It was like a stream*
> *running into the dry bed*
> *of a lake,*
> *like rain pouring on plants*
> *parched to sticks.*
> *It was like this world's pleasure*
> *and the way to the other,*
> *both walking towards me.*
> *Seeing the feet of the master,*
> *O lord white as jasmine*
> *I was made worthwhile.*[8]

© William J. Duiker

Dancing Shiva. From the tenth to the twelfth centuries C.E., the southern kingdom of Chola excelled in the use of the lost-wax technique to make portable bronze statues of Hindu gods. Bathed, clothed, and decorated with flowers, these Chola bronzes were then paraded in religious ceremonies. One of the most numerous and iconic of these bronze deities was the dancing Shiva. As shown here, the statue portrays Shiva performing a cosmic dance in which he simultaneously creates and destroys the universe. While his upper right hand creates the cosmos, his upper left hand reduces it in flames. With his right foot, Shiva crushes the back of the dwarf of ignorance. Shiva's dancing statues visually convey to his followers the message of his power and compassion.

The great secular literature of traditional India was also written in Sanskrit in the form of poetry, drama, and prose. Some of the best medieval Indian poetry is found in single-stanza poems, which create an entire emotional scene in just four lines. Witness this poem by the poet Amaru (am-uh-ROO):

We'll see what comes of it, I thought,
and I hardened my heart against her.
What, won't the villain speak to me? She
thought, flying into a rage.
And there we stood, sedulously refusing to look one
another in the face,
Until at last I managed an unconvincing laugh,
and her tears robbed me of my resolution.[9]

One of India's most famous authors, Kalidasa (kah-lee-DAH-suh), lived during the Gupta dynasty. Although little is known of him, including his dates, he probably wrote for the court of Chandragupta II (r. 375–415 C.E.). Even today Kalidasa's hundred-verse poem, *The Cloud Messenger*, remains one of the most popular Sanskrit poems. In addition to poetry, Kalidasa wrote three plays, all dramatic romances that blend the erotic with the heroic and the comic. *Shakuntala*, perhaps the best-known play in Indian literature, tells the story of a king who falls in love with the maiden Shakuntala. He asks her to marry him but is suddenly recalled to his kingdom before their wedding. Shakuntala, who is pregnant, goes to him, but the king has been cursed and no longer recognizes her. With the help of the gods, the king eventually recalls their love and is reunited with Shakuntala and their son.

Like poetry, prose developed in India from the Vedic period and was established by the sixth and seventh centuries C.E.—a full millennium before the novel developed in seventeenth-century Europe. One of the greatest masters of Sanskrit prose was Dandin (DUN-din), who lived during the seventh century. In *The Ten Princes*, he created a fantastic world that fuses history and fiction. His keen powers of observation, details of low life, and humor give his writing considerable vitality.

MUSIC Indian music also developed during this era. Ancient Indian music had come from the chanting of the Vedic hymns and thus had a strong metaphysical and spiritual flavor. The actual physical vibrations of music (*nada*) were considered to be related to the spiritual world. An off-key or sloppy rendition of a sacred text could upset the harmony and balance of the entire universe.

In form, Indian classical music is based on a scale, called a *raga* (RAH-guh). There are dozens, if not hundreds, of separate scales, which are grouped into separate categories depending on the time of day during which they are to be performed. The performers use a stringed instrument called a *sitar* (si-TAHR) and various types of wind instruments and drums. The performers select a basic *raga* and then are free to improvise the melodic structure and rhythm. A good performer never performs a particular *raga* the same way twice. As with jazz music in the West, creativity rather than faithful reproduction is the primary concern.

The Golden Region: Early Southeast Asia

FOCUS QUESTION: What were the main characteristics of Southeast Asian social and economic life, culture, and religion before 1500 C.E.?

Between China and India lies the region that today is called Southeast Asia. It has two major components: a mainland region extending southward from the Chinese border to the tip of the Malay peninsula and an extensive archipelago, most of which is part of present-day Indonesia and the Philippines. Travel between the islands and regions to the west, north, and east was not difficult, so Southeast Asia has historically served as a vast land bridge for the movement of peoples between China, the Indian subcontinent, and the more than 25,000 islands of the South Pacific. The first arrivals probably appeared as long as 40,000 years ago, as part of the initial exodus of *Homo sapiens* from Africa. The final destination for some of these peoples was Australia, where their descendants, known today as aborigines, still live.

Mainland Southeast Asia consists of several north-south mountain ranges, separated by river valleys that run in a southerly or southeasterly direction. Several groups of migrants came down the valleys in search of new homelands. First were **Malayo-Polynesian** (muh-LAY-oh-pah-leh-NEE-zhun) speakers who originated on the island of Taiwan or the southeastern coast of China. Most of them settled in the southern part of the mainland or on the islands to the south. Then came the Thai (TY) from southwestern China and the Burmese from the Tibetan highlands. Once in Southeast Asia, most of these migrants settled in the fertile deltas of the rivers—the Irrawaddy (ir-uh-WAH-dee) and the Salween (SAL-ween) in Burma, the Chao Phraya (chow PRY-uh) in Thailand, and the Red River and the Mekong (MAY-kahng) in Vietnam—or in lowland areas on the islands to the south.

Although the river valleys facilitated north-south travel on the Southeast Asian mainland, the mountains made movement between east and west relatively difficult. Consequently, the lowland peoples in the river valleys were often isolated from each other and had only limited contacts with the upland peoples in the mountains. These geographic barriers may help explain why Southeast Asia is one of the few regions in Asia that was never unified under a single government.

Given Southeast Asia's location between China and India, it is not surprising that both civilizations influenced developments in the region. In 111 B.C.E., Vietnam was conquered by the Han dynasty and remained under Chinese control for more than a millennium (see Chapter 11). The Indian states never exerted much political control over Southeast Asia, but their influence was pervasive nevertheless. The first contacts had taken place by the fourth century B.C.E., when Indian merchants began sailing to Southeast Asia; they were soon followed by Buddhist and Hindu missionaries. Indian influence can be seen in many aspects of Southeast Asian culture, from political institutions to religion, architecture, language, and literature.

Paddy Fields and Spices: The States of Southeast Asia

The traditional states of Southeast Asia can generally be divided between agricultural societies and trading societies. Whereas the trading societies were located on the trade routes that crisscrossed the region, the agricultural societies—notably, Vietnam, Angkor (AN-kor) in what is now Cambodia, and the Burmese state of Pagan (puh-GAHN)—were situated in fertile river deltas that were conducive to the development of a wet rice economy (see Map 9.6). As in India and China, the cultivation of wet rice led to an expanding population and eventually to the formation of states. Although all produced some goods for regional markets, commerce never became an important source of income for them.

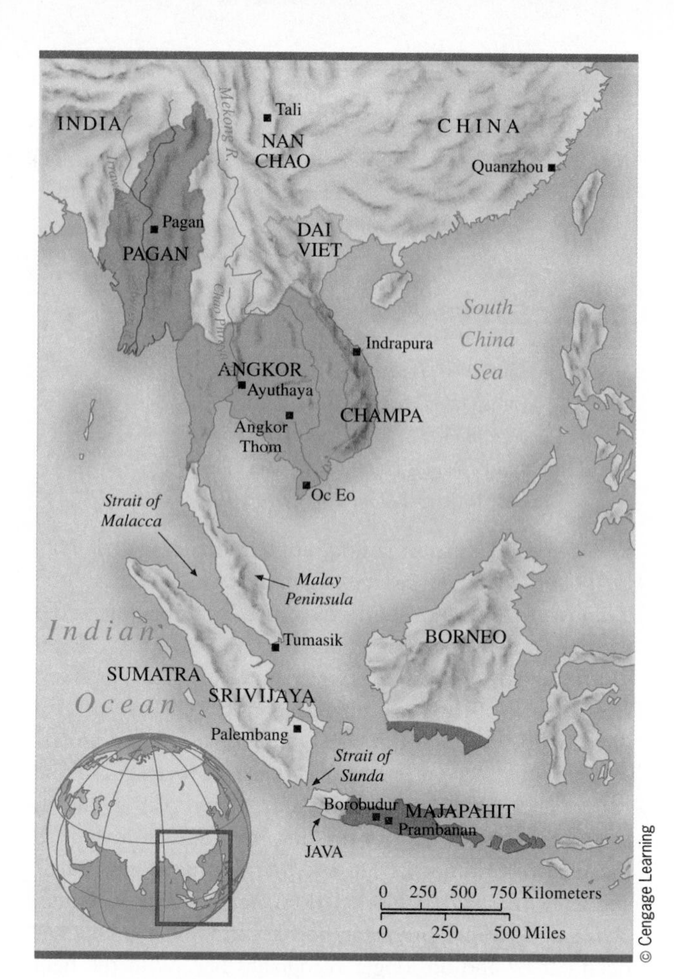

© Cengage Learning

MAP 9.6 Southeast Asia in the Thirteenth Century. This map shows the major states that arose in Southeast Asia after 1000 C.E. Some, like Angkor and Dai Viet, were predominantly agricultural. Others, like Srivijaya and Champa, were commercial.

How did geography influence whether states were primarily agricultural or commercial?

THE MAINLAND STATES One exception to this general rule was the kingdom of Funan (FOO-nan), which arose in the fertile valley of the lower Mekong River in the second century C.E. At that time, much of the regional trade between India and the South China Sea moved across the narrow neck of the Malay peninsula. With access to copper, tin, and iron, as well as a variety of tropical agricultural products, Funan played an active role in this process, and Oc Eo (ohk EEOH), on the Gulf of Thailand, became one of the primary commercial ports in the region. Funan declined in the fifth century when trade began to pass through the Strait of Malacca and was eventually replaced by the agricultural state of Chenla (CHEEN-luh) and then, three hundred years later, by the great kingdom of Angkor.

Angkor was the most powerful state to emerge in mainland Southeast Asia before the sixteenth century (see the box on p. 242). The remains of its capital city, Angkor Thom (AN-kor TOHM), give a sense of the magnificence of Angkor civilization. The city formed a square 2 miles on each side. Its massive stone walls were several feet thick and were surrounded by a moat. Four main gates led into the city, which at its height had a substantial population. As in its predecessor, the wealth of Angkor was based primarily on the cultivation of wet rice, which had been introduced to the Mekong River valley from China in the third millennium B.C.E. Other products were honey, textiles, fish, and salt. By the fourteenth century, however, Angkor had begun to decline, a product of incessant wars with its neighbors and the silting up of its irrigation system. In 1432, Angkor Thorn was destroyed by the Thai, who had migrated into the region from southwestern China in the thirteenth

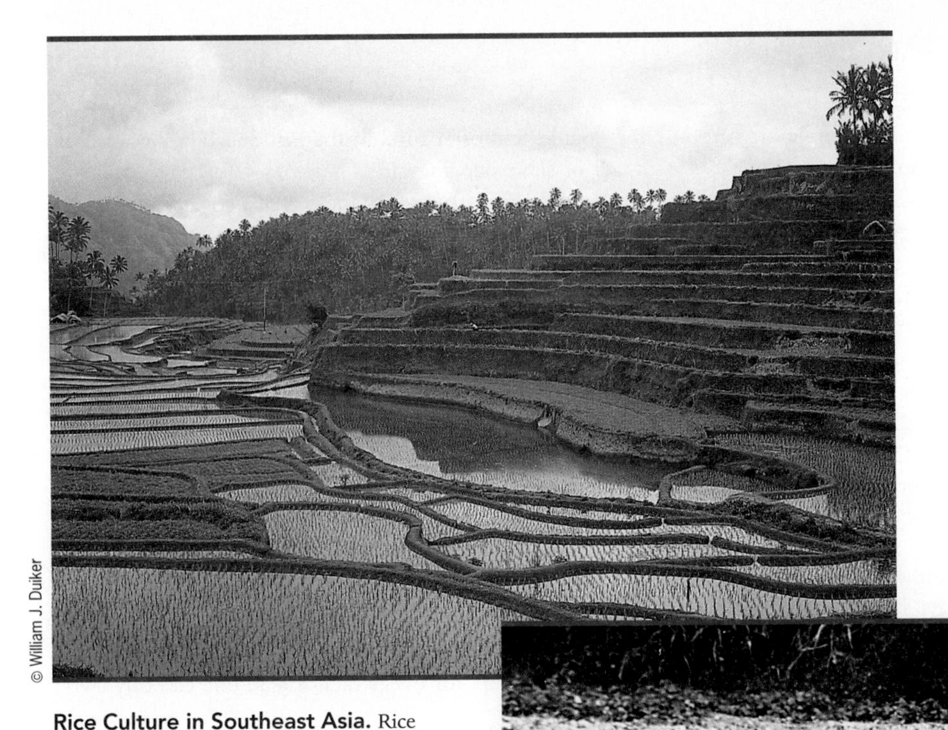

© William J. Duiker

© William J. Duiker

Rice Culture in Southeast Asia. Rice was first cultivated in southern Asia seven or eight thousand years ago. It is a labor-intensive crop that requires many workers to plant the seedlings and organize the distribution of water. Initially, the fields are flooded to facilitate the rooting of the rice seedlings and add nutrients to the soil. The upper photo shows terracing on a hillside in Bali, and in the lower photo workers are performing the backbreaking task of transplanting rice seedlings in a flooded field in modern Vietnam.

The significance of rice in Southeast Asia is reflected in the elaborate rituals in honor of the rice goddess that all cultures in the region have traditionally observed. In Indonesia, the worship of Dewi Sri has long been essential to assure a good harvest.

century and established their capital at Ayuthaya (ah-yoo-TY-yuh), in lower Thailand, in 1351.

As the Thai expanded southward, however, their main competition came from the west, where the Burmese peoples had formed their own agricultural society in the valleys of the Salween and Irrawaddy Rivers. Like the Thai, they were relatively recent arrivals in the area, having migrated southward from the highlands of Tibet beginning in the seventh century C.E. After subjugating weaker societies already living in the area, in the eleventh century they founded the first great Burmese state, the kingdom of Pagan. Like the Thai, they quickly converted to Buddhism and adopted Indian political institutions and culture. For a while, they were a major force in the western part of Southeast Asia, but attacks from the Mongols in the late thirteenth century (see Chapter 10) weakened Pagan, and the resulting vacuum may have benefited the Thai as they moved into areas occupied by Burmese migrants in the Chao Phraya valley.

THE MALAY WORLD In the Malay peninsula and the Indonesian archipelago, a different pattern emerged. For centuries, this area had been linked to regional trade networks, and much of its wealth had come from the export of tropical products to China, India, and the Middle East. The vast majority of the inhabitants were of Malay ethnic stock, a people who spread from their original homeland

The Kingdom of Angkor

INTERACTION & EXCHANGE

Angkor (known to the Chinese as Chen-la) was the greatest kingdom of its time in Southeast Asia. This passage was probably written in the thirteenth century by Chau Ju-kua (zhow RU-gwah), an inspector of foreign trade in the city of Quanzhou (CHWAHN-JOE) (sometimes called Zayton) on the southern coast of China. His account, compiled from reports of seafarers, includes a brief description of the capital city, Angkor Thom, which is still one of the great archaeological sites of the region. Angkor was already in decline when Chau Ju-kua described the kingdom, and the capital was later abandoned in 1432.

Chau Ju-kua, *Records of Foreign Nations*

The officials and the common people dwell in houses with sides of bamboo matting and thatched with reeds. Only the king resides in a palace of hewn stone. It has a granite lotus pond of extraordinary beauty with golden bridges, some three hundred odd feet long. The palace buildings are solidly built and richly ornamented. The throne on which the king sits is made of gharu wood and the seven precious substances; the dais is jeweled, with supports of veined wood [ebony?]; the screen [behind the throne] is of ivory.

When all the ministers of state have audience, they first make three full prostrations at the foot of the throne; they then kneel and remain thus, with hands crossed on their breasts, in a circle round the king, and discuss the affairs of state. When they have finished, they make another prostration and retire. . . .

[The people] are devout Buddhists. There are serving [in the temples] some three hundred foreign women; they dance and offer food to the Buddha. They are called *a-nan* or slave dancing girls.

As to their customs, lewdness is not considered criminal; theft is punished by cutting off a hand and a foot and by branding on the chest.

The incantations of the Buddhist and Taoist priests [of this country] have magical powers. Among the former those who wear yellow robes may marry, while those who dress in red lead ascetic lives in temples. The Taoists clothe themselves with leaves; they have a deity called P'o-to-li which they worship with great devotion.

[The people of this country] hold the right hand to be clean, the left unclean, so when they wish to mix their rice with any kind of meat broth, they use the right hand to do so and also to eat with.

The soil is rich and loamy; the fields have no bounds. Each one takes as much as he can cultivate. Rice and cereals are cheap; for every tael of lead one can buy two bushels of rice.

The native products comprise elephants' tusks, the *chan* and *su* [varieties of gharu wood], good yellow wax, kingfisher's feathers, . . . resin, foreign oils, ginger peel, gold-colored incense, . . . raw silk and cotton fabrics.

The foreign traders offer in exchange for these gold, silver, porcelainware, sugar, preserves, and vinegar.

Because of the paucity of written records about Angkor society, much of our knowledge about local conditions comes from documents such as this one by a Chinese source. What does this excerpt tell us about the political system, religious beliefs, and land use in thirteenth-century Angkor?

Source: Excerpt from Chau Ju-Kua: *His Work on the Chinese and Arab Trade in the Twelfth and Thirteenth Centuries*, entitled *Chu-fanchi*, Friedrich Hirth and W. W. Rockhill, eds., copyright © 1966 by Paragon Reprint.

in southeastern China into island Southeast Asia and even to more distant locations in the South Pacific.

Eventually, the islands of the Indonesian archipelago gave rise to two of the region's most notable trading societies—Srivijaya (sree-vih-JAH-yuh) and Majapahit (mah-jah-PAH-hit). Both were based in large part on spices. As the wealth of the Arab Empire in the Middle East and then of western Europe increased, so did the demand for the products of East Asia. Merchant fleets from India and the Arabian peninsula sailed to the Indonesian islands to buy cloves, pepper, nutmeg, cinnamon, precious woods, and other exotic products coveted by the wealthy. In the eighth century, Srivijaya, which had been established along the eastern coast of Sumatra around 670, became a powerful commercial state that dominated the trade route passing through the Strait of Malacca (muh-LAK-uh), at that time the most convenient route from East Asia into the Indian Ocean. The rulers of Srivijaya had helped bring the route to prominence by controlling the pirates who had previously preyed on shipping in the strait. Another inducement was Srivijaya's capital at Palembang (pah-lem-BAHNG), a deepwater port where sailors could wait out the change in the monsoon season before making their return voyage. In 1025, however, Chola, one of the kingdoms of southern India and a commercial rival of Srivijaya, inflicted a devastating defeat on the island kingdom. Although Srivijaya survived, it was unable to regain its former dominance, in part because the main trade route had shifted to the east, through the Strait of Sunda (SOON-duh) and directly out into the Indian Ocean. In the late thirteenth century, this shift in trade patterns led to the founding of a new kingdom of Majapahit on the island of Java. In the mid-fourteenth century, Majapahit succeeded in uniting most of the archipelago and perhaps even part of the Southeast Asian mainland under its rule.

THE ROLE OF INDIA Indian influence was evident in all of these societies to various degrees. Based on models from the kingdoms of southern India, Southeast Asian kings were believed to possess special godlike qualities that set them apart from ordinary people. In some societies such as Angkor, the most prominent royal advisers constituted a *brahmin* class on the Indian model. In Pagan and Angkor, some division of the population into separate classes based on occupation and ethnic background seems to have occurred, although with less rigidity than the Indian class system.

India also supplied Southeast Asians with a writing system. The societies of the region had no written scripts for their spoken languages before the arrival of the Indian merchants and missionaries. Indian phonetic symbols were borrowed and used to record the spoken language. Initially, Southeast Asian literature was written in the Indian Sanskrit but eventually came to be written in the local languages. Southeast Asian authors borrowed popular Indian themes, such as stories from the Buddhist scriptures and tales from the Ramayana.

A popular form of entertainment among the common people, the *wayang kulit* (WAH-yahng KOO-lit), or shadow play, may have come originally from India or possibly China, but it became a distinctive art form in Java and other islands of the Indonesian archipelago. In a shadow play, flat leather puppets were manipulated behind an illuminated screen while the narrator recited tales from the Indian classics. The plays were often accompanied by a gamelan (GA-muh-lan), an orchestra composed primarily of percussion instruments such as gongs and drums that apparently originated in Java.

CHRONOLOGY Early Southeast Asia

Chinese conquest of Vietnam	111 B.C.E.
Arrival of Burmese peoples	c. seventh century C.E.
Formation of Srivijaya	c. 670
Construction of Borobudur	c. eighth century
Creation of Angkor kingdom	c. ninth century
Thai migrations into Southeast Asia	c. thirteenth century
Rise of Majapahit empire	Late thirteenth century
Fall of Angkor kingdom	1432

Daily Life

Because of the diversity of ethnic backgrounds, religions, and cultures, making generalizations about daily life in Southeast Asia during the early historical period is difficult. Nevertheless, it appears that Southeast Asian societies did not always apply the social distinctions that were sometimes imported from India.

SOCIAL STRUCTURES Still, traditional societies in Southeast Asia had some clearly hierarchical characteristics. At the top of the social ladder were the hereditary aristocrats, who monopolized both political power and economic wealth and enjoyed a borrowed aura of charisma by virtue of their proximity to the ruler. Most aristocrats lived in the major cities, which were the main source of power, wealth, and foreign influence. Beyond the major cities lived the mass of the population, composed of farmers, fishers, artisans, and merchants. In most Southeast Asian societies, the vast majority were probably rice farmers, living at a bare subsistence level and paying heavy rents or taxes to a landlord or a local ruler.

The average Southeast Asian peasant was not actively engaged in commerce, but accounts by foreign visitors indicate that in the Malay world, some were growing or mining products for export, such as tropical food products, precious woods, tin, and gems. Most of the regional trade was carried on by local merchants, who purchased products from local growers and then transported them by small boats down the rivers to the major port cities. There the goods were loaded onto larger ships for delivery outside the region. Growers of export goods in areas near the coast were thus indirectly involved in the regional trade network but received few economic benefits from the relationship.

Social structures differed significantly from country to country. In the Indianized states on the mainland, the tradition of a hereditary tribal aristocracy was probably accentuated by the Hindu practice of dividing the population into separate classes, called *varna* in imitation of the Indian model. In Angkor and Pagan, for example, the divisions were based on occupation or ethnic background. Some people were considered free subjects of the king, although there may have been legal restrictions against changing occupations. Others, however, may have been indentured to an employer. Each community was under a chieftain, who in turn was subordinated to a higher official responsible for passing on the tax revenues of each group to the central government.

In the kingdoms in the Malay peninsula and the Indonesian archipelago, social relations were generally less formal. Most of the people in the region, whether farmers, fishers, or artisans, lived in small *kampongs* (KAHM-pahngs) (Malay for "villages") in wooden houses built on stilts to avoid flooding during the monsoon season. Some of the farmers were probably sharecroppers who paid a part of their harvest to a landlord, who was often a member of the aristocracy. But in other areas, the tradition of free farming was strong.

WOMEN AND THE FAMILY The women of Southeast Asia during this era have been described as the most fortunate in the world. Although most women worked side by side with men in the fields, as in Africa they also often actively engaged in trading activities. Not only did this lead to a higher literacy rate among women than among men, but it also allowed them more financial independence than their counterparts in China and India, a fact that was noticed by the Chinese traveler Zhou Daguan (JOE dah-GWAHN) at the end of the thirteenth century: "In Cambodia it is the women who take charge of trade. For this reason a Chinese arriving in the country loses no time in getting himself a mate, for he will find her commercial instincts a great asset."[10]

Although, as elsewhere, warfare was normally part of the male domain, women sometimes played a role as bodyguards as well. According to Zhou Daguan, women were used to protect the royal family in Angkor, as well as in kingdoms located on the islands of Java and Sumatra. Though there is no evidence that such female units ever engaged in battle, they did give rise to wondrous tales of Amazon warriors in the writings of foreign travelers such as the fourteenth-century Muslim adventurer Ibn Battuta.

One reason for the enhanced status of women in traditional Southeast Asia is that the nuclear family was more common than the joint family system prevalent in China and the Indian subcontinent. Throughout the region, wealth in marriage was passed from the male to the female, in contrast to the dowry system used in China and India. Most societies usually did not put a high value on virginity in brokering a marriage, and divorce proceedings could be initiated by either party. Still, most marriages were monogamous, and marital fidelity was taken seriously.

The relative availability of cultivable land in the region may help explain the absence of joint families. Joint families under patriarchal leadership tend to be found in areas where land is scarce and individual families must work together to conserve resources and maximize income. With the exception of a few crowded river valleys, few areas in Southeast Asia had a high population density. Throughout most of the area, water was plentiful, and the land was relatively fertile.

World of the Spirits: Religious Belief

Indian religions also had a profound effect on Southeast Asia. Traditional religious beliefs in the region took the familiar form of spirit worship and animism that we have seen in other cultures. Southeast Asians believed that spirits dwelled in the mountains, rivers, streams, and other sacred places in their environment. Mountains were probably particularly sacred, since they were considered to be the abode of ancestral spirits, the place to which the souls of all the departed would retire after death.

When Hindu and Buddhist ideas began to penetrate the area early in the first millennium C.E., they exerted a strong appeal among local elites. Not only did the new doctrines offer a more convincing explanation of the nature of the cosmos, but they also provided local rulers with a means of enhancing their prestige and power and conferred an aura of legitimacy on their relations with their subjects. In Angkor, the king's duties included performing sacred rituals on the mountain in the capital city; in time, the ritual became a state cult uniting Hindu gods with local nature deities and ancestral spirits in a complex pantheon.

This state cult, financed by the royal court, eventually led to the construction of temples throughout the country. Many of these temples housed thousands of priests and retainers and amassed great wealth, including vast estates farmed by local peasants. It has been estimated that there were as many as 300,000 priests in Angkor at the height of its power. This vast wealth, which was often exempt from taxes, may be one explanation for the gradual decline of Angkor in the thirteenth and fourteenth centuries.

Initially, the spread of Hindu and Buddhist doctrines took place mostly among the elite. Although the common people participated in the state cult and helped construct the temples, they did not give up their traditional beliefs in local deities and ancestral spirits. A major transformation began in the eleventh century, however, when

© William J. Duiker

Angkor Wat. The Khmer (kuh-MEER) rulers of Angkor constructed a number of remarkable temples and palaces. Devised as either Hindu or Buddhist shrines, the temples also reflected the power and sanctity of the king. This twelfth-century temple known as Angkor Wat is renowned both for its spectacular architecture and for the thousands of fine bas-reliefs relating Hindu legends and Khmer history. Most memorable are the heavenly dancing maidens and the royal processions with elephants and soldiers.

Theravada Buddhism began to penetrate the kingdom of Pagan in mainland Southeast Asia from the island of Sri Lanka. From Pagan, it spread rapidly to other areas in Southeast Asia and eventually became the religion of the masses throughout the mainland west of the Annamite Mountains.

Theravada's appeal to the peoples of Southeast Asia is reminiscent of the original attraction of Buddhist thought centuries earlier on the Indian subcontinent. By teaching that individuals could seek Nirvana through their own actions rather than through the intercession of the ruler or a priest, Theravada was more accessible to the masses than the state cults promoted by the rulers. During the next centuries, Theravada gradually undermined the influence of state-supported religions and became the dominant faith in several mainland societies, including Burma, Thailand, Laos, and Cambodia.

Theravada did not penetrate far into the Malay peninsula or the Indonesian island chain, perhaps because it entered Southeast Asia through Burma farther to the north. But the Malay world found its own popular alternative to state religions when Islam began to enter the area in the thirteenth and fourteenth centuries. Because Islam's expansion into Southeast Asia took place for the most part after 1500, its emergence as a major force in the region will be discussed in a later chapter.

Not surprisingly, Indian influence extended to the Buddhist and Hindu temples of Southeast Asia. Temple architecture reflecting Gupta or southern Indian styles began to appear in Southeast Asia during the first centuries C.E. Most famous is the Buddhist temple at Borobudur (boh-roh-buh-DOOR), in central Java. Begun in the late eighth century at the behest of a king of Sailendra (SY-len-druh) (an agricultural kingdom based in eastern Java), Borobudur is a massive stupa with nine terraces. Sculpted on the sides of each terrace are bas-reliefs depicting the nine stages in the life of Siddhartha Gautama, from childhood to his final release from the chain of human existence. Surmounted by hollow bell-like towers containing representations of the Buddha and capped by a single stupa, the structure dominates the landscape for miles around.

Second only to Borobudur in technical excellence and even more massive in size are the ruins of the old capital

The Temple of Borobudur. The colossal pyramid temple at Borobudur, on the island of Java, is one of the greatest Buddhist monuments. Constructed in the eighth century C.E., it depicts the path to spiritual enlightenment in stone. Sculptures and relief portrayals of the life of the Buddha at the lower level depict the world of desire. At higher elevations, they give way to empty bell towers (see the inset) and culminate at the summit with an empty and closed stupa, signifying the state of Nirvana. Shortly after it was built, Borobudur was abandoned when a new ruler switched his allegiance to Hinduism and ordered the erection of the Hindu temple of Prambanan nearby. Buried for a thousand years under volcanic ash and jungle, Borobudur was rediscovered in the nineteenth century and has recently been restored to its former splendor.

city of Angkor Thom. The temple of Angkor Wat (AN-kor WAHT) is the most famous and arguably the most beautiful of all the existing structures at Angkor Thom. Built on the model of the legendary Mount Meru (the home of the gods in Hindu tradition), it combines Indian architectural techniques with native inspiration in a structure of impressive delicacy and grace. In existence for more than eight hundred years, Angkor Wat serves as a bridge between the Hindu and Buddhist architectural styles.

Expansion into the Pacific

One of the great maritime feats of human history was the penetration of the islands of the Pacific Ocean by Malayo-Polynesian-speaking peoples. By 2000 B.C.E., these seafarers had migrated as far as the Bismarck Archipelago, northeast of the island of New Guinea, where they encountered Melanesian peoples whose ancestors had taken part in the first wave of human settlement into the region 30,000 years previously.

From there, the Polynesian peoples—as they are now familiarly known—continued their explorations eastward in large sailing canoes up to 100 feet long that carried more than forty people and many of their food staples, such as chickens, chili peppers, and a tuber called taro, the source of poi. Stopping in Fiji, Samoa, and the Cook Islands during the first millennium C.E., their descendants pressed onward, eventually reaching Tahiti, Hawaii, and even Easter Island, one of the most remote sites of human habitation in the world. Eventually, one group of Polynesians, now known as the Maori (MAU-ree), sailed southwestward from the island of Rarotonga and settled in New Zealand, off the coast of Australia. The final frontier of human settlement had been breached.

CHAPTER SUMMARY

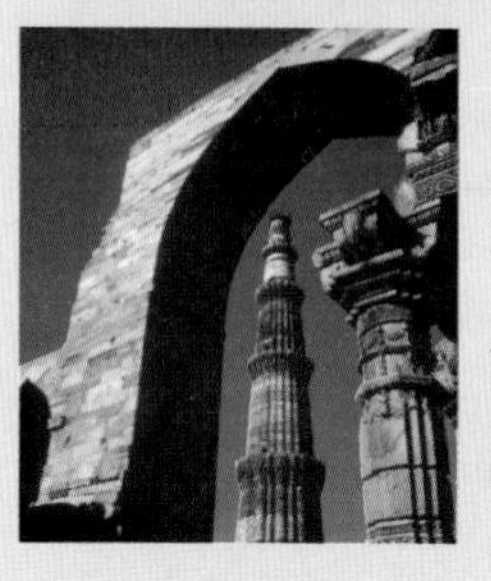

During the more than 1,500 years from the fall of the Mauryas to the rise of the Mughals, Indian civilization faced a number of severe challenges. One challenge was primarily external and took the form of a continuous threat from beyond the mountains in the northwest. As a result of the foreign conquest of northern India, Islam was introduced into the region. The new religion soon became a serious rival to traditional beliefs among the people of India. Another challenge had internal causes, stemming from the tradition of factionalism and internal rivalry that had marked relations within the aristocracy since the Aryan influx in the second millennium B.C.E. (see Chapter 2). Despite the abortive efforts of the Guptas, that tradition continued almost without interruption down to the founding of the Mughal Empire in the sixteenth century.

During the same period that Indian civilization faced these challenges at home, it was having a profound impact on the emerging states of Southeast Asia. Situated at the crossroads between two oceans and two great civilizations, Southeast Asia has long served as a bridge linking peoples and cultures, and as complex societies began to develop in the area, it is not surprising that they were strongly influenced by the older civilizations of neighboring China and India. At the same time, the Southeast Asian peoples put their own unique stamp on the ideas that they adopted and eventually rejected those that were inappropriate to local conditions.

The result was a region characterized by an almost unparalleled cultural richness and diversity, reflecting influences from as far away as the Middle East yet preserving indigenous elements that were deeply rooted in the local culture. Unfortunately, that very diversity posed potential problems for the peoples of Southeast Asia as they faced a new challenge from beyond the horizon. We shall deal with that challenge when we return to the region later in the book. In the meantime, we must turn our attention to the other major civilization that spread its shadow over the societies of southern Asia—China.

CHAPTER TIMELINE

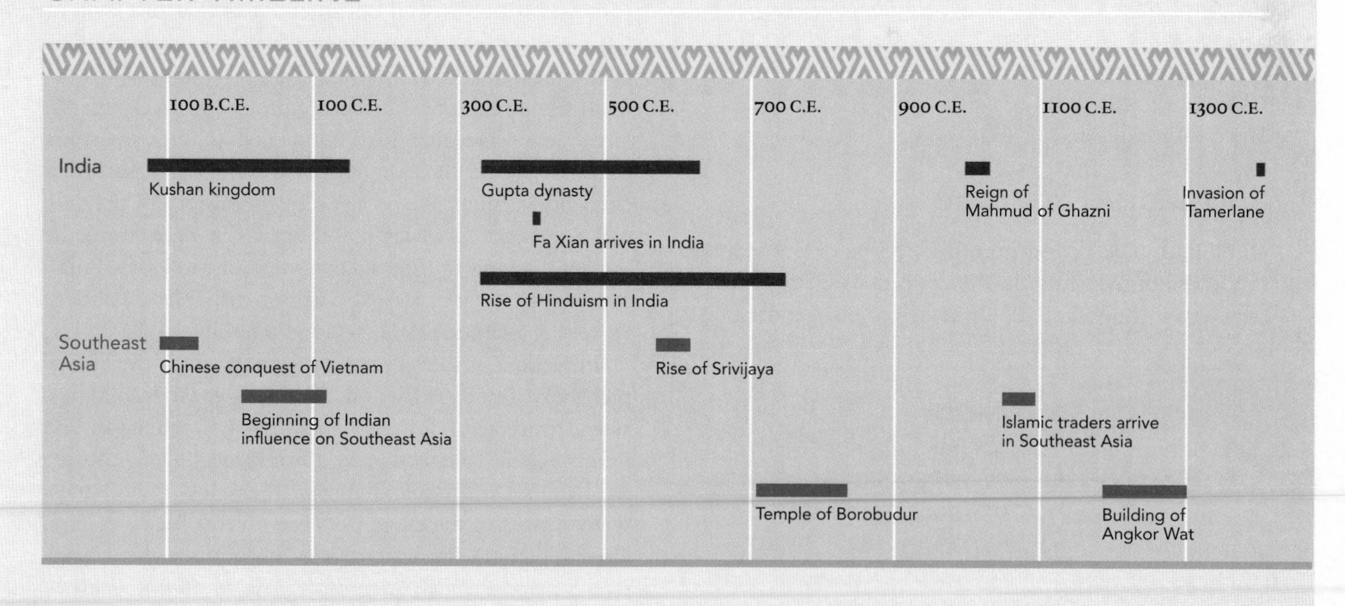

CHAPTER REVIEW

Upon Reflection

Q How does the religion known today as Hinduism compare in its essential respects with the Brahmanical faith from which it emerged in the first millennium C.E.? What may explain the differences?

Q The Indian social system has been characterized by the existence of extensive lineage groups—known as *jati*—that are larger than the traditional joint and nuclear families found in many other societies. What are the most prominent features of such lineage groups, and why have they endured for so long in Indian society?

Q Many of the states that were formed in Southeast Asia during the first millennium C.E. absorbed strong influences from merchants and missionaries arriving from India. What political, social, and religious characteristics of Indian civilization were adopted by the indigenous states in Southeast Asia, and how were they applied in their new environment?

Key Terms

Theravada (p. 225)
Mahayana (p. 225)
Hinayana (p. 225)
bodhisattva (p. 225)
Hinduism (p. 227)
bhakti (p. 227)
puja (p. 228)
purdah (p. 232)
Sikhism (p. 233)
Malayo-Polynesian (p. 239)

Suggested Reading

GENERAL The period from the decline of the Mauryas to the rise of the Mughals in India is not especially rich in materials in English. Still, a number of the standard texts on Indian history contain useful sections on the period. Particularly good are **B. and T. Metcalf, *A Concise History of India*** (Cambridge, 2001), and **S. Wolpert, *India*,** 3rd ed. (New York, 2005).

INDIAN SOCIETY AND CULTURE A number of studies of Indian society and culture deal with this period. See, for example, **R. Thapar, *Early India, from the Origins to A.D. 1300*** (London, 2002), for an authoritative interpretation of Indian culture during the medieval period. On Buddhism, see **H. Nakamura, *Indian Buddhism: A Survey with Bibliographical Notes*** (Delhi, 1987), and **H. Akira, *A History of Indian Buddhism from Sakyamuni to Early Mahayana*** (Honolulu, 1990).

WOMEN'S ISSUES For a discussion of women's issues, see **S. Hughes** and **B. Hughes, *Women in World History*,** vol. 1 (Armonk, N.Y., 1995), and **V. Dehejia, *Devi: The Great Goddess*** (Washington, D.C., 1999).

CENTRAL ASIA For an overview of events in Central Asia during this period, see **D. Christian, *Inner Eurasia from Prehistory to the Mongol Empire*** (Oxford, 1998). On the career of Tamerlane, see **B. F. Manz, *The Rise and Rule of Tamerlane*** (Cambridge, 1989).

MEDIEVAL INDIAN ART On Indian art during the medieval period, see **V. Dehejia, *Indian Art*** (London, 1997).

EARLY SOUTHEAST ASIA The early history of Southeast Asia is not as well documented as that of China or India. Except for Vietnam, where histories written in Chinese appeared shortly after the Chinese conquest, written materials on societies in the region are relatively sparse. Historians were therefore compelled to rely on stone inscriptions and the accounts of travelers and historians from other countries. As a result, the history of precolonial Southeast Asia was presented, as it were, from the outside looking in. For an overview of modern scholarship on the region, see **N. Tarling, ed., *The Cambridge History of Southeast Asia*,** vol. 1 (Cambridge, 1999).

Impressive advances are now being made in the field of prehistory. See **P. Bellwood, *Prehistory of the Indo-Malaysian Archipelago*** (Honolulu, 1997), and **C. Higham, *The Bronze Age of Southeast Asia*** (Cambridge, 1996). Also see the latter's ***Civilization of Angkor*** (Berkeley, Calif., 2001), which discusses the latest evidence on that major empire. On the region's impact on world history, see the impressive ***Strange Parallels: Southeast Asia in Global Context, c. 800–1300*,** vol. 1, by **V. Lieberman** (Cambridge, 2003).

Visit the CourseMate website at **www.cengagebrain.com** for additional study tools and review materials for this chapter.

The Flowering of Traditional China

© Pierre Colombel/CORBIS

Detail of a Chinese scroll, Spring Festival on the River

CHAPTER OUTLINE AND FOCUS QUESTIONS

China After the Han

Q Why did China go through several centuries of internal division after the decline of the Han dynasty, and what impact did this have on Chinese society?

China Reunified: The Sui, the Tang, and the Song

Q What major changes in political structures and social and economic life occurred during the Sui, Tang, and Song dynasties?

Explosion in Central Asia: The Mongol Empire

Q Why were the Mongols able to amass an empire, and what were the main characteristics of their rule in China?

The Ming Dynasty

Q What were the chief initiatives taken by the early rulers of the Ming dynasty to enhance the role of China in the world? Why did the imperial court order the famous voyages of Zhenghe, and why were they discontinued?

In Search of the Way

Q What roles did Buddhism, Daoism, and Neo-Confucianism play in Chinese intellectual life in the period between the Sui dynasty and the Ming?

The Apogee of Chinese Culture

Q What were the main achievements in Chinese literature and art in the period between the Tang dynasty and the Ming, and what technological innovations and intellectual developments contributed to these achievements?

CRITICAL THINKING

Q The civilization of ancient China fell under the onslaught of nomadic invasions, as had some of its counterparts elsewhere in the world. But China, unlike other ancient empires, was later able to reconstitute itself on the same political and cultural foundations. How do you account for the difference?

ON HIS FIRST VISIT to the city, the traveler was mightily impressed. Its streets were so straight and wide that he could see through the city from one end to the other. Along the wide boulevards were beautiful palaces and inns in great profusion. The city was laid out in squares like a chessboard, and within each square were spacious courts and gardens. Truly, said the visitor, this must be one of the largest and wealthiest cities on earth—a city "planned out to a degree of precision and beauty impossible to describe."

The visitor was Marco Polo (MAR-koh POH-loh), and the city was Khanbaliq (kahn-bah-LEEK) (later known as Beijing), capital of the Yuan (YOO-enn *or* YWAHN) dynasty (1279–1368) and one of the great urban centers of the Chinese Empire. Marco Polo was an Italian merchant who had traveled to China in the late thirteenth century and then served as an official at the court of Khubilai Khan (KOO-blah KAHN). In later travels in China, Polo visited a number of other great cities, including the commercial hub of Kaifeng (KY-fuhng) (Ken-Zan-fu) on the Yellow River. It is a city, he remarked,

> of great commerce, and eminent for its manufactures. Raw silk is produced in large quantities, and tissues of gold and every other kind of silk are woven there. At this place likewise they prepare every article necessary for the equipment of an army. All species of provisions are in abundance, and to be procured at a moderate price.[1]

Polo's diary, published after his return to Italy almost twenty years later, astonished readers with tales of this magnificent but unknown civilization far to the east. In fact, many of his European contemporaries were skeptical and suspected that he was a charlatan seeking to win fame and fortune with a fictional account of his travels to fantastic lands.

Readers of Marco Polo's memoirs in other parts of the world, however, undoubtedly would have found his account of the wonders of the East more credible, for evidence of the greatness of the Chinese Empire—now under the domination of a fearsome Central Asian people called Mongols—was all around them. Indeed, after the decline of the Abbasids in the eleventh and twelfth centuries, China had clearly emerged as the richest and most powerful empire on the Eurasian supercontinent.

China After the Han

FOCUS QUESTION: Why did China go through several centuries of internal division after the decline of the Han dynasty, and what impact did this have on Chinese society?

After the collapse of the Han dynasty at the beginning of the third century C.E., China fell into an extended period of division and civil war. Taking advantage of the absence of organized government in China, nomadic forces from the Gobi Desert penetrated south of the Great Wall and established their own rule over northern China. In the Yangtze valley and farther to the south, native Chinese rule was maintained, but the constant civil war and instability led later historians to refer to the period as the "era of the six dynasties."

The collapse of the Han Empire had a marked effect on the Chinese psyche. The Confucian principles that emphasized hard work, subordination of the individual to community interests, and belief in the essentially rational order of the universe came under severe challenge, and many Chinese intellectuals began to reject the stuffy moralism and complacency of State Confucianism as they sought emotional satisfaction in hedonistic pursuits or philosophical Daoism.

Eccentric behavior and a preference for philosophical Daoism became a common response to a corrupt age. A group of writers known as the "seven sages of the bamboo forest" exemplified the period. Among the best known was the poet Liu Ling (lyoo LING), whose odd behavior is described in this oft-quoted passage:

> Liu Ling was an inveterate drinker and indulged himself to the full. Sometimes he stripped off his clothes and sat in his room stark naked. Some men saw him and rebuked him. Liu Ling said, "Heaven and earth are my dwelling, and my house is my trousers. Why are you all coming into my trousers?"[2]

But neither popular beliefs in the supernatural nor philosophical Daoism could satisfy deeper emotional needs or provide solace in time of sorrow or the hope of a better life in the hereafter. Instead Buddhism filled that gap.

Buddhism was brought to China in the first or second century C.E., probably by missionaries and merchants traveling over the Silk Road. The concept of rebirth was probably unfamiliar to most Chinese, and the intellectual hairsplitting that often accompanied discussion of the Buddha's message in India was somewhat esoteric for Chinese tastes. Still, in the difficult years of the Han dynasty's decline, Buddhist ideas, especially those of the Mahayana school, began to find adherents among intellectuals and ordinary people alike. As Buddhism increased in popularity, it was frequently attacked by supporters of Confucianism and Daoism for its foreign origins. But such sniping did not halt the progress of Buddhism, and eventually the new faith was assimilated into Chinese culture, assisted by the efforts of such tireless advocates as the missionaries Fa Xian and Xuan Zang and the support of ruling elites in both northern and southern China (see "The Rise and Decline of Buddhism and Daoism" later in this chapter).

China Reunified: The Sui, the Tang, and the Song

FOCUS QUESTION: What major changes in political structures and social and economic life occurred during the Sui, Tang, and Song dynasties?

After nearly four centuries of internal division, China was unified once again in 581 C.E. when Yang Jian (yahng JEE-YEN) (Yang Chien), a member of a respected aristocratic family in northern China, founded a new dynasty, known as the Sui (SWAY) (581–618). Yang Jian, who is also known by his reign title of Sui Wendi (SWAY wen-DEE) (Sui Wen Ti), established his capital at the historic metropolis of Chang'an (CHENG-AHN) (Ch'ang-an) and began to extend his authority throughout the Chinese heartland.

The Sui Dynasty

Like his predecessors, the new emperor sought a unifying ideology to enhance the state's efficiency. But whereas Liu Bang, the founder of the Han dynasty, had adopted Confucianism as the official doctrine to hold the empire together, Yang Jian turned to Daoism and Buddhism. He founded monasteries for both doctrines and appointed Buddhist monks to key positions as political advisers.

Yang Jian was a builder as well as a conqueror, ordering the construction of a new canal from the capital to the confluence of the Wei and Yellow Rivers nearly 100 miles to the east. His son, Sui Yangdi (SWAY yahng-DEE) (Sui Yang Ti), continued the process, and the 1,400-mile-long Grand Canal, linking the Yellow and Yangtze Rivers, was completed during his reign. The new canal facilitated the shipment of grain from the rice-rich southern provinces to the densely populated north and also served as an imperial highway for dispatching troops to troubled provinces.

Despite these achievements, the Sui dynasty came to an end immediately after Sui Yangdi's death. The Sui emperor was a tyrannical ruler, and his expensive military campaigns aroused widespread unrest. After his return from a failed campaign against Korea in 618, the emperor was murdered in his palace. One of his generals, Li Yuan (lee YWAHN), took advantage of the ensuing instability and founded a new dynasty, known as the Tang (TAHNG) (T'ang). Building on the successes of its predecessor, the Tang lasted for three hundred years, until 907.

The Tang Dynasty

After only a brief reign, Li Yuan was elbowed aside by his son, who assumed the reign title Tang Taizong (tahng ty-ZOONG) (T'ang T'ai-tsung). Under his leadership, the Tang launched a program of internal renewal and external expansion that would make it one of the greatest Chinese dynasties (see Map 10.1). The northwest was pacified and given the name of Xinjiang (SHIN-jyahng), or "new region." A long conflict with Tibet led for the first time to the extension of Chinese control over the vast and desolate plateau north of the Himalaya Mountains. The southern provinces below the Yangtze were fully assimilated into the Chinese Empire, and the imperial court established commercial and diplomatic relations with the states of Southeast Asia. With reason, China now claimed to be the foremost power in East Asia, and the emperor demanded fealty and tribute from all his fellow rulers beyond the frontier. Korea accepted tribute status and attempted to adopt the Chinese model, and the Japanese dispatched official missions

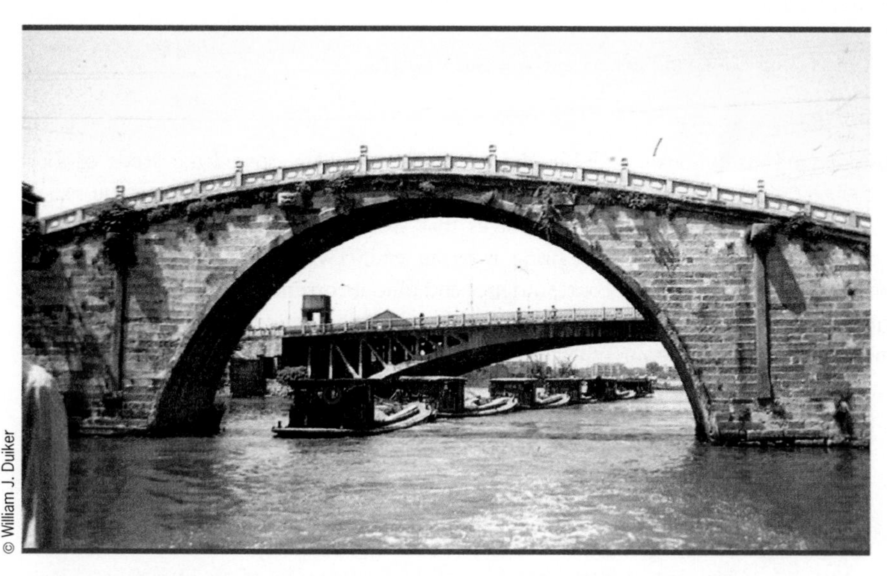

© William J. Duiker

The Grand Canal. Built over centuries, the Grand Canal is one of the engineering wonders of the world and a crucial conduit for carrying goods between northern and southern China. During the Song dynasty, when the region south of the Yangtze River became the heartland of the empire, the canal was used to carry rice and other agricultural products to the food-starved northern provinces. Many of the towns and cities located along the canal became famous for their wealth and cultural achievements. Among the most renowned was Suzhou (soo-JOE), a center for silk manufacture, which is sometimes described as the "Venice of China" because of its many canals. Shown here is a classic example of a humpback bridge crossing an arm of the canal in downtown Suzhou. Chinese engineers discovered how to construct such bridges several hundred years before their counterparts in Europe mastered the technique.

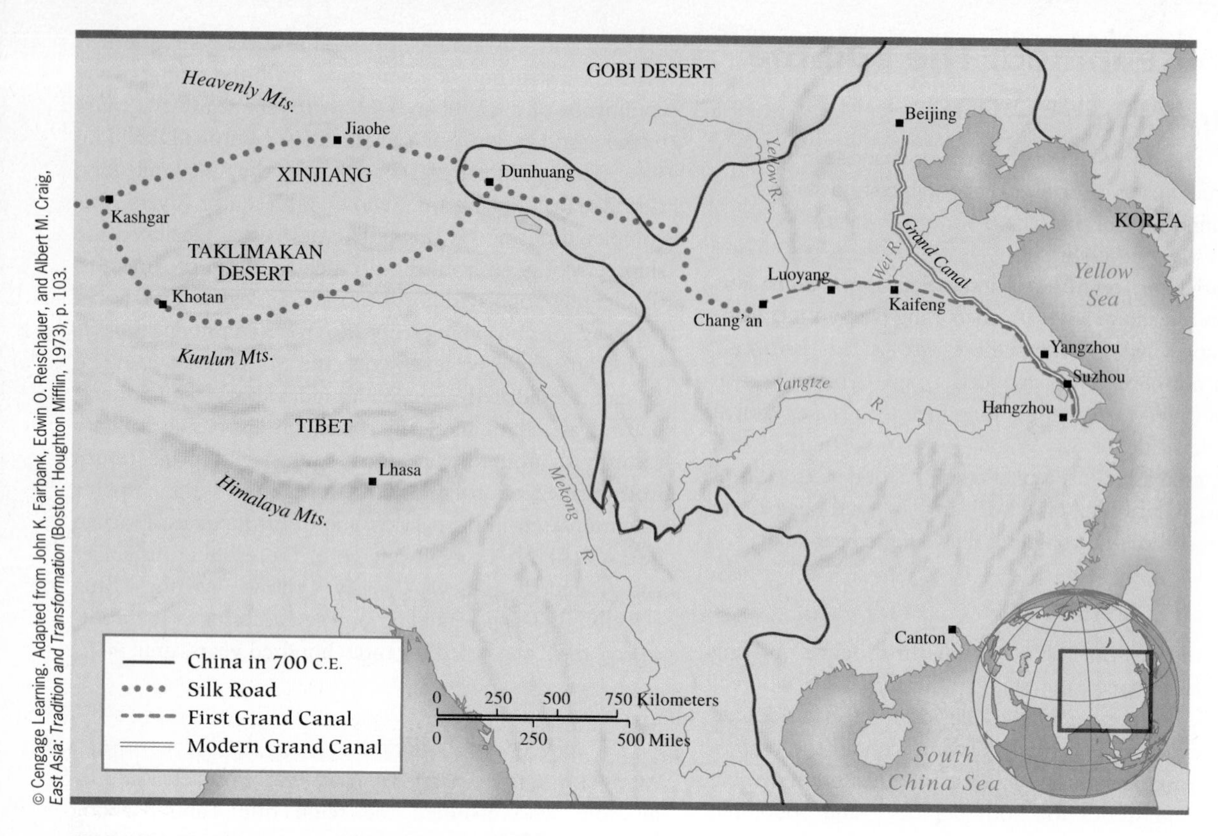

© Cengage Learning. Adapted from John K. Fairbank, Edwin O. Reischauer, and Albert M. Craig, *East Asia: Tradition and Transformation* (Boston: Houghton Mifflin, 1973), p. 103.

MAP 10.1 China Under the Tang. The era of the Tang dynasty was one of the greatest periods in the long history of China. Tang influence spread from the Chinese heartland into neighboring regions, including Central and Southeast Asia.

Q *What was the main function of the Grand Canal during this period, and why was it built?*

to China to learn more about its customs and institutions (see Chapter 11).

Finally, the Tang dynasty witnessed a flowering of culture, often regarded as the apogee of Chinese creativity in poetry and sculpture. One reason for this explosion of culture was the influence of Buddhism, which affected art, literature, and philosophy, as well as religion and politics. Monasteries sprang up throughout China, and (as under the Sui) Buddhist monks served as advisers at the imperial court. The city of Chang'an once again became the seat of the empire. With a population estimated at nearly 2 million, it was possibly the greatest city in the world.

© Cengage Learning. Albert Hermann, *An Historical Atlas of China* (Chicago: Aldine, 1966), p. 13.

Chang'an Under the Sui and the Tang

But the Tang, like the Han, sowed the seeds of their own destruction. Tang rulers could not prevent the rise of internal forces that would ultimately weaken the dynasty and bring it to an end. Two ubiquitous problems were court intrigues and official corruption. A prolonged drought may also have played a role in the dynasty's decline. In 755, rebellious forces briefly seized control of Chang'an itself. Although the revolt was eventually suppressed, the Tang never fully recovered. The loss of power by the central government led to increased influence by great landed families inside China and chronic instability along the northern and western frontiers, where local military commanders ruled virtually without central government interference. It was an eerie repetition of the final decades of the Han.

The end finally came in the early tenth century, when border troubles with northern nomadic peoples called the Khitan (KEE-tan) caused the Tang to follow the classic Chinese strategy of "using a barbarian to oppose a barbarian" by allying with the Uighurs (WEE-gurz), a Turkic-speaking people who had taken over many of the caravan routes along the Silk Road. But yet another nomadic people called the Kirghiz (keer-GEEZ) defeated the Uighurs and then turned on the Tang government in its moment of weakness and overthrew it.

The Song Dynasty

China slipped once again into chaos. This time, the period of foreign invasion and division was much shorter. In 960, a new dynasty, known as the Song (SOONG) (960–1279), rose to power. From the start, however, the Song (Sung) rulers encountered more problems in defending their territory than their predecessors. The founding emperor, Song Taizu (soong ty-DZOO) (Sung T'ai-tsu), was unable to reconquer the northwestern part of the country from the nomadic Khitan peoples and therefore established his capital farther to the east, at Kaifeng, where the Grand Canal intersected the Yellow River. Later, when pressures from the nomads in the north increased, the court was forced to move the capital even farther south, to Hangzhou (HAHNG-joe) (Hangchow), on the coast just south of the Yangtze River delta; the emperors who ruled from Hangzhou are known as the southern Song (1127–1279). Despite its political and military weaknesses, the dynasty nevertheless ruled during a period of economic expansion, prosperity, and cultural achievement and is therefore considered among the more successful Chinese dynasties. The empire's population, estimated at 40 million, was slightly higher than that of the continent of Europe.

Yet the Song were never able to surmount the external challenge from the north, and that failure eventually brought about the end of the dynasty. During its final decades, the Song rulers were forced to pay tribute to the Jurchen (roor-ZHEN) peoples from Manchuria (man-CHUR-ee-uh). In the early thirteenth century, the Song, ignoring precedent and the fate of the Tang, formed an alliance with the Mongols, a new and obscure nomadic people from the Gobi Desert. As under the Tang, the decision proved to be a disaster. Within a few years, the Mongols had become a much more serious threat to China than the Jurchen. After defeating the Jurchen, the Mongols turned their attention to the Song, advancing on Song territory from both the north and the west. By this time, the Song empire had been weakened by internal factionalism and a loss of tax revenues. After a series of battles and sieges marked by the use of catapults and gunpowder, the Song were defeated, and the conquerors announced the creation of a new Yuan (Mongol) dynasty. Ironically, the Mongols had first learned about gunpowder from the Chinese.

CHRONOLOGY Medieval China

Arrival of Buddhism in China	c. first century C.E.
Fall of the Han dynasty	220 C.E.
Sui dynasty	581–618
Tang dynasty	618–907
Li Bo (Li Po) and Du Fu (Tu Fu)	700s
Song dynasty	960–1279
Wang Anshi	1021–1086
Southern Song dynasty	1127–1279
Mongol conquest of China	1279
Reign of Khubilai Khan	1260–1294
Fall of the Yuan dynasty	1368
Ming dynasty	1369–1644

Political Structures: The Triumph of Confucianism

During the nearly seven hundred years from the Sui to the end of the Song, a mature political system based on principles originally established during the Qin and Han dynasties gradually emerged in China. After the Tang dynasty's brief flirtation with Buddhism, State Confucianism became the ideological cement that held the system together (see the box on p. 254). The development of this system took several centuries, and it did not reach its height until the period of the Song dynasty.

EQUAL OPPORTUNITY IN CHINA: THE CIVIL SERVICE EXAMINATION At the apex of the government hierarchy was the **Grand Council**, assisted by a secretariat and a chancellery; it included representatives from all three authorities—civil, military, and censorate. Under the Grand Council was the Department of State Affairs, composed of ministries responsible for justice, military affairs, personnel, public works, revenue, and rites (ritual).

The Tang dynasty adopted the practice of selecting some officials through periodic civil service examinations. The effectiveness of this merit system was limited, however, because it was dominated by the great aristocratic clans, who had mastered the technique of preparing candidates for the exams. According to one source, fully one-third of those who succeeded on the examinations during the Tang era came from the great families.

The Song were more successful at limiting aristocratic control over the bureaucracy, in part because the nobility had been weakened during the final years of the Tang dynasty and the interregnum that followed its collapse. Making the civil service examination system the primary route to an official career was a way of strengthening the power of the central administration. To reduce the power of the noble families, relatives of individuals serving in the imperial court were prohibited from taking the examinations. But if the objective was to make the bureaucracy more subservient to the court, the Song rulers may have been disappointed. The rising professionalism and influence of the bureaucracy, which numbered about

OPPOSING ✂ VIEWPOINTS

Action or Inaction: An Ideological Dispute in Medieval China

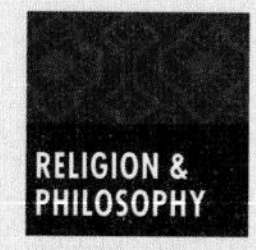

During the four hundred years between the fall of the Han dynasty in 220 C.E. and the rise of the Tang, Daoist critics lampooned the hypocrisy of the "Confucian gentleman" and the Master's emphasis on ritual and the maintenance of proper relations among individuals in society. In the first selection, a third-century Daoist launches an attack on the pompous and hypocritical Confucian gentleman who feigns high moral principles while secretly engaging in corrupt and licentious behavior.

By the eighth century, the tables had turned. In the second selection, Han Yu (hahn YOO) (768–824), a key figure in the emergence of Neo-Confucian thought as the official ideology of the state, responds to such remarks with a withering analysis of the dangers of "doing nothing"—a clear reference to the famous Daoist doctrine of "inaction."

Biography of a Great Man

What the world calls a gentleman [*chun-tzu*] is someone who is solely concerned with moral law [*fa*], and cultivates exclusively the rules of propriety [*li*]. His hand holds the emblem of jade [authority]; his foot follows the straight line of the rule. He likes to think that his actions set a permanent example; he likes to think that his words are everlasting models. In his youth, he has a reputation in the villages of his locality; in his later years, he is well known in the neighboring districts. Upward, he aspires to the dignity of the Three Dukes; downward, he does not disdain the post of governor of the nine provinces.

Have you ever seen the lice that inhabit a pair of trousers? They jump into the depths of the seams, hiding themselves in the cotton wadding, and believe they have a pleasant place to live. Walking, they do not risk going beyond the edge of the seam; moving, they are careful not to emerge from the trouser leg; and they think they have kept to the rules of etiquette. But when the trousers are ironed, the flames invade the hills, the fire spreads, the villages are set on fire and the towns burned down; then the lice that inhabit the trousers cannot escape. What difference is there between the gentleman who lives within a narrow world and the lice that inhabit trouser legs?

Han Yu, *Essentials of the Moral Way*

In ancient times men confronted many dangers. But sages arose who taught them the way to live and to grow together. They served as rulers and as teachers. They drove out reptiles and wild beasts and had the people settle the central lands. The people were cold, and they clothed them; hungry, and they fed them. Because the people dwelt in trees and fell to the ground, dwelt in caves and became ill, the sages built houses for them.

They fashioned crafts so the people could provide themselves with implements. They made trade to link together those who had and those who had not and medicine to save them from premature death. They taught the people to bury and make sacrifices [to the dead] to enlarge their sense of gratitude and love. They gave rites to set order and precedence, music to vent melancholy, government to direct idleness, and punishments to weed out intransigence. When the people cheated each other, the sages invented tallies and seals, weights and measures to make them honest. When they attacked each other, they fashioned walls and towns, armor and weapons for them to defend themselves. So when dangers came, they prepared the people; and when calamity arose, they defended the people. But now the Daoists maintain:

Till the sages are dead,
theft will not end . . .
so break the measures, smash the scales,
and the people will not contend.

These are thoughtless remarks indeed, for humankind would have died out long ago if there had been no sages in antiquity. Men have neither feathers nor fur, neither scales nor shells to ward off heat and cold, neither talons nor fangs to fight for food. . . .

But now the Daoists advocate "doing nothing" as in high antiquity. Such is akin to criticizing a man who wears furs in winter by asserting that it is easier to make

(Continued)

linen, or akin to criticizing a man who eats when he is hungry by asserting that it is easier to take a drink. . . .

This being so, what can be done? Block them or nothing will flow; stop them or nothing will move. Make humans of these people, burn their books, make homes of their dwellings, make clear the way of the former kings to guide them, and "the widowers, the widows, the orphans, the childless, and the diseased all shall have care." This can be done.

How might the author of the first selection have responded to Han Yu's arguments? Which author appears to make the better case for his chosen ideological preference?

Sources: Biography of a Great Man. From *Chinese Civilization and Bureaucracy,* by Etienne Balasz. Copyright © 1964 by Yale University Press. Used with permission. Han Yu, *Essentials of the Moral Way.* Excerpt from *Sources of Chinese Tradition,* by William Theodore de Bary. Copyright © 1960 by Columbia University Press. Reprinted with the permission of the publisher.

20,000 in total, with 10,000 in the imperial capital, sometimes enabled it to resist the whims of individual emperors.

Under the Song, the examination system attained the form that it would retain in later centuries. Three levels of examinations were administered. The first was a qualifying examination given annually at the provincial capital. Candidates who succeeded at this stage normally could only obtain positions at the local level. Candidates who wished to go on could take a second examination given at the capital every three years. Successful candidates could apply for an official position. Those who passed the final examination, which was given in the imperial palace once every three years, were eligible for high positions in the central bureaucracy or for appointments as district magistrates.

The examinations were based entirely on the Confucian classics. Candidates were expected to memorize passages and to be able to explain the moral lessons they contained. The system guaranteed that successful candidates—and therefore officials—would have received a full dose of Confucian political and social ethics. Many students complained about the rigors of memorization and the irrelevance of the process. Others brought crib notes into the examination hall (one enterprising candidate concealed an entire Confucian text in the lining of his cloak).

The Song authorities ignored such criticisms, but they did open the exams to almost all males except criminals and set up training academies at the provincial and district level. Without such academies, only individuals with access to family-run schools could have passed the examinations. In time, the majority of candidates came from the landed gentry, nonaristocratic landowners who controlled much of the wealth in the countryside. Because the gentry prized education and became the primary upholders of the Confucian tradition, they were often called the **scholar-gentry**.

Nevertheless, the system still did not truly provide equal opportunity to all. Not only were only males eligible, but the Song never attempted to establish a system of universal elementary education. In practice, only those who had been given a basic education in the classics at home were able to enter the state-run academies and compete for a position in the bureaucracy. Hence, the poor had little chance.

Nor could the system guarantee an honest, efficient bureaucracy. Official arrogance, bureaucratic infighting, and corruption were as prevalent in medieval China as in bureaucracies the world over. Nepotism was a particular problem, since many Chinese, following Confucius, held that filial duty transcended loyalty to the community.

Despite such weaknesses, the civil service examination system was an impressive achievement for its day and probably provided a more efficient government and more opportunity for upward mobility than existed in any other civilization of the time. Most Western governments, for example, did not begin to recruit officials on the basis of merit until the nineteenth century. Furthermore, by regulating the content of the examinations, the system helped provide China with a cultural uniformity lacking in empires elsewhere in Asia.

LOCAL GOVERNMENT The Song dynasty maintained the local government institutions that it had inherited from its predecessors. At the base of the government pyramid was the district (or county), governed by a magistrate who was responsible for maintaining law and order and collecting taxes within his district, which could exceed 100,000 people. Below the district was the basic unit of Chinese government, the village. Villages were allowed to administer themselves, normally through a council of elders. The council, usually made up of the heads of influential families in the village, maintained the local irrigation and transportation network, adjudicated disputes, organized a militia, and assisted in collecting taxes (usually paid in grain).

The Economy

During the long period between the Sui and the Song, the Chinese economy, like the government, grew considerably in size and complexity. China was still an agricultural society, but major changes were taking place. The urban sector was becoming increasingly important, new social classes were beginning to appear, and the economic focus of the empire was beginning to shift from the Yellow River valley in the north to the Yangtze River valley in the center—a process that was encouraged both by the expansion of cultivation in the Yangtze delta and by the control exerted over the north by nomadic peoples during the Song.

LAND REFORM The economic revival began shortly after the rise of the Tang. During the long period of internal division, land had become concentrated in the hands of aristocratic families, with most peasants reduced to serfdom or slavery. The early Tang tried to reduce the power of the landed nobility and maximize tax revenues by adopting the ancient "well-field" system, in which land was allocated to farmers for life in return for an annual tax payment and three weeks of conscript labor.

At first, the new system led to increased rural prosperity and government revenue, but eventually, the rich and politically influential, including some of the largest Buddhist monasteries, learned to manipulate the system and accumulated huge tracts of land. The growing population also put steady pressure on the system. Finally, the government abandoned the effort to equalize landholdings and returned the land to private hands while attempting to prevent inequalities through the tax system. The failure to resolve the land problem contributed to the fall of the Tang dynasty in the early tenth century, although the reversion of farmlands to private hands did result in more efficient production in some instances as well as increased long-distance trade in food products.

The Song tried to resolve the land problem by returning to the successful programs of the early Tang and reducing the power of the landed aristocrats. During the late eleventh century, the reformist official Wang Anshi (WAHNG ahn-SHEE) (Wang An-shih) (1021–1086) attempted to limit the size of landholdings through progressive land taxes and provided cheap credit to poor farmers to help them avoid bankruptcy. His reforms met with some success, but other developments probably contributed more to the general agricultural prosperity under the Song. These included the opening of new lands in the Yangtze River valley, technological improvements such as the chain pump (a circular chain of square pallets on a treadmill that enabled farmers to lift water to a higher level), and the introduction of a quick-growing rice from Southeast Asia, which allowed two crops to be produced each year. It was during the Song dynasty that rice became the main food crop for the Chinese people.

AN INCREASE IN MANUFACTURING Major changes also took place in the urban economy, which witnessed a significant increase in trade and manufacturing, helped by several technological developments (see the comparative essay "The Spread of Technology" on p. 257). During the Tang, the Chinese mastered the art of manufacturing steel by mixing cast iron and wrought iron. Blast furnaces were heated to a high temperature by burning coal. The resulting product was used for swords, sickles, and even suits of armor. By the eleventh century, more than 35,000 tons of steel were being produced annually. The introduction of cotton offered new opportunities in textile manufacturing. Gunpowder was invented by the Chinese during the late Tang dynasty and was used primarily for explosives and a primitive form of flamethrower; it reached the West via the Arabs in the twelfth century.

THE EXPANSION OF COMMERCE The nature of trade was also changing. In the past, most long-distance trade had been undertaken by state monopoly, but by the time of the Song, private commerce was being actively encouraged. Guilds began to appear, along with a new money economy. Paper currency began to be used in the eighth and ninth centuries and led to the development of banking as merchants found that strings of copper coins were too cumbersome for their increasingly complex operations. Credit (at first called "flying money") also made its appearance during the Tang. The invention of the abacus, an early form of calculator, simplified the calculations needed for commercial transactions.

THE SILK ROAD Long-distance trade, both overland and by sea, expanded under the Tang and the Song. Trade with countries and peoples to the west had been carried on for centuries (see Chapter 3), but it had declined dramatically between the fourth and sixth centuries C.E. as a result of the collapse of the Han and Roman Empires. It began to revive with the rise of the Tang and the simultaneous unification of much of the Middle East under the Arabs. During the Tang era, the route that we call the Silk Road reached its zenith. Along the Silk Road to China came raw hides, furs, and horses. Much of the trade was carried by the Turkic-speaking Uighurs or Iranian-speaking Sogdians (SAHG-dee-unz) from Central Asia. During the Tang, Uighur caravans of two-humped Bactrian camels carried goods between China and the countries of South Asia and the Middle East.

In actuality, the Silk Road was composed of a number of separate routes. The first to be used, probably because of the jade found in the mountains south of Khotan (koh-TAHN), ran along the southern rim of the Taklimakan (tah-kluh-muh-KAHN) Desert and thence through the Pamir (pah-MEER) Mountains into Bactria. The first Buddhist missionaries traveled this route from India to

COMPARATIVE ESSAY

The Spread of Technology

From the invention of stone tools and the discovery of fire to the introduction of agriculture and writing systems, mastery of technology has been a driving force in human history. But why do some societies appear to be much more advanced in their use of technology than others? People living on the island of New Guinea, for example, began cultivating local crops like taro and bananas as early as ten thousand years ago but never took the next steps toward creating a complex society until the arrival of Europeans many millennia later. Advanced societies began to emerge in the Western Hemisphere during the ancient era, but none discovered the use of the wheel or the smelting of metals for toolmaking. Writing also remained in its infancy there.

Technological advances appear to take place for two reasons: need and opportunity. Farming peoples throughout the world needed to control the flow of water, so in areas where water was scarce or unevenly distributed, they developed irrigation techniques to make resources available throughout the region. Sometimes, however, opportunity strikes by accident (as in the legendary story of the Chinese princess who dropped a silkworm cocoon into her cup of hot tea, thereby initiating a series of discoveries that resulted in the manufacture of silk) or when new technology is introduced from a neighboring region (as when the discovery of tin in Anatolia launched the Bronze Age throughout the Middle East).

The most important factor enabling societies to keep abreast of the latest advances in technology, it would appear, is participation in the global trade and communications network. In this respect, the Abbasid Empire enjoyed a major advantage because the relative ease of communications between the Mediterranean region and the Indus River valley gave the empire rapid access to all the resources and technological advances in that part of the world. China was more isolated from such developments because of distance and barriers such as the Himalaya Mountains. But with its size and high level of cultural achievement, China was almost a continent in itself and was able to communicate with countries to the west via the Silk Road.

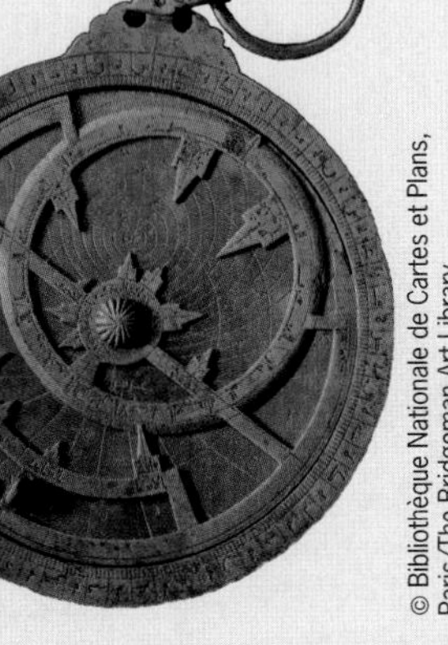

A copper astrolabe from the Middle East, circa the ninth century C.E.

© Bibliothèque Nationale de Cartes et Plans, Paris/The Bridgeman Art Library

Societies that were not linked to this vast network were at an enormous disadvantage in keeping up with new developments in technology. The peoples of New Guinea, at the far end of the Indonesian archipelago, had little or no contact with the outside world. In the Western Hemisphere, a trade network did begin to take shape between societies in the Andes and their counterparts in Mesoamerica. But because of difficulties in communication (see Chapter 6), contacts were intermittent. Not until the arrival of the conquistadors did technological developments taking place in distant Eurasia reach the Americas.

In what ways did China contribute to the spread of technology and ideas throughout the world during the period from the Sui dynasty to the rise of the Ming? How did China benefit from the process?

China. Eventually, however, this area began to dry up, and traders were forced to seek other routes. The route to the north of the Tian Shan (TEE-en SHAHN) (Heavenly Mountains) offered pastures where animals could graze, but the area was frequently infested by bandits, so most caravans followed the southern route, which passed along the northern fringes of the Taklimakan Desert to Kashgar (KASH-gahr) and down into northwestern India. Travelers avoided the direct route through the desert (in the Uighur language, the name means "go in and you won't come out") and trudged from oasis to oasis along the southern slopes of the Tian Shan.

The eastern terminus of the Silk Road was the city of Chang'an, perhaps the wealthiest city in the world during the Tang era. Its days as China's foremost metropolis were numbered, however. Chronic droughts throughout

© The Philadelphia Museum of Art/Art Resource, NY

Tang Camel. During the Tang dynasty, trade between China, India, and the Middle East along the famous Silk Road increased rapidly and introduced new Central Asian motifs to Chinese culture. As seen in this sturdy example, the Bactrian two-humped camel played a major role in carrying goods along the trade route, since its ability to withstand long periods without water enabled it to survive the grueling trek across the Central Asian deserts. Numerous ceramic studies of horses and camels, along with officials, court ladies, and servants, painted in brilliant gold, green, and blue lead glazes, were created as tomb figures and therefore are preserved for us today.

the region made it more and more difficult to supply the city with food, and the growing power of nomadic peoples in the hinterlands made the city increasingly vulnerable to attack. During the later Tang, the imperial court was periodically shifted to the old capital of Luoyang (LWOH-yahng). The Song dynasty, a product of the steady drift of the national center of gravity toward the south, was forced to abandon Chang'an altogether.

THE MARITIME ROUTE The Silk Road was so hazardous that shipping goods by sea became increasingly popular. China had long been engaged in sea trade with other countries in the region, but most of the commerce was originally in the hands of Korean, Japanese, Southeast Asian, or Middle Eastern merchants. Under the Song, however, Chinese maritime trade was stimulated by the invention of the compass and technical improvements in shipbuilding such as the sternpost rudder. If Marco Polo's observations can be believed, by the thirteenth century, Chinese junks (a type of seagoing ship with square sails and a flat bottom) had multiple sails and were up to 2,000 tons in size, much larger than contemporary ships in the West. The Chinese governor of Canton (KAN-tahn) in the early twelfth century remarked:

> According to the government regulations concerning seagoing ships, the larger ones can carry several hundred men, and the smaller ones may have more than a hundred men on board. . . . The ship's pilots are acquainted with the configuration of the coasts; at night they steer by the stars, and in the daytime by the Sun. In dark weather they look at the south-pointing needle. They also use a line a hundred feet long with a hook at the end, which they let down to take samples of mud from the sea-bottom; by its appearance and smell they can determine their whereabouts.[3]

A wide variety of goods passed through Chinese ports. The Chinese exported tea, silk, and porcelain to the countries beyond the South China Sea, receiving exotic woods, precious stones, cotton from India, and various tropical goods in exchange. The major southern port was Canton, home to an estimated 100,000 merchants. Chinese aristocrats, their appetite for material consumption stimulated by the affluence of much of the Tang and Song periods, were fascinated by the exotic goods shipped from the tropical lands of the South Seas and the flora and fauna of the desert that arrived via the Silk Road.

Some of this trade was a product of the tribute system. The Chinese viewed the outside world as they viewed their own society—in a hierarchical manner. Rulers of smaller countries along the periphery were viewed as "younger brothers" of the Chinese emperor and owed fealty to him. Foreign rulers who accepted the relationship were required to pay tribute and to promise not to harbor enemies of the Chinese Empire. In return, they obtained legitimacy and access to the vast Chinese market.

Society in Traditional China

These political and economic changes affected Chinese society during the Tang and Song eras. For one thing, it became much more complex. Whereas previously China had been almost exclusively rural, with a small urban class of merchants and artisans almost entirely dependent on the state, the cities had now grown into an important, if statistically still insignificant, part of the population. Cities were no longer primarily administrative centers but now included a much broader mix of officials, merchants, artisans, touts, and entertainers. Unlike European cities, however, Chinese cities did not possess special privileges that protected their residents from the rapacity of the central government.

© Burstein Collection/CORBIS

Court Ladies Preparing Silk. Since antiquity, human beings have fashioned textiles out of hemp, flax, wool, cotton, and silk. The Shang dynasty produced both hemp and silk cloth, whereas wool was prominent in the Middle East and Greece. Linen, woven in Egypt, was used by the Roman Empire to clothe its army. Fine Indian cotton was introduced to China along the Silk Road, just as Chinese satin was carried by Mongol warriors to Europe, where it was used for making banners. Sometimes the Chinese government demanded bolts of cloth as well as grain as a tax from peasants. Although most silk was produced by peasants as an agricultural by-product, it was also woven by the elegant court ladies of the Song dynasty, as seen here, and its use as a fabric was restricted to the elite classes until the nineteenth century.

In the countryside, equally significant changes were taking place, as the relatively rigid demarcation between the landed aristocracy and the mass of the rural population gave way to a more complex mixture of landed gentry, free farmers, sharecroppers, and landless laborers. There was also a class of "base people," consisting of actors, butchers, and prostitutes, who possessed only limited legal rights and were not permitted to take the civil service examination.

THE RISE OF THE GENTRY Under the early Tang, powerful noble families not only possessed a significant part of the national wealth, but also dominated high positions in the imperial government, just as they had at the end of the Han dynasty four hundred years earlier. The soaring ambitions and arrogance of China's great families are evident in the following wish list set in poetry by a young bridegroom of the Tang dynasty:

Chinese slaves to take charge of treasury and barn,
Foreign slaves to take care of my cattle and sheep.
Strong-legged slaves to run by saddle and stirrup
when I ride,
Powerful slaves to till the fields with might
and main,
Handsome slaves to play the harp and hand
the wine;
Slim-waisted slaves to sing me songs, and dance;
Dwarfs to hold the candle by my dining-couch.[4]

Some Tang rulers, notably Empress Wu Zhao (WOO ZHOW) in the late seventh century, sought to limit the power of the great families by recruiting officials through the civil service examinations, but in the end it was the expansion of regional power—often under non-Chinese military governors—after the revolt in 755 that sounded the death knell to the aristocratic system.

Perhaps the most significant development during the Song dynasty was the rise of the landed gentry as the most influential force in Chinese society. The gentry controlled much of the wealth in the rural areas and produced the majority of the candidates for the bureaucracy. By virtue of their possession of land and specialized knowledge of the Confucian classics, the gentry had replaced the aristocracy as the political and economic elite of Chinese society. Unlike the aristocracy, however, the gentry did not form an exclusive class. Upward and downward mobility between the scholar-gentry and the remainder of the population was not uncommon and may have been a key factor in the stability of the system. A position in the bureaucracy opened the doors to wealth and prestige for the individual and his family but was no guarantee of success, and the fortunes of individual families might experience a rapid rise and fall.

For affluent Chinese in this era, life offered many more pleasures than had been available to their ancestors. There were new forms of entertainment, such as playing cards and chess (brought from India, although an early form had been invented in China during the Zhou dynasty); new forms of transportation, such as the paddle-wheel boat and horseback riding (made possible by the introduction of the stirrup); and better means of communication (block printing was first invented in the eighth century C.E.). Tea, which had been introduced from the Burmese frontier by monks as early as the Han dynasty, began to emerge as a national drink, and brandy and other distilled spirits made their appearance in the seventh century.

VILLAGE AND FAMILY The vast majority of the Chinese people still lived in rural villages. Their lives were bounded by their village. Although many communities were connected to the outside world by roads or rivers, most Chinese rarely left their native village except for an occasional visit to a nearby market town.

An even more basic unit than the village for most Chinese, of course, was the family. The ideal was the joint family with at least three generations under one roof. Because of the heavy labor requirements of rice farming, the tradition of the joint family was especially prevalent in the south. When a son married, he was expected to bring his new wife back to live in his parents' home.

Chinese village architecture reflected these traditions. Most family dwellings were simple, consisting of one or two rooms. They were usually constructed of dried mud, stone, or brick, depending on available materials and the family's prosperity. Roofs were of thatch or tile, and the floors were usually of packed dirt. Large houses were often built in a square around an inner courtyard.

Within the family unit, the eldest male theoretically ruled as an autocrat. He was responsible for presiding over ancestral rites at an altar, usually in the main room of the house. He had traditional legal rights over his wife, and if she did not provide him with a male heir, he was permitted to take a second wife. The wife, however, had no recourse to divorce. As the old saying went, "Marry a chicken, follow the chicken; marry a dog, follow the dog." Wealthy Chinese might keep concubines, who lived in a separate room in the house and sometimes competed with the legal wife for precedence.

In accordance with Confucian tradition, children were expected, above all, to obey their parents, who not only determined their children's careers but also selected their marriage partners. Filial piety was viewed as an absolute moral good, above virtually all other moral obligations.

THE ROLE OF WOMEN The tradition of male superiority continued from ancient times into the medieval era, especially under the southern Song when it was reinforced by Neo-Confucianism (see the box on p. 261). Female children were considered less desirable than males because they could not undertake heavy work in the fields or carry on the family traditions. Poor families often sold their daughters to wealthy villagers to serve as concubines, and in times of famine, female infanticide was not uncommon to ensure that there would be food for the remainder of the family.

During the Song era, two new practices emerged that changed the equation for women seeking to obtain a successful marriage contract. First, a new form of dowry appeared. Whereas previously the prospective husband offered the bride's family a bride price, now the reverse became the norm, with the bride's parents paying the groom's family a dowry. With the prosperity that characterized much of the Song era, affluent parents sought to buy a satisfactory husband for their daughter, preferably one with a higher social standing and good prospects for an official career.

A second source of marital bait during the Song period was the promise of a bride with tiny bound feet. The process of **foot binding**, carried out on girls aged five to thirteen, was excruciatingly painful, as it bent and compressed the foot to half its normal size by imprisoning it in restrictive bandages. But the procedure was often performed by ambitious mothers intent on assuring their daughters of the best possible prospects for marriage. Bound feet represented submissiveness and self-discipline, two attributes of the ideal Confucian wife.

Throughout northern China, foot binding became common for women of all social classes. It was less common in southern China, where the cultivation of wet rice could not be carried out with bandaged feet; there it tended to be limited to the scholar-gentry. Still, most Chinese women with bound feet contributed to the labor force to supplement the family income. Although foot binding was eventually prohibited, the practice lasted into the twentieth century, particularly in rural villages.

As in most traditional societies, there were exceptions to the low status of women in Chinese society. Women had substantial property rights and retained control over their dowries even after divorce or the death of the husband. Wives were frequently an influential force within the home, often handling the accounts and taking primary responsibility for raising the children. Some were active in politics. The outstanding example was Wu Zhao (c. 625–c. 706), popularly known as Empress Wu. Selected by Emperor Tang Taizong as a concubine, after his death she rose to a position of supreme power at court. At first, she was content to rule through her sons, but in 690, she declared herself empress of China. For her presumption, she has been vilified by later Chinese historians, but she was actually a quite capable ruler. She was responsible for giving meaning to the civil service examination system and was the first to select graduates of the examinations for the highest positions in government. During her last years, she reportedly fell under the influence of courtiers and was deposed in 705, when she was probably around eighty.

The Saintly Miss Wu

The idea that a wife should sacrifice her wants to the needs of her husband and family was deeply embedded in traditional Chinese society. Widows in particular had few rights, and their remarriage was strongly condemned. In this account from a story by Hung Mai (hoong MY), a twelfth-century writer, the widowed Miss Wu wins the respect of the entire community by faithfully serving her mother-in-law.

Hung Mai, *A Song Family Saga*

Miss Wu served her mother-in-law very filially. Her mother-in-law had an eye ailment and felt sorry for her daughter-in-law's solitary and poverty-stricken situation, so she suggested that they call in a son-in-law for her and thereby get an adoptive heir. Miss Wu announced in tears, "A woman does not serve two husbands. I will support you. Don't talk this way." Her mother-in-law, seeing that she was determined, did not press her. Miss Wu did spinning, washing, sewing, cooking, and cleaning for her neighbors, earning perhaps a hundred cash a day, all of which she gave to her mother-in-law to cover the cost of firewood and food. If she was given any meat, she would wrap it up to take home. . . .

Once when her mother-in-law was cooking rice, a neighbor called to her, and to avoid overcooking the rice she dumped it into a pan. Owing to her bad eyes, however, she mistakenly put it in the dirty chamber pot. When Miss Wu returned and saw it, she did not say a word. She went to a neighbor to borrow some cooked rice for her mother-in-law and took the dirty rice and washed it to eat herself.

One day in the daytime neighbors saw [Miss Wu] ascending into the sky amid colored clouds. Startled, they told her mother-in-law, who said, "Don't be foolish. She just came back from pounding rice for someone, and is lying down on the bed. Go and look." They went to the room and peeked in and saw her sound asleep. Amazed, they left.

When Miss Wu woke up, her mother-in-law told her what happened, and she said, "I just dreamed of two young boys in blue clothes holding documents and riding on the clouds. They grabbed my clothes and said the Emperor of Heaven had summoned me. They took me to the gate of heaven and I was brought in to see the emperor, who was seated beside a balustrade. He said 'Although you are just a lowly ignorant village woman, you are able to serve your old mother-in-law sincerely and work hard. You really deserve respect.' He gave me a cup of aromatic wine and a string of cash, saying, 'I will supply you. From now on you will not need to work for others.' I bowed to thank him and came back, accompanied by the two boys. Then I woke up."

There was in fact a thousand cash on the bed, and the room was filled with a fragrance. They then realized that the neighbors' vision had been a spirit journey. From this point on even more people asked her to work for them, and she never refused. But the money that had been given to her she kept for her mother-in-law's use. Whatever they used promptly reappeared, so the thousand cash was never exhausted. The mother-in-law also regained her sight in both eyes.

What is the moral of this story? How do the supernatural elements in the account strengthen the lesson intended by the author?

Source: From *The Inner Quarters: Marriage and the Lives of Chinese Women in the Sung Period,* Patricia Ebrey (Berkeley, University of California Press, 1993), pp. 197–198.

Explosion in Central Asia: The Mongol Empire

FOCUS QUESTION: Why were the Mongols able to amass an empire, and what were the main characteristics of their rule in China?

The Mongols, who succeeded the Song as the rulers of China in 1279, rose to power in Asia with stunning rapidity. In the latter half of the twelfth century, the Mongols were a relatively obscure pastoral people in the region of modern Outer Mongolia. Like most of the nomadic peoples in the region, they were organized loosely into clans and tribes and even lacked a common name for themselves. Rivalry among the various tribes over pasture, livestock, and booty was intense and increased at the end of the twelfth century as a result of a growing population and the consequent overgrazing of pastures.

This challenge was met by Temuchin (TEM-yuh-jin) (or Temujin), who became the great Mongol chieftan

Genghis Khan (JING-uss *or* GENG-uss KAHN) (also known as Chinggis Khan) (c. 1162–1227). When Temuchin was still a child, his father was murdered by a rival, and the boy was forced to seek refuge in the wilderness. Described as tall, adroit, and vigorous, young Temuchin gradually unified the Mongol tribes through his prowess and the power of his personality. In 1206, he was elected Genghis Khan ("universal ruler") at a massive tribal meeting in the Gobi Desert. From that time on, he devoted himself to military pursuits. "Man's highest joy," Genghis Khan reportedly remarked, "is in victory: to conquer one's enemies, to pursue them, to deprive them of their possessions, to make their beloved weep, to ride on their horses, and to embrace their wives and daughters."[5]

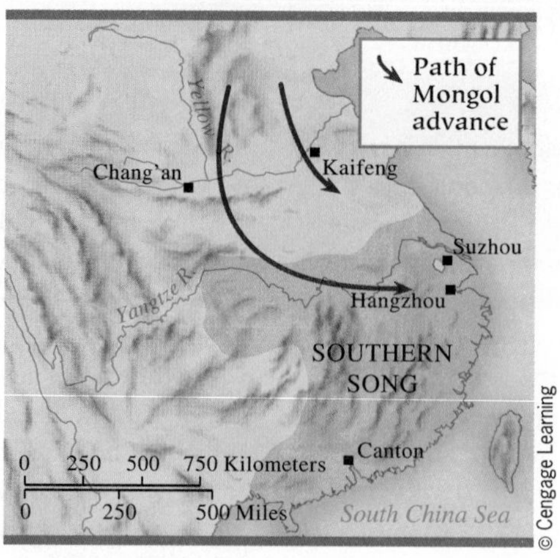

The Mongol Conquest of China

The army that Genghis Khan unleashed on the world was not exceptionally large—totaling less than 130,000 in 1227, at a time when the total Mongol population numbered between 1 and 2 million. But their mastery of military tactics set the Mongols apart. Their tireless flying columns of mounted warriors surrounded their enemies and harassed them like cattle, luring them into pursuit and then ambushing them with flank attacks.

The Mongols first defeated tribal groups to their west and then turned their attention to the seminomadic non-Chinese kingdoms of northern China. There they discovered that their adversaries were armed with a weapon called a firelance, an early form of flame-thrower that could spew out flames and projectiles a distance of 30 or 40 yards. By the end of the thirteenth century, the firelance had evolved into the much more effective handgun and cannon. These inventions came too late to save China from the Mongols, however, and were transmitted to Europe by the early fourteenth century by foreigners employed by the Mongol rulers of China.

While some Mongol armies were engaged in the conquest of northern China, others traveled farther afield and advanced as far as central Europe. Only the death of Genghis Khan in 1227 may have prevented an all-out Mongol attack on western Europe (see the box on p. 263). In 1231, the Mongols attacked Persia and then defeated the Abbasids at Baghdad in 1258 (see Chapter 7). Mongol forces attacked the Song from the west in the 1260s and finally defeated the remnants of the Song navy in 1279.

By then, the Mongol Empire was quite different from what it had been under its founder. Prior to the conquests of Genghis Khan, the Mongols had been purely nomadic. They spent their winters in the southern plains, where they found pasture for their cattle, and traveled north in the summer. They lived in round, felt-covered tents (called yurts), which were lightly constructed so that they could be easily transported. For food, the Mongols depended on milk and meat from their herds and game from hunting.

To administer the new empire, Genghis Khan had set up a capital city at Karakorum (kah-rah-KOR-um), in present-day Outer Mongolia, but prohibited his fellow Mongols from practicing sedentary occupations or living in cities. But under his successors, the Mongols began to adapt to their conquered areas. As one khan remarked, quoting his Chinese adviser, "Although you inherited the Chinese Empire on horseback, you cannot rule it from that position." Mongol aristocrats began to enter administrative positions, while commoners took up sedentary occupations as farmers or merchants.

The territorial nature of the empire also changed. Following tribal custom, at the death of the ruling khan, the territory was distributed among his heirs. The once-united empire of Genghis Khan was thus divided into several separate **khanates** (KHAH-nayts), each ruled by one of his sons by his principal wife. One son was awarded the khanate of Chaghadai (chag-huh-DY) in Central Asia with its capital at Samarkand; another ruled Persia from Baghdad; a third received the khanate of Kipchak (KIP-chahk), commonly known as the Golden Horde. But it was one of his grandsons, named Khubilai Khan (1215–1294), who completed the conquest of the Song and established a new Chinese dynasty, called the Yuan (from a phrase in the *Book of Changes* referring to the "original creative force" of the universe). Khubilai moved the capital of China northward from Hangzhou to Khanbaliq ("city of the khan"), which was located on a major trunk route from the Great Wall to the plains of northern China (see Map 10.2). Later the city would be known by the Chinese name Beijing (bay-ZHING), or Peking (pee-KING) ("northern capital").

OPPOSING ≺ VIEWPOINTS

A Meeting of Two Worlds

In 1245, Pope Innocent IV dispatched the Franciscan friar John Plano Carpini (PLAN-oh car-PEE-nee) to the Mongol headquarters at Karakorum with a written appeal to the great khan Kuyuk (koo-YOOK) to cease his attacks on Christians. After a considerable wait, Plano Carpini was given the following reply, which could not have pleased the pope. The letter was discovered recently in the Vatican archives.

A Letter from Pope Innocent IV to Kuyuk Khan

It is not without cause that we are driven to express in strong terms our amazement that you, as we have heard, have invaded many countries belonging to Christians and to others and are laying them waste in a horrible desolation. . . . Following the example of the King of Peace, and desiring that all men should live united in concord in the fear of God, we do admonish, beg, and earnestly beseech all of you that for the future you desist entirely from assaults of this kind and especially from the persecution of Christians, and that after so many and such grievous offenses you conciliate by a fitting penance the wrath of Divine Majesty. . . . On this account we have thought fit to send to you our beloved son [Friar John] and his companions, the bearers of this letter. . . . When you have had profitable discussions with them concerning the aforesaid affairs, especially those pertaining to peace, make fully known to us through these same friars what moved you to destroy other nations and what your intentions are for the future.

A Letter from Kuyuk Khan to Pope Innocent IV

By the power of the Eternal Heaven, We are the all-embracing Khan of all the Great Nations. It is our command:

This is a decree, sent to the great Pope that he may know and pay heed.

After holding counsel with the monarchs under your suzerainty, you have sent us an offer of subordination, which we have accepted from the hands of your envoy.

If you should act up to your word, then you, the great Pope, should come in person with the monarchs to pay us homage and we should thereupon instruct you concerning the commands of the Yasak.

Furthermore, you have said it would be well for us to become Christians. You write to me in person about this matter, and have addressed to me a request. This, your request, we cannot understand.

Furthermore, you have written me these words: "You have attacked all the territories of the Magyars and other Christians, at which I am astonished. Tell me, what was their crime?" These, your words, we likewise cannot understand. Jenghiz Khan and Ogatai Khakan revealed the commands of Heaven. But those whom you name would not believe the commands of Heaven. Those of whom you speak showed themselves highly presumptuous and slew our envoys. Therefore, in accordance with the commands of the Eternal Heaven the inhabitants of the aforesaid countries have been slain and annihilated. If not by the command of Heaven, how can anyone slay or conquer out of his own strength?

And when you say: "I am a Christian. I pray to God. I arraign and despise others," how do you know who is pleasing to God and to whom He allots His grace? How can you know it, that you speak such words?

Thanks to the power of the Eternal Heaven, all lands have been given to us from sunrise to sunset. How could anyone act other than in accordance with the commands of Heaven? Now your own upright heart must tell you: "We will become subject to you, and will place our powers at your disposal." You in person, at the head of the monarchs, all of you, without exception, must come to tender us service and pay us homage, then only will we recognize your submission. But if you do not obey the commands of Heaven, and run counter to our orders, we shall know that you are our foe.

That is what we have to tell you. If you fail to act in accordance therewith, how can we foresee what will happen to you? Heaven alone knows.

Based on these selections, what message was the pope seeking to convey to the great khan in Karakorum? What was the nature of the latter's reply?

Sources: A Letter from Pope Innocent IV to Kuyuk Khan. From I. Rachewiltz, *Papal Envoys to the Great Khans* (Stanford, 1971). A Letter from Kuyuk Khan to Pope Innocent IV. From Prawdin, Michael, *The Mongol Empire: Its Rise and Legacy* (Free Press, 1961), pp. 280–281.

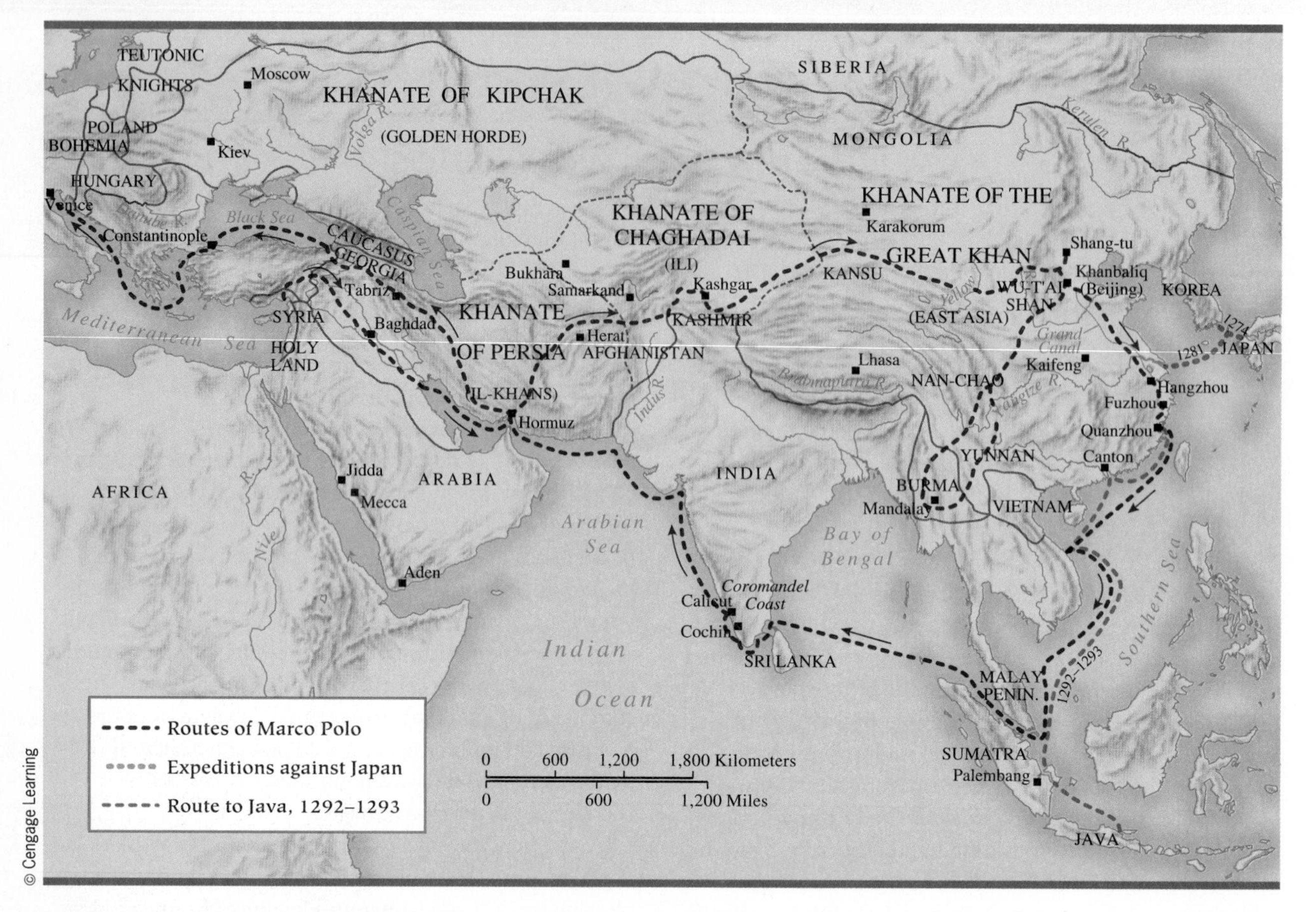

© Cengage Learning

MAP 10.2 Asia Under the Mongols. This map traces the expansion of Mongol power throughout Eurasia in the thirteenth century. After the death of Genghis Khan in 1227, the empire was divided into four separate khanates.

Why was the Mongol Empire divided into four separate khanates?

Mongol Rule in China

At first, China's new rulers exhibited impressive vitality. Under Khubilai Khan, the Yuan continued to flex their muscles by attempting to expand their empire. Mongol armies advanced into the Red River valley and reconquered Vietnam, which had declared its independence after the fall of the Tang three hundred years earlier. Mongol fleets were launched against Malay kingdoms in Java and Sumatra and also against Japan. Only the expedition against Vietnam succeeded, however, and even that success was temporary. The Vietnamese counterattacked and eventually drove the Mongols back across the border. The attempted conquest of Japan was even more disastrous. On one occasion, a massive storm destroyed the Mongol fleet, killing thousands (see Chapter 11).

The Mongols had more success in governing China. After a failed attempt to administer their conquest as they had ruled their own tribal society (some advisers reportedly even suggested that the plowed fields be transformed into pastures), Mongol rulers adapted to the Chinese political system and made use of local talents in the bureaucracy. The tripartite division of the administration into civilian, military, and censorate was retained, as were the six ministries. The civil service system, which had been abolished in the north in 1237 and in the south forty years later, was revived in the early fourteenth century. The state cult of Confucius was also restored, although Khubilai Khan himself remained a Buddhist.

But there were some key differences. Culturally, the Mongols were nothing like the Chinese and remained a separate class with their own laws. The highest positions in the bureaucracy were usually staffed by Mongols. Although some leading Mongols followed their ruler in converting to Buddhism, most commoners retained their traditional religion.

FILM & HISTORY

The Adventures of Marco Polo (1938) and *Marco Polo* (2007)

Courtesy The Everett Collection, Inc.

Scene from *The Adventures of Marco Polo* (1938). Marco Polo (Gary Cooper, gesturing on the right) confers with Kaidu (Alan Hale), leader of the Mongols.

The famous story of Marco Polo's trip to East Asia in the late thirteenth century has sparked the imagination of Western readers ever since. The son of an Italian merchant from Venice, Polo went to China in 1270 and did not return for twenty-four years, traveling east via the Silk Road and returning by sea across the Indian Ocean. Captured by the Genoese in 1298 and tossed into prison, he recounted his experiences to a professional writer known as Rusticello of Pisa. Copies of the resulting book were soon circulating throughout Europe, and one even found its way into the hands of Christopher Columbus, who used it as a source for information on the eastern lands he sought during his own travels. Marco Polo's adventures have been translated into numerous languages, thrilling readers around the world.

But did Marco Polo actually visit China, or was the book an elaborate hoax? In recent years, some historians have expressed doubts about the veracity of his account. Frances Wood, author *of Did Marco Polo Go to China?* (1996), provoked a lively debate in academic circles with the suggestion that he might have simply recounted tales that he heard from contemporaries.

Such reservations aside, filmmakers have long been fascinated by Marco Polo's story. The first Hollywood production, *The Adventures of Marco Polo* (1938), starred Gary Cooper, with Basil Rathbone as his evil nemesis in China. Like many film epics of the era, it was highly entertaining but not historically accurate. The most recent version, a Hallmark Channel production called *Marco Polo*, appeared in 2007 and starred the young American actor Ian Somerhalder in the title role. The film is a reasonably faithful rendition of the book, with stirring battle scenes, the predictable "cast of thousands," and a somewhat unlikely love interest between Marco Polo and a Mongol princess thrown in. Although Somerhalder is not particularly convincing in the title role—after two grueling decades in Asia, he still bears a striking resemblance to a teenage surfing idol—the filmmakers should be credited for their efforts to portray China as the most advanced civilization of its day. A number of Chinese inventions then unknown in Europe, such as paper money, explosives, and the compass, appear in the film.

Despite these differences, some historians believe that the Mongol dynasty won considerable support from the majority of the Chinese. The people of the north, after all, were used to foreign rule, and although those living farther to the south may have resented their alien conquerors, they probably came to respect the stability, unity, and economic prosperity that the Mongols initially brought to China.

Indeed, the Mongols' greatest achievement may have been the prosperity they fostered. At home, they continued the relatively tolerant economic policies of the southern Song, and by bringing much of the Eurasian landmass under a single rule, they encouraged long-distance trade, particularly along the Silk Road, now dominated by Muslim merchants from Central Asia. To promote trade, the Grand Canal was extended from the Yellow River to the capital. Adjacent to the canal, a paved highway was constructed that extended all the way from the Song capital of Hangzhou to its Mongol counterpart at Khanbaliq.

The capital was a magnificent city. According to the Italian merchant Marco Polo, who resided there during the reign of Khubilai Khan, it was 24 miles in diameter and surrounded by thick walls of earth (see the Film & History feature above). He described the old Song capital of Hangzhou as a noble city where "so many pleasures may be found that one fancies himself to be in Paradise."

But the Yuan eventually fell victim to the same fate that had afflicted other powerful dynasties in China. Excessive spending on foreign campaigns, inadequate tax revenues, and factionalism and corruption at court and in the bureaucracy all contributed to the dynasty's demise. Khubilai Khan's successors lacked his administrative genius, and by the middle of the fourteenth century, the Yuan dynasty in China, like the Mongol khanates elsewhere in Central Asia, had fallen into a rapid decline.

The immediate instrument of Mongol defeat was Zhu Yuanzhang (JOO yoo-wen-JAHNG) (Chu Yuan-chang), the son of a poor peasant in the lower Yangtze valley. After losing most of his family during a famine, Zhu became the leader of a band of bandits. In the 1360s, unrest spread throughout the country, and after defeating a number of rivals, Zhu Yuanzhang put an end to the disintegrating Yuan regime and declared the foundation of a new Ming (MING) ("bright") dynasty (1369–1644).

The Mongols' Place in History

The Mongols were the last, and arguably the greatest, of the nomadic peoples who came out of the steppes of Central Asia, pillaging and conquering the territories of their adversaries. What caused this burst of energy, and why were the Mongols so much more successful than their predecessors? Some historians have suggested that drought and overpopulation may have depleted the available pasture on the steppes. Others have cited the genius of Genghis Khan and his ability to arouse a sense of personal loyalty. Still others point to his reliance on the organizational unit known as the *ordos* (OR-dohz), described by historian Samuel Adshead as "a system of restructuring tribes into decimal units whose top level of leadership was organized on bureaucratic lines."[6] Although other nomadic peoples had also used the *ordos*, the Mongols applied it to create disciplined and highly effective military units. Once organized, the Mongols used their superior horsemanship and blitzkrieg tactics effectively, while taking advantage of divisions within the enemy ranks and borrowing more advanced military technology.

Once in power, however, the Mongols' underlying weaknesses eventually proved fatal. The Mongols had difficulty making the transition from the nomadic life of the steppes to the sedentary life, and their unwieldy system of royal succession led to instability. Still, although the Mongol era was brief, it was rich in consequences.

THE MONGOLS: A REPUTATION UNDESERVED? The era of Mongol expansion has usually been portrayed as a tragic period in human history. Certainly, the Mongols' conquests resulted in widespread death and destruction throughout the civilized world. And the Black Death (bubonic plague), probably carried by lice hidden in the saddlebags of Mongol horsemen, decimated the population of Europe and the Middle East (see Chapter 13), with severe economic consequences.

Few modern historians would dispute the brutality that characterized Mongol expansion. But some now point out that beyond the legacy of death and destruction, the Mongols also brought an era of widespread peace, known as the *Pax Mongolica* (PAKS *or* PAHKS mahn-GOH-lik-uh), to much of the Eurasian supercontinent and inaugurated what one scholar has described as "the idea of the unified conceptualization of the globe," creating a "basic information circuit" that spread commodities, ideas, and inventions from one end of the Eurasian supercontinent to the other. That being said, there is no denying that the Mongol invasions resulted in widespread suffering and misfortune. If there was a Mongol peace, it was, for many, the peace of death.

The Ming Dynasty

FOCUS QUESTIONS: What were the chief initiatives taken by the early rulers of the Ming dynasty to enhance the role of China in the world? Why did the imperial court order the famous voyages of Zhenghe, and why were they discontinued?

The Ming inaugurated a new era of greatness in Chinese history. Under a series of strong rulers, China extended its rule into Mongolia and Central Asia. The Ming even briefly reconquered Vietnam. Along the northern frontier, the emperor Yongle (YOONG-luh) (Yung Lo, 1402–1424) strengthened the Great Wall and pacified the nomadic tribespeople who had troubled China in previous centuries (see the comparative illustration on p. 267). A tributary relationship was established with the Yi (YEE) dynasty in Korea.

The internal achievements of the Ming were equally impressive. When they replaced the Mongols in the fourteenth century, the Ming turned to traditional Confucian institutions as a means of ruling their vast empire. These included the six ministries at the apex of the bureaucracy, the use of civil service examinations to select members of the bureaucracy, and the division of the empire into provinces, districts, and counties.

The society that was governed by this vast hierarchy of officials was a far cry from the predominantly agrarian society that had been ruled by the Han. In the burgeoning cities near the coast and along the Yangtze River valley, factories and workshops were vastly increasing the

© Robert Harding Picture Library/SuperStock
© William J. Duiker

COMPARATIVE ILLUSTRATION

The Great Walls of China. Although the Great Wall is popularly believed to be more than two thousand years old, the part of the wall that is most frequently visited by tourists today was a reconstruction undertaken during the early Ming dynasty to protect against invasion from the north. Part of that wall, which was built to protect the imperial capital of Beijing, is shown at the top. The original walls, which stretched from the shores of the Pacific Ocean to the deserts of Central Asia, were often composed of loose stone, dirt, or piled rubble. The section shown in the inset is located north of the Turfan Depression in Xinjiang Province.

What were the major reasons for building the Great Wall? To what degree was the wall successful in achieving these objectives?

variety and output of their manufactured goods. The population had doubled, and new crops had been introduced, greatly expanding the food output of the empire.

The Voyages of Zhenghe

In 1405, in a splendid display of Chinese maritime might, Yongle sent a fleet of Chinese trading ships under the eunuch admiral Zhenghe (JEHNG-huh) (Cheng Ho) through the Strait of Malacca and out into the Indian Ocean; there they traveled as far west as the east coast of Africa, stopping on the way at ports in South Asia. The size of the fleet was impressive: it included nearly 28,000 sailors on sixty-two ships, some of them junks larger by far than any other oceangoing vessels the world had yet seen. China seemed about to become a direct participant in the vast trade network that extended as far west as the Atlantic Ocean.

Why the expeditions were undertaken has been a matter of some debate. Some historians assume that economic profit was the main reason. Others point to Yongle's native curiosity and note that the voyage—and the six others that followed it—returned not only with goods but also with a plethora of information about the outside world as well as with some items unknown in China (the emperor was especially intrigued by the giraffes and installed them in the imperial zoo).

Whatever the case, the voyages resulted in a dramatic increase in Chinese knowledge about the world and the nature of ocean travel. They also brought massive profits for their sponsors, including individuals connected with

Admiral Zhenghe at court. This aroused resentment among conservatives within the bureaucracy, some of whom viewed commercial activities with a characteristic measure of Confucian disdain.

Shortly after Yongle's death, the voyages were discontinued, never to be revived. The decision had long-term consequences and in the eyes of many modern historians marks a turning inward of the Chinese state, away from commerce and toward a more traditional emphasis on agriculture, away from the exotic lands to the south and toward the heartland of the country in the Yellow River valley. The imperial capital was moved from Nanjing (nahn-JING), in central China, back to Beijing.

WHY WERE ZHENGHE'S VOYAGES ABANDONED? Why the Ming government discontinued Zhenghe's explorations has long been a quandary. Was it simply a consequence of court intrigues or the replacement of one emperor by another, or were deeper issues involved? Some scholars speculate that the real purpose of the voyages was "power projection" and that when local rulers throughout the South Seas had been sufficiently intimidated to accept a tributary relationship with their "elder brother" in China, such expensive voyages were no longer necessary.

One recent theory that has spurred scholarly debate contends that the fleets actually circled the earth and discovered the existence of the Western Hemisphere. Although that theory has won few scholarly adherents, the voyages, and their abrupt discontinuance, remain one of the most fascinating enigmas in the history of China.

In Search of the Way

FOCUS QUESTION: What roles did Buddhism, Daoism, and Neo-Confucianism play in Chinese intellectual life in the period between the Sui dynasty and the Ming?

By the time of the Sui dynasty, Buddhism and Daoism had emerged as major rivals of Confucianism as the ruling ideology of the state. But during the last half of the Tang dynasty, Confucianism revived and once again became dominant at court, a position it would retain to the end of the dynastic period in the early twentieth century. Buddhist and Daoist beliefs, however, remained popular at the local level.

The Rise and Decline of Buddhism and Daoism

As noted earlier, Buddhism arrived in China with merchants from India and found its first adherents among the merchant community and intellectuals. During the chaotic centuries following the collapse of the Han dynasty, Buddhism and Daoism appealed to those who were searching for more emotional and spiritual satisfaction than Confucianism could provide. Both faiths reached beyond the common people and found support among the ruling classes as well.

THE SINIFICATION OF BUDDHISM As Buddhism attracted more followers, it began to take on Chinese characteristics and divided into a number of separate sects. Some, like the **Chan** (Zen in Japanese) sect, called for mind training and a strict regimen as a means of seeking enlightenment (see the box on p. 269). Others, like the **Pure Land** sect, stressed the role of devotion, an approach that was more appealing to ordinary Chinese, who lacked the time and inclination for strict monastic discipline. Still others were mystical sects, like **Tantrism** (TUHN-tri-zum), which emphasized the importance of magical symbols and ritual. Some Buddhist groups, like their Daoist counterparts, had political objectives. The **White Lotus** sect, founded in 1133, often adopted the form of a rebel movement, seeking political reform or the overthrow of a dynasty and forecasting a new era when a "savior Buddha" would come to earth to herald the advent of a new age. Most believers, however, assimilated Buddhism into their daily lives, where it joined Confucian ideology and spirit worship as an element in the highly eclectic and tolerant Chinese worldview.

The burgeoning popularity of Buddhism continued into the early years of the Tang dynasty. Early Tang rulers lent their support to the Buddhist monasteries that had been established throughout the country. But ultimately, Buddhism and Daoism lost favor at court. Daoists and Confucianists made a point of criticizing the foreign origins of Buddhist doctrines, which one prominent Confucian scholar characterized as nothing but "silly relics." But another reason for this change of heart may have been financial. The great Buddhist monasteries had accumulated thousands of acres of land and serfs that were exempt from paying taxes. As the state attempted to eliminate the great landholdings of the aristocracy, the large monasteries also attracted its attention. During the later Tang, countless temples and monasteries were destroyed, and more than 100,000 monks were compelled to leave the monasteries and return to secular life.

BUDDHISM UNDER THREAT Yet there were probably deeper political and ideological reasons for the growing antagonism between Buddhism and the state. By preaching the illusory nature of the material world, Buddhism was denying the essence of Confucian teachings—the necessity for filial piety and hard work. By encouraging young Chinese to abandon their fields and seek wisdom in the monasteries, Buddhism was undermining the foundation stones of Chinese society—the family unit and the work ethic. Ultimately, Buddhism was incompatible with the activist element in Chinese society. In the

The Way of the Great Buddha

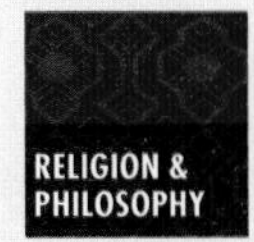
RELIGION & PHILOSOPHY

According to Buddhists, it is impossible to describe the state of Nirvana, which is sometimes depicted as an extinction of self. Yet Buddhist scholars found it difficult to avoid trying to interpret the term for their followers. The following passage by the Chinese monk Shen-Hui (shun-HWEE), one of the leading exponents of Chan Buddhism, dates from the eighth century and attempts to describe the means by which an individual may hope to seek enlightenment. There are clear similarities with philosophical Daoism.

Shen-Hui, *Elucidating the Doctrine*

"Absence of thought" is the doctrine.

"Absence of action" is the foundation.

True Emptiness is the substance.

And all wonderful things and beings are the function.

True Thusness is without thought; it cannot be known through conception and thought.

The True State is noncreated—can it be seen in matter and mind?

There is no thought except that of True Thusness.

There is no creation except that of the True State.

Abiding without abiding, forever abiding in Nirvana.

Acting without acting, immediately crossing to the Other Shore.

Thusness does not move, but its motion and functions are inexhaustible.

In every instant of thought, there is no seeking; the seeking itself is no thought.

Perfect wisdom is not achieved, and yet the Five Eyes all become pure and the Three Bodies are understood.

Great Enlightenment has no knowledge, and yet the Six Supernatural Powers of the Buddha are utilized and the Four Wisdoms of the Buddha are made great.

Thus, we know that calmness is at the same time no calmness, wisdom at the same time no wisdom, and action at the same time no action.

The nature is equivalent to the void and the substance is identical with the Realm of Law.

In this way, the Six Perfections are completed.

None of the ways to arrive at Nirvana is wanting.

Thus, we know that the ego and the dharmas are empty in reality and being and nonbeing are both obliterated.

The mind is originally without activity; the Way is always without thought.

No thought, no reflection, no seeking, no attainment;

No this, no that, no coming, no going.

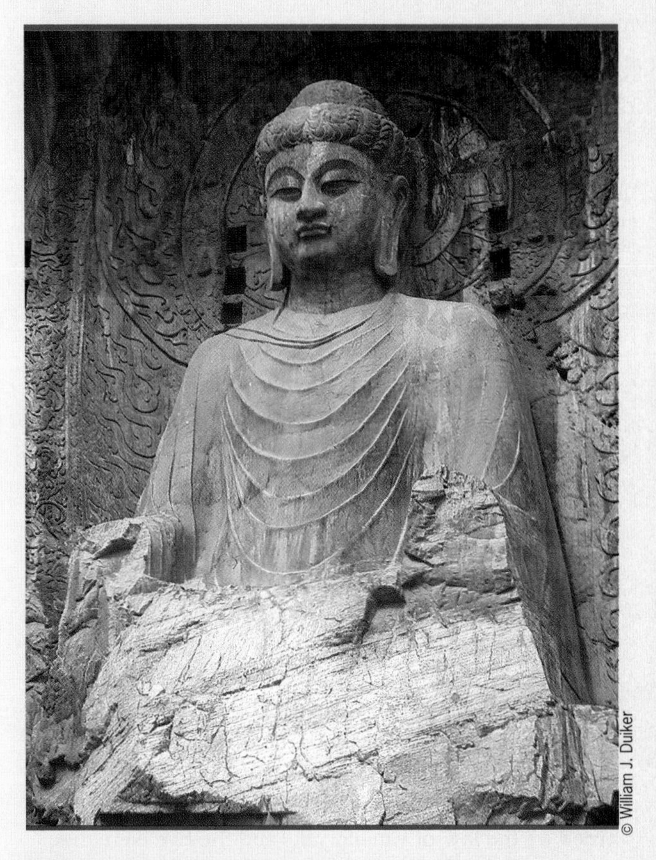
© William J. Duiker

Buddhist Sculpture at Longmen. In the seventh century, the Tang emperor Gaozong (gow-ZOONG) commissioned this massive cliffside carving as part of a large complex of cave art devoted to the Buddha at Longmen (LAHNG-mun) in central China. Bold and grandiose in its construction, this towering statue of the Buddha, surrounded by temple guardians and bodhisattvas, reflects the glory of the Tang dynasty.

With such reality one understands the True Insight [into previous and future mortal conditions and present mortal suffering].

With such a mind one penetrates the Eight Emancipations [through the eight stages of mental concentration].

By merits one accomplishes the Ten Powers of the Buddha.

What similarities with philosophical Daoism are expressed in this passage? Compare and contrast the views expressed here with the Neo-Confucian worldview.

Source: Excerpt from *Sources of Chinese Tradition*, by William Theodore de Bary. Copyright © 1960 by Columbia University Press. Reprinted with the permission of the publisher.

competition with Confucianism for support by the state, Buddhism, like Daoism, was almost certain to lose.

Neo-Confucianism: The Investigation of Things

Into the vacuum left by the decline of Buddhism and Daoism stepped a revived Confucianism. Challenged by Buddhist and Daoist ideas about the nature of the universe, Confucian thinkers began to flesh out the spare metaphysical structure of classical Confucian doctrine with a set of sophisticated theories about the nature of the cosmos and humans' place in it.

The fundamental purpose of **Neo-Confucianism**, as the new doctrine was called, was to unite the metaphysical speculations of Buddhism and Daoism with the pragmatic Confucian approach to society. In response to Buddhism and Daoism, Neo-Confucianism maintained that the world is real, not illusory, and that fulfillment comes from participation, not withdrawal.

The primary contributor to this intellectual effort was the philosopher Zhu Xi (JOO SHEE) (Chu Hsi). Raised during the southern Song era, Zhu Xi accepted the division of the world into a material world and a transcendent world, called the **Supreme Ultimate**, or *Tai Ji* (TY JEE), which was roughly equivalent to the *Dao*, or Way, in classical Confucian philosophy. To Zhu Xi, this Supreme Ultimate was a set of abstract principles governed by the law of *yin* and *yang* and the five elements.

Human beings served as a link between the two halves of this universe. Although human beings live in the material world, each individual has an identity that is linked with the Supreme Ultimate, and the goal of individual action is to transcend the material world in a Buddhist sense to achieve an essential identity with the Supreme Ultimate. According to Zhu Xi and his followers, this transcendence occurs through self-cultivation, which is achieved by the "investigation of things."

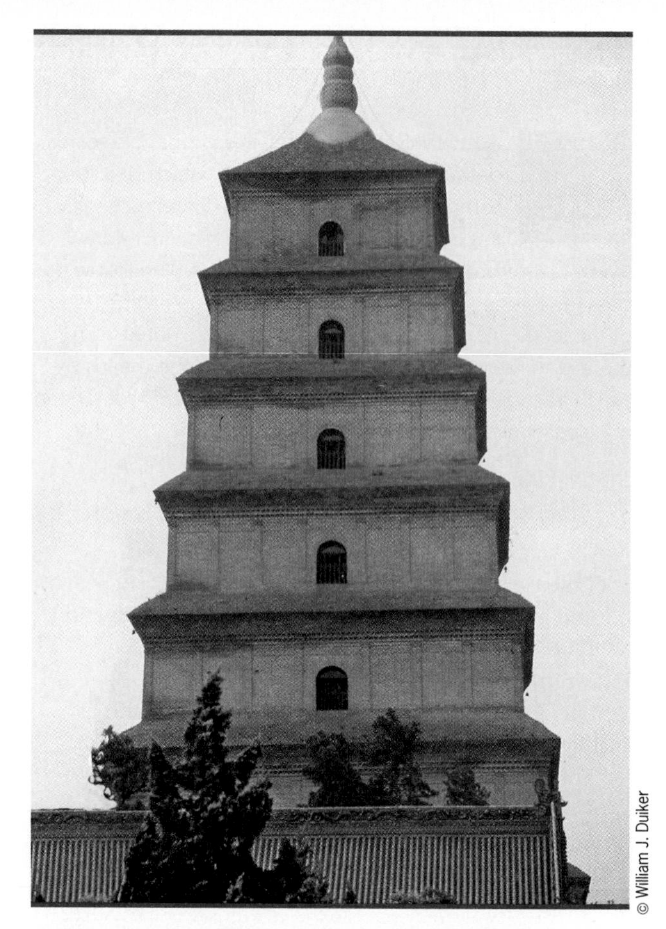

© William J. Duiker

The Big Goose Pagoda. When the Buddhist pilgrim Xuan Zang returned to China from India in the mid-seventh century C.E., he settled in the capital of Chang'an, where, under orders from the Tang emperor, he began to translate Buddhist texts in his possession from Sanskrit into Chinese. The Big Goose Pagoda, shown here, was erected shortly afterward to house them. Originally known as the Pagoda of the Classics, the structure consists of seven stories and is more than 240 feet high.

THE SCHOOL OF MIND During the remainder of the Song dynasty and into the early years of the Ming, Zhu Xi's ideas became the core of Confucian ideology and a favorite source of questions for the civil service examinations. But during the mid-Ming era, his ideas came under attack from a Confucian scholar named Wang Yangming (WAHNG yahng-MING). Wang and his supporters disagreed with Zhu Xi's focus on learning through an investigation of the outside world and asserted that the correct way to transcend the material world was through an understanding of self. According to this so-called **School of Mind**, the mind and the universe were a single unit. Knowledge was thus intuitive rather than empirical and was obtained through internal self-searching rather than through an investigation of the outside world. The debate is reminiscent of a similar disagreement between followers of the ancient Greek philosophers Plato and Aristotle. Plato had argued that all knowledge comes from within, while Aristotle argued that knowledge resulted from an examination of the external world. Wang Yangming's ideas attracted many followers during the Ming dynasty, and the school briefly rivaled that of Zhu Xi in popularity. Nevertheless, it never won official acceptance, probably because it was too much like Buddhism in denying the importance of a life of participation and social action.

For the average Chinese, of course, an instinctive faith in the existence of household deities or nature spirits continued to take precedence over the intellectual ruminations of Buddhist monks or Confucian scholars. But a prevailing belief in the concept of *karma* and possible rebirth in a next life was one important legacy of the Buddhist connection, while a new manifestation of the Confucian concept of hierarchy was the village god—often believed to live in a prominent tree in the vicinity—who protected the community from wandering evil spirits.

The Apogee of Chinese Culture

FOCUS QUESTION: What were the main achievements in Chinese literature and art in the period between the Tang dynasty and the Ming, and what technological innovations and intellectual developments contributed to these achievements?

The period between the Tang and the Ming dynasties was in many ways the great age of Chinese literature and art. Enriched by Buddhist and Daoist images and themes, Chinese poetry and painting reached the pinnacle of their creativity. Porcelain emerged as the highest form of Chinese ceramics, and sculpture flourished under the influence of styles imported from India and Central Asia.

Literature

The development of Chinese literature was stimulated by two technological innovations: the invention of paper during the Han dynasty and the invention of woodblock printing during the Tang. At first, paper was used for clothing, wrapping material, toilet tissue, and even armor, but by the first century B.C.E., it was being used for writing as well.

In the seventh century C.E., the Chinese developed the technique of carving an entire page of text into a wooden block, inking it, and then pressing it onto a sheet of paper. Ordinarily, a text was printed on a long sheet of paper like a scroll. Then the paper was folded and stitched together to form a book. The earliest printed book known today is a Buddhist text published in 868 C.E.; it is more than 16 feet long. Although the Chinese eventually developed movable type as well, block printing continued to be used until relatively modern times because of the large number of Chinese characters needed to produce a lengthy text. Even with printing, books remained too expensive for most Chinese, but they did help popularize all forms of literary writing among the educated elite.

POETRY Although historical writing and essays continued to be popular, it was in poetry that Chinese from the Tang to the Ming dynasties most effectively expressed their literary talents. Chinese poems celebrated the beauty of nature, the changes of the seasons, and the joys of friendship; others expressed sadness at the brevity of life, old age, and parting. Love poems existed but were neither as intense as Western verse nor as sensual as Indian poetry.

The nature of the Chinese language imposed certain characteristics on Chinese poetry, the first being compactness. The most popular forms were four-line and eight-line poems, with five or seven words in each line. Because Chinese grammar does not rely on case or gender and makes no distinction between verb tenses, five-character Chinese poems were not only brief but often cryptic and ambiguous.

Two eighth-century Tang poets, Li Bo (LEE BOH) (Li Po, sometimes known as Li Bai or Li Taibo) and Du Fu (DOO FOO) (Tu Fu), symbolized the genius of the era. Li Bo was a free spirit whose writing often shifted easily between moods of revelry and melancholy. One of his best-known poems is *Drinking Alone in Moonlight*:

Among the flowers, with a jug of wine,
I drink all alone—no one to share.
Raising my cup, I welcome the moon.
And my shadow joins us, making a threesome.
Alas! the moon won't take part in the drinking,
And my shadow just does whatever I do.
But I'm friends for a while with the moon and
my shadow.[7]

Whereas Li Bo was a carefree Daoist, Du Fu was a sober Confucian whose poems often dealt with historical or ethical issues. Many of his works reflect a concern with social injustice and the plight of the unfortunate rarely found in the writings of his contemporaries.

Neither the poetry nor the prose of the great writers of the Tang and Song dynasties was written for or ever reached the majority of the Chinese population. Chinese peasants and artisans acquired their knowledge of Chinese history, Confucian moralisms, and even Buddhist scripture from a rich oral tradition passed down by storytellers, wandering minstrels, and itinerant monks. One exception is the popular poem *Song of Lasting Pain* by the Tang poet Bo Ju-yi (BOH joo-YEE) (772–846) (see the box on p. 272).

THE CHINESE NOVEL During the Yuan dynasty, new forms of literary creativity, including popular theater and the novel, began to appear. One of the most famous novels was *Tale of the Marshes*, an often violent tale of bandit heroes who at the end of the northern Song banded together to oppose government taxes and official oppression. They stole from those in power to share with the poor. *Tale of the Marshes* is the first prose fiction that describes the daily ordeal of ordinary Chinese people in their own language.

Art

Although painting flourished in China under the Han and reached a level of artistic excellence under the Tang, little remains from those periods. The painting of the Song and the Yuan, however, is considered the apogee of painting in traditional China.

Beautiful Women: The Scapegoats of Legends

One of the most famous episodes in Chinese history occurred during the Tang dynasty when the emperor Xuanzong (shyahn-ZOONG) became infatuated with a beautiful concubine Yang Guifei (yahng gway-FAY). She was put to death after one of her protégés launched a rebellion in 755. Although for centuries Chinese historians have blamed Yang Guifei for distracting the emperor from his imperial duties, the Chinese people have always been fascinated by her passion, her beauty, and her dramatic downfall.

One who sought to capture her story was the Tang poet Bo Ju-yi, whose famous work *Song of Lasting Pain* has captivated Chinese readers for more than 1,300 years. After describing her brutal murder and Xuanzong's inconsolable grief, the poem ends with the emperor and his lover united in everlasting sorrow.

Bo Ju-yi, *Song of Lasting Pain*

Han's sovereign prized the beauty of flesh,
he longed for such as ruins domains;
for many years he ruled the Earth
and sought for one in vain.
A daughter there was of the house of Yang,
just grown to maturity,
raised deep in the women's quarters
where no man knew of her.
When Heaven begets beauteous things,
it is loath to let them be wasted,
so one morning this maiden was chosen
to be by the ruler's side.
When she turned around with smiling glance,
she exuded every charm;
in the harem all who wore powder and paint
of beauty then seemed barren.

In springtime's chill he let her bathe
in Hua-qing Palace's pools
whose warm springs' glistening waters
washed flecks of dried lotions away.
Those in attendance helped her rise,
in helplessness so charming—
this was the moment when first she enjoyed
the flood of royal favor.

She waited his pleasure at banquets,
with never a moment's peace,
their springs were spent in outings of spring,
he was sole lord of her nights.
In the harems there were beauties,
three thousand there were in all,
but the love that was due to three thousand
was spent on one body alone.

Tresses like cloud, face like flower,
gold pins that swayed to her steps;
it was warm in the lotus-embroidered tents
where they passed the nights of spring.
And the nights of spring seemed all too short,
the sun would too soon rise,
from this point on our lord and king
avoided daybreak court.

. . . .

If in Heaven, may we become
those birds that fly on shared wing;
or on Earth, then may we become
branches that twine together.
Heaven lasts, the Earth endures
yet a time will come when they're gone,
yet this pain of ours will continue
and never finally end.

Like Yang Guifei, a number of other beautiful women in history and legend, including Helen of Troy, Cleopatra, and Rama's wife Sita, have been blamed for the downfall of states and other misfortunes. Why is this is such a familiar theme in many cultures around the world? Can you think of other examples?

Source: Appears in *An Anthology of Chinese Literature*,(trans. S. Owen, (New York, 1996), pp. 442–447

Like literature, Chinese painting found inspiration in Buddhist and Daoist sources. Some of the best surviving examples of the Tang period are the Buddhist wall paintings in the caves at Dunhuang (doon-HWAHNG), in Central Asia. Like the few surviving Tang scroll paintings, these wall paintings display a love of color and refinement that are reminiscent of styles in India and Persia (see the comparative illustration on p. 273).

British Museum, London//© The Art Archive at Art Resource, NY

© William J. Duiker

COMPARATIVE ILLUSTRATION

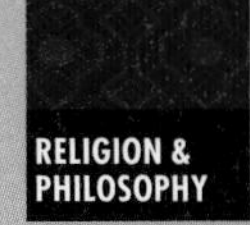

The Two Worlds of Tang China. In Tang dynasty China, the arts often reflected influences from a wide variety of cultures. On the left is an eighth-century wall painting from a cliffside cave at Dunhuang, a major rest stop on the Silk Road. The portrait of the Buddha clearly reflects Indian influence. The illustration on the right is a stone rubbing of Confucius based on a painting by the Tang dynasty artist Wu Daozi (woo DOW-ZEE) (c. 685–758). Although the original painting is not extant, this block print of a stone copy of Wu Daozi's work, showing Confucius in his flowing robe, reflects the indigenous style for which the painter was famous. It became the iconic portrait of the Master for millions of later Chinese. The Chinese government recently commissioned a copy based on Wu's original painting to serve as the standard portrait of Confucius for people around the world.

How do the two portraits shown here differ in the way their creators seek to present the character and the underlying philosophy of the Buddha and Confucius?

Daoism ultimately had a greater influence than Buddhism on Chinese painting. From early times, Chinese artists retreated to the mountains to write and paint and find the *Dao*, or Way, in nature. In the fifth century, one Chinese painter, who was too old to travel, began to paint mountain scenes from memory and announced that depicting nature could function as a substitute for contemplating it. Painting, he said, could be the means of realizing the *Dao*. This explains in part the emphasis on nature in traditional Chinese painting. The word *landscape* in Chinese means "mountain-water," and the Daoist search for balance between earth and water, hard and soft, *yang* and *yin*, is at play in the tradition of Chinese painting.

To represent nature, Chinese artists attempted to reveal the quintessential forms of the landscape. Rather than depicting a specific mountain, they tried to portray the idea of "mountain." Empty spaces were left in the paintings because in the Daoist vision, one cannot know the whole truth. Daoist influence was also evident in the tendency to portray human beings as insignificant in the midst of nature. In contrast to Western art with its focus on the human body and personality, Chinese art presented people as tiny figures fishing in a small boat, meditating on a cliff, or wandering up a hillside trail, coexisting with but not dominating nature.

The Chinese displayed their paintings on long scrolls of silk or paper that were attached to a wooden cylindrical bar at the

National Palace Museum, Taipei//© The Art Archive at Art Resource, NY

Emperor Ming-huang Traveling to Shu. Although the Tang dynasty was a prolific period in the development of Chinese painting, few examples have survived. Fortunately, the practice of copying the works of previous masters was a common tradition in China. Here we see an eleventh-century copy of an eighth-century painting depicting the precipitous journey of Emperor Ming-huang after a revolt forced him to flee from the capital into the mountains of southwest China. Rather than portraying the bitterness of the emperor's precarious escape, however, the artist reflected the confidence and brilliance of the Tang dynasty through cheerful color and an idyllic landscape.

bottom. Varying in length from 3 to 20 feet, the paintings were unfolded slowly so that the eye could enjoy each segment, beginning at the bottom with water or a village and moving upward into the hills to the mountain peaks and the sky.

By the tenth century, Chinese painters began to eliminate color from their paintings, preferring to capture the distilled essence of a landscape in washes of black ink on white silk. Borrowing from calligraphy, now a sophisticated and revered art, they emphasized the brush stroke and created black-and-white landscapes characterized by a gravity of mood and dominated by overpowering mountains.

Second only to painting in creativity was the field of ceramics, notably, the manufacture of porcelain. Made of fine clay baked at unusually high temperatures in a kiln, porcelain was first produced during the period after the fall of the Han and became popular during the Tang era. During the Song, porcelain came into its own. The translucence of Chinese porcelain represented the final product of a technique that did not reach Europe until the eighteenth century.

CHAPTER SUMMARY

Traditionally Chinese historians believed that Chinese history tended to be cyclical driven by the dynamic interplay of the forces of good and evil, *yang* and *yin*, growth and decay. Beyond the forces of conflict and change lay the essential continuity of Chinese history, based on timeless principles established by Confucius and other thinkers during the Zhou dynasty in antiquity.

This view of the dynamic forces of Chinese history was long accepted as valid by historians in the West and led many to assert that Chinese history was unique and could not be placed in a European or universal framework. Whereas Western history was linear, leading steadily away from the past, China's always returned to its moorings and was rooted in the values and institutions of antiquity.

In recent years, however, this traditional view of a changeless China has come under increasing challenge from historians who see patterns of change that made the China of the late fifteenth century a very different place from the country that had existed at the rise of the Tang dynasty in 600. To these scholars, China had passed through its own version of the "middle ages" and was on the verge of beginning a linear evolution into a posttraditional society.

As we have seen, China at the beginning of the Ming had advanced in many ways since the end of the great Han dynasty more than a thousand years earlier. The industrial and commercial sector had grown considerably in size, complexity, and technological capacity, while in the countryside, the concentration of political and economic power in the hands of the aristocracy had been replaced by a more stable and more equitable mixture of landed gentry, freehold farmers, and sharecroppers. The civil service provided an avenue of upward mobility that was unavailable elsewhere in the world, and the state tolerated a diversity of beliefs that responded to the emotional needs and preferences of the Chinese people. In many respects, China's achievements were unsurpassed throughout the world and marked a major advance beyond the world of antiquity.

Yet there were also some key similarities between the China of the Ming and the China of late antiquity. Ming China was still a predominantly agrarian society, with wealth based primarily on the ownership of land. Commercial activities flourished but remained under a high level of government regulation and by no means represented a major proportion of the national income. China also remained a relatively centralized empire based on an official ideology that stressed the virtue of hard work, social conformity, and hierarchy.

Thus, the significant change that China experienced during its medieval era can probably be best described as change within continuity, an evolutionary working out of trends that had first become visible during the Han dynasty or even earlier. The result was a civilization that was the envy of its neighbors and of the world. It also influenced other states in the region, including Japan, Korea, and Vietnam. It is to these societies along the Chinese rimlands that we now turn.

CHAPTER TIMELINE

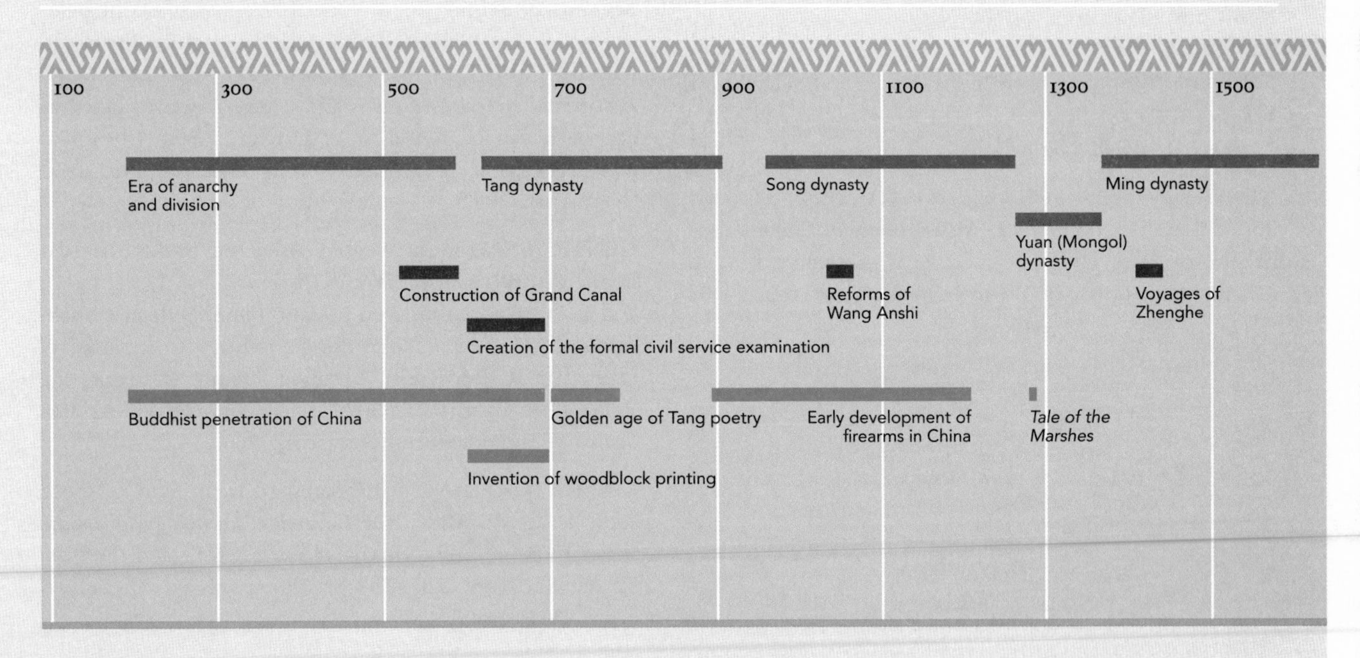

CHAPTER REVIEW

Upon Reflection

Q Why is the Tang dynasty often described as the greatest and most glorious era in Chinese history, and do you think that its reputation is justified?

Q What impact did the era of Mongol rule have on societies that were affected by it? Do you agree that some of the consequences ultimately had beneficial effects on world history? If so, why?

Q What are the arguments on both sides of the debate over whether Chinese society underwent fundamental changes during the period discussed in this chapter? Which arguments do you find more persuasive, and why?

Key Terms

Grand Council (p. 253)
scholar-gentry (p. 255)
foot binding (p. 260)
khanates (p. 262)
Chan (p. 268)
Pure Land (p. 268)
Tantrism (p. 268)
White Lotus (p. 268)
Neo-Confucianism (p. 270)
Supreme Ultimate (p. 270)
School of Mind (p. 270)

Suggested Reading

GENERAL For an authoritative overview of the early imperial era in China, see **F. Mote, *Imperial China*** (Cambridge, 1999). A global perspective is presented in **S. A. M. Adshead, *China in World History*** (New York, 2000).

Visit the CourseMate website at **www.cengagebrain.com** for additional study tools and review materials for this chapter.

For an informative treatment of China's relations with its neighbors, see **C. Holcombe, *The Genesis of East Asia, 220 B.C.–A.D. 907*** (Honolulu, 2001).

FROM THE HAN TO THE MING For a readable treatment of the period from the Han to the Ming dynasties by reputable scholars, see the several volumes in the series published by the Belknap Press at Harvard: **M. E. Lewis, *China Between Empires: The Northern and Southern Dynasties*** (Cambridge, Mass., 2009) and ***China's Cosmopolitan Empire: The Tang Dynasty*** (Cambridge, Mass., 2009); **D. Kuhn, *The Age of Confucian Rule: The Song Transformation of China*** (Cambridge, Mass., 2009); and **T. Brook, *The Troubled Empire: China in the Yuan and Ming Dynasties*** (Cambridge, Mass., 2010). Also see **C. Benn, *China's Golden Age: Everyday Life in the Tang Dynasty*** (Oxford, 2004).

MISCELLANEOUS TOPICS The emergence of urban culture during the Mongol era is analyzed in **C. K. Heng, *Cities of Aristocrats and Bureaucrats: The Development of Medieval Chinese Cityscapes*** (Honolulu, 1999). For perspectives on China as viewed from the outside, see **J. Spence, *The Chan's Great Continent: China in a Western Mirror*** (New York, 1998). China's contacts with foreign cultures are discussed in **J. Waley-Cohen, *The Sextants of Beijing*** (New York, 1999). On the controversial belief that Chinese fleets circled the globe in the fifteenth century, see **G. Menzies, *1421: The Year China Discovered America*** (New York, 2002). A more judicious approach can be found in **E. Dreyer, *Zheng He: China and the Oceans in the Early Ming Dynasty, 1405–1433*** (New York, 2007).

CENTRAL ASIA On Central Asia, see **S. A. M. Adshead, *Central Asia in World History*** (New York, 1993), and **E. T. Grotenhuis, ed., *Along the Silk Road*** (Washington, D.C., 2002). Xuan Zang's journey to India is recreated in **R. Bernstein, *Ultimate Journey: Retracing the Path of an Ancient Buddhist Monk Who Crossed Asia in Search of Enlightenment*** (New York, 2000).

LITERATURE AND ART Standard treatments of these subjects are **V. Mair, *The Columbia Anthology of Traditional Chinese Literature*** (New York, 1994), and the classic **M. Sullivan, *The Arts of China,*** 4th ed. (Berkeley, Calif., 1999).

CHAPTER

11

The East Asian Rimlands: Early Japan, Korea, and Vietnam

© William J. Duiker

Turtle Island, Hanoi

CHAPTER OUTLINE AND FOCUS QUESTIONS

Japan: Land of the Rising Sun

Q How did Japan's geographic location affect the course of early Japanese history, and how did the location influence the political structures and social institutions that arose there?

Korea: Bridge to the East

Q What were the main characteristics of economic and social life in early Korea?

Vietnam: The Smaller Dragon

Q What were the main developments in Vietnamese history before 1500? Why were the Vietnamese able to restore their national independence after a millennium of Chinese rule?

CRITICAL THINKING

Q How did Chinese civilization influence the societies that arose in Japan, Korea, and Vietnam during their early history?

THERE IS A SMALL body of water in the heart of the Vietnamese national capital of Hanoi (ha-NOY) that is known affectionately to local city-dwellers as Returned Sword Lake. The lake owes its name to a legend that Le Loi (LAY LOY), founder of the later Le (LAY) dynasty in the fifteenth century, drew a magic sword from the lake that enabled him to achieve a great victory over Chinese occupation forces. Thus, to many Vietnamese the lake symbolizes their nation's historical resistance to domination by its powerful northern neighbor.

Ironically, however, a temple that was later erected on tiny Turtle Island in the middle of the lake reflects the strong influence that China continued to exert on traditional Vietnamese culture. After Le Loi's victory, according to the legend, the sword was returned to the water, and the Vietnamese ruler accepted a tributary relationship to his "elder brother," the Chinese emperor in Beijing. China's philosophy, political institutions, and social mores served as hallmarks for the Vietnamese people down to the early years of the twentieth century. That is why for centuries Vietnam was known as "the smaller dragon."

Le Loi's deferential attitude toward his larger neighbor should not surprise us. During ancient times, China was the most technologically advanced society in East Asia. To its north and west were pastoral peoples whose military exploits were often impressive but whose political and cultural attainments were still limited, at least by comparison with the great river valley civilizations of the day. In inland areas south of the Yangtze River were scattered clumps of rice farmers and hill peoples, most of whom had not yet entered the era of state building and had little knowledge of the niceties of Confucian ethics. Along the fringes of Chinese civilization were a number of other agricultural societies that were beginning to follow a pattern of development similar to that of China, although somewhat later in time. One of these was in the Red River valley, heartland of early Vietnamese civilization, where a relatively advanced agricultural civilization had been in existence for several hundred years before the area was finally conquered by the Han dynasty in the second century C.E. Another was in the islands of Japan, where an organized society was beginning to take shape just as Chinese administrators were attempting to consolidate imperial rule over the Vietnamese people. On the Korean peninsula, an advanced Neolithic society had already begun to develop a few centuries earlier.

All of these early agricultural societies were eventually influenced to some degree by their great neighbor, China. Vietnam remained under Chinese rule for a thousand years. Korea retained its separate existence but was long a tributary state of China and in many ways followed the cultural example of its larger patron. Only Japan retained both its political independence and its cultural uniqueness. Yet even the Japanese were strongly influenced by the glittering culture of their powerful neighbor, and today many Japanese institutions and customs still bear the imprint of several centuries of borrowing from China. In this chapter, we will take a closer look at these emerging societies along the Chinese rimlands and consider how their cultural achievements reflected or contrasted with those of the Chinese Empire.

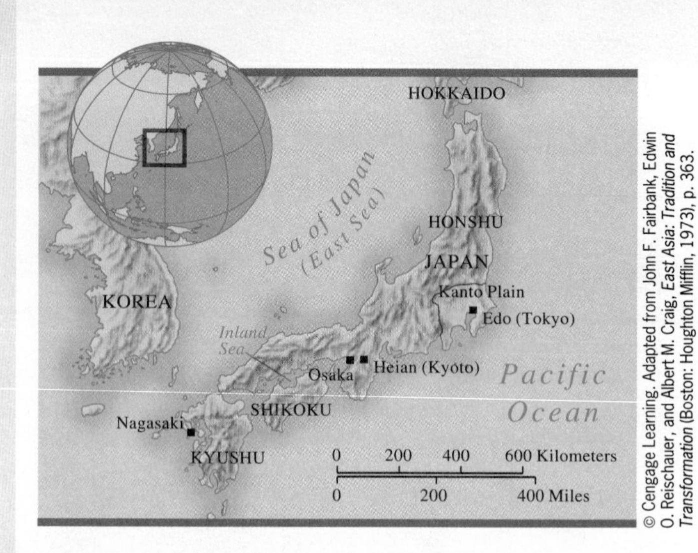

© Cengage Learning, Adapted from John F. Fairbank, Edwin O. Reischauer, and Albert M. Craig, *East Asia: Tradition and Transformation* (Boston: Houghton Mifflin, 1973), p. 363.

MAP 11.1 Early Japan. This map shows key cities in Japan during the early development of the Japanese state.

Where was the original heartland of Japanese civilization on the main island of Honshu?

Japan: Land of the Rising Sun

FOCUS QUESTION: How did Japan's geographic location affect the course of early Japanese history, and how did the location influence the political structures and social institutions that arose there?

Geography accounts for some of the historical differences between Chinese and Japanese society. Whereas China is a continental civilization, Japan is an island country. It consists of four main islands (see Map 11.1): Hokkaido (hoh-KY-doh) in the north, the main island of Honshu (HAHN-shoo) in the center, and the two smaller islands of Kyushu (KYOO-shoo) and Shikoku (shee-KOH-koo) in the southwest. Its total land area is about 146,000 square miles, about the size of the state of Montana. Japan's main islands are at approximately the same latitude as the eastern seaboard of the United States. Like the eastern United States, Japan is blessed with a temperate climate. It is slightly warmer on the east coast, which is washed by the Pacific current that sweeps up from the south, and has a number of natural harbors that provide protection from the winds and high waves of the Pacific Ocean. As a consequence, in recent times, the majority of the Japanese people have tended to live along the east coast, especially in the flat plains surrounding the cities of Tokyo (TOH-kee-oh), Osaka (oh-SAH-kuh), and Kyoto (KYOH-toh). In these favorable environmental conditions, Japanese farmers have been able to harvest two crops of rice annually since early times.

By no means, however, is Japan an agricultural paradise. Like China, much of the country is mountainous, so only about 20 percent of the total land area is suitable for cultivation. These mountains are of volcanic origin, since the Japanese islands are located at the juncture of the Asian and Pacific tectonic plates. This location is both an advantage and a disadvantage. Volcanic soils are extremely fertile, which helps explain the exceptionally high productivity of Japanese farmers. At the same time, the area is prone to earthquakes, such as the famous earthquake of 1923, which destroyed almost the entire city of Tokyo, and the massive earthquake just offshore in 2011, which triggered a devastating tsunami along the east coast of northern Honshu island.

The fact that Japan is an island country has had a significant impact on Japanese history. As we have seen, the continental character of Chinese civilization, with its constant threat of invasion from the north, had a number of consequences for Chinese history. One effect was to make the Chinese more sensitive to the preservation of their culture from destruction at the hands of non-Chinese invaders. As one fourth-century C.E. Chinese ruler remarked when he was forced to move his capital southward under pressure from nomadic incursions, "The King takes All Under Heaven as his home."[1] Proud of their considerable cultural achievements and their dominant position throughout the region, the Chinese have traditionally been reluctant to dilute the purity of their culture with foreign innovations. Culture more than race is a determinant of the Chinese sense of identity.

By contrast, the island character of Japan probably had the effect of strengthening the Japanese sense of ethnic and cultural distinctiveness. Although the Japanese view of themselves as the most ethnically homogeneous people in East Asia may not be entirely accurate (modern Japanese probably represent a mix of peoples, much like their neighbors on the continent), their sense of racial and cultural homogeneity has enabled them to import ideas from abroad without worrying that the borrowings will destroy the uniqueness of their own culture.

A Gift from the Gods: Prehistoric Japan

According to an ancient legend recorded in historical chronicles written in the eighth century C.E., the islands of Japan were formed as a result of the marriage of the god Izanagi (ee-zah-NAH-gee) and the goddess Izanami (ee-zah-NAH-mee). After giving birth to Japan, Izanami gave birth to a sun goddess whose name was Amaterasu (ah-mah-teh-RAH-soo). A descendant of Amaterasu later descended to earth and became the founder of the Japanese nation (see the box on p. 280). This Japanese creation myth is reminiscent of similar beliefs in other ancient societies, which often saw themselves as the product of a union of deities. What is interesting about the Japanese version is that it has survived into modern times as an explanation for the uniqueness of the Japanese people and the divinity of the Japanese emperor, who is still believed by some Japanese to be a direct descendant of the sun goddess Amaterasu. Modern scholars have a more prosaic explanation for the origins of Japanese civilization. According to archaeological evidence, the Japanese islands have been occupied by human beings for at least 100,000 years. The earliest known Neolithic inhabitants, known as the Jomon (JOH-mahn) people from the cord pattern of their pottery, lived in the islands as early as 8000 B.C.E. They lived by hunting, fishing, and food gathering and probably had not mastered the techniques of agriculture.

Agriculture probably first appeared in Japan sometime during the first millennium B.C.E., although some archaeologists believe that the Jomon people had already learned how to cultivate some food crops considerably earlier than that. About 400 B.C.E., rice cultivation was introduced, probably by immigrants from the mainland by way of the Korean peninsula. Until recently, historians believed that these immigrants drove out the existing inhabitants of the area and gave rise to the emerging Yayoi (yah-YOH-ee) culture (named for the site near Tokyo where pottery from the period was found). It is now thought, however, that Yayoi culture was a product of a mixture between the Jomon people and the new arrivals, enriched by imports such as wet-rice agriculture, which had been brought by the immigrants from the mainland. In any event, it seems clear that the Yayoi peoples were the ancestors of the vast majority of present-day Japanese (see the comparative illustration on p. 287).

At first, the Yayoi lived primarily on the southern island of Kyushu, but eventually they moved northward onto the main island of Honshu, conquering, assimilating, or driving out the previous inhabitants of the area, some of whose descendants, known as the Ainu (Y-nyoo), still live in the northern islands. Finally, in the first centuries C.E., the Yayoi settled in the Yamato (YAH-mah-toh) plain in the vicinity of the modern cities of Osaka and Kyoto. Japanese legend recounts the story of a "divine warrior," *Jimmu* (JIH-moo), who led his people eastward from the island of Kyushu to establish a kingdom in the Yamato plain.

In central Honshu, the Yayoi set up a tribal society based on a number of clans, called ***uji*** (oo-JEE). Each *uji* was ruled by a hereditary chieftain, who provided protection to the local population in return for a proportion of the annual harvest. The population itself was divided between a small aristocratic class and the majority of the population, composed of rice farmers, artisans, and other household servants of the aristocrats. Yayoi society was highly decentralized, although eventually the chieftain of the dominant clan in the Yamato region, who claimed to be descended from the sun goddess Amaterasu, achieved a kind of titular primacy. There is no evidence, however, of a central ruler equivalent in power to the Chinese rulers of the Shang and the Zhou eras.

The Rise of the Japanese State

Although the Japanese had been aware of China for centuries, they paid relatively little attention to their more advanced neighbor until the early seventh century, when the rise of the centralized and expansionistic Tang dynasty presented a challenge. The Tang began to

How the Earth Was Formed

RELIGION & PHILOSOPHY

When Japanese accounts about the creation of the earth and the emergence of human society began to be recorded in the eighth century C.E., the early chroniclers had already been exposed to Chinese writings on the subject and were very likely influenced by Chinese founding myths such as those we discussed in Chapter 3. Yet there are significant differences in the Japanese approach, which places more emphasis on the role of nature deities than on sage-kings. The Japanese account also links the creation of the Japanese islands directly with the emergence of the imperial line. The following selection is from the *Kojiki* (koh-JIK-ee), an eighth-century chronicle known in English translation as *Records of Ancient Matters.*

Records of Ancient Matters

Now when chaos had begun to condense but force and form were not yet manifest and there was nought named, nought done, who could know its shape? Nevertheless Heaven and Earth first parted, and the Three Deities performed the commencement of creation; yin and yang then developed; and the Two Spirits [Izanagi and Izanami] became the ancestors of all things. Therefore with [Izanagi's] entering obscurity and emerging into light, the sun and moon were revealed by the washing of his eyes; he floated on and plunged into the seawater, and heavenly and earthly deities appeared through the ablutions of his person. So in the dimness of the great commencement, we, by relying on the original teaching, learn the time of the conception of the earth and of the birth of islands; in the remoteness of the original beginning, we, by trusting the former sages, perceive the era of the genesis of deities and of the establishment of men. Truly we do know that a mirror was hung up, that jewels were spat out, and that then a hundred kings succeeded each other; that a blade was bitten and a serpent cut in pieces, so that the myriad deities did flourish. By deliberations in the Tranquil River the empire was pacified; by discussions on the Little Shore the land was purified. Wherefore His Augustness Ho-no-ni-ni-gi [grandson of the sun goddess] first descended to the Peak of Takachi, and the Heavenly Sovereign Kamu-Yamato [Jimmu, the founding emperor of Japan] did traverse the Island of the Dragon-Fly. A weird bear put forth its claws, and a heavenly saber was obtained at Takakura. They with tails obstructed the path and a great crow guided him to Eshinu. Dancing in rows they destroyed the brigands, and listening to a song they vanquished the foeman. Being instructed in a dream, he was reverent to the heavenly and earthly deities and was therefore styled the Wise Monarch; having gazed on the smoke, he was benevolent to the black-haired people, and is therefore remembered as the Emperor-Sage. Determining the frontiers and civilizing the country, he issued laws, reform[ed] the surnames and select[ed] the [clan] names. . . . Though each differed in caution and in ardor, though all were unlike in accomplishments and in intrinsic worth, yet was there none who did not by contemplating antiquity correct manners that had fallen to ruin and, by illumining modern times, repair laws that were approaching dissolution.

How does this account of the founding of the earth compare with the Mayan creation myth in Popul Vuh, presented in Chapter 6?

Source: W. de Bary, et al., *Sources of Japanese Tradition (from earliest times to 1600)*, vol. I, 2nd ed. (New York, 2001), pp. 15–16.

meddle in the affairs of the Korean peninsula, conquering the southwestern coast and arousing anxiety in Japan. Yamato rulers attempted to deal with the potential threat posed by the Chinese in two ways. First, they sought alliances with the remaining Korean states. Second, they attempted to centralize their authority so that they could mount a more effective resistance in the event of a Chinese invasion. The key figure in this effort was Shotoku Taishi (shoh-TOH-koo ty-EE-shee) (572–622), a leading aristocrat in one of the dominant clans in the Yamato region. Prince Shotoku sent missions to the Tang capital of Chang'an to learn about the political institutions already in use in the relatively centralized Tang kingdom (see Map 11.2).

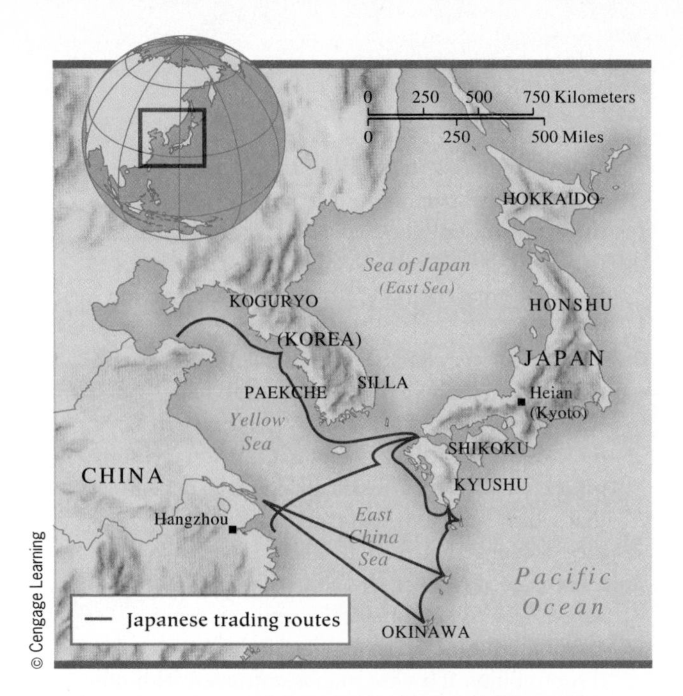

© Cengage Learning

MAP 11.2 Japan's Relations with China and Korea. This map shows the Japanese islands at the time of the Yamato state. Maritime routes taken by Japanese traders and missions to China are indicated.

Where did Japanese traders travel after reaching the mainland?

EMULATING THE CHINESE MODEL Shotoku Taishi then launched a series of reforms to create a new system based roughly on the Chinese model. In the so-called seventeen-article constitution, he called for the creation of a centralized government under a supreme ruler and a merit system for selecting and ranking public officials (see the box on p. 282). His objective was to limit the powers of the hereditary nobility and enhance the prestige and authority of the Yamato ruler, who claimed divine status and was now emerging as the symbol of the unique character of the Japanese nation. In reality, there is evidence that places the origins of the Yamato clan on the Korean peninsula.

After Shotoku Taishi's death in 622, his successors continued to introduce reforms to make the government more efficient. In the series of so-called **Taika reforms**—*taika* (TY-kuh) means "great change"—that began in the mid-seventh century, the Grand Council of State was established to preside over a cabinet of eight ministries. To the traditional six ministries of Tang China were added ministers representing the central secretariat and the imperial household. The territory of Japan was divided into administrative districts on the Chinese pattern. The rural village, composed ideally of fifty households, was the basic unit of government. The village chief was responsible for "the maintenance of the household registers, the assigning of the sowing of crops and the cultivation of mulberry trees, the prevention of offenses, and the requisitioning of taxes and forced labor." A law code was introduced, and a new tax system was established; now all farmland technically belonged to the state, so taxes were paid directly to the central government rather than through the local nobility, as had previously been the case.

As a result of their new acquaintance with China, the Japanese also developed a strong interest in Buddhism. Some of the first Japanese to travel to China during this period were Buddhist pilgrims hoping to learn more about the exciting new doctrine and bring back scriptures. By the seventh century C.E., Buddhism had become quite popular among the aristocrats, who endowed wealthy monasteries that became active in Japanese politics. At first, the new faith did not penetrate to the masses, but eventually, popular sects such as the Pure Land sect, an import from China, won many adherents among the common people.

THE NARA PERIOD Initial efforts to build a new state modeled roughly after the Tang state were successful. After Shotoku Taishi's death in 622, political influence fell into the hands of the powerful Fujiwara (foo-jee-WAH-rah) clan, which managed to marry into the ruling family and continue the reforms Shotoku had begun. In 710, a new capital, laid out on a grid similar to the great Tang city of Chang'an, was established at Nara (NAH-rah), on the eastern edge of the Yamato plain. The Yamato ruler began to use the title "son of Heaven" in the Chinese fashion. In deference to the belief in the ruling family's divine character, the mandate remained in perpetuity in the imperial house rather than being bestowed on an individual who was selected by Heaven because of his talent and virtue, as was the case in China.

Had these reforms succeeded, Japan might have followed the Chinese pattern and developed a centralized bureaucratic government. But as time passed, the central government proved unable to curb the power of the aristocracy. Unlike in Tang China, the civil service examinations in Japan were not open to all but were restricted to individuals of noble birth. Leading officials were awarded large tracts of land, and they and other powerful families were able to keep the taxes from the lands for themselves. Increasingly starved for revenue, the central government steadily lost power and influence.

THE HEIAN PERIOD The influence of powerful Buddhist monasteries in the city of Nara soon became oppressive, and in 794 the emperor moved the capital to his family's original power base at nearby Heian (hay-AHN), on the site of present-day Kyoto. The new capital

The Seventeen-Article Constitution

POLITICS & GOVERNMENT

The following excerpt from the *Nihon Shoki* (nee-HAHN SHOH-kee) (*The Chronicles of Japan*) is a passage from the seventeen-article constitution promulgated in 604 C.E. Although the opening section reflects Chinese influence in its emphasis on social harmony, there is also a strong focus on obedience and hierarchy. The constitution was put into practice during the reign of the famous Prince Shotoku.

The Chronicles of Japan

Summer, 4th month, 3rd day [12th year of Empress Suiko, 604 C.E.]. The Crown Prince personally drafted and promulgated a constitution consisting of seventeen articles, which are as follows:

I. Harmony is to be cherished, and opposition for opposition's sake must be avoided as a matter of principle. Men are often influenced by partisan feelings, except a few sagacious ones. Hence there are some who disobey their lords and fathers, or who dispute with their neighboring villages. If those above are harmonious and those below are cordial, their discussion will be guided by a spirit of conciliation, and reason shall naturally prevail. There will be nothing that cannot be accomplished.

II. With all our heart, revere the three treasures. The three treasures, consisting of Buddha, the Doctrine, and the Monastic Order, are the final refuge of the four generated beings, and are the supreme objects of worship in all countries. Can any man in any age ever fail to respect these teachings? Few men are utterly devoid of goodness, and men can be taught to follow the teachings. Unless they take refuge in the three treasures, there is no way of rectifying their misdeeds.

III. When an imperial command is given, obey it with reverence. The sovereign is likened to heaven, and his subjects are likened to earth. With heaven providing the cover and earth supporting it, the four seasons proceed in orderly fashion, giving sustenance to all that which is in nature. If earth attempts to overtake the functions of heaven, it destroys everything. . . . If there is no reverence shown to the imperial command, ruin will automatically result. . . .

IV. Every man must be given his clearly delineated responsibility. If a wise man is entrusted with office, the sound of praise arises. If a wicked man holds office, disturbances become frequent. . . . In all things, great or small, find the right man, and the country will be well governed. . . . In this manner, the state will be lasting and its sacerdotal functions will be free from danger.

What are the key components in this first constitution in the history of Japan? To what degree do its provisions conform to Chinese Confucian principles?

Source: Excerpt from *Sources of Japanese History*, David Lu, ed. (New York: McGraw-Hill, 1974), I, p. 7.

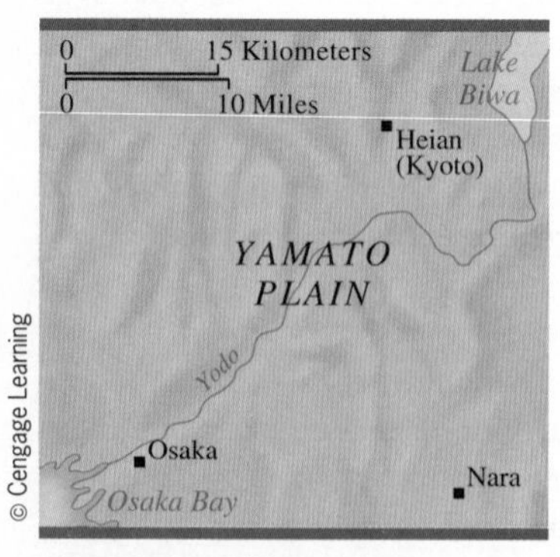

The Yamato Plain

was laid out in the now familiar Chang'an checkerboard pattern, but on a larger scale than at Nara. Now increasingly self-confident, the rulers ceased to emulate the Tang and sent no more missions to Chang'an. At Heian, the emperor—as the head of the royal line descended from the sun goddess was now officially styled—continued to rule in name, but actual power was in the hands of the Fujiwara clan, which had managed through intermarriage to link its fortunes closely with the imperial family. A senior member of the clan began to serve as regent (in practice, the chief executive of the government) for the emperor.

What was occurring was a return to the decentralization that had existed prior to Shotoku Taishi. The central government's attempts to impose taxes directly on the rice lands failed, and rural areas came under the control of powerful families whose wealth was based on the ownership of tax-exempt farmland called *shoen*

© William J. Duiker

A Worship Hall in Nara. Buddhist temple compounds in Japan traditionally offered visitors an escape from the tensions of the outside world. The temple site normally included an entrance gate, a central courtyard, a worship hall, a pagoda, and a cloister, as well as support buildings for the monks. The pagoda, a multitiered tower, harbored a sacred relic of the Buddha and served as the East Asian version of the Indian stupa. The worship hall corresponded to the Vedic carved chapel. Here we see the Todaiji (toh-DY-jee) worship hall in Nara. Originally constructed in the mid-eighth century C.E., it is reputed to be the largest wooden structure in the world and is the centerpiece of a vast temple complex on the outskirts of the old capital city.

(SHOH-en). To avoid paying taxes, peasants would often surrender their lands to a local aristocrat, who would then allow the peasants to cultivate the lands in return for the payment of rent. To obtain protection from government officials, these local aristocrats might in turn grant title of their lands to a more powerful aristocrat with influence at court. In return, these individuals would receive inheritable rights to a portion of the income from the estate (see the comparative essay "Feudal Orders Around the World" on p. 284).

With the decline of central power at Heian, local aristocrats tended to take justice into their own hands and increasingly used military force to protect their interests. A new class of military retainers called the **samurai** (SAM-uh-ry) emerged whose purpose was to protect the security and property of their patron. They frequently drew their leaders from disappointed aristocratic office seekers, who thus began to occupy a prestigious position in local society, where they often served an administrative as well as a military function. The samurai lived a life of simplicity and self-sacrifice and were expected to maintain an intense and unquestioning loyalty to their lord. Bonds of loyalty were also quite strong among members of the samurai class, and homosexuality was common. Like the knights of medieval Europe, the samurai fought on horseback (although a samurai carried a sword and a bow and arrows rather than lance and shield) and were supposed to live by a strict warrior code, known in Japan as **Bushido** (BOO-shee-doh), or "way of the warrior" (see the box on p. 285). As time went on, they became a major force and almost a surrogate government in much of the Japanese countryside.

THE KAMAKURA SHOGUNATE AND AFTER By the end of the twelfth century, as rivalries among noble families led to almost constant civil war, once again centralizing forces asserted themselves. This time the instrument was a powerful noble from a warrior clan named Minamoto Yoritomo (mee-nah-MOH-toh yoh-ree-TOH-moh) (1142–1199), who defeated several rivals and set up his power base on the Kamakura (kah-mah-KOO-rah) peninsula, south of the modern city of Tokyo. To strengthen the state, he created a more centralized government—the ***bakufu*** (buh-KOO-foo *or* bah-KOO-fuh) or "tent government"—under a powerful military leader, known as the **shogun** (SHOH-gun) (general). The shogun attempted to increase the powers of the central government while reducing rival aristocratic clans to vassal status. This **shogunate system**, in which the emperor was the titular authority while the shogun exercised actual power, served as the political system in Japan until the second half of the nineteenth century.

The shogunate (SHOH-gun-ut *or* SHOH-gun-ayt) system worked effectively, and it was fortunate that it did, because during the next century, Japan faced the most serious challenge it had yet confronted. The Mongols, who had destroyed the Song dynasty in China, were now attempting to assert their hegemony throughout all of Asia (see Chapter 10). In 1266, Emperor Khubilai Khan demanded tribute from Japan. When the Japanese refused, he invaded with an army of more than 30,000 troops. Bad weather and difficult conditions forced a retreat, but the Mongols tried again in 1281. An army nearly 150,000 strong landed on the northern coast of Kyushu. The Japanese were able to contain them for two months until virtually the entire Mongol fleet was destroyed by a massive typhoon—a "divine wind," or *kamikaze* (kah-mi-KAH-zee). Japan would not face a foreign invader again until American forces landed on the Japanese islands in the summer of 1945.

COMPARATIVE ESSAY

Feudal Orders Around the World

The word *feudalism* usually conjures up images of European knights on horseback clad in armor and wielding a sword and lance. Between 800 and 1500, however, a form of social organization that modern historians have called feudalism developed in different parts of the world. By the term *feudalism*, these historians mean a decentralized political order in which local lords owed loyalty and provided military service to a king or more powerful lord. In Europe, a feudal order based on lords and vassals arose between 800 and 900 and flourished for the next four hundred years.

In Japan, a feudal order much like that found in Europe developed between 800 and 1500. By the end of the ninth century, powerful nobles in the countryside, while owing a loose loyalty to the Japanese emperor, began to exercise political and legal power in their own extensive lands. To protect their property and security, these nobles retained samurai, warriors who owed loyalty to the nobles and provided military service for them. Like knights in Europe, the samurai followed a warrior code and fought on horseback, clad in armor. They carried a sword and bow and arrow, however, rather than a sword and lance.

Eisei-bunko, Japan//© Sakamoto Photo Research Laboratory/CORBIS

Samurai. During the Kamakura period, painters began to depict the adventures of the new warrior class. Here is an imposing mounted samurai warrior, the Japanese equivalent of the medieval knight in fief-holding Europe. Like his European counterpart, the samurai was supposed to live by a strict moral code and to maintain unquestioning loyalty to his liege lord. Above all, a samurai's life was one of simplicity and self-sacrifice.

In some respects, the political relationships among the Indian states beginning in the fifth century took on the character of the feudal order that emerged in Europe in the Middle Ages. Like medieval European lords, local Indian rajas were technically vassals of the king, but unlike in European feudalism, the relationship was not a contractual one. Still, the Indian model became highly complex, with "inner" and "outer" vassals, depending on their physical or political proximity to the king, and "greater" or "lesser" vassals, depending on their power and influence. As in Europe, the vassals themselves often had vassals.

In the Valley of Mexico, between 1300 and 1500 the Aztecs developed a political system that bore some similarities to the Japanese, Indian, and European feudal orders. Although the Aztec king was a powerful, authoritarian ruler, the local rulers of lands outside the capital city were allowed considerable freedom. Nevertheless, they paid tribute to the king and also provided him with military forces. Unlike the knights and samurai of Europe and Japan, however, Aztec warriors were armed with sharp knives made of stone and spears of wood fitted with razor-sharp blades cut from stone.

What were the key characteristics of the political order we know as feudalism? To what degree did Japanese feudalism exhibit these characteristics?

The resistance to the Mongols had put a heavy strain on the system, however, and in 1333, the Kamakura shogunate was overthrown by a coalition of powerful clans. A new shogun, supplied by the Ashikaga (ah-shee-KAH-guh) family, arose in Kyoto and attempted to continue the shogunate system. But the Ashikaga were unable to restore the centralized power of their predecessors. With the central government reduced to a shell, the power of the local landed aristocracy increased to an unprecedented degree. Heads of great noble families, now called **daimyo** (DYM-yoh)

Japan's Warrior Class

The samurai was the Japanese equivalent of the medieval European knight. Like the knights, the samurai fought on horseback and were expected to adhere to a strict moral code. Although this selection comes from a document dating only to the 1500s, a distinct mounted warrior class had already begun to emerge in Japan as early as the tenth century. This passage shows the importance of hierarchy and duty in a society influenced by the doctrine of Confucius.

The Way of the Samurai

The master once said: . . . Generation after generation men have taken their livelihood from tilling the soil, or devised and manufactured tools, or produced profit from mutual trade, so that people's needs were satisfied. Thus, the occupations of farmer, artisan, and merchant necessarily grew up as complementary to one another. However, the samurai eats food without growing it, uses utensils without manufacturing them, and profits without buying or selling. . . . The samurai is one who does not cultivate, does not manufacture, and does not engage in trade, but it cannot be that he has no function at all as a samurai. . . .

If one deeply fixes [one's] attention on what I have said and examines closely one's own function, it will become clear what the business of the samurai is. The business of the samurai consists in reflecting on his own station in life, in discharging loyal service to his master if he has one, in deepening his fidelity in associations with friends, and, with due consideration of his own position, in devoting himself to duty above all. . . . The samurai dispenses with the business of the farmer, artisan, and merchant and confines himself to practicing this Way; should there be someone in the three classes of the common people who transgresses against these moral principles, the samurai summarily punishes him and thus upholds proper moral principles in the land. . . . Outwardly he stands in physical readiness for any call to service, and inwardly he strives to fulfill the Way of the lord and subject, friend and friend, father and son, older and younger brother, and husband and wife. Within his heart he keeps to the ways of peace, but without he keeps his weapons ready for use. The three classes of the common people make him their teacher and respect him. By following his teachings, they are enabled to understand what is fundamental and what is secondary.

Herein lies the Way of the samurai, the means by which he earns his clothing, food, and shelter; and by which his heart is put at ease, and he is enabled to pay back at length his obligation to his lord and the kindness of his parents. Were there no such duty, it would be as though one were to steal the kindness of one's parents, greedily devour the income of one's master, and make one's whole life a career of robbery and brigandage. This would be very grievous.

In what ways were the duties of a samurai similar to those of an Indian warrior, as expressed by Krishna in Chapter 2? How do they compare with the responsibilities of a Confucian "gentleman" in China? What might account for the similarities and differences?

Source: From *Sources of Japanese Tradition* by William Theodore de Bary, Carol Gluck, and Arthur E. Tiedemann. Copyright © 2005 by Columbia University Press. Reprinted with permission of the publisher.

("great names"), controlled vast landed estates that owed no taxes to the government or to the court in Kyoto. As clan rivalries continued, the daimyo relied increasingly on the samurai for protection, and political power came into the hands of a loose coalition of noble families.

By the end of the fifteenth century, Japan was again close to anarchy. A disastrous civil conflict known as the Onin War (1467–1477) led to the virtual destruction of the capital city of Kyoto and the disintegration of the shogunate. With the disappearance of any central authority, powerful aristocrats in rural areas now seized total control over large territories and ruled as independent great lords. Territorial rivalries and claims of precedence led to almost constant warfare in this period of "warring states," as it is called (in obvious parallel with a similar era during the Zhou dynasty in China). The trend back toward central authority did not begin until the last quarter of the sixteenth century.

WAS JAPAN A FEUDAL SOCIETY? That question has aroused vigorous debate among historians in recent years. Few would dispute that political, social, and

Museum of Fine Arts, Boston/© Werner Forman/Art Resource, NY

The Burning of the Palace. The Kamakura era is represented in this action-packed thirteenth-century scene from the *Scroll of the Heiji Period*, which depicts the burning of a retired emperor's palace in the middle of the night. Servants and ladies of the court flee the massive flames; confusion and violence reign. The determined faces of the samurai warriors only add to the ferocity of the attack.

economic conditions in Japan were similar in a number of respects to those in medieval Europe, to which the term was first applied (see the comparative essay "Feudal Orders Around the World" on p. 284 and Chapter 12). But some European historians worry that the term *feudalism* has been overused; they argue that it should be narrowly defined, based on conditions that existed in Europe during a specific time period.

For the student of world history, the term obviously has some comparative value, in that the broad conditions that are normally considered to be characteristic of a feudal society can be found in a number of areas around the world. Still, it is important to remember that, under the surface, there were often profound differences between one "feudal" society and another. With that in mind, the term can be a highly useful teaching tool for world historians.

CHRONOLOGY **Formation of the Japanese State**	
Shotoku Taishi	572–622
Era of Taika reforms	Mid-seventh century
Nara period	710–784
Heian (Kyoto) period	794–1185
Murasaki Shikibu	978–c. 1016
Minamoto Yoritomo	1142–1199
Kamakura shogunate	1185–1333
Mongol invasions	Late thirteenth century
Ashikaga period	1333–1600
Onin War	1467–1477

Economic and Social Structures

From the time the Yayoi culture was first established on the Japanese islands, Japan was a predominantly agrarian society. Although Japan lacked the spacious valleys and deltas of the river valley societies, its inhabitants were able to take advantage of their limited amount of tillable land and plentiful rainfall to create a society based on the cultivation of wet rice.

TRADE AND MANUFACTURING As in China, commerce was slow to develop in Japan. During ancient times, each *uji* had a local artisan class, composed of weavers, carpenters, and ironworkers, but trade was essentially local and was regulated by the local clan leaders. With the rise of the Yamato state, a money economy gradually began to develop, although most trade was still conducted through barter until the twelfth century, when metal coins introduced from China became more popular.

Trade and manufacturing began to develop more rapidly during the Kamakura period, with the appearance of trimonthly markets in the larger towns and the emergence of such industries as paper, iron casting, and porcelain. Foreign trade, mainly with Korea and China, began during the eleventh century. Japan exported raw

© William J. Duiker

© William J. Duiker

© William J. Duiker

COMPARATIVE ILLUSTRATION

SCIENCE & TECHNOLOGY

The Longhouse. Many early peoples built longhouses of wood and thatch to store their goods and carry on community activities. Many such structures were erected on heavy pilings to protect the interior from flooding, insects, or wild animals. On the left is a model of a sixth-century C.E. warehouse in Osaka, Japan. The original was apparently used by local residents to store grain and other foodstuffs. In the center is a reconstruction of a similar structure built originally by Vikings in Denmark. The longhouses on the right are still occupied by families living on Nias, a small island off the coast of Sumatra. The outer walls were built to resemble the hulls of Dutch galleons that plied the seas near Nias during the seventeenth and eighteenth centuries.

Q *The longhouse served as a communal structure in many human communities in early times. What types of structures serve communities in modern societies today?*

materials, paintings, swords, and other manufactured items in return for silk, porcelain, books, and copper cash. Some Japanese traders were so aggressive in pressing their interests that authorities in China and Korea attempted to limit the number of Japanese commercial missions that could visit each year. Such restrictions were often ignored, however, and encouraged some Japanese traders to turn to piracy.

Significantly, manufacturing and commerce developed rapidly during the more decentralized period of the Ashikaga shogunate and the era of the warring states, perhaps because of the rapid growth in the wealth and autonomy of local daimyo families. Market towns, now operating on a full money economy, began to appear, and local manufacturers formed guilds to protect their mutual interests. Sometimes local peasants would sell products made in their homes, such as clothing made of silk or hemp, household items, or food products, at the markets. In general, however, trade and manufacturing remained under the control of the local daimyo, who would often provide tax breaks to local guilds in return for other benefits. Although Japan remained a primarily agricultural society, it was on the verge of a major advance in manufacturing.

DAILY LIFE One of the first descriptions of the life of the Japanese people comes from a Chinese dynastic history from the third century C.E. It describes lords and peasants living in an agricultural society that was based on the cultivation of wet rice. Laws had been enacted to punish offenders, local trade was conducted in markets, and government granaries stored the grain that was paid as taxes.

Life for the common people probably changed very little over the next several hundred years. Most were peasants who worked on land owned by their lord or, in some cases, by the state or by Buddhist monasteries. By no means, however, were all peasants equal either economically or socially. Although in ancient times, all land was owned by the state and peasants working the land were taxed at an equal rate depending on the nature of the crop, after the Yamato era variations began to develop. At the top were local officials who were often well-to-do peasants. They were responsible for organizing collective labor services and collecting tax grain from the peasants and in turn were exempt from such obligations themselves (see the comparative illustration above).

The mass of the peasants were under the authority of these local officials. In theory, peasants were free to dispose of their harvest as they saw fit after paying their tax quota, but in practical terms, their freedom was limited. Those who were unable to pay the tax sank to the level of ***genin*** (GAY-nin), or landless laborers, who could be bought and sold by their proprietors like slaves along with the land on which they worked. Some fled to escape such a fate and attempted to survive by clearing plots of land in the mountains or by becoming bandits.

In addition to the *genin*, the bottom of the social scale was occupied by the ***eta*** (AY-tuh), a class of hereditary slaves who were responsible for what were considered degrading occupations, such as curing leather and burying the dead. The origins of the *eta* are not entirely clear, but they probably were descendants of prisoners of war, criminals, or mountain dwellers who were not related to the dominant Yamato peoples. As we shall see, the *eta* are still a distinctive part of Japanese society, and although their full legal rights are guaranteed under the current constitution, discrimination against them is not uncommon.

Daily life for ordinary people in early Japan resembled that of their counterparts throughout much of Asia. The vast majority lived in small villages, several of which normally made up a single *shoen*. Housing was simple. Most lived in small two-room houses of timber, mud, or thatch, with dirt floors covered by straw or woven mats—the origin, perhaps, of the well-known *tatami* (tuh-TAH-mee), or woven-mat floor, of more modern times. Their diet consisted of rice (if some was left after the payment of the grain tax), wild grasses, millet, roots, and some fish and birds. Life must have been difficult at best; as one eighth-century poet lamented:

Here I lie on straw
Spread on bare earth,
With my parents at my pillow,
My wife and children at my feet,
All huddled in grief and tears.
No fire sends up smoke
At the cooking place,
And in the cauldron
A spider spins its web.[2]

THE ROLE OF WOMEN Evidence about the relations between men and women in early Japan presents a mixed picture (see the Film & History feature on p. 289). The Chinese dynastic history reports that "in their meetings and daily living, there is no distinction between . . . men and women." It notes that a woman "adept in the ways of shamanism" had briefly ruled Japan in the third century C.E. But it also remarks that polygyny was common, with nobles normally having four or five wives and commoners two or three.[3] An eighth-century law code guaranteed the inheritance rights of women, and wives abandoned by their husbands were permitted to obtain a divorce and remarry. A husband could divorce his wife if she did not produce a male child, committed adultery, disobeyed her parents-in-law, talked too much, engaged in theft, was jealous, or had a serious illness.[4]

When Buddhism was introduced, women were initially relegated to a subordinate position in the new faith. Although they were permitted to take up monastic life—often a widow entered a monastery on the death of her husband—they were not permitted to visit Buddhist holy places, nor were they even (in the accepted wisdom) equal with men in the afterlife. One Buddhist commentary from the late thirteenth century said that a woman could not attain enlightenment because "her sin is grievous, and so she is not allowed to enter the lofty palace of the great Brahma, nor to look upon the clouds which hover over his ministers and people."[5] Other Buddhist scholars were more egalitarian: "Learning the Law of Buddha and achieving release from illusion have nothing to do with whether one happens to be a man or a woman."[6] Such views ultimately prevailed, and women were eventually allowed to participate fully in Buddhist activities in medieval Japan.

Although women did not possess the full legal and social rights of their male counterparts, they played an active role at various levels of Japanese society. Aristocratic women were prominent at court, and some, such as the author Murasaki Shikibu (MOO-rah-SAH-kee SHEE-kee-boo), known as Lady Murasaki (978–c. 1016), became renowned for their artistic or literary talents. Though few commoners could aspire to such prominence, women often appear in the scroll paintings of the period along with men, doing the spring planting, threshing and hulling the rice, and acting as carriers, peddlers, salespersons, and entertainers.

In Search of the Pure Land: Religion in Early Japan

In Japan, as elsewhere, religious belief began with the worship of nature spirits. Early Japanese worshiped spirits, called ***kami*** (KAH-mi), who resided in trees, rivers and streams, and mountains. They also believed in ancestral spirits present in the atmosphere. In Japan, these beliefs eventually evolved into a kind of state religion called **Shinto** (SHIN-toh) (the "Sacred Way" or the "Way of the Gods"), which is still practiced today. Shinto serves as an ideological and emotional force that knits the Japanese into a single people and nation.

Shinto does not have a complex metaphysical superstructure or an elaborate moral code. It does require certain ritual acts, usually undertaken at a shrine, and a process of purification, which may have originated in

FILM & HISTORY

Rashomon (1950)

The Japanese director Akira Kurosawa (ah-KEE-rah KOO-rah-SAW-wah) was one of the most respected filmmakers of the second half of the twentieth century. In a series of films produced after World War II, he sought to evoke the mood of a long-lost era—medieval Japan. The first to attract world attention was *Rashomon* (rah-SHOH-muhn), released in 1950, in which Kurosawa used an unusual technique to explore the ambiguity of truth. The film became so famous that the expression "Rashomon effect" has come to stand for the difficulty of establishing the veracity of an incident.

In the movie, a woman is accosted and raped in a forest glen by the local brigand Tajomaru, and her husband is killed in the encounter. The true facts remain obscure, however, as the testimony of each of the key figures in the story—including the ghost of the deceased—seems to present a different version of the facts. Was the husband murdered by the brigand, or did he commit suicide in shame for failing to protect his wife's virtue? Did she herself kill her husband in anger after he rejected her as soiled goods, or is it even possible that she actually hoped to run away with the bandit?

Although the plot line in *Rashomon* is clearly fictional, the film sheds light on several key features of life in medieval Japan. The hierarchical nature of the class system provides a fascinating backdrop, as the traveling couple are members of the aristocratic elite while the bandit—played by the director's favorite actor, Toshiro Mifune (toh-SHEE-roh mi-FOO-neh)—is a rough-hewn commoner. The class distinctions between the two men are evident during their physical confrontation, which includes a lengthy bout of spirited swordplay A second theme centers on the question of honor. Though the husband's outrage at the violation of his wife is quite understandable, his anger is directed primarily at her because her reputation has been irreparably tarnished. She in turn harbors a deep sense of shame that she has been physically possessed by two men, one in the presence of the other.

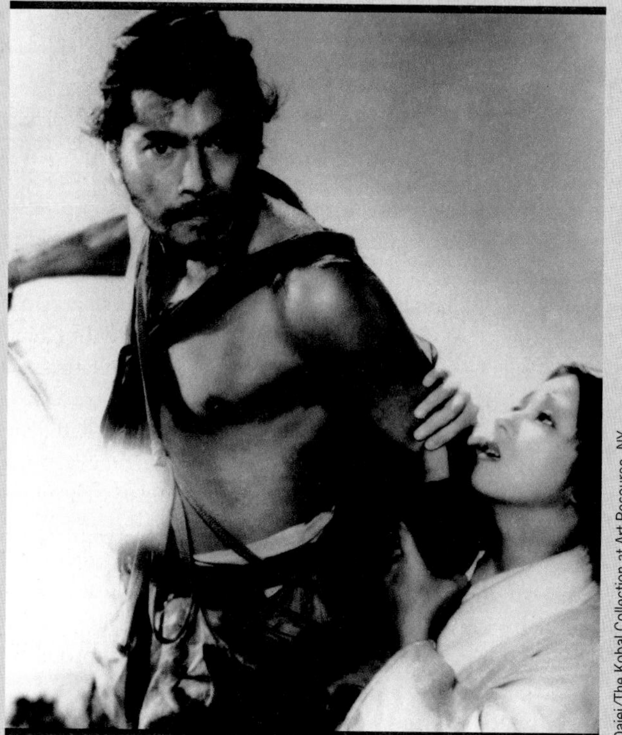

Daiei/The Kobal Collection at Art Resource, NY

In this still from Kurosawa's *Rashomon*, the samurai' wife, Masako (Machiko Kyo), pleads with the brigand Tajomaru (Toshiro Mifune).

Over the years, Kurosawa followed his success in *Rashomon* with a series of films based on themes from premodern Japanese history. In *The Seven Samurai* (1954), a village hires a band of warriors to provide protection against nearby bandits. The warrior-for-hire theme reappears in the satirical film *Yojimbo* (1961), while *Ran* (1985) borrows from Shakespeare's play *King Lear* in depicting a power struggle among the sons of an aging warlord. Hollywood has in turn paid homage to Kurosawa in a number of films that borrow from his work, including *Ocean's Eleven*, *The Magnificent Seven*, and *Hostage*.

primitive concerns about death, childbirth, illness, and menstruation. This traditional concern about physical purity may help explain the strong Japanese emphasis on personal cleanliness and the practice of denying women entrance to the holy places.

Another feature of Shinto is its stress on the beauty of nature and the importance of nature itself in Japanese life. Shinto shrines are usually located in places of exceptional beauty and are often dedicated to a nearby physical feature. As time passed, such primitive beliefs contributed to the characteristic Japanese love of nature. In this sense, early Shinto beliefs have been incorporated into the lives of all Japanese.

In time, Shinto evolved into a state doctrine that was linked with belief in the divinity of the emperor and the sacredness of the Japanese nation. A national shrine was established at Ise (EE-say), north of the early capital of Nara, where the emperor annually paid tribute to the sun goddess. But although Shinto had evolved well beyond its primitive origins, like its counterparts elsewhere it could not satisfy all the religious and emotional needs of the Japanese people. For those needs, the Japanese turned to Buddhism.

BUDDHISM As we have seen, Buddhism was introduced into Japan from China during the sixth century C.E. and had begun to spread beyond the court to the general population by the eighth century. As in China, most Japanese saw no contradiction between worshiping both the Buddha and their local nature gods (*kami*), many of whom were considered to be later manifestations of the Buddha. Most of the Buddhist sects that had achieved popularity in China were established in Japan, and many of them attracted powerful patrons at court. Great monasteries were established that competed in wealth and influence with the noble families that had traditionally ruled the country.

Perhaps the two most influential Buddhist sects were the **Pure Land** (Jodo) sect and **Zen** (in Chinese, Chan or Ch'an). The Pure Land sect, which taught that devotion alone could lead to enlightenment and release, was very popular among the common people, for whom monastic life was one of the few routes to upward mobility. Among the aristocracy, the most influential school was Zen, which exerted a significant impact on Japanese life and culture during the era of the warring states. In its emphasis on austerity, self-discipline, and communion with nature, Zen complemented many traditional beliefs in Japanese society and became an important component of the samurai warrior's code.

In Zen teachings, there were various ways to achieve enlightenment—***satori*** (suh-TAWR-ee) in Japanese. Some stressed that it could be achieved suddenly. One monk, for example, reportedly achieved *satori* by listening to the sound of a bamboo striking against roof tiles; another, by carefully watching the opening of peach blossoms in the spring. But other practitioners, sometimes called adepts, said that enlightenment could come only through studying the scriptures and arduous self-discipline, known as *zazen* (ZAH-ZEN), or "seated Zen." Seated Zen involved a lengthy process of meditation that cleansed the mind of all thoughts so that it could concentrate on the essential.

Sources of Traditional Japanese Culture

Nowhere is the Japanese genius for blending indigenous and imported elements into an effective whole better demonstrated than in culture. In such widely diverse fields as art, architecture, sculpture, and literature, the Japanese from early times showed an impressive capacity to borrow selectively from abroad without destroying essential native elements.

Growing contact with China during the period of the rise of the Yamato state stimulated Japanese artists. Missions sent to China and Korea during the seventh and eighth centuries returned with examples of Tang literature, sculpture, and painting, all of which influenced the Japanese.

LITERATURE Borrowing from Chinese models was somewhat complicated, however, since the early Japanese had no writing system for recording their own spoken language and initially adopted the Chinese written language for writing. But resourceful Japanese soon began to adapt the Chinese written characters so that they could be used for recording the Japanese language. In some cases, Chinese characters were given Japanese pronunciations. But Chinese characters ordinarily could not be used to record Japanese words, which normally contain more than one syllable. Sometimes the Japanese simply used Chinese characters as phonetic symbols that were combined to form Japanese words. Later they simplified the characters into phonetic symbols that were used alongside Chinese characters. This hybrid system continues to be used today. At first, most educated Japanese preferred to write in Chinese, and a court literature—consisting of essays, poetry, and official histories—appeared in the classical Chinese language. But spoken Japanese never totally disappeared among the educated classes and eventually became the instrument of a unique literature. With the lessening of Chinese cultural influence in the tenth century, Japanese verse resurfaced. Between the tenth and fifteenth centuries, twenty imperial anthologies of poetry were compiled. Initially, they were written primarily by courtiers, but with the fall of the Heian court and the rise of the warrior and merchant classes, all literate segments of society began to produce poetry.

Japanese poetry is unique. It expresses its themes in a simple form, a characteristic stemming from traditional Japanese aesthetics, Zen religion, and the language itself. The aim of the Japanese poet was to create a mood, perhaps the melancholic effect of gently falling cherry blossoms or leaves. With a few specific references, the poet suggested a whole world, just as Zen Buddhism sought enlightenment from a sudden perception. Poets often alluded to earlier poems by repeating their images with small changes, a technique that was viewed not as plagiarism but as an elaboration on the meaning of the earlier poem.

By the fourteenth century, the technique of the "linked verse" had become the most popular form of Japanese poetry. Known as *haiku* (HY-koo), it is composed of seventeen syllables divided into lines of five, seven, and five syllables, respectively. The poems usually focused on images from nature and the mutability of life. Often the poetry was written by several individuals alternately composing verses and linking them together into long sequences of hundreds and even thousands of lines. The following example, by three poets named Sogi (SOH-gee), Shohaku (shoh-HAH-koo), and Socho (SOH-choh), is one of the most famous of the period:

Snow clinging to slope, — Sogi
On mist-enshrouded mountains
At eveningtime.

In the distance flows — Shohaku
Through plum-scented villages.

Willows cluster — Socho
In the river breeze
As spring appears.[7]

Poetry served a unique function at the Heian court, where it was the initial means of communication between lovers. By custom, aristocratic women were isolated from all contact with men outside their immediate family and spent their days hidden behind screens. Some amused themselves by writing poetry. When courtship began, poetic exchanges were the only means a woman had to attract her prospective lover, who would be enticed solely by her poetic art.

During the Heian period, male courtiers wrote in Chinese, believing that Chinese civilization was superior and worthy of emulation. Like the Chinese, they viewed prose fiction as "vulgar gossip." Nevertheless, from the ninth century to the twelfth, Japanese women were prolific writers of prose fiction in Japanese. Excluded from school, they learned to read and write at home and wrote diaries and stories to pass the time. Some of the most talented women were invited to court as authors in residence.

In the increasingly pessimistic world of the warring states of the Kamakura period (1185–1333), Japanese novels typically focused on a solitary figure who is aloof from the refinements of the court and faces battle and possibly death. Another genre, that of the heroic war tale, came out of the new warrior class. These works described the military exploits of warriors, coupled with an overwhelming sense of sadness and loneliness.

The famous classical Japanese drama known as *No* (NOH) also originated during this period. *No* developed out of a variety of entertainment forms, such as dancing and juggling, that were part of the native tradition or had been imported from China and other regions of Asia. The plots were normally based on stories from Japanese history or legend. Eventually, *No* evolved into a highly stylized drama in which the performers wore masks and danced to the accompaniment of instrumental music. Like much of Japanese culture, *No* was restrained, graceful, and refined.

ART AND ARCHITECTURE In art and architecture, as in literature, the Japanese pursued their interest in beauty, simplicity, and nature. To some degree, Japanese artists and architects were influenced by Chinese forms. As they became familiar with Chinese architecture, Japanese rulers and aristocrats tried to emulate the splendor of Tang civilization and began constructing their palaces and temples in Chinese style.

During the Heian period (794–1185), the search for beauty was reflected in various art forms, such as narrative hand scrolls, screens, sliding door panels, fans, and lacquer decoration. As in literature, nature themes dominated, such as seashore scenes, a spring rain, moon and mist, or flowering wisteria and cherry blossoms. All were intended to evoke an emotional response on the part of the viewer. Japanese painting suggested the frail beauty of nature by presenting it on a smaller scale. The majestic

© William J. Duiker

The Golden Pavilion in Kyoto. Gardens, water, and architecture combine to create a magnificient setting for the Golden Pavilion. Constructed in the fourteenth century as a retreat where the shoguns could withdraw from their administrative chores, the pavilion derived its name from the gold foil that covered its exterior. Completely destroyed by an arsonist in 1950 as a protest against the commercialism of modern Buddhism, it was rebuilt and reopened in 1987. The use of water as a backdrop is especially noteworthy in Chinese and Japanese landscapes, as well as in the Middle East.

mountain in a Chinese painting became a more intimate Japanese landscape with rolling hills and a rice field. Faces were rarely shown, and human drama was indicated by a woman lying prostrate or hiding her face in her sleeve. Tension was shown by two people talking at a great distance or with their backs to one another.

During the Kamakura period (1185–1333), the hand scroll with its physical realism and action-packed paintings of the new warrior class achieved great popularity. Reflecting these chaotic times, the art of portraiture flourished, and a scroll would include a full gallery of warriors and holy men in starkly realistic detail, including such unflattering features as stubble, worry lines on a forehead, and crooked teeth. Japanese sculptors also produced naturalistic wooden statues of generals, nobles, and saints. By far the most distinctive, however, were the fierce heavenly "guardian kings," who still intimidate the viewer today.

© William J. Duiker

Guardian Kings. Larger than life and intimidating in its presence, this thirteenth-century wooden statue departs from the refined atmosphere of the Heian court and pulsates with the masculine energy of the Kamakura period. Placed strategically at the entrance to Buddhist shrines, guardian kings such as this one protected the temple and the faithful. In contrast to the refined atmosphere of the Fujiwara court, the Kamakura era was a warrior's world.

Zen Buddhism, an import from China in the thirteenth century, also influenced Japanese aesthetics. With its emphasis on immediate enlightenment without recourse to intellectual analysis and elaborate ritual, Zen reinforced the Japanese predilection for simplicity and self-discipline. During this era, Zen philosophy found expression in the Japanese garden, the tea ceremony, the art of flower arranging, pottery and ceramics, and miniature plant display—the famous ***bonsai*** (bon-SY), literally "pot scenery."

Landscapes served as an important means of expression in both Japanese art and architecture. Japanese gardens were initially modeled on Chinese examples. Early court texts during the Heian period emphasized the importance of including a stream or pond when creating a garden. The landscape surrounding the fourteenth-century Golden Pavilion in Kyoto displays a harmony of garden, water, and architecture that makes it one of the treasures of the world. Because of the shortage of water in the city, later gardens concentrated on rock compositions, using white pebbles to represent water (see the comparative illustration on p. 293).

Like the Japanese garden, the tea ceremony represents the fusion of Zen and aesthetics. Developed in the fifteenth century, it was practiced in a simple room devoid of external ornament except for a *tatami* floor, sliding doors, and an alcove with a writing desk and asymmetrical shelves. The participants could therefore focus completely on the activity of pouring and drinking tea. "Tea and Zen have the same flavor," goes the Japanese saying. Considered the ultimate symbol of spiritual deliverance, the tea ceremony had great aesthetic value and moral significance in traditional times just as it does today.

Japan and the Chinese Model

Few societies in Asia have historically been as isolated as Japan. Cut off from the mainland by 120 miles of frequently turbulent ocean, the Japanese had only minimal contact with the outside world during most of their early development.

Whether this isolation was ultimately beneficial to Japanese society cannot be determined. On the one hand, the lack of knowledge of developments taking place elsewhere probably delayed the process of change in Japan. On the other hand, the Japanese were spared the

© William J. Duiker

© Kaz Mori/Getty Images

COMPARATIVE ILLUSTRATION

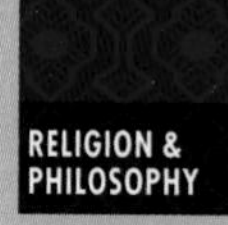

In the Garden. In traditional China and Japan, gardens were meant to free the observer's mind from mundane concerns, offering spiritual refreshment in the quiet of nature. Chinese gardens were designed to reconstruct an orderly microcosm of nature, where the harassed Confucian official could find spiritual renewal. Wandering through constantly changing perspectives of ponds, trees, rocks, and pavilions, he could imagine himself immersed in a monumental landscape. In the garden in Suzhou on the left, the rocks represent towering mountains to suggest a Daoist sense of withdrawal and eternity, reducing the viewer to a tiny speck in the grand flow of life.

In Japan, the traditional garden reflected the Zen Buddhist philosophy of simplicity, restraint, allusion, and tranquillity. In this garden at the Ryoanji (RYOH-ahn-jee) temple in Kyoto, the rocks are meant to suggest mountains rising from a sea of pebbles. Such gardens served as an aid to meditation, inspiring the viewer to join with comrades in composing "linked verse" (see the poetry on p. 291).

How do gardens in traditional China and Japan differ in form and purpose from gardens in Western societies? Why do you think this is the case?

destructive invasions that afflicted other ancient civilizations. Certainly, once the Japanese became acquainted with Chinese culture at the height of the Tang era, they were quick to take advantage of the opportunity. In the space of a few decades, the young state adopted many aspects of Chinese society and culture and thereby introduced major changes into Japanese life.

Nevertheless, Japanese political institutions failed to follow all aspects of the Chinese pattern. Despite Prince Shotoku's effort to make effective use of the imperial traditions of Tang China, the decentralizing forces inside Japanese society remained dominant throughout the period under discussion in this chapter. Adoption of the Confucian civil service examination did not lead to a breakdown of Japanese social divisions; instead the examination was administered in a manner that preserved and strengthened them. Although Buddhist and Daoist doctrines made a significant contribution to Japanese religious practices, Shinto beliefs continued to play a major role in shaping the Japanese worldview.

Why Japan did not follow the Chinese road to centralized authority has been the subject of some debate among historians. Some argue that the answer lies in differing cultural traditions, while others suggest that Chinese institutions and values were introduced too rapidly to be assimilated effectively by Japanese society. One factor may have been the absence of a foreign threat (except for the Mongols) in Japan. A recent view holds that diseases (such as smallpox and measles) imported inadvertently from China led to a marked decline in the population of the islands, reducing the food output and preventing the population from coalescing in more compact urban centers.

In any event, Japan was not the only society in Asia to assimilate ideas from abroad while at the same time preserving customs and institutions inherited from the past. Across the Sea of Japan to the west and several thousand miles to the south, other Asian peoples were embarked on a similar journey. We now turn to their experience.

Korea: Bridge to the East

FOCUS QUESTION: What were the main characteristics of economic and social life in early Korea?

Few of the societies on the periphery of China have been as directly influenced by the Chinese model as Korea. Nevertheless, the relationship between China and Korea has often been characterized by tension and conflict, and Koreans have often resented what they perceive to be Chinese chauvinism and arrogance.

A graphic example of this attitude has occurred in recent years as officials and historians in both countries have vociferously disputed differing interpretations of the early history of the Korean people. Slightly larger than the state of Minnesota, the Korean peninsula was probably first settled by Altaic-speaking fishing and hunting peoples from neighboring Manchuria during the Neolithic Age. Because the area is relatively mountainous (only about one-fifth of the peninsula is adaptable to cultivation), farming was apparently not practiced until about 2000 B.C.E. At that time, the peoples living in the area began to form organized communities.

It is this period that gives rise to scholarly disagreement. In 2004, official Chinese sources claimed that the first organized kingdom in the area, known as Koguryo (koh-GOOR-yoh) (37 B.C.E.–668 C.E.), occupied a wide swath of Manchuria as well as the northern section of the Korean peninsula and was thus an integral part of Chinese history. Korean scholars, basing their contentions on both legend and scattered historical evidence, countered that the first kingdom established on the peninsula, known as Gojoseon (goh-joh-SHAWN), was created by the Korean ruler Dangun (dan-GOON) in or about 2333 B.C.E. and was ethnically Korean. It was at that time, these scholars maintain, that the Bronze Age got under way in northeastern Asia.

Although this issue continues to be in dispute, most scholars today do agree that in 109 B.C.E., the northern part of the peninsula came under direct Chinese rule. During the next several generations, the area was ruled by the Han dynasty, which divided the territory into provinces and introduced Chinese institutions. With the decline of the Han in the third century C.E., power gradually shifted to local tribal leaders, who drove out the Chinese administrators but continued to absorb Chinese cultural influence. Eventually, three separate kingdoms emerged on the peninsula: Koguryo in the north, Paekche (bayk-JEE) in the southwest, and Silla (SIL-uh) in the southeast. The Japanese, who had recently established their own state on the Yamato plain, may have maintained a small colony on the southern coast.

The Three Kingdoms

From the fourth to the seventh centuries, the three kingdoms were bitter rivals for influence and territory on the peninsula. At the same time, all began to absorb Chinese political and cultural institutions. Chinese influence was most notable in Koguryo, where Buddhism was introduced in the late fourth century C.E. and the first Confucian academy on the peninsula was established in the capital at Pyongyang (pyahng-YANG). All three kingdoms also appear to have accepted a tributary relationship with one or another of the squabbling states that emerged in China after the fall of the Han. The kingdom of Silla, less exposed than its two rivals to Chinese influence, was at first the weakest of the three, but eventually its greater internal cohesion—perhaps a consequence of the tenacity of its tribal traditions—enabled it to become the dominant power on the peninsula. Then the rulers of Silla forced the Chinese to withdraw from all but the area adjacent to the Yalu (YAH-loo) River. To pacify the haughty Chinese, Silla accepted tributary status under the Tang dynasty. The remaining Japanese colonies in the south were eliminated.

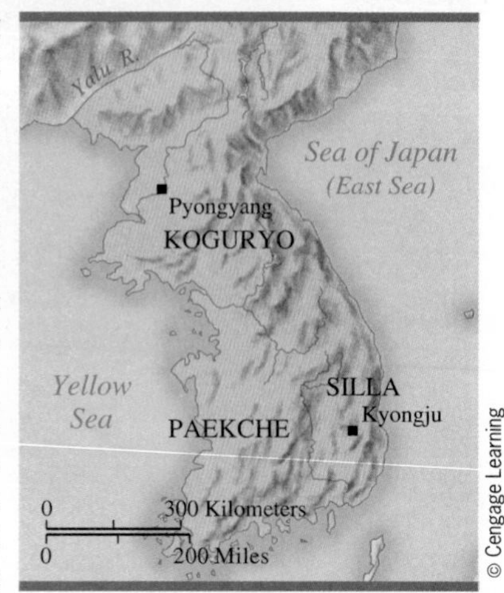

Korea's Three Kingdoms

With the country unified for the first time, the rulers of Silla attempted to use Chinese political institutions and ideology to forge a centralized state. Buddhism, now rising in popularity, became the state religion, and Korean monks followed the paths of their Japanese counterparts on journeys to the Middle Kingdom. Chinese architecture and art became dominant in the capital at Kyongju (KEE-yahng-joo) and other urban centers, and the written Chinese language became the official means of communication at court. But powerful aristocratic families, long dominant in the southeastern part of the peninsula, were still influential at court. They were able to prevent the adoption of the Tang civil service examination system and resisted the distribution of manorial lands to the poor. The failure to adopt the Chinese model was fatal. Squabbling among noble families steadily increased, and after the assassination of the king of Silla in 780, civil war erupted.

The Rise of the Koryo Dynasty

In the early tenth century, a new dynasty called Koryo (KAWR-yoh) (the root of the modern word for Korea) arose in the north. The new kingdom adopted Chinese political institutions in an effort to strengthen its power and unify its territory. The civil service examination system was introduced in 958, but as in Japan, the bureaucracy continued to be dominated by influential aristocratic families.

The Koryo dynasty remained in power for four hundred years, protected from invasion by the absence of a

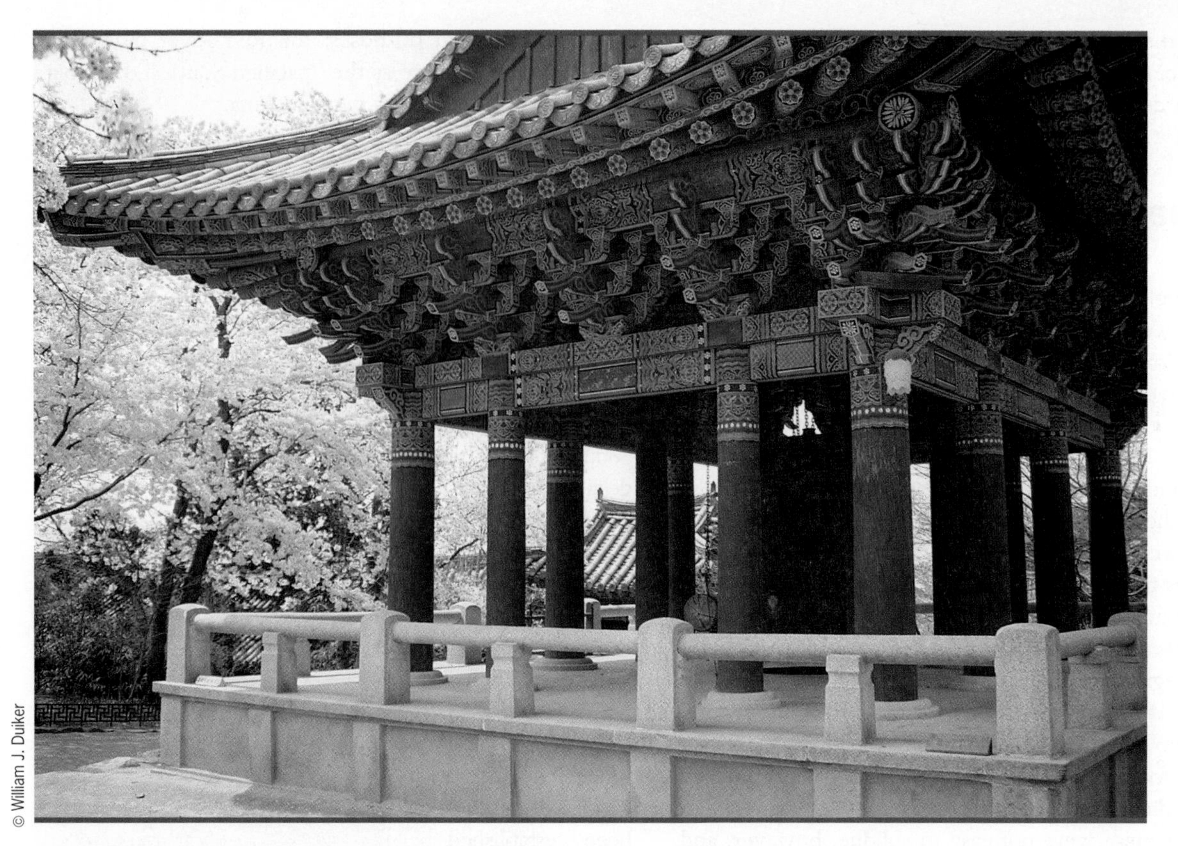
© William J. Duiker

Pulguksa Bell Tower. Among the greatest architectural achievements on the Korean peninsula is the Pulguksa (Monastery of the Land of Buddha), built near Kyongju, the ancient capital of Silla, in the eighth century C.E. Shown here is the bell tower, located in the midst of beautiful parklands on the monastery grounds. In 1966, a scroll was discovered inside a stone stupa adjacent to the monastery. Dating from the early eighth century C.E., it is believed to be the oldest printed text extant in the world today.

strong dynasty in neighboring China. Under the Koryo, industry and commerce slowly began to develop, but as in China, agriculture was the prime source of wealth. In theory, all land was the property of the king, but in actuality, noble families controlled their holdings. The lands were worked by peasants who were subject to burdens similar to those of European serfs. At the bottom of society was a class of ***chonmin*** (CHAWN-min), or "base people," composed of slaves, artisans, and other specialized workers.

From a cultural perspective, the Koryo era was one of high achievement. Buddhist monasteries, run by sects introduced from China, including Pure Land and Zen (Chan), controlled vast territories, while their monks served as royal advisers at court. At first, Buddhist themes dominated in Korean art and sculpture, and the entire Tripitaka (tri-pih-TAH-kah) (the "three baskets" of the Buddhist canon) was printed using wooden blocks. Eventually, however, with the appearance of landscape painting and porcelain, Confucian themes began to predominate.

Under the Mongols

Like its predecessor in Silla, the kingdom of Koryo was unable to overcome the power of the nobility and the absence of a reliable tax base. In the thirteenth century, the Mongols seized the northern part of the country and assimilated it into the Yuan Empire. The weakened kingdom of Koryo became a tributary of the Great Khan in Khanbaliq (see Chapter 10).

The era of Mongol rule was one of profound suffering for the Korean people, especially the thousands of peasants and artisans who were compelled to perform forced labor to help build the ships in preparation for Khubilai Khan's invasion of Japan. On the positive side, the Mongols introduced many new ideas and technology from China and farther afield. The Koryo dynasty had managed to survive, but only by accepting Mongol authority, and when the power of the Mongols declined, the kingdom declined with it. With the rise to power of the Ming in China, Koryo collapsed, and power was seized by the military commander Yi Song-gye (YEE-song-YEE), who declared the founding of the new Yi (YEE) dynasty in 1392. Once again, the Korean people were in charge of their own destiny.

Vietnam: The Smaller Dragon

FOCUS QUESTIONS: What were the main developments in Vietnamese history before 1500? Why were the Vietnamese able to restore their national independence after a millennium of Chinese rule?

While the Korean people were attempting to establish their own identity in the shadow of the powerful Chinese Empire, the peoples of Vietnam, on China's southern frontier, were seeking to do the same. The Vietnamese (known as the Yueh in Chinese, from the peoples of that name inhabiting the southeastern coast of mainland China) began to practice irrigated agriculture in the flooded regions of the Red River delta at an early date and entered the Bronze Age sometime during the second millennium B.C.E. By about 200 B.C.E., a young state had begun to form in the area but immediately encountered the expanding power of the Qin Empire (see Chapter 3). The Vietnamese were not easy to subdue, however, and the collapse of the Qin dynasty temporarily enabled them to preserve their independence (see the box on p. 297). Nevertheless, a century later, they were absorbed into the Han Empire.

At first, the Han were content to rule the delta as an autonomous region under the administration of the local landed aristocracy. But Chinese taxes were oppressive, and in 39 C.E., a revolt led by the Trung sisters (widows of local nobles who had been executed by the Chinese) briefly brought Han rule to an end. The Chinese soon suppressed the rebellion, however, and began to rule the area directly through officials dispatched from China. The first Chinese officials to serve in the region became exasperated at the uncultured ways of the locals, who wandered around "naked without shame."[8] In time, however, these foreign officials began to intermarry with the local nobility and form a Sino-Vietnamese ruling class who, though trained in Chinese culture, began to identify with the cause of Vietnamese autonomy.

For nearly a thousand years, the Vietnamese were exposed to the art, architecture, literature, philosophy, and written language of China as the Chinese attempted to integrate the area culturally as well as politically and administratively into their empire. It was a classic case of the Chinese effort to introduce advanced Confucian civilization to the "backward peoples" along the perimeter. To all intents and purposes, the Red River delta, then known to the Chinese as the "pacified South," or Annam (ahn-NAHM), became a part of China.

The Rise of Great Viet

Despite the Chinese efforts to assimilate Vietnam, the Vietnamese sense of ethnic and cultural identity proved inextinguishable, and in 939, the Vietnamese took advantage of the collapse of the Tang dynasty in China to overthrow Chinese rule.

The new Vietnamese state, which called itself Dai Viet (dy VEE-et) (Great Viet), became a dynamic new force on the Southeast Asian mainland. As the population of the Red River delta expanded, Dai Viet soon came into conflict with Champa (CHAHM-puh), its neighbor to the south. Located along the central coast of modern Vietnam, Champa was a trading society based on Indian cultural traditions that had been established earlier in 192 C.E. Over the next several centuries, the two states fought on numerous occasions. Finally, in 1471, Dai Viet succeeded in conquering Champa. The Vietnamese then resumed their march southward, establishing agricultural settlements in the newly conquered territory. By the seventeenth century, the Vietnamese had reached the Gulf of Siam.

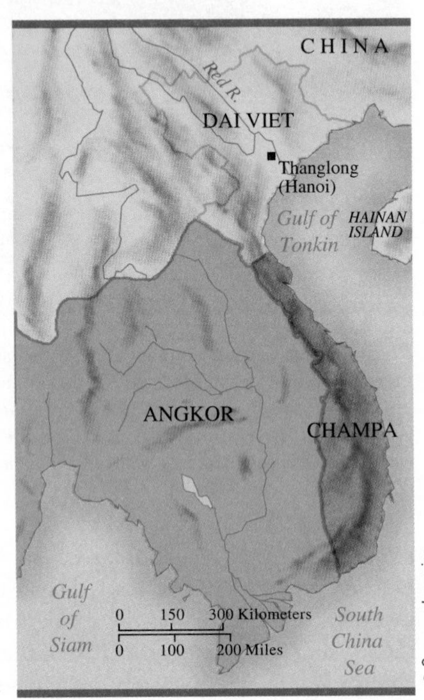

The Kingdom of Dai Viet, 1100

The Vietnamese faced an even more serious challenge from the north. The Song dynasty in China, beset with its own problems on the northern frontier, eventually accepted the Dai Viet ruler's offer of tribute status, but later dynasties attempted to reintegrate the Red River delta into the Chinese Empire. The first effort was made in the late thirteenth century by the Mongols, who attempted on two occasions to conquer the Vietnamese. After a series of bloody battles, during which the Vietnamese displayed an impressive capacity for guerrilla warfare, the invaders were driven out. A little over a century later,

The First Vietnam War

POLITICS & GOVERNMENT

In the third century B.C.E., the armies of the Chinese state of Qin (Ch'in) invaded the Red River delta to launch an attack on the small Vietnamese state located there. As this passage from a Han dynasty philosophical text shows, the Vietnamese were not easy to conquer, and the new state soon declared its independence from the Qin. It was a lesson that was too often forgotten by would-be conquerors in later centuries.

Masters of Huai Nan

Ch'in Shih Huang Ti [the first emperor of Qin] was interested in the rhinoceros horn, the elephant tusks, the kingfisher plumes, and the pearls of the land of Yueh [Viet]; he therefore sent Commissioner T'u Sui at the head of five hundred thousand men divided into five armies. . . . For three years the sword and the crossbow were in constant readiness. Superintendent Lu was sent; there was no means of assuring the transport of supplies so he employed soldiers to dig a canal for sending grain, thereby making it possible to wage war on the people of Yueh. The lord of Western Ou, I Hsu Sung, was killed; consequently, the Yueh people entered the wilderness and lived there with the animals; none consented to be a slave of Ch'in; choosing from among themselves men of valor, they made them their leaders and attacked the Ch'in by night, inflicting on them a great defeat and killing Commissioner T'u Sui; the dead and wounded were many. After this, the emperor deported convicts to hold the garrisons against the Yueh people.

The Yueh people fled into the depths of the mountains and forests, and it was not possible to fight them. The soldiers were kept in garrisons to watch over the abandoned territories. This went on for a long time, and the soldiers grew weary. Then the Yueh came out and attacked; the Ch'in soldiers suffered a great defeat. Subsequently, convicts were sent to hold the garrisons against the Yueh.

How would the ancient Chinese military strategist Sun Tzu, mentioned in Chapter 3, have advised the Qin military commanders to carry out their operations? Would he have approved of the tactics adopted by the Vietnamese?

Source: From Keith W. Taylor, *The Birth of Vietnam* (Berkeley, 1983), p. 18.

the Ming dynasty tried again, and for twenty years Vietnam was once more under Chinese rule. In 1428, the Vietnamese evicted the Chinese again, but the experience had contributed to the strong sense of Vietnamese identity.

THE CHINESE LEGACY Despite their stubborn resistance to Chinese rule, after the restoration of independence in the tenth century, Vietnamese rulers quickly discovered the convenience of the Confucian model in administering a river valley society and therefore attempted to follow Chinese practice in forming their own state. The ruler styled himself an emperor like his counterpart to the north (although he prudently termed himself a king in his direct dealings with the Chinese court), adopted Chinese court rituals, claimed the mandate of Heaven, and arrogated to himself the same authority and privileges in his dealings with his subjects. But unlike a Chinese emperor, who had no particular symbolic role as defender of the Chinese people or Chinese culture, a Vietnamese monarch was viewed, above all, as the symbol and defender of Vietnamese independence.

Like their Chinese counterparts, Vietnamese rulers fought to preserve their authority from the challenges of powerful aristocratic families and turned to the Chinese

CHRONOLOGY Early Korea and Vietnam	
Foundation of Gojoseon state in Korea	c. 2333 B.C.E.
Chinese conquest of Korea and Vietnam	Second century B.C.E.
Trung Sisters' Revolt	39 C.E.
Founding of Champa	192
Era of Three Kingdoms in Korea	300s–600s
Restoration of Vietnamese independence	939
Mongol invasions of Korea and Vietnam	1257–1285
Founding of Yi dynasty in Korea	1392
Vietnamese conquest of Champa	1471

© William J. Duiker

The One-Pillar Pagoda, Hanoi. This eleventh-century pagoda was built at the order of a Vietnamese monarch who had dreamed that the Buddhist goddess of mercy, known in China as Guan Yin, while seated on a lotus, had promised him a son. Shortly after the dream, the emperor fathered a son. In gratitude, he constructed this distinctive pagoda on one pillar, resembling a lotus blossom, the Buddhist symbol of purity, rising out of the mud.

bureaucratic model, including civil service examinations, as a means of doing so. Under the pressure of strong monarchs, the concept of merit eventually took hold, and the power of the landed aristocracy was weakened if not entirely broken. The Vietnamese adopted much of the Chinese administrative structure, including the six ministries, the censorate, and the various levels of provincial and local administration.

Another aspect of the Chinese legacy was the spread of Buddhist, Daoist, and Confucian ideas, which supplemented the traditional Vietnamese belief in nature spirits. Buddhist precepts became popular among the local population, who integrated the new faith into their existing belief system by founding Buddhist temples dedicated to the local village deity in the hope of guaranteeing an abundant harvest. Upper-class Vietnamese educated in the Confucian classics tended to follow the more agnostic Confucian doctrine, but some joined Buddhist monasteries. Daoism also flourished at all levels of society and, as in China, provided a structure for animistic beliefs and practices that still predominated at the village level.

During the early period of independence, Vietnamese culture also borrowed liberally from its larger neighbor. Educated Vietnamese tried their hand at Chinese poetry, wrote dynastic histories in the Chinese style, and followed Chinese models in sculpture, architecture, and porcelain. Many of the notable buildings of the medieval period, such as the Temple of Literature and the famous One-Pillar Pagoda in Hanoi, are classic examples of Chinese architecture.

But there were signs that Vietnamese creativity would eventually transcend the bounds of Chinese cultural norms. Although most classical writing was undertaken in literary Chinese, the only form of literary expression deemed suitable by Confucian conservatives, an adaptation of Chinese written characters, called ***chu nom*** (CHOO nahm) ("southern characters"), was devised to provide a written system for spoken Vietnamese. In use by the early ninth century, it eventually began to be used for the composition of essays and poetry in the Vietnamese language. Such pioneering efforts would lead in later centuries to the emergence of a vigorous national literature totally independent of Chinese forms.

Society and Family Life

Vietnamese social institutions and customs were also strongly influenced by those of China. As in China, the introduction of a Confucian system and the adoption of civil service examinations undermined the role of the old landed aristocrats and led eventually to their replacement by the scholar-gentry class. Also as in China, the examinations were open to most males, regardless of family background, which opened the door to a degree of social mobility unknown in most of the states elsewhere in the region. Candidates for the bureaucracy read many of the same Confucian classics and absorbed the same ethical principles as their counterparts in China. At the same time, they were also exposed to the classic works of Vietnamese history, which strengthened their sense that Vietnam was a distinct culture similar to, but separate from, that of China.

The vast majority of the Vietnamese people, however, were peasants. Most were small landholders or sharecroppers who rented their plots from wealthier farmers, but large estates were rare due to the systematic efforts of the central government to prevent the rise of a powerful local landed elite.

Family life in Vietnam was similar in many respects to that in China. The Confucian concept of family took hold during the period of Chinese rule, along with the related concepts of filial piety and gender inequality. Perhaps the most striking difference between family traditions in China and Vietnam was that Vietnamese women possessed more rights both in practice and by law. Since ancient times, wives had been permitted to own property and initiate divorce proceedings. One consequence of Chinese rule was a growing emphasis on male dominance, but the tradition of women's rights was never totally extinguished and was legally recognized in a law code promulgated in 1460.

Moreover, Vietnam had a strong historical tradition associating heroic women with the defense of the homeland. The Trung sisters were the first but by no means the only example. In the following passage, a Vietnamese historian of the eighteenth century recounts their story:

> The imperial court was far away; local officials were greedy and oppressive. At that time the country of one hundred sons was the country of the women of Lord To. The ladies [the Trung sisters] used the female arts against their irreconcilable foe; skirts and hairpins sang of patriotic righteousness, uttered a solemn oath at the inner door of the ladies' quarters, expelled the governor, and seized the capital. . . . Were they not grand heroines? . . . Our two ladies brought forward an army of all the people, and, establishing a royal court that settled affairs in the territories of the sixty-five strongholds, shook their skirts over the Hundred Yueh [the Vietnamese people].[9]

CHAPTER SUMMARY

Like many other great civilizations, the Chinese were traditionally convinced of the superiority of their culture and, when the opportunity arose, sought to introduce it to neighboring peoples. Although the latter were viewed with a measure of condescension, Confucian teachings suggested the possibility of redemption. As the Master had remarked in the *Analects*, "By nature, people are basically alike; in practice they are far apart."[10] As a result, Chinese policies in the region were often shaped by the desire to introduce Chinese values and institutions to non-Chinese peoples living on the periphery.

As this chapter has shown, when conditions were right, China's "civilizing mission" sometimes had some marked success. All three countries that we have dealt with here borrowed liberally from the Chinese model. At the same time, all adapted Chinese institutions and values to the conditions prevailing in their own societies. Though all expressed admiration and respect for China's achievement, all sought to keep Chinese power at a distance.

As an island nation, Japan was the most successful of the three in protecting its political sovereignty and its cultural identity. Both Korea and Vietnam were compelled on various occasions to defend their independence by force of arms. That experience may have shaped their strong sense of national distinctiveness, which we shall discuss further in a later chapter.

The appeal of Chinese institutions can undoubtedly be explained by the fact that Japan, Korea, and Vietnam were all agrarian societies, much like their larger neighbor. But it is undoubtedly significant that the aspect of Chinese political culture that was least amenable to adoption abroad was the civil service examination system. The Confucian concept of meritocracy ran directly counter to the strong aristocratic tradition that flourished in all three societies during their early stage of development. Even when the system was adopted, it was put to quite different uses. Only in Vietnam did the concept of merit eventually triumph over that of birth, as strong rulers of Dai Viet attempted to initiate the Chinese model as a means of creating a centralized system of government.

CHAPTER TIMELINE

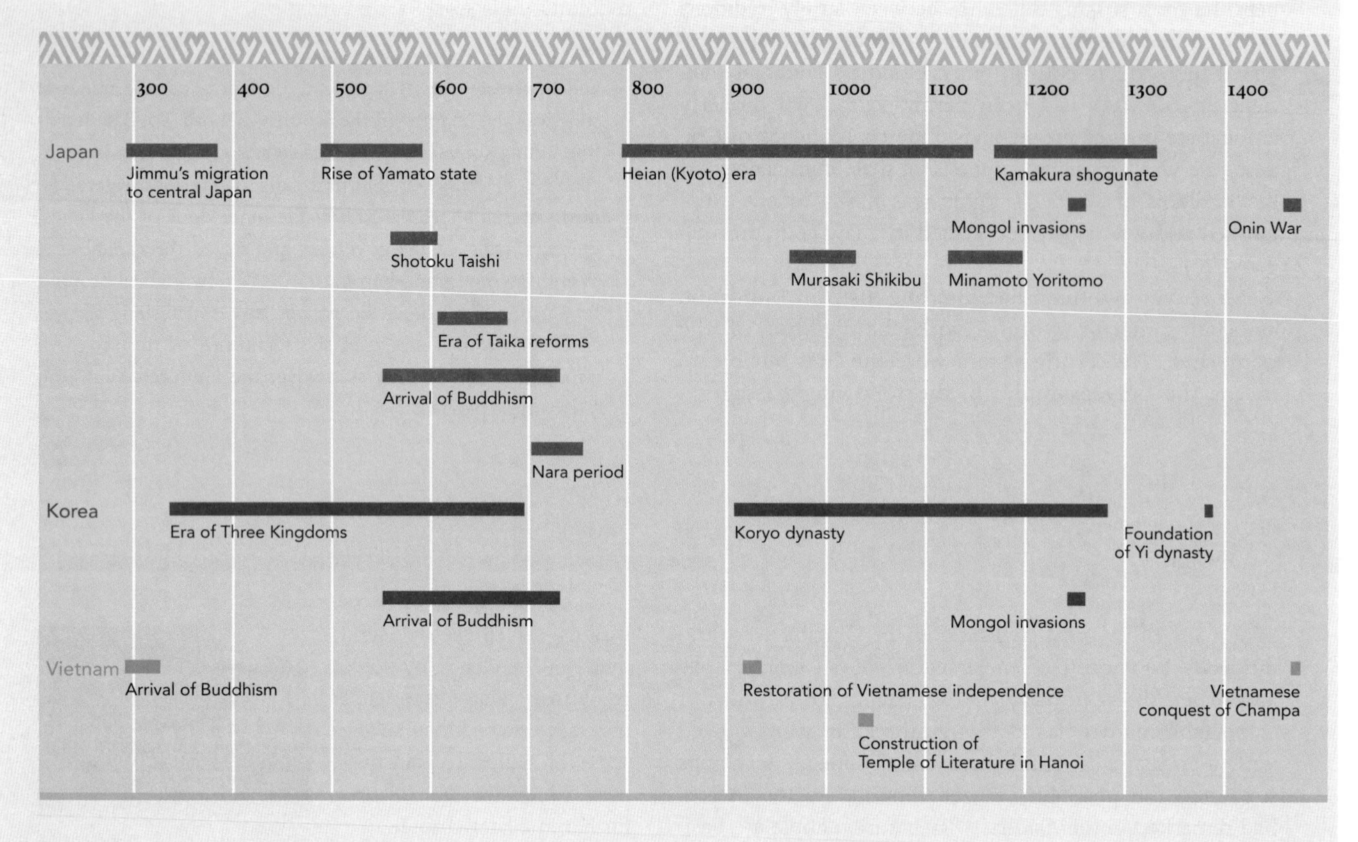

CHAPTER REVIEW

Upon Reflection

Q To what degree did the institutions and values of medieval Japan conform to the Chinese model? What factors explain the key differences?

Q How did the Korean peninsula fit into the overall history of East Asia during the period under discussion in this chapter and the previous chapter?

Q In what ways was Vietnam's relationship with China during the early historical period similar to the relationship between China and the other two major civilizations in the region—Japan and Korea? In what ways was the Vietnamese relationship with China different?

Key Terms

uji (p. 279)
Taika reforms (p. 281)
samurai (p. 283)
Bushido (p. 283)
bakufu (p. 283)
shogun (p. 283)
shogunate system (p. 283)
daimyo (p. 284)
genin (p. 288)
eta (p. 288)
kami (p. 288)
Shinto (p. 288)
Pure Land (p. 290)
Zen (p. 290)
satori (p. 290)
bonsai (p. 292)
chonmin (p. 295)
chu nom (p. 298)

Suggested Reading

RISE OF JAPANESE CIVILIZATION Some of the standard treatments of the rise of Japanese civilization appear in textbooks dealing with the early history of East Asia. Two of the best are **J. K. Fairbank, E. O. Reischauer,** and **A. M. Craig,** ***East Asia: Tradition and Transformation*** (Boston, 1989), and **C. Schirokauer et al.,** ***A Brief History of Chinese and Japanese Civilizations,*** 4th ed.

(Boston, 2013). For the latest scholarship on the early period, see the first three volumes of ***The Cambridge History of Japan,*** **ed. J. W. Hall, M. B. Jansen, M. Kanai,** and **D. Twitchett** (Cambridge, 1988).

EARLY HISTORY OF JAPAN The best available collection of documents on the early history of Japan is **W. T. de Bary et al., eds.,** ***Sources of Japanese Tradition,*** vol. 1 (New York, 2001).

For specialized books on the early historical period, see **J. Mass, ed.,** ***The Origins of Japan's Medieval World: Courtiers, Clerics, Warriors, and Peasants in the Fourteenth Century*** (Stanford, Calif., 1997); **K. Friday,** ***Samurai, Warfare and the State in Early Medieval Japan*** (New York, 2004); and **P. Valrey,** ***Japanese Culture,*** 4th ed. (Honolulu, 2000).

WOMEN'S ISSUES IN EARLY JAPAN A concise and provocative introduction to women's issues during this period in Japan, as well as in other parts of the world, can be found in **S. S. Hughes** and **B. Hughes,** ***Women in World History*** (Armonk, N.Y., 1995). For a tenth-century account of daily life for women at the Japanese court, see **I. Morris, trans. and ed.,** ***The Pillow Book of Sei Shonagon*** (New York, 1991).

JAPANESE LITERATURE The best introduction to Japanese literature for college students is still the concise and insightful **D. Keene,** ***Seeds in the Heart: Japanese Literature from Earlier Times to the Late Sixteenth Century*** (New York, 1993).

KOREA For an excellent recent survey of Korean history, see **M. J. Seth,** ***A Concise History of Korea: From the Neolithic Period Through the Nineteenth Century*** (Lanham, Mass., 2006). For documents, see **P. H. Lee, ed.,** ***Sourcebook of Korean Civilization,*** vols. 1 and 2 (New York, 1996).

VIETNAM Vietnam often receives little attention in general studies of Southeast Asia because it was part of the Chinese Empire for much of the traditional period. For a detailed investigation of the origins of Vietnamese civilization, see **K. W. Taylor,** ***The Birth of Vietnam*** (Berkeley, Calif., 1983).

Visit the CourseMate website at **www.cengagebrain.com** for additional study tools and review materials for this chapter.

CHAPTER

12

The Making of Europe

Bibliothèque de l'Arsenal, Paris//© Scala/Art Resource, NY

A medieval French manuscript illustration of the coronation of Charlemagne by Pope Leo III

CHAPTER OUTLINE AND FOCUS QUESTIONS

The Emergence of Europe in the Early Middle Ages

Q What contributions did the Romans, the Christian church, and the Germanic peoples make to the new civilization that emerged in Europe after the collapse of the Western Roman Empire? What was the significance of Charlemagne's coronation as emperor?

Europe in the High Middle Ages

Q What roles did aristocrats, peasants, and townspeople play in medieval European civilization, and how did their lifestyles differ? How did cities in Europe compare with those in China and the Middle East? What were the main aspects of the political, economic, spiritual, and cultural revivals that took place in Europe during the High Middle Ages?

Medieval Europe and the World

Q In what ways did Europeans begin to relate to peoples in other parts of the world after 1000 C.E.? What were the reasons for the Crusades, and who or what benefited the most from the experience of the Crusades?

CRITICAL THINKING

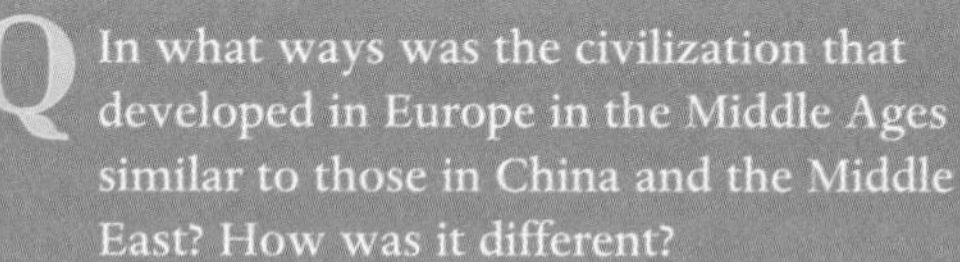
Q In what ways was the civilization that developed in Europe in the Middle Ages similar to those in China and the Middle East? How was it different?

IN 800, CHARLEMAGNE, the king of the Franks, journeyed to Rome to help Pope Leo III, head of the Catholic Church, who was barely clinging to power in the face of rebellious Romans. On Christmas Day, Charlemagne and his family, attended by Romans and Franks, crowded into Saint Peter's Basilica to hear Mass. Quite unexpectedly, according to a Frankish writer, "as the king rose from praying before the tomb of the blessed apostle Peter, Pope Leo placed a golden crown on his head." The people in the church shouted, "Long life and victory to Charles Augustus, crowned by God the great and peace-loving Emperor of the Romans." Seemingly, the Roman Empire in the west had been reborn, and Charles had become the first Roman emperor since 476. But this "Roman emperor" was actually a German king, and he had been crowned by the head of the western Christian church. In truth, the coronation of Charlemagne was a sign not of the rebirth of the Roman Empire but of the emergence of a new European civilization that came into being in western Europe after the collapse of the Western Roman Empire.

This new civilization—European civilization—was formed by the coming together of three major elements: the legacy of the Romans, the Christian church, and the Germanic peoples who moved in and settled the western empire. European civilization developed during a period that historians call the Middle Ages, or the medieval period, which lasted from about 500 to about 1500. To the historians who first used the name, the Middle Ages was a middle period between the ancient world and the modern world. During the Early Middle Ages, from about 500 to 1000 C.E., the Roman world of the western empire was slowly transformed into a new Christian European society.

The Emergence of Europe in the Early Middle Ages

FOCUS QUESTIONS: What contributions did the Romans, the Christian church, and the Germanic peoples make to the new civilization that emerged in Europe after the collapse of the Western Roman Empire? What was the significance of Charlemagne's coronation as emperor?

As we saw in Chapter 10, China descended into political chaos and civil wars after the end of the Han Empire, and it was almost four hundred years before a new imperial dynasty established political order. Similarly, after the collapse of the Western Roman Empire in the fifth century, it would also take hundreds of years to establish a new society.

The New Germanic Kingdoms

Already in the third century C.E., Germanic peoples in large numbers had begun to move into the lands of the Roman Empire, and by 500, the Western Roman Empire had been replaced politically by a series of successor states ruled by German kings. The fusion of Romans and Germans took different forms in the various Germanic kingdoms. Both the kingdom of the Ostrogoths in Italy and the kingdom of the Visigoths in Spain (see Map 12.1) maintained the Roman structure for the larger native Roman populations, while a Germanic warrior caste came to dominate. Over a period of time, Germans and natives began to fuse. In Britain, however, after the Roman armies withdrew at the beginning of the fifth century, the Angles and Saxons, Germanic tribes from Denmark and northern Germany, moved in and settled there.

Only one of the German states on the European continent proved long-lasting—the kingdom of the Franks. The establishment of a Frankish kingdom was the work of Clovis (KLOH-viss) (c. 482–511), who became a Catholic Christian around 500. By 510, Clovis had established a powerful new Frankish kingdom stretching from the Pyrenees in the west to German lands in the east (modern France and western Germany). After Clovis's death, however, as was the Frankish custom, his sons divided his newly created kingdom, and during the sixth and seventh centuries, the once-united Frankish kingdom came to be divided into three major areas: Neustria NOO-stree-uh) in northern Gaul, Austrasia (awss-TRAY-zhuh), consisting of the ancient Frankish lands on both sides of the Rhine, and the former kingdom of Burgundy.

The Role of the Christian Church

By the end of the fourth century, Christianity had become the predominant religion of the Roman Empire. As the official Roman state disintegrated, the Christian church played an increasingly important role in the growth of the new European civilization.

THE ORGANIZATION OF THE CHURCH By the fourth century, the Christian church had developed a system of government. The Christian community in each city was headed by a bishop, whose area of jurisdiction was known as a bishopric, or **diocese**; the bishoprics of each Roman province were joined together under the direction of an archbishop. The bishops of four great cities—Rome, Jerusalem, Alexandria, and Antioch—held positions of special power in church affairs. Soon, however, one of them—the bishop of Rome—claimed that he was the sole leader of the western Christian church, which came to be known as the Roman Catholic Church. According to church tradition, Jesus had given the keys to the kingdom of heaven to Peter, who was considered the chief apostle and the first bishop of Rome. Subsequent bishops of Rome were considered Peter's successors and came to be known as popes (from the Latin word *papa*, meaning "father"). By the sixth century, popes had been successful in extending papal authority over the Christian church in the west and converting the pagan peoples of Germanic Europe. Their primary instrument of conversion was the monastic movement.

THE MONKS AND THEIR MISSIONS A **monk** (in Latin, *monachus*, meaning "someone who lives alone") was a man who sought to live a life divorced from the world, cut off from ordinary human society, in order to pursue an ideal of total dedication to God. As the monastic ideal spread, a new form of **monasticism** based on living together in a community soon became the dominant

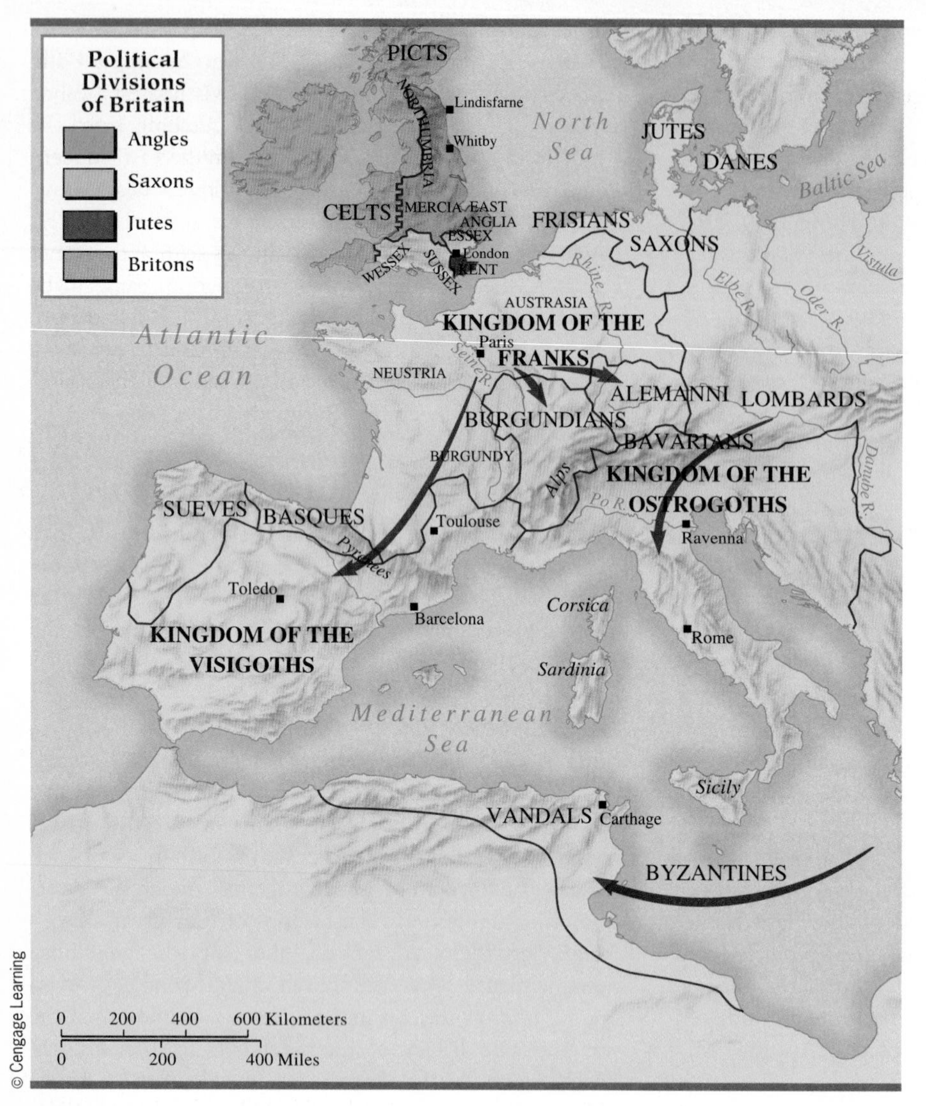

© Cengage Learning

MAP 12.1 The Germanic Kingdoms of the Old Western Empire. The Germanic tribes filled the power vacuum caused by the demise of the Western Roman Empire, building states that blended elements of Germanic customs and laws with those of Roman culture, including large-scale conversions to Christianity. The Franks established the most durable of these Germanic states.

Q *Which Germanic tribes settled in the present-day countries of Europe?*

form. Saint Benedict (c. 480–c. 543), who founded a monastic house and wrote a set of rules for it, established the basic form of monastic life in the western Christian church.

Benedict's rule divided each day into a series of activities. All monks were required to do physical work of some kind for several hours a day because idleness was "the enemy of the soul." At the very heart of community practice was prayer, the proper "work of God." Although this included private meditation and reading, all of the monks gathered together seven times during the day for common prayer and chanting of psalms. The Benedictine life was a communal one. Monks ate, worked, slept, and worshiped together.

Each Benedictine monastery was strictly ruled by an **abbot**, or "father" of the monastery, who had complete authority over his fellow monks. Unquestioning obedience to the will of the abbot was expected of every monk. Each Benedictine monastery held lands that enabled it to be a self-sustaining community, isolated from and independent of the world surrounding it. Within the monastery, however, monks were to fulfill their vow of poverty: "Let all things be common to all, as it is written, lest anyone should say that anything is his own."[1] Only men could be monks, but women, called **nuns**, also began to withdraw from the world to dedicate themselves to God.

Monasticism played an indispensable role in early medieval civilization. Monks became the new heroes of Christian civilization, and their dedication to God became the highest ideal of Christian life. They were the social workers of their communities: monks provided schools for the young, hospitality for travelers, and hospitals for the sick. Monks also copied Latin works and passed on the legacy of the ancient world to the new European civilization. Monasteries became centers of learning wherever they were located, and monks worked to spread Christianity to all of Europe.

Women played an important role in the monastic missionary movement and the conversion of the Germanic kingdoms. Some served as **abbesses** (an abbess was the head of a monastery for nuns, known as a *convent*); many abbesses came from aristocratic families, especially in Anglo-Saxon England. In the kingdom of Northumbria, for example, Saint Hilda founded the monastery of Whitby in 657. As abbess, she was responsible for making learning an important part of the life of the monastery.

Charlemagne and the Carolingians

During the seventh and eighth centuries, as the kings of the Frankish kingdom gradually lost their power, the mayors of the palace—the chief officers of the king's household—assumed more control of the kingdom. One of these mayors, Pepin (PEP-in *or* pay-PANH), finally took the logical step of assuming the kingship of the Frankish state for himself and his family. Upon his death in 768, his son came to the throne of the Frankish kingdom.

This new king was the dynamic and powerful ruler known to history as Charles the Great (768–814), or Charlemagne (SHAR-luh-mayn) (from the Latin for Charles the Great, *Carolus Magnus*). He was determined and decisive, intelligent and inquisitive, a strong statesman, and a pious Christian. Though he himself was unable to read or write, he was a wise patron of learning. In a series of military campaigns, he greatly expanded the territory he had inherited and created what came to be known as the Carolingian Empire. At its height, Charlemagne's empire covered much of western and central Europe (see the box on p. 306).

© Cengage Learning

Charlemagne's Empire

THE SIGNIFICANCE OF CHARLEMAGNE As Charlemagne's power grew, so did his prestige as the most powerful Christian ruler of what one monk even called the "kingdom of Europe." In 800, Charlemagne acquired a new title: emperor of the Romans. The significance of this imperial coronation has been much debated by historians. We are not even sure if the pope or Charlemagne initiated the idea when they met in the summer of 799 in Paderborn in German lands or whether he was pleased or displeased.

In any case, Charlemagne's coronation as Roman emperor demonstrated the strength, even after three hundred years, of the concept of an enduring Roman Empire. More important, it symbolized the fusion of Roman, Christian, and Germanic elements: a Germanic king had been crowned emperor of the Romans by the spiritual leader of western Christendom. Charlemagne had assembled an empire that stretched from the North Sea to Italy and from the Atlantic Ocean to the Danube River. This differed significantly from the Roman Empire, which encompassed much of the Mediterranean world. Had a new civilization emerged? And should Charlemagne be regarded, as one of his biographers has argued, as the "father of Europe"?[2]

The World of Lords and Vassals

The Carolingian Empire began to disintegrate soon after Charlemagne's death in 814, and less than thirty years later, in 843, it was divided among his grandsons into three major sections. Invasions in different parts of the old Carolingian world added to the process of disintegration.

INVASIONS OF THE NINTH AND TENTH CENTURIES In the ninth and tenth centuries, western Europe was beset by a wave of invasions. Muslims attacked the southern coasts of Europe and sent raiding parties into southern France. The Magyars (MAG-yarz), a people from western Asia, moved into central Europe at the end of the ninth century and settled on the plains of Hungary; from there they made forays into western Europe. Finally crushed at the Battle of Lechfeld (LEK-feld) in Germany in 955, the Magyars converted to Christianity, settled down, and created the kingdom of Hungary.

The most far-reaching attacks of the time came from the Northmen or Norsemen of Scandinavia, also known to us as the Vikings. The Vikings were warriors whose love of adventure and search for booty and new avenues of trade may have led them to invade other areas of Europe. Viking ships were the best of the period. Their shallow draft enabled them to sail up European rivers and attack places at some distance inland. In the ninth century, Vikings sacked villages and towns, destroyed churches, and easily defeated small local armies.

By the middle of the ninth century, the Northmen had begun to build winter settlements in different areas of Europe. By 850, groups of Norsemen from Norway had settled in Ireland, and Danes occupied northeastern England by 878. Beginning in 911, the ruler of the western Frankish lands gave one band of Vikings land at the mouth of the Seine River, forming a section of France that came to be known as Normandy. This policy of settling the Vikings and converting them to Christianity was a deliberate one; by their conversion to Christianity, the Vikings were soon made a part of European civilization.

THE DEVELOPMENT OF FIEF-HOLDING The disintegration of central authority in the Carolingian world and the invasions by Muslims, Magyars, and Vikings led to the emergence of a new type of relationship between free individuals. When governments ceased to be able to defend

The Achievements of Charlemagne

Einhard (YN-hart), the biographer of Charlemagne, was born in the valley of the Main River in Germany about 775. Raised and educated in the monastery of Fulda, an important center of learning, he arrived at the court of Charlemagne in 791 or 792. Although he did not achieve high office under Charlemagne, he served as private secretary to Louis the Pious, Charlemagne's son and successor. In this selection, Einhard discusses some of Charlemagne's accomplishments.

Einhard, *Life of Charlemagne*

Such are the wars, most skillfully planned and successfully fought, which this most powerful king waged during the forty-seven years of his reign. He so largely increased the Frank kingdom, which was already great and strong when he received it at his father's hands, that more than double its former territory was added to it. . . . He subdued all the wild and barbarous tribes dwelling in Germany between the Rhine and the Vistula, the Ocean and the Danube, all of which speak very much the same language, but differ widely from one another in customs and dress. . . .

He added to the glory of his reign by gaining the good will of several kings and nations; so close, indeed, was the alliance that he contracted with Alfonso, King of Galicia and Asturias, that the latter, when sending letters or ambassadors to Charles, invariably styled himself his man. . . . The Emperors of Constantinople [the Byzantine emperors] sought friendship and alliance with Charles by several embassies; and even when the Greeks [the Byzantines] suspected him of designing to take the empire from them, because of his assumption of the title Emperor, they made a close alliance with him, that he might have no cause of offense. In fact, the power of the Franks was always viewed with a jealous eye, whence the Greek proverb, "Have the Frank for your friend, but not for your neighbor."

This King, who showed himself so great in extending his empire and subduing foreign nations, and was constantly occupied with plans to that end, undertook also very many works calculated to adorn and benefit his kingdom, and brought several of them to completion. Among these, the most deserving of mention are the basilica of the Holy Mother of God at Aix-la-Chapelle [Aachen], built in the most admirable manner, and a bridge over the Rhine River at Mainz, half a mile long, the breadth of the river at this point. . . . Above all, sacred buildings were the object of his care throughout his whole kingdom; and whenever he found them falling to ruin from age, he commanded the priests and fathers who had charge of them to repair them, and made sure by commissioners that his instructions were obeyed. . . . Thus did Charles defend and increase as well as beautify his kingdom. . . .

He cherished with the greatest fervor and devotion the principles of the Christian religion, which had been instilled into him from infancy. Hence it was that he built the beautiful church at Aix-la-Chapelle, which he adorned with gold and silver and lamps, and with rails and doors of solid brass. He had the columns and marbles for this structure brought from Rome and Ravenna, for he could not find such as were suitable elsewhere. He was a constant worshiper at this church as long as his health permitted, going morning and evening, even after nightfall, besides attending mass. . . .

He was very forward in caring for the poor, so much so that he not only made a point of giving in his own country and his own kingdom, but when he discovered that there were Christians living in poverty in Syria, Egypt, and Africa, at Jerusalem, Alexandria, and Carthage, he had compassion on their wants, and used to send money over the seas to them. . . . He sent great and countless gifts to the popes, and throughout his whole reign the wish that he had nearest at heart was to reestablish the ancient authority of the city of Rome under his care and by his influence, and to defend and protect the Church of St. Peter, and to beautify and enrich it out of his own store above all other churches.

How long did Einhard know Charlemagne? Does this excerpt reflect close, personal knowledge of the man, his court, and his works or hearsay and legend?

Source: From Einhard, *The Life of Charlemagne*, translated by S. E. Turner, pp. 50–54. Copyright © 1960 by The University of Michigan. Translated from the *Monumenta Germanie*.

© The Pierpont Morgan Library, New York/Art Resource, NY

© Robert Harding Picture Library Ltd (G. Richardson)/Alamy

The Vikings Attack England. The illustration on the left, from an eleventh-century English manuscript, depicts a band of armed Vikings invading England. Two ships have already reached the shore, and a few Vikings are shown walking down a long gangplank onto English soil. On the right is a replica of a well-preserved Viking ship found at Oseberg, Norway. The Oseberg ship was one of the largest Viking ships of its day.

their subjects, it became important to find some powerful lord who could offer protection in return for service. The contract sworn between a lord and his subordinate (known as a **vassal**) is the basis of a form of social organization that modern historians called *feudalism*. But feudalism was never a cohesive system, and many historians today prefer to avoid using the term (see the comparative essay "Feudal Orders Around the World" on p. 284 in Chapter 11).

With the breakdown of royal governments, powerful nobles took control of large areas of land. They needed men to fight for them, so the practice arose of giving grants of land to vassals who in return would fight for their lord. The Frankish army had originally consisted of foot soldiers, dressed in coats of mail and armed with swords. But in the eighth century, a military change began to occur when larger horses and the stirrup were introduced. Earlier, horsemen had been throwers of spears. Now they came to be armored in coats of mail (the larger horse could carry the weight) and wielded long lances that enabled them to act as battering rams (stirrups kept them on their horses). For almost five hundred years, warfare in Europe would be dominated by heavily armored cavalry, or *knights*, as they were called. The knights came to have the greatest social prestige and formed the backbone of the European aristocracy.

Of course, a horse, armor, and weapons were expensive, and it took time and much practice to learn to wield these instruments skillfully from horseback. Consequently, lords who wanted men to fight for them had to grant each vassal a piece of land that provided for the support of the vassal and his family. In return for the land, the vassal provided his lord with his fighting skills. Each needed the other. In the society of the Early Middle Ages, where there was little trade and wealth was based primarily on land, land became the most important gift a lord could give to a vassal in return for his loyalty and military service (see the box on p. 308).

OPPOSING VIEWPOINTS

Lords and Vassals in Europe and Japan

Between 800 and 900 in Europe, as royal governments proved unable to provide protection against the invaders and turbulence of the time, a social order based on lords and vassals arose and flourished for the next four hundred years. In exchange for protection and grants of land from the lord, the vassals would provide the lord with military service. But Europe was not the only part of the world where a form of social organization based on lords and vassals emerged. In Japan, a social order much like that found in Europe developed between 800 and 1500. The first selection is the classic statement by Bishop Fulbert of Chartres in 1020 on the mutual obligations between lord and vassals. The second selection is taken from *Tale of the Heike*, a Japanese tale written in the first half of the thirteenth century about military struggles that took place at the end of the twelfth century.

Bishop Fulbert of Chartres

Asked to write something concerning the form of fealty, I have noted briefly for you, on the authority of the books, the things which follow. He who swears fealty to his lord ought always to have these six things in memory: what is harmless, safe, honorable, useful, easy, practicable. *Harmless*, that is to say, that he should not injure his lord in his body; *safe*, that he should not injure him by betraying his secrets or the defenses upon which he relies for safety; *honorable*, that he should not injure him in his justice or in other matters that pertain to his honor; *useful*, that he should not injure him in his possessions; *easy* and *practicable*, that that good which his lord is able to do easily he make not difficult, nor that which is practicable he make not impossible to him.

That the faithful vassal should avoid these injuries is certainly proper, but not for this alone does he deserve his holding; for it is not sufficient to abstain from evil, unless what is good is done also. It remains, therefore, that in the same six things mentioned above he should faithfully counsel and aid his lord, if he wishes to be looked upon as worthy of his benefice [fief] and to be safe concerning the fealty which he has sworn.

The lord also ought to act toward his faithful vassal reciprocally in all these things. And if he does not do this, he will be justly considered guilty of bad faith, just as the former, if he should be detected in avoiding or consenting to the avoidance of his duties, would be perfidious and perjured.

Tale of the Heike

Recognizing each other, master and retainer spurred their horses to join each other. Seizing Kanehira's hands, Yoshinaka said: "I would have fought to the death on the banks of the Kamo at Rokujō. Simply because of you, however, I have galloped here through the enemy swarms."

"It was very kind of you, my lord," replied Kanehira. "I too would have fought to the death at Seta. But in fear of your uncertain fate, I have come this way."

"We are still tied by karma," said Yoshinaka. "There must be more of my men around here, for I have seen them scattered among the hills. Unroll the banner and raise it high!"

As soon as Kanehira unfurled the banner, many men who had been in flight from the capital and Seta saw it and rallied. They soon numbered more than three hundred.

"Since we still have so many men, let us try one last fight!" shouted Yoshinaka jubilantly. . . .

Shouting, Yoshinaka dashed ahead. That day he wore armor laced with twilled silk cords over a red battle robe. His helmet was decorated with long golden horns. At his side hung a great sword studded with gold. He carried his quiver a little higher than usual on his back. Some eagle-feathered arrows still remained. Gripping his rattan-bound bow, he rode his famous horse, Oniashige.

Rising high in his stirrups, he roared at the enemy: "You have often heard of me. Now take a good look at the captain of the Imperial Stables of the Left and governor of Iyo Province—Rising-Sun General Minamoto no Yoshinaka, that is who I am! I know that among you is Kai no Ichijōjirō Tadayori. We are fit opponents for each other. Cut off my head and show it to Yoritomo!"

At this challenge, Tadayori shouted to his men: "Now, hear this! He is the commander of our enemy. Let him not escape! All men—to the attack!"

According to Bishop Fulbert, what were the mutual obligations of lords and vassals? Why were these important in the practice of fief-holding? The lord-vassal relationship was based on loyalty. What differences and similarities do you see in the loyalty between lord and vassals in Europe and Japan? How did the weapons used by a European knight and a Japanese warrior differ?

Sources: Bishop Fulbert of Chartres. From *Readings in European History*, vol. 1, by James Harvey Robinson (Lexington, Mass.: Ginn and Co., 1904). *Tale of the Heike*. From Hiroski Kitagawa and Bruce T. Tsuchida, trans., THE TALE OF THE HEIKE (Tokyo: University of Tokyo Press, 1975), p. 52.

By the ninth century, the grant of land made to a vassal had become known as a **fief** (FEEF). A fief was a piece of land held from the lord by a vassal in return for military service, but vassals who held such grants of land also came to exercise rights of jurisdiction or political and legal authority within their fiefs. As the Carolingian world disintegrated politically under the impact of internal dissension and invasions, an increasing number of powerful lords arose who were now responsible for keeping order.

Fief-holding came to be characterized by a set of practices that determined the relationship between a lord and his vassal. The major obligation of a vassal to his lord was to perform military service, usually about forty days a year. A vassal was also required to appear at his lord's court when summoned to give advice to the lord. He might also be asked to sit in judgment in a legal case, since the important vassals of a lord were peers and only they could judge each other. Finally, vassals were also responsible for aids, or financial payments to the lord, on a number of occasions. In turn, a lord also had responsibilities toward his vassals. His major obligation was to protect his vassal, either by defending him militarily or by taking his side in a court of law. The lord was also responsible for the maintenance of the vassal, usually by granting him a fief.

THE MANORIAL SYSTEM The landholding class of nobles and knights contained a military elite whose ability to function as warriors depended on having the leisure time to pursue the arts of war. Landed estates, or manors, located on the fiefs given to a vassal by his lord and worked by a dependent peasant class, provided the economic sustenance that made this way of life possible. A **manor** was an agricultural estate operated by a lord and worked by peasants. Although a large class of free peasants continued to exist, increasing numbers of free peasants became **serfs**—persons bound to the land and required to provide labor services, pay rents, and be subject to the lord's jurisdiction. By the ninth century, probably 60 percent of the population of western Europe had become serfs.

Labor services involved working the lord's **demesne** (duh-MAYN *or* duh-MEEN), the land retained by the lord, which might consist of one-third to one-half of the cultivated lands scattered throughout the manor. The rest would be used by the peasants for themselves. Building barns and digging ditches were also part of the labor services. Serfs usually worked about three days a week for their lord and paid rents by giving the lord a share of every product they raised.

Serfs were legally bound to the lord's lands and could not leave without his permission. Although free to marry, serfs could not marry anyone outside their manor without the lord's approval. Moreover, some lords exercised public rights or political authority on their lands, which gave a lord the right to try peasants in his own courts.

Europe in the High Middle Ages

FOCUS QUESTIONS: What roles did aristocrats, peasants, and townspeople play in medieval European civilization, and how did their lifestyles differ? How did cities in Europe compare with those in China and the Middle East? What were the main aspects of the political, economic, spiritual, and cultural revivals that took place in Europe during the High Middle Ages?

The new European civilization that had emerged in the Early Middle Ages began to flourish in the High Middle Ages (1000–1300). New agricultural practices that increased the food supply spurred commercial and urban expansion. Both lords and vassals recovered from the invasions and internal dissension of the Early Middle Ages, and medieval kings began to exert a centralizing authority. The recovery of the Catholic Church made it a forceful presence in every area of life. The High Middle Ages also gave birth to a cultural revival.

Land and People

In the Early Middle Ages, Europe had a relatively small population of about 38 million, but in the High Middle Ages, the number of people nearly doubled to 74 million. What accounted for this dramatic increase? For one thing, conditions in Europe were more settled and more peaceful after the invasions of the Early Middle Ages had ended. For another, agricultural production surged after 1000.

THE NEW AGRICULTURE During the High Middle Ages, Europeans began to farm in new ways. An improvement in climate resulted in better growing conditions, but an important factor in increasing food production was the expansion of cultivated or arable land, accomplished by clearing forested areas. Peasants of the eleventh and twelfth centuries cut down trees and drained swamps.

Technological changes also furthered improvements in farming. The Middle Ages saw an explosion of labor-saving devices, many of which were made from iron, which was mined in different areas of Europe. Iron was used to make scythes, axes, and hoes for use on farms as well as saws, hammers, and nails for building purposes. Iron was crucial in making the *carruca* (kuh-ROO-kuh), a heavy, wheeled plow with an iron plowshare pulled by teams of horses, which could turn over the heavy clay soil found north of the Alps.

COMPARATIVE ILLUSTRATION

The New Agriculture in the Medieval World. New agricultural methods and techniques in the Middle Ages enabled peasants in both Europe and China to increase food production. This general improvement in diet was a factor in supporting noticeably larger populations in both areas. At the bottom, a thirteenth-century illustration shows a group of English peasants harvesting grain. Overseeing their work is a bailiff, or manager. At the right, a thirteenth-century painting shows Chinese peasants harvesting rice, which became the staple food in China.

How important were staple foods (such as wheat and rice) in the diet and health of people in Europe and China during the Middle Ages?

Freer Gallery of Art, Washington, DC//© The Art Archive at Art Resource, NY

© British Library/The Art Archive at Art Resource, NY

Besides using horsepower, the High Middle Ages harnessed the power of water and wind to do jobs formerly done by humans or animals. Located along streams, mills powered by water were used to grind grains and produce flour. Where rivers were lacking or not easily dammed, Europeans developed windmills to harness the power of the wind.

The shift from a two-field to a three-field system also contributed to the increase in food production (see the comparative illustration above). In the Early Middle Ages, peasants planted one field while another of equal size was allowed to lie fallow to regain its fertility. Now estates were divided into three parts. One field was planted in the fall with winter grains, such as rye and wheat, and spring grains, such as oats or barley, and vegetables, such as peas or beans, were planted in the second field. The third was allowed to lie fallow. By rotating their use, only one-third rather than one-half of the land lay fallow at any time. The rotation of crops also kept the soil from being exhausted so quickly, and more crops could now be grown.

DAILY LIFE OF THE PEASANTRY The lifestyle of the peasants was quite simple. Their cottages were made of wood frames surrounded by sticks with the space between them filled with rubble and then plastered over with clay. Roofs were simply thatched. The houses of poorer peasants consisted of a single room, but others had at least two rooms—a main room for cooking, eating, and other activities and another room for sleeping.

Peasant women occupied both an important and a difficult position in manorial society. They were expected to carry and bear their children and at the same time fulfill their obligation to labor in the fields. Their ability to manage the household might determine whether a peasant family would starve or survive in difficult times.

Though simple, a peasant's daily diet was adequate when food was available. The staple of the peasant diet, and the medieval diet in general, was bread. Women made the dough for the bread at home and then brought their loaves to be baked in community ovens, which were owned by the lord of the manor. Peasant bread was highly nutritious, containing not only wheat and rye but also barley, millet, and oats, giving it a dark appearance and a very heavy, hard texture. Bread was supplemented by numerous vegetables from the household gardens, cheese from cow's or goat's milk, nuts and berries from woodlands, and fruits, such as apples, pears, and cherries. Chickens provided eggs and sometimes meat.

THE NOBILITY OF THE MIDDLE AGES In the High Middle Ages, European society, like that of Japan during the same period, was dominated by men whose chief concern was warfare. Like the Japanese samurai, many nobles loved war. As one nobleman wrote:

> *And well I like to hear the call of "Help" and see the wounded fall,*
> *Loudly for mercy praying,*
> *And see the dead, both great and small,*
> *Pierced by sharp spearheads one and all.*[3]

The men of war were the lords and vassals of medieval society.

The lords were the kings, dukes, counts, barons, and viscounts (and even bishops and archbishops) who had extensive landholdings and wielded considerable political influence. They formed an **aristocracy** or nobility of people who held real political, economic, and social power. Both the great lords and ordinary knights were warriors, and the institution of knighthood united them. But there were also social divisions among them based on extremes of wealth and landholdings.

Although aristocratic women could legally hold property, most women remained under the control of men—their fathers until they married and their husbands after that. Nevertheless, these women had many opportunities for playing important roles. Because the lord was often away at war or at court, the lady of the castle had to manage the estate. Households could include large numbers of officials and servants, so this was no small responsibility.

Although women were expected to be subservient to their husbands, there were many strong women who advised and sometimes even dominated their husbands. Perhaps the most famous was Eleanor of Aquitaine (c. 1122–1204). Married to King Louis VII of France, Eleanor accompanied her husband on a Crusade, but her alleged affair with her uncle during the Crusade led Louis to have their marriage annulled. Eleanor then married Henry, duke of Normandy and count of Anjou (AHN-zhoo), who became King Henry II of England in 1154. She took an active role in politics, even assisting her sons in rebelling against Henry in 1173 and 1174.

The New World of Trade and Cities

Medieval Europe was overwhelmingly agrarian, with most people living in small villages. In the eleventh and twelfth centuries, however, new elements were introduced that began to transform the economic foundation of European civilization: a revival of trade, the emergence of specialized craftspeople and artisans, and the growth and development of towns.

THE REVIVAL OF TRADE The revival of trade was a gradual process. During the chaotic conditions of the Early Middle Ages, large-scale trade had declined in western Europe except for Byzantine contacts with Italy and the Jewish traders who moved back and forth between the Muslim and Christian worlds. By the end of the tenth century however, people were emerging in Europe with both the skills and the products for commercial activity. Cities in northern Italy took the lead in this revival of trade.

While the northern Italian cities were busy trading in the Mediterranean, the towns of Flanders were doing likewise in northern Europe. Flanders, the area along the coast of present-day Belgium and northern France, was known for its high-quality woolen cloth. The location of Flanders made it an ideal center for the traders of northern Europe. Merchants from England, Scandinavia, France, and Germany converged there to trade their goods for woolen cloth. Flanders prospered in the eleventh and twelfth centuries. By the twelfth century, a regular exchange of goods had developed between Flanders and Italy, the two major centers of northern and southern European trade.

As trade increased, both gold and silver came to be in demand at fairs and trading markets of all kinds. Slowly, a money economy began to emerge. New trading companies and banking firms were set up to manage the exchange and sale of goods. All of these new practices were part of the rise of **commercial capitalism**, an economic system in which people invested in trade and goods in order to make profits.

TRADE OUTSIDE EUROPE In the High Middle Ages, Italian merchants became even more daring in their trade activities. They established trading posts in Cairo, Damascus, and a number of Black Sea ports, where they acquired spices, silks, jewelry, dyestuffs, and other goods brought by Muslim merchants from India, China, and Southeast Asia.

The spread of the Mongol Empire in the thirteenth century (see Chapter 10) also opened the door to Italian merchants in the markets of Central Asia, India, and China. As nomads who relied on trade with settled communities, the Mongols maintained safe trade routes for merchants moving through their lands. Two Venetian merchants, Niccolò and Maffeo Polo, began to travel in the Mongol Empire around 1260.

The creation of the crusader states in Syria and Palestine in the twelfth and thirteenth centuries (discussed later in this chapter) was especially favorable for Italian merchants. In return for taking the crusaders to the east, Italian merchant fleets received trading concessions in Syria and Palestine. Venice, for example, which profited the most from this trade, was given a quarter, soon known as "a little Venice in the east," in Tyre on the coast of what is now Lebanon. Such quarters here and in other cities soon became bases for carrying on lucrative trade.

THE GROWTH OF CITIES The revival of trade led to a revival of cities. Towns had experienced a great decline in the Early Middle Ages, especially in Europe north of the Alps. Old Roman cities continued to exist but had dwindled in size and population. With the revival of trade, merchants began to settle in these old cities, followed by craftspeople or artisans, people who on manors or elsewhere had developed skills and now saw an opportunity to ply their trade and make goods that could be sold by the merchants. In the course of the eleventh and twelfth centuries, the old Roman cities came alive with new populations and growth.

Beginning in the late tenth century, many new cities or towns were also founded, particularly in northern Europe. Usually, a group of merchants established a settlement near some fortified stronghold, such as a castle or monastery. (This explains why so many place names in Europe end in *borough*, *burgh*, *burg*, or *bourg*, all of which mean "fortress" or "walled enclosure.") Castles were particularly favored because they were generally located along trade routes; the lords of the castle also offered protection. If the settlement prospered and expanded, new walls were built to protect it.

Although lords wanted to treat towns and townspeople as they would their vassals and serfs, cities had totally different needs and a different perspective. Townspeople needed mobility to trade. Consequently, these merchants and artisans (who came to be called *burghers* or *bourgeois*, from the same root as *borough* and *burg*) needed their own unique laws to meet their requirements and were willing to pay for them. In many instances, lords and kings saw that they could also make money and were willing to sell to the townspeople the liberties they were beginning to demand, including the right to bequeath goods and sell property, freedom from any military obligation to the lord, and written urban laws that guaranteed their freedom. Some towns also obtained the right to govern themselves by choosing their own officials and administering their own courts of law.

As time went on, medieval cities developed their own governments for running the affairs of the community. Only males who were born in the city or had lived there for a certain length of time could be citizens. In many cities, these citizens elected members of a city council who served as judges and city officials and passed laws.

Medieval cities remained relatively small in comparison to either ancient or modern cities (see the comparative essay "Cities in the Medieval World" on p. 313). A large trading city might have about 5,000 inhabitants. By 1200, London was the largest city in England with 30,000 people. On the Continent north of the Alps, only a few urban centers of commerce, such as Bruges and Ghent, had populations close to 40,000. Italian cities tended to be larger, with Venice, Florence, Genoa, Milan, and Naples numbering almost 100,000. Even the largest European city, however, seemed small alongside the Byzantine capital of Constantinople or the Arab cities of Damascus, Baghdad, and Cairo.

DAILY LIFE IN THE MEDIEVAL CITY Medieval towns were surrounded by stone walls that were expensive to build, so the space within was precious. Consequently, most medieval cities featured narrow, winding streets with houses crowded against each other and second and third stories extending out over the streets. Because dwellings were built mostly of wood before the fourteenth century and candles and wood fires were used for light and heat, fire was a constant threat. Medieval cities burned rapidly once a fire started.

Most of the people who lived in cities were merchants involved in trade and artisans engaged in manufacturing a wide range of goods, such as cloth, metalwork, shoes, and leather goods. Generally, merchants and artisans had their own sections within a city. The merchant area included warehouses, inns, and taverns. Artisan sections were usually divided along craft lines. From the twelfth century on, craftspeople began to organize themselves into **guilds**, and by the thirteenth century, virtually every craft had its own individual guild, as well as its own street where its activity was pursued.

The physical environment of medieval cities was not pleasant. They were dirty and smelled from animal and human wastes deposited in backyard privies or on the streets. The rivers near most cities were polluted with wastes, especially from the tanning and butchering industries. Because of the pollution, cities did not use the rivers for drinking water but relied instead on wells.

COMPARATIVE ESSAY

Cities in the Medieval World

The exchange of goods between societies was a feature of both the ancient and medieval worlds. Trade routes crisscrossed the lands of the medieval world, and with increased trade came the growth of cities. In Europe, towns had undergone a significant decline after the collapse of the Western Roman Empire, but with the revival of trade in the eleventh and twelfth centuries, the cities came back to life. This revival occurred first in the old Roman cities, but soon new cities arose as merchants and artisans sought additional centers for their activities. As cities grew, so did the number of fortified houses, town halls, and churches whose towers punctuated the urban European skyline. Nevertheless, in the Middle Ages, cities in western Europe, especially north of the Alps, remained relatively small. Even the larger cities of Italy, with populations of 100,000, seemed insignificant in comparison with Constantinople and the great cities of the Middle East and China.

With a population of possibly 300,000, Constantinople, the capital city of the Byzantine Empire (see Chapter 13), was the largest city in Europe in the Early and High Middle Ages, and until the twelfth century, it was Europe's greatest commercial center, important for the exchange of goods between west and east. Although it had its share of palaces, cathedrals, and monastic buildings, Constantinople also had numerous gardens and orchards that occupied large areas inside its fortified walls. Despite the extensive open and cultivated spaces, the city was not self-sufficient and relied on imports of food under close government direction.

As trade flourished in the Islamic world, cities prospered. When the Abbasids were in power, Baghdad, with a population close to 700,000, was probably the largest city in the empire and one of the greatest cities in the world. After the rise of the Fatimids in Egypt, however, the focus of trade shifted to Cairo. Islamic cities had a distinctive physical appearance. Usually, the most impressive urban buildings were the palaces for the caliphs or the local governors and the great mosques for worship. There were also public buildings with fountains and secluded courtyards, public baths, and bazaars. The bazaar, a covered market, was a crucial part of every Muslim settlement and an important trading center where goods from all the known world were available. Food prepared for sale at the market was carefully supervised. A rule in one Muslim city stated, "Grilled meats should only be made with fresh meat and not with meat coming from a sick animal and bought for its cheapness." The merchants were the greatest beneficiaries of the growth of cities in the Islamic world.

© British Library, London//HIP/Art Resource, NY

Crime and Punishment in the Medieval City. Violence was a common feature of medieval life. Criminals, if apprehended, were punished quickly and severely, and public executions, like the one seen here, were considered a deterrent to crime.

During the medieval period, the largest cities in the world were in China. The southern port of Hangzhou had at least a million residents by the year 1000, and a number of other cities, including Chang'an and Kaifeng, may also have reached that size. Chinese cities were known for their broad canals and wide, tree-lined streets. They were no longer administrative centers dominated by officials and their families but now included a broader mix of officials, merchants, artisans, and entertainers. The prosperity of Chinese cities was well known. Marco Polo, in describing Hangzhou to unbelieving Europeans in the late thirteenth century, said, "So many pleasures can be found that one fancies himself to be in Paradise."

Based on a comparison of their cities, which of these civilizations do you think was the most advanced during the medieval period? Why?

Bibliothèque de l'Arsenal, Paris//© Snark/Art Resource, NY

Shops in a Medieval Town. Most urban residents were merchants involved in trade and artisans who manufactured a wide variety of products. Master craftsmen had their workshops in the ground-level rooms of their homes. In this illustration, two well-dressed burghers are touring the shopping district of a French town. Tailors, furriers, a barber, and a grocer (from left to right) are visible at work in their shops.

In medieval cities, women, in addition to supervising the household, purchasing food, preparing meals, raising the children, and managing the family finances, were also often expected to help their husbands in their trades. Some women also developed their own trades to earn extra money. When some master craftsmen died, their widows even carried on their trades. Some women in medieval towns were thus able to lead lives of considerable independence.

Evolution of the European Kingdoms

The recovery and growth of European civilization in the High Middle Ages also affected the state. Although lords and vassals seemed forever mired in endless petty conflicts, some medieval kings inaugurated the process of developing new kinds of monarchical states that were based on the centralization of power rather than the decentralized political order that was characteristic of fief-holding. By the thirteenth century, European monarchs were solidifying their governmental institutions in pursuit of greater power.

ENGLAND IN THE HIGH MIDDLE AGES In late September 1066, an army of heavily armed knights under William of Normandy landed on the coast of England, and a few weeks later, on October 14, they soundly defeated King Harold and his Anglo-Saxon foot soldiers in the Battle of Hastings. William (1066–1087) was crowned king of England at Christmastime in London and promptly began a process of combining Anglo-Saxon and Norman institutions that would change England forever. Many of the Norman knights were given parcels of land that they held as fiefs from the new English king. William made all nobles swear an oath of loyalty to him as sole ruler of England and insisted that all people owed loyalty to the king. All in all, William of Normandy established a strong, centralized monarchy.

In the twelfth century, the power of the English monarchy was greatly enlarged during the reign of Henry II (1154–1189; see the Film & History feature on p. 315). The new king was particularly successful in strengthening the royal courts. By increasing the number of criminal cases to be tried in the king's courts and taking other steps to expand the power of the royal courts, he expanded the power of the king. Moreover, since the royal courts were now found throughout England, a body of **common law** (law that was common to the whole kingdom) began to replace the different law codes that often varied from place to place.

Many English nobles came to resent the ongoing growth of the king's power and rose in rebellion during the reign of King John (1199–1216). At Runnymede in 1215, John was forced to accept Magna Carta (the Great Charter) guaranteeing feudal liberties. Feudal custom had always recognized that the relationship between king and vassals was based on mutual rights and obligations. Magna Carta gave written recognition to that fact and was used in later years to support the idea that a monarch's power was limited.

During the reign of Edward I (1272–1307), an institution of great importance in the development of representative government—the English Parliament—emerged. Originally, the word *parliament* was applied to meetings of the king's Great Council, in which the greater barons and chief prelates of the church met with the king's judges and principal advisers to deal with judicial affairs. But needing money, in 1295 Edward I invited two knights from every county and two residents from each town to meet with the Great Council to consent to new taxes. This was the first Parliament.

Thus, the English Parliament came to be composed of two knights from every county and two burgesses from every borough as well as the barons and ecclesiastical lords. Eventually, the barons and church lords formed the House of Lords; the knights and burgesses, the House of Commons. The Parliaments of Edward I approved taxes, discussed politics, passed laws, and handled

FILM & HISTORY

The Lion in Winter (1968)

Avco Embassy/The Kobal Collection at Art Resource, NY

Eleanor of Aquitaine (Katharine Hepburn) and Henry II (Peter O'Toole) at dinner at Henry's palace in Chinon, France.

Directed by Anthony Harvey, *The Lion in Winter* is based on a play by James Goldman, who also wrote the script for the movie and won an Oscar for best adapted screenplay for it. The action takes place in a castle in Chinon, France, over the Christmas holidays in 1183. The setting is realistic: medieval castles had dirt floors covered with rushes, under which lay, according to one observer, "an ancient collection of grease, fragments, bones, excrement of dogs and cats, and everything that is nasty." The powerful but world-weary King Henry II (played by Peter O'Toole), ruler of England and a number of French lands (the "Angevin Empire"), wants to establish his legacy and plans a Christmas gathering to decide which of his sons should succeed him. He favors his overindulged youngest son John (Nigel Terry), but he is opposed by his strong-willed and estranged wife, Eleanor of Aquitaine (Katharine Hepburn). She has been imprisoned by the king for leading a rebellion against him but has been temporarily freed for the holidays. Eleanor favors their son Richard (Anthony Hopkins), the most military minded of the brothers. The middle brother, Geoffrey (John Castle), is not a candidate but manipulates the other brothers to gain his own advantage. All three sons are portrayed as treacherous and traitorous, and Henry is distrustful of them. At one point, he threatens to imprison and even kill his sons; marry his mistress Alais (Jane Merrow), who is also the sister of the king of France; and have a new family to replace them.

In contemporary terms, Henry and Eleanor are an unhappily married couple, and their family is acutely dysfunctional. Sparks fly as family members plot against each other, using intentionally cruel comments and sarcastic responses to wound each other as much as possible. When Eleanor says to Henry, "What would you have me do? Give up? Give in?" he responds, "Give me a little peace." To which Eleanor replies, "A little? Why so modest? How about eternal peace? Now there's a thought." At one point, John responds to bad news about his chances for the throne with "Poor John. Who says poor John? Don't everybody sob at once. My God, if I went up in flames, there's not a living soul who'd pee on me to put the fire out!" His brother Richard replies, "Let's strike a flint and see." Henry can also be cruel to his sons: "You're not mine! We're not connected! I deny you! None of you will get my crown. I leave you nothing, and I wish you plague!"

In developing this well-written, imaginative re-creation of a royal family's hapless Christmas gathering, James Goldman had a great deal of material to use. Henry II was one of the most powerful monarchs of his day, and Eleanor of Aquitaine was one of the most powerful women. She had first been queen of France, but that marriage was annulled. Next she married Henry, who was then count of Anjou, and became queen of England when he became king in 1154. During their stormy marriage, Eleanor and Henry had five sons and three daughters. She is supposed to have murdered Rosamond, one of her husband's mistresses, and aided her sons in a rebellion against their father in 1173, causing Henry to distrust his sons ever after. But Henry struck back, imprisoning Eleanor for sixteen years. After his death, however, Eleanor returned to Aquitaine and lived on to play an influential role in the reigns of her two sons, Richard and John, who succeeded their father.

judicial business. The law of the realm was beginning to be determined not by the king alone but by the king in consultation with representatives of various groups that constituted the community.

GROWTH OF THE FRENCH KINGDOM In 843, the Carolingian Empire had been divided into three major sections. The western Frankish lands formed the core of the eventual kingdom of France. In 987, after the death of the last Carolingian king, the western Frankish nobles chose Hugh Capet (YOO ka-PAY) as the new king, thus establishing the Capetian (kuh-PEE-shun) dynasty of French kings. Although they carried the title of kings, the Capetians had little real power. They controlled as the royal domain only the lands around Paris known as the Île-de-France (EEL-duh-fronhss). As kings of France, the Capetians were formally the overlords of the great lords of France, such as the dukes of Normandy, Brittany, Burgundy, and Aquitaine. In reality, however, many of the dukes were considerably more powerful than the Capetian kings. All in all, it would take the Capetian dynasty hundreds of years to create a truly centralized monarchical authority in France.

The reign of King Philip II Augustus (1180–1223) was an important turning point in the growth of the French monarchy. Philip II waged war against the Plantagenet (plan-TAJ-uh-net) rulers of England, who also ruled the French territories of Normandy, Maine, Anjou, and Aquitaine, and was successful in gaining control of most of these territories, therby enlarging the power of the French monarchy (see Map 12.2). To administer justice and collect royal revenues in his new territories, Philip appointed new royal officials, thus inaugurating a French royal bureaucracy in the thirteenth century.

Capetian rulers after Philip II continued to add lands to the royal domain. Philip IV the Fair (1285–1314) was especially effective in strengthening the French monarchy. He reinforced the royal bureaucracy and also brought a French parliament into being by asking representatives of the three estates, or classes—the clergy (First Estate), the nobles (Second Estate), and the townspeople (Third Estate)—to meet with him. They did so in 1302, inaugurating the Estates-General, the first French

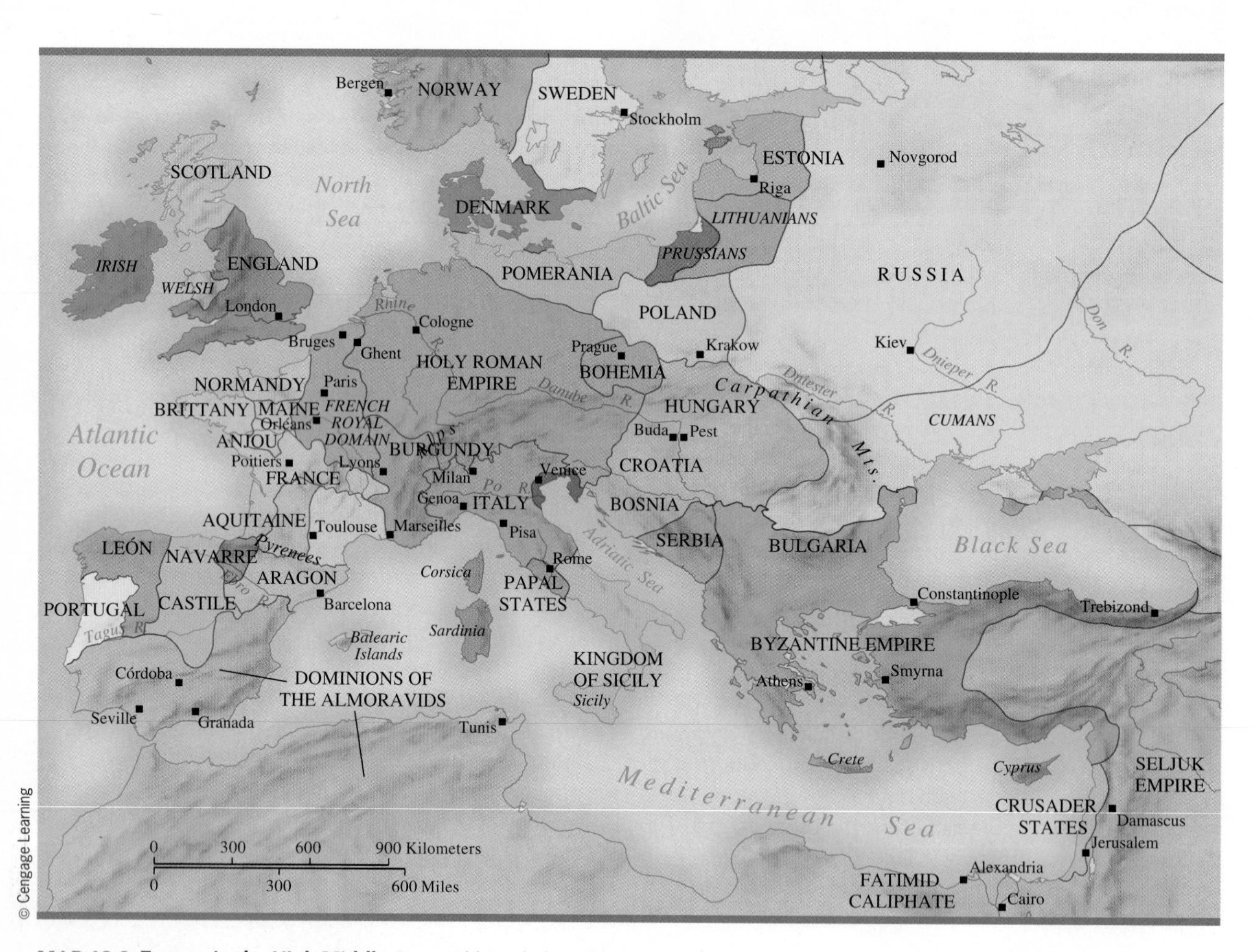

© Cengage Learning

MAP 12.2 Europe in the High Middle Ages. Although the nobility dominated much of European society in the High Middle Ages, kings began the process of extending their power in more effective ways, creating the monarchies that would form the European states.

Q *Which were the strongest monarchical states by 1300? Why?*

parliament, although it had little real power. By the end of the thirteenth century, France was the largest, wealthiest, and best-governed monarchical state in Europe.

CHRISTIAN RECONQUEST: THE IBERIAN KINGDOMS Much of Spain had been part of the Islamic world since the eighth century. Starting in the tenth century, however, the most noticeable feature of Spanish history was the weakening of Muslim power and the beginning of a Christian reconquest that lasted until the final expulsion of the Muslims at the end of the fifteenth century.

A number of small Christian kingdoms were established in northern Spain in the eleventh century, and within a hundred years, they had been consolidated into the Christian kingdoms of Castile (ka-STEEL), Navarre, Aragon, and Portugal, which first emerged as a separate kingdom in 1139. The southern half of Spain still remained under the control of the Muslims.

In the thirteenth century, Aragon, Castile, and Portugal made significant conquests of Muslim territory. The Muslims remained ensconced only in the kingdom of Granada in the southeast of the Iberian peninsula, which remained an independent Muslim state until its final conquest by the forces of Ferdinand of Aragon and Isabella of Castile in 1492.

The Spanish kingdoms did not follow a consistent policy in their treatment of the conquered Muslim population. In Aragon, Muslim farmers continued to work the land but were forced to pay very high rents. In Castile, King Alfonso X (1252–1284), who called himself the "King of Three Religions," encouraged the continued development of a cosmopolitan culture shared by Christians, Jews, and Muslims.

THE LANDS OF THE HOLY ROMAN EMPIRE In the tenth century, the powerful dukes of the Saxons became kings of the eastern Frankish kingdom (or Germany, as it came to be called). The best known of the Saxon kings of Germany was Otto I (936–973), who intervened in Italian politics and for his efforts was crowned emperor of the Romans by the pope in 962, reviving a title that had not been used since the time of Charlemagne.

As leaders of a new Roman Empire, the German kings attempted to rule both German and Italian lands. Frederick I Barbarossa (bar-buh-ROH-suh) (1152–1190) and Frederick II (1212–1250) tried to create a new kind of empire. Previous German kings had focused on building a strong German kingdom, but Frederick I planned to get his chief revenues from Italy as the center of a "holy empire," as he called it (hence the name *Holy Roman Empire*). But his attempt to conquer northern Italy ran into severe opposition from the pope and the cities of northern Italy. An alliance of these cities and the pope defeated Frederick's forces in 1176.

The main goal of Frederick II was the establishment of a strong centralized state in Italy, but he too became involved in a deadly conflict with the popes and the north Italian cities. Frederick waged a bitter struggle in northern Italy, winning many battles but ultimately losing the war.

The struggle between popes and emperors had dire consequences for the Holy Roman Empire. By spending their time fighting in Italy, the German emperors left Germany in the hands of powerful German lords who ignored the emperor and created their own independent kingdoms. This ensured that the German monarchy would remain weak and incapable of building a centralized monarchical state; thus, the German Holy Roman Emperor had no real power over either Germany or Italy. Unlike France and England, neither Germany nor Italy created a centralized national monarchy in the Middle Ages. Both of these regions consisted of many small, independent states, a situation that changed little until the nineteenth century.

THE SLAVIC PEOPLES OF CENTRAL AND EASTERN EUROPE The Slavs were originally a single people in central Europe, but they gradually divided into three major groups: the western, southern, and eastern Slavs (see Map 12.3). The western Slavs eventually formed the Polish and Bohemian kingdoms. German Christian missionaries converted both the Czechs in Bohemia and the Slavs in Poland by the tenth century. German Christians also converted the non-Slavic kingdom of Hungary, which emerged after the Magyars settled down after their defeat in 955. The Poles, Czechs, and Hungarians all accepted Catholic or western Christianity and became closely tied to the Roman Catholic Church and its Latin culture.

The southern and eastern Slavic populations took a different path: the Slavic peoples of Moravia were converted to the Orthodox Christianity of the Byzantine Empire (see Chapter 13) by two Byzantine missionary brothers, Cyril and Methodius (muh-THOH-dee-uss), who began their activities in 863. The southern Slavic peoples included the Croats, Serbs, and Bulgarians. For the most part, they too embraced Eastern Orthodoxy, although the Croats came to accept the Roman Catholic Church. The acceptance of Eastern Orthodoxy by the Serbs and Bulgarians tied their cultural life to the Byzantine state.

The eastern Slavic peoples, from whom the modern Russians and Ukrainians are descended, had settled in the territory of present-day Ukraine and European Russia. There, beginning in the late eighth century, they began to encounter Swedish Vikings who moved down the extensive network of rivers into the lands of the eastern

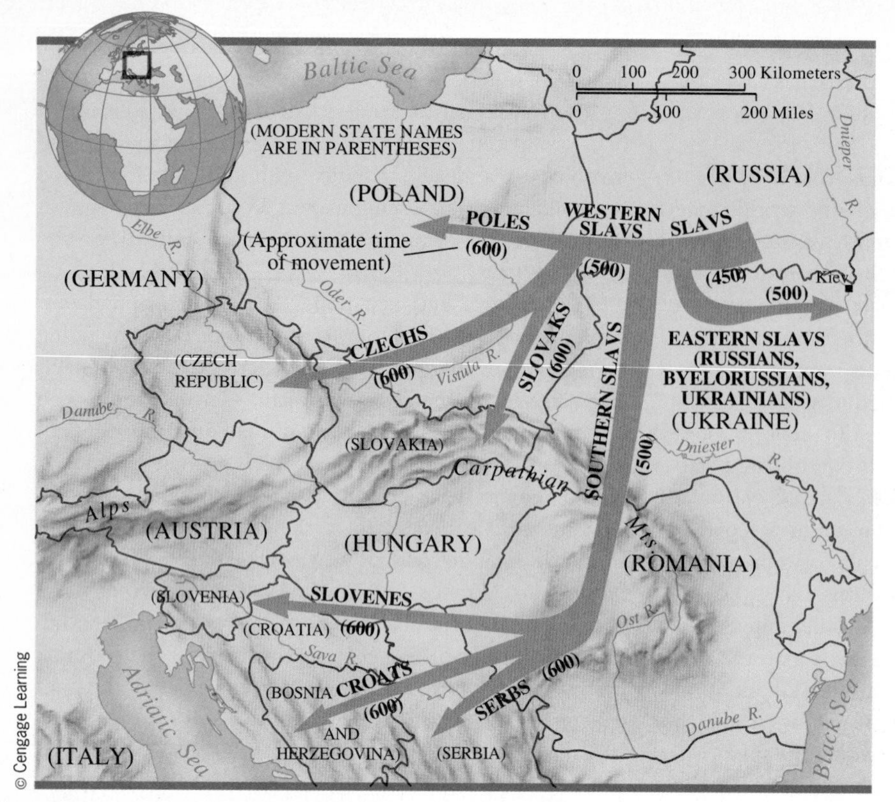

© Cengage Learning

MAP 12.3 The Migrations of the Slavs. Originally from east-central Europe, the Slavic people broke into three groups. The western Slavs converted to Catholic Christianity, while most of the eastern Slavs and southern Slavs, under the influence of the Byzantine Empire, embraced the Eastern Orthodox faith.

Q *What connections do these Slavic migrations have with what we today characterize as eastern Europe?*

Slavs in search of booty and new trade routes (see the box on p. 319). These Vikings built trading settlements and eventually came to dominate the native peoples, who called them "the Rus" (ROOSS *or* ROOSH), from which the name *Russia* is derived.

THE DEVELOPMENT OF RUSSIA: IMPACT OF THE MONGOLS A Viking leader named Oleg (c. 873–913) settled in Kiev (KEE-yev) at the beginning of the tenth century and created the Rus state known as the principality of Kiev. His successors extended their control over the eastern Slavs and expanded the territory of Kiev until it included the territory between the Baltic and Black Seas and the Danube and Volga Rivers. By marrying Slavic wives, the Viking ruling class was gradually assimilated into the Slavic population.

The growth of the principality of Kiev attracted religious missionaries, especially from the Byzantine Empire. One Rus ruler, Vladimir (VLAD-ih-meer) (c. 980–1015), married the Byzantine emperor's sister and officially accepted Christianity for himself and his people in 987. By the end of the tenth century, Byzantine Christianity had become the model for Russian religious life.

The Kievan Rus state prospered and reached its high point in the first half of the eleventh century. But civil wars and new invasions by Asiatic nomads caused the principality of Kiev to collapse, and the sack of Kiev by north Russian princes in 1169 brought an end to the first Russian state, which had remained closely tied to the Byzantine Empire, not to Europe. In the thirteenth century, the Mongols conquered Russia and cut it off even more from Europe.

The Mongols had exploded onto the scene in the thirteenth century, moving east into China and west into the Middle East and central Europe. Although they conquered Russia, they were not numerous enough to settle the vast Russian lands. They occupied only part of Russia but required the Russian princes to pay tribute to them. One Russian prince soon emerged as more powerful than the others. Alexander Nevsky (NYEF-skee) (c. 1220–1263), prince of Novgorod (NAHV-guh-rahd), defeated a German invading army in northwestern Russia in 1242. His cooperation with the Mongols won him their favor. The khan, leader of the western part of the Mongol Empire, rewarded Alexander Nevsky with the title of grand-prince, enabling his descendants to become the princes of Moscow and eventually leaders of all Russia.

Christianity and Medieval Civilization

Christianity was an integral part of the fabric of European society and the consciousness of Europe. Papal directives affected the actions of kings and princes alike, and Christian teachings and practices touched the lives of all Europeans.

REFORM OF THE PAPACY Since the fifth century, the popes of the Catholic Church had reigned supreme over church affairs. They had also come to exercise control over the territories in central Italy that came to be known as the Papal States, which kept the popes involved in political matters, often at the expense of their spiritual

A Muslim's Description of the Rus

INTERACTION & EXCHANGE

Despite the difficulties that travel presented, early medieval civilization did witness some contact among the various cultures. This might occur through trade, diplomacy, or the conquest and migration of peoples. This document is a description of the Swedish Rus, who eventually merged with the native Slavic peoples to form the principality of Kiev, commonly regarded as the first Russian state. It was written by Ibn Fadlan, a Muslim diplomat sent from Baghdad in 921 to a settlement on the Volga River. His comments on the filthiness of the Rus reflect the Muslim emphasis on cleanliness.

Ibn Fadlan, Description of the Rus

I saw the Rus folk when they arrived on their trading mission and settled at the river Atul [Volga]. Never had I seen people of more perfect physique. They are tall as date palms, and reddish in color. They wear neither coat nor kaftan, but each man carried a cape which covers one half of his body, leaving one hand free. No one is ever parted from his axe, sword, and knife. Their swords are Frankish in design, broad, flat, and fluted. Each man has a number of trees, figures, and the like from the fingernails to the neck. Each woman carried on her bosom a container made of iron, silver, copper, or gold—its size and substance depending on her man's wealth. They [the Rus] are the filthiest of God's creatures. They do not wash after discharging their natural functions, neither do they wash their hands after meals. They are as lousy as donkeys. They arrive from their distant lands and lay their ships alongside the banks of the Atul, which is a great river, and there they build big houses on its shores. Ten or twenty of them may live together in one house, and each of them has a couch of his own where he sits and diverts himself with the pretty slave girls whom he had brought along for sale. He will make love with one of them while a comrade looks on; sometimes they indulge in a communal orgy, and, if a customer should turn up to buy a girl, the Rus man will not let her go till he has finished with her.

They wash their hands and faces every day in incredibly filthy water. Every morning the girl brings her master a large bowl of water in which he washes his hands and face and hair, then blows his nose into it and spits into it. When he has finished the girl takes the bowl to his neighbor—who repeats the performance. Thus, the bowl goes the rounds of the entire household. . . .

If one of the Rus folk falls sick they put him in a tent by himself and leave bread and water for him. They do not visit him, however, or speak to him, especially if he is a serf. Should he recover he rejoins the others; if he dies they burn him. But if he happens to be a serf they leave him for the dogs and vultures to devour. If they catch a robber they hang him to a tree until he is torn to shreds by wind and weather.

What was Ibn Fadlan's impression of the Rus? Why do you think he was so critical of their behavior?

Source: From *The Vikings*, by Johannes Brøndsted, translated by Kalle Skov (Penguin Books, 1965) copyright © Johannes Brøndsted, 1960, 1965. Reproduced by permission of Penguin Books Ltd.

obligations. At the same time, the church became increasingly entangled in the evolving feudal relationships. High officials of the church, such as bishops and abbots, came to hold their offices as fiefs from nobles. As vassals, they were obliged to carry out the usual duties, including military service. Of course, lords assumed the right to choose their vassals and thus came to appoint bishops and abbots.

In the eleventh century, church leaders realized the need to free the church from the interference of lords in the appointment of church officials. **Lay investiture** was the practice by which secular rulers both chose nominees to church offices and invested them with (bestowed upon them) the symbols of their office. Pope Gregory VII (1073–1085) decided to fight this practice. Gregory claimed that he, as pope, was God's "vicar on earth" and that the pope's authority extended over all of Christendom, including its rulers. In 1075, he issued a decree forbidding high-ranking clerics from receiving their investiture from lay leaders.

Gregory VII soon found himself in conflict with the king of Germany over his actions. King Henry IV (1056–1106) of Germany was also a determined man who had appointed high-ranking clerics, especially bishops, as his vassals in order to use them as administrators.

CHRONOLOGY The European Kingdoms	
England	
Norman conquest	1066
William the Conqueror	1066–1087
Henry II	1154–1189
John	1199–1216
Magna Carta	1215
Edward I	1272–1307
First Parliament	1295
France	
Philip II Augustus	1180–1223
Philip IV	1285–1314
First Estates-General	1302
Germany and the Empire	
Otto I	936–973
Frederick I Barbarossa	1152–1190
Frederick II	1212–1250
The Eastern World	
Mongol conquest of Russia	1230s
Alexander Nevsky, prince of Novgorod	c. 1220–1263

Henry had no intention of obeying a decree that challenged the very heart of his administration.

The struggle between Henry IV and Gregory VII, which is known as the Investiture Controversy, was one of the great conflicts between church and state in the High Middle Ages. It dragged on until a new German king and a new pope reached a compromise in 1122 called the Concordat of Worms (kun-KOR-dat of WURMZ *or* VORMPS). Under this agreement, a bishop in Germany was first elected by church officials. After election, the nominee paid homage to the king as his lord, who then invested him with the symbols of temporal office. A representative of the pope, however, then invested the new bishop with the symbols of his spiritual office.

THE CHURCH SUPREME: THE PAPAL MONARCHY The popes of the twelfth century did not abandon the reform ideals of Pope Gregory VII, but they were more inclined to consolidate their power and build a strong administrative system. During the papacy of Pope Innocent III (1198–1216), the Catholic Church reached the height of its power. At the beginning of his pontificate, in a letter to a priest, the pope made a clear statement of his views on papal supremacy:

> As God, the creator of the universe, set two great lights in the firmament of heaven, the greater light to rule the day, and the lesser light to rule the night, so He set two great dignities in the firmament of the universal church, . . . the greater to rule the day, that is, souls, and the lesser to rule the night, that is, bodies. These dignities are the papal authority and the royal power. And just as the moon gets her light from the sun, and is inferior to the sun . . . so the royal power gets the splendor of its dignity from the papal authority.[4]

Innocent III's actions were those of a man who believed that he, as pope, was the supreme judge of European affairs. To achieve his political ends, he did not hesitate to use the spiritual weapons at his command, especially the **interdict**, which forbade priests to dispense the **sacraments** of the church in the hope that the people, deprived of the comforts of religion, would exert pressure against their ruler.

NEW RELIGIOUS ORDERS AND NEW SPIRITUAL IDEALS Between 1050 and 1150, a wave of religious enthusiasm seized Europe, leading to a spectacular growth in the number of monasteries and the emergence of new monastic orders. Most important was the Cistercian (sis-TUR-shun) order, founded in 1098 by a group of monks dissatisfied with the moral degeneration and lack of strict discipline at their own Benedictine monastery. The Cistercians were strict. They ate a simple diet and possessed only a single robe apiece. More time for prayer and manual labor was provided by shortening the number of hours spent at religious services. The Cistercians played a major role in developing a new, activist spiritual model for twelfth-century Europe. A Benedictine monk often spent hours in prayer to honor God. The Cistercian ideal had a different emphasis: "Arise, soldier of Christ, arise! Get up off the ground and return to the battle from which you have fled! Fight more boldly after your flight, and triumph in glory!"[5]

Women were also actively involved in the spiritual movements of the age. The number of women joining religious houses grew dramatically in the High Middle Ages. Most nuns were from the ranks of the landed aristocracy. Convents were convenient for families unable or unwilling to find husbands for their daughters and for aristocratic women who did not wish to marry. Female intellectuals found them a haven for their activities. Most of the learned women of the Middle Ages were nuns.

In the thirteenth century, two new religious orders emerged that had a profound impact on the lives of ordinary people. Like their founder, Saint Francis of Assisi (uh-SEE-zee) (1182–1226), the Franciscans lived among the people, preaching repentance and aiding the poor. Their calls for a return to the simplicity and poverty of the early church, reinforced by their own example, were especially effective and made them very popular.

The Dominicans arose out of the desire of a Spanish priest, Dominic de Guzmán (DAH-muh-nik duh gooz-MAHN) (1170–1221), to defend church teachings from **heresy**—beliefs

© Musée de l'Assistance Publique, Hopitaux de Paris//Archives Charmet/The Bridgeman Art Library

A Group of Nuns. Although still viewed by the medieval church as inferior to men, women were as susceptible to the spiritual fervor of the twelfth century as men, and female monasticism grew accordingly. This manuscript illustration shows at the left a group of nuns welcoming a novice (dressed in white) to their order. At the right, a nun receives a sick person on a stretcher for the order's hospital care.

contrary to official church doctrine. Dominic was an intellectual who came to believe that a new religious order of men who lived lives of poverty but were learned and capable of preaching effectively would best be able to attack heresy. The Dominicans became especially well known for their roles as the inquisitors of the papal Inquisition.

The Holy Office, as the papal Inquisition was formally called, was a court established by the church to find and try heretics. Anyone accused of heresy who refused to confess was still considered guilty and was turned over to the state for execution. To the Christians of the thirteenth century, who believed that there was only one path to salvation, heresy was a crime against God and against humanity. In their minds, force should be used to save souls from damnation.

The Culture of the High Middle Ages

The High Middle Ages was a time of extraordinary intellectual and artistic vitality. It witnessed the birth of universities and a building spree that left Europe bedecked with churches and cathedrals.

THE RISE OF UNIVERSITIES The university as we know it—with faculty, students, and degrees—was a product of the High Middle Ages. The word *university* is derived from the Latin word *universitas* (yoo-nee-VAYR-see-tahss), meaning a corporation or guild, and referred to either a corporation of teachers or a corporation of students. Medieval universities were educational guilds or corporations that produced educated and trained individuals.

The first European university appeared in Bologna (boh-LOHN-yuh), Italy, where a great teacher named Irnerius (ur-NEER-ee-uss) (1088–1125), who taught Roman law, attracted students from all over Europe. To protect themselves, students at Bologna formed a guild or *universitas*, which was recognized by Emperor Frederick Barbarossa and given a charter in 1158. Kings, popes, and princes soon competed to found new universities, and by the end of the Middle Ages, there were eighty universities in Europe, most of them in England, France, Italy, and Germany (see the box on p. 322).

University students (all men—women did not attend universities in the Middle Ages) began their studies with the traditional **liberal arts** curriculum, which consisted of grammar, rhetoric, logic, arithmetic, geometry, music, and astronomy. Teaching was done by the lecture method. The word *lecture* is derived from the Latin verb for "read." Before the development of the printing press in the fifteenth century, books were expensive and few students could afford them, so teachers read from a basic text (such as a collection of laws if the subject was law) and then added their explanations. No exams were given after a series of lectures, but when a student applied for a degree, he was given a comprehensive oral examination by a committee of teachers. The exam was taken after a four- or six-year period of study. The first degree a student could earn was a bachelor of arts; later he might receive a master of arts.

After completing the liberal arts curriculum, a student could go on to study law, medicine, or theology. A student who passed his final oral examinations was granted a doctor's degree, which officially enabled him to teach his subject. Students who received degrees from medieval universities could pursue other careers besides teaching that proved to be much more lucrative. A law degree was necessary for those who wished to serve as advisers to kings and princes.

THE DEVELOPMENT OF SCHOLASTICISM The importance of Christianity in medieval society ensured that theology would play a central role in the European

University Students and Violence at Oxford

Medieval universities shared in the violent atmosphere of their age. Town and gown quarrels often resulted in bloody conflicts, especially during the universities' formative period. This selection is taken from an anonymous description of a student riot at Oxford at the end of the thirteenth century.

A Student Riot at Oxford

They [the townsmen] seized and imprisoned all scholars on whom they could lay hands, invaded their inns [halls of residence], made havoc of their goods and trampled their books under foot. In the face of such provocation the proctors [university officials] sent their assistants about the town, forbidding the students to leave their inns. But all commands and exhortations were in vain. By nine o'clock next morning, bands of scholars were parading the streets in martial array. If the proctors failed to restrain them, the mayor was equally powerless to restrain his townsmen. The great bell of St. Martin's rang out an alarm; oxhorns were sounded in the streets; messengers were sent into the country to collect rustic allies. The clerks [students and teachers], who numbered 3,000 in all, began their attack simultaneously in various quarters. They broke open warehouses in the Spicery, the Cutlery and elsewhere. Armed with bow and arrows, swords and bucklers, slings and stones, they fell upon their opponents. Three they slew, and wounded fifty or more. One band . . . took up a position in High Street between the Churches of St. Mary and All Saints' and attacked the house of a certain Edward Hales. This Hales was a longstanding enemy of the clerks. There were no half measures with him. He seized his crossbow, and from an upper chamber sent an unerring shaft into the eye of the pugnacious rector. The death of their valiant leader caused the clerks to lose heart. They fled, closely pursued by the townsmen and country-folk. Some were struck down in the streets, and others who had taken refuge in the churches were dragged out and driven mercilessly to prison, lashed with thongs and goaded with iron spikes.

Complaints of murder, violence and robbery were lodged straightway with the king by both parties. The townsmen claimed 3,000 pounds' damage. The commissioners, however, appointed to decide the matter, condemned them to pay 200 marks, removed the bailiffs, and banished twelve of the most turbulent citizens from Oxford.

Who do you think was responsible for this conflict between town and gown? Why? Why do you think the king supported the university?

Source: From *The Story of Oxford* by Cecil Headlam, 1907.

intellectual world. Theology, the formal study of religion, was "queen of the sciences" in the new universities.

Beginning in the eleventh century, the effort to apply reason or logical analysis to the church's basic theological doctrines had a significant impact on the study of theology. The philosophical and theological system of the medieval schools is known as **scholasticism** (skoh-LAS-tih-siz-uhm). Scholasticism tried to reconcile faith and reason, to demonstrate that what was accepted on faith was in harmony with what could be learned by reason.

The overriding task of scholasticism was to harmonize Christian teachings with the work of the Greek philosopher Aristotle. In the twelfth century, due largely to the work of Muslim and Jewish scholars in Spain, western Europe was introduced to a large number of Greek scientific and philosophical works, including the works of Aristotle. Aristotle's works threw many theologians into consternation, however. Aristotle had arrived at his conclusions by rational thought, not by faith, and some of his doctrines contradicted the teachings of the church. The most famous attempt to reconcile Aristotle and the doctrines of Christianity was that of Saint Thomas Aquinas (uh-KWY-nuss) (1225–1274).

Aquinas's reputation derives from his masterful attempt to reconcile faith and reason. He took it for granted that there were truths derived by reason and truths derived by faith. He was certain, however, that the two truths could not be in conflict. The natural mind, unaided by faith, could arrive at truths concerning the physical universe. Without the help of God's grace, however, reason alone could not grasp spiritual truths, such as the Trinity (the manifestation of God in three separate yet identical persons—Father, Son, and Holy Spirit) or the Incarnation (Jesus's simultaneous identity as God and human).

THE GOTHIC CATHEDRAL Begun in the twelfth century and brought to perfection in the thirteenth, the **Gothic** cathedral remains one of the greatest artistic triumphs of the High Middle Ages. Soaring skyward, as if to reach heaven, it was a fitting symbol for medieval people's preoccupation with God.

Two fundamental innovations of the twelfth century made Gothic cathedrals possible. The combination of ribbed vaults and pointed arches replaced the barrel vault of earlier churches and enabled builders to make Gothic churches higher. The use of pointed arches and ribbed vaults created an impression of upward movement. Another technical innovation, the flying buttress, basically a heavy arched pier of stone built onto the outside of the walls, made it possible to distribute the weight of the church's vaulted ceilings outward and down and thus eliminate the heavy walls used in earlier churches to hold the weight of the massive barrel vaults. Thus, Gothic cathedrals could be built with thin walls containing magnificent stained-glass windows, which created a play of light inside that varied with the sun at different times of the day. The use of light reflected the belief that natural light was a symbol of the divine light of God.

The first fully Gothic church was the abbey of Saint-Denis (san-duh-NEE) near Paris, inspired by its famous Abbot Suger (soo-ZHAYR) (1122–1151) and built between 1140 and 1150. By the mid-thirteenth century, French Gothic architecture, most brilliantly executed in cathedrals in Paris (Notre-Dame), Reims, Amiens, and Chartres, had spread to virtually all of Europe.

A Gothic cathedral was the work of the entire community. All classes contributed to its construction. Master masons, who were both architects and engineers, designed the cathedrals, and stonemasons and other craftspeople were paid a daily wage and provided the skilled labor to build them. A Gothic cathedral symbolized the chief preoccupation of a medieval Christian community, its dedication to a spiritual ideal. As we have observed before, the largest buildings of an era reflect the values of its society. The Gothic cathedral, with its towers soaring toward heaven, gave witness to an age when a spiritual impulse underlay most aspects of its existence.

© Adam Sylvester/Photo Researchers

The Gothic Cathedral. The Gothic cathedral was one of the great artistic triumphs of the High Middle Ages. Shown here is the cathedral of Notre-Dame in Paris. Begun in 1163, it was not completed until the beginning of the fourteenth century.

Medieval Europe and the World

FOCUS QUESTIONS: In what ways did Europeans begin to relate to peoples in other parts of the world after 1000 C.E.? What were the reasons for the Crusades, and who or what benefited the most from the experience of the Crusades?

As it developed, European civilization remained largely confined to its home continent, although Europe was never completely isolated. Some Europeans, especially merchants, had contacts with parts of Asia and Africa, and the goods of those lands made their way into medieval castles. The Vikings were also daring explorers. After 860, they sailed westward in their long ships across the North Atlantic, reaching Iceland in 874. Erik the Red, a Viking exiled from Iceland, traveled even farther west and discovered Greenland in 985. Some Vikings even reached North America, landing in Newfoundland, the only known Viking site in North America, but it proved to be short-lived as Viking expansion drew to a close by the end of the tenth century. Only at the end of the eleventh century did Europeans begin their first concerted attempt to expand beyond the frontiers of Europe by conquering the land of Palestine.

The First Crusades

The Crusades were based on the idea of a holy war against the infidels (unbelievers). Christian wrath was directed against the Muslims, and at the end of the eleventh century, Christian Europe found itself with a glorious opportunity to attack them. The immediate impetus for the Crusades came when the Byzantine emperor, Alexius I, asked Pope Urban II for help against the Seljuk Turks, who were Muslims (see Chapter 13). The pope saw this as a chance to to rally the warriors of Europe for the liberation of Jerusalem and the Holy Land of Palestine from the infidel. At the Council of Clermont in southern France near the end of 1095, Urban II challenged Christians to take up their weapons and join in a holy war to recover the Holy Land.

Three organized crusading bands of noble warriors, most of them French, made their way eastward. After the capture of Antioch in 1098, much of the crusading host proceeded down the Palestinian coast, evading the well-defended coastal cities, and reached Jerusalem in June 1099. After a five-week siege, the Holy City was taken amid a horrible massacre of the inhabitants—men, women, and children (see the box on p. 181 in Chapter 7).

After further conquest of Palestinian lands, the crusaders ignored the wishes of the Byzantine emperor and organized four Latin crusader states. Because the crusader kingdoms were surrounded by Muslims hostile to them, they grew increasingly dependent on the Italian commercial cities for supplies from Europe. Some Italian cities, such as Genoa, Pisa, and, above all, Venice, grew rich and powerful in the process.

But it was not easy for the crusader kingdoms to maintain themselves. Already by the 1120s, the Muslims had begun to strike back. The fall of one of the Latin kingdoms in 1144 led to renewed calls for another Crusade, especially from the monastic firebrand Saint Bernard of Clairvaux (klayr-VOH). He exclaimed: "Now, on account of our sins, the enemies of the cross have begun to show their faces. . . . What are you doing, you servants of the cross? Will you throw to the dogs that which is most holy? Will you cast pearls before swine?"[6] Bernard even managed to enlist two powerful rulers, but the Second Crusade proved to be a total failure.

The Third Crusade was a reaction to the fall of the Holy City of Jerusalem to the Muslim forces under Saladin in 1187. Now all of Christendom was ablaze with calls for a new Crusade. Three major monarchs agreed to lead their forces in person: Emperor Frederick Barbarossa of Germany, Richard I the Lionhearted of England (1189–1199), and Philip II Augustus, king of France. Some of the crusaders finally arrived in the Holy Land by 1189 only to encounter problems. Frederick Barbarossa drowned while swimming in a local river, and his army quickly disintegrated. The English and French arrived by sea and met with success against the coastal cities, where they had the support of their fleets, but when they moved inland, they failed miserably. Eventually, after Philip went home, Richard the Lionhearted negotiated a settlement whereby Saladin agreed to allow Christian pilgrims free access to Jerusalem.

The Later Crusades

After the death of Saladin in 1193, Pope Innocent III initiated the Fourth Crusade. On its way to the east, the crusading army became involved in a dispute over the succession to the Byzantine throne. The Venetian leaders

Bibliothèque de l'Arsenal, Paris//© Scala/Art Resource, NY

The First Crusade: The Capture of Jerusalem. Recruited from the noble class of western Europe, the first crusading army reached Constantinople by 1097. By 1098, the crusaders had taken Antioch. Working down the coast of Palestine, they captured Jerusalem in 1099. Shown here in a fifteenth-century French manuscript illustration is a fanciful re-creation of the capture and sack of Jerusalem. A crusader in the center is shown wearing the crusading cross on his back.

of the Fourth Crusade saw an opportunity to neutralize their greatest commercial competitor, the Byzantine Empire. Diverted to Constantinople, the crusaders sacked the great capital city of Byzantium in 1204 and set up the new Latin Empire of Constantinople (see Chapter 13). Not until 1261 did a Byzantine army recapture Constantinople. In the meantime, additional Crusades were undertaken to reconquer the Holy Land. All of them were largely disasters, and by the end of the thirteenth century, the European military effort to capture Palestine was recognized as a complete failure.

What Were the Effects of the Crusades?

Whether the Crusades had much effect on European civilization is debatable. The only visible remains are the European castles that began to incorporate features adopted from fortresses that the crusaders observed in the east (see the comparative illustration on p. 180 in Chapter 7). Although there may have been some broadening of perspective from the exchange between two cultures, the interaction of Christian Europe with the Muslim world was actually both more intense and more meaningful in Spain and Sicily than in the Holy Land.

Did the Crusades help stabilize European society by removing large numbers of young warriors who would have fought each other in Europe? Some historians think so and believe that Western monarchs established their control more easily as a result. There is no doubt that the Crusades did contribute to the economic growth of the Italian port cities, especially Genoa, Pisa, and Venice. But it is important to remember that the growing wealth and population of twelfth-century Europe had made the Crusades possible in the first place. The Crusades may have enhanced the revival of trade, but they certainly did not cause it. Even without the Crusades, Italian merchants would have pursued new trade contacts with the Eastern world.

Did the Crusades have side effects that would haunt European society for generations? Some historians have argued that the Crusades might be considered a "Christian holy war," whose memories still trouble the relationship between the Muslim world and the West today. Other historians argue that the early crusaders were motivated as much by economic and political reasons as religious ones.

Another possible side effect is more apparent. The first widespread attacks on the Jews began with the Crusades. As some Christians argued, it was unthinkable to undertake holy wars against infidel Muslims while the "murderers of Christ" ran free at home. With the Crusades, the massacre of Jews became a regular feature of medieval European life.

CHAPTER SUMMARY

After the collapse of the Han Dynasty in the third century C.E., China experienced nearly four centuries of internal chaos until the Tang dynasty in the seventh century C.E. attempted to follow the pattern of the Han dynasty and restore the power of the Chinese Empire. The fall of the Western Roman Empire in the fifth century brought a quite different result as three new civilizations emerged out of the collapse of Roman power in the Mediterranean. A new world of Islam emerged in the east; it occupied large parts of the old Roman Empire and created its own flourishing civilization. As we shall see in Chapter 13, the eastern part of the old Roman Empire, increasingly Greek in culture, continued to survive as the Christian Byzantine Empire. At the same time, a new Christian European civilization was establishing its roots in the West. By the eleventh and twelfth centuries, these three heirs of Rome began their own conflict for control of the lands of the eastern Mediterranean.

The coronation of Charlemagne, the descendant of a Germanic tribe converted to Christianity, as emperor of the Romans in 800 symbolized the fusion of the three chief components of the new European civilization: the German tribes, the Roman legacy, and the Christian church. Charlemagne's Carolingian Empire fostered the idea of a distinct European identity. With the disintegration of that empire, however, power fell into the hands of many different lords, who came to constitute a nobility that dominated Europe's political, economic and social life. But within this world of castles and private power, during the High Middle Ages, kings gradually began to develop the machinery of government and accumulate political authority. Although they could not know it then, the actions of these medieval monarchs laid the foundation for the European states that in one form or another have dominated the European political scene ever since.

European civilization began to flourish in the High Middle Ages. The revival of trade, the expansion of towns and cities, and the development of a money economy did not mean the end of a predominantly rural European society, but they did open the door to new ways to make a living and new opportunities for people to expand and enrich their lives. At the same time, the High Middle Ages also gave birth to a cultural revival that led to new centers of learning in the universities, to the use of reason to systematize the study of theology, and to a dramatic increase in the number and size of churches.

The Catholic Church shared in the challenge of new growth by reforming itself and striking out on a path toward greater papal power, both within the church and over European society. The High Middle Ages witnessed a spiritual renewal that enhanced papal leadership and the religious life of the clergy and laity. At the same time, this spiritual renewal also gave rise to the crusading "holy warrior," thereby creating an animosity between Christians and Muslims that still has repercussions to this day.

CHAPTER TIMELINE

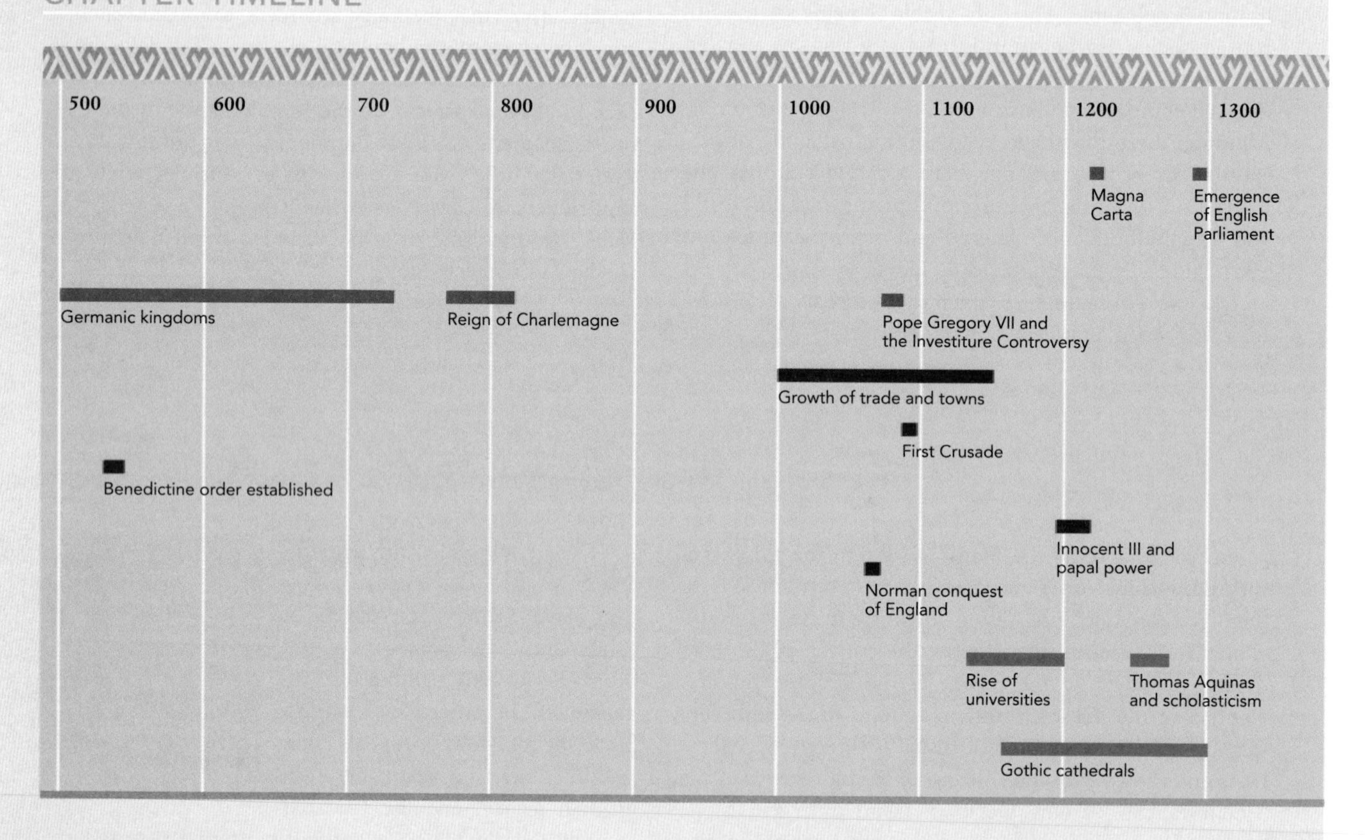

CHAPTER REVIEW

Upon Reflection

Q What impact did the Vikings have on the history and culture of medieval Europe?

Q How did the revival of trade and cities affect the economy and society of Europe in the High Middle Ages?

Q The medieval Catholic Church developed along new institutional lines in the High Middle Ages. What are the most important features of this development?

Key Terms

diocese (p. 303)
monk (p. 303)

monasticism (p. 303)
abbot (p. 304)
nuns (p. 304)
abbesses (p. 304)
vassal (p. 307)
fief (p. 309)
manor (p. 309)
serfs (p. 309)
demesne (p. 309)
aristocracy (p. 311)
commercial capitalism (p. 311)
guild (p. 312)
common law (p. 314)
lay investiture (p. 319)
interdict (p. 320)
sacraments (p. 320)
heresy (p. 320)
liberal arts (p. 321)
scholasticism (p. 322)
Gothic (p. 323)

Suggested Reading

EARLY MIDDLE AGES For general histories of the Middle Ages, see **J. M. Riddle, *A History of the Middle Ages, 300–1500*** (New York, 2008), and **B. Rosenwein, *A Short History of the Middle Ages*** (Orchard Park, N.Y., 2002). A brief history of the Early Middle Ages can be found in **R. Collins, *Early Medieval Europe, 300–1000*** (New York, 1991). On Charlemagne, see **A. Barbero, *Charlemagne: Father of a Continent,*** trans. **A. Cameron** (Berkeley, Calif., 2004).

The Vikings are examined in **M. Arnold, *The Vikings: Culture and Conquest*** (London, 2006). For an important revisionist view of feudalism, see **S. Reynolds, *Fiefs and Vassals*** (Oxford, 1994).

HIGH MIDDLE AGES For a good introduction to the High Middle Ages, see **W. C. Jordan, *Europe in the High Middle Ages*** (New York, 2003).

Urban history is covered in **D. Nicholas, *The Growth of the Medieval City: From Late Antiquity to the Early Fourteenth Century*** (New York, 1997). On women, see **L. Bitel, *Women in Early Medieval Europe, 400–1100*** (Cambridge, 2002). On daily life, see **R. Fossier, *The Axe and the Oath*** (Princeton, N.J., 2010).

For a general survey of Christianity in the Middle Ages, see **F. D. Logan, *A History of the Church in the Middle Ages*** (London, 2002). For a superb introduction to early Christianity, see **P. Brown, *The Rise of Western Christendom: Triumph and Adversity, A.D. 200–1000,*** 2nd ed. (Oxford, 2002). On the papacy in the High Middle Ages, see **I. S. Robinson, *The Papacy*** (Cambridge, 1990). On monasticism, see **C. H. Lawrence, *Medieval Monasticism,*** 3rd ed. (London, 2000), a good general account.

On medieval intellectual life, see **M. L. Colish, *Medieval Foundations of the Western Intellectual Tradition, 400–1400*** (New Haven, Conn., 1997). A good introduction to Romanesque style is **A. Petzold, *Romanesque Art,*** rev. ed. (New York, 2003). On the Gothic movement, see **M. Camille, *Gothic Art: Glorious Visions,*** rev. ed. (New York, 2003).

MEDIEVAL EUROPE AND THE WORLD For a detailed survey of the Crusades, see **C. Tyerman, *God's War: A New History of the Crusades*** (Cambridge, Mass., 2006). Also see **J. Riley-Smith, ed., *The Oxford Illustrated History of the Crusades*** (New York, 1995).

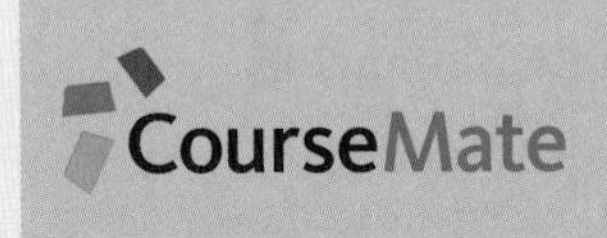

Visit the CourseMate website at **www.cengagebrain.com** for additional study tools and review materials for this chapter.

CHAPTER

13

The Byzantine Empire and Crisis and Recovery in the West

S. Vitale, Ravenna//© Scala/Art Resource, NY

Justinian and Theodora

CHAPTER OUTLINE AND FOCUS QUESTIONS

From Eastern Roman to Byzantine Empire

Q How did the Byzantine Empire that had emerged by the eighth century differ from the empire of Justinian and from the Germanic kingdoms in the west? How were they alike?

The Zenith of Byzantine Civilization (750–1025)

Q What were the chief developments in the Byzantine Empire between 750 and 1025?

The Decline and Fall of the Byzantine Empire (1025–1453)

Q What impact did the Crusades have on the Byzantine Empire? How and why did Constantinople and the Byzantine Empire fall?

The Crises of the Fourteenth Century

Q What impact did the Black Death have on Europe and Asia in the fourteenth century? What problems did Europeans face during the fourteenth century, and what impact did these crises have on European economic, social, and religious life?

Recovery: The Renaissance

Q What were the main features of the Renaissance in Europe, and how did it differ from the Middle Ages?

CRITICAL THINKING

Q In what ways did the Byzantine, European, and Islamic civilizations resemble and differ from each other? Were their relationships overall based on cooperation or conflict?

AT THE SAME TIME that medieval European civilization was emerging in the west, the eastern part of the Late Roman Empire, increasingly Greek in culture, continued to survive. While serving as a buffer between Europe and the peoples to the east, especially the growing empire of Islam, the Late Roman Empire in the east (Byzantine Empire) also preserved the intellectual and legal accomplishments of the Greeks and Romans.

In its early decades, the Eastern Roman Empire was beset by crises. Soon after the beginning of his reign, the emperor Justinian was faced with a serious revolt in the capital city of Constantinople. In 532, two factions, called the Blues and the Greens because they supported chariot teams bearing those colors when they competed in the Hippodrome (a huge amphitheater), joined together and rioted to protest the emperor's taxation policies. The riots soon became a revolt as insurgents burned and looted the center of the city, shouting "*Nika!*" (victory), the word normally used to cheer on their favorite teams. Aristocratic factions joined the revolt and put forward a nobleman named Hypatius as a new emperor. Justinian seemed ready to flee, but his wife, the empress Theodora, strengthened his resolve by declaring, according to the historian Procopius, "If now, it is your wish to save yourself, O Emperor, there is no difficulty. For we have much money, and there is the sea, here the boats. However, consider whether it will not come about after you have been saved that you would gladly exchange that safety for death. As for myself, I approve a certain ancient saying that royalty is a good burial shroud."[1] Shamed by his wife's words, Justinian resolved to fight. He ordered troops, newly returned from fighting the Persians, to attack a large crowd that had gathered in the Hippodrome to acclaim Hypatius as emperor. In the ensuing massacre, the imperial troops slaughtered 30,000 of the insurgents, about 5 percent of the city's population. After crushing the Nika Revolt, Justinian began a massive rebuilding program and continued the autocratic reign that established the foundations of the Byzantine Empire (as it came to known beginning in the eighth century).

Despite the early empire's reversals, the Macedonian emperors in the ninth, tenth, and eleventh centuries enlarged the empire, achieved economic prosperity, and expanded its cultural influence to eastern Europe and Russia. But after the Macedonian dynasty ended in 1056 C.E., the empire began a slow but steady decline. Involvement in the Crusades proved especially disastrous, leading to the occupation of Constantinople by western crusading forces in 1204. Byzantine rule was restored in 1261, and the empire survived in a weakened condition for another 190 years until the Ottoman Turks finally conquered it in 1453.

In the fourteenth century, Europe, too, sustained a series of crises and reversals after flourishing during the three centuries of the High Middle Ages. Unlike the Byzantine Empire, however, European civilization rebounded in the fifteenth century, experiencing an artistic and intellectual revival in the Renaissance as well as a renewal of monarchical authority among the western European states. Europe was poised to begin its dramatic entry into world affairs.

From Eastern Roman to Byzantine Empire

FOCUS QUESTIONS: How did the Byzantine Empire that had emerged by the eighth century differ from the empire of Justinian and from the Germanic kingdoms in the west? How were they alike?

As noted earlier, the western and eastern parts of the Roman Empire began to drift apart in the fourth century. As the Germanic peoples moved into the western part of the empire and established various kingdoms over the course of the fifth century, the Late Roman Empire in the east solidified and prospered.

Constantinople, the imperial capital, viewed itself not only as the center of a world empire but also as a special Christian city. The inhabitants believed that the city was under the protection of God and the Virgin Mary. One thirteenth-century Byzantine said: "About our city you shall know: until the end she will fear no nation whatsoever, for no one will entrap or capture her, not by any means, for she has been given to the Mother of God and no one will snatch her out of Her hands. Many nations will break their horns against her walls and withdraw with shame."[2] The Byzantines saw their state as a Christian empire.

The Reign of Justinian (527–565)

In the sixth century, the empire in the east came under the control of one of its most remarkable rulers, the emperor Justinian (juh-STIN-ee-un). He married Theodora (thee-uh-DOR-uh), daughter of a lower-class circus trainer, who proved to be a remarkably strong-willed woman and played a critical role, as we have seen, in giving Justinian the determination to crush a revolt against his rule in 532. Justinian was determined to reestablish the Roman Empire in the entire Mediterranean world and began his attempt to reconquer the west within a year after the revolt had failed.

Justinian's army under Belisarius (bell-uh-SAH-ree-uss), probably the best general of the late Roman world, presented a formidable force. Belisarius sailed to North Africa and quickly defeated the Vandals in two major battles. From North Africa, he led his forces onto the Italian peninsula after occupying Sicily in 535. But it was not until 552 that the Ostrogoths in Italy were finally defeated. Justinian appeared to have achieved his goals. He had restored the imperial Mediterranean world; his empire included Italy, part of Spain, North Africa, Asia Minor, Palestine, and Syria. But the conquest of the western empire proved fleeting. Only three years after

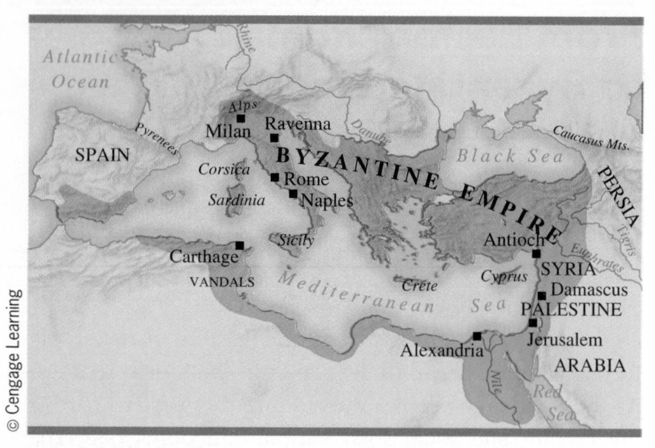

© Cengage Learning

The Byzantine Empire in the Time of Justinian

Justinian's death, another Germanic people, the Lombards, entered Italy. Although the eastern empire maintained the fiction of Italy as a province, it controlled only a few small pockets here and there.

THE CODIFICATION OF ROMAN LAW Though his conquests proved short-lived, Justinian made a lasting contribution to Western civilization through his codification of Roman law. The eastern empire was heir to a vast quantity of materials connected to the development of Roman law. Justinian had been well trained in imperial government and was thoroughly acquainted with Roman law. He wished to codify and simplify this mass of materials.

To accomplish his goal, Justinian authorized the jurist Trebonian (tre-BOHN-ee-un) to make a systematic compilation of imperial edicts. The result was the Code of Law, the first part of the *Corpus Iuris Civilis* (KOR-pus YOOR-iss SIV-i-liss) (Body of Civil Law), completed in 529. Four years later, two other parts of the *Corpus* appeared: the *Digest*, a compendium of writings of Roman jurists, and the *Institutes*, a brief summary of the chief principles of Roman law that could be used as a textbook. The fourth part of the *Corpus* was the *Novels*, a compilation of the most important new edicts issued during Justinian's reign.

Justinian's codification of Roman law became the basis of imperial law in the Byzantine Empire until its end in 1453. More important, however, since it was written in Latin (it was, in fact, the last product of eastern Roman culture to be written in Latin, which was soon replaced by Greek), it was also eventually used in the west and became the basis of the legal systems of all of continental Europe.

THE EMPEROR'S BUILDING PROGRAM After the riots destroyed much of Constantinople, Justinian rebuilt the city and gave it the appearance it would keep for almost a thousand years. Earlier, Emperor Theodosius (thee-uh-DOH-shuss) II (408–450) had constructed an enormous defensive wall to protect the capital on its land side. The city was dominated by an immense palace complex, the huge arena known as the Hippodrome, and hundreds of churches. Justinian added many new buildings. His public works projects included roads, bridges, walls, public baths, law courts,

S. Vitale, Ravenna//© Scala/Art Resource, NY

The Emperor Justinian and His Court. As the seat of late Roman power in Italy, the town of Ravenna was adorned with late Roman art. The Church of San Vitale at Ravenna contains some of the finest examples of sixth-century mosaics. Small pieces of colored glass were set in mortar on the wall to form these figures and their surroundings. The emperor is depicted as both head of state (he wears a jeweled crown and a purple robe) and head of the church (he carries a gold bowl symbolizing the body of Jesus).

and colossal underground reservoirs to hold the city's water supply. He also built hospitals, schools, monasteries, and churches. Churches were his special passion, and in Constantinople he built or rebuilt thirty-four of them. His greatest achievement was the famous Hagia Sophia (HAH-yuh soh-FEE-uh), the Church of the Holy Wisdom.

Completed in 537, Hagia Sophia was designed by two Greek scientists who departed radically from the simple, flat-roofed basilica of western architecture. The center of Hagia Sophia consisted of four huge piers crowned by an enormous dome, which seemed to be floating in space. This effect was emphasized by Procopius (pruh-KOH-pee-uss), the court historian, who at Justinian's request wrote a treatise on the emperor's building projects: "From the lightness of the building, it does not appear to rest upon a solid foundation, but to cover the place beneath as though it were suspended from heaven by the fabled golden chain." In part, this impression was created by putting forty-two windows around the base of the dome, which allowed an incredible play of light within the cathedral. Light served to remind the worshipers of God; as Procopius commented:

> Whoever enters there to worship perceives at once that it is not by any human strength or skill, but by the favor of God that this work has been perfected; his mind rises sublime to commune with God, feeling that He cannot be far off, but must especially love to dwell in the place which He has chosen; and this takes place not only when a man sees it for the first time, but it always makes the same impression upon him, as though he had never beheld it before.[3]

As darkness is illuminated by invisible light, so too, it was believed, the world is illuminated by invisible spirit.

The royal palace complex, Hagia Sophia, and the Hippodrome were the three greatest buildings in Constantinople. This last was a huge amphitheater, constructed of brick covered by marble, holding as many as 60,000 spectators. The main events were the chariot races; twenty-four would usually be presented in one day. The citizens of Constantinople were passionate fans of chariot racing. Crowds in the Hippodrome also took on political significance. Being a member of the two chief factions of charioteers—the Blues or the Greens—was the only real outlet for political expression. Even emperors had to be aware of their demands and attitudes: the loss of a race in the Hippodrome frequently resulted in bloody riots that could threaten the emperor's power.

A New Kind of Empire

Justinian's accomplishments had been spectacular, but when he died, he left the Eastern Roman Empire with serious problems: too much distant territory to protect, an empty treasury, a smaller population after a devastating plague, and renewed threats to the frontiers. The seventh century proved to be an important turning point in the history of the empire.

© Robert Harding/Getty Images

Interior View of Hagia Sophia. Pictured here is the interior of the Church of the Holy Wisdom in Constantinople (modern Istanbul), constructed under Justinian by Anthemius of Tralles (an-THEE-mee-uss of TRAL-leez) and Isidore of Miletus (IH-zuh-dor of mih-LEE-tuss). Some of the stones used in the construction of the church had been plundered from the famous Classical Temple of Diana, near Ephesus, in Asia Minor (modern Turkey). This view gives an idea of how the windows around the base of the dome produced a special play of light within the cathedral. The pulpits and plaques bearing inscriptions from the Qur'an were introduced when the Turks converted the church to a mosque in the fifteenth century.

PROBLEMS OF THE SEVENTH CENTURY In the first half of the century, during the reign of Heraclius (he-ruh-KLY-uss *or* huh-RAK-lee-uss) (610–641), the empire faced attacks from the Persians to the east and the Slavs to the north. A new system of defense was put in place, using a new and larger administrative unit, the *theme*, which combined civilian and military offices in the hands of the same person. Thus, the civil governor was also the military leader of the area. Although this innovation helped the empire survive, it also fostered an increased militarization of the empire. By the mid-seventh century, it had become apparent that a restored Mediterranean empire was simply beyond the resources of the eastern empire, which now increasingly turned its back on the Latin west. A renewed series of external threats in the second half of the seventh century strengthened this development.

The most serious challenge to the empire was the rise of Islam, which unified the Arab tribes and created a powerful new force that swept through the region (see Chapter 7). The defeat of an eastern Roman army near the Yarmuk River in 636 meant the loss of the provinces of Syria and Palestine. The Arabs also moved into the old Persian Empire and conquered it. An Arab attempt to besiege Constantinople in 717 failed, leaving Arabs and eastern Roman forces facing each other along a frontier in southern Asia Minor.

Problems also arose along the northern frontier, especially in the Balkans, where an Asiatic people known as the Bulgars had arrived earlier in the sixth century. In 679, the Bulgars defeated the eastern Roman forces and took possession of the lower Danube valley, setting up a strong Bulgarian kingdom. By the beginning of the eighth century, the Eastern Roman Empire was greatly diminished in size, consisting only of a portion of the Balkans and Asia Minor.

© Cengage Learning

The Byzantine Empire, c. 750

It was now an eastern Mediterranean state. These external challenges had important internal repercussions as well. By the eighth century, the Eastern Roman Empire had been transformed into what historians call the Byzantine Empire, a civilization with its own unique character that would last until 1453 (Constantinople was built on the site of an older city named Byzantium—hence the name *Byzantine*).

THE BYZANTINE EMPIRE IN THE EIGHTH CENTURY The Byzantine Empire was a Greek state. Latin fell into disuse as Greek became not only the common language of the empire but its official language as well.

The Byzantine Empire was also a Christian state, built on a faith in Jesus that was shared in a profound way by almost all its citizens. An enormous amount of artistic talent was poured into the construction of churches, church ceremonies, and church decoration. Spiritual principles deeply permeated Byzantine art. The importance of religion to the Byzantines explains why theological disputes took on an exaggerated form. The most famous of these disputes, the so-called iconoclastic controversy, threatened the stability of the empire in the first half of the eighth century.

Beginning in the sixth century, the use of religious images, especially in the form of icons or pictures of sacred figures, became so widespread that charges of idolatry, the worship of images, began to be heard. The use of images or icons had been justified by the argument that icons were not worshiped but were simply used to help illiterate people understand their religion. This argument failed to stop the **iconoclasts**, as the opponents of icons were called. **Iconoclasm** was not unique to the Byzantine Empire. In the neighboring Islamic empire, religious art did not include any physical representations of Muhammad (see the comparative illustration on p. 333).

Beginning in 730, the Byzantine emperor Leo III (717–741) outlawed the use of icons. Strong resistance ensued, especially from monks. Leo also used the iconoclastic controversy to add to the prestige of the patriarch of Constantinople, the highest church official in the east and second in dignity only to the bishop of Rome. The Roman popes were opposed to the iconoclastic edicts, and their opposition created considerable dissension between the popes and the Byzantine emperors. Late in the eighth century, the Byzantine rulers reversed their stand on the use of images, but not before considerable damage had been done to the unity of the Christian church. Although the final separation between Roman Catholicism and Greek Orthodoxy (as the Christian church in the Byzantine Empire was called) did not occur until 1054, the iconoclastic controversy was important in moving both sides in that direction.

The emperor occupied a crucial position in the Byzantine state. Portrayed as chosen by God, the Byzantine emperor was crowned in elaborate sacred ceremonies, and his subjects were expected to prostrate themselves in his presence. The emperor's power was considered absolute and was limited in practice only by deposition or assassination. Because the emperor appointed the patriarch, he also exercised control over both church and state. The Byzantines believed that God had commanded their state to preserve the true faith, Orthodox Christianity. Emperor, clergy, and civic officials were all bound together in service to this ideal. It can be said that spiritual values truly held the Byzantine state together.

By 750, it was apparent that two of Rome's heirs, the Germanic kingdoms and the Byzantine Empire, were moving in different directions. Nevertheless, Byzantine influence on the Western world was significant. The images of a Roman imperial state that continued to haunt the west lived on in Byzantium. As noted, the legal systems of the west came to owe much to Justinian's codification of Roman law. In addition, the Byzantine Empire served in part as a buffer state, protecting the west for a long time from incursions from the east.

INTELLECTUAL LIFE The intellectual life of the Byzantine Empire was greatly influenced by the traditions of Classical civilization. Scholars actively strived to preserve the works of the ancient Greeks and based a great deal of

Trinity College, Dublin//© Art Resource, NY

St. Catherine Monastery, Mount Sinai, Sinai Desert//© Erich Lessing/Art Resource, NY

Patio De Los Arrayanes, Alhambra, Granada//© Vanni/Art Resource, NY

COMPARATIVE ILLUSTRATION

ART & IDEAS

Religious Imagery in the Medieval World. The Middle Ages was a golden age of religious art, reflecting the important role of religion itself in medieval society. These three illustrations show different aspects of medieval religious imagery. In Europe, much Christian art appeared in illuminated manuscripts. The illustration at the top left shows a page depicting the figure of Jesus from *The Book of Kells*, a richly decorated illuminated manuscript of the Christian gospels produced by the monks of Iona in the British Isles. Byzantine art was also deeply religious, as was especially evident in icons. At the top right is an icon of the Virgin and Child (Mary and Jesus) from the monastery of Saint Catherine at Mount Sinai in Egypt dating to around the year 600. Painted on wood, this icon shows the enthroned Virgin and Child between Saints Theodore and George with two angels behind them looking upward to a beam of light containing the hand of God. The figures are not realistic; the goal of the icon was to bridge the gap between the divine and the outer material world. Artists in the Muslim world faced a different challenge—Muslims warned against imitating God by creating pictures of living beings, thus effectively prohibiting the representation of humans, especially Muhammad. Islamic religious artists therefore used decorative motifs based on geometric patterns and the Arabic script. The scriptural panel in the lower illustration is an artistic presentation of a verse from the Qur'an, thus blending the spiritual and artistic spheres.

Q *How is the importance of religious imagery in the Middle Ages evident in these three illustrations?*

their own literature on Classical models. Although the Byzantines produced a substantial body of literature, much of it was of a very practical nature, focusing on legal, military, and administrative matters. The most outstanding literary achievements of the early Byzantine Empire, however, were historical and religious works.

The empire's best-known historian was Procopius (c. 500–c. 562), court historian during the reign of Justinian. Procopius served as secretary to the great general Belisarius and accompanied him on his wars on behalf of Justinian. Procopius's best historical work, the *Wars*, is a firsthand account of Justinian's wars of reconquest in the western Mediterranean and his wars against the Persians in the east. Deliberately modeled after the work of his hero, the Greek historian Thucydides (see Chapter 4), Procopius's narrative features vivid descriptions of battle scenes, clear judgment, and noteworthy objectivity.

LIFE IN CONSTANTINOPLE: THE IMPORTANCE OF TRADE With a population in the hundreds of thousands, Constantinople was the largest city in Europe during the Middle Ages. Until the twelfth century, Constantinople was also Europe's greatest commercial center. The city was the chief entrepôt for the exchange of products between west and east, and trade formed the basis for its fabulous prosperity. This trade, however, was largely carried on by foreign merchants. As one contemporary said:

> All sorts of merchants come here from the land of Babylon, from . . . Persia, Media, and all the sovereignty of the land of Egypt, from the lands of Canaan, and from the empire of Russia, from Hungaria, Khazaria [the Caspian region], and the land of Lombardy and Sepharad [Spain]. It is a busy city, and merchants come to it from every country by sea or land, and there is none like it in the world except Baghdad, the great city of Islam.[4]

Highly desired in Europe were the products of the east: silk from China, spices from Southeast Asia and India, jewelry and ivory from India (used by artisans for church items), wheat and furs from southern Russia, and flax and honey from the Balkans. Many of these eastern goods were then shipped to the Mediterranean area and northern Europe. Despite the Germanic incursions, trade with Europe never entirely ended.

Moreover, imported raw materials were used in Constantinople for local industries. During Justinian's reign, two Christian monks smuggled silkworms from China to begin a silk industry. The state had a monopoly on the production of silk cloth, and the workshops themselves were housed in Constantinople's royal palace complex. European demand for silk cloth made it the city's most lucrative product. It is interesting to note that the upper classes, including emperors and empresses, were not discouraged from making money through trade and manufacturing. Indeed, one empress even manufactured perfumes in her bedroom.

The Zenith of Byzantine Civilization (750–1025)

FOCUS QUESTION: What were the chief developments in the Byzantine Empire between 750 and 1025?

In the seventh and eighth centuries, the Byzantine Empire lost much of its territory to Slavs, Bulgars, and Muslims. By 750, the empire consisted only of Asia Minor, some lands in the Balkans, and a small amount of territory in Italy. Although Byzantium was beset with internal dissension and invasions in the ninth century, it was able to deal with them and not only endured but even expanded, reaching its high point in the tenth century, which some historians have called the golden age of Byzantine civilization.

The Beginning of a Revival

During the reign of Michael III (842–867), the Byzantine Empire began to experience a revival. Iconoclasm was finally abolished in 843, and reforms were made in education, church life, the military, and the peasant economy. There was a noticeable intellectual renewal. But the empire was still plagued by persistent problems. The Bulgars mounted new attacks, and the Arabs continued to harass the periphery. Moreover, a new religious dispute with political repercussions erupted over differences between the pope as leader of the western Christian church and the patriarch of Constantinople as leader of the eastern Christian church. Patriarch Photius (FOH-shuss) condemned the pope as a heretic for accepting a revised form of the Nicene Creed stating that the Holy Spirit proceeded from the Father and the Son instead of from the Father alone. A council of eastern bishops followed Photius's wishes and excommunicated the pope, creating the so-called Photian schism. Although the differences were later papered over, this controversy inserted a greater wedge between the eastern and western Christian churches.

The Macedonian Dynasty

The problems that arose during Michael's reign were effectively dealt with by a new dynasty of Byzantine emperors known as the Macedonians (867–1056). The Macedonian dynasty managed to hold off Byzantium's external enemies and reestablish domestic order. Supported by the church, the emperors thought of the Byzantine Empire as a continuation of the Christian Roman Empire of late antiquity. Although for diplomatic reasons they occasionally recognized the imperial titles of earlier western emperors, such as Charlemagne and Otto I, they still regarded them as little more than barbarian parvenus.

ECONOMIC AND RELIGIOUS POLICIES The Macedonian emperors could boast of a remarkable number of

A Western View of the Byzantine Empire

Bishop Liudprand of Cremona (LOO-id-prand of kray-MOH-nuh) undertook diplomatic missions to Constantinople on behalf of two western kings, Berengar of Italy and Otto I of Germany. This selection is taken from his description of his mission to the Byzantine emperor Constantine VII in 949 as an envoy for Berengar, king of Italy from 950 until his overthrow by Otto I of Germany in 964. Liudprand had mixed feelings about Byzantium: admiration, yet also envy and hostility because of its superior wealth.

Liudprand of Cremona, *Antapodosis*

Next to the imperial residence at Constantinople there is a palace of remarkable size and beauty which the Greeks call Magnavra . . . the name being equivalent to "Fresh breeze." In order to receive some Spanish envoys, who had recently arrived, as well as myself . . . , Constantine gave orders that this palace should be got ready. . . .

Before the emperor's seat stood a tree, made of bronze gilded over, whose branches were filled with birds, also made of gilded bronze, which uttered different cries, each according to its varying species. The throne itself was so marvelously fashioned that at one moment it seemed a low structure, and at another it rose high into the air. It was of immense size and was guarded by lions, made either of bronze or of wood covered over with gold, who beat the ground with their tails and gave a dreadful roar with open mouth and quivering tongue. Leaning upon the shoulders of two eunuchs I was brought into the emperor's presence. At my approach the lions began to roar and the birds to cry out, each according to its kind; but I was neither terrified nor surprised, for I had previously made enquiry about all these things from people who were well acquainted with them. So after I had three times made obeisance to the emperor with my face upon the ground, I lifted my head, and behold! The man whom just before I had seen sitting on a moderately elevated seat had now changed his raiment and was sitting on the level of the ceiling. How it was done I could not imagine, unless perhaps he was lifted up by some such sort of device as we use for raising the timbers of a wine press. On that occasion he did not address me personally, . . . but by the intermediary of a secretary he enquired about Berengar's doings and asked after his health. I made a fitting reply and then, at a nod from the interpreter, left his presence and retired to my lodging.

It would give me some pleasure also to record here what I did then for Berengar. . . . The Spanish envoys . . . had brought handsome gifts from their masters to the emperor Constantine. I for my part had brought nothing from Berengar except a letter and that was full of lies. I was very greatly disturbed and shamed at this and began to consider anxiously what I had better do. In my doubt and perplexity it finally occurred to me that I might offer the gifts, which on my account I had brought for the emperor, as coming from Berengar, and trick out my humble present with fine words. I therefore presented him with nine excellent cuirasses, seven excellent shields with gilded bosses, two silver gilt cauldrons, some swords, spears, and spits, and what was more precious to the emperor than anything, four carzimasia; that being the Greek name for young eunuchs who have had both their testicles and their penis removed. This operation is performed by traders at Verdun, who take the boys into Spain and make a huge profit.

What impressions of the Byzantine court do you get from Liudprand's account? What is the modern meaning of the word byzantine*? How does this account help explain the modern meaning of the word?*

Source: Excerpt from *Works of Liudprand of Cremona* by F. A. Wright, 1930, Routledge and Kegan Paul Publishers.

achievements in the late ninth and tenth centuries. They worked to strengthen the position of the free farmers, who felt threatened by the attempts of landed aristocrats to expand their estates at the farmers' expense. The emperors were well aware that the free farmers made up the rank and file of the Byzantine cavalry and provided the military strength of the empire.

The Macedonian emperors also fostered a burst of economic prosperity by expanding trade relations with western Europe, especially by selling silks and metalwork, and the city of Constantinople flourished. Foreign visitors continued to be astounded by its size, wealth, and physical surroundings. To western Europeans, it was the stuff of legends and fables (see the box above).

Hagia Sophia, Istanbul//© Erich Lessing/Art Resource, NY

Emperor Leo VI. Under the Macedonian dynasty, the Byzantine Empire achieved economic prosperity through expanded trade and gained new territories through military victories. This mosaic over the western door of Hagia Sophia in Constantinople depicts the Macedonian emperor Leo VI prostrating himself before Jesus. This act of humility symbolized the emperor's role as an intermediary between God and the people. Leo's son characterized him as the "Christ-loving and glorious emperor."

In this period of prosperity, Byzantine cultural influence expanded due to the active missionary efforts of eastern Byzantine Christians. Eastern Orthodox Christianity was spread to eastern European peoples, such as the Bulgars and Serbs. Perhaps the greatest missionary success occurred when the prince of Kiev in Russia converted to Christianity in 987.

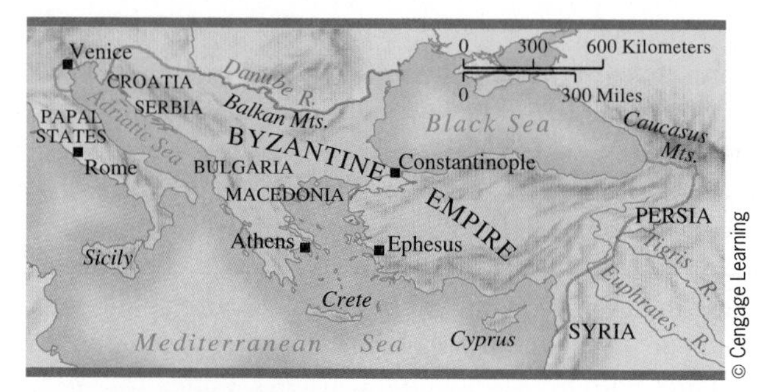

© Cengage Learning

The Byzantine Empire, 1025

POLITICAL AND MILITARY ACHIEVEMENTS Under the Macedonian rulers, Byzantium enjoyed a strong civil service, talented emperors, and military advances. The Byzantine civil service was staffed by well-educated, competent aristocrats from Constantinople who oversaw the collection of taxes, domestic administration, and foreign policy. At the same time, the Macedonian dynasty produced some truly outstanding emperors skilled in administration and law. Leo VI (886–912), known as Leo the Wise, composed works on politics and theology, systematized rules for regulating both trade and court officials, and arranged for a new codification of all Byzantine law.

In the tenth century, competent emperors combined with a number of talented generals to mobilize the empire's military resources and take the offensive. Especially important was Basil II (976–1025), who defeated the Bulgars and annexed Bulgaria to the empire (see the box on p. 337). After his final victory over the Bulgars in 1014, Basil blinded 14,000 Bulgar captives before allowing them to return to their homes. The Byzantines went on to add the islands of Crete and Cyprus to the empire and to defeat the Muslim forces in Syria, expanding the empire to the upper Euphrates. By the end of Basil's reign in 1025, the Byzantine Empire was the largest it had been since the beginning of the seventh century.

The Achievements of Basil II

Basil II came to power at the age of eighteen and during his long reign greatly enlarged the Byzantine Empire. During his reign, an alliance with the Russian prince Vladimir was instrumental in bringing Orthodox Christianity to the Russians. We know a great deal about Basil II from an account by Michael Psellus (SELL-uss) (1018–c. 1081), one of the foremost Byzantine historians. He wrote the *Chronographia*, a series of biographies of the Byzantine emperors from 976 to 1078, much of it based on his own observations. In this selection, Psellus discusses the qualities of Basil as a leader.

Michael Psellus, *Chronographia*

In his dealings with his subjects, Basil behaved with extraordinary circumspection. It is perfectly true that the great reputation he built up as a ruler was founded rather on terror than on loyalty. As he grew older and became more experienced he relied less on the judgment of men wiser than himself. He alone introduced new measures, he alone disposed his military forces. As for the civil administration, he governed, not in accordance with the written laws, but following the unwritten dictates of his own intuition, which was most excellently equipped by nature for the purpose. . . .

Having purged the empire of the barbarians [Bulgars] he dealt with his own subjects and completely subjugated them too—I think "subjugate" is the right word to describe it. He decided to abandon his former policy, and after the great families had been humiliated and put on an equal footing with the rest, Basil found himself playing the game of power-politics with considerable success. He surrounded himself with favorites who were neither remarkable for brilliance of intellect, nor of noble lineage, nor too learned. . . .

By humbling the pride or jealousy of his people, Basil made his own road to power an easy one. He was careful, moreover, to close the exit-doors on the monies contributed to the treasury. So a huge sum of money was built up, partly by the exercise of strict economy, partly by fresh additions from abroad. . . . He himself took no pleasure in any of it: quite the reverse indeed, for the majority of the precious stones, both the white ones (which we call pearls) and the colored brilliants, far from being inlaid in diadems or collars, were hidden away in his underground vaults. . . .

On his expedition against the barbarians, Basil did not follow the customary procedure of other emperors, setting out at the middle of spring and returning home at the end of summer. For him the time to return was when the task in hand was accomplished. He endured the rigors of winter and the heat of summer with equal indifference. He disciplined himself against thirst. In fact, all his natural desires were kept under stern control, and the man was as hard as steel. . . . He professed to conduct his wars and draw up the troops in line of battle, himself planning each campaign, but he preferred not to engage in combat personally. A sudden retreat might otherwise prove embarrassing. . . .

Basil's character was two-fold, for he readily adapted himself no less to the crises of war than to the calm of peace. Really, if the truth be told, he was more of a villain in wartime, more of an emperor in time of peace. Outbursts of wrath he controlled and like the proverbial "fire under the ashes," kept anger hid in his heart, but if his orders were disobeyed in war, on his return to the palace he would kindle his wrath and reveal it. Terrible then was the vengeance he took on the miscreant. Generally, he persisted in his opinions, but there were occasions when he did change his mind. . . . He was slow to adopt any course of action, but never would he willingly alter the decision, once it was [made].

Based on this account, what were the personal qualities that made Basil II successful, and how would you characterize the nature of the Byzantine government? Compare the achievements of Basil II with those of Charlemagne as described by Einhard on page 306. How were the two rulers alike? How were they different? How do you explain the differences?

Source: E. R. A. Sewter, trans. *The Chronographia of Michael Psellus* (Yale University Press, 1953), pp. 23–27.

The Decline and Fall of the Byzantine Empire (1025–1453)

FOCUS QUESTIONS: What impact did the Crusades have on the Byzantine Empire? How and why did Constantinople and the Byzantine Empire fall?

The Macedonian dynasty of the tenth and eleventh centuries had restored much of the power of the Byzantine Empire; its incompetent successors, however, reversed most of the gains.

New Challenges and New Responses

After the Macedonian dynasty was extinguished in 1056, the empire was beset by internal struggles for power between ambitious military leaders and aristocratic families who bought the support of the great landowners of Anatolia by allowing them greater control over their peasants. This policy was self-destructive, however, because the peasant-warrior was an important source of military strength in the Byzantine state. By the middle of the eleventh century, the Byzantine army began to decline.

A CHRISTIAN SCHISM The growing division between the Roman Catholic Church of the west and the Eastern Orthodox Church of the Byzantine Empire also weakened the Byzantine state. The Eastern Orthodox Church was unwilling to accept the pope's claim that he was the sole head of the Christian church. This dispute reached a climax in 1054 when Pope Leo IX and Patriarch Michael Cerularius (sayr-yuh-LAR-ee-uss), head of the Byzantine church, formally excommunicated each other, initiating a schism between the two branches of Christianity that has not been healed to this day.

ISLAM AND THE SELJUK TURKS The Byzantine Empire faced external threats to its security as well. In the west, the Normans were menacing the remaining Byzantine possessions in Italy. A much greater threat, however, came from the world of Islam.

A nomadic people from Central Asia, the Seljuk Turks had been converted to Islam. As their numbers increased, they moved into the eastern provinces of the Abbasid Empire (see Chapter 7), and in 1055 they captured Baghdad and occupied the rest of the empire. When they moved into Asia Minor—the heartland of the Byzantine Empire and its main source of food and manpower—the Byzantines were forced to react. Emperor Romanus IV led an army of recruits and mercenaries into Asia Minor in 1071 and met the Turkish forces at Manzikert (MANZ-ih-kurt), where the Byzantines were soundly defeated. The Seljuk Turks then went on to occupy much of Anatolia, where many peasants, already disgusted by their exploitation at the hands of Byzantine landowners, readily accepted Turkish control (see Map 7.4 on p. 178).

A NEW DYNASTY After the loss at Manzikert, factional fighting erupted over the emperorship until the throne was seized by Alexius Comnenus (kahm-NEE-nuss) (1081–1118), who established a dynasty that breathed new life into the Byzantine Empire. Under Alexius, the Byzantines were victorious on the Greek Adriatic coast against the Normans, defeated their enemies in the Balkans, and stopped the Turks in Anatolia. In the twelfth century, the Byzantine Empire experienced a cultural revival and a period of prosperity, fueled by an expansion of trade. But both the Comneni dynasty and the revival of the twelfth century were ultimately threatened by Byzantium's encounters with crusaders from the west.

Impact of the Crusades

Lacking the resources to undertake additional campaigns against the Turks, Emperor Alexius turned to the west for military assistance and asked Pope Urban II for help against the Seljuk Turks. Instead of the military aid Alexius had expected, the pope set in motion the First Crusade (see Chapter 12), a decision that created enormous difficulties for the Byzantines.

Alexius requested that the military leaders of the First Crusade take an oath of loyalty to him and promise that any territory they conquered would be under Byzantine control. The crusaders ignored the emperor's wishes, and after conquering Antioch, Jerusalem, and additional Palestinian lands, they organized the four crusading states of Edessa, Antioch, Tripoli, and Jerusalem. The Byzantines now had to worry not only about the Turks in Anatolia but also about westerners in the crusading states.

Even more disastrous was the Fourth Crusade. After the death of Saladin in 1193 (see Chapter 7), Pope Innocent III launched the Fourth Crusade. On its way to Palestine, however, the new crusading army became involved in a dispute over the succession to the Byzantine throne. The Venetian leaders of the Fourth Crusade saw an opportunity to neutralize their greatest commercial competitor, the Byzantine Empire. Diverted to Constantinople, the crusaders sacked the great capital city in 1204 (see the box on p. 339).

The Byzantine Empire now disintegrated into a series of petty states ruled by crusading barons and Byzantine princes. The chief state was the new Latin Empire of Constantinople led by Count Baldwin of Flanders as emperor. The Venetians seized the island of Crete and assumed control of Constantinople's trade.

Christian Crusaders Capture Constantinople

POLITICS & GOVERNMENT

Pope Innocent III inaugurated the Fourth Crusade after Saladin's empire began to disintegrate. Tragically, however, the crusading army of mostly French nobles was diverted to Constantinople to intervene in Byzantine politics. In 1204, the Christian crusaders stormed and sacked one of Christendom's greatest cities. This description of the conquest of Constantinople is taken from a contemporary account by Geoffrey de Villehardouin (VEEL-ar-dwahn), a participant in the struggle.

Geoffrey de Villehardouin, *The Conquest of Constantinople*

The moment the knights aboard the transports saw this happen, they landed, and raising their ladders against the wall, climbed to the top, and took four more towers. Then all the rest of the troops started to leap out of warships, galleys, and transports, helter-skelter, each as fast as he could. They broke down about three of the gates and entered the city. The horses were then taken out of the transports; the knights mounted and rode straight towards the place where the Emperor had his camp. He had his battalions drawn up in front of the tents; but as soon as his men saw the knights charging towards them on horseback, they retreated in disorder. The Emperor himself fled through the streets of the city to the castle of Bucoleon.

Then followed a scene of massacre and pillage: on every hand the Greeks [Byzantines] were cut down, their horses, mules, and other possessions snatched as booty. So great was the number of killed and wounded that no man could count them. A great part of the Greek nobles had fled towards the gate of Blachernae; but by this time it was past six o'clock, and our men had grown weary of fighting and slaughtering. The troops began to assemble in a great square inside Constantinople . . . [and] decided to settle down near the walls and towers they had already captured. . . .

That night passed, and the next day came. . . . Early that morning all the troops, knights and sergeants alike, armed themselves, and each man went to join his division. They left their quarters thinking to meet with stronger resistance than they had encountered the day before, since they did not know that the Emperor had fled during the night. But they found no one to oppose them.

The Marquis de Montferrat rode straight along the shore to the palace of Bucoleon. As soon as he arrived there the place was surrendered to him, on condition that the lives of all the people in it should be spared. Among these were very many ladies of the highest rank who had taken refuge there. . . . Words fail me when it comes to describing the treasures found in the palace, for there was such a store of precious things that one could not possibly count them. . . .

The rest of the army, scattered throughout the city, also gained much booty, so much, indeed, that no one could estimate its amount or its value. It included gold and silver, table-services and precious stones, satin and silk, mantles of squirrel fur, ermine and miniver, and every choicest thing to be found on this earth. . . .

Everyone took quarters where he pleased, and there was no lack of fine dwellings in that city. So the troops of the Crusaders and the Venetians were duly housed. They all rejoiced and gave thanks to our Lord for the honor and the victory he had granted them, so that those who had been poor now lived in wealth and luxury. Thus, they celebrated Palm Sunday and the Easter Day following, with hearts full of joy for the benefits our Lord and Savior had bestowed on them. And well might they praise Him, since the whole of their army numbered no more than twenty thousand, or more, and with His help they had conquered four hundred thousand, or more, and that in the greatest, most powerful, and most strongly fortified city in the world.

What does this account reveal about the crusading ideals and practices of the Europeans?

Source: Villehardouin, *The Conquest of Constaninople* is reprinted from *Chronicles of the Crusades* by Joinville and Villehardouin, translated by M. R. B. Shaw (Penguin Classics, 1963), copyright © M. R. B. Shaw 1963. Reprinted with permission.

REVIVAL OF THE BYZANTINE EMPIRE The west was unable to maintain the Latin Empire, however, for the western rulers of the newly created principalities were soon engrossed in fighting each other. Some parts of the Byzantine Empire had managed to survive under Byzantine princes. In 1259, Michael Paleologus (pay-lee-AWL-uh-guss), a Greek military leader, took control of the kingdom of Nicaea in western Asia Minor, led a Byzantine army to recapture Constantinople two years later, and then established a new Byzantine dynasty, the Paleologi.

The Byzantine Empire had been saved, but it was no longer a Mediterranean power. The restored empire was a badly truncated entity, consisting of the city of Constantinople and its surrounding territory, some lands in Asia Minor, and part of Thessalonica. It was surrounded by enemies—Bulgarians, Mongols, Turks, and westerners, especially the resentful Venetians. Even in its reduced size, the empire limped along for another 190 years, but its enemies continued to multiply. The threat from the Turks finally doomed the aged empire.

The Ottoman Turks and the Fall of Constantinople

Beginning in northeastern Asia Minor in the thirteenth century, the Ottoman Turks spread rapidly, seizing the lands of the Seljuk Turks and the Byzantine Empire. In 1345, they bypassed Constantinople and moved into the Balkans. Under Sultan Murad (moo-RAHD), Ottoman forces moved through Bulgaria and into the lands of the Serbs; in 1389, at the Battle of Kosovo (KAWSS-suh-voh), Ottoman forces defeated the Serbs. By the beginning of the fifteenth century, the Byzantine Empire had been reduced to little more than Constantinople, now surrounded on all sides by the Ottomans. When Mehmet (meh-MET) II came to the throne in 1451 at the age of only nineteen, he was determined to capture Constantinople and complete the demise of the Byzantine Empire.

The siege began in April 1453 when Mehmet moved his forces—probably about 80,000 men—within striking distance of the 13-mile-long land walls along the western edge of the city. The Ottomans' main attack came against these walls. On April 6, the artillery onslaught began. The Ottoman invaders had a distinct advantage with their cannons. One of them, constructed by a Hungarian engineer, had a 26-foot barrel that fired stone balls weighing 1,200 pounds. It took 60 oxen and 2,000 men to pull the great cannon into position. On May 29, Mehmet decided on a final assault and focused against the areas where the walls had been breached. When Ottoman forces broke into the city, the emperor became one of the first casualties. About 4,000 defenders were killed, and thousands of the inhabitants were sold into slavery. Early in the afternoon, Mehmet II rode into the city, exalted the power of Allah from the pulpit in the cathedral of Hagia Sophia, and ordered that it be converted into a mosque. He soon began rebuilding the city as the capital of the Ottoman Empire. The Byzantine Empire had come to an end.

CHRONOLOGY **The Byzantine Empire, 750–1453**	
Revival under Michael III	842–867
Macedonian dynasty	867–1056
Leo VI	886–912
Basil II	976–1025
Schism between Eastern Orthodox Church and Roman Catholic Church	1054
Turkish defeat of the Byzantines at Manzikert	1071
Revival under Alexius Comnenus	1081–1118
Latin Empire of Constantinople	1204–1261
Revival of Byzantine Empire	1261
Turkish defeat of Serbs at Kosovo	1389
Fall of the empire	1453

The Crises of the Fourteenth Century

FOCUS QUESTIONS: What impact did the Black Death have on Europe and Asia in the fourteenth century? What problems did Europeans face during the fourteenth century, and what impact did these crises have on European economic, social, and religious life?

At the beginning of the fourteenth century, changes in global weather patterns ushered in what has been called a "little ice age." Shortened growing seasons and disastrous weather conditions, including heavy storms and constant rain, led to widespread famine and hunger. Soon an even greater catastrophe struck.

The Black Death: From Asia to Europe

In the mid-fourteenth century, a disaster known as the Black Death struck in Asia, North Africa, and Europe. Bubonic plague was the most common and most important form of plague in the diffusion of the Black Death and was spread by black rats infested with fleas who were host to the deadly bacterium *Yersinia pestis* (yur-SIN-ee-uh PES-tiss).

ROLE OF THE MONGOLS This great plague originated in Asia. After disappearing from Europe and the Middle East in the Middle Ages, bubonic plague continued to haunt areas of southwestern China. In the early 1300s, rats accompanying Mongol troops spread the plague into central China and by 1331 to northeastern China. In one province near Beijing, it was reported that 90 percent of the population died. Overall, China's population may have declined from 120 million in the mid-1300s to 80 million by 1400.

In the thirteenth century, the Mongols had brought much of the Eurasian landmass under a single rule, which in turn facilitated long-distance trade, particularly along the Silk Road, now dominated by Muslim merchants from Central Asia (see Chapter 10). The flow of people and goods throughout this Eurasian landmass also facilitated the spread of the plague.

In the 1330s, the plague had spread to Central Asia; by 1339 it had reached Samarkand, a caravan stop on the Silk Road. From Central Asia, trading caravans brought the plague to Caffa, on the Black Sea, in 1346 and to Constantinople by the following year (see the comparative essay "The Role of Disease in History" on p. 342). Its arrival in the Byzantine Empire was noted in a work by Emperor John VI, who lost a son: "Upon arrival in Constantinople she [the empress] found Andronikos, the youngest born, dead from the invading plague, which . . . attacked almost all the sea coasts of the world and killed most of their people."[5] By 1348, the plague had spread to Egypt and also to Mecca and Damascus and other parts of the Middle East. The Muslim historian Ibn Khaldun (IB-un kahl-DOON), writing in the fourteenth century, commented, "Civilization in the East and West was visited by a destructive plague which devastated nations and caused populations to vanish. It swallowed up many of the good things of civilization and wiped them out."[6]

THE BLACK DEATH IN EUROPE The **Black Death** of the mid-fourteenth century was the most devastating natural disaster in European history. The plague reached Europe in October 1347 when Genoese merchants brought it from Caffa to the island of Sicily off the coast of Italy. It quickly spread to southern Italy and southern France by the end of 1347. Diffusion of the Black Death followed commercial trade routes. In 1348, it spread through Spain, France, and the Low Countries and into Germany. By the end of that year, it had moved to England, ravaging it in 1349. By the end of 1349, the plague had reached northern Europe and Scandinavia. Eastern Europe and Russia were affected by 1351.

Mortality figures for the Black Death were incredibly high. Especially hard hit were Italy's crowded cities, where 50 to 60 percent of the people died. One citizen of Florence wrote, "A great many breathed their last in the public streets, day and night; a large number perished in their homes, and it was only by the stench of their decaying bodies that they proclaimed their deaths to their neighbors. Everywhere the city was teeming with corpses."[7] In England and Germany, entire villages simply disappeared. It has been estimated that out of a total European population of 75 million, as many as 38 million people may have died of the plague between 1347 and 1351.

As contemporaries attempted to explain the Black Death and mitigate its harshness, some turned to extreme sorts of behavior. Many believed that the plague either had been sent by God as a punishment for humans' sins or had been caused by the devil (see the box on p. 343). Some, known as flagellants (FLAJ-uh-lunts), resorted to extreme measures to gain God's forgiveness. Groups of flagellants, both men and women, wandered from town to town, flogging each other with whips to beg the forgiveness of a God who, they felt, had sent the plague to punish humans for their sinful ways. One contemporary chronicler described their activities:

> The penitents went about, coming first out of Germany. They were men who did public penance and scourged themselves with whips of hard knotted leather with little iron spikes. Some made themselves bleed very badly between the shoulder blades and some foolish women had cloths ready to catch the blood and smear it on their eyes, saying it was miraculous blood. While they were doing penance, they sang very mournful songs about the nativity and the passion of Our Lord. The object of this penance was to put a stop to the mortality, for in that time . . . at least a third of all the people in the world died.[8]

The flagellants created mass hysteria wherever they went, and authorities worked overtime to crush the movement. An outbreak of virulent anti-Semitism also accompanied the Black Death. Jews were accused of causing the plague by poisoning town wells. The worst **pogroms** against this minority were carried out in Germany, where more than sixty major Jewish communities had been exterminated by 1351. Many Jews fled eastward to Russia and especially to Poland, where the king offered them protection. Eastern Europe became home to large Jewish communities.

Economic Dislocation and Social Upheaval

The deaths of so many people in the fourteenth century had severe economic consequences. Trade declined, and some industries suffered greatly. A shortage of workers caused a dramatic rise in the price of labor, while the decline in the number of people lowered the demand for

COMPARATIVE ESSAY

The Role of Disease in History

Bibliothèque Royale Albert I, Brussels//© Snark/Art Resource, NY

Mass Burial of Plague Victims. The Black Death had spread to northern Europe by the end of 1348. Shown here is a mass burial of victims of the plague in Tournai, located in modern Belgium. As is evident in the illustration, at this stage of the plague, there was still time to make coffins for the victims' burial. Later, as the plague intensified, the dead were thrown into open pits.

When Hernán Cortés and his fellow conquistadors arrived in Mesoamerica in 1519, the local inhabitants were frightened of the horses and the firearms that accompanied the Spaniards. What they did not know was that the most dangerous enemies brought by these strange new arrivals were invisible—the disease-bearing microbes that would soon kill them by the millions.

Diseases have been the scourge of animal species since the dawn of prehistory, making the lives of human beings, in the words of the English philosopher Thomas Hobbes, "nasty, brutish, and short." With the increasing sophistication of forensic evidence, archaeologists today are able to determine from recently discovered human remains that our immediate ancestors were plagued by such familiar ailments as anemia, arthritis, tuberculosis, and malaria.

With the explosive growth of the human population brought about by the agricultural revolution, the problems posed by the presence of disease intensified. As people began to congregate in villages and cities, bacteria settled in their piles of refuse and were carried by lice and fleas in their clothing. The domestication of animals made humans more vulnerable to diseases carried by their livestock. As population density increased, the danger of widespread epidemics increased with it.

As time went on, succeeding generations gradually developed partial or complete immunity to many of these diseases, which became chronic rather than fatal to their victims, as occurred with malaria in parts of Africa, for example, and chicken pox in the Americas. But when a disease was introduced to a particular society that had not previously been exposed to it, the consequences were often devastating. The most dramatic example was the famous Black Death, the plague that ravaged Europe and China during the fourteenth century, killing one-fourth to one-half of the inhabitants in the affected regions (and even greater numbers in certain areas). Smallpox had the same impact in the Americas after the arrival of Christopher Columbus, and malaria was fatal to many Europeans on their arrival in West Africa.

How were these diseases transmitted? In most instances, they followed the trade routes. Such was the case with the Black Death, which was initially carried by fleas living in the saddlebags of Mongol warriors as they advanced toward Europe in the thirteenth and fourteenth centuries and thereafter by rats in the holds of cargo ships. Smallpox and other diseases were brought to the Americas by the conquistadors. Epidemics, then, are a price that humans pay for having developed the network of rapid communication that has accompanied the evolution of human society.

What role has disease played in human history?

food, resulting in falling prices. Landlords were now paying more for labor at the same time that their rental income was declining. Concurrently, the decline in the number of peasants after the Black Death made it easier for some to convert their labor services to rent, thus freeing them from serfdom. But there were limits to how much the peasants could advance. They faced the same economic hurdles as the lords, who also attempted to

OPPOSING ✕ VIEWPOINTS

Causes of the Black Death: Contemporary Views

The Black Death was the most terrifying natural calamity of the Middle Ages and affected wide areas of Europe, North Africa, and Asia. People were often baffled by the plague, especially its causes, and tried to find an explanation. The first selection is taken from the preface to the *Decameron* by the fourteenth-century Italian writer Giovanni Boccaccio (joh-VAH-nee boh-KAH-choh). The next two selections are from contemporary treatises that offered very different explanations for the great plague.

Giovanni Boccaccio, *Decameron*

In the year of Our Lord 1348 the deadly plague broke out in the great city of Florence, most beautiful of Italian cities. Whether through the operation of the heavenly bodies or because of our own iniquities which the just wrath of God sought to correct, the plague had arisen in the East some years before, causing the death of countless human beings. It spread without stop from one place to another, until, unfortunately, it swept over the West. Neither knowledge nor human foresight availed against it, though the city was cleansed of much filth by chosen officers in charge and sick persons were forbidden to enter it, while advice was broadcast for the preservation of health. Nor did humble supplications serve. Not once but many times they were ordained in the form of processions and other ways for the propitiation of God by the faithful, but, in spite of everything, toward the spring of the year the plague began to show its ravages.

On Earthquakes as the Cause of Plague

There is a fourth opinion, which I consider more likely than the others, which is that insofar as the mortality arose from natural causes its immediate cause was a corrupt and poisonous earthy exhalation, which infected the air in various parts of the world and, when breathed in by people, suffocated them and suddenly snuffed them out. . . .

It is a matter of scientific fact that earthquakes are caused by the exhalation of fumes enclosed in the bowels of the earth. When the fumes batter against the sides of the earth, and cannot get out, the earth is shaken and moves. I say that it is the vapor and corrupted air which has been vented—or so to speak purged—in the earthquake which occurred on St Paul's day, 1347, along with the corrupted air vented in other earthquakes and eruptions, which has infected the air above the earth and killed people in various parts of the world; and I can bring various reasons in support of this conclusion.

Herman Gigas on Well Poisoning

In 1347 there was such a great pestilence and mortality throughout almost the whole world that in the opinion of well-informed men scarcely a tenth of mankind survived. . . . Some say that it was brought about by the corruption of the air; others that the Jews planned to wipe out all the Christians with poison and had poisoned wells and springs everywhere. And many Jews confessed as much under torture: that they had bred spiders and toads in pots and pans, and had obtained poison from overseas; and that not every Jew knew about this wickedness, only the more powerful ones, so that it would not be betrayed. As evidence of this heinous crime, men say that the bags full of poison were found in many wells and springs, and as a result, in cities, towns and villages throughout Germany, and in fields and woods too, almost all the wells and springs have been blocked up or built over, so that no one can drink from them or use the water for cooking, and men have to use rain or river water instead. God, the lord of vengeance, has not suffered the malice of the Jews to go unpunished. Throughout Germany, in all but a few places, they were burnt. For fear of that punishment many accepted baptism and their lives were spared. This action was taken against the Jews in 1349, and it still continues unabated, for in a number of regions many people, noble and humble alike, have laid plans against them and their defenders, which they will never abandon until the whole Jewish race has been destroyed.

What were the different explanations for the causes of the Black Death? How do you explain the differences, and what do these explanations tell you about the level of scientific knowledge in the Later Middle Ages? Why do you think Jews became scapegoats?

Sources: Giovanni Boccaccio, *Decameron.* From *The Decameron* by Giovanni Boccaccio, trans by Frances Winwar, pp. xxii. Reprinted by permission of The Limited Editions Club. On Earthquakes as the Cause of Plague and Herman Gigas on Well Poisoning. Two excerpts from Rosemary Horrox, ed., *The Black Death* (Manchester: Manchester University Press, 1994), pp. 167, 169, 171, 177–178, 207.

impose wage restrictions and reinstate old forms of labor service. Peasant complaints became widespread and soon gave rise to rural revolts.

Although the peasant revolts sometimes resulted in short-term gains for the participants, the uprisings were easily crushed and their gains quickly lost. Accustomed to ruling, the established classes easily combined and stifled dissent.

Political Instability

Famine, plague, economic turmoil, and social upheaval were not the only problems of the fourteenth century. War and political instability must also be added to the list. And of all the struggles that ensued in the fourteenth century, the Hundred Years' War was the most violent.

THE HUNDRED YEARS' WAR In the thirteenth century, England still held one small possession in France known as the duchy of Gascony. As duke of Gascony, the English king pledged loyalty as a vassal to the French king, but when King Philip VI of France (1328–1350) seized Gascony in 1337, the duke of Gascony—King Edward III of England (1327–1377)—declared war on Philip.

The Hundred Years' War began in a burst of knightly enthusiasm. The French army of 1337 still relied largely on heavily armed noble cavalrymen, who looked with contempt on foot soldiers and crossbowmen, whom they regarded as social inferiors. The English, too, used heavily armed cavalry, but they relied even more on large numbers of paid foot soldiers. Armed with pikes, many of these soldiers had also adopted the longbow, invented by the Welsh. The longbow had a longer range and more rapid speed of fire than the crossbow.

The first major battle of the war occurred in 1346 at Crécy (kray-SEE), just south of Flanders. The larger French army followed no battle plan but simply attacked the English lines in a disorderly fashion. The arrows of the English archers decimated the French cavalry. As the chronicler Froissart (frwah-SAR) described it, "[With their longbows] the English continued to shoot into the thickest part of the crowd, wasting none of their arrows. They impaled or wounded horses and riders, who fell to the ground in great distress, unable to get up again without the help of several men."[9] It was a stunning victory for the English and the foot soldier.

The Battle of Crécy was not decisive, however. The English simply did not possess the resources to subjugate all of France, but they continued to try. The English king, Henry V (1413–1422), was especially eager to achieve victory. At the Battle of Agincourt (AH-zhen-koor) in 1415, the heavy, armor-plated French knights attempted to attack across a field turned to mud by heavy rain; the result was a disastrous French defeat and the death of 1,500 French nobles. The English were masters of northern France.

The seemingly hopeless French cause then fell into the hands of the dauphin (DAH-fin *or* doh-FAN) Charles, the heir to the throne, who governed the southern two-thirds of French lands. Charles's cause seemed doomed until a French peasant woman quite unexpectedly saved the timid monarch. Born in 1412, the daughter of well-to-do peasants, Joan of Arc was a deeply religious person who came to believe that her favorite saints had commanded her to free France. In February 1429, Joan made her way to the dauphin's court and persuaded Charles to allow her to accompany a French army to Orléans (or-lay-AHN). Apparently inspired by the faith of the peasant girl called "the Maid of Orléans," the French armies found new confidence in themselves and liberated Orléans and the entire Loire valley.

But Joan did not live to see the war concluded. Captured in 1430, she was turned over to the Inquisition on charges of witchcraft. In the fifteenth century, spiritual visions were thought to be inspired by either God or the devil. Joan was condemned to death as a heretic and burned at the stake in 1431.

Joan of Arc's accomplishments proved decisive. Although the war dragged on for another two decades, defeats of English armies in Normandy and Aquitaine led to French victory by 1453. Important to the French success was the use of the cannon, a new weapon made possible by the invention of gunpowder. The Chinese had invented gunpower in the tenth century and devised a simple cannon by the thirteenth century. The Mongols greatly improved this technology, developing more accurate cannons and cannonballs; both spread to the Middle East in the thirteenth century and to Europe by the fourteenth. The use of gunpowder eventually brought drastic changes to European warfare by making castles, city walls, and armored knights obsolete.

POLITICAL DISINTEGRATION By the fourteenth century, the feudal order had begun to break down. With money from taxes, kings could now hire professional soldiers, who tended to be more reliable than feudal knights anyway. Fourteenth-century kings had their own problems, however. Many dynasties in Europe failed to produce male heirs, and the founders of new dynasties had to fight for their positions as groups of nobles, trying to gain advantages for themselves, supported opposing candidates. Rulers encountered financial problems, too. Hiring professional soldiers left them always short of cash, adding yet another element of uncertainty and confusion to fourteenth-century politics.

The Decline of the Church

The papacy of the Roman Catholic Church reached the height of its power in the thirteenth century. But crises in the fourteenth century led to a serious decline for the church. By that time, the monarchies of Europe were no longer willing to accept papal claims of temporal supremacy, as is evident in the struggle between Pope Boniface VIII (1294–1303) and King Philip IV (1285–1314) of France. In his desire to acquire new revenues, Philip claimed the right to tax the clergy of France, but Boniface VIII insisted that the clergy of any state could not pay taxes to their secular ruler without the consent of the pope, who, he argued, was supreme over both the church and the state.

Philip IV refused to accept the pope's position and sent a small contingent of French forces to capture Boniface and bring him back to France for trial. The pope escaped but soon died from the shock of his experience. To ensure his position, Philip IV engineered the election of a Frenchman, Clement V (1305–1314), as pope. The new pope took up residence in Avignon (ah-veen-YOHN) on the east bank of the Rhône River.

From 1305 to 1377, the popes resided in Avignon, leading to an increase in antipapal sentiment. The city of Rome was the traditional capital of the universal church. The pope was the bishop of Rome, and it was unseemly that the head of the Catholic Church should reside in Avignon instead of Rome. Moreover, the splendor in which the pope and cardinals were living in Avignon led to highly vocal criticism of both clergy and papacy. At last, Pope Gregory XI (1370–1378), perceiving the disastrous decline in papal prestige, returned to Rome in 1377, but died there the spring after his return.

When the college of cardinals met to elect a new pope, the citizens of Rome threatened that the cardinals would not leave Rome alive unless they elected an Italian as pope. Wisely, the terrified cardinals duly elected the Italian archbishop of Bari as Pope Urban VI (1378–1389). Five months later, however, a group of dissenting cardinals—the French ones—declared Urban's election invalid and chose one of their number as pope, who promptly returned to Avignon. Because Urban remained in Rome, there were now two popes, beginning a crisis that has been called the Great Schism of the church.

The Great Schism divided Europe. France and its allies supported the pope in Avignon, whereas France's enemy England and its allies supported the pope in Rome. The Great Schism was also damaging to the faith of Christian believers. The pope was widely believed to be the true leader of Christendom; when both lines of popes denounced the other as the Antichrist, people's faith in the papacy and the church was undermined. Finally, a church council met at Constance, Switzerland, in 1417. After the competing popes resigned or were deposed, a new pope was elected who was acceptable to all parties.

By the mid-fifteenth century, as a result of these crises, the church had lost much of its temporal power. Even worse, the papacy and the church had also lost much of their moral prestige.

Recovery: The Renaissance

FOCUS QUESTION: What were the main features of the Renaissance in Europe, and how did it differ from the Middle Ages?

People who lived in Italy between 1350 and 1550 or so believed that they were witnessing a rebirth of Classical antiquity—the world of the Greeks and Romans. To them, this marked a new age, which historians later called the **Renaissance** (French for "rebirth") and viewed as a distinct period of European history, which began in Italy and then spread to the rest of Europe.

Renaissance Italy was largely an urban society. The city-states became the centers of Italian political, economic, and social life. Within this new urban society, a secular spirit emerged as increasing wealth created new possibilities for the enjoyment of worldly things.

The Renaissance was also an age of recovery from the disasters of the fourteenth century, including the Black Death, political disorder, and economic recession. In pursuing that recovery, Italian intellectuals became intensely interested in the glories of their own past, the Greco-Roman culture of antiquity.

A new view of human beings emerged as people in the Italian Renaissance began to emphasize individual ability. The fifteenth-century Florentine architect Leon Battista Alberti (LAY-un buh-TEESS-tuh al-BAYR-tee) expressed the new philosophy succinctly: "Men can do all things if they will."[10] This high regard for human worth and for individual potentiality gave rise to a new social ideal of the well-rounded personality or "universal person"—*l'uomo universale* (LWOH-moh OO-nee-ver-SAH-lay)—who was capable of achievements in many areas of life.

The Intellectual Renaissance

The emergence and growth of individualism and secularism as characteristics of the Italian Renaissance are most noticeable in the intellectual and artistic realms. The most important literary movement associated with the Renaissance was humanism.

Renaissance humanism was an intellectual movement based on the study of the classics, the literary works of Greece and Rome. Humanists studied the liberal arts—grammar, rhetoric, poetry, moral philosophy or ethics, and history—all based on the writings of ancient Greek and Roman authors. We call these subjects the humanities.

Petrarch (PEE-trark *or* PET-trark) (1304–1374), who has often been called the father of Italian Renaissance humanism, did more than any other individual in the fourteenth century to foster its development. Petrarch sought to find forgotten Latin manuscripts and also began the humanist emphasis on the use of pure Classical Latin. Humanists used the works of Cicero as a model for prose and those of Virgil for poetry. As Petrarch said, "Christ is my God; Cicero is the prince of the language."

In Florence, the humanist movement took a new direction at the beginning of the fifteenth century. Fourteenth-century humanists such as Petrarch had described the intellectual life as one of solitude. Now, however, the humanists who worked as secretaries for the city council of Florence took a new interest in civic life. They came to believe that intellectuals had a duty to live an active life for their state and that their study of the humanities should be put to the service of the state.

Also evident in the humanism of the first half of the fifteenth century was a growing interest in Classical Greek civilization. One of the first Italian humanists to gain a thorough knowledge of Greek was Leonardo Bruni (leh-ah-NAHR-doh BROO-nee), who became an enthusiastic pupil of the Byzantine scholar Manuel Chrysoloras (man-WEL kriss-uh-LAHR-uss), who taught in Florence from 1396 to 1400.

WAS THERE A RENAISSANCE FOR WOMEN? Historians have disagreed over whether women benefited from the Renaissance. Some maintain that during the Middle Ages upper-class women in particular had greater freedom to satisfy their emotional needs, whereas upper-class women in the Renaissance experienced a contraction of both social and personal options as they became even more subject to male authority. Other historians have argued that although conditions remained bleak for most women, some women, especially those in courtly, religious, and intellectual environments, found ways to develop a new sense of themselves as women. This may be especially true of women who were educated in the humanist fashion and went on to establish their own literary careers. Isotta Nogarola (ee-ZAHT-uh noh-guh-ROH-luh), for example, born to a noble family in Verona, mastered Latin and wrote numerous letters and treatises that brought her praise from male Italian intellectuals.

The Artistic Renaissance

Renaissance artists sought to imitate nature in their works of art. Their search for naturalism became an end in itself: to persuade onlookers of the reality of the object or event they were portraying. At the same time, the new artistic standards reflected the new attitude of mind in which human beings became the focus of attention, the "center and measure of all things," as one artist proclaimed.

This new Renaissance style was developed by Florentine painters in the fifteenth century. Especially important

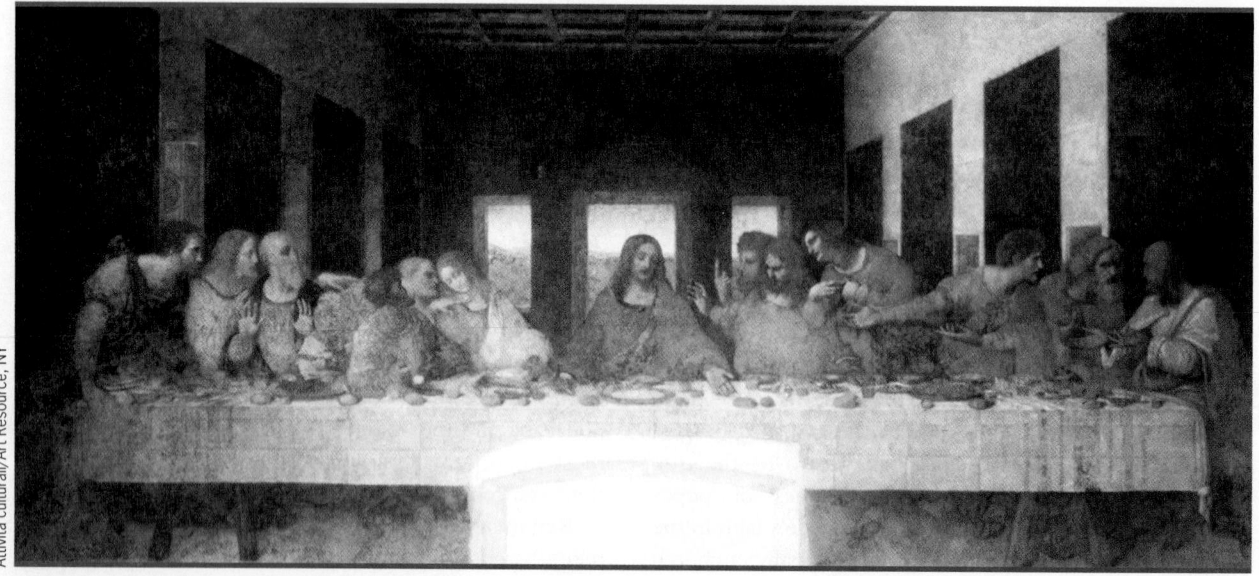

S. Maria delle Grazie, Milan//© Scala/Ministero per i Beni e le Attività culturali/Art Resource, NY

Leonardo da Vinci, *The Last Supper*. Leonardo da Vinci was the impetus behind the High Renaissance interest in the idealization of nature, moving from a realistic portrayal of the human figure to an idealized form. Evident in Leonardo's *Last Supper* is his effort to depict a person's character and inner nature by the use of gesture and movement. Unfortunately, Leonardo used an experimental technique in this fresco, which soon led to its physical deterioration.

were two major developments. One emphasized the technical side of painting—understanding the laws of perspective and the geometrical organization of outdoor space and light. The second development was the investigation of movement and anatomical structure. The realistic portrayal of the human nude became one of the foremost preoccupations of Italian Renaissance art.

By the end of the fifteenth century, Italian artists had mastered the new techniques for scientific observation of the world around them and were ready to move into new forms of creative expression. This marked the shift to the High Renaissance, which was dominated by the work of three artistic giants, Leonardo da Vinci (leh-ah-NAHR-doh dah VEEN-chee) (1452–1519), Raphael (RAFF-ee-ul) (1483–1520), and Michelangelo (my-kuh-LAN-juh-loh) (1475–1564). Leonardo carried on the fifteenth-century experimental tradition by studying everything and even dissecting human bodies in order to see how nature worked. But Leonardo also stressed the need to advance beyond such realism and initiated the High Renaissance's preoccupation with the idealization of nature, an attempt to generalize from realistic portrayal to an ideal form.

At twenty-five, Raphael was already regarded as one of Italy's best painters. He was acclaimed for his numerous madonnas, in which he attempted to achieve an ideal of beauty far surpassing human standards. He is well known for his frescoes in the Vatican Palace, which reveal a world of balance, harmony, and order—the underlying principles of the Classical art of Greece and Rome.

Michelangelo, an accomplished painter, sculptor, and architect, was fiercely driven by a desire to create, and he worked with great passion and energy on a remarkable number of projects. Michelangelo was influenced by Neoplatonism, which viewed the ideal beauty of the human form as a reflection of divine beauty; the more beautiful the body, the more God-like the figure. Another manifestation of Michelangelo's search for ideal beauty was his *David*, a colossal marble statue commissioned by the government of Florence in 1501 and completed in 1504.

Accademia, Florence//© Scala/Art Resource, NY

Michelangelo, *David*. This statue of David, cut from an 18-foot-high block of marble, exalts the beauty of the human body and is a fitting symbol of the Italian Renaissance's affirmation of human power. Completed in 1504, *David* was moved by Florentine authorities to a special location in front of the Palazzo Vecchio, the seat of the Florentine government.

The State in the Renaissance

In the second half of the fifteenth century, attempts were made to reestablish the centralized power of monarchical governments after the political disasters of the fourteenth century. Some historians called these states the "new monarchies," especially those of France, England, and Spain.

THE ITALIAN STATES The Italian states provided the earliest examples of state building in the fifteenth century. During the Middle Ages, Italy had failed to develop a centralized territorial state, and by the fifteenth century five major powers dominated the Italian peninsula: the duchy of Milan, the republics of Florence and Venice, the Papal States, and the kingdom of Naples.

Milan, Florence, and Venice proved especially adept at building strong, centralized states. Under a series of dukes, Milan became a highly centralized territorial state whose rulers devised systems of taxation that generated enormous revenues for the government. The maritime republic of Venice remained an extremely stable political entity governed by a small oligarchy of merchant-aristocrats. Its commercial empire brought in vast revenues and gave it the status of an international power. In Florence, Cosimo de' Medici (KAH-zee-moh duh MED-ih-chee) took control of the merchant oligarchy in 1434. Through lavish patronage and careful courting of political allies, he and his family dominated the city at a time when Florence was the center of the cultural Renaissance.

As strong as these Italian states became, they still could not compete with the powerful monarchical states to the north and west. Beginning in 1494, Italy became a battlefield for the great power struggle between the French and Spanish monarchies, a conflict that led to Spanish domination of Italy in the sixteenth century.

WESTERN EUROPE The Hundred Years' War left France prostrate. But it had also engendered a certain degree of French national feeling toward a common enemy that the kings could use to reestablish monarchical power. The development of a French territorial state was greatly advanced by King Louis XI (1461–1483), who strengthened the use of the ***taille*** (TY)—an annual direct tax usually on land or property—as a permanent tax imposed by royal authority, giving him a sound, regular source of income and creating the foundations of a strong French monarchy.

As the first Tudor king, Henry VII (1485–1509) worked to establish a strong monarchical government in England. Henry ended the petty wars of the nobility by abolishing their private armies. He was also very thrifty. By not overburdening the nobility and the middle class with taxes, Henry won their favor, and they provided him much support.

Spain, too, experienced the growth of a strong national monarchy by the end of the fifteenth century. During the Middle Ages, several independent Christian kingdoms had emerged in the course of the long reconquest of the Iberian peninsula from the Muslims. Two of the strongest were Aragon and Castile. The marriage of Isabella of Castile (1474–1504) and Ferdinand of Aragon (1479–1516) in 1469 was a major step toward unifying Spain. The two rulers worked to strengthen royal control of government. They filled the royal council with middle-class lawyers who operated on the belief that the monarchy embodied the power of the state. Ferdinand and Isabella also reorganized the military forces of Spain, making the new Spanish army the best in Europe by the sixteenth century.

CENTRAL AND EASTERN EUROPE Unlike France, England, and Spain, the Holy Roman Empire failed to develop a strong monarchical authority. The failure of the German emperors in the thirteenth century ended any chance of centralized monarchical authority, and Germany became a land of hundreds of virtually independent states. After 1438, the position of Holy Roman emperor was held by members of the Habsburg (HAPS-burg) dynasty. Having gradually acquired a number of possessions along the Danube, known collectively as Austria, the house of Habsburg had become one of the wealthiest landholders in the empire.

In eastern Europe, rulers struggled to achieve the centralization of the territorial states. Religious differences troubled the area, as Roman Catholics, Eastern Orthodox Christians, and other groups, including the Mongols, confronted each other. In Poland, the nobles gained the upper hand and established the right to elect their kings, a policy that drastically weakened royal authority.

Since the thirteenth century, Russia had been under the domination of the Mongols. Gradually, the princes of Moscow rose to prominence by using their close relationship to the Mongol khans to increase their wealth and expand their possessions. During the reign of the great Prince Ivan III (1462–1505), a new Russian state was born. Ivan annexed other Russian principalities and took advantage of dissension among the Mongols to throw off their yoke by 1480.

CHAPTER SUMMARY

After the collapse of Roman power in the west, the Late Roman Empire in the east or the Eastern Roman Empire, centered on Constantinople, continued in the eastern Mediterranean and eventually emerged as the Byzantine Empire, which flourished for hundreds of years. While a new Christian civilization arose in Europe, the Byzantine Empire created its own unique Christian civilization. And while western Europe struggled in the Early Middle Ages, the Byzantine world continued to prosper and flourish. Especially during the ninth, tenth, and eleventh centuries, under the Macedonian emperors, the Byzantine Empire expanded and achieved an economic prosperity that was evident to foreign visitors who frequently praised the size, wealth, and physical surroundings of Constantinople.

During its heyday, Byzantium was a multicultural and multiethnic world empire that ruled a remarkable number of peoples who spoke different languages. Byzantine cultural and religious forms spread to the Balkans, parts of central Europe, and Russia. Byzantine scholars eventually spread the study of the Greek language to Italy, fostering the Renaissance humanists' interest in Classical Greek civilization. The Byzantine Empire also interacted with the world of Islam to its east and the new European civilization of the west. Both interactions proved costly and ultimately fatal. Although European civilization and Byzantine civilization shared a common bond in Christianity, it proved incapable of keeping them in harmony politically. Indeed, the west's Crusades to Palestine, ostensibly for religious motives, led to western control of the Byzantine Empire from 1204 to 1261. Although the empire was restored, it limped along until its interaction with its other neighbor—the Muslim world—led to its demise in 1453 when the Ottoman Turks conquered the city of Constantinople and made it the center of their new empire.

While Byzantium was declining in the twelfth and thirteenth centuries, Europe was achieving new levels of growth and optimism. In the fourteenth century, however, Europe too experienced a time of troubles, as it was devastated by the Black Death, economic dislocation, political chaos, and religious decline. But in the fifteenth century, while Constantinople and the remnants of the Byzantine Empire finally fell to the world of Islam, Europe experienced a dramatic revival. Elements of recovery in the age of the Renaissance made the fifteenth century a period of significant artistic, intellectual, and political change in Europe. By the second half of the fifteenth century, as we shall see in the next chapter, the growth of strong, centralized monarchical states made possible the dramatic expansion of Europe into other parts of the world.

CHAPTER TIMELINE

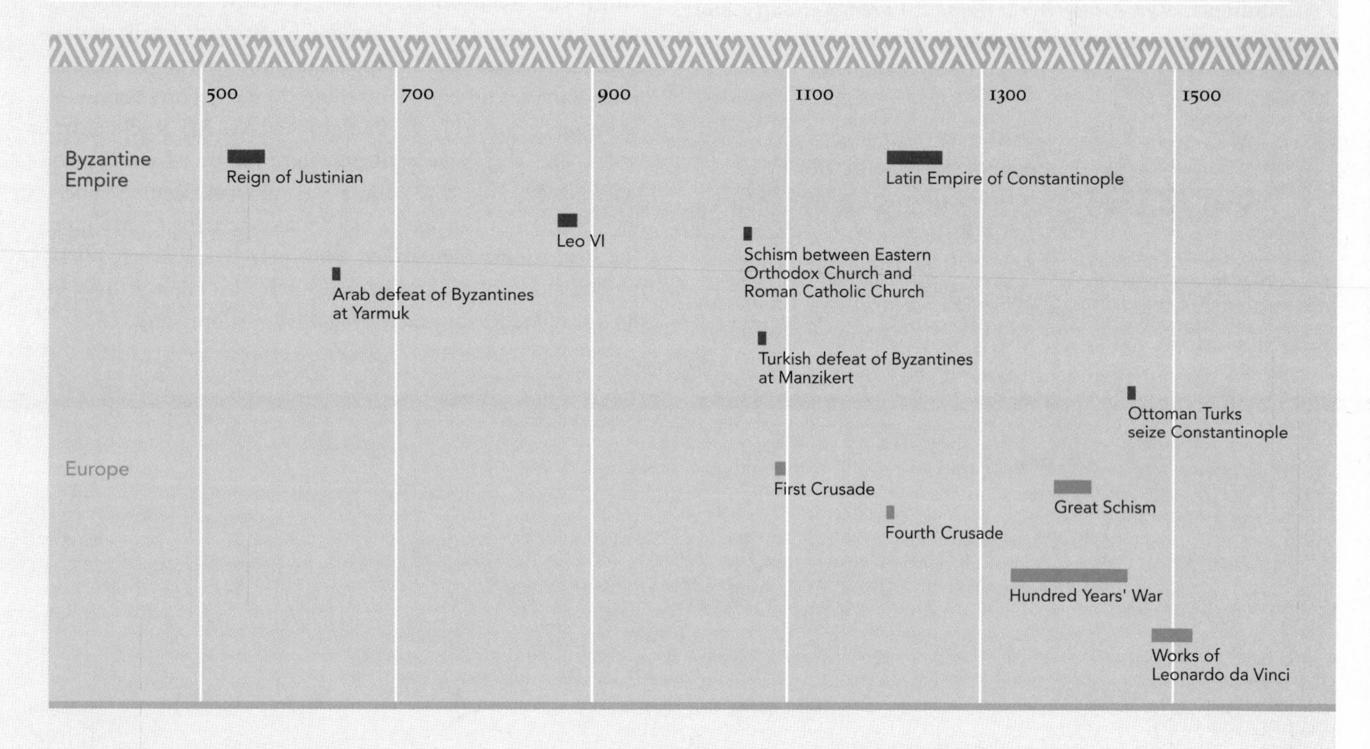

CHAPTER REVIEW

Upon Reflection

Q What were Justinian's major goals and how did he try to achieve them? How successful was he in actually achieving these goals?

Q Why does the chapter use the phrase "zenith of Byzantine civilization" to describe the period from 750 to 1025?

Q What was the relationship between Italian Renaissance humanism and Italian Renaissance art?

Key Terms

iconoclasts (p. 332)
iconoclasm (p. 332)
Black Death (p. 341)
pogroms (p. 341)
Renaissance (p. 345)
Renaissance humanism (p. 345)
taille (p. 348)

Suggested Reading

GENERAL HISTORIES OF THE BYZANTINE EMPIRE For comprehensive surveys of the Byzantine Empire, see **T. E. Gregory,** ***A History of Byzantium*** (Oxford, 2005), and **W. Treadgold,** ***A History of the Byzantine State and Society*** (Stanford, Calif., 1997). For a thematic approach, see **A. Cameron,** ***The Byzantines*** (Oxford, 2006).

THE EARLY EMPIRE (TO 1025) On Justinian, see **J. A. S. Evans,** ***The Age of Justinian*** (New York, 1996). On Constantinople, see **J. Harris,** ***Constantinople: Capital of Byzantium*** (London, 2007). Women in the Byzantine Empire are examined in **C. L. Connor,** ***Women of Byzantium*** (New Haven, Conn., 2004). Art is examined in **T. F. Mathews,** ***The Art of Byzantium: Between Antiquity and the Renaissance*** (London, 1998).

Visit the CourseMate website at **www.cengagebrain.com** for additional study tools and review materials for this chapter.

THE LATE EMPIRE (1025–1453) The impact of the Crusades on the Byzantine Empire is examined in **J. Harris,** ***Byzantium and the Crusades*** (London, 2003). The disastrous Fourth Crusade is examined in **J. Philips,** ***The Fourth Crusade and the Sack of Constantinople*** (New York, 2004). On the fall of Constantinople, see **D. Nicolle, J. Haldon,** and **S. Turnbull,** ***The Fall of Constantinople: The Ottoman Conquest of Byzantium*** (Oxford, 2007).

CRISES OF THE FOURTEENTH CENTURY On the Black Death, see **J. Kelly,** ***The Great Mortality*** (New York, 2005). A worthy account of the Hundred Years' War is **A. Curry,** ***The Hundred Years' War,*** 2nd ed. (New York, 2004).

THE RENAISSANCE On the Renaissance, see **M. L. King,** ***The Renaissance in Europe*** (New York, 2004). A brief introduction to Renaissance humanism can be found in **C. G. Nauert Jr.,** ***Humanism and the Culture of Renaissance Europe,*** 2nd ed. (Cambridge, 2006). A good survey of Renaissance art is **J. T. Paoletti** and **G. M. Radke,** ***Art, Power, and Patronage in Renaissance Italy,*** 3rd ed. (Upper Saddle River, N.J., 2003). For a general work on the political development of Europe in the Renaissance, see **C. Mulgan,** ***The Renaissance Monarchies, 1469–1558*** (Cambridge, 1998). A good study of the Italian states is **J. M. Najemy,** ***Italy in the Age of the Renaissance, 1300–1550*** (Oxford, 2004).

PART III

The Emergence of New World Patterns (1500–1800)

Historians often refer to the period from the sixteenth through eighteenth centuries as the early modern era. During these years, several factors were at work that created the conditions of our own time.

From a global perspective, perhaps the most noteworthy event of the period was the extension of the maritime trade network throughout the entire populated world. The Chinese had inaugurated the process with their groundbreaking voyages to East Africa in the early fifteenth century. The primary instrument of that expansion, however, was a resurgent Europe, which exploded onto the world scene with the initial explorations of the Portuguese and the Spanish at the end of the fifteenth century and then gradually came to dominate shipping on international trade routes during the next three centuries.

Some contemporary historians argue that it was this sudden burst of energy from Europe that created the first truly global economic network. According to Immanuel Wallerstein, one of the leading proponents of this theory, the Age of Exploration led to the creation of a new "world system" characterized by the emergence of global trade networks dominated by the rising force of European capitalism, which now began to scour the periphery of the system for access to markets and cheap raw materials.

Many historians, however, qualify Wallerstein's view and point to the Mongol expansion beginning in the thirteenth century or even to the rise of the Arab Empire in the Middle East a few centuries earlier as signs of the creation of a global communications network enabling goods and ideas to travel from one end of the Eurasian supercontinent to the other.

Whatever the truth of this debate, there are still many reasons for considering the end of the fifteenth century to be a crucial date in world history. In the first place, it marked the end of the long isolation of the Western Hemisphere from the rest of the inhabited world. This in turn led to the creation of the first truly global network of ideas and commodities, which would introduce plants, ideas, and (unfortunately) many new diseases to all humanity (see the comparative essay in Chapter 14). Second, the period gave birth to a stunning increase in trade and manufacturing that stimulated major economic changes not only in Europe but in other parts of the world as well.

The period from 1500 to 1800, then, was an incubation period for the modern world and the launching pad for an era of European domination that would reach fruition in the nineteenth century. To understand why the West emerged as the leading force in the world at that time, it is necessary to grasp the factors that were at work in Europe and why they were absent in other major civilizations around the globe.

Historians have identified improvements in navigation, shipbuilding, and weaponry that took place in Europe in the early modern era as essential elements in the Age of Exploration. As we have seen, many of these technological advances were based on earlier discoveries that had taken place elsewhere—in China, India, and the Middle East—and

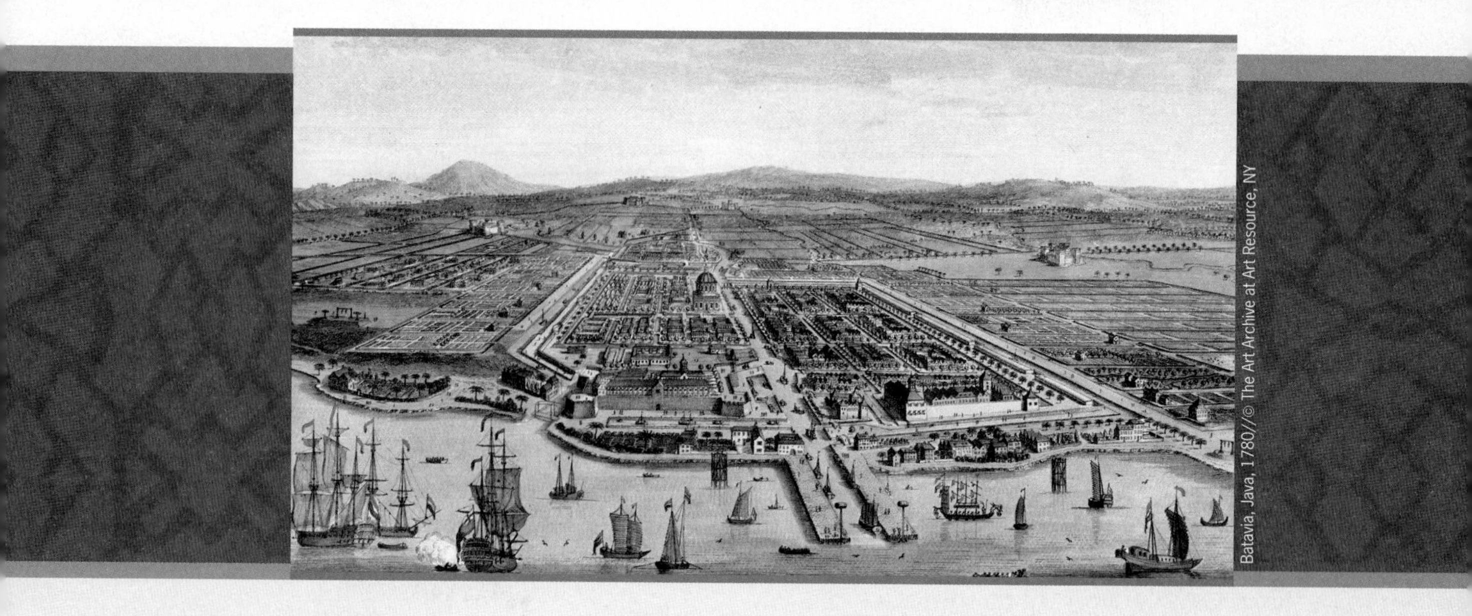
Batavia, Java, 1780// © The Art Archive at Art Resource, NY

had then been brought to Europe on Muslim ships or along the trade routes through Central Asia. But it was the capacity and the desire of the Europeans to enhance their wealth and power by making practical use of the discoveries of others that was the significant factor in the equation and enabled them to dominate international sea lanes and create vast colonial empires in the Western Hemisphere.

European expansion was not fueled solely by economic considerations, however. As in the rise of Islam, religion played a major role in motivating the European Age of Exploration in the early modern era. Although Christianity was by no means a new faith in the sixteenth century (as Islam had been at the moment of Arab expansion), the world of Christendom was in the midst of a major period of conflict with the forces of Islam, a rivalry that had been exacerbated by the conquest of the Byzantine Empire by the Ottoman Turks in 1453.

Although the claims of Portuguese and Spanish adventurers that their activities were motivated primarily by a desire to bring the word of God to non-Christian peoples certainly included a considerable measure of self-delusion and hypocrisy, there seems no reason to doubt that religious motives played a meaningful role in the European Age of Exploration. Religious motives were perhaps less evident in the activities of the non-Catholic powers that entered the competition beginning in the seventeenth century. English and Dutch merchants and officials were more inclined to be motivated purely by the pursuit of economic profit.

Conditions in many areas of Asia were less conducive to these economic and political developments. In China, a centralized monarchy continued to rely on a prosperous agricultural sector as the economic foundation of the empire. In Japan, power was centralized under the powerful Tokugawa shogunate, and the era of peace and stability that ensued saw an increase in manufacturing and commercial activity. But Japanese elites, after initially expressing interest in the outside world, abruptly shut the door on European trade and ideas in an effort to protect Japan from external contamination.

In the societies of India and the Middle East, commerce and manufacturing had played a vital role in the life of societies since the emergence of the Indian Ocean trade network in the first centuries C.E. But beginning in the eleventh century, the area had suffered through an extended period of political instability, marked by invasions by nomadic peoples from Central Asia. The violence of the period and the local rulers' lack of experience in promoting maritime commerce had a severe depressing effect on urban manufacturing and commerce.

In the early modern era, then, Europe was best placed to take advantage of the technological innovations that had become increasingly available. With its political stability, sources of capital, and a "modernizing elite," it was well equipped to wrest the greatest benefit from the new conditions. Whereas other regions were beset by internal obstacles or had deliberately turned inward to seek their destiny, Europe now turned outward to seek a new and dominant position in the world. Nevertheless, significant changes were taking place in other parts of the world as well, and many of these changes had relatively little to do with the situation in the West. As we shall see, the impact of European expansion on the rest of the world was still limited at the end of the eighteenth century. Though European political authority was firmly established in a few key areas, such as the Spice Islands and Latin America, traditional societies remained relatively intact in most regions of Africa and Asia. And processes at work in these societies were often operating independently of events in Europe and would later give birth to forces that acted to restrict or shape the Western impact. One of these forces was the progressive emergence of centralized states, some of them built on the concept of ethnic unity. ◆

New Encounters: The Creation of a World Market

© Mary Evans Picture Library/The Image Works

The port of Calicut in the mid-1500s

CHAPTER OUTLINE AND FOCUS QUESTIONS

An Age of Exploration and Expansion

Q How did Muslim merchants expand the world trade network at the end of the fifteenth century?

The Portuguese Maritime Empire

Q Why were the Portuguese so successful in taking over the spice trade?

The Conquest of the "New World"

Q How did Portugal and Spain acquire their empires in the Americas, and how did their methods of governing their colonies differ?

Africa in Transition

Q What were the main features of the African slave trade, and what effects did European participation have on traditional African practices?

Southeast Asia in the Era of the Spice Trade

Q What were the main characteristics of Southeast Asian societies, and how were they affected by the coming of Islam and the Europeans?

CRITICAL THINKING

Q How was European expansion into the rest of the world both a positive and a negative experience for Europeans and non-Europeans?

WHEN THE PORTUGUESE FLEET arrived at the town of Calicut (KAL-ih-kuht) (now known as Kozhikode) on the western coast of India, in the spring of 1498, fleet commander Vasco da Gama (VAHSH-koh dah GAHM-uh) ordered a landing party to go ashore to contact the local authorities. The first to greet them, a Muslim merchant from Tunisia, said, "May the Devil take thee! What brought thee hither?" "Christians and spices," replied the visitors. "A lucky venture, a lucky venture," replied the Muslim. "Plenty of rubies, plenty of emeralds! You owe great thanks to God, for having brought you to a country holding such riches!"[1]

Such words undoubtedly delighted the Portuguese, who concluded that the local population appeared to be Christians. Although it later turned out that they were mistaken—the local faith was a form of Hinduism—their spirits were probably not seriously dampened, for God was undoubtedly of less immediate importance than gold and glory to sailors who had become the first Europeans since the ancient Greeks to sail across the Indian Ocean. They left two months later with a cargo of spices and the determination to return soon with a larger fleet.

Vasco da Gama's voyage to India inaugurated a period of European expansion into Asia that lasted several hundred years and had effects that are still felt today. Eventually, it resulted in a Western takeover of existing trade routes in the Indian Ocean and the establishment of colonies throughout Asia, Africa, and Latin America. In later years, Western historians would describe the era as an "Age of Discovery" that significantly broadened the maritime trade network and set the stage for the emergence of the modern world.

In fact, however, the voyages of Vasco da Gama and his European successors were only the latest stage in a process that had begun generations earlier, at a time when European explorations were still restricted to the North Atlantic. As we saw in Chapter 10, Chinese fleets under Admiral Zhenghe had roamed the Indian Ocean for several years during the early fifteenth century, linking the Middle Kingdom with societies as distant as the Middle East and the coast of East Africa. Although the Chinese voyages were short in duration and had few lasting effects, the world of Islam was also expanding its reach, as Muslim traders blazed new trails into Southeast Asia and across the Sahara to the civilizations along the banks of the Niger River. It was, after all, a Muslim from North Africa who greeted the Portuguese when they first appeared off the coast of India. In this chapter, we turn our attention to the stunning expansion in the scope and volume of commercial and cultural contacts that took place in the generations preceding and following da Gama's historic voyage to India, as well as to the factors that brought about this expansion.

An Age of Exploration and Expansion

FOCUS QUESTION: How did Muslim merchants expand the world trade network at the end of the fifteenth century?

The voyage of Vasco da Gama has customarily been seen as a crucial step in the opening of trade routes to the East. In the sense that the voyage was a harbinger of future European participation in the spice trade, this view has merit. In fact, however, as has been pointed out in earlier chapters, the Indian Ocean had been a busy thoroughfare for centuries. The spice trade had been carried on by sea in the region since the days of the legendary Queen of Sheba, and Chinese junks had sailed to the area in search of cloves and nutmeg since the Tang dynasty (see Chapter 10).

Islam and the Spice Trade

By the fourteenth century, Muslim ships were transporting a growing percentage of the spice trade. Muslims, either Arabs or Indian converts, had taken part in the Indian Ocean trade for centuries, and by the thirteenth century Islam had established a presence in seaports on the islands of Sumatra and Java. In 1292, the Venetian traveler Marco Polo observed that Muslims were engaging in missionary activity in Sumatra: "This kingdom is so much frequented by the Saracen merchants that they have converted the natives to the Law of Mahomet—I mean the townspeople only, for the hill people live for all the world like beasts, and eat human flesh, as well as other kinds of flesh, clean or unclean."[2]

But the major impetus for the spread of Islam in Southeast Asia came in the early fifteenth century, with the foundation of a new sultanate at Malacca (muh-LAK-uh). The founder was Paramesvara (pahr-uh-muss-VAHR-uh), a vassal of the Hindu state of Majapahit (mah-jah-PAH-hit) on Java, who had been based first on Sumatra and then at Tumasik (tuh-MAH-sik) (modern Singapore), at the tip of the Malay peninsula. In the early fifteenth century, Paramesvara moved to Malacca to take advantage of its strategic location. As a sixteenth-century visitor from Portugal would observe, Malacca "is a city that was made for commerce; . . . the trade and commerce between the different nations for a thousand leagues on every hand must come to Malacca."[3]

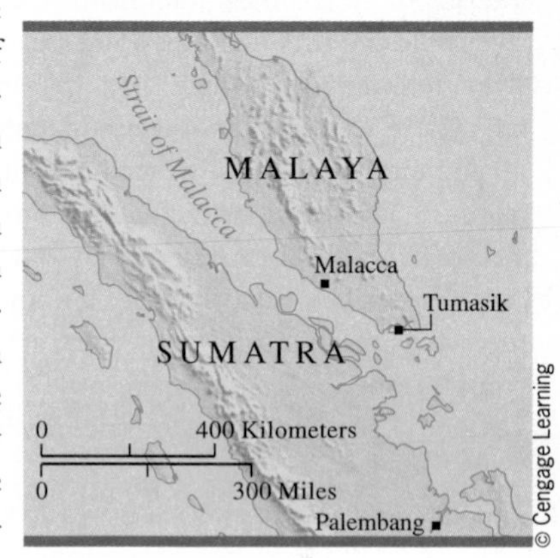

The Strait of Malacca

Shortly after its founding, Malacca was visited by a Chinese fleet under the command of Admiral Zhenghe (see Chapter 10). To protect his patrimony from local rivals, Paramesvara accepted Chinese vassalage and cemented the new relationship by making an official visit to the Ming emperor in Beijing (see the box on p. 356). More importantly, perhaps, he also converted to Islam, a move that would have enhanced Malacca's ability to participate in the trade that passed through the strait, much of which was dominated by Muslim merchants. Within a few years, Malacca had become the leading economic power in the region and helped to promote the spread of Islam to trading ports throughout the islands of Southeast Asia, including Java, Borneo, Sulawesi (soo-lah-WAY-see), and the Philippines.

A Chinese Description of Malacca

Malacca, located on the west coast of the Malay peninsula, first emerged as a major trading port in the early fifteenth century, when its sultan, Paramesvara, avoided Thai rule with the aid of the emperor of China. This description of the area was written by a naval officer who served in one of the famous Chinese fleets that visited the city in the early fifteenth century.

Ma Huan, *Description of a Starry Raft*

This place did not formerly rank as a kingdom. It can be reached from Palembang on the monsoon in eight days. The coast is rocky and desolate, the population sparse. The country [used to] pay an annual tax of 40 taels of gold to Siam. The soil is infertile and yields low. In the interior there is a mountain from [the slopes of] which a river takes its rise. The [local] folk pan the sands [of this river] to obtain tin, which they melt into ingots called *tou*. These weigh 1 kati 4 taels standard weight. [The inhabitants] also weave banana fiber into mats. Apart from tin, no other product enters into [foreign] trade. The climate is hot during the day but cool at night. [Both] sexes coil their hair into a knot. Their skin resembles black lacquer, but there are [some] white-complexioned folk among them who are of Chinese descent. The people esteem sincerity and honesty. They make a living by panning tin and catching fish. Their houses are raised above the ground. [When constructing them] they refrain from joining planks and restrict the building to the length of a [single] piece of timber. When they wish to retire, they spread their bedding side by side. They squat on their haunches when taking their meals. The kitchen and all its appurtenances is [also] raised [on the stilts]. The goods [used in trading at Malacca] are blue and white porcelain, colored beads, colored taffetas, gold and silver. In the seventh year of Yung-lo [1409], the imperial envoy, the eunuch Cheng-Ho [Zhenghe], and his lieutenants conferred [on the ruler], by Imperial command, a pair of silver seals, and a headdress, girdle and robe. They also set up a tablet [stating that] Malacca had been raised to the rank of a kingdom, but at first Siam refused to recognize it. In the thirteenth year [of Yung-lo] [1415], the ruler [of Malacca, desirous of] showing his gratitude for the Imperial bounty, crossed the ocean and, accompanied by his consort and son, came to court with tribute. The Emperor rewarded him [appropriately], whereupon [the ruler of Malacca] returned to his [own] country.

Why was Malacca such an important center of world trade?

Source: From Harry J. Banda and John A. Larkin, eds. *The World of Southeast Asia: Selected Historical Readings*, Harper & Row, 1967.

The Spread of Islam in West Africa

In the meantime, Muslim trade and religious influence continued to expand south of the Sahara into the Niger River valley in West Africa. Muslim traders—first Arabs and later African converts—crossed the desert carrying Islamic values, political culture, and legal traditions along with their goods. The early stage of state formation had culminated with the kingdom of Mali under the renowned Mansa Musa (see Chapter 8).

THE EMPIRE OF SONGHAI With the decline of Mali in the late fifteenth century, a new power eventually appeared: the empire of Songhai (song-GY). Its founder was Sonni Ali, a local chieftain who seized Timbuktu from its Berber overlords in 1468 and then sought to restore the formidable empire of his predecessors. Sonni Ali was criticized by Muslim scholars for supporting traditional religious practices, but under his rule, Songhai emerged as a major trading state (see Map 14.1). Shortly after his death in 1492, one of his military commanders seized power as king under the name Askia Mohammed (r. 1493–1528).

The new ruler, a fervent Muslim, increasingly relied on Islamic institutions and ideology to strengthen national unity and centralize authority. After his return from a pilgrimage to Mecca, Askia Mohammed tried to revive Timbuktu as a major center of Islamic learning, although many of his subjects—especially in rural

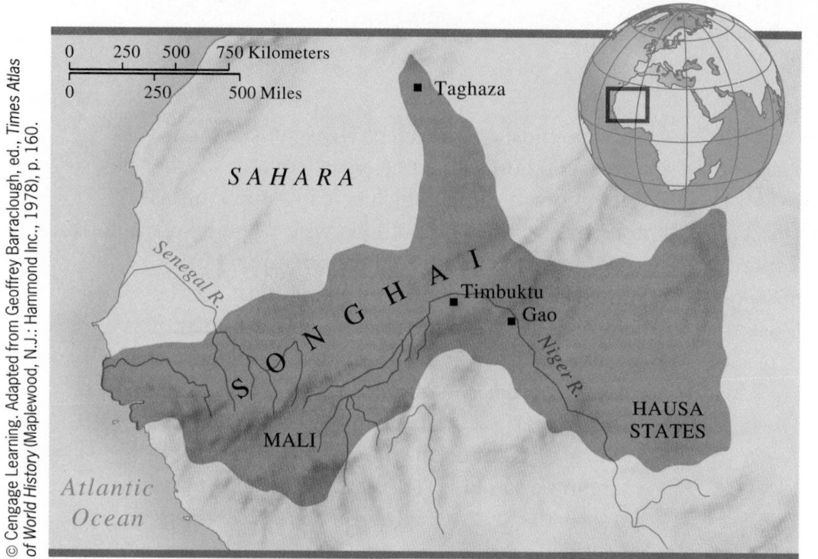

© Cengage Learning. Adapted from Geoffrey Barraclough, ed., *Times Atlas of World History* (Maplewood, N.J.: Hammond Inc., 1978), p. 160.

MAP 14.1 The Songhai Empire. Songhai was the last of the great states to dominate the region of the Niger River valley prior to the European takeover in the nineteenth century.

What were the predecessors of the Songhai Empire in the region? What explains the importance of the area in African history?

areas—continued to resist conversion to Islam. He did preside over a significant increase in trans-Saharan trade (notably in salt and gold), which provided a steady source of income to Songhai (see the box on p. 358). After his death, however, centrifugal forces within Songhai eventually led to its breakup. In 1591, Moroccan forces armed with firearms conquered the city to gain control over the gold trade in the region.

A New Player: Europe

For almost a millennium, Catholic Europe had largely been confined to one area. Its one major attempt to expand beyond those frontiers, the Crusades, ultimately had failed. Of course, Europe had never completely lost contact with the outside world: in particular, with the revival of trade in the High Middle Ages, European merchants began to travel more frequently to Asia and Africa. Nevertheless, Europe's contacts with non-European civilizations remained limited until the fifteenth century, when Europeans began to embark on a remarkable series of overseas journeys. What caused European seafarers to undertake such dangerous voyages to the ends of the earth?

Europeans had long been attracted to the East. Myths and legends of an exotic land of great riches were widespread in the Middle Ages, but the most informative description of the East was provided by Marco Polo of Venice, who wrote an account of his experiences at the court of the great Mongol ruler Khubilai Khan in the thirteenth century (see Chapter 10). In the fourteenth century, however, the conquests of the Ottoman Turks and then the breakup of the Mongol Empire reduced Western traffic to the East. With the closing of the overland routes, a number of people in Europe became interested in the possibility of reaching Asia by sea.

THE MOTIVES An economic motive thus looms large in Renaissance European expansion (see Chapter 13). Merchants, adventurers, and government officials had high hopes of finding precious metals and a direct source for the spices of the East, which continued to be transported to Europe via Arab intermediaries but were outrageously expensive. Europeans did not hesitate to express their desire to share in the wealth. As one Spanish conquistador (kahn-KEES-tuh-dor) explained, he and his kind went to the Americas to "serve God and His Majesty, to give light to those who were in darkness, and to grow rich, as all men desire to do."[4]

This statement expresses another major reason for the overseas voyages—religious zeal. A crusading mentality was particularly strong in Portugal and Spain, where the Muslims had largely been driven out in the Middle Ages. Prince Henry the Navigator of Portugal, an outspoken advocate of European expansion, was said to be motivated by "his great desire to make increase in the faith of our Lord Jesus Christ and to bring him all the souls that should be saved." Although most scholars believe that the religious motive was secondary to economic considerations, it would be foolish to overlook the genuine desire to convert the heathen to Christianity. Hernán Cortés (hayr-NAHN kor-TAYSS *or* kor-TEZ), the conqueror of Mexico, asked his Spanish rulers if it was not their duty to ensure that the native Mexicans were "introduced into and instructed in the holy Catholic faith."[5]

THE MEANS If "God, glory, and gold" were the primary motives, what made the voyages possible? First of all, the expansion of Europe was a state enterprise, tied to the growth of centralized monarchies during the Renaissance. By the second half of the fifteenth century, European monarchies had increased both their authority and their resources and were in a position to turn their energies beyond their borders. That meant the invasion of Italy for France, but for Portugal, a state not strong enough to pursue power in Europe, it meant going abroad. The Spanish scene was more complex, since the Spanish monarchy was strong enough by the sixteenth century to pursue power both on the Continent and beyond.

The Great City of Timbuktu

After its founding in the twelfth century, Timbuktu became a great center of Islamic learning and a fabled city of mystery and riches to Europeans. In the sixteenth century, Timbuktu was still a major commercial center on the trade route through the Sahara. This description of the city was written in 1526 by Leo Africanus, a Muslim from the Islamic state of Granada and one of the great travelers of his time.

Leo Africanus, *History and Description of Africa*

Here are many shops of artificers and merchants, and especially of such as weave linen and cotton cloth. And hither do the Barbary merchants bring cloth of Europe. All the women of this region, except the maid-servants, go with their faces covered, and sell all necessary victuals. The inhabitants, and especially strangers there residing, are exceeding rich, insomuch that the king that now is, married both his daughters to rich merchants. Here are many wells containing sweet water; and so often as the river Niger overfloweth, they convey the water thereof by certain sluices into the town. Corn, cattle, milk, and butter this region yieldeth in great abundance: but salt is very scarce here; for it is brought hither by land from Taghaza which is 500 miles distant. When I myself was here, I saw one camel's load of salt sold for 80 ducats. The rich king of Timbuktu hath many plates and scepters of gold, some whereof weigh 1,300 pounds: and he keeps a magnificent and well-furnished court. When he travelleth any whither he rideth upon a camel which is led by some of his noblemen; and so he doth likewise when he goeth forth to warfare, and all his soldiers ride upon horses. Whoever will speak unto this king must first fall down before his feet, and then taking up earth must first sprinkle it upon his own head and shoulders: which custom is ordinarily observed by . . . ambassadors from other princes. He hath always 3,000 horsemen, and a number of footmen that shoot poisoned arrows, attending upon him. They have often skirmishes with those that refuse to pay tribute, and so many as they take, they sell unto the merchants of Timbuktu. . . . Here are great store of doctors, judges, priests, and other learned men, that are bountifully maintained at the king's cost and charges, and hither are brought divers manuscripts or written books out of Barbary, which are sold for more money than any other merchandise. The coin of Timbuktu is of gold without any stamp or superscription but in matters of small value they use certain shells brought hither out of the kingdom of Persia. . . . The inhabitants are people of gentle and cheerful disposition, and spend a great part of the night singing and dancing through all the streets of the city.

What role did the city of Timbuktu play in regional commerce, according to this author? What were the chief means of payment?

Source: From *The History and Description of Africa*, by Leo Africanus (New York: Burt Franklin).

At the same time, by the end of the fifteenth century European states had a level of knowledge and technology that enabled them to regularly engage in voyages beyond Europe. In the thirteenth and fourteenth centuries, navigators and mathematicians began to produce ***portolani*** (pohr-tuh-LAH-nee), detailed charts that provided information on coastal contours, distances between ports, and compass readings. The *portolani* were valuable for voyages in European waters, but because they were drawn on a flat surface and did not account for the curvature of the earth, they were of little use for longer overseas voyages. Only when seafarers began to venture beyond the coasts of Europe did they begin to accumulate information about the actual shape of the earth and how to measure it. By the end of the fifteenth century, cartography had developed to the point that Europeans possessed fairly accurate maps of the known world.

In addition, Europeans had developed remarkably seaworthy ships as well as new navigational techniques. European shipbuilders had mastered the use of the sternpost rudder (an import from China) and learned how to combine the use of lateen sails with a square rig. With these innovations, they could construct ships mobile enough to sail against the wind and engage in naval warfare and also large enough to be armed with heavy cannons and carry a substantial amount of goods. In addition, new navigational aids such as the compass (a Chinese invention) and the astrolabe (an instrument, reportedly

Museo de la Torre del Oro, Seville//© Gianni Dagli Orti/
The Art Archive at Art Resource, NY

Marine Museum, Lisbon//© Gianni Dagli Orti/
The Art Archive at Art Resource, NY

European Warships During the Age of Exploration. Prior to the fifteenth century, most European ships were either small craft with triangular, lateen sails used in the Mediterranean or slow, unwieldy square-rigged vessels operating in the North Atlantic. By the sixteenth century, European naval architects began to build **caravels** (KER-uh-velz) (left), which combined the maneuverability and speed offered by lateen sails (widely used by sailors in the Indian Ocean) with the carrying capacity and seaworthiness of the square-riggers. For a century, caravels were the feared "raiders of the oceans." Eventually, as naval technology progressed, European warships developed in size and firepower, as the illustration of Portuguese carracks on the right shows.

devised by Arab sailors, that was used to measure the altitude of the sun and the stars above the horizon) enabled sailors to explore the high seas with confidence.

The Portuguese Maritime Empire

FOCUS QUESTION: Why were the Portuguese so successful in taking over the spice trade?

Portugal took the lead in exploration when it began exploring the coast of Africa under the sponsorship of Prince Henry the Navigator (1394–1460), who hoped both to find a Christian kingdom to be an ally against the Muslims and to acquire new trade opportunities for Portugal. In 1419, he founded a school for navigators, and shortly thereafter, Portuguese fleets began probing southward along the western coast of Africa in search of gold. In 1441, Portuguese ships reached the Senegal River, just north of Cape Verde. They found no gold, but brought home a cargo of black Africans, most of whom were sold as slaves to wealthy buyers elsewhere in Europe. Within a few years, an estimated thousand slaves were shipped annually from the area back to Lisbon.

Continuing southward, in 1471 the Portuguese discovered a new source of gold along the southern coast of the hump of West Africa (an area henceforth known to Europeans as the Gold Coast). A few years later, they established contact with the state of Kongo, near the mouth of the Congo River in Central Africa, and with the inland state of Benin, north of the Gold Coast.

The Portuguese in India

Hearing reports of a route to India around the southern tip of Africa, Portuguese sea captains continued their probing (see Map 14.2). In 1487, Bartolomeu Dias (bar-toh-loh-MAY-oo DEE-uhs) rounded the Cape of Good Hope, but fearing a mutiny from his crew, he returned home without continuing onward. Ten years later, a fleet under the command of Vasco da Gama rounded the cape and stopped at several ports controlled by Muslim merchants along the coast of East Africa, including Sofala, Kilwa, and Mombasa. Then da Gama's fleet crossed the Arabian Sea and arrived at Calicut on the Indian coast on May 18, 1498. The Portuguese crown had sponsored the voyage with the clear objective of destroying the Muslim monopoly over the spice trade, which had intensified since the Ottoman conquest of Constantinople in 1453 (see Chapter 13). Calicut was a major entrepôt (ON-truh-poh) on the route from the Spice Islands to the Mediterranean, but the ill-informed Europeans believed it was the source of the spices themselves. Da Gama returned to Europe with a cargo of ginger and cinnamon that earned the investors a profit of several thousand percent.

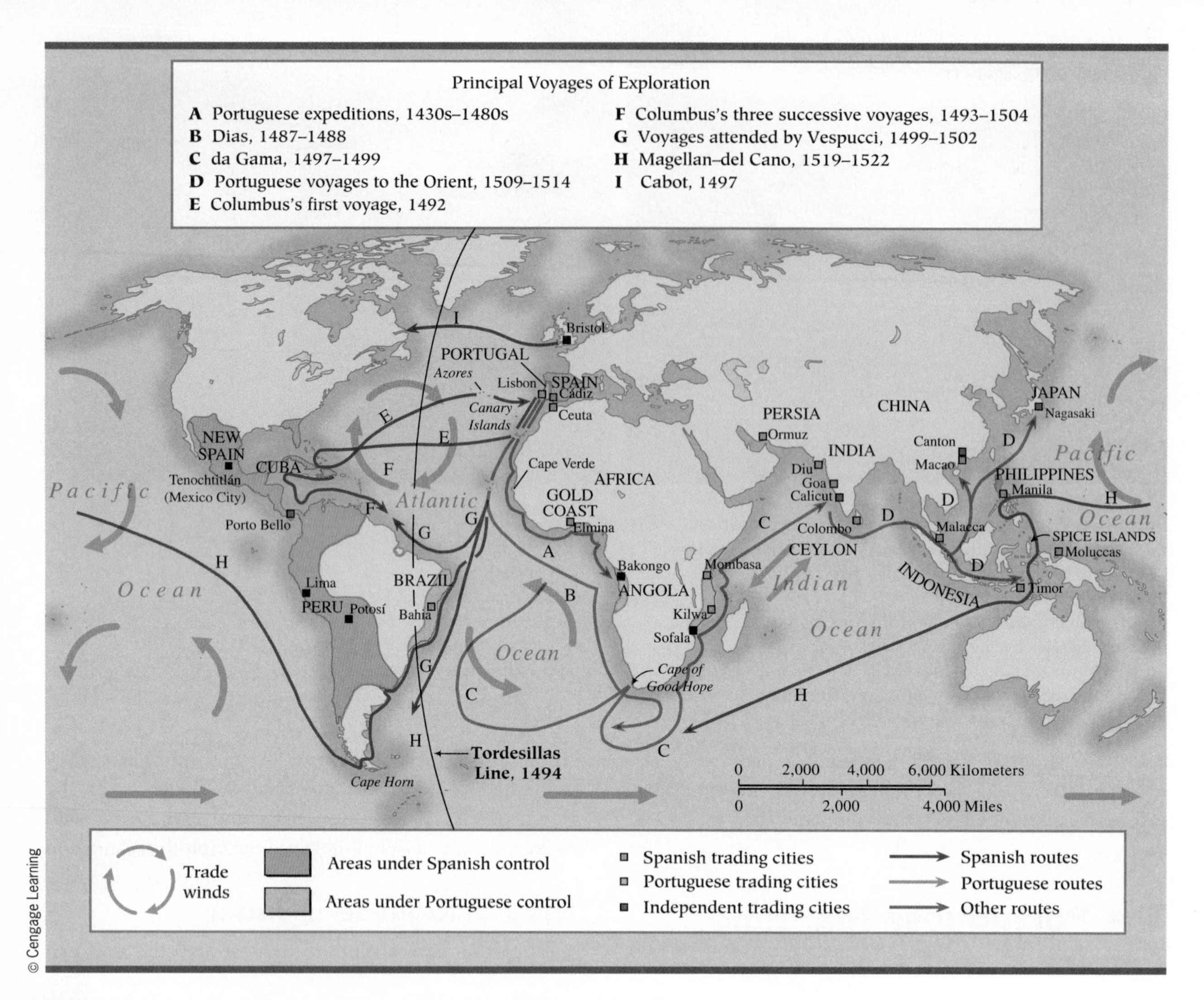

© Cengage Learning

MAP 14.2 European Voyages and Possessions in the Sixteenth and Seventeenth Centuries. This map indicates the most important voyages launched by Europeans during their momentous Age of Exploration in the sixteenth and seventeenth centuries.

Why did Vasco da Gama sail so far into the South Atlantic on his voyage to Asia?

The Search for Spices

During the next years, the Portuguese set out to gain control of the spice trade. In 1510, Admiral Afonso de Albuquerque (ah-FAHN-soh day AL-buh-kur-kee) established his headquarters at Goa (GOH-uh), on the western coast of India. From there, the Portuguese raided Arab shippers, provoking the following comment from an Arab source: "[The Portuguese] took about seven vessels, killing those on board and making some prisoner. This was their first action, may God curse them."[6] In 1511, Albuquerque seized Malacca and put the local Muslim population to the sword. Control of Malacca not only provided the Portuguese with a way station en route to the Spice Islands, known today as the Moluccas (muh-LUHK-uhz), but also gave them a means to destroy the Arab spice trade network by blocking passage through the Strait of Malacca.

From Malacca, the Portuguese sent

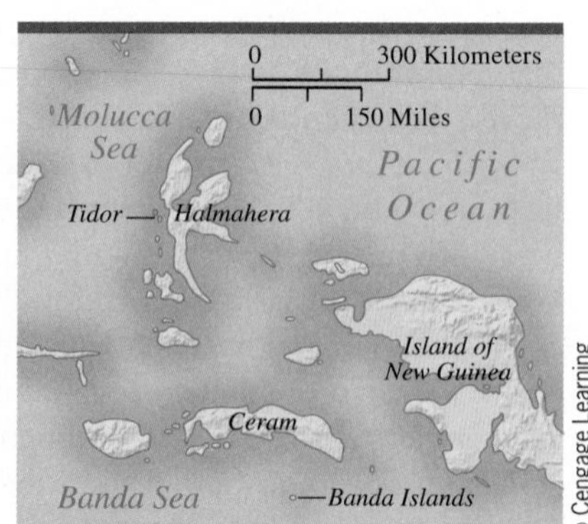

© Cengage Learning

The Spice Islands

expeditions farther east, to China in 1514 and to the Spice Islands. There they signed a treaty with a local sultan for the purchase of cloves for the European market. Within a few years, they had managed to seize control of the spice trade from Muslim traders and had garnered substantial profits for the Portuguese monarchy.

Why were the Portuguese so successful? Basically, their success was a matter of guns and seamanship. The Portuguese by no means possessed a monopoly on the use of firearms and explosives, but they used the maneuverability of their light ships to maintain their distance while bombarding the enemy with their powerful cannons. Such tactics gave them a military superiority over lightly armed rivals that they were able to exploit until the arrival of other European forces several decades later.

New Rivals Enter the Scene

Portugal's efforts to dominate the trade of the Indian Ocean were never totally successful, however. The Portuguese lacked both the numbers and the wealth to overcome local resistance and colonize the Asian regions. Moreover, their massive investments in ships and laborers for their empire (hundreds of ships and hundreds of thousands of workers in shipyards and overseas bases) proved very costly. The empire was simply too large and Portugal too small to maintain it, and by the end of the sixteenth century, the Portuguese were being severely challenged by rivals.

THE SPANISH First came the Spanish, whose desire to find a westward route to the East Indies had already led Queen Isabella to sponsor the voyage of Christopher Columbus across the Atlantic in 1492. Two years later, in an effort to head off conflict between the two countries, the Treaty of Tordesillas (tor-day-SEE-yass) divided the newly discovered world into Portuguese and Spanish spheres of influence. Thereafter, the route east around the Cape of Good Hope was reserved for the Portuguese, while the route across the Atlantic (except for the eastern hump of South America) was assigned to Spain (see Map 14.2 on p. 360).

Eventually convinced that the lands Columbus had reached were not the Indies, the Spanish continued to seek a route to the Spice Islands. In 1519, a Spanish fleet under the command of the Portuguese sea caption Ferdinand Magellan sailed around the southern tip of South America, proceeded across the Pacific Ocean, and landed in the Philippine Islands. Although Magellan and some forty of his crew were killed in a skirmish with the local population, one of the two remaining ships sailed on to the Moluccas and thence around the world via the Cape of Good Hope. In the words of a contemporary historian, they arrived in Cádiz "with precious cargo and fifteen men surviving out of a fleet of five sail."[7]

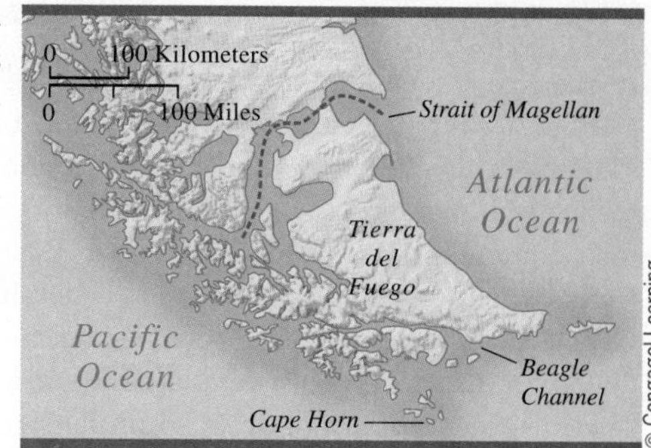

Cape Horn and the Strait of Magellan

As it turned out, the Spanish could not follow up on Magellan's accomplishment, and in 1529, they sold their rights in the Moluccas to the Portuguese. But Magellan's voyage was not a total loss. The Spanish managed to consolidate their control over the Philippines, which eventually became a major Spanish base in the carrying trade across the Pacific. Spanish galleons carried silk and other luxury goods to Acapulco in exchange for silver from the mines of Mexico.

THE ENGLISH AND THE DUTCH The primary threat to the Portuguese toehold in Southeast Asia, however, came from the English and the Dutch. In 1591, the first English expedition to the Indies through the Indian Ocean returned to London with a cargo of pepper. Nine years later, a private joint-stock company, the East India Company, was founded to provide a stable source of capital for future voyages. In 1608, an English fleet landed at Surat (SOOR-et), on the northwestern coast of India. Trade with Southeast Asia soon followed.

The Dutch were quick to follow suit, and the first Dutch fleet arrived in India in 1595. In 1602, the Dutch East India Company was established under government sponsorship and was soon actively competing with the English and the Portuguese. In 1641, the Dutch seized Malacca, one of the linchpins of Portugal's trading empire in Asia.

The Conquest of the "New World"

FOCUS QUESTION: How did Portugal and Spain acquire their empires in the Americas, and how did their methods of governing their colonies differ?

While the Portuguese were seeking access to the spice trade by sailing eastward through the Indian Ocean, the Spanish attempted to reach the same destination by sailing westward across the Atlantic. Although the Spanish came to overseas discovery and exploration later than the Portuguese, their greater resources enabled them to establish a far grander overseas empire.

The Voyages

In the late fifteenth century, knowledgeable Europeans were aware that the earth was round but had little understanding of its size or the extent of the continent of Asia. Convinced that the earth's circumference was smaller than contemporaries believed and that Asia was larger, Christopher Columbus (1451–1506), an Italian from Genoa, maintained that Asia could be reached by sailing due west instead of eastward around Africa. He persuaded Queen Isabella of Spain to finance an expedition, which reached the Americas in October 1492 and explored the coastline of Cuba and the neighboring island of Hispaniola (his-puhn-YOH-luh *or* ees-pahn-YAH-luh). Columbus believed that he had reached Asia and in three subsequent voyages (1493, 1498, and 1502) sought in vain to find a route through the outer islands to the Asian mainland.

Other navigators, however, realized that Columbus had discovered a new frontier altogether. State-sponsored explorers joined the race to what Europeans called the "New World." A Venetian, John Cabot, explored the New England coastline under a license from King Henry VII of England. The continent of South America was discovered accidentally by the Portuguese captain Pedro Cabral (PAY-droh kuh-BRAHL) in 1500. Amerigo Vespucci (ahm-ay-REE-goh vess-POO-chee), a Florentine, accompanied several voyages and wrote a series of letters describing the lands he observed. The publication of these letters led to the name "America" (after Amerigo) for the new lands.

The Conquests

The territories that Europeans referred to as the New World actually contained flourishing civilizations populated by millions of people. But the Americas were new to the Europeans, who quickly saw opportunities for conquest and exploitation. With Portugal clearly in the lead in the race to exploit the riches of the Indies, the importance of these lands was magnified in the minds of the Spanish.

The Spanish **conquistadors** were a hardy lot of mostly upper-class individuals motivated by a typical sixteenth-century blend of glory, greed, and religious zeal. Although sanctioned by the Castilian crown, these groups were financed and outfitted privately, not by the government.

Their superior weapons, organizational skills, and determination brought the conquistadors incredible success. In 1519, a Spanish expedition led by Hernán Cortés landed at Veracruz, on the Gulf of Mexico. Marching to Tenochtitlán (teh-nahch-teet-LAHN) with a small contingent of troops, Cortés received a friendly welcome from the Aztec monarch Moctezuma Xocoyotzin (mahk-tuh-ZOO-muh shoh-koh-YAHT-seen) (often called Montezuma).

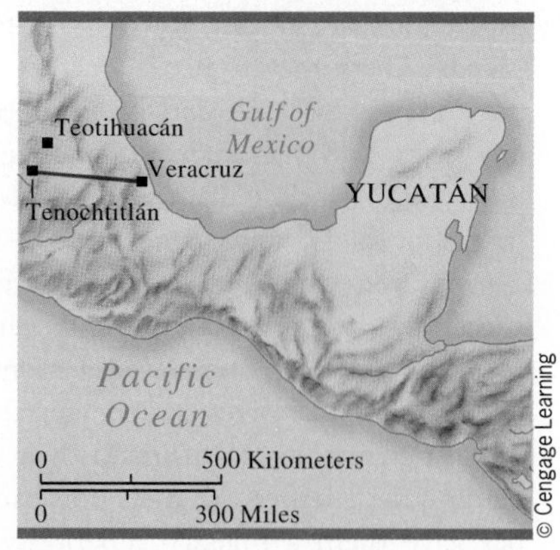

The Arrival of Hernán Cortés in Mexico

But tensions soon erupted between the Spaniards and the Aztecs. When the Spanish took Moctezuma hostage and began to destroy Aztec religious shrines, the local population revolted and drove the invaders from the city. Meanwhile, the Aztecs were beginning to suffer the first effects of the diseases brought by the Europeans, which would eventually wipe out the majority of the local population. With assistance from the state of Tlaxcallan (tuh-lah-SKAH-lahn), Cortés finally succeeded in vanquishing the Aztecs (see the comparative illustration on p. 363). Within months, their magnificent city and its temples, believed by the conquerors to be the work of Satan, had been destroyed.

A similar fate awaited the powerful Inka Empire in South America. Between 1531 and 1536, an expedition led by Francisco Pizarro (frahn-CHESS-koh puh-ZAHR-oh) (1470–1541) destroyed Inka power high in the Peruvian Andes. Here, too, the Spanish conquests were undoubtedly facilitated by the previous arrival of European diseases, which had decimated the local population.

THE PORTUGUESE IN BRAZIL Meanwhile, the Portuguese crown had established the colony of Brazil, basing its claim on the Treaty of Tordesillas, which had allocated the eastern coast of South America to the Portuguese sphere of influence. Like their Spanish rivals, the Portuguese initally saw their new colony as a source of gold and silver, but they soon discovered that profits could be made in other ways as well. A formal administrative system was instituted in Brazil in 1549, and Portuguese migrants arrived to establish plantations to produce sugar, coffee, and other tropical products for export to Europe.

Governing the Empires

While Portugal came to dominate Brazil, Spain established a colonial empire that included Central America, most of South America, and parts of North America. Within the lands of Central and South America, a new civilization arose that we have come to call Latin America (see Map 14.3).

Latin America rapidly became a multiracial society. Already by 1501, Spanish rulers allowed intermarriage between Europeans and the inhabitants of the Americas,

© North Wind Picture Archives

COMPARATIVE ILLUSTRATION

POLITICS & GOVERNMENT

The Spaniards Conquer a New World. The Spanish perception of their arrival in the Americas was quite different from that of the indigenous peoples. In the European painting shown above, the encounter was a peaceful one, and the upturned eyes of Columbus and his fellow voyagers imply that their motives were spiritual rather than material. The image below, drawn by an Aztec artist, expresses a dramatically different point of view, as the Spanish invaders, assisted by their Indian allies, use superior weapons against the bows and arrows of their adversaries to bring about the conquest of Mexico.

What does the Aztec painting show the viewer about the nature of the conflict between the two contending armies?

© bpk, Berlin/Ibero-Amerikanisches Institut/Art Resource, NY

whom the Europeans called Indians. Their offspring were known as **mestizos** (mess-TEE-zohz). In addition, over three centuries, as many as 8 million African slaves were brought to Spanish and Portuguese America to work the plantations (see "The Slave Trade" later in this chapter). **Mulattoes** (muh-LAH-tohz)—the offspring of Africans and whites—joined mestizos and descendants of whites, Africans, and local Indians to produce a unique multiracial society.

THE STATE AND THE CHURCH IN COLONIAL LATIN AMERICA In administering their colonial empires in the Americas, both Portugal and Spain tried to keep the most important posts of colonial government in the hands of Europeans. Nevertheless, the distance from the home countries meant that colonial officials would have considerable autonomy in implementing their monarchs' policies.

At the head of the administrative system that the Portuguese established for Brazil was the position of governor-general. The governor-general developed a bureaucracy but had at best only loose control over the captains-general, who were responsible for governing the districts into which Brazil was divided.

To rule his American empire, the king of Spain appointed **viceroys**. The first viceroyalties were established for New Spain (Mexico) in 1535 and for Peru in 1543. Viceroyalties were in turn subdivided into smaller units. All of the major government positions were held by Spaniards. For **creoles**—American-born descendants of Europeans—the chief opportunity to hold a government post was in city councils.

From the beginning, the Spanish and Portuguese rulers were determined to convert the indigenous peoples of the Americas to Christianity. Consequently, the Catholic

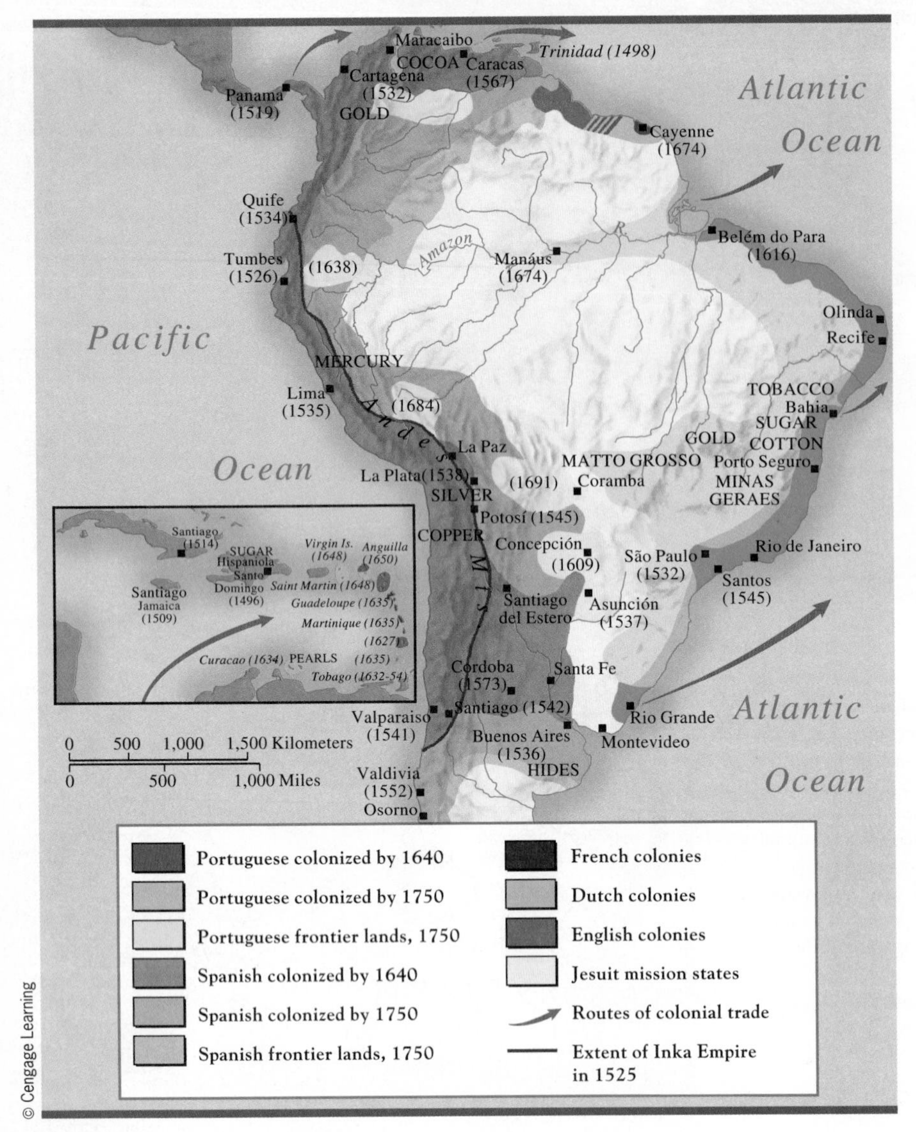

© Cengage Learning

MAP 14.3 Latin America from c. 1500 to 1750. From the sixteenth century, Latin America was largely the colonial preserve of the Spanish, although Portugal dominated Brazil. The Latin American colonies supplied the Spanish and Portuguese with gold, silver, sugar, tobacco, cotton, and animal hides.

How do you explain the ability of Europeans to dominate such large areas of Latin America?

Church played an important role in the colonies—a role that added considerably to church power. As Catholic missionaries fanned out across the Spanish Empire, the church built hospitals, orphanages, and schools to instruct the Indians in the rudiments of reading, writing, and arithmetic. To facilitate their efforts, missionaries often brought Indians to live in mission villages where they could be converted, taught trades, and encouraged to grow crops, all under the control of the church.

For women in the colonies, Catholic nunneries provided outlets other than marriage. Women in religious orders, many of them of aristocratic background, often operated outside their establishments by running schools and hospitals. The nun Sor Juana Inés de la Cruz (SAWR HWAH-nuh ee-NAYSS day lah KROOZ) (1651–1695) became one of seventeenth-century Latin America's best-known literary figures. She wrote poetry and prose and urged that women be educated.

EXPLOITING THE RICHES OF THE AMERICAS Both the Portuguese and the Spanish sought to profit economically from their colonies. One source of wealth came from the gold and silver that the Europeans sought so avidly. One Aztec observer commented that the Spanish conquerors "longed and lusted for gold. Their bodies swelled with greed, and their hunger was ravenous; they hungered like pigs for that gold."[8] Rich silver deposits were exploited in Mexico and southern Peru (modern Bolivia). When the mines at Potosí (poh-toh-SEE) in Peru were opened in 1545, the value of precious metals imported into Europe quadrupled. Between 1503 and 1650, an estimated 16 million kilograms (17,500 tons) of silver and 185,000 kilograms (200 tons) of gold entered the port of Seville in Spain.

In the long run, however, agriculture proved to be more rewarding. The American colonies became sources of raw materials for Spain and Portugal as sugar, tobacco, chocolate, precious woods, animal hides, and other natural products made their way to Europe. In turn, the mother countries supplied their colonists with manufactured goods (see Map 14.4).

To produce these goods, colonial authorities initially tried to rely on local sources of human labor. Spanish policy toward the Indians was a combination of confusion, misguided paternalism, and cruel exploitation. Queen Isabella declared the Indians to be subjects of Castile and instituted the ***encomienda* system**, under which European settlers received grants of land and could collect tribute from the indigenous peoples and use them as laborers. In return, the holders of an ***encomienda*** (en-koh-MYEN-duh) were supposed to protect the Indians and supervise their spiritual and material needs. In practice, this meant that the settlers were free to implement the system as they pleased. Spanish settlers largely ignored their distant government and brutally used the Indians to pursue their own economic interests. Indians were put to work on sugar plantations and in the gold and silver mines.

Forced labor, starvation, and especially disease took a fearful toll on Indian lives. With little or no natural resistance to European diseases, the Indians were ravaged by smallpox, measles, and typhus brought by the Europeans. Although estimates vary, in some areas at least half of the local population probably died of European diseases. On Hispaniola alone, out of an initial population of 100,000 when Columbus arrived in 1493, only 300 Indians survived by 1570. In 1542, largely in response to the publications of Bartolomé de Las Casas (bahr-toh-loh-MAY day lahs KAH-sahs), the government abolished the *encomienda* system and provided more protection for the Indians (see the box on p. 366). By then, however, the indigenous population had been decimated by disease, causing the Spanish

CHRONOLOGY Spanish and Portuguese Activities in the Americas

Christopher Columbus's first voyage to the Americas	1492
Portuguese fleet arrives in Brazil	1500
Columbus's last voyages	1502–1504
Spanish conquest of Mexico	1519–1522
Francisco Pizarro's conquest of the Inkas	1531–1536
Viceroyalty of New Spain established	1535
Formal colonial administrative system established in Brazil	1549

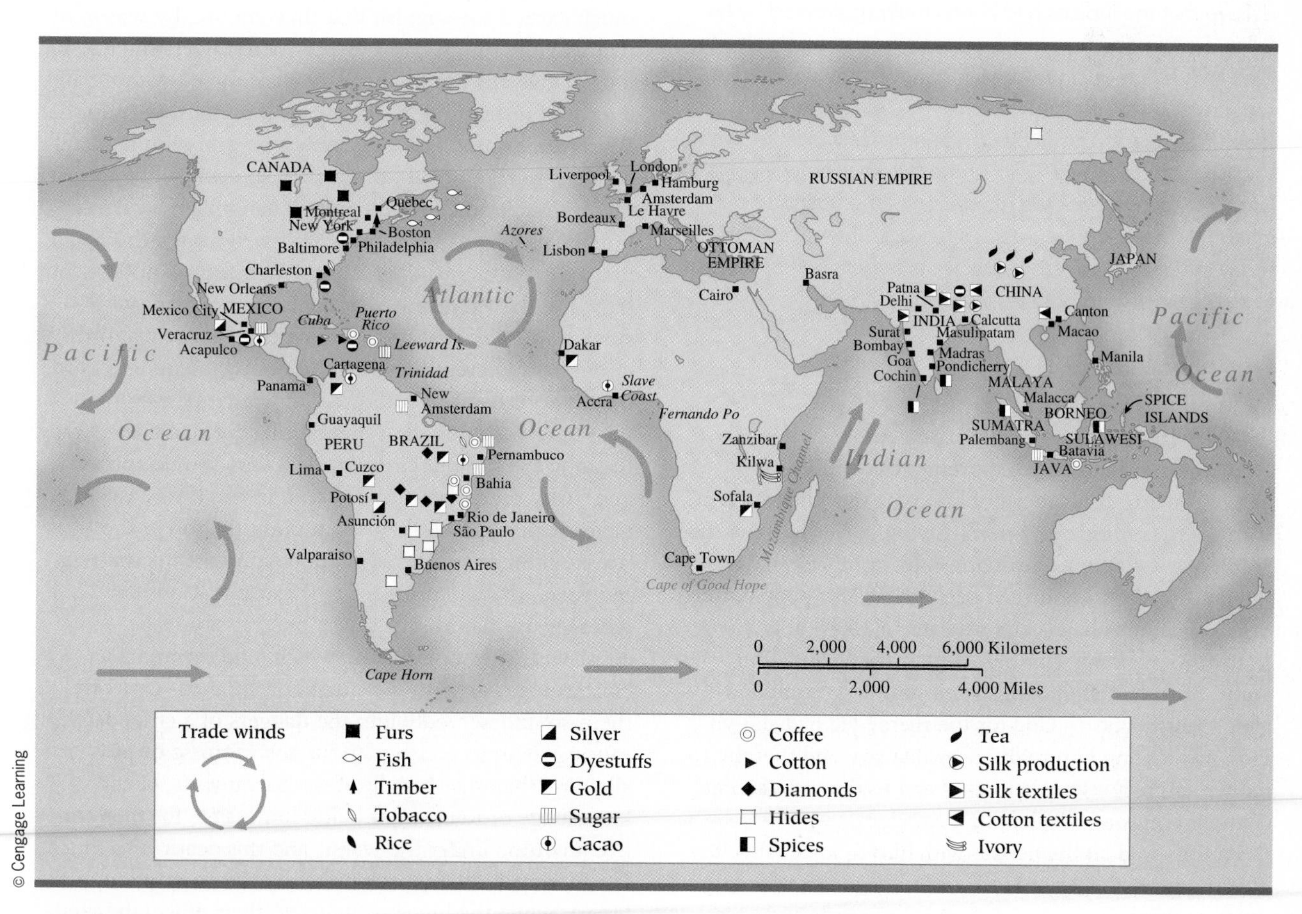

© Cengage Learning

MAP 14.4 Patterns of World Trade Between 1500 and 1800. This map shows the major products that were traded by European merchants throughout the world during the era of European exploration.

Q *What were the primary sources of gold and silver, so sought after by Columbus and his successors?*

OPPOSING ≺ VIEWPOINTS

The March of Civilization

INTERACTION & EXCHANGE

As Europeans began to explore new parts of the world in the fifteenth century, they were convinced that it was their duty to introduce civilized ways to the heathen peoples they encountered. This attitude is reflected in the first selection, which describes the Spanish captain Vasco Núñez de Balboa (BAHS-koh NOON-yez day bal-BOH-uh) in 1513, when from a hill on the Isthmus of Panama he first laid eyes on the Pacific Ocean.

Bartolomé de Las Casas (1474–1566) was a Dominican monk who participated in the conquest of Cuba and received land and Indians in return for his efforts. But in 1514, he underwent a radical transformation that led him to believe that the Indians had been cruelly mistreated by his fellow Spaniards. He spent the remaining years of his life (he lived to the age of ninety-two) fighting for the Indians. The second selection is taken from his most influential work, *Brevísima Relación de la Destrucción de las Indias*, known to English readers as *The Tears of the Indians*. This work was largely responsible for the reputation of the Spanish as inherently "cruel and murderous fanatics." Many scholars today feel that Las Casas may have exaggerated his account to shock his contemporaries into action.

Gonzalo Fernández de Ovieda, *Historia General y Natural de las Indias*

On Tuesday, the twenty-fifth of September of the year 1513, at ten o'clock in the morning, Captain Vasco Núñez, having gone ahead of his company, climbed a hill with a bare summit, and from the top of this hill saw the South Sea. Of all the Christians in his company, he was the first to see it. He turned back toward his people, full of joy, lifting his hands and his eyes to Heaven, praising Jesus Christ and his glorious Mother the Virgin, Our Lady. Then he fell upon his knees on the ground and gave great thanks to God for the mercy He had shown him, in allowing him to discover that sea, and thereby to render so great a service to God and to the most serene Catholic Kings of Castile, our sovereigns. . . .

And he told all the people with him to kneel also, to give the same thanks to God, and to beg Him fervently to allow them to see and discover the secrets and great riches of that sea and coast, for the greater glory and increase of the Christian faith, for the conversion of the Indians, natives of those southern regions, and for the fame and prosperity of the royal throne of Castile and of its sovereigns present and to come. All the people cheerfully and willingly did as they were bidden; and the Captain made them fell a big tree and make from it a tall cross, which they erected in that same place, at the top of the hill from which the South Sea had first been seen.

Bartolomé de Las Casas, *The Tears of the Indians*

There is nothing more detestable or more cruel than the tyranny which the Spaniards use toward the Indians for the getting of pearl. Surely the infernal torments cannot much exceed the anguish that they endure, by reason of that way of cruelty; for they put them under water some four or five ells deep, where they are forced without any liberty of respiration, to gather up the shells wherein the Pearls are; sometimes they come up again with nets full of shells to take breath, but if they stay any while to rest themselves, immediately comes a hangman row'd in a little boat, who as soon as he hath well beaten them, drags them again to their labor. Their food is nothing but filth, and the very same that contains the Pearl, with small portion of that bread which that Country affords; in the first whereof there is little nourishment; and as for the latter, it is made with great difficulty, besides that they have not enough of that neither for sustenance; they lie upon the ground in fetters, lest they should run away; and many times they are drown'd in this labor, and are never seen again till they swim upon the top of the waves; oftentimes they also are devoured by certain sea monsters, that are frequent in those seas. Consider whether this hard usage of the poor creatures be consistent with the precepts which God commands concerning charity to our neighbor, by those that cast them so undeservedly into the dangers of a cruel death, causing them to perish without any remorse or pity, or allowing them the benefit of the Sacraments, or the knowledge of Religion; it being impossible for them to live any time under the water; and this death is so much the more painful, by reason that by the coarctation of the breast, while the lungs strive to do their office, the vital parts are so afflicted that they die vomiting the blood out of their mouths.

(Continued)

(Opposing Viewpoints Continued)

Their hair also, which is by nature black, is hereby changed and made of the same color with that of the sea Wolves; their bodies are also so besprinkled with the froth of the sea, that they appear rather like monsters than men.

Can the sentiments expressed by Vasco Núñez be reconciled with the treatment accorded to the Indians as described by Las Casas? Which selection do you think better describes the behavior of the Spaniards in the Americas? Compare the treatment of the Indians described here with the treatment of African slaves described in the selection on p. 373.

Sources: Gonzalo Fernández de Ovieda, *Historia General y Natural de las Indias*. From *The Age of Reconnaissance* by J.H. Parry (International Thomson Publishing, 1969), p. 233–234. Bartolomé de Las Casas, *The Tears of the Indians*. From *The Tears of the Indians*, Bartolome de Las Casas. Copyright © 1970 by The John Lilburne Company Publishers.

and eventually the Portuguese to import African slaves to replace the Indians in the sugar fields.

The Competition Intensifies

The success of the Spanish and the Portuguese in exploiting the riches of the Americas soon attracted competition from other European states. The Dutch formed the Dutch West India Company in 1621, but although it made some inroads in Brazil and the Caribbean (see Map 14.3), the company's profits were never large enough to cover its expenditures. Dutch settlements were also established in North America. The colony of New Netherland stretched from the mouth of the Hudson River as far north as present-day Albany, New York.

By the second half of the seventeenth century, however, the Dutch commercial empire in the Americas had begun to decline as years of rivalry and warfare with the English and French took their toll. In 1664, the English seized New Netherland and renamed it New York, and the Dutch West India Company soon went bankrupt. In 1663, Canada became the property of the French crown and was administered as a French province. But the French never provided adequate men or money for their North American possessions and, by the early eighteenth century, had begun to cede some of them to the English.

The English, meanwhile, had proceeded to create a colonial empire along the Atlantic seaboard of North America. Although their early efforts did not lead to quick profits, the desire to escape from religious oppression combined with economic interests could result in successful colonization, as the Massachusetts Bay Company demonstrated. The Massachusetts colony had only 4,000 settlers in its early years, but by 1660, their numbers had swelled to 40,000.

Christopher Columbus: Hero or Villain?

For centuries, Christopher Columbus has generally been viewed in a positive light. By discovering the Western Hemisphere, he opened up the world and laid the foundations for the modern global economy. Recently, however, some historians have begun to challenge the image of Columbus as a heroic figure and view him instead as a symbol of European colonial repression and a prime mover in the virtual extinction of the peoples and cultures of the Americas (see the comparative essay "The Columbian Exchange" on p. 368).

Certainly, they have a point. As we have seen, the immediate consequences of Columbus's voyages were tragic for countless peoples. Columbus himself viewed the indigenous peoples that he encountered with condescension, describing them as naíve innocents who could be exploited to increase the wealth and power of Spain. As a consequence, his men frequently treated the local population brutally.

But is it fair to blame Columbus for possessing many of the character traits and prejudices common to his era? To do so is to demand that an individual transcend the limitations of his time and adopt the values of a future generation. Perhaps it is better to note simply that Columbus and his contemporaries showed relatively little understanding and sympathy for the cultural values of peoples who lived beyond the borders of their own civilization, a limitation that would probably apply to one degree or another to all generations, including our own. Whether Columbus was a hero or a villain will remain a matter of debate. That he and his contemporaries played a key role in the emergence of the modern world is a matter on which there can be no doubt.

COMPARATIVE ESSAY

The Columbian Exchange

In the Western world, the discovery of the Americas has traditionally been viewed in a largely positive sense, as the first step in a process that expanded the global trade network and eventually led to increased economic well-being and the spread of civilization throughout the world. In recent years, however, that view has come under sharp attack from some observers, who point out that for the peoples of the Americas, the primary legacy of the European conquest was not improved living standards but harsh colonial exploitation and the spread of pestilential diseases that devastated local populations.

Certainly, the record of the European conquistadors leaves much to be desired, and the voyages of Columbus were not of universal benefit to his contemporaries or to later generations. They not only resulted in the destruction of vibrant civilizations in the Americas but also led ultimately to the enslavement of millions of Africans.

But to focus solely on the evils committed in the name of exploration and civilization misses a larger point and obscures the long-term ramifications of the Age of Exploration. The age of European expansion that began with Prince Henry the Navigator and Christopher Columbus was only the latest in a series of population movements that included the spread of nomadic peoples across Central Asia and the expansion of Islam out of the Middle East. In fact, the migration of peoples in search of a better livelihood has been a central theme since the dawn of prehistory. Virtually all of the migrations involved acts of unimaginable cruelty and the forcible displacement of peoples and societies.

In retrospect, it seems clear that the consequences of such broad population movements are too complex to be summed up in moral or ideological simplifications. The Mongol invasions and the expansion of Islam are two examples of movements that brought benefits as well as costs for the affected peoples. By the same token, the European conquest of the Americas not only brought the destruction of cultures and dangerous new diseases but also initiated an exchange of plant and animal species that has been beneficial for peoples throughout the globe. The introduction of the horse, the cow, and various grain crops vastly increased food production in the Americas. The cultivation of corn, manioc, and the potato, all of them products of the Western Hemisphere, has had the same effect in Asia, Africa, and Europe. The **Columbian Exchange**, as it is sometimes called, has had far-reaching consequences that transcend facile moral judgments.

Collections of the Library of Congress, Washington, DC

Massacre of the Indians. This sixteenth-century engraving is an imaginative treatment of what was probably an all-too-common occurrence as the Spanish attempted to enslave the American peoples and convert them to Christianity.

The opening of the Americas had other long-term ramifications as well. The importation of vast amounts of gold and silver fueled a price revolution that for years distorted the Spanish economy. At the same time, the increase in liquid capital was a crucial factor in the growth of commercial capitalism that set the stage for the global economy of the modern era. Some have even suggested that the precious metals that flowed into European treasuries may have helped finance the Industrial Revolution (see Chapter 19).

Viewed in that context, the Columbian Exchange, whatever its moral failings, ultimately brought benefits to peoples throughout the world. For some, the costs were high, and it can be argued that the indigenous peoples of the Americas might have better managed the transformation on their own. But the "iron law" of history operates at its own speed and does not wait for laggards. For good or ill, the Columbian Exchange marks a major stage in the transition between the traditional and the modern world.

How can the costs and benefits of the Columbian Exchange be measured? What standards would you apply in attempting to measure them?

Africa in Transition

FOCUS QUESTION: What were the main features of the African slave trade, and what effects did European participation have on traditional African practices?

Although the primary objective of the Portuguese in rounding the Cape of Good Hope was to find a sea route to the Spice Islands, they soon discovered that profits were to be made en route, along the eastern coast of Africa.

Europeans in Africa

In the early sixteenth century, a Portuguese fleet seized a number of East African port cities, including Kilwa, Sofala, and Mombasa, and built forts along the coast in an effort to control the trade in the area (see Map 14.2 on p. 360). Above all, the Portuguese wanted to monopolize the trade in gold, which was mined by Bantu workers in the hills and then shipped to Sofala on the coast (see Chapter 8). For centuries, the gold trade had been monopolized by local Bantu-speaking Shona peoples at Zimbabwe. In the fifteenth century, it had come under the control of a Shona dynasty known as the Mwene Mutapa (MWAY-nay moo-TAH-puh). At first, the Mwene Mutapa found the Europeans useful as an ally against local rivals, but by the end of the sixteenth century, the Portuguese had forced the local ruler to grant them large tracts of land. The Portuguese lacked the personnel, the capital, and the expertise to dominate the local trade, however, and in the late seventeenth century, a vassal of the Mwene Mutapa succeeded in driving them from the plateau.

The first Europeans to settle in southern Africa were the Dutch. In 1652, the Dutch set up a way station at the Cape of Good Hope to serve as a base for their fleets en route to the East Indies. Eventually, the settlement developed into a permanent colony as Dutch farmers, known as **Boers** (BOORS *or* BORS) and speaking a Dutch dialect that evolved into Afrikaans, began to settle outside the city of Cape Town. With its temperate climate and absence of tropical diseases, the territory was practically the only land south of the Sahara that the Europeans had found suitable for habitation.

The Slave Trade

The European exploration of the African coastline had little apparent significance for most peoples living in the interior of the continent, except for a few who engaged in direct or indirect trade with the foreigners. But for peoples living on or near the coast, the impact was often great indeed. As the trade in slaves increased during the sixteenth through the eighteenth centuries, thousands, and then millions, were removed from their homes and forcibly exported to plantations in the Western Hemisphere.

THE ARRIVAL OF THE EUROPEANS As we saw in Chapter 8, there were different forms of slavery in Africa before the arrival of the Europeans. For centuries, slaves—often captives seized in battle—had been used in many African societies as agricultural laborers or as household servants. After the expansion of Islam south of the Sahara in the eighth century, a vigorous traffic in slaves developed, as Arab merchants traded for slaves to be transported to the Middle East. Slavery also existed in many European countries, where a few slaves from Africa or Slavic-speaking peoples captured in war in the regions near the Black Sea (the English word *slave* derives from "Slav") were used for domestic purposes or as agricultural workers.

With the arrival of the Europeans in the fifteenth century, the African slave trade changed dramatically, although the shift did not occur immediately. At first, the Portuguese simply replaced European slaves with African ones. But the discovery of the Americas in the 1490s and the planting of sugarcane in South America and the islands of the Caribbean changed the situation. Cane sugar was native to Indonesia and had first been introduced to Europeans from the Middle East during the Crusades. But when the Ottoman Empire seized much of the eastern Mediterranean (see Chapter 16), the Europeans needed to seek out new areas suitable for cultivation.

The primary impetus to the sugar industry came from the colonization of the Americas. During the sixteenth century, plantations were established along the eastern coast of Brazil and on several Caribbean islands. Because the cultivation of cane sugar is an arduous process demanding large quantities of labor, the new plantations required more workers than could be provided by the local Indian population, many of whom had died of diseases as described earlier. Since the climate and soil of much of West Africa were not especially conducive to the cultivation of sugar, African slaves began to be shipped to Brazil and the Caribbean to work on the plantations. The first were sent from Portugal, but in 1518, a Spanish ship carried the first boatload of African slaves directly from Africa to the Americas.

GROWTH OF THE SLAVE TRADE During the next two centuries, the trade in slaves increased by massive proportions. An estimated 275,000 enslaved Africans were exported to other countries during the sixteenth century, with 2,000 going annually to the Americas alone. The total climbed to over a million during the next century and jumped to 6 million in the eighteenth century, when the trade spread from West and Central Africa to East Africa. It has been estimated that altogether as many as

A Sugar Plantation. To meet the growing European demand for sugar in the sixteenth century, sugar plantations were established in suitable areas throughout South America and the Caribbean islands. Shown here is a plantation established by the French on the island of Hispaniola. The backbreaking nature of the work is evident, as slaves imported from Africa cut the sugarcane and bring it to the mill for crushing and transformation into raw sugar. The inset shows a contemporary sugar plantation on the island of St. Kitts.

10 million African slaves were transported to the Americas between the early sixteenth and the late nineteenth centuries (see Map 14.5). As many as 2 million were exported to other areas during the same period.

THE MIDDLE PASSAGE One reason for these astonishing numbers was the tragically high death rate. In what is often called the **Middle Passage**, the arduous voyage from Africa to the Americas, losses were frequently appalling. Although figures on the number of slaves who died on the journey are almost entirely speculative, during the first shipments, up to one-third may have died of disease or malnourishment. Even among crew members, mortality rates were sometimes as high as one in four. Later merchants became more efficient and reduced losses to about 10 percent. Still, the future slaves were treated inhumanely, chained together in the holds of ships reeking with the stench of human waste and diseases carried by vermin.

Ironically, African slaves who survived the brutal voyage fared somewhat better than whites after their arrival. Mortality rates for Europeans in the West Indies were ten to twenty times higher than in Europe, and death rates for new arrivals in the islands averaged more than 125 per 1,000 annually. But the figure for Africans, many of whom had developed at least a partial immunity to yellow fever, was only about 30 per 1,000.

The reason for these staggering death rates was clearly more than maltreatment, although that was certainly a factor. As we have seen, the transmission of diseases from one continent to another brought high death rates among those lacking immunity. African slaves were somewhat less susceptible to European diseases than the American Indian populations. Indeed, they seem to have possessed a degree of immunity, perhaps because their ancestors had developed antibodies to diseases common to the Old World from centuries of contact via the trans-Saharan trade. The Africans would not have had immunity to native American diseases, however.

SOURCES OF SLAVES Slaves were obtained by traditional means. When Europeans first began to take part in the slave trade, they would normally purchase slaves from local African merchants at the infamous slave markets in exchange for gold, guns, or other European manufactured goods such as textiles or copper or iron utensils. At first, local slave traders obtained their supply from immediately surrounding regions, but as demand increased, they had to move farther inland to locate their victims. A few local rulers became concerned about the

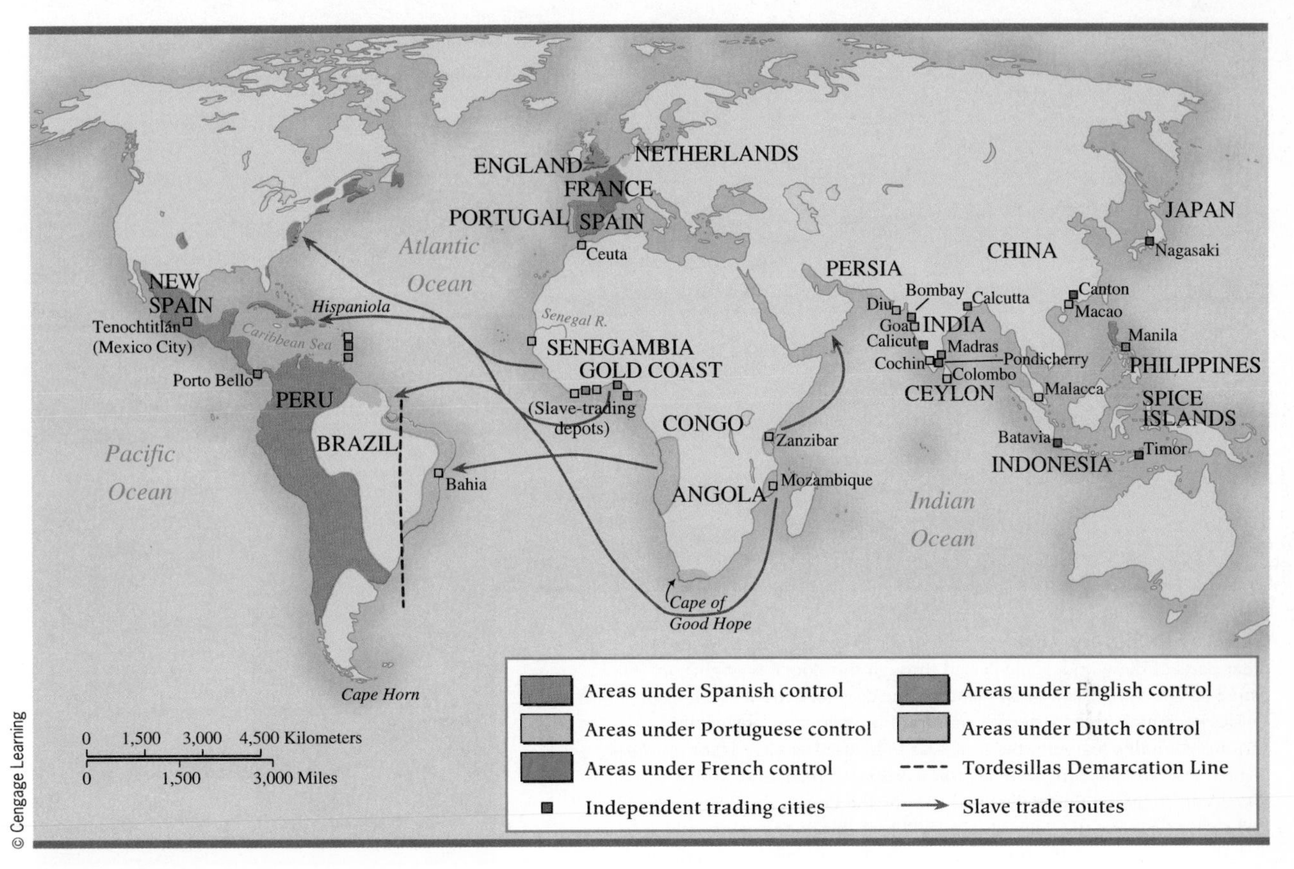

© Cengage Learning

MAP 14.5 The Slave Trade. Beginning in the sixteenth century, the trade in African slaves to the Americas became a major source of profit for European merchants. This map traces the routes taken by slave-trading ships, as well as the territories and ports of call of European powers in the seventeenth century.

What were the major destinations for the slave trade?

impact of the slave trade on their societies. In a letter to the king of Portugal in 1526, King Afonso of Kongo complained that "so great, Sire, is the corruption and licentiousness that our country is being completely depopulated."[9] More frequently, however, local monarchs viewed the slave trade as a source of income, and many launched forays against defenseless villages in search of victims (see the box on p. 373).

THE EFFECTS OF THE SLAVE TRADE The effects of the slave trade varied from area to area. It might be assumed that the practice would have led to the depopulation of vast areas of the continent. This did occur in some areas, notably in modern Angola, south of the mouth of the Congo River, and in thinly populated areas in East Africa, but it was less true in West Africa. There high birthrates were often able to counterbalance the loss of able-bodied adults, and the introduction of new crops from the Western Hemisphere, such as maize, peanuts, and manioc, led to an increase in food production that made it possible to support a larger population. One of the many cruel ironies of history is that while the institution of slavery was a tragedy for many, it benefited others.

Still, there is no denying that from a moral point of view, the slave trade represented a tragic loss for millions of Africans, for families as well as individuals. As many as 20 percent of those sold to European slavers were children, a statistic that may be partly explained by the fact that many European countries had enacted regulations that permitted more children than adults to be transported aboard the ships.

How did Europeans justify cruelty of such epidemic proportions? Some rationalized that slave traders were only carrying on a tradition that had existed for centuries throughout the Mediterranean and African world. In fact, African intermediaries were active in the process and were often able to dictate the price, volume, and availability of

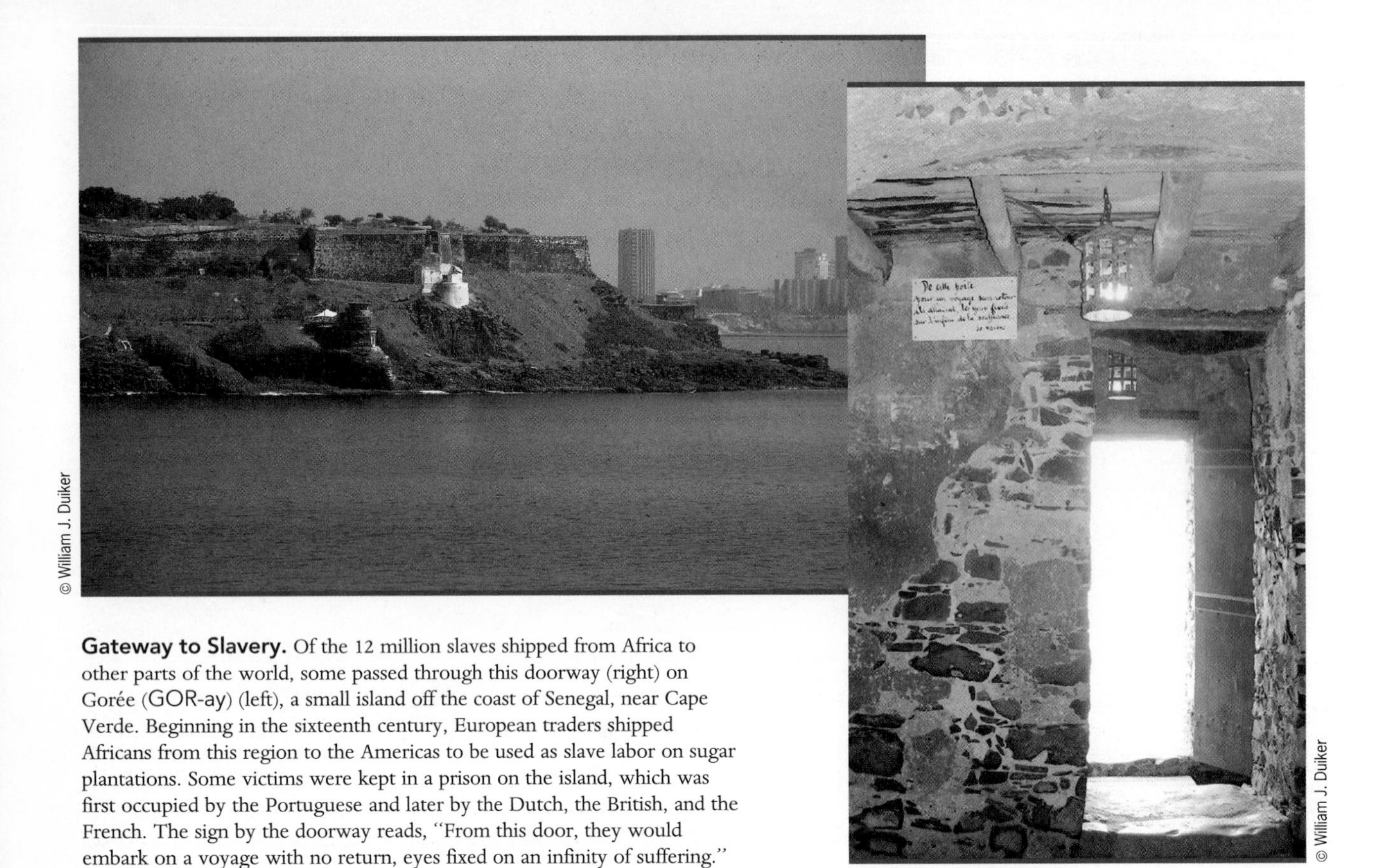
© William J. Duiker
© William J. Duiker

Gateway to Slavery. Of the 12 million slaves shipped from Africa to other parts of the world, some passed through this doorway (right) on Gorée (GOR-ay) (left), a small island off the coast of Senegal, near Cape Verde. Beginning in the sixteenth century, European traders shipped Africans from this region to the Americas to be used as slave labor on sugar plantations. Some victims were kept in a prison on the island, which was first occupied by the Portuguese and later by the Dutch, the British, and the French. The sign by the doorway reads, "From this door, they would embark on a voyage with no return, eyes fixed on an infinity of suffering."

slaves to European purchasers. Other Europeans eased their consciences by noting that slaves would now be exposed to the Christian faith.

Political and Social Structures in a Changing Continent

Of course, the Western economic penetration of Africa had other dislocating effects. The importation of manufactured goods from Europe undermined the foundations of local cottage industry and impoverished countless families. The introduction of firearms intensified political instability and civil strife. As the European demand for slaves increased, African slave traders began to use their newly purchased guns to raid neighboring villages in search of captives, initiating a chain of violence that created a climate of fear and insecurity. Old polities were undermined, and new regimes ruled by rapacious "merchant princes" began to proliferate on the coast.

At the same time, the impact of the Europeans should not be exaggerated. Only in a few isolated areas, such as South Africa and Mozambique, were permanent European settlements established. Elsewhere, at the insistence of African rulers and merchants, European influence generally did not penetrate beyond the coastal regions. Nevertheless, inland areas were often affected by events taking place elsewhere. In the western Sahara, for example, the diversion of trade routes toward the coast led to the weakening of the old Songhai trading empire and its eventual conquest by a vigorous new Moroccan dynasty in the late sixteenth century.

European influence had a more direct impact along the coast of West Africa, but no European colonies were established there before 1800. Most of the numerous African states in the area from Cape Verde to the delta of the Niger River were sufficiently strong to resist Western encroachments. Some, like the powerful Ashanti kingdom, established in 1680 on the Gold Coast, profited substantially from the rise in seaborne commerce. Some states, particularly along the so-called Slave Coast, in what is now Benin and Togo, or in the densely populated Niger River delta, took an active part in the slave trade. The demands of slavery and the temptations to profit, however, also contributed to the increase in conflict among the states in the area.

A Slave Market in Africa

Traffic in slaves had been carried on in Africa since the kingdom of the pharaohs in ancient Egypt. But the slave trade increased dramatically after the arrival of the Europeans. The following passage by a Dutch observer describes a slave market in Africa and the conditions on the ships that carried the slaves to the Americas.

Slavery in Africa: A Firsthand Report

Not a few in our country fondly imagine that parents here sell their children, men their wives, and one brother the other. But those who think so deceive themselves, for this never happens on any other account but that of necessity, or some great crime; most of the slaves that are offered to us are prisoners of war, who are sold by the victors as their booty.

When these slaves come to Fida, they are put in prison all together; and when we treat concerning buying them, they are brought out into a large plain. There, by our surgeons, whose province it is, they are thoroughly examined, even to the smallest member, and that naked too, both men and women, without the least distinction or modesty. Those that are approved as good are set on one side; and the lame or faulty are set by as invalids. . . .

The invalids and the maimed being thrown out, . . . the remainder are numbered, and it is entered who delivered them. In the meanwhile, a burning iron, with the arms or name of the companies, lies in the fire, with which ours are marked on the breast. This is done that we may distinguish them from the slaves of the English, French, or others (which are also marked with their mark), and to prevent the Negroes exchanging them for worse, at which they have a good hand.

I doubt not but this trade seems very barbarous to you, but since it is followed by mere necessity, it must go on; but we take all possible care that they are not burned too hard, especially the women, who are more tender than the men.

When we have agreed with the owners of the slaves, they are returned to their prison. There from that time forward they are kept at our charge, costing us two pence a day a slave; which serves to subsist them, like our criminals, on bread and water. To save charges, we send them on board our ships at the very first opportunity, before which their masters strip them of all they have on their backs so that they come aboard stark naked, women as well as men. In this condition they are obliged to continue, if the master of the ship is not so charitable (which he commonly is) as to bestow something on them to cover their nakedness.

You would really wonder to see how these slaves live on board, for though their number sometimes amounts to six or seven hundred, yet by the careful management of our masters of ships, they are so regulated that it seems incredible. And in this particular our nation exceeds all other Europeans, for the French, Portuguese and English slave ships are always foul and stinking; on the contrary, ours are for the most part clean and neat.

The slaves are fed three times a day with indifferent good victuals, and much better than they eat in their own country. Their lodging place is divided into two parts, one of which is appointed for the men, the other for the women, each sex being kept apart. Here they lie as close together as it is possible for them to be crowded.

We are sometimes sufficiently plagued with a parcel of slaves which come from a far inland country who very innocently persuade one another that we buy them only to fatten and afterward eat them as a delicacy. When we are so unhappy as to be pestered with many of this sort, they resolve and agree together (and bring over the rest to their party) to run away from the ship, kill the Europeans, and set the vessel ashore, by which means they design to free themselves from being our food.

I have twice met with this misfortune; and the first time proved very unlucky to me, I not in the least suspecting it, but the uproar was quashed by the master of the ship and myself by causing the abettor to be shot through the head, after which all was quiet.

What is the author's overall point of view with respect to the institution of slavery? Does he justify the practice? How does he think Dutch behavior compares with that of other European countries?

Source: From *The Great Travelers*, vol. I, Milton Rugoff, ed. Copyright © 1960 by Simon & Schuster. Used with permission of Milton Rugoff.

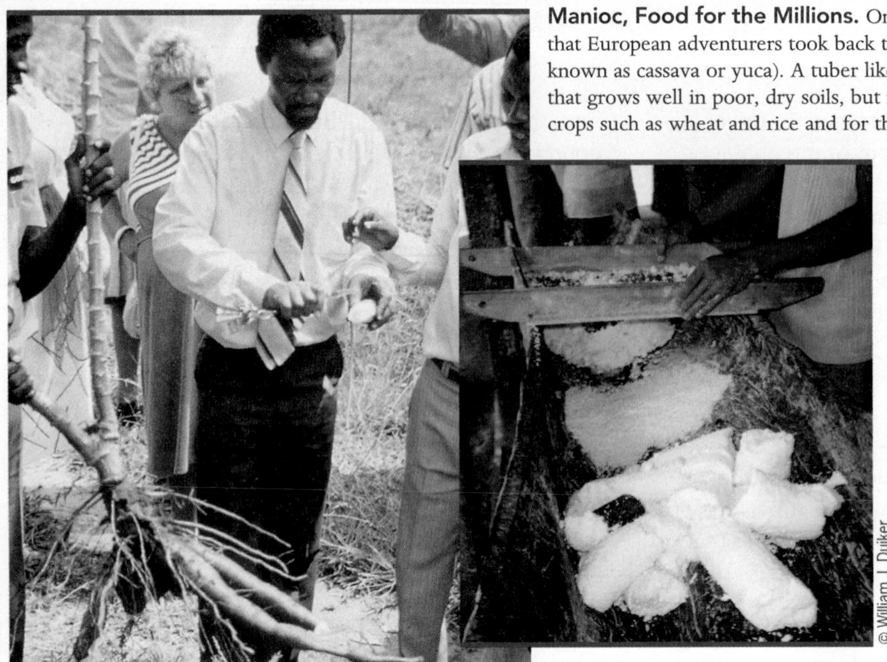
© William J. Duiker
© William J. Duiker

Manioc, Food for the Millions. One of the plants native to the Americas that European adventurers took back to the Old World was manioc (also known as cassava or yuca). A tuber like the potato, manioc is a prolific crop that grows well in poor, dry soils, but it lacks the high nutrient value of grain crops such as wheat and rice and for that reason never became popular in Europe (except as a source of tapioca). It was introduced to Africa in the seventeenth century. Because it flourishes in dry climates and can be preserved easily for consumption at a later date, it eventually became a staple food for up to one-third of the population of that continent. Shown at the left is a manioc plant growing in East Africa. On the right, a Brazilian farmer on the Amazon River sifts peeled lengths of manioc into fine grains that will be dried into flour.

This was especially true in the region of the Congo River, where Portuguese activities eventually led to the splintering of the Kongo Empire and two centuries of strife among its successor states. Similarly, in East Africa, Portuguese activities led to the decline and eventual collapse of the Mwene Mutapa. Northward along the coast, in present-day Kenya and Tanzania, African rulers, assisted by Arab forces from the Arabian peninsula, expelled the Portuguese from Mombasa in 1728. Swahili culture now regained some of its earlier dynamism, but with much shipping now diverted to the route around the Cape of Good Hope, the area never completely recovered and was increasingly dependent on the export of slaves and ivory obtained through contacts with African states in the interior.

CHRONOLOGY **The Penetration of Africa**	
Life of Prince Henry the Navigator	1394–1460
Portuguese ships reach the Senegal River	1441
Bartolomeu Dias sails around the tip of Africa	1487
First boatload of slaves to the Americas	1518
Dutch way station established at Cape of Good Hope	1652
Ashanti kingdom established in West Africa	1680
Portuguese expelled from Mombasa	1728

Southeast Asia in the Era of the Spice Trade

FOCUS QUESTION: What were the main characteristics of Southeast Asian societies, and how were they affected by the coming of Islam and the Europeans?

As noted earlier, Southeast Asia would be affected in various ways by the expansion of the global trade network that began to accelerate in the fifteenth century. Not only did the Muslim faith begin to make inroads in the region, but the seizure of Malacca by the Portuguese in 1511 inaugurated a period of conflict among various European competitors for control of the spice trade. At first, the rulers of most of the local states were able to fend off these challenges and maintain their independence. As we shall see in a later chapter, however, the reprieve was only temporary.

The Arrival of the West

As we have seen, the Spanish soon followed the Portuguese into Southeast Asia. By the seventeenth century, the Dutch, English, and French had begun to join the scramble for rights to the lucrative spice trade.

Within a short time, the Dutch, through the well-financed Dutch East India Company (Vereenigde Oost-Indische Compagnie, or VOC), succeeded in elbowing

© William J. Duiker

© William J. Duiker

COMPARATIVE ILLUSTRATION

Bringing Lumber to Java. Long before the Europeans arrived, a brisk trade was taking place throughout the Indonesian islands and the South China Sea. Many of the goods were carried on sturdy boats—called pinisi—that were manned by the Bugi (BOO-gih), a trading people who lived mainly in the eastern islands. The trade continues today, as these cargo ships in the harbor of Jakarta attest. The Bugi were also feared as pirates, giving rise to the once-familiar parental admonition to children, "Don't let the bogyman get you!" The bas-relief in the inset from the temple of Borobudur, is a rare example of a sailing vessel in the ninth century C.E.

What role did Southeast Asia play in the global trade network?

their rivals out of the spice trade and began to consolidate their control over the area. On the island of Java, where they established a fort at Batavia (buh-TAY-vee-uh) (today's Jakarta) in 1619 (see the illustration on p. 353), the Dutch found it necessary to bring the inland regions under their control to protect their position. Rather than establishing a formal colony, however, they tried to rule through the local aristocracy. On Java and Sumatra, the VOC established pepper plantations, which became the source of massive profits for Dutch merchants in Amsterdam. Elsewhere they attempted to monopolize the clove trade by limiting cultivation of the crop to one island. By the end of the eighteenth century, the Dutch had succeeded in bringing almost the entire Indonesian archipelago under their control.

Competition among the European naval powers for territory and influence continued to intensify throughout the region, however, and prospects for the future were ominous. In island groups scattered throughout the Pacific Ocean, local rulers were already finding it difficult to resist the growing European presence. The results were sometimes tragic, as indigenous cultures were overwhelmed under the impact of Western material civilization, which often left a sense of rootlessness and psychic stress in its wake.

The arrival of the Europeans had somewhat less impact in the Indian subcontinent and in mainland Southeast Asia, where cohesive monarchies in Burma, Thailand, and Vietnam resisted foreign encroachment. In addition, the coveted spices did not thrive on the mainland, so the Europeans' efforts were far less determined

© William J. Duiker

© Claire L. Duiker

COMPARATIVE ILLUSTRATION

RELIGION & PHILOSOPHY

The Face of Christianity in America and Asia. As Europeans began to spread through the Americas and Asia in the sixteenth and seventeenth centuries, the churches that they built reflected the styles that had become popular in their own countries. The photograph on the left shows a Baroque cathedral in Mexico City, the headquarters of Spanish rule in Central America. It was erected on the site of the Aztec temple to the sun god at Tenochtitlán, using materials from the dismantled Aztec pyramids. The Dutch preferred a less ornate approach, as seen in the rose-colored church in Malacca shown at the right, erected after their takeover of that trading port in 1641.

How did the spread of Christianity in America and Asia in the sixteenth and seventeenth centuries compare with the expansion of Islam in earlier times?

Buddhism and Islam also helped shape Southeast Asian political institutions. As the political systems began to mature, they evolved into four main types: Buddhist kings, Javanese kings, Islamic sultans, and Vietnamese emperors (for Vietnam, which was strongly influenced by China, see Chapter 11). In each case, institutions and concepts imported from abroad were adapted to local circumstances.

The Buddhist style of kingship took shape between the eleventh and the fifteenth centuries. It became the predominant political system in the mainland Buddhist states—Burma, Ayuthaya, Laos, and Cambodia. Its dominant feature was the godlike character of the monarch, who was considered by virtue of his *karma* to be innately superior to other human beings and served as a link between humans and the cosmos.

The Javanese model was a blend of Buddhist and Islamic political traditions. Like their Buddhist counterparts, Javanese monarchs possessed a sacred quality and maintained the balance between the sacred and the material world.

The Islamic model was found mainly on the Malay peninsula and along the coast of the Indonesian archipelago. In this pattern, the head of state was a sultan, who was viewed as a mortal, although he still possessed some magical qualities.

THE ECONOMY During the early period of European penetration, the economy of most Southeast Asian societies was still based on agriculture, although by the sixteenth century, commerce was growing, especially in the cities that were beginning to proliferate along the coasts or on navigable rivers. In part, this was because agriculture itself was becoming more commercialized as cash crops like sugar and spices replaced subsistence farming in rice or other cereals in some areas.

Regional and interregional trade were already expanding before the coming of the Europeans. Southeast Asia's location enabled it to become a focal point in a widespread trading network. Spices, of course, were the mainstay of the interregional trade, but other products were exchanged as well. Tin (mined in Malaya since the tenth century), copper, gold, tropical fruits and other agricultural products, cloth, gems, and luxury goods were exported in exchange for manufactured goods, ceramics, and high-quality textiles such as silk from China.

Society

In general, Southeast Asians probably enjoyed a higher living standard than most of their contemporaries elsewhere in Asia. Although most of the population was poor by modern Western standards, hunger was not widespread. Several factors help explain this relative prosperity. First, most of Southeast Asia has been blessed by a salubrious climate. The uniformly high temperatures and the abundant rainfall enable as many as two or even three crops to be grown each year. Second, although the soil in some areas is poor, the alluvial deltas on the mainland are fertile, and the volcanoes of Indonesia periodically spew forth rich volcanic ash that renews the soil of Sumatra and Java. Finally, with some exceptions, most of Southeast Asia was relatively thinly populated.

Social institutions tended to be fairly homogeneous throughout Southeast Asia. Compared with China and India, there was little social stratification, and the nuclear family predominated. In general, women fared better in the region than elsewhere in Asia. Daughters often had the same inheritance rights as sons, and family property was held jointly between husband and wife. Wives were often permitted to divorce their husbands, and monogamy was the rule rather than the exception. Although women were usually restricted to specialized work, such as making ceramics, weaving, or transplanting the rice seedlings into the main paddy fields, and rarely possessed legal rights equal to those of men, they enjoyed a comparatively high degree of freedom and status in most societies in the region and were sometimes involved in commerce.

CHAPTER SUMMARY

During the fifteenth century, the pace of international commerce increased dramatically. Chinese fleets visited the Indian Ocean while Muslim traders extended their activities into the Spice Islands and sub-Saharan West Africa. Then the Europeans burst onto the world scene. Beginning with the seemingly modest ventures of the Portuguese ships that sailed southward along the West African coast, the process accelerated with the epoch-making voyages of Christopher Columbus to the Americas and Vasco da Gama to the Indian Ocean in the 1490s. Soon a number of other European states had entered the fray, and by the end of the eighteenth century, they had created a global trade network dominated by Western ships and Western power that distributed foodstuffs, textile goods, spices, and precious minerals from one end of the globe to the other.

In less than three hundred years, the European Age of Exploration changed the face of the world. In some areas, such as the Americas and the Spice Islands, it led to the destruction of indigenous civilizations and the establishment of European colonies. In others, as in Africa, South Asia, and mainland Southeast Asia, it left local regimes intact but had a strong impact on local societies and regional trade patterns. In some areas, it led to an irreversible decline in traditional institutions and values, setting in motion a corrosive process that has not been reversed to this day.

At the time, many European observers viewed the process in a favorable light. Not only did it expand world trade and foster the exchange of new crops and discoveries between the Old and New Worlds, but it also introduced Christianity to "heathen peoples" around the globe. Many modern historians have been much more critical, concluding that European activities during the sixteenth and seventeenth centuries created a "tributary mode of production" based on European profits from unequal terms of trade that foreshadowed the exploitative relationship characteristic of the later colonial period. Other scholars have questioned

that contention, however, and argue that although Western commercial operations had a significant impact on global trade patterns, they did not—at least not before the nineteenth century—usher in an era of dominance over the rest of the world. Muslim merchants were long able to evade European efforts to eliminate them from the spice trade, and the trans-Saharan caravan trade was relatively unaffected by European merchant shipping along the West African coast. In the meantime, powerful empires continued to hold sway over the lands washed by the Muslim faith. Beyond the Himalayas, Chinese emperors in their new northern capital of Beijing retained proud dominion over all the vast territory of continental East Asia. We shall deal with these regions, and how they confronted the challenges of a changing world, in Chapters 16 and 17.

CHAPTER TIMELINE

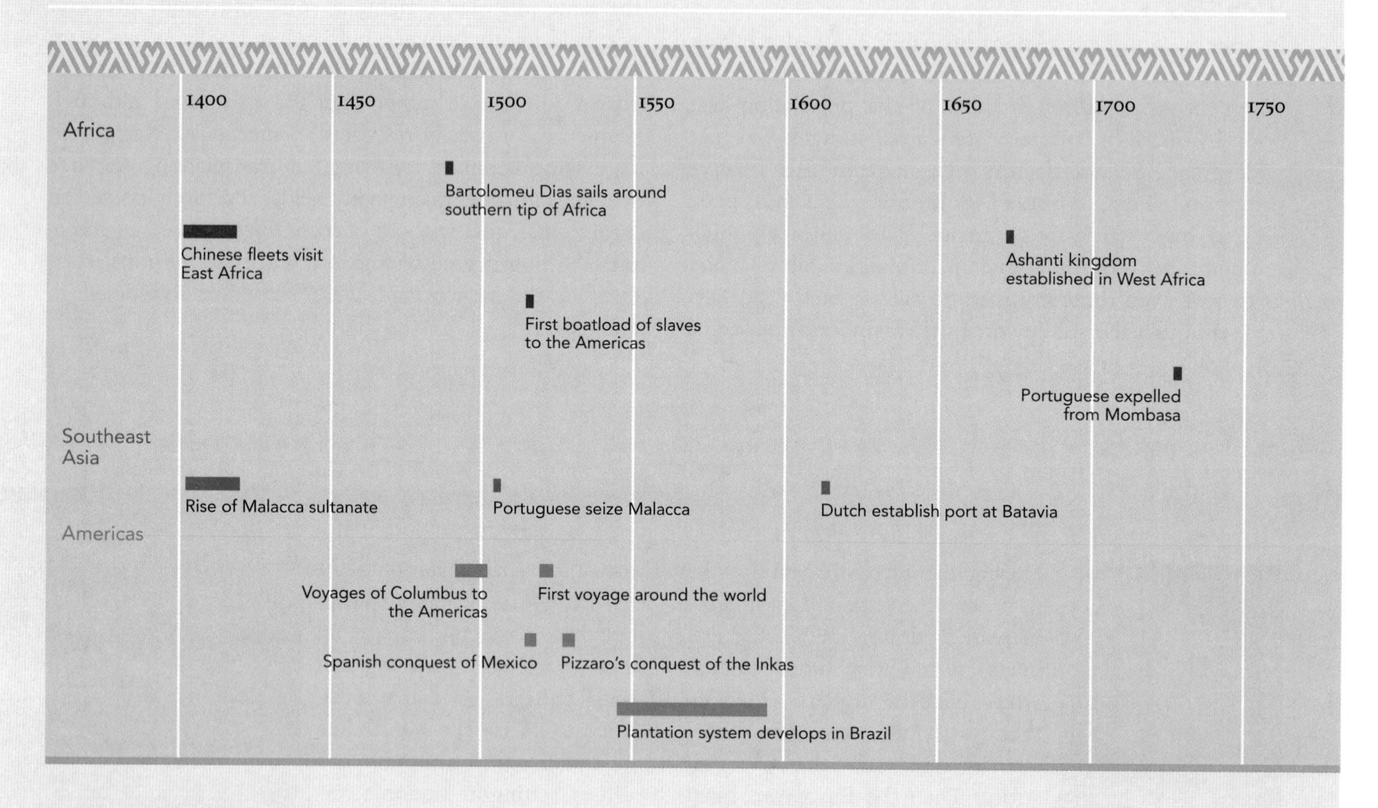

CHAPTER REVIEW

Upon Reflection

Q What were some of the key features of the Columbian Exchange, and what effects did they have on the world trade network?

Q How did the expansion of European power during the Age of Exploration compare with the expansion of the Islamic empires in the Middle East a few centuries earlier?

Q Why were the Spanish conquistadors able to complete their conquest of Latin America so quickly when their contemporaries failed to do so in Africa and Southeast Asia?

Key Terms

portolani (p. 358)
caravels (p. 359)
conquistadors (p. 362)
mestizos (p. 363)
mulattoes (p. 363)
viceroys (p. 363)
creoles (p. 363)
***encomienda* system** (p. 364)
encomienda (p. 365)
Columbian Exchange (p. 368)
Boers (p. 369)
Middle Passage (p. 370)

Suggested Reading

EUROPEAN EXPANSION On the technological aspects of European expansion, see **F. Fernandez-Armesto, ed., *The Times Atlas of World Exploration*** (New York, 1991), and **R. C. Smith, *Vanguard of Empire: Ships of Exploration in the Age of Columbus*** (Oxford, 1993). Also see **A. Pagden, *Lords of All the World: Ideologies of Empire in Spain, Britain, and France, c. 1500–c. 1800*** (New Haven, Conn., 1995). For an overview of the advances in map making that accompanied the Age of Exploration, see **T. Lester, *The Fourth Part of the World: The Race to the Ends of the Earth, and the Epic Story of the Map That Gave America Its Name*** (New York, 2009). Also see **A. Gurney, *Compass: A Story of Exploration and Innovation*** (New York, 2004), and **W. Bernstein's** impressive ***A Splendid Exchange: How Trade Shaped the World*** (New York, 2008).

COUNTRY-SPECIFIC STUDIES A gripping work on the conquistadors is **H. Thomas, *Conquest: Montezuma, Cortés, and the Fall of Old Mexico*** (New York, 1993). On the Dutch, see **J. I. Israel, *Dutch Primacy in World Trade, 1585–1740*** (Oxford, 1989). British activities are chronicled in **S. Sen, *Empire of Free Trade: The East India Company and the Making of the Colonial Marketplace*** (Philadelphia, 1998), and **Anthony Wild's** elegant work ***The East India Company: Trade and Conquest from 1600*** (New York, 2000).

THE SPICE TRADE The effects of European trade in Southeast Asia are discussed in **A. Reid, *Southeast Asia in the Age of Commerce, 1450–1680*** (New Haven, Conn., 1989). On the spice trade, see **A. Dalby, *Dangerous Tastes: The Story of Spices*** (Berkeley, Calif., 2000), and **J. Turner, *Spice: The History of a Temptation*** (New York, 2004).

THE SLAVE TRADE On the African slave trade, see **P. E. Lovejoy, *Transformations in Slavery: A History of Slavery in Africa*** (Cambridge, 1983), and **P. Manning, *Slavery and African Life*** (Cambridge, 1990). **H. Thomas, *The Slave Trade*** (New York, 1997), provides a useful overview.

WOMEN For a brief introduction to women's experiences during the Age of Exploration and global trade, see **S. Hughes** and **B. Hughes, *Women in World History,*** vol. 2 (Armonk, N.Y., 1997). The native American female experience with the European encounter is presented in **R. Gutierrez, *When Jesus Came the Corn Mothers Went Away: Marriage, Sexuality, and Power in New Mexico, 1500–1846*** (Stanford, Calif., 1991).

Visit the CourseMate website at **www.cengagebrain.com** for additional study tools and review materials for this chapter.

CHAPTER 15

Europe Transformed: Reform and State Building

© bpk, Berlin/Art Resource, NY

A nineteenth-century engraving showing Martin Luther before the Diet of Worms

CHAPTER OUTLINE AND FOCUS QUESTIONS

The Reformation of the Sixteenth Century

Q What were the main tenets of Lutheranism and Calvinism, and how did they differ from each other and from Catholicism?

Europe in Crisis, 1560–1650

Q Why is the period between 1560 and 1650 in Europe considered an age of crisis?

Response to Crisis: The Practice of Absolutism

Q What was absolutism, and what were the main characteristics of the absolute monarchies that emerged in France, Prussia, Austria, and Russia?

England and Limited Monarchy

Q How and why did England avoid the path of absolutism?

The Flourishing of European Culture

Q How did the artistic and literary achievements of this era reflect the political and economic developments of the period?

CRITICAL THINKING

Q What was the relationship between European overseas expansion (as traced in Chapter 14) and political, economic, and social developments in Europe?

ON APRIL 18, 1521, A LOWLY MONK stood before the emperor and princes of Germany in the city of Worms (VAWRMZ). He had been called before this august gathering to answer charges of heresy, charges that could threaten his very life. The monk was confronted with a pile of his books and asked if he wished to defend them all or reject a part. Courageously, Martin Luther defended them all and asked to be shown where any part was in error on the basis of "Scripture and plain reason." The emperor was outraged by Luther's response and made his own position clear the next day: "Not only I, but you of this noble German nation, would be forever disgraced if by our negligence not only heresy but the very suspicion of heresy were to survive. After having heard yesterday the obstinate defense of Luther, I regret that I have so long delayed in proceeding against him and his false teaching. I will have no more to do with him." Luther's appearance at Worms set the stage for a serious challenge to the authority of the Catholic Church. This was by no means the first crisis in the church's 1,500-year history, but its consequences were more far-reaching than anyone at Worms in 1521 could have imagined.

After the disintegrative patterns of the fourteenth century, Europe began a remarkable recovery that encompassed a revival of arts and letters in the fifteenth century, known as the Renaissance, and a religious renaissance in the sixteenth century, known as the Reformation. The resulting religious division of Europe (Catholics versus Protestants) was instrumental in beginning a series of wars that dominated much of European history from 1560 to 1650 and exacerbated the economic and social crises that were besetting the region.

One of the responses to the crises of the seventeenth century was a search for order. The most general trend was an extension of monarchical power as a stablizing force. This development, which historians have called **absolutism** or *absolute monarchy*, was most evident in France during the flamboyant reign of Louis XIV, regarded by some as the perfect embodiment of an absolute monarch.

But absolutism was not the only response to the search for order in the seventeenth century. Other states, such as England, reacted very differently to domestic crises, and another system emerged in which monarchs were limited by the power of their representative assemblies. Absolute and limited monarchy were the two poles of seventeenth-century state building.

The Reformation of the Sixteenth Century

FOCUS QUESTION: What were the main tenets of Lutheranism and Calvinism, and how did they differ from each other and from Catholicism?

The **Protestant Reformation** is the name given to the religious reform movement that divided the western Christian church into Catholic and Protestant groups. Although the Reformation began with Martin Luther in the early sixteenth century, several earlier developments had set the stage for religious change.

Background to the Reformation

Changes in the fifteenth century—the age of the Renaissance—helped prepare the way for the dramatic upheavals in sixteenth-century Europe.

THE GROWTH OF STATE POWER In the first half of the fifteenth century, European states had continued the disintegrative patterns of the previous century. In the second half of the fifteenth century, however, recovery had set in, and attempts had been made to reestablish the centralized power of monarchical governments. To characterize the results, some historians have used the label "Renaissance states"; others have spoken of the "**new monarchies**," especially those of France, England, and Spain at the end of the fifteenth century (see Chapter 13).

What was new about these Renaissance monarchs was their concentration of royal authority, their attempts to suppress the nobility, their efforts to control the church in their lands, and their desire to obtain new sources of revenue in order to increase royal power and enhance the military forces at their disposal. Like the rulers of fifteenth-century Italian states, the Renaissance monarchs were often crafty men obsessed with the acquisition and expansion of political power. Of course, none of these characteristics was entirely new; a number of medieval monarchs, especially in the thirteenth century, had also exhibited them. Nevertheless, the Renaissance period marks a significant expansion of centralized royal authority.

No one gave better expression to the Renaissance preoccupation with political power than Niccolò Machiavelli (nee-koh-LOH mahk-ee-uh-VEL-ee) (1469–1527), an Italian who wrote *The Prince* (1513), one of the most influential works on political power in the Western world. Machiavelli's major concerns in *The Prince* were the acquisition, maintenance, and expansion of political power as the means to restore and maintain order. In the Middle Ages, many political theorists stressed the ethical side of a prince's activity—how a ruler ought to behave based on Christian moral principles. Machiavelli bluntly contradicted this approach: "For the gap between how people actually behave and how they ought to behave is so great that anyone who ignores everyday reality in order to live up to an ideal will soon discover he had been taught how to destroy himself, not how to preserve himself."[1] Machiavelli was among the first Western thinkers to abandon morality as the basis for the analysis of political activity. The same emphasis on the ends justifying the means, or on achieving results regardless of the methods employed, had in fact been expressed a thousand years earlier by a court official in India named Kautilya (kow-TIL-yuh) in his treatise on politics, the *Arthasastra* (ar-thuh-SAS-truh) (see Chapter 2).

SOCIAL CHANGES IN THE RENAISSANCE Social changes in the fifteenth century also helped to create an environment in which the Reformation of the sixteenth century could occur. After the severe economic reversals and social upheavals of the fourteenth century, the European economy gradually recovered as manufacturing and trade increased in volume.

As noted in Chapter 12, society in the Middle Ages was divided into three estates: the clergy, or First Estate, whose preeminence was grounded in the belief that people should be guided to spiritual ends; the nobility, or Second Estate, whose privileges rested on the principle that nobles provided security and justice for society; and the peasants and inhabitants of the towns and cities, the Third Estate. Although this social order continued into the Renaissance, some changes also became evident.

Throughout much of Europe, the landholding nobles faced declining real incomes during most of the fourteenth and fifteenth centuries. Many members of the old nobility survived, however, and new blood also infused their ranks. By 1500, the nobles, old and new, who constituted between 2 and 3 percent of the population in most countries, still dominated society, as they had done in the Middle Ages, holding important political posts and serving as advisers to the king.

Except in the heavily urban areas of northern Italy and Flanders, peasants made up the overwhelming mass of the Third Estate—they constituted 85 to 90 percent of the total European population. Serfdom had decreased as the manorial system continued to decline. Increasingly, the labor dues owed by peasants to their lord were converted into rents paid in money. By 1500, especially in western Europe, more and more peasants were becoming legally free. At the same time, peasants in many areas resented their social superiors and sought a greater share of the benefits coming from their labor. In the sixteenth century, the grievances of the peasants, especially in Germany, led many of them to support religious reform movements.

Inhabitants of towns and cities, originally merchants and artisans, constituted the remainder of the Third Estate. But by the fifteenth century, the Renaissance town or city had become more complex. At the top of urban society were the patricians, whose wealth from capitalistic enterprises in trade, industry, and banking enabled them to dominate their urban communities economically, socially, and politically. Below them were the petty burghers—the shopkeepers, artisans, guildmasters, and guildsmen—who were largely concerned with providing goods and services for local consumption. Below these two groups were the propertyless workers earning pitiful wages and the unemployed, living squalid and miserable lives. These poor city-dwellers made up 30 to 40 percent of the urban population. The pitiful conditions of the lower groups in urban society often led them to support calls for radical religious reform in the sixteenth century.

THE IMPACT OF PRINTING The Renaissance witnessed the development of printing, which made an immediate impact on European intellectual life and thought. Printing from hand-carved wooden blocks had been done in the West since the twelfth century and in China even before that. What was new in the fifteenth century in Europe was multiple printing with movable metal type. The development of printing from movable type was a gradual process that culminated sometime between 1445 and 1450; Johannes Gutenberg (yoh-HAH-nuss GOO-ten-bayrk) of Mainz (MYNTS) played an important role in bringing the process to completion. Gutenberg's Bible, completed in 1455 or 1456, was the first true book produced from movable type.

By 1500, there were more than a thousand printers in Europe, who collectively had published almost 40,000 titles (between 8 and 10 million copies). Probably half of these books were religious—Bibles and biblical commentaries, books of devotion, and sermons.

The printing of books encouraged scholarly research and the desire to attain knowledge. Printing also stimulated the development of an ever-expanding lay reading public, a development that had an enormous impact on European society. Indeed, without the printing press, the new religious ideas of the Reformation would never have spread as rapidly as they did in the sixteenth century. Moreover, printing allowed European civilization to compete for the first time with the civilization of China.

PRELUDE TO REFORMATION During the second half of the fifteenth century, the new Classical learning of the Italian Renaissance spread to the European countries north of the Alps and spawned a movement called **Christian humanism** or **northern Renaissance humanism**, whose major goal was the reform of Christendom. The Christian humanists believed in the ability of human beings to reason and improve themselves and thought that through education in the sources of Classical, and especially Christian, antiquity, they could instill an inner piety or an inward religious feeling that would bring about a reform of the church and society. To change society, then, they believed they must first change the human beings who composed it.

The most influential of all the Christian humanists was Desiderius Erasmus (dez-i-DEER-ee-us i-RAZZ-mus) (1466–1536), who formulated and popularized the reform program of Christian humanism. He called his conception of religion "the philosophy of Christ," by which he meant that Christianity should be a guiding philosophy for the direction of daily life rather than the system of dogmatic beliefs and practices that the medieval church seemed to stress. No doubt his work helped prepare the way for the Reformation; as contemporaries proclaimed, "Erasmus laid the egg that Luther hatched."

CHURCH AND RELIGION ON THE EVE OF THE REFORMATION Corruption in the Catholic Church was another factor that encouraged people to want reform. Between 1450 and 1520, a series of popes—called the Renaissance popes—failed to meet the church's spiritual needs. The popes were supposed to be the spiritual leaders of the Catholic Church, but as rulers of the Papal States, they were all too often involved in worldly concerns. Julius II (1503–1513), the fiery "warrior-pope," personally led armies against his enemies, much to the disgust of pious Christians, who viewed the pope as a spiritual leader. As one intellectual wrote, "How, O bishop standing in the room of the Apostles, dare you teach the people the things that pertain to war?" Many high church officials regarded their church offices mainly as opportunities to advance their careers and their wealth, and many ordinary parish priests seemed ignorant of their spiritual duties.

While the leaders of the church were failing to meet their responsibilities, ordinary people were clamoring for meaningful religious expression and certainty of salvation. As a result, for some the process of salvation became almost mechanical. As more and more people sought certainty of salvation through veneration of **relics** (bones or other objects intimately association with the saints), collections of relics grew. Frederick the Wise, elector of Saxony and Martin Luther's prince, had amassed nearly 19,000 relics to which were attached **indulgences** that could reduce one's time in purgatory by 1,443 years. (An indulgence is a remission, after death, of all or part of the punishment due to sin.) Other people sought certainty of salvation in more spiritual terms by participating in the popular mystical movement known as the Modern Devotion, which downplayed religious dogma and stressed the need to follow the teachings of Jesus.

Martin Luther and the Reformation in Germany

Martin Luther (1483–1546) was a monk and a professor at the University of Wittenberg (VIT-ten-bayrk), where he lectured on the Bible. Probably sometime between 1513 and 1516, through his study of the Bible, he arrived at an answer to a problem—the assurance of salvation—that had disturbed him since his entry into the monastery.

Catholic doctrine had emphasized that both faith and good works were required for a Christian to achieve personal salvation. In Luther's eyes, human beings, weak and powerless in the sight of an almighty God, could never do enough good works to merit salvation. Through his study of the Bible, Luther came to believe that humans are saved not through their good works but through faith in the promises of God, made possible by the sacrifice of Jesus on the cross. This doctrine of salvation, or justification by grace through faith alone, became the primary doctrine of the Protestant Reformation (**justification by faith** is the act by which a person is made deserving of salvation). Because Luther had arrived at this doctrine from his study of the Bible, the Bible became for Luther, as for all other Protestants, the chief guide to religious truth.

Luther did not see himself as a rebel, but he was greatly upset by the widespread selling of indulgences. Especially offensive in his eyes was the monk Johann Tetzel, who hawked indulgences with the slogan: "As soon as the coin in the coffer [money box] rings, the soul from purgatory springs." Greatly angered, in 1517 Luther issued a stunning indictment of the abuses in the sale of indulgences, known as the Ninety-Five Theses. Thousands of copies were printed and quickly spread to all parts of Germany.

Unable to accept Luther's ideas, the church excommunicated him in January 1521. He was also summoned to appear before the imperial diet or Reichstag (RYKHSS-tahk) of the Holy Roman Empire, convened by the newly elected Emperor Charles V (1519–1556). Ordered to recant the heresies he had espoused, Luther refused and made the famous reply that became the battle cry of the Reformation:

> Unless I am convicted by Scripture and plain reason—I do not accept the authority of popes and councils, for they have contradicted each other—my conscience is captive to the Word of God. I cannot and I will not recant anything, for to go against conscience is neither right nor safe. Here I stand, I cannot do otherwise. God help me. Amen.[2]

Members of the Reichstag were outraged and demanded that Luther be arrested and delivered to the emperor. But Luther's ruler, Elector Frederick of Saxony, stepped in and protected him.

During the next few years, Luther's movement began to grow and spread. As it made an impact on the common people, it also created new challenges. This was especially true when the Peasants' War erupted in 1524. Social discontent created by their pitiful conditions became entangled with religious revolt as the German peasants looked to Martin Luther for support. But when the peasants took up arms and revolted against their landlords, Luther turned against them and called on the German princes, who in Luther's eyes were ordained by God to maintain peace and order, to crush the rebels. By May 1525, the German princes had ruthlessly suppressed the peasant hordes. By this time, Luther found himself dependent on the state authorities for the growth of his reformed church.

Luther now succeeded in gaining the support of many of the rulers of the three hundred or so German states that made up the Holy Roman Empire. These rulers quickly took control of the churches in their territories. The Lutheran churches in Germany (and later in Scandinavia) became territorial or state churches in which the state supervised the affairs of the church. As part of the development of these state-dominated churches, Luther also instituted new religious services to replace the Catholic Mass. These focused on Bible reading, preaching the word of God, and singing hymns.

POLITICS AND RELIGION IN THE GERMAN REFORMATION From its very beginning, the fate of Luther's movement was closely tied to political affairs. In 1519, Charles I, king of Spain and the grandson of Emperor Maximilian, was elected Holy Roman Emperor as Charles V. Charles V ruled over an immense empire, consisting of Spain and its

© bpk, Berlin/Kupferstichkabinett/Jörg P. Anders/Art Resource, NY

A Reformation Woodcut. In the 1520s, after Luther's return to Wittenberg, his teachings began to spread rapidly, ending ultimately in a reform movement supported by state authorities. Pamphlets containing picturesque woodcuts were important in the spread of Luther's ideas. In the woodcut shown here, the crucified Jesus attends Luther's service on the left, while on the right the pope is at a table selling indulgences.

overseas possessions, the traditional Austrian Habsburg lands, Bohemia, Hungary, the Low Countries, and the kingdom of Naples in southern Italy. Politically, Charles wanted to maintain his enormous empire; religiously, he hoped to preserve the unity of his empire in the Catholic faith.

The internal political situation in the Holy Roman Empire was not in Charles's favor, however. Although all the German states owed loyalty to the emperor, in the Middle Ages these states had become quite independent of imperial authority. By the time Charles V was able to bring military forces to Germany in 1546, Lutheranism had become well established, and the Lutheran princes were well organized. Unable to defeat them, Charles was forced to negotiate a truce. Religious warfare in Germany came to an end in 1555 with the Peace of Augsburg (OUKS-boork). The division of Christianity was formally acknowledged; Lutheran states were to have the same legal rights as Catholic states. Although the German states were now free to choose between Catholicism and Lutheranism, the peace settlement did not recognize the principle of religious toleration for individuals. The right of each German ruler to determine the religion of his subjects was accepted, but not the right of the subjects to choose their own religion. With the Peace of Augsburg, what had at first been merely feared was now certain: the ideal of Christian unity was forever lost. The rapid spread of new Protestant groups made this a certainty.

The Spread of the Protestant Reformation

Switzerland was home to two major Reformation movements: Zwinglianism and Calvinism. Ulrich Zwingli (OOL-rikh TSFING-lee) (1484–1531) was ordained a priest in 1506 and accepted an appointment as a cathedral priest in the Great Minster of Zürich (ZOOR-ik *or* TSIH-rikh) in 1518. Zwingli's preaching of the Gospel caused such unrest that in 1523 the city council decided to institute evangelical reforms. Relics and images were abolished; all paintings and decorations were removed from the churches and replaced by whitewashed walls. The Mass was replaced by a new liturgy consisting of Scripture reading, prayer, and sermons. Monasticism, pilgrimages, the veneration of saints, clerical celibacy, and the pope's authority were all abolished as remnants of papal Christianity.

As his movement began to spread to other cities in Switzerland, Zwingli sought an alliance with Martin Luther and the German reformers. Although both the German and the Swiss reformers realized the need for unity to defend against the opposition of the Catholic authorities, they were unable to agree on the interpretation of the Lord's Supper, the sacrament of Communion (see the box on p. 387). Zwingli believed that the scriptural words "This is my body, this is my blood" should be taken figuratively, not literally, and refused to accept

OPPOSING ≺ VIEWPOINTS

A Reformation Debate: Conflict at Marburg

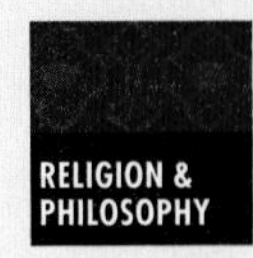

RELIGION & PHILOSOPHY

Debates played a crucial role in the Reformation period. They were a primary instrument for introducing the Reformation in innumerable cities as well as a means of resolving differences among like-minded Protestant groups. This selection contains an excerpt from the vivacious and often brutal debate between Luther and Zwingli over the sacrament of the Lord's Supper at Marburg in 1529. The two protagonists failed to reach agreement.

The Marburg Colloquy, 1529

THE HESSIAN CHANCELLOR FEIGE: My gracious prince and lord [Landgrave Philip of Hesse] has summoned you for the express and urgent purpose of settling the dispute over the sacrament of the Lord's Supper. . . . Let everyone on both sides present his arguments in a spirit of moderation, as becomes such matters. . . . Now then, Doctor Luther, you may proceed.

LUTHER: Noble prince, gracious lord! Undoubtedly the colloquy is well intentioned. . . . Although I have no intention of changing my mind, which is firmly made up, I will nevertheless present the grounds of my belief and show where the others are in error. . . . Your basic contentions are these: In the last analysis you wish to prove that a body cannot be in two places at once, and you produce arguments about the unlimited body which are based on natural reason. I do not question how Christ can be God and man and how the two natures can be joined. For God is more powerful than all our ideas, and we must submit to his word. Prove that Christ's body is not there where the Scripture says, "This is my body!" Rational proofs I will not listen to. . . . God is beyond all mathematics and the words of God are to be revered and carried out in awe. It is God who commands, "Take, eat, this is my body."
I request, therefore, valid scriptural proof to the contrary.

Luther writes on the table in chalk, "This is my body," and covers the words with a velvet cloth.

OECOLAMPADIUS [leader of the reform movement in Basel and a Zwinglian partisan]: The sixth chapter of John clarifies the other scriptural passages. Christ is not speaking there about a local presence. "The flesh is of no avail," he says. It is not my intention to employ rational, or geometrical, arguments—neither am I denying the power of God—but as long as I have the complete faith I will speak from that. For Christ is risen; he sits at the right hand of God; and so he cannot be present in the bread. Our view is neither new nor sacrilegious, but is based on faith and Scripture. . . .

ZWINGLI: I insist that the words of the Lord's Supper must be figurative. This is ever apparent, and even required by the article of faith: "taken up into heaven, seated at the right hand of the Father." Otherwise, it would be absurd to look for him in the Lord's Supper at the same time that Christ is telling us that he is in heaven. One and the same body cannot possibly be in different places. . . .

LUTHER: I call upon you as before: your basic contentions are shaky. Give way, and give glory to God!

ZWINGLI: And we call upon you to give glory to God and to quit begging the question! The issue at stake is this: Where is the proof of your position? I am willing to consider your words carefully—no harm meant! You're trying to outwit me. I stand by this passage in the sixth chapter of John, verse 63, and shall not be shaken from it. You'll have to sing another tune.

LUTHER: You're being obnoxious.

ZWINGLI: (*excitedly*) Don't you believe that Christ was attempting in John 6 to help those who did not understand?

LUTHER: You're trying to dominate things! You insist on passing judgment! Leave that to someone else! . . . It is your point that must be proved, not mine. But let us stop this sort of thing. It serves no purpose.

ZWINGLI: It certainly does! It is for you to prove that the passage in John 6 speaks of a physical repast.

LUTHER: You express yourself poorly and make about as much progress as a cane standing in a corner. You're going nowhere.

ZWINGLI: NO, no, no! This is the passage that will break your neck!

(Continued)

LUTHER: Don't be so sure of yourself. Necks don't break this way. You're in Hesse, not Switzerland.

How did the positions of Zwingli and Luther on the sacrament of the Lord's Supper differ? What was the purpose of this debate? Based on this example, why did many Reformation debates lead to further hostility rather than compromise and unity between religious and sectarian opponents? What implication did this have for the future of the Protestant Reformation?

Source: "The Marburg Colloquy," edited by Donald Ziegler, from GREAT DEBATES OF THE REFORMATION, edited by Donald Ziegler, copyright © 1969 by Donald Ziegler.

Luther's insistence on the real presence of the body and blood of Christ "in, with, and under the bread and wine." In October 1531, war erupted between the Swiss Protestant and Catholic states. Zürich's army was routed, and Zwingli was found wounded on the battlefield. His enemies killed him, cut up his body, burned the pieces, and scattered the ashes. The leadership of Swiss Protestantism now passed to John Calvin, the systematic theologian and organizer of the Protestant movement.

CALVIN AND CALVINISM John Calvin (1509–1564) was educated in his native France, but after converting to Protestantism, he was forced to flee to the safety of Switzerland. In 1536, he published the first edition of the *Institutes of the Christian Religion*, a masterful synthesis of Protestant thought that immediately secured his reputation as one of the new leaders of Protestantism.

On most important doctrines, Calvin stood very close to Luther. He adhered to the doctrine of justification by faith alone to explain how humans achieved salvation. But Calvin also placed much emphasis on the absolute sovereignty of God or the all-powerful nature of God—what Calvin called the "power, grace, and glory of God." One of the ideas derived from his emphasis on the absolute sovereignty of God—**predestination**—gave a unique cast to Calvin's teachings. This "eternal decree," as Calvin called it, meant that God had predestined some people to be saved (the elect) and others to be damned (the reprobate). According to Calvin, "He has once for all determined, both whom He would admit to salvation, and whom He would condemn to destruction."[3] Although Calvin stressed that there could be no absolute certainty of salvation, his followers did not always make this distinction. The practical psychological effect of predestination was to give later Calvinists an unshakable conviction that they were doing God's work on earth, making Calvinism a dynamic and activist faith.

In 1536, Calvin began working to reform the city of Geneva. He was able to fashion a tightly organized church order that employed both clergy and laymen in the service of the church. The Consistory, a special body for enforcing moral discipline, functioned as a court to oversee the moral life, daily behavior, and doctrinal orthodoxy of Genevans and to admonish and correct deviants. Citizens of Geneva were punished for such varied "crimes" as dancing, singing obscene songs, drunkenness, swearing, and playing cards.

Calvin's success in Geneva enabled the city to become a vibrant center of Protestantism. Following Calvin's lead, missionaries trained in Geneva were sent to all parts of Europe. Calvinism became established in France, the Netherlands, Scotland, and central and eastern Europe, and by the mid-sixteenth century, Calvin's Geneva stood as the fortress of the Reformation.

THE ENGLISH REFORMATION The English Reformation was rooted in politics, not religion. King Henry VIII (1509–1547) had a strong desire to divorce his first wife, Catherine of Aragon, with whom he had a daughter, Mary, but no male heir. The king wanted to marry Anne Boleyn (BUH-lin *or* buh-LIN), with whom he had fallen in love. Impatient with the pope's unwillingness to grant him an annulment of his marriage, Henry turned to England's own church courts. As archbishop of Canterbury and head of the highest church court in England, Thomas Cranmer ruled in May 1533 that the king's marriage to Catherine was "absolutely void." At the beginning of June, Anne was crowned queen, and three months later, a child was born; much to the king's disappointment, the baby was a a girl (the future Queen Elizabeth I).

In 1534, at Henry's request, Parliament moved to finalize the break of the Church of England with Rome. The Act of Supremacy of 1534 declared that the king was "the only supreme head on earth of the Church of England," a position that gave him control of doctrine, clerical appointments, and discipline. Although Henry VIII had broken with the papacy, little change occurred in matters of doctrine, theology, and ceremony. Some of his supporters, including Archbishop Cranmer, sought a religious reformation as well as an administrative one, but Henry was unyielding. But he died in 1547 and was succeeded by his son, the underage and sickly Edward VI (1547–1553), and during Edward's reign, Cranmer and others inclined toward Protestant doctrines were able to move the Church of England (or Anglican Church) in a more Protestant direction. New acts of Parliament gave the clergy the right to marry and created a new Protestant church service.

Edward VI was succeeded by Mary (1553–1558), a Catholic who attempted to return England to Catholicism. Her actions aroused much anger, however, especially when "bloody Mary" burned more than three hundred Protestant heretics. By the end of Mary's reign, England was more Protestant than it had been at the beginning.

The Social Impact of the Protestant Reformation

The Protestants were especially important in developing a new view of the family. Because Protestantism had eliminated any idea of special holiness for celibacy and had abolished both monasticism and a celibate clergy, the family could be placed at the center of human life, and a new stress on "mutual love between man and wife" could be extolled (see the comparative essay "Marriage in the Early Modern World" on p. 390).

But were doctrine and reality the same? Most often, reality reflected the traditional roles of husband as the ruler and wife as the obedient servant whose chief duty was to please her husband. Luther stated it clearly:

> The rule remains with the husband, and the wife is compelled to obey him by God's command. He rules the home and the state, wages war, defends his possessions, tills the soil, builds, plants, etc. The woman on the other hand is like a nail driven into the wall . . . so the wife should stay at home and look after the affairs of the household, as one who has been deprived of the ability of administering those affairs that are outside and that concern the state. She does not go beyond her most personal duties.[4]

Obedience to her husband was not a wife's only role; her other important duty was to bear children. To Calvin and Luther, this function of women was part of the divine plan, and for most Protestant women, family life was their only destiny. Overall, the Protestant Reformation did not noticeably alter women's subordinate place in society.

The Catholic Reformation

By the mid-sixteenth century, Lutheranism had become established in Germany and Scandinavia and Calvinism in Scotland, Switzerland, France, the Netherlands, and eastern Europe. In England, the split from Rome had resulted in the creation of a national church. The situation in Europe did not look particularly favorable for the Roman Catholic Church. Nevertheless, the Catholic Church underwent a revitalization in the sixteenth century that gave it new strength.

CATHOLIC REFORMATION OR COUNTER-REFORMATION?

But was this revitalization a **Catholic Reformation** or a Counter-Reformation? Some historians prefer the term *Counter-Reformation* to focus on the aspects that were a direct reaction against the Protestant movement. Historians who prefer the term *Catholic Reformation* point out that elements of reform were already present in the Catholic Church at the end of the fifteenth century and the beginning of the sixteenth century. Especially noticeable were the calls for reform from the religious orders of the Franciscans, Dominicans, and Augustinians. Members of these groups put particular emphasis on preaching to laypeople. Another example was the Oratory of Divine Love. First organized in Italy in 1497, the Oratory was an informal group of clergy and laymen who worked to foster reform by emphasizing personal spiritual development and outward acts of charity. Its members included a Spanish archbishop, Cardinal Ximenes (khee-MAY-ness), who was especially active in using Christian humanism to reform the church in Spain.

No doubt, both positions on the nature of the reformation of the Catholic Church contain elements of truth. The Catholic Reformation revived the best features of medieval Catholicism and then adjusted them to meet new conditions, as is most apparent in the emergence of a new mysticism, closely tied to the traditions of Catholic piety, and the revival of monasticism by the regeneration of older religious orders and the founding of new orders.

THE SOCIETY OF JESUS Of all the new religious orders, the most important was the Society of Jesus, known as the Jesuits; it was founded by a Spanish nobleman, Ignatius of Loyola (ig-NAY-shuss of loi-OH-luh) (1491–1556). Loyola brought together a small group of individuals who were recognized as a religious order by the pope in 1540. The new order was grounded on the principles of absolute obedience to the papacy, a strict hierarchical order for the society, the use of education to achieve its goals, and a dedication to engage in "conflict for God." A special vow of absolute obedience to the pope made the Jesuits an important instrument for papal policy. Jesuit missionaries proved singularly successful in restoring Catholicism to parts of Germany and eastern Europe.

Another prominent Jesuit activity was the propagation of the Catholic faith among non-Christians. Francis Xavier (ZAY-vee-ur) (1506–1552), one of the original members of the Society of Jesus, carried the message of

COMPARATIVE ESSAY

Marriage in the Early Modern World

Marriage is an ancient institution. In China, myths about the beginnings of Chinese civilization maintained that the rites of marriage began with the primordial couple Fuxi and Nugun and that these rites actually preceded such discoveries as fire, farming, and medicine. In the early modern world, family and marriage were inseparable and at the center of all civilizations.

In the early modern period, the family was still at the heart of Europe's social organization. For the most part, people viewed the family in traditional terms, as a patriarchal institution in which the husband dominated his wife and children. The upper classes in particular thought of the family as a "house," an association whose collective interests were more important than those of its individual members. Parents (especially fathers) generally selected marriage partners for their children, based on the interests of the family. When the son of a French noble asked about his upcoming marriage, the father responded, "Mind your own business." Details were worked out well in advance, sometimes when children were only two or three years old, and were set out in a legally binding contract. An important negotiating point was the size of the dowry, money presented by the wife's family to the groom upon marriage. The dowry could be a large sum, and all families were expected to provide dowries for their daughters.

Arranged marriages were not unique to Europe but were common throughout the world. In China, marriages were normally arranged for the benefit of the family, often by a go-between, and the groom and bride were usually not consulted. Frequently, they did not meet until the marriage ceremony. Love was obviously not a reason for marriage and in fact was often viewed as a detriment because it could distract the married couple from their responsibility to the larger family unit. In Japan too, marriages were arranged, often by the heads of dominant families in rural areas, and the new wife moved in with the family of her husband. In India, not only were marriages arranged, but it was not uncommon

Marriage Ceremonies. At the left is a detail of a marriage ceremony in Italy from a fresco painted by Domenico di Bartolo in 1443. At the right is a seventeenth-century Mughal painting from India showing Shah Jahan, the Mughal emperor (with halo). He is riding to the wedding celebration of his son, who rides before him.

Santa Maria della Scala Hospital, Siena//© Alfredo Dagli Orti/The Art Archive at Art Resource, NY

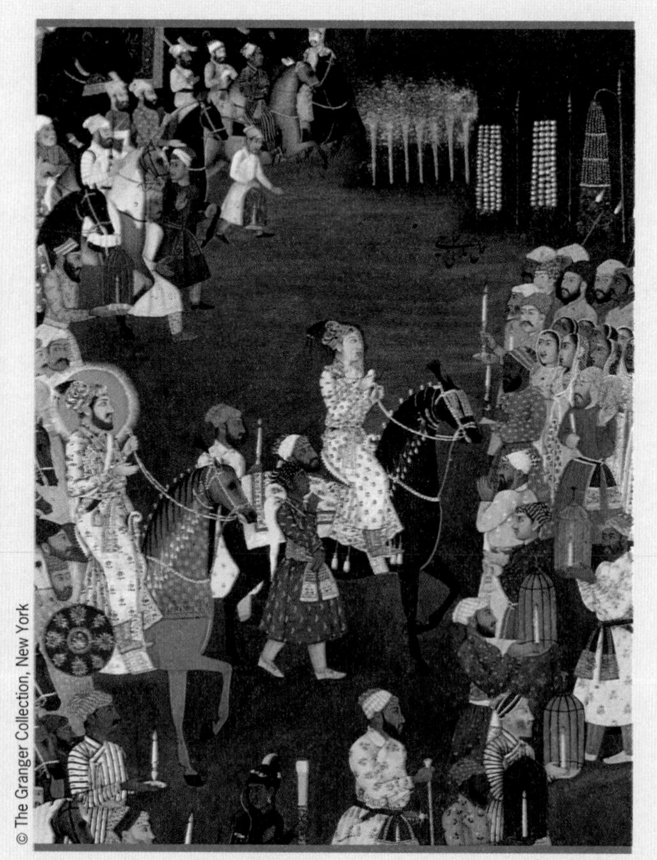

© The Granger Collection, New York

(Continued)

(Comparative Essay Continued)

for women to be married before the age of ten. In colonial Latin America, parents selected marriage partners for their children and often chose a dwelling for the couple as well. In many areas, before members of the lower classes could marry, they had to offer gifts to the powerful noble landlords in the region and obtain their permission. These nobles often refused to allow women to marry in order to keep them as servants.

Arranged marriages were the logical result of a social system in which men dominated and women's primary role was to bear children, manage the household, and work in the fields. Not until the nineteenth century did a feminist movement emerge in Europe to improve the rights of women. By the beginning of the twentieth century, that movement had spread to other parts of the world. The New Culture Movement in China, for example, advocated the free choice of spouses. Although the trend throughout the world is toward allowing people to choose their mates, in some places, especially in rural communities, families continue to play an active role in selecting marriage partners.

In what ways were marriage practices similar in the West and East during the early modern period? Were there any significant differences?

Catholic Christianity to the East. After attracting tens of thousands of converts in India, he traveled to Malacca and the Moluccas before finally reaching Japan in 1549. He spoke highly of the Japanese: "They are a people of excellent morals—good in general and not malicious."[5] Thousands of Japanese, especially in the southernmost islands, became Christians. In 1552, Xavier set out for China but died of fever before he reached the mainland.

Although conversion efforts in Japan proved short-lived, Jesuit activity in China, especially that of the Italian Matteo Ricci (ma-TAY-oh REE-chee), was more long-lasting. Recognizing the Chinese pride in their own culture, the Jesuits attempted to draw parallels between Christian and Confucian concepts and to show the similarities between Christian morality and Confucian ethics. For their part, the missionaries were much impressed with many aspects of Chinese civilization, and reports of their experiences heightened European curiosity about this great society on the other side of the world.

A REFORMED PAPACY A reformed papacy was another important factor in the development of the Catholic Reformation. The involvement of Renaissance popes in dubious finances and Italian political and military affairs had created numerous sources of corruption. It took the jolt of the Protestant Reformation to bring about serious reform. Pope Paul III (1534–1549) perceived the need for change and took the audacious step of appointing a reform commission to ascertain the church's ills. The commission's report in 1537 blamed the church's problems on the corrupt policies of popes and cardinals. Paul III also formally recognized the Jesuits and summoned the Council of Trent.

THE COUNCIL OF TRENT In March 1545, a group of high church officials met in the city of Trent on the border between Germany and Italy and initiated the Council of Trent, which met intermittently from 1545 to 1563 in three major sessions. The final decrees of the Council of Trent reaffirmed traditional Catholic teachings in opposition to Protestant beliefs. Scripture and tradition were affirmed as equal authorities in religious matters; only the church could interpret Scripture. Both faith and good works were declared necessary for salvation. Belief in purgatory and in the use of indulgences was strengthened, although the selling of indulgences was prohibited.

After the Council of Trent, the Roman Catholic Church possessed a clear body of doctrine and a unified structure under the acknowledged supremacy of the popes. Although the Roman Catholic Church had become one Christian denomination among many, the church entered a new phase of its history with a spirit of confidence.

Europe in Crisis, 1560–1650

FOCUS QUESTION: Why is the period between 1560 and 1650 in Europe considered an age of crisis?

Between 1560 and 1650, Europe experienced religious wars, revolutions and constitutional crises, economic and social disintegration, and a witchcraft craze. It was truly an age of crisis.

Politics and the Wars of Religion in the Sixteenth Century

By 1560, Calvinism and Catholicism had become activist religions dedicated to spreading the word of God as they interpreted it. Although their struggle for the minds and hearts of Europeans was at the center of the religious wars of the sixteenth century, economic, social, and political forces also played important roles in these conflicts.

THE FRENCH WARS OF RELIGION (1562–1598) Religion was central to the French civil wars of the sixteenth century. The growth of Calvinism had led to persecution by the French kings, but the latter did little to stop the spread of Calvinism. Huguenots (HYOO-guh-nots) (as the French Calvinists were called) constituted only about 7 percent of the population, but 40 to 50 percent of the French nobility became Huguenots, including the house of Bourbon (boor-BOHN), which stood next to the Valois (val-WAH) in the royal line of succession. The conversion of so many nobles made the Huguenots a potentially dangerous political threat to monarchical power. Still, the Calvinist minority was greatly outnumbered by the Catholic majority, and the Valois monarchy was staunchly Catholic.

For thirty years, battles raged in France between Catholic and Calvinist parties. Finally, in 1589, Henry of Navarre, the political leader of the Huguenots and a member of the Bourbon dynasty, succeeded to the throne as Henry IV (1589–1610). Realizing, however, that he would never be accepted by Catholic France, Henry converted to Catholicism. With his coronation in 1594, the Wars of Religion had finally come to an end. The Edict of Nantes (NAHNT) in 1598 solved the religious problem by acknowledging Catholicism as the official religion of France while guaranteeing the Huguenots the right to worship and to enjoy all political privileges, including the holding of public offices.

PHILIP II AND MILITANT CATHOLICISM The greatest advocate of militant Catholicism in the second half of the sixteenth century was King Philip II of Spain (1556–1598), the son and heir of Charles V. Philip's reign ushered in an age of Spanish greatness, both politically and culturally. Philip II had inherited from his father Spain, the Netherlands, and possessions in Italy and the Americas. To strengthen his control, Philip insisted on strict conformity to Catholicism and strong monarchical authority. Achieving the latter was not an easy task, because each of the lands of his empire had its own structure of government.

Philip's attempt to strengthen his control over the Spanish Netherlands, which consisted of seventeen provinces (the modern Netherlands and Belgium), soon led to a revolt. The nobles, who stood to lose the most politically, strongly opposed Philip's efforts. Religion also became a major catalyst for rebellion when Philip attempted to crush Calvinism. Violence erupted in 1566, and the revolt became organized, especially in the northern provinces, where the Dutch, under the leadership of William of Nassau, the prince of Orange, offered growing resistance. The struggle dragged on for decades until 1609, when the war ended with a twelve-year truce that virtually recognized the independence of the northern provinces. These seven northern provinces, which called themselves the United Provinces of the Netherlands, became the core of the modern Dutch state.

To most Europeans at the beginning of the seventeenth century, Spain still seemed the greatest power of the age, but the reality was quite different. The Spanish treasury was empty, the armed forces were obsolescent, and the government was inefficient. Spain continued to play the role of a great power, but real power had shifted to England.

THE ENGLAND OF ELIZABETH When Elizabeth Tudor, the daughter of Henry VIII and Anne Boleyn, ascended the throne in 1558, England was home to fewer than 4 million people. Yet during her reign (1558–1603), the small island kingdom became the leader of the Protestant nations of Europe and laid the foundations for a world empire.

Intelligent, cautious, and self-confident, Elizabeth moved quickly to solve the difficult religious problem she inherited from her half-sister, Queen Mary. Elizabeth's religious policy was based on moderation and compromise. She repealed the Catholic laws of Mary's reign, and a new Act of Supremacy designated Elizabeth as "the only supreme governor" of both church and state. The Church of England under Elizabeth was basically Protestant, but it was of a moderate bent that kept most people satisfied.

Caution and moderation also dictated Elizabeth's foreign policy. Nevertheless, Elizabeth was gradually drawn into conflict with Spain. Having resisted for years the idea of invading England as too impractical, Philip II of Spain was finally persuaded to do so by advisers who assured him that the people of England would rise against their queen when the Spaniards arrived. A successful invasion of England would mean the overthrow of heresy and the return of England to Catholicism. Philip ordered preparations for a fleet of warships, the *armada*, to spearhead the invasion of England.

The armada was a disaster. The Spanish fleet that finally set sail had neither the ships nor the manpower that Philip had planned to send. Battered by a number of encounters with the English, the Spanish fleet sailed back to Spain by a northward route around Scotland and Ireland, where it was further pounded by storms.

Economic and Social Crises

The period of European history from 1560 to 1650 witnessed severe economic and social crises as well as political upheaval. Economic contraction began to be evident

© Stapleton Collection/CORBIS

Procession of Queen Elizabeth I. Intelligent and learned, Elizabeth Tudor was familiar with Latin and Greek and spoke several European languages. Served by able administrators, Elizabeth ruled for nearly forty-five years and generally avoided open military action against any major power. This picture, painted near the end of her reign, shows the queen in a ceremonial procession.

in some parts of Europe by the 1620s. In the 1630s and 1640s, as imports of silver from the Americas declined, economic recession intensified, especially in the Mediterranean area.

POPULATION DECLINE Population trends of the sixteenth and seventeenth centuries also reveal Europe's worsening conditions. The population of Europe increased from 60 million in 1500 to 85 million by 1600, the first major recovery of the European population since the devastation of the Black Death in the mid-fourteenth century. By 1650, however, records indicate a decline in the population, especially in central and southern Europe. Europe's longtime adversaries—war, famine, and plague—continued to affect population levels. These problems created social tensions, some of which were manifested in an obsession with witches.

WITCHCRAFT MANIA Hysteria over witchcraft affected the lives of many Europeans in the sixteenth and seventeenth centuries. Perhaps more than 100,000 people were prosecuted throughout Europe on charges of witchcraft. As more and more people were brought to trial, the fear of witches, as well as the fear of being accused of witchcraft, escalated to frightening levels (see the box on p. 394).

Common people—usually those who were poor and without property—were more likely to be accused of witchcraft. Indeed, where lists are given, those mentioned most often are milkmaids, peasant women, and servant girls. In the witchcraft trials of the sixteenth and seventeenth centuries, more than 75 percent of the accused were women, most of them single or widowed and many over fifty years old.

That women should be the chief victims of witchcraft trials was hardly accidental. Nicholas Rémy (nee-koh-LAH ray-MEE), a witchcraft judge in France in the 1590s, found it "not unreasonable that this scum of humanity, i.e., witches, should be drawn chiefly from the feminine sex." To another judge, it came as no surprise that witches would confess to sexual experiences with Satan: "The Devil uses them so, because he knows that women love carnal pleasures, and he means to bind them to his allegiance by such agreeable provocations."[6]

By the mid-seventeenth century the witchcraft hysteria had begun to subside. As governments grew stronger, fewer magistrates were willing to accept the unsettling

A Witchcraft Trial in France

Persecutions for witchcraft reached their high point in the sixteenth and seventeenth centuries, when tens of thousands of people were brought to trial. In this excerpt from the minutes of a trial in France in 1652, we can see why the accused witch stood little chance of exonerating herself.

The Trial of Suzanne Gaudry

28 May, 1652. . . . Interrogation of Suzanne Gaudry, prisoner at the court of Rieux. . . . During interrogations on May 28 and May 29, the prisoner confessed to a number of activities involving the devil.

Deliberation of the Court—June 3, 1652

The undersigned advocates of the Court have seen these interrogations and answers. They say that the aforementioned Suzanne Gaudry confesses that she is a witch, that she had given herself to the devil, that she had renounced God, Lent, and baptism, that she has been marked on the shoulder, that she has cohabited with the devil and that she has been to the dances, confessing only to have cast a spell upon and caused to die a beast of Philippe Cornié. . . .

Third Interrogation, June 27

This prisoner being led into the chamber, she was examined to know if things were not as she had said and confessed at the beginning of her imprisonment.

—Answers no, and that what she has said was done so by force.

Pressed to say the truth, that otherwise she would be subjected to torture, having pointed out to her that her aunt was burned for this same subject.

—Answers that she is not a witch. . . .

She was placed in the hands of the officer in charge of torture, throwing herself on her knees, struggling to cry, uttering several exclamations, without being able, nevertheless, to shed a tear. Saying at every moment that she is not a witch.

The Torture

On this same day, being at the place of torture.

This prisoner, before being strapped down, was admonished to maintain herself in her first confessions and to renounce her lover.

—Says that she denies everything she has said, and that she has no lover. Feeling herself being strapped down, says that she is not a witch, while struggling to cry . . . and upon being asked why she confessed to being one, said that she was forced to say it.

Told that she was not forced, that on the contrary she declared herself to be a witch without any threat.

—Says that she confessed it and that she is not a witch, and being a little stretched [on the rack] screams ceaselessly that she is not a witch.

Asked if she did not confess that she had been a witch for twenty-six years.

—Says that she said it, that she retracts it, crying that she is not a witch.

Asked if she did not make Philippe Cornié's horse die, as she confessed.

—Answers no, crying Jesus-Maria, that she is not a witch.

The mark having been probed by the officer, in the presence of Doctor Bouchain, it was adjudged by the aforesaid doctor and officer truly to be the mark of the devil.

Being more tightly stretched upon the torture rack, urged to maintain her confessions.

—Said that it was true that she is a witch and that she would maintain what she had said.

Asked how long she has been in subjugation to the devil.

—Answers that it was twenty years ago that the devil appeared to her, being in her lodgings in the form of a man dressed in a little cowhide and black breeches. . . .

Verdict

July 9, 1652. In the light of the interrogations, answers, and investigations made into the charge against Suzanne Gaudry, . . . seeing by her own confessions that she is said to have made a pact with the devil, received the mark from him, . . . and that following this, she had renounced God, Lent, and baptism and had let herself be known carnally by him, in which she received satisfaction. Also, seeing that she is said to have been a part of nocturnal carols and dances.

For expiation of which the advice of the undersigned is that the office of Rieux can legitimately condemn the aforesaid Suzanne Gaudry to death, tying her to a gallows, and strangling her to death, then burning her body and burying it here in the environs of the woods.

Why were women, particularly older women, especially vulnerable to accusations of witchcraft? What "proofs" are offered here that Suzanne Gaudry had consorted with the devil? What does this account tell us about the spread of witchcraft persecutions in the seventeenth century?

Source: From *Witchcraft in Europe, 1100–1700: A Documentary History* by Alan Kors and Edward Peters (Philadelphia: University of Pennsylvania Press, 1972), pp. 266–275. Used with permission of the publisher.

and divisive conditions generated by the trials of witches. Moreover, by the beginning of the eighteenth century, more and more people were questioning altogether their old attitudes toward religion and found it especially contrary to reason to believe in the old view of a world haunted by evil spirits.

ECONOMIC TRENDS IN THE SEVENTEENTH CENTURY

In the course of the seventeenth century, new economic trends also emerged. Historians refer to the economic practices of the seventeenth century as **mercantilism**. According to the mercantilists, the prosperity of a nation depended on a plentiful supply of bullion (gold and silver). For this reason, it was desirable to achieve a favorable balance of trade in which goods exported were of greater value than those imported, promoting an influx of gold and silver payments that would increase the quantity of bullion. Furthermore, to encourage exports, governments should stimulate and protect export industries and trade by granting trade monopolies, encouraging investment in new industries through subsidies, importing foreign artisans, and improving transportation systems by building roads, bridges, and canals. By placing high tariffs on foreign goods, a government could reduce imports and prevent them from competing with domestic industries. Colonies were also deemed valuable as sources of raw materials and markets for finished goods.

Mercantilist theory on the role of colonies was matched in practice by Europe's overseas expansion. With the development of colonies and trading posts in the Americas and the East, Europeans embarked on an adventure in international commerce in the seventeenth century. Although some historians speak of a nascent world economy, we should remember that local, regional, and intra-European trade still predominated. At the end of the seventeenth century, for example, English imports totaled 360,000 tons, but only 5,000 tons came from the East Indies. What made the transoceanic trade rewarding, however, was not the volume but the value of its goods. Dutch, English, and French merchants were bringing back products that were still consumed largely by the wealthy but were beginning to make their way into the lives of artisans and merchants. Pepper and spices from the Indies, West Indian and Brazilian sugar, and Asian coffee and tea were becoming more readily available to European consumers.

The commercial expansion of the sixteenth and seventeenth centuries was made easier by new forms of commercial organization, especially the **joint-stock company**. Individuals bought shares in a company and received dividends on their investment while a board of directors ran the company and made the important business decisions. The return on investments could be spectacular. The joint-stock company made it easier to raise large amounts of capital for world trading ventures.

Despite the growth of commercial capitalism, most of the European economy still depended on an agricultural system that had experienced few changes since the thirteenth century. At least 80 percent of Europeans still worked on the land. Almost all of the peasants of western Europe were free of serfdom, although many still owed a variety of feudal dues to the nobility. Despite the expanding markets and rising prices, European peasants saw little or no improvement in their lot as they faced increased rents and fees and higher taxes imposed by the state.

Seventeenth-Century Crises: Revolution and War

During the first half of the seventeenth century, a series of rebellions and civil wars rocked the domestic stability of many European governments. A devastating war that affected much of Europe also added to the sense of crisis.

THE THIRTY YEARS' WAR (1618–1648) The Thirty Years' War began in 1618 in the Germanic lands of the Holy Roman Empire as a struggle between Catholic forces, led by the Habsburg Holy Roman Emperors, and Protestant—primarily Calvinist—nobles in Bohemia who rebelled against Habsburg authority (see Map 15.1). What began as a struggle over religious issues soon became a wider conflict perpetuated by political motivations as both minor and major European powers—Denmark, Sweden, France, and Spain—entered the war. The competition for European leadership between the Bourbon dynasty of France and the Habsburg dynasties of Spain and the Holy Roman Empire was an especially important factor. Nevertheless, most of the battles were fought on German soil (see the box on p. 397).

The war in Germany was officially ended in 1648 by the Peace of Westphalia, which proclaimed that all German states, including the Calvinist ones, were free to determine their own religion. The major contenders gained new territories, and France emerged as the dominant nation in Europe. The more than three hundred entities that made up the Holy Roman Empire were recognized as independent states, and each was given the power to conduct its own foreign policy; this brought an end to the Holy Roman Empire and ensured German disunity for another two hundred years. The Peace of Westphalia made it clear that political motives, not religious convictions, had become the guiding force in public affairs.

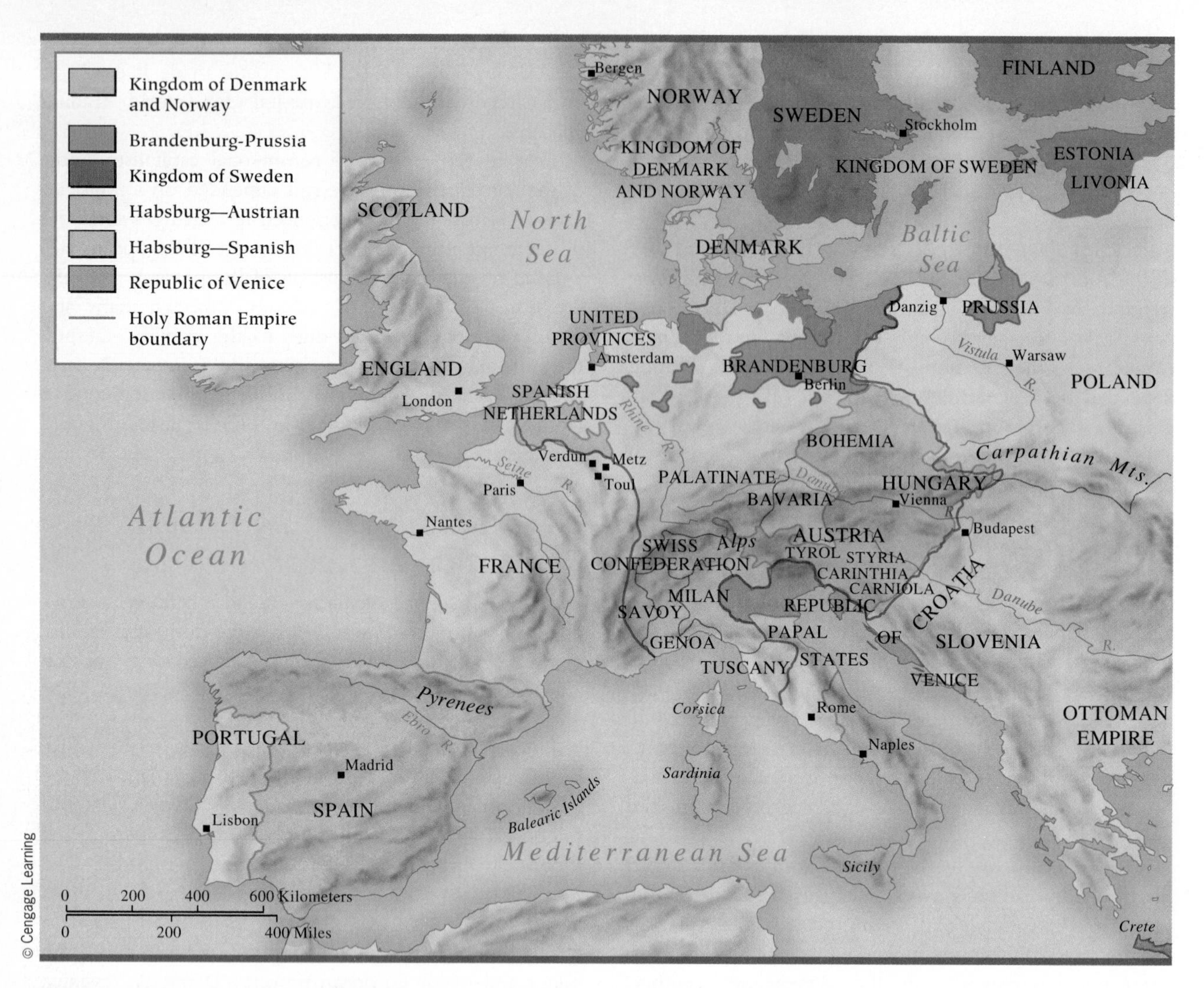

MAP 15.1 Europe in the Seventeenth Century. This map shows Europe at the time of the Thirty Years' War (1618–1648). Although the struggle began in Bohemia and much of the fighting took place in the Germanic lands of the Holy Roman Empire, the conflict became a Europe-wide struggle.

Q *Which countries engaged in the war were predominantly Protestant, which were Catholic, and which were mixed?*

A MILITARY REVOLUTION? By the seventeenth century, war was playing an increasingly important role in European affairs. Military power was considered essential to a ruler's reputation and power; thus, the pressure to build an effective military machine was intense. Some historians believe that the changes that occurred in the science of warfare between 1560 and 1650 constituted a military revolution.

These changes included increased use of firearms and cannons, greater flexibility and mobility in tactics, and better-disciplined and better-trained armies. These innovations necessitated standing armies, based partly on conscription, which grew ever larger and more expensive as the seventeenth century progressed. Such armies could be maintained only by levying heavier taxes, making war an economic burden and an ever more important part of the early modern European state. The creation of large bureaucracies to supervise the military resources of the state contributed to the growth in the power of governments.

The Face of War in the Seventeenth Century

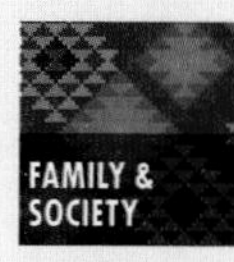

We have a firsthand account of the face of war in Germany from a picaresque novel called *Simplicius Simplicissimus*, written by Jakob von Grimmelshausen (YAH-kop fun GRIM-ulz-how-zun). The author's experiences as a soldier in the Thirty Years' War give his descriptions of the effect of the war on ordinary people a certain vividness and reality. This selection describes the fate of a peasant farm, an experience all too familiar to thousands of German peasants between 1618 and 1648.

Jakob von Grimmelshausen, *Simplicius Simplicissimus*

The first thing these horsemen did in the nice back rooms of the house was to put in their horses. Then everyone took up a special job, one having to do with death and destruction. Although some began butchering, heating water, and rendering lard, as if to prepare for a banquet, others raced through the house, ransacking upstairs and down; not even the privy chamber was safe, as if the golden fleece of Jason might be hidden there. Still others bundled up big packs of cloth, household goods, and clothes, as if they wanted to hold a rummage sale somewhere. What they did not intend to take along they broke and spoiled. Some ran their swords into the hay and straw, as if there hadn't been hogs enough to stick. Some shook the feathers out of beds and put bacon slabs, hams, and other stuff in the ticking, as if they might sleep better on these. Others knocked down the hearth and broke the windows, as if announcing an everlasting summer. They flattened out copper and pewter dishes and baled the ruined goods. They burned up bedsteads, tables, chairs, and benches, though there were yards and yards of dry firewood outside the kitchen. Jars and crocks, pots and casseroles all were broken, either because they preferred their meat broiled or because they thought they'd eat only one meal with us. In the barn, the hired girl was handled so roughly that she was unable to walk away, I am ashamed to report. They stretched the hired man out flat on the ground, stuck a wooden wedge in his mouth to keep it open, and emptied a milk bucket full of stinking manure drippings down his throat; they called it a Swedish cocktail. He didn't relish it and made a very wry face. By this means they forced him to take a raiding party to some other place where they carried off men and cattle and brought them to our farm. Among those were my father, mother, and [sister] Ursula.

Then they used thumbscrews, which they cleverly made out of their pistols, to torture the peasants, as if they wanted to burn witches. Though he had confessed to nothing as yet, they put one of the captured hayseeds in the bake-oven and lighted a fire in it. They put a rope around someone else's head and tightened it like a tourniquet until blood came out of his mouth, nose, and ears. In short, every soldier had his favorite method of making life miserable for peasants, and every peasant had his own misery. My father was, as I thought, particularly lucky because he confessed with a laugh what others were forced to say in pain and martyrdom. No doubt because he was the head of the household, he was shown special consideration; they put him close to a fire, tied him by his hands and legs, and rubbed damp salt on the bottoms of his feet. Our old nanny goat had to lick it off and this so tickled my father that he could have burst laughing. This seemed so clever and entertaining to me—I had never seen or heard my father laugh so long—that I joined him in laughter, to keep him company or perhaps to cover up my ignorance. In the midst of such glee he told them the whereabouts of hidden treasure much richer in gold, pearls, and jewelry than might have been expected on a farm.

I can't say much about the captured wives, hired girls, and daughters because the soldiers didn't let me watch their doings. But I do remember hearing pitiful screams from various dark corners and I guess that my mother and our Ursula had it no better than the rest.

What does this document reveal about the effect of war on ordinary Europeans?

Source: Excerpt from *The Adventure of Simplicius Simplissimus* by Hans Jacob Chistoffel von Grimmelshausen, translated by George Schulz-Behren, © 1993 Camden House/Boydell & Brewer, Rochester, New York.

Response to Crisis: The Practice of Absolutism

FOCUS QUESTION: What was absolutism, and what were the main characteristics of the absolute monarchies that emerged in France, Prussia, Austria, and Russia?

Many people responded to the crises of the seventeenth century by searching for order. An increase in monarchical power became an obvious means for achieving stability. The result was what historians have called absolutism or absolute monarchy, in which the sovereign power or ultimate authority in the state rested in the hands of a king who claimed to rule by divine right—the idea that kings received their power from God and were responsible to no one but God. Late-sixteenth-century political theorists believed that sovereign power consisted of the authority to make laws, levy taxes, administer justice, control the state's administrative system, and determine foreign policy.

France Under Louis XIV

France during the reign of Louis XIV (1643–1715) has traditionally been regarded as the best example of the practice of absolute or **divine-right monarchy** in the seventeenth century. French culture, language, and manners reached into all levels of European society. French diplomacy and wars overwhelmed the political affairs of western and central Europe. The court of Louis XIV seemed to be imitated everywhere in Europe (see the comparative illustration on p. 399).

POLITICAL INSTITUTIONS One of the keys to Louis's power was his ability to control the central policy-making machinery of government because it was part of his own court and household. The royal court, located in the magnificent palace at Versailles (vayr-SY) served three purposes simultaneously: it was the personal household of the king, the location of central governmental machinery, and the place where powerful subjects came to find favors and offices for themselves and their clients. The greatest danger to Louis's personal rule came from the very high nobles and princes of the blood (the royal princes), who considered it their natural role to assert the policy-making role of royal ministers. Louis eliminated this threat by removing them from the royal council, the chief administrative body of the king, and enticing them to his court at Versailles, where he could keep them preoccupied with court life and out of politics. Instead of the high nobility and royal princes, Louis relied for his ministers on nobles who came from relatively new aristocratic families. His ministers were expected to be subservient: "I had no intention of sharing my authority with them," Louis said.

Louis's domination of his ministers and secretaries gave him control of the central policy-making machinery of government and thus authority over the traditional areas of monarchical power: the formulation of foreign policy, the making of war and peace, the assertion of the secular power of the crown against any religious authority, and the ability to levy taxes to fulfill these functions. Louis had considerably less success with the internal administration of the kingdom, however.

THE ECONOMY AND THE MILITARY The cost of building palaces, maintaining his court, and pursuing his wars made finances a crucial issue for Louis XIV. He was most fortunate in having the services of Jean-Baptiste Colbert (ZHAHN-bap-TEEST kohl-BAYR) (1619–1683) as controller general of finances. Colbert sought to increase the wealth and power of France by general adherence to mercantilism, which advocated government intervention in economic activities for the benefit of the state. To decrease imports and increase exports, Colbert granted subsidies to individuals who established new industries. To improve communications and the transportation of goods internally, he built roads and canals. To decrease imports directly, Colbert raised tariffs on foreign goods.

The increase in royal power that Louis pursued led the king to develop a professional army numbering 100,000 men in peacetime and 400,000 in time of war. To achieve the prestige and military glory befitting an absolute monarch as well as to ensure the domination of his Bourbon dynasty over European affairs, Louis waged four wars between 1667 and 1713. His ambitions roused much of Europe to form coalitions that were determined to prevent the certain destruction of the European balance of power by Bourbon hegemony. Although Louis added some territory to France's northeastern frontier and established a member of his own Bourbon dynasty on the throne of Spain, he also left France impoverished and surrounded by enemies.

Absolutism in Central and Eastern Europe

During the seventeenth century, a development of great importance for the modern Western world took place with the appearance in central and eastern Europe of three new powers: Prussia, Austria, and Russia.

PRUSSIA Frederick William the Great Elector (1640–1688) laid the foundation for the Prussian state. Realizing that the land he had inherited, known as Brandenburg-Prussia, was a small, open territory with no natural frontiers for defense, Frederick William built an army of

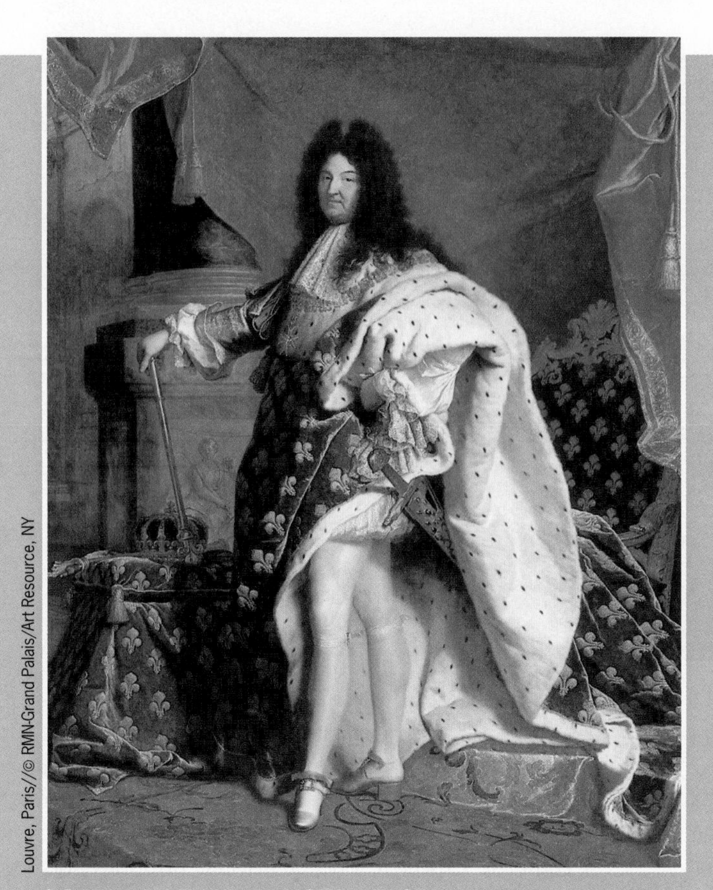

Louvre, Paris//© RMN-Grand Palais/Art Resource, NY

© Hu Weibiao/Panorama/The Image Works

COMPARATIVE ILLUSTRATION

POLITICS & GOVERNMENT

Sun Kings, West and East. At the end of the seventeenth century, two powerful rulers held sway in kingdoms that dominated the affairs of the regions around them. Both rulers saw themselves as favored by divine authority—Louis XIV of France as a divine-right monarch and Kangxi (KANG-shee) of China as possessing the mandate of Heaven. Thus, both rulers saw themselves not as divine beings but as divinely ordained beings whose job was to govern organized societies. On the left, Louis XIV, who ruled France from 1643 to 1715, is seen in a portrait by Hyacinthe Rigaud (ee-ah-SANT ree-GOH) that captures the king's sense of royal dignity and grandeur. One person at court said of Louis XIV: "Louis XIV's vanity was without limit or restraint." On the right, Kangxi, who ruled China from 1661 to 1722, is seen in a nineteenth-century portrait that shows him seated in majesty on his imperial throne. A dedicated ruler, Kangxi once wrote, "One act of negligence may cause sorrow all through the country, and one moment of negligence may result in trouble for hundreds and thousands of generations."

Although these rulers practiced very different religions, why did they justify their powers in such a similar fashion?

40,000 men, the fourth largest in Europe. To sustain this force, he established the General War Commissariat to levy taxes for the army and oversee its growth. The Commissariat soon evolved into an agency for civil government as well. The new bureaucratic machine became the elector's chief instrument for governing the state. Many of its officials were members of the Prussian landed aristocracy, the Junkers (YOONG-kers), who also served as officers in the all-important army.

In 1701, Frederick William's son Frederick (1688–1713) officially gained the title of king. Elector Frederick III became King Frederick I, and Brandenburg-Prussia simply Prussia. In the eighteenth century, Prussia emerged as a great power in Europe.

AUSTRIA The Austrian Habsburgs had long played a significant role in European politics as Holy Roman Emperors, but by the end of the Thirty Years' War, their hopes of creating an empire in Germany had been dashed. In the seventeenth century, the house of Austria created a new empire in eastern and southeastern Europe.

The nucleus of the new Austrian Empire remained the traditional Austrian hereditary possessions: Lower and Upper Austria, Carinthia, Carniola, Styria, and Tyrol. To these had been added the kingdom of Bohemia and parts of northwestern Hungary. After the defeat of the Turks in 1687 (see Chapter 16), Austria took control of all of Hungary, Transylvania, Croatia, and Slovenia, thus establishing the Austrian Empire in southeastern Europe.

Chateaux de Versailles et de Trianon, Versailles//© RMN-Grand Palais/Art Resource, NY

Interior of Versailles: The Hall of Mirrors. Pictured here is the exquisite Hall of Mirrors in King Louis XIV's palace at Versailles. Located on the second floor, the hall overlooks the park below. Three hundred and fifty-seven mirrors were placed on the wall opposite the windows to create an illusion of even greater width. Careful planning went into every detail of the interior decoration. Even the doorknobs were specially designed to reflect the magnificence of Versailles. This photo shows the Hall of Mirrors after the restoration work that was completed in June 2007, a project that took three years, cost 12 million euros (more than $16 million), and included the restoration of the Bohemian crystal chandeliers.

By the beginning of the eighteenth century, the house of Austria had assembled an empire of considerable size.

The Austrian monarchy, however, never became a highly centralized, absolutist state, primarily because it contained so many different national groups. The Austrian Empire remained a collection of territories held together by the Habsburg emperor, who was archduke of Austria, king of Bohemia, and king of Hungary. Each of these regions had its own laws and political life.

FROM MUSCOVY TO RUSSIA A new Russian state had emerged in the fifteenth century under the leadership of the principality of Muscovy and its grand dukes. In the sixteenth century, Ivan IV (1533–1584) became the first ruler to take the title of *tsar* (the Russian word for *Caesar*). Ivan expanded the territories of Russia eastward and crushed the power of the Russian nobility. He was known as Ivan the Terrible because of his ruthless deeds, among them stabbing his son to death in a heated argument. When Ivan's dynasty came to an end in 1598, it was followed by a period of anarchy that did not end until the Zemsky Sobor (ZEM-skee suh-BOR), or national assembly, chose Michael Romanov (ROH-muh-nahf) as the new tsar, establishing a dynasty that lasted more than three hundred years. One of its most prominent members was Peter the Great.

Peter the Great (1689–1725) was an unusual character. A towering, strong man at 6 feet 9 inches tall, Peter enjoyed a low kind of humor—belching contests and crude jokes—and vicious punishments, including floggings, impalings, and roastings. Peter got a firsthand view of the West when he made a trip there in 1697–1698 and returned to Russia with a firm determination to westernize or Europeanize Russia. He was especially eager to borrow European technology in order to create the army and navy he needed to make Russia a great power.

As could be expected, one of his first priorities was the reorganization of the army and the creation of a navy. Employing both Russians and Europeans as officers, he conscripted peasants for twenty-five-year stints of service to build a standing army of 210,000 men and at the same time formed the first navy Russia had ever had.

To impose the rule of the central government more effectively throughout the land, Peter divided Russia into provinces. Although he hoped to create a "police state," by which he meant a well-ordered community governed in accordance with law, few of his bureaucrats shared his concept of loyalty to the state. Peter hoped to evoke a sense of civic duty among his people, but his own forceful personality created an atmosphere of fear that prevented any such sentiment.

The object of Peter's domestic reforms was to make Russia into a great state and military power. His primary goal was to "open a window to the west," meaning an ice-free port easily accessible to Europe. This could only be achieved on the Baltic, but at that time, the Baltic coast was controlled by Sweden, the most important power in northern Europe. A long and hard-fought war with Sweden won Peter the lands he sought. In 1703, Peter began the construction of a new city, Saint Petersburg, his window to the west and a symbol that Russia was looking westward to Europe. Under Peter, Russia became a great military power and, by his death in 1725, an important European state.

England and Limited Monarchy

FOCUS QUESTION: How and why did England avoid the path of absolutism?

Not all states were absolutist in the seventeenth century. One of the most prominent examples of resistance to absolute monarchy came in England, where king and Parliament struggled to determine the roles each should play in governing England.

Conflict Between King and Parliament

With the death of Queen Elizabeth I in 1603, the Tudor dynasty became extinct, and the Stuart line of rulers was inaugurated with the accession to the throne of Elizabeth's cousin, King James VI of Scotland, who became James I (1603–1625) of England. James espoused the divine right of kings, a viewpoint that alienated Parliament, which had grown accustomed under the Tudors to act on the premise that monarch and Parliament together ruled England as a "balanced polity." Then, too, the Puritans—Protestants within the Anglican Church who, inspired by Calvinist theology, wished to eliminate every trace of Roman Catholicism from the Church of England—were alienated by the king's strong defense of the Anglican Church. Many of England's gentry, mostly well-to-do landowners, had become Puritans, and they formed an important and substantial part of the House of Commons, the lower house of Parliament. It was not wise to alienate these men.

The conflict that had begun during the reign of James came to a head during the reign of his son Charles I (1625–1649). Like his father, Charles believed in divine-right monarchy, and religious differences also added to the hostility between Charles I and Parliament. The king's attempt to impose more ritual on the Anglican Church struck the Puritans as a return to Catholic practices. When Charles tried to force the Puritans to accept his religious policies, thousands of them went off to the "howling wildernesses" of America.

Civil War and Commonwealth

Grievances mounted until England finally slipped into a civil war (1642–1648) won by the parliamentary forces, due largely to the New Model Army of Oliver Cromwell, the only real military genius of the war. The New Model Army was composed primarily of more extreme Puritans known as the Independents, who, in typical Calvinist fashion, believed they were doing battle for God. As Cromwell wrote in one of his military reports, "Sir, this is none other but the hand of God; and to Him alone belongs the glory." We might give some credit to Cromwell; his soldiers were well trained in the new military tactics of the seventeenth century.

After the execution of Charles I on January 30, 1649, Parliament abolished the monarchy and the House of Lords and proclaimed England a republic or commonwealth. But Cromwell and his army, unable to work effectively with Parliament, dispersed it by force and established a military dictatorship. After Cromwell's death in 1658, the army decided that military rule was no longer feasible and restored the monarchy in the person of Charles II (1660–1685), the son of Charles I.

Restoration and a Glorious Revolution

Charles II was sympathetic to Catholicism, and Parliament's suspicions were aroused in 1672 when he took the audacious step of issuing the Declaration of Indulgence, which suspended the laws that Parliament had passed against Catholics and Puritans after the restoration of the monarchy. Parliament forced the king to suspend the declaration.

The accession of James II (1685–1688) to the crown virtually guaranteed a new constitutional crisis for England. An open and devout Catholic, his attempt to further Catholic interests made religion once more a primary cause of conflict between king and Parliament. James named Catholics to high positions in the government, army, navy, and universities. Parliamentary outcries against James's policies stopped short of rebellion because the members knew that he was an old man and that his successors were his Protestant daughters Mary and

CHRONOLOGY Absolute and Limited Monarchy

France	
Louis XIV	1643–1715
Brandenburg-Prussia	
Frederick William the Great Elector	1640–1688
Elector Frederick III (King Frederick I)	1688–1713
Russia	
Ivan IV the Terrible	1533–1584
Peter the Great	1689–1725
First trip to the West	1697–1698
Construction of Saint Petersburg begins	1703
England	
Civil wars	1642–1648
Commonwealth	1649–1653
Charles II	1660–1685
Declaration of Indulgence	1672
James II	1685–1688
Glorious Revolution	1688
Bill of Rights	1689

The Bill of Rights

In 1688, the English experienced a bloodless revolution in which the Stuart king James II was replaced by Mary, James's daughter, and her husband, William of Orange. After William and Mary had assumed power, Parliament passed a Bill of Rights that specified the rights of Parliament and laid the foundation for a constitutional monarchy.

The Bill of Rights

Whereas the said late King James II having abdicated the government, and the throne being thereby vacant, his Highness the prince of Orange (whom it hath pleased Almighty God to make the glorious instrument of delivering this kingdom from popery and arbitrary power) did (by the device of the lords spiritual and temporal, and diverse principal persons of the Commons) cause letters to be written to the lords spiritual and temporal, being Protestants, and other letters to the several counties, cities, universities, boroughs, and Cinque Ports, for the choosing of such persons to represent them, as were of right to be sent to parliament, to meet and sit at Westminster upon the two and twentieth day of January, in this year 1689, in order to such an establishment as that their religion, laws, and liberties might not again be in danger of being subverted; upon which letters elections have been accordingly made.

And thereupon the said lords spiritual and temporal and Commons, pursuant to their respective letters and elections, being now assembled in a full and free representation of this nation, taking into their most serious consideration the best means for attaining the ends aforesaid, do in the first place (as their ancestors in like case have usually done), for the vindication and assertion of their ancient rights and liberties, declare:

1. That the pretended power of suspending laws, or the execution of laws, by regal authority, without consent of parliament is illegal.
2. That the pretended power of dispensing with the laws, or the execution of law by regal authority, as it hath been assumed and exercised of late, is illegal.
3. That the commission for erecting the late court of commissioners for ecclesiastical causes, and all other commissions and courts of like nature, are illegal and pernicious.
4. That levying money for or to the use of the crown by pretense of prerogative, without grant of parliament, for longer time or in other manner than the same is or shall be granted, is illegal.
5. That it is the right of the subjects to petition the king, and all commitments and prosecutions for such petitioning are illegal.
6. That the raising or keeping a standing army within the kingdom in time of peace, unless it be with consent of parliament, is against law.
7. That the subjects which are Protestants may have arms for their defense suitable to their conditions, and as allowed by law.
8. That election of members of parliament ought to be free.
9. That the freedom of speech, and debates or proceedings in parliament, ought not to be impeached or questioned in any court or place out of parliament.
10. That excessive bail ought not to be required, nor excessive fines imposed, nor cruel and unusual punishments inflicted.
11. That jurors ought to be duly impaneled and returned, and jurors which pass upon men in trials for high treason ought to be freeholders.
12. That all grants and promises of fines and forfeitures of particular persons before conviction are illegal and void.
13. And that for redress of all grievances, and for the amending, strengthening, and preserving of the laws, parliament ought to be held frequently.

How did the Bill of Rights lay the foundation for a constitutional monarchy in England?

Source: From *The Statutes: Revised Edition* (London: Eyre & Spottiswoode, 1871), Vol. 2, pp. 10–12.

Anne, born to his first wife. But on June 10, 1688, a son was born to James II's second wife, also a Catholic. Suddenly, the specter of a Catholic hereditary monarchy loomed large. A group of prominent English noblemen invited the Dutch chief executive, William of Orange, husband of James's daughter Mary, to invade England. William and Mary raised an army and invaded England while James, his wife, and their infant son fled to France. With little bloodshed, England had undergone its "Glorious Revolution."

In January 1689, Parliament offered the throne to William and Mary, who accepted it along with the provisions of the Bill of Rights (see the box above). The Bill of Rights affirmed Parliament's right to make laws and levy taxes. The rights of citizens to keep arms and have a jury trial were also confirmed. By deposing one king and establishing another, Parliament had destroyed the divine-right theory of kingship (William was, after all, king by grace of Parliament, not God) and asserted its right to participate in the government. Parliament did not have complete control of the government, but it now had the right to participate in affairs of state. Over the next century, it would gradually prove to be the real authority in the English system of **limited (constitutional) monarchy**.

The Flourishing of European Culture

FOCUS QUESTION: How did the artistic and literary achievements of this era reflect the political and economic developments of the period?

Despite religious wars and the growth of absolutism, European culture continued to flourish. The era was blessed with a number of prominent artists and writers.

Art: The Baroque

The artistic movement known as the **Baroque** (buh-ROHK) dominated the Western artistic world for a century and a half. The Baroque began in Italy in the last quarter of the sixteenth century and spread to the rest of Europe and Latin America. Baroque artists sought to harmonize the Classical ideals of Renaissance art with the spiritual feelings of the sixteenth-century religious revival. In large part, Baroque art and architecture reflected the search for power that was characteristic of much of the seventeenth century. Baroque churches and palaces featured richly ornamented facades, sweeping staircases, and an overall splendor meant to impress people. Kings and princes wanted not only their subjects, but also other kings and princes to be in awe of their power.

Baroque painting was known for its use of dramatic effects to arouse the emotions, especially evident in the works of Peter Paul Rubens (1577–1640), a prolific artist and an important figure in the spread of the Baroque from Italy to other parts of Europe. In his artistic masterpieces, bodies in violent motion, heavily fleshed nudes, a dramatic use of light and shadow, and rich sensuous pigments converge to express intense emotions.

Louvre, Paris//© RMN-Grand Palais/Art Resource, NY

Peter Paul Rubens, *The Landing of Marie de' Medici at Marseilles.* The Flemish painter Peter Paul Rubens played a key role in spreading the Baroque style from Italy to other parts of Europe. In *The Landing of Marie de' Medici at Marseilles*, Rubens made dramatic use of light and color, bodies in motion, and luxurious nudes to heighten the emotional intensity of the scene. This was one of a cycle of twenty-one paintings dedicated to the queen mother of France.

Art: Dutch Realism

The supremacy of Dutch commerce in the seventeenth century was paralleled by a brilliant flowering of Dutch painting. Wealthy patricians and burghers of Dutch urban society commissioned works of art for their guildhalls, town halls, and private dwellings. The interests of this burgher society were reflected in the subject matter of many Dutch paintings: portraits of themselves, group portraits of their military companies and guilds, landscapes, seascapes, genre scenes, still lifes, and the interiors of their residences. Neither Classical nor Baroque, Dutch painters were primarily interested in the realistic portrayal of secular everyday life.

A Golden Age of Literature in England

In England, writing for the stage reached new heights between 1580 and 1640. The golden age of English literature is often called the Elizabethan Era because much of the English cultural flowering occurred during Elizabeth's reign. Elizabethan literature exhibits the exuberance and pride associated with English exploits at the time. Of all the forms of Elizabethan literature, none expressed the energy and intellectual versatility of the era better than drama. And no dramatist is more famous or more accomplished than William Shakespeare (1564–1614).

Shakespeare was a "complete man of the theater." Although best known for writing plays, he was also an actor and a shareholder in the chief acting company of the time, the Lord Chamberlain's Company, which played in various London theaters. Shakespeare is to this day hailed as a genius. A master of the English language, he imbued its words with power and majesty. And his technical proficiency was matched by incredible insight into human psychology. Whether writing tragedies or comedies, Shakespeare exhibited a remarkable understanding of the human condition.

CHAPTER SUMMARY

In the last chapter, we observed how the movement of Europeans beyond Europe began to change the shape of world history. But what had made this development possible? After all, the Reformation of the sixteenth century, initially begun by Martin Luther, had brought about the religious division of Europe into Protestant and Catholic camps. By the middle of the sixteenth century, it was apparent that the religious passions of the Reformation era had brought an end to the religious unity of medieval Europe. The religious division (Catholics versus Protestants) was instrumental in beginning a series of religious wars that were complicated by economic, social, and political forces that also played a role.

The crises of the sixteenth and seventeenth centuries soon led to a search for a stable, secular order of politics and made possible the emergence of a system of nation-states in which power politics took on an increasing significance. Within those states, there slowly emerged some of the machinery that made possible a growing centralization of power. In those states called absolutist, strong monarchs with the assistance of their aristocracies took the lead in providing the leadership for greater centralization. In this so-called age of absolutism, Louis XIV, the Sun King of France, was the model for other rulers. Strong monarchy also prevailed in central and eastern Europe, where three new powers made their appearance: Prussia, Austria, and Russia.

But not all European states followed the pattern of absolute monarchy. Especially important were developments in England, where a series of struggles between king and Parliament took place in the seventeenth century. In the long run, the landed aristocracy gained power at the expense of the monarchs, thus laying the foundations for a constitutional government in which Parliament provided the focus for the institutions of centralized power.

In all the major European states, a growing concern for power and dynamic expansion led to larger armies and greater conflict, stronger economies, and more powerful governments. From a global point of view, Europeans—with their strong governments, prosperous economies, and strengthened military forces—were beginning to dominate other parts of the world, leading to a growing belief in the superiority of their civilization.

Yet despite Europeans' increasing domination of global trade markets, they had not achieved their goal of diminishing the power of Islam, first pursued during the Crusades. In fact, as we shall see in the next chapter, in the midst of European expansion and exploration, three new and powerful Muslim empires were taking shape in the Middle East and South Asia.

CHAPTER TIMELINE

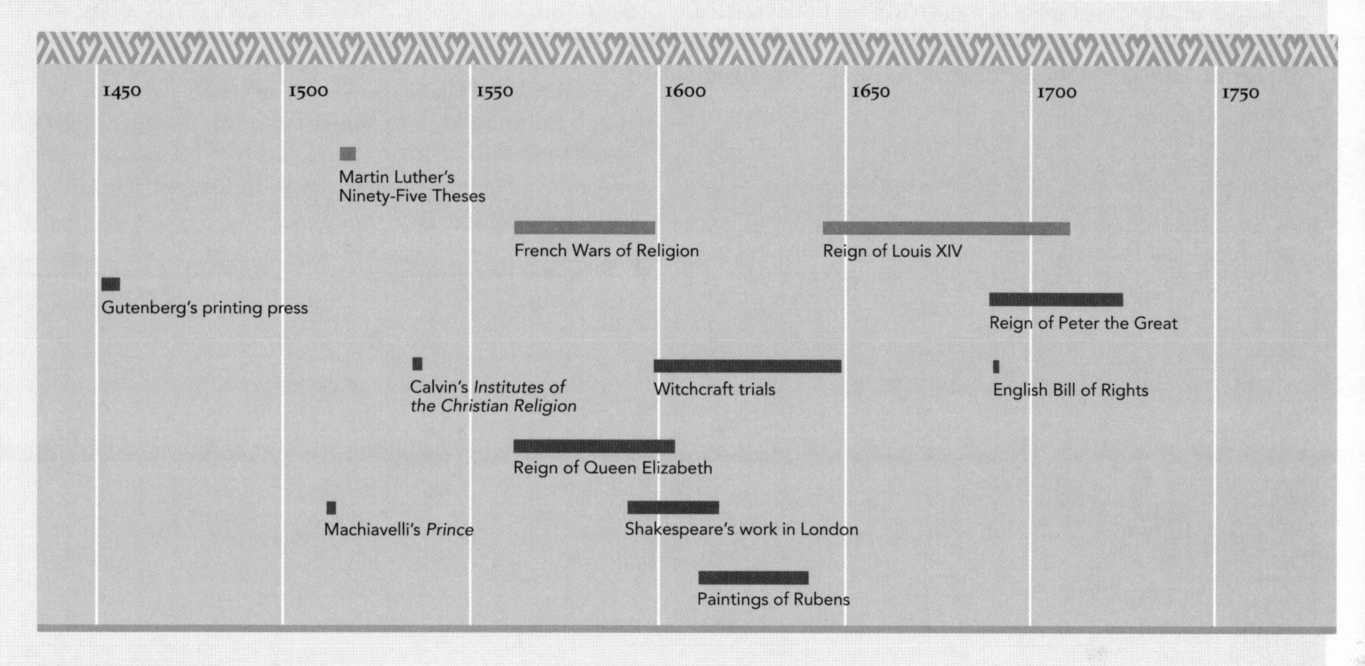

CHAPTER REVIEW

Upon Reflection

Q What role did politics play in the success of the Protestant Reformation?

Q What did Louis XIV hope to accomplish in his domestic and foreign policies? To what extent did he succeed?

Q What role did the gentry play in seventeenth-century England?

Key Terms

absolutism (p. 383)
Protestant Reformation (p. 383)
new monarchies (p. 383)
Christian humanism (northern Renaissance humanism) (p. 384)
relics (p. 385)
indulgences (p. 385)
justification by faith (p. 385)
predestination (p. 388)
Catholic Reformation (p. 389)
mercantilism (p. 395)
joint-stock company (p. 395)
divine-right monarchy (p. 398)
limited (constitutional) monarchy (p. 403)
Baroque (p. 403)

Suggested Reading

THE REFORMATION: GENERAL WORKS Basic surveys of the Reformation period include **J. D. Tracy, *Europe's Reformations, 1450–1650*** (Oxford, 1999), and **D. MacCulloch, *The Reformation*** (New York, 2003). Also see the brief work by **U. Rublack, *Reformation Europe*** (Cambridge, 2005).

THE PROTESTANT AND CATHOLIC REFORMATIONS On Martin Luther's life, see **H. A. Oberman, *Luther: Man Between God and the Devil*** (New York, 1992), and the brief biography by **M. Marty, *Martin Luther*** (New York, 2004). A good survey of the English Reformation is **A. G. Dickens, *The English Reformation*,** 2nd ed. (New York, 1989). On John Calvin, see **W. G. Naphy, *Calvin and the Consolidation of the Genevan Reformation*** (Philadelphia, 2003). A good introduction to the Catholic Reformation can be found in **R. P. Hsia, *The World of Catholic Renewal, 1540–1770*** (Cambridge, 1998).

EUROPE IN CRISIS, 1560–1650 On the French Wars of Religion, see **R. J. Knecht, *The French Wars of Religion, 1559–1598*,** 2nd ed. (New York, 1996). The fundamental study of the Thirty Years' War is **P. H. Wilson, *The Thirty Years War, Europe's Tragedy*** (Cambridge, Mass., 2009). Witchcraft hysteria can be examined in **R. Briggs, *Witches and Neighbours: The Social and Cultural Context of European Witchcraft*,** 2nd ed. (Oxford, 2002).

ABSOLUTE AND LIMITED MONARCHY A solid and very readable biography of Louis XIV is **J. Levi, *Louis XIV*** (New York, 2004). See **P. H. Wilson, *Absolutism in Central Europe*** (New York, 2000), on both Prussia and Austria. On Peter the Great, see **P. Bushkovitz, *Peter the Great*** (Oxford, 2001). On the English Civil War, see **D. Purkiss, *The English Civil War*** (New York, 2006).

EUROPEAN CULTURE For a general survey of Baroque culture, see **F. C. Marchetti et al., *Baroque, 1600–1770*** (New York, 2005). The literature on Shakespeare is enormous. For a biography, see **A. L. Rowse, *The Life of Shakespeare*** (New York, 1963).

CourseMate

Visit the CourseMate website at **www.cengagebrain.com** for additional study tools and review materials for this chapter.

The Muslim Empires

Topkapi Museum, Istanbul/© Gianni Dagli Orti/The Art Archive at Art Resource, NY

Turks fight Christians at the Battle of Mohács.

CHAPTER OUTLINE AND FOCUS QUESTIONS

The Ottoman Empire

Q What was the ethnic composition of the Ottoman Empire, and how did the government of the sultan administer such a diverse population? How did Ottoman policy in this regard compare with the policies applied in Europe and Asia?

The Safavids

Q How did the Safavid Empire come into existence, and what led to its collapse?

The Grandeur of the Mughals

Q What role did Islam play in the Mughal Empire, and how did the Mughals' approach to religion compare with that of the Ottomans and the Safavids? What might explain the differences?

CRITICAL THINKING

Q What were the main characteristics of each of the Muslim empires, and in what ways did they resemble each other? How were they distinct from their European counterparts?

THE OTTOMAN ARMY, led by Sultan Suleyman the Magnificent, arrived at Mohács, on the plains of Hungary, on an August morning in 1526. The Turkish force numbered about 100,000 men, and its weapons included three hundred new long-range cannons. Facing them was a somewhat larger European force, clothed in heavy armor but armed with only one hundred older cannons.

The battle began at noon and was over in two hours. The flower of the Hungarian cavalry had been destroyed, and 20,000 foot soldiers had drowned in a nearby swamp. The Ottomans had lost fewer than two hundred men. Two weeks later, they seized the Hungarian capital at Buda and prepared to lay siege to the nearby Austrian city of Vienna. Europe was in a panic, but Mohács was to be the high point of Turkish expansion in Europe.

In launching their Age of Exploration, European rulers had hoped that by controlling global markets, they could cripple the power of Islam and reduce its threat to the security of Europe. But the Christian nations' dream of expanding their influence around the globe at the expense of their great Muslim rival had not entirely been achieved. On the contrary, the Muslim world, which appeared to have entered a period of decline with the collapse of the Abbasid caliphate during the era of the Mongols, managed to revive in the shadow of Europe's Age of Exploration, a period that also saw the rise of three great Muslim empires. These powerful Muslim states—those of the Ottomans, the Safavids, and the Mughals—dominated the Middle East and the South Asian subcontinent and brought a measure of stability to a region that had been in turmoil for centuries.

The Ottoman Empire

FOCUS QUESTIONS: What was the ethnic composition of the Ottoman Empire, and how did the government of the sultan administer such a diverse population? How did Ottoman policy in this regard compare with the policies applied in Europe and Asia?

The Ottoman Turks were among the various Turkic-speaking nomadic peoples who had spread westward from Central Asia in the ninth, tenth, and eleventh centuries. The first to appear were the Seljuk Turks, who initially attempted to revive the declining Abbasid caliphate in Baghdad. Later they established themselves in the Anatolian peninsula at the expense of the Byzantine Empire. Turks served as warriors or administrators, while the peasants who tilled the farmland were mainly Greek.

The Rise of the Ottoman Turks

In the late thirteenth century, a new group of Turks under the tribal leader Osman (os-MAHN) (1280–1326) began to consolidate their power in the northwestern corner of the Anatolian peninsula. At first, the Osman Turks were relatively peaceful and engaged in pastoral pursuits, but as the Seljuk Empire began to disintegrate in the early fourteenth century, they began to expand and founded the Osmanli (os-MAHN-lee) dynasty, with its capital at Bursa (BURR-suh). The Osmanlis later came to be known as the Ottomans.

The Ottomans gained a key advantage by seizing the Bosporus and the Dardanelles, between the Mediterranean and the Black Seas. The Byzantine Empire, of course, had controlled the area for centuries, serving as a buffer between the Muslim Middle East and the Latin West. The Byzantines, however, had been severely weakened by the sack of Constantinople in the Fourth Crusade in 1204 and the Western occupation of much of the empire for the next half century. In 1345, Ottoman forces under their leader Orkhan (or-KHAHN) I (1326–1360) crossed the Bosporus for the first time to support a usurper against the Byzantine emperor in Constantinople. Setting up their first European base at Gallipoli (gah-LIP-poh-lee) at the Mediterranean entrance to the Dardanelles, Turkish forces expanded gradually into the Balkans and allied with fractious Serbian and Bulgar forces against the Byzantines. In these unstable conditions, the Ottomans gradually established permanent settlements throughout the area, where Turkish provincial governors, called **beys** (BAYS) (from the Turkish *beg*, "knight"), drove out the previous landlords and collected taxes from the local Slavic peasants. The Ottoman leader now began to claim the title of **sultan** (SUL-tun) or sovereign of his domain.

In 1360, Orkhan was succeeded by his son Murad I (moo-RAHD) (1360–1389), who consolidated Ottoman power in the Balkans and gradually reduced the Byzantine emperor to a vassal. Murad now began to build up a strong military administration based on the recruitment of Christians into an elite guard. Called **Janissaries** (JAN-nih-say-reez) (from the Turkish *yeni chert*, "new troops"), they were recruited from the local Christian population in the Balkans and then converted to Islam and trained as foot soldiers or administrators. One of the major advantages of the Janissaries was that they were directly subordinated to the sultanate and therefore owed their loyalty to the person of the sultan. Other military forces were organized by the beys and were thus loyal to their local tribal leaders.

The Janissary corps also represented a response to changes in warfare. As the knowledge of firearms spread in the late fourteenth century, the Turks began to master the new technology, including siege cannons and muskets (see the comparative essay "The Changing Face of War" on p. 409). The traditional nomadic cavalry charge was now outmoded and was superseded by infantry forces armed with muskets. Thus, the Janissaries provided a well-armed infantry who served both as an elite guard to protect the palace and as a means of extending Turkish control in the Balkans. With his new forces, Murad defeated the Serbs at the famous Battle of Kosovo (KAWSS-suh-voh) in 1389 and ended Serbian hegemony in the area.

Expansion of the Empire

Under Murad's successor, Bayazid (by-uh-ZEED) I (1389–1402), the Ottomans advanced northward, annexed Bulgaria, and slaughtered the French cavalry at a major battle on the Danube. When Mehmet (meh-MET) II (1451–1481) succeeded to the throne, he was determined to capture Constantinople. Already in control of the Dardanelles, he ordered the construction of a major fortress on the Bosporus just north of the city, which put the Turks in a position to strangle the Byzantines.

THE FALL OF CONSTANTINOPLE The last Byzantine emperor issued a desperate call for help from the Europeans, but only the Genoese came to his defense. With 80,000 troops ranged against only 7,000 defenders,

COMPARATIVE ESSAY

The Changing Face of War

"War," as the renowned French historian Fernand Braudel once observed, "has always been a matter of arms and techniques. Improved techniques can radically alter the course of events." Braudel's remark was directed to the situation in the Mediterranean region during the sixteenth century, when the adoption of artillery changed the face of warfare and gave enormous advantages to the countries that stood at the head of the new technological revolution. But it could as easily have been applied to the present day, when potential adversaries possess weapons capable of reaching across oceans and continents.

© William J. Duiker

Roman troops defeat Celtic warriors in this detail from the Great Altar of Pergamum.

One crucial aspect of military superiority, of course, lies in the nature of weaponry. From the invention of the bow and arrow to the advent of the atomic era, the possession of superior instruments of war has provided a distinct advantage against a poorly armed enemy. It was at least partly the possession of bronze weapons, for example, that enabled the invading Hyksos to conquer Egypt during the second millennium B.C.E.

Mobility is another factor of vital importance. During the second millennium B.C.E., horse-drawn chariots revolutionized the art of war from the Mediterranean Sea to the Yellow River valley in northern China. Later, the invention of the stirrup enabled mounted warriors to shoot bows and arrows from horseback, a technique applied with great effect by the Mongols as they devastated civilizations across the Eurasian supercontinent.

To protect themselves from marauding warriors, settled societies began to erect massive walls around their cities and fortresses. That in turn led to the invention of siege weapons like the catapult and the battering ram. The Mongols allegedly even came up with an early form of chemical warfare, hurling human bodies infected with the plague into the bastions of their enemies.

The invention of explosives launched the next great revolution in warfare. First used as a weapon of war by the Tang dynasty in China, explosives were brought to the West by the Turks, who used them with great effectiveness in the fifteenth century against the Byzantine Empire. But the Europeans quickly mastered the new technology and took it to new heights, inventing handheld firearms and mounting iron cannons on their warships. The latter represented a significant advantage to European fleets as they began to compete with rivals for control of the Indian and Pacific Oceans.

The twentieth century saw revolutionary new developments in the art of warfare, from armored vehicles to airplanes to nuclear arms. But as weapons grow ever more fearsome, they are more risky to use, resulting in the paradox of the Vietnam War, when lightly armed Viet Cong guerrilla units were able to fight the world's mightiest army to a virtual standstill. As the Chinese military strategist Sun Tzu had long ago observed, victory in war often goes to the smartest, not the strongest.

Why were the Europeans, rather than other peoples, able to make effective use of firearms to expand their influence throughout the rest of the world?

Mehmet laid siege to Constantinople in 1453. In their attack on the city, the Turks made use of massive cannons with 26-foot barrels that could launch stone balls weighing up to 1,200 pounds each. The Byzantines stretched heavy chains across the Golden Horn, the inlet that forms the city's harbor, to prevent a naval attack

© Bibliothèque Nationale, Paris/The Bridgeman Art Library

The Turkish Conquest of Constantinople. Mehmet II put a stranglehold on the Byzantine capital of Constantinople with a surprise attack by Turkish ships, which were dragged overland and placed in the water behind the Byzantines' defense lines. In addition, the Turks made use of massive cannons that could launch stone balls weighing up to 1,200 pounds each. The heavy bombardment of the city walls presaged a new kind of warfare in Europe. Notice the fanciful Gothic interpretation of the city in this contemporary French miniature of the siege.

from the north and prepared to make their final stand behind the 13-mile-long wall along the western edge of the city. But Mehmet's forces seized the tip of the peninsula north of the Golden Horn and then dragged their ships overland across the peninsula from the Bosporus and put them into the water behind the chains. Finally, the walls were breached; the Byzantine emperor died in the final battle.

THE ADVANCE INTO WESTERN ASIA AND AFRICA With their new capital at Constantinople, renamed Istanbul, the Ottoman Turks had become a dominant force in the Balkans and the Anatolian peninsula. They now began to advance to the east against the Shi'ite kingdom of the Safavids (sah-FAH-weeds) in Persia (see "The Safavids" later in this chapter), which had been promoting rebellion among the Anatolian tribal population and disrupting Turkish trade through the Middle East. After defeating the Safavids at a major battle in 1514, Emperor Selim (seh-LEEM) I (1512–1520) consolidated Turkish control over the territory that had been ancient Mesopotamia and then turned his attention to the Mamluks (MAM-looks) in Egypt, who had failed to support the Ottomans in their struggle against the Safavids. The Mamluks were defeated in Syria in 1516; Cairo fell a year later. Now controlling several of the holy cities of Islam, including Jerusalem, Mecca, and Medina, Selim declared himself to be the new caliph, or successor to Muhammad. During the next few years, Turkish armies and fleets advanced westward along the African coast, occupying Tripoli, Tunis, and Algeria and eventually penetrating almost to the Strait of Gibraltar (see Map 16.1).

The impact of Turkish rule on the peoples of North Africa was relatively light. Like their predecessors, the Turks were Muslims, and they preferred where possible to administer their conquered regions through local rulers. The central government appointed **pashas** (PAH-shuz) who collected taxes (and then paid a fixed percentage as tribute to the central government), maintained law and order, and were directly responsible to Istanbul. The Turks ruled from coastal cities like Algiers, Tunis, and Tripoli and made no attempt to control the interior beyond maintaining the trade routes through the Sahara to the trading centers along the Niger River. Meanwhile, local pirates along the Barbary Coast—the northern coast of Africa from Egypt to the Atlantic Ocean—competed with their Christian rivals in raiding shipping in the Mediterranean.

By the seventeenth century, the links between the imperial court in Istanbul and its appointed representatives in North Africa had begun to decline. Some pashas were dethroned by local elites, while others, such as the bey of Tunis, became hereditary rulers. Even Egypt, whose agricultural wealth and control over the route to the Red Sea made it the most important country in the area to the Turks, gradually became autonomous under a new official class of Janissaries.

TURKISH EXPANSION IN EUROPE After their conquest of Constantinople in 1453, the Turks tried to extend their territory in Europe. Under the leadership of Suleyman (SOO-lay-mahn) I the Magnificent (1520–1566), Turkish forces advanced up the Danube, seizing Belgrade in 1521 and winning a major victory over the Hungarians at the Battle of Mohács (MOH-hach) on the Danube in 1526. Subsequently, the Turks overran most of Hungary, moved into Austria, and advanced as far as Vienna, where they were finally repulsed in 1529. At the

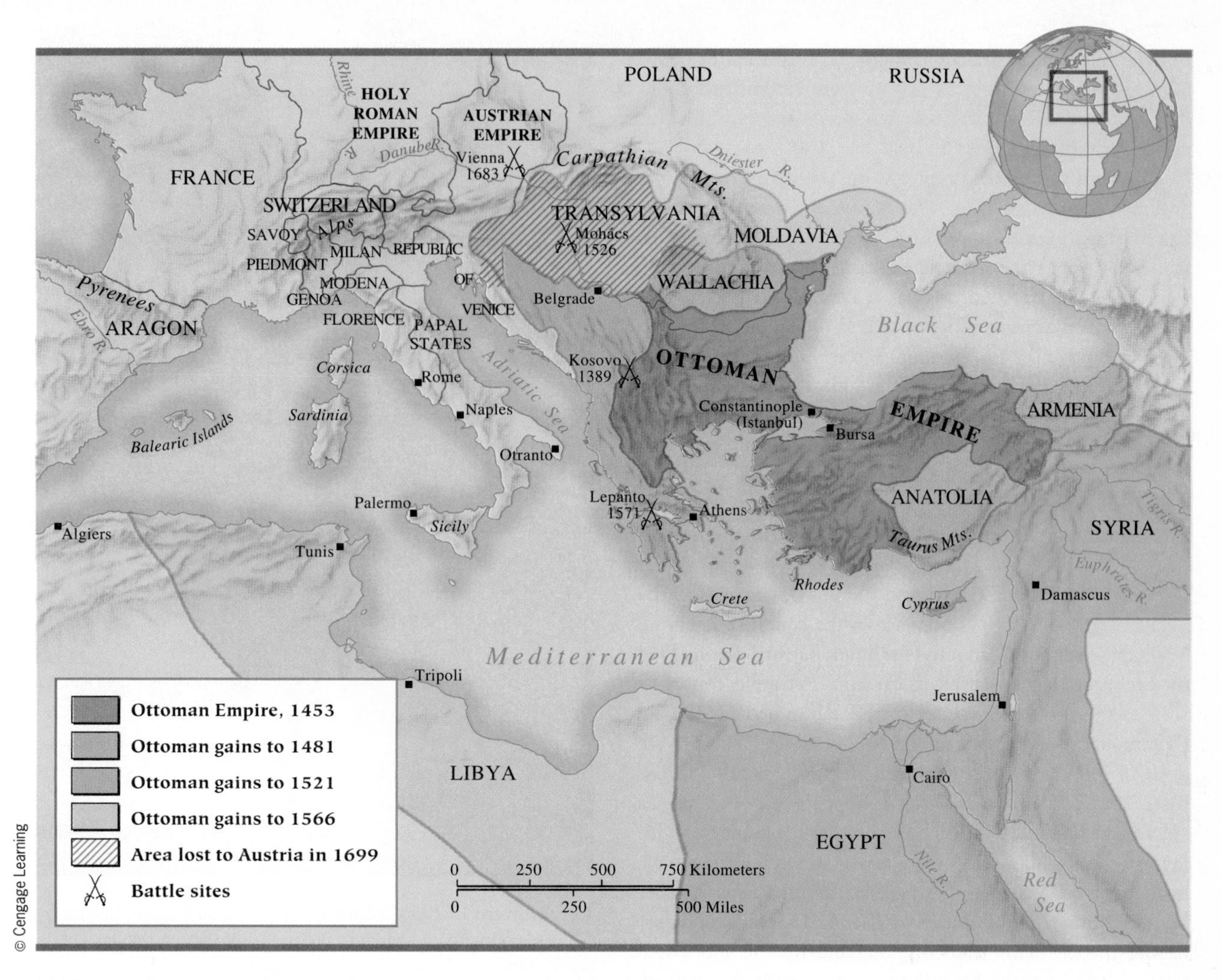

© Cengage Learning

MAP 16.1 The Ottoman Empire. This map shows the territorial growth of the Ottoman Empire from the eve of the conquest of Constantinople in 1453 to the end of the seventeenth century, when a defeat at the hands of Austria led to the loss of a substantial portion of central Europe.

Q *Where did the Ottomans come from?*

same time, they extended their power into the western Mediterranean and threatened to turn it into a Turkish lake until a large Turkish fleet was destroyed by the Spanish at Lepanto (LEH-pahn-toh *or* LIH-pan-toh) in 1571.

In the second half of the seventeenth century, the Ottoman Empire again took the offensive. By mid-1683, the Ottomans had marched through the Hungarian plain and laid siege to Vienna. Repulsed by a mixed army of Austrians, Poles, Bavarians, and Saxons, the Turks retreated and were pushed out of Hungary by a new European coalition. Although they retained the core of their empire, the Ottoman Turks would never again be a threat to Europe. The Turkish empire held together for the rest of the seventeenth and the eighteenth centuries, but it faced new challenges from the ever-growing Austrian Empire in southeastern Europe and the new Russian giant to the north.

The Nature of Turkish Rule

Like other Muslim empires in Persia and India, the Ottoman political system was the result of the evolution of tribal institutions into a sedentary empire. At the apex of the Ottoman system was the sultan, who was the supreme authority in both a political and a military sense. The origins of this system can be traced back to the bey, who as tribal leader was a first among equals, who could claim loyalty from his chiefs only as long as he could provide them with booty and grazing lands. Disputes were settled by tribal law, while Muslim laws were secondary. Tribal leaders collected taxes—or booty—from areas under their control and sent one-fifth on to the bey. Both administrative and military power were centralized under the bey, and the capital was wherever the bey and his administration happened to be.

But with the rise of empire came the adoption of Byzantine traditions of rule. The status and prestige of the sultan now increased relative to the subordinate tribal leaders. Court rituals inherited from the Byzantines and Persians were adopted, as was a centralized administrative system that increasingly isolated the sultan in his palace. The position of the sultan was hereditary, with a son, although not necessarily the eldest, always succeeding the father. This practice led to chronic succession struggles upon the death of individual sultans, and the losers were often executed (strangled with a silk bowstring) or imprisoned. Heirs to the throne were assigned as provincial governors to provide them with experience.

THE HAREM The heart of the sultan's power was in the Topkapi (tahp-KAH-pee) Palace in the center of Istanbul. Topkapi (meaning "cannon gate") was constructed in 1459 by Mehmet II and served as an administrative center as well as the private residence of the sultan and his family. Eventually, it had a staff of 20,000 employees. The private domain of the sultan was called the **harem** ("sacred place"). Here he resided with his concubines. Normally, a sultan did not marry but chose several concubines as his favorites; they were accorded this status after they gave birth to sons. When a son became a sultan, his mother became known as the queen mother and served as adviser to the throne. This tradition, initiated by the influential wife of Suleyman the Magnificent, often resulted in considerable authority for the queen mother in affairs of state.

Members of the harem, like the Janissaries, were often of slave origin and formed an elite element in Ottoman society. Since the enslavement of Muslims was forbidden, slaves were taken among non-Islamic peoples. Some concubines were prisoners selected for the position, while others were purchased or offered to the sultan as a gift. They were then trained and educated like the Janissaries in a system called ***devshirme*** (dev-SHEER-may) ("collection"). *Devshirme* had originated in the practice of requiring local clan leaders to provide prisoners to the sultan as part of their tax obligation. Talented males were given special training for eventual placement in military or administrative positions, while their female counterparts were trained for service in the harem, with instruction in reading, the Qur'an, sewing and embroidery, and musical performance. They were ranked according to their status, and some were permitted to leave the harem to marry officials.

Unique to the Ottoman Empire from the fifteenth century onward was the exclusive use of slaves to produce its royal heirs. Contrary to myth, few of the women of the imperial harem were used for sexual purposes, as the majority were members of the sultan's extended family—sisters, daughters, widowed mothers, and in-laws, with their own personal slaves and entourage. Contemporary European observers compared the atmosphere in the Topkapi harem to a Christian nunnery, with its hierarchical organization, enforced chastity, and rule of silence.

© Topkapi Palace Museum, Istanbul/The Bridgeman Art Library

Recruitment of the Children. The Ottoman Empire, like its Chinese counterpart, sought to recruit its officials on the basis of merit. Through the *devshirme* system, youthful candidates were selected from the non-Muslim population in villages throughout the empire. In this painting, an imperial officer is counting coins to pay for the children's travel expenses to Istanbul, where they will undergo extensive academic and military training. Note the concern of two of the mothers and a priest as they question the official, who undoubtedly underwent the process himself as a child. As they leave their family and friends, the children carry their worldly possessions in bags slung over their shoulders.

Because of their proximity to the sultan, the women of the harem often wielded so much political power that the era has been called "the sultanate of women." Queen mothers administered the imperial household and engaged in diplomatic relations with other countries while controlling the marital alliances of their daughters with senior officials or members of other royal families in the region. One princess was married seven separate times from the age of two after her previous husbands died either in battle or by execution.

ADMINISTRATION OF THE GOVERNMENT The sultan ruled through an imperial council that met four days a week and was chaired by the chief minister known as the **grand vizier** (veh-ZEER) (Turkish *vezir*). The sultan often attended behind a screen, whence he could privately indicate his desires to the grand vizier. The latter presided over the imperial bureaucracy. Like the palace guard, the bureaucrats were not an exclusive group but were chosen at least partly by merit from a palace school for training officials. Most officials were Muslims by birth, but some talented Janissaries became senior members of the bureaucracy, and almost all the later grand viziers came from the *devshirme* system.

Local administration during the imperial period was a product of Turkish tribal tradition and was similar in some respects to fief-holding in Europe. The empire was divided into provinces and districts governed by officials who, like their tribal predecessors, combined civil and military functions. Senior officials were assigned land in fief by the sultan and were then responsible for collecting taxes and supplying armies to the empire. These lands were then farmed out to the local cavalry elite called the ***sipahis*** (suh-pah-heez), who obtained their salaries by exacting taxes from all peasants in their fiefdoms.

Religion and Society in the Ottoman World

Like most Turkic-speaking peoples throughout the Middle East, the Ottoman ruling elites were Sunni Muslims. Ottoman sultans had claimed the title of caliph ("defender of the faith") since the early sixteenth century and thus were theoretically responsible for guiding the flock and maintaining Islamic law, the *Shari'a*. In practice, the sultan assigned these duties to a supreme religious authority, who administered the law and maintained schools for educating Muslims. Islamic law and customs were applied to all Muslims in the empire. Like their rulers, most Turkic-speaking people were Sunni Muslims, but some communities were attracted to Sufism (see Chapter 7) or other heterodox doctrines. The government tolerated such activities as long as their practitioners remained loyal, but in the early sixteenth century, unrest among these groups—some of whom converted to the Shi'ite version of Islam—outraged the conservative *ulama* and eventually led to war against the Safavids (see "The Safavids" later in this chapter).

THE TREATMENT OF MINORITIES Non-Muslims—mostly Orthodox Christians (Greeks and Slavs), Jews, and Armenian Christians—formed a significant minority within the empire, which treated them with relative tolerance. Non-Muslims were compelled to pay a head tax (because of their exemption from military service), and they were permitted to practice their religion or convert to Islam, although Muslims were prohibited from adopting another faith. Most of the population in European areas of the empire remained Christian, but in some places, such as the territory now called Bosnia, substantial numbers converted to Islam.

CHRONOLOGY The Ottoman Empire

Reign of Osman I	1280–1326
Ottoman Turks cross the Bosporus	1345
Murad I consolidates Turkish power in the Balkans	1360
Ottomans defeat the Serbian army at Kosovo	1389
Reign of Mehmet II the Conqueror	1451–1481
Turkish conquest of Constantinople	1453
Turks defeat the Mamluks in Syria and seize Cairo	1516–1517
Reign of Suleyman I the Magnificent	1520–1566
Turks defeat the Hungarians at Battle of Mohács	1526
Defeat of the Turks at Vienna	1529
Battle of Lepanto	1571
Second siege of Vienna	1683

Technically, women in the Ottoman Empire were subject to the same restrictions that afflicted their counterparts in other Muslim societies, but their position was ameliorated to some degree by various factors. In the first place, non-Muslims were subject to the laws and customs of their own religions; thus, Orthodox Christian, Jewish, and Armenian Christian women were spared some of the restrictions applied to their Muslim sisters. In the second place, Islamic laws as applied in the Ottoman Empire defined the legal position of women comparatively tolerantly. Women were permitted to own and inherit property, including their dowries. They could not be forced into marriage and in certain cases were permitted to seek a divorce. As we have seen, women often exercised considerable influence in the palace and in a few instances even served as senior officials, such as governors of provinces. The relatively tolerant attitude toward women in Ottoman-held territories has been ascribed by some to Turkish tribal traditions, which took a more egalitarian view of gender roles than the sedentary societies of the region did.

The Ottomans in Decline

By the seventeenth century, signs of internal rot had begun to appear in the empire, although the first loss of

A Turkish Discourse on Coffee

Coffee was first introduced to Turkey from the Arabian peninsula in the mid-sixteenth century and supposedly came to Europe during the Turkish siege of Vienna in 1529. The following account was written by Katib Chelebi (kah-TEEB CHEL-uh-bee), a seventeenth-century Turkish author who, among other things, compiled an extensive encyclopedia and bibliography. Here, in *The Balance of Truth*, he describes how coffee entered the empire and the problems it caused for public morality. (In the Muslim world, as in Europe and later in colonial America, the drinking of coffee was associated with coffeehouses, where rebellious elements often gathered to promote antigovernment activities.) Chelebi died in Istanbul in 1657, reportedly while drinking a cup of coffee.

Katib Chelebi, *The Balance of Truth*

[Coffee] originated in Yemen and has spread, like tobacco, over the world. Certain sheikhs, who lived with their dervishes in the mountains of Yemen, used to crush and eat the berries . . . of a certain tree. Some would roast them and drink their water. Coffee is a cold dry food, suited to the ascetic life and sedative of lust. . . .

It came to Asia Minor by sea, about 1543, and met with a hostile reception, *fetwas* [decrees] being delivered against it. For they said, Apart from its being roasted, the fact that it is drunk in gatherings, passed from hand to hand, is suggestive of loose living. It is related of Abul-Suud Efendi that he had holes bored in the ships that brought it, plunging their cargoes of coffee into the sea. But these strictures and prohibitions availed nothing. . . . One coffeehouse was opened after another, and men would gather together, with great eagerness and enthusiasm, to drink. Drug addicts in particular, finding it a life-giving thing, which increased their pleasure, were willing to die for a cup.

Storytellers and musicians diverted the people from their employments, and working for one's living fell into disfavor. Moreover the people, from prince to beggar, amused themselves with knifing one another. Toward the end of 1633, the late Ghazi Gultan Murad, becoming aware of the situation, promulgated an edict, out of regard and compassion for the people, to this effect: Coffeehouses throughout the Guarded Domains shall be dismantled and not opened hereafter. Since then, the coffeehouses of the capital have been as desolate as the heart of the ignorant. . . . But in cities and towns outside Istanbul, they are opened just as before. As has been said above, such things do not admit of a perpetual ban.

Why did coffee come to be regarded as a dangerous substance in the Ottoman Empire? Were the authorities successful in suppressing its consumption?

Source: From *The Balance of Truth* by Katib Chelebi, translated by G.L. Lewis, copyright 1927.

imperial territory did not occur until 1699, when Transylvania and much of Hungary were ceded to Austria in the Treaty of Karlowitz (KARL-oh-vits). Apparently, a number of factors were involved. In the first place, the administrative system inherited from the tribal period began to break down. Although the *devshirme* system of training officials continued, *devshirme* graduates were now permitted to marry and inherit property and to enroll their sons in the palace corps. Thus, they were gradually transformed from a meritocratic administrative elite into a privileged and often degenerate hereditary caste. Local administrators were corrupted and taxes rose as the central bureaucracy lost its links with rural areas. Constant wars depleted the treasury, and transport and communications were neglected. Interest in science and technology, once a hallmark of the Arab Empire, was in decline. In addition, the empire was beset by economic difficulties caused by the diversion of trade routes away from the eastern Mediterranean and the price inflation brought about by the influx of cheap American silver.

Other signs of change were the increasing material affluence and the impact of Western ideas and customs. Sophisticated officials and merchants began to mimic the habits and lifestyles of their European counterparts, dressing in the European fashion, purchasing Western furniture and art objects, and ignoring Muslim strictures against the consumption of alcohol and sexual activities outside marriage. During the sixteenth and early seventeenth centuries, coffee and tobacco were introduced into polite Ottoman society, and cafés for their consumption began to appear in the major cities (see the box above). One sultan in the early seventeenth century issued a decree prohibiting the

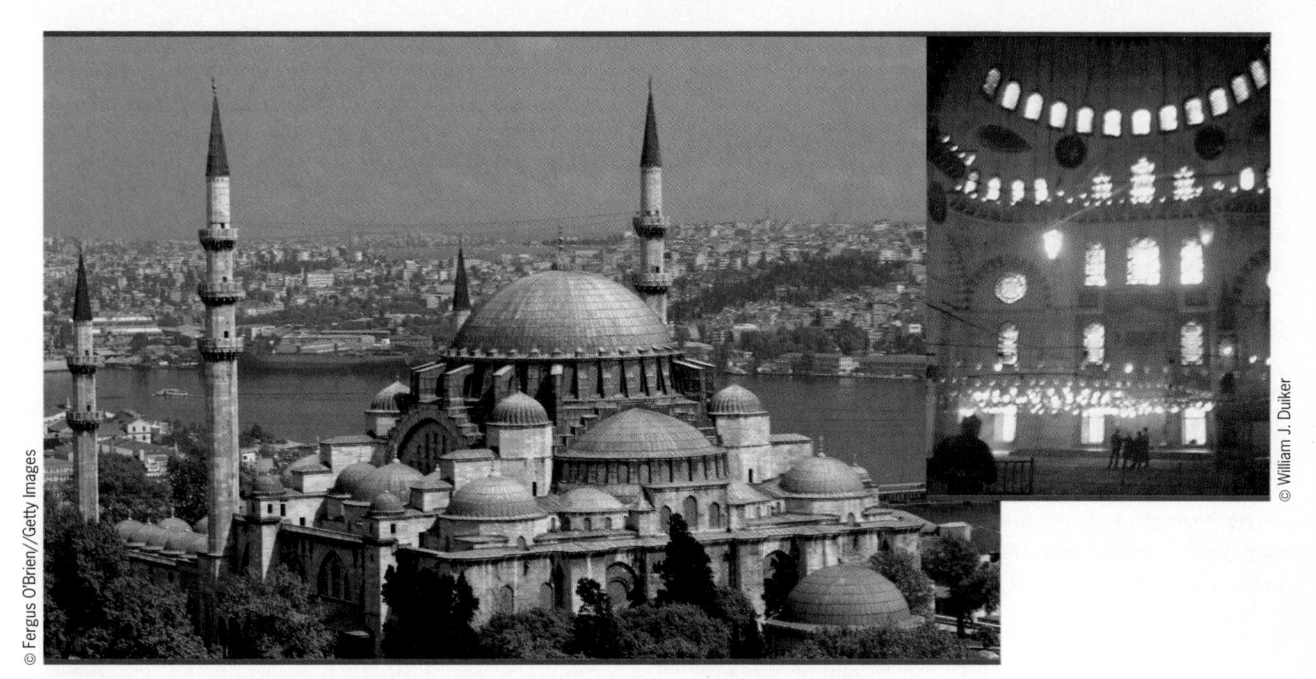

The Suleymaniye Mosque, Istanbul. The magnificent mosques built under the patronage of Suleyman the Magnificent are a great legacy of the Ottoman Empire and a fitting supplement to Hagia Sophia, the cathedral built by the Byzantine emperor Justinian in the sixth century C.E. Towering under a central dome, these mosques seem to defy gravity and, like European Gothic cathedrals, convey a sense of weightlessness. The Suleymaniye (soo-lay-MAHN-ee-eh) Mosque is one of the most impressive and most graceful in Istanbul. A far cry from the seventh-century desert mosques constructed of palm trunks, the Ottoman mosques stand among the architectural wonders of the world. Under the massive dome, the interior of the Suleymaniye Mosque offers a quiet refuge for prayer and reflection, bathed in muted sunlight and the warmth of plush carpets, as shown in the inset photo.

consumption of both coffee and tobacco, arguing (correctly, no doubt) that many cafés were nests of antigovernment intrigue. He even began to wander incognito through the streets of Istanbul at night. Any of his subjects detected in immoral or illegal acts were summarily executed and their bodies left on the streets as an example to others.

There were also signs of a decline in competence within the ruling family. Whereas the first sultans reigned twenty-seven years on average, later ones averaged only thirteen years, suggesting an increase in turmoil within the ruling cliques. The throne now went to the oldest surviving male, while his rivals were kept secluded in a latticed cage and thus had no governmental experience if they succeeded to rule. Later sultans also became less involved in government, and more power flowed to the office of the grand vizier, called the **Sublime Porte** (PORT), or to eunuchs and members of the harem. Palace intrigue increased as a result.

Ottoman Art

The Ottoman sultans were enthusiastic patrons of the arts and maintained large ateliers of artisans and artists, primarily at the Topkapi Palace in Istanbul but also in other important cities of the vast empire. The period from Mehmet II in the fifteenth century to the early eighteenth century witnessed the flourishing of pottery, rugs, silk and other textiles, jewelry, arms and armor, and calligraphy. All adorned the palaces of the rulers, testifying to their opulence and exquisite taste. The artists came from all parts of the realm and beyond.

ARCHITECTURE By far the greatest contribution of the Ottoman Empire to world art was its architecture, especially the magnificent mosques of the second half of the sixteenth century. Traditionally, prayer halls in mosques were divided by numerous pillars that supported small individual domes, creating a private, forestlike atmosphere. The Turks, however, modeled their new mosques on the open floor plan of the Byzantine church of Hagia Sophia (completed in 537), which had been turned into a mosque by Mehmet II, and began to push the pillars toward the outer wall to create a prayer hall with an uninterrupted central area under one large dome. With this plan, large numbers of believers could worship in unison in accordance with Muslim preference. By the mid-sixteenth century, the greatest of all Ottoman architects, Sinan (si-NAHN), began erecting the first of his eighty-one mosques with an uncluttered prayer area. Each was topped by an imposing dome, and often, as at Edirne, the entire building was framed with four towering narrow minarets. By emphasizing its vertical lines, the minarets camouflaged the massive stone bulk of the structure and gave it a feeling of incredible lightness. These four graceful minarets would find new expression sixty years later in India's white marble Taj Mahal (see "Mughal Culture" later in this chapter).

Earlier, in the thirteenth-century the Seljuk Turks of Anatolia had created beautiful tile decorations with two-color mosaics. Now Ottoman artists invented a new glazed tile art with painted flowers and geometrical designs in brilliant blue, green, yellow, and their own secret "tomato red." Entire walls, both interior and exterior, were covered with the painted tiles, which adorned palaces as well as mosques.

TEXTILES The sixteenth century also witnessed the flourishing of textiles and rugs. The Byzantine emperor Justinian had introduced the cultivation of silkworms to the West in the sixth century, and the silk industry resurfaced under the Ottomans. Perhaps even more famous than Turkish silks are the rugs. But whereas silks were produced under the patronage of the sultans, rugs were a peasant industry. Each village boasted its own distinctive design and color scheme for the rugs it produced.

The Safavids

FOCUS QUESTION: How did the Safavid Empire come into existence, and what led to its collapse?

After the collapse of the empire of Tamerlane in the early fifteenth century, the area extending from Persia into Central Asia lapsed into anarchy. The Uzbeks (ooz-BEKS), Turkic-speaking peoples from Central Asia, were the chief political and military force in the area. From their capital at Bukhara (boh-KAHR-uh *or* boo-KAH-ruh), east of the Caspian Sea, they maintained a semblance of control over the highly fluid tribal alignments until the emergence of the Safavid dynasty in Persia at the beginning of the sixteenth century.

The Safavid dynasty was founded by Shah Ismail (IS-mah-eel) (1487–1524), the descendant of Sheikh Safi al-Din (SAH-fee ul-DIN) (hence the name *Safavid*), who traced his origins to Ali, the fourth *imam* of the Muslim faith. In the early fourteenth century, Safi had been the leader of a community of Turkic-speaking tribespeople in Azerbaijan, near the Caspian Sea. Safi's community was only one of many Sufi mystical religious groups throughout the area. In time, the doctrine spread among nomadic groups throughout the Middle East and was transformed into the more activist Shi'ite version of Islam. Its adherents were known as "red heads" because they wore a distinctive red cap with twelve folds, meant to symbolize allegiance to the twelve *imams* of the Shi'ite faith.

In 1501, after Ismail's forces seized much of Iran and Iraq, he proclaimed himself the shah of a new Persian state. Baghdad was subdued in 1508 and the Uzbeks and their capital at Bokhara shortly thereafter. Ismail now sent Shi'ite preachers into Anatolia to proselytize and promote rebellion among Turkish tribal peoples in the Ottoman Empire. In retaliation, the Ottoman sultan, Selim I, advanced against the Safavids in Iran and won a major battle near Tabriz (tah-BREEZ) in 1514. But Selim could not maintain control of the area, and Ismail regained Tabriz a few years later.

The Ottomans returned to the attack in the 1580s and forced the new Safavid shah, Abbas (uh-BAHS) I the Great (1587–1629), to sign a punitive peace acceding to the loss of much territory. The capital was subsequently moved from Tabriz in the northwest to Isfahan (is-fah-HAHN) in the south. Still, it was under Shah Abbas that the Safavids reached the zenith of their glory. He established a system similar to the Janissaries in Turkey to train administrators to replace the traditional warrior elite. He also used the period of peace to strengthen his army, now armed with modern weapons, and in the early seventeenth century, he attempted to regain the lost territories. Although he had some initial success, war resumed in the 1620s, and a lasting peace was not achieved until 1638 (see Map 16.2).

Abbas the Great had managed to strengthen the dynasty significantly, and for a time after his death in 1629, it remained stable and vigorous. But succession conflicts plagued the dynasty. Partly as a result, the power of the more militant Shi'ites began to increase at court and in Safavid society at large. The intellectual freedom that had characterized the empire at its height was curtailed under the pressure of religious orthodoxy, and Iranian women, who had enjoyed considerable freedom and influence during the early empire, were forced to withdraw into seclusion and behind the veil. Meanwhile, attempts to suppress the religious beliefs of minorities led to increased popular unrest. In the early eighteenth century, Afghan warriors took advantage of local revolts to seize the capital of Isfahan, forcing the remnants of the Safavid ruling family to retreat to Azerbaijan, their original homeland. As the Ottomans seized territories along the western border, the empire finally collapsed in 1723. Eventually, order was restored by the military adventurer Nadir Shah Afshar (NAH-der shah ahf-SHAR), who launched an extended series of campaigns that restored the country's borders and even occupied the Mughal capital of Delhi (see "The Shadows Lengthen" later in this

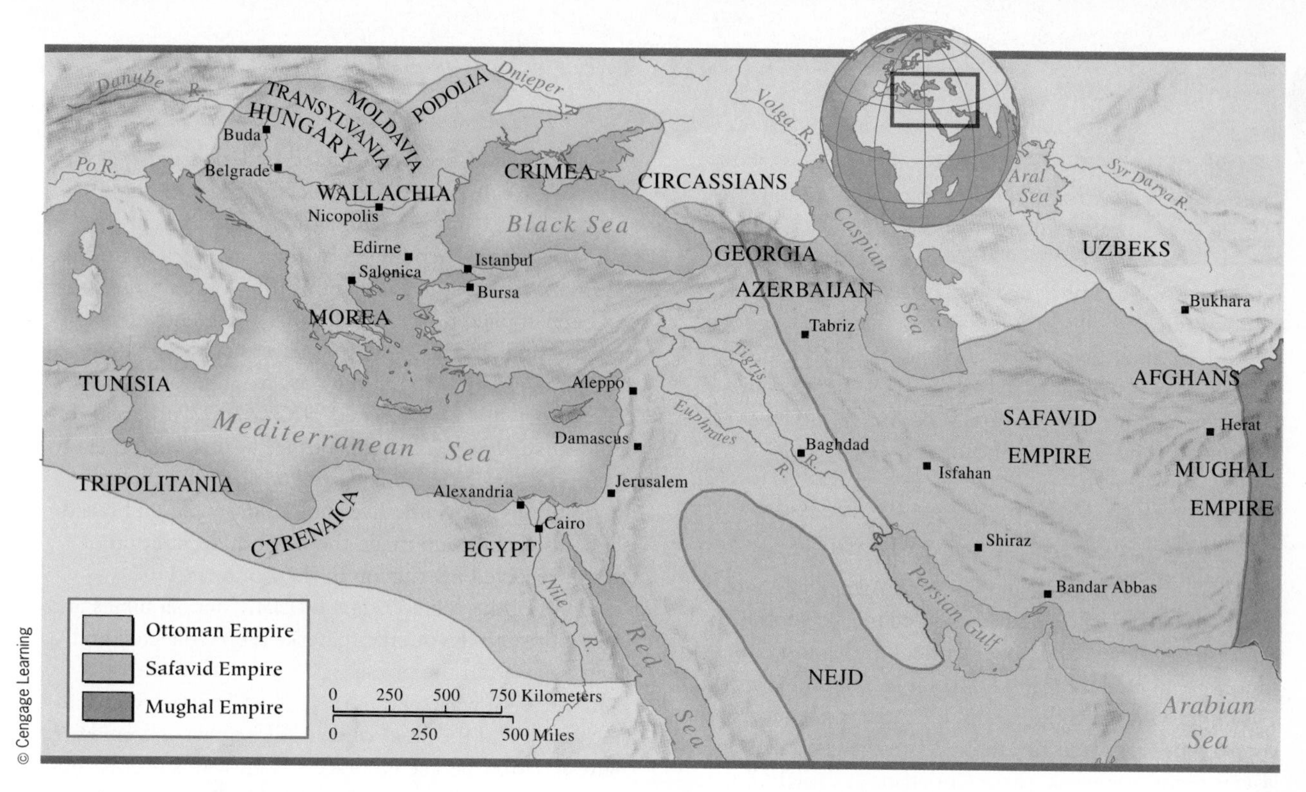

© Cengage Learning

MAP 16.2 The Ottoman and Safavid Empires, c. 1683. During the seventeenth century, the Ottoman and Safavid Empires contested vigorously for hegemony in the eastern Mediterranean and the Middle East. This map shows the territories controlled by each state in the late seventeenth century.

Q *Which states shared control over the ancient lands in the Tigris and Euphrates valleys? In which modern-day countries are those lands?*

chapter). After his death, the Zand dynasty ruled until the end of the eighteenth century.

Safavid Politics and Society

Like the Ottoman Empire, Persia under the Safavids was a mixed society The Safavids had come to power with the support of nomadic Turkic-speaking tribal groups, and leading elements from those groups retained considerable influence. But the majority of the population were Iranian; most were farmers or townspeople, with attitudes inherited from the relatively sophisticated and urbanized culture of pre-Safavid Iran. Faced with the problem of integrating unruly Turkic-speaking tribal peoples with the sedentary Persian-speaking population of the urban areas, the Safavids used the Shi'ite faith as a unifying force (see the box on p. 418). The shah himself acquired an almost divine quality and claimed to be the spiritual leader of all Islam. Shi'ism was declared the state religion.

Although there was a landed aristocracy, aristocratic power and influence were firmly controlled by strong-minded shahs, who confiscated aristocratic estates when possible and brought them under the control of the crown. Appointment to senior positions in the bureaucracy was by merit rather than birth.

The Safavid shahs took a direct interest in the economy and actively engaged in commercial and manufacturing activities, although there was also a large and affluent urban bourgeoisie. Like the Ottoman sultan, one shah regularly traveled the city streets incognito to check on the honesty of his subjects. When he discovered that a baker and butcher were overcharging for their products, he had the baker cooked in his own oven and the butcher roasted on a spit.

At its height, Safavid Iran was a worthy successor to the great Persian empires of the past, although it was

CHRONOLOGY The Safavids	
Ismail seizes Iran and Iraq and becomes shah of Persia	1501
Ismail conquers Baghdad and defeats Uzbeks	1508
Reign of Shah Abbas I	1587–1629
Truce achieved between Ottomans and Safavids	1638
Collapse of the Safavid Empire	1723

The Religious Zeal of Shah Abbas the Great

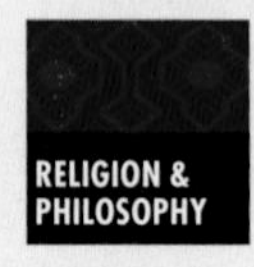

Shah Abbas I, probably the greatest of the Safavid rulers, expanded the borders of his empire into areas of the southern Caucasus inhabited by Christians and other non-Muslim peoples. After Persian control was assured, he instructed that the local populations be urged to convert to Islam for their own protection and the glory of God. In this passage, his biographer, the Persian historian Eskander Beg Monshi (es-KAHN-der bayg MAHN-shee), recounts the story of that effort.

Eskander Beg Monshi, "The Conversion of a Number of Christians to Islam"

This year the Shah decreed that those Armenians and other Christians who had been settled in [the southern Caucasus] and had been given agricultural land there should be invited to become Muslims. Life in this world is fraught with vicissitudes, and the Shah was concerned lest, in a period when the authority of the central government was weak, these Christians . . . might be subjected to attack by the neighboring Lor tribes (who are naturally given to causing injury and mischief), and their women and children carried off into captivity. In the areas in which these Christian groups resided, it was the Shah's purpose that the places of worship which they had built should become mosques, and the muezzin's call should be heard in them, so that these Christians might assume the guise of Muslims, and their future status accordingly be assured. . . .

Some of the Christians, guided by God's grace, embraced Islam voluntarily; others found it difficult to abandon their Christian faith and felt revulsion at the idea. They were encouraged by their monks and priests to remain steadfast in their faith. After a little pressure had been applied to the monks and priests, however, they desisted, and these Christians saw no alternative but to embrace Islam, though they did so with reluctance. The women and children embraced Islam with great enthusiasm, vying with one another in their eagerness to abandon their Christian faith and declare their belief in the unity of God. Some five thousand people embraced Islam. As each group made the Muslim declaration of faith, it received instruction in the Koran and the principles of the religious law of Islam, and all bibles and other Christian devotional material were collected and taken away from the priests.

In the same way, all the Armenian Christians who had been moved to [the area] were also forcibly converted to Islam. . . . Most people embraced Islam with sincerity, but some felt an aversion to making the Muslim profession of faith. True knowledge lies with God! May God reward the Shah for his action with long life and prosperity!

How do Shah Abbas's efforts to convert nonbelievers to Islam compare with similar programs by Muslim rulers in India, as described in Chapter 9? What did the author of this selection think about the conversions?

Source: From Eskander Beg Monshi in *History of Shah Abbas The Great*, Vol. II by Roger M. Savory by Westview Press, 1978.

probably not as wealthy as its Mughal and Ottoman neighbors to the east and west. Hemmed in by the sea power of the Europeans to the south and by the land power of the Ottomans to the west, the early Safavids had no navy and were forced to divert overland trade with Europe through southern Russia to avoid an Ottoman blockade. In the early seventeenth century, the situation improved when Iranian forces, in cooperation with the English, seized the island of Hormuz (hawr-MOOZ) from Portugal and established a new seaport on the southern coast at Bandar Abbas (BUHN-der uh-BAHS). As a consequence, commercial ties with Europe began to increase.

Safavid Art and Literature

Persia witnessed an extraordinary flowering of the arts during the reign of Shah Abbas I. His new capital of Isfahan was a grandiose planned city with wide visual perspectives and a sense of order almost unique in the region. Shah Abbas ordered his architects to position his palaces, mosques, and bazaars around a massive rectangular polo ground. Much of the original city is still in good condition and remains the gem of modern Iran. The immense mosques are richly decorated with elaborate blue tiles. The palaces are delicate structures with unusual

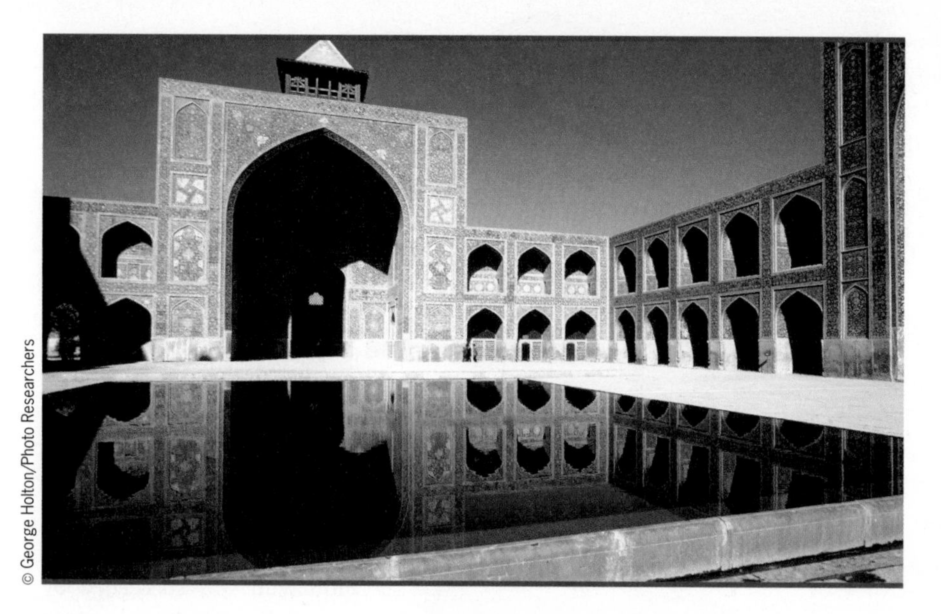

© George Holton/Photo Researchers

The Royal Academy of Isfahan. Along with institutions such as libraries and hospitals, theological schools were often included in the mosque compound. One of the most sumptuous was the Royal Academy of Isfahan, built by the shah of Persia in the early eighteenth century. This view shows the large courtyard surrounded by arcades of student rooms, reminiscent of the arrangement of monks' cells in European cloisters.

slender wooden columns. These architectural wonders of Isfahan epitomize the grandeur, delicacy, and color that defined the Safavid golden age. To adorn the splendid buildings, Safavid artisans created imaginative metalwork, tile decorations, and original and delicate glass vessels.

Textiles, however, were the area of greatest productivity. Silk weaving based on new techniques became a national industry. The silks depicted birds, animals, and flowers in a brilliant mass of color with silver and gold threads. Above all, carpet weaving flourished, stimulated by the great demand for Persian carpets in the West.

The long tradition of Persian painting continued into the Safavid era, but changed dramatically in two ways during the second half of the sixteenth century. First, taking advantage of the growing official toleration of portraiture, painters began to highlight the inner character of their subjects. Secondly, since royal patronage was not always forthcoming, artists sought to attract a larger audience by producing individual paintings that promoted their own distinctive styles and proudly bore their own signature.

The Grandeur of the Mughals

FOCUS QUESTIONS: What role did Islam play in the Mughal Empire, and how did the Mughals' approach to religion compare with that of the Ottomans and the Safavids? What might explain the differences?

In retrospect, the period from the sixteenth to the eighteenth centuries can be viewed as a high point of traditional culture in India. The era began with the creation of one of the subcontinent's greatest empires—that of the Mughals (MOO-guls). For the first time since the Mauryan dynasty, the entire subcontinent was united under a single government, with a common culture that inspired admiration and envy throughout the entire region.

The Mughal Empire reached its peak in the sixteenth century under the famed Emperor Akbar (AK-bar) and maintained its vitality under a series of strong rulers for another century (see Map 16.3). Then the dynasty began to weaken, a process that was hastened by the challenge of the foreigners arriving by sea. The Portuguese, who first arrived in 1498, were little more than an irritant. Two centuries later, however, Europeans began to seize control of regional trade routes and to meddle in the internal politics of the subcontinent. By the end of the eighteenth century, nothing remained of the empire but a shell. But some historians see the seeds of decay less in the challenge from abroad than in internal weakness—in the very nature of the empire itself, which was always more a heterogeneous collection of semiautonomous political forces than a centralized empire in the style of neighboring China.

The Founding of the Empire

When the Portuguese fleet led by Vasco da Gama arrived at the port of Calicut in 1498, the Indian subcontinent was still divided into a number of Hindu and Muslim kingdoms. But it was on the verge of a new era of unity that would be brought about by a foreign dynasty—the Mughals. Like so many recent rulers of northern India, the founders of the Mughal Empire were not natives of India but came from the mountainous region north of the Ganges River. The founder of the dynasty, known to history as Babur (BAH-burr) (1483–1530), had an illustrious pedigree. His father was descended from the great Asian conqueror Tamerlane, his mother from the Mongol conqueror Genghis Khan.

Babur had inherited a fragment of Tamerlane's empire in a valley of the Syr Darya (SEER DAHR-yuh) River

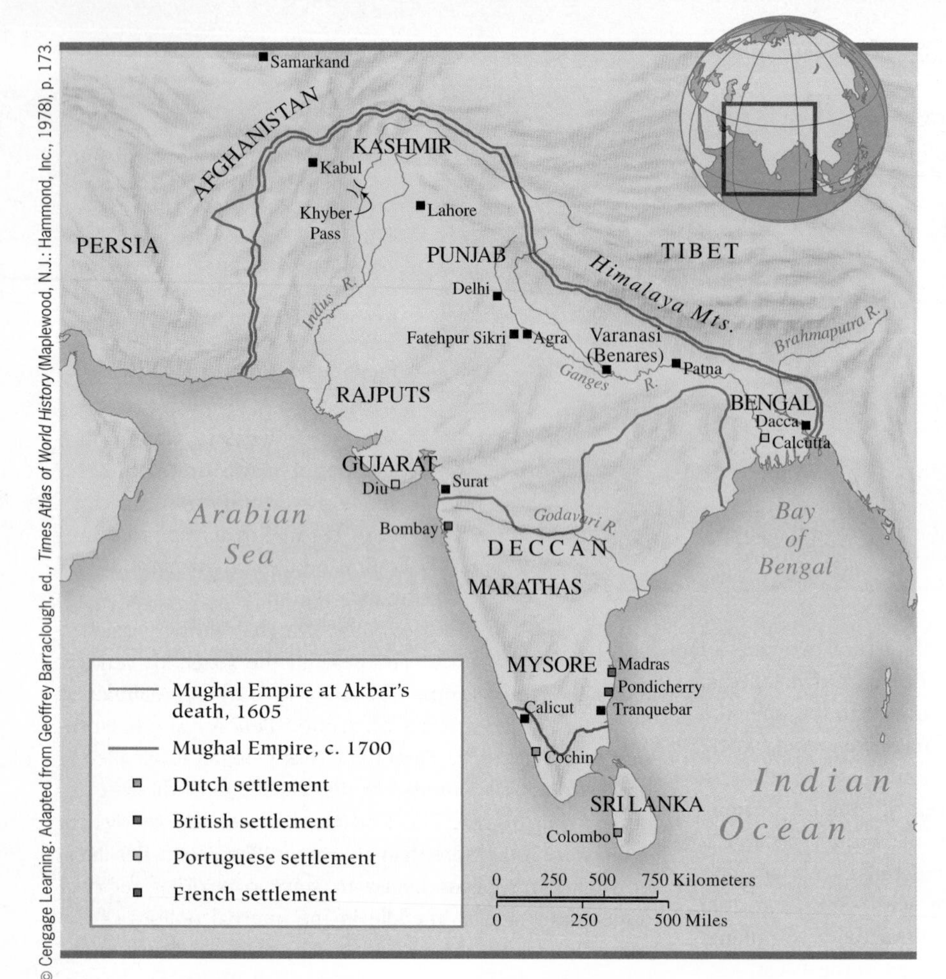

© Cengage Learning. Adapted from Geoffrey Barraclough, ed., *Times Atlas of World History* (Maplewood, N.J.: Hammond, Inc., 1978), p. 173.

MAP 16.3 The Mughal Empire. This map shows the expansion of the Mughal Empire from the death of Akbar in 1605 to the rule of Aurangzeb at the end of the seventeenth century.

In which cities on the map were European settlements located? When did each group of Europeans arrive, and how did the settlements spread?

(see Map 16.2 on p. 417). Driven south by the rising power of the Uzbeks and then the Safavid dynasty in Persia, Babur and his warriors seized Kabul in 1504 and, thirteen years later, crossed the Khyber Pass to India.

Following a pattern that we have seen before, Babur began his rise to power by offering to help an ailing dynasty against its opponents. Although his own forces were far smaller than those of his adversaries, he possessed advanced weapons, including artillery, and used them to great effect. His use of mobile cavalry was particularly successful against the massed forces, supplemented by mounted elephants, of his enemy. In 1526, with only 12,000 troops against an enemy force nearly ten times that size, Babur captured Delhi (DEL-ee). Over the next years, he continued his conquests in northern India, until his early death in 1530 at the age of forty-seven.

Babur's success was due in part to his vigor and his charismatic personality, which earned him the undying loyalty of his followers. His son and successor Humayun (hoo-MY-yoon) (1530–1556) was, in the words of one British historian, "intelligent but lazy." In 1540, he was forced to flee to Persia, where he lived in exile for sixteen years. Finally, with the aid of the Safavid shah of Persia, he returned to India and reconquered Delhi in 1555 but died the following year, reportedly from injuries suffered in a fall after smoking opium.

Humayun was succeeded by his son Akbar (1556–1605). Born while his father was in exile, Akbar was only fourteen when he mounted the throne. Illiterate but highly intelligent and industrious, Akbar set out to extend his domain, then limited to the Punjab (puhn-JAHB) and the upper Ganges River valley. "A monarch," he remarked, "should be ever intent on conquest, otherwise his neighbors rise in arms against him. The army should be exercised in warfare, lest from want of training they become self-indulgent."[1] By the end of his life, he had brought Mughal rule to most of the subcontinent, from the Himalaya Mountains to the Godavari (goh-DAH-vuh-ree) River in central India and from Kashmir to the mouths of the Brahmaputra (brah-muh-POO-truh) and the Ganges. In so doing, Akbar had created the greatest Indian empire since the Mauryan dynasty nearly two thousand years earlier. Though it appeared highly centralized from the outside, the empire was actually a collection of semiautonomous principalities ruled by provincial elites and linked together by the overarching majesty of the Mughal emperor.

Akbar and Indo-Muslim Civilization

Although Akbar was probably the greatest of the conquering Mughal monarchs, like his famous predecessor

Asoka, he is best known for the humane character of his rule. Above all, he accepted the diversity of Indian society and took steps to reconcile his Muslim and Hindu subjects.

RELIGION AND THE STATE Though raised an orthodox Muslim, Akbar had been exposed to other beliefs during his childhood and had little patience with the pedantic views of Muslim scholars at court. As emperor, he displayed a keen interest in other religions, not only tolerating Hindu practices and taking a Hindu princess as one of his wives but also welcoming the expression of Christian views by his Jesuit advisers (the Jesuits first sent a mission to Agra in 1580). He patronized classical Indian arts and architecture and abolished many of the restrictions faced by Hindus in a Muslim-dominated society.

During his later years, Akbar became steadily more hostile to Islam. To the dismay of many Muslims at court, he sponsored a new form of worship called the Divine Faith (*Din-i-Ilahi*), which combined characteristics of several religions with a central belief in the infallibility of all decisions reached by the emperor. The new faith aroused deep hostility in Muslim circles and rapidly vanished after his death.

ADMINISTRATIVE REFORMS Akbar also extended his innovations to the imperial administration. The empire was divided into provinces, and the administration of each province was modeled after the central government, with departments for military, financial, commercial, and legal affairs. Senior officials in each department reported directly to their counterparts in the capital city.

Although the upper ranks of the government continued to be dominated by nonnative Muslims, a substantial proportion of lower-ranking officials were Hindus, and a few Hindus were appointed to positions of importance. At first, most officials were paid salaries, but later they were ordinarily assigned sections of land for their temporary use; they kept a portion of the taxes paid by the local peasants in lieu of a salary. These local officials, known as ***zamindars*** (zuh-meen-DAHRZ), were expected to forward the rest of the taxes from the lands under their control to the central government. *Zamindars* often recruited a number of military and civilian retainers and accumulated considerable power in their localities.

The same tolerance that marked Akbar's attitude toward religion and administration extended to the legal system. While Muslims were subject to the Islamic codes (the *Shari'a*), Hindu law applied in areas settled by Hindus, who after 1579 were no longer required to pay the unpopular *jizya* (JIZ-yuh), or poll tax on non-Muslims. Punishments for crime were mild by the standards of the day, and justice was administered in a relatively impartial and efficient manner.

A HARMONIOUS SOCIETY A key element in Akbar's vision of the ideal social order was the concept of harmony, meaning that each individual and group within the empire would play their assigned role and contribute to the welfare of society as a whole. This concept of social harmony was based in part on his vision of a world shaped by the laws of Islam as transmitted by Muhammad (*Shari'a*), but it also corresponded to the deep-seated indigenous belief in the importance of class hierarchy, as expressed in the Indian class and caste system (see the box on p. 422). In its overall conception, it bears a clear resemblance to the social structure adopted by the Mughals' contemporaries to the west, the Ottoman Empire.

Overall, Akbar's reign was a time of peace and prosperity. Although all Indian peasants were required to pay about one-third of their annual harvest to the state through the *zamindars*, in general the system was applied fairly, and when drought struck in the 1590s, the taxes were reduced or even suspended altogether. Thanks to a long period of relative peace and political stability, commerce and manufacturing flourished. Foreign trade, in particular, thrived as Indian goods, notably textiles, tropical food products, spices, and precious stones, were exported in exchange for gold and silver. Tariffs on imports were low. Much of the foreign commerce was handled by Arab traders, since the Indians, like their Mughal rulers, did not care for travel by sea. Internal trade, however, was dominated by large merchant castes, who also were active in banking and handicrafts.

Akbar's Successors

Akbar died in 1605 and was succeeded by his son Jahangir (juh-HAHN-geer) (1605–1628). During the early years of his reign, Jahangir continued to strengthen central control over the vast empire. Eventually, however, his grip began to weaken (according to his memoirs, he "only wanted a bottle of wine and a piece of meat to make merry"), and the court fell under the influence of one of his wives, the Persian-born Nur Jahan (NOOR juh-HAHN) (see the box on p. 423). The empress took advantage of her position to enrich her own family and arranged for her niece Mumtaz Mahal (MOOM-tahz muh-HAHL) to marry her husband's third son and ultimate successor, Shah Jahan (1628–1657). When Shah Jahan succeeded to the throne, he quickly demonstrated the single-minded quality of his grandfather (albeit in a much more brutal manner), ordering the assassination of all of his rivals in order to secure his position.

THE REIGN OF SHAH JAHAN During a reign of three decades, Shah Jahan maintained the system established by his predecessors while expanding the boundaries of the empire by successful campaigns in the Deccan

Designing the Perfect Society

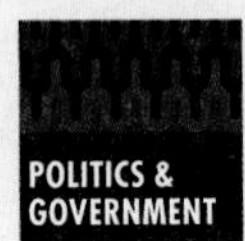
POLITICS & GOVERNMENT

In the late fifteenth century, the Persian author Muhammad ibn Asad Jalal ud-din al-Dawwani (al-da-WAH-nee) (1427–1501) wrote an essay on the ideal society entitled *Jalali's Ethics*. The work later attracted favorable notice at the Mughal court in India and eventually was paraphrased by Emperor Akbar's famous adviser Abu'l Fazl Allami (uh-BUL FAYZ-ul ahl-LAHM-mee). It thus provides insight into the political and social views of key officials in Mughal India during the reign of its most famous ruler.

Jalali's Ethics

In order to preserve this political equipoise, there is a correspondence to be maintained between the various classes. Like as the equipoise of bodily temperament is affected by intermixture and correspondence of four elements, the equipoise of the political temperament is to be sought for in the correspondence of four classes.

1. *Men of the pen*, such as lawyers, divines, judges, bookmen, statisticians, geometricians, astronomers, physicians, poets. In these and their exertions in the use of their delightful pens, the subsistence of the faith and of the world itself is vested and bound up. They occupy the place in politics that water does among the elements. Indeed, to persons of ready understanding, the similarity of knowledge and water is as clear as water itself, and as evident as the sun that makes it so.
2. *Men of the sword*, such as soldiers, fighting zealots, guards of forts and passes, etc.; without whose exercise of the impetuous and vindictive sword, no arrangement of the age's interests could be effected; without the havoc of whose tempest-like energies, the materials of corruption, in the shape of rebellious and disaffected persons, could never be dissolved and dissipated. These then occupy the place of fire, their resemblance to it is too plain to require demonstration; no rational person need call in the aid of fire to discover it.
3. *Men of business*, such as merchants, capitalists, artisans, and craftsmen by whom the means of emolument and all other interests are adjusted; and through whom the remotest extremes enjoy the advantage and safeguard of each other's most peculiar commodities. The resemblance of these to air—the auxiliary of growth and increase in vegetables—the reviver of spirit in animal life—the medium of the undulation and movement of which all sorts of rare and precious things traverse the hearing to arrive at the headquarters of human nature—is exceedingly manifest.
4. *Husbandmen*, such as seedsmen, bailiffs, and agriculturists—the superintendents of vegetation and preparers of provender; without whose exertions the continuance of the human kind must be cut short. These are, in fact, the only producers of what had no previous existence; the other classes adding nothing whatever to subsisting products, but only transferring what subsists already from person to person, from place to place, and from form to form. How close these come to the soil and surface of the earth—the point to which all the heavenly circles refer—the scope to which all the luminaries of the purer world direct their rays—the stage on which wonders are displayed—the limit to which mysteries are confined—must be universally apparent.

In like manner then as in the composite organizations the passing of any element beyond its proper measure occasions the loss of equipoise, and is followed by dissolution and ruin, in political coalition, no less, the prevalence of any one class over the other three overturns the adjustment and dissolves the junction. Next attention is to be directed to the condition of the individuals composing them, and the place of every one determined according to his right.

How does the social class system described here compare with the traditional division of classes in premodern India?

Source: A. T. Embree (ed.), *Sources of Indian Tradition: From the Beginning to 1800*, Vol. I, 2nd ed. (New York, 1988), pp. 431–432.

The Power Behind the Throne

POLITICS & GOVERNMENT

During his reign, the Mughal emperor Jahangir became addicted to alcohol and opium. Because of his weakened condition, his Persian wife, Nur Jahan, began to rule on his behalf. She served as the de facto ruler of India, exerting influence in both internal and foreign affairs. Although the extent of Nur Jahan's influence was often criticized at court, her performance impressed many European observers, as these remarks by an English visitor attest.

Nur Jahan, Empress of Mughal India

If anyone with a request to make at Court obtains an audience or is allowed to speak, the King hears him indeed, but will give no definite answer of Yes or No, referring him promptly to Asaf Khan, who in the same way will dispose of no important matter without communicating with his sister, the Queen, and who regulates his attitude in such a way that the authority of neither of them may be diminished. Anyone then who obtains a favour must thank them for it, and not the King. . . .

Her abilities were uncommon; for she rendered herself absolute, in a government in which women are thought incapable of bearing any part. Their power, it is true, is sometimes exerted in the harem; but, like the virtues of the magnet, it is silent and unperceived. Nur Jahan stood forth in public; she broke through all restraint and custom, and acquired power by her own address, more than by the weakness of Jahangir. . . .

Her former and present supporters have been well rewarded, so that now most of the men who are near the King owe their promotion to her, and are consequently under . . . obligations to her. . . . Many misunderstandings result, for the King's orders or grants of appointments, etc., are not certainties, being of no value until they have been approved by the Queen.

Based on this description, how does the position that Nur Jahan occupied in Mughul government compare with the roles played by other female political figures in China, Africa, and Europe? What do all of these women have in common?

Source: From *Nur Jahan: Empress of Mughal India* by Ellison Banks Findly. Oxford University Print on Demand, 1993.

Plateau and against Samarkand, north of the Hindu Kush. But Shah Jahan's rule was marred by his failure to deal with the growing domestic problems. He had inherited a nearly empty treasury because of Empress Nur Jahan's penchant for luxury and ambitious charity projects. Though the majority of his subjects lived in grinding poverty, Shah Jahan's frequent military campaigns and expensive building projects put a heavy strain on the imperial finances and compelled him to raise taxes. At the same time, the government did little to improve rural conditions. In a country where transport was primitive (it often took three months to travel the 600 miles between Patna, in the middle of the Ganges River valley, and Delhi) and drought conditions frequent, the dynasty made few efforts to increase agricultural efficiency or to improve the roads, although a grand trunk road was eventually constructed between the capital Agra (AH-gruh) and Lahore (luh-HOHR), a growing city several hundred miles to the northwest. A Dutch merchant in Gujarat (goo-juh-RAHT) described conditions during a famine in the mid-seventeenth century:

> As the famine increased, men abandoned towns and villages and wandered helplessly. It was easy to recognize their condition: eyes sunk deep in head, lips pale and covered with slime, the skin hard, with the bones showing through, the belly nothing but a pouch hanging down empty, knuckles and kneecaps showing prominently. One would cry and howl for hunger, while another lay stretched on the ground dying in misery; wherever you went, you saw nothing but corpses.[2]

In 1648, Shah Jahan moved his capital from Agra to Delhi and built the famous Red Fort in his new capital city. But he is best known for the Taj Mahal (tahj muh-HAHL) in Agra, widely considered to be the most beautiful building in India, if not in the entire world (see the comparative illustration on p. 430). The story is a romantic one—that the Taj was built by the emperor in memory of his wife Mumtaz Mahal, who had died giving birth to her thirteenth child at the age of thirty-nine. But the reality has a less attractive side: the expense of the building, which employed 20,000 masons over twenty years, forced the government to raise agricultural taxes, further impoverishing many Indian peasants.

RULE OF AURANGZEB Succession struggles returned to haunt the dynasty in the mid-1650s when Shah Jahan's illness led to a struggle for power between his sons Dara Shikoh (DA-ruh SHIH-koh) and Aurangzeb (ow-rang-ZEB). Dara Shikoh was described by his contemporaries as progressive and humane, but he apparently lacked political acumen and was outmaneuvered by Aurangzeb (1658–1707), who had Dara Shikoh put to death and then imprisoned his father in the fort at Agra.

Aurangzeb is one of the most controversial individuals in the history of India. A man of high principle, he attempted to eliminate many of what he considered to be India's social evils, prohibiting the immolation of widows on their husband's funeral pyre (*sati*), the castration of eunuchs, and the exaction of illegal taxes. With less success, he tried to forbid gambling, drinking, and prostitution. But Aurangzeb, a devout and somewhat doctrinaire Muslim, also adopted a number of measures that reversed the policies of religious tolerance established by his predecessors. The building of new Hindu temples was prohibited, and the Hindu poll tax was restored. Forced conversions to Islam were resumed, and non-Muslims were driven from the court. Aurangzeb's heavy-handed religious policies led to a revival of Hindu fervor. The last years of his reign saw considerable domestic unrest and a number of revolts against imperial authority.

THE SHADOWS LENGTHEN During the eighteenth century, Mughal power was threatened from both within and without. Fueled by the growing power and autonomy of the local gentry and merchants, rebellious groups throughout the empire, from the Deccan to the Punjab, began to reassert local authority and reduce the power of the Mughal emperor to that of a "tinsel sovereign." Increasingly divided, India was vulnerable to attack from abroad. In 1739, Delhi was sacked by the Persians, who left it in ashes.

A number of obvious reasons for the virtual collapse of the Mughal Empire can be identified, including the draining of the imperial treasury and the decline in competence of the Mughal rulers. But it should also be noted that even at its height under Akbar, the empire was a loosely knit collection of heterogeneous principalities held together by the authority of the throne, which tried to combine Persian concepts of kingship with the Indian tradition of decentralized power. Decline set in when centrifugal forces gradually began to predominate over centripetal ones.

The Impact of European Power in India

As we have seen, the first Europeans to arrive were the Portuguese. Although they established a virtual monopoly over regional trade in the Indian Ocean, they did not seek to penetrate the interior of the subcontinent but focused on establishing way stations en route to China and the Spice Islands. The situation changed at the end of the sixteenth century, when the English and the Dutch appeared on the scene. Soon both powers were in active competition with Portugal, and with each other, for trading privileges in the region (see the box on p. 425).

Penetration of the new market was not easy. When the first English fleet arrived at Surat (SOOR-et), a thriving port on the northwestern coast of India, in 1608, their request for trading privileges was rejected by Emperor Jahangir. Needing lightweight Indian cloth to trade for spices in the East Indies, the English persisted, and in 1616, they were finally permitted to install their own ambassador at the imperial court in Agra. Three years later, the first English factory (trading station) was established at Surat.

During the next several decades, the English presence in India steadily increased while Mughal power gradually waned. By midcentury, additional English factories had been established at Fort William (now the great city of Kolkata, formerly Calcutta) on the Hoogly River near the Bay of Bengal and in 1639 at Madras (muh-DRAS *or* muh-DRAHS) (Chennai) on the southeastern coast. From there, English ships carried Indian-made cotton goods to the East Indies, where they were bartered for spices, which were shipped back to England.

English success in India attracted rivals, including the Dutch and the French. The Dutch abandoned their interests to concentrate on the spice trade in the mid-seventeenth century, but the French were more persistent and established factories of their own. For a brief period, under the ambitious empire builder Joseph François Dupleix (zho-ZEF frahn-SWAH doo-PLAY), the French competed successfully with the British, even capturing Madras from a British garrison in 1746. But the military genius of Sir Robert Clive (CLYV), an aggressive British administrator and empire builder who eventually became the chief representative of the East India Company in the subcontinent, and the refusal of the French government to provide financial support for Dupleix's efforts eventually left the French with only their fort at Pondicherry (pon-duh-CHEH-ree) and a handful of small territories on the southeastern coast.

OPPOSING ✂ VIEWPOINTS

The Capture of Port Hoogly

In 1632, the Mughal ruler, Shah Jahan, ordered an attack on the city of Hoogly (HOOG-lee), a fortified Portuguese trading post on the northeastern coast of India. For the Portuguese, who had profited from half a century of triangular trade involving India, China, and various countries in the Middle East and Southeast Asia, the loss of Hoogly hastened the decline of their influence in the region. Presented here are two contemporary versions of the battle. The first, from the *Padshahnama* (pad-shah-NAHM-uh) (*Book of Kings*), relates the course of events from the Mughal point of view. The second account is by John Cabral, a Jesuit missionary who was resident in Hoogly at the time.

The *Padshahnama*

During the reign of the Bengalis, a group of Frankish [European] merchants . . . settled in a place one *kos* from Satgaon . . . and, on the pretext that they needed a place for trading, they received permission from the Bengalis to construct a few edifices. Over time, due to the indifference of the governors of Bengal, many Franks gathered there and built dwellings of the utmost splendor and strength, fortified with cannons, guns, and other instruments of war. It was not long before it became a large settlement and was named Hoogly. . . . The Franks' ships trafficked at this port, and commerce was established, causing the market at the port of Satgaon to slump. . . . Of the peasants of those places, they converted some to Christianity by force and others through greed and sent them off to Europe in their ships. . . .

Since the improper actions of the Christians of Hoogly Port toward the Muslims were accurately reflected in the mirror of the mind of the Emperor before his accession to the throne, when the imperial banners cast their shadows over Bengal, and inasmuch as he was always inclined to propagate the true religion and eliminate infidelity, it was decided that when he gained control over this region he would eradicate the corruption of these abominators from the realm.

John Cabral, *Travels of Sebastian Manrique, 1629–1649*

Hugli continued at peace all the time of the great King Jahangir. For, as this Prince, by what he showed, was more attached to Christ than to Mohammad and was a Moor in name and dress only. . . . Sultan Khurram [Shah Jahan] was in everything unlike his father, especially as regards the latter's leaning towards Christianity. . . . He declared himself the mortal enemy of the Christian name and the restorer of the law of Mohammad. . . . He sent a *firman* [order] to the Viceroy of Bengal, commanding him without reply or delay, to march upon the Bandel of Hugli and put it to fire and the sword. He added that, in doing so, he would render a signal service to God, to Mohammad, and to him. . . .

Consequently, on a Friday, September 24, 1632, . . . all the people [the Portuguese] embarked with the utmost secrecy. . . . Learning what was going on, and wishing to be able to boast that they had taken Hugli by storm, they [the imperialists] made a general attack on the Bandel by Saturday noon. They began by setting fire to a mine, but lost in it more men than we. Finally, however, they were masters of the Bandel.

How do these two accounts of the Battle of Hoogly differ? Is there any way to reconcile the two accounts into a single narrative?

Source: From *King of the World: a Mughal manuscript from the Royal Library*, Windsor Castle, trans. by Wheeler Thackston, text by Milo Cleveland Beach and Ebba Koch (London: Thames and Hudson, 1997), p. 59.

In the meantime, Clive began to consolidate British control in Bengal (ben-GAHL), where the local ruler had attacked Fort William and imprisoned the local British population in the infamous Black Hole of Calcutta (an underground prison for holding the prisoners, many of whom died in captivity). In 1757, a small British force numbering about three thousand defeated a Mughal-led army over ten times that size in the Battle of Plassey (PLASS-ee). As part of the spoils of victory, the British East India Company exacted from the now-decrepit Mughal court the authority to collect taxes from extensive lands in the area surrounding Calcutta. Less than ten

Bibliothèque Nationale, Paris//© The Art Archive at Art Resource, NY

A Pepper Plantation. During the Age of Exploration, pepper was one of the spices most sought by European adventurers. Unlike cloves and nutmeg, it was found in other areas in Asia besides the Indonesian archipelago. Shown here is a French pepper plantation in southern India. Eventually, the French were driven out of the Indian subcontinent by the British and retained only a few tiny enclaves along the coast.

years later, British forces seized the reigning Mughal emperor in a skirmish at Buxar (buk-SAHR), and the British began to consolidate their economic and administrative control over Indian territory through the surrogate power of the now powerless Mughal court (see Map 16.4).

To officials of the East India Company, the expansion of their authority into the interior of the subcontinent probably seemed like a simple commercial decision, a way to obtain guaranteed revenues to pay for the increasingly expensive military operations in India. To historians, it marks a major step in the gradual transfer of all of the Indian subcontinent to the British East India Company and later, in 1858, to the British crown. The process was more haphazard than deliberate.

ECONOMIC DIFFICULTIES The company's takeover of vast landholdings, notably in the eastern Indian states of Orissa (uh-RIH-suh) and Bengal, may have been a windfall for enterprising British officials, but it was a disaster for the Indian economy. In the first place, it resulted in the transfer of capital from the local Indian aristocracy to company officials, most of whom sent their profits back to Britain. Second, it hastened the destruction of once healthy local industries because British goods such as machine-made textiles were imported duty-free into India to compete against local products. Finally, British expansion hurt the peasants. As the British took over the administration of the land tax, they also applied British law, which allowed the lands of those unable to pay the tax to be confiscated. In the 1770s, a series of massive famines led to the death of an estimated one-third of the population in the areas under company administration. The British government attempted to resolve the problem by assigning tax lands to the local revenue collectors (*zamindars*) in the hope of transforming them into English-style rural gentry, but many collectors themselves fell into bankruptcy and sold their lands to absentee bankers while the now landless peasants remained in abject poverty. It was hardly an auspicious beginning to "civilized" British rule.

RESISTANCE TO THE BRITISH As a result of such problems, Britain's rise to power in India did not go unchallenged. Astute Indian commanders avoided pitched battles with the well-armed British troops but harassed and ambushed them in the manner of guerrillas in our time. Haidar Ali (HY-dur AH-lee), one of Britain's primary rivals for control in southern India, said:

> You will in time understand my mode of warfare. Shall I risk my cavalry which cost a thousand rupees each horse, against your cannon ball which cost two pice? No! I will march your troops until their legs swell to the size of their bodies. You shall not have a blade of grass, nor a drop of water. I will hear of you every time your drum beats, but you shall not know where I am once a month. I will give your army battle, but it must be when I please, and not when you choose.[3]

motivated by religious zeal, were at least equally important.

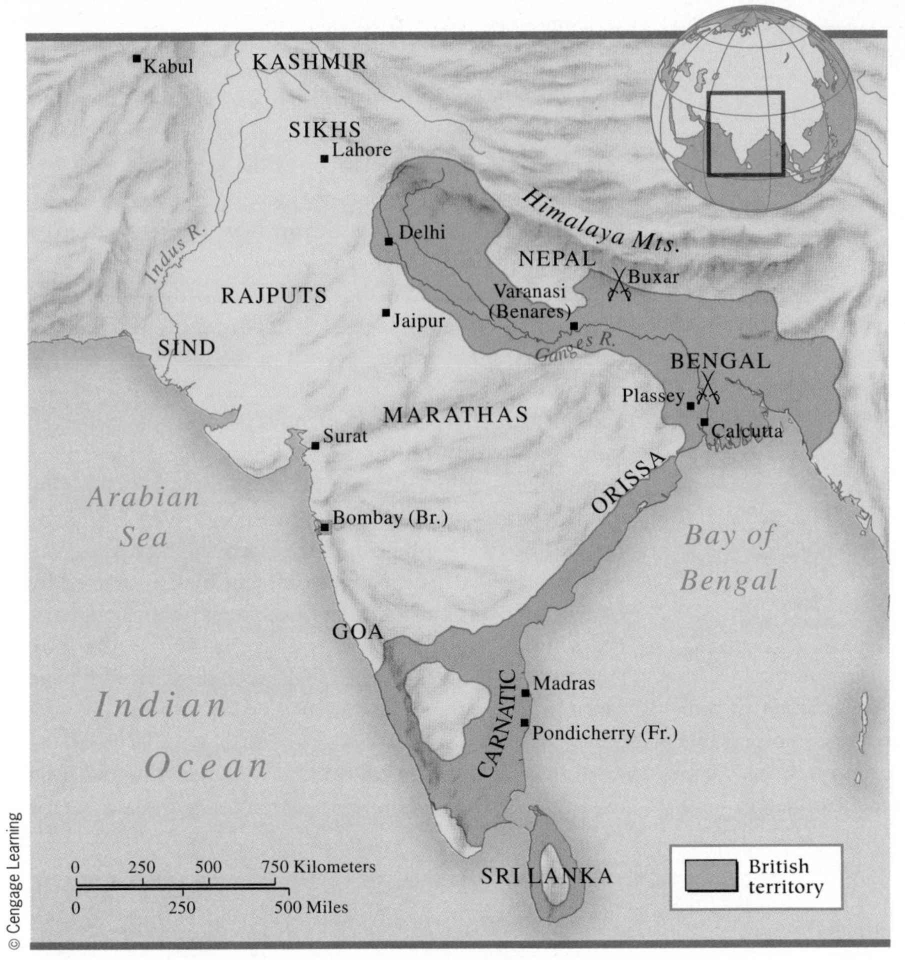

© Cengage Learning

MAP 16.4 India in 1805. By the early nineteenth century, much of the Indian subcontinent had fallen under British domination.

 *Where was the capital of the Mughal Empire located?*

In the case of the Mughals, the "gunpowder empire" thesis has been challenged by historian Douglas Streusand, who argues that the Mughals used "the carrot and the stick" to extend their authority, relying not just on heavy artillery but also on other forms of siege warfare and the offer of negotiations. Once in power, the Mughals created an empire in which the semiautonomous provinces were held together as much by the majesty of the Mughal emperor as by the barrel of a gun. Even today, many Indians regard Akbar as the country's greatest ruler, a tribute not only to his military success but also to the humane policies adopted during his reign.

Society Under the Mughals: A Synthesis of Cultures

The Mughals were the last of the great traditional Indian dynasties. Like so many of their predecessors since the fall of the Guptas nearly a thousand years before, the Mughals were Muslims. But like the Ottoman Turks, the best Mughal rulers did not simply impose Islamic institutions and beliefs on the predominantly Hindu population; they combined Muslim with Hindu and even Persian concepts and cultural values in a unique social and cultural synthesis. The new faith of Sikhism, founded in the early sixteenth century in an effort to blend both faiths (see Chapter 9), undoubtedly benefited from the mood of syncretism promoted by the Mughal court.

To be sure, Hindus sometimes attempted to defend themselves and their religious practices against the efforts of some Mughal monarchs to impose the Islamic religion and Islamic mores on the indigenous population. In some cases, despite official prohibitions, Hindu men forcibly married Muslim women and then converted them to the native faith, while converts to Islam normally lost all of their inheritance rights within the Indian family. Government orders to destroy Hindu temples were often

Unfortunately for India, not all of its commanders were as astute as Haidar Ali. In the last years of the eighteenth century, the stage was set for the final consolidation of British rule over the subcontinent.

The Mughal Dynasty: A "Gunpowder Empire"?

To some recent historians, the success of the Mughals, like that of the Ottomans and the Safavids, was due to their mastery of the techniques of modern warfare, especially the use of firearms. In this view, firearms played a central role in the rise of all three empires to regional hegemony. Accordingly, some scholars have labeled them "gunpowder empires." Although technical prowess in the art of warfare was undoubtedly a key element in their success, we should not forget that other factors, such as dynamic leadership, political acumen, and ardent followers

CHRONOLOGY **The Mughal Era**	
Arrival of Vasco da Gama at Calicut	1498
Babur seizes Delhi	1526
Death of Babur	1530
Humayun recovers throne in Delhi	1555
Death of Humayun and accession of Akbar	1556
First Jesuit mission to Agra	1580
Death of Akbar and accession of Jahangir	1605
Arrival of English at Surat	1608
English embassy to Agra	1616
Reign of Emperor Shah Jahan	1628–1657
Foundation of English factory at Madras	1639
Aurangzeb succeeds to the throne	1658
Death of Aurangzeb	1707
Sack of Delhi by the Persians	1739
French capture Madras	1746
Battle of Plassey	1757

ignored by local officials, sometimes as the result of bribery or intimidation. Although the founding emperor Babur expressed little admiration for the country he had subjected to his rule, ultimately Indian practices had an influence on the Mughal elites, as many Mughal chieftains married Indian women and adopted Indian forms of dress.

In some areas, Emperor Akbar's tireless effort to bring about a blend of Middle Eastern and South Asian religious and cultural values paid rich dividends, as substantial numbers of Indians decided to convert to the Muslim faith during the centuries of Mughal rule. Some were undoubtedly attracted to the egalitarian characteristics of Islam, but others found that the mystical and devotional qualities promoted by Sufi missionaries corresponded to local traditions. This was especially true in Bengal, on the eastern edge of the Indian subcontinent, where Hindu practices were not as well established and where forms of religious devotionalism had long been popular.

THE ECONOMY Although much of the local population in the subcontinent lived in grinding poverty, punctuated by occasional periods of widespread famine, the first centuries of Mughal rule were in some respects a period of relative prosperity for the region. India was a leading participant in the growing foreign trade that crisscrossed the Indian Ocean from the Red Sea and the Persian Gulf to the Strait of Malacca and the Indonesian archipelago. High-quality cloth from India was especially prized, and the country's textile industry made it, in the words of one historian, "the industrial workshop of the world."

Long-term stability led to increasing commercialization and the spread of wealth to new groups within Indian society. The Mughal era saw the emergence of an affluent landed gentry and a prosperous merchant class. Members of prestigious castes from the pre-Mughal period reaped many of the benefits of the increasing wealth, but some of these changes transcended caste boundaries and led to the emergence of new groups who achieved status and wealth on the basis of economic achievement rather than traditional kinship ties. During the late eighteenth century, this economic prosperity was shaken by the decline of the Mughal Empire and the increasing European presence. But many prominent Indians reacted by establishing commercial relationships with the foreigners. For a time, such relationships often worked to the Indians' benefit. Later, as we shall see, they would have cause to regret the arrangement.

THE POSITION OF WOMEN Whether Mughal rule had much effect on the lives of ordinary Indians seems

© Ian Bell

The Palace of the Winds at Jaipur. Built by the maharaja of Jaipur (JY-poor) in 1799, this imposing building, part of a palace complex, is today actually only a facade. Behind the intricate pink sandstone window screens, the women of the palace were able to observe city life while at the same time remaining invisible to prying eyes. The palace, like most of the buildings in the city of Jaipur, was constructed of sandstone, a product of the nearby desert of Rajasthan (RAH-juh-stahn).

somewhat problematic. The treatment of women is a good example. Women had traditionally played an active role in Mongol tribal society—many actually fought on the battlefield alongside the men—and Babur and his successors often relied on the women in their families for political advice. Women from aristocratic families were often awarded honorific titles, received salaries, and were permitted to own land and engage in business. Women at court sometimes received an education, and aristocratic women often expressed their creative talents by writing poetry, painting, or playing music. Women of all classes were adept at spinning thread, either for their own use or to sell to weavers to augment the family income. They sold simple cloth to local villages and fine cottons, silks, and wool to the Mughal court.

To a certain degree, these Mughal attitudes toward women may have had an impact on Indian society. Women were allowed to inherit land, and some even possessed *zamindar* rights. Women from mercantile castes sometimes took an active role in business activities. At the same time, however, as Muslims, the Mughals subjected women to certain restrictions under Islamic law. On the whole, these Mughal practices coincided with and even accentuated existing tendencies in Indian society. The Muslim practice of isolating women and preventing them from associating with men outside the home (***purdah***) was adopted by many upper-class Hindus as a means of enhancing their status or protecting their women from unwelcome advances by Muslims in positions of authority. In other ways, Hindu practices were unaffected. The custom of *sati* continued to be practiced despite efforts by the Mughals to abolish it, and child marriage (most women were betrothed before the age of ten) remained common. Women were still instructed to obey their husbands without question and to remain chaste.

Mughal Culture

The era of the Mughals was one of synthesis in culture as well as in politics and religion. The Mughals combined Islamic themes with Persian and indigenous motifs to produce a unique style that enriched and embellished Indian art and culture. The Mughal emperors were zealous patrons of the arts and enticed painters, poets, and artisans from as far away as the Mediterranean. Apparently, the generosity of the Mughals made it difficult to refuse a trip to India. It was said that they would reward a poet with his weight in gold.

ARCHITECTURE Undoubtedly, the Mughals' most visible achievement was in architecture. Here they integrated Persian and Indian styles in a new and sometimes breathtakingly beautiful form best symbolized by the Taj Mahal, built by the emperor Shah Jahan in the mid-seventeenth century (see the comparative illustration on p. 430). Although the human and economic cost of the Taj tarnishes the romantic legend of its construction, there is no denying the beauty of the building. It had evolved from a style that originated several decades earlier with the tomb of Humayun.

Humayun's mausoleum had combined Persian and Islamic motifs ina square building finished in red sandstone and topped with a dome. The Taj brought the style to perfection. Working with a model created by his Persian architect, Shah Jahan raised the dome and replaced the red sandstone with brilliant white marble. The entire surface of the exterior and interior is decorated with cut-stone geometrical patterns, delicate black stone tracery, or intricate inlay of colored precious stones in floral and Qur'anic arabesques. The technique of creating dazzling floral mosaics of lapis lazuli, malachite, carnelian, turquoise, and mother of pearl may have been introduced by Italian artists at the Mughal court. Shah Jahan spent his last years imprisoned in a room in the Red Fort at Agra; from his windows, he could see the beautiful memorial to his beloved wife.

The Taj was by no means the only magnificent building erected during the Mughal era. Akbar, who, in the words of a contemporary, "[dressed] the work of his mind and heart in the garment of stone and clay," was the first of the great Mughal builders. His first palace at Agra, the Red Fort, was begun in 1565. A few years later, he ordered the construction of a new palace at Fatehpur Sikri (fah-tay-POOR SIK-ree), 26 miles west of Agra. The new palace was built in honor of a Sufi mystic who had correctly forecast the birth of a son to the emperor. In gratitude, Akbar decided to build a new capital city and palace on the site of the mystic's home in the village of Sikri. Over a period of fifteen years, from 1571 to 1586, a magnificent new city in red sandstone was constructed. Although the city was abandoned before completion and now stands almost untouched, it is a popular destination for tourists and pilgrims.

PAINTING The other major artistic achievement of the Mughal period was painting. Like so many other aspects of Mughal India, painting blended two cultures. While living in exile, Emperor Humayun had learned to admire Persian miniatures. On his return to India in 1555, he invited two Persian masters to live in his palace and introduce the technique to his adopted land. His successor, Akbar, appreciated the new style and popularized it with his patronage. He established a state workshop at Fatehpur Sikri for two hundred artists, mostly Hindus, who worked under the guidance of the Persian masters to create the Mughal school of painting.

The "Akbar style" combined Persian with Indian motifs, such as the use of extended space and the

© Steve Vidler/SuperStock

© Carol C. Coffin

© William J. Duiker

COMPARATIVE ILLUSTRATION

The Taj Mahal: Symbol of the Exotic East. The Taj Mahal, completed in 1653, was built by the Mughal emperor Shah Jahan as a tomb to glorify the memory of his beloved wife. Raised on a marble platform above the Jumna River, the Taj is dramatically framed by contrasting twin red sandstone mosques, magnificent gardens, and a long reflecting pool that mirrors and magnifies its beauty. The effect is one of monumental size, near blinding brilliance, and delicate lightness, a startling contrast to the heavier and more masculine Baroque style then popular in Europe. The inset at the upper right shows an example of the exquisite inlay of precious stones that adorns the façade. The Taj Mahal inspired many imitations, including the Royal Pavilion at Brighton, England (inset at lower right), constructed in 1815 to commemorate the British victory over Napoleon at Waterloo. The Pavilion is a good example of the way Europeans portrayed the "exotic" East.

How does Mughal architecture, as exemplified by the Taj Majal, compare with the mosques erected by builders such as Sinan in the Ottoman Empire?

portrayal of physical human action, characteristics not usually seen in Persian art. Akbar also apparently encouraged the imitation of European art forms, including the portrayal of Christian subjects, the use of perspective, lifelike portraits, and the shading of colors in the Renaissance style. The depiction of the human figure in Mughal painting outraged orthodox Muslims at court, but Akbar argued that the painter, "in sketching anything that has life . . . must come to feel that he cannot bestow individuality upon his work, and is thus forced to think of God, the Giver of Life, and will thus increase in knowledge."[4]

LITERATURE The development of Indian literature was held back by the absence of printing, which was not introduced until the end of the Mughal era. Literary works were inscribed by calligraphers, and one historian has estimated that the library of Agra contained more than 24,000 volumes. Poetry, in particular, flourished under the Mughals, who established poet laureates at court. Poems were written in the Persian style and in the Persian language. In fact, Persian became the official language of the court until the sack of Delhi in 1739.

Another aspect of the long Mughal reign was a revival of Hindu devotional literature, much of it dedicated to Krishna and Rama. The retelling of the Ramayana in the vernacular culminated in the sixteenth-century Hindi version by the great poet Tulsidas (tool-see-DAHSS) (1532–1623). His *Ramcaritmanas* (RAM-kah-rit-MAH-nuz) presents the devotional story with a deified Rama and Sita. Tulsidas's genius was in combining the conflicting cults of Vishnu and Shiva into a unified and overwhelming love for the divine, which he expressed in some of the most moving of all Indian poetry. The *Ramcaritmanas* has eclipsed its two-thousand-year-old Sanskrit ancestor in popularity and even became the basis of an Indian television series in the late 1980s.

CHAPTER SUMMARY

The three empires discussed in this chapter exhibited a number of striking similarities. First of all, they were Muslim in their religious affiliation, although the Safavids were Shi'ite rather than Sunni, a distinction that often led to mutual tensions and conflict. More important, perhaps, they were all of nomadic origin, and the political and social institutions that they adopted carried the imprint of their preimperial past. Once they achieved imperial power, however, all three ruling dynasties displayed an impressive capacity to administer a large empire and brought a degree of stability to peoples who had all too often lived in conditions of internal division and war.

The rise of these powerful Muslim states coincided with the opening period of European expansion at the end of the fifteenth century and the beginning of the sixteenth. The military and political talents of these empires helped protect much of the Muslim world from the resurgent forces of Christianity. In fact, the Ottoman Turks carried their empire into the heart of Christian Europe and briefly reached the gates of the great city of Vienna. By the end of the eighteenth century, however, the Safavid dynasty had imploded, and the powerful Mughal Empire was in a state of virtual collapse. Only the Ottoman Empire was still functioning. Yet it too had lost much of its early expansionistic vigor and was showing signs of internal decay.

The reasons for the decline of these empires have inspired considerable debate among historians. One factor was undoubtedly the expansion of European power into the Indian Ocean and the Middle East. But internal causes were probably more important in the long run. All three empires experienced growing factionalism within the ruling elite, incompetent leadership, and the emergence of divisive forces in the empire at large—factors that have marked the passing of traditional empires since early times. Climate change (the region was reportedly hotter and drier after the beginning of the seventeenth century) may have been a contributing factor. Paradoxically, one of the greatest strengths of these empires—their mastery of gunpowder—may have simultaneously been a serious weakness in that it allowed them to develop a complacent sense of security. With little incentive to turn their attention to new developments in science and technology, they were increasingly vulnerable to attack by the advanced nations of the West.

The Muslim empires, however, were not the only states in the Old World that were able to resist the first outward thrust of European expansion. Farther to the east, the mature civilizations in China and Japan faced down a similar challenge from Western merchants and missionaries. Unlike their counterparts in South Asia and the Middle East, as the nineteenth century dawned, they continued to thrive.

CHAPTER TIMELINE

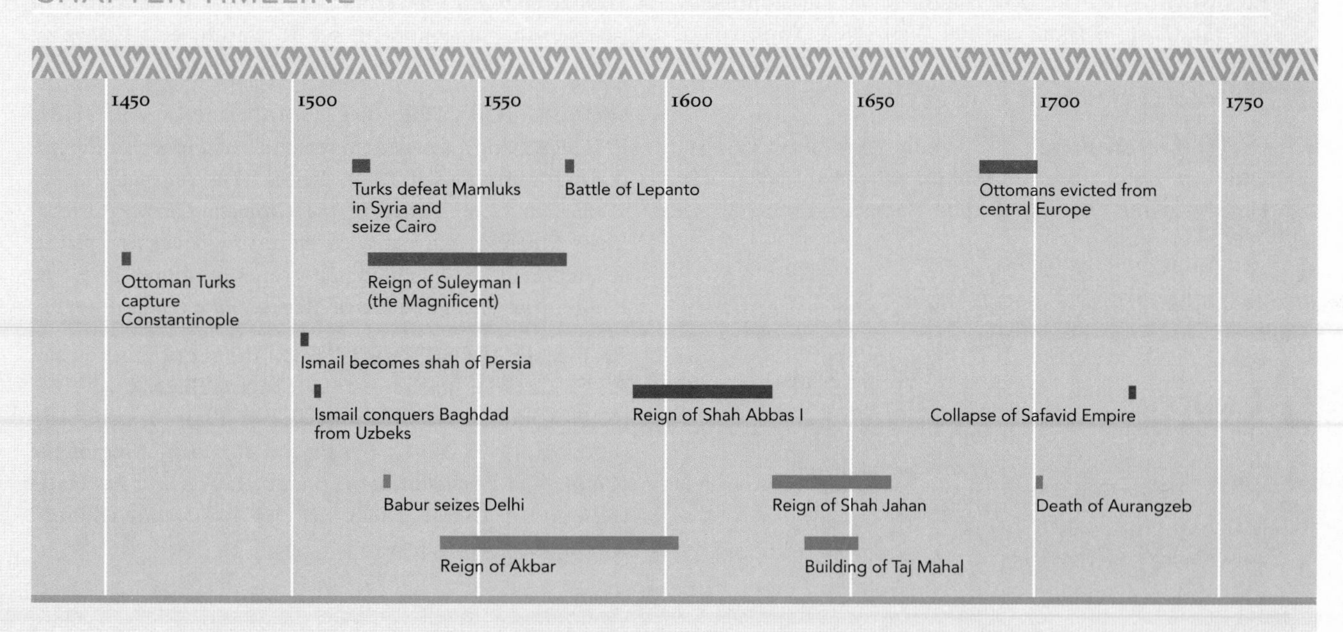

Upon Reflection

Q How did the social policies adopted by the Ottomans compare with those of the Mughals? What similarities and differences do you detect, and what might account for them?

Q What is meant by the phrase "gunpowder empires," and to what degree did the Muslim states discussed here conform to this description?

Q What role did women play in the Ottoman, Safavid, and Mughal Empires? What might explain the similarities and differences? How did the treatment of women in these states compare with their treatment in other parts of the world?

Key Terms

bey (p. 408)
sultan (p. 408)
Janissaries (p. 408)
pashas (p. 410)
harem (p. 412)
devshirme (p. 412)
grand vizier (p. 413)
sipahis (p. 413)
Sublime Porte (p. 415)
zamindars (p. 421)
purdah (p. 429)

Suggested Reading

CONSTANTINOPLE A dramatic recent account of the Muslim takeover of Constantinople is provided by **R. Crowley** in ***1453: The Holy War for Constantinople and the Clash of Islam and the West*** (New York, 2005). Crowley acknowledges his debt to the classic by **S. Runciman, *The Fall of Constantinople, 1453*** (Cambridge, 1965).

OTTOMAN EMPIRE Two useful general surveys of Ottoman history are **C. Finkel, *Osman's Dream: The History of the Ottoman Empire*** (Jackson, Tenn., 2006), and **J. Goodwin, *Lords of the Horizons: A History of the Ottoman Empire*** (London, 2002).

For the argument that the decline of the Ottoman Empire was not inevitable, see **E. Karsh et al., *Empires of the Sand: The Struggle for Mastery in the Middle East, 1789–1923*** (Cambridge, Mass., 2001).

THE SAFAVIDS On the Safavids, see **R. M. Savory, *Iran Under the Safavids*** (Cambridge, 1980). For a thoughtful if scholarly account of the reasons for the rise of the Safavid Empire, see **R. J. Abisaab, *Converting Persia: Shia Islam and the Safavid Empire, 1501–1736*** (London, 2004).

THE MUGHALS For an elegant overview of the Mughal Empire and its cultural achievements, see **A. Schimmel, *The Empire of the Great Mughals: History, Art and Culture,*** trans. **C. Attwood** (London, 2004). The Mughal Empire is analyzed in a broad Central Asian context in **R. C. Foltz, *Mughal India and Central Asia*** (Karachi, 1998).

There are a number of specialized works on various aspects of the period. The concept of "gunpowder empires" is persuasively analyzed in **D. E. Streusand, *The Formation of the Mughal Empire*** (Delhi, 1989). Economic issues predominate in much recent scholarship. For example, see **O. Prakash, *European Commercial Enterprise in Pre-Colonial India*** (Cambridge, 1998). Finally, **K. N. Chaudhuri, *Trade and Civilization in the Indian Ocean: An Economic History from the Rise of Islam to 1750*** (Cambridge, 1985), views Indian commerce in the perspective of the regional trade network throughout the Indian Ocean.

For treatments of all three Muslim empires in a comparative context, see **J. J. Kissling et al., *The Last Great Muslim Empires*** (Princeton, N.J., 1996). On the impact of Islam in the subcontinent, see **R. Eaton, ed., *Essays on Islam and Indian History*** (New Delhi, 2000).

WOMEN OF THE OTTOMAN AND MUGHAL EMPIRES For a detailed presentation of women in the imperial harem, consult **L. P. Peirce, *The Imperial Harem: Women and Sovereignty in the Ottoman Empire*** (Oxford, 1993). The fascinating story of the royal woman who played an important role behind the scenes is found in **E. B. Findly, *Nur Jahan: Empress of Mughal India*** (Oxford, 1993).

ART AND ARCHITECTURE On the art of this era, see **R. C. Craven, *Indian Art: A Concise History,*** rev. ed. (New York, 1997); **J. Bloom** and **S. Blair, *Islamic Arts*** (London, 1997); **M. C. Beach** and **E. Koch, *King of the World: The Padshahnama*** (London, 1997); and **M. Hattstein** and **P. Delius, *Islam: Art and Architecture*** (Königswinter, Germany, 2004).

Visit the CourseMate website at **www.cengagebrain.com** for additional study tools and review materials for this chapter.

CHAPTER 17

The East Asian World

© Hu Weibiao/Panorama/The Image Works

Emperor Kangxi

CHAPTER OUTLINE AND FOCUS QUESTIONS

China at Its Apex

Q Why were the Manchus so successful at establishing a foreign dynasty in China, and what were the main characteristics of Manchu rule?

Changing China

Q How did the economy and society of China change during the Ming and Qing eras, and to what degree did these changes seem to be leading toward an industrial revolution on the European model?

Tokugawa Japan

Q How did the society and economy of Japan change during the Tokugawa era, and how did Japanese culture reflect those changes?

Korea and Vietnam

Q To what degree did developments in Korea during this period reflect conditions in China and Japan? What were the unique aspects of Vietnamese civilization?

CRITICAL THINKING

Q How did China and Japan respond to the coming of the Europeans, and what explains the differences in their approach? What impact did European contacts have on these two East Asian civilizations through the end of the eighteenth century?

IN DECEMBER 1717, Emperor Kangxi (KANG-shee) returned from a hunting trip north of the Great Wall and began to suffer from dizzy spells. Conscious of his approaching date with mortality—he was now nearly seventy years of age—the emperor called together his sons and leading government officials in the imperial palace and issued an edict summing up his ideas on the art of statecraft. Rulers, he declared, should sincerely revere Heaven's laws as their fundamental strategy for governing the country. Among other things, those laws required that the ruler show concern for the welfare of the people, practice diligence, protect the state from its enemies, choose able advisers, and strike a careful balance between leniency and strictness, principle and expedience. That, he concluded, was all there was to it.[1]

Any potential successor to the throne would have been well advised to attend to the emperor's advice. Kangxi was not only one of the longest reigning of all Chinese rulers but also one of the wisest. His era was one of peace and prosperity, and after a half century of his rule, the empire was now at the zenith of its power and influence. As his life approached its end, Heaven must indeed have been pleased at the quality of his stewardship.

As for the emperor's edict, it clearly reflected the genius of Confucian teachings at their best and, with its emphasis on prudence, compassion, and tolerance, has a timeless quality that applies to our age as well as to the golden age of the Qing (CHING) dynasty.

Kangxi reigned during one of the most glorious eras in the long history of China. Under the Ming (MING) and the early Qing dynasties, the empire expanded its borders to a degree not seen since the Han and the Tang. Chinese culture was the envy of its neighbors and earned the admiration of many European visitors, including Jesuit priests and Enlightenment philosophes.

On the surface, China appeared to be an unchanging society patterned after the Confucian vision of a "golden age" in the remote past. This indeed was the image presented by China's rulers, who referred constantly to tradition as a model for imperial institutions and cultural values. Although few observers could have been aware of it at the time, however, China was changing—and rather rapidly.

A similar process was under way in neighboring Japan. A vigorous new shogunate (SHOH-gun-ut *or* SHOH-gun-ayt) called the Tokugawa (toh-goo-GAH-wah) rose to power in the early seventeenth century and managed to revitalize the traditional system in a somewhat more centralized form that enabled it to survive for another 250 years. But major structural changes were taking place in Japanese society, and by the nineteenth century, tensions were growing as the gap between theory and reality widened.

One of the many factors contributing to the quickening pace of change in both countries was contact with the West, which began with the arrival of Portuguese ships in Chinese and Japanese ports in the first half of the sixteenth century. The Ming and the Tokugawa initially opened their doors to European trade and missionary activity. Later, however, Chinese and Japanese rulers became concerned about the corrosive effects of Western ideas and practices and attempted to protect their traditional societies from external intrusion. But neither could forever resist the importunities of Western trading nations; nor were they able to inhibit the societal shifts that were taking place within their borders. When the doors to the West were finally reopened in the mid-nineteenth century, both societies were ripe for radical change.

China at Its Apex

FOCUS QUESTION: Why were the Manchus so successful at establishing a foreign dynasty in China, and what were the main characteristics of Manchu rule?

In 1514, a Portuguese fleet dropped anchor off the coast of China, just south of the Pearl River estuary and present-day Hong Kong. It was the first direct contact between the Chinese Empire and the West since the arrival of the Venetian adventurer Marco Polo two centuries earlier, and it opened an era that would eventually change the face of China and, indeed, all the world.

From the Ming to the Qing

Marco Polo had reported on the magnificence of China after visiting Beijing (bay-ZHING) during the reign of Khubilai Khan, the great Mongol ruler. By the time the Portuguese fleet arrived off the coast of China, of course, the Mongol Empire had long since disappeared. It had gradually weakened after the death of Khubilai Khan and was finally overthrown in 1368 by a massive peasant rebellion under the leadership of Zhu Yuanzhang (JOO yoo-wen-JAHNG), who had declared himself the founding emperor of a new Ming (Bright) dynasty (1369–1644).

As we have seen, the Ming inaugurated a period of territorial expansion westward into Central Asia and southward into Vietnam while consolidating control over China's vast heartland. At the same time, between 1405 and 1433 the dynasty sponsored a series of voyages under Admiral Zhenghe (JEHNG-huh) that spread Chinese influence far into the Indian Ocean. Then suddenly the voyages were discontinued, and the dynasty turned its attention to domestic concerns (see Chapter 10).

FIRST CONTACTS WITH THE WEST Despite the Ming's retreat from active participation in maritime trade, when the Portuguese arrived in 1514, China was in command of a vast empire that stretched from the steppes of Central Asia to the China Sea, from the Gobi Desert to the tropical rain forests of Southeast Asia. From the lofty perspective of the imperial throne in Beijing, the Europeans could only have seemed like an unusually exotic form of barbarian to be placed within the familiar framework of the tributary system, the hierarchical arrangement in which rulers of all other countries were regarded as "younger brothers" of the Son of Heaven. Indeed, the bellicose and uncultured behavior of the Portuguese so outraged Chinese officials that they expelled the Europeans, but after further negotiations, the Portuguese were permitted to occupy the tiny territory of Macao (muh-KOW), a foothold they would retain until the end of the twentieth century.

Initially, the arrival of the Europeans did not have much impact on Chinese society. Direct trade between Europe and China was limited, and Portuguese ships became involved in the regional trade network, carrying silk from China to Japan in return for Japanese silver. Eventually, the Spanish also began to participate, using the Philippines as an anchor in the galleon trade between China and the great silver mines in the Americas.

More influential than trade, perhaps, were the ideas introduced by Christian missionaries, who first received permission to reside in China in the last quarter of the sixteenth century. Among the most active and the most effective were highly educated Jesuits, who were familiar with European philosophical and scientific developments. Court officials were particularly impressed by the visitors' ability to predict the exact time of a solar eclipse, an event that the Chinese viewed with extreme reverence.

Recognizing the Chinese pride in their own culture, the Jesuits attempted to draw parallels between Christian and Confucian concepts (for example, they identified the Western concept of God with the Chinese character for Heaven) and to show the similarities between Christian morality and Confucian ethics. European inventions such as the clock, the prism, and various astronomical and musical instruments impressed Chinese officials, hitherto deeply imbued with a sense of the superiority of Chinese civilization, and helped Western ideas win acceptance at court. An elderly Chinese scholar expressed his wonder at the miracle of eyeglasses:

White glass from across the Western Seas
Is imported through Macao:
Fashioned into lenses big as coins,
They encompass the eyes in a double frame.
I put them on—it suddenly becomes clear;
I can see the very tips of things!
And read fine print by the dim-lit window
Just like in my youth.[2]

For their part, the missionaries were much impressed with many aspects of Chinese civilization, and reports of their experiences heightened European curiosity about this great society on the other side of the world (see the box on p. 436). By the late seventeenth century, European philosophers and political thinkers had begun to praise Chinese civilization and to hold up Confucian institutions and values as a mirror to criticize their counterparts in the West.

THE MING BROUGHT TO EARTH During the late sixteenth century, the Ming began to decline as a series of weak rulers led to an era of corruption, concentration of landownership, and ultimately peasant rebellions and tribal unrest along the northern frontier. The inflow of vast amounts of foreign silver to pay for Chinese goods resulted in an alarming increase in inflation. Then the arrival of the English and the Dutch, whose ships preyed on the Spanish galleon trade between Asia and the Americas, disrupted the silver trade; silver imports plummeted, severely straining the Chinese economy by raising the value of the metal relative to that of copper. Crop yields declined due to harsh weather, and the resulting scarcity made it difficult for the government to provide food in times of imminent starvation. High taxes, necessitated in part because corrupt officials siphoned off revenues, led to rural unrest and violent protests among urban workers.

As always, internal problems were accompanied by unrest along the northern frontier. Following long precedent, the Ming had attempted to pacify the frontier tribes by forging alliances with them and granting trade privileges. One of the alliances was with the Manchus (man-CHOOZ)—also known as the Jurchen (roor-ZHEN)—the descendants of peoples who had briefly established a kingdom in northern China during the early thirteenth century. The Manchus, a mixed agricultural and hunting people, lived northeast of the Great Wall in the area known today as Manchuria (man-CHUR-ee-uh).

At first, the Manchus were satisfied with consolidating their territory and made little effort to extend their rule south of the Great Wall. But during the first decades of the seventeenth century, a major epidemic devastated the population in many areas of the country. The suffering brought on by the epidemic helped spark a vast peasant revolt led by Li Zicheng (lee zuh-CHENG) (Li Tzu-ch'eng) (1604–1651), a postal worker in central China who had been dismissed from his job as part of a cost-saving measure by the imperial court. In the 1630s, Li managed to extend the revolt throughout the country, and his forces finally occupied the capital of Beijing in 1644. The last Ming emperor committed suicide by hanging himself from a tree in the palace gardens.

But Li was unable to hold his conquest. The overthrow of the Ming dynasty presented a great temptation to the Manchus. With the assistance of many military commanders who had deserted from the Ming, they conquered Beijing on their own (see Map 17.1). Li Zicheng's army disintegrated, and the Manchus declared the creation of a new dynasty: the Qing (Ch'ing, or Pure), which lasted from 1644 until 1911. Once again, China was under foreign rule.

The Greatness of the Qing

The accession of the Manchus to power in Beijing was not universally applauded. Some Ming loyalists fled to

The Art of Printing

ART & IDEAS

Europeans obtained much of their early information about China from the Jesuits who served at the Ming court in the sixteenth and seventeenth centuries. Clerics such as the Italian Matteo Ricci (ma-TAY-oh REE-chee) (1552–1610), who arrived in China in 1601, found much to admire in Chinese civilization. Here Ricci expresses a keen interest in Chinese printing methods, which at that time were well in advance of the techniques used in the West. Later Christian missionaries expressed strong interest in Confucian philosophy and Chinese ideas of statecraft.

Matteo Ricci, *The Diary of Matthew Ricci*

The art of printing was practiced in China at a date somewhat earlier than that assigned to the beginning of printing in Europe, which was about 1405. It is quite certain that the Chinese knew the art of printing at least five centuries ago, and some of them assert that printing was known to their people before the beginning of the Christian era, about 50 B.C.E. Their method of printing differs widely from that employed in Europe, and our method would be quite impracticable for them because of the exceedingly large number of Chinese characters and symbols. . . .

Their method of making printed books is quite ingenious. The text is written in ink, with a brush made of very fine hair, on a sheet of paper which is inverted and pasted on a wooden tablet. When the paper has become thoroughly dry, its surface is scraped off quickly and with great skill, until nothing but a fine tissue bearing the characters remains on the wooden tablet. Then, with a steel graver, the workman cuts away the surface following the outlines of the characters until these alone stand out in low relief. From such a block a skilled printer can make copies with incredible speed, turning out as many as fifteen hundred copies in a single day. . . . This scheme of engraving wooden blocks is well adapted for the large and complex nature of the Chinese characters, but I do not think it would lend itself very aptly to our European type, which could hardly be engraved upon wood because of its small dimensions.

Their method of printing has one decided advantage, namely, that once these tablets are made, they can be preserved and used for making changes in the text as often as one wishes. Additions and subtractions can also be made as the tablets can be readily patched. . . . We have derived great benefit from this method of Chinese printing, as we employ the domestic help in our homes to strike off copies of the books on religious and scientific subjects which we translate into Chinese from the languages in which they were written originally. In truth, the whole method is so simple that one is tempted to try it for himself after once having watched the process. The simplicity of Chinese printing is what accounts for the exceedingly large numbers of books in circulation here and the ridiculously low prices at which they are sold.

How did the Chinese method of printing differ from that used in Europe at that time? What were its advantages?

Source: From *China in the Sixteenth Century*, by Matthew Ricci, translated by Louis J. Gallagher. Copyright © 1942 and renewed 1970 by Louis J. Gallagher, S.J.

Southeast Asia, but others continued their resistance to the new rulers from inside the country. To make it easier to identify the rebels, the government ordered all Chinese to adopt Manchu dress and hairstyles. All Chinese males were to shave their foreheads and braid their hair into a queue (KYOO); those who refused were to be executed. As a popular saying put it, "Lose your hair or lose your head."[3]

But the Manchus eventually proved to be more adept at adapting to Chinese conditions than their predecessors, the Mongols. Unlike the latter, who had tried to impose their own methods of ruling, the Manchus adopted the Chinese political system (although, as we shall see, they retained their distinct position within it) and were gradually accepted by most Chinese as the legitimate rulers of the country.

Like all of China's great dynasties, the Qing was blessed with a series of strong early rulers who pacified the country, rectified many of the most obvious social and economic inequities, and restored peace and prosperity. For the Ming dynasty, these strong emperors had been Zhu Yuanzhang and Yongle (YOONG-luh); under

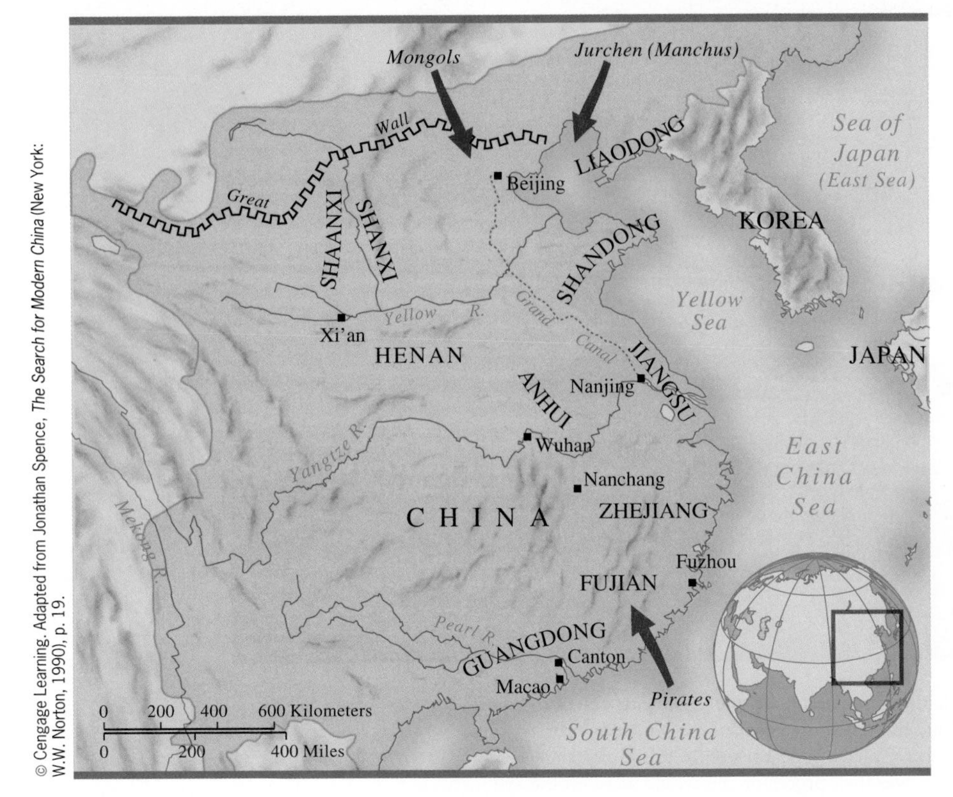

© Cengage Learning. Adapted from Jonathan Spence, *The Search for Modern China* (New York: W.W. Norton, 1990), p. 19.

MAP 17.1 China and Its Enemies During the Late Ming Era. During the seventeenth century, the Ming dynasty faced challenges on two fronts: from China's traditional adversaries, nomadic groups north of the Great Wall, and from new arrivals, European merchants who had begun to press for trading privileges along the southern coast.

How did these threats differ from those faced by previous dynasties in China?

the Qing, they would be Kangxi (K'ang Hsi) and Qianlong (CHAN-loong) (Chien Lung). The two Qing monarchs ruled China for well over a century, from the middle of the seventeenth century to the end of the eighteenth, and were responsible for much of the greatness of Manchu China.

THE REIGN OF KANGXI Kangxi (1661–1722) was arguably the greatest ruler in Chinese history. Ascending to the throne at the age of seven, he was blessed with diligence, political astuteness, and a strong character and began to take charge of Qing administration while still an adolescent. During the six decades of his reign, Kangxi not only stabilized imperial rule by pacifying the restive peoples along the northern and western frontiers but also managed to make the dynasty acceptable to the general population. As an active patron of arts and letters, he cultivated the support of scholars through a number of major projects.

During Kangxi's reign, the activities of the Western missionaries, Dominicans and Franciscans as well as Jesuits, reached their height. The emperor was quite tolerant of the Christians, and several Jesuit missionaries became influential at court. Several hundred court officials converted to Christianity, as did an estimated 300,000 ordinary Chinese. But the Christian effort was ultimately undermined by squabbling among the Western religious orders over the Jesuit policy of accommodating local beliefs and practices in order to facilitate conversion. Jealous Dominicans and Franciscans complained to the pope, who issued an edict ordering all missionaries and converts to conform to the official orthodoxy set forth in Europe. At first, Kangxi attempted to resolve the problem by appealing directly to the Vatican, but the pope was uncompromising. After Kangxi's death, his successor began to suppress Christian activities throughout China.

THE REIGN OF QIANLONG Kangxi's achievements were carried on by his successors, Yongzheng (YOONG-jehng) (Yung Cheng, 1722–1736) and Qianlong (1736–1795). Like Kangxi, Qianlong was known for his diligence, tolerance, and intellectual curiosity, and he too combined vigorous military action against the unruly tribes along the frontier with active efforts to promote economic prosperity, administrative efficiency, and scholarship and artistic excellence. The result was continued growth for the Manchu Empire throughout much of the eighteenth century.

But it was also under Qianlong that the first signs of the internal decay of the Manchu dynasty began to appear. The clues were familiar ones. Qing military campaigns along the frontier were expensive and placed heavy demands on the imperial treasury. As the emperor aged, he became less astute in selecting his subordinates and fell under the influence of corrupt elements at court.

Corruption at the center led inevitably to unrest in rural areas, where higher taxes, bureaucratic venality, and rising pressure on the land because of the growing population had produced economic hardship. The heart of the unrest was in central China, where discontented peasants who had recently been settled on infertile land launched

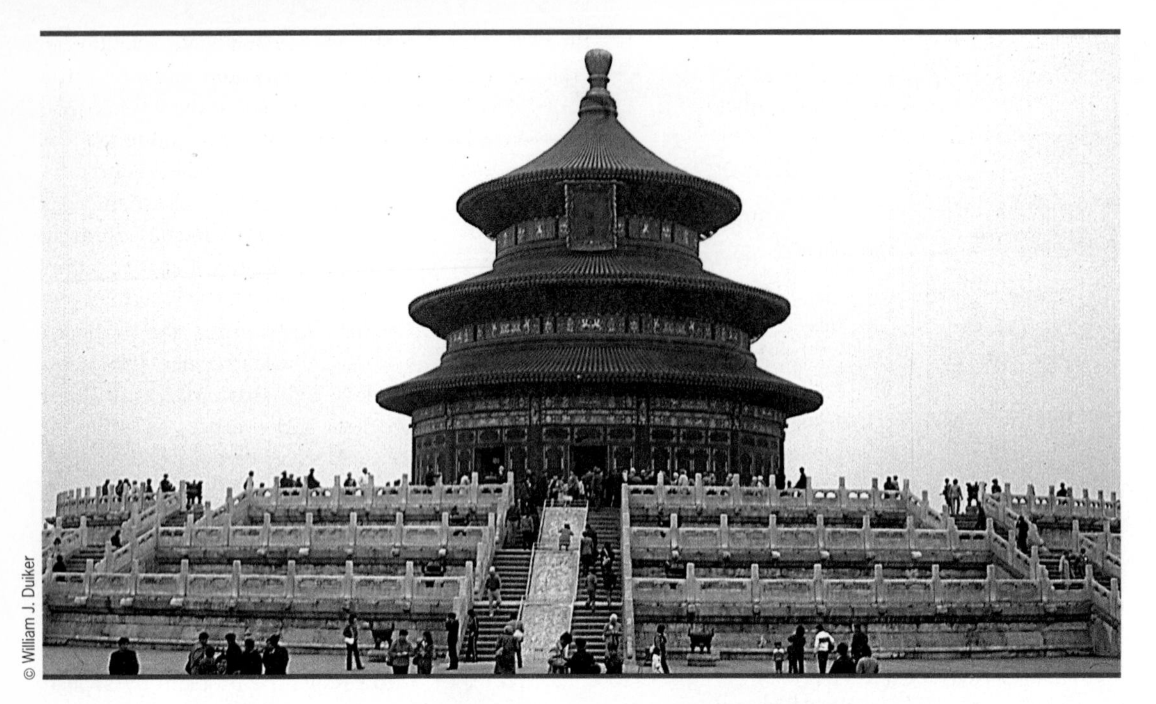
© William J. Duiker

The Temple of Heaven. This temple, located in the capital city of Beijing, is one of the most significant historical structures in China. Built in 1420 at the order of the Ming emperor Yongle, it was the site of the emperor's annual appeal to Heaven for a good harvest. In this important ceremony, the emperor demonstrated to his subjects that he was their protector and would ward off the evil forces in nature. Yongle's temple burned to the ground in 1889 but was immediately rebuilt following the original design.

a revolt known as the White Lotus Rebellion (1796–1804). The revolt was eventually suppressed but at great expense.

QING POLITICS One reason for the success of the Manchus was their ability to adapt to their new environment. They retained the Ming political system with relatively few changes. They also tried to establish their legitimacy as China's rightful rulers by stressing their devotion to the principles of Confucianism. Emperor Kangxi ostentatiously studied the sacred Confucian classics and issued a "sacred edict" that proclaimed to the entire empire the importance of the moral values established by the master (see the box on p. 452).

CHRONOLOGY China During the Early Modern Era	
Rise of Ming dynasty	1369
Voyages of Zhenghe	1405–1433
Portuguese arrive in southern China	1514
Matteo Ricci arrives in China	1601
Li Zicheng occupies Beijing	1644
Manchus seize China	1644
Reign of Kangxi	1661–1722
Treaty of Nerchinsk	1689
First English trading post at Canton	1699
Reign of Qianlong	1736–1795
Lord Macartney's mission to China	1793
White Lotus Rebellion	1796–1804

Still, the Manchus, like the Mongols, were ethnically, linguistically, and culturally different from their subject population. The Qing attempted to cope with this reality by adopting a two-pronged strategy. As one part of this strategy, the Manchus, representing less than 2 percent of the entire population, were legally defined as distinct from everyone else in China. The Manchu nobles retained their aristocratic privileges, while their economic base was protected by extensive landholdings and revenues provided from the state treasury. Other Manchus were assigned farmland and organized into military units, called **banners**, which were stationed as separate units in various strategic positions throughout China. These "bannermen" were the primary fighting force of the empire. Ethnic Chinese were prohibited from settling in Manchuria and were still compelled to wear their hair in a queue as a sign of submission to the ruling dynasty.

But while the Qing attempted to protect their distinct identity within an alien society, they also recognized the need to bring ethnic Chinese into the top ranks of imperial administration. Their solution was to create a **dyarchy**, a system in which all important administrative positions were shared equally by Chinese and Manchus. Meanwhile, the Manchus themselves, despite official efforts to preserve their separate language and culture, were increasingly assimilated into Chinese civilization.

CHINA ON THE EVE OF THE WESTERN ONSLAUGHT Unfortunately for China, the decline of the Qing dynasty occurred just as China's modest relationship with the West was about to give way to a new era of military confrontation and increased pressure for trade. The first problems came in the north, where Russian traders seeking skins and furs began to penetrate the region between Siberian Russia and Manchuria. Earlier the Ming dynasty had attempted to deal with the Russians by the traditional method of placing them in a tributary relationship. But the tsar refused to play by Chinese rules. His envoys to Beijing ignored the tribute system and refused to perform the **kowtow** (the ritual of prostration and touching the forehead to the ground before the emperor), the classic symbol of fealty demanded of all foreign ambassadors to the Chinese court. Formal diplomatic relations were finally established in 1689, when the Treaty of Nerchinsk (ner-CHINSK) settled the boundary dispute and provided for regular trade between the two countries. Through such arrangements, the Manchus were able not only to pacify the northern frontier but also to extend their rule over Xinjiang (SHIN-jyahng) and Tibet to the west and southwest (see Map 17.2).

Dealing with the foreigners who arrived by sea was more difficult. By the end of the seventeenth century, the English had replaced the Portuguese as the dominant force in European trade. Operating through the East India

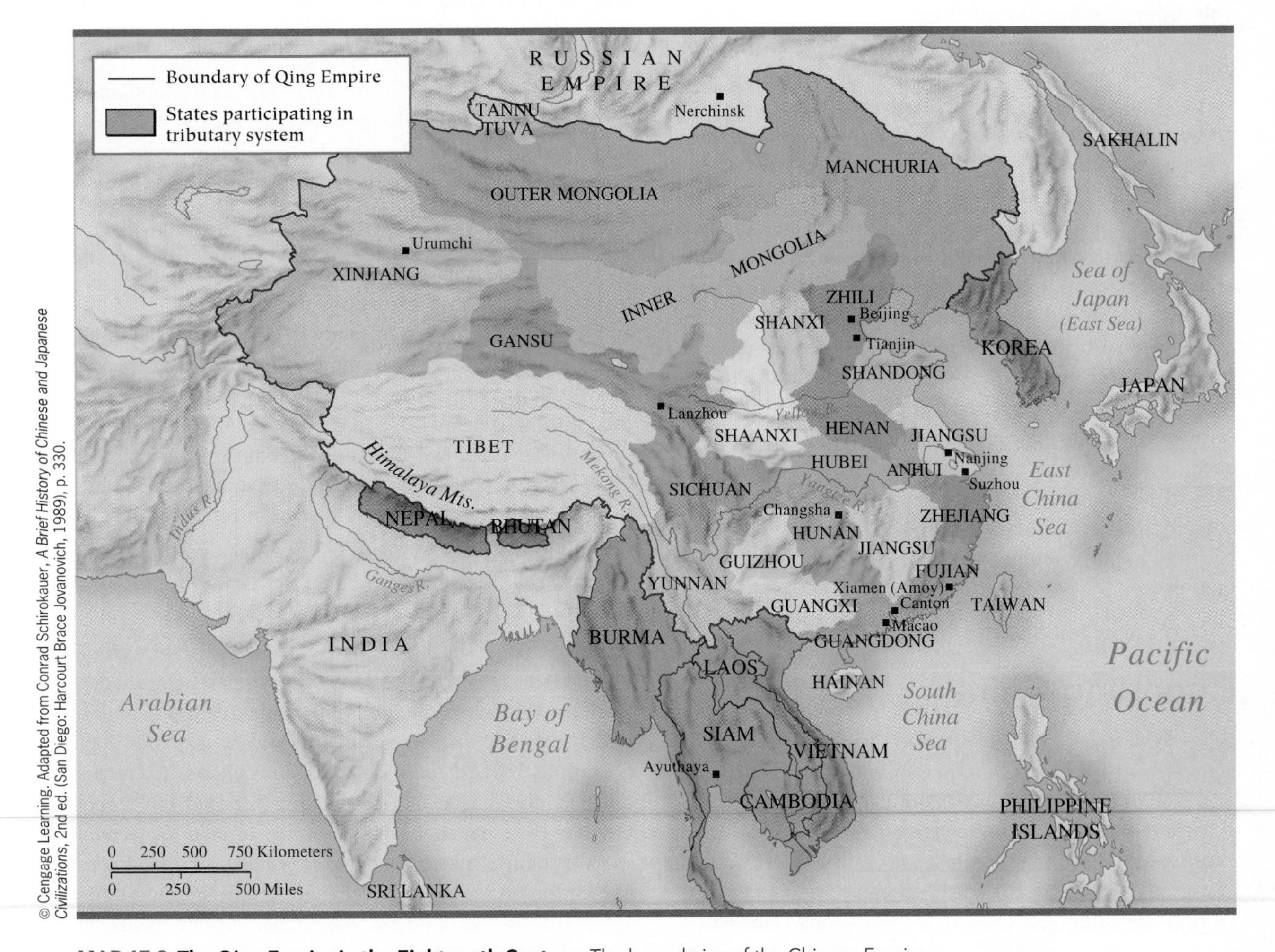

© Cengage Learning. Adapted from Conrad Schirokauer, *A Brief History of Chinese and Japanese Civilizations*, 2nd ed. (San Diego: Harcourt Brace Jovanovich, 1989), p. 330.

MAP 17.2 The Qing Empire in the Eighteenth Century. The boundaries of the Chinese Empire at the height of the Qing dynasty in the eighteenth century are shown on this map.

Q *What areas were linked in tributary status to the Chinese Empire, and how did they benefit the empire?*

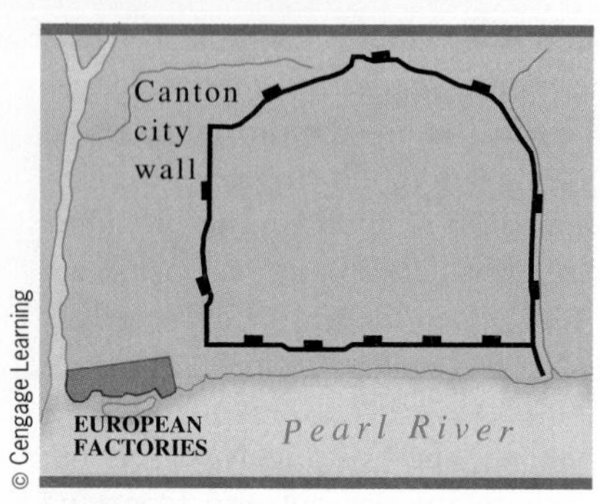

Canton in the Eighteenth Century

Company, which served as both a trading unit and the administrator of English territories in Asia, the English established their first trading post at Canton (KAN-tun) in 1699. Over the next decades, trade with China, notably the export of tea and silk to England, increased rapidly. To limit contact between Chinese and Europeans, the Qing licensed Chinese trading firms at Canton to be the exclusive conduit for trade with the West. Eventually, the Qing confined the Europeans to a small island just outside the city wall and permitted them to reside there only from October through March.

For a while, the British tolerated this system, but by the end of the eighteenth century, the British government became restive at the uneven balance of trade between the two countries, which forced the British to ship vast amounts of silver bullion to China in exchange for its silks, porcelains, and teas. In 1793, a mission under Lord Macartney visited Beijing to press for liberalization of trade restrictions. A compromise was reached on the kowtow (Macartney was permitted to bend on one knee as was the British custom), but Qianlong expressed no interest in British manufactured products (see the box on p. 441). An exasperated Macartney compared the Chinese Empire to "an old, crazy, first-rate man-of-war" that had once awed its neighbors "merely by her bulk and appearance" but was now destined under incompetent leadership to be "dashed to pieces on the shore."[4] With his contemptuous dismissal of the British request, the emperor had inadvertently sowed the seeds for a century of humiliation.

Changing China

FOCUS QUESTION: How did the economy and society of China change during the Ming and Qing eras, and to what degree did these changes seem to be leading toward an industrial revolution on the European model?

During the Ming and Qing dynasties, China remained a predominantly agricultural society; nearly 85 percent of its people were farmers. But although most Chinese still lived in rural villages, the economy was undergoing a number of changes.

The Population Explosion

In the first place, the center of gravity was continuing to shift steadily from the north to the south. In the early centuries of Chinese civilization, the administrative and economic center of gravity was clearly in the north. By the early Qing, the economic breadbasket of China was located along the Yangtze River and regions to the south. One concrete indication of this shift occurred during the Ming dynasty, when Emperor Yongle ordered the renovation of the Grand Canal to facilitate the shipment of rice from the Yangtze delta to the food-starved north.

Moreover, the population was beginning to increase rapidly (see the comparative essay "The Population Explosion" on p. 442). For centuries, China's population had remained within a range of 50 to 100 million, rising in times of peace and prosperity and falling in periods of foreign invasion and internal anarchy. During the Ming and the early Qing, however, the population increased from an estimated 70 to 80 million in 1390 to more than 300 million at the end of the eighteenth century. There were probably several reasons for this population increase: the relatively long period of peace and stability under the early Qing; the introduction of new crops from the Americas, including peanuts, sweet potatoes, and maize; and the planting of a new species of faster-growing rice from Southeast Asia.

Of course, this population increase meant much greater population pressure on the land, smaller farms, and a razor-thin margin of safety in case of climatic disaster. The imperial court attempted to deal with the problem through various means, most notably by preventing the concentration of land in the hands of wealthy landowners. Nevertheless, by the eighteenth century, almost all the land that could be irrigated was already under cultivation, and the problems of rural hunger and landlessness became increasingly serious.

Seeds of Industrialization

Another change during the early modern period in China was the steady growth of manufacturing and commerce. Taking advantage of the long era of peace and prosperity, merchants and manufacturers began to expand their operations beyond their immediate provinces. Commercial networks began to operate on a regional and sometimes even a national basis, as trade in silk, metal and wood products, porcelain, cotton goods, and cash crops like cotton and tobacco developed rapidly. Foreign trade also expanded as Chinese merchants set up extensive contacts with countries in Southeast Asia. As Chinese tea, silk, and porcelain became ever more popular in other parts of the world, the trade surplus grew as the country's exports greatly outnumbered its imports.

The Tribute System in Action

In 1793, the British emissary Lord Macartney visited the Qing Empire to request the opening of formal diplomatic and trading relations between his country and China. Emperor Qianlong's reply, addressed to King George III of Britain, illustrates how the imperial court in Beijing viewed the world. King George could not have been pleased. The document provides a good example of the complacency with which the Celestial Empire viewed the world beyond its borders.

A Decree of Emperor Qianlong

An Imperial Edict to the King of England: You, O King, are so inclined toward our civilization that you have sent a special envoy across the seas to bring to our Court your memorial of congratulations on the occasion of my birthday and to present your native products as an expression of your thoughtfulness. On perusing your memorial, so simply worded and sincerely conceived, I am impressed by your genuine respectfulness and friendliness and greatly pleased.

As to the request made in your memorial, O King, to send one of your nationals to stay at the Celestial Court to take care of your country's trade with China, this is not in harmony with the state system of our dynasty and will definitely not be permitted. Traditionally people of the European nations who wished to render some service under the Celestial Court have been permitted to come to the capital. But after their arrival they are obliged to wear Chinese court costumes, are placed in a certain residence, and are never allowed to return to their own countries. This is the established rule of the Celestial Dynasty with which presumably you, O King, are familiar. Now you, O King, wish to send one of your nationals to live in the capital, but he is not like the Europeans who come to Peking [Beijing] as Chinese employees, live there, and never return home again, nor can he be allowed to go and come and maintain any correspondence. This is indeed a useless undertaking.

Moreover the territory under the control of the Celestial Court is very large and wide. There are well-established regulations governing tributary envoys from the outer states to Peking, giving them provisions (of food and traveling expenses) by our post-houses and limiting their going and coming. There has never been a precedent for letting them do whatever they like. Now if you, O King, wish to have a representative in Peking, his language will be unintelligible and his dress different from the regulations; there is no place to accommodate him. . . .

The Celestial Court has pacified and possessed the territory within the four seas. Its sole aim is to do its utmost to achieve good government and to manage political affairs, attaching no value to strange jewels and precious objects. The various articles presented by you, O King, this time are accepted by my special order to the office in charge of such functions in consideration of the offerings having come from a long distance with sincere good wishes. As a matter of fact, the virtue and prestige of the Celestial Dynasty having spread far and wide, the kings of the myriad nations come by land and sea with all sorts of precious things. Consequently there is nothing we lack, as your principal envoy and others have themselves observed. We have never set much store on strange or ingenious objects, nor do we need any more of your country's manufactures.

What reasons did the emperor give for refusing Macartney's request to have a permanent British ambassador in Beijing? How did the tribute system differ from the principles of international relations as practiced in the West?

Source: Reprinted by permission of the publisher from *China's Response to the West: A Documentary Survey, 1839–1923*, by Ssu-yu Teng and John King Fairbank, pp. 24–27, Cambridge, Mass.: Harvard University Press, copyright © 1954, 1979 by the President and Fellows of Harvard College, copyright renewed 1982 by Ssu-yu Teng and John King Fairbank.

THE QING ECONOMY: READY FOR TAKEOFF? In recent years, a number of historians have suggested that because of these impressive advances, by the end of the eighteenth century China was poised to make the transition from an agricultural to a predominantly manufacturing and commercial economy—a transition that began to take place in western Europe with the onset of the Industrial Revolution in the late eighteenth century (see Chapter 19).

Certainly, in most respects the Chinese economy in the mid-Qing era was as advanced as any of its counterparts around the world. China's achievements in technology

COMPARATIVE ESSAY

The Population Explosion

Between 1700 and 1800, Europe, China, and, to a lesser degree, India and the Ottoman Empire experienced a dramatic growth in population. In Europe, the population grew from 120 million people to almost 200 million by 1800; China, from less than 200 million to 300 million during the same period.

Four factors were important in causing this population explosion. First, better growing conditions, made possible by an improvement in climate, affected wide areas of the world and enabled people to produce more food. Summers in both China and Europe became warmer beginning in the early eighteenth century. Second, by the eighteenth century, people had begun to develop immunities to the epidemic diseases that had caused such widespread loss of life between 1500 and 1700. The movements of people by ship after 1500 had led to devastating epidemics. For example, the arrival of Europeans in Mexico introduced smallpox, measles, and chicken pox to a native population that had no immunities to European diseases. In 1500, between 11 and 20 million people lived in the area of Mexico; by 1650, only 1.5 million remained. Gradually, however, people developed immunities to these diseases.

A third factor in the population increase was the availability of new foods. As a result of the Columbian Exchange (see the box on p. 368 in Chapter 14), American food crops—such as corn, potatoes, and sweet potatoes—were carried to other parts of the world, where they became important food sources. China had imported a new species of rice from Southeast Asia that had a shorter harvest cycle than that of existing varieties. These new foods provided additional sources of nutrition that enabled more people to live for a longer time. At the same time, land development and canal building in the eighteenth century also enabled government authorities to move food supplies to areas threatened with crop failure and famine.

Finally, the use of new weapons based on gunpowder allowed states to control larger territories and maintain a new degree of order. The early rulers of the Qing dynasty, for example, pacified the Chinese Empire and ensured a long period of peace and stability. Absolute monarchs achieved similar goals in a number of European states. Thus, in the eighteenth century, deaths from violence and from diseases were declining at the same time that food supplies were increasing, thereby making possible the beginning of the world population explosion that persists to this day.

© Lambeth Palace Library, London/The Bridgeman Art Library

Festival of the Yam. With the spread of a few major food crops, new sources of nutrition became available to feed more people. The importance of the yam to the Ashanti people of West Africa is evident in this celebration of a yam festival at harvest time in 1817.

What were the main reasons for the dramatic expansion in the world's population during the early modern era?

over the past centuries were unsurpassed, and a perceptive observer at the time might well have concluded that the Manchu Empire would be highly competitive with the most advanced nations around the world for the indefinite future.

Nevertheless, a number of factors made it unlikely that China would advance rapidly into the industrial age. In the first place, the mercantile class was not as independent in China as in some European societies. Trade and manufacturing in China remained under the firm control of the state. In addition, political and social prejudices against commercial activity remained strong. Reflecting an ancient preference for agriculture over manufacturing and trade, the state levied heavy taxes on manufacturing and commerce while attempting to keep agricultural taxes low.

© Peabody Essex Museum, Salem/The Bridgeman Art Library International

Haggling Over the Price of Tea. An important item in the China trade of the eighteenth and early nineteenth centuries was tea, which had become extremely popular in Great Britain. This painting depicts the various stages of growing, processing, and marketing tea leaves. In the background, workers are removing tender young leaves from the bushes. In the foreground, British and Chinese merchants bargain over the price. After being dried, the leaves are packed into chests and loaded on vessels for shipment abroad.

To a considerable degree, these views were shared by the population at large, as the scholar-gentry continued to dominate intellectual fashions in China throughout the early Qing period. Chinese elites in general had little interest in the natural sciences or economic activities and often viewed them as a threat to their own dominant status within Chinese society as a whole. The commercial middle class, lacking social status and an independent position in society, had little say in intellectual matters.

At the root of such attitudes was the lingering influence of Neo-Confucianism, which remained the official state doctrine in China down to the end of the Qing dynasty. Although the founding fathers of Neo-Confucianism had originally focused on the "investigation of things," as time passed its practitioners tended to emphasize the elucidation of moral principles rather than the expansion of scientific knowledge. Though the Chinese economy was gradually being transformed from an agricultural to a commercial and industrial giant, scholars tended to look back to antiquity, rather than to empirical science, as the prime source for knowledge of the natural world and human events. The result was an intellectual environment that valued continuity over change and tradition over innovation.

The Chinese reaction to European clock-making techniques provides an example. In the early seventeeth century, the Jesuit priest Matteo Ricci introduced advanced European clocks driven by weights or springs. The emperor was fascinated and found the clocks more reliable than Chinese timekeepers. Over the next decades, European timepieces became a popular novelty at court, but the Chinese expressed little curiosity about the technology involved, provoking one European observer to remark that playthings like cuckoo clocks "will be received here with much greater interest than scientific instruments or *objets d'art*."[5]

Daily Life in Qing China

Daily life under the Ming and early Qing dynasties continued to follow traditional patterns. As in earlier periods, Chinese society was organized around the family. The ideal family unit in Qing China was the joint family, in which as many as three or even four generations lived under the same roof. When sons married, they brought their wives to live with them in the family homestead. Unmarried daughters would also remain in the house. Aging parents and grandparents remained under the same roof and were cared for by younger members of the household until they died. This ideal did not always correspond to reality, however, since many families did not possess sufficient land to support a large household.

THE FAMILY The family continued to be important in early Qing times for much the same reasons as in earlier times. As a labor-intensive society based primarily on the cultivation of rice, China needed large families to help with the harvest and to provide security for parents too old to work in the fields. Sons were particularly prized, not only because they had strong backs but also because they would raise their own families under the parental roof. With few opportunities for employment outside the family, sons had little choice but to remain with their parents and help on the land. Within the family, the oldest male was king, and his wishes theoretically had to be obeyed by all family members. Arranged marriages were the norm, and the primary consideration in selecting a spouse was whether the union would benefit the family as a whole. The couple themselves usually had no say in the matter and might not even meet until the marriage ceremony. Not only was love considered unimportant in marriage, but it was often viewed as undesirable because it would draw the attention of the husband and wife away from their primary responsibility to the larger family unit.

Although this emphasis on filial piety might seem to represent a blatant disregard for individual rights, the obligations were not all on the side of the children. The father was expected to provide support for his wife and children and, like the ruler, was supposed to treat those in his care with respect and compassion. All too often, however, the male head of the family was able to exact his privileges without performing his responsibilities in return.

Beyond the joint family was the clan. Sometimes called a lineage, a clan was an extended kinship unit consisting of dozens or even hundreds of joint and nuclear families linked together by a clan council of elders and a variety of other common social and religious functions. The clan served a number of useful purposes. Some clans possessed lands that could be rented out to poorer families, or richer families within the clan might provide land for the poor. Since there was no general state-supported educational system, sons of poor families might be invited to study in a school established in the home of a more prosperous relative. If the young man succeeded in becoming an official, he would be expected to provide favors and prestige for the clan as a whole.

THE ROLE OF WOMEN In traditional China, the role of women had always been inferior to that of men. A sixteenth-century Spanish visitor to South China observed that Chinese women were "very secluded and virtuous, and it was a very rare thing for us to see a woman in the cities and large towns, unless it was an old crone."[6] Women were more visible, he said, in rural areas, where they frequently could be seen working in the fields.

The concept of female inferiority had deep roots in Chinese history. This view was embodied in the belief that only a male would carry on sacred family rituals and that men alone had the talent to govern others. Only males could aspire to a career in government or scholarship. Within the family system, the wife was clearly subordinated to the husband. Legally, she could not divorce her husband or inherit property. The husband, however, could divorce his wife if she did not produce male heirs, or he could take a second wife as well as a concubine for his pleasure. A widow suffered especially because she had to either raise her children on a single income or fight off her former husband's greedy relatives, who would coerce her to remarry since, by law, they would then inherit all of her previous property and her original dowry.

Female children were less desirable because of their limited physical strength and because a girl's parents would have to pay a dowry to the parents of her future husband. Female children normally did not receive an education, and in times of scarcity when food was in short supply, daughters might even be put to death.

Though women were clearly inferior to men in theory, this was not always the case in practice. Capable women often compensated for their legal inferiority by playing a strong role within the family. Women were often in charge of educating the children and handled the family budget. Some privileged women also received training in the Confucian classics, although their schooling was generally for a shorter time and less rigorous than that of their male counterparts. A few produced significant works of art and poetry.

Cultural Developments

During the late Ming and the early Qing dynasties, traditional culture in China reached new heights of achievement. With the rise of a wealthy urban class, the demand for art, porcelain, textiles, and literature grew significantly.

THE RISE OF THE CHINESE NOVEL During the Ming dynasty, a new form of literature appeared that eventually evolved into the modern Chinese novel. Although considered less respectable than poetry and nonfiction prose, these groundbreaking works (often written anonymously or under pseudonyms) were enormously popular, especially among well-to-do urban dwellers.

Written in a colloquial style, the new fiction was characterized by a realism that resulted in vivid portraits of Chinese society. Many of the stories sympathized with society's downtrodden—often helpless maidens—and dealt with such crucial issues as love, money, marriage, and power. Adding to the realism were sexually explicit passages that depicted the private side of Chinese life. Readers delighted in sensuous tales that, no matter how pornographic, always professed a moral lesson; the villains were punished and the virtuous rewarded.

The Dream of the Red Chamber is generally considered China's most distinguished popular novel. Published in 1791, it tells of the tragic love between two young people caught in the financial and moral disintegration of a powerful Chinese clan. The hero and the heroine, both sensitive and spoiled, represent the inevitable decline of the Chia family and come to an equally inevitable tragic end, she in death and he in an unhappy marriage to another.

THE ART OF THE MING AND THE QING During the Ming and the early Qing, China produced its last outpouring of traditional artistic brilliance. Although most of the creative work was modeled on past examples, the art of this period is impressive for its technical perfection and breathtaking quantity.

In architecture, the most outstanding example is the Imperial City in Beijing. Building on the remnants of the palace of the Yuan dynasty, the Ming emperor Yongle ordered renovations when he returned the capital to Beijing in 1421. Succeeding emperors continued to add to the palace, but the basic design has not changed since the Ming era. Surrounded by high walls, the immense compound is divided into a maze of private apartments and offices and an imposing ceremonial quadrangle with a series of stately halls for imperial audiences and banquets. The grandiose scale, richly carved marble, spacious gardens, and graceful upturned roofs all contribute to the splendor of the "Forbidden City."

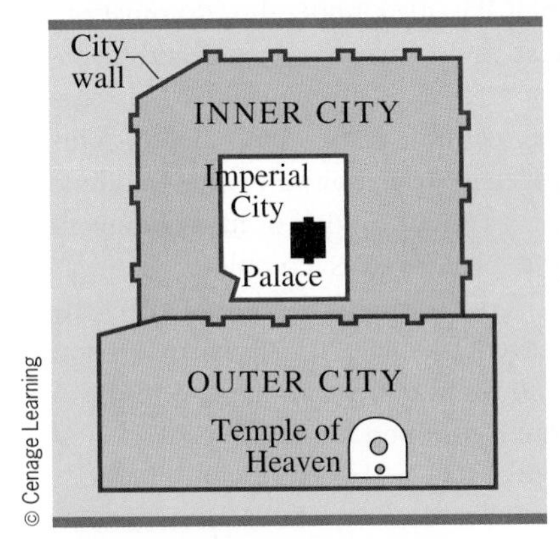

Beijing Under the Ming and the Manchus, 1400–1911

The decorative arts flourished in this period, especially the intricately carved lacquerware and the boldly shaped and colored cloisonné (kloi-zuh-NAY *or* KLWAH-zuh-nay), a type of enamelwork in which thin metal bands separate the areas of colored enamel. Silk production reached its zenith, and the best-quality silks were highly prized in Europe, where chinoiserie (sheen-wah-zuh-REE *or* shee-nwahz-REE), as Chinese art of all kinds was called, was in vogue. Perhaps the most famous of all the achievements of the Ming era was its blue-and-white porcelain, still prized by collectors throughout the world.

During the Qing dynasty, artists produced great quantities of paintings, mostly for home consumption. Inside the Forbidden City in Beijing, court painters worked alongside Jesuit artists and experimented with Western techniques. Most scholarly painters and the literati, however, totally rejected foreign techniques and became obsessed with traditional Chinese styles. As a result, Qing painting became progressively more repetitive and stale.

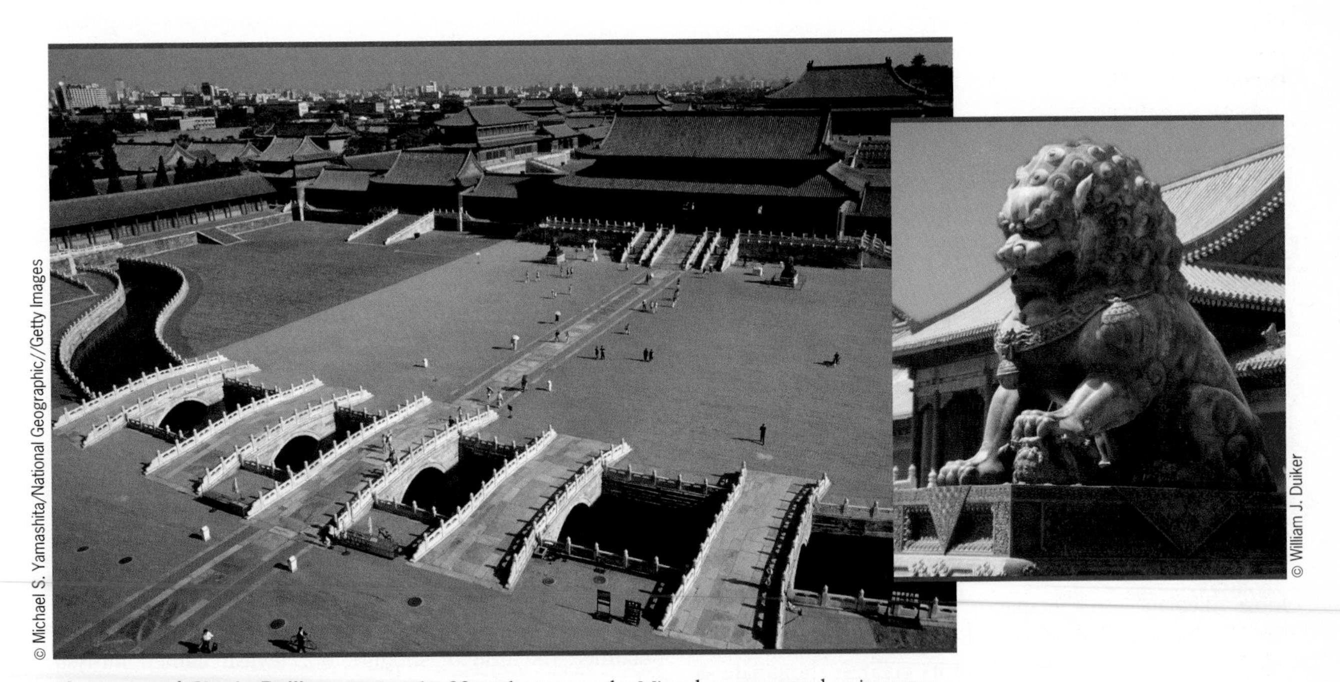

The Imperial City in Beijing. During the fifteenth century, the Ming dynasty erected an immense imperial city on the remnants of the palace of Khubilai Khan in Beijing. Surrounded by 6½ miles of walls, the enclosed compound is divided into a maze of private apartments and offices; it also includes an imposing ceremonial quadrangle with stately halls for imperial audiences and banquets. Because it was off-limits to commoners, the compound was known as the Forbidden City. The fearsome lion shown in the inset, representing the omnipotence of the Chinese Empire, guards the entrance to the private apartments of the palace.

© William J. Duiker

World-Class China Ware. Ming porcelain was desired throughout the world for its delicate blue-and-white floral decorations. The blue coloring was produced with cobalt that had originally been brought from the Middle East along the Silk Road and was known in China as "Mohammedan blue." In the early seventeenth century, the first Ming porcelain arrived in the Netherlands, where it was called *kraak* because it had been loaded on two Portuguese ships known as carracks seized by the Dutch fleet. It took Dutch artisans more than a century to learn how to produce a porcelain as fine as the examples brought from China.

Tokugawa Japan

FOCUS QUESTION: How did the society and economy of Japan change during the Tokugawa era, and how did Japanese culture reflect those changes?

At the end of the fifteenth century, the traditional Japanese system was at a point of near anarchy. With the decline in the authority of the Ashikaga (ah-shee-KAH-guh) shogunate at Kyoto (KYOH-toh), clan rivalries had exploded into an era of warring states. Even at the local level, power was frequently diffuse. The typical daimyo (DYM-yoh) (great lord) domain had often become little more than a coalition of fief-holders held together by a loose allegiance to the manor lord. Nevertheless, Japan was on the verge of an extended era of national unification and peace under the rule of its greatest shogunate—the Tokugawa.

The Three Great Unifiers

The process began in the mid-sixteenth century with the emergence of three very powerful political figures, Oda Nobunaga (1568–1582), Toyotomi Hideyoshi (1582–1598), and Tokugawa Ieyasu (1598–1616). In 1568, Oda Nobunaga (OH-dah noh-buh-NAH-guh), the son of a samurai (SAM-uh-ry) and a military commander under the Ashikaga shogunate, seized the imperial capital of Kyoto and placed the reigning shogun (SHOH-gun) under his domination. During the next few years, the brutal and ambitious Nobunaga attempted to consolidate his rule throughout the central plains by defeating his rivals and suppressing the power of the Buddhist estates, but he was killed by one of his generals in 1582 before the process was complete. He was succeeded by Toyotomi Hideyoshi (toh-yoh-TOH-mee hee-day-YOH-shee), a farmer's son who had worked his way up through the ranks to become a military commander. Hideyoshi located his capital at Osaka (oh-SAH-kuh), where he built a castle to accommodate his headquarters, and gradually extended his power outward to the southern islands of Shikoku (shee-KOH-koo) and Kyushu (KYOO-shoo) (see Map 17.3). By 1590, he had persuaded most of the daimyo on the Japanese islands to accept his authority and created a national currency. Then he invaded Korea in an abortive effort to export his rule to the Asian mainland (see "Korea: In a Dangerous Neighborhood" later in this chapter).

Despite their efforts, however, neither Nobunaga nor Hideyoshi was able to eliminate the power of the local daimyo. Both were compelled to form alliances with some daimyo in order to destroy other more powerful rivals. At the conclusion of his conquests in 1590, Toyotomi Hideyoshi could claim to be the supreme proprietor of all registered lands in areas under his authority. But he then reassigned those lands as fiefs to the local daimyo, who declared their allegiance to him. The daimyo in turn began to pacify the countryside, carrying out extensive "sword hunts" to disarm the population and attracting samurai to their service. The Japanese tradition of decentralized rule had not yet been overcome.

After Hideyoshi's death in 1598, Tokugawa Ieyasu (toh-koo-GAH-wah ee-yeh-YAH-soo), the powerful daimyo of Edo (EH-doh) (modern Tokyo), moved to fill the vacuum. Neither Hideyoshi nor Oda Nobunaga had claimed the title of shogun, but Ieyasu named himself shogun in 1603, initiating the most powerful and long-lasting of all Japanese shogunates. The Tokugawa rulers completed the restoration of central authority begun by Nobunaga and Hideyoshi and remained in power until 1868, when a war dismantled the entire system. As a contemporary phrased it, "Oda pounds the national rice

CHINA
Hokkaido
Hakodate
Sea of Japan
(East Sea)
KOREA
Seoul
Honshu
Nikko
Lake Biwa
Kanto Plain
Edo
Yokohama
Nagoya
Kobe
Kyoto
Himeji
Osaka
Hiroshima
Tsushima
Shimonoseki
Inland Sea
Shikoku
Pacific Ocean
Nagasaki
Kyushu
East China Sea
Kagoshima
0 100 200 300 Kilometers
0 100 200 Miles

© Cengage Learning. Adapted from John K. Fairbank, Edwin O. Reischauer, and Albert M. Craig, *East Asia: Tradition and Transformation* (Boston: Houghton Mifflin, 1973), pp. 402–403.

MAP 17.3 Tokugawa Japan. This map shows the Japanese islands during the long era of the Tokugawa shogunate. Key cities, including the shogun's capital of Edo (Tokyo), are shown.

Where was the imperial court located?

cake, Hideyoshi kneads it, and in the end Ieyasu sits down and eats it."[7]

Opening to the West

The unification of Japan took place almost simultaneously with the coming of the Europeans. Portuguese traders sailing in a Chinese junk that may have been blown off course by a typhoon had landed on the islands in 1543. Within a few years, Portuguese ships were stopping at Japanese ports on a regular basis to take part in the regional trade between Japan, China, and Southeast Asia. The first Jesuit missionary, Francis Xavier (ZAY-vee-ur), arrived in 1549.

Initially, the visitors were welcomed. The curious Japanese were fascinated by tobacco, clocks, spectacles, and other European goods, and local daimyo were interested in purchasing all types of European weapons and armaments (see the box on p. 448). Oda Nobunaga and Toyotomi Hideyoshi found the new firearms helpful in defeating their enemies and unifying the islands. The effect on Japanese military architecture was particularly striking as local lords began to erect castles on the European model, many of which still exist today.

Musée des Arts Asiatiques-Guimet, Paris//© RMN-Grand Palais/Art Resource, NY

Arrival of the Portuguese at Nagasaki. Portuguese traders, dressed in billowing pantaloons and broad-brimmed hats, landed in Japan by accident in 1543. In a few years, they were arriving regularly, taking part in a regional trade network involving Japan, China, and Southeast Asia. In these panels done in black lacquer and gold leaf, we see a late-sixteenth-century Japanese interpretation of Portuguese merchants at Nagasaki. Normally, Japanese screens are read from right to left, but this one is read left to right. Having arrived by ship, the Portuguese proceed in splendor to the Jesuit priests waiting in a church on the right.

A Present For Lord Tokitaka

SCIENCE & TECHNOLOGY

The Portuguese introduced firearms to Japan in the sixteenth century, and Japanese warriors were quick to explore the possibilities of these new weapons. In this passage, the daimyo of a small island off the southern tip of Japan receives an explanation of how to use the new weapons and is fascinated by the results. Note how Lord Tokitaka (toh-kuh-TAH-kuh) attempts to understand the procedures in terms of traditional Daoist beliefs.

The Japanese Discover Firearms

"There are two leaders among the traders, the one called Murashusa, and the other Christian Mota. In their hands they carried something two or three feet long, straight on the outside with a passage inside, and made of a heavy substance. The inner passage runs through it although it is closed at the end. At its side there is an aperture which is the passageway for fire. Its shape defies comparison with anything I know. To use it, fill it with powder and small lead pellets. Set up a small . . . target on a bank. Grip the object in your hand, compose your body, and closing one eye, apply fire to the aperture. Then the pellet hits the target squarely. The explosion is like lightning and the report like thunder. Bystanders must cover their ears. . . . This thing with one blow can smash a mountain of silver and a wall of iron. If one sought to do mischief in another man's domain and he was touched by it, he would lose his life instantly. Needless to say this is also true for the deer and stag that ravage the plants in the fields."

Lord Tokitaka saw it and thought it was the wonder of wonders. He did not know its name at first nor the details of its use. Then someone called it "iron-arms," although it was not known whether the Chinese called it so, or whether it was so called only on our island. Thus, one day, Tokitaka spoke to the two alien leaders through an interpreter: "Incapable though I am, I should like to learn about it." Whereupon, the chiefs answered, also through an interpreter: "If you wish to learn about it, we shall teach you its mysteries." Tokitaka then asked, "What is its secret?" The chief replied: "The secret is to put your mind aright and close one eye." Tokitaka said: "The ancient sages have often taught how to set one's mind aright, and I have learned something of it. If the mind is not set aright, there will be no logic for what we say or do. Thus, I understand what you say about setting our minds aright. However, will it not impair our vision for objects at a distance if we close an eye? Why should we close an eye?" To which the chiefs replied: "That is because concentration is important in everything. When one concentrates, a broad vision is not necessary. To close an eye is not to dim one's eyesight but rather to project one's concentration farther. You should know this." Delighted, Tokitaka said: "That corresponds to what Lao Tzu has said, 'Good sight means seeing what is very small.'"

That year the festival day of the Ninth Month fell on the day of the Metal and the Boar. Thus, one fine morning the weapon was filled with powder and lead pellets, a target was set up more than a hundred paces away, and fire was applied to the weapon. At first the people were astonished; then they became frightened. But in the end they all said in unison: "We should like to learn!" Disregarding the high price of the arms, Tokitaka purchased from the aliens two pieces of the firearms for his family treasure. As for the art of grinding, sifting, and mixing of the powder, Tokitaka let his retainer, Shinokawa Shoshiro, learn it. Tokitaka occupied himself, morning and night, and without rest in handling the arms. As a result, he was able to convert the misses of his early experiments into hits—a hundred hits in a hundred attempts.

How did Lord Tokitaka use Daoist concepts to explain something unfamiliar to him? What impact did the introduction of firearms have on Japanese society at the time?

Source: From *Sources of Japanese Tradition* by William Theodore de Bary, Carol Gluck, and Arthur E. Tiedemann. Copyright © 2005 by Columbia University Press. Reprinted with permission of the publisher.

The missionaries also had some success in converting a number of local daimyo, some of whom may have been motivated in part by the desire for commercial profits. By the end of the sixteenth century, thousands of Japanese in the southernmost islands of Kyushu and Shikoku had become Christians. But papal claims to the loyalty of all Japanese Christians and the European habit of intervening in local politics soon began to arouse suspicion in official circles. Missionaries added to the problem by deliberately destroying local idols and shrines and turning some temples into Christian schools or churches.

THE CHRISTIANS ARE EXPELLED Inevitably, the local authorities reacted. In 1587, Toyotomi Hideyoshi issued an edict prohibiting further Christian activities within his domains. Japan, he declared, was "the land of the Gods," and the destruction of shrines by the foreigners was "something unheard of in previous ages."[8] The Jesuits were ordered to leave the country within twenty days. Hideyoshi was careful to distinguish missionary from trading activities, however, and merchants were permitted to continue their operations.

The Jesuits protested the expulsion, and eventually Hideyoshi relented, permitting them to continue proselytizing as long as they were discreet. But he refused to repeal the edicts, and when the aggressive activities of newly arrived Spanish Franciscans aroused his ire, he ordered the execution of nine missionaries and a number of their Japanese converts. When the missionaries continued to interfere in local politics, Tokugawa Ieyasu ordered the eviction of all missionaries in 1612.

At first, Japanese authorities hoped to maintain commercial relations with European countries even while suppressing the Western religion, but eventually they decided to regulate foreign trade more closely and closed the two major foreign factories on the island of Hirado (heh-RAH-doh) and at Nagasaki (nah-gah-SAH-kee). The sole remaining opening to the West was at the island of Deshima (deh-SHEE-muh *or* deh-JEE-muh) in Nagasaki harbor, where in 1609 a small Dutch community was given permission to engage in limited trade with Japan (the Dutch, unlike the Portuguese and the Spanish, had not allowed missionary activities to interfere with their commercial interests). Dutch ships were permitted to dock at Nagasaki harbor only once a year and, after close inspection, were allowed to remain for two or three months. Conditions on the island of Deshima itself were quite confining: the Dutch physician Engelbert Kaempfer complained that the Dutch lived in "almost perpetual imprisonment."[9] Nor were the Japanese free to engage in foreign trade. A small amount of commerce took place with China and other parts of Asia, but Japanese subjects of the shogunate were forbidden to leave the country on penalty of death.

The Tokugawa "Great Peace"

Once in power, the Tokugawa attempted to strengthen the system that had governed Japan for more than three hundred years. They followed precedent in ruling through the *bakufu* (buh-KOO-foo *or* bah-KOO-fuh), composed now of a coalition of daimyo, and a council of elders. But the system was more centralized than it had been previously. Now the shogunate government played a dual role. It set national policy on behalf of the emperor in Kyoto while simultaneously governing the shogun's own domain, which included about one-quarter of the national territory as well as the three great cities of Edo, Kyoto, and Osaka. As before, the state was divided into separate territories, called domains (***han***), which were ruled by a total of about 250 individual daimyo.

In theory, the daimyo were essentially autonomous in that they were able to support themselves from taxes on their lands (the shogunate received its own revenues from its extensive landholdings). In actuality, the shogunate was able to guarantee their loyalty by compelling the daimyo to maintain two residences, one in their own domains and the other at Edo, and to leave their families in Edo as hostages for the daimyo's good behavior. Keeping up two residences also put the Japanese nobility in a difficult economic position. Some were able to defray the high costs by concentrating on cash crops such as sugar, fish, and forestry products; but most were rice producers, and their revenues remained roughly the same throughout the period. The daimyo were also able to protect their economic interests by depriving their samurai retainers of their proprietary rights over the land and transforming them into salaried officials. The fief thus became a stipend, and the personal relationship between the daimyo and his retainers gradually gave way to a bureaucratic authority.

CHRONOLOGY Japan and Korea During the Early Modern Era

First phonetic alphabet in Korea	Fifteenth century
Portuguese merchants arrive in Japan	1543
Francis Xavier arrives in Japan	1549
Rule of Oda Nobunaga	1568–1582
Seizure of Kyoto	1568
Rule of Toyotomi Hideyoshi	1582–1598
Edict prohibiting Christianity in Japan	1587
Japan invades Korea	1592
Death of Hideyoshi and withdrawal of the Japanese army from Korea	1598
Rule of Tokugawa Ieyasu	1598–1616
Creation of Tokugawa shogunate	1603
Dutch granted permission to trade at Nagasaki	1609
Order evicting Christian missionaries	1612
Yi dynasty of Korea declares fealty to China	1630s

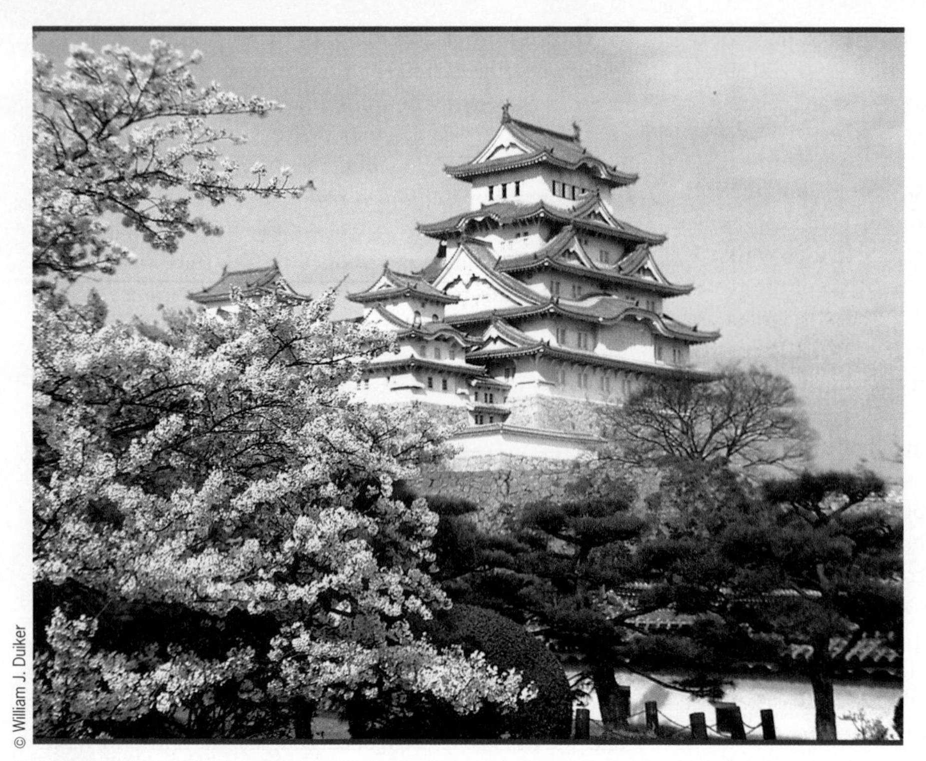

© William J. Duiker

A Japanese Castle. In imitation of European castle architecture, the Japanese perfected a new type of fortress-palace in the early seventeenth century. Strategically placed high on a hilltop, constructed of heavy stone with tiny windows, and fortified by numerous watchtowers and massive walls, these strongholds were impregnable to arrows and catapults. They served as a residence for the local daimyo, while the castle compound also housed his army and contained the seat of local government. Himeji (HEE-meh-jee) Castle, shown here, is one of the most beautiful in Japan.

The Tokugawa also tinkered with the social system by limiting the size of the samurai class and reclassifying samurai who supported themselves by tilling the land as commoners. In fact, with the long period of peace brought about by Tokugawa rule, the samurai gradually ceased to be a warrior class and were required to live in the castle towns. As a gesture to their glorious past, samurai were still permitted to wear their two swords, and a rigid separation was maintained between persons of samurai status and the nonaristocratic segment of the population.

SEEDS OF CAPITALISM The long period of peace under the Tokugawa shogunate made possible a dramatic rise in commerce and manufacturing, especially in the growing cities of Edo, Kyoto, and Osaka. By the mid-eighteenth century, Edo, with a population of more than one million, was one of the largest cities in the world. The growth of trade and industry was stimulated by a rising standard of living—driven in part by technological advances in agriculture and an expansion of arable land—and the voracious appetites of the aristocrats for new products.

Most of this commercial expansion took place in the major cities and the castle towns, where the merchants and artisans lived along with the samurai, who were clustered in neighborhoods surrounding the daimyo's castle. Banking flourished, and paper money became the normal medium of exchange in commercial transactions. Merchants formed guilds not only to control market conditions but also to facilitate government control and the collection of taxes. Under the benign if somewhat contemptuous supervision of Japan's noble rulers, a Japanese merchant class gradually began to emerge from the shadows to play a significant role in the life of the Japanese nation. Some historians view the Tokugawa era as the first stage in the rise of an indigenous form of capitalism.

Eventually, the increased pace of industrial activity spread beyond the cities into rural areas. As in Great Britain, cotton was a major factor. Cotton had been introduced to China during the Song dynasty and had spread to Korea and Japan shortly thereafter. Traditionally, cotton cloth had been too expensive for the common people, who instead wore clothing made of hemp. Imports increased during the sixteenth century, however, when cotton cloth began to be used for uniforms, matchlock fuses, and sails. Eventually, technological advances reduced the cost, and specialized communities for producing cotton cloth began to appear in the countryside and were gradually transformed into towns. By the eighteenth century, cotton had firmly replaced hemp as the cloth of choice for most Japanese.

Not everyone benefited from the economic changes of the seventeenth and eighteenth centuries, however, notably the samurai, who were barred by tradition and prejudice from commercial activities. Most samurai still relied on their revenues from rice lands, which were often insufficient to cover their rising expenses; consequently, they fell heavily into debt. Others were released from servitude to their lord and became "masterless samurai." Occasionally, these unemployed warriors—known as ***ronin*** (ROH-nihn), or "wave men"—revolted or plotted against the local authorities.

LAND PROBLEMS The effects of economic developments on the rural population during the Tokugawa era are harder to estimate. Some farm families benefited by exploiting the growing demand for cash crops. But not all prospered. Most peasants continued to rely on rice cultivation and were whipsawed between declining profits and rising costs and taxes (as daimyo expenses increased, land taxes often took up to 50 percent of the annual harvest). Many were forced to become tenants or to work as wage laborers on the farms of wealthy neighbors or in village industries. When rural conditions in some areas became desperate, peasant revolts erupted. According to one estimate, nearly seven thousand disturbances took place during the Tokugawa era.

Some Japanese historians, influenced by a Marxist view of history, have interpreted such evidence as an indication that the Tokugawa economic system was highly exploitative, with feudal aristocrats oppressing powerless peasants. Recent scholars, however, have tended to adopt a more balanced view, maintaining that in addition to agriculture, manufacturing and commerce experienced extensive growth. Some point out that although the population doubled in the seventeenth century, a relatively low rate for the time period, so did the amount of cultivable land, while agricultural technology made significant advances.

The relatively low rate of population growth probably meant that Japanese peasants were spared the kind of land hunger that many of their counterparts in China faced. Recent evidence indicates that the primary reasons for the relatively low rate of population growth were late marriage, abortion, and infanticide.

Life in the Village

The changes that took place during the Tokugawa era had a major impact on the lives of ordinary Japanese. In some respects, the result was an increase in the power of the central government at the village level. The shogunate increasingly relied on Confucian maxims advocating obedience and hierarchy to enhance its authority with the general population. Decrees from the *bakufu* instructed the peasants on all aspects of their lives, including their eating habits and their behavior (see the box on p. 452). At the same time, the increased power of the government led to more autonomy from the local daimyo for the peasants. Villages now had more control over their local affairs.

At the same time, the Tokugawa era saw the emergence of the nuclear family (*ie*) as the basic unit in Japanese society. In previous times, Japanese peasants had few legal rights. Most were too poor to keep their conjugal family unit intact or to pass property on to their children. Many lived at the manorial residence or worked as servants in the households of more affluent villagers. Now, with farm income on the rise, the nuclear family took on the same form as in China, although without the joint family concept. The Japanese system of inheritance was based on primogeniture (pry-moh-JEN-ih-chur). Family property was passed on to the eldest son, although younger sons often received land from their parents to set up their own families after marriage.

THE ROLE OF WOMEN Another result of the changes under the Tokugawa was that women were somewhat more restricted than they had been previously. The rights of females were especially restricted in the samurai class, where Confucian values were highly influential. Male heads of households had broad authority over property, marriage, and divorce; wives were expected to obey their husbands on pain of death. Males often took concubines or homosexual partners, while females were expected to remain chaste. The male offspring of samurai parents studied the Confucian classics in schools established by the daimyo, while females were reared at home, where only the fortunate might receive a rudimentary training in reading and writing Chinese characters. Nevertheless, some women were able to become accomplished poets and painters since, in aristocratic circles, female literacy was prized for enhancing the refinement, social graces, and moral virtue of the home.

Women were similarly at a disadvantage among the common people. Marriages were arranged, and as in China, the new wife moved in with the family of her husband. A wife who did not meet the expectations of her spouse or his family was likely to be divorced. Still, gender relations were more egalitarian than among the nobility. Women were generally valued as childbearers and homemakers, and both men and women worked in the fields. Coeducational schools were established in villages and market towns, and about one-quarter of the students were female. Poor families, however, often put infant daughters to death or sold them into prostitution.

Such attitudes toward women operated within the context of the increasingly rigid stratification of Japanese society. Deeply conservative in their social policies, the Tokugawa rulers established strict legal distinctions between the four main classes in Japan (warriors, artisans, peasants, and merchants). Intermarriage between classes was forbidden in theory, although sometimes the prohibitions were ignored in practice. Below these classes were Japan's outcasts, the ***eta*** (AY-tuh). Formerly, they were permitted to escape their status, at least in theory. The Tokugawa made their status hereditary and enacted severe discriminatory laws against them, regulating their place of residence, their dress, and even their hairstyles.

OPPOSING ≺ VIEWPOINTS

Some Confucian Commandments

Although the Qing dynasty was of foreign origin, its rulers found Confucian maxims convenient for maintaining the social order. In 1670, the great emperor Kangxi issued the Sacred Edict to popularize Confucian values among the common people. The edict was read publicly at periodic intervals in every village in China and set the standard for behavior throughout the empire. Like the Qing dynasty in China, the Tokugawa shoguns attempted to keep their subjects in line with decrees that carefully prescribed all kinds of behavior. Yet a subtle difference in tone can be detected in these two documents. Whereas Kangxi's edict tended to encourage positive behavior, the decree of the Tokugawa shogunate focused more on actions that were prohibited or discouraged.

Kangxi's Sacred Edict

1. Esteem most highly filial piety and brotherly submission, in order to give due importance to the social relations.
2. Behave with generosity toward your kindred, in order to illustrate harmony and benignity.
3. Cultivate peace and concord in your neighborhoods, in order to prevent quarrels and litigations.
4. Recognize the importance of husbandry and the culture of the mulberry tree, in order to ensure a sufficiency of clothing and food.
5. Show that you prize moderation and economy, in order to prevent the lavish waste of your means.
6. Give weight to colleges and schools, in order to make correct the practice of the scholar.
7. Extirpate strange principles, in order to exalt the correct doctrine.
8. Lecture on the laws, in order to warn the ignorant and obstinate.
9. Elucidate propriety and yielding courtesy, in order to make manners and customs good.
10. Labor diligently at your proper callings, in order to stabilize the will of the people.
11. Instruct sons and younger brothers, in order to prevent them from doing what is wrong.
12. Put a stop to false accusations, in order to preserve the honest and good.
13. Warn against sheltering deserters, in order to avoid being involved in their punishment.
14. Fully remit your taxes, in order to avoid being pressed for payment.
15. Unite in hundreds and tithing, in order to put an end to thefts and robbery.
16. Remove enmity and anger, in order to show the importance due to the person and life.

Maxims for Peasant Behavior in Tokugawa Japan

1. Young people are forbidden to congregate in great numbers.
2. Entertainments unsuited to peasants, such as playing the samisen or reciting ballad dramas, are forbidden.
3. Staging sumo matches is forbidden for the next five years.
4. The edict on frugality issued by the *han* at the end of last year must be observed.
5. Social relations in the village must be conducted harmoniously.
6. If a person has to leave the village for business or pleasure, that person must return by ten at night.
7. Father and son are forbidden to stay overnight at another person's house. An exception is to be made if it is to nurse a sick person.
8. Corvée [obligatory labor] assigned by the *han* must be performed faithfully.
9. Children who practice filial piety must be rewarded.
10. One must never get drunk and cause trouble for others.
11. Peasants who farm especially diligently must be rewarded.
12. Peasants who neglect farm work and cultivate their paddies and upland fields in a slovenly and careless fashion must be punished.
13. The boundary lines of paddy and upland fields must not be changed arbitrarily.
14. Recognition must be accorded to peasants who contribute greatly to village political affairs.
15. Fights and quarrels are forbidden in the village.
16. The deteriorating customs and morals of the village must be rectified.

(Continued)

17. Peasants who are suffering from poverty must be identified and helped.
18. This village has a proud history compared to other villages, but in recent years bad times have come upon us. Everyone must rise at six in the morning, cut grass, and work hard to revitalize the village.
19. The punishments to be meted out to violators of the village code and gifts to be awarded the deserving are to be decided during the last assembly meeting of the year.

In what ways did Kangxi's set of commandments conform to the principles of State Confucianism? How do these standards compare with those applied in Japan?

Sources: Kangxi's Sacred Edict. From *Popular Culture in Late Imperial China* by David Johnson et al. Copyright © 1985 The Regents of the University of California. Maxims for Peasant Behavior in Tokugawa Japan. From Chi Nakane and Oishi Shinsabura, *Tokugawa Japan: The Social and Economic Antecedents of Modern Japan* (Japan, University of Tokyo, 1990), pp. 51–52. Translated by Conrad Totman. Copyright 1992 by Columbia University Press.

Tokugawa Culture

Under the Tokugawa, a vital new set of cultural values began to appear, especially in the cities. This innovative era witnessed the rise of popular literature written by and for the townspeople. With the development of woodblock printing in the early seventeenth century, literature became available to the common people, literacy levels rose, and lending libraries increased the accessibility of the printed word.

THE LITERATURE OF THE NEW MIDDLE CLASS The best examples of this new urban fiction are the works of Saikaku (SY-kah-koo) (1642–1693), considered one of Japan's finest novelists. Saikaku's greatest novel, *Five Women Who Loved Love*, relates the amorous exploits of five women of the merchant class. Based partly on real-life experiences, it broke from the Confucian ethic of wifely fidelity to her husband and portrayed women who were willing to die for love—and all but one eventually did. Despite the tragic circumstances, the tone of the novel is upbeat and sometimes comic, and the author's wry comments prevent the reader from becoming emotionally involved with the heroines' misfortunes.

In the theater, the rise of Kabuki (kuh-BOO-kee) threatened the long dominance of the *No* (NOH) play, replacing the somewhat restrained and elegant thematic and stylistic approach of the classical drama with a new emphasis on violence, music, and dramatic gestures. Significantly, the new drama emerged not from the rarefied world of the court but from the new world of entertainment and amusement (see the comparative illustration on p. 454). Its very commercial success, however, led to difficulties with the government, which periodically attempted to restrict or even suppress it. Early Kabuki was often performed by prostitutes, and shogunate officials, fearing that such activities could have a corrupting effect on the nation's morals, prohibited women from appearing on the stage; at the same time, they attempted to create a new professional class of male actors to impersonate female characters on stage.

In contrast to the popular literature of the Tokugawa period, poetry persevered in its more serious tradition. The most exquisite poetry was produced in the seventeenth century by the greatest of all Japanese poets, Basho (BAH-shoh) (1644–1694). He was concerned with the search for the meaning of existence and the poetic expression of his experience. With his love of Daoism and Zen Buddhism, Basho found answers to his quest for the meaning of life in nature, and his poems are grounded in seasonal imagery. The following are among his most famous poems:

The ancient pond
A frog leaps in
The sound of the water.

On the withered branch
A crow has alighted—
The end of autumn.

His last poem, dictated to a disciple only three days before his death, succinctly expressed his frustration with the unfinished business of life:

On a journey, ailing—
my dreams roam about
on a withered moor.

Like all great artists, Basho made his poems seem effortless and simple. He speaks directly to everyone, everywhere.

TOKUGAWA ART Art also reflected the dynamism and changes in Japanese culture under the Tokugawa regime. The shogun's order that all daimyo and their families live every other year in Edo set off a burst of building as provincial rulers competed to erect the most magnificent mansion. Furthermore, the shoguns themselves constructed splendid castles adorned with sumptuous, almost ostentatious decor and furnishings. And the prosperity of

© The Newark Museum, NJ/Art Resource, NY

Museo di Firenze com'era, Florence//©Scala/Art Resource, NY

COMPARATIVE ILLUSTRATION

Popular Culture: East and West. By the seventeenth century, a popular culture distinct from the elite culture of the nobility was beginning to emerge in the urban worlds of both the East and the West. At the top is a festival scene from the pleasure district of Kyoto known as the Gion. Spectators on a balcony are enjoying a colorful parade of floats and costumed performers. The festival originated as a celebration of the passing of a deadly epidemic in medieval Japan. On the right below is a scene from the celebration of Carnival on the Piazza Sante Croce in Florence, Italy. Carnival was a period of festivities before Lent, celebrated primarily in Roman Catholic countries. It became an occasion for indulgence in food, drink, games, and practical jokes as a prelude to the austerity of the forty-day Lenten season from Ash Wednesday to Easter.

Do festivals such as these still exist in our own day? What purpose might they serve?

the newly rising merchant class added fuel to the fire. Japanese paintings, architecture, textiles, and ceramics all flourished during this affluent era.

Although Japan was isolated from the Western world during much of the Tokugawa era, Japanese art was enriched by ideas from other cultures. Japanese pottery makers borrowed both techniques and designs from Korea to produce handsome ceramics. The passion for "Dutch learning" inspired Japanese to study Western medicine, astronomy, and languages and also led to experimentation with oil painting and Western ideas of perspective and the interplay of light and dark. Europeans desired Japanese lacquerware and metalwork, inlaid with ivory and mother-of-pearl, and especially the ceramics, which were now as highly prized as those of the Chinese.

Perhaps the most famous of all Japanese art of the Tokugawa era is the woodblock print. Genre painting, or representations of daily life, began in the sixteenth century and found its new mass-produced form in the eighteenth-century woodblock print. The now literate mercantile class was eager for illustrated texts of the amusing and bawdy tales that had circulated in oral tradition. Some prints depict entire city blocks filled with people, trades, and festivals, while others show the interiors of houses; thus, they provide us with excellent visual documentation of the times. Others portray the "floating

© The Art Institute of Chicago/The Bridgeman Art Library

Evening Bell at the Clock. As woodblock prints became a popular form of pictorial expression in Tokugawa Japan, the painter Suzuki Haranobu (SOO-ZOO-kee hah-ROO-noh-boo) (c. 1725–1770) used the technique to portray scenes of daily life in the homes of ordinary Japanese. In the print shown here, a Japanese woman dries herself with a towel, while her companion looks up at a chiming clock on the dresser.

world" of the entertainment quarter, with scenes of carefree revelers enjoying the pleasures of life.

One of the most renowned of the numerous block-print artists was Utamaro (OO-tah-mah-roh) (1754–1806), who painted erotic and sardonic women in everyday poses, such as walking down the street, cooking, or drying their bodies after a bath. Hokusai (HOH-kuh-sy) (1760–1849) was famous for *Thirty-Six Views of Mount Fuji*, a new and bold interpretation of the Japanese landscape.

Korea and Vietnam

FOCUS QUESTIONS: To what degree did developments in Korea during this period reflect conditions in China and Japan? What were the unique aspects of Vietnamese civilization?

On the fringes of the East Asian mainland, two of China's close neighbors sought to preserve their fragile independence from the expansionistic tendencies of the powerful Ming and Qing dynasties.

Korea: In a Dangerous Neighborhood

While Japan under the Tokugawa shogunate moved steadily out from the shadows of the Chinese Empire by creating a unique society with its own special characteristics, the Yi (YEE) dynasty in Korea continued to pattern itself, at least on the surface, after the Chinese model. The dynasty had been founded by the military commander Yi Song Gye (YEE song yee) in the late fourteenth century and immediately set out to establish close political and cultural relations with the Ming dynasty. From their new capital at Seoul (SOHL), located on the Han (HAHN) River in the center of the peninsula, the Yi rulers accepted a tributary relationship with their powerful neighbor and engaged in the wholesale adoption of Chinese institutions and values. As in China, the civil service examinations tested candidates on their knowledge of the Confucian classics, and success was viewed as an essential step toward upward mobility.

There were differences, however. As in Japan, the dynasty continued to restrict entry into the bureaucracy to members of the aristocratic class, known in Korea as the ***yangban*** (YAHNG-ban) (or "two groups," civilian and military). At the same time, the peasantry remained in serflike conditions, working on government estates or on the manor holdings of the landed elite. A class of slaves, called ***chonmin*** (CHAWN-min), labored on government plantations or served in certain occupations, such as butchers and entertainers, considered beneath the dignity of other groups in the population.

Eventually, Korean society began to show signs of independence from Chinese orthodoxy. In the fifteenth century, a phonetic alphabet for writing the Korean spoken language (*hangul*) was devised. Although it was initially held in contempt by the elites and used primarily as a teaching device, eventually it became the medium for private correspondence and the publishing of fiction for a popular audience. At the same time, changes were taking place in the economy, where rising agricultural production contributed to a population increase and the appearance of a small urban industrial and commercial sector, and in society, where the long domination of the *yangban* class began to weaken. As their numbers increased and their power and influence declined, some *yangban* became merchants or even moved into the ranks of the peasantry, further blurring the distinction between the aristocratic class and the common people.

Meanwhile, the Yi dynasty faced continual challenges to its independence from its neighbors. Throughout much of the sixteenth century, the main threat came from the north, where Manchu forces harassed Korean lands just south of the Yalu (YAH-loo) River (see Map 17.3 on p. 447). By the 1580s, however, the larger threat

Be My Brother, or I'll Bash Your Head In!

In 1590, Toyotomi Hideyoshi defeated the last of his enemies and brought the islands of Japan under his rule. Shortly thereafter, an emissary from the Yi dynasty in Korea presented him with a letter congratulating him on his success. In his reply, presented here, Hideyoshi disclosed his plan to conquer the Chinese mainland and bring all of East Asia under his control. In a thinly veiled warning, which disclosed his megalomaniacal ambition, he demanded that the Yi ruler support his forthcoming attack on China. If not, he declared, Japan would exact terrible revenge. But the Korean king was more fearful of his powerful neighbor to the west and rejected Hideyoshi's demand for an alliance with Japan. Thereupon Hideyoshi attacked Korea in the so-called Imjin (IM-jin) War (1592–1598), which caused tremendous hardship throughout the peninsula.

Hideyoshi, Imperial Regent of Japan, to His Excellency the King of Korea

I read your epistle from afar with pleasure, opening and closing the scroll again and again to savor the aroma of your distinguished presence.

Now, then: This empire is composed of more than sixty provinces, but for years the country was divided, the polity disturbed, civility abandoned, and the realm unresponsive to imperial rule. Unable to stifle my indignation at this, I subjugated the rebels and struck down the bandits within the span of three or four years. As far away as foreign regions and distant islands, all is now in my grasp.

As I privately consider the facts of my background, I recognize it to be that of a rustic and unrefined minor retainer. Nevertheless: As I was about to be conceived, my dear mother dreamt that the wheel of the sun had entered her womb. The diviner declared, "As far as the sun shines, so will the brilliance of his rule extend. When he reaches his prime, the Eight Directions will be enlightened through his benevolence and the Four Seas replete with the glory of his name. How could anyone doubt this?" As a result of this miracle, anyone who turned against me was automatically crushed. Whomever I fought, I never failed to conquer. Now that the realm has been thoroughly pacified, I caress and nourish the people, solacing the orphaned and the desolate. Hence my subjects live in plenty and the revenue produced by the land has increased ten-thousand-fold over the past. Since this empire originated, never has the imperial court seen such prosperity or the capital city such grandeur as now.

Man born on this earth, though he live to a ripe old age, will as a rule not reach a hundred years. Why should I rest, then, grumbling in frustration, where I am? Disregarding the distance of the sea and mountain reaches that lie in between, I shall in one fell swoop invade Great Ming. I have in mind to introduce Japanese customs and values to the four hundred and more provinces of that country and bestow upon it the benefits of imperial rule and culture for the coming hundred million years.

Your esteemed country has done well to make haste in attending on our court. Where there is farsightedness, grief does not come near. Those who lag behind [in offering homage], however, will not be granted pardon, even if this is a distant land of little islands lying in the sea. When the day comes for my invasion of Great Ming and I lead my troops to the staging area, that will be the time to make our neighborly relations flourish all the more. I have no other desire but to spread my fame throughout the Three Countries, this and no more.

I have received your regional products as itemized. Stay healthy and take care.

Hideyoshi
Imperial Regent of Japan

How did Hideyoshi justify his ambitious plan to bring all of eastern Asia under his control?

Source: From W. T. de Bary, et al., *Sources of Japanese Tradition* 2nd ed., Vol. I (New York, 2001), pp. 466–467, citing Zoku Zenrin Kokuho Ki xxx, in Zoku gunsho ruiju, demivol. I, fasc. 881, 404, JSAE.

came from the east in the form of a newly united Japan. During much of the sixteenth century, leading Japanese daimyo had been involved in a protracted civil war, as Oda Nobunaga, Toyotomi Hideyoshi, and Tokugawa Ieyasu strove to solidify their control over the islands. Of the three, only Hideyoshi lusted for an empire beyond the seas. Although born to a commoner family, he harbored visions of grandeur and in the late 1580s announced plans to attack the Ming Empire (see the box above). When the Korean king Sonjo (SOHN-joe) (1567–1608) refused

Hideyoshi's offer of an alliance, in 1592 the latter launched an invasion of the Korean peninsula.

At first the campaign went well, and Japanese forces, wreaking death and devastation throughout the countryside, advanced as far as the Korean capital at Seoul. But eventually the Koreans, under the inspired leadership of the military commander Yi Sunshin (YEE-soon-SHIN) (1545–1598), who designed fast but heavily armed ships that could destroy the more cumbersome landing craft of the invading forces, managed to repel the attack and safeguard their independence. The respite was brief, however. By the 1630s, a new threat from the Manchus had emerged from across the northern border. A Manchu force invaded northern Korea in the 1630s and eventually compelled the Yi dynasty to promise allegiance to the new imperial government in Beijing. Korea was relatively untouched by the arrival of European merchants and missionaries, although information about Christianity was brought to the peninsula by Koreans returning from tribute missions to China, and a small Catholic community was established there in the late eighteenth century.

Vietnam: The Perils of Empire

Vietnam—or Dai Viet (dy VEE-et), as it was known at the time—had managed to avoid the fate of many of its neighbors during the seventeenth and eighteenth centuries. Isolated from the major maritime routes that passed through the region, the country was only peripherally involved in the spice trade with the West and had not suffered the humiliation of losing territory to European colonial powers. In fact, Dai Viet followed an imperialist path of its own, defeating the trading state of Champa to the south and imposing its suzerainty over the rump of the old Angkor empire—today known as Cambodia. The state of Dai Viet now extended from the Chinese border to the shores of the Gulf of Siam.

But expansion undermined the cultural integrity of traditional Vietnamese society, as those migrants who settled in the marshy Mekong River delta developed a "frontier spirit" far removed from the communal values long practiced in the old national heartland of the Red River valley. By the seventeenth century, a civil war had split Dai Viet into two squabbling territories in the north and south, providing European powers with the opportunity to meddle in the country's internal affairs to their own benefit. In 1802, with the assistance of a French adventurer long active in the region, a member of the southern royal family managed to reunite the country under the new Nguyen (NGWEN) dynasty, which lasted until 1945.

To placate China, the country was renamed Vietnam (South Viet), and the new imperial capital was established in the city of Hué (HWAY), a small river port roughly equidistant from the two rich river valleys that provided the country with its chief sustenance, wet rice. The founder of the new dynasty, who took the reign title of Gia Long, fended off French efforts to promote Christianity among his subjects and sought to promote traditional Confucian values among an increasingly diverse population.

CHAPTER SUMMARY

When Christopher Columbus sailed from southern Spain in his three ships in August 1492, he was seeking a route to China and Japan. He did not find it, but others eventually did. In 1514, Portuguese ships arrived on the coast of southern China. Thirty years later, a small contingent of Portuguese merchants became the first Europeans to set foot on the islands of Japan.

At first, the new arrivals were welcomed, if only as curiosities. Eventually, several European nations established trade relations with China and Japan, and Christian missionaries of various religious orders were active in both countries and in Korea as well. But their success was short-lived. Europeans eventually began to be perceived as detrimental to law and order, and during the seventeenth century, the majority of the foreign merchants and missionaries were evicted from all three countries. From that time until the middle of the nineteenth century, China, Japan, and Korea were relatively little affected by events taking place beyond their borders.

That fact led many observers to assume that the societies of East Asia were essentially stagnant, characterized by agrarian institutions and values reminiscent of those of the feudal era in Europe. As we have seen, however, that picture is misleading, for all three countries were evolving and by the early nineteenth century were quite different from what they had been three centuries earlier.

Ironically, these changes were especially marked in Tokugawa Japan, a seemingly "closed" country, but one where traditional classes and institutions were under increasing strain, not only from the emergence of a new merchant class but also from the centralizing tendencies of the powerful Tokugawa shogunate. On the mainland as well, the popular image in the West of a "changeless China" was increasingly divorced from reality, as social and economic conditions were marked by a growing complexity, giving birth to tensions that by the middle of the nineteenth century would strain the Qing dynasty to its very core.

By the beginning of the nineteenth century, then, powerful tensions, reflecting a growing gap between ideal and reality, were at work in both Chinese and Japanese society. Under these conditions, both countries were soon forced to face a new challenge from the aggressive power of an industrializing Europe.

CHAPTER TIMELINE

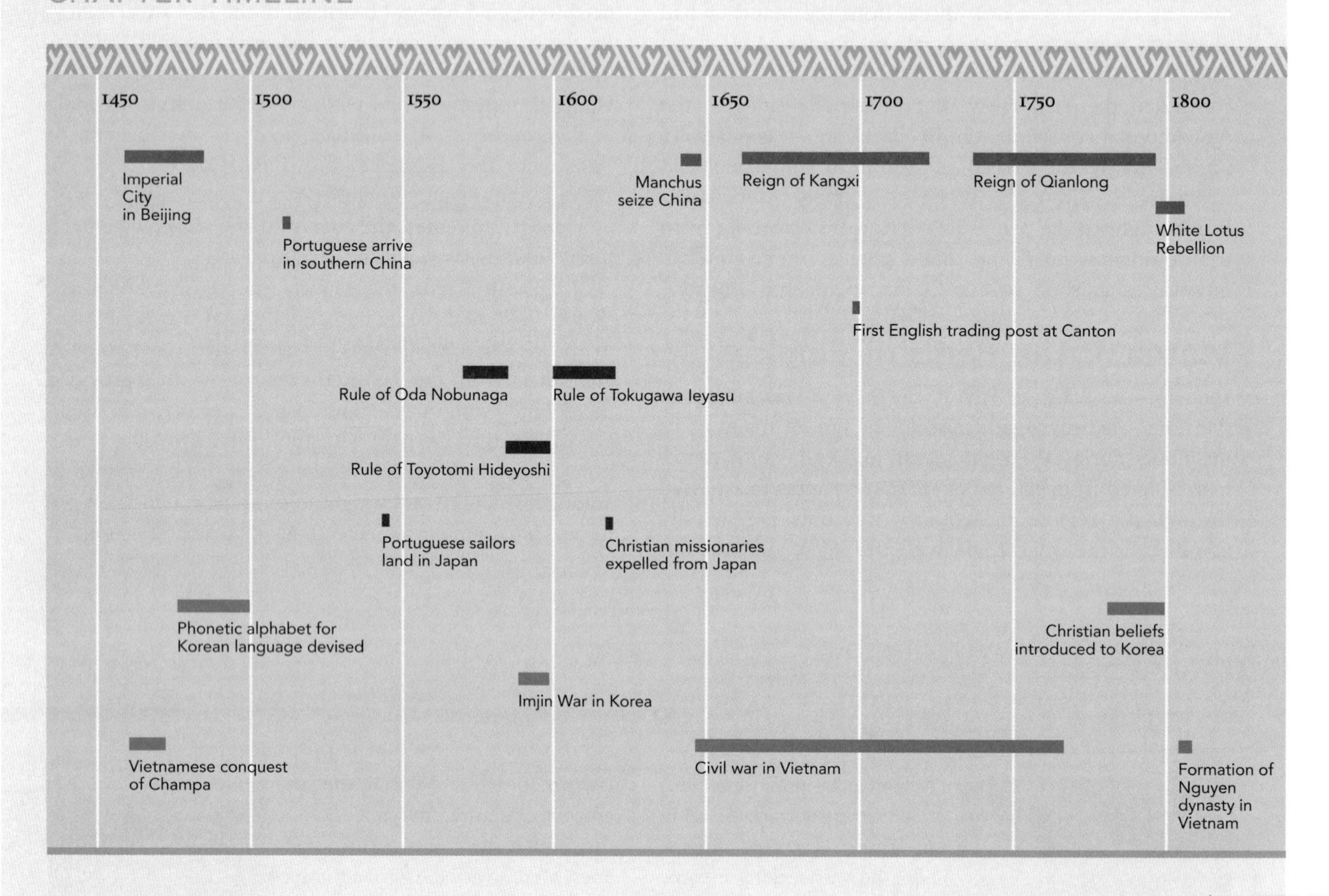

CHAPTER REVIEW

Upon Reflection

Q What factors at the end of the eighteenth century might have served to promote or to impede China's transition to an advanced industrial and market economy? Which factors do you think were the most important? Why?

Q Some historians have declared that during the Tokugawa era the Japanese government essentially sought to close the country to all forms of outside influence. Is that claim justified? Why or why not?

Q What was the nature of Sino-Korean relations during the early modern era? How did they compare with Chinese policies toward Vietnam?

Key Terms

banners (p. 438)
dyarchy (p. 439)
kowtow (p. 439)
han (p. 449)
ronin (p. 450)
eta (p. 451)
yangban (p. 455)
chonmin (p. 455)

Suggested Reading

CHINA UNDER THE MING AND QING DYNASTIES Reliable surveys with a readable text are **T. Brook, *The Troubled Empire: China in the Yuan and Ming Dynasties*** (Cambridge, Mass., 2010), and **W. Rowe, *China's Last Empire: Great Qing*** (Cambridge, Mass., 2009). For fascinating vignettes of Chinese social conditions, see **J. Spence, *Return to Dragon Mountain: Memories of a Late Ming Man*** (New York, 2007) and ***Treason by the Book*** (New York, 2001).

L. Brockey, *Journey to the East: The Jesuit Mission to China, 1579–1724* (Cambridge, Mass., 2007), is an account of China's first encounter with Europe. For a defense of Chinese science, see **B. Elman, *On Their Own Terms: Science in China, 1550–1900*** (Cambridge, Mass., 2005). **J. E. Wills Jr., *Mountains of Fame: Portraits in Chinese History*** (Princeton, N.J., 1994), is an interesting collection of biographies from across the gamut of Chinese history.

CHINESE LITERATURE AND ART The best surveys of Chinese literature are **S. Owen, *An Anthology of Chinese Literature: Beginnings to 1911*** (New York, 1996), and **V. Mair, *The Columbia Anthology of Traditional Chinese Literature*** (New York, 1994). For a comprehensive introduction to the Chinese art of this period, see **M. Sullivan, *The Arts of China,*** 4th ed. (Berkeley, Calif., 1999), and **C. Clunas, *Art in China*** (Oxford, 1997). For the best introduction to the painting of this era, see **J. Cahill, *Chinese Painting*** (New York, 1977).

JAPAN AND KOREA C. Totman, *A History of Japan,* 2nd ed. (Cambridge, Mass., 2005), is a reliable survey of Japanese history. For a more detailed analysis, see **J. W. Hall, ed., *The Cambridge History of Japan,*** vol. 4 (Cambridge, 1991). Social issues are explored in **W. Farris, *Japan's Medieval Population*** (Honolulu, 2006). **B. Bodart-Baily, *Kaempfer's Japan: Tokugawa Culture Observed*** (Honolulu, 1999), is a first-hand account by a Western visitor to Tokugawa Japan. On Korea, see **M. Seth, *A Concise History of Korea: From the Neolithic Period Through the Nineteenth Century*** (Lanham, Md., 2006).

WOMEN IN CHINA AND JAPAN For a brief introduction to women in the Ming and Qing dynasties as well as the Tokugawa era, see **S. Hughes** and **B. Hughes, *Women in World History,*** vol. 2 (Armonk, N.Y., 1997), and **S. Mann** and **Y. Cheng, eds., *Under Confucian Eyes: Writings on Gender in Chinese History*** (Berkeley, Calif., 2001). Also see **D. Ko, J. K. Haboush,** and **J. R. Piggott, eds., *Women and Confucian Culture in Premodern China, Korea, and Japan*** (Berkeley, Calif., 2003). On women's literacy in seventeenth-century China, see **D. Ko, *Teachers of the Inner Chambers: Women and Culture in Seventeenth-Century China*** (Stanford, Calif., 1994). Most valuable is the collection of articles edited by **G. L. Bernstein, *Re-Creating Japanese Women, 1600–1945*** (Berkeley, Calif., 1991).

JAPANESE LITERATURE AND ART Of specific interest on Japanese literature of the Tokugawa era is **D. Keene, *World Within Walls: Japanese Literature of the Pre-Modern Era, 1600–1867*** (New York, 1976). For the most comprehensive and accessible overview of Japanese art, see **P. Mason, *Japanese Art*** (New York, 1993).

Visit the CourseMate website at **www.cengagebrain.com** for additional study tools and review materials for this chapter.

CHAPTER

18

The West on the Eve of a New World Order

© Marc Charmet/The Art Archive at Art Resource, NY

The storming of the Bastille

CHAPTER OUTLINE AND FOCUS QUESTIONS

Toward a New Heaven and a New Earth: An Intellectual Revolution in the West

Q Who were the leading figures of the Scientific Revolution and the Enlightenment, and what were their main contributions?

Economic Changes and the Social Order

Q What changes occurred in the European economy in the eighteenth century, and to what degree were these changes reflected in social patterns?

Colonial Empires and Revolution in the Americas

Q What colonies did the British and French establish in the Americas, and how did their methods of administering their colonies differ?

Toward a New Political Order and Global Conflict

Q What do historians mean by the term *enlightened absolutism*, and to what degree did eighteenth-century Prussia, Austria, and Russia exhibit its characteristics?

The French Revolution

Q What were the causes, the main events, and the results of the French Revolution?

The Age of Napoleon

Q Which aspects of the French Revolution did Napoleon preserve, and which did he destroy?

CRITICAL THINKING

Q In what ways were the American Revolution, the French Revolution, and the seventeenth-century English revolutions alike? In what ways were they different?

IN PARIS ON THE MORNING of **July 14, 1789**, a mob of eight thousand men and women in search of weapons streamed toward the Bastille (bass-STEEL), a royal armory filled with arms and ammunition. The Bastille was also a state prison, and although it held only seven prisoners at the time, in the eyes of these angry Parisians, it was a glaring symbol of the government's despotic policies. It was defended by the marquis de Launay (mar-KEE duh loh-NAY) and a small garrison of 114 men. The attack on the Bastille began in earnest in the early afternoon, and after three hours of fighting, de Launay and the garrison surrendered. Angered by the loss of ninety-eight protesters, the victors beat de Launay to death, cut off his head, and carried it aloft in triumph through the streets of Paris. When King Louis XVI was told the news of the fall of the Bastille by the duc de La Rochefoucauld-Liancourt (dook duh lah-RUSH-foo-koh-lee-ahn-KOOR), he exclaimed, "Why, this is a revolt." "No, Sire," replied the duc. "It is a revolution."

The French Revolution was a key factor in the emergence of a new world order. Historians have often portrayed the eighteenth century as the final phase of an old Europe that would be forever changed by the violent upheaval and reordering of society associated with the French Revolution. Before the Revolution, the old order—still largely agrarian, dominated by kings and landed aristocrats, and grounded in privileges for nobles, clergy, towns, and provinces—seemed to continue a basic pattern that had prevailed in Europe since medieval times. As the century drew to a close, however, a new intellectual order based on rationalism and secularism emerged, and demographic, economic, social, and political patterns were beginning to change in ways that proclaimed the arrival of a new and more modern order.

The French Revolution demolished the institutions of the old regime and established a new order based on individual rights, representative institutions, and a concept of loyalty to the nation rather than to the monarch. The revolutionary upheavals of the era, especially in France, created new liberal and national political ideals, summarized in the French revolutionary slogan, "Liberty, Equality, Fraternity," that transformed France and then spread to other European countries and the rest of the world.

Toward a New Heaven and a New Earth: An Intellectual Revolution in the West

FOCUS QUESTION: Who were the leading figures of the Scientific Revolution and the Enlightenment, and what were their main contributions?

In the seventeenth century, a group of scientists set the Western world on a new path known as the **Scientific Revolution**, which gave Europeans a new way of viewing the universe and their place in it. The Scientific Revolution affected only a small number of Europe's educated elite. But in the eighteenth century, this changed dramatically as a group of intellectuals popularized the ideas of the Scientific Revolution and used them to undertake a dramatic reexamination of all aspects of life. The widespread impact of these ideas on their society has caused historians ever since to call the eighteenth century in Europe the Age of Enlightenment.

The Scientific Revolution

The Scientific Revolution ultimately challenged conceptions and beliefs about the nature of the external world that had become dominant by the Late Middle Ages.

TOWARD A NEW HEAVEN: A REVOLUTION IN ASTRONOMY Medieval philosophers had used the ideas of Aristotle, Ptolemy (the greatest astronomer of antiquity, who lived in the second century C.E.), and Christianity to form the Ptolemaic (tahl-uh-MAY-ik) or **geocentric theory** of the universe. In this conception, the universe was seen as a series of concentric spheres with a fixed or motionless earth at its center. Composed of material substance, the earth was imperfect and constantly changing. The spheres surrounding the earth were made of a crystalline, transparent substance and moved in circular orbits around the earth. The heavenly bodies, believed to number ten in 1500, were pure orbs of light, embedded in the moving, concentric spheres. Working outward from the earth, the first eight spheres contained the moon, Mercury, Venus, the sun, Mars, Jupiter, Saturn, and the fixed stars. The ninth sphere imparted to the eighth sphere of the fixed stars its daily motion, while the tenth sphere was frequently described as the prime mover that moved itself and imparted motion to the other spheres. Beyond the tenth sphere was the Empyrean Heaven—the location of God and all the saved souls. Thus, God and the saved souls were at one end of the universe and humans were at the center.

Nicolaus Copernicus (NEE-koh-lowss kuh-PURR-nuh-kuss) (1473–1543), a Polish mathematician, felt that Ptolemy's geocentric system failed to accord with the observed motions of the heavenly bodies and offered his **heliocentric** (sun-centered) **theory** as a more accurate explanation. Copernicus argued that the sun was motionless at the center of the universe. The planets revolved around the sun in the order of Mercury, Venus, the earth, Mars, Jupiter, and Saturn. The moon, however, revolved around the earth. Moreover, what appeared to be the movement of the sun around the earth was really explained by the earth's daily rotation on its axis and its journey around the sun each year. But Copernicus did not reject the idea that the heavenly spheres moved in circular orbits.

The next step in destroying the geocentric conception and supporting the Copernican system was taken by Johannes Kepler (yoh-HAHN-us KEP-lur) (1571–1630). A brilliant German mathematician and astronomer, Kepler arrived at laws of planetary motion that confirmed Copernicus's heliocentric theory. In his first law, however, he revised Copernicus by showing that the orbits of the planets around the sun were not circular but elliptical, with the sun at one focus of the ellipse rather than at the center.

Kepler's work destroyed the basic structure of the Ptolemaic system. People could now think in new terms of the actual paths of planets revolving around the sun in elliptical orbits. But important questions remained. For example, what were the planets made of? An Italian

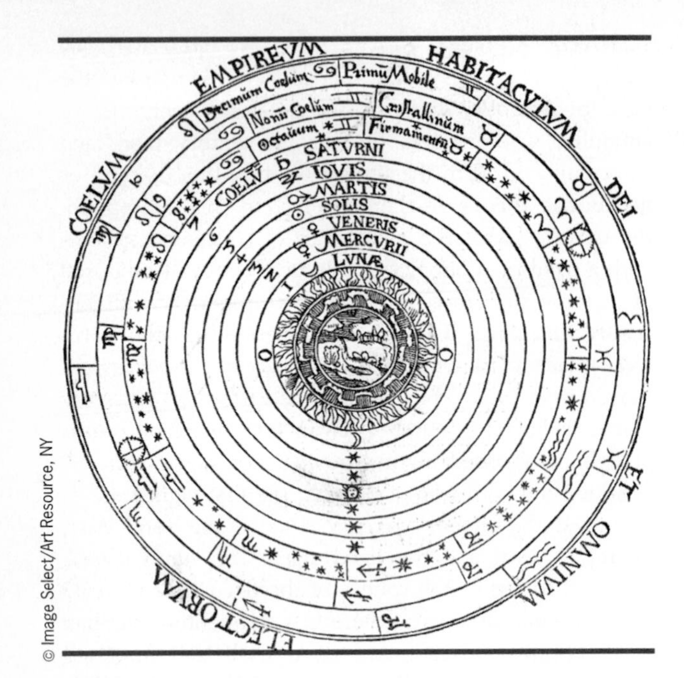

© Image Select/Art Resource, NY

Medieval Conception of the Universe. As this sixteenth-century illustration shows, the medieval cosmological view placed the earth at the center of the universe, surrounded by a series of concentric spheres. The earth was imperfect and constantly changing, while the heavenly bodies that surrounded it were perfect and incorruptible. Beyond the tenth and final sphere was heaven, where God and all the saved souls were located. (The circles read, from the center outward: 1. Moon, 2. Mercury, 3. Venus, 4. Sun, 5. Mars, 6. Jupiter, 7. Saturn, 8. Firmament of the Stars, 9. Crystalline Sphere, 10. Prime Mover, and at the end, Empyrean Heaven—Home of God and All the Elect, that is, saved souls.)

© Image Select/Art Resource, NY

The Copernican System. The Copernican system was presented in *On the Revolutions of the Heavenly Spheres*, published shortly before Copernicus's death. As shown in this illustration from the first edition, Copernicus maintained that the sun was the center of the universe while the planets, including the earth, revolved around it. Moreover, the earth rotated daily on its axis. (The circles read, from the center outward: Sun; VII. Mercury, orbit of 80 days; VI. Venus; V. Earth, with the moon, orbit of one year; IIII. Mars, orbit of 2 years; III. Jupiter, orbit of 12 years; II. Saturn, orbit of 30 years; I. Immobile Sphere of the Fixed Stars.)

scientist achieved the next important breakthrough to a new cosmology by answering that question.

Galileo Galilei (gal-li-LAY-oh GAL-li-lay) (1564–1642) taught mathematics and was the first European to make systematic observations of the heavens by means of a telescope, inaugurating a new age in astronomy. Galileo turned his telescope to the skies and made a remarkable series of discoveries: mountains on the moon, four moons revolving around Jupiter, and sunspots. Galileo's observations seemed to destroy yet another aspect of the traditional cosmology in that the universe seemed to be composed of material similar to that of earth rather than a perfect, unchanging substance.

Galileo's revelations, published in *The Starry Messenger* in 1610, made Europeans aware of a new picture of the universe. But the Catholic Church condemned Copernicanism and ordered Galileo to abandon the Copernican thesis. The church attacked the Copernican system because it threatened not only Scripture but also an entire conception of the universe. The heavens were no longer a spiritual world but a world of matter.

By the 1630s and 1640s, most astronomers had come to accept the new conception of the universe. Nevertheless, the problem of explaining motion in the universe and tying together the ideas of Copernicus, Galileo, and Kepler had not yet been done. This would be the work of an Englishman who has long been considered the greatest genius of the Scientific Revolution.

Isaac Newton (1642–1727) taught at Cambridge University, where he wrote his major work, *Mathematical Principles of Natural Philosophy*, known simply as the *Principia* (prin-SIP-ee-uh) by the first word of its Latin title. In the *Principia*, Newton defined the three laws of motion that govern the planetary bodies, as well as objects on earth. Crucial to his argument was the universal law of gravitation, which explained why the planetary bodies did not go off in straight lines but continued in elliptical orbits about the sun. In mathematical terms, Newton explained that every object in the universe is attracted to every other object by a force called gravity.

Newton had demonstrated that one mathematically proven universal law could explain all motion in the

COMPARATIVE ESSAY

The Scientific Revolution

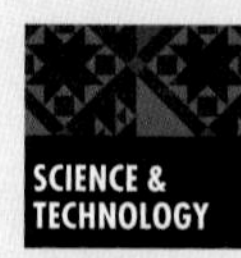

When Catholic missionaries began to arrive in China during the sixteenth century, they marveled at the many accomplishments of Chinese civilization, including woodblock printing and the civil service examination system. In turn, their hosts were impressed with European inventions such as the spring-driven clock and eyeglasses.

It is not surprising that the Western visitors were impressed with what they saw in China, for that country had long been at the forefront of human achievement. After the sixteenth century, however, Europe would take the lead in science and technology, a phenomenon that would ultimately bring about the Industrial Revolution and begin a transformation of human society that would lay the foundations of the modern world.

© Iberfoto/The Image Works

The telescope—a European invention.

Why did Europe suddenly become the engine for rapid change in the seventeenth and eighteenth centuries? One factor was the shift in the European worldview from a metaphysical to a materialist perspective and the growing inclination among European intellectuals to question first principles. In contrast to China, where, for example, Song dynasty thinkers had used the "investigation of things" to analyze and confirm principles first established by Confucius and his contemporaries, empirical scientists in early modern Europe rejected received religious ideas, developed a new conception of the universe, and sought ways to improve material conditions around them.

Why were European thinkers more interested in practical applications of their discoveries than their counterparts elsewhere? No doubt the literate mercantile and propertied elites of Europe were attracted to the new science because it offered new ways to exploit resources for profit. Some early scientists made it easier for these groups to accept the new ideas by showing how they could be applied to specific industrial and technological needs. Galileo, for example, consciously appealed to the material interests of the educated elite when he explained that the science of mechanics would be quite useful "when it becomes necessary to build bridges or other structures over water, something occurring mainly in affairs of great importance."

Finally, the political changes taking place in Europe may also have contributed. Many European states enlarged their bureaucratic machinery and consolidated their governments in order to collect the revenues and amass the armies needed to compete militarily with rivals. Political leaders desperately sought ways to enhance their wealth and power and grasped eagerly at new tools that might guarantee their survival and prosperity.

Why did the Scientific Revolution emerge in Europe and not in China?

universe. At the same time, the Newtonian synthesis created a new cosmology in which the universe was seen as one huge, regulated machine that operated according to natural laws in absolute time, space, and motion. Newton's **world-machine** concept dominated the modern worldview until the twentieth century, when Albert Einstein's concept of relativity created a new picture of the universe.

EUROPE, CHINA, AND SCIENTIFIC REVOLUTIONS A question that arises is why the Scientific Revolution occurred in Europe and not in China. In the Middle Ages, China had been the most technologically advanced civilization in the world. After 1500, that distinction passed to the West (see the comparative essay "The Scientific Revolution" above). Historians are not sure why. Some have contrasted the sense of order in Chinese society with the competitive spirit existing in Europe. Others have emphasized China's ideological viewpoint that favored living in harmony with nature rather than trying to dominate it.

One historian has even suggested that China's civil service system drew the "best and the brightest" into government service, to the detriment of other occupations.

Background to the Enlightenment

The impetus for political and social change in the eighteenth century stemmed in part from the **Enlightenment**. The Enlightenment was a movement of intellectuals who were greatly impressed with the accomplishments of the Scientific Revolution. When they used the word *reason*—one of their favorite words—they were advocating the application of the **scientific method** to the understanding of all life. All institutions and all systems of thought were subject to the rational, scientific way of thinking if people would only free themselves from the shackles of outmoded traditions, especially religious ones. If Isaac Newton could discover the natural laws regulating the world of nature, they too, by using reason, could find the laws that governed human society. This belief in turn led them to hope that they could create a better society than the one they had inherited. *Reason, natural law, hope, progress*—these were the buzzwords in the heady atmosphere of eighteenth-century Europe.

Major sources of inspiration for the Enlightenment were Isaac Newton and his fellow Englishman John Locke (1632–1704). Newton had contended that the world and everything in it worked like a giant machine. Enchanted by the grand design of this world-machine, the intellectuals of the Enlightenment were convinced that by following Newton's rules of reasoning, they could discover the natural laws that governed politics, economics, justice, and religion.

John Locke's theory of knowledge also made a great impact. In his *Essay Concerning Human Understanding* (1690), Locke denied the existence of innate ideas and argued that every person was born with a *tabula rasa* (TAB-yuh-luh RAH-suh), a blank mind:

> Let us then suppose the mind to be, as we say, white paper, void of all characters, without any ideas. How comes it to be furnished? Whence comes it by that vast store which the busy and boundless fancy of man has painted on it with an almost endless variety? Whence has it all the materials of reason and knowledge? To this I answer, in one word, from experience. . . . Our observation, employed either about external sensible objects or about the internal operations of our minds perceived and reflected on by ourselves, is that which supplies our understanding with all the materials of thinking.[1]

By denying innate ideas, Locke implied that people were molded by their environment, by whatever they perceived through their senses from their surrounding world. By changing the environment and subjecting people to proper influences, they could be changed and a new society created. And how should the environment be changed? Newton had paved the way: reason enabled enlightened people to discover the natural laws to which all institutions should conform.

The Philosophes and Their Ideas

The intellectuals of the Enlightenment were known by the French term *philosophes* (fee-loh-ZAHFS), although they were not all French and few were philosophers in the strict sense of the term. The **philosophes** were literary people, professors, journalists, economists, political scientists, and, above all, social reformers. Although it was a truly international and cosmopolitan movement, the Enlightenment also enhanced the dominant role being played by French culture; Paris was its recognized capital. Most of the leaders of the Enlightenment were French. The French philosophes, in turn, affected intellectuals elsewhere and created a movement that touched the entire Western world, including the British and Spanish colonies in the Americas. (The terms *British* and *British* began to be used after 1707 when the Act of Union united England and Scotland.)

To the philosophes, the role of philosophy was not just to discuss the world but to change it. A spirit of rational criticism was to be applied to everything, including religion and politics. Spanning almost a century, the Enlightenment evolved with each succeeding generation, becoming more radical as new thinkers built on the contributions of their predecessors. A few individuals, however, dominated the landscape so completely that we can gain insight into the core ideas of the philosophes by focusing on the three French giants—Montesquieu, Voltaire, and Diderot.

MONTESQUIEU Charles de Secondat (SHARL duh suh-KAHN-da), the baron de Montesquieu (MOHN-tess-kyoo) (1689–1755), came from the French nobility. In his most famous work, *The Spirit of the Laws* (1748), Montesquieu attempted to apply the scientific method to the comparative study of governments to ascertain the "natural laws" governing the social and political relationships of human beings. Montesquieu distinguished three basic kinds of governments: republic, monarchy, and despotism.

Montesquieu used England as an example of monarchy, and his analysis of England's constitution led to his most lasting contribution to political thought—the importance of checks and balances achieved by means of a **separation of powers**. He believed that England's system, with its separate executive, legislative, and judicial powers that served to limit and control each other, provided the greatest freedom and security for a state. His work was eventually read by American political leaders, who incorporated its principles into the U.S. Constitution.

VOLTAIRE The greatest figure of the Enlightenment was François-Marie Arouet (frahn-SWAH-ma-REE ahr-WEH), known simply as Voltaire (vohl-TAYR) (1694–1778). Son of a prosperous middle-class family from Paris, he studied law, but achieved his first success as a playwright. Voltaire was a prolific author and wrote an almost endless stream of pamphlets, novels, plays, letters, philosophical essays, and histories.

Voltaire was especially well known for his criticism of traditional religion and his strong attachment to the ideal of religious toleration. As he grew older, Voltaire became ever more strident in his denunciations. "Crush the infamous thing," he thundered—the infamous thing being religious fanaticism, intolerance, and superstition.

Throughout his life, Voltaire championed not only religious tolerance but also **deism**, a religious outlook shared by most other philosophes. Deism was built on the Newtonian world-machine, which implied the existence of a mechanic (God) who had created the universe. To Voltaire, the universe was like a clock, and God was the clockmaker who had created it, set it in motion, and allowed it to run according to its own natural laws.

DIDEROT Denis Diderot (duh-NEE dee-DROH) (1713–1784), the son of a skilled craftsman, became a writer so that he could be free to study many subjects and languages. One of Diderot's favorite topics was Christianity, which he condemned as fanatical and unreasonable.

Diderot's most famous contribution was the *Encyclopedia*, or *Classified Dictionary of the Sciences, Arts, and Trades*, a twenty-eight-volume compendium of knowledge that he edited and referred to as the "great work of his life." Its purpose, according to Diderot, was to "change the general way of thinking." It did precisely that, becoming a major weapon of the philosophes' crusade against the old French society. The contributors included many philosophes who attacked religious intolerance and advocated social, legal, and political improvements that would lead to a society that was more cosmopolitan, more tolerant, more humane, and more reasonable. The *Encyclopedia* was sold to doctors, clergymen, teachers, lawyers, and even military officers, thus spreading the ideas of the Enlightenment.

TOWARD A NEW "SCIENCE OF MAN" The Enlightenment belief that Newton's scientific methods could be used to discover the natural laws underlying all areas of human life led to the emergence of what the philosophes called a "science of man," or what we would call the social sciences. In a number of areas, such as economics, politics, and education, the philosophes arrived at natural laws that they believed governed human actions.

Adam Smith (1723–1790), often viewed as one of the founders of the discipline of economics, believed that individuals should be free to pursue their own economic self-interest. Through their actions, all society would ultimately benefit. Consequently, the state should in no way interrupt the free play of natural economic forces by imposing government regulations on the economy but should leave it alone, a doctrine that subsequently became known as ***laissez-faire*** (less-ay-FAYR) (French for "leave it alone"). In Smith's view, government had only three basic functions: it should protect society from invasion (army), defend its citizens from injustice (police), and keep up certain public works, such as roads and canals, that private individuals could not afford.

THE LATER ENLIGHTENMENT By the late 1760s, a new generation of philosophes began to move beyond their predecessors' beliefs. Most famous was Jean-Jacques Rousseau (ZHAHNH-ZHAHK roo-SOH) (1712–1778), whose political beliefs were presented in two major works. In his *Discourse on the Origins of the Inequality of Mankind*, Rousseau argued that people had adopted laws and governors in order to preserve their private property. In the process, they had become enslaved by government. What, then, should people do to regain their freedom? In his celebrated treatise *The Social Contract* (1762), Rousseau found an answer in the concept of the social contract whereby an entire society agreed to be governed by its general will. Each individual might have a particular will contrary to the general will, but if the individual put his particular will (self-interest) above the general will, he should be forced to abide by the general will. "This means nothing less than that he will be forced to be free," said Rousseau, because the general will, being ethical and not just political, represented what the entire community ought to do.

Another influential treatise by Rousseau was his novel *Émile*, one of the Enlightenment's most important works on education. Rousseau's fundamental concern was that education should foster, rather than restrict, children's natural instincts. Rousseau's own experiences had shown him the importance of the emotions. He sought a balance between heart and mind, between emotion and reason.

But Rousseau did not necessarily practice what he preached. His own children were sent to orphanages, where many children died at a young age. Rousseau also viewed women as "naturally" different from men. In *Émile*, Sophie, Émile's intended wife, was educated for her role as wife and mother by learning obedience and nurturing skills that would enable her to provide loving care for her husband and children. Not everyone in the eighteenth century, however, agreed with Rousseau.

THE "WOMAN QUESTION" IN THE ENLIGHTENMENT For centuries, many male intellectuals had argued that the nature of women made them inferior to men and made

The Rights of Women

Mary Wollstonecraft responded to an unhappy childhood in a large family by seeking to lead an independent life. Few occupations were available for middle-class women in her day, but she survived by working as a governess to aristocratic children. All the while, she wrote and developed her ideas on the rights of women. This excerpt is taken from her *Vindication of the Rights of Woman*, written in 1792. This work established her reputation as the foremost British feminist thinker of the eighteenth century.

Mary Wollstonecraft, *Vindication of the Rights of Woman*

It is a melancholy truth—yet such is the blessed effect of civilization—the most respectable women are the most oppressed; and, unless they have understandings far superior to the common run of understandings, taking in both sexes, they must, from being treated like contemptible beings, become contemptible. How many women thus waste life away the prey of discontent, who might have practiced as physicians, regulated a farm, managed a shop, and stood erect, supported by their own industry, instead of hanging their heads surcharged with the dew of sensibility, that consumes the beauty to which it at first gave luster. . . .

Proud of their weakness, however, [women] must always be protected, guarded from care, and all the rough toils that dignify the mind. If this be the fiat of fate, if they will make themselves insignificant and contemptible, sweetly to waste "life away," let them not expect to be valued when their beauty fades, for it is the fate of the fairest flowers to be admired and pulled to pieces by the careless hand that plucked them. In how many ways do I wish, from the purest benevolence, to impress this truth on my sex; yet I fear that they will not listen to a truth that dear-bought experience has brought home to many an agitated bosom, nor willingly resign the privileges of rank and sex for the privileges of humanity, to which those have no claim who do not discharge its duties. . . .

Would men but generously snap our chains, and be content with rational fellowship instead of slavish obedience, they would find us more observant daughters, more affectionate sisters, more faithful wives, and more reasonable mothers—in a word, better citizens. We should then love them with true affection, because we should learn to respect ourselves; and the peace of mind of a worthy man would not be interrupted by the idle vanity of his wife.

What picture did Wollstonecraft paint of the women of her day? Why were they in such a deplorable state? Why did Wollstonecraft suggest that both women and men were at fault for the "slavish" situation of females?

Source: From *First Feminists: British Women, 1578–1799* by Moira Ferguson. Copyright © 1985. Reprinted with permission of Indiana University Press.

male domination of women necessary and right. In the Scientific Revolution, however, some women had made notable contributions. Maria Winkelmann (VINK-ul-mahn) in Germany, for example, was an outstanding practicing astronomer. Nevertheless, when she applied for a position as assistant astronomer at the Berlin Academy, for which she was highly qualified, she was denied the post by the academy's members, who feared that hiring her would establish a precedent ("mouths would gape").

Female thinkers in the eighteenth century disagreed with this attitude and offered suggestions for improving conditions for women. The strongest statement of the rights of women was advanced by the English writer Mary Wollstonecraft (WULL-stun-kraft) (1759–1797), viewed by many as the founder of modern European **feminism**.

In her *Vindication of the Rights of Woman* (1792), Wollstonecraft pointed out two contradictions in the views of women held by such Enlightenment thinkers as Rousseau. To argue that women must obey men, she said, was contrary to the beliefs of those same individuals that a system based on the arbitrary power of monarchs over their subjects or slave owners over their slaves was wrong. The subjection of women to men was equally wrong. Furthermore, the Enlightenment was based on an ideal of reason innate in all human beings. If women have reason, then they should have the same rights as men to obtain an education and engage in economic and political life (see the box above).

Louvre, Paris//© RMN-Grand Palais/Art Resource, NY

Antoine Watteau, *The Pilgrimage to Cythera.* Antoine Watteau was one of the most gifted painters in eighteenth-century France. His portrayal of aristocratic life reveals a world of elegance, wealth, and pleasure. In this painting, Watteau depicts a group of aristocratic lovers about to depart from the island of Cythera, where they have paid homage to Venus, the goddess of love.

Culture in an Enlightened Age

Although the Baroque style that had dominated the seventeenth century continued to be popular, by the 1730s, a new style of decoration and architecture known as **Rococo** (ruh-KOH-koh) had spread throughout Europe. Unlike the Baroque, which stressed power, grandeur, and movement, Rococo emphasized grace, charm, and gentle action. Rococo rejected strict geometrical patterns and had a fondness for curves; it liked to follow the wandering lines of natural objects, such as seashells and flowers. Highly secular, its lightness and charm spoke of the pursuit of pleasure, happiness, and love.

Some of Rococo's appeal is evident in the work of Antoine Watteau (AHN-twahn wah-TOH) (1684–1721), whose lyrical views of aristocratic life, refined, sensual, and civilized, with gentlemen and ladies in elegant dress, revealed a world of upper-class pleasure and joy. Underneath that exterior, however, was an element of sadness as the artist revealed the transitory nature of pleasure, love, and life.

HIGH CULTURE Historians have grown accustomed to distinguishing between a civilization's high culture and its popular culture. **High culture** is the literary and artistic culture of the educated and wealthy ruling classes; **popular culture** is the written and unwritten culture of the masses, most of which has traditionally been passed down orally. By the eighteenth century, the two forms were beginning to blend, owing to the expansion of both the reading public and publishing. Whereas French publishers issued 300 titles in 1750, about 1,600 were being published yearly in the 1780s. Although many of these books were still aimed at small groups of the educated elite, many were also directed to the new reading public of the middle classes, which included women and even urban artisans.

POPULAR CULTURE The distinguishing characteristic of popular culture is its collective nature. Group activity was especially common in the *festival*, a broad name used to cover a variety of celebrations: community festivals; annual festivals, such as Christmas and Easter; and the ultimate festival, Carnival, which was celebrated in the Mediterranean world of Spain, Italy, and France as well as in Germany and Austria.

Carnival began after Christmas and lasted until the start of Lent, the forty-day period of fasting and purification leading up to Easter. Because people were expected to abstain from meat, sex, and most recreations during Lent, Carnival was a time of great indulgence when heavy consumption of food and drink was the norm. It was a time of intense sexual activity as well. Songs with double meanings that would ordinarily be considered offensive could be sung publicly at this time of year. A float of Florentine "keymakers," for example, sang this ditty to the ladies: "Our tools are fine, new and useful. We always carry them with us. They are good for anything. If you want to touch them, you can."[2]

Economic Changes and the Social Order

FOCUS QUESTION: What changes occurred in the European economy in the eighteenth century, and to what degree were these changes reflected in social patterns?

The eighteenth century in Europe witnessed the beginning of economic changes that ultimately had a strong impact on the rest of the world.

New Economic Patterns

Europe's population began to grow around 1750 and continued to increase steadily. The total European population was probably around 120 million in 1700, 140 million in 1750, and 190 million in 1790. A falling death rate was perhaps the most important reason for this population growth. Of great significance in lowering death rates was the disappearance of bubonic plague, but so was diet. More plentiful food and better transportation of food supplies led to improved nutrition and relief from devastating famines.

More plentiful food was in part a result of improvements in agricultural practices and methods in the eighteenth century, especially in Britain, parts of France, and the Low Countries. Food production increased as more land was farmed, yields per acre increased, and climate improved. Also important to the increased yields was the cultivation of new vegetables, including two important American crops, the potato and maize (Indian corn). Both had been brought to Europe from the Americas in the sixteenth century.

In European industry in the eighteenth century, textiles were the most important product and were still mostly produced by master artisans in guild workshops. But in many areas textile production was shifting to the countryside through the "putting-out" or "domestic" system. A merchant-capitalist entrepreneur bought the raw materials, mostly wool and flax, and "put them out" to rural workers who spun them into yarn and then wove the yarn into cloth on simple looms. The entrepreneurs sold the finished product, made a profit, and used it to purchase more raw materials. This system also became known as the **cottage industry** because the spinners and weavers did their work in their own cottages.

Overseas trade boomed in the eighteenth century. Some historians speak of the emergence of a true global economy, with patterns of trade that interlocked Europe, Africa, the East, and the Americas (see Map 18.1). One important pattern involved the influx of gold and silver into Spain from its colonial American empire. Much of this gold and silver made its way to Britain, France, and the Netherlands in return for manufactured goods. British, Dutch, and French merchants in turn used their profits to buy tea, spices, silk, and cotton goods from China and India to sell in Europe.

Commercial capitalism created enormous prosperity for some European countries. By 1700, Spain, Portugal, and the Dutch Republic, which had earlier monopolized overseas trade, found themselves increasingly overshadowed by France and England, which built enormously profitable colonial empires in the course of the eighteenth century. After the French lost the Seven Years' War in 1763, Britain emerged as the world's strongest overseas trading nation, and London became the world's greatest port.

European Society in the Eighteenth Century

The pattern of Europe's social organization, first established in the Middle Ages, continued well into the eighteenth century. Society was still divided into the traditional "orders" or "estates" determined by heredity.

Because society was still mostly rural in the eighteenth century, the peasantry constituted the largest social group, about 85 percent of Europe's population. There were rather wide differences within this group, however, especially between free peasants and serfs. In eastern Germany, eastern Europe, and Russia, serfs remained tied to the lands of their noble landlords. In contrast, peasants in Britain, northern Italy, the Low Countries, Spain, most of France, and some areas of western Germany were largely free.

The nobles, who constituted only 2 to 3 percent of the European population, played a dominating role in society. Being born a noble automatically guaranteed a place at the top of the social order, with all its attendant privileges and rights. Nobles, for example, were exempt from many forms of taxation. Since medieval times, landed aristocrats had functioned as military officers, and eighteenth-century nobles held most of the important offices in the administrative machinery of state and controlled much of the life of their local districts.

Townspeople were still a distinct minority of the total population except in the Dutch Republic, Britain, and parts of Italy. At the end of the eighteenth century, about one-sixth of the French population lived in towns of two thousand people or more. The biggest city in Europe was London, with a million inhabitants; Paris was a little more than half that size.

Many cities in western and even central Europe had a long tradition of **patrician** oligarchies that dominated town and city councils. Just below the patricians stood

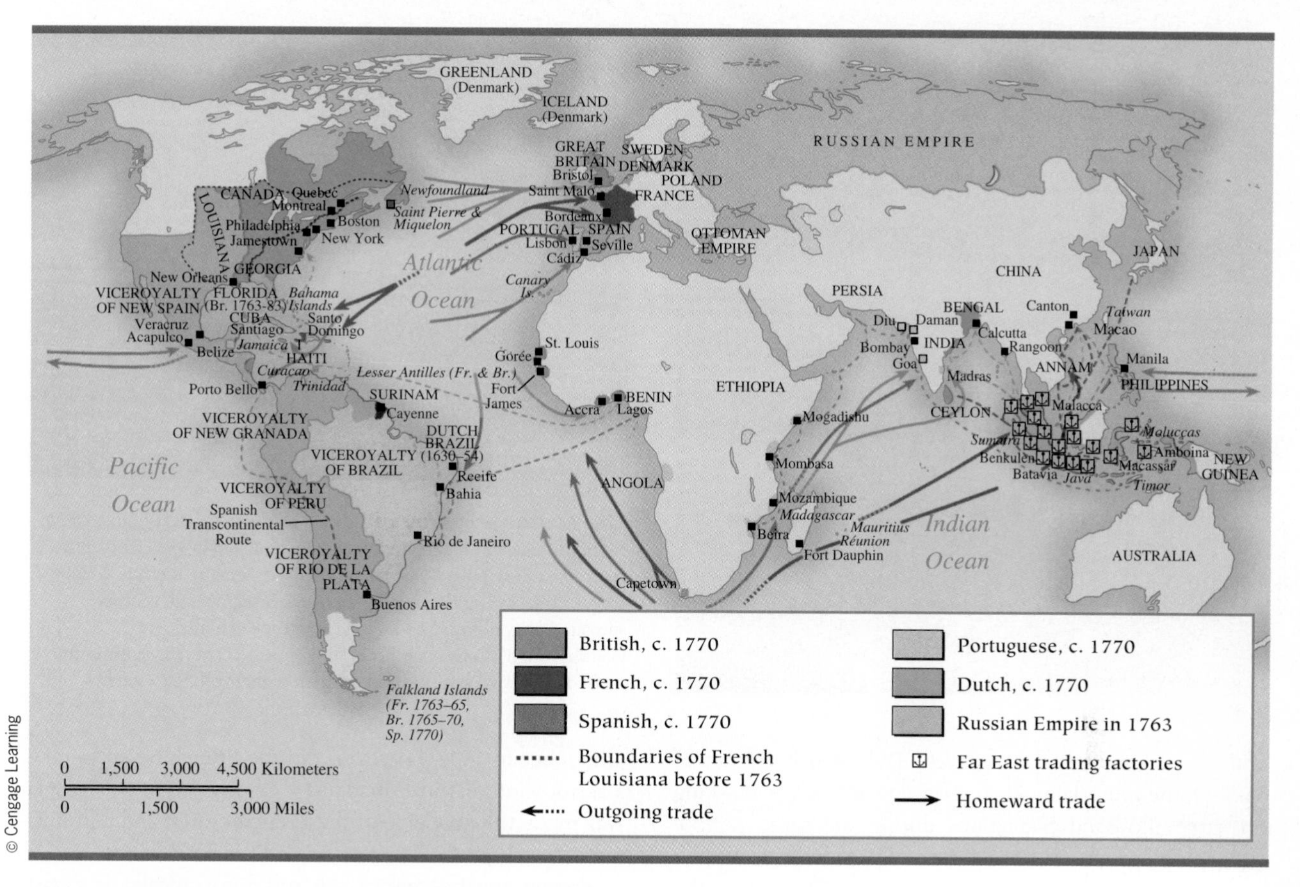

© Cengage Learning

MAP 18.1 Global Trade Patterns of the European States in the Eighteenth Century. New patterns of trade interlocked Europe, Africa, the East, and the Americas. Dutch, English, French, Spanish, and Portuguese colonies had been established in North and South America, and the ships of these nations followed the trade routes across the Atlantic, Pacific, and Indian Oceans.

With what regions did Britain conduct most of its trade?

the upper crust of the middle classes: nonnoble officeholders, financiers and bankers, merchants, wealthy ***rentiers*** (rahn-TYAYS) who lived off their investments, and important professionals, including lawyers. Another large urban group consisted of the lower middle class, made up of master artisans, shopkeepers, and small traders. Below them were the laborers or working classes and a large group of unskilled workers who served as servants, maids, and cooks at pitifully low wages.

Colonial Empires and Revolution in the Americas

FOCUS QUESTION: What colonies did the British and French establish in the Americas, and how did their methods of administering their colonies differ?

The first colonial empires in the Americas had been established in the sixteenth century by Spain and Portugal (see Chapter 14). By the early seventeenth century, however, both Portugal and Spain were facing challenges from the Dutch, English, and French, who sought to create their own colonial empires in the Western Hemisphere, both in the West Indies and on the North American continent.

The West Indies

Both the French and British colonial empires in the Americas ultimately included large parts of the West Indies. The British held Barbados, Jamaica, and Bermuda, and the French possessed Saint-Dominique, Martinique, and Guadeloupe. On these tropical islands, both the British and the French developed plantations, worked by African slaves, to produce tobacco, cotton, coffee, and sugar, all products increasingly in demand in Europe.

The "sugar factories," as the sugar plantations in the Caribbean were called, played an especially prominent role. By the 1780s, Jamaica, one of Britain's most important colonies, was producing 50,000 tons of sugar annually

© Louvre, Paris//Peter Willi/The Bridgeman Art Library

© Collection of the Earl of Pembroke, Wilton House, UK/The Bridgeman Art Library

The Aristocratic Way of Life. The desire of British aristocrats for both elegance and greater privacy was fulfilled by the eighteenth-century country house. The painting on the right, by Richard Wilson, shows a typical English country house of the eighteenth century, surrounded by a simple and serene landscape. Thomas Gainsborough's *Coversation in the Park*, shown at the left, captures the relaxed life of two aristocrats in the park of their country estate.

with the labor of 200,000 slaves. The French colony of Saint-Dominique (later Haiti) had 500,000 slaves working on three thousand plantations during the same period. This colony produced 100,000 tons of sugar a year, supplying 40 percent of the world's sugar by 1789, but at the expense of a high death rate from the brutal treatment of the slaves. It is not surprising that Saint-Dominique saw the first successful slave uprising in 1793.

British North America

Although Spain had claimed all of North America as part of its empire, other nations largely ignored its claims. The first permanent English settlement in North America was established in 1607 at Jamestown, in what is now Virginia. The settlers barely survived, making it clear that colonizing American lands was not necessarily conducive to quick profits. The Massachusetts colony fared much better; its initial 4,000 settlers had increased to 40,000 by 1660. By the eighteenth century, British North America consisted of thirteen colonies. They were thickly populated, containing about 1.5 million people by 1750, and were also prosperous.

French North America

The French also established a colonial empire in North America. In 1534, the French explorer Jacques Cartier (ZHAHK kar-TYAY) had discovered the Saint Lawrence River and laid claim to Canada as a French possession. Not until Samuel de Champlain (sa-my-ELL duh shahm-PLAN *or* SHAM-playn) established a settlement at Quebec in 1608, however, did the French begin to take a serious interest in Canada as a colony. In 1663, Canada was made the property of the French crown and administered by a French governor like a French province.

French North America was run autocratically as a vast trading area, where valuable furs, leather, fish, and timber were acquired. The inability of the French state to persuade its people to emigrate to its Canadian possessions, however, left the territory thinly populated. Already in 1713, the French began to cede some of their American possessions to their British rival. As a result of the Seven Years' War, they surrendered the rest of their Canadian lands to Britain in 1763 (see "Changing Patterns of War: Global Confrontation" later in this chapter).

The American Revolution

By the mid-eighteenth century, increasing trade and industry had led to a growing middle class in Britain that favored expansion of trade and world empire. These people found a spokesman in William Pitt the Elder (1708–1778), who became prime minister in 1757 and began to expand the British Empire. In North America, after the end of the Seven Years' War, Great Britain controlled Canada and the lands east of the Mississippi.

The Americans and the British had different conceptions of how the empire should be governed, however. In eighteenth-century Britain, the king or queen and Parliament shared power, with Parliament gradually gaining the upper hand. The monarch chose ministers who were responsible to the crown and who set policy and guided Parliament. Parliament had the power to make laws, levy taxes, pass budgets, and indirectly influence the ministers. The British envisioned Parliament as the supreme authority throughout the empire, but the Americans had their own representative assemblies. They believed that neither king nor Parliament should interfere in their internal affairs and that no tax could be levied without the consent of their own assemblies. After the Seven Years' War, when the British tried to obtain new revenues from the colonies to pay for the cost of defending them, the colonists resisted. An attempt to levy new taxes by the Stamp Act of 1765 led to riots and the law's quick repeal.

Crisis followed crisis until 1776, when the colonists declared their independence from Great Britain. On July 4, 1776, the Second Continental Congress approved a declaration of independence drafted by Thomas Jefferson. A stirring political document, the Declaration of Independence affirmed the Enlightenment's natural rights of "life, liberty, and the pursuit of happiness" and declared the colonies to be "free and independent states absolved from all allegiance to the British crown." The war for American independence had formally begun.

Of great importance to the colonies' cause was support from foreign countries eager to gain revenge for earlier defeats at the hands of the British. French officers and soldiers served in the American Continental Army under George Washington as commander in chief. When the British army of General Cornwallis was forced to surrender to a combined American and French army and French fleet under Washington at Yorktown in 1781, the British decided to call it quits. The Treaty of Paris, signed in 1783, recognized the independence of the American colonies and granted the Americans control of the territory from the Appalachians to the Mississippi River.

BIRTH OF A NEW NATION The thirteen American colonies had gained their independence, but fear of concentrated power caused them to have little enthusiasm for establishing a strong central government, and so the Articles of Confederation, ratified in 1781, did not create one. A movement for a different form of national government soon arose. In the summer of 1787, fifty-five delegates—wealthy, politically experienced, and well educated—convened in Philadelphia to revise the Articles of Confederation, but decided instead to devise a new constitution.

The proposed U.S. Constitution established a central government distinct from and superior to governments of the individual states. The central or federal government was divided into three branches, each with some power to check the others. A president would serve as the chief executive with the power to execute laws, veto the legislature's acts, supervise foreign affairs, and direct military forces. Legislative power was vested in the second branch of government, a bicameral legislature composed of the Senate, elected by the state legislatures, and the House of Representatives, elected directly by the people. A supreme court and other courts "as deemed necessary" by Congress provided the third branch of government. They would enforce the Constitution as the "supreme law of the land."

The Constitution was approved by the states—by a slim margin. Important to its success was a promise to add a bill of rights as the new government's first piece of business. Accordingly, in March 1789, the new Congress enacted the first ten amendments to the Constitution, known as the Bill of Rights. These guaranteed freedom of religion, speech, press, petition, and assembly, as well as the right to bear arms, protection against unreasonable searches and arrests, trial by jury, due process of law, and protection of property rights. Many of these rights were derived from the **natural rights** philosophy of the eighteenth-century philosophes. Is it any wonder that many European intellectuals saw the American Revolution as the embodiment of the Enlightenment's political dreams?

Toward a New Political Order and Global Conflict

FOCUS QUESTION: What do historians mean by the term *enlightened absolutism*, and to what degree did eighteenth-century Prussia, Austria, and Russia exhibit its characteristics?

There is no doubt that Enlightenment thought had some impact on the political development of European states in the eighteenth century. The philosophes believed there were certain natural rights, which should not be withheld from any person. These rights included equality before the law, freedom of religious worship, freedom of speech and press, and the rights to assemble, hold property, and pursue happiness. But how were these natural rights to be established and preserved? Most philosophes believed that people needed to be ruled by an enlightened ruler, by which they meant a ruler who would allow religious toleration, freedom of speech and press, and the rights of private property; foster the arts, sciences, and education; and, above all, obey the laws and enforce them fairly. Only strong monarchs seemed capable of overcoming vested interests and effecting the needed reforms. Therefore, reforms should come from above (from absolute rulers) rather than from below (from the people).

Many historians once assumed that a new type of monarchy emerged in the later eighteenth century, which they called *enlightened despotism* or **enlightened absolutism**. Monarchs such as Frederick II of Prussia, Catherine the Great of Russia, and Joseph II of Austria supposedly followed the philosophes' advice and ruled by enlightened principles. Recently, however, scholars have questioned the usefulness of the concept of enlightened absolutism. We can determine the extent to which it can be applied by examining the major "enlightened absolutists" of the late eighteenth century.

Prussia

Frederick II, known as Frederick the Great (1740–1786), was one of the best-educated and most cultured monarchs of the eighteenth century. He was well versed in Enlightenment thought and even invited Voltaire to live at his court for several years. A believer in the king as the "first servant of the state," Frederick was a conscientious ruler who enlarged the Prussian army (to 200,000 men) and kept a strict watch over the bureaucracy.

For a time, Frederick seemed quite willing to make enlightened reforms. He abolished the use of torture except in treason and murder cases and also granted limited freedom of speech and press, as well as complete religious toleration. His efforts were limited, however, as he kept Prussia's rigid social structure and serfdom intact and avoided any additional reforms.

The Austrian Empire of the Habsburgs

The Austrian Empire had become one of the great European states by the beginning of the eighteenth century. Yet it was difficult to rule because it was a sprawling conglomerate of nationalities, languages, religions, and cultures (see Map 18.2).

© Cengage Learning

MAP 18.2 Europe in 1763. By the mid-eighteenth century, five major powers dominated Europe—Prussia, Austria, Russia, Britain, and France. Each sought to enhance its power both domestically, through a bureaucracy that collected taxes and ran the military, and internationally, by capturing territory or preventing other powers from doing so.

Q *Given the distribution of Prussian and Habsburg holdings, in what areas of Europe were they most likely to compete for land and power?*

Joseph II (1780–1790) believed in the need to sweep away anything standing in the path of reason. As he said, "I have made Philosophy the lawmaker of my empire; her logical applications are going to transform Austria." Joseph's reform program was far-reaching. He abolished serfdom, abrogated the death penalty, and established the principle of equality of all before the law. Joseph instituted drastic religious reforms as well, including complete religious toleration.

Joseph's program proved overwhelming for Austria, however. He alienated the nobility by freeing the serfs and alienated the church by his attacks on the monastic establishment. Joseph realized his failure when he wrote the epitaph for his own gravestone: "Here lies Joseph II, who was unfortunate in everything that he undertook." His successors undid many of his reforms.

Russia Under Catherine the Great

Catherine II the Great (1762–1796) was an intelligent woman who was familiar with the works of the philosophes and seemed to favor enlightened reforms. But she was skeptical about impractical theories. She did consider the idea of a new law code that would recognize the principle of the equality of all people in the eyes of the law. But in the end she did nothing, knowing that her success depended on the support of the Russian nobility. In 1785, she gave the nobles a charter that exempted them from taxes. Catherine's policy of favoring the landed nobility led to even worse conditions for the Russian peasants and sparked a rebellion, but it soon faltered and collapsed. Catherine responded with even harsher measures against the peasantry.

Above all, Catherine proved a worthy successor to Peter the Great in her policies of territorial expansion westward into Poland and southward to the Black Sea. Russia spread southward by defeating the Turks. Russian expansion westward occurred at the expense of neighboring Poland. In three partitions of Poland, Russia gained about 50 percent of Polish territory.

Enlightened Absolutism Reconsidered

Of the rulers we have discussed, only Joseph II sought truly radical changes based on Enlightenment ideas. Both Frederick II and Catherine II liked to talk about enlightened reforms, and they even attempted some. But neither ruler's policies seemed seriously affected by Enlightenment thought. Necessities of state and maintenance of the existing system took precedence over reform. Indeed, many historians maintain that Joseph, Frederick, and Catherine were all primarily concerned for the power and well-being of their states. In the final analysis, heightened state power was used to create armies and wage wars to gain more power.

At the same time, the ability of enlightened rulers to make reforms was limited by political and social realities. Everywhere in Europe, the hereditary aristocracy was still the most powerful class. As the chief beneficiaries of a system based on traditional rights and privileges, the nobles were not willing to support a political ideology that trumpeted the principle of equal rights for all. The first serious challenge to their supremacy would come with the French Revolution, an event that blew open the door to the world of modern politics.

Changing Patterns of War: Global Confrontation

The philosophes condemned war as a foolish waste of life and resources. Despite their words, the rivalries and costly struggles among the European states continued unabated in the eighteenth century. Europe consisted of a number of self-governing, individual states that were chiefly guided by the self-interest of the ruler. And as Frederick the Great of Prussia said, "The fundamental rule of governments is the principle of extending their territories."

By far the most dramatic confrontation was the Seven Years' War. Although it began in Europe, it soon turned into a global conflict fought in Europe, India, and North America. In Europe, the British and Prussians fought the Austrians, Russians, and French. With his superb army and military skill, Frederick the Great of Prussia was able for some time to defeat the Austrian, French, and Russian armies. Eventually, however, his forces were gradually worn down and faced utter defeat until a new Russian tsar withdrew Russia's troops from the conflict. A stalemate ensued, ending the European conflict in 1763.

The struggle between Britain and France in the rest of the world had more decisive results. In India, local rulers allied with British and French troops fought a number of battles. Ultimately, the British under Robert Clive won out, not because they had better forces but because they were more persistent (see the box on p. 474). By the Treaty of Paris in 1763, the French withdrew and left India to the British.

The greatest conflicts of the Seven Years' War took place in North America, where it was known as the French and Indian War. Despite initial French successes, the British went on to seize Montreal, the Great Lakes area, and the Ohio valley. The French were forced to make peace. By the Treaty of Paris, they ceded Canada and the lands east of the Mississippi to Britain. Their ally Spain transferred Spanish Florida to British control; in return, the French gave their Louisiana territory to the Spanish. By 1763, Great Britain had become the world's greatest colonial power. For France, the loss of its empire was soon followed by an even greater internal upheaval.

British Victory in India

The success of the British against the French in India was due to Robert Clive, who, in this excerpt from one of his letters, describes his famous victory at Plassey, north of Calcutta, on June 23, 1757. This battle demonstrated the inability of native Indian soldiers to compete with Europeans and signified the beginning of British control in Bengal. Clive claimed to have a thousand Europeans, two thousand sepoys (local soldiers), and eight cannons available for this battle.

Robert Clive's Account of His Victory at Plassey

At daybreak we discovered the [governor's army] moving toward us, consisting, as we since found, of about fifteen thousand horse and thirty-five thousand foot, with upwards of forty pieces of cannon. They approached apace, and by six began to attack with a number of heavy cannon, supported by the whole army, and continued to play on us very briskly for several hours, during which our situation was of the utmost service to us, being lodged in a large grove with good mud banks. To succeed in an attempt on their cannon was next to impossible, as they were planted in a manner round us and at considerable distances from each other. We therefore remained quiet in our post, in expectation of a successful attack upon their camp at night. About noon the enemy drew off their artillery and retired to their camp. . . .

On finding them make no great effort to dislodge us, we proceeded to take possession of one or two more eminences lying very near an angle of their camp, from whence, and an adjacent eminence in their possession, they kept a smart fire of musketry upon us. They made several attempts to bring out their cannon, but our advanced fieldpieces played so warmly and so well upon them that they were always driven back. Their horse exposing themselves a good deal on this occasion, many of them were killed, and among the rest four or five officers of the first distinction; by which the whole army being visibly dispirited and thrown into some confusion, we were encouraged to storm both the eminence and the angle of their camp, which were carried at the same instant, with little or no loss; though the latter was defended (exclusively of blacks) by forty French and two pieces of cannon; and the former by a large body of blacks, both horse and foot. On this a general rout ensued, and we pursued the enemy six miles, passing upwards of forty pieces of cannon they had abandoned, with an infinite number of carts and carriages filled with baggage of all kinds. . . . It is computed there are killed of the enemy about five hundred.

Our loss amounted to only twenty-two killed and fifty wounded, and those chiefly blacks.

In what ways, if any, would Clive's account likely have been different if the Battle of Plassey had occurred in Europe? According to the letter, what role did native Indians seemingly play in the battle? Why does Clive give them such little mention?

Source: From *Readings in European History*, vol. 2, by James Harvey Robinson (Lexington, Mass.: Ginn and Co., 1906).

The French Revolution

FOCUS QUESTION: What were the causes, the main events, and the results of the French Revolution?

The year 1789 witnessed two far-reaching events, the beginning of a new United States of America under its revamped constitution and the eruption of the French Revolution. Compared with the American Revolution a decade earlier, the French Revolution was more complex, more violent, and far more radical in its attempt to construct both a new political and a new social order.

Background to the French Revolution

The root causes of the French Revolution must be sought in the condition of French society. Before the Revolution, France was a society grounded in privilege and inequality. Its population of 27 million was divided, as it had been since the Middle Ages, into three orders or estates.

SOCIAL STRUCTURE OF THE OLD REGIME The first estate consisted of the clergy and numbered about 130,000 people who owned approximately 10 percent of the land. Clergy were exempt from the *taille* (TY), France's chief tax. Clergy were also radically divided: the higher clergy, stemming from aristocratic families, shared the interests of the nobility, while the parish priests were often poor commoners.

The second estate consisted of the nobility, composed of about 350,000 people who owned about 25 to 30 percent of the land. The nobility continued to play an important role in French society, holding many of the leading positions in the government, the military, the law courts, and the higher church offices. The nobles sought to expand their power at the expense of the monarchy and to maintain their positions in the military, church, and government. Common to all nobles were tax exemptions, especially from the *taille*.

The third estate, or the commoners, constituted the overwhelming majority of the French population. They were divided by vast differences in occupation, level of education, and wealth. The peasants, who constituted 75 to 80 percent of the total population, were by far the largest segment of the third estate. They owned about 35 to 40 percent of the land, although more than half had little or no land on which to survive. Serfdom no longer existed on any large scale in France, but French peasants still had obligations to their local landlords that they deeply resented. These "relics of feudalism," or aristocratic privileges, had survived from an earlier age and included the payment of fees for the use of village facilities, such as the flour mill, community oven, and winepress.

Another part of the third estate consisted of skilled craftspeople, shopkeepers, and other urban wage earners. In the eighteenth century, these groups suffered a decline in purchasing power as consumer prices rose faster than wages. Their daily struggle for survival led many of these people to play an important role in the Revolution, especially in Paris.

About 8 percent of the population, or 2.3 million people, constituted the bourgeoisie or middle class, who owned about 20 to 25 percent of the land. This group included merchants, industrialists, and bankers who had benefited from the economic prosperity after 1730. The bourgeoisie also included professional people—lawyers, holders of public offices, doctors, and writers. Many members of the bourgeoisie had their own grievances because they were often excluded from the social and political privileges monopolized by nobles.

Moreover, the new political ideas of the Enlightenment proved attractive to both the aristocracy and the bourgeoisie. Both elites, long accustomed to a new socioeconomic reality based on wealth and economic achievement, were increasingly frustrated by a monarchical system resting on privileges and on an old and rigid social order based on the concept of estates. The opposition of these elites to the **old order** led them ultimately to drastic action against the monarchical **old regime**. In a real sense, the Revolution had its origins in political grievances.

OTHER PROBLEMS FACING THE FRENCH MONARCHY Although France had enjoyed fifty years of economic expansion, bad harvests in 1787 and 1788 and the beginnings of a manufacturing depression had resulted in food shortages, rising prices for food and other goods, and unemployment in the cities. The number of poor, estimated at almost one-third of the population, reached crisis proportions on the eve of the Revolution.

The French monarchy seemed incapable of dealing with the new social realities. Louis XVI (1774–1792) had become king in 1774 at the age of twenty; he knew little about the operations of the French government and lacked the energy to deal decisively with state affairs. His wife, Marie Antoinette (ma-REE ahn-twahn-NET), was a spoiled Austrian princess who devoted much of her time to court intrigues (see the Film & History feature on p. 476). As France's crises worsened, neither Louis nor his queen seemed able to fathom the depths of despair and discontent that soon led to violent revolution.

The immediate cause of the French Revolution was the near collapse of government finances. Costly wars and royal extravagance drove French governmental expenditures ever higher. On the verge of a complete financial collapse, the government of Louis XVI was finally forced to call a meeting of the Estates-General, the French parliamentary body that had not met since 1614. The Estates-General consisted of representatives from the three orders of French society. In the elections for the Estates-General, the government had ruled that the third estate should get double representation (it did, after all, constitute 97 percent of the population). Consequently, while both the first estate (the clergy) and the second estate (the nobility) had about three hundred delegates each, the third estate had almost six hundred representatives, most of whom were lawyers from French towns.

From Estates-General to National Assembly

The Estates-General opened at Versailles on May 5, 1789. The first issue was whether voting should be by order or by head (each delegate having one vote). Traditionally, each order would vote as a group and have one vote. That meant that the first and second estates could outvote the third estate two to one. The third estate demanded that each deputy have one vote. With the assistance of liberal nobles and clerics, that would give the

FILM & HISTORY

Marie Antoinette (2006)

The film *Marie Antoinette* (2006), directed by Sofia Coppola, is based on Antonia Fraser's book, *Marie Antoinette: A Journey* (2001). The film begins in 1770 with the marriage of Marie Antoinette (Kirsten Dunst), the daughter of Empress Maria Theresa of Austria (Marianne Faithful), to Louis (Jason Schwartzman), the heir to the French throne. Four years later, Marie Antoinette became queen of France, and in 1793, she would go to the guillotine. Although the Revolution is briefly mentioned near the end, the majority of the film focuses on the early experiences of a young woman thrust into the court of Versailles.

Perhaps the best part of the film is the portrayal of life at Versailles. Under intense scrutiny due to her Austrian heritage and unfamiliar with court protocol, Marie Antoinette makes several early missteps. She refuses to speak to Louis XV's mistress, the comtesse du Barry (Asia Argento), because the comtesse threatens Marie Antoinette's position as the highest-ranking woman at court. By ignoring the king's mistress, however, she appears to insult the king.

Columbia/American Zoetrope/Sony/The Kobal Collection at Art Resource, NY

Marie Antoinette (Kirsten Dunst) at Versailles.

An even greater challenge for Marie Antoinette is her need to produce an heir to the French throne. Her young husband, whose interests include hunting and lock making, fails to consummate their marriage for seven years. During this time, Marie Antoinette faces increasing pressure from her mother, who has produced sixteen children while ruling the Austrian Empire. Bored but aware that she must remain chaste, Marie Antoinette turns to frivolous pursuits—outings in Paris, gambling, and, above all, buying clothes. In 1782 alone, she commissions ninety-three gowns made of silk and other expensive fabrics.

After the birth of her first child in 1777, Marie Antoinette begins to withdraw from the court. After 1783, she spends most of time in the Petit Trianon, a small palace on the grounds of Versailles. Although she is spending more time with her children and less on frivolity, her estrangement from the court only worsens her reputation with the French public.

Filmed at Versailles, the film captures the grandeur and splendor of eighteenth-century royal life. But the movie received unfavorable reviews when it opened in France, in part because it uses contemporary music by artists such as The Cure and The Strokes and includes modern products such as Converse sneakers. Although the flurry of costumes and music can be distracting, they also convey the rebelliousness of a young woman, frustrated and bored, isolated yet always on display.

third estate a majority. When the first estate declared in favor of voting by order, the third estate responded dramatically. On June 17, 1789, the third estate declared itself the "National Assembly" and prepared to draw up a constitution. This was the first step in the French Revolution because the third estate had no legal right to act as the National Assembly. Louis XVI sided with the first estate and prepared to use force to dissolve the Estates-General.

The common people, however, saved the third estate from the king's forces. On July 14, a mob of Parisians stormed the Bastille, a royal armory, and proceeded to dismantle it, brick by brick. Louis XVI was soon informed that the royal troops were unreliable. Louis's acceptance of that reality signaled the collapse of royal authority; the king could no longer enforce his will.

At the same time, popular revolts broke out throughout France, both in the cities and in the countryside

© School of Oriental and African Studies, London/Eileen Tweedy/ The Art Archive at Art Resource, NY

© Musée de la Revolution Francaise, Vizille/The Bridgeman Art Library

COMPARATIVE ILLUSTRATION

Revolution and Revolt in France and China. Both France and China experienced revolutionary upheaval in the late eighteenth and nineteenth centuries. In both countries, common people often played an important role. At the right is a scene from the storming of the Bastille in 1789. This early action by the people of Paris ultimately led to the overthrow of the French monarchy. At the top is an episode during the Taiping Rebellion, a major peasant revolt in the mid-nineteenth century in China. An imperial Chinese army is shown recapturing the city of Nanjing from Taiping rebels in 1864.

Q *What role did common people play in revolutionary upheavals in France and China in the eighteenth and nineteenth centuries?*

(see the comparative illustration above). Behind the popular uprising was a growing resentment of the entire landholding system, with its fees and obligations. The fall of the Bastille and the king's apparent capitulation to the demands of the third estate now led peasants to take matters into their own hands. The peasant rebellions that occurred throughout France had a great impact on the National Assembly meeting at Versailles.

Destruction of the Old Regime

One of the first acts of the National Assembly was to abolish the rights of landlords and the fiscal exemptions of nobles, clergy, towns, and provinces. Three weeks later, the National Assembly adopted the Declaration of the Rights of Man and the Citizen. This charter of basic liberties proclaimed freedom and equal rights for all men and access to public office based on talent. All citizens were to have the right to take part in the legislative process. Freedom of speech and the press was coupled with the outlawing of arbitrary arrests.

But did the declaration's ideal of equal rights for "all men" also include women? Many deputies insisted that it did, provided that, as one said, "women do not hope to exercise political rights and functions." Olympe de Gouges (oh-LAMP duh GOOZH), a playwright, refused to accept this exclusion of women from political rights. Echoing the words of the official declaration, she penned the Declaration of the Rights of Woman and the Female Citizen, in which she insisted that women should have all the same rights as men (see the box on p. 478). The National Assembly ignored her demands.

OPPOSING ≺ VIEWPOINTS

The Natural Rights of the French People: Two Views

One of the important documents of the French Revolution, the Declaration of the Rights of Man and the Citizen was adopted on August 26, 1789, by the National Assembly. The declaration affirmed that "men are born and remain free and equal in rights," that governments must protect these natural rights, and that political power is derived from the people.

Olympe de Gouges (the pen name used by Marie Gouze) was a butcher's daughter who wrote plays and pamphlets. She argued that the Declaration of the Rights of Man and the Citizen did not apply to women and composed her own Declaration of the Rights of Woman and the Female Citizen in 1791.

Declaration of the Rights of Man and the Citizen

1. Men are born and remain free and equal in rights. Social distinctions can only be founded upon the general good.
2. The aim of all political association is the preservation of the natural and imprescriptible rights of man. These rights are liberty, property, security, and resistance to oppression.
3. The principle of all sovereignty resides essentially in the nation. No body or individual may exercise any authority which does not proceed directly from the nation.
4. Liberty consists in being able to do everything which injures no one else. . . .

6. Law is the expression of the general will. Every citizen has a right to participate personally or through his representative in its formation. It must be the same for all, whether it protects or punishes. All citizens being equal in the eyes of the law are equally eligible to all dignities and to all public positions and occupations according to their abilities and without distinction except that of their virtues and talents.
7. No person shall be accused, arrested, or imprisoned except in the cases and according to the forms prescribed by law. . . .

10. No one shall be disturbed on account of his opinions, including his religious views, provided their manifestation does not disturb the public order established by law.
11. The free communication of ideas and opinions is one of the most precious of the rights of man. Every citizen may, accordingly, speak, write and print with freedom, being responsible, however, for such abuses of this freedom as shall be defined by law.
12. The security of the rights of man and of the citizen requires public military force. These forces are, therefore, established for the good of all and not for the personal advantage of those to whom they shall be entrusted.

14. All the citizens have a right to decide either personally or by their representatives as to the necessity of the public contribution, to grant this freely, to know to what uses it is put, and to fix the proportion, the mode of assessment, and of collection, and the duration of the taxes.
15. Society has the right to require of every public agent an account of his administration.
16. A society in which the observance of the law is not assured nor the separation of powers defined has no constitution at all.
17. Property being an inviolable and sacred right, no one shall be deprived thereof except where public necessity, legally determined, shall clearly demand it, and then only on condition that the owner shall have been previously and equitably indemnified.

Declaration of the Rights of Woman and the Female Citizen

Mothers, daughters, sisters and representatives of the nation demand to be constituted into a national assembly. Believing that ignorance, omission, or scorn for the rights of woman are the only causes of public misfortunes and of the corruption of governments, the women have resolved to set forth in a solemn declaration the natural, inalienable, and sacred rights of woman in order that this declaration, constantly exposed before all the members of the society, will ceaselessly remind them of their rights and duties. . . .

Consequently, the sex that is as superior in beauty as it is in courage during the sufferings of maternity recognizes and declares in the presence and under the

(Continued)

(Opposing Viewpoints Continued)

auspices of the Supreme Being, the following Rights of Woman and of Female Citizens.

1. Woman is born free and lives equal to man in her rights. Social distinctions can be based only on the common utility.
2. The purpose of any political association is the conservation of the natural and imprescriptible rights of woman and man; these rights are liberty, property, security, and especially resistance to oppression.
3. The principle of all sovereignty rests essentially with the nation, which is nothing but the union of woman and man; no body and no individual can exercise any authority which does not come expressly from [the nation].
4. Liberty and justice consist of restoring all that belongs to others; thus, the only limits on the exercise of the natural rights of woman are perpetual male tyranny; these limits are to be reformed by the laws of nature and reason. . . .
6. The law must be the expression of the general will; all female and male citizens must contribute either personally or through representatives to its formation; it must be the same for all: male and female citizens, being equal in the eyes of the law, must be equally admitted to all honors, positions, and public employment according to their capacity and without other distinctions besides those of their virtues and talents.
7. No woman is an exception; she is accused, arrested, and detained in cases determined by law. Women, like men, obey this rigorous law. . . .
10. No one is to be disquieted for his very basic opinions; woman has the right to mount the scaffold; she must equally have the right to mount the rostrum, provided that her demonstrations do not disturb the legally established public order.
11. The free communication of thought and opinions is one of the most precious rights of woman, since that liberty assured the recognition of children by their fathers. . . .
12. The guarantee of the rights of woman and the female citizen implies a major benefit; this guarantee must be instituted for the advantage of all, and not for the particular benefit of those to whom it is entrusted. . . .
14. Female and male citizens have the right to verify, either by themselves or through their representatives, the necessity of the public contribution. This can only apply to women if they are granted an equal share, not only of wealth, but also of public administration, and in the determination of the proportion, the base, the collection, and the duration of the tax.
15. The collectivity of women, joined for tax purposes to the aggregate of men, has the right to demand an accounting of his administration from any public agent.
16. No society has a constitution without the guarantee of rights and the separation of powers; the constitution is null if the majority of individuals comprising the nation have not cooperated in drafting it.
17. Property belongs to both sexes whether united or separate; for each it is an inviolable and sacred right; no one can be deprived of it, since it is the true patrimony of nature, unless the legally determined public need obviously dictates it, and then only with a just and prior indemnity.

What "natural rights" does the first document proclaim? To what extent was this document influenced by the writings of the philosophes? What rights for women does the second document enunciate? Given the nature and scope of the arguments in favor of natural rights and women's rights in these two documents, what key effects on European society would you attribute to the French Revolution?

Sources: Declaration of the Rights of Man and the Citizen. Excerpt from THOMAS CARLYLE,THE FRENCH REVOLUTION: A HISTORY, VOL. I, (GEORGE BELL AND SONS, LONDON, 1902), PP. 346–348. Declaration of the Rights of Woman and the Female Citizen. From *Women in Revolutionary Paris, 1789–1795: Selected Documents Translated with Notes and Commentary.* Translated with notes and commentary by Darline Gay Levy, Harriet Branson Applewhite, and Mary Durham Johnson. Copyright © 1979 by the Board of Trustees of the University of Illinois. Used with permission of the editors and the University of Illinois Press.

Because the Catholic Church was seen as an important pillar of the old order, it too was reformed. Most of the lands of the church were seized. Under the Civil Constitution of the Clergy, which was adopted on July 12, 1790, bishops and priests were to be elected by the people and paid by the state. The Catholic Church, still an important institution in the life of the French people, now became an enemy of the Revolution.

By 1791, the National Assembly had completed a new constitution that established a limited constitutional monarchy. There was still a monarch (now called "king of the French"), but sovereign power was vested in the new Legislative Assembly, which would make the laws. The Legislative Assembly was to sit for two years and consist of 745 representatives elected by an indirect system that preserved power in the hands of the more affluent members of society. A small group of 50,000 electors chose the deputies.

Thus, the old order had been destroyed, but the new order had many opponents—Catholic priests, nobles, lower classes hurt by the rising cost of living, peasants opposed to dues that had still not been eliminated, and political clubs like the Jacobins (JAK-uh-binz) that offered more radical solutions. The king also made things difficult for the new government when he sought to flee France in June 1791 and almost succeeded before being recognized, captured, and brought back to Paris. In this unsettled situation, under a discredited and seemingly disloyal monarch, the new Legislative Assembly held its first session in October 1791. France's relations with the rest of Europe soon led to Louis's downfall.

On August 27, 1791, the monarchs of Austria and Prussia, fearing that revolution would spread to their countries, invited other European monarchs to use force to reestablish monarchical authority in France. The French fared badly in the fighting in the spring of 1792, and a frantic search for scapegoats began. As one observer noted, "Everywhere you hear the cry that the king is betraying us, the generals are betraying us, that nobody is to be trusted; . . . that Paris will be taken in six weeks by the Austrians. . . . We are on a volcano ready to spout flames."[3] Defeats in war coupled with economic shortages led to renewed political demonstrations, especially against the king. In August 1792, radical political groups in Paris took the king captive and forced the Legislative Assembly to suspend the monarchy and call for a national convention, chosen on the basis of universal male suffrage, to decide on the future form of government. The French Revolution was about to enter a more radical stage.

The Radical Revolution

In September 1792, the newly elected National Convention began its sessions. Dominated by lawyers and other professionals, two-thirds of its deputies were under forty-five, and almost all had gained political experience as a result of the Revolution. Almost all distrusted the king. As a result, the convention's first step on September 21 was to abolish the monarchy and establish a republic. On January 21, 1793, the king was executed, and the destruction of the old regime was complete. But the execution of the king created new enemies for the Revolution both at home and abroad.

In Paris, the local government, known as the Commune, whose leaders came from the working classes, favored radical change and put constant pressure on the convention, pushing it to ever more radical positions. Meanwhile, peasants in the west and inhabitants of the major provincial cities refused to accept the authority of the convention.

A foreign crisis also loomed. By the beginning of 1793, after the king had been executed, most of Europe—an informal coalition of Austria, Prussia, Spain, Portugal, Britain, the Dutch Republic, and even Russia—aligned militarily against France. Grossly overextended, the French armies began to experience reverses, and by late spring, France was threatened with invasion.

A NATION IN ARMS To meet these crises, the convention gave broad powers to an executive committee of twelve known as the Committee of Public Safety, which came to be dominated by Maximilien Robespierre (mak-see-meel-YENH ROHBZ-pyayr). For a twelve-month period, from 1793 to 1794, the Committee of Public Safety took control of France. To save the Republic from its foreign foes, on August 23, 1793, the committee decreed a levy-in-mass, or universal mobilization of the nation:

> Young men will fight, young men are called to conquer. Married men will forge arms, transport military baggage and guns and will prepare food supplies. Women, who at long last are to take their rightful place in the revolution and follow their true destiny, will forget their futile tasks: their delicate hands will work at making clothes for soldiers; they will make tents and they will extend their tender care to shelters where the defenders of the *Patrie* [nation] will receive the help that their wounds require. Children will make lint of old cloth. It is for them that we are fighting: children, those beings destined to gather all the fruits of the revolution, will raise their pure hands toward the skies. And old men, performing their missions again, as of yore, will be guided to the public squares of the cities where they will kindle the courage of young warriors and preach the doctrines of hate for kings and the unity of the Republic.[4]

In less than a year, the French revolutionary government had raised an army of 650,000, and by 1795 it had pushed the allies back across the Rhine and even conquered the Austrian Netherlands.

The French revolutionary army was an important step in the creation of modern **nationalism**. Previously, wars had been fought between governments or ruling dynasties by relatively small armies of professional soldiers.

The new French army was the creation of a "people's" government; its wars were now "people's" wars, involving the entire nation. But when dynastic wars became people's wars, warfare increased in ferocity and lack of restraint. The wars of the French revolutionary era opened the door to the total war of the modern world.

REIGN OF TERROR To meet the domestic crisis, the National Convention and the Committee of Public Safety launched the Reign of Terror. Revolutionary courts were instituted to protect the Republic from its internal enemies. In the course of nine months, 16,000 people were officially killed under the blade of the guillotine—a revolutionary device designed for the quick and efficient separation of heads from bodies.

Revolutionary armies were set up to bring recalcitrant cities and districts back under the control of the National Convention. The Committee of Public Safety decided to make an example of Lyons (LYOHNH), which had defied the authority of the National Convention. By April 1794, some 1,880 citizens of Lyons had been executed. When the guillotine proved too slow, cannon fire was used to blow condemned men into open graves. A German observed:

> Whole ranges of houses, always the most handsome, burnt. The churches, convents, and all the dwellings of the former patricians were in ruins. When I came to the guillotine, the blood of those who had been executed a few hours beforehand was still running in the street. . . . I said to a group of [radicals] that it would be decent to clear away all this human blood. Why should it be cleared? one of them said to me. It's the blood of aristocrats and rebels. The dogs should lick it up.[5]

EQUALITY AND SLAVERY: REVOLUTION IN HAITI Early in the French Revolution, the desire for equality led to a discussion of what to do about slavery. A club called Friends of the Blacks advocated the abolition of slavery, which was achieved in France in September 1791. But French planters in the West Indies, who profited greatly from the use of slaves on their sugar plantations, opposed the abolition of slavery in the French colonies. On February 4, 1794, however, the National Convention, guided by ideals of equality, abolished slavery in the colonies.

In one French colony, slaves had already rebelled. In 1791, black slaves in the French colony of Saint-Domingue (the western third of the island of Hispaniola), inspired by the revolution in France, revolted against French plantation owners. Led by Toussaint L'Ouverture (too-SANH loo-vayr-TOOR) (1746–1803), a son of African slaves, more than 100,000 black slaves rose in revolt and seized control of Hispaniola. Later, an army sent by Napoleon captured L'Ouverture, who died in captivity in France. But the French soldiers, weakened by disease, soon succumbed to the slave forces. On January 1, 1804, the western part of Hispaniola, now called Haiti, became the first independent state in Latin America. One of the French revolutionary ideals had triumphed abroad.

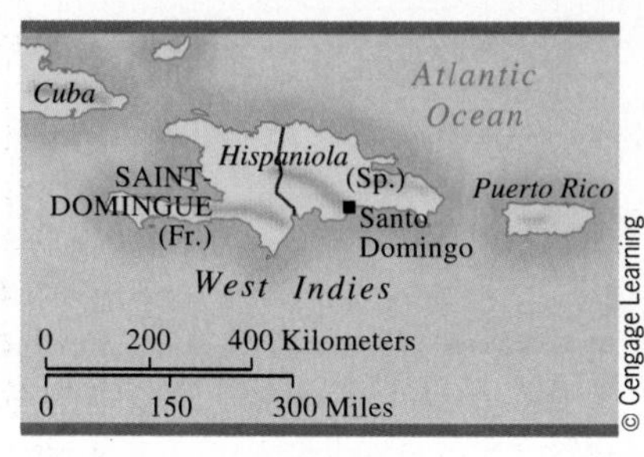

Revolt in Saint-Dominique

Reaction and the Directory

By the summer of 1794, the French had been successful on the battlefield against their foreign foes, making the Terror less necessary. But the Terror continued because Robespierre, who had come to dominate the Committee of Public Safety, became obsessed with purifying the body politic of all the corrupt. Many deputies in the National Convention began to fear that they were not safe while Robespierre was free to act and gathered enough votes to condemn him. Robespierre was guillotined on July 28, 1794.

After the death of Robespierre, a reaction set in as more moderate middle-class leaders took control. The Reign of Terror came to a halt, and the National Convention reduced the power of the Committee of Public Safety. In August, a new constitution was drafted that reflected the desire for a stability that did not sacrifice the ideals of 1789. Five directors—the Directory—acted as the executive authority.

The period of the Revolution under the Directory (1795–1799) was an era of stagnation and corruption. At the same time, the Directory faced political enemies from both the left and the right of the political spectrum. On

CHRONOLOGY The French Revolution

Meeting of Estates-General	May 5, 1789
Formation of National Assembly	June 17, 1789
Fall of the Bastille	July 14, 1789
Declaration of the Rights of Man and the Citizen	August 26, 1789
Civil Constitution of the Clergy	July 12, 1790
Flight of the king	June 20–21, 1791
Attack on the royal palace	August 10, 1792
Abolition of the monarchy	September 21, 1792
Execution of the king	January 21, 1793
Levy-in-mass	August 23, 1793
Execution of Robespierre	July 28, 1794
Adoption of Constitution of 1795 and the Directory	August 22, 1795

Napoleon and Psychological Warfare

In 1796, at the age of twenty-seven, Napoleon Bonaparte was given command of the French army in Italy, where he won a series of stunning victories. His use of speed, deception, and surprise to overwhelm his opponents is well known. In this selection from a proclamation to his troops in Italy, Napoleon also appears as a master of psychological warfare.

Napoleon Bonaparte, Proclamation to French Troops in Italy (April 26, 1796)

Soldiers:

In a fortnight you have won six victories, taken twenty-one standards [flags of military units], fifty-five pieces of artillery, several strong positions, and conquered the richest part of Piedmont [in northern Italy]; you have captured 15,000 prisoners and killed or wounded more than 10,000 men You have won battles without cannon, crossed rivers without bridges, made forced marches without shoes, camped without brandy and often without bread. Soldiers of liberty, only republican troops could have endured what you have endured. Soldiers, you have our thanks! The grateful *Patrie* [nation] will owe its prosperity to you.

The two armies which but recently attacked you with audacity are fleeing before you in terror; the wicked men who laughed at your misery and rejoiced at the thought of the triumphs of your enemies are confounded and trembling.

But, soldiers, as yet you have done nothing compared with what remains to be done. . . . Undoubtedly the greatest obstacles have been overcome; but you still have battles to fight, cities to capture, rivers to cross. Is there one among you whose courage is abating? No. . . . All of you are consumed with a desire to extend the glory of the French people; all of you long to humiliate those arrogant kings who dare to contemplate placing us in fetters; all of you desire to dictate a glorious peace, one which will indemnify the *Patrie* for the immense sacrifices it has made; all of you wish to be able to say with pride as you return to your villages, "I was with the victorious army of Italy!"

What themes did Napoleon use to play on the emotions of his troops and inspire them to greater efforts? Do you think Napoleon believed these words? Why or why not?

Source: From *A Documentary Survey of the French Revolution* by John Hall Stewart, ed. Copyright © 1951 by Macmillan College Publishing Company, renewed 1979 by John Hall Stewart.

the right, royalists continued their efforts to restore the monarchy. On the left, radical hopes of power were revived by continuing economic problems. Battered from both sides, unable to solve the country's economic problems, and still carrying on the wars inherited from the Committee of Public Safety, the Directory increasingly relied on the military to maintain its power. This led to a coup d'état in 1799 in which the popular military general Napoleon Bonaparte seized power.

The Age of Napoleon

FOCUS QUESTION: Which aspects of the French Revolution did Napoleon preserve, and which did he destroy?

Napoleon dominated both French and European history from 1799 to 1815. He had been born in Corsica in 1769 shortly after France had annexed the island. The young Napoleone Buonaparte (his birth name) was sent to France to study in one of the new military schools and was a lieutenant when the Revolution broke out in 1789. The Revolution and the European war that followed gave him new opportunities, and Napoleon rose quickly through the ranks. In 1794, at the age of only twenty-five, he was made a brigadier general. Two years later, he commanded the French armies in Italy, where he won a series of victories and returned to France as a conquering hero (see the box above). After a disastrous expedition to Egypt, Napoleon returned to Paris, where he participated in the coup that gave him control of France. He was only thirty years old.

After the coup of 1799, a new form of the Republic—called the Consulate—was proclaimed in which Napoleon, as first consul, controlled the entire executive authority of government. He had overwhelming influence over the

Chateaux de Versailles et de Trianon, Versailles//© RMN-Grand Palais/Art Resource, NY

The Coronation of Napoleon. In 1804, Napoleon restored monarchy to France when he became Emperor Napoleon I. In the coronation scene painted by Jacques-Louis David, Napoleon is shown crowning his wife, the empress Josephine, while the pope looks on. The painting shows Napoleon's mother seated in the box in the background, even though she was not at the ceremony.

legislature, appointed members of the administrative bureaucracy, commanded the army, and conducted foreign affairs. In 1802, Napoleon was made consul for life, and in 1804, he returned France to monarchy when he became Emperor Napoleon I.

Domestic Policies

One of Napoleon's first domestic policies was to establish peace with the oldest and most implacable enemy of the Revolution, the Catholic Church. In 1801, Napoleon arranged a concordat with the pope that recognized Catholicism as the religion of a majority of the French people. In return, the pope agreed not to challenge the confiscation of church lands during the Revolution.

Napoleon's most enduring domestic achievement was his codification of the laws. Before the Revolution, France had some three hundred local legal systems. During the Revolution, efforts were made to prepare a single code of laws for the nation, but it remained for Napoleon to bring the work to completion in the famous Civil Code. It preserved most of the revolutionary gains by recognizing the equality of all citizens before the law, the abolition of serfdom and feudalism, and religious toleration. Property rights were also protected.

Napoleon also developed a powerful, centralized administration and worked hard to develop a bureaucracy of capable officials. Early on, the regime showed that it cared little whether officials had acquired their expertise in royal or revolutionary bureaucracies. Promotion, whether in civil or military offices, was based not on rank or birth but on ability only. This principle of a government career open to talent was, of course, what many bourgeois had wanted before the Revolution.

In his domestic policies, then, Napoleon both destroyed and preserved aspects of the Revolution. Although equality was preserved in the law code and the opening of careers to talent, the creation of a new aristocracy, the strong protection accorded to property rights, and the use of conscription for the military made it clear that much equality had been lost. Liberty was replaced by an initially benevolent despotism that grew increasingly arbitrary. Napoleon shut down sixty of France's seventy-three newspapers.

Napoleon's Empire

When Napoleon became consul in 1799, France was at war with a second European coalition of Russia, Great Britain, and Austria. Napoleon realized the need for a pause and made a peace treaty in 1802. But in 1803 war was renewed with Britain, which was soon joined by Austria, Russia, and Prussia in the Third Coalition. In a series of battles from 1805 to 1807, Napoleon's Grand Army defeated the Austrian, Prussian, and Russian armies, giving Napoleon the opportunity to create a new European order.

THE GRAND EMPIRE From 1807 to 1812, Napoleon was the master of Europe. His Grand Empire was composed of three major parts: the French Empire, dependent states, and allied states (see Map 18.3). Dependent states were under the rule of Napoleon's relatives; these came to include Spain, the Netherlands, the kingdom of Italy, the Swiss Republic, the Grand Duchy of Warsaw, and the Confederation of the Rhine (a union of all German states except Austria and Prussia). Allied states were those defeated by Napoleon and forced to join his struggle against Britain; these included Prussia, Austria, Russia, and Sweden.

Within his empire, Napoleon sought acceptance of certain revolutionary principles, including legal equality, religious toleration, and economic freedom. In the inner core and dependent states of his Grand Empire, Napoleon tried to destroy the old order. Nobility and clergy

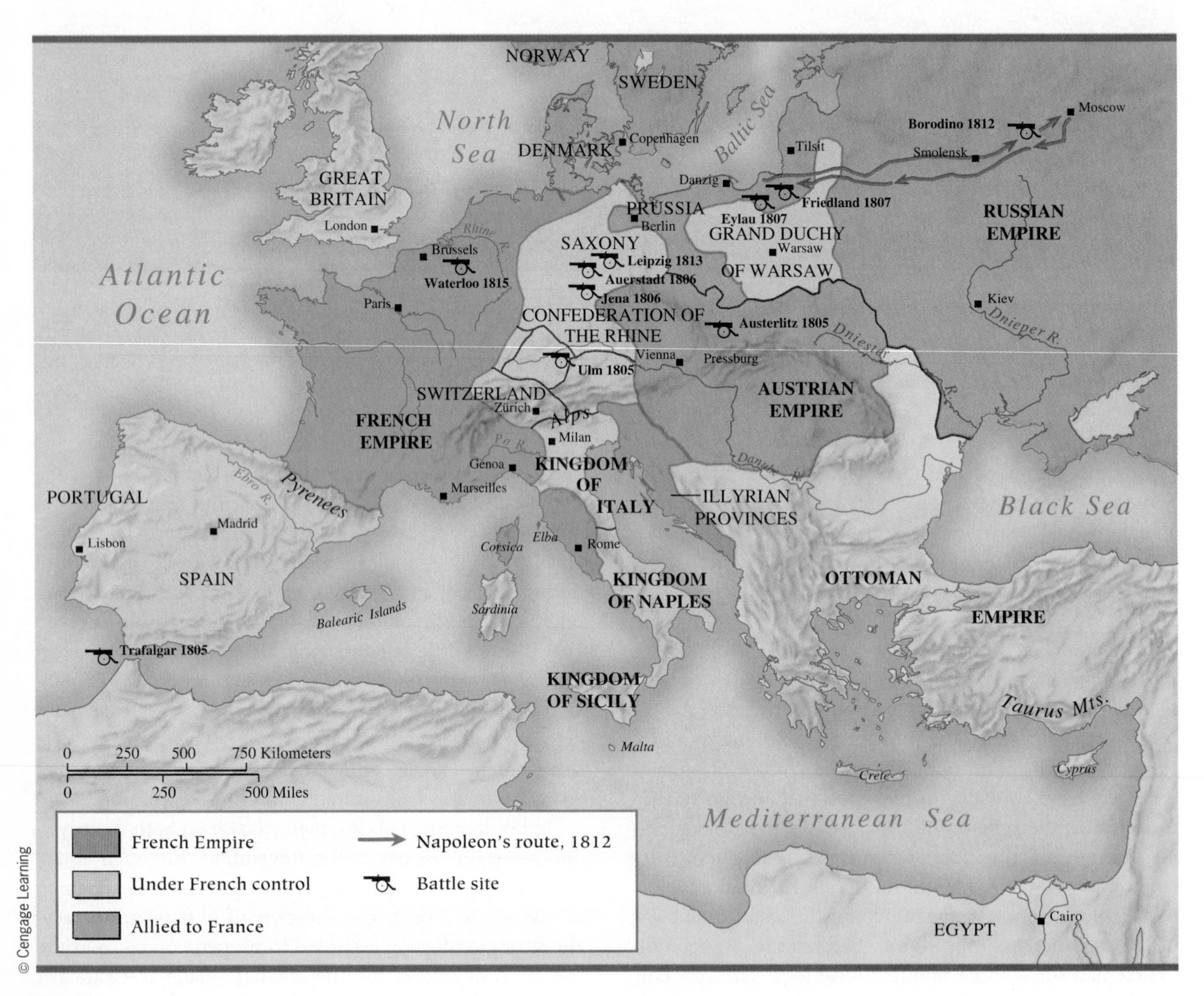

© Cengage Learning

MAP 18.3 Napoleon's Grand Empire. Napoleon's Grand Army won a series of victories against Austria, Prussia, and Russia that gave the French emperor full or partial control over much of Europe by 1807.

On the Continent, what was the overall relationship between distance from France and degree of French control, and how can you account for this?

everywhere in these states lost their special privileges. He decreed equality of opportunity with offices open to talent, equality before the law, and religious toleration.

Napoleon hoped that his Grand Empire would last for centuries, but it collapsed almost as rapidly as it had been formed. As long as Britain ruled the waves, it was not subject to military attack. Napoleon hoped to invade Britain, but he could not overcome the British navy's decisive defeat of a combined French-Spanish fleet at Trafalgar in 1805. To defeat Britain, Napoleon turned to his **Continental system**. An alliance put into effect between 1806 and 1808, it attempted to prevent British goods from reaching the European continent in order to weaken Britain economically and destroy its capacity to wage war. But the Continental system failed. Allied states resented it; some began to cheat and others to resist.

Napoleon also encountered new sources of opposition. His conquests made the French hated oppressors and aroused the patriotism of the conquered people. A Spanish uprising, aided by the British, kept a French force of 200,000 pinned down for years.

THE FALL OF NAPOLEON The beginning of Napoleon's downfall came in 1812 with his invasion of Russia. The refusal of the Russians to remain in the Continental system left Napoleon with little choice. Although aware of the risks in invading such a huge country, he knew that if the Russians were allowed to challenge the Continental system unopposed, others would follow suit. In June 1812, he led his Grand Army of more than 600,000 men into Russia. His hopes for victory depended on quickly defeating the Russian armies, but the Russian forces retreated and refused to give battle, torching their own villages to keep Napoleon's army from finding food. When the Russians did stop to fight at Borodino, Napoleon won an indecisive and costly victory. When the remaining troops of the Grand Army arrived in Moscow, they found the city ablaze. Lacking food and supplies, Napoleon abandoned Moscow late in October and made a retreat across Russia in terrible winter conditions. Only 40,000 of the original 600,000 men arrived back in Poland in January 1813.

This military disaster led other European states to rise up and attack the crippled French army. Paris was captured in March 1814, and Napoleon was sent into exile on the island of Elba, off the coast of Italy. Meanwhile, the Bourbon monarchy was restored in the person of Louis XVIII, brother of the executed king. (Louis XVII, son of Louis XVI, had died in prison at age ten.) Napoleon, bored on Elba, slipped back into France. When troops were sent to capture him, Napoleon opened his coat and addressed them: "Soldiers of the 5th regiment, I am your Emperor. . . . If there is a man among you would kill his Emperor, here I am!" No one fired a shot. Shouting "Vive l'Empereur! Vive l'Empereur," the troops went over to his side, and Napoleon entered Paris in triumph on March 20, 1815. The powers that had defeated him pledged once more to fight him. Napoleon raised another army and moved to attack the allied forces stationed in what is now Belgium. At Waterloo on June 18, Napoleon met a combined British and Prussian army under the duke of Wellington and suffered a bloody defeat. This time, the victorious allies exiled him to Saint Helena, a small, forsaken island in the South Atlantic, off the coast of Africa. Only Napoleon's memory continued to haunt French political life.

CHAPTER SUMMARY

In the Scientific Revolution, the Western world overthrew the medieval, Ptolemaic worldview and arrived at a new conception of the universe: the sun at the center, the planets as material bodies revolving around the sun in elliptical orbits, and an infinite rather than finite world. With the changes in the conception of "heaven" came changes in the conception of "earth." Highly influenced by the new worldview created by the Scientific Revolution, the philosophes of the eighteenth century hoped to create a new society by using reason to discover the natural laws that governed it. They attacked traditional religion as the enemy and developed the new "sciences of man" in economics, politics, and education. Together, the Scientific Revolution of the seventeenth century and the Enlightenment of the eighteenth century constituted an intellectual revolution that laid the foundations for a modern worldview based on rationalism and secularism.

Everywhere in Europe at the beginning of the eighteenth century, the old order remained strong. Nobles, clerics, towns, and provinces all had privileges. Everywhere in the eighteenth century, monarchs sought to enlarge their bureaucracies to raise taxes to support large standing armies. The existence of these armies led to wars on a worldwide scale. Although the wars resulted in few changes in Europe, British victories enabled Great Britain to emerge as the world's greatest naval and colonial power. Meanwhile, in Europe increased demands for taxes to support these wars led to attacks on the old order and a desire for change not met by the ruling monarchs. At the same time, a growing population as well as changes in finance, trade, and industry created tensions that undermined the foundations of the old order. Its inability to deal with these changes led to a revolutionary outburst at the end of the eighteenth century that marked the beginning of the end for the old order.

The revolutionary era of the late eighteenth century was a time of dramatic political transformations. Revolutionary upheavals, beginning in North America and continuing in France, spurred movements for political liberty and equality. The documents promulgated by these revolutions, the Declaration of Independence and the Declaration of the Rights of Man and the Citizen, embodied the fundamental ideas of the Enlightenment and created a liberal political agenda based on a belief in popular sovereignty—the people as the source of political power—and the principles of liberty and equality. Liberty meant, in theory, freedom from arbitrary power as well as the freedom to think, write, and worship as one chose. Equality meant equality in rights, although it did not include equality between men and women.

CHAPTER TIMELINE

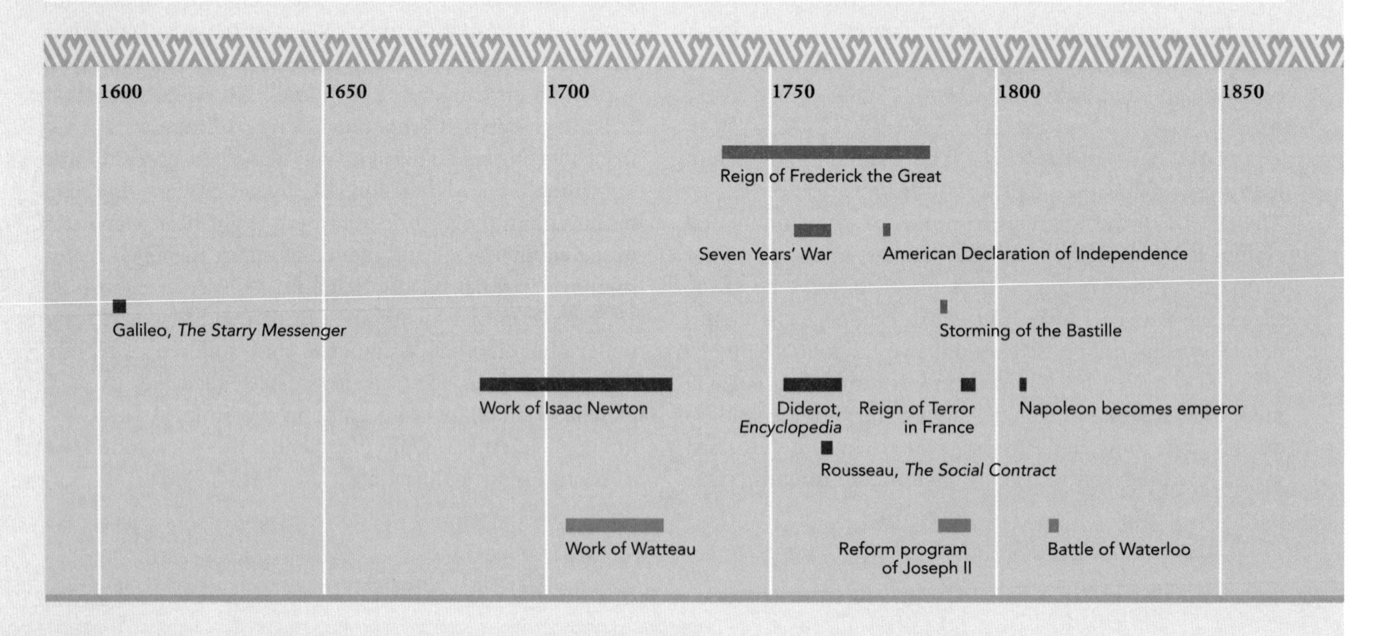

CHAPTER REVIEW

Upon Reflection

Q What was the impact of the intellectual revolution of the seventeenth and eighteenth centuries on European society?

Q How was France changed by the revolutionary events between 1789 and 1799, and who benefited the most from these changes?

Q In what ways did Napoleon's policies reject the accomplishments of the French Revolution? In what ways did his policies strengthen those accomplishments?

Key Terms

Scientific Revolution (p. 461)
geocentric theory (p. 461)
heliocentric theory (p. 461)
world-machine (p. 463)
Enlightenment (p. 464)
scientific method (p. 464)
philosophes (p. 464)
separation of powers (p. 464)
deism (p. 465)
laissez-faire (p. 465)
feminism (p. 466)

Rococo (p. 467)
high culture (p. 467)
popular culture (p. 467)
cottage industry (p. 468)
patrician (p. 468)
rentiers (p. 469)
natural rights (p. 471)
enlightened absolutism (p. 472)
old order (p. 475)
old regime (p. 475)
nationalism (p. 480)
Continental system (p. 485)

Suggested Reading

INTELLECTUAL REVOLUTION IN THE WEST Two general surveys of the Scientific Revolution are **J. R. Jacob, *The Scientific Revolution: Aspirations and Achievements, 1500–1700*** (Atlantic Highlands, N.J., 1998), and **J. Henry, *The Scientific Revolution and the Origins of Modern Science,*** 2nd ed. (New York, 2002). Good introductions to the Enlightenment can be found in **U. Im Hof, *The Enlightenment*** (Oxford, 1994), and **D. Outram, *The Enlightenment,*** 2nd ed. (Cambridge, 2005). See also the beautifully illustrated work by **D. Outram, *Panorama of the Enlightenment*** (Los Angeles, 2006). See also **P. H. Reill** and **E. J. Wilson, eds., *Encylopedia of the Enlightenment,*** rev. ed. (New York, 2004). On women in the eighteenth century, see **M. E. Wiesner-Hanks, *Women and Gender in Early Modem Europe*** (Cambridge, 2000).

THE SOCIAL ORDER On the European nobility in the eighteenth century, see **J. Dewald, *The European Nobility, 1400–1800,*** 2nd ed. (Cambridge, 2004).

ENLIGHTENED ABSOLUTISM AND GLOBAL CONFLICT On enlightened absolutism, see **D. Beales, *Enlightenment and Reform in Eighteenth-Century Europe*** (New York, 2005).

THE FRENCH REVOLUTION A well-written, up-to-date introduction to the French Revolution can be found in **W. Doyle, *The Oxford History of the French Revolution,*** 2nd ed. (Oxford, 2003). On the entire revolutionary and Napoleonic eras, see **O. Connelly, *The French Revolution and Napoleonic Era,*** 3rd ed. (Fort Worth, Tex., 2000). On the radical stage of the French Revolution, see **D. Andress, *The Terror: The Merciless War for Freedom in Revolutionary France*** (New York, 2005). On the role of women in revolutionary France, see **O. Hufton, *Women and the Limits of Citizenship in the French Revolution*** (Toronto, 1992).

THE AGE OF NAPOLEON The best biography of Napoleon is **S. Englund, *Napoleon: A Political Life*** (New York, 2004). On Napoleon's wars, see **D. A. Bell, *The First Total War: Napoleon's Europe and the Birth of Warfare as We Know It*** (Boston 2007).

Visit the CourseMate website at **www.cengagebrain.com** for additional study tools and review materials for this chapter.

PART IV

Modern Patterns of World History (1800–1945)

THE PERIOD OF WORLD HISTORY from 1800 to 1945 was characterized by three major developments: the growth of industrialization, Western domination of the world, and the rise of nationalism. The three developments were, of course, interconnected. The Industrial Revolution became one of the major forces of change in the nineteenth century as it led Western civilization into the industrial era that has characterized the modern world. Beginning in Britain, it spread to the Continent and the Western Hemisphere in the course of the nineteenth century. At the same time, the Industrial Revolution created the technological means, including new weapons, by which the West achieved domination over much of the rest of the world by the end of the nineteenth century. Moreover, the existence of competitive European nation-states after 1870 was undoubtedly a major determinant in the European states' intense scramble for overseas territory.

The advent of the industrial age had a number of lasting consequences for the modern world. On the one hand, the nations that successfully passed through the process experienced a significant increase in material wealth. In many cases, the creation of advanced industrial societies led to stronger democratic institutions and enabled the majority of the population to enjoy a higher standard of living. On the other hand, not all the consequences of the Industrial Revolution were beneficial. In the industrializing societies themselves, rapid economic change often led to widening disparities in the distribution of wealth and, with the decline in the pervasiveness of religious belief, a sense of rootlessness and alienation among much of the population.

A second development that had a major impact on the era was the rise of nationalism. Like the Industrial Revolution, nationalism originated in eighteenth-century Europe, where it was a product of the secularization of the age and the experience of the French revolutionary and Napoleonic eras. Although the concept provided the basis for a new sense of community and the rise of the modern nation-state, it also gave birth to ethnic tensions and hatreds that led to bitter disputes and civil strife and contributed to the competition that eventually erupted into world war.

© Art Media, Victoria and Albert Museum, London/HIP/The Image Works

Industrialization and the rise of national consciousness also transformed the nature of war itself. New weapons of mass destruction created the potential for a new kind of warfare that reached beyond the battlefield into the very heartland of the enemy's territory, while the concept of nationalism transformed war from the sport of kings to a matter of national honor and commitment. Since the French Revolution, governments had relied on mass conscription to defend the nation, while their engines of destruction reached far into enemy territory to destroy the industrial base and undermine the will to fight. This trend was amply demonstrated in the two world wars of the twentieth century.

In the end, then, industrial power and nationalism, the very factors that had created the conditions for European global dominance, contained the seeds for the decline of that dominance. These seeds germinated during the 1930s, when the Great Depression sharpened international competition and mutual antagonism, and then sprouted in the ensuing conflict, which spanned the entire globe. By the time World War II came to an end, the once powerful countries of Europe were exhausted, leaving the door ajar for the emergence of two new global superpowers, the United States and the Soviet Union, and for the collapse of the Europeans' colonial empires.

Europeans had begun to explore the world in the fifteenth century, but even as late as 1870, they had not yet completely penetrated North America, South America, Australia, or most of Africa. In Asia and Africa, with few exceptions, the Western presence was limited to trading posts. Between 1870 and 1914, Western civilization expanded into the rest of the Americas and Australia, while the bulk of Africa and Asia was divided into European colonies or spheres of influence. Two major events explain this remarkable expansion: the migration of many Europeans to other parts of the world due to population growth and the revival of imperialism, which was made possible by the West's technological advances. Beginning in the 1880s, European states began an intense scramble for overseas territory. This revival of imperialism—the "new imperialism," some have called it—led Europeans to carve up Asia and Africa.

What was the overall economic effect of imperialism on the subject peoples? For most of the population in colonial areas, Western domination was rarely beneficial and often destructive. Although some merchants, large landowners, and traditional hereditary elites undoubtedly prospered under the expanding imperialistic economic order, the majority of colonial peoples, urban and rural alike, probably suffered considerable hardship as a result of the policies adopted by their foreign rulers.

Some historians point out, however, that for all its inequities, there was a positive side to the colonial system as well. The expansion of markets and the beginnings of a modern transportation and communications network, while bringing few immediate benefits to the colonial peoples, offered considerable promise for future economic growth. At the same time, colonial peoples soon learned the power of nationalism, and in the twentieth century, nationalism would become a powerful force in the rest of the world as nationalist revolutions moved through Asia, Africa, and the Middle East. Moreover, the exhaustive struggles of two world wars sapped the power of the European states, and the colonial powers no longer had the energy or the wealth to maintain their colonial empires after World War II. ◆

CHAPTER

19

The Beginnings of Modernization: Industrialization and Nationalism in the Nineteenth Century

Museo del Risorgimento, Milan//© Scala/Art Resource, NY

A meeting of the Congress of Vienna

CHAPTER OUTLINE AND FOCUS QUESTIONS

The Industrial Revolution and Its Impact

Q What were the basic features of the new industrial system created by the Industrial Revolution, and what effects did the new system have on urban life, social classes, family life, and standards of living?

The Growth of Industrial Prosperity

Q What was the Second Industrial Revolution, and what effects did it have on economic and social life? What were the main ideas of Karl Marx, and what role did they play in politics and the union movement in the late nineteenth and early twentieth centuries?

Reaction and Revolution: The Growth of Nationalism

Q What were the major ideas associated with conservatism, liberalism, and nationalism, and what role did each ideology play in Europe between 1800 and 1850? What were the causes of the revolutions of 1848, and why did these revolutions fail?

National Unification and the National State, 1848–1871

Q What actions did Cavour and Bismarck take to bring about unification in Italy and Germany, respectively, and what role did war play in their efforts?

The European State, 1871–1914

Q What general political trends were evident in the nations of western Europe in the late nineteenth and early twentieth centuries, and to what degree were those trends also apparent in the nations of central and eastern Europe? How did the growth of nationalism affect international affairs during the same period?

CRITICAL THINKING

Q In what ways was the development of industrialization related to the growth of nationalism?

IN SEPTEMBER 1814, hundreds of foreigners began to converge on Vienna, the capital of the Austrian Empire. Many were members of European royalty—kings, archdukes, princes, and their wives—accompanied by their diplomatic advisers and scores of servants. Their congenial host was the Austrian emperor, Francis I, who never tired of regaling his guests with concerts, glittering balls, and sumptuous feasts. One participant remembered, "Eating, fireworks, public illuminations. For eight or ten days, I haven't been able to work at all. What a life!" Of course, not every waking hour was spent in pleasure during this gathering of notables, known to history as the Congress of Vienna. The guests were also representatives of all the states that had fought Napoleon, and their real business was to arrange a peace settlement after almost a decade of war. On June 8, 1815, they finally completed their task.

The forces of upheaval unleashed during the French revolutionary and Napoleonic wars were temporarily quieted in 1815 as rulers sought to restore stability by reestablishing much of the old order to a Europe ravaged by war. But the Western world had been changed, and it would not readily go back to the old system. New ideologies, especially liberalism and nationalism, products of the upheaval initiated in France, had become too powerful to be contained. The forces of change called forth revolts that periodically shook the West and culminated in a spate of revolutions in 1848. Some of the revolutions were successful; most were not. And yet by 1870, many of the goals sought by the liberals and nationalists during the first half of the nineteenth century seemed to have been achieved. National unity became a reality in Italy and Germany, and many Western states developed parliamentary features. Between 1870 and 1914, these newly constituted states experienced a time of great tension. Europeans engaged in a race for colonies that intensified existing antagonisms among the European states, while the creation of huge conscript armies and enormous military establishments heightened tensions among the major powers.

During the late eighteenth and early nineteenth centuries, another revolution—an industrial one—transformed the economic and social structure of Europe and spawned the industrial era that has characterized modern world history.

The Industrial Revolution and Its Impact

FOCUS QUESTION: What were the basic features of the new industrial system created by the Industrial Revolution, and what effects did the new system have on urban life, social classes, family life, and standards of living?

During the Industrial Revolution, Europe shifted from an economy based on agriculture and handicrafts to an economy based on manufacturing by machines and automated factories. The Industrial Revolution triggered an enormous leap in industrial production that relied largely on coal and steam, which replaced wind and water as new sources of energy to drive laborsaving machines. In turn, these machines called for new ways of organizing human labor to maximize the benefits and profits from the new machines. As factories replaced shop and home workrooms, large numbers of people moved from the countryside to the cities to work in the new factories. The creation of a wealthy industrial middle class and a huge industrial working class (or proletariat) substantially transformed traditional social relationships. Finally, the Industrial Revolution altered how people related to nature, ultimately creating an environmental crisis that in the twentieth century came to be recognized as a danger to human existence itself.

The Industrial Revolution in Great Britain

The Industrial Revolution began in Britain in the 1780s. Improvements in agricultural practices in the eighteenth century led to a significant increase in food production. British agriculture could now feed more people at lower prices with less labor; even ordinary families did not have to use most of their income to buy food, giving them the wherewithal to purchase manufactured goods. At the same time, rapid population growth in the second half of the eighteenth century provided a pool of surplus labor for the new factories of the emerging British industry.

In the course of its eighteenth-century wars, Great Britain had assembled a vast colonial empire at the expense of its leading rivals, the Dutch Republic and France. That empire's many markets gave British industrialists a ready outlet for their manufactured goods. British exports quadrupled from 1660 to 1760. Crucial to Britain's successful industrialization was the ability to produce cheaply the articles in greatest demand. The traditional methods of cottage industry could not keep up with the growing demand for cotton clothes throughout Britain and its vast colonial empire. Faced with this problem, British cloth manufacturers readily adopted the new methods of manufacturing that a series of inventions provided. In so doing, these individuals ignited the Industrial Revolution.

CHANGES IN TEXTILE PRODUCTION The invention of the flying shuttle enabled weavers to weave faster on a loom, thereby doubling their output. This created shortages of yarn until James Hargreaves's spinning jenny, perfected by 1768, allowed spinners to produce more yarn. Edmund Cartwright's loom, powered by water and invented in 1787, allowed the weaving of cloth to catch up with the spinning of yarn. It was now more efficient to bring workers to the machines and organize their labor collectively in factories located next to rivers, the source of power for these early machines.

The invention of the steam engine pushed the cotton industry to even greater heights of productivity. In the 1760s, a Scottish engineer, James Watt (1736–1819), built an engine powered by steam that could pump water from mines three times as quickly as previous engines. In 1782, Watt developed a rotary engine that could turn a shaft and thus drive machinery. Steam power could now be applied to spinning and weaving cotton, and before long, cotton mills using steam engines were multiplying across Britain. Fired by coal, these steam engines could be located anywhere.

The boost given to cotton textile production by these technological changes was readily apparent. In 1760, Britain had imported 2.5 million pounds of raw cotton, which was farmed out to cottage industries. In 1787, the British imported 22 million pounds of cotton; most of it was spun on machines, some powered by water in large mills. By 1840, some 366 million pounds of cotton—now Britain's most important product in value—were being imported. By this time, British cotton goods were sold everywhere in the world.

OTHER TECHNOLOGICAL CHANGES The British iron industry was also radically transformed. Britain had always had large reserves of iron ore, but at the beginning of the eighteenth century, iron production had changed little since the Middle Ages and still depended heavily on charcoal. In the 1780s, Henry Cort developed a system called puddling, in which coke, derived from coal, was used to burn away impurities in pig iron (crude iron) and produce an iron of high quality. A boom then ensued in the British iron industry. By 1852, Britain was producing almost 3 million tons of iron annually, more than the rest of the world combined.

The new high-quality wrought iron was in turn used to build new machines and ultimately new industries. In 1804, Richard Trevithick (TREV-uh-thik) pioneered the first steam-powered locomotive on an industrial rail line in southern Wales. It pulled 10 tons of ore and seventy people at 5 miles per hour. Better locomotives soon followed. Engines built by George Stephenson and his son proved superior, and it was Stephenson's *Rocket* that was used on the first public railway line, which opened in 1830, extending 32 miles from Liverpool to Manchester. *Rocket* sped along at 16 miles per hour. Within twenty years, locomotives were traveling at 50 miles per hour. By 1840, Britain had almost 6,000 miles of railroads.

The railroad was important to the success and maturing of the Industrial Revolution. The availability of a cheaper and faster means of transportation had a ripple effect on the growth of the industrial economy. As the prices of goods fell, markets grew larger; increased sales meant more factories and more machinery, thereby reinforcing the self-sustaining aspect of the Industrial Revolution—a development that marked a fundamental break with the traditional European economy. Continuous, self-sustaining economic growth came to be a fundamental characteristic of the new economy.

THE INDUSTRIAL FACTORY Another visible symbol of the Industrial Revolution was the factory (see the comparative illustration on p. 493). From its beginning, the factory created a new labor system. Factory owners wanted to use their new machines constantly. Workers were therefore obliged to work regular hours and in shifts to keep the machines producing at a steady rate. Early factory workers, however, came from rural areas, where they were used to a different pace of life. Peasant farmers worked hard, especially at harvest time, but they were also used to periods of inactivity.

Early factory owners therefore had to institute a system of work discipline that would accustom employees to working regular hours and doing the same work over and over. Of course, such work was boring, and factory owners resorted to detailed regulations and tough methods to accomplish their goals. Adult workers were fined for a wide variety of minor infractions, such as being a few minutes late for work, and dismissed for more serious misdoings, especially drunkenness, which courted disaster in the midst of dangerous machinery. Employers found that dismissals and fines worked well for adult employees; in a time when great population growth had produced large masses of unskilled labor, dismissal meant disaster. Children were less likely to understand the implications of dismissal, so they were disciplined more directly—often by beating. As the nineteenth century progressed, the second and third generations of workers came to view a regular workweek as a natural way of life.

By the mid-nineteenth century, Great Britain had become the world's first and richest industrial nation. Britain was the "workshop, banker, and trader of the world." It produced half of the world's coal and manufactured goods; in 1850, its cotton industry alone was equal in size to the industries of all other European countries combined.

The Spread of Industrialization

From Britain, industrialization spread to the continental countries of Europe and the United States, though at different times and speeds. First to be industrialized on the Continent were Belgium, France, and the German states. Their governments actively encouraged industrialization by, among other things, setting up technical schools to train engineers and mechanics and providing funds to build roads, canals, and railroads. By 1850, a network of iron rails had spread across Europe.

COMPARATIVE ILLUSTRATION

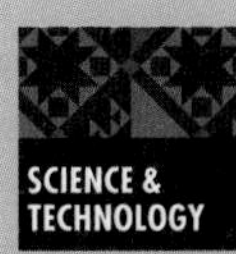

Textile Factories, West and East. The development of the factory changed the relationship between workers and employers as workers had to adjust to a new system of discipline that required them to work regular hours under close supervision. At the top is an 1851 illustration that shows women working in a British cotton factory. The factory system came later to the rest of the world than it did to Britain. Shown at the bottom is one of the earliest industrial factories in Japan, the Tomioka silk factory, built in the 1870s. Note that although women are doing the work in both factories, the managers are men.

What do you think were the major differences and similarities between British and Japanese factories (see also the box on p. 496)?

© Corbis

© The Granger Collection, New York

The Industrial Revolution also transformed the new nation in North America, the United States. In 1800, six out of every seven American workers were farmers, and there were no cities with more than 100,000 people. By 1860, the population had sextupled to 30 million people (larger than Great Britain), nine U.S. cities had populations over 100,000, and only 50 percent of American workers were farmers.

In sharp contrast to Britain, the United States was a large country. Thousands of miles of roads and canals were built linking east and west. The steamboat facilitated transportation on the Great Lakes, Atlantic coastal waters, and rivers. Most important in the development of an American transportation system was the railroad, which was needed to transport the abundant raw materials found throughout the country. Beginning with 100 miles in 1830, by 1865 the United States was crisscrossed by more than 35,000 miles of railroad track. This transportation revolution turned the United States into a single massive market for the manufactured goods of the Northeast, the early center of American industrialization. By the end of the nineteenth century, with its growing manufacturing sector, abundant raw materials, and elaborate transportation system, the United States had become the world's second-largest industrial nation.

Limiting the Spread of Industrialization to the Rest of the World

Before 1870, the industrialization that was transforming western and central Europe and the United States did not extend in any significant way to the rest of the world (see the comparative essay "The Industrial Revolution" on p. 494). Even in eastern Europe, industrialization

COMPARATIVE ESSAY

The Industrial Revolution

Why some societies were able to embark on the road to industrialization during the nineteenth century and others were not has long been debated. Some historians have pointed to the cultural characteristics of individual societies, such as the Protestant work ethic in parts of Europe or the tradition of social discipline and class hierarchy in Japan. Others have placed more emphasis on practical reasons. To the historian Peter Stearns, for example, the availability of capital, natural resources, a network of trade relations, and navigable rivers all helped stimulate industrial growth in nineteenth-century Britain. By contrast, the lack of urban markets for agricultural goods (which reduced landowners' incentives to introduce mechanized farming) is sometimes cited as a reason for China's failure to set out on its own path toward industrialization.

To some observers, the ability of western European countries to exploit the resources of their colonies in Asia, Africa, and Latin America was crucial to their industrial success. In this view, the Age of Exploration led to the creation of a new "world system" characterized by the emergence of global trade networks, propelled by the rising force of European capitalism in pursuit of precious metals, markets, and cheap raw materials.

These views are not mutually exclusive. In his recent book *The Great Divergence: China, Europe, and the Making of the Modern World Economy*, Kenneth Pomeranz argued that coal resources and access to the cheap raw materials of the Americas were both assets for Great Britain as it became the first to industrialize.

© Oxford Science Archive, Oxford//HIP/Art Resource, NY

The Steam Engine. Pictured here is an early steam engine developed by James Watt. The steam engine revolutionized the production of cotton goods and helped usher in the factory system.

Clearly, this controversy has no single answer. In any event, the coming of the industrial age had a number of lasting consequences for the world at large. On the one hand, the material wealth of the nations that successfully passed through the process increased significantly. In many cases, the creation of advanced industrial societies strengthened democratic institutions and led to a higher standard of living for the majority of the population. It also helped reduce class barriers and bring about the emancipation of women from many of the legal and social restrictions that had characterized the previous era.

On the other hand, not all the consequences of the Industrial Revolution were beneficial. In the industrializing societies themselves, rapid economic change often led to widening disparities in wealth and a sense of rootlessness and alienation among much of the population. Although some societies were able to manage these problems with a degree of success, others experienced a breakdown of social values and widespread political instability. In the meantime, the transformation of Europe into a giant factory sucking up raw materials and spewing manufactured goods out to the entire world had a wrenching impact on traditional societies whose own economic, social, and cultural foundations were forever changed by absorption into the new world order.

What were the positive and negative consequences of the Industrial Revolution?

lagged far behind. Russia, for example, was still largely rural and agricultural, ruled by an autocratic regime that preferred to keep the peasants in serfdom.

In other parts of the world where they had established control (see Chapter 21), newly industrialized European states pursued a deliberate policy of preventing the growth of mechanized industry. India provides an excellent example. In the eighteenth century, India had been one of the world's greatest exporters of cotton cloth produced by hand labor. In the first half of the nineteenth century, much of India fell under the control of the British East India Company. With British control came inexpensive textiles produced in British factories. As the indigenous Indian textile industry declined, thousands of Indian spinners and handloom weavers lost their jobs, forcing many to turn to growing raw materials, such as cotton, wheat, and tea, for export to Britain, while buying British-made finished goods. In a similar fashion elsewhere, the rapidly industrializing nations of Europe worked to thwart the spread of the Industrial Revolution to their colonial dominions.

Social Impact of the Industrial Revolution

Eventually, the Industrial Revolution revolutionized the social life of Europe and the world. This change was already evident in the first half of the nineteenth century in the growth of cities and the emergence of new social classes.

POPULATION GROWTH AND URBANIZATION The European population had already begun to increase in the eighteenth century, but the pace accelerated in the nineteenth century. Between 1750 and 1850, the total European population almost doubled, rising from 140 million to 266 million. The key to this population growth was a decline in death rates as wars and major epidemic diseases, such as plague and smallpox, became less frequent. Thanks to the increase in the food supply, more people were also better fed and more resistant to disease.

Throughout Europe, cities and towns grew dramatically in the first half of the nineteenth century, a phenomenon related to industrialization. By 1850, especially in Great Britain and Belgium, cities were rapidly becoming home to many industries. With the steam engine, factories could be located in urban centers where they had ready access to transportation facilities and large numbers of new arrivals from the country looking for work.

In 1800, Great Britain had one major city, London, with a population of one million, and six cities with populations between 50,000 and 100,000. Fifty years later, London's population had swelled to 2,363,000, and there were nine cities with populations over 100,000 and eighteen cities with populations between 50,000 and 100,000. More than 50 percent of the British population lived in towns and cities by 1850. Urban populations also grew on the Continent, but less dramatically.

The dramatic growth of cities in the first half of the nineteenth century resulted in miserable living conditions for many of the inhabitants. Located in the center of most industrial towns were the row houses of the industrial workers. Rooms were small and frequently overcrowded, as a government report of 1838 in Britain revealed: "There were 63 families where there were at least five persons to one bed; and there were some in which even six were packed in one bed, lying at the top and bottom—children and adults."[1]

Sanitary conditions were appalling; sewers and open drains were common on city streets: "In the centre of this street is a gutter, into which the refuse of animal and vegetable matters of all kinds, the dirty water from the washing of clothes and of the houses, are all poured, and there they stagnate and putrefy."[2] Unable to deal with human excrement, early industrial cities smelled horrible and were extraordinarily unhealthy. Towns and cities were death traps: deaths outnumbered births in most large cities in the first half of the nineteenth century; only a constant influx of people from the country kept them alive and growing.

NEW SOCIAL CLASSES: THE INDUSTRIAL MIDDLE CLASS The rise of industrial capitalism produced a new middle-class group. The bourgeoisie was not new; it had existed since the emergence of cities in the Middle Ages. Originally, the bourgeois or burgher was a town dweller, active as a merchant, official, artisan, lawyer, or man of letters. As wealthy townspeople bought land, the original meaning of the word *bourgeois* became lost, and the term came to include people involved in commerce, industry, and banking as well as professionals such as teachers, physicians, and government officials.

The new industrial middle class was made up of the people who constructed the factories, purchased the machines, and figured out where the markets were (see the box on p. 496). Their qualities included resourcefulness, single-mindedness, resolution, initiative, vision, ambition, and often, of course, greed. As Jedediah Strutt, a cotton manufacturer said, "Getting of money . . . is the main business of the life of men."

Members of the industrial middle class sought both to reduce the barriers between themselves and the landed elite and at the same time to separate themselves from the laboring classes below. In the first half of the nineteenth century, the working class was actually a mixture of different groups, but in the course of the century, factory workers came to form an industrial **proletariat** that constituted a majority of the working class.

NEW SOCIAL CLASSES: THE INDUSTRIAL WORKING CLASS Early industrial workers faced wretched working conditions. Work shifts ranged from twelve to sixteen hours a day, six days a week, with a half hour for lunch and dinner. Workers had no security of employment and no minimum wage. The worst conditions were in the cotton mills, where temperatures were especially debilitating.

Attitudes of the Industrial Middle Class in Britain and Japan

In the nineteenth century, a new industrial middle class in Great Britain took the lead in creating the Industrial Revolution. Japan did not begin to industrialize until after 1870 (see Chapter 22). There, too, an industrial middle class emerged, although there were also important differences in the attitudes of business leaders in Britain and Japan. Some of these differences can be seen in these documents. The first is an excerpt from the book *Self-Help* (1859) by Samuel Smiles, who believed that people succeed through "individual industry, energy, and uprightness." The other two selections are by Shibuzawa Eiichi (shih-boo-ZAH-wah EH-ee-chee), a Japanese industrialist who supervised textile factories. Although his business career began in 1873, he did not write his autobiography, the source of his first excerpt, until 1927.

Samuel Smiles, *Self-Help*

"Heaven helps those who help themselves" is a well-worn maxim, embodying in a small compass the results of vast human experience. The spirit of self-help is the root of all genuine growth in the individual; and, exhibited in the lives of many, it constitutes the true source of national vigor and strength. Help from without is often enfeebling in its effects, but help from within invariably invigorates. Whatever is done for men or classes, to a certain extent takes away the stimulus and necessity of doing for themselves; and where men are subjected to overguidance and overgovernment, the inevitable tendency is to render them comparatively helpless. . . .

National progress is the sum of individual industry, energy, and uprightness, as national decay is of individual idleness, selfishness, and vice. . . . If this view be correct, then it follows that the highest patriotism and philanthrophy consist, not so much in altering laws and modifying institutions as in helping and stimulating men to elevate and improve themselves by their own free and independent action as individuals. . . .

Many popular books have been written for the purpose of communicating to the public the grand secret of making money. But there is no secret whatever about it, as the proverbs of every nation abundantly testify. . . . "A penny saved is a penny gained."— "Diligence is the mother of good-luck."—"No pains no gains."—"No sweat no sweet."—"Sloth, the key of poverty"—"Work, and thou shalt have."—"He who will not work, neither shall he eat."—"The world is his, who has patience and industry."

Shibuzawa Eiichi, *Autobiography*

I . . . felt that it was necessary to raise the social standing of those who engaged in commerce and industry. By way of setting an example, I began studying and practicing the teachings of the *Analects of Confucius*. It contains teachings first enunciated more than twenty-four hundred years ago. Yet it supplies the ultimate in practical ethics for all of us to follow in our daily living. It has many golden rules for businessmen. For example, there is a saying: "Wealth and respect are what men desire, but unless a right way is followed, they cannot be obtained; poverty and lowly position are what men despise, but unless a right way is found, one cannot leave that status once reaching it." It shows very clearly how a businessman must act in this world.

Shibuzawa Eiichi on Progress

One must beware of the tendency of some to argue that it is through individualism or egoism that the State and society can progress most rapidly. They claim that under individualism, each individual competes with the others, and progress results from this competition. But this is to see merely the advantages and ignore the disadvantages, and I cannot support such a theory. Society exists, and a State has been founded. Although people desire to rise to positions of wealth and honor, the social order and the tranquillity of the State will be disrupted if this is done egoistically. Men should not do battle in competition with their fellow men. Therefore, I believe that in order to get along together in society and serve the State, we must by all means abandon this idea of independence and self-reliance and reject egoism completely.

What are the major similarities and differences between the business attitudes of Samuel Smiles and Shibuzawa Eiichi? How do you explain the differences?

Sources: Samuel Smiles, *Self-Help*. From Samuel Smiles, *Self-Help*, London, 1859. Shibuzawa Eiichi, *Autobiography* and Shibuzawa Eiichi on Progress. Shibuzawa Eiichi, *The Autobiography of Shibusawa Eiichi: From Peasant to Entrepreneur*, 1927 (Tokyo: University of Tokyo Press, 1994).

One report noted that "in the cotton-spinning work, these creatures are kept, fourteen hours in each day, locked up, summer and winter, in a heat of from eighty to eighty-four degrees." Mills were also dirty, dusty, and unhealthy.

Conditions in the coal mines were also harsh. Although steam-powered engines were used to lift coal to the top of the mines, inside the mines, men still had to dig the coal out while horses, mules, women, and children pulled coal carts on rails to the lift. Cave-ins, explosions, and gas fumes were a way of life. The cramped conditions—tunnels were often only 3 or 4 feet high—and constant dampness led to deformed bodies and ruined lungs.

Both children and women worked in large numbers in early factories and mines. Children had been an important part of the family economy in preindustrial times, working in the fields or carding and spinning wool at home. In the Industrial Revolution, however, child labor was exploited more than ever. The owners of cotton factories found child labor very helpful. Children had a particular delicate touch as spinners of cotton, and their small size enabled them to crawl under machines to gather loose cotton. Moreover, children were more easily trained to do factory work. Above all, children were a cheap supply of labor. In 1821, about half of the British population was under twenty years of age. Hence, children made up an abundant supply of labor, and they were paid only about one-sixth to one-third of what a man was paid. Children as young as seven worked twelve to fifteen hours per day, six days a week, in the cotton mills.

By 1830, women and children made up two-thirds of the cotton industry's labor. Under the Factory Act of 1833, however, which prohibited employment of children under the age of nine and restricted the working hours of those under eighteen, child labor declined but did not disappear. In 1838, children under eighteen still made up 29 percent of the total workforce in the cotton mills. As the number of children employed declined, women came to dominate the labor forces of the early factories, making up 50 percent of the labor force in textile (cotton and woolen) factories before 1870. They were mostly unskilled laborers and were paid half or less of what men received.

DID INDUSTRIALIZATION BRING AN IMPROVED STANDARD OF LIVING? During the first half of the nineteenth century, industrialization altered the lives of Europeans, especially the British, as they left their farms and moved to cities to work in factories. But did they experience a higher standard of living during this time? Some historians argue that industrialization increased employment and lowered the price of consumer goods, thus improving the way people lived. They also maintain that household income rose because several family members could now hold wage-paying jobs. Other historians argue that wage labor initially made life worse for many families. They maintain that employment in the early factories was highly volatile as employers quickly dismissed workers whenever demand declined. Wages were not uniform, and families lived in cramped and unsanitary conditions in the early industrial cities. Families continued to spend most of their income on food and clothing. Most historians agree that members of the middle class were the real gainers in the early Industrial Revolution and that industrial workers had to wait until the second half of the nineteenth century to begin to reap the benefits of industrialization.

The Growth of Industrial Prosperity

FOCUS QUESTIONS: What was the Second Industrial Revolution, and what effects did it have on economic and social life? What were the main ideas of Karl Marx, and what role did they play in politics and the union movement in the late nineteenth and early twentieth centuries?

After 1870, the Western world experienced a dynamic age of material prosperity. The new industries, new sources of energy, and new goods of the Second Industrial Revolution led people to believe that their material progress reflected human progress.

New Products

The first major change in industrial development between 1870 and 1914 was the substitution of steel for iron. New methods of shaping steel made it useful for constructing lighter, smaller, and faster machines and engines, as well as railways, ships, and armaments. In 1860, Great Britain, France, Germany, and Belgium produced 125,000 tons of steel; by 1913, the total was 32 million tons.

Electricity was a major new form of energy that could be easily converted into other forms of energy—such as heat, light, and motion—and moved relatively effortlessly through space over transmitting wires. In the 1870s, the first commercially practical generators of electrical current were developed, and by 1910, hydroelectric power stations and coal-fired steam-generating plants enabled homes and factories in whole neighborhoods to be tied into a single, common source of power.

Electricity spawned a number of inventions. The lightbulb, developed independently by the American Thomas Edison and the Briton Joseph Swan, permitted homes and cities to be illuminated by electric lights. By the 1880s, streetcars and subways powered by electricity had appeared in major European cities. Electricity also

Photo courtesy private collection

An Age of Progress. Between 1871 and 1914, the Second Industrial Revolution led many Europeans to believe that they were living in an age of progress when science would solve most human problems. This illustration is taken from a special issue of *The Illustrated London News* celebrating the Diamond Jubilee of Queen Victoria in 1897. On the left are scenes from 1837, when Victoria came to the British throne; on the right are scenes from 1897. The vivid contrast underscored the magazine's conclusion: "The most striking . . . evidence of progress during the reign is the ever increasing speed which the discoveries of physical science have forced into everyday life. Steam and electricity have conquered time and space to a greater extent during the last sixty years than all the preceding six hundred years witnessed."

transformed the factory. Conveyor belts, cranes, machines, and machine tools could all be powered by electricity and located anywhere. Similarly, a revolution in communications began when Alexander Graham Bell invented the telephone in 1876 and Guglielmo Marconi (gool-YEL-moh mahr-KOH-nee) sent the first radio waves across the Atlantic in 1901.

The development of the internal combustion engine, fired by oil and gasoline, provided a new source of power and gave rise to ocean liners as well as to the airplane and the automobile. In 1900, world production stood at 9,000 cars, but an American, Henry Ford, revolutionized the automotive industry with the mass production of the Model T. By 1916, Ford's factories were producing 735,000 cars a year. In 1903, at Kitty Hawk, North Carolina, brothers Orville and Wilbur Wright made the first flight in a fixed-wing airplane. The first regular passenger air service was established in 1919.

New Patterns

Industrial production grew rapidly at this time because of the greatly increased sales of manufactured goods. An increase in real wages for workers after 1870, combined with lower prices for manufactured goods because of reduced transportation costs, made it easier for Europeans to buy consumer products. In the cities, the first department stores began to sell a host of new consumer goods made possible by the development of the steel and electrical industries. The desire to own sewing machines, clocks, bicycles, electric lights, and typewriters was rapidly generating a new consumer ethic that has been a crucial part of the modern economy.

Not all nations benefited from the Second Industrial Revolution. Between 1870 and 1914, Germany replaced Great Britain as the industrial leader of Europe. Moreover, by 1900, Europe was divided into two economic zones. Great Britain, Belgium, France, the Netherlands, Germany, the western part of the Austro-Hungarian Empire, and northern Italy constituted an advanced industrialized core that had a high standard of living, decent systems of transportation, and relatively healthy and educated peoples (see Map 19.1). Another part of Europe, the backward and little industrialized area to the south and east, consisting of southern Italy, most of Austria-Hungary, Spain, Portugal, the Balkan kingdoms, and Russia, was still largely agricultural and relegated by the industrial countries to providing food and raw materials.

Emergence of a World Economy

The economic developments of the late nineteenth century, combined with the transportation revolution that saw the growth of marine transport and railroads, fostered a true world economy. By 1900, Europeans were receiving beef and wool from Argentina and Australia, coffee from Brazil, iron ore from Algeria, and sugar from Java. Until the Industrial Revolution, European countries had imported more from Asia than they had exported, but now foreign countries provided markets for the surplus manufactured goods of Europe. European capital was also invested abroad to develop railways, mines, electrical power plants, and banks. With its capital, industries, and military might, Europe dominated the world economy by the beginning of the twentieth century.

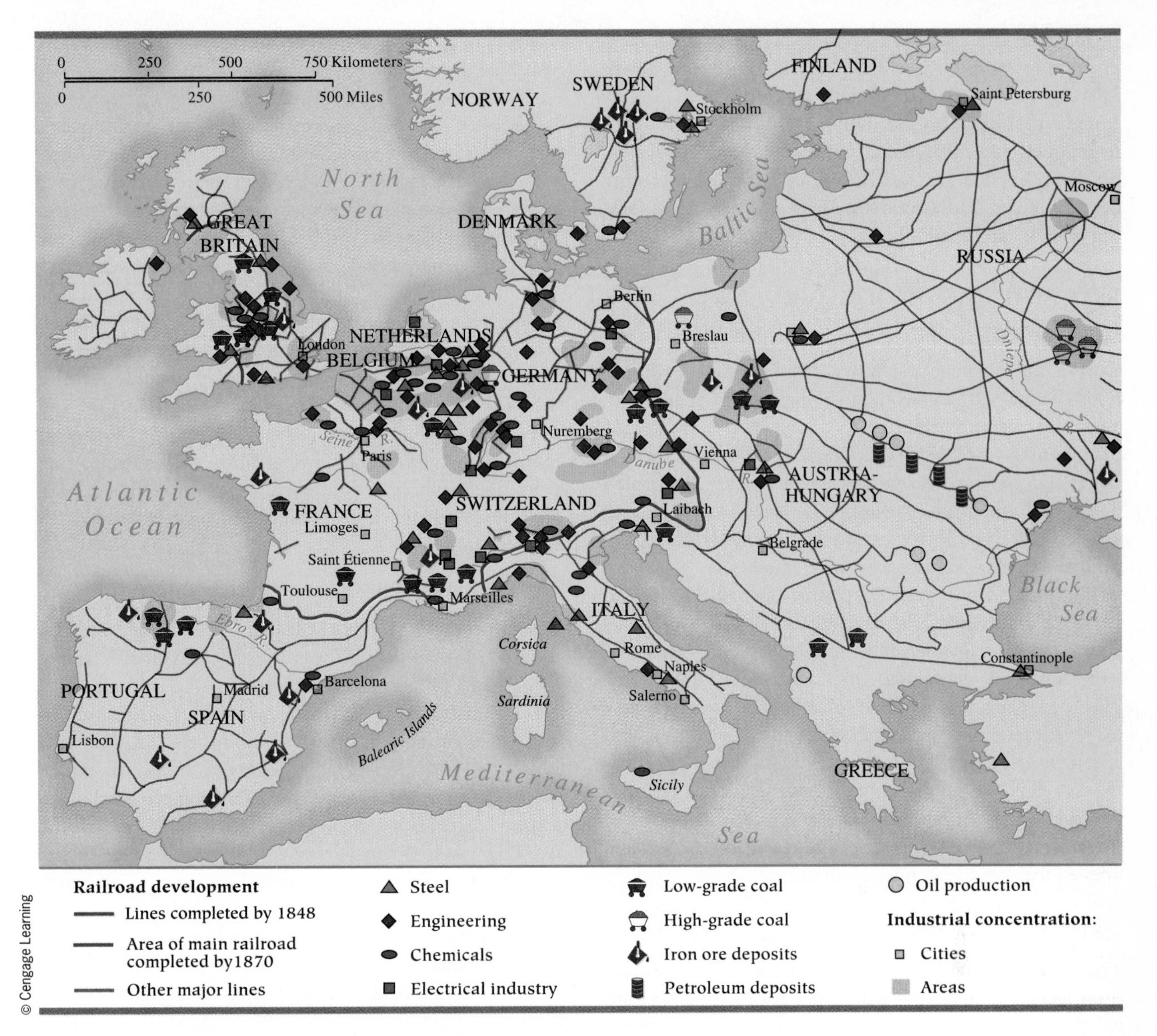

MAP 19.1 The Industrial Regions of Europe at the End of the Nineteenth Century. By the end of the nineteenth century, the Second Industrial Revolution—in steelmaking, electricity, petroleum, and chemicals—had spurred substantial economic growth and prosperity in western and central Europe; it also sparked economic and political competition between Great Britain and Germany.

What correlation, if any, was there between industrial growth and political developments in the nineteenth century?

The Spread of Industrialization

After 1870, industrialization began to spread beyond western and central Europe and North America. Especially noticeable was its rapid development, fostered by governments, in Russia and Japan. A surge of industrialization began in Russia in the 1890s under the guiding hand of Sergei Witte (syir-GYAY VIT-uh), the minister of finance. Witte pushed the government to support massive railroad construction. By 1900, 35,000 miles of track had been laid. Witte's program also made possible the rapid growth of a modern steel and coal industry, making Russia by 1900 the fourth-largest producer of steel, behind the United States, Germany, and Great Britain. At the same time, Russia was also turning out half of the world's oil production.

In Japan, the imperial government took the lead in promoting industry (see Chapter 22). The government financed industries, built railroads, brought foreign experts to train Japanese employees in new industrial techniques, and instituted a universal educational system based on applied science. By the end of the nineteenth century, Japan had developed key industries in tea, silk, armaments, and shipbuilding.

Women and Work: New Job Opportunities

During the nineteenth century, working-class organizations maintained that women should remain at home to bear and nurture children. Working-class men argued that keeping women out of industrial work would ensure the moral and physical well-being of families. In reality, however, when their husbands were unemployed, women had to do low-wage work at home or labor part-time in sweatshops to support their families.

The Second Industrial Revolution opened the door to new jobs for women. The development of larger industrial plants and the expansion of government services created a large number of service and white-collar jobs. The increased demand for white-collar workers at relatively low wages coupled with a shortage of male workers led employers to hire women. Women found new opportunities as telephone operators, typists, secretaries, file clerks, and salesclerks. Compulsory education necessitated more teachers, and the development of modern hospital services opened the way for an increase in nurses.

Organizing the Working Classes

The desire to improve their working and living conditions led many industrial workers to form socialist political parties and socialist trade unions. These emerged after 1870, but the theory that made them possible had been developed more than two decades earlier in the work of Karl Marx. **Marxism** made its first appearance on the eve of the revolutions of 1848 with the publication of a short treatise titled *The Communist Manifesto*, written by two Germans, Karl Marx (1818–1883) and Friedrich Engels (FREE-drikh ENG-ulz) (1820–1895).

MARXIST THEORY Marx and Engels began their treatise with the statement that "the history of all hitherto existing society is the history of class struggles." Throughout history, oppressor and oppressed have "stood in constant opposition to one another."[3] One group of people—the oppressors—owned the means of production and thus had the power to control government and society. Indeed, government itself was but an instrument of the ruling class. The other group, which depended on the owners of the means of production, were the oppressed.

The **class struggle** continued in the industrialized societies of Marx's day. According to Marx, "Society as a whole is more and more splitting up into two great hostile camps, into two great classes directly facing each other: Bourgeoisie and Proletariat." Marx predicted that the struggle between the bourgeoisie and the proletariat would ultimately break into open revolution, "where the violent overthrow of the bourgeoisie lays the foundation for the sway of the proletariat." The fall of the bourgeoisie "and the victory of the proletariat are equally inevitable."[4] For a while, the proletariat would form a dictatorship to reorganize the means of production, but then the state—itself an instrument of the bourgeois interests—would wither away. Since classes had arisen from the economic differences that would have been abolished, the end result would be a classless society (see the box on p. 501).

SOCIALIST PARTIES In time, Marx's ideas were picked up by working-class leaders who formed socialist parties. Most important was the German Social Democratic Party (SPD), which emerged in 1875 and espoused revolutionary Marxist rhetoric while organizing itself as a mass political party competing in elections for the Reichstag (RYKHSS-tahk), the lower house of parliament. Once in the Reichstag, SPD delegates worked to achieve legislation to improve the condition of the working class. When it received 4 million votes in the 1912 elections, the SPD became the largest single party in Germany.

Socialist parties also emerged in other European states. In 1889, leaders of the various socialist parties formed the Second International, an association of national socialist groups to fight against capitalism worldwide. (The First International had failed in 1872.) The Second International took some coordinated actions—May Day (May 1), for example, was made an international labor holiday—but differences often wreaked havoc at the organization's congresses.

Marxist parties divided over the issue of **revisionism**. Pure Marxists believed in violent revolution that would bring the collapse of capitalism and socialist ownership of the means of production. But others, called revisionists, rejected **revolutionary socialism** and argued that workers must organize mass political parties and work with other progressive elements to gain reforms. Evolution by democratic means, not revolution, would achieve the desired goal of socialism.

Another force working for evolutionary rather than revolutionary socialism was the development of trade unions. In Great Britain, unions won the right to strike in

The Classless Society

In *The Communist Manifesto*, Karl Marx and Friedrich Engels projected that the struggle between the bourgeoisie and the proletariat would end with the creation of a classless society. In this selection, they discuss the steps by which that classless society would be reached.

Karl Marx and Friedrich Engels, *The Communist Manifesto*

We have seen . . . that the first step in the revolution by the working class is to raise the proletariat to the position of ruling class. . . . The proletariat will use its political supremacy to wrest, by degrees, all capital from the bourgeoisie, to centralize all instruments of production in the hands of the State, i.e., of the proletariat organized as the ruling class; and to increase the total of productive forces as rapidly as possible.

Of course, in the beginning, this cannot be effected except by means of despotic inroads on the rights of property, and on the conditions of bourgeois production; by means of measures, therefore, which appear economically insufficient and untenable, but which, in the course of the movement, outstrip themselves, necessitate further inroads upon the old social order, and are unavoidable as a means of entirely revolutionizing the mode of production.

These measures will of course be different in different countries.

Nevertheless, in the most advanced countries, the following will be pretty generally applicable:

1. Abolition of property in land and application of all rents of land to public purposes.
2. A heavy progressive or graduated income tax.
3. Abolition of all right of inheritance. . . .
5. Centralization of credit in the hands of the State, by means of a national bank with State capital and an exclusive monopoly.
6. Centralization of the means of communication and transport in the hands of the State.
7. Extension of factories and instruments of production owned by the State. . . .
8. Equal liability of all to labor. Establishment of industrial armies, especially for agriculture.
9. Combination of agriculture with manufacturing industries; gradual abolition of the distinction between town and country, by a more equable distribution of the population over the country.
10. Free education for all children in public schools. Abolition of children's factory labor in its present form. . . .

When, in the course of development, class distinctions have disappeared, and all production has been concentrated in the whole nation, the public power will lose its political character. Political power, properly so called, is merely the organized power of one class for oppressing another. If the proletariat during its contest with the bourgeoisie is compelled, by the force of circumstances, to organize itself as a class, if, by means of a revolution, it makes itself the ruling class, and, as such, sweeps away by force the old conditions of production, then it will, along with these conditions, have swept away the conditions for the existence of class antagonisms and of classes generally, and will thereby have abolished its own supremacy as a class.

In place of the old bourgeois society, with its classes and class antagonisms, we shall have an association, in which the free development of each is the condition for the free development of all.

How did Marx and Engels define the proletariat? The bourgeoisie? Why did Marxists come to believe that this distinction was paramount for understanding history? For shaping the future?

Source: From *The Communist Manifesto* by Karl Marx and Friedrich Engels.

the 1870s. Soon after, factory workers began to organize into trade unions so that they could use the strike to improve their conditions. By 1900, British trade unions had 2 million members; by 1914, the number had risen to almost 4 million. Trade unions in the rest of Europe had varying degrees of success, but by the outbreak of World War I, they had made considerable progress in bettering the living and working conditions of the laboring classes.

Reaction and Revolution: The Growth of Nationalism

FOCUS QUESTIONS: What were the major ideas associated with conservatism, liberalism, and nationalism, and what role did each ideology play in Europe between 1800 and 1850? What were the causes of the revolutions of 1848, and why did these revolutions fail?

Industrialization was a major force for change as it led the West into the machine-dependent modern world. Another major force for change was nationalism, which transformed the political map of Europe in the nineteenth century.

The Conservative Order

After the defeat of Napoleon, European rulers moved to restore much of the old order. This was the goal of the great powers—Great Britain, Austria, Prussia, and Russia—when they met at the Congress of Vienna in 1814 to arrange a final peace settlement after the Napoleonic wars. The leader of the congress was the Austrian foreign minister, Prince Klemens von Metternich (KLAY-menss fun MET-ayr-nikh) (1773–1859), who claimed that he was guided at Vienna by the principle of **legitimacy**. To reestablish peace and stability in Europe, he considered it necessary to restore the legitimate monarchs who would preserve traditional institutions. This had already been done in France with the restoration of the Bourbon monarchy and in a number of other states, but it did not stop the great powers from grabbing territory, often from the smaller, weaker states (see Map 19.2).

The peace arrangements of 1815 were only the beginning of a conservative reaction determined to contain the liberal and nationalist forces unleashed by the French Revolution. Metternich and his kind were representatives of the ideology known as **conservatism**. Most conservatives favored obedience to political authority, believed that organized religion was crucial to social order, hated revolutionary upheavals, and were unwilling to accept either the liberal demands for civil liberties and representative governments or the nationalistic aspirations generated

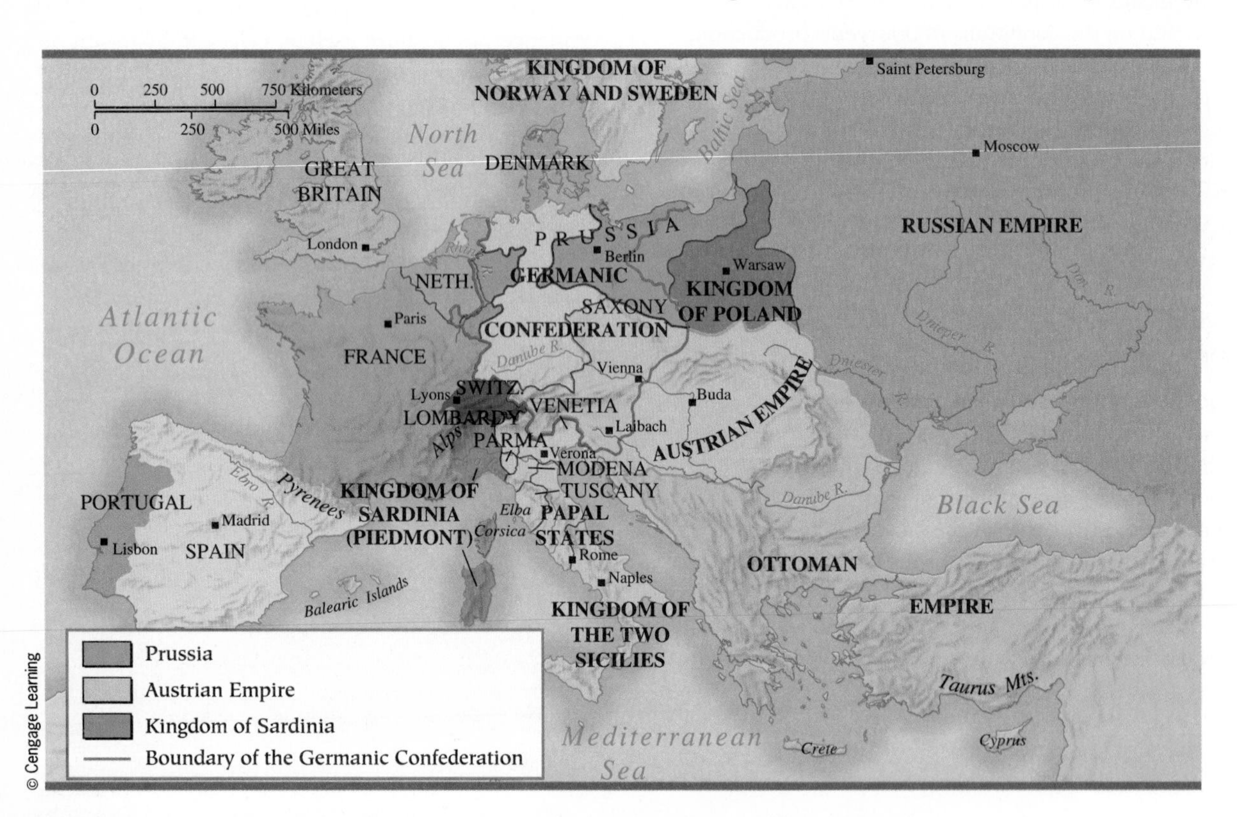

© Cengage Learning

MAP 19.2 Europe After the Congress of Vienna, 1815. The Congress of Vienna imposed order on Europe based on the principles of monarchical government and a balance of power. Monarchs were restored in France, Spain, and other states recently under Napoleon's control, and much territory changed hands, often at the expense of the small, weak states.

How did Europe's major powers manipulate territory to decrease the probability that France could again threaten the Continent's stability?

by the French revolutionary era. After 1815, the political philosophy of conservatism was supported by hereditary monarchs, government bureaucracies, landowning aristocracies, and revived churches, both Protestant and Catholic. The conservative forces were dominant after 1815.

One method used by the great powers to maintain the new status quo they had constructed was the Concert of Europe, according to which Great Britain, Russia, Prussia, and Austria (and later France) agreed to convene periodically to take steps that would maintain the peace in Europe. Eventually, the great powers adopted a principle of **intervention**, asserting that they had the right to send armies into countries where there were revolutions to restore legitimate monarchs to their thrones.

Forces for Change

Although conservative governments throughout Europe strived to restore the old order after 1815, powerful forces for change—liberalism and nationalism—were also at work. **Liberalism** owed much to the eighteenth-century Enlightenment and the American and French Revolutions; it was based on the idea that people should be as free from restraint as possible.

Politically, liberals came to hold a common set of beliefs. Chief among them was the protection of civil liberties, or the basic rights of all people, which included equality before the law; freedom of assembly, speech, and the press; and freedom from arbitrary arrest. All of these freedoms should be guaranteed by a written document, such as the American Bill of Rights. In addition to religious toleration for all, most liberals advocated separation of church and state. Liberals also demanded the right of peaceful opposition to the government in and out of parliament and the making of laws by a representative assembly (legislature) elected by qualified voters. Thus, many liberals believed in a constitutional monarchy or constitutional state with limits on the powers of government to prevent despotism and in written constitutions that would guarantee these rights. Liberals were not democrats, however. They thought that the right to vote and hold office should be open only to men of property. Liberals also believed in *laissez-faire* economic principles that rejected state interference in the regulation of wages and work hours. As a political philosophy, liberalism was adopted by middle-class men, especially industrial middle-class men, who favored voting rights for themselves so that they could share power with the landowning classes.

Nationalism was an even more powerful ideology for change. Nationalism arose out of an awareness of being part of a community that has common institutions, traditions, language, and customs. This community constitutes a "nation," and it would be the focus of the individual's primary loyalty. Nationalism did not become a popular force for change until the French Revolution. From then on, nationalists came to believe that each nationality should have its own government. Thus, the Germans, who were not united, wanted national unity in a German nation-state with one central government. Subject peoples, such as the Hungarians, wanted to establish their own autonomy rather than be subject to a German minority in the multinational Austrian Empire.

Nationalism thus posed a threat to the existing political order. A united Germany, for example, would upset the balance of power established at Vienna in 1815, and an independent Hungarian state would mean the breakup of the Austrian Empire. Because many European states were multinational, conservatives tried hard to repress the radical threat of nationalism. The conservative order dominated much of Europe after 1815, but the forces of liberalism and nationalism, first generated by the French Revolution, continued to grow as that second great revolution, the Industrial Revolution, expanded and brought in new groups of people who wanted change. In 1848, these forces for change erupted.

The Revolutions of 1848

Revolution in France was the spark for revolts in other countries. While the lower middle class, workers, and peasants were suffering from a severe industrial and agricultural depression, the government's persistent refusal to lower the property qualification for voting angered the disenfranchised members of the middle class. When the government of King Louis-Philippe (1830–1848) refused to make changes, opposition grew and finally overthrew the monarchy on February 24, 1848. A group of moderate and radical republicans established a provisional government and called for the election by universal male suffrage of a "constituent assembly" to draw up a new constitution.

The new constitution, ratified on November 4, 1848, established the Second Republic, with a single legislature elected to three-year terms by universal male suffrage and a president, also elected by universal male suffrage to a four-year term. In the elections for the presidency held in December 1848, Charles Louis Napoleon Bonaparte (1808–1873), the nephew of the famous French ruler, won a resounding victory. Within four years, President Louis Napoleon would become Emperor Napoleon III and establish an authoritarian regime.

News of the 1848 revolution in France led to upheaval in central Europe as well (see the box on p. 504). The Vienna settlement in 1815 had recognized the existence of thirty-eight sovereign states (called the Germanic Confederation) in what had once been the Holy Roman

OPPOSING VIEWPOINTS

Response to Revolution: Two Perspectives

Based on their political beliefs, Europeans responded differently to the specter of revolution that haunted Europe in the first half of the nineteenth century. The first excerpt is taken from a speech by Thomas Babington Macaulay (muh-KAHL-lee) (1800–1859), a historian and a member of the British Parliament. Macaulay spoke in Parliament on behalf of the Reform Act of 1832, which extended the right to vote to the industrial middle classes of Britain. A revolution in France in 1830 that had resulted in some gains for the upper bourgeoisie had influenced his belief that it was better to reform than to have a political revolution.

The second excerpt is taken from the *Reminiscences* of Carl Schurz (SHOORTS) (1829–1906). Like many liberals and nationalists in Germany, Schurz received the news of the 1848 revolution in France with great expectations for change in the German states. After the failure of the German revolution, Schurz emigrated to the United States and eventually became a U.S. senator.

Thomas Babington Macaulay, Speech of March 2, 1831

My hon[orable] friend the member of the University of Oxford tells us that, if we pass this law, England will soon be a Republic. The reformed House of Commons will, according to him, before it has sat ten years, depose the King, and expel the Lords from their House. . . . His proposition is, in fact, this—that our monarchical and aristocratical institutions have no hold on the public mind of England; that these institutions are regarded with aversion by a decided majority of the middle class. . . . Now, sir, if I were convinced that the great body of the middle class in England look with aversion on monarchy and aristocracy, I should be forced, much against my will, to come to this conclusion, that monarchical and aristocratical institutions are unsuited to this country. Monarchy and aristocracy, valuable and useful as I think them, are still valuable and useful as means, and not as ends. The end of government is the happiness of the people; and I do not conceive that, in a country like this, the happiness of the people can be promoted by a form of government in which the middle classes place no confidence. . . . But, sir, I am fully convinced that the middle classes sincerely wish to uphold the royal prerogatives, and the constitutional rights of the Peers. . . .

But let us know our interest and our duty better. Turn where we may—within, around—the voice of great events is proclaiming to us, "Reform, that you may preserve." Now, therefore, while everything at home and abroad forebodes ruin to those who persist in a hopeless struggle against the spirit of the age; now, . . . take counsel, not of prejudice, not of party spirit . . . but of history, of reason. . . . Save property divided against itself. Save the multitude, endangered by their own ungovernable passions. Save the aristocracy, endangered by its own unpopular power. Save the greatest, and fairest, and most highly civilized community that ever existed, from calamities which may in a few days sweep away all the rich heritage of so many ages of wisdom and glory. The danger is terrible. The time is short. If this Bill should be rejected, I pray to God that none of those who concur in rejecting it may ever remember their votes with unavailing regret, amidst the wreck of laws, the confusion of ranks, the spoliation of property, and the dissolution of social order.

Carl Schurz, *Reminiscences*

One morning, toward the end of February, 1848, I sat quietly in my attic-chamber, . . . when suddenly a friend rushed breathlessly into the room, exclaiming: "What, you sitting here! Do you not know what has happened?"

"No; what?"

"The French have driven away Louis Philippe and proclaimed the republic."

. . . We tore down the stairs, into the street, to the market-square. . . . Although it was still forenoon, the market was already crowded with young men talking excitedly. . . What did we want there? This probably no one knew. But since the French had driven away Louis Philippe and proclaimed the republic, something of course must happen here, too. . . .

The next morning . . . [we were] impelled by a feeling that now we had something more important [than our classes] to do—to devote ourselves to the affairs of the fatherland. And this we did by seeking as quickly as

(Continued)

possible again the company of our friends, in order to discuss what had happened and what was to come.

In these conversations, excited as they were, certain ideas and catchwords worked themselves to the surface, which expressed more or less the feelings of the people. Now had arrived in Germany the day for the establishment of "German Unity," and the founding of a great, powerful national German Empire. In the first line the convocation of a national parliament. Then the demands for civil rights and liberties, free speech, free press, the right of free assembly, equality before the law, a freely elected representation of the people with legislative power, responsibility of ministers, self-government of the communes, the right of the people to carry arms, the formation of a civic guard with elective officers, and so on—in short, that which was called a "constitutional form of government on a broad democratic basis." Republican ideas were at first only sparingly expressed. But the word *democracy* was soon on all tongues, and many, too, thought it a matter of course that if the princes should try to withhold from the people the rights and liberties demanded, force would take the place of mere petition. Of course the regeneration of the fatherland must, if possible, be accomplished by peaceable means. . . . I was dominated by the feeling that at last the great opportunity had arrived for giving to the German people the liberty which was their birthright and to the German fatherland its unity and greatness, and that it was now the first duty of every German to do and to sacrifice everything for this sacred object.

What arguments did Macaulay use to support the Reform Act of 1832? Was he correct? Why or why not? Why was Carl Schurz so excited when he heard the news about the revolution in France? Do you think being a university student helps explain his reaction? Why or why not? What differences do you see in the approaches of these two writers? What do these selections tell you about the development of politics in the German states and Britain in the nineteenth century?

Sources: Thomas Babington Macaulay, Speech of March 2, 1831. From *Speeches, Parliamentary and Miscellaneous* by Thomas B. Macaulay (New York: Hurst Co., 1853), vol. 1, pp. 20–21, 25–26. Carl Schurz, *Reminiscences*. From *The Reminiscences of Carl Schurz* by Carl Schurz (New York: The McClure Co., 1907), vol. 1, pp. 112–113.

Empire. Austria and Prussia were the two great powers; the other states varied considerably in size. In 1848, cries for change caused many German rulers to promise constitutions, a free press, jury trials, and other liberal reforms. In Prussia, King Frederick William IV (1840–1861) agreed to establish a new constitution and work for a united Germany.

The promise of unity reverberated throughout the German states as governments allowed elections by universal male suffrage for deputies to an all-German parliament called the Frankfurt Assembly. Its purpose was to fulfill a liberal and nationalist dream—the preparation of a constitution for a new united Germany. But the assembly failed to achieve its goal. The members had no real means of compelling the German rulers to accept the constitution they had drawn up. German unification was not achieved; the revolution had failed.

The Austrian Empire needed only the news of the revolution in Paris to erupt in flames in March 1848. The Austrian Empire was a multinational state, containing at least eleven ethnically distinct peoples, including Germans, Czechs, Magyars (Hungarians), Slovaks, Romanians, Serbians, and Italians. The Germans, though only a quarter of the population, were economically dominant and played a leading role in government. The Hungarians, however, wanted their own legislature. In March, demonstrations in Buda, Prague, and Vienna led to the dismissal of Metternich, the Austrian foreign minister and archsymbol of the conservative order, who fled abroad. In Vienna, revolutionary forces took control of the capital and demanded a liberal constitution. Hungary was given its own legislature and a separate national army.

Austrian officials had made concessions to appease the revolutionaries, but they were determined to reestablish firm control. As in the German states, they were increasingly encouraged by the divisions between radical and moderate revolutionaries. By the end of October 1848, Austrian military forces had crushed the rebels in Vienna, but it was only with the assistance of a Russian army of 140,000 men that the Hungarian revolution was finally put down in 1849. The revolutions in the Austrian Empire had failed.

Revolutions in Italy also failed. The Congress of Vienna had established nine states in Italy, including the kingdom of Sardinia in the north, ruled by the house of Savoy; the kingdom of the Two Sicilies (Naples and

Wien Museum Karlsplatz, Vienna//© Erich Lessing/Art Resource, NY

Austrian Students in the Revolutionary Civil Guard. In 1848, revolutionary fervor swept the European continent and toppled governments in France, central Europe, and Italy. In the Austrian Empire, students joined the revolutionary civil guard in taking control of Vienna and forcing the Austrian emperor to call a constituent assembly to draft a liberal constitution.

Sicily); the Papal States; a handful of small duchies; and the important northern provinces of Lombardy and Venetia (vuh-NEE-shuh), which were part of the Austrian Empire. Italy was largely under Austrian domination, but a new movement for Italian unity known as Young Italy led to initially successful revolts in 1848. By 1849, however, the Austrians had reestablished complete control over Lombardy and Venetia, and the old order also prevailed in the rest of Italy.

Throughout Europe in 1848–1849, moderate, middle-class liberals and radical workers soon divided over their aims, and the failure of the revolutionaries to stay united soon led to the reestablishment of authoritarian regimes. In other parts of the Western world, revolutions took somewhat different directions (see Chapter 20).

Nationalism in the Balkans: The Ottoman Empire and the Eastern Question

The Ottoman Empire had long been in control of much of the Balkans in southeastern Europe. By the beginning of the nineteenth century, however, the Ottoman Empire was in decline, and authority over its outlying territories in the Balkans waned. As a result, European governments, especially those of Russia and Austria, began to take an active interest in the disintegration of the empire. The "Eastern Question," as it came to be called, troubled European diplomats throughout the century.

When the Russians invaded the Ottoman provinces of Moldavia (mohl-DAY-vee-uh) and Wallachia (wah-LAY-kee-uh), the Ottoman Turks declared war on Russia on October 4, 1853. In the following year, on March 28, Great Britain and France, fearful of Russian gains, declared war on Russia. The Crimean War, as the conflict came to be called, was poorly planned and poorly fought. Heavy losses caused the Russians to sue for peace. By the Treaty of Paris in 1856, Russia agreed to allow Moldavia and Wallachia to be placed under the protection of all the great powers.

The Crimean War destroyed the Concert of Europe. Austria and Russia, the chief powers maintaining the status quo in the first half of the nineteenth century, were now enemies because Austria had failed to support Russia in the war. Russia, defeated and humiliated by the obvious failure of its armies, withdrew from European affairs for the next two decades. Great Britain, disillusioned by its role in the war, also pulled back from continental affairs. Austria, paying the price for its neutrality, was now without friends among the great powers. This new international situation opened the door for the unification of Italy and Germany.

National Unification and the National State, 1848–1871

FOCUS QUESTION: What actions did Cavour and Bismarck take to bring about unification in Italy and Germany, respectively, and what role did war play in their efforts?

The revolutions of 1848 had failed, but within twenty-five years, many of the goals sought by liberals and nationalists during the first half of the nineteenth century were achieved. Italy and Germany became nations, and many European states were led by constitutional monarchs.

The Unification of Italy

The Italians were the first to benefit from the breakdown of the Concert of Europe. In 1850, Austria was still the dominant power on the Italian peninsula. After the failure of the revolution of 1848–1849, more and more Italians looked to the northern Italian state of Piedmont, ruled by the house of Savoy, as their best hope to achieve the unification of Italy. It was, however, doubtful that the little state could provide the necessary leadership until King Victor Emmanuel II (1849–1878; 1861–1878 as king of Italy) named Count Camillo di Cavour (kuh-MEEL-oh dee kuh-VOOR) (1810–1861) prime minister in 1852.

Cavour pursued a policy of economic expansion that increased government revenues and enabled Piedmont to equip a large army. Then, allied with the French emperor, Napoleon III, Cavour defeated the Austrians and gained control of Lombardy. Cavour's success caused nationalists in some northern Italian states (Parma, Modena, and Tuscany) to overthrow their governments and join Piedmont.

Meanwhile, in southern Italy, Giuseppe Garibaldi (joo-ZEP-pay gar-uh-BAHL-dee) (1807–1882), a dedicated Italian patriot, raised an army of a thousand volunteers called Red Shirts because of the color of their uniforms. Garibaldi's forces swept through Sicily and then crossed over to the mainland and began a victorious march up the Italian peninsula. Naples, and with it the kingdom of the Two Sicilies, fell in September 1860. Ever the patriot, Garibaldi chose to turn over his conquests to Cavour's Piedmontese forces. On March 17, 1861, the new kingdom of Italy was proclaimed under a centralized government subordinated to the control of Piedmont and King Victor Emmanuel II. The task of unification was not yet complete, however. Venetia in the north was taken from Austria in 1866. The Italian army annexed the city of Rome on September 20, 1870, and it became the new capital of the united Italian state.

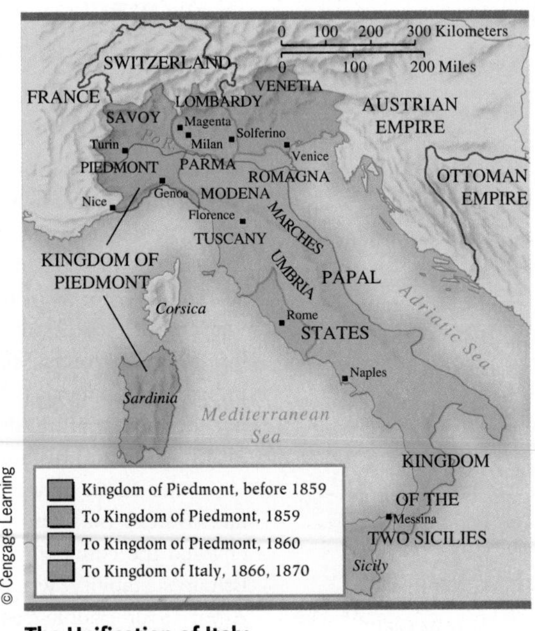

© Cengage Learning

The Unification of Italy

CHRONOLOGY **The Unification of Italy**	
Victor Emmanuel II	1849–1878
Count Cavour becomes prime minister of Piedmont	1852
Garibaldi's invasion of the Two Sicilies	1860
Kingdom of Italy is proclaimed	March 17, 1861
Italy's annexation of Venetia	1866
Italy's annexation of Rome	1870

The Unification of Germany

After the failure of the Frankfurt Assembly to achieve German unification in 1848–1849, Germans increasingly looked to Prussia for leadership in the cause of German unification. Prussia had become a strong, prosperous, and authoritarian state, with the Prussian king in firm control of both the government and the army. In 1862, King William I (1861–1888) appointed a new prime minister, Count Otto von Bismarck (OT-toh fun BIZ-mark) (1815–1898). Bismarck has often been portrayed as the ultimate realist, the foremost nineteenth-century practitioner of ***Realpolitik*** (ray-AHL-poh-lee-teek)—the "politics of reality." He said, "Not by speeches and majorities will the great questions of the day be decided—that was the mistake of 1848–1849—but by iron and blood."[5] Opposition to his domestic policy determined Bismarck on an active foreign policy, which led to war and German unification.

After defeating Denmark with Austrian help in 1864 and gaining control over the duchies of Schleswig (SHLESS-vik) and Holstein (HOHL-shtyn), Bismarck goaded the Austrians into a war on June 14, 1866. The Austrians were barely defeated at Königgrätz (kur-nig-GRETS) on July 3, but Prussia now organized the northern German states into the North German Confederation. The southern German states, largely Catholic, remained independent but signed military alliances with Prussia due to their fear of France, their western neighbor.

Prussia now dominated all of northern Germany, but Bismarck realized that France would never be content with a strong German state to its east because of the potential threat to French security. Bismarck goaded the French into declaring war on Prussia on July 15, 1870. The Prussian armies advanced into France, and at Sedan (suh-DAHN) on September 2, 1870, they captured an entire French army and the French emperor Napoleon III himself. Paris capitulated on January 28, 1871. France had to give up the provinces of Alsace (al-SASS) and Lorraine (luh-RAYN) to the new German state, a loss that left the French burning for revenge.

Even before the war had ended, the southern German states had agreed to enter the North German Confederation. On January 18, 1871, in the Hall of Mirrors in Louis XIV's palace at Versailles, William I was proclaimed kaiser (KY-zur) (emperor) of the Second German Empire

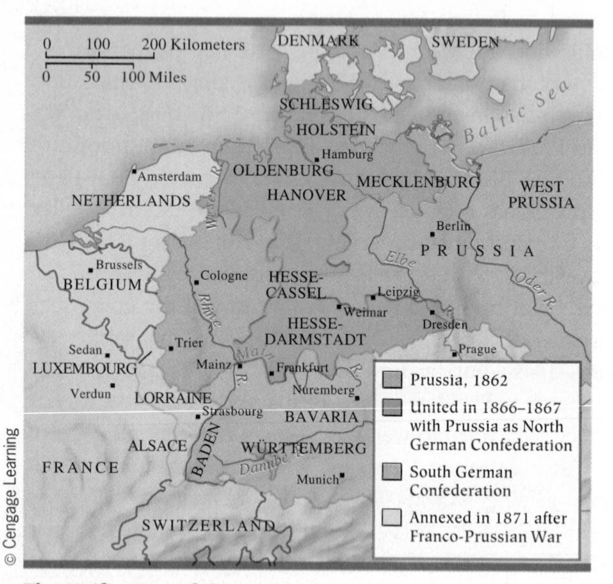

© Cengage Learning

The Unification of Germany

(the first was the medieval Holy Roman Empire). German unity had been achieved by the Prussian monarchy and the Prussian army. The Prussian leadership of German unification meant the triumph of authoritarian, militaristic values over liberal, constitutional sentiments in the development of the new German state. With its industrial resources and military might, the new state had become the strongest power on the Continent. A new European balance of power was at hand.

CHRONOLOGY The Unification of Germany	
King William I of Prussia	1861–1888
Danish War	1864
Austro-Prussian War	1866
Franco-Prussian War	1870–1871
German Empire is proclaimed	January 18, 1871

© bpk, Berlin/Bismarck Museum, Friedrichsruh/Art Resource, NY

The Unification of Germany. Under Prussian leadership, a new German empire was proclaimed on January 18, 1871, in the Hall of Mirrors in the palace of Versailles. King William of Prussia became Emperor William I of the Second German Empire. Otto von Bismarck, who had been so instrumental in creating the new German state, is shown here, resplendently attired in his white uniform, standing at the foot of the throne.

Nationalism and Reform: The European National State at Mid-Century

Unlike nations on the Continent, Great Britain managed to avoid the revolutionary upheavals of the first half of the nineteenth century. In the early part of the century, Great Britain was governed by the aristocratic landowning classes that dominated both houses of Parliament. But in 1832, to avoid turmoil like that on the Continent, Parliament passed a reform bill that increased the number of male voters, chiefly by adding members of the industrial middle class (see the box on p. 504). By allowing the industrial middle class to join the landed interests in ruling Britain, Britain avoided revolution in 1848.

In the 1850s and 1860s, the British liberal parliamentary system made both social and political reforms that enabled the country to remain stable. Another reason for Britain's stability was its continuing economic growth. After 1850, middle-class prosperity was at last coupled with improvements for the working classes as real wages for laborers increased more than 25 percent between

FILM & HISTORY

The Young Victoria (2009)

Directed by Jean-Marc Vallée, *The Young Victoria* is an imaginative and yet relatively realistic portrayal of the early years of the young woman who became Britain's longest-reigning monarch. The film begins in 1836 when the seventeen-year-old Victoria (Emily Blunt) is the heir to the throne. Her controlling mother, the duchess of Kent (Miranda Richardson), schemes to prevent her daughter from ascending the throne by trying to create a regency for herself and her paramour, Sir John Conroy (Mark Strong). The mother and Conroy fail, and Victoria succeeds to the throne after the death of her uncle, King William IV (Jim Broadbent), in 1837. The movie also shows the impact that Lord Melbourne (Paul Bettany), the prime minister, had on the young queen. Indeed, Victoria's attachment to Melborne led to considerable discontent among her subjects. Central to the film, however, is the romantic portrayal of the wooing of Victoria by her young German cousin, Prince Albert of Sax-Coburg-Gotha (Rupert Friend). The film accurately conveys the deep and abiding love that developed between Victoria and Albert.

GK Films/The Kobal Collection at Art Resource, NY

The coronation of Victoria (Emily Blunt) as queen of England

With its castle and cathedral settings, the film is a visual treat but also contains some inaccuracies. Victoria is shown painting with her right hand, although she was actually left-handed. The facts are also embellished at times for dramatic effect. Although there was an assassination attempt on the queen, Prince Albert was not shot while trying to protect her. Both shots fired by the would-be assassin went wide of the mark. The banquet scene in which King William IV insults the duchess of Kent is accurate and uses many of the king's actual words, but its consequences are not. The duchess did not leave the room, and Victoria did not remain calm, but broke into tears. Finally, except for a passing reference to Victoria's concern for workers' housing conditions, this romantic movie makes no attempt to portray the political and social issues of Victoria's time.

1850 and 1870. The British sense of national pride was well reflected in Queen Victoria (1837–1901), whose sense of duty and moral respectability reflected the attitudes of her age, which has ever since been known as the Victorian Age (see the Film & History feature above)

After the revolution of 1848, France moved toward the restoration of monarchy. Four years after his election as president, Louis Napoleon restored an authoritarian empire. On December 2, 1852, he assumed the title of Napoleon III (the first Napoleon had abdicated in favor of his son, Napoleon II, in 1814). The Second Empire had begun.

The first five years of Napoleon III's reign were a spectacular success. He took many steps to expand industrial growth. Government subsidies fostered the rapid construction of railroads as well as harbors, roads, and canals. The major French railway lines were completed during Napoleon III's reign, and iron production tripled. Napoleon III also undertook a vast reconstruction of the city of Paris. The medieval Paris of narrow streets and old city walls was destroyed and replaced by a modern Paris of broad boulevards, spacious buildings, an underground sewage system, a new public water supply, and gas streetlights.

In the 1860s, as opposition to his rule began to mount, Napoleon III began to liberalize his regime. He gave the Legislative Corps more say in affairs of state, including debate over the budget. Liberalization policies worked initially; in a plebiscite in May 1870 on whether to accept a new constitution that might have inaugurated a parliamentary regime, the French people gave Napoleon III a resounding victory. This triumph was short-lived, however. War with Prussia in 1870 brought Napoleon III's ouster, and a republic was proclaimed.

Although nationalism was a major force in nineteenth-century Europe, one of the most powerful states, the Austrian Empire, managed to frustrate the desire of its numerous ethnic groups for self-determination. After the

Emancipation: Serfs and Slaves

Although overall their histories have been quite different, Russia and the United States shared a common feature in the 1860s. They were the only states in the Western world that still had large enslaved populations (the Russian serfs were virtually slaves). The leaders of both countries issued emancipation proclamations within two years of each other. The first excerpt is taken from the imperial decree of March 3, 1861, which freed the Russian serfs. The second excerpt is from Abraham Lincoln's Emancipation Proclamation, issued on January 1, 1863.

Alexander II's Imperial Decree, March 3, 1861

By the grace of God, we, Alexander II, Emperor and Autocrat of all the Russias, King of Poland, Grand Duke of Finland, etc., to all our faithful subjects, make known:

Called by Divine Providence and by the sacred right of inheritance to the throne of our ancestors, we took a vow in our innermost heart to respond to the mission which is intrusted to us as to surround with our affection and our Imperial solicitude all our faithful subjects of every rank and of every condition, from the warrior, who nobly bears arms for the defense of the country, to the humble artisan devoted to the works of industry; from the official in the career of the high offices of the State to the laborer whose plough furrows the soil. . . .

We thus came to the conviction that the work of a serious improvement of the condition of the peasants was a sacred inheritance bequeathed to us by our ancestors, a mission which, in the course of events, Divine Providence called upon us to fulfill. . . .

In virtue of the new dispositions above mentioned, the peasants attached to the soil will be invested within a term fixed by the law with all the rights of free cultivators. . . .

At the same time, they are granted the right of purchasing their close, and, with the consent of the proprietors, they may acquire in full property the arable lands and other appurtenances which are allotted to them as a permanent holding. By the acquisition in full property of the quantity of land fixed, the peasants are free from their obligations toward the proprietors for land thus purchased, and they enter definitely into the condition of free peasant-landholders.

Lincoln's Emancipation Proclamation, January 1, 1863

Now therefore, I, Abraham Lincoln, President of the United States, by virtue of the power in me vested as Commander-in-Chief of the Army and Navy of the United States in time of actual armed rebellion against the authority and government of the United States, and as a fit and necessary war measure for suppressing such rebellion, do, on this 1st day of January, A.D. 1863, and in accordance with my purpose to do so, . . . order and designate as the States and parts of States wherein the people thereof, respectively, are this day in rebellion against the United States the following, to wit:

Arkansas, Texas, Louisiana, . . . Mississippi, Alabama, Florida, Georgia, South Carolina, North Carolina, and Virginia. . . .

And by virtue of the power for the purpose aforesaid, I do order and declare that all persons held as slaves within said designated States and parts of States are, and henceforward shall be free; and that the Executive Government of the United States, including the military and naval authorities thereof, will recognize and maintain the freedom of said persons.

What changes did Tsar Alexander II's emancipation of the serfs initiate in Russia? What effect did Lincoln's Emancipation Proclamation have on the southern "armed rebellion"? What reasons did each leader give for his action?

Sources: Alexander II's Imperial Decree, March 3, 1861. From Annual Register (New York: Longmans, Green, 1861), p. 207. Lincoln's Emancipation Proclamation, January 1, 1863. From *U.S. Statutes at Large* (Washington, D.C., Government Printing Office, 1875), vol. 12, pp. 1268–1269.

Habsburgs had crushed the revolutions of 1848–1849, they restored centralized, autocratic government. But Austria's defeat at the hands of the Prussians in 1866 forced the Austrians to deal with the fiercely nationalistic Hungarians.

The result was the negotiated ***Ausgleich*** (OWSS-glykh), or Compromise, of 1867, which created the dual monarchy of Austria-Hungary. Each part of the empire now had its own constitution, its own legislature, its own governmental bureaucracy, and its own capital (Vienna for Austria and Budapest for Hungary). Holding the two states together were a single monarch—Francis Joseph (1848–1916) was emperor of Austria and king of Hungary—and a common army, foreign policy, and system of finances. The *Ausgleich* did not, however, satisfy the other nationalities that make up the Austro-Hungarian Empire.

At the beginning of the nineteenth century, Russia was overwhelmingly rural, agricultural, and autocratic. The Russian imperial autocracy, based on soldiers, secret police, and repression, withstood the revolutionary fervor of the first half of the nineteenth century. But defeat in the Crimean War in 1856 led even staunch conservatives to realize that Russia was falling hopelessly behind the western European powers. Tsar Alexander II (1855–1881) decided to make serious reforms.

Serfdom was Russia's most burdensome problem. On March 3, 1861, Alexander issued his emancipation edict (see the box on p. 510). Peasants were now free to own property and marry as they chose. But the redistribution of land instituted after emancipation was not favorable to them. The government provided land for the peasants by purchasing it from the landlords, but the landowners often kept the best lands. The peasants soon found that they had inadequate amounts of arable land to support themselves.

Nor were the peasants completely free. The state compensated the landowners for the land given to the peasants, but the peasants were to repay the state in long-term installments. To ensure that the payments were made, peasants were subjected to the authority of their *mir* (MEER), or village commune, which was collectively responsible for the payments to the government. Since the communes were responsible for the payments, they were reluctant to allow peasants to leave. Emancipation, then, led not to free, landowning peasants on the Western model but to unhappy, land-starved peasants who largely followed the old ways of agricultural production.

The European State, 1871–1914

FOCUS QUESTIONS: What general political trends were evident in the nations of western Europe in the late nineteenth and early twentieth centuries, and to what degree were those trends also apparent in the nations of central and eastern Europe? How did the growth of nationalism affect international affairs during the same period?

Throughout much of Europe by 1870, the national state had become the focus of people's loyalties. Only in Russia, eastern Europe, Austria-Hungary, and Ireland did national groups still struggle for independence.

Within the major European states, considerable progress was made in achieving such liberal practices as constitutions and parliaments, but it was largely in the western European states that **mass politics** became a reality. Reforms encouraged the expansion of political democracy through voting rights for men and the creation of mass political parties. At the same time, however, similar reforms were strongly resisted in parts of Europe where the old political forces remained strong.

Western Europe: The Growth of Political Democracy

By 1871, Great Britain had a functioning two-party parliamentary system. For the next fifty years, Liberals and Conservatives alternated in power. Both parties were dominated by aristocratic landowners and upper-middle-class businesspeople. The parties competed in passing laws that expanded the right to vote. By 1918, all males over twenty-one and women over thirty could vote. Political democracy was soon accompanied by social welfare measures for the working class.

The growth of trade unions, which advocated more radical economic change, and the emergence in 1900 of the Labour Party, which dedicated itself to workers' interests, caused the Liberals, who held the government from 1906 to 1914, to realize that they would have to create a program of social welfare or lose the workers' support. Therefore, they voted for a series of social reforms. The National Insurance Act of 1911 provided benefits for workers in case of sickness and unemployment. Additional legislation provided a small pension for those over seventy. Although both the benefits and the tax increase were modest, they were the first hesitant steps toward the future British welfare state.

In France, the confusion that ensued after the collapse of the Second Empire finally ended in 1875 when an improvised constitution established the Third Republic, which lasted sixty-five years. France's parliamentary system was weak, however, because the existence of a dozen political parties forced the premier (or prime minister) to depend on a coalition of parties to stay in power. The Third Republic was notorious for its changes of government. Nevertheless, by 1914, the Third Republic commanded the loyalty of most French people.

Central and Eastern Europe: Persistence of the Old Order

The constitution of the new imperial Germany begun by Chancellor Otto von Bismarck in 1871 provided for a bicameral legislature. The lower house of the German parliament, the Reichstag, was elected by universal male suffrage, but it did not have ministerial responsibility. Government ministers were responsible to the emperor, not the parliament. The emperor also commanded the armed forces and controlled foreign policy and the bureaucracy.

During the reign of Emperor William II (1888–1918), Germany continued to be an "authoritarian, conservative, military-bureaucratic power state." By the end of William's reign, Germany had become the strongest military and industrial power on the Continent, but the rapid change had also helped produce a society torn between modernization and traditionalism. With the expansion of industry and cities came demands for true democracy. Conservative forces, especially the landowning nobility and industrialists, tried to block the movement for democracy by supporting William II's activist foreign policy. Expansion abroad, they believed, would divert people's attention from the yearning for democracy at home.

After the creation of the dual monarchy of Austria-Hungary in 1867, the Austrian part received a constitution that theoretically established a parliamentary system. In practice, however, Emperor Francis Joseph largely ignored parliament, ruling by decree when parliament was not in session. The problem of the various nationalities also remained unsolved. The German minority that governed Austria felt increasingly threatened by the Czechs, Poles, and other Slavic groups within the empire. Their agitation in the parliament for autonomy led prime ministers after 1900 to ignore the parliament and rely increasingly on imperial decrees to govern.

In Russia, the assassination of Alexander II in 1881 convinced his son and successor, Alexander III (1881–1894), that reform had been a mistake, and he lost no time in persecuting both reformers and revolutionaries. When Alexander III died, his weak son and successor, Nicholas II (1894–1917), began his rule with his father's conviction that the absolute power of the tsars should be preserved: "I shall maintain the principle of autocracy just as firmly and unflinchingly as did my unforgettable father."[6] But conditions were changing.

Industrialization progressed rapidly in Russia after 1890, and with industrialization came factories, an industrial working class, and the development of socialist parties, including the Marxist Social Democratic Party and the Social Revolutionaries. Although repression forced both parties to go underground, the growing opposition to the regime finally exploded into revolution in 1905.

The defeat of the Russians by the Japanese in 1904–1905 encouraged antigovernment groups to rebel against the tsarist regime. Nicholas II granted civil liberties and created a legislative assembly, the Duma (DOO-muh), elected directly by a broad franchise. But real constitutional monarchy proved short-lived. By 1907, the tsar had curtailed the power of the Duma and relied again on the army and bureaucracy to rule Russia.

CHRONOLOGY **The National State, 1870–1914**	
Great Britain	
Formation of Labour Party	1900
National Insurance Act	1911
France	
Republican constitution (Third Republic)	1875
Germany	
Bismarck as chancellor	1871–1890
Emperor William II	1888–1918
Austria-Hungary	
Emperor Francis Joseph	1848–1916
Russia	
Tsar Alexander III	1881–1894
Tsar Nicholas II	1894–1917
Russo-Japanese War	1904–1905
Revolution	1905

International Rivalries and the Winds of War

Between 1871 and 1914, Europe was mostly at peace. Wars did occur (including wars of conquest in the non-Western world), but none involved the great powers. Bismarck had realized in 1871 that the emergence of a unified Germany as the most powerful state on the Continent (see Map 19.3) had upset the balance of power established at Vienna in 1815. Fearful of a possible anti-German alliance between France and Russia, and possibly even Austria, Bismarck made a defensive alliance with Austria in 1879. Three years later, this alliance was enlarged with the addition of Italy, angry with the French over conflicting colonial ambitions in North Africa. The Triple Alliance of 1882—Germany, Austria-Hungary, and Italy—committed the three powers to a defensive alliance against France. At the same time, Bismarck maintained a separate treaty with Russia.

When Emperor William II cashiered Bismarck in 1890 and took over direction of Germany's foreign policy, he embarked on an activist foreign policy dedicated to enhancing German power by finding, as he put it, Germany's rightful "place in the sun." One of his changes in Bismarck's foreign policy was to drop the treaty with Russia, which he viewed as being at odds with Germany's alliance with Austria. The ending of the alliance brought France and Russia together, and in 1894, the two powers concluded a military alliance. During the next ten years, German policies caused the British to draw closer

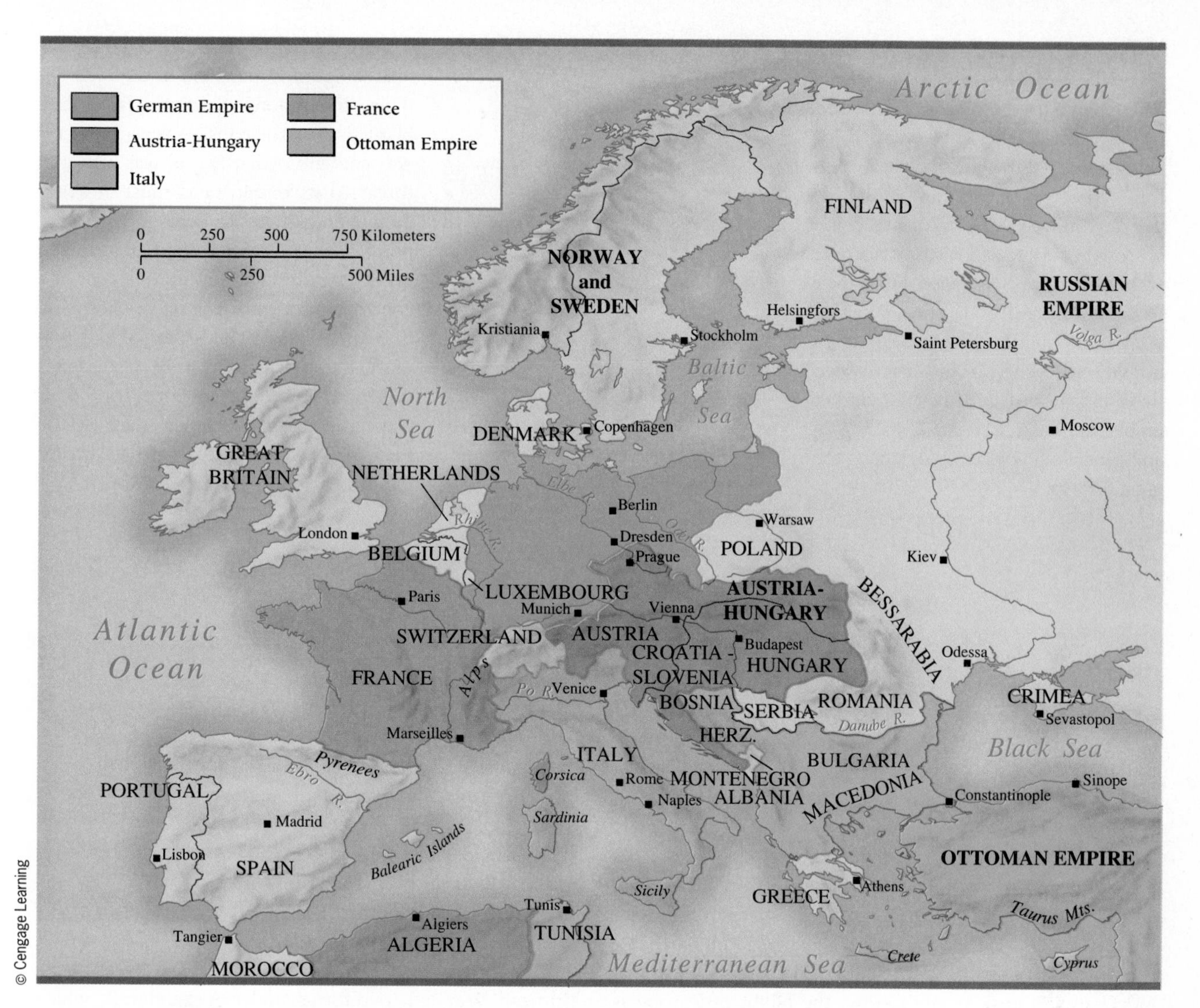

© Cengage Learning

MAP 19.3 Europe in 1871. German unification in 1871 upset the balance of power established at Vienna in 1815 and eventually led to a realignment of European alliances. By 1907, Europe was divided into two opposing camps: the Triple Entente of Great Britain, Russia, and France and the Triple Alliance of Germany, Austria-Hungary, and Italy.

How was Germany affected by the formation of the Triple Entente?

to France. By 1907, an alliance of Great Britain, France, and Russia—known as the Triple Entente (ahn-TAHNT)—stood opposed to the Triple Alliance of Germany, Austria-Hungary, and Italy. Europe became divided into two opposing camps that became more and more inflexible and unwilling to compromise. A series of crises in the Balkans between 1908 and 1913 set the stage for World War I.

CRISIS IN THE BALKANS During the nineteenth century, the Balkan provinces of the Ottoman Empire had gradually gained their freedom, although the rivalry between Austria and Russia complicated the process. By 1878, Greece, Serbia, Romania, and Montenegro (mahn-tuh-NEE-groh) had become independent. Bulgaria, though not totally independent, was allowed to operate autonomously under Russian protection. Bosnia and Herzegovina (HAYRT-suh-guh-VEE-nuh) were placed under Austrian protection; Austria could occupy but not annex them.

Nevertheless, in 1908, Austria did annex the two Slavic-speaking territories. Serbia was outraged because the annexation dashed the Serbs' hopes of creating a large Serbian kingdom that would unite most of the southern

Slavs. The Russians, as protectors of their fellow Slavs, supported the Serbs and opposed the Austrian action. Backed by the Russians, the Serbs prepared for war against Austria. At this point, William II intervened and demanded that the Russians accept Austria's annexation of Bosnia and Herzegovina or face war with Germany. Weakened from their defeat in the Russo-Japanese War in 1904–1905, the Russians backed down but vowed revenge. Two wars between the Balkan states in 1912–1913 further embittered the inhabitants of the region and generated more tensions among the great powers.

The Balkans in 1913

Serbia's desire to create a large Serbian kingdom remained unfulfilled. In their frustration, Serbian nationalists blamed the Austrians. Austria-Hungary was convinced that Serbia was a mortal threat to its empire and must at some point be crushed. As Serbia's chief supporters, the Russians were determined not to back down again in the event of a confrontation with Austria or Germany in the Balkans. The allies of Austria-Hungary and Russia were also determined to be more supportive of their respective allies in another crisis. By the beginning of 1914, two armed camps viewed each other with suspicion.

CHAPTER SUMMARY

In 1815, a conservative order had been reestablished throughout Europe, but the forces of liberalism and nationalism, unleashed by the French Revolution and now reinforced by the spread of industrialization, were pushing Europe into a new era of political and social change. Industrialization spread rapidly from Great Britain to the Continent and United States. As cities grew, the plight of Europe's new working class became the focus of new political philosophies, notably the work of Karl Marx who sought to liberate the oppressed proletariat. At the same time, middle-class industrialists adopted the political philosophy of liberalism, espousing freedom in politics and in economic activity. By the mid-nineteenth century, nationalism threatened the status quo in divided Germany and Italy and the multiethnic Austrian Empire.

In 1848, revolutions erupted across the Continent. A republic with universal manhood suffrage was established in France, but within four years, it had given way to the Second Empire. The Frankfurt Assembly worked to create a unified Germany, but it also failed. In the Austrian Empire, the liberal demands of the Hungarians and other nationalities were eventually put down, In Italy, too, uprisings against Austrian rule failed when conservatives regained control.

By 1871, nationalist forces had prevailed in Germany and Italy. The combined activities of Count Cavour and Giuseppe Garibaldi finally led to the unification of Italy in 1870. Under the guidance of Otto von Bismarck, Prussia engaged in wars with Denmark, Austria, and France before it finally achieved the goal of Germany national unification in 1871. Reform characterized developments in other Western states. Austria created the dual monarchy of Austria-Hungary. Russia's defeat in the Crimean War led to reforms under Alexander II, which included the freeing of the Russian serfs.

Between 1871 and 1914, the functions of the national state began to expand as social insurance measures such as protection against illnesses and old age were adopted to appease the working masses. Liberal and democratic reforms, especially in western Europe, brought the possibility for greater participation in the political process. Nevertheless, large minorities, especially in the multiethnic empires controlled by the Austrians, Ottomans, and Russians, had not achieved the goal of their own national states. Meanwhile, the collapse of the Ottoman Empire caused Russia and Austria to set their sights on territories in the Balkans. As Germany's power increased, the European nations formed new alliances that helped maintain a balance of power but also led to the creation of large armies. The alliances also generated tensions that were unleashed when Europeans were unable to resolve a series of crises in the Balkans and rushed into the catastrophic carnage of World War I.

CHAPTER TIMELINE

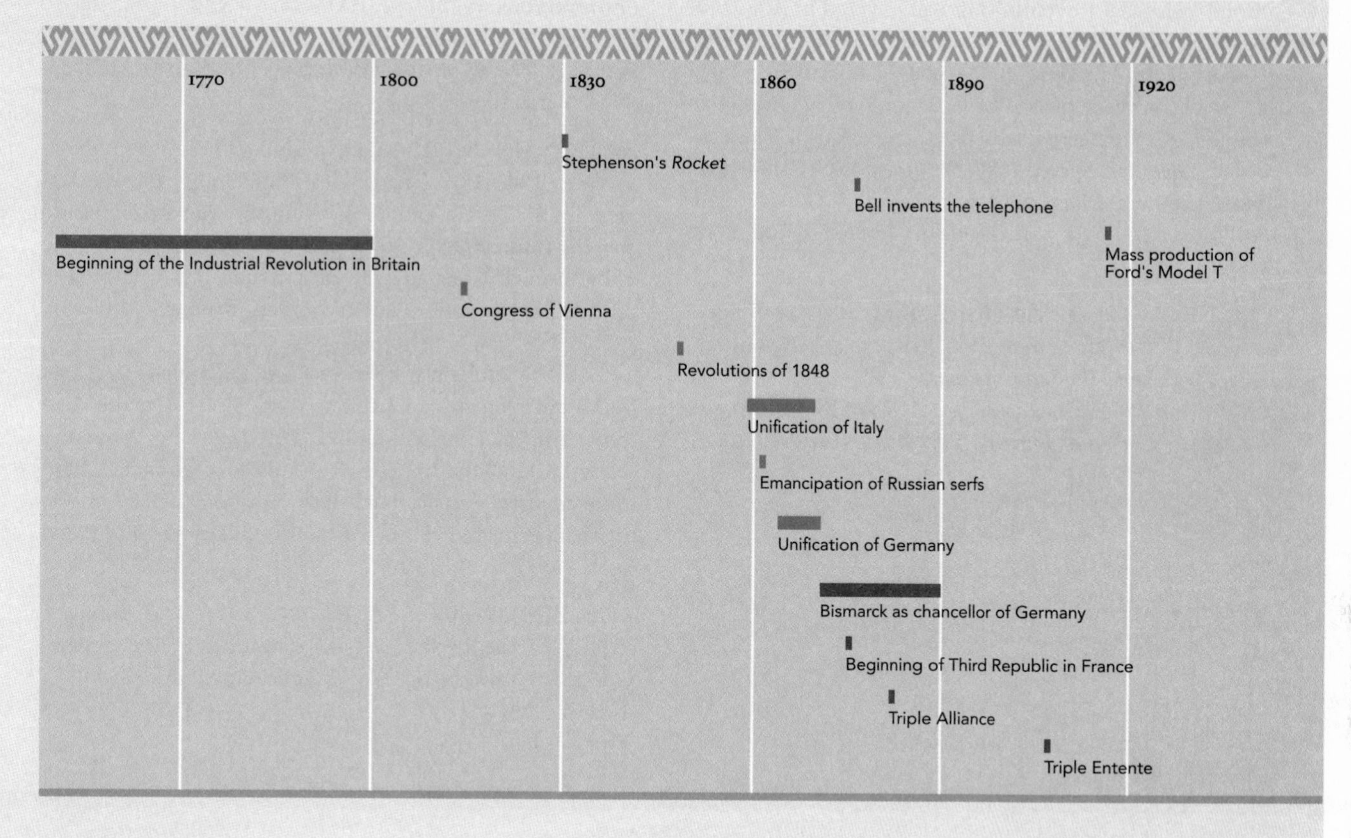

CHAPTER REVIEW

Upon Reflection

Q What are the major similarities and differences between the First and Second Industrial Revolutions?

Q What were the chief ideas associated with liberalism and nationalism, and how were these ideas put into practice in the first half of the nineteenth century?

Q To what extent were the major goals of establishing liberal practices and achieving the growth of political democracy realized in Great Britain, France, Germany, Austria-Hungary, and Russia between 1871 and 1914?

Key Terms

proletariat (p. 495)
Marxism (p. 500)
class struggle (p. 500)
revisionism (p. 500)
revolutionary socialism (p. 500)
legitimacy (p. 502)
conservatism (p. 502)
intervention (p. 503)
liberalism (p. 503)
nationalism (p. 503)
Realpolitik (p. 507)
Ausgleich (p. 510)
mass politics (p. 511)

Suggested Reading

THE INDUSTRIAL REVOLUTION AND ITS IMPACT A good introduction to the Industrial Revolution is **J. Horn, *The Industrial Revolution*** (Westport, Conn., 2007). On the role of the British, see **K. Morgan, *The Birth of Industrial Britain: Social Change, 1750–1850*** (New York, 2004). A work on female labor patterns is **J. Rendall, *Women in an Industrializing Society: England, 1750–1880*** (Oxford, 2002).

For a global approach to the modern economy, see **K. Pomeranz, *The Great Deliverance: China, Europe, and the Making of the Modern World Economy*** (Princeton, N.J., 2002).

THE GROWTH OF INDUSTRIAL PROSPERITY The Second Industrial Revolution is well covered in **A. S. Milward** and **S. B. Saul, *The Development of the Economies of Continental Europe, 1850–1914*** (Cambridge, Mass., 1977). The impact of the new technology on European thought is imaginatively discussed in **S. Kern, *The Culture of Time and Space, 1880–1914,*** rev. ed. (Cambridge, Mass., 2003). On Marx, the standard work is **D. McLellan, *Karl Marx: His Life and Thought,*** 4th ed. (New York, 2006).

THE GROWTH OF NATIONALISM, 1814–1848 For a good survey of the nineteenth century, see **R. Gildea, *Barricades and Borders: Europe, 1800–1914,*** 3rd ed. (Oxford, 2003). Also valuable is **T. C. W. Blanning, ed., *Nineteenth Century: Europe, 1789–1914*** (Oxford, 2000). For a survey of the period 1814–1848, see **M. Lyons, *Postrevolutionary Europe, 1815–1856*** (New York, 2006). The best introduction to the revolutions of 1848 is **J. Sperber, *The European Revolutions, 1848–1851,*** 2nd ed. (New York, 2005).

NATIONAL UNIFICATION AND THE NATIONAL STATE, 1848–1871 The unification of Italy can be examined in **B. Derek** and **E. F. Biagini**, ***The Risorgimento and the Unification*** of ***Italy,*** 2nd ed. (London, 2002). The unification of Germany can be pursued first in a biography of Bismarck, **E. Feuchtwanger, *Bismarck*** (London, 2002).

Louis Napoleon's role can be examined in **J. F. McMillan, *Napoleon III*** (New York, 1991). On the Austrian Empire, see **R. Okey, *The Habsburg Monarchy*** (New York, 2001). Imperial Russia is covered in **T. Chapman, *Imperial Russia, 1801–1905*** (London, 2001). On Victorian Britain, see **W. L. Arnstein, *Queen Victoria*** (New York, 2005).

THE EUROPEAN STATE, 1871–1914 The domestic politics of the period can be examined in the general works listed above. See also **J. Sperber, *Europe 1850–1914*** (New York, 2009).

CourseMate

Visit the CourseMate website at **www.cengagebrain.com** for additional study tools and review materials for this chapter.

The Americas and Society and Culture in the West

© North Wind Picture Archives

A portrait of Toussaint L'Ouverture, leader of the Haitian independence movement

CHAPTER OUTLINE AND FOCUS QUESTIONS

Latin America in the Nineteenth and Early Twentieth Centuries

Q What role did liberalism and nationalism play in Latin America between 1800 and 1870? What were the major economic, social, and political trends in Latin America in the late nineteenth and early twentieth centuries?

The North American Neighbors: The United States and Canada

Q What role did nationalism and liberalism play in the United States and Canada between 1800 and 1870? What economic, social, and political trends were evident in the United States and Canada between 1870 and 1914?

The Emergence of Mass Society

Q What is meant by the term *mass society*, and what were its main characteristics?

Cultural Life: Romanticism and Realism in the Western World

Q What were the main characteristics of Romanticism and Realism?

Toward the Modern Consciousness: Intellectual and Cultural Developments

Q What intellectual and cultural developments in the late nineteenth and early twentieth centuries "opened the way to a modern consciousness," and how did this consciousness differ from earlier worldviews?

CRITICAL THINKING

Q In what ways were the intellectual and cultural developments in the Western world between 1800 and 1914 related to the economic, social, and political developments?

NATIONALISM—one of the major forces for change in Europe in the nineteenth century—also affected Latin America as the colonial peoples there overthrew their Spanish and Portuguese masters and began the process of creating new national states. An unusual revolution in Haiti preceded the main independence movements. François-Dominique Toussaint L'Ouverture (frahn-SWAH-doh-muh-NEEK too-SANH loo-vayr-TOOR), the grandson of an African king, was born a slave in Saint-Domingue (san doh-MAYNG)—the western third of the island of Hispaniola, a French sugar colony—in 1746. Educated by his godfather, Toussaint was able to amass a small private fortune through his own talents and the generosity of his French master. When black slaves in Saint-Domingue, inspired by news of the French Revolution, revolted in 1791, Toussaint became their leader. For years, Toussaint and his ragtag army struck at the French. By 1801, after his army had come to control Saint-Domingue, Toussaint assumed the role of ruler and issued a constitution that freed all slaves.

But Napoleon Bonaparte refused to accept Toussaint's control of France's richest colony and sent a French army of 23,000 men under General Leclerc (luh-KLAHR), his brother-in-law, to crush the rebellion. Although yellow fever took its toll on the French, their superior numbers and weapons enabled them to gain the upper hand. Toussaint was tricked into surrendering in 1802 by Leclerc's promise: "You will not find a more sincere friend than myself." Instead, Toussaint was arrested, put in chains, and shipped to France, where he died a year later in a dungeon. The western part of Hispaniola, now called Haiti, however, became the first independent state in Latin America when Toussaint's lieutenants drove out the French forces in 1804. Haiti was only one of a number of places in the Americas where new nations were formed during the nineteenth century. Indeed, nation building was prominent in North America as the United States and Canada expanded.

As national states in both the Western Hemisphere and Europe were evolving in the nineteenth century, significant changes were occurring in society and culture. The rapid economic changes of the nineteenth century led to the emergence of mass society in the Western world, which meant improvements for the lower classes, who benefited from the extension of voting rights, a better standard of living, and universal education. The coming of mass society also created new roles for the governments of nation-states, which now fostered national loyalty, created mass armies by conscription, and took more responsibility for public health and housing in their cities. Cultural and intellectual changes paralleled these social developments, and after 1870, Western philosophers, writers, and artists began exploring modern cultural expressions that questioned traditional ideas and increasingly provoked a crisis of confidence.

Latin America in the Nineteenth and Early Twentieth Centuries

FOCUS QUESTIONS: What role did liberalism and nationalism play in Latin America between 1800 and 1870? What were the major economic, social, and political trends in Latin America in the late nineteenth and early twentieth centuries?

The Spanish and Portuguese colonial empires in Latin America had been integrated into the traditional monarchical structure of Europe for centuries. When that structure was challenged, first by the ideas of the Enlightenment and then by the upheavals of the Napoleonic era, Latin America encountered the possibility of change. How it responded to that possibility, however, was determined in part by conditions unique to the region.

The Wars for Independence

By the end of the eighteenth century, the ideas of the Enlightenment and the new political ideals stemming from the successful revolution in North America were beginning to influence the creole elites (descendants of Europeans who became permanent inhabitants of Latin America). The principles of the equality of all people in the eyes of the law, free trade, and a free press proved very attractive. Sons of creoles, such as Simón Bolívar (see-MOHN boh-LEE-var) (1783–1830) and José de San Martín (hoh-SAY day san mar-TEEN) (1778–1850) who became leaders of the independence movement, even went to European universities, where they imbibed the ideas of the Enlightenment. These Latin American elites, joined by a growing class of merchants, especially resented the domination of their trade by Spain and Portugal.

NATIONALISTIC REVOLTS IN LATIN AMERICA The creole elites soon began to use their new ideas to denounce the rule of the Iberian monarchs and the peninsulars (Spanish and Portuguese officials who resided in Latin America for political and economic gain). As Bolívar said in 1815, "It would be easier to have the two continents meet than to reconcile the spirits of Spain and America."[1] When Napoleon Bonaparte toppled the monarchies of Spain and Portugal, the authority of the Spaniards and Portuguese in their colonial empires was weakened, and between 1807 and 1825, a series of revolts enabled most of Latin America to become independent.

As described in the chapter-opening vignette, the first revolt was actually a successful slave rebellion. Led by Toussaint L'Ouverture (1746–1803), the revolt resulted in the formation of Haiti as the first independent postcolonial state in Latin America in 1804.

Beginning in 1810, Mexico, too, experienced a revolt, fueled initially by the desire of the creole elites to overthrow the rule of the peninsulars. The first real hero of Mexican independence was Miguel Hidalgo y Costilla (mee-GEL ee-THAHL-goh ee kahs-TEE-yuh), a parish priest in a small village about 100 miles from Mexico City. Hidalgo, who had studied the French Revolution, roused the local Indians and mestizos, many of whom were suffering from a major famine, to free themselves from the Spanish. On September 16, 1810, a crowd of Indians and mestizos, armed with clubs, machetes, and a few guns, quickly formed a mob army and attacked the Spaniards, shouting, "Long live independence and death to the Spaniards." But Hidalgo was not a good organizer, and his forces were soon crushed. A military court sentenced Hidalgo to death, but his memory lived on. In fact, September 16, the first day of the uprising, is celebrated as Mexico's Independence Day.

The participation of Indians and mestizos in Mexico's revolt against Spanish control frightened both creoles and peninsulars. Fearful of the masses, they cooperated in defeating the popular revolutionary forces. The elites—both creoles and peninsulars—then decided to overthrow Spanish rule as a way of preserving their own power. They selected a creole military leader, Augustín de Iturbide (ah-goo-STEEN day ee-tur-BEE-day), as their leader and the first emperor of Mexico in 1821. The new government fostered neither political nor economic changes, and it soon became apparent that Mexican independence had benefited primarily the creole elites.

Independence movements elsewhere in Latin America were likewise the work of elites—primarily creoles—who overthrew Spanish rule and set up new governments that they could dominate. José de San Martín of Argentina and Simón Bolívar of Venezuela, leaders of the independence movement, were both members of the creole elite, and both were hailed as the liberators of South America.

THE EFFORTS OF BOLÍVAR AND SAN MARTÍN Simón Bolívar has long been regarded as the George Washington of Latin America. Born into a wealthy Venezuelan family, he was introduced as a young man to the ideas of the Enlightenment. While in Rome in 1805 to witness the coronation of Napoleon as king of Italy, he committed himself to free his people from Spanish control. He vowed, "I swear before the God of my fathers, by my fathers themselves, by my honor and by my country, that my arm shall not rest nor my mind be at peace until I have broken the chains that bind me by the will and power of Spain."[2] When he returned to South America, Bolívar began to lead the bitter struggle for independence in Venezuela as well as other parts of northern South America. Although he was acclaimed as the "liberator" of Venezuela in 1813 by the people, it was not until 1821 that he definitively defeated Spanish forces there. He went on to liberate Colombia, Ecuador, and Peru. Already in 1819, he had become president of Venezuela, at the time part of a federation that included Colombia and Ecuador. Bolívar was well aware of the difficulties in establishing stable republican governments in Latin America (see the box on p. 520).

While Bolívar was busy liberating northern South America from the Spanish, José de San Martín was concentrating his efforts on the southern part of the continent. Son of a Spanish army officer in Argentina, San Martín himself went to Spain and pursued a military career in the Spanish army. In 1811, after serving twenty-two years, he learned of the liberation movement in his native Argentina, abandoned his military career in Spain, and returned to his homeland in March 1812. Argentina had already been freed from Spanish control, but San Martín believed that the Spaniards must be removed from all of South America if any nation was to remain free. In January 1817, he led his forces over the high Andes Mountains, an amazing feat in itself. Two-thirds of their pack mules and horses died during the difficult journey. Many of the soldiers suffered from lack of oxygen and severe cold while crossing mountain passes more than 2 miles above sea level. The arrival of San Martín's troops in Chile completely surprised the Spaniards, whose forces were routed at the Battle of Chacabuco (chahk-ah-BOO-koh) on February 12, 1817.

In 1821, San Martín moved on to Lima, Peru, the center of Spanish authority. Convinced that he would be unable to complete the liberation of all of Peru, San Martín welcomed the arrival of Bolívar and his forces. As he wrote to Bolívar, "For me it would have been the height of happiness to end the war of independence under the orders of a general to whom [South] America owes its freedom. Destiny orders it otherwise, and one must resign oneself to it."[3] Highly disappointed, San Martín left South America for Europe, where he remained until his death in 1850. Meanwhile, Bolívar took on the task of crushing the last significant Spanish army at Ayacucho (ah-ya-KOO-choh) on December 9, 1824. By then, Peru, Uruguay, Paraguay, Colombia, Venezuela, Argentina, Bolivia, and Chile had all become free states. In 1823, the Central American states became independent

Simón Bolívar on Government in Latin America

POLITICS & GOVERNMENT

Simón Bolívar is acclaimed as the man who liberated Latin America from Spanish control. His interest in history and the ideas of the Enlightenment also led him to speculate on how Latin American nations would be governed after their freedom was obtained. This selection is taken from a letter that he wrote to the British governor of Jamaica.

Simón Bolívar, *The Jamaica Letter*

It is . . . difficult to foresee the future fate of the New World, to set down its political principles, or to prophesy what manner of government it will adopt. . . . We inhabit a world apart, separated by broad seas. We are young in the ways of almost all the arts and sciences, although in a certain manner, we are old in the ways of civilized society. . . . But we scarcely retain a vestige of what once was; we are, moreover, neither Indian nor European, but a species midway between the legitimate proprietors of this country and the Spanish usurpers. In short, though Americans by birth we derive our rights from Europe, and we have to assert these rights against the rights of the natives, and at the same time we must defend ourselves against the invaders. This places us in a most extraordinary and involved situation. . . .

The role of the inhabitants of the American hemisphere has for centuries been purely passive. Politically they were nonexistent. We are still in a position lower than slavery, and therefore it is more difficult for us to rise to the enjoyment of freedom. . . . States are slaves because of either the nature or the misuse of their constitutions; a people is therefore enslaved when the government, by its nature or its vices, infringes on and usurps the rights of the citizen or subject. Applying these principles, we find that America was denied not only its freedom but even an active and effective tyranny. . . .

It is harder, Montesquieu has written, to release a nation from servitude than to enslave a free nation. This truth is proven by the annals of all times, which reveal that most free nations have been put under the yoke, but very few enslaved nations have recovered their liberty. Despite the convictions of history, South Americans have made efforts to obtain liberal, even perfect, institutions, doubtless out of that instinct to aspire to the greatest possible happiness, which, common to all men, is bound to follow in civil societies founded on the principles of justice, liberty, and equality. But are we capable of maintaining in proper balance the difficult charge of a republic? Is it conceivable that a newly emancipated people can soar to the heights of liberty . . . ? Such a marvel is inconceivable and without precedent. There is no reasonable probability to bolster our hopes.

More than anyone, I desire to see America fashioned into the greatest nation in the world, greatest not so much by virtue of her area and wealth as by her freedom and glory. Although I seek perfection for the government of my country, I cannot persuade myself that the New World can, at the moment, be organized as a great republic. Since it is impossible, I dare not desire it; yet much less do I desire to have all America a monarchy because this plan is not only impracticable but also impossible. Wrongs now existing could not be righted, and our emancipation would be fruitless. The American states need the care of paternal governments to heal the sores and wounds of despotism and war.

What problems did Bolívar foresee for Spanish America's political future? Do you think he believed in democracy? Why or why not?

Source: Simón Bolívar, *Selected Writings*, ed. H. A. Bierck, trans. L Berrand (New York, 1951), pp. 106, 108, 112–114.

and in 1838–1839 divided into five republics (Guatemala, El Salvador, Honduras, Costa Rica, and Nicaragua). Earlier, in 1822, the prince regent of Brazil had declared Brazil's independence from Portugal.

INDEPENDENCE AND THE MONROE DOCTRINE In the early 1820s, only one major threat remained to the newly won independence of the Latin American states. Reveling in their success in crushing rebellions in Spain and Italy, the victorious continental European powers favored the use of troops to restore Spanish control in Latin America. This time, Britain's opposition to intervention prevailed. Eager to gain access to an entire continent for investment and trade, the British proposed joint

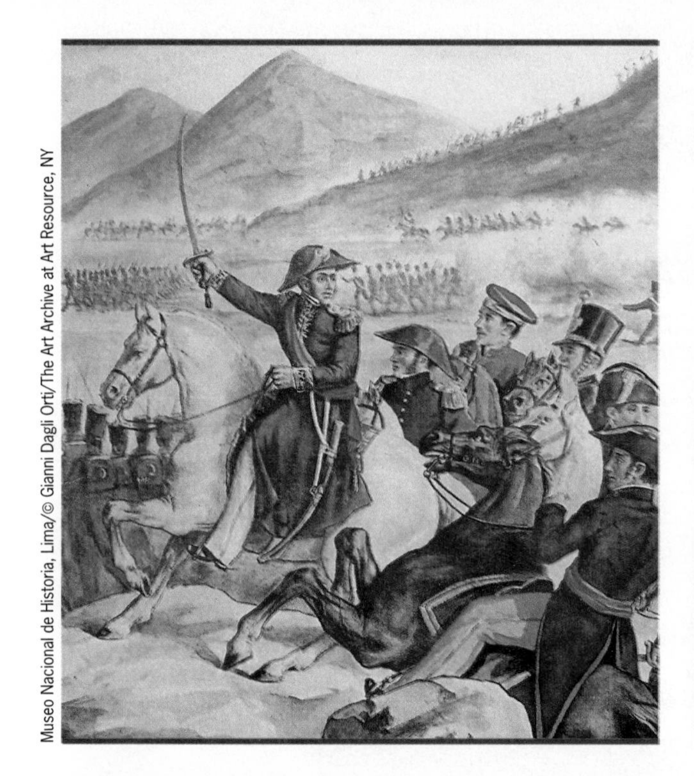

Museo Nacional de Historia, Lima/© Gianni Dagli Orti/The Art Archive at Art Resource, NY

© SuperStock

The Liberators of South America. José de San Martín and Simón Bolívar are hailed as the leaders of the South American independence movement. In the painting on the left, by Théodore Géricault (zhay-rih-KOH), a French Romantic painter, San Martín is shown leading his troops at the Battle of Chacabuco in Chile in 1817. The painting on the right shows Bolívar leading his troops across the Andes in 1823 to fight in Peru. This depiction of impeccably uniformed troops moving in perfect formation through the snow of the Andes, by the Chilean artist Franco Gomez, is, of course, highly unrealistic.

action with the United States against European interference in Latin America. Distrustful of British motives, President James Monroe acted alone in 1823, guaranteeing the independence of the new Latin American nations and warning against any further European intervention in the Americas under what is known as the Monroe Doctrine. Even more important to Latin American independence than American words was Britain's navy. All of the continental European powers were reluctant to challenge British naval power, which stood between Latin America and any European invasion force.

The Difficulties of Nation Building

As Simón Bolívar had foreseen, the new Latin American nations (see Map 20.1), most of which began as republics, faced a number of serious problems between 1830 and 1870. The wars for independence themselves had resulted in a staggering loss of population, property, and livestock. At the same time, disputes arose between nations over their precise boundaries.

POLITICAL DIFFICULTIES The new nations of Latin America established republican governments, but they had had no experience in ruling themselves. Due to the insecurities prevalent after independence, strong leaders known as **caudillos** (kah-DEEL-yohz *or* kow-THEEL-yohz) came to power. Caudillos at the national level were generally one of two types. One group, who supported the elites, consisted of autocrats who controlled (and often abused) state revenues, centralized power, and kept the new national states together. Sometimes they were also modernizers who built roads and canals, ports, and schools. These caudillos were usually supported by the Catholic Church, the rural aristocracy, and the army, which emerged from the wars of independence as a powerful political force that often made and deposed governments. Many caudillos, in fact, were former army leaders.

In contrast, other caudillos were supported by the masses, became extremely popular, and served as instruments for radical change. Juan Manuel de Rosas (WAHN mahn-WEL day ROH-sas), for example, who led

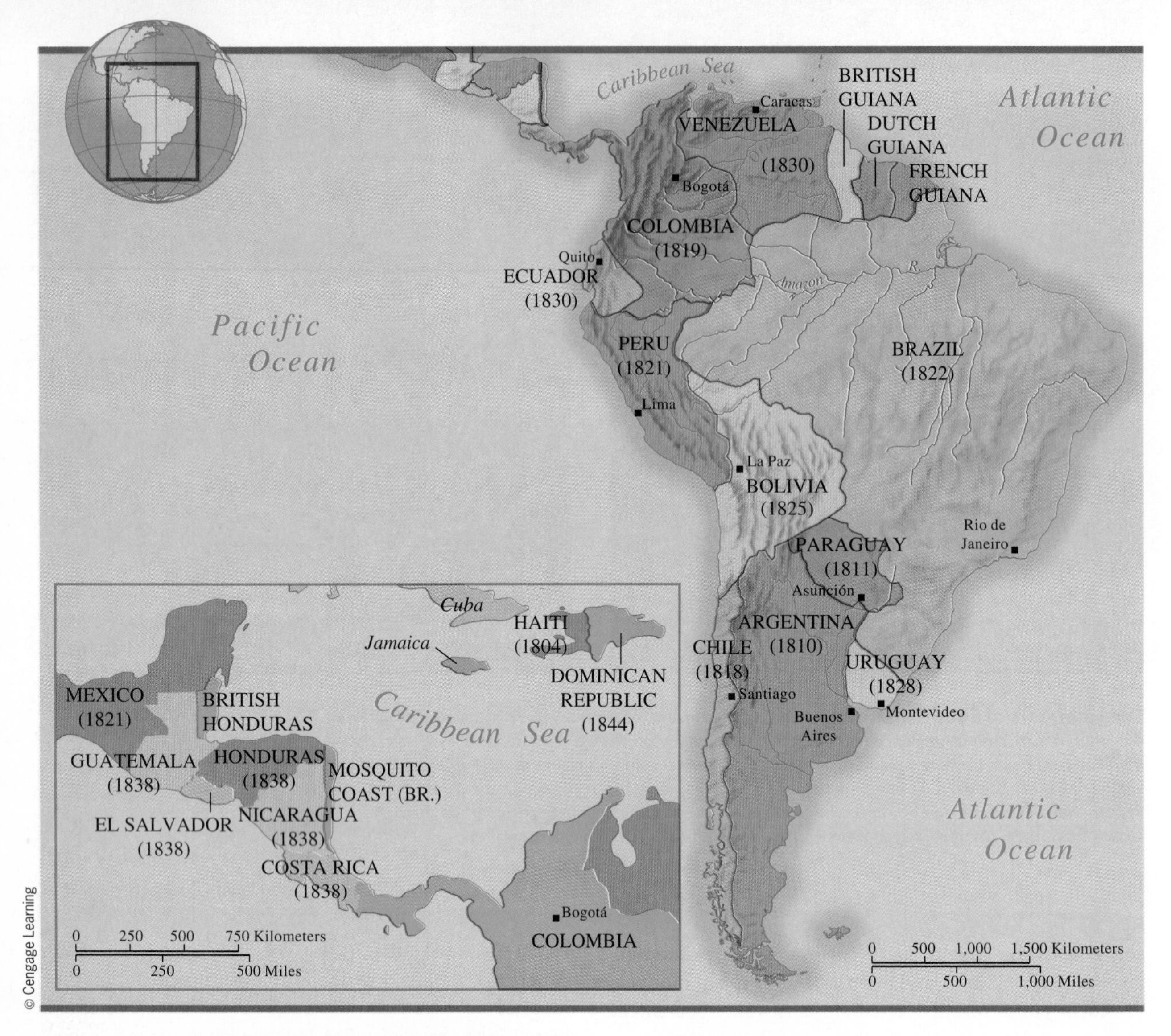

© Cengage Learning

MAP 20.1 Latin America in the First Half of the Nineteenth Century. Latin American colonies took advantage of Spain's weakness during the Napoleonic wars to fight for independence, beginning with Argentina in 1810 and spreading throughout the region over the next decade with the help of leaders like Simón Bolívar and José de San Martín.

How many South American countries are sources of rivers that feed the Amazon, and roughly what percentage of the continent is contained within the Amazon's watershed?

Argentina from 1829 to 1852, became very popular by favoring Argentine interests against foreigners.

ECONOMIC PATTERNS Although political independence brought economic independence, old patterns were quickly reestablished. Instead of Spain and Portugal, Great Britain now dominated the Latin American economy. British merchants arrived in large numbers, and British investors poured in funds, especially into the mining industry. Old trade patterns soon reemerged. Since Latin America served as a source of raw materials and foodstuffs for the industrializing nations of Europe and the United States, exports—especially wheat, tobacco, wool, sugar, coffee, and hides—to the North Atlantic countries increased noticeably. At the same time, finished consumer goods, especially textiles, were imported in increasing quantities, causing a decline in industrial production in Latin America. The emphasis on exporting raw materials and importing finished products ensured the ongoing domination of the Latin American economy by foreigners.

SOCIAL CONDITIONS A fundamental underlying problem for all of the new Latin American nations was the persistent domination of society by the landed elites. Large estates remained an important aspect of Latin America's economic and social life. After independence, the size of these estates expanded even more. By 1848, the Sánchez Navarro (SAHN-ches nuh-VAH-roh) family in Mexico owned seventeen haciendas (hah-see-EN-duhz), or plantations, covering 16 million acres. Estates were often so large that they could not be farmed efficiently. As one Latin American newspaper put it, "The huge fortunes have the unfortunate tendency to grow even larger, and their owners possess vast tracts of land, which lie fallow and abandoned. Their greed for land does not equal their ability to use it intelligently and actively."[4]

Land remained the basis of wealth, social prestige, and political power throughout the nineteenth century. The Latin American elites tended to identify with European standards of progress, which worked to their benefit, while the masses gained little. Landed elites ran governments, controlled courts, and maintained the system of debt peonage that provided large landowners with a supply of cheap labor. These landowners made enormous profits by concentrating on specialized crops for export, such as coffee, while the masses, left without land to grow basic food crops, lived in dire poverty.

Tradition and Change in the Latin American Economy and Society

After 1870, Latin America began to experience an era of rapid economic growth based to a large extent on the export of a few basic commodities, such as wheat and beef from Argentina, coffee from Brazil, nitrates from Chile, coffee and bananas from Central America, and sugar and silver from Peru. These foodstuffs and raw materials were exchanged for finished goods—textiles, machines, and luxury goods—from Europe and the United States. Despite their economic growth, Latin American nations remained economic colonies of Western nations.

Old patterns also still largely prevailed in society. Rural elites dominated their estates and their workers. Although slavery was abolished by 1888, former slaves and their descendants were at the bottom of their society. The Indians remained poverty-stricken.

One result of the new prosperity that came from increased exports was growth in the middle sectors of Latin American society—lawyers, merchants, shopkeepers, businesspeople, schoolteachers, professors, bureaucrats, and military officers. These middle sectors, which made up only 5 to 10 percent of the population, depending on the country, were hardly large enough in numbers to constitute a true middle class. Nevertheless, after 1900, the middle sectors continued to expand. They lived in the cities, sought education and decent incomes, and increasingly saw the United States as the model to emulate, especially in regard to industrialization and education.

As Latin American exports increased, so did the working class, and that in turn led to the growth of labor unions, especially after 1914. Radical unions often advocated the use of the general strike as an instrument for change. By and large, however, the governing elites succeeded in stifling the political influence of the working class by restricting workers' right to vote.

The need for industrial labor also led Latin American countries to encourage immigration from Europe. Between 1880 and 1914, 3 million Europeans, primarily Italians and Spaniards, settled in Argentina. More than 100,000 Europeans, mostly Italian, Portuguese, and Spanish, arrived in Brazil each year between 1891 and 1900.

As in Europe and the United States, industrialization led to urbanization, evident in both the emergence of new cities and the rapid growth of old ones. Buenos Aires (the "Paris" of South America) had 750,000 inhabitants by 1900 and 2 million by 1914—a fourth of Argentina's population.

Political Change in Latin America

Latin America also experienced a political transformation after 1870. Large landowners began to take a more direct interest in national politics and even in governing. In Argentina and Chile, for example, landholding elites controlled the governments, and although they produced constitutions similar to those of the United States and European nations, they ensured that they would maintain power by restricting voting rights.

In some countries, large landowners supported dictators who would protect their interests. José de la Cruz Porfirio Díaz (hoh-SAY day lah KROOZ por-FEER-yoh DEE-ahs) (1830–1915), who ruled Mexico from 1876 to 1910, created a conservative, centralized government with the support of the army, foreign capitalists, large landowners, and the Catholic Church. Nevertheless, there were forces for change in Mexico that led to revolution in 1910.

During Díaz's dictatorial regime, the real wages of the working class declined. Moreover, 95 percent of the rural population owned no land, while about a thousand families owned almost all of Mexico. When a liberal landowner, Francisco Madero (frahn-SEES-koh muh-DERR-oh) (1873–1913), forced Díaz from power, he opened the door to a wider revolution. Madero's ineffectiveness triggered a demand for agrarian reform led by

CHRONOLOGY Latin America	
Revolt in Mexico	1810
Bolívar and San Martín free most of South America	1810–1824
Augustín de Iturbide becomes emperor of Mexico	1821
Brazil gains independence from Portugal	1822
Monroe Doctrine	1823
Rule of Porfirio Díaz in Mexico	1876–1910
Mexican Revolution begins	1910

Emiliano Zapata (eh-mee-LYAH-noh zup-PAH-tuh) (1873–1919), who aroused the masses of landless peasants and began to seize the estates of the wealthy landholders. The ensuing revolution caused untold destruction to the Mexican economy. Finally, a new constitution in 1917 established a strong presidency, initiated land reform policies, established limits on foreign investors, and set an agenda for social welfare for workers.

© Snark/Art Resource, NY

Emiliano Zapata. The inability of Francisco Madero to carry out far-reaching reforms led to a more radical upheaval in the Mexican countryside. Emiliano Zapata led a band of Indians in a revolt against the large landowners of southern Mexico and issued his own demands for land reform.

By this time, a new power had begun to wield its influence over Latin America. By 1900, the United States, which had begun to emerge as a great world power, began to interfere in the affairs of its southern neighbors. As a result of the Spanish-American War (1898), Cuba became a U.S. protectorate, and Puerto Rico was annexed outright by the United States. American investments in Latin America soon followed; so did American resolve to protect these investments. Between 1898 and 1934, American military forces were sent to Cuba, Mexico, Guatemala, Honduras, Nicaragua, Panama, Colombia, Haiti, and the Dominican Republic to protect American interests. At the same time, the United States became the chief foreign investor in Latin America.

The North American Neighbors: The United States and Canada

Q FOCUS QUESTIONS: What role did nationalism and liberalism play in the United States and Canada between 1800 and 1870? What economic, social, and political trends were evident in the United States and Canada between 1870 and 1914?

Whereas Latin America had been colonized by Spain and Portugal, the colonies established in North America were part of the British Empire and thus differed in various ways from their southern neighbors. Although they gained their freedom from the British at different times, both the United States and Canada emerged as independent and prosperous nations whose political systems owed much to British political thought. In the nineteenth century, both the United States and Canada faced difficult obstacles in achieving national unity.

The Growth of the United States

The U.S. Constitution, ratified in 1789, committed the United States to two of the major influences of the first half of the nineteenth century, liberalism and nationalism. Initially, this constitutional commitment to national unity was challenged by divisions over the power of the federal government versus the individual states. A strong force for national unity came from the Supreme Court while John Marshall (1755–1835) was chief justice from 1801 to 1835. Marshall made the Supreme Court into an important national institution by asserting the right of the Court to overrule an act of Congress if the Court found it to be in violation of the Constitution. Under Marshall, the Supreme Court contributed further to establishing the supremacy of the national government by curbing the actions of state courts and legislatures.

The election of Andrew Jackson (1767–1845) as president in 1828 opened a new era in American politics, the era of mass democracy. The electorate was expanded by dropping property qualifications; by the 1830s, suffrage had been extended to almost all adult white males. During the period from 1815 to 1850, the traditional liberal belief in the improvement of human beings was also given concrete expression through the establishment of detention schools for juvenile delinquents and new penal institutions, both motivated by the liberal belief that the right kind of environment would rehabilitate wayward individuals.

SLAVERY AND THE COMING OF WAR By the mid-nineteenth century, however, American national unity was increasingly threatened by the issue of slavery. Both North and South had grown dramatically in population during the first half of the nineteenth century, but in different ways. The cotton economy and social structure of the South were based on the exploitation of enslaved black Africans and their descendants. Although the importation of new slaves had been barred in 1808, there were 4 million slaves in the South by 1860—four times the number sixty years earlier. The cotton economy depended on plantation-based slavery, and the South was determined to maintain its slaves. In the North, many people feared the spread of slavery into western territories. The issue first arose in the 1810s as new states were being created by the rush of settlers beyond the Mississippi. The free states of the North feared the prospect of a slave-state majority in the national government.

As polarization over the issue of slavery intensified, compromise became less feasible. When Abraham Lincoln, the man who had said in a speech in Illinois in 1858 that "this government cannot endure permanently half slave and half free," was elected president in November 1860, the die was cast. Lincoln, the Republicans' second presidential candidate, carried only 2 of the 1,109 counties in the South; the Republican Party was not even on the ballot in ten southern states. On December 20, 1860, a South Carolina convention voted to repeal the state's ratification of the U.S. Constitution. In February 1861, six more southern states did the same, and a rival nation, the Confederate States of America, was formed. In April, fighting erupted between North and South.

THE CIVIL WAR The American Civil War (1861–1865) was an extraordinarily bloody struggle, a foretaste of the total war to come in the twentieth century. More than 600,000 soldiers died, either in battle or from deadly infectious diseases spawned by filthy camp conditions. The northern, or Union, forces enjoyed a formidable advantage in numbers of troops and material resources, but to southerners, those assets were not decisive. As they saw it, the Confederacy only had to defend the South from invasion, whereas the Union had to conquer the South. Southerners also believed that the dependence of manufacturers in the North and the European countries on southern raw cotton would lead to antiwar sentiment in the North and support abroad for the South.

All these southern calculations meant little in the long run. Over a period of four years, the Union states of the North mobilized their superior assets and gradually wore down the Confederate forces of the South. As the war dragged on, it had the effect of radicalizing public opinion in the North. What began as a war to save the Union became a war against slavery. On January 1, 1863, Lincoln issued his Emancipation Proclamation, declaring most of the nation's slaves "forever free" (see the box on p. 510 in Chapter 19). An increasingly effective Union blockade of the ports of the South, combined with a shortage of fighting men, made the Confederate cause desperate by the end of 1864. The final push of Union troops under General Ulysses S. Grant forced General Robert E. Lee's Confederate Army to surrender on April 9, 1865. Although problems lay ahead, the Union victory reunited the country and confirmed that the United States would thereafter again be "one nation, indivisible."

The Rise of the United States

Four years of bloody civil war had restored American national unity. The old South had been destroyed; one-fifth of its adult white male population had been killed, and 4 million black slaves had been freed. For a while at least, a program of radical change in the South was attempted. Slavery was formally abolished by the Thirteenth Amendment to the Constitution in 1865, and the Fourteenth and Fifteenth Amendments extended citizenship to blacks and gave black men the right to vote. Radical Reconstruction in the early 1870s tried to create a new South based on the principle of the equality of black and white people, but the changes were soon mostly undone. Militia organizations, such as the Ku Klux Klan, used violence to discourage blacks from voting. A new system of sharecropping made blacks once again economically dependent on white landowners. New state laws made it nearly impossible for blacks to exercise their right to vote. By the end of the 1870s, supporters of white supremacy were back in power everywhere in the South.

© Peter Newark Military Pictures/The Bridgeman Art Library

The Dead at Antietam. National unity in the United States dissolved over the issue of slavery and led to a bloody civil war that cost 600,000 American lives. This photograph shows the southern dead after the Battle of Antietam on September 17, 1862. The invention of photography in the 1830s made it possible to document the horrors of war in the most graphic manner.

PROSPERITY AND PROGRESSIVISM Between 1860 and 1914, the United States made the shift from an agrarian to a mighty industrial nation. American heavy industry stood unchallenged in 1900. In that year, the Carnegie Steel Company alone produced more steel than Great Britain's entire steel industry. Industrialization also led to urbanization. Whereas 20 percent of Americans lived in cities in 1860, more than 40 percent did in 1900. Four-fifths of the population growth came from migration. Eight to 10 million Americans moved from rural areas into the cities, and 14 million foreigners came from abroad.

The United States had become the world's richest nation and greatest industrial power. Yet serious questions remained about the quality of American life. In 1890, the richest 9 percent of Americans owned an incredible 71 percent of all the wealth. Labor unrest over unsafe working conditions, strict work discipline, and periodic cycles of devastating unemployment led workers to organize. By the turn of the century, one national organization, the American Federation of Labor, had emerged as labor's dominant voice. Its lack of real power, however, was reflected in its membership figures. In 1900, it included only 8.4 percent of the American industrial labor force.

During the so-called Progressive Era after 1900, reform swept the United States. Efforts to improve living conditions in the cities included attempts to eliminate corrupt machine politics. At the state level, reforming governors sought to achieve clean government by introducing elements of direct democracy, such as direct primaries for selecting nominees for public office. State governments also enacted economic and social legislation, such as laws that governed hours, wages, and working conditions, especially for women and children.

State laws were ineffective in dealing with nationwide problems, however, and a Progressive movement soon developed at the national level. The Meat Inspection Act and Pure Food and Drug Act of 1906 provided for a limited degree of federal regulation of industrial practices. The presidency of Woodrow Wilson (1913–1921) witnessed the enactment of a graduated federal income tax and the establishment of the Federal Reserve System, which permitted the national government to play a role in important economic decisions formerly made by bankers. Like European nations, the United States was slowly adopting policies that broadened the functions of the state.

THE UNITED STATES AS A WORLD POWER At the end of the nineteenth century, the United States began to expand abroad. The Samoan Islands in the Pacific became the first important American colony; the Hawaiian Islands were next. By 1887, American settlers had gained control of the sugar industry on the Hawaiian Islands. As more Americans settled in Hawaii, they sought political power. When Queen Liliuokalani (LIL-ee-uh-woh-kuh-LAH-nee) (1838–1917) tried to strengthen the monarchy in order to keep the islands for the Hawaiian people, the U.S. government sent Marines to "protect" American lives. The queen was deposed, and Hawaii was annexed by the United States in 1898.

The defeat of Spain in the Spanish-American War in 1898 expanded the American empire to include Cuba, Puerto Rico, Guam, and the Philippines. Although the Filipinos appealed for independence, the Americans refused to grant it. As President William McKinley said, the United States had a duty "to educate the Filipinos and uplift and Christianize them," a remarkable statement in view of the fact that most of them had been Roman Catholics for centuries. It took three years and 60,000 troops to pacify the Philippines and establish U.S. control. By the beginning of the twentieth century, the United States had become another Western imperialist power.

The Making of Canada

North of the United States, the process of nation building was also making progress. Under the Treaty of Paris in 1763, Canada—or New France, as it was called—passed into the hands of the British. By 1800, most Canadians favored more autonomy, although the colonists disagreed on the form this autonomy should take. Upper Canada (now Ontario) was predominantly English speaking, whereas Lower Canada (now Quebec) was dominated by French Canadians. A dramatic increase in immigration to Canada from Great Britain (almost one million immigrants between 1815 and 1850) also fueled the desire for self-government.

In 1837, a number of Canadian groups rose in rebellion against British authority. Although the rebellions were crushed by the following year, the British government now began to seek ways to satisfy some of the Canadian demands. The U.S. Civil War proved to be a turning point. Fearful of American designs on Canada during the war, the British government finally capitulated to Canadian demands. In 1867, Parliament established the Dominion of Canada, with its own constitution. Canada now possessed a parliamentary system and ruled itself, although foreign affairs still remained under the control of the British government.

Canada faced problems of national unity between 1870 and 1914. At the beginning of 1870, the Dominion of Canada had only four provinces: Quebec, Ontario, Nova Scotia, and New Brunswick. With the addition of two more provinces in 1871—Manitoba and British Columbia—the Dominion now extended from the Atlantic Ocean to the Pacific. As the first prime minister, John Macdonald (1815–1891) moved to strengthen Canadian unity. He pushed for the construction of a transcontinental railroad, which was completed in 1885 and opened the western lands to industrial and commercial development. This also led to the incorporation of two more provinces—Alberta and Saskatchewan—into the Dominion of Canada in 1905.

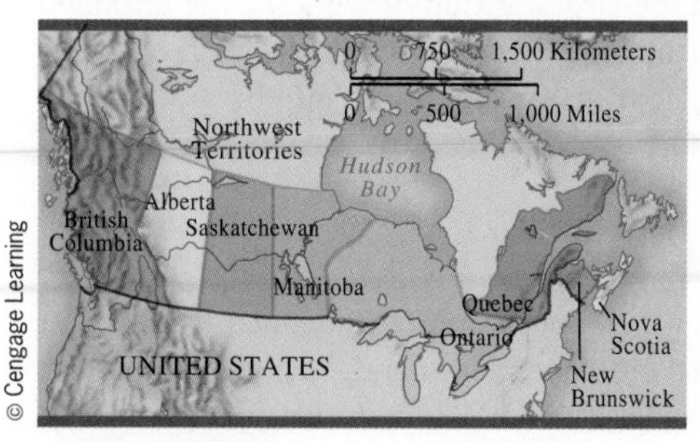

© Cengage Learning

Canada, 1914

CHRONOLOGY The United States and Canada	
United States	
Election of Andrew Jackson	1828
Election of Abraham Lincoln and secession of South Carolina	1860
Civil War	1861–1865
Lincoln's Emancipation Proclamation	1863
Surrender of Robert E. Lee's Confederate Army	April 9, 1865
Spanish-American War	1898
Presidency of Woodrow Wilson	1913–1921
Canada	
Rebellions	1837–1838
Formation of the Dominion of Canada	1867
Transcontinental railroad	1885
Wilfred Laurier as prime minister	1896

Real unity was difficult to achieve, however, because of the distrust between the English-speaking majority and the French-speaking Canadians living primarily in Quebec. Wilfred Laurier (LOR-ee-ay), who became the first French Canadian prime minister in 1896, was able to reconcile Canada's two major groups and resolve the issue of separate schools for French Canadians. During Laurier's administration, industrialization boomed, especially the production of textiles, furniture, and railway equipment. Hundreds of thousands of immigrants, primarily from central and eastern Europe, also flowed into Canada. Many settled on lands in the west, thus helping populate Canada's vast territories.

The Emergence of Mass Society

FOCUS QUESTION: What is meant by the term *mass society*, and what were its main characteristics?

While new states were developing in the Western Hemisphere in the nineteenth century, a new kind of society—a **mass society**—was emerging in Europe, especially in the second half of the nineteenth century, as a result of rapid economic and social changes. For the lower classes, mass society brought voting rights, an improved standard of living, and access to education. At the same time, however, mass society also made possible the development of organizations that manipulated the populations of the **nation-states**. To understand this mass society, we need to examine some aspects of its structure.

The New Urban Environment

One of the most important consequences of industrialization and the population explosion of the nineteenth century was urbanization. In the course of the nineteenth century, more and more people came to live in cities. In 1800, city dwellers constituted 40 percent of the population in Britain, 25 percent in France and Germany, and only 10 percent in eastern Europe. By 1914, urban residents had increased to 80 percent of the population in Britain, 45 percent in France, 60 percent in Germany, and 30 percent in eastern Europe. The size of cities also expanded dramatically, especially in industrialized countries. Between 1800 and 1900, London's population grew from 960,000 to 6.5 million and Berlin's from 172,000 to 2.7 million.

Urban populations grew faster than the general population primarily because of the vast migration from rural areas to cities. But cities also grew faster in the second half of the nineteenth century because health and living conditions were improving as urban reformers and city officials used new technology to improve urban life. Following the reformers' advice, city governments set up boards of health to improve the quality of housing and instituted regulations requiring all new buildings to have running water and internal drainage systems.

Middle-class reformers also focused on the housing needs of the working class. Overcrowded, disease-ridden slums were seen as dangerous not only to physical health but also to the political and moral health of the entire nation. V. A. Huber, a German housing reformer, wrote in 1861: "Certainly it would not be too much to say that the home is the communal embodiment of family life. Thus, the purity of the dwelling is almost as important for the family as is the cleanliness of the body for the individual."[5] To Huber, good housing was a prerequisite for stable family life, and without stable family life, society would fall apart.

Early efforts to attack the housing problem emphasized the middle-class, liberal belief in the power of private enterprise. By the 1880s, as the number and size of cities continued to mushroom, governments concluded that private enterprise could not solve the housing crisis. In 1890, a British law empowered local town councils to construct cheap housing for the working classes. More and more, governments were stepping into areas of activity that they would not have touched earlier.

The Social Structure of Mass Society

At the top of European society stood a wealthy elite, constituting but 5 percent of the population while controlling between 30 and 40 percent of its wealth. In the course of the nineteenth century, landed aristocrats had joined with the most successful industrialists, bankers, and merchants (the wealthy upper middle class) to form a new elite. Marriage also united the two groups. Daughters of business tycoons gained titles, while aristocratic heirs gained new sources of cash. Members of this elite, whether aristocratic or middle class in background, assumed leadership roles in government bureaucracies and military hierarchies.

The middle classes included a variety of groups. Below the upper middle class was a group that included lawyers, doctors, and members of the civil service, as well as business managers, engineers, architects, accountants, and chemists benefiting from industrial expansion. Beneath this solid and comfortable middle group was a lower middle class of small shopkeepers, traders, manufacturers, and prosperous peasants.

Standing between the lower middle class and the lower classes were new groups of white-collar workers who were the product of the Second Industrial Revolution. They were the salespeople, bookkeepers, bank tellers, telephone operators, and secretaries. Though often paid little more than skilled laborers, these white-collar workers were committed to middle-class ideals of hard work, Christian morality, and propriety.

Below the middle classes on the social scale were the working classes, who constituted almost 80 percent of the European population. Many of them were landholding peasants, agricultural laborers, and sharecroppers, especially in eastern Europe. The urban working class included skilled artisans in such traditional trades as cabinetmaking, printing, and jewelry making, along with semiskilled laborers, such as carpenters, bricklayers, and many factory workers. At the bottom of the urban working class stood the largest group of workers, the unskilled laborers. They included day laborers, who worked irregularly for very low wages, and large numbers of domestic servants, most of whom were women.

The Experiences of Women

In the nineteenth century, women remained legally inferior, economically dependent, and largely defined by family and household roles. Women struggled to change their status throughout the century.

MARRIAGE AND THE FAMILY Many women in the nineteenth century aspired to the ideal of femininity popularized by writers and poets. Alfred Lord Tennyson's poem *The Princess* expressed it well:

> *Man for the field and woman for the hearth:*
> *Man for the sword and for the needle she:*
> *Man with the head and woman with the heart:*
> *Man to command and woman to obey;*
> *All else confusion.*

This traditional characterization of the sexes, based on socially defined gender roles, was elevated to the status of universal male and female attributes in the nineteenth century. As the chief family wage earners, men worked outside the home for pay, while women were left with the care of the family, for which they were paid nothing. For most of the century, marriage was viewed as the only honorable career available to most women.

The most significant development in the modern family was the decline in the number of offspring born to the average woman. While some historians attribute the decline to more widespread use of coitus interruptus, or male withdrawal before ejaculation, others have emphasized female control of family size through abortion and even infanticide or abandonment. That a change in attitude occurred was apparent in the development of a movement to increase awareness of birth control methods. Europe's first birth control clinic opened in Amsterdam in 1882.

The family was the central institution of middle-class life. Men provided the family income while women focused on household and child care. The use of domestic servants in many middle-class homes, made possible by an abundant supply of cheap labor, reduced the amount of time middle-class women had to spend on household chores. At the same time, by reducing the number of children in the family, mothers could devote more time to child care and domestic leisure.

The middle-class family fostered an ideal of togetherness. The Victorians created the family Christmas with its Yule log, Christmas tree, songs, and exchange of gifts. In the United States, Fourth of July celebrations changed from drunken revels to family picnics by the 1850s.

Women in working-class families were more accustomed to hard work. Daughters in working-class families were expected to work until they married; even after marriage, they often did piecework at home to help support the family. For the children of the working classes, childhood was over by the age of nine or ten, when they became apprentices or were employed at odd jobs.

Between 1890 and 1914, however, family patterns among the working class began to change. High-paying jobs in heavy industry and improvements in the standard of living made it possible for working-class families to depend on the income of husbands and the wages of grown children. By the early twentieth century, some working-class mothers could afford to stay at home, following the pattern of middle-class women.

© Harrogate Museums and Arts, UK/The Bridgeman Art Library

A Middle-Class Family. Nineteenth-century middle-class moralists considered the family the fundamental pillar of a healthy society. The family was a crucial institution in middle-class life, and togetherness constituted one of the important ideals of the middle-class family. This painting by William P. Frith, titled *Many Happy Returns of the Day*, shows a family birthday celebration for a little girl in which grandparents, parents, and children are taking part. The servant at the left holds the presents for the little girl.

THE MOVEMENT FOR WOMEN'S RIGHTS Modern European feminism, or the movement for women's rights, had its beginnings during the French Revolution, when some women advocated equality for women based on the doctrine of natural rights. In the 1830s, a number of women in the United States and Europe, who worked together in several reform movements, argued for the right of women to divorce and own property. These early efforts were not overly successful; women did not gain the right to their own property until 1870 in Britain, 1900 in Germany and 1907 in France.

Divorce and property rights were only a beginning for the women's movement, however. Some middle- and upper-middle-class women gained access to higher education, and others sought entry into occupations dominated by men. The first to fall was teaching. As medical training was largely closed to women, they sought alternatives in the development of nursing. Nursing pioneers included the British nurse Florence Nightingale, whose efforts during the Crimean War (1854–1856), along with those of Clara Barton in the American Civil War (1861–1865), transformed nursing into a profession of trained, middle-class "women in white."

By the 1840s and 1850s, the movement for women's rights had entered the political arena with the call for equal political rights. Many feminists believed that the right to vote was the key to all other reforms to improve the position of women. **Suffragists** had one basic aim: the right of women to full citizenship in the nation-state.

The British women's movement was the most vocal and active in Europe. In 1903, Emmeline Pankhurst (PANK-hurst) (1858–1928) and her daughters, Christabel and Sylvia, founded the Women's Social and Political Union, which enrolled mostly middle- and upper-class women. The members of Pankhurst's organization realized the value of the media and staged unusual publicity stunts to call attention to their demands. Derisively labeled "suffragettes" by male politicians, they pelted government officials with eggs, chained themselves to lampposts, smashed the windows of department stores on fashionable shopping streets, burned railroad cars, and went on hunger strikes in jail.

Before World War I, the demands for women's rights were being heard throughout Europe and the United States, although only in Norway and some American states did women receive the right to vote before 1914. It would take the dramatic upheaval of World War I before male-dominated governments capitulated on this basic issue. At the same time, at the turn of the twentieth century, a number of "new women" became prominent. These women rejected traditional feminine roles (see the box on p. 531) and sought new freedom outside the household and new roles other than those of wives and mothers.

Education in an Age of Mass Society

Education in the early nineteenth century was primarily for the elite or the wealthier middle class, but between 1870 and 1914, most Western governments began to offer at least primary education to both boys and girls between the ages of six and twelve. States also assumed responsibility for better training of teachers by establishing teacher-training schools. By the beginning of the twentieth century, many European states, especially in northern and western Europe, were providing state-financed primary schools, salaried and trained teachers, and free, compulsory elementary education.

Why did Western nations make this commitment to **mass education**? One reason was industrialization. The new firms of the Second Industrial Revolution demanded skilled labor. Both boys and girls with an elementary education had new possibilities of jobs beyond their villages or small towns, including white-collar jobs in railways and subways, post offices, banking and shipping firms, teaching, and nursing. Mass education furnished the trained workers industrialists needed. For most students, elementary education led to apprenticeship and a job.

The chief motive for mass education, however, was political. The expansion of suffrage created the need for a more educated electorate. In parts of Europe where the Catholic Church remained in control of education, implementing a mass education system reduced the influence of the church over the electorate. Even more important, however, mass compulsory education instilled patriotism and nationalized the masses, providing an opportunity for even greater national integration. As people lost their ties to local regions and even to religion, nationalism supplied a new faith (see the comparative essay "The Rise of Nationalism" on p. 533).

Compulsory elementary education created a demand for teachers, and most of them were women. Many men viewed the teaching of children as an extension of women's "natural role" as nurturers of children. Moreover, females were paid lower salaries, in itself a considerable incentive for governments to encourage the establishment of teacher-training institutes for women. The first female colleges were really teacher-training schools. It was not until the beginning of the twentieth century that women were permitted to enter the male-dominated universities.

Leisure in an Age of Mass Society

With the Industrial Revolution came new forms of leisure. Work and leisure became opposites as leisure came to be viewed as what people do for fun after work. The new leisure hours created by the industrial system—evening hours after work, weekends, and eventually a week or two in the summer—largely determined the contours of the new **mass leisure**.

New technology created novel experiences for leisure, such as the Ferris wheel at amusement parks, while the subways and streetcars of the 1880s meant that even the working classes were no longer dependent on neighborhood facilities but could make their way to athletic games, amusement parks, and dance halls. Railroads could take people to the beaches on weekends.

By the late nineteenth century, team sports had also developed into another important form of mass leisure. Unlike the old rural games, which were spontaneous and

OPPOSING VIEWPOINTS

Advice to Women: Two Views

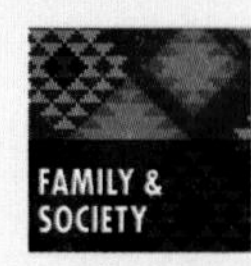

Industrialization had a strong impact on middle-class women as strict gender-based social roles became the norm. Men worked outside the home to support the family, while women provided for the needs of their children and husband at home. In the first selection, *Woman in Her Social and Domestic Character* (1842), Elizabeth Poole Sanford gives advice to middle-class women on their proper role and behavior.

Although a majority of women probably followed the nineteenth-century middle-class ideal, an increasing number of women fought for women's rights. The second selection is taken from the third act of Henrik Ibsen's 1879 play *A Doll's House*, in which the character Nora Helmer declares her independence from her husband's control.

Elizabeth Poole Sanford, *Woman in Her Social and Domestic Character*

The changes wrought by Time are many. . . .

It is thus that the sentiment for woman has undergone a change. The romantic passion which once almost deified her is on the decline; and it is by intrinsic qualities that she must now inspire respect. She is no longer the queen of song and the star of chivalry. But if there is less of enthusiasm entertained for her, the sentiment is more rational, and, perhaps, equally sincere; for it is in relation to happiness that she is chiefly appreciated.

And in this respect it is, we must confess, that she is most useful and most important. Domestic life is the chief source of her influence; and the greatest debt society can owe to her is domestic comfort. . . .
A woman may make a man's home delightful, and may thus increase his motives for virtuous exertion. She may refine and tranquilize his mind—may turn away his anger or allay his grief. Her smile may be the happy influence to gladden his heart, and to disperse the cloud that gathers on his brow. And in proportion to her endeavors to make those around her happy, she will be esteemed and loved. She will secure by her excellence that interest and that regard which she might formerly claim as the privilege of her sex, and will really merit the deference which was then conceded to her as a matter of course. . . .

Nothing is so likely to conciliate the affections of the other sex as a feeling that woman looks to them for support and guidance. In proportion as men are themselves superior, they are accessible to this appeal. On the contrary, they never feel interested in one who seems disposed rather to offer than to ask assistance. There is, indeed, something unfeminine in independence. It is contrary to nature, and therefore it offends. We do not like to see a woman affecting tremors, but still less do we like to see her acting the amazon. A really sensible woman feels her dependence. She does what she can; but she is conscious of inferiority, and therefore grateful for support. She knows that she is the weaker vessel, and that as such she should receive honor. In this view, her weakness is an attraction, not a blemish.

Henrik Ibsen, *A Doll's House*

NORA: Yes, it's true, Torvald. When I was living at home with Father, he told me his opinions and mine were the same. If I had different opinions, I said nothing about them, because he would not have liked it. He used to call me his doll-child and played with me as I played with my dolls. Then I came to live in your house.

HELMER: What a way to speak of our marriage!

NORA *(Undisturbed)*: I mean that I passed from Father's hands into yours. You arranged everything to your taste and I got the same tastes as you; or pretended to—I don't know which—both, perhaps; sometimes one, sometimes the other. When I look back on it now, I seem to have been living here like a beggar, on handouts. I lived by performing tricks for you, Torvald. . . . I must stand quite alone if I am ever to know myself and my surroundings; so I cannot stay with you.

HELMER: You are mad! I shall not allow it! I forbid it!

NORA: It's no use your forbidding me anything now. I shall take with me only what belongs to me; from you I will accept nothing, either now or later. . . .

HELMER: Forsake your home, your husband, your children! And you don't consider what the world will say.

NORA: I can't pay attention to that. I only know that I must do it.

(Continued)

(*Opposing Viewpoints Continued*)

HELMER: This is monstrous! Can you forsake your holiest duties?
NORA: What do you consider my holiest duties?
HELMER: Need I tell you that? Your duties to your husband and children.
NORA: I have other duties equally sacred.
HELMER: Impossible! What do you mean?
NORA: My duties toward myself.
HELMER: Before all else you are a wife and a mother.
NORA: That I no longer believe. Before all else I believe I am a human being just as much as you are—or at least that I should try to become one. I know that most people agree with you, Torvald, and that they say so in books. But I can no longer be satisfied with what most people say and what is in books. I must think things out for myself and try to get clear about them.

According to Elizabeth Sanford, what is the proper role of women? What forces in nineteenth-century European society merged to shape Sanford's understanding of "proper" gender roles? In Ibsen's play, what challenges does Nora Helmer make to Sanford's view of the proper role and behavior of wives? Why is her husband so shocked? Why did Ibsen title this play A Doll's House*?*

Sources: Elizabeth Poole Sanford, *Woman in Her Social and Domestic Character*. From Elizabeth Poole Sanford, *Woman in Her Social and Domestic Character* (Boston: Otis, Broaders & Co., 1842), pp. 5–7, 15–16. Henrik Ibsen, *A Doll's House*. From Henrik Ibsen, *A Doll's House*, Act III, 1879, as printed in *Roots of Western Civilization* by Wesley D. Camp, John Wiley & Sons, 1983.

often chaotic activities, the new sports were strictly organized with sets of rules and officials to enforce them. These rules were the products of organized athletic groups, such as the English Football Association (1863) and the American Bowling Congress (1895). The development of urban transportation systems made possible the construction of stadiums where thousands could attend, making mass spectator sports into a big business.

Cultural Life: Romanticism and Realism in the Western World

FOCUS QUESTION: What were the main characteristics of Romanticism and Realism?

At the end of the eighteenth century, a new intellectual movement known as **Romanticism** emerged to challenge the ideas of the Enlightenment. The Enlightenment stressed reason as the chief means for discovering truth. Although the Romantics by no means disparaged reason, they tried to balance its use by stressing the importance of feeling, emotion, and imagination as sources of knowing.

The Characteristics of Romanticism

Many Romantics had a passionate interest in the past. They revived medieval Gothic architecture and left European countrysides adorned with pseudo-medieval castles and cities bedecked with grandiose neo-Gothic cathedrals, city halls, and parliamentary buildings. Literature, too, reflected this historical consciousness. The novels of Walter Scott (1771–1832) became European best-sellers in the first half of the nineteenth century. *Ivanhoe*, in which Scott sought to evoke the clash between Saxon and Norman knights in medieval England, became one of his most popular works.

Many Romantics also had a deep attraction to the exotic and unfamiliar. In an exaggerated form, this preoccupation gave rise to so-called **Gothic literature**, chillingly evident in Mary Shelley's *Frankenstein* and Edgar Allan Poe's short stories of horror (see the box on p. 534). Some Romantics even tried to bring the unusual into their own lives by experimenting with cocaine, opium, and hashish to achieve drug-induced altered states of consciousness.

To the Romantics, poetry was the direct expression of the soul and therefore ranked above all other literary forms. Romantic poetry gave full expression to one of the most important characteristics of Romanticism: love of nature, especially evident in the poetry of William Wordsworth (1770–1850). His experience of nature was almost mystical as he claimed to receive "authentic tidings of invisible things":

One impulse from a vernal wood
May teach you more of man,
Of Moral Evil and of good,
Than all the sages can.[6]

Romantics believed that nature served as a mirror into which humans could look to learn about themselves.

COMPARATIVE ESSAY

The Rise of Nationalism

Like the Industrial Revolution, the concept of nationalism originated in eighteenth-century Europe, where it was the product of a variety of factors, including the spread of printing and the replacement of Latin with vernacular languages, the secularization of the age, and the experience of the French revolutionary and Napoleonic eras. The French were the first to show what a nation in arms could accomplish, but peoples conquered by Napoleon soon created their own national armies. At the beginning of the nineteenth century, peoples who had previously focused their identity on a locality or a region, on loyalty to a monarch or to a particular religious faith, now shifted their political allegiance to the idea of a nation, based on ethnic, linguistic, or cultural factors. The idea of the nation had explosive consequences: by 1920, the world's three largest multiethnic states—imperial Russia, Austria-Hungary, and the Ottoman Empire—had all given way to a number of individual nation-states.

Museo Civico, Modigliana/© Alfredo Dagli Orti/The Art Archive at Art Resource, NY

Garibaldi. Giuseppe Garibaldi was a dedicated patriot and an outstanding example of the Italian nationalism that led to the unification of Italy by 1870.

The idea of establishing political boundaries on the basis of ethnicity, language, or culture had a broad appeal throughout Western civilization, but it also had unintended consequences. Although the concept provided the basis for a new sense of community that was tied to liberal thought in the first half of the nineteenth century, it also gave birth to ethnic tensions and hatred in the second half of the century that resulted in bitter disputes and contributed to the competition between nation-states that eventually erupted into world war. Governments, following the lead of the radical government in Paris during the French Revolution, took full advantage of the rise of a strong national consciousness and transformed war into a demonstration of national honor and commitment. Universal schooling enabled states to arouse patriotic enthusiasm and create national unity. Most soldiers who joyfully went to war in 1914 were convinced that their nation's cause was just.

Although the concept of nationalism was initially the product of conditions in modern Europe, it soon spread to other parts of the world. A few societies, such as Vietnam, had already developed a strong sense of national identity, but most of the peoples in Asia and Africa lived in multiethnic and multireligious communities and were not yet ripe for the spirit of nationalism. As we shall see, the first attempts to resist European colonial rule were often based on religious or ethnic identity, rather than on the concept of denied nationhood. But the imperialist powers, which at first benefited from the lack of political cohesion among their colonial subjects, eventually reaped what they had sowed. As the colonial peoples became familiar with Western concepts of democracy and self-determination, they too began to manifest a sense of common purpose that helped knit together the different elements in their societies to oppose colonial regimes and create the conditions for the emergence of future nations. For good or ill, the concept of nationalism had now achieved global proportions. We shall explore such issues, and their consequences, in greater detail in the chapters that follow.

What is nationalism? How did it arise, and what impact did it have on the history of the nineteenth and twentieth centuries?

Gothic Literature: Edgar Allan Poe

American writers and poets made significant contributions to the movement of Romanticism. Although Edgar Allan Poe (1809–1849) was influenced by the German Romantic school of mystery and horror, many literary historians give him the credit for pioneering the modern short story. This selection from the conclusion of "The Fall of the House of Usher" gives a feeling for the nature of so-called Gothic literature.

Edgar Allan Poe, "The Fall of the House of Usher"

No sooner had these syllables passed my lips, than—as if a shield of brass had indeed, at the moment, fallen heavily upon a floor of silver—I became aware of a distinct, hollow, metallic, and clangorous, yet apparently muffled, reverberation. Completely unnerved, I leaped to my feet; but the measured rocking movement of Usher was undisturbed. I rushed to the chair in which he sat. His eyes were bent fixedly before him, and throughout his whole countenance there reigned a stony rigidity. But, as I placed my hand upon his shoulder, there came a strong shudder over his whole person; a sickly smile quivered about his lips; and I saw that he spoke in a low, hurried, and gibbering murmur, as if unconscious of my presence. Bending closely over him, I at length drank in the hideous import of his words.

"Not hear it?—yes, I hear it, and have heard it. Long-long-long-many minutes, many hours, many days, have I heard it—yet I dared not—oh, pity me, miserable wretch that I am!—I dared not—I *dared* not speak! *We have put her living in the tomb!* Said I not that my senses were acute? I now tell you that I heard her first feeble movements in the hollow coffin. I heard them—many, many days ago—yet I dared not—*I dared not speak!* And now—to-night— . . . the rending of her coffin, and the grating of the iron hinges of her prison, and her struggles within the coppered archway of the vault! Oh whither shall I fly? Will she not be here anon? Is she not hurrying to upbraid me for my haste? Have I not heard her footstep on the stair? Do I not distinguish that heavy and horrible beating of her heart? MADMAN!"—here he sprang furiously to his feet, and shrieked out his syllables, as if in the effort he were giving up his soul—"MADMAN! I TELL YOU THAT SHE NOW STANDS WITHOUT THE DOOR!" As if in the superhuman energy of his utterance there had been found the potency of a spell, the huge antique panels to which the speaker pointed threw slowly back, upon the instant, their ponderous and ebony jaws. It was the work of the rushing gust—but then without those doors there DID stand the lofty and enshrouded figure of the lady Madeline of Usher. There was blood upon her white robes, and the evidence of some bitter struggle upon every portion of her emaciated frame. For a moment she remained trembling and reeling to and fro upon the threshold, then, with a low moaning cry, fell heavily inward upon the person of her brother, and in her violent and now final death-agonies, bore him to the floor a corpse, and a victim to the terrors he had anticipated.

What were the aesthetic aims of Gothic literature? How did it come to be called "Gothic"? How did its values relate to those of the Romantic movement as a whole?

Source: From *Selected Prose and Poetry*, Edgar Allan Poe, copyright © 1950 by Holt, Rinehart, and Winston, Inc.

Like the literary arts, the visual arts were also deeply affected by Romanticism. To Romantic artists, all artistic expression was a reflection of the artist's inner feelings; a painting should mirror the artist's vision of the world and be the instrument of his own imagination.

Eugène Delacroix (oo-ZHEN duh-lah-KRWAH) (1798–1863) was one of the most famous French exponents of the Romantic school of painting. Delacroix visited North Africa in 1832 and was strongly impressed by its vibrant colors and the brilliant dress of the people. His paintings came to exhibit two primary characteristics—a fascination with the exotic and a passion for color. Both are apparent in his *Women of Algiers*. In Delacroix, theatricality and movement combined with a daring use of color. Many of his works reflect his own belief that "a painting should be a feast to the eye."

Louvre, Paris//© Erich Lessing/Art Resource, NY

Eugène Delacroix, *Women of Algiers*. A characteristic of Romanticism was its love of the exotic and unfamiliar. In his *Women of Algiers*, Delacroix reflected this fascination with the exotic. In this portrayal of harem concubines from North Africa, the clothes and jewelry of the women combine with their calm facial expressions to create an atmosphere of peaceful sensuality. At the same time, Delacroix's painting reflects his preoccupation with light and color.

A New Age of Science

With the Industrial Revolution came a renewed interest in basic scientific research. By the 1830s, new scientific discoveries led to many practical benefits that caused science to have an ever-greater impact on European life.

In biology, the Frenchman Louis Pasteur (LWEE pass-TOOR) (1822–1895) discovered the germ theory of disease, which had enormous practical applications in the development of modern scientific medical practices. In chemistry, the Russian Dmitri Mendeleev (di-MEE-tree men-duh-LAY-ef) (1834–1907) in the 1860s classified all the material elements then known on the basis of their atomic weights and provided the systematic foundation for the periodic law.

The popularity of scientific and technological achievement produced a widespread acceptance of the **scientific method** as the only path to objective truth and objective reality. This in turn undermined the faith of many people in religious revelation. It is no accident that the nineteenth century was an age of increasing **secularization**, evident in the belief that truth was to be found in the concrete material existence of human beings. No one did more to create a picture of humans as material beings that were simply part of the natural world than Charles Darwin.

In 1859, Charles Darwin (1809–1882) published *On the Origin of Species by Means of Natural Selection*. The basic idea of this book was that all plants and animals had evolved over a long period of time from earlier and simpler forms of life, a principle known as **organic evolution**. In every species, he argued, "many more individuals of each species are born than can possibly survive." This results in a "struggle for existence." Darwin believed that some organisms were more adaptable to the environment than others, a process that he called **natural selection**. Those that were naturally selected for survival ("survival of the fit") reproduced and thrived. The unfit did not and became extinct. The fit who survived passed on small variations that enhanced their survival until, from Darwin's point of view, a new and separate species emerged. In *The Descent of Man*, published in 1871, he argued for the animal origins of human beings. Humans were not an exception to the rule governing other species.

Realism in Literature and Art

The name **Realism** was first applied in 1850 to describe a new style of painting and soon spread to literature. The literary Realists of the mid-nineteenth century rejected Romanticism. They wanted to deal with ordinary characters from actual life rather than Romantic heroes in exotic settings. They also sought to avoid emotional language by using close observation and precise description, an approach that led them to write novels rather than poems.

The leading novelist of the 1850s and 1860s, the Frenchman Gustave Flaubert (goo-STAHV floh-BAYR) (1821–1880), perfected the Realist novel. His *Madame Bovary* (1857) was a straightforward description of barren and sordid provincial life in France. Emma Bovary is trapped in a marriage to a drab provincial doctor. Impelled by the images of romantic love she has read

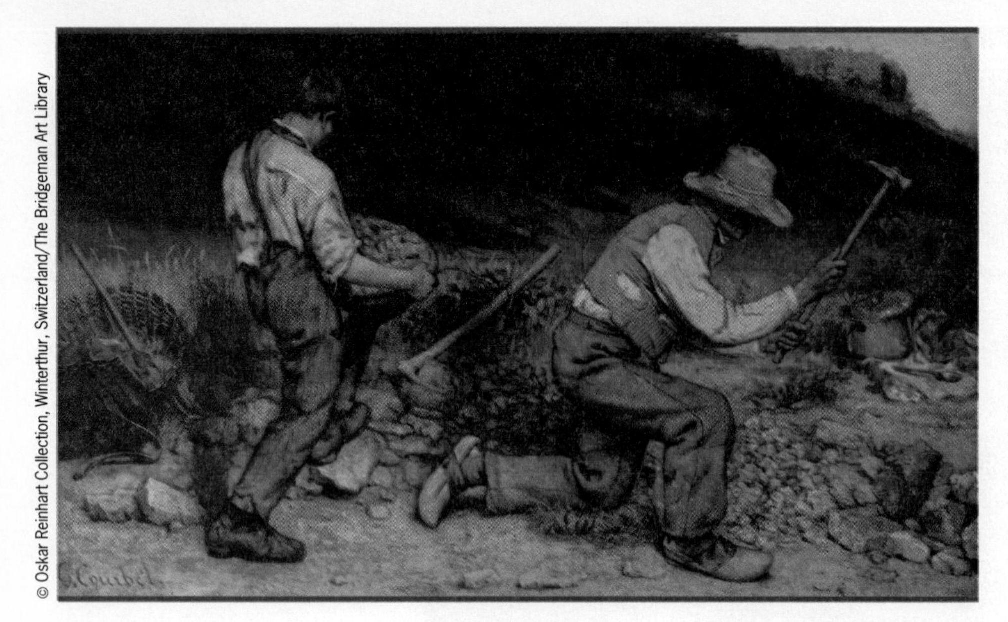

© Oskar Reinhart Collection, Winterthur, Switzerland/The Bridgeman Art Library

Gustave Courbet, *The Stonebreakers*. Realism, largely developed by French painters, aimed at a lifelike portrayal of the daily activities of ordinary people. Gustave Courbet was the most famous of the Realist artists. As is evident in *The Stonebreakers*, he sought to portray things as they really appear. He shows an old road builder and his young assistant in their tattered clothes, engrossed in their dreary work of breaking stones to construct a road.

about in novels, she seeks the same thing for herself in adulterous love affairs but is ultimately driven to suicide.

By the second half of the nineteenth century, Realism had also made inroads into the Latin American literary scene. There, Realist novelists focused on the injustices of their society, evident in the work of Clorinda Matto de Turner (kloh-RIN-duh MAH-toh day TUR-nerr) (1852–1909). Her *Aves sin Nido* (*Birds Without a Nest*) was a brutal revelation of the pitiful living conditions of the Indians in Peru. She blamed the Catholic Church in particular for much of their misery.

In art, too, Realism became dominant after 1850. Gustave Courbet (goo-STAHV koor-BAY) (1819–1877), the most famous artist of the Realist school, reveled in realistic portrayals of everyday life. His subjects were factory workers, peasants, and the wives of saloonkeepers. "I have never seen either angels or goddesses, so I am not interested in painting them," he exclaimed. One of his famous works, *The Stonebreakers*, painted in 1849, shows two road workers engaged in the deadening work of breaking stones to build a road.

Toward the Modern Consciousness: Intellectual and Cultural Developments

FOCUS QUESTION: What intellectual and cultural developments in the late nineteenth and early twentieth centuries "opened the way to a modern consciousness," and how did this consciousness differ from earlier worldviews?

Before 1914, many people in the Western world continued to believe in the values and ideals that had been generated by the Scientific Revolution and the Enlightenment. The idea that human beings could improve themselves and achieve a better society seemed to be proved by a rising standard of living, urban comforts, and mass education. It was easy to think that the human mind could make sense of the universe. Between 1870 and 1914, though, radically new ideas challenged these optimistic views and opened the way to a modern consciousness.

A New Physics

Science was one of the chief pillars underlying the optimistic and rationalistic view of the world that many Westerners shared in the nineteenth century. Supposedly based on hard facts and cold reason, science offered a certainty of belief in the orderliness of nature. The new physics dramatically altered that perspective.

Throughout much of the nineteenth century, Westerners adhered to the mechanical conception of the universe postulated by the classic physics of Isaac Newton. In this perspective, the universe was viewed as a giant machine in which time, space, and matter were objective realities that existed independently of the observers. Matter was thought to be composed of indivisible and solid material bodies called atoms.

Albert Einstein (YN-styn) (1879–1955), a German-born patent officer working in Switzerland, questioned this view of the universe. In 1905, Einstein published his special theory of relativity, which stated that space and time are not absolute but relative to the observer. Neither space nor time had an existence independent of human experience. As Einstein later explained simply to a journalist: "It was formerly believed that if all material things disappeared out of the universe, time and space would be left. According to the **relativity theory**, however, time and space disappear together with the things."[7] Einstein concluded that matter was nothing but another form of energy. His epochal formula $E = mc^2$—stating that each particle of matter is equivalent to its mass times the square of the velocity of light—was the key theory explaining the vast energies contained within the atom. It led to the atomic age.

Sigmund Freud and the Emergence of Psychoanalysis

At the turn of the twentieth century, the Viennese physician Sigmund Freud (SIG-mund *or* ZIG-munt FROID) (1856–1939) advanced a series of theories that undermined optimism about the rational nature of the human mind. Freud's thought, like the new physics, added to the uncertainties of the age. His major ideas were published in 1900 in *The Interpretation of Dreams*.

According to Freud, human behavior was strongly determined by the unconscious, by past experiences and internal forces of which people were largely oblivious. For Freud, human behavior was no longer truly rational but rather instinctive or irrational. He argued that painful and unsettling experiences were blotted from conscious awareness but still continued to influence behavior since they had become part of the unconscious (see the box on p. 538). Repression of these thoughts began in childhood. Freud devised a method, known as **psychoanalysis**, by which a psychotherapist and patient could probe deeply into the memory and retrace the chain of repression all the way back to its childhood origins. By making the conscious mind aware of the unconscious and its repressed contents, the patient's psychic conflict was resolved.

The Impact of Darwin: Social Darwinism and Racism

In the second half of the nineteenth century, scientific theories were sometimes wrongly applied to achieve other ends. For example, Charles Darwin's principle of organic evolution was applied to the social order as **social Darwinism**, the belief that societies were organisms that evolved through time from a struggle with their environment. Such ideas were used in a radical way by rabid nationalists and racists. In their pursuit of national greatness, extreme nationalists insisted that nations, too, were engaged in a "struggle for existence" in which only the fittest survived.

ANTI-SEMITISM Anti-Semitism had a long history in European civilization, but in the nineteenth century, as a result of the ideals of the Enlightenment and the French Revolution, Jews were increasingly granted legal equality in many European countries. Many Jews now left the ghetto and became assimilated into the cultures around them. Many became successful as bankers, lawyers, scientists, scholars, journalists, and stage performers.

These achievements represent only one side of the picture, however. In Germany and Austria during the 1880s and 1890s, conservatives founded right-wing anti-Jewish parties that used anti-Semitism to win the votes of traditional lower-middle-class groups who felt threatened by the new economic forces of the times. The worst treatment of Jews at the turn of the century, however, occurred in eastern Europe, where 72 percent of the entire world Jewish population lived. Russian Jews were forced to live in certain regions of the country, and persecutions and pogroms were widespread. Hundreds of thousands of Jews decided to emigrate to escape the persecution.

Many Jews went to the United States, although some moved to Palestine, which soon became the focus of a Jewish nationalist movement called **Zionism**. For many Jews, Palestine, the land of ancient Israel, had long been the land of their dreams. Settlement in Palestine was difficult, however, because it was then part of the Ottoman Empire, which was opposed to Jewish immigration. Despite the problems, the First Zionist Congress, which met in Switzerland in 1897, proclaimed as its aim the creation of a "home in Palestine secured by public law" for the Jewish people. In 1900, around a thousand Jews migrated to Palestine, and the trickle rose to about three thousand a year between 1904 and 1914, keeping the Zionist dream alive.

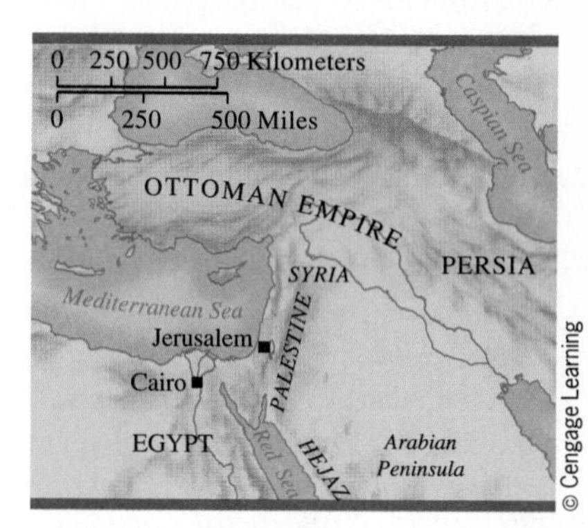

© Cengage Learning

Palestine in 1900

The Culture of Modernity

The revolution in physics and psychology was paralleled by a revolution in literature and the arts. Before 1914, writers and artists were rebelling against the traditional literary and artistic styles that had dominated European cultural life since the Renaissance. The changes that they produced have since been called **Modernism**.

At the beginning of the twentieth century, a group of writers known as the Symbolists caused a literary revolution. Primarily interested in writing poetry and strongly influenced by the ideas of Freud, the Symbolists believed

Freud and the Concept of Repression

Freud's psychoanalytical theories resulted from his attempt to understand the world of the unconscious. This excerpt is taken from a lecture given in 1909 in which Freud described how he arrived at his theory of the role of repression.

Sigmund Freud, *Five Lectures on Psychoanalysis*

I did not abandon [the technique of encouraging patients to reveal forgotten experiences], however, before the observations I made during my use of it afforded me decisive evidence. I found confirmation of the fact that the forgotten memories were not lost. They were in the patient's possession and were ready to emerge in association to what was still known by him; but there was some force that prevented them from becoming conscious and compelled them to remain unconscious. The existence of this force could be assumed with certainty, since one became aware of an effort corresponding to it if, in opposition to it, one tried to introduce the unconscious memories into the patient's consciousness. The force which was maintaining the pathological condition became apparent in the form of resistance on the part of the patient.

It was on this idea of resistance, then, that I based my view of the course of psychical events in hysteria. In order to effect a recovery, it had proved necessary to remove these resistances. Starting out from the mechanism of cure, it now became possible to construct quite definite ideas of the origin of the illness. The same forces which, in the form of resistance, were now offering opposition to the forgotten material's being made conscious, must formerly have brought about the forgetting and must have pushed the pathogenic experiences in question out of consciousness. I gave the name of "repression" to this hypothetical process, and I considered that it was proved by the undeniable existence of resistance.

The further question could then be raised as to what these forces were and what the determinants were of the repression in which we now recognized the pathogenic mechanism of hysteria. A comparative study of the pathogenic situations which we had come to know through the cathartic procedure made it possible to answer this question. All these experiences had involved the emergence of a wishful impulse which was in sharp contrast to the subject's other wishes and which proved incompatible with the ethical and aesthetic standards of his personality. There had been a short conflict, and the end of this internal struggle was that the idea which had appeared before consciousness as the vehicle of this irreconcilable wish fell a victim to repression, was pushed out of consciousness with all its attached memories, and was forgotten. Thus, the incompatibility of the wish in question with the patient's ego was the motive for the repression; the subject's ethical and other standards were the repressing forces. An acceptance of the incompatible wishful impulse or a prolongation of the conflict would have produced a high degree of unpleasure; this unpleasure was avoided by means of repression, which was thus revealed as one of the devices serving to protect the mental personality.

According to Freud, how did he discover the existence of repression? What function does repression perform?

Source: Reprinted from *Five Lectures on Psychoanalysis* by Sigmund Freud. Translated and edited by James Strachey, W. W. Norton & Company, Inc. Copyright 1909, 1910 by Sigmund Freud. Copyright © 1961 by James Strachey. Copyright renewed 1989.

that an objective knowledge of the world was impossible. The external world was not real but only a collection of symbols that reflected the true reality of the individual human mind.

The period from 1870 to 1914 was one of the most fertile in the history of art. By the late nineteenth century, artists were seeking new forms of expression. The preamble to modern painting can be found in **Impressionism**, a movement that originated in France in the 1870s when a group of artists rejected the studios and museums and went out into the countryside to paint nature directly.

An important Impressionist painter was Berthe Morisot (BAYRT mor-ee-ZOH) (1841–1895), who believed

Musée Fabre, Montpellier//© Erich Lessing/Art Resource, NY

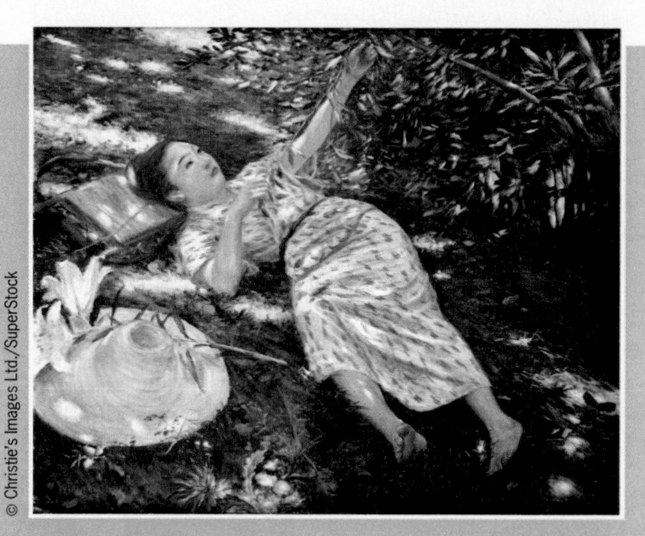
© Christie's Images Ltd./SuperStock

COMPARATIVE ILLUSTRATION

Painting—West and East. Berthe Morisot, the first female painter to join the Impressionists, developed her own unique style. Her gentle colors and strong use of pastels are especially evident in *Young Girl by the Window*, seen at the left. The French Impressionist style also spread abroad. One of the most outstanding Japanese artists of the time was Kuroda Seiki (koor-OH-duh SAY-kee) (1866–1924), who returned from nine years in Paris to open a Western-style school of painting in Tokyo. Shown at the right is his *Under the Trees*, an excellent example of the fusion of contemporary French Impressionist painting with the Japanese tradition of courtesan prints.

What differences and similarities do you notice in these two paintings?

that women had a special vision that she described as "more delicate than that of men." She made use of lighter colors and flowing brushstrokes (see the comparative illustration above). Near the end of her life, she lamented the refusal of men to take her work seriously: "I don't think there has ever been a man who treated a woman as an equal, and that's all I would have asked, for I know I'm worth as much as they."[8]

In the 1880s, a new movement known as **Post-Impressionism** arose in France and soon spread to other European countries. A famous Post-Impressionist was the tortured and tragic figure Vincent van Gogh (van GOH *or* vahn GOK) (1853–1890). For van Gogh, art was a spiritual experience. He was especially interested in color and believed that it could act as its own form of language.

By the beginning of the twentieth century, the belief that the task of art was to represent "reality" had lost much of its meaning. The growth of photography gave artists one reason to reject Realism. Invented in the 1830s, photography became popular and widespread after 1888 when George Eastman created the first Kodak camera for the mass market. What was the point of an artist's doing what the camera did better? Unlike the camera, which could only mirror reality, artists could create reality.

By 1905, one of the most important figures in modern art was just beginning his career. Pablo Picasso (PAHB-loh pi-KAH-soh) (1881–1973) was from Spain but settled in Paris in 1904. Picasso was extremely flexible and painted in a remarkable variety of styles. He was instrumental in the development of a new style called **Cubism** that used geometrical designs as visual stimuli to re-create reality in the viewer's mind.

The modern artist's flight from "visual reality" reached a high point in 1910 with the beginning of **abstract painting**. A Russian who worked in Germany, Vasily Kandinsky (vus-YEEL-yee kan-DIN-skee) (1866–1944) was one of its founders. Kandinsky sought to avoid representation altogether. He believed that art should speak directly to the soul. To do so, it must avoid any reference to visual reality and concentrate on line and color.

Pablo Picasso, *Les Demoiselles d'Avignon.* Pablo Picasso, a major pioneer and activist of modern art, experimented with a remarkable variety of modern styles. *Les Demoiselles d'Avignon* (lay dem-wah-ZEL dah-vee-NYONH) was the first great example of Cubism, which one art historian called "the first style of this [twentieth] century to break radically with the past." Geometrical shapes replace traditional forms, forcing the viewer to re-create reality in his or her own mind. The head at the upper right of the painting reflects Picasso's attraction to aspects of African art, as is evident from the mask included at the left.

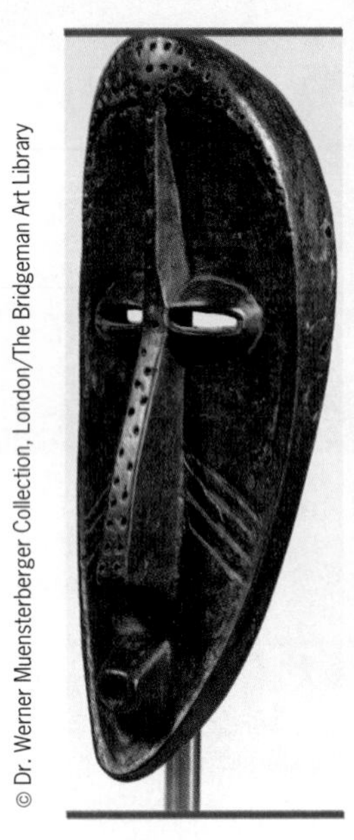

© Dr. Werner Muensterberger Collection, London/The Bridgeman Art Library

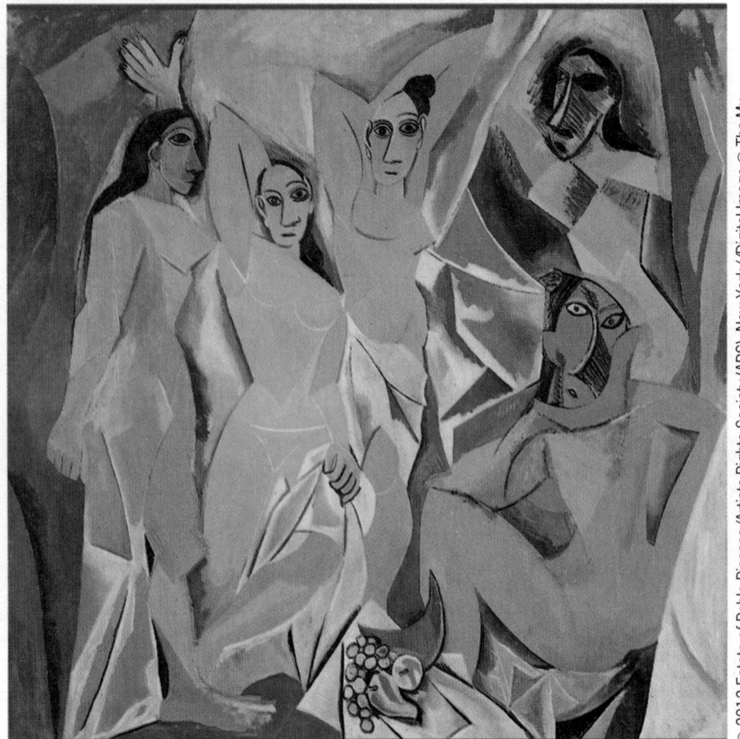

© 2012 Estate of Pablo Picasso/Artists Rights Society (ARS), New York/Digital Image © The Museum of Modern Art/Licensed by Scala/Art Resource, NY

CHAPTER SUMMARY

Since the sixteenth century, much of the Western Hemisphere had been under the control of Great Britain, Spain, and Portugal. But between 1776 and 1826, an age of revolution in the Atlantic world led to the creation of the United States and nine new nations in Latin America. Canada and other nations in Latin America followed in the course of the nineteenth century. This age of revolution was an expression of the force of nationalism, which had first emerged as a political ideology at the end of the eighteenth century. Influential, too, were the ideas of the Enlightenment that had made an impact on intellectuals and political leaders in both North and South America.

The new nations that emerged in the Western Hemisphere did not, however, develop without challenges to their national unity. Latin American nations often found it difficult to establish stable republics and resorted to strong leaders who used military force to govern. And although Latin American nations had achieved political independence, they found themselves economically dependent on Great Britain as well as their northern neighbor. The United States dissolved into four years of bloody civil war before reconciling, and Canada achieved only questionable unity owing to distrust between the English-speaking majority and the French-speaking minority.

By the second half of the nineteenth century, much of the Western world was experiencing a new mass society in which the lower classes in particular benefited from the right to vote, a higher standard of living, and new schools that provided them with some education. New forms of mass transportation, combined with new work patterns, enabled large numbers of people to enjoy weekend trips to amusement parks and seaside resorts, as well as to participate in new mass leisure activities.

The cultural revolutions before 1914 produced anxiety and a crises of confidence in Western civilization. Albert Einstein showed that time and space were relative to the observer, that matter was simply another form of energy, and that the old Newtonian view of the universe was no longer valid. Sigmund Freud added to the uncertainties of the age with his argument that human behavior was governed not by reason but by the unconscious. Some intellectuals used the ideas of Charles Darwin to argue that in the struggle of race and nations, only the fittest survive. Collectively, these new ideas helped create a modern consciousness that questioned most Europeans' optimistic faith in reason, the rational structure of nature, and the certainty of progress. As we shall see in Chapter 23, the devastating experiences of World War I would turn this culture of uncertainty into a way of life after 1918.

CHAPTER TIMELINE

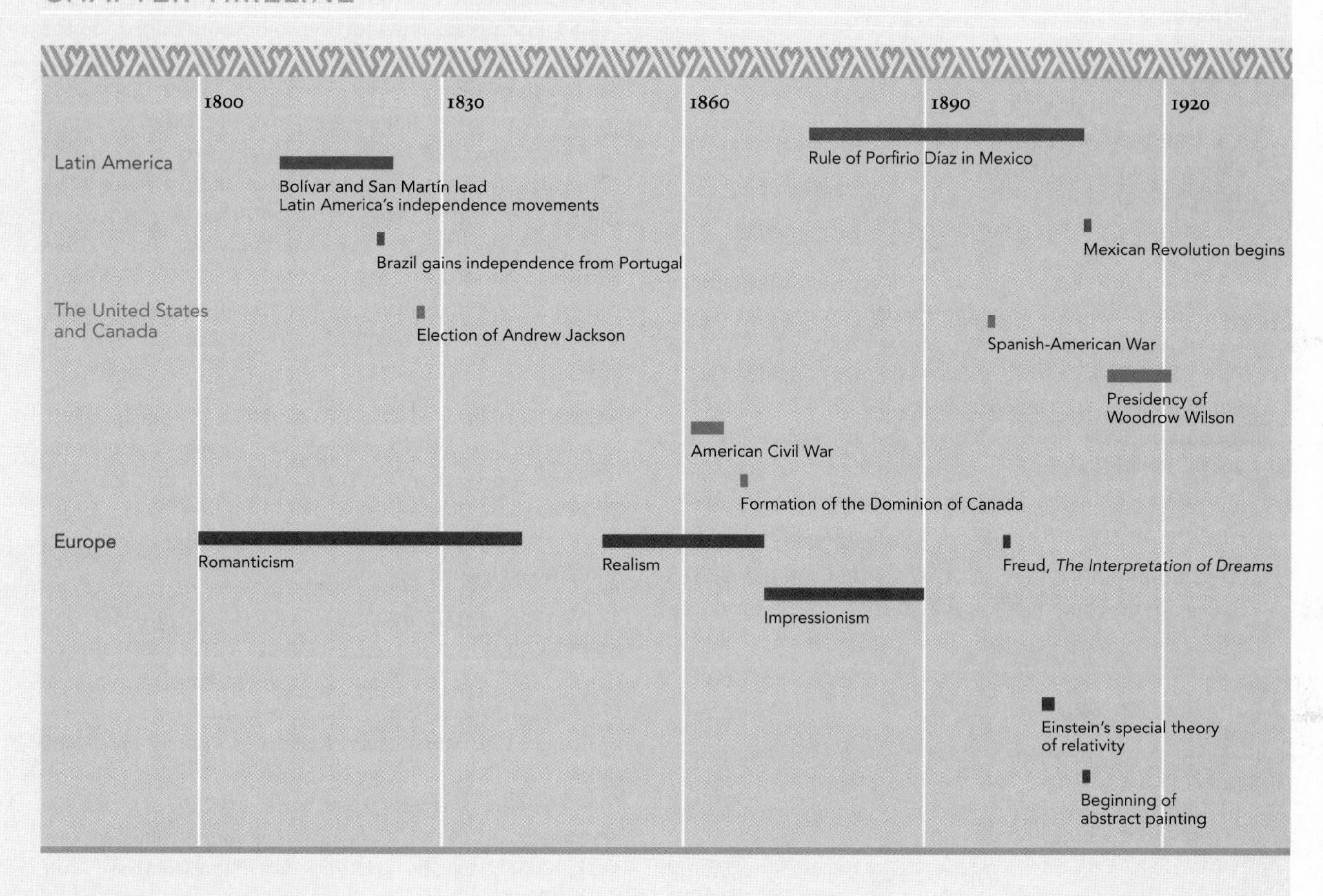

CHAPTER REVIEW

Upon Reflection

Q What were the similarities and dissimilarities in the development of Latin American nations, the United States, and Canada in the nineteenth century?

Q How were the promises and problems of the new mass society reflected in education, leisure, and the experiences of women?

Q How is Modernism evident in literature and the arts between 1870 and 1914? How do these literary and artistic products reflect the political and social developments of the age?

Key Terms

caudillos (p. 521)
mass society (p. 527)
nation-states (p. 528)
suffragists (p. 530)
mass education (p. 530)
mass leisure (p. 530)

Romanticism (p. 532)
Gothic literature (p. 532)
scientific method (p. 535)
secularization (p. 535)
organic evolution (p. 535)
natural selection (p. 535)
Realism (p. 535)
relativity theory (p. 537)
psychoanalysis (p. 537)
social Darwinism (p. 537)
Zionism (p. 537)
Modernism (p. 537)
Impressionism (p. 538)
Post-Impressionism (p. 539)
Cubism (p. 539)
abstract painting (p. 539)

Suggested Reading

LATIN AMERICA For general surveys of Latin American history, see **M. C. Eakin,** ***The History of Latin America: Collision of Cultures*** (New York, 2007), and **P. Bakewell,** ***A History of Latin America*** (Oxford, 1997). On the wars for independence, see **J. C. Chasteen,** ***Americanos: Latin America's Struggle for Independence*** (Oxford, 2008). On the economic history of Latin America, see **V. Bulmer-Thomas,** ***The Economic History of Latin America Since Independence,*** 2nd ed. (New York, 2003).

THE UNITED STATES AND CANADA On the United States in the first half of the nineteenth century, see **D. W. Howe,** ***What God Hath Wrought: The Transformation of America, 1815–1848*** (Oxford, 2007). The definitive one-volume history of the American Civil War is **J. M. McPherson,** ***Battle Cry of Freedom: The Civil War Era*** in the Oxford History of the United States series (New York, 2003). On the second half of the nineteenth century, see **L. Gould,** ***America in the Progressive Era, 1890–1914*** (New York, 2001). For a general history of Canada, see **S. W. See,** ***History of Canada*** (Westport, N.Y., 2001).

THE EMERGENCE OF MASS SOCIETY IN THE WEST For a good introduction to housing reform on the Continent, see **N. Bullock** and **J. Read,** ***The Movement for Housing Reform in Germany and France, 1840–1914*** (Cambridge, 1985). There are good overviews of women's experiences in the nineteenth century in **B. Smith,** ***Changing Lives: Women in European History Since 1700,*** rev. ed. (Lexington, Mass., 2005). On various aspects of education, see **M. J. Maynes,** ***Schooling in Western Europe: A Social History*** (Albany, N.Y., 1985). A concise and well-presented survey of leisure patterns is **G. Cross,** ***A Social History of Leisure Since 1600*** (State College, Pa., 1989).

ROMANTICISM AND REALISM On the ideas of the Romantics, see **M. Cranston,** ***The Romantic Movement*** (Oxford, 1994). For an introduction to the arts, see **W. Vaughan,** ***Romanticism and Art*** (New York, 1994). On Realism, **J. Malpas,** ***Realism*** (Cambridge, 1997), is a good introduction.

TOWARD THE MODERN CONSCIOUSNESS: INTELLECTUAL AND CULTURAL DEVELOPMENTS On Freud, see **P. D. Kramer,** ***Sigmund Freud: Inventor of the Modem Mind*** (New York, 2006). European racism is analyzed in **N. MacMaster,** ***Racism in Europe, 1870–2000*** (New York, 2001). On Modernism, see **P. Gay,** ***Modernism: The Lure of Heresy*** (New York, 2007). Very valuable on modern art are **G. Crepaldi,** ***The Impressionists*** (New York, 2002), and **B. Denvir,** ***Post-Impressionism*** (New York, 1992).

CourseMate

Visit the CourseMate website at **www.cengagebrain.com** for additional study tools and review materials for this chapter.

CHAPTER

21

The High Tide of Imperialism

© Time Life Pictures/Getty Images

Revere the conquering heroes: Establishing British rule in Africa

CHAPTER OUTLINE AND FOCUS QUESTIONS

The Spread of Colonial Rule

Q What were the causes of the new imperialism of the nineteenth century, and how did it differ from European expansion in earlier periods?

The Colonial System

Q What types of administrative systems did the various colonial powers establish in their colonies, and how did these systems reflect the general philosophy of colonialism?

India Under the British Raj

Q What were some of the major consequences of British rule in India, and how did they affect the Indian people?

Colonial Regimes in Southeast Asia

Q Which Western countries were most active in seeking colonial possessions in Southeast Asia, and what were their motives in doing so?

Empire Building in Africa

Q What factors were behind the "scramble for Africa," and what impact did it have on the continent?

The Emergence of Anticolonialism

Q How did the subject peoples respond to colonialism, and what role did nationalism play in their response?

CRITICAL THINKING

Q What were the consequences of the new imperialism of the nineteenth century for the colonies of the European powers? How should the motives and stated objectives of the imperialist countries be evaluated?

IN 1877, THE BRITISH empire builder Cecil Rhodes drew up his last will and testament. He bequeathed his fortune, achieved as a diamond magnate in South Africa, to two of his close friends. He instructed them to use the inheritance to form a secret society aimed at bringing about "the extension of British rule throughout the world, the perfecting of a system of emigration from the United Kingdom . . . especially the occupation by British settlers of the entire continent of Africa, the Holy Land, the valley of the Euphrates, the Islands of Cyprus and Candia [Crete], the whole of South America. . . . The ultimate recovery of the United States of America as an integral part of the British Empire . . . then finally the foundation of so great a power as to hereafter render wars impossible and promote the best interests of humanity."[1]

Preposterous as such ideas sound today, they serve as a graphic reminder of the hubris that characterized the worldview of Rhodes and many of his contemporaries during the age of imperialism, as well as the complex union of moral concern and vaulting ambition that motivated their actions on the world stage.

Through their efforts, Western colonialism spread throughout much of the non-Western world during the nineteenth and early twentieth centuries. Spurred by the demands of the Industrial Revolution, a few powerful Western states—notably, Great Britain, France, Germany, Russia, and the United States—competed avariciously for consumer markets and raw materials for their expanding economies. By the end of the nineteenth century, virtually all of the traditional societies in Asia and Africa were under direct or indirect colonial rule. As the new century began, the Western imprint on Asian and African societies, for better or for worse, appeared to be a permanent feature of the political and cultural landscape.

The Spread of Colonial Rule

FOCUS QUESTION: What were the causes of the new imperialism of the nineteenth century, and how did it differ from European expansion in earlier periods?

In the nineteenth century, a new phase of Western expansion into Asia and Africa began. Whereas before 1800 European aims in the East could be summed up as "Christians and spices" and Western gold and silver were exchanged for cloves, silk, and porcelain, now European nations began to view Asian and African societies as markets for the prodigious output of European factories and as sources of the raw materials needed to fuel the Western industrial machine. This relationship between the West and African and Asian societies has been called the **new imperialism** (see the comparative essay on p. 545).

The Motives

The reason for this change, of course, was the Industrial Revolution. Now industrializing countries in the West needed vital raw materials that were not available at home, as well as reliable markets for the goods produced in their factories. The latter factor became increasingly crucial as producers discovered that their home markets could not absorb their entire output and that they had to export to make a profit. When consumer demand lagged, economic depression threatened.

The relationship between colonialism and national survival was expressed directly by the French politician Jules Ferry (ZHOOL feh-REE) in 1885. A policy of "containment or abstinence," he warned, would set France on "the broad road to decadence" and initiate its decline into a "third- or fourth-rate power." British imperialists, convinced by the theory of social Darwinism that in the struggle between nations, only the fit are victorious and survive, agreed. As the British professor of mathematics Karl Pearson argued in 1900, "The path of progress is strewn with the wrecks of nations; traces are everywhere to be seen of the [slaughtered remains] of inferior races.... Yet these dead people are, in very truth, the stepping stones on which mankind has arisen to the higher intellectual and deeper emotional life of today."[2]

For some, colonialism had a moral purpose, whether to promote Christianity or to build a better world. The British colonial official Henry Curzon (CURR-zun) declared that the British Empire "was under Providence, the greatest instrument for good that the world has seen." To Cecil Rhodes, the most famous empire builder of his day, the extraction of material wealth from the colonies was only a secondary matter. "My ruling purpose," he remarked, "is the extension of the British Empire."[3] That British Empire, on which, as the saying went, "the sun never set," was the envy of its rivals and was viewed as the primary source of British global dominance during the second half of the nineteenth century.

The Tactics

With the change in European motives for colonization came a shift in tactics. Earlier, European states had generally been satisfied to deal with existing independent states rather than attempting to establish direct control over vast territories. There had been exceptions where state power was at the point of collapse (as in India), where European economic interests were especially intense (as in Latin America and the East Indies), or where there was no centralized authority (as in North America and the Philippines). But for the most part, the Western presence had been limited to controlling regional trade networks and establishing a few footholds where the foreigners could carry on trade and missionary activity.

After 1800, the demands of industrialization in Europe created a new set of dynamics. Maintaining access to raw materials such as tin and rubber and setting up markets for European products required more extensive control over colonial territories. As competition for colonies increased, the colonial powers sought to solidify their hold over their territories to protect them from attack by their rivals. After 1880, the quest for colonies became a scramble as all the major European states, now joined by the United States and Japan, engaged in a global land grab. In many cases, economic interests were secondary to security concerns or the demands of national prestige. In Africa, for example, the British engaged in a struggle with their rivals to protect their interests in the Suez Canal and the Red Sea.

COMPARATIVE ESSAY

Imperialisms Old and New

INTERACTION & EXCHANGE

Originally, the word *imperialism* (derived from the Latin meaning "to command") was used to describe certain types of political entities. An empire was larger than a kingdom and comprised more than one nation or people, all ruled by an emperor who represented one dominant ethnic or religious group within the territory. Good examples include the Roman Empire, the Chinese Empire, the Mongol Empire in Central Asia, the empires of Ghana and Mali in West Africa, and perhaps the Inkan Empire in South America.

In the nineteenth century, as Western expansion into Asia and Africa gathered strength, it became fashionable to call that process "imperialism" as well. In this instance, the expansion was motivated by the efforts of capitalist states in the West to seize markets, cheap raw materials, and lucrative avenues for investment in the countries beyond Western civilization. Eventually, it resulted in the creation of colonies ruled by the imperialist powers. In this interpretation, the primary motives behind imperial expansion were economic. In his influential book *Imperialism: A Study*, published in 1902, the British political economist John A. Hobson promoted this view, maintaining that modern imperialism was a direct consequence of the modern industrial economy.

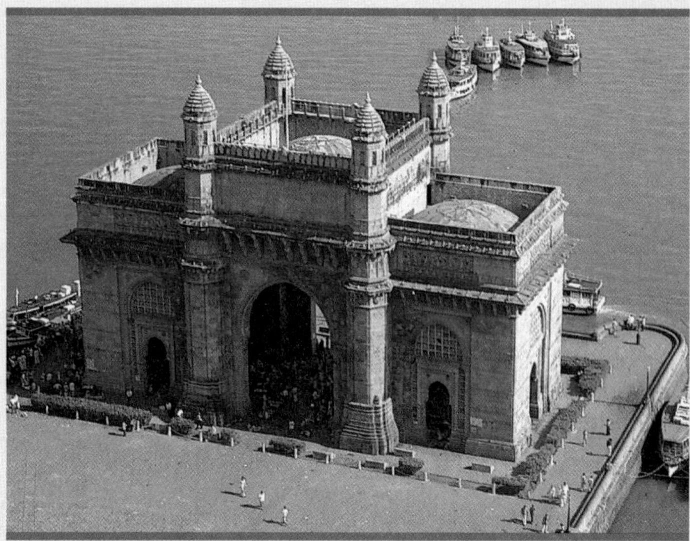

© William J. Duiker

Gateway to India. Built in the Roman imperial style by the British to commemorate the visit to India of King George V and Queen Mary in 1911, the Gateway to India was erected at the water's edge in the harbor of Bombay (now Mumbai), India's greatest port city. For thousands of British citizens arriving in India, the Gateway to India was the first view of their new home and a symbol of the power and majesty of the British raj.

As historians began to analyze the phenomenon, however, many became convinced that the motivations of the imperial powers were not simply economic. As Hobson himself conceded, economic concerns were inevitably tinged with political overtones and questions of national grandeur and moral purpose. To nineteenth-century Europeans, economic wealth, national status, and political power went hand in hand with the possession of a colonial empire. To global strategists, colonies brought tangible benefits in balance-of-power politics as well as economic profits, and many nations pursued colonies as much to gain advantage over their rivals as to acquire territory for its own sake.

After World War II, when colonies throughout Asia and Africa were replaced by independent nations, a new term *neocolonialism* appeared to describe the situation in which imperialist nations cede formal political independence to their former colonies, but continue to exercise control by various political and economic means. Hence, many critics argue, Western imperialism has not disappeared in the former colonial territories but has simply found other ways to maintain its influence. We will discuss this issue further in Part V.

What were the principal motives of the major trading nations for seizing colonies in Asia and Africa in the late nineteenth century?

By 1900, almost all the societies of Africa and Asia were either under full colonial rule or, as in China and the Ottoman Empire, at a point of virtual collapse. Only a handful of states, including Thailand, Afghanistan, Iran, Ethiopia, and Japan, managed to escape internal disintegration or subjection to colonial rule. For the most part, the exceptions were the result of good fortune rather than design. Thailand escaped subjugation primarily because officials in London and Paris found it more convenient to transform the country into a buffer state than to fight over it. Ethiopia and Afghanistan survived not only because of their long tradition of fierce resistance to outside threats, but also because of their remote location and mountainous terrain. Only Japan managed to avoid the common fate through a concerted strategy of political and economic reform.

The Colonial System

FOCUS QUESTION: What types of administrative systems did the various colonial powers establish in their colonies, and how did these systems reflect the general philosophy of colonialism?

Now that they had control of most of the world, what did the colonial powers do with it? As we have seen, their primary objective was to exploit the natural resources of the subject areas and to open up markets for manufactured goods and capital investment from the mother country. In some cases, that goal could be realized in cooperation with local political elites, whose loyalty could be earned, or purchased, by economic rewards or by confirming them in their positions of authority and status in a new colonial setting. Sometimes, however, this policy of **indirect rule** was not feasible because local leaders refused to cooperate with their colonial masters or even actively resisted. In such cases, the imperialists resorted to **direct rule**, removing the local elites from power and replacing them with officials from the mother country.

In general, the societies most likely to actively resist colonial conquest were those with a long tradition of national cohesion and independence, such as Burma and Vietnam in Asia and the African Muslim states in northern Nigeria and Morocco. In those areas, the colonial powers encountered more resistance and consequently tended to dispense with local collaborators and govern directly. In some parts of Africa, the Indian subcontinent, and the Malay peninsula, where the local authorities, for whatever reason, were willing to collaborate with the imperialist powers, indirect rule was more common.

Overall, colonialism in India, Southeast Asia, and Africa exhibited many similarities but also some differences. Some of these variations can be traced to differences among the colonial powers themselves. The French, for example, often tried to impose a centralized administrative system on their colonies that mirrored the system in use in France, while the British sometimes attempted to transform local aristocrats into the equivalent of the landed gentry at home in Britain. Other differences stemmed from conditions in the colonies themselves.

The Philosophy of Colonialism

To justify their rule, the colonial powers appealed in part to the time-honored maxim of "might makes right." That attitude received pseudoscientific validity from the concept of social Darwinism, which maintained that only societies that aggressively adapted to changing circumstances would survive and prosper in a world governed by the Darwinian law of "survival of the fittest."

Some people, however, were uncomfortable with such a brutal view and sought a moral justification that appeared to benefit the victim. Here again, social Darwinism pointed the way. By bringing the benefits of Western democracy, capitalism, and Christianity to tradition-ridden societies, the colonial powers were enabling primitive peoples to adapt to the challenges of the modern world. Buttressed by such comforting theories, sensitive Westerners could ignore the brutal aspects of colonialism and persuade themselves that in the long run, the results would be beneficial for both sides (see the box on p. 547). Few were

© Art Media, Victoria and Albert Museum, London/HIP/The Image Works

The Company Resident and His Puppet. The British East India Company gradually replaced the sovereigns of the once independent Indian states with puppet rulers who carried out the company's policies. Here we see the company's resident dominating a procession in Tanjore in 1825, while the Indian ruler, Sarabhoji, follows like an obedient shadow. As a boy, Sarabhoji had been educated by European tutors and had filled his life and home with English books and furnishings.

OPPOSING ≺ VIEWPOINTS

White Man's Burden, Black Man's Sorrow

One of the justifications for imperialism was that the "more advanced" white peoples had a moral responsibility to raise "ignorant" indigenous peoples to a higher level of civilization. Few captured this notion better than the British poet Rudyard Kipling (1865–1936) in his poem *The White Man's Burden*. Directed to the United States, it became famous throughout the English-speaking world.

That moral responsibility, however, was often misplaced or, even worse, laced with hypocrisy. Few observers described the destructive effects of Western imperialism on the African people as well as Edmund Morel, a British journalist whose book *The Black Man's Burden* pointed out some of the more harmful aspects of colonialism in the Belgian Congo.

Rudyard Kipling, *The White Man's Burden*

Take up the White Man's burden—
Send forth the best ye breed—
Go bind your sons to exile
To serve your captives' need;
To wait in heavy harness,
On fluttered folk and wild—
Your new-caught sullen peoples,
Half-devil and half-child.

Take up the White Man's burden—
In patience to abide,
To veil the threat of terror
And check the show of pride;
By open speech and simple,
An hundred times made plain
To seek another's profit,
And work another's gain.

Take up the White Man's burden—
The savage wars of peace—
Fill full the mouth of Famine
And bid the sickness cease;
And when your goal is nearest
The end for others sought,
Watch Sloth and heathen Folly
Bring all your hopes to nought.

Edmund Morel, *The Black Man's Burden*

It is [the Africans] who carry the "Black man's burden." They have not withered away before the white man's occupation. Indeed . . . Africa has ultimately absorbed within itself every Caucasian and, for that matter, every Semitic invader, too. In hewing out for himself a fixed abode in Africa, the white man has massacred the African in heaps. The African has survived, and it is well for the white settlers that he has. . . .

What the partial occupation of his soil by the white man has failed to do; what the mapping out of European political "spheres of influence" has failed to do; what the Maxim and the rifle, the slave gang, labour in the bowels of the earth and the lash, have failed to do; what imported measles, smallpox and syphilis have failed to do; whatever the overseas slave trade failed to do; the power of modern capitalistic exploitation, assisted by modern engines of destruction, may yet succeed in accomplishing.

For from the evils of the latter, scientifically applied and enforced, there is no escape for the African. Its destructive effects are not spasmodic; they are permanent. In its permanence resides its fatal consequences. It kills not the body merely, but the soul. It breaks the spirit. It attacks the African at every turn, from every point of vantage. It wrecks his polity, uproots him from the land, invades his family life, destroys his natural pursuits and occupations, claims his whole time, enslaves him in his own home.

According to Kipling, why should Western nations take up the "white man's burden"? What was the "black man's burden," in the eyes of Edmund Morel?

Sources: Rudyard Kipling, *The White Man's Burden*. From Rudyard Kipling, "The White Man's Burden," *McClure's Magazine* 12 (Feb. 1899). Edmund Morel, *The Black Man's Burden*. Edmund Morel, *Black Man's Burden*, Metro Books, 1972.

as adept at describing this "civilizing mission" as the French governor-general of French Indochina Albert Sarraut (ahl-BAYR sah-ROH). While admitting that colonialism was originally an "act of force" undertaken for profit, he insisted that by redistributing the wealth of the earth, the colonial process would result in a better life for all: "Is it just, is it legitimate that such [an uneven distribution of resources] should be indefinitely prolonged? . . . No! . . . Humanity is distributed throughout the globe. No race, no people has the right or power to isolate itself egotistically from the movements and necessities of universal life."[4]

But what if historically and culturally the societies of Asia and Africa were fundamentally different from those of the West and could not, or would not, be persuaded to transform themselves along Western lines? In that case, a policy of cultural transformation could not be expected to succeed and could even lead to disaster.

ASSIMILATION OR ASSOCIATION? In fact, colonial theorists never decided the issue. The French, who were most inclined to philosophize about the problem, adopted the terms **assimilation** (which implied an effort to transform colonial societies in the Western image) and **association** (implying collaboration with local elites while leaving local traditions alone) to describe the two alternatives and then proceeded to vacillate between them. French policy in Indochina, for example, began as one of association but switched to assimilation under pressure from those who felt that colonial powers owed a debt to their subject peoples. But assimilation (which in any case was never accepted as feasible or desirable by many colonial officials) aroused resentment among the local population, many of whom opposed the destruction of their native traditions. In the end, the French abandoned the attempt to justify their presence and resorted to ruling by force of arms.

Other colonial powers had little interest in the issue. The British, whether out of a sense of pragmatism or of racial superiority, refused to entertain the possibility of assimilation and treated their subject peoples as culturally and racially distinct.

India Under the British Raj

FOCUS QUESTION: What were some of the major consequences of British rule in India, and how did they affect the Indian people?

By 1800, the once glorious empire of the Mughals (MOO-guls) had been reduced by British military power to a shadow of its former greatness. During the next decades, the British consolidated their control over the Indian subcontinent. Some territories were taken over directly, first by the East India Company and later by the British crown; others were ruled indirectly through their local maharajas (mah-huh-RAH-juhs) and rajas (RAH-juhs).

Colonial Reforms

Not all of the effects of British rule were bad. British governance over the subcontinent brought order and stability to a society that had been rent by civil war. By the early nineteenth century, British control had led to a relatively honest and efficient government that in many respects operated to the benefit of the average Indian. One benefit was the heightened attention given to education. Through the efforts of the British administrator Thomas Babington Macaulay (muh-KAHL-lee) (1800–1859), a new school system was established to train the children of Indian elites, and the British civil service examination was introduced (see the box on p. 549). The instruction of young girls also expanded, primarily in order to make them better wives and mothers for the educated male population. In 1875, a Madras (muh-DRAS *or* muh-DRAHS) medical college accepted its first female student.

British rule also brought an end to some of the more inhumane aspects of Indian tradition. The practice of *sati* (suh-TEE) was outlawed, and widows were legally permitted to remarry. The British also attempted to put an end to the endemic brigandage (known as *thuggee*, which gave rise to the English word *thug*) that had plagued travelers in India since time immemorial. Railroads, the telegraph, and the postal service were introduced to India shortly after they appeared in Great Britain. Work began on the main highway from Calcutta to Delhi (DEL-ee) in 1839 (see Map 21.1), and the first rail network in northern India was opened in 1853.

The Costs of Colonialism

But the Indian people paid a high price for the peace and stability brought by the British **raj** (RAHJ) (from the Indian *raja*, or prince). Perhaps the most flagrant cost was economic. While British entrepreneurs and a small percentage of the local population reaped financial benefits from British rule, it brought hardship to millions in both the cities and the rural areas. The introduction of British textiles put thousands of Bengali women out of work and severely damaged the local textile industry.

In rural areas, the British introduced the *zamindar* (zuh-meen-DAHR) system (see Chapter 16) in the misguided expectation that it would facilitate the collection of taxes and create a new landed gentry, who could, as in Britain, become the conservative foundation of imperial rule. But the local gentry took advantage of this new authority to increase taxes and force the less fortunate peasants to become tenants or lose their land entirely. British officials

Indian in Blood, English in Taste and Intellect

As a member of the Supreme Council of India in the early 1830s, Thomas Babington Macaulay drew up an educational policy for Britain's Indian subjects. In his *Minute on Education*, he considered the claims of English and various local languages to become the vehicle for educational training and decided in favor of the former. If Indian elites were taught about Western civilization, he argued, they would "form a class who may be interpreters between us and the millions whom we govern; a class of persons, Indian in blood and color, but English in taste, in opinions, in morals, and in intellect." Later Macaulay became a prominent historian. The debate over the relative benefits of English and the various Indian languages continues today.

Thomas Babington Macaulay, *Minute on Education*

We have a fund to be employed as government shall direct for the intellectual improvement of the people of this country. The simple question is, what is the most useful way of employing it?

All parties seem to be agreed on one point, that the dialects commonly spoken among the natives of this part of India contain neither literary or scientific information, and are, moreover so poor and rude that, until they are enriched from some other quarter, it will not be easy to translate any valuable work into them. . . .

What, then, shall the language [of education] be? One half of the Committee maintain that it should be the English. The other half strongly recommend the Arabic and Sanskrit. The whole question seems to me to be, which language is the best worth knowing?

I have no knowledge of either Sanskrit or Arabic—but I have done what I could to form a correct estimate of their value. I have read translations of the most celebrated Arabic and Sanskrit works. I have conversed both here and at home with men distinguished by their proficiency in the Eastern tongues. I am quite ready to take the Oriental learning at the valuation of the Orientalists themselves. I have never found one among them who could deny that a single shelf of a good European library was worth the whole native literature of India and Arabia. . . .

It is, I believe, no exaggeration to say, that all the historical information which has been collected from all the books written in the Sanskrit language is less valuable than what may be found in the most paltry abridgments used at preparatory schools in England. In every branch of physical or moral philosophy the relative position of the two nations is nearly the same.

How did Macaulay justify the teaching of the English language in India? How might a critic have responded?

Source: From Speeches by *Lord Macaulay, With His Minute on Indian Education* by Thomas B. MacAuley. AMS Press, 1935.

also made few efforts during the nineteenth century to introduce democratic institutions or values. As one senior political figure remarked in Parliament in 1898, democratic institutions "can no more be carried to India by Englishmen . . . than they can carry ice in their luggage."[5]

The British also did little to bring modern science and technology to India. Some limited industrialization took place, notably in the manufacturing of textiles and jute (used in making rope). The first textile mill opened in 1856. Seventy years later, there were eighty mills in the city of Bombay (now Mumbai) alone. Nevertheless, the lack of local capital and the advantages given to British imports prevented the emergence of other vital new commercial and manufacturing operations.

Foreign rule also had a psychological effect on the Indian people. Although many British colonial officials sincerely tried to improve the lot of the people under their charge, British arrogance and contempt for native tradition cut deeply into the pride of many Indians, especially those of high caste, who were accustomed to a position of superior status in India. Educated Indians trained in the Anglo-Indian school system for a career in the civil service, as well as Eurasians born to mixed marriages, often imitated the behavior and dress of their rulers, speaking English, eating Western food, and taking up European leisure activities, but many rightfully wondered where their true cultural loyalties lay (see the comparative illustration on p. 551).

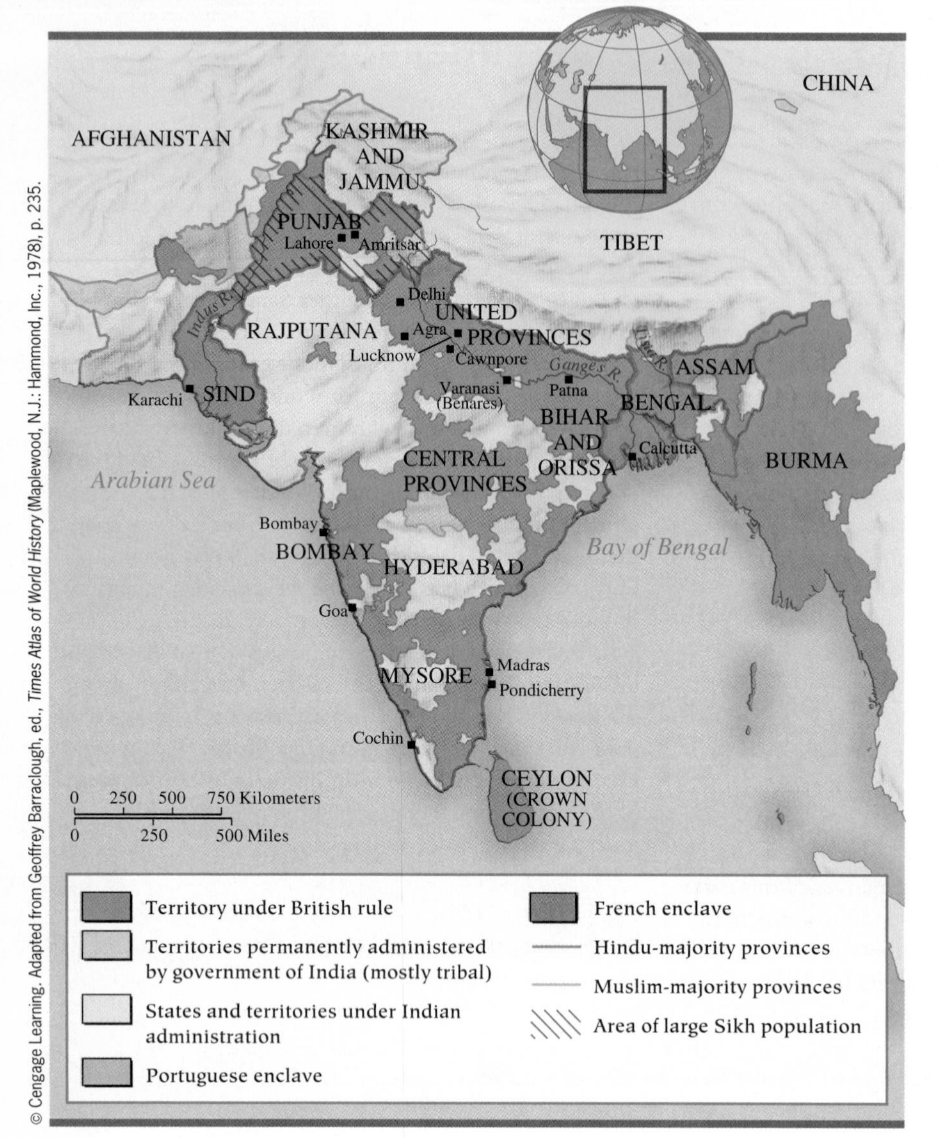

© Cengage Learning. Adapted from Geoffrey Barraclough, ed., *Times Atlas of World History* (Maplewood, N.J.: Hammond, Inc., 1978), p. 235.

MAP 21.1 India Under British Rule, 1805–1931. This map shows the different forms of rule that the British applied in India under their control.

Q *Where were the major cities of the subcontinent located, and under whose rule did they fall?*

Colonial Regimes in Southeast Asia

FOCUS QUESTION: Which Western countries were most active in seeking colonial possessions in Southeast Asia, and what were their motives in doing so?

In 1800, only two societies in Southeast Asia were under effective colonial rule: the Spanish Philippines and the Dutch East Indies. During the nineteenth century, however, European interest in Southeast Asia increased rapidly, and by 1900, virtually the entire area was under colonial rule (see Map 21.2).

"Opportunity in the Orient": The Colonial Takeover in Southeast Asia

The process began after the Napoleonic wars, when the British, by agreement with the Dutch, abandoned their claims to territorial possessions in the East Indies in return for a free hand in the Malay peninsula. In 1819, the colonial administrator Stamford Raffles founded a new British colony on the island of Singapore at the tip of the peninsula. Singapore became a major stopping point for traffic en route to and from China and other commercial centers in the region.

During the next decades, the pace of European penetration into Southeast Asia accelerated. The British attacked Burma in 1826 and eventually established control there, arousing fears in France that the British might acquire a monopoly of trade in South China. In 1858, the French launched an attack against Vietnam. Though it was not a total success, the Nguyen (NGWEN) dynasty in Vietnam was ultimately forced to cede some territories. A generation later, French rule was extended over the remainder of the country. By 1900, French seizure of neighboring Cambodia and Laos had led to the creation of the French-ruled Indochinese Union.

After the French conquest of Indochina, Thailand was the only remaining independent state on the Southeast Asian mainland. Under the astute leadership of two remarkable rulers, King Mongkut (MAHNG-koot) (1851–1868) and his son, King Chulalongkorn (CHOO-luh-lahng-korn) (1868–1910), the Thai attempted to introduce Western learning and maintain relations with the

École Francaise d'Extreme Orient, Paris//© Archives Charmet/The Bridgeman Art Library

British Library, London//© Werner Forman/Art Resource, NY

COMPARATIVE ILLUSTRATION

Cultural Influences—East and West. When Europeans moved into Asia in the nineteenth century, some Asians began to imitate European customs for prestige or social advancement. Seen at the left, for example, is a young Vietnamese during the 1920s dressed in Western sports clothes, learning to play tennis. Sometimes, however, the cultural influence went the other way. At the right, an English nabob, as European residents in India were often called, apes the manner of an Indian aristocrat, complete with harem and hookah, the Indian water pipe. The paintings on the wall, however, are in the European style.

Compare and contrast the artistic styles of these two paintings. What message do they send to the viewer?

major European powers without undermining internal stability or inviting an imperialist attack. In 1896, the British and the French agreed to preserve Thailand as an independent buffer zone between their possessions in Southeast Asia.

The final piece in the colonial edifice in Southeast Asia was put in place during the Spanish-American War in 1898 (see Chapter 20), when U.S. naval forces under Commodore George Dewey defeated the Spanish fleet in Manila Bay. President William McKinley agonized over the fate of the Philippines but ultimately decided that the moral thing to do was to turn the islands into an American colony to prevent them from falling into the hands of the Japanese. In fact, the Americans (like the Spanish before them) found the islands a convenient jumping-off point for the China trade (see Chapter 22). The mixture of moral idealism and desire for profit was reflected in a speech given in the U.S. Senate in January 1900 by Senator Albert Beveridge of Indiana:

> Mr. President, the times call for candor. The Philippines are ours forever, "territory belonging to the United States," as the Constitution calls them. And just beyond the Philippines are China's illimitable markets. We will not retreat from either. . . . We will not renounce our part in the mission of our race, trustee, under God, of the civilization of the world. And we will move forward to our work, not howling out regrets like slaves whipped to their burdens, but with gratitude for a task worthy of our strength, and thanksgiving to Almighty God that He has marked us as His chosen people, henceforth to lead in the regeneration of the world.[6]

Not all Filipinos agreed with Beveridge's portrayal of the situation. Under the leadership of Emilio Aguinaldo (ay-MEEL-yoh ah-gwee-NAHL-doh), guerrilla forces fought bitterly against U.S. troops to establish their independence from both Spain and the United States. But America's first war against guerrilla forces in Asia was a success, and the bulk of the resistance collapsed in 1901. President McKinley had his stepping-stone to the rich markets of China.

The Nature of Colonial Rule

In Southeast Asia, the colonial powers were primarily concerned with economic profit and tried wherever possible to work with local elites to facilitate the exploitation

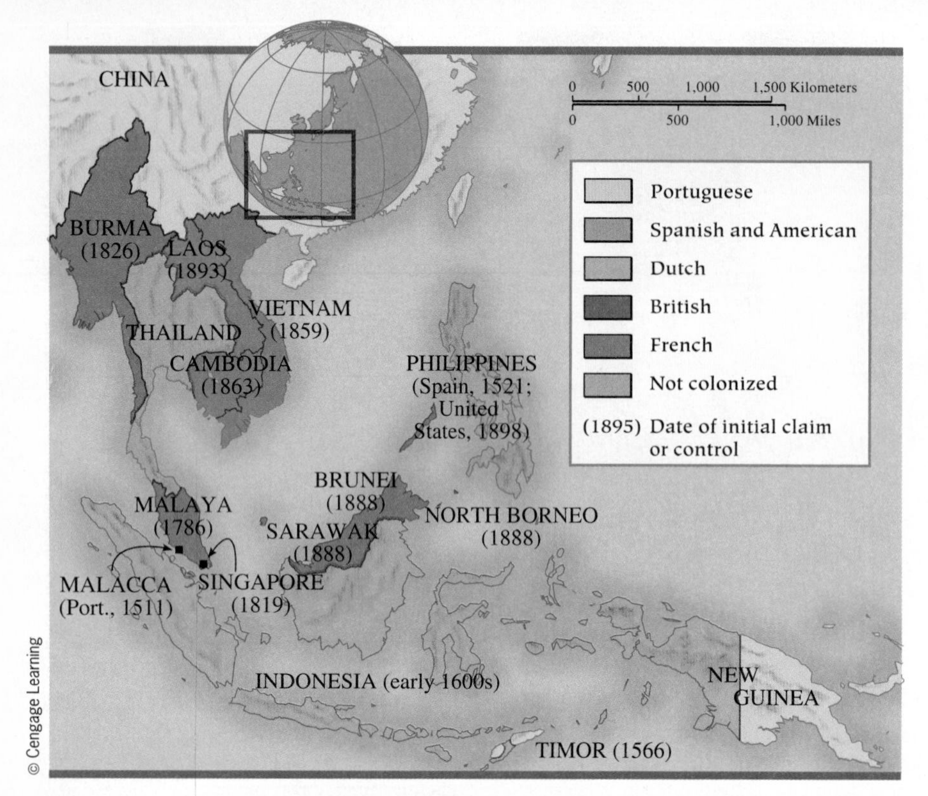

© Cengage Learning

MAP 21.2 Colonial Southeast Asia. This map shows the spread of European colonial rule into Southeast Asia from the sixteenth century to the end of the nineteenth. Malacca, initially seized by the Portuguese in 1511, was taken by the Dutch in the seventeenth century and then by the British one hundred years later.

Q *What was the significance of Malacca?*

of natural resources. Indirect rule was less costly than training European administrators and had a less corrosive impact on the local culture. In the Dutch East Indies, for example, officials of the Dutch East India Company (or VOC, the initials of its Dutch name) entrusted local administration to the indigenous aristocracy, who maintained law and order and collected taxes in return for a payment from the VOC. The British followed a similar practice in Malaya. While establishing direct rule over the crucial commercial centers of Singapore and Malacca, the British allowed local Muslim rulers to maintain power in the interior of the peninsula.

ADMINISTRATION AND EDUCATION Indirect rule, though convenient and inexpensive, was not always feasible. In some instances, local resistance to the colonial conquest made such a policy impossible. In Burma, the staunch opposition of the monarchy and other traditionalist forces caused the British to abolish the monarchy and administer the country directly through their colonial government in India. In Indochina, the French used both direct and indirect means. They imposed direct rule on the southern provinces in the Mekong delta but governed the north as a protectorate, with the emperor retaining titular authority from his palace in Hué (HWAY). The French adopted a similar policy in Cambodia and Laos, where local rulers were left in charge with French advisers to counsel them.

Whatever method was used, the colonial regimes were slow to create democratic institutions. The first legislative councils and assemblies were composed almost exclusively of European residents in the colonies. The first representatives from the indigenous population were wealthy and politically conservative. When Southeast Asians complained, the French official Albert Sarraut advised patience: "I will treat you like my younger brothers, but do not forget that I am the older brother. I will slowly give you the dignity of humanity."[7] Only gradually and reluctantly did colonial officials begin to broaden the franchise.

Colonial officials were also slow to adopt educational reforms. Although the introduction of Western education was one of the justifications of colonialism, officials soon discovered that educating local elites could backfire. Colonial societies often had few jobs for lawyers, engineers, and architects, leading to a mass of unemployed intellectuals ready to take out their frustrations on the colonial regime. As one French official noted in voicing his opposition to increasing the number of schools in Vietnam, educating the locals meant not "one coolie less, but one rebel more."

ECONOMIC DEVELOPMENT Colonial powers were equally reluctant to take up the "white man's burden" in the area of economic development. As we have seen, their primary goals were to secure cheap raw materials and to maintain markets for manufactured goods. Colonial policy therefore concentrated on exporting raw materials—teakwood from Burma; rubber and tin from Malaya; spices, tea and coffee, and palm oil from the East Indies; and sugar and copra (the meat of a coconut) from the Philippines.

In some Southeast Asian colonial societies, a measure of industrial development did take place to meet the

© British Library, London//HIP/Art Resource, NY

Government Hill in Singapore. After occupying Singapore early in the nineteenth century, the British turned what was once a pirate lair into an important commercial seaport. Like other colonial port cities, Singapore became home to a rich mixture of peoples, who came to work as merchants, urban laborers, and craftsmen in the new imperial marketplace. The multiracial character of the colony is evident in this mid-nineteenth-century painting by a British artist. People of various ethnic backgrounds stroll on Government Hill, with the busy harbor in the background.

© William J. Duiker

© William J. Duiker

A Rubber Plantation. Natural rubber was one of the most important cash crops in European colonies in Asia. Rubber trees, native to the Amazon River basin in Brazil, were transplanted to Southeast Asia, where they became a major source of profit. Workers on the plantations received few benefits, however. Once the sap of the tree (known as latex and shown on the left) was extracted, it was hardened and pressed into sheets (shown on the right) and then sent to Europe for refining.

needs of the European population and local elites. Major manufacturing cities like Rangoon in lower Burma, Batavia (buh-TAY-vee-uh) on the island of Java, and Saigon (sy-GAHN) in French Indochina grew rapidly. Most large industrial and commercial establishments were owned and managed by Europeans, however, or, in some cases, by Indian or Chinese merchants.

COLONIALISM AND THE COUNTRYSIDE Despite the growth of an urban economy, the vast majority of people continued to farm the land. Many continued to live by subsistence agriculture, but the colonial policy of emphasizing cash crops for export also led to the creation of a plantation agriculture in which peasants worked for poverty-level wages on rubber and tea plantations owned by Europeans. Many laborers were "shanghaied" (the English term originated from the practice of recruiting workers, often from the docks and streets of Shanghai, by the use of force, alcohol, or drugs) to work on the plantations, where conditions were often so inhumane that thousands died. High taxes, imposed by colonial governments to pay for administrative costs or improvements in the local infrastructure, were a heavy burden for poor peasants.

The situation was made even more difficult by the dramatic growth of the population as improved sanitation and medical treatment resulted in lower rates of infant mortality. The population of the island of Java, for example, increased from about a million in the precolonial era to about 40 million at the end of the nineteenth century. Under these conditions, the rural areas could no longer support the growing populations, and many young people fled to the cities to seek jobs in factories or shops.

As in India, colonial rule brought some benefits to Southeast Asia. It led to the beginnings of a modern economic infrastructure and to what is sometimes called a "modernizing elite" dedicated to the creation of an advanced industrialized society. The development of an export market helped create an entrepreneurial class in rural areas. This happened, for example, on the outer islands of the Dutch East Indies (such as Borneo and Sumatra), where small growers of rubber trees, palm trees for oil, coffee, tea, and spices began to share in the profits of the colonial enterprise.

CHRONOLOGY Imperialism in Asia	
Stamford Raffles arrives in Singapore	1819
British attack lower Burma	1826
British rail network opens in northern India	1853
Sepoy Rebellion	1857
French attack Vietnam	1858
British and French agree to neutralize Thailand	1896
Commodore Dewey defeats Spanish fleet in Manila Bay	1898
French create Indochinese Union	1900

Empire Building in Africa

FOCUS QUESTION: What factors were behind the "scramble for Africa," and what impact did it have on the continent?

Before 1800, European economic interests in Africa had been relatively limited, providing little incentive for the penetration of the interior or the political takeover of the coastal areas. The slave trade, the main source of European profit during the eighteenth century, could be carried on by using African rulers and merchants as intermediaries. Disease, political instability, the lack of transportation, and the generally unhealthy climate all deterred Europeans from more extensive efforts in Africa. The situation began to change in the nineteenth century, as the growing need for industrial materials created a reason for the imperialist countries to increase their economic presence in the continent.

The Growing European Presence in West Africa

As the new century dawned, the slave trade was in decline, in part because of the efforts of humanitarians in several European countries. Dutch merchants effectively ceased trafficking in slaves in 1795, and the Danes stopped in 1803. In 1808, the slave trade was declared illegal in both Great Britain and the United States. The British began to apply pressure on other nations to follow suit, and most did so after the end of the Napoleonic wars in 1815, leaving only Portugal and Spain as practitioners of the trade south of the equator. In the meantime, the demand for slaves began to decline in the Western Hemisphere. When slavery was abolished in the United States in 1863 and in Cuba and Brazil seventeen years later, the slave trade across the Atlantic was effectively brought to an end. It continued to exist, although at a reduced rate, along the Swahili coast in East Africa.

As the Atlantic slave trade declined, Europeans became more interested in so-called legitimate trade. Exports of peanuts, timber, hides, and palm oil from West Africa increased substantially during the first decades of the nineteenth century, while imports of textile goods and other manufactured products rose.

European governments also began to push for a more permanent presence along the coast. During the early nineteenth century, the British established settlements along the Gold Coast and in Sierra Leone, where they set up agricultural plantations for freed slaves who had returned from the Western Hemisphere or had been liberated by British ships while en route to the Americas. A similar haven for ex-slaves was developed with the assistance of the United States in Liberia. The French occupied the area around the Senegal River near Cape Verde, where they attempted to develop peanut plantations.

The European presence in West Africa led to the emergence of a new class of Africans educated in Western culture and often employed by Europeans. Many became Christians, and some studied in European or American universities. At the same time, tensions were increasing between Europeans and African governments. Most African states were able to maintain their independence from this creeping European encroachment, called "**informal empire**" by some historians, but the prospects for the future were ominous. When local groups attempted to organize to protect their interests, the British stepped in and annexed the coastal states as the British colony of Gold Coast in 1874. At about the same time, the British extended an informal protectorate over warring ethnic groups in the Niger delta (see Map 21.3).

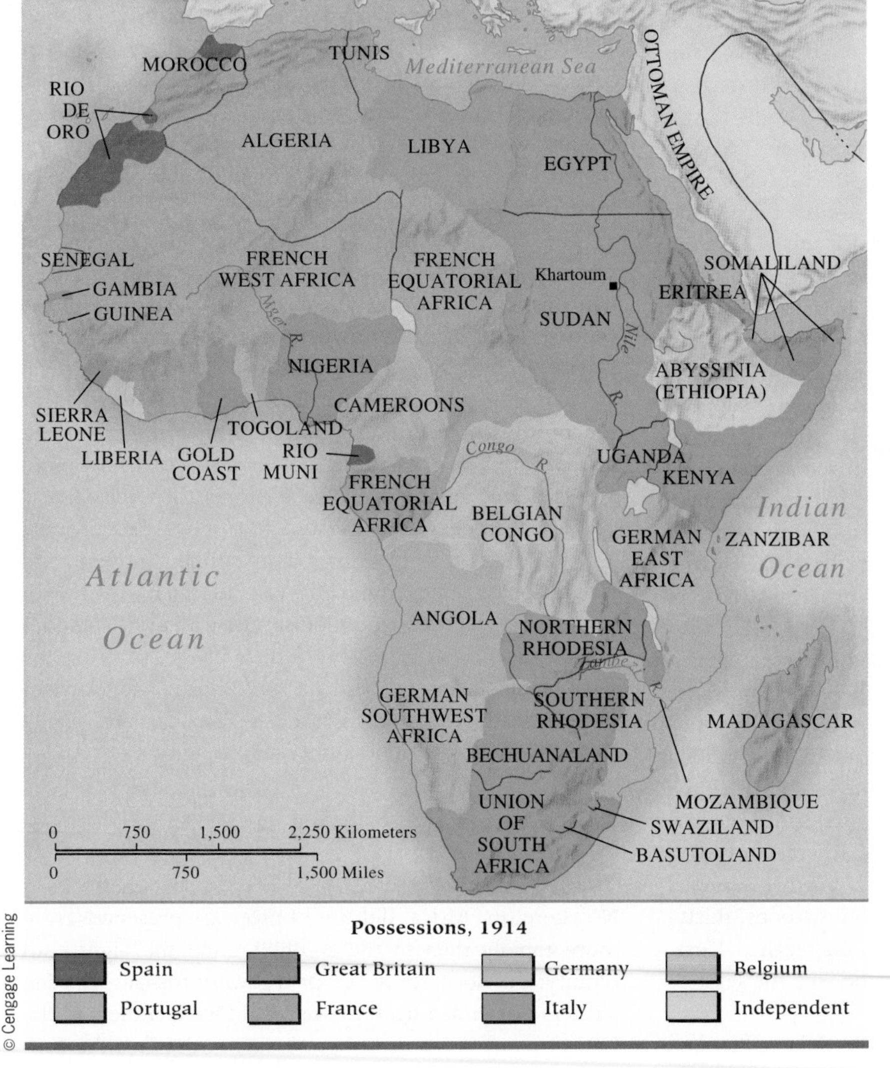

© Cengage Learning

MAP 21.3 Africa in 1914. By the start of the twentieth century, virtually all of Africa was under some form of European rule. The territorial divisions established by colonial powers on the continent of Africa on the eve of World War I are shown here.

Q *Which European countries possessed the most colonies in Africa? Why did Ethiopia remain independent?*

Imperialist Shadow over the Nile

A similar process was under way in the Nile valley. There had long been interest in shortening the trade route to the East by digging a canal across the isthmus separating the Mediterranean from the Red Sea. In 1798, Napoleon had unsuccessfully invaded Egypt in an effort to cement French power in the eastern Mediterranean and open a faster route to India. French troops landed in Egypt and destroyed the ramshackle Mamluk (MAM-look) regime, but the British counterattacked and destroyed the French fleet. The British restored the Mamluks to power, but in 1805 Muhammad Ali (1769–1849), an Ottoman army officer, seized control.

During the next three decades, Muhammad Ali introduced a series of reforms to bring Egypt into the modern world. He modernized the army, set up a public education system (supplementing the traditional religious education provided in Muslim schools), and sponsored the creation of a small industrial sector producing refined sugar, textiles, munitions, and even ships. Muhammad Ali also extended

Egyptian authority southward into the Sudan and eastward into Arabia, Syria, and northern Iraq and even threatened to seize Istanbul itself. To prevent the possible collapse of the Ottoman Empire, the British and the French recognized Muhammad Ali as the hereditary **pasha** (PAH-shuh) of Egypt under the loose authority of the Ottoman government.

The growing economic importance of the Nile valley, along with the development of steam navigation, made the heretofore visionary plans for a Suez canal more urgent. In 1869, construction of the canal was completed under the direction of Ferdinand de Lesseps (fer-DEE-nahn duh le-SEPS), a French entrepreneur. The project brought little immediate benefit to Egypt, however. The construction cost thousands of lives and left the Egyptian government deep in debt, forcing it to depend increasingly on foreign financial support. When an army revolt against growing foreign influence broke out in 1881, the British stepped in to protect their investment (they had bought Egypt's canal company shares in 1875) and established an informal protectorate that would last until World War I.

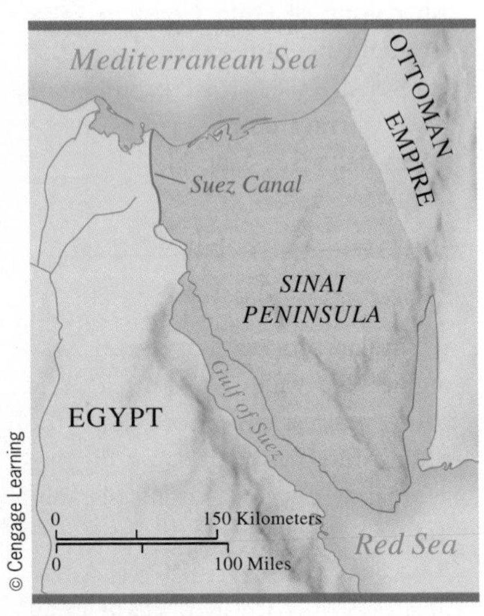

The Suez Canal

Rising discontent in the Sudan added to Egypt's growing internal problems. In 1881, the Muslim cleric Muhammad Ahmad (AH-mahd) (1844–1885), known as the Mahdi (MAH-dee) (in Arabic, the "rightly guided one"), led a religious revolt that brought much of the upper Nile under his control. The famous British general Charles Gordon led a military force to Khartoum (kahr-TOOM) to restore Egyptian authority, but his besieged army was captured in 1885 by the Mahdi's troops, thirty-six hours before a British rescue mission reached Khartoum. Gordon himself died in the battle (see the Film & History feature on p. 557).

The weakening of Turkish rule in the Nile valley had a parallel to the west, where local viceroys in Tripoli, Tunis, and Algiers had begun to establish their autonomy. In 1830, the French, on the pretext of protecting shipping from pirates, seized the area surrounding Algiers and integrated it into the French Empire. In 1881, the French imposed a protectorate on neighboring Tunisia; only Tripoli and Cyrenaica (seer-uh-NAY-uh-kuh), the territories comprising modern Libya, remained under Turkish rule.

Arab Merchants and European Missionaries in East Africa

As always, events in East Africa followed their own distinctive pattern. Whereas the Atlantic slave trade was in decline, demand for slaves was increasing on the other side of the continent due to the growth of plantation agriculture in the region. The French introduced sugar to the island of Réunion (ray-yoo-NYAHN) early in the century, and plantations of cloves (introduced from the Moluccas) were established under Omani Arab ownership on the island of Zanzibar (ZAN-zi-bar). Zanzibar itself became the major shipping port along the east coast during the early nineteenth century, and the sultan of Oman, who had reasserted Arab suzerainty over the region after the collapse of Portuguese authority, established his capital there in 1840.

The tenacity of the slave trade in East Africa—Zanzibar was now the largest slave market in Africa—drew Christian missionaries to the region during the middle of the century. The most renowned was the Scottish doctor David Livingstone (LIV-ing-stuhn) (1813–1873), who arrived in Africa in 1841. Because Livingstone spent much of his time exploring the interior of the continent, discovering Victoria Falls in the process, he was occasionally criticized for being more explorer than missionary. But Livingstone was convinced that it was his divinely appointed task to bring Christianity to the continent, and his passionate opposition to slavery did much to win public support for the abolitionist cause. Public outcries caused the British to redouble their efforts to bring the slave trade to an end, and in 1873 shortly after Livingstone's death, the slave market at Zanzibar was finally closed as the result of pressure from London.

Bantus, Boers, and British in the South

Nowhere in Africa did the European presence grow more rapidly than in the south. During the eighteenth century, the Boers (BOORS *or* BORS), Afrikaans-speaking farmers descended from the original Dutch settlers of the Cape Colony, began to migrate eastward. After the British seized the cape during the Napoleonic wars, the Boers' eastward migration intensified, culminating in the Great Trek of the mid-1830s. In part, the Boers' departure was provoked by the British attitude toward the local population. Slavery was abolished in the British Empire in 1834, and the British government was

FILM & HISTORY

Khartoum (1966)

The mission of General Charles Gordon to Khartoum in 1884 was one of the most dramatic news stories of the late nineteenth century. Gordon was already renowned for his successful efforts to bring an end to the practice of slavery in North Africa and his role in helping suppress the Taiping Rebellion in China in the 1860s (see Chapter 22). But the Khartoum affair not only marked the culmination of his storied career but also symbolized the struggle in Britain between advocates and opponents of imperial expansion. The battle for Khartoum became an object lesson in modern British history.

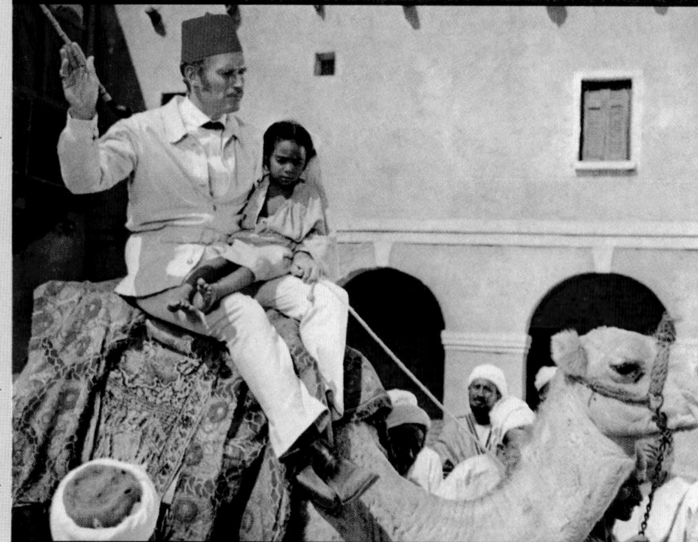
Cinerama/United Artists/The Kobal Collection at Art Resource, NY

General Charles Gordon (Charlton Heston) astride his camel in Khartoum, Sudan.

Proponents of British imperial expansion argued that the country must project its power in the Nile valley to protect the Suez Canal, its main trade route to the East. Critics argued that imperial overreach would inevitably entangle the country in unwinnable wars in far-off places. The movie *Khartoum,* filmed in Egypt and London, captures the ferocity of the battle for the Nile as well as its significance for the future of the British Empire. General Gordon, stoically played by the American actor Charlton Heston, is a devout Christian who has devoted his life to carrying out the moral imperative of imperialism. When peace in the Sudan (then a British protectorate) is threatened by the forces of the Muslim mystic Muhammad Ahmad—known as the Mahdi—Gordon leads a mission to Khartoum under orders to prevent catastrophe there. But Prime Minister William Ewart Gladstone, admirably portrayed by the British actor Ralph Richardson, fears that Gordon's messianic desire to save the Sudan will entrap the government in an unwinnable war; he thus orders Gordon to evacuate the city. The most fascinating character in the film is the Mahdi (played brilliantly by Sir Laurence Olivier), who believes that he has a sacred mandate to carry the Prophet's words to the global Muslim community.

The film reaches a climax with the clash of wills in the battle for control of Khartoum. Although the film's portrayal of a face-to-face meeting between Gordon and the Mahdi is not based on fact, the narrative serves as an object lesson on the dangers of imperial overreach and as an eerie foretaste of the clash between Islam and Christendom in our own day.

generally more sympathetic to the rights of the local African population than were the Afrikaners (ah-fri-KAH-nurz), many of whom believed that white superiority was ordained by God. Eventually, the Boers formed their own independent republics—the Orange Free State and the South African Republic, usually called the Transvaal (trans-VAHL) (see Map 21.4).

Although the Boer occupation of the eastern territory was initially facilitated by internecine warfare among the local inhabitants, the new settlers met some resistance. In the early nineteenth century, the Zulus (ZOO-looz), a Bantu people led by a talented ruler named Shaka (SHAH-kuh), engaged in a series of wars with the Europeans that ended only when Shaka was overthrown.

The Scramble for Africa

At the beginning of the 1880s, most of Africa was still independent. European rule was limited to the fringes of the continent, such as Algeria, the Gold Coast, and South Africa. Other areas like Egypt, lower Nigeria, Senegal (sen-ni-GAHL), and Mozambique (moh-zam-BEEK) were under loose protectorates. But the pace of European penetration was accelerating.

The scramble began in the mid-1880s when several European states, including Belgium, France, Germany, and Great Britain, engaged in a feeding frenzy to seize a piece of the African cake before the plate had been picked clean. By 1900, virtually all of the continent had

© Mary Evans Picture Library/Courtesy The Everett Collection, Inc.

The Sunday Battle. When Boer "trekkers" arrived in the Transvaal in the 1830s and 1840s, they were bitterly opposed by the Zulus, a Bantu-speaking people who resisted European encroachments on their territory for decades. This 1847 lithograph depicted thousands of Zulu warriors engaged in battle with their European rivals. Zulu resistance was not finally quelled until the end of the nineteenth century.

been placed under some form of European rule. The British consolidated their authority over the Nile valley and seized additional territories in East Africa (see Map 21.3 on p. 555). The French advanced eastward from Senegal into the central Sahara. They also occupied Madagascar and other territories in West and Central Africa. The Germans claimed the hinterland opposite Zanzibar, as well as coastal strips in West and Southwest Africa, and King Leopold (LAY-oh-polt) II (1835–1909) of Belgium claimed the Congo for his own personal use. Italy entered the contest in 1911–1912 and seized the territories that comprise modern Libya.

What had sparked the imperialist hysteria that brought an end to African independence? Although trade between Europe and Africa had increased, it was probably not sufficient, by itself, to justify the risks and expense of conquest. More important than economic interests were the rivalries among the European states that led them to engage in imperialist takeovers out of fear that if they did not, another state would. As one British diplomat remarked, a protectorate at the mouth of the Niger River would be an "unwelcome burden," but a French protectorate there would be "fatal." Hence, as in Southeast Asia, statesmen felt compelled to obtain colonies as a hedge against future actions by rivals. Notably, the British solidified their control over the entire Nile valley to protect the Suez Canal from the French.

Another consideration might be called the "missionary factor," as European missionaries lobbied for colonial takeovers to facilitate their efforts to convert the African population. The concept of social Darwinism and the "white man's burden" persuaded many that they had a duty to introduce the African people to the benefits of Western civilization. Even David Livingstone believed that missionary work and economic development had to go hand in hand, pleading with his fellow Europeans to introduce the "three Cs" (Christianity, commerce, and civilization) to the continent. How much easier that task would be if African peoples were under benevolent European rule!

There were more prosaic reasons as well. Advances in Western technology and European superiority in firearms made it easier than ever for a small European force to defeat superior numbers (see the box on p. 560). Furthermore, life expectancy for Europeans living in Africa had improved. With the discovery that quinine (from the bark of the cinchona tree) could provide partial immunity from malaria, the mortality rate for Europeans living in Africa dropped dramatically. By the end of the century, European residents in tropical Africa faced only slightly higher risks of death by disease than individuals living in Europe.

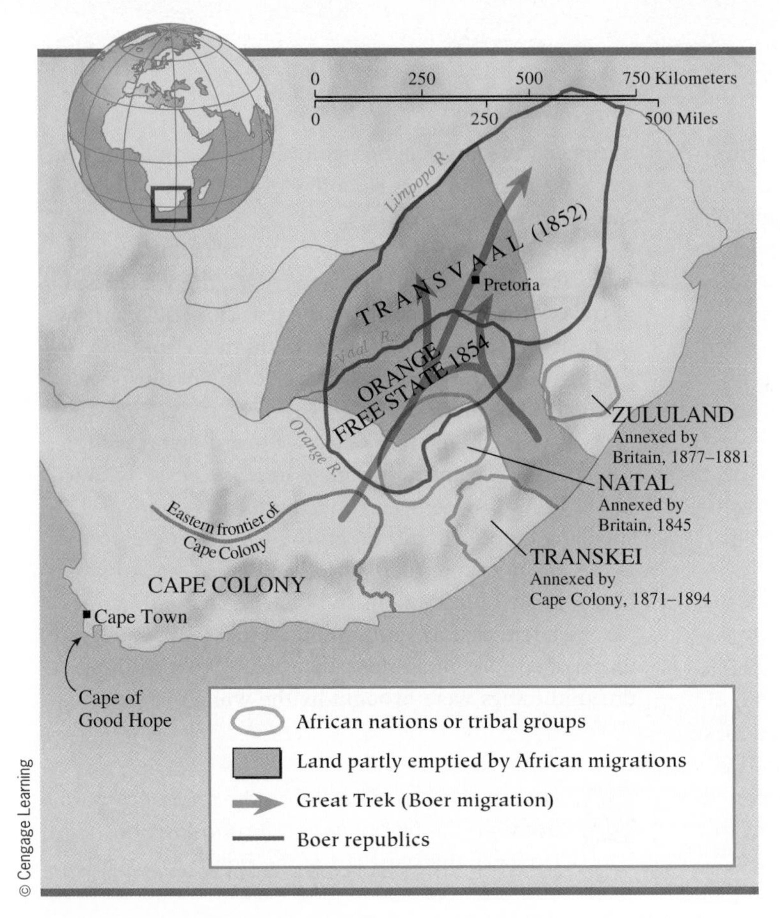

© Cengage Learning

MAP 21.4 The Struggle for Southern Africa. European settlers from the Cape Colony expanded into adjacent areas of southern Africa during the nineteenth century. The arrows indicate the routes taken by the Afrikaans-speaking Boers.

Who were the Boers, and why did they migrate eastward?

Under these circumstances, King Leopold of Belgium used missionary activities as an excuse to claim vast territories in the Congo River basin—Belgium, he said, as "a small country, with a small people," needed a colony to enhance its image.[8] The royal land grab set off a race among European nations to stake claims throughout sub-Saharan Africa. Leopold ended up with the territories south of the Congo River, while France occupied areas to the north. Rapacious European adventurers established plantations in the new Belgian Congo to grow rubber, palm oil, and other valuable export products. Conditions for African workers were so abysmal that an international outcry led in 1903 to the formation of a commission under British consul Roger Casement to investigate. The commission's report, issued in 1904, helped to bring about reforms.

Meanwhile, in East Africa, Germany annexed the colony of Tanganyika (tan-gan-YEE-kuh). To avert violent clashes among the great powers, the German chancellor, Otto von Bismarck, convened a conference in Berlin in 1884 to set ground rules for future annexations of African territory. Like the famous Open Door Notes fifteen years later (see Chapter 22), the conference combined high-minded resolutions with a hardheaded recognition of practical interests. The delegates called for free commerce in the Congo and along the Niger River as well as for further efforts to end the slave trade. At the same time, the participants recognized the inevitability of the imperialist dynamic, agreeing only that future annexations of African territory should not be recognized until effective occupation had been demonstrated. No African delegates were present at the conference.

During the next few years, African territories were annexed without provoking a major confrontation between the Western powers, but in 1898, Britain and France reached the brink of conflict at Fashoda (fuh-SHOH-duh), a small town in the Sudan. The French had been advancing eastward across the Sahara with the objective of controlling the regions around the upper Nile. British and Egyptian troops then marched southward to head off the French. After a tense face-off, the French government backed down, and British authority over the area was secured.

Colonialism in Africa

Having seized Africa in what could almost be described as a fit of hysteria, the European powers had to decide what to do with it. With economic concerns relatively limited except for isolated areas like the gold mines in the Transvaal and copper deposits in the Belgian Congo, interest in Africa declined, and most European governments settled down to govern their new territories with the least effort and expense possible. In many cases, this meant a form of indirect rule similar to what the British used in the princely states in India.

INDIRECT RULE IN WEST AFRICA For British administrators, the stated goal of indirect rule was to preserve African political traditions. The desire to limit cost was one reason for this approach, but it may also have been due to the conviction that Africans were inherently inferior and thus incapable of adopting European customs and institutions. In any event, indirect rule entailed relying on existing political elites and institutions. In some areas, the British simply asked a local ruler to formally accept British authority. Sometimes the Africans did the

The Ndebele Rebellion

As British forces advanced northward from the Cape Colony toward the Zambezi River in the 1890s, they overran the Ndebele (uhn-duh-BEE-lee) people, who occupied rich lands near the site of the ruins of Great Zimbabwe (zim-BAHB-way). Angered by British brutality, Ndebele warriors revolted in 1896 to throw off their oppressors. Despite the Ndebele's great superiority in numbers, British units possessed the feared Maxim gun, which mowed down African attackers by the hundreds. Faced with defeat, the Ndebele king, Lobengula (loh-beng-GOO-luh), fled into the hills and committed suicide. In the following account, a survivor describes the conflict.

Ndansi Kumalo, *A Personal Account*

We surrendered to the white people and were told to go back to our homes and live our usual lives and attend to our crops. But the white men sent native police who did abominable things; they were cruel and assaulted a lot of our people and helped themselves to our cattle and goats. . . . They interfered with our wives and molested them. . . . We thought it best to fight and die rather than bear it. . . .

We knew that we had very little chance because their weapons were so much superior to ours. But we meant to fight to the last, feeling that even if we could not beat them we might at least kill a few of them and so have some sort of revenge. . . .

I remember a fight . . . when we charged the white men. There were some hundreds of us; the white men also were many. We charged them at close quarters: we thought we had a good chance to kill them but the Maxims were too much for us. . . . Many of our people were killed in this fight. . . .

We were still fighting when we heard that [Cecil] Rhodes was coming and wanted to make peace with us. It was best to come to terms he said, and not go shedding blood like this on both sides. . . . So peace was made. Many of our people had been killed, and now we began to die of starvation; and then came the rinderpest [an infectious disease] and the cattle that were still left to us perished. We could not help thinking that all these dreadful things were brought by the white people.

How would you characterize the relationship between the Ndebele people and the British? How can the behavior of the British as described in this account be reconciled with the concept of the "white man's burden"?

Source: From Margery Perham, *Ten Africans* (London: Faber & Faber, 1963), pp. 72–75.

asking, as in the case of the African leaders in Cameroons who wrote to Queen Victoria:

> We *wish* to have your laws in our towns. We want to have every *fashion* altered; also we will do according to your Consul's *word*. Plenty wars here in our country. Plenty murder and plenty idol worshippers. Perhaps these *lines* of our writing will look to you as an *idle* tale.
>
> We have *spoken* to the English consul plenty times about having an English *government* here. We never have answer from you, so we wish to write you *ourselves*.[9]

Nigeria offers a typical example of British indirect rule. British officials maintained the central administration, but local authority was assigned to local chiefs, with British district officers serving as intermediaries. The local authorities were expected to maintain law and order and to collect taxes. Local customs were generally left undisturbed, although slavery was abolished. A dual legal system was instituted that applied African laws to Africans and European laws to foreigners.

Although such a system did not severely disrupt local institutions, it had some undesirable consequences. It was essentially a fraud since British administrators made all major decisions and the local authorities merely enforced them. Moreover, indirect rule served to perpetuate the autocratic system often in use prior to colonial takeover.

THE BRITISH IN EAST AFRICA The situation was somewhat different in East Africa, especially in Kenya, which had a relatively large European population. The local government had encouraged white settlers to

© Universal Images Group/Getty Images

Legacy of Shame. By the mid-nineteenth century, most European nations had prohibited the trade in African slaves, but slavery continued to exist in Africa well into the next century. The most flagrant example was in the Belgian Congo, where the mistreatment of conscript laborers led to a popular outcry and the formation of a commission to investigate and recommend reforms. Shown here are two members of a chain gang in the Belgian Congo. The photograph was taken in 1904.

CHRONOLOGY Imperialism in Africa

Dutch abolish slave trade in Africa	1795
Napoleon invades Egypt	1798
Slave trade declared illegal in Great Britain	1808
French seize Algeria	1830
Boers' Great Trek in southern Africa	1830s
Sultan of Oman establishes capital at Zanzibar	1840
David Livingstone arrives in Africa	1841
Slavery abolished in the United States	1863
Suez Canal completed	1869
Zanzibar slave market closed	1873
British establish Gold Coast colony	1874
British establish informal protectorate over Egypt	1881
Berlin Conference on Africa	1884
Charles Gordon killed at Khartoum	1885
Confrontation at Fashoda	1898
Boer War	1899–1902
Casement Commission report on the Belgian Congo	1904
Union of South Africa established	1910

migrate to the area as a means of promoting economic development. Fertile farmlands in the central highlands were reserved for Europeans, while specified reserve lands were set aside for Africans. The presence of a substantial European minority (although, in fact, they represented only about 1 percent of the entire population) affected Kenya's political development. The white settlers sought self-government and dominion status similar to that granted to Canada and Australia. The British government, however, was not willing to risk provoking racial tensions with the African majority and agreed only to establish separate government organs for the European and African populations.

BRITISH RULE IN SOUTH AFRICA The British used a different system in southern Africa, which had a high percentage of European settlers. The situation was complicated by the division between the English-speaking and Afrikaner elements, which intensified after gold and diamonds were discovered in the Boer republic of the Transvaal. After Cecil Rhodes, prime minister of the Cape Colony, attempted to bring the Transvaal under British rule, the so-called Boer War broke out between Britain and the Boer republics in 1899. Guerrilla resistance by the Boers was fierce, but the vastly superior forces of the British were able to prevail by 1902. To compensate the Afrikaners for the loss of independence, the British government agreed that only whites would vote in the now essentially self-governing colony. Nevertheless, the brutalities committed during the war (the British introduced an institution later known as the concentration camp) had left bitterness on both sides.

In 1910, the British agreed to the creation of the independent Union of South Africa, which combined the old Cape Colony and Natal (nuh-TAHL) with the Boer republics. The new union adopted a representative government, but only for the European population, while the African reserves of Basutoland (buh-SOO-toh-land), now Lesotho (luh-SOH-toh); Bechuanaland (bech-WAH-nuh-land), now Botswana (baht-SWAH-nuh); and Swaziland (SWAH-zee-land) were subordinated directly to the crown. The union was free to manage its domestic affairs and possessed considerable autonomy in foreign relations. Formal British rule was also extended to the lands south of the Zambezi River, which were eventually divided into the territories of Northern and Southern Rhodesia. Southern Rhodesia attracted many British immigrants, and in 1922, after a popular referendum, it became a crown colony.

DIRECT RULE Most other European nations governed their African possessions through a form of direct rule. The prototype was the French system, which reflected the centralized administrative system used in France. At the top was a French governor-general, who was appointed from Paris. At the provincial level, French commissioners were assigned to deal with local administrators, who were required to be conversant in French.

The French ideal was to assimilate their African subjects into French culture rather than preserving their local traditions. Africans were eligible to run for office and to serve in the French National Assembly, and a few were appointed to high positions in the colonial administration. Such policies reflected the relative absence of racist attitudes in French society, as well as the conviction among the French of the superiority of Gallic culture.

After World War I, European colonial policy in Africa entered a more formal phase that specialists in African studies call "**high colonialism**." The administrative network was extended into outlying areas, where it was represented by a district official and defended by a small African army under European command. The colonial system was viewed more formally as a moral and social responsibility, a "sacred trust" to be maintained by the civilized countries until the Africans became capable of self-government. Greater attention was given to improving social services, including education, medicine and sanitation, and communications. More emphasis was placed on economic development to enable the colonies to become self-sufficient. More Africans served in colonial administrations, although rarely in positions of responsibility. At the same time, race consciousness probably increased. Segregated clubs, schools, and churches were established as more European officials brought their wives and began to raise families in the colonies. European feelings of superiority to their African subjects led to countless examples of cruelty. Although the institution of slavery was discouraged, African workers were often subjected to harsh conditions as they were put to use in promoting the cause of imperialism.

WOMEN IN COLONIAL AFRICA The colonial era had a mixed impact on the rights and status of women in Africa. Sexual relationships changed profoundly, sometimes in ways that could justly be described as beneficial. Colonial governments attempted to bring an end to forced marriage, bodily mutilation such as clitoridectomy (clit-er-ih-DEK-toh-mee), and polygamy. Missionaries introduced women to Western education and encouraged them to organize to defend their interests.

But the colonial system had some unfavorable consequences as well. Previously, African women had benefited from the matrilineal system and their traditional role as the primary agricultural producers. Under colonialism, European settlers not only took the best land for themselves but also tended to deal exclusively with males, encouraging them to develop lucrative cash crops using new techniques, while women were restricted to traditional farming methods. African men applied chemical fertilizer to the fields, but women continued to use manure. Men began to use bicycles and eventually trucks for transport, but women still carried goods on their heads. In British colonies, Victorian attitudes of female subordination led to restrictions on women's freedom, and positions in government that they had formerly held were now closed to them.

The Emergence of Anticolonialism

FOCUS QUESTION: How did the subject peoples respond to colonialism, and what role did nationalism play in their response?

Thus far we have looked at the colonial experience primarily from the point of view of the colonial powers. Equally important is the way the subject peoples reacted to the experience. In this chapter, we will deal with the initial response, which can be described in most cases as "traditional resistance." Later, however, many people in the colonized societies began to turn to nationalism as a means of preserving their ethnic, cultural, or religious identity. We will deal with that stage in more detail in Chapter 24.

Stirrings of Nationhood

As noted earlier, nationalism involves an awareness of being part of a community that possesses common institutions, traditions, language, and customs (see the comparative essay "The Rise of Nationalism" in Chapter 20). In the nineteenth century, few societies met such criteria. Even today, most modern states contain a variety of ethnic, religious, and linguistic communities, each with its own sense of cultural and national identity. Another question is how nationalism differs from other forms of tribal, religious, or linguistic affiliation. Should every group that resists assimilation into a larger political entity be called nationalist?

Such questions complicate the study of nationalism and make agreement on a definition elusive. The dilemmas are especially complex when discussing Asia and Africa, where most societies are deeply divided by ethnic, linguistic, and religious differences and the very term *nationalism* is a foreign concept imported from the West. Before the colonial era, most traditional societies in Africa and Asia were formed on the basis of religious beliefs, ethnic loyalties, or devotion to hereditary monarchies. Although some individuals may have identified themselves as members of a particular national group, others viewed themselves as subjects of a king, members of a lineage group, or adherents to a particular religion.

The advent of European colonialism brought the consciousness of modern nationhood to many of these societies. The creation of colonies with defined borders and a powerful central government led to the weakening of local ethnic and religious loyalties. The introduction of Western ideas of citizenship and representative government—even though they usually were not replicated in the colonies themselves—produced a desire for participation in the affairs of government. At the same time, the appearance of a new elite class based on alleged racial or cultural superiority aroused a shared sense of resentment among the subject peoples. By the first quarter of the twentieth century, political movements dedicated to the overthrow of colonial rule and the creation of modern nations had arisen throughout much of the non-Western world.

Modern nationalism, then, was both a product of colonialism and a reaction to it. But a sense of nationhood does not emerge full-blown in a society. The rise of modern nationalism is a process that begins among a few members of the educated elite (most commonly among articulate professionals such as lawyers, teachers, journalists, and doctors) and then spreads gradually to the mass of the population. Even after national independence has been realized, it is often questionable whether a mature sense of nationhood has been created, since local ethnic, linguistic, or religious ties often continue to predominate over loyalty to the larger community (see Chapter 29).

Traditional Resistance: A Precursor to Nationalism

The beginnings of modern nationalism can be found in the initial resistance by the indigenous peoples to the colonial conquest. Although such resistance was essentially motivated by the desire to defend traditional institutions and thus was not strictly "nationalist," it did reflect a primitive concept of nationhood in that it aimed at protecting the homeland from the invader. After independence was achieved, governments of new nations often hailed early resistance movements as the precursors of twentieth-century nationalist movements. Thus, traditional resistance to colonial conquest may be viewed as the first stage in the development of modern nationalism.

Such resistance took various forms. For the most part, it was led by the existing ruling class, although in some instances traditionalists continued their opposition even after resistance by the rulers had ceased. In India, Tipu Sultan (tih-POO SUL-tun) fought the British in the Deccan after the collapse of the Mughal dynasty. Similarly, after the decrepit monarchy in Vietnam had bowed to French pressure, civilian and military officials set up an organization called Can Vuong (kahn VWAHNG) (literally, "save the king") and continued their own resistance campaign without imperial sanction.

Sometimes traditional resistance to Western penetration took the form of peasant revolts. In traditional Asian societies, peasant discontent with high taxes, official corruption, rising debt, and famine had often led to uprisings. Under colonialism, rural conditions frequently deteriorated as population density increased and peasants were driven off the land to make way for plantation agriculture. Angry peasants then vented their frustration at the foreign invaders. For example, in Burma, the Buddhist monk Saya San (SAH-yuh SAHN) led a peasant uprising against the British. Similar unrest occurred in India, where *zamindars* and rural villagers alike resisted government attempts to increase tax revenues. A peasant uprising took place in Algeria in 1840.

OPPOSITION TO COLONIAL RULE IN AFRICA Because of Africa's size and its ethnic, religious, and linguistic diversity, resistance to the European invaders was often sporadic and uncoordinated, but fierce nonetheless. The uprising led by the Mahdi in the Sudan was only the most dramatic example. In South Africa, the Zulus engaged in a bitter war of resistance to Boer colonists arriving from the Cape Colony. Later they fought against the British occupation of their territory and were not finally subdued until the end of the century. In West Africa, the Ashanti ruling class led a bitter struggle against the British with broad-based popular support. The lack of modern weapons was decisive, however, and African resistance forces eventually suffered defeat throughout the continent (see the box on p. 560). The one exception was Ethiopia where, at the Battle of Adowa (AH-doo-wah) in 1896, the modernized army created by Emperor Menelik (MEN-il-ik), who had prudently purchased modern European weapons, was able to fend off an Italian invasion force and preserve the country's national independence well into the next century.

THE SEPOY REBELLION Perhaps the most famous uprising against European authority in the mid-nineteenth century was the revolt of the **sepoys** (SEE-poiz) in India. The sepoys (from the Turkish *sipahis*, cavalrymen or soldiers) were Indian troops hired by the East India Company to protect British interests. Unrest within Indian units of the colonial army had been common since early in the century, when it had been sparked by economic issues, religious sensitivities, or nascent anticolonial sentiment. In 1857, tension erupted when the British adopted the new Enfield rifle for use by sepoy infantrymen. The rifle was a muzzleloader that used paper cartridges covered with animal fat and lard; because the cartridge had to be bitten off, it broke strictures against high-class Hindus' eating animal products and Muslim prohibitions against eating pork. Protests among sepoy units in northern India turned into a full-scale mutiny, supported by uprisings in rural districts in various parts of the country. But the revolt lacked clear goals, and discord between Hindus and Muslims prevented them from coordinating operations. Although the Indian troops fought bravely and outnumbered the British six to one, they were poorly organized, and the British forces (often supplemented by sepoy troops) suppressed the rebellion.

Still, the revolt frightened the British and led to a number of reforms. The proportion of Indian troops in the army was reduced, and precedence was given to ethnic groups likely to be loyal to the British, such as the Sikhs (SEEKS *or* see-ikhz) of Punjab (pun-JAHB) and the Gurkhas (GUR-kuhz), an upland people from Nepal (nuh-PAHL). The British also decided to suppress the final remnants of the hapless Mughal dynasty, which had supported the mutiny, and turned responsibility for the administration of the subcontinent over to the crown.

Like the Sepoy Rebellion, traditional resistance movements usually met with little success. Peasants armed with pikes and spears were no match for Western armies possessing the most terrifying weapons then known to human society. In a few cases, such as the revolt of the Mahdi at Khartoum, the local peoples were able to defeat the invaders temporarily. But such successes were rare, and the late nineteenth century witnessed the seemingly inexorable march of the Western powers, armed with the Gatling gun (the first rapid-fire weapon and the precursor of the modern machine gun), to mastery of the globe.

THE PATH OF COLLABORATION Not all Asians and Africans reacted to a colonial takeover by choosing the path of violent resistance. Some found elements to admire in Western civilization and compared it favorably with their own traditional practices and institutions (see the box on p. 565). Even in sub-Saharan Africa, where the colonial record was often at its most brutal, some elites supported the imposition of colonial authority.

The decision to collaborate with the colonial administration was undoubtedly often motivated by self-interest. In those cases, the collaborators might be treated with scorn or even hostility by their contemporaries, especially those who had chosen resistance. On occasion, however, the decision was reached only after painful consideration of the alternatives. Whatever the circumstances, the decision often divided friends and families, as occurred with two onetime childhood friends in central Vietnam, when one chose resistance and the other collaboration (see the box on p. 566).

Not all colonial subjects, of course, felt required to choose between resistance and collaboration. Most simply lived out their lives without engaging in the political arena. Even so, in some cases their actions had an impact on their country's future. A prime example was Ram Mohan Roy (RAHM moh-HUHN ROI). A *brahmin* from Bengal (ben-GAHL), Roy founded the Brahmo Samaj (BRAH-moh suh-MAHJ) (Society of Brahma) in 1828 to help his fellow Hindus defend their faith against verbal attacks from British acquaintances. Roy was by no means a hidebound traditionalist. He opposed such practices as *sati* and recognized the benefit of introducing the best aspects of European culture into Indian society. He probably had no intention of promoting Indian independence by his action, but by encouraging his countrymen to defend their traditional values against the onslaught of Western civilization, he helped to promote the first stirrings of nationalist sentiment in nineteenth-century India.

Imperialism: The Balance Sheet

Few periods of history are as controversial as the era of imperialism. To defenders of the colonial enterprise like the poet Rudyard Kipling, imperialism was the "white man's burden," a disagreeable but necessary phase in the evolution of human society (see the box on p. 547).

Critics disagree, portraying imperialism as a tragedy of major proportions. The insatiable drive of the advanced economic powers for access to raw materials and markets created an exploitative environment that transformed the vast majority of colonial peoples into a permanent underclass while restricting the benefits of modern technology to a privileged few. In this view, Kipling's "white man's burden" was a hypocritical gesture to hoodwink the naive and salve the guilty feelings of those who recognized imperialism for what it was—a savage act of rape. In the blunt words of two Western critics of imperialism: "Why is Africa (or for that matter Latin America and much of Asia) so poor? . . . The answer is very brief: we have made it poor."[10]

The Civilizing Mission in Egypt

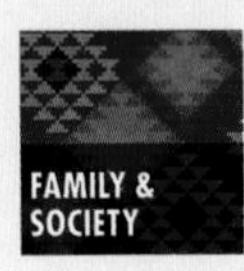
FAMILY & SOCIETY

In many cases, European occupation served to sharpen class divisions in traditional societies. This occurred in Egypt, where many elites benefited after the British protectorate was established in the early 1880s. Ordinary Egyptians, less inclined to adopt foreign ways, seldom profited from the European presence. In response, British administrators showed little patience for those who failed to recognize the superiority of Western civilization. The governor-general, Lord Cromer (KROH-mer), remarked in exasperation, "The mind of the Oriental, . . . like his picturesque streets, is eminently wanting in symmetry. His reasoning is of the most slipshod description." Cromer was especially irritated at the treatment of women, arguing that the seclusion of women and the wearing of the veil were the chief causes of Islamic backwardness.

Such views were echoed by some Egyptian elites, who embraced the colonialists' condemnation of traditional ways. The French-educated lawyer Qassim Amin was an example. His book *The Liberation of Women*, published in 1899 and excerpted here, precipitated a heated debate between those who considered Western nations the liberators of Islam and those who reviled them as oppressors.

Qassim Amin, *The Liberation of Women*

European civilization advances with the speed of steam and electricity, and has even overspilled to every part of the globe so that there is not an inch that he [European man] has not trodden underfoot. Any place he goes he takes control of its resources . . . and turns them into profit . . . and if he does harm to the original inhabitants, it is only that he pursues happiness in this world and seeks it wherever he may find it. . . . For the most part he uses his intellect, but when circumstances require it, he deploys force. He does not seek glory from his possessions and colonies, for he has enough of this through his intellectual achievements and scientific inventions. What drives the Englishman to dwell in India and the French in Algeria . . . is profit and the desire to acquire resources in countries where the inhabitants do not know their value or how to profit from them.

When they encounter savages they eliminate them or drive them from the land, as happened in America . . . and is happening now in Africa. . . . When they encounter a nation like ours, with a degree of civilization, with a past, and a religion . . . and customs and . . . institutions . . . they deal with its inhabitants kindly. But they do soon acquire its most valuable resources, because they have greater wealth and intellect and knowledge and force. . . . [The veil constituted] a huge barrier between woman and her elevation, and consequently a barrier between the nation and its advance.

Why did Qassim Amin believe that Western culture would be beneficial to Egyptian society? How might a critic of colonialism have responded?

Source: From Leila Ahmen, *Women and Gender in Islam* (New Haven, CT: Yale University Press, 1992), pp. 152–160.

Defenders of the colonial enterprise sometimes concede that there were gross inequities in the system but point out that there was a positive side as well. The expansion of markets and the beginnings of a modern transportation and communications network, while bringing few immediate benefits to the colonial peoples, laid the groundwork for future economic growth. The introduction of new ways of looking at human freedom, the relationship between the individual and society, and democratic principles set the stage for the adoption of such ideas after the restoration of independence following World War II. Finally, the colonial experience offered a new approach to the traditional relationship between men and women. Although colonial rule was by no means uniformly beneficial to women in African and Asian societies, their growing awareness of the struggle for equality by women in the West gave them a weapon to use against long-standing barriers of custom and legal discrimination.

Between these two irreconcilable views, where does the truth lie? This chapter has contended that neither extreme position is justified. The consequences of

OPPOSING ✕ VIEWPOINTS

To Resist or Not to Resist

How to respond to colonial rule could be an excruciating problem for political elites in many Asian countries. Not only did resistance often seem futile but it could even add to the suffering of the indigenous population. Hoang Cao Khai (HWANG cow KY) and Phan Dinh Phung (FAN din FUNG) were members of the Confucian scholar-gentry from the same village in Vietnam. Yet they reacted in dramatically different ways to the French conquest of their country. Their exchange of letters, reproduced here, illustrates the dilemmas they faced.

Hoang Cao Khai's Letter to Phan Dinh Phung

Soon, it will be seventeen years since we ventured upon different paths of life. How sweet was our friendship when we both lived in our village. . . . At the time when the capital was lost and after the royal carriage had departed, you courageously answered the appeals of the King by raising the banner of righteousness. It was certainly the only thing to do in those circumstances. No one will question that.

But now the situation has changed and even those without intelligence or education have concluded that nothing remains to be saved. How is it that you, a man of vast understanding, do not realize this? . . . You are determined to do whatever you deem righteous. . . . But though you have no thoughts for your own person or for your own fate, you should at least attend to the sufferings of the population of a whole region. . . .

Until now your actions have undoubtedly accorded with your loyalty. May I ask however what sin our people have committed to deserve so much hardship? I would understand your resistance, did you involve but your family for the benefit of a large number. As of now, hundreds of families are subject to grief; how do you have the heart to fight on? I venture to predict that, should you pursue your struggle, not only will the population of our village be destroyed but our entire country will be transformed into a sea of blood and a mountain of bones. It is my hope that men of your superior morality and honesty will pause a while to appraise the situation.

Reply of Phan Dinh Phung to Hoang Cao Khai

In your letter, you revealed to me the causes of calamities and of happiness. You showed me clearly where advantages and disadvantages lie. All of which sufficed to indicate that your anxious concern was not only for my own security but also for the peace and order of our entire region. I understood plainly your sincere arguments.

I have concluded that if our country has survived these past thousand years when its territory was not large, its army not strong, its wealth not great, it was because the relationships between king and subjects, fathers and children, have always been regulated by the five moral obligations. In the past, the Han, the Sung, the Yuan, the Ming time and again dreamt of annexing our country and of dividing it up into prefectures and districts within the Chinese administrative system. But never were they able to realize their dream. Ah! if even China, which shares a common border with our territory, and is a thousand times more powerful than Vietnam, could not rely upon her strength to swallow us, it was surely because the destiny of our country had been willed by Heaven itself.

The French, separated from our country until the present day by I do not know how many thousand miles, have crossed the oceans to come to our country. Wherever they came, they acted like a storm, so much so that the Emperor had to flee. The whole country was cast into disorder. Our rivers and our mountains have been annexed by them at a stroke and turned into a foreign territory.

Moreover, if our region has suffered to such an extent, it was not only from the misfortunes of war. You must realize that wherever the French go, there flock around them groups of petty men who offer plans and tricks to gain the enemy's confidence. . . . They use every expedient to squeeze the people out of their possessions. That is how hundreds of misdeeds, thousands of offenses have been perpetrated. How can the French not be aware of all the suffering that the rural population has had to endure? Under these

(Continued)

circumstances, is it surprising that families should be disrupted and the people scattered?

My friend, if you are troubled about our people, then I advise you to place yourself in my position and to think about the circumstances in which I live. You will understand naturally and see clearly that I do not need to add anything else.

Explain briefly the reasons advanced by each writer to justify his actions. Which argument do you think would have earned more support from contemporaries? Why?

Source: From Truong Buu Lam, *Patterns of Vietnamese Response to Foreign Intervention*, Monograph Series No. 11. Southeast Asian Studies, Yale University, 1967. Dist. By Celler Book Shop, Detroit, MI.

colonialism have been more complex than either its defenders or its critics would have us believe. While the colonial peoples received little immediate benefit, overall the imperialist era brought about a vast expansion of the international trade network and created at least the potential for societies throughout Africa and Asia to play an active and rewarding role in the new global economic arena. If, as the historian William McNeill believes, the introduction of new technology through cross-cultural encounters is the driving force of change in world history, then Western imperialism, whatever its faults, helped to open the door to such change, much as the rise of the Arab empire and the Mongol invasions hastened the process of global economic development in an earlier time.

Still, the critics have a point. Although colonialism introduced the peoples of Asia and Africa to new technology and the expanding global marketplace, it was unnecessarily brutal and all too often failed to realize the exalted claims of its promoters. Existing economic networks—often potentially valuable as a foundation for later economic development—were ruthlessly swept aside to provide markets for Western manufactured goods. Potential sources of local industrialization were nipped in the bud to avoid competition for factories in Amsterdam, London, Pittsburgh, or Manchester. Training in Western democratic ideals and practices was ignored out of fear that the recipients might use them as weapons against the ruling authorities.

The fundamental weakness of colonialism, then, was that it was ultimately based on the self-interests of the colonial powers. When those interests collided with the needs of the colonial peoples, those of the former always triumphed. However sincerely the David Livingstones, Albert Sarrauts, and William McKinleys of the world were convinced of the rightness of their civilizing mission, the ultimate result was to deprive the colonial peoples of the right to make their own choices about their own destiny. Sophisticated, age-old societies that could have been left to respond to the technological revolution in their own way were squeezed dry of precious national resources under the false guise of a "civilizing mission." As the sociologist Clifford Geertz remarked in his book *Agricultural Involution: The Processes of Ecological Change in Indonesia*, the tragedy is not that the colonial peoples suffered through the colonial era but that they suffered for nothing.

CHAPTER SUMMARY

By the first quarter of the twentieth century, virtually all of Africa and a good part of South and Southeast Asia were under some form of colonial rule. With the advent of the age of imperialism, a global economy was finally established, and the domination of Western civilization over the civilizations of Africa and Asia appeared to be complete.

The imperialist rush for colonies did not take place without opposition. In most areas of the world, local governments and peoples resisted the onslaught, sometimes to the bitter end. But with few exceptions, they were unable to overcome the fearsome new warships and firearms that the Industrial Revolution in Europe had brought into being.

Although the material benefits and democratic values of the occupying powers aroused admiration from observers in much of the colonial world, in the end it was weapons, more than ideas, that ushered in the age of imperialism.

Africa and southern Asia were not the only areas of the world that were buffeted by the winds of Western expansionism in the late nineteenth century. The nations of eastern Asia, and those of Latin America and the Middle East as well, were also affected in significant ways. The consequences of Western political, economic, and military penetration varied substantially from one region to another, however, and therefore require separate treatment. The experience of East Asia will be dealt with in the next chapter. That of Latin America and the Middle East will be discussed in Chapter 24. In these areas, new rivals—notably the United States, Russia, and Japan—entered the scene and played an active role in the process. By the end of the nineteenth century, the rush to secure colonies had circled the world.

CHAPTER TIMELINE

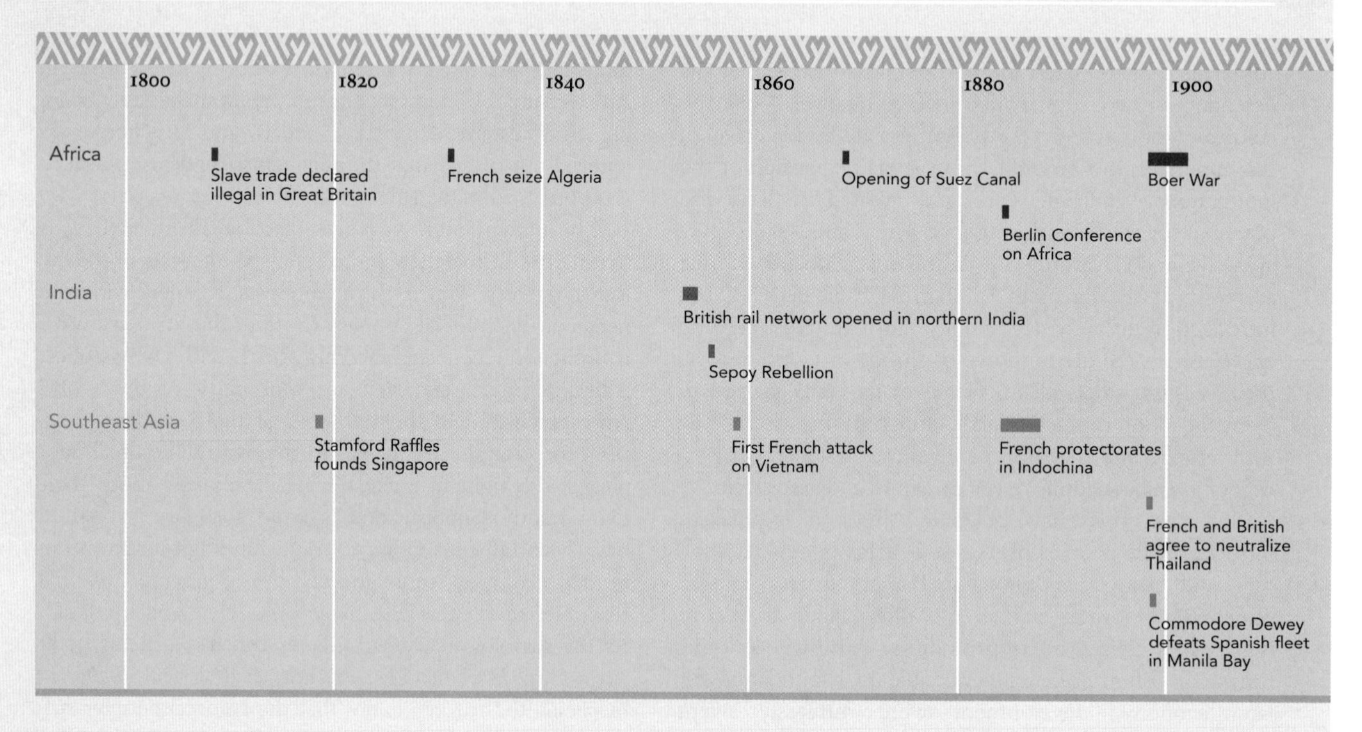

CHAPTER REVIEW

Upon Reflection

Q What arguments have been advanced to justify the European takeover of societies in Asia and Africa during the latter part of the nineteenth century? To what degree are such arguments justified?

Q The colonial powers adopted two basic philosophies in seeking to govern their conquered territories in Asia and Africa—assimilation and association. What were the principles behind these philosophies, and how did they work in practice? Which do you believe was more successful?

Q What was the purpose of the Berlin Conference of 1884, and how successful was it at achieving that purpose? What was the impact of the conference for the European powers and for Africa?

Key Terms

imperialism (p. 544)
indirect rule (p. 546)
direct rule (p. 546)
assimilation (p. 548)
association (p. 548)
raj (p. 548)
informal empire (p. 555)
pasha (p. 556)
high colonialism (p. 562)
sepoys (p. 564)

Suggested Reading

IMPERIALISM AND COLONIALISM There are a number of good works on the subject of imperialism and colonialism. For a study that directly focuses on the question of whether colonialism was beneficial to subject peoples, see **D. K. Fieldhouse, *The West and the Third World: Trade, Colonialism, Dependence, and Development*** (Oxford, 1999). Also see **D. B. Abernathy, *Global Dominance: European Overseas Empires, 1415–1980*** (New Haven, Conn., 2000). For a defense of the British imperial mission, see **N. Ferguson, *Empire: The Rise and Demise of the British World Order*** (New York, 2003).

IMPERIALIST AGE IN AFRICA On the imperialist age in Africa, above all see **B. Vandervoort, *Wars of Imperial Conquest in Africa, 1830–1914*** (Bloomington, Ind., 1998), and **T. Pakenham, *The Scramble for Africa*** (New York, 1991). The three-sided conflict in South Africa is ably analyzed in **M. Meredith, *Diamonds, Gold, and War: The British, the Boers, and the Making of South Africa*** (New York, 2007). The scandal in the Belgian Congo is chronicled in **A. Hothschild, *King Leopold's Ghost: A Story of Greed, Terror, and Heroism in Central Africa*** (New York, 1999). Also informative is **R. O. Collins, ed., *Historical Problems of Imperial Africa*** (Princeton, N.J., 1994).

INDIA For an overview of the British takeover and administration of India, see **S. Wolpert, *A New History of India*,** 8th ed. (New York, 2008). **C. A. Bayly, *Indian Society and the Making of the British Empire*** (Cambridge, 1988), is a scholarly analysis of the impact of British conquest on the Indian economy. Also see **A. Wild's** elegant ***East India Company: Trade and Conquest from 1600*** (New York, 2000). In a provocative work, ***Ornamentalism: How the British Saw Their Empire*** (Oxford, 2000), **D. Cannadine** argues that it was class and not race that motivated British policy in the subcontinent. In ***The Last Mughal: The Fall of a Dynasty: Delhi 1857*** (New York, 2007), **W. Dalrymple** argues that religion was the key issue in provoking the Sepoy Rebellion. Also see **N. Dirks, *The Scandal of Empire: India and the Creation of Imperial Britain*** (Cambridge, Mass., 2007).

COLONIAL AGE IN SOUTHEAST ASIA General studies of the colonial period in Southeast Asia are rare because most authors focus on specific areas. For an overview by several authors, see **N. Tarling, ed., *The Cambridge History of Southeast Asia*,** vol. 3 (Cambridge, 1992).

Visit the CourseMate website at **www.cengagebrain.com** for additional study tools and review materials for this chapter.

CHAPTER 22

Shadows over the Pacific: East Asia Under Challenge

British Museum, London/© Eileen Tweedy/The Art Archive at Art Resource, NY

The Macartney mission to China, 1793

CHAPTER OUTLINE AND FOCUS QUESTIONS

The Decline of the Manchus

Q Why did the Qing dynasty decline and ultimately collapse, and what role did the Western powers play in this process?

Chinese Society in Transition

Q What political, economic, and social reforms were instituted by the Qing dynasty during its final decades, and why were they not more successful in reversing the decline of Manchu rule?

A Rich Country and a Strong State: The Rise of Modern Japan

Q To what degree was the Meiji Restoration a "revolution," and to what extent did it succeed in transforming Japan?

CRITICAL THINKING

Q How did China and Japan each respond to Western pressures in the nineteenth century, and what were the implications of their different responses for each nation's history?

THE BRITISH EMISSARY Lord Macartney had arrived in Beijing in 1793 with a caravan loaded with gifts for the emperor. Flags provided by the Chinese proclaimed in Chinese characters that the visitor was an "ambassador bearing tribute from the country of England." But the tribute was in vain, for Macartney's request for an increase in trade between the two countries was flatly rejected, and he left Beijing with nothing to show for his efforts. Not until half a century later would the Qing dynasty—at the point of a gun—agree to the British demand for an expansion of commercial ties.

In fact, the Chinese emperor Qianlong had responded to his visitor's requests with polite but poorly disguised condescension. To Macartney's proposal that a British ambassador be stationed in Beijing, the emperor replied that such a request was "not in harmony with the state system of our dynasty and will definitely not be permitted." He also rejected the British envoy's suggestion that regular trade relations be established between the two countries. We receive all sorts of precious things as gifts from the myriad nations, replied the Celestial Emperor. "Consequently," he added, "there is nothing we lack, as your principal envoy and others have themselves observed. We have never set much store on strange or ingenious objects, nor do we need more of your country's manufactures."

Historians have often viewed the failure of Macartney's mission as a reflection of the disdain of Chinese rulers toward their counterparts in other countries and their serene confidence in the superiority of Chinese civilization in a world inhabited by barbarians. If that was the case, Qianlong's confidence was misplaced, for as the eighteenth century came to an end, China faced a growing challenge not only from the escalating power and ambitions of the West, but also from its own internal weakness. When British demands for the right to carry out trade and missionary activities in China were rejected, Britain resorted to force and in the Opium War, which broke out in 1839, gave Manchu troops a sound thrashing. A humiliated China was finally forced to open its doors.

The Decline of the Manchus

FOCUS QUESTION: Why did the Qing dynasty decline and ultimately collapse, and what role did the Western powers play in this process?

In 1800, the Qing (CHING) (Ch'ing) or Manchu dynasty was at the height of its power. China had experienced a long period of peace and prosperity under the rule of two great emperors, Kangxi (kang-SHEE) and Qianlong (CHAN-loong). Its borders were secure, and its culture and intellectual achievements were the envy of the world. Its rulers, hidden behind the walls of the Forbidden City in Beijing (bay-ZHING), had every reason to describe their patrimony as the "Central Kingdom." But a little over a century later, humiliated and harassed by the black ships and big guns of the Western powers, the Qing dynasty, the last in a series that had endured for more than two thousand years, collapsed in the dust (see Map 22.1).

Historians once assumed that the primary reason for the rapid decline and fall of the Manchu dynasty was the intense pressure applied by the Western powers. Now, however, most historians believe that internal changes played a major role in the dynasty's collapse and that at least some of its problems during the nineteenth century were self-inflicted.

Both explanations have some validity. Like so many of its predecessors, after an extended period of growth, the Qing dynasty began to suffer from the familiar dynastic ills of official corruption, peasant unrest, and incompetence at court. Such weaknesses were probably exacerbated by the rapid growth in population. The long era of peace, the introduction of new crops from the Americas, and the cultivation of new, fast-ripening strains of rice enabled the Chinese population to double between 1550 and 1800 and to reach the unprecedented level of 400 million by the end of the nineteenth century. Even without the Western powers, the Manchus were probably destined to repeat the fate of their imperial predecessors. The ships, guns, and ideas of the foreigners simply highlighted the growing weakness of the dynasty and likely hastened its demise. In doing so, Western imperialism exerted an indelible impact on the history of modern China—but as a contributing, not a causal, factor.

Opium and Rebellion

By 1800, Westerners had been in contact with China for more than two hundred years, but Western traders were limited to a small commercial outlet at Canton. This arrangement was not acceptable to the British, however. Not only did they chafe at being restricted to a tiny enclave, but the growing British appetite for Chinese tea created a severe balance-of-payments problem. After the failure of Macartney's mission in 1793, Lord Amherst led another mission to China in 1816, but it managed only to worsen the already strained relations between the two countries. The British solution was opium, which was grown in northeastern India and then shipped to China. Opium had been grown in southwestern China for several hundred years but had been used primarily for medicinal purposes. Now, as imports increased, popular demand for the addictive product in southern China became insatiable despite an official prohibition on its use. Soon bullion was flowing out of the Chinese imperial treasury into the pockets of British merchants.

The Chinese became concerned and tried to negotiate. In 1839, Lin Zexu (LIN dzeh-SHOO) (Lin Tse-hsu; 1785–1850), a Chinese official appointed to curtail the opium trade, appealed to Queen Victoria on both moral and practical grounds and threatened to prohibit the sale of rhubarb (widely used as a laxative in nineteenth-century Europe) to Great Britain if she did not respond (see the box on p. 573). But moral principles paled before the lure of commercial profits, and the British continued to promote the opium trade, arguing that if the Chinese did not want the opium, they did not have to buy it. Lin Zexu attacked on three fronts, imposing penalties on smokers, arresting dealers, and seizing supplies from importers as they attempted to smuggle the drug into China. The last tactic caused his downfall. When he blockaded the foreign factory area in Canton to force traders to hand over their opium, the British government, claiming that it could not permit British subjects "to be exposed to insult and injustice," launched a naval expedition to punish the Manchus and force them to open China to foreign trade.[1]

THE OPIUM WAR The Opium War (1839–1842) lasted three years and demonstrated the superiority of British firepower and military tactics. British warships destroyed Chinese coastal and river forts and seized the offshore

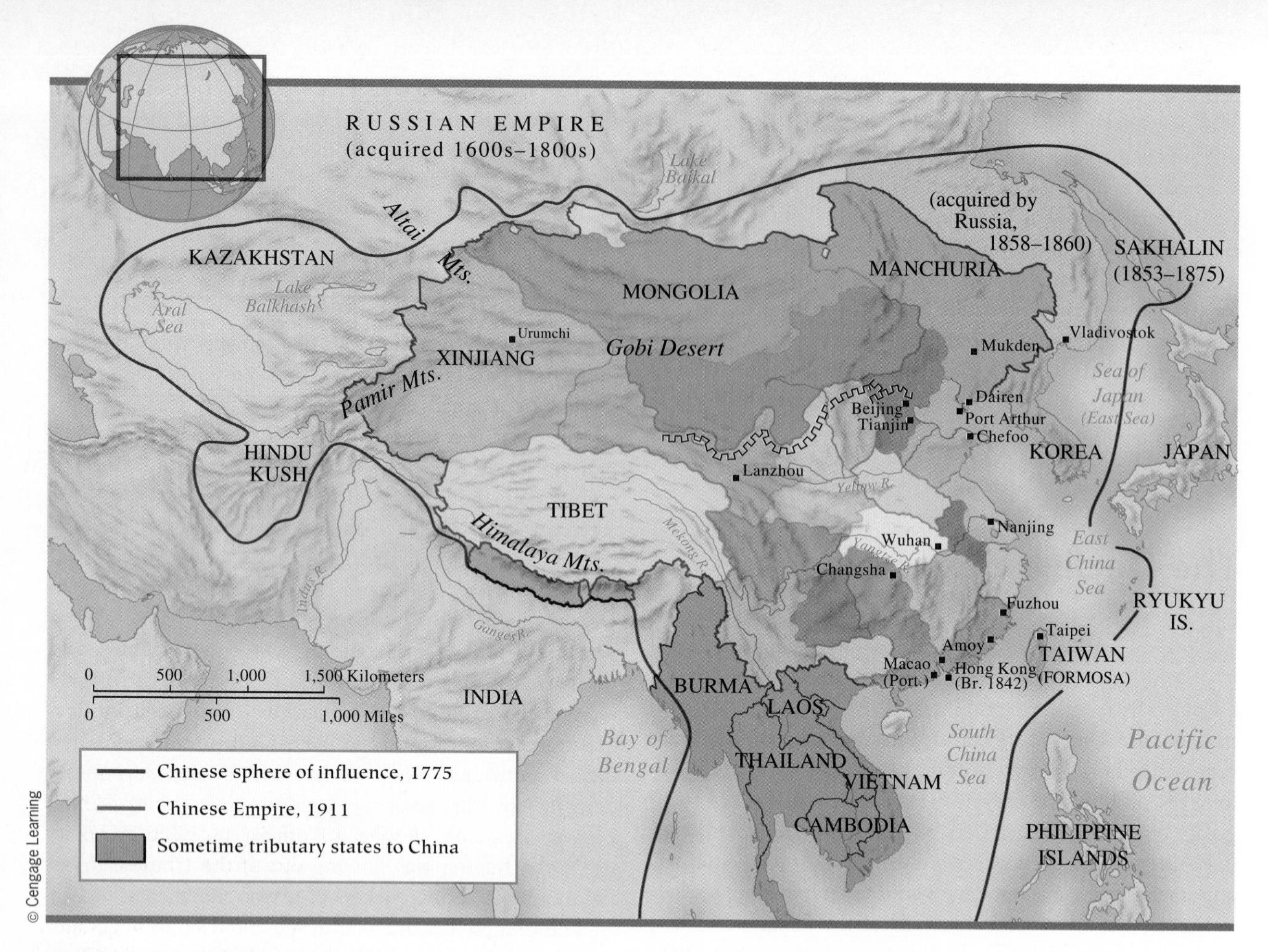

© Cengage Learning

MAP 22.1 The Qing Empire. Shown here is the Qing Empire at the height of its power in the late eighteenth century, together with its shrunken boundaries at the moment of dissolution in 1911.

Q *How do China's tributary states on this map differ from those in Map 17.2? Which of them fell under the influence of foreign powers during the nineteenth century?*

island of Zhoushan (JOE-shahn), near the mouth of the Yangtze River. When a British fleet sailed virtually unopposed up the Yangtze to Nanjing (nan-JING) and cut off the supply of "tribute grain" from southern to northern China, the Qing finally agreed to British terms. In the Treaty of Nanjing in 1842, the Chinese agreed to open five coastal ports to British trade, limit tariffs on imported British goods, grant extraterritorial rights to British citizens in China, and pay a substantial indemnity to cover the costs of the war. China also agreed to cede the island of Hong Kong (dismissed by a senior British official as a "barren rock") to Great Britain. Nothing was said in the treaty about the opium trade, which continued unabated until it was brought under control through Chinese government efforts in the early twentieth century.

Although the Opium War has traditionally been considered the beginning of modern Chinese history, probably few Chinese at the time viewed it that way. This was not the first time that a ruling dynasty had been forced to make concessions to foreigners, and the opening of five coastal ports to the British hardly constituted a serious threat to the empire. Although a few concerned Chinese argued that the court should learn more about European civilization, others contended that China had nothing to learn from the barbarians and that borrowing foreign ways would undercut the purity of Confucian civilization.

For the time being, the Manchus attempted to deal with the foreigners in the traditional way of playing them off against each other. Concessions granted to the British were offered to other Western nations, including the United States, and soon foreign concession areas were operating in treaty ports along the Chinese coast from Canton to Shanghai (SHANG-hy).

A Letter of Advice to the Queen

Lin Zexu was the Chinese imperial commissioner in Canton at the time of the Opium War. Prior to the conflict, he attempted to use reason and the threat of retaliation to persuade the British to stop smuggling opium into China. The following selection is from a letter that he wrote to Queen Victoria. In it, he appeals to her conscience while showing the condescension that the Chinese traditionally displayed to the rulers of other countries.

Lin Zexu, Letter to Queen Victoria

The kings of your honorable country by a tradition handed down from generation to generation have always been noted for their politeness and submissiveness. . . . Privately we are delighted with the way in which the honorable rulers of your country deeply understand the grand principles and are grateful for the Celestial grace. . . . The profit from trade has been enjoyed by them continuously for two hundred years. This is the source from which your country has become known for its wealth.

But after a long period of commercial intercourse, there appear among the crowd of barbarians both good persons and bad, unevenly. Consequently there are those who smuggle opium to seduce the Chinese people and so cause the spread of the poison to all provinces. . . .

The wealth of China is used to profit the barbarians. That is to say, the great profit made by barbarians is all taken from the rightful share of China. By what right do they then in return use the poisonous drug to injure the Chinese people? . . . Let us ask, where is your conscience? I have heard that the smoking of opium is very strictly forbidden by your country; that is because the harm caused by opium is clearly understood. Since it is not permitted to do harm to your own country, then even less should you let it be passed on to the harm of other countries—how much less to China! Of all that China exports to foreign countries, there is not a single thing which is not beneficial to people. . . . Take tea and rhubarb, for example; the foreign countries cannot get along for a single day without them. . . . On the other hand, articles coming from the outside to China can only be used as toys. We can take them or get along without them. Nevertheless our Celestial Court lets tea, silk, and other goods be shipped without limit and circulated everywhere without begrudging it in the slightest. This is for no other reason but to share the benefit with the people of the whole world. . . .

May you, O King, check your wicked and sift your vicious people before they come to China, in order to guarantee the peace of your nation, to show further the sincerity of your politeness and submissiveness, and to let the two countries enjoy together the blessings of peace. . . . After receiving this dispatch will you immediately give us a prompt reply regarding the details and circumstances of your cutting off the opium traffic. Be sure not to put this off.

How did Lin Zexu seek to persuade Queen Victoria to prohibit the sale of opium in China? To what degree are his arguments persuasive?

Source: Reprinted by permission of the publisher from *China's Response to the West: A Documentary Survey, 1839–1923,* by Ssu-yu Teng and John K. Fairbank, pp. 19, 24–27, Cambridge, Mass.: Harvard University Press. Copyright © 1954, 1979 by the President and Fellows of Harvard College, copyright © renewed 1982 by Ssu-yu Teng and John King Fairbank.

THE TAIPING REBELLION In the meantime, the Qing's failure to deal with internal economic problems led to a major peasant revolt that shook the foundations of the empire. On the surface, the Taiping (TY-ping) (T'ai p'ing) Rebellion owed something to the Western incursion; the leader of the uprising, Hong Xiuquan (HOONG shee-oo-CHWAHN) (Hung Hsiu-ch'uan), a failed examination candidate, was a Christian convert who viewed himself as a younger brother of Jesus and hoped to establish what he referred to as a "Heavenly Kingdom of Supreme Peace." But there were many local causes as well. The rapid increase in population forced millions of peasants to eke out a living as sharecroppers or landless laborers. Official corruption and incompetence led to the whipsaw of increased taxes and a decline in government services; even the Grand Canal was allowed to silt up, hindering the shipment of grain. In 1853, the rebels seized

© Eileen Tweedy/The Art Archive at Art Resource, NY

The Opium War. The Opium War, waged between China and Great Britain between 1839 and 1842, was China's first conflict with a European power. Lacking modern military technology, the Chinese suffered a humiliating defeat. In this painting, heavily armed British steamships destroy unwieldy Chinese junks. China's humiliation at sea was a legacy of its rulers' lack of interest in maritime matters since the mid-fifteenth century, when Chinese junks were among the most advanced ships in the world.

Nanjing, but that proved to be their high-water mark. Plagued by factionalism, the rebellion gradually lost momentum and was finally suppressed in 1864, but by then more than 25 million people had been killed, the vast majority of them civilians.

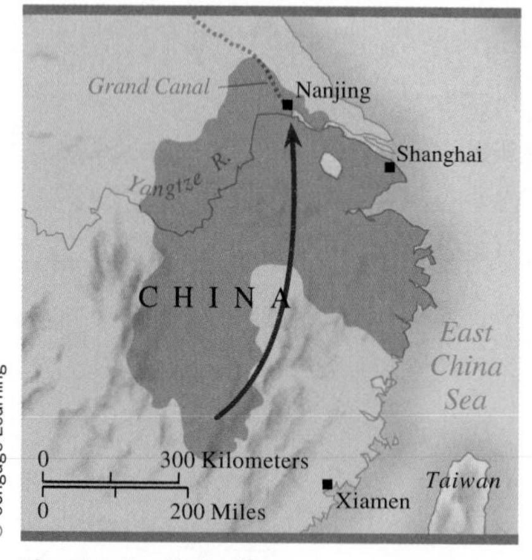

© Cengage Learning

The Taiping Rebellion

One reason for the dynasty's failure to deal effectively with the internal unrest was its continuing difficulties with the Western imperialists. In 1856, the British and the French, still smarting from the restrictions on trade and on their missionary activities, launched a new series of attacks and seized Beijing in 1860. As punishment, British troops destroyed the imperial summer palace outside the city. In the ensuing Treaty of Tianjin (TYAHN-jin) (Tientsin), the Qing agreed to humiliating new concessions: the legalization of the opium trade, the opening of additional ports to foreign trade, and the cession of the peninsula of Kowloon (KOW-loon) (opposite the island of Hong Kong) to the British (see Map 22.2). Additional territories in the north were ceded to Russia.

Efforts at Reform

By the late 1870s, the old dynasty was well on the road to internal disintegration. To fend off the Taiping Rebellion, the Manchus had had to rely on armed forces under regional command, but now many of these regional commanders refused to disband their units and continued to collect local taxes for their own use. The dreaded pattern of imperial breakdown, so familiar in Chinese history, was beginning to appear again.

Finally, the court began to listen to reform-minded officials, who advocated a new policy called **self-strengthening**, in which Western technology would be adopted while Confucian principles and institutions were maintained intact. This policy, popularly known by its slogan "East for Essence, West for Practical Use," remained China's guiding standard for nearly a quarter of a century. Some even called for reforms in education and

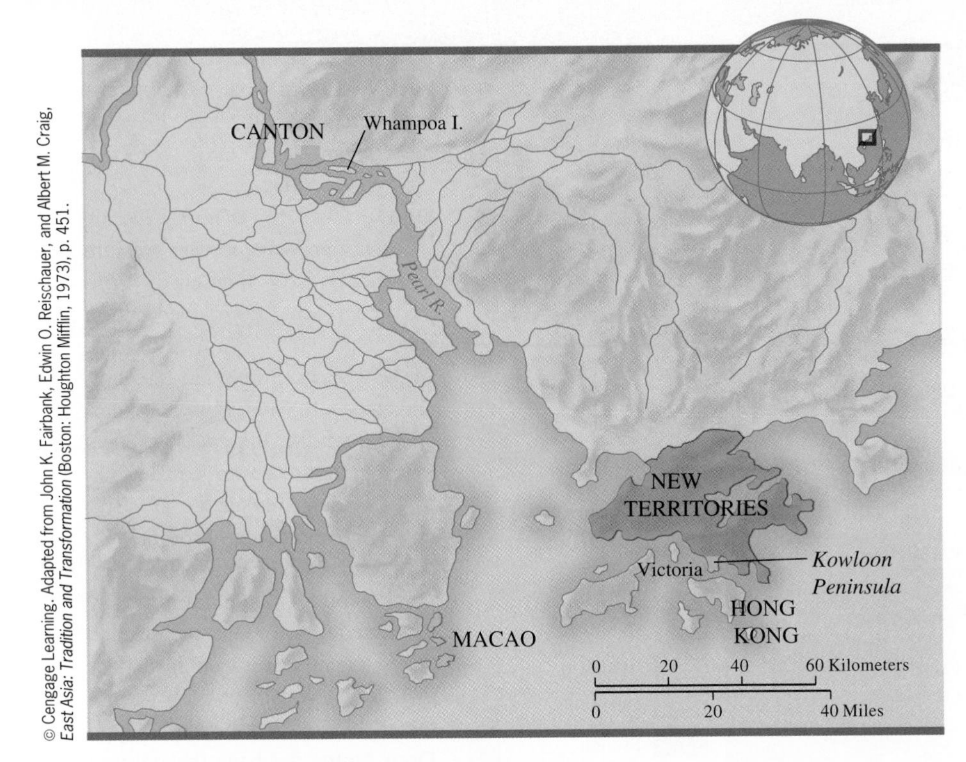

© Cengage Learning. Adapted from John K. Fairbank, Edwin O. Reischauer, and Albert M. Craig, *East Asia: Tradition and Transformation* (Boston: Houghton Mifflin, 1973), p. 451.

MAP 22.2 Canton and Hong Kong. This map shows the estuary of the Pearl River in southern China, an important area of early contact between China and Europe.

What was the importance of Canton? What were the New Territories, and when were they annexed by the British?

in China's hallowed political institutions. Pointing to British power and prosperity, the journalist Wang Tao (wahng TOW ["ow" as in "how"]) (Wang T'ao, 1828–1897) remarked, "The real strength of England . . . lies in the fact that there is a sympathetic understanding between the governing and the governed, a close relationship between the ruler and the people. . . . My observation is that the daily domestic political life of England actually embodies the traditional ideals of our ancient Golden Age."[2] Such democratic ideas were too radical for most moderate reformers, however. Zhang Zhidong (JANG jee-DOONG) (Chang Chih-tung), a leading court official, countered:

> The doctrine of people's rights will bring us not a single benefit but a hundred evils. Are we going to establish a parliament? . . . Even supposing the confused and clamorous people are assembled in one house, for every one of them who is clear-sighted, there will be a hundred others whose vision is beclouded; they will converse at random and talk as if in a dream—what use will it be?[3]

The Climax of Imperialism

For the time being, Zhang Zhidong's arguments won the day. During the last quarter of the nineteenth century, the Manchus attempted to modernize the military and build an industrial base without disturbing the essential elements of traditional Chinese civilization. Railroads, weapons arsenals, and shipyards were built, but the value system remained unchanged.

In the end, the results spoke for themselves. During the last decades of the century, the European penetration of China intensified. Rapacious imperialists began to bite off the outer edges of the empire. The Gobi Desert north of the Great Wall, Central Asia, and Tibet, all inhabited by non-Chinese peoples and never fully assimilated into the Chinese Empire, were gradually lost. In the north and northwest, the main beneficiary was Russia, which forced the court to cede territories north of the Amur (ah-MOOR) River in Siberia. Competition between Russia and Great Britain prevented either power from seizing Tibet outright but enabled Tibetan authorities to revive their local autonomy. In the south, British and French advances in mainland Southeast Asia removed Burma and Vietnam from their traditional status as vassals to the Manchu court. Even more ominous were the foreign spheres of influence in the Chinese heartland, where local commanders were willing to sell exclusive commercial, railroad-building, or mining privileges.

The disintegration of the Manchu dynasty accelerated as the century came to an end. In 1894, the Qing went to war with Japan over Japanese incursions into the Korean peninsula, which threatened China's long-held suzerainty over the area (see "Joining the Imperialist Club" later in this chapter). The Chinese were roundly defeated, confirming to some critics the failure of the policy of self-strengthening by halfway measures. In 1897, Germany, a new entry in the race for spoils in East Asia, used the murder of two German missionaries by Chinese rioters as a pretext to demand territories in the Shandong (SHAHN-doong) (Shantung) peninsula. The imperial court granted the demand, setting off a scramble for territory (see Map 22.3). Russia demanded the Liaodong (LYOW-doong) peninsula with its ice-free port at Port Arthur, and Great Britain obtained a hundred-year lease on the New Territories, adjacent to Hong Kong, as well as a coaling station in northern China.

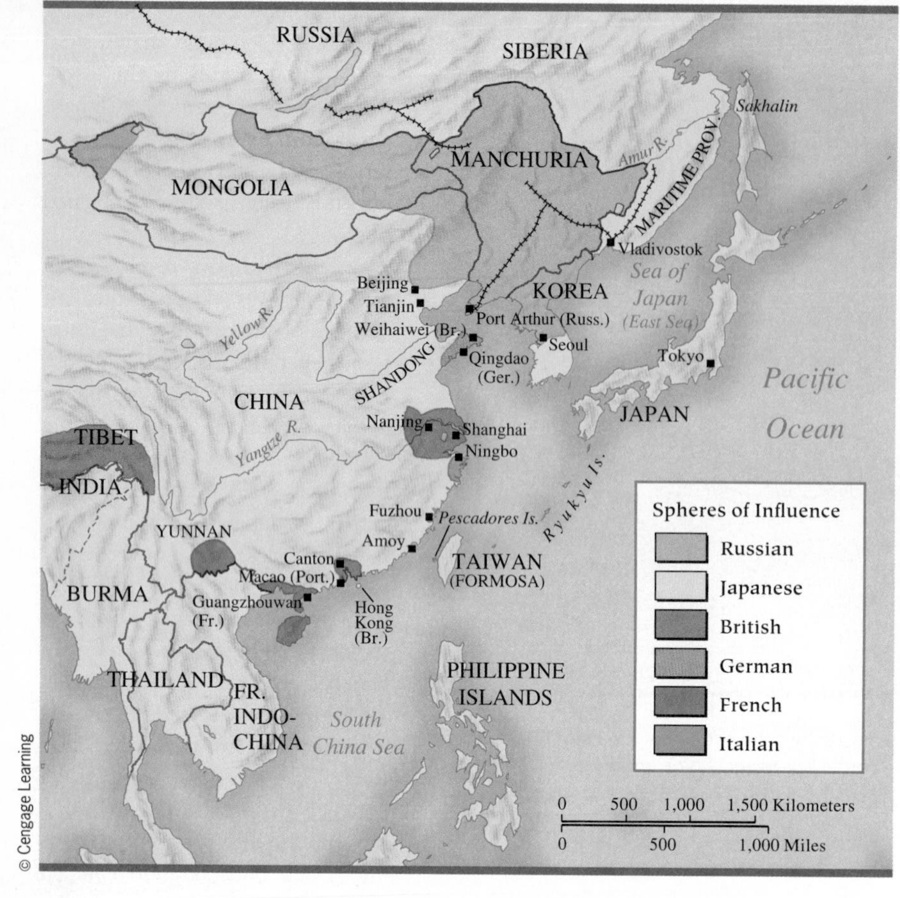

© Cengage Learning

MAP 22.3 Foreign Possessions and Spheres of Influence About 1900. At the end of the nineteenth century, China was being carved up like a melon by foreign imperialist powers.

Which of the areas marked on the map were removed from Chinese control during the nineteenth century?

The government responded with yet another effort at reform. In 1898, the progressive Confucian scholar Kang Youwei (KAHNG yow-WAY) (K'ang Yu-wei) won the support of the young Guangxu (gwahng-SHOO) (Kuang Hsu) emperor for a comprehensive reform program patterned after recent measures in Japan. During the next several weeks, the emperor issued edicts calling for political, administrative, and educational reforms. Not surprisingly, Kang's proposals were opposed by conservatives, who saw little advantage and much risk in copying the West. More important, the new program was opposed by the emperor's aunt, the Empress Dowager Cixi (TSE-shee) (Tz'u Hsi; 1835–1908), the real power at court. Cixi had begun her career as a concubine to an earlier emperor. After his death, she became a dominant force at court and in 1878 placed her infant nephew, the future Guangxu emperor, on the throne. For two decades, she ruled in his name as regent. With the aid of conservatives in the army, she arrested and executed several of the reformers and had the emperor incarcerated in the palace. With Cixi's palace coup, the so-called One Hundred Days of reform came to an end.

OPENING THE DOOR During the next two years, foreign pressure on the dynasty intensified. With encouragement from the British, who hoped to avert a total collapse of the Manchu Empire, in 1899 U.S. Secretary of State John Hay proposed that the imperialist powers join together to ensure equal access to the China market for all states and to guarantee the territorial and administrative integrity of the Chinese Empire. Though probably motivated more by the United States' preference for open markets than by a benevolent wish to protect China, the so-called **Open Door Notes** did have the practical effect of reducing the imperialist hysteria over access to China. The "gentlemen's agreement" about the Open Door (it was not a treaty, but merely a nonbinding expression of intent) quelled fears in Britain, France, Germany, and Russia that other powers would take advantage of the dynasty's weakness to dominate the China market.

Although the Open Door brought a measure of sanity to imperialist meddling in East Asia, it unfortunately came too late to stop the explosion known as the Boxer Rebellion. The Boxers, so-called because of the physical exercises they performed (similar to the more martial forms of tai chi), were a secret society operating primarily in rural areas in northern China. Provoked by a damaging drought and high unemployment caused in part by

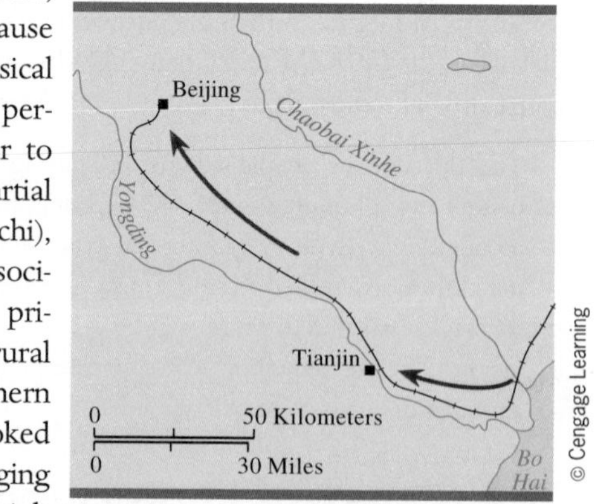

© Cengage Learning

The International Expeditionary Force Advances to Beijing to Suppress the Boxers

Leslie's Illustrated Newspaper, October 14, 1900

Justice or Mercy? Uncle Sam Decides. In the summer of 1900, Chinese rebels known as Boxers besieged Western embassies in the imperial capital of Beijing. Western nations, including the United States, dispatched troops to North China to rescue their compatriots. In this cartoon, which appeared in a contemporary American newsmagazine, China figuratively seeks pardon from a stern Uncle Sam.

CHRONOLOGY **China in the Era of Imperialism**	
Lord Macartney's mission to China	1793
Opium War	1839–1842
Taiping rebels seize Nanjing	1853
Taiping Rebellion suppressed	1864
Cixi becomes regent for nephew, the Guangxu emperor	1878
Sino-Japanese War	1894–1895
One Hundred Days reform	1898
Open Door policy	1899
Boxer Rebellion	1900
Commission to study constitution formed	1905
Deaths of Cixi and the Guangxu emperor	1908
Revolution in China	1911

foreign activity (the introduction of railroads and steamships, for example, undercut the livelihood of barge workers on the rivers and canals), the Boxers attacked foreign residents and besieged the foreign legation quarter in Beijing until an international expeditionary force arrived in the late summer of 1900. As punishment, the foreign troops destroyed temples in the capital suburbs, and the Chinese government was compelled to pay a heavy indemnity to the foreign governments involved in suppressing the uprising.

The Collapse of the Old Order

During the next few years, the old dynasty tried desperately to reform itself. The empress dowager, who had long resisted change, now embraced a number of reforms. The venerable civil service examination system was replaced by a new educational system based on the Western model. In 1905, a commission was formed to study constitutional changes; over the next years, legislative assemblies were established at the provincial level, and elections for a national assembly were held in 1910.

Such moves helped shore up the dynasty temporarily, but history shows that the most dangerous period for an authoritarian system is when it begins to reform itself, because change breeds instability and performance rarely matches rising expectations. Such was the case in China. The new provincial elite, composed of merchants, professionals, and reform-minded gentry, became impatient with the slow pace of change and were disillusioned to find that the new assemblies were to be primarily advisory. The reforms also had little meaning for peasants, artisans, miners, and transportation workers, whose standard of living was being eroded by rising taxes and official venality. Rising rural unrest was an ominous sign of deep-seated resentment.

THE RISE OF SUN YAT-SEN The first physical manifestations of future revolution appeared during the last decade of the nineteenth century with the formation of the Revive China Society by the young radical Sun Yat-sen (SOON yaht-SEN) (1866–1925). Born in a village south of Canton, Sun was educated in Hawaii and returned to China to practice medicine. Soon he turned his full attention to the ills of Chinese society.

At first, Sun's efforts yielded few positive results, but in 1905, he managed to unite radical groups from across China in the so-called Revolutionary Alliance, or Tongmenghui (toong-meng-HWAY) (T'ung Meng Hui). Its program was based on Sun's "**three people's principles**" of nationalism (meaning primarily the elimination of Manchu rule over China), democracy, and people's livelihood. It called for a three-stage process beginning with a military takeover and ending with a constitutional democracy (see the box on p. 578). Although the organization was small and relatively inexperienced, it benefited from rising popular discontent.

Program for a New China

In 1905, Sun Yat-sen united a number of anti-Manchu groups into a single organization called the Revolutionary Alliance (Tongmenghui). The new organization eventually formed the core of his Guomindang (gwoh-min-DAHNG), or Nationalist Party. This excerpt is from the organization's manifesto, published in 1905 in Tokyo. Note that Sun believed that the Chinese people were not ready for democracy and required a period of tutelage to prepare them for constitutional government. This formula would be adopted by many other political leaders in Asia and Africa after World War II.

Sun Yat-sen, *Manifesto for the Tongmenghui*

By order of the Military Government, . . . the Commander-in-Chief of the Chinese National Army proclaims the purposes and platform of the Military Government to the people of the nation:

Therefore we proclaim to the world in utmost sincerity the outline of the present revolution and the fundamental plan for the future administration of the nation.

1. *Drive out the Tartars:* The Manchus of today were originally the eastern barbarians beyond the Great Wall. . . . when China was in a disturbed state they came inside Shanhaikuan, conquered China, and enslaved our Chinese people. The extreme cruelties and tyrannies of the Manchu government have now reached their limit. With the righteous army poised against them, we will overthrow that government, and restore our sovereign rights.
2. *Restore China:* China is the China of the Chinese. The government of China should be in the hands of the Chinese. After driving out the Tartars we must restore our national state. . . .
3. *Establish the Republic:* Now our revolution is based on equality, in order to establish a republican government. All our people are equal and all enjoy political rights. . . .
4. *Equalize land ownership:* The good fortune of civilization is to be shared equally by all the people of the nation. We should improve our social and economic organization, and assess the value of all the land in the country. Its present price shall be received by the owner, but all increases in value resulting from reform and social improvements after the revolution shall belong to the state, to be shared by all the people, in order to create a socialist state, where each family within the empire can be well supported, each person satisfied, and no one fail to secure employment. . . .

The above four points will be carried out in three steps in due order. The first period is government by military law. When the righteous army has arisen, various places will join the cause. . . . Evils like the oppression of the government, the greed and graft of officials, . . . the cruelty of tortures and penalties, the tyranny of tax collections, the humiliation of the queue [the requirement that all Chinese males braid their hair]—shall all be exterminated together with the Manchu rule. Evils in social customs, such as the keeping of slaves, the cruelty of foot binding, the spread of the poison of opium, should also all be prohibited. . . .

The second period is that of government by a provisional constitution. When military law is lifted in each *hsien* [district], the Military Government shall return the right of self-government to the local people. . . .

The third period will be government under the constitution. Six years after the provisional constitution has been enforced a constitution shall be made. The military and administrative powers of the Military Government shall be annulled; the people shall elect the president, and elect the members of parliament to organize the parliament.

What were Sun Yat-sen's key proposals to transform China into a modern society? How does his program compare with the so-called Meiji reforms in Japan, discussed later in this chapter?

Source: Excerpt from *Sources of Chinese Tradition* by William Theodore De Bary. Copyright © 1960 by Columbia University Press, New York. Reprinted with permission of the publisher.

FILM & HISTORY

The Last Emperor (1987)

On November 14, 1908, the Chinese emperor Guangxu died in Beijing. One day later, Empress Dowager Cixi passed away as well. A three-year-old boy, to be known in history as Henry Puyi, ascended the throne. Three years later, the Qing dynasty collapsed, and the deposed monarch lived out the remainder of his life in a China lashed by political turmoil and violence.

The Last Emperor (1987), directed by the Italian filmmaker Bernardo Bertolucci, is a brilliant portrayal of the experience of one hapless individual in a nation caught up in a seemingly endless revolution. The film evokes the fading majesty of the last days of imperial China, the chaos of the warlord era, and the terrors of the Maoist period, when the last shreds of Puyi's personality are shattered under the pressure of Communist brainwashing. The main character, who never appears to grasp what is happening to his country, lives and dies a nonentity.

The film, based on Puyi's autobiography, benefits from having been filmed partly onsite in the Imperial City. The only major Western actor in the movie is the veteran film star Peter O'Toole, who plays Puyi's tutor.

Yanco/Tao/Recorded Picture Co/The Kobal Collection at Art Resource, NY

Three-year-old Puyi (Richard Vuu), the last emperor of China, watches an emissary approach at the Imperial Palace.

THE REVOLUTION OF 1911 In October 1911, Sun's followers launched an uprising in the industrial center of Wuhan (WOO-HAHN), in central China. With Sun traveling in the United States, the insurrection lacked leadership, but the decrepit government's inability to react quickly encouraged political forces at the provincial level to take measures into their own hands. The dynasty was now in a state of virtual collapse: the empress dowager had died in 1908, one day after her nephew; the throne was occupied by China's "last emperor," the infant Puyi (POO-YEE) (P'u Yi). Sun's party lacked the military strength and political base needed to seize the initiative, however, and was forced to turn to a representative of the old order, General Yuan Shikai (yoo-AHN shee-KY) (Yuan Shih-k'ai). Yuan had been put in charge of the imperial forces sent to suppress the rebellion, but now he abandoned the Manchus and acted on his own behalf. In negotiations with Sun Yat-sen's party (Sun himself had arrived in China in January 1912), he agreed to serve as president of a new Chinese republic. The old dynasty and the age-old system that it had attempted to preserve were no more (see the Film & History feature above).

Although the dynasty was gone, Sun and his followers were unable to consolidate their gains. Their program was based on Western liberal democratic principles aimed at the urban middle class, but the middle class in China was too small to form the basis for a new political order. The vast majority of the Chinese people still lived on the land. Sun had hoped to win their support with a land reform program, but few peasants had participated in the revolution. In failing to create new institutions and values to provide a framework for change, the events of 1911 were less a revolution than a collapse of the old order. Under the weight of imperialism and its own internal weaknesses, the old dynasty had crumbled before new political and social forces were ready to fill the vacuum.

What China had experienced was part of a historical process that was bringing down traditional empires across the globe, both in regions threatened by Western imperialism and in Europe itself, where tsarist Russia, the Austro-Hungarian Empire, and the Ottoman Empire all came to an end not long after the collapse of the Qing. The circumstances of their demise differed. The

Austro-Hungarian Empire was dismembered by the victorious allies after World War I, and the fate of tsarist Russia was directly linked to that conflict. Still, all four regimes bore some responsibility for their fate in that they had failed to meet the challenges posed by the times. All had responded to the forces of industrialization and popular participation in the political process with hesitation and reluctance, and their attempts at reform were too little and too late. All paid the supreme price for their folly.

Chinese Society in Transition

FOCUS QUESTION: What political, economic, and social reforms were instituted by the Qing dynasty during its final decades, and why were they not more successful in reversing the decline of Manchu rule?

The growing Western presence in China during the late nineteenth and early twentieth centuries obviously had a major impact on Chinese society. Hence, until recently historians commonly asserted that the arrival of the Europeans shook China out of centuries of slumber and launched it on the road to revolutionary change. As we now know, however, Chinese society was already in a state of transition when the European penetration began to accelerate in the mid-nineteenth century. The growth of industry and trade was particularly noticeable in the cities, where a national market for such commodities as oil, copper, salt, tea, and porcelain had developed. The foundation of an infrastructure more conducive to the rise of a money economy appeared to be in place. In the countryside, new crops introduced from abroad significantly increased food production and aided population growth. The Chinese economy had never been more productive or more complex.

The Economy: The Drag of Tradition

Whether these changes by themselves in the absence of outside intervention would have led to an industrial revolution and a capitalist economy on the Western model is impossible to know. Certainly, a number of obstacles would have made it difficult for China to embark on the Western path if it had wished to do so.

Although industrial production was on the rise, it was still based almost entirely on traditional methods. There was no uniform system of weights and measures, and the banking system was still primitive by European standards. The use of paper money, invented by the Chinese centuries earlier, was still relatively limited. The transportation system, which had been neglected since the end of the Yuan dynasty, was increasingly chaotic. There were few paved roads, and the Grand Canal, long the most efficient means of carrying goods from north to south, was silting up.

The Chinese also borrowed less Western technology than they might have. Foreign manufacturing enterprises could not legally operate in China until the last decade of the nineteenth century, and their methods had little influence beyond the concession areas in the coastal cities. Chinese efforts to imitate Western methods, notably in shipbuilding and weapons manufacture, were dominated by the government and often suffered from mismanagement.

Equally serious problems persisted in the countryside. The rapid increase in population had led to smaller plots and burgeoning numbers of tenant farmers. Rice as a staple of the diet was increasingly being replaced by less nutritious foods, many of which depleted the soil, already under pressure from the dramatic increase in population. Some farmers benefited from switching to commercial agriculture to supply the markets of the growing coastal cities, but the shift entailed a sizable investment. Many farmers went so deeply into debt that they eventually lost their land. In the meantime, the traditional patron-client relationship was frayed as landlords moved to the cities to take advantage of the glittering urban lifestyle introduced by the West.

Some of these problems can undoubtedly be ascribed to the growing Western presence. But the court's hesitant efforts to cope with these challenges suggest that the most important obstacle was at the top: Qing officials often seemed overwhelmed by the combination of external pressure and internal strife. At a time when other traditional societies, such as Russia, the Ottoman Empire, and Japan, were making vigorous attempts to modernize their economies, the Manchu court, along with much of the elite class, still exhibited an alarming degree of complacency.

THE IMPACT OF IMPERIALISM In any event, with the advent of the imperialist era the question of whether China left to itself would have experienced an industrial revolution became academic. Imperialism created serious distortions in the local economy that resulted in massive changes in Chinese society during the twentieth century. Whether the Western intrusion was beneficial or harmful is debated to this day. The Western presence undoubtedly accelerated the development of the Chinese economy in some ways: the introduction of modern means of production, transport, and communications; the creation of an export market; and the steady integration of the Chinese market into the global economy. To many Westerners at the time, it was self-evident that such changes would ultimately benefit the Chinese people (see the comparative essay "Imperialism and the Global Environment" on p. 581). In their view, by supplying (in the

COMPARATIVE ESSAY

Imperialism and the Global Environment

Beginning in the 1870s, European states engaged in an intense scramble for territory in Asia and Africa. Within the empires created by this "new imperialism," the Western powers redrew political boundaries to meet their needs and paid no attention to existing political, linguistic, or religious divisions. In Africa, for example, the Europeans often drew boundaries that divided distinctive communities between colonies or included two hostile communities within the same colony; those boundaries often became the boundaries of the countries of modern Africa.

Similarly, Europeans paid little heed to the requirements of their colonial subjects but instead organized the economies of their empires to meet their own needs in the world market. In the process, Europeans often dramatically altered the global environment. Westerners built railways and ports, drilled for oil, and dug mines for gold, tin, iron ore, and copper. Although the extraction of such resources often resulted in enormous profits, the colonial powers, not the indigenous population, were the prime beneficiaries. At the same time, these projects transformed and often scarred the natural landscape.

Landscapes were even more dramatically altered by Europe's demand for cash crops. Throughout vast regions of Africa and Asia, woodlands were cleared to make way for plantations. In Ceylon (modern Sri Lanka) and India, the British cut down vast tropical forests to plant row upon row of tea bushes. The Dutch razed forests in the East Indies to plant cinchona trees imported from Peru. (Quinine, used to treat malaria, was derived from the trees' bark.) In Indochina, the French replaced extensive forests with rubber, sugar, and coffee plantations. Local workers provided the labor for these vast plantations, usually at pitiful wages.

In many areas, precious farmland was turned over to the cultivation of cash crops. In the Dutch East Indies, farmers were forced to plow up rice fields to make way for the cultivation of sugar. In West Africa, overplanting of cash crops damaged fragile grasslands and turned parts of the Sahel (suh-HAYL *or* suh-HEEL) into a wasteland.

European states greatly profited from this transformed environment, however. To the British botanist John Christopher Willis, their actions were entirely justified. In *Agriculture in the Tropics: An Elementary Treatise*, written in 1909, he commented:

> Whether planting in the tropics will always continue to be under European management is another question, but the northern powers will not permit that the rich and as yet comparatively undeveloped countries of the tropics should be entirely wasted by being devoted merely to the supply of the food and clothing wants of their own people, when they can also supply the wants of the colder zones in so many indispensable products.

How did the effects of imperialism on the environment in colonial countries compare with the impact of the Industrial Revolution in Europe and North America?

© Transcendental Graphics/Getty Images

Picking Tea Leaves in Ceylon. In this 1900 photograph, women on a plantation in Ceylon (Sri Lanka) pick tea leaves for shipment abroad. The British cut down vast stands of tropical forests in Ceylon and India to grow tea to satisfy demand back home.

catch phrase of the day) "oil for the lamps of China," the West was providing a backward society with an opportunity to move up a notch or two on the ladder of human evolution.

Not everyone agreed. The Russian Marxist Vladimir Lenin contended that Western imperialists hindered the process of structural change in preindustrial societies by thwarting the rise of a local industrial and commercial sector in order to maintain colonies as markets for Western manufactured goods and sources of cheap labor and materials. Fellow Marxists in China such as Mao Zedong (see Chapter 24) later asserted that if the West had not intervened, China would have found its own road to capitalism and thence to socialism and communism.

Many historians today would say that such explanations are too simplistic. By shaking China out of its traditional mind-set, imperialism accelerated the change that had begun in the late Ming and early Qing periods and forced the Chinese to adopt new ways of thinking and acting. At the same time, China paid a heavy price in the destruction of its local industry while many of the profits flowed abroad. Although industrial revolution is inevitably a painful process, the Chinese found the experience doubly painful because it was foisted on them from the outside.

Daily Life in Qing China

In 1800, daily life for most Chinese was not substantially different from what it had been centuries earlier. Most were farmers, whose lives were governed by the harvest cycle, village custom, and family ritual. Their roles in society were fixed by the time-honored principles of Confucian social ethics. Male children, at least the more fortunate ones, were educated in the Confucian classics, while females remained in the home or in the fields. All children were expected to obey their parents, and all wives to submit to their husbands.

A visitor to China a hundred years later would have seen a very different society, although one still recognizably Chinese. Change was most striking in the coastal cities, where the educated and affluent had been affected by the Western presence. Confucian social institutions and behavioral norms were declining rapidly in influence, while those of Europe and North America were on the ascendant. Change was much less noticeable in the countryside, but even there, the customary bonds had been frayed.

Some of the change can be traced to the educational system. During the nineteenth century, the importance of a Confucian education steadily declined as up to half of the degree holders had purchased their degrees. After 1906, when the government abolished the civil service examinations, a Confucian education ceased to be the key to a successful career, and Western-style education became more desirable. The old dynasty attempted to establish an educational system on the Western model with universal education at the elementary level. The effect was greatest in the cities, where public schools, missionary schools, and other private institutions educated a new generation of Chinese with little knowledge of or respect for the past.

CHANGING ROLES FOR WOMEN The status of women was also in transition. During the mid-Qing era, women were still expected to remain in the home. Their status as useless sex objects was painfully symbolized by the practice of foot binding, which had probably originated among court entertainers in the Tang dynasty. By the mid-nineteenth century, more than half of all adult women probably had bound feet.

© Royal Geographical Society/Alamy

Women with Bound Feet. To provide the best possible marriage for their daughters, upper-class families began to perform foot binding during the Song dynasty. Eventually, the practice spread to all social classes. Although small feet were supposed to denote a woman of leisure, most Chinese women with bound feet worked, mainly in textiles and handicrafts, to supplement the family income.

During the second half of the century, signs of change began to appear. Women began to seek employment in factories—notably in cotton mills and in the silk industry. Some women participated in the Taiping Rebellion and the Boxer movement, and a few fought beside men in the 1911 revolution. Qiu Jin (chee-oo JIN), a well-known female revolutionary, wrote a manifesto calling for women's liberation and then organized a revolt against the Manchu government, only to be captured and executed at the age of thirty-two in 1907.

By the end of the century, educational opportunities for women began to appear for the first time. Christian missionaries opened some girls' schools, mainly in the foreign concession areas. Although only a small number of women were educated in these schools, they had a significant impact as progressive intellectuals began to argue that ignorant women produced ignorant children. In 1905, the court announced plans to open public schools for girls, but few such schools ever materialized. The government also began to take steps to discourage foot binding, initially with only minimal success.

A Rich Country and a Strong State: The Rise of Modern Japan

FOCUS QUESTION: To what degree was the Meiji Restoration a "revolution," and to what extent did it succeed in transforming Japan?

When the nineteenth century began, the Tokugawa (toh-KOO-gah-wah) shogunate had ruled the Japanese islands for two hundred years. It had revitalized the old governmental system, which had virtually disintegrated under its predecessors. It had driven out the foreign traders and missionaries and reduced its contacts with the Western world. The Tokugawa maintained formal relations only with Korea, although informal trading links with Dutch and Chinese merchants continued at Nagasaki (nah-gah-SAH-kee). Isolation, however, did not mean stagnation. Although the vast majority of Japanese still depended on agriculture for their livelihood, a vigorous manufacturing and commercial sector had begun to emerge during the long period of peace and prosperity. As a result, Japanese society had begun to undergo deep-seated changes, and traditional class distinctions were becoming blurred. Eventually, these changes would end Tokugawa rule and destroy the traditional feudal system.

Some historians speculate that the Tokugawa system was beginning to come apart, just as the medieval order in Europe had started to disintegrate at the beginning of the Renaissance. Factionalism and corruption plagued the central bureaucracy, while rural unrest, provoked by a series of poor harvests brought about by bad weather, swept the countryside. Farmers fled to the towns, where anger was already rising as a result of declining agricultural incomes and shrinking stipends for the samurai. Many samurai lashed out at the perceived incompetence and corruption of the government. In response, the *bakufu* (buh-KOO-foo *or* bah-KOO-fuh) became increasingly rigid, persecuting its critics and attempting to force fleeing peasants back to their lands.

The government also intensified its efforts to limit contacts with the outside world, driving away the foreign ships that were prowling along the Japanese coast in increasing numbers. For years, Japan had financed its imports of silk and other needed products from other countries in Asia with the output of its silver and copper mines. But as these mines became exhausted during the eighteenth century, the *bakufu* cut back on foreign trade, while encouraging the domestic production of goods that had previously been imported. Thus, the Tokugawa sought to adopt a policy of ***sakoku*** (sah-KOH-koo), or closed country, even toward the Asian neighbors with which Japan had once had active relations.

Opening to the World

To the Western powers, Japan's refusal to open its doors to Western goods was an affront and a challenge. Convinced that the expansion of trade would benefit all nations, Western nations began to approach Japan in the hope of opening up the kingdom to foreign interests.

The first to succeed was the United States. American steamships crossing the northern Pacific needed a fueling station before going on to China. In 1853, four American warships under Commodore Matthew C. Perry arrived in Edo Bay (now Tokyo Bay) with a letter from President Millard Fillmore asking for the opening of foreign relations between the two countries. A few months later, Perry returned with a larger fleet for an answer. In his absence, Japanese officials had hotly debated the issue. Some argued that contacts with the West would be politically and morally disadvantageous to Japan, while others pointed to U.S. military superiority and recommended concessions. For the shogunate in Edo (EH-doh), the black guns of Perry's ships proved decisive, and Japan agreed to the Treaty of Kanagawa (kah-nah-GAH-wah), which provided for the return of shipwrecked American sailors, the opening of two ports, and the establishment of a U.S. consulate in Japan. In 1858, U.S. consul Townsend Harris negotiated a more elaborate commercial treaty calling for the opening of several more ports, the exchange of ministers, and the granting of extraterritorial privileges for U.S. residents in Japan. Similar treaties were soon signed with several European nations.

The opening of relations with the Western barbarians was highly unpopular in some quarters, particularly in regions distant from the shogunate headquarters in Edo. Resistance was especially strong in the key southern territories of Satsuma (sat-SOO-muh) and Choshu (CHOH-shoo), both of which had strong military traditions. In 1863, the "Sat-Cho" alliance forced the hapless shogun to promise to end relations with the West. The shogun eventually reneged on the agreement, but the rebels soon had their own problems. When Choshu troops fired on Western ships in the Strait of Shimonoseki (shee-moh-noh-SEK-ee), the Westerners fired back and destroyed the Choshu fortifications. The incident reinforced the rebellious samurai's antagonism toward the West and convinced them of the need to build up their own military. Having done so, they demanded the shogun's resignation and the restoration of the emperor's power. In January 1868, rebel armies attacked the shogun's palace in Kyoto and proclaimed the restored authority of the emperor.

British Museum, London/© The Art Archive at Art Resource, NY

Black Ships in Tokyo Bay. The arrival of a U.S. fleet commanded by Commodore Matthew Perry in 1853 caused consternation among many Japanese observers, who were intimidated by the size and ominous presence of the American ships. This nineteenth-century woodblock print shows curious Japanese paddling out to greet the arrivals.

After a few weeks, resistance collapsed, and the venerable shogunate system came to an end.

The Meiji Restoration

Although the victory of the Sat-Cho faction appeared on the surface to be a triumph of tradition over change, the new leaders soon realized that Japan must change to survive. Accordingly, they embarked on a policy of comprehensive reform that would lay the foundations of a modern industrial nation within a generation.

The symbol of the new era was the young emperor himself, who had taken the reign name Meiji (MAY-jee) ("enlightened rule") on ascending the throne in 1867. Although the post-Tokugawa period was termed a "restoration," the Meiji ruler, who shared the Sat-Cho group's newly adopted modernist outlook, was controlled by the new leadership just as the shogun had controlled his predecessors. In tacit recognition of the real source of political power, the new capital was located at Edo (now renamed Tokyo, "eastern capital"), and the imperial court was moved to the shogun's palace in the center of the city.

THE TRANSFORMATION OF JAPANESE POLITICS The new leaders launched a comprehensive reform of Japanese political, social, economic, and cultural institutions. They moved first to abolish the remnants of the old order and strengthen executive power in their hands. To undercut the power of the daimyo (DYM-yoh), hereditary privileges were abolished in 1871, and the great lords lost title to their lands. As compensation, they were given government bonds and were named governors of the territories formerly under their control. The samurai, comprising about 8 percent of the total population, received a lump-sum payment to replace their traditional stipends, but they were forbidden to wear the sword, the symbol of their hereditary status.

The Meiji modernizers also set out to create a modern political system on the Western model. In the Charter Oath of 1868, they promised to create a new deliberative assembly within the framework of continued imperial rule. They also called for the elimination of the "evil customs" of the past and the implementation of reforms based on international practices to "strengthen the foundations of imperial rule." The key posts in the new government were dominated by modernizing samurai, eventually known as the ***genro*** (gen-ROH *or* GEN-roh), or elder statesmen, from the Sat-Cho clique.

During the next two decades, the Meiji government undertook a systematic study of Western political systems. A commission under Ito Hirobumi (ee-TOH HEE-roh-BOO-mee) traveled to several Western countries, including Great Britain, Germany, Russia, and the United States, to observe their systems. Eventually, several factions appeared, each representing different

Collection Ministry of Foreign Affairs, Tokyo//© Art Resource, NY

Emperor Meiji and the Charter Oath. In 1868, reformist elements overthrew the Tokugawa shogunate and initiated an era of rapid modernization. Their intentions were announced in a charter oath of five articles promulgated in April 1868. In this contemporary print, the young Emperor Meiji listens to the reading of the Charter Oath in his palace in Kyoto.

political ideas. The Liberal Party favored a model that would vest supreme authority in the parliament as the representative of the people. The Progressive Party called for the distribution of power between the legislative and executive branches, with a slight nod to the latter.

THE CONSTITUTION OF 1890 During the 1870s and 1880s, these factions competed for preeminence. In the end, the Progressives emerged victorious. The Meiji Constitution, which was adopted in 1890, was based on the Bismarckian model with authority vested in the executive branch; the imperialist faction was pacified by the statement that the constitution was the gift of the emperor. The Meiji oligarchs would handpick the cabinet. The upper house of parliament would be appointed and have equal legislative powers with the lower house, called the Diet, whose members would be elected. The core ideology of the state, called the ***kokutai*** (koh-kuh-TY), or national polity, embodied the concept of the uniqueness of the Japanese system based on the supreme authority of the emperor. The ancient practice of Shinto was transformed into a virtual national religion, and its traditional ceremonies were performed at all important events in the imperial court.

The result was a system that was democratic in form but despotic in practice, modern in appearance but still traditional in that power remained in the hands of a ruling oligarchy. The system permitted the traditional ruling class to retain its influence and economic power while acquiescing in the emergence of new institutions and values.

MEIJI ECONOMICS With the end of the daimyo domains, the government needed a new system of landownership that would transform the rural population from indentured serfs into citizens. To do so, it enacted a land reform program that redefined the domain lands as the private property of the tillers while compensating the previous owners with government bonds. A new land tax, set at an annual rate of 3 percent of the land's estimated value, was then imposed to raise revenue for the government. The tax proved to be a lucrative source of income for the government, but it was onerous for the farmers, who had previously paid a fixed percentage of their harvest to the landowner. In bad years, many peasants were unable to pay their taxes and were forced to sell their lands to wealthy neighbors. Eventually, the government reduced the tax to 2.5 percent of the land value. Still, by the end of the century, about 40 percent of all farmers were tenants.

With its budget needs secured, the government turned to the promotion of industry with the objective of guaranteeing Japan's survival against the challenge of Western imperialism. Building on the small but growing industrial economy that existed under the Tokugawa, the Meiji reformers provided massive stiumulus in the form of financial subsidies, training, foreign advisers, improved transport and communications, and a universal educational system emphasizing applied science. Unlike China, Japan relied very little on foreign capital.

During the late Meiji era, Japan's industrial sector began to grow. Besides tea and silk, key industries included weaponry, shipbuilding, and sake (SAH-kee) (fermented rice wine). From the start, the distinctive feature of the Meiji model was the intimate relationship between government and private business. Once an individual enterprise or industry was on its feet, it was turned over entirely to private ownership, although the government often continued to play some role. One historian has explained the process:

> [The Meiji government] pioneered many industrial fields and sponsored the development of others, attempting to cajole businessmen into new and risky kinds of endeavor, helping assemble the necessary capital, forcing weak companies to merge into stronger units, and providing private entrepreneurs with aid and privileges of a sort that would be corrupt favoritism today. All this was in keeping with Tokugawa traditions that business operated under the tolerance and patronage of government. Some of the political leaders even played a dual role in politics and business.[4]

From the workers' perspective, the Meiji reforms had a less attractive side. Industrial growth was subsized by funds provided by the new land tax, but the tax imposed severe hardships on the peasants, many of whom fled to the cities, where they provided an abundant source of cheap labor. As in Europe during the early Industrial Revolution, workers toiled for long hours in the coal mines and textile mills, often under horrendous conditions. Reportedly, coal miners on a small island in Nagasaki harbor worked naked in temperatures up to 130 degrees Fahrenheit. If they tried to escape, they were shot.

BUILDING A MODERN SOCIAL STRUCTURE By the late Tokugawa era, the rigidly hierarchical social order was beginning to disintegrate. Rich merchants were buying their way into the ranks of the samurai, and Japanese of all classes were abandoning their rice fields and moving into the cities. Nevertheless, community and hierarchy still formed the basis of society. The lives of all Japanese were determined by their membership in various social organizations—their family, village, and social class. Membership in a particular social class determined a person's occupation and social relationships with others. Women in particular were constrained by the "**three obediences**": child to father, wife to husband, and widow to son. Husbands could easily obtain a divorce, but wives could not (allegedly, a husband could divorce his wife if she drank too much tea or talked too much). Marriages were arranged, and the average age at marriage for females was sixteen years. Females did not share inheritance rights with males, and few received any education outside the family.

The Meiji reformers destroyed much of the traditional social system. With the abolition of hereditary rights in 1871, the legal restrictions of the past were brought to an end with a single stroke. Special privileges for the aristocracy were abolished, as were the legal restrictions on the ***eta*** (AY-tuh), the traditional slave class (numbering about 400,000 in the 1870s). Another key focus of the reformers was the army. The Sat-Cho reformers had been struck by the weakness of the Japanese forces in clashes with Western powers and set out to create a military that could compete in the modern world. The old feudal army based on the traditional warrior class was abolished, and an imperial army based on universal conscription was formed in 1871.

Education also underwent major changes. Recognizing the need for universal education including technical subjects, the Meiji leaders adopted the American model of a three-tiered system culminating in a series of universities and specialized institutes. They also sent bright students to study abroad and brought foreign scholars to Japan to teach in the new schools, where much of the content was inspired by Western models. In another break with tradition, women for the first time were given an opportunity to get an education.

These changes were included in the Imperial Rescript on Education that was issued in 1890, but the rescript also emphasized the traditional Confucian virtues of filial piety and loyalty to the state. One reason for issuing the Imperial Rescript was concern that Western individualistic ideas might dilute the traditional Japanese emphasis on responsibility to the community.

Indeed, Western ideas and fashions had become the rage in elite circles, and the ministers of the first Meiji government were known as the "dancing cabinet" because of their addiction to Western-style ballroom dancing. Young people began to imitate the clothing styles, eating habits, and social practices of their European and American counterparts (see the box on p. 587).

TRADITIONAL VALUES AND WOMEN'S RIGHTS Nevertheless, the self-proclaimed transformation of Japan into a "modern society" by no means detached the country entirely from its traditional moorings. Although an educational order in 1872 increased the percentage of Japanese women exposed to public education, conservatives soon began to impose restrictions and bring about a return to more traditional social relationships. As we have seen, the Imperial Rescript on Education in 1890 stressed the Confucian virtues of filial piety, patriotism, and loyalty to the family and community. Traditional values were given a firm legal basis in the Constitution of 1890, which restricted the franchise to males and defined individual liberties as "subject to the limitations imposed by law," and by the Civil Code of 1898, which de-emphasized individual rights and treated women within the context of their role in the family.

By the end of the century, however, changes were under way as women began to play a crucial role in the nation's effort to modernize. Urged by their parents to augment the family income, as well as by the government to fulfill their patriotic duty, young girls went en

OPPOSING VIEWPOINTS

The Wonders of Western Civilization: Two Views

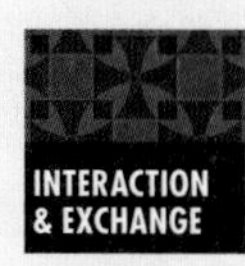

As information about the West began to penetrate East Asian societies during the nineteenth century, it aroused considerable interest and discussion. Some found much to admire in Western science and democracy, as the first selection demonstrates. Published in 1891 by the Chinese intellectual Wang Xiji (wahng SHEE-jee) (Wang Hsi-ch'i), it is a generally laudatory description of European society written by a hypothetical Chinese visitor.

Other Asian observers, however, found the lavish praise and imitation of Western ways somewhat ridiculous. In the second selection, published in 1871, the Japanese writer Kanagaki Rebun (REE-bun) mocks his compatriots who imitate Western practices. He begins by heaping scorn on those Japanese who now eat beef simply because it is popular in the West.

Wang Xiji, *A Chinese Description of Europe*

Europe (*Ou-lo-pa*) is one of the five great continents. . . . Though it is smaller than the other four continents, its soil is fertile, its products are plentiful, it has many talented people and many famous places. For this reason, Europe's power in the present world is pre-eminent, and it has become a leading force in the five continents. Yet in ancient times its people hunted for a living, ate meat, and wore skins. Their customs were barbaric, and their spirit was wild and free. But during our own Shang period (2000 B.C.E.) Greece and other countries gradually came under the influence of the Orient. For the first time they began to till fields and manufacture products, build cities, and dig lakes. . . . Before long, writing and civilization began to flourish. Thus, they became beautiful like the countries of the East. . . .

Now for their machines. When they first invented them, they just relied on common sense. They tried this and rejected that, without ever finding out from anyone else how it ought to be done. However, they did some research and found people who investigated the fine points and propagated their usage. In this way they gradually developed all their machines such as steamships, steam trains, spinning machines, mining and canal-digging machines, and all machines for making weapons and gunpowder. Things improved day to day and helped enrich the nation and benefit the people. Day by day they became more prosperous and will keep on becoming so.

Kanagaki Rebun, *The Beefeater*

Excuse me, but the beef is certainly a most delicious thing, isn't it? Once you get accustomed to its taste, you can never go back to deer or wild boar again. I wonder why we in Japan haven't eaten such a clean thing before? For over 1,620—or is it 1,630—years people in the West have been eating huge quantities of beef. . . . We really should be grateful that even people like ourselves can now eat beef, thanks to the fact that Japan is steadily becoming a truly civilized country.

In the West they're free of superstitions. There it's the custom to do everything scientifically, and that's why they've invented amazing things like the steamship and the steam engine. Did you know that . . . they bring down wind from the sky with balloons? . . . Of course, there are good reasons behind these inventions. If you look at a map of the world you'll see some countries marked "tropical," which means that's where the sun shines closest. The people in those countries are all burnt black by the sun. The king of that part of the world tried all kinds of schemes before he hit on what is called a balloon. That's a big round bag they fill with air high up in the sky. They bring the bag down and open it, causing the cooling air inside the bag to spread out all over the country. That's a great invention. On the other hand, in Russia, which is a cold country where the snow falls even in summer and the ice is so thick that people can't move, they invented the steam engine. You've got to admire them for it. I understand that they modeled the steam engine after the flaming chariot of hell, but anyway, what they do is to load a crowd of people on a wagon and light a fire in a pipe underneath. They keep feeding the fire inside the pipe with a coal, so that the people riding on top can travel a great distance completely oblivious to the cold. Those people in the West can think up inventions like that, one after the other.

Which of these two views of European society in the late nineteenth century appears to be more accurate? Why?

Sources: Wang Xiji, *A Chinese Description of Europe*. A Chinese Description of Europe. Kanagaki Rebun, *The Beefeater*. Excerpt from *Modern Japanese Literature*, Donald Keene, ed. (New York: Grove Press, 1960), pp. 32–33.

"In the Beginning, We Were the Sun"

One aspect of Western thought that the Meiji reformers did not seek to imitate was the idea of gender equality. Although Japanese women sometimes tried to be "modern" like their male counterparts, Japanese society as a whole continued to treat women differently. In 1911, a young woman named Hiratsuka Raicho (hee-RAHT-soo-kuh RAY-choh) founded a journal named *Seito* (SAY-toh) (Blue Stockings) to promote the liberation of women in Japan. Her goal was to encourage women to develop their own latent talents, rather than to demand legal changes. The following document is the proclamation that was issued at the creation of the Seito Society. Compare it with Mary Wollstonecraft's discussion of the rights of women in Chapter 18.

Hiratsuka Raicho, Proclamation at the Founding of the Seito Society

Freedom and Liberation! Oftentimes we have heard the term "liberation of women." But what is it then? . . . Assuming that women are freed from external oppression, liberated from constraint, given the so-called higher education, employed in various occupations, given [the] franchise, and provided an opportunity to be independent from the protection of their parents and husbands, and to be freed from the little confinement of their homes, can all of these be called liberation of women? They may provide proper surroundings and opportunities to let us fulfill the true goal of liberation. Yet they remain merely the means, and do not represent our goal or ideals.

However, I am unlike many intellectuals in Japan who suggest that higher education is not necessary for women. Men and women are endowed by nature to have equal faculties. Therefore, it is odd to assume that one of the sexes requires education while the other does not. This may be tolerated in a given country and in a given age, but it is fundamentally a very unsound proposition.

I bemoan the facts that there is only one private college for women in Japan, and that there is no tolerance on man's part to permit entrance of women into many universities maintained for men. However, what benefit is there when the intellectual level of women becomes similar to that of men? Men seek knowledge in order to escape from their lack of wisdom and lack of enlightenment. They want to free themselves. . . . Yet multifarious thought can darken true wisdom, and lead men away from nature. . . .

Now, what is the true liberation which I am seeking? It is none other than to provide an opportunity for women to develop fully their hidden talents and hidden abilities. We must remove all the hindrances that stand in the way of women's development, whether they be external oppression or lack of knowledge. And above and beyond these factors, we must realize that we are the masters in possession of great talents, for we are the bodies which enshrine the great talents.

What did Hiratsuka Raicho think was necessary to bring about the liberation of women in Meiji Japan? Were her proposals similar to those set forth by her counterparts in the West?

Source: From John David Lu, *Sources of Japanese Tradition* (New York: McGraw-Hill, 1974), vol II, pp. 118–119, from CHUO KOREN, November 1965, pp. 354–357.

masse to work in textile mills. From 1894 to 1912, women represented 60 percent of the Japanese labor force. Thanks to them, by 1914, Japan was the world's leading exporter of silk and dominated cotton manufacturing. Without the revenues earned from textile exports, Japan might have required an infusion of foreign capital to develop its heavy industry and military.

Japanese women received few rewards for their contribution, however. In 1900, new regulations prohibited women from joining political organizations or attending public meetings. Beginning in 1905, a group of independent-minded women petitioned the Japanese parliament to rescind this restriction. Although the regulation was not repealed until 1922, calls for women's rights increasingly were heard (see the box above).

Joining the Imperialist Club

Traditionally, Japan had not been an expansionist country, but now the Japanese began to emulate the Western approach to foreign affairs as well as Western domestic policies. This is perhaps not surprising. The Japanese felt particularly vulnerable in the world economic arena. Their territory was small, lacking in resources, and densely populated, and they had no natural outlet for expansion. To observant Japanese, the lessons of history were clear. Western nations had amassed wealth and power not only because of their democratic systems and high level of education but also because of their colonies. The Japanese began their program of territorial expansion close to home (see Map 22.4). In 1874, after a brief conflict with China, Japan was able to claim suzerainty over the Ryukyu (RYOO-kyoo) Islands, long tributary to the Chinese Empire. Two years later, Japanese naval pressure forced Korea to open three ports to Japanese commerce.

During the early nineteenth century, Korea had followed Japan's example and attempted to isolate itself from outside contact except for periodic tribute missions to China. Christian missionaries, mostly Chinese or French, were vigorously persecuted. But Korea's problems were basically internal. In the early 1860s, a peasant revolt, inspired in part by the Taiping Rebellion in China, caused considerable devastation before being crushed in 1864. In succeeding years, the Yi (YEE) dynasty sought to strengthen the country by returning to traditional values and fending off outside intrusion, but rural poverty and official corruption remained rampant. A U.S. fleet sought to open the country in 1871 but was driven off with considerable loss of life.

Korea's most persistent suitor, however, was Japan, which was determined to bring an end to Korea's dependency status with China and modernize it along Japanese lines. In 1876, Korea agreed to open three ports to Japanese commerce in return for Japanese recognition of Korean independence. During the 1880s, Sino-Japanese rivalry over Korea intensified. When a new peasant rebellion broke out in Korea in 1894, China and Japan intervened on opposite sides (see the box on p. 590). During the war, the Japanese navy destroyed the Chinese fleet and seized the Manchurian city of Port Arthur. In the Treaty of Shimonoseki, the Chinese were forced to recognize the independence of Korea and cede Taiwan (TY-WAHN) and the Liaodong peninsula with its strategic naval base at Port Arthur to Japan.

Shortly thereafter, under pressure from the European powers, the Japanese returned the Liaodong peninsula to China, but in the early twentieth century, they went back on the offensive. Rivalry with Russia over influence in Korea led to increasingly strained relations between the two countries. In 1904, Japan launched a surprise attack on the Russian naval base at Port Arthur, which Russia had taken from China in 1898. The Japanese armed forces were weaker, but Russia faced difficult logistical problems along its new Trans-Siberian Railway and severe political instability at home. In 1905, after Japanese warships sank almost the entire Russian fleet off the coast of Korea, the Russians agreed to a humiliating peace, ceding the Liaodong peninsula back to Japan, as well as southern Sakhalin (SAK-uh-leen) and the Kurile (KOOR-il *or* koo-REEL) Islands. Russia also agreed to abandon its political and economic influence in Korea and southern Manchuria, which now came increasingly under Japanese control. The Japanese victory stunned the world, including the colonial peoples of Southeast Asia, who now began to realize that the white race was not necessarily invincible.

During the next few years, the Japanese consolidated their position in northeastern Asia, annexing Korea in 1908 as an integral part of Japan. When the Koreans protested, Japanese reprisals resulted in thousands of deaths. The United States was the first to recognize the annexation in return for Tokyo's declaration of respect for U.S. authority in the Philippines. In 1908, the United States recognized Japanese interests in the region in return for Japanese acceptance of the principles of the Open Door. But mutual suspicion between the two countries was growing, sparked in part by U.S. efforts to restrict immigration from all Asian countries.

© Cengage Learning

MAP 22.4 Japanese Overseas Expansion During the Meiji Era. Beginning in the late nineteenth century, Japan ventured beyond its home islands and became an imperialist power. The extent of Japanese colonial expansion through World War I is shown here.

Which parts of imperial China came under Japanese influence?

OPPOSING VIEWPOINTS

Two Views of the World

During the nineteenth century, China's hierarchical way of looking at the outside world came under severe challenge, not only from Western countries but also from the rising power of Japan, which accepted the Western view that a colonial empire was the key to national greatness. Japan's first objective was Korea, long a dependency of China, and in 1894, the competition between China and Japan in the Korean peninsula led to war. The following declarations of war by the rulers of the two countries are revealing. Note the Chinese use of the derogatory term *Wojen* ("dwarf people") in referring to the Japanese.

Declaration of War Against China

Korea is an independent state. She was first introduced into the family of nations by the advice and guidance of Japan. It has, however, been China's habit to designate Korea as her dependency, and both openly and secretly to interfere with her domestic affairs. At the time of the recent insurrection in Korea, China despatched troops thither, alleging that her purpose was to afford a succor to her dependent state. We, in virtue of the treaty concluded with Korea in 1882, and looking to possible emergencies, caused a military force to be sent to that country.

Wishing to procure for Korea freedom from the calamity of perpetual disturbance, and thereby to maintain the peace of the East in general, Japan invited China's cooperation for the accomplishment of the object. But China, advancing various pretexts, declined Japan's proposal. . . . Such conduct on the part of China is not only a direct injury to the rights and interests of this Empire, but also a menace to the permanent peace and tranquility of the Orient. . . . In this situation, . . . we find it impossible to avoid a formal declaration of war against China.

Declaration of War Against Japan

Korea has been our tributary for the past two hundred odd years. She has given us tribute all this time, which is a matter known to the world. For the past dozen years or so Korea has been troubled by repeated insurrections and we, in sympathy with our small tributary, have as repeatedly sent succor to her aid. . . . This year another rebellion was begun in Korea, and the King repeatedly asked again for aid from us to put down the rebellion. We then ordered Li Hung-chang to send troops to Korea; and they having barely reached Yashan the rebels immediately scattered. But the *Wojen*, without any cause whatever, suddenly sent their troops to Korea, and entered Seoul, the capital of Korea, reinforcing them constantly until they have exceeded ten thousand men. In the meantime the Japanese forced the Korean king to change his system of government, showing a disposition every way of bullying the Koreans. . . .

As Japan has violated the treaties and not observed international laws, and is now running rampant with her false and treacherous actions commencing hostilities herself, and laying herself open to condemnation by the various powers at large, we therefore desire to make it known to the world that we have always followed the paths of philanthropy and perfect justice throughout the whole complications, while the *Wojen*, on the other hand, have broken all the laws of nations and treaties which it passes our patience to bear with. Hence we commanded Li Hung-chang to give strict orders to our various armies to hasten with all speed to root the *Wojen* out of their lairs.

Compare the worldviews of China and Japan at the end of the nineteenth century as reflected in these declarations. Which point of view do you find more persuasive?

Source: From MacNair, *Modern Chinese History*, pp. 530–534, quoted in Franz Schurmann and Orville Schell, eds., *The China Reader: Imperial China* (New York: Vintage, 1967), pp. 251–259.

Japanese Culture in Transition

The wave of Western technology and ideas that entered Japan in the second half of the nineteenth century greatly altered traditional Japanese culture. Literature in particular was affected as European models eclipsed the repetitive and frivolous tales of the Tokugawa era. Dazzled by this "new" literature, Japanese authors began translating and imitating the imported models. Experimenting with Western verse, Japanese poets were influenced by such styles as Symbolism, and in later decades by Dadaism

(DAH-duh-iz-um) and Surrealism, although some traditional poetry was still composed.

As the Japanese invited technicians, engineers, architects, and artists from Europe and the United States to teach their "modern" skills to a generation of eager students, Western artistic techniques and styles were adopted on a massive scale. Japanese architects and artists created huge buildings of steel and reinforced concrete adorned with Greek columns and cupolas, oil paintings reflecting the European concern with depth perception and shading, and bronze sculptures of secular subjects.

Cultural exchange also went the other way as Japanese arts and crafts, porcelains, textiles, fans, folding screens, and woodblock prints became the vogue in Europe and North America. Japanese art influenced Western painters such as Vincent van Gogh, Edgar Degas (duh-GAH), and James Whistler, who experimented with flatter compositional perspectives and unusual poses. Japanese gardens, with their exquisite attention to the positioning of rocks and falling water, became especially popular.

After the initial period of mass absorption of Western art, a reaction occurred at the end of the nineteenth century as many artists returned to pre-Meiji techniques. In 1889, the Tokyo School of Fine Arts (today the Tokyo National University of Fine Arts and Music) was founded to promote traditional Japanese art. Over the next decades, Japanese art underwent a dynamic resurgence, reflecting the nation's emergence as a prosperous and powerful state. While some Japanese artists attempted to synthesize native and foreign techniques, others found inspiration in past artistic traditions.

CHRONOLOGY **Japan and Korea in the Era of Imperialism**	
Commodore Perry arrives in Tokyo Bay	1853
Townsend Harris Treaty	1858
Fall of Tokugawa shogunate	1868
U.S. fleet fails to open Korea	1871
Feudal titles abolished in Japan	1871
Japanese imperial army formed	1871
Meiji Constitution adopted	1890
Imperial Rescript on Education	1890
Treaty of Shimonoseki awards Taiwan to Japan	1895
Russo-Japanese War	1904–1905
Korea annexed by Japan	1908

The Meiji Restoration: A Revolution from Above

Japan's transformation from a feudal, agrarian society to an industrializing, technologically advanced society in little more than half a century has frequently been described by outside observers (if not by the Japanese themselves) in almost miraculous terms. Some historians have questioned this characterization, pointing out that

Collection Ministry of Foreign Affairs, Tokyo//© Art Resource, NY

The Ginza in Downtown Tokyo. This 1877 woodblock print shows the Ginza, a major commercial thoroughfare in downtown Tokyo, with modern brick buildings and a horse-drawn streetcar. The focus of public attention is a new electric streetlight. In combining traditional form with modern content, this print symbolizes the unique ability of the Japanese to borrow ideas from abroad while preserving much of the essence of their traditional culture.

the achievements of the Meiji leaders were spotty. In *Japan's Emergence as a Modern State,* the Canadian historian E. H. Norman lamented that the **Meiji Restoration** was an "incomplete revolution" because it did not end the economic and social inequities of feudal society or enable the common people to participate fully in the governing process. Although the *genro* were enlightened in many respects, they were also despotic and elitist, and the distribution of wealth remained as unequal as it had been under the old system.[5]

Moreover, Japan's transformation into a major industrial nation was by no means complete by the beginning of the new century. Until at least the outbreak of World War I in 1914, the majority of manufactured goods were produced by traditional cottage industries, rather than by modern factories. The integration of the Japanese economy into the global marketplace was also limited, and foreign investment played a much smaller role than in most comparable economies in the West.

These criticisms are persuasive, although most of them could also be applied to most other societies going through the early stages of industrialization. In any event, from an economic perspective, the Meiji Restoration was certainly one of the great success stories of modern times. Not only did the Meiji leaders put Japan firmly on the path to economic and political development, but they also managed to remove the unequal treaty provisions that had been imposed at mid-century. Japanese achievements are especially impressive when compared with the difficulties experienced by China, which was not only unable to bring about significant changes in its traditional society but had not even reached a consensus on the need for doing so. Japan's achievements more closely resemble those of Europe, but whereas the West needed a century and a half to achieve significant industrial development, the Japanese realized it in forty years.

One of the distinctive features of Japan's transition from a traditional to a modern society was that it took place for the most part without violence or the kind of social or political revolution that occurred in so many other countries. The Meiji Restoration, which began the process, has been called a "revolution from above," a comprehensive restructuring of Japanese society by its own ruling group.

WHAT EXPLAINS JAPANESE UNIQUENESS? The differences between the Japanese response to the West and the responses of China and many other nations in the region have sparked considerable debate among students of comparative history. In this and previous chapters, we have already discussed some of the reasons why China—along with most other countries in Asia and Africa—had not begun to enter an industrial revolution of its own by the end of the nineteenth century. The puzzle then becomes, why was Japan apparently uniquely positioned to make the transition to an advanced industrial economy?

A number of explanations have been offered. Some have argued that Japan's success was partly due to good fortune. Lacking abundant natural resources, it was exposed to less pressure from the West than many of its neighbors. That argument is problematic, however, and would probably not have been accepted by Japanese observers at the time. Nor does it explain why nations under considerably less pressure, such as Laos and Nepal, did not advance even more quickly. All in all, the luck hypothesis is not very persuasive.

Some explanations have already been suggested in this book. Japan's unique geographic position was certainly a factor. China, a continental nation with a heterogeneous ethnic composition, was distinguished from its neighbors by its Confucian culture. By contrast, Japan was an island nation, ethnically and linguistically homogeneous, and had never been conquered. Unlike the Chinese or many other peoples in the region, the Japanese had little to fear from cultural change in terms of its effect on their national identity. The fact that the emperor, the living symbol of the nation, had adopted change ensured that his subjects could follow in his footsteps without fear.

In addition, a number of other factors may have played a role. Japanese values, with their emphasis on practicality and military achievement, may have contributed. Finally, the Meiji also benefited from the fact that the pace of urbanization and commercial and industrial development had already begun to quicken under the Tokugawa. Having already lost their traditional feudal role and much of the revenue from their estates, the Japanese aristocracy—daimyo and samurai alike—could discard sword and kimono and don modern military uniforms or Western business suits and still feel comfortable in both worlds.

Whatever the case, as the historian W. G. Beasley has noted, the Meiji Restoration was possible because aristocratic and capitalist elements managed to work together to bring about drastic change. Japan, it was said, was ripe for change, and nothing could have been more suitable as an antidote for the collapsing old system than the Western emphasis on wealth and power. It was a classic example of challenge and response.

THE FUSION OF EAST AND WEST The final product was an amalgam of old and new, Japanese and foreign, forming a new civilization that was still uniquely Japanese. There were some undesirable consequences, however. Because Meiji politics was essentially despotic,

Japanese leaders were able to fuse key traditional elements such as the warrior ethic and the concept of feudal loyalty with the dynamics of modern industrial capitalism to create a state totally dedicated to the possession of material wealth and national power. This combination of *kokutai* and capitalism, which one scholar has described as a form of "Asian fascism," was highly effective but explosive in its international manifestation. Like modern Germany, which also entered the industrial age directly from feudalism, Japan eventually engaged in a policy of repression at home and expansion abroad to achieve its national objectives. In Japan, as in Germany, it took defeat in war to disconnect the drive for national development from the feudal ethic and bring about the transformation to a pluralistic society dedicated to living in peace and cooperation with its neighbors.

CHAPTER SUMMARY

Few areas of the world resisted the Western incursion as stubbornly and effectively as East Asia. Although military, political, and economic pressure by the European powers was relatively intense during this era, two of the main states in the area were able to retain their independence while the third—Korea—was temporarily absorbed by one of its larger neighbors. Why the Chinese and the Japanese were able to prevent a total political and military takeover by foreign powers is an interesting question. One key reason was that both had a long history as well-defined states with a strong sense of national community and territorial cohesion. Although China had frequently been conquered, it had retained its sense of unique culture and identity. Geography, too, was in its favor. As a continental nation, China was able to survive partly because of its sheer size. Japan possessed the advantage of an island location.

Even more striking, however, are the different ways in which the two states attempted to deal with the challenge. While the Japanese chose to face the problem in a pragmatic manner, borrowing foreign ideas and institutions that appeared to be of value and at the same time were not in conflict with traditional attitudes and customs, China agonized over the issue for half a century while conservative elements fought a desperate battle to retain a maximum of the traditional heritage intact.

This chapter has discussed some of the possible reasons for those differences. In retrospect, it is difficult to avoid the conclusion that the Japanese approach was more effective. Whereas the Meiji leaders were able to set in motion an orderly transition from a traditional to an advanced society, in China the old system collapsed in disorder, leaving chaotic conditions that were still not rectified a generation later. China would pay a heavy price for its failure to respond coherently to the challenge.

But the Japanese "revolution from above" was by no means an unalloyed success. Ambitious efforts by Japanese leaders to carve out a share in the spoils of empire led to escalating conflict with China as well as with rival Western powers and in the early 1940s to global war. We will deal with that issue in Chapter 25. Meanwhile, in Europe, a combination of old rivalries and the effects of the Industrial Revolution were leading to a bitter regional conflict that eventually engulfed the entire world.

CHAPTER TIMELINE

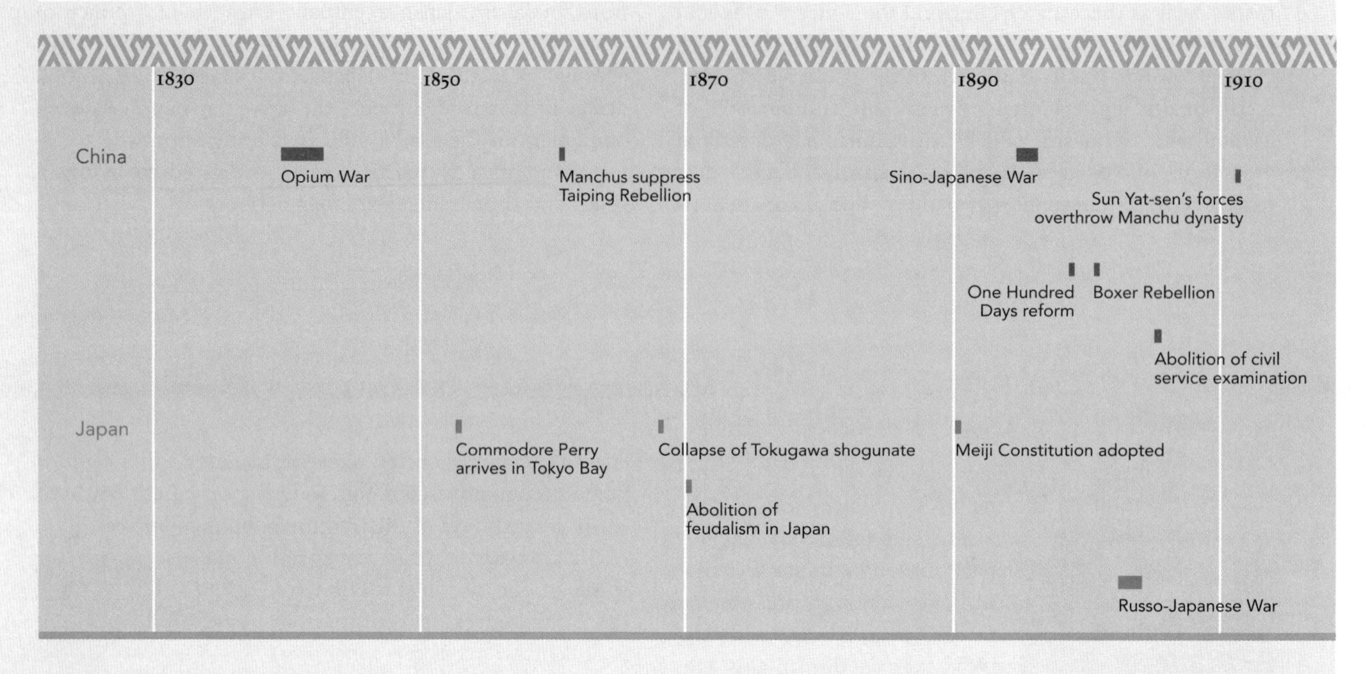

CHAPTER REVIEW

Upon Reflection

Q What were some of the key reasons why the Meiji reformers were so successful in launching Japan on the road to industrialization? Which of those reasons also applied to China under the Manchus?

Q What impact did colonial rule have on the environment in the European colonies in Asia and Africa during the nineteenth century? Did some of these same factors apply in China and Japan?

Q How did Western values and institutions influence Chinese and Japanese social mores and traditions during the imperialist era?

Key Terms

self-strengthening (p. 574)
Open Door Notes (p. 576)
three people's principles (p. 577)
sakoku (p. 583)
genro (p. 584)
kokutai (p. 585)
three obediences (p. 586)
eta (p. 586)
Meiji Restoration (p. 592)

Suggested Reading

CHINA For a general overview of modern Chinese history, see **I. C. Y. Hsu, *The Rise of Modern China,*** 6th ed. (Oxford, 2000). Also see **J. Spence's** stimulating ***The Search for Modern China*** (New York, 1990).

On the Taiping Rebellion, **J. Spence, *God's Chinese Son: The Taiping Heavenly Kingdom of Hong Xiuquan*** (New York, 1996), has become a classic. Social issues are dealt with in **E. S. Rawski, *The Last Emperors: A Social History of Qing Imperial Institutions*** (Berkeley, Calif., 1998). On the Manchus' attitude toward modernization, see **D. Pong, *Shen Pao-chen and China's Modernization in the Nineteenth Century*** (New York, 1994). For a series of stimulating essays on various aspects of China's transition to modernity, see **Wenhsin Yeh, ed., *Becoming Chinese: Passages to Modernity and Beyond*** (Berkeley, Calif., 2000).

Sun Yat-sen's career is explored in **M. C. Bergère, *Sun Yat-sen,*** trans. **J. Lloyd** (Stanford, Calif., 2000). **S. Seagraves's *Dragon Lady: The Life and Legend of the Last Empress of China*** (New York, 1992), is a revisionist treatment of Empress Dowager Cixi. On the Boxer Rebellion, see **D. Preston, *The Boxer Rebellion: The Dramatic Story of China's War on Foreigners That Shook the World in the Summer of 1900*** (Berkeley, Calif., 2001).

JAPAN The Meiji period of modern Japan is covered in **M. B. Jansen, ed., *The Emergence of Meiji Japan*** (Cambridge, 1995). Also see **D. Keene, *Emperor of Japan: Meiji and His World, 1852–1912*** (New York, 2000). See also **C. Gluck, *Japan's Modern Myths: Ideology in the Late Meiji Period*** (Princeton, N.J., 1985). To understand the role of the samurai in the Meiji Revolution, see **E. Ikegami, *The Taming of the Samurai: Honorific Individualism and the Making of Modern Japan*** (Cambridge, 1995).

On the international scene, **W. Lafeber, *The Clash: U.S.-Japanese Relations Throughout History*** (New York, 1997), is slow reading but a good source of information. The U.S. role in opening Japan to the West is analyzed in **G. Feifer, *Breaking Open Japan: Commodore Perry, Lord Abe, and American Imperialism in 1853*** (Washington, D.C., 2007). On the Russo-Japanese War, **R. Connaughton, *Rising Sun and Tumbling Bear: Russia's War with Japan*** (London, 2003), is one of several good offerings. The best introduction to Japanese art is **P. Mason, *History of Japanese Art*** (New York, 1993).

Visit the CourseMate website at **www.cengagebrain.com** for additional study tools and review materials for this chapter.

CHAPTER 23

The Beginning of the Twentieth-Century Crisis: War and Revolution

© Hulton Archive/Getty Images

Canadian soldiers prepare for an attack at the Battle of the Somme.

CHAPTER OUTLINE AND FOCUS QUESTIONS

The Road to World War I

Q What were the long-range and immediate causes of World War I?

The Great War

Q Why did the course of World War I turn out to be so different from what the belligerents had expected? How did World War I affect the belligerents' governmental and political institutions, economic affairs, and social life?

Crisis in Russia and the End of the War

Q What were the causes of the Russian Revolution of 1917, and why did the Bolsheviks prevail in the civil war and gain control of Russia?

An Uncertain Peace

Q What problems did Europe and the United States face in the 1920s?

In Pursuit of a New Reality: Cultural and Intellectual Trends

Q How did the cultural and intellectual trends of the post–World War I years reflect the crises of the time as well as the lingering effects of the war?

CRITICAL THINKING

Q What was the relationship between World War I and the Russian Revolution?

ON JULY 1, 1916, BRITISH and French infantry forces attacked German defensive lines along a 25-mile front near the Somme (SUHM) River in France. Each soldier carried almost 70 pounds of equipment, making it "impossible to move much quicker than a slow walk." German machine guns soon opened fire: "We were able to see our comrades move forward in an attempt to cross No-Man's Land, only to be mown down like meadow grass," recalled one British soldier. "I felt sick at the sight of this carnage and remember weeping." In one day, more than 21,000 British soldiers died. After six months of fighting, the British had advanced 5 miles; one million British, French, and German soldiers had been killed or wounded.

Philip Gibbs, an English war correspondent, described what he saw in the German trenches that the British forces overran: "Victory! . . . Some of the German dead were young boys, too young to be killed for old men's crimes, and others might have been old or young. One could not tell because they had no faces, and were just masses of raw flesh in rags of uniforms. Legs and arms lay separate without any bodies thereabout."

World War I (1914–1918) was the defining event of the twentieth-century Western world. Overwhelmed by the size of its battles, the extent of its casualties, and its impact on all facets of life, contemporaries referred to it simply as the "Great War." The Great War was all the more disturbing to Europeans because it came after a period that many believed to have been an age of progress. Material prosperity and a fervid belief in scientific and technological advances had convinced many people that the world stood on the verge of creating the utopia that humans had dreamed of for centuries. The historian Arnold Toynbee expressed what the era before the war had meant to his generation:

> [We had expected] that life throughout the world would become more rational, more humane, and more democratic and that, slowly, but surely, political democracy would produce greater social justice. We had also expected that the progress of science and technology would make mankind richer, and that this increasing wealth would gradually spread from a minority to a majority. We had expected that all this would happen peacefully. In fact we thought that mankind's course was set for an earthly paradise.[1]

After 1918, it was no longer possible to maintain naive illusions about the progress of Western civilization. As World War I was followed by revolutionary upheavals, the mass murder machines of totalitarian regimes, and the destructiveness of World War II, it became all too apparent that instead of a utopia, Western civilization had become a nightmare. World War I and the revolutions it spawned can properly be seen as the first stage in the crisis of the twentieth century.

The Road to World War I

FOCUS QUESTION: What were the long-range and immediate causes of World War I?

On June 28, 1914, the heir to the Austrian throne, Archduke Francis Ferdinand, was assassinated in the Bosnian city of Sarajevo (sar-uh-YAY-voh). Although this event precipitated the confrontation between Austria and Serbia that led to World War I, underlying forces had been propelling Europeans toward armed conflict for a long time.

Nationalism and Internal Dissent

The system of nation-states that had emerged in Europe in the second half of the nineteenth century (see Map 23.1) had led to intense competition. Rivalries over colonies and trade intensified during an era of frenzied imperialist expansion, while the division of Europe's great powers into two loose alliances (Germany, Austria, and Italy on one side and France, Great Britain, and Russia on the other) only added to the tensions. The series of crises that tested these alliances in the 1900s and early 1910s had left European states embittered, eager for revenge, and willing to go to war to preserve the power of their national states.

The growth of nationalism in the nineteenth century had yet another serious consequence. Not all ethnic groups had achieved the goal of nationhood. Slavic minorities in the Balkans and the multiethnic Habsburg Empire, for example, still dreamed of creating their own national states. So did the Irish in the British Empire and the Poles in the Russian Empire.

National aspirations, however, were not the only source of internal strife at the beginning of the twentieth century. Socialist labor movements had grown more powerful and were increasingly inclined to use strikes, even violent ones, to achieve their goals. Some conservative leaders, alarmed at the increase in labor strife and class division, even feared that European nations were on the verge of revolution. Did these statesmen opt for war in 1914 because they believed that "prosecuting an active foreign policy," as some Austrian leaders expressed it, would smother "internal troubles"? Some historians have argued that the desire to suppress internal disorder may have encouraged some leaders to take the plunge into war in 1914.

Militarism

The growth of large mass armies after 1900 not only heightened the existing tensions in Europe but also made it inevitable that if war did come, it would be extremely destructive. **Conscription**—obligatory military service—had been established as a regular practice in most Western countries before 1914 (the United States and Britain were major exceptions). European military machines had doubled in size between 1890 and 1914. The Russian army was the largest, with 1.3 million men, but the French and Germans were not far behind, with 900,000 each. The British, Italian, and Austrian armies numbered between 250,000 and 500,000 soldiers.

Militarism, however, involved more than just large armies. As armies grew, so did the influence of military leaders, who drew up vast and complex plans for quickly mobilizing millions of men and enormous quantities of supplies in the event of war. Fearful that changing these plans would cause chaos in the armed forces, military leaders insisted that the plans could not be altered. In the crises during the summer of 1914, the generals' lack of flexibility forced European political leaders to make decisions for military instead of political reasons.

© Cengage Learning

MAP 23.1 Europe in 1914. By 1914, two alliances dominated Europe: the Triple Entente of Britain, France, and Russia and the Triple Alliance of Germany, Austria-Hungary, and Italy. Russia sought to bolster fellow Slavs in Serbia, whereas Austria-Hungary was intent on increasing its power in the Balkans and thwarting Serbia's ambitions. Thus, the Balkans became the flash point for World War I.

Q *Which nonaligned nations were positioned between the two alliances?*

The Outbreak of War: Summer 1914

Militarism, nationalism, and the desire to stifle internal dissent may all have played a role in the coming of World War I, but the decisions made by European leaders in the summer of 1914 directly precipitated the conflict. It was another crisis in the Balkans that forced this predicament on European statesmen.

As we have seen, states in southeastern Europe had struggled to free themselves from Ottoman rule in the course of the nineteenth and early twentieth centuries. But the rivalry between Austria-Hungary and Russia for domination of these new states created serious tensions in the region. By 1914, Serbia, supported by Russia, was determined to create a large, independent Slavic state in the Balkans, while Austria-Hungary, which had its own Slavic minorities to contend with, was equally set on preventing that possibility. Many Europeans perceived the inherent dangers in this explosive situation. The British ambassador to Vienna wrote in 1913:

> Serbia will some day set Europe by the ears, and bring about a universal war on the Continent. . . . I cannot tell you how exasperated people are getting here at the continual worry which that little country causes to Austria under encouragement from Russia. . . . It will be lucky if Europe succeeds in avoiding war as a result of the present crisis. The next time a Serbian crisis arises . . . , I feel sure that Austria-Hungary will refuse to admit of any Russian interference in the dispute and that she will proceed to settle her differences with her little neighbor by herself.[2]

It was against this backdrop of mutual distrust and hatred that the events of the summer of 1914 were played out.

THE ASSASSINATION OF FRANCIS FERDINAND: A "BLANK CHECK"? The assassination of the Austrian Archduke Francis Ferdinand and his wife, Sophia, on June 28, 1914, was carried out by a Bosnian activist who worked for the Black Hand, a Serbian terrorist organization dedicated to the creation of a pan-Slavic kingdom. Although the Austrian government did not know whether the Serbian government had been directly involved in the archduke's assassination, it saw an opportunity to "render Serbia innocuous once and for all by a display of force," as the Austrian foreign minister put it. Fearful of Russian intervention on Serbia's behalf, Austrian leaders sought the backing of their German allies. Emperor William II and his chancellor responded with the infamous "blank check," their assurance that Austria-Hungary could rely on Germany's "full support," even if "matters went to the length of a war between Austria-Hungary and Russia." Much historical debate has focused on this "blank check" extended to the Austrians. Did the Germans realize that an Austrian-Serbian war could lead to a wider war? If so, did they actually want one? Historians are still divided on the answers to these questions.

DECLARATIONS OF WAR Strengthened by German support, Austrian leaders issued an ultimatum to Serbia on July 23 in which they made such extreme demands that Serbia had little choice but to reject some of them in order to preserve its sovereignty. Austria then declared war on Serbia on July 28. Although the Austrians had hoped to keep the war limited to Serbia and Austria in order to ensure their success in the Balkans, Russia was determined to support Serbia's cause. Thus, on July 28, Tsar Nicholas II ordered partial mobilization of the Russian army against Austria. The Russian General Staff informed the tsar that their mobilization plans were based on a war against both Germany and Austria simultaneously. They could not execute partial mobilization without creating chaos in the army. Consequently, the Russian government ordered full mobilization of the Russian army on July 29, knowing that the Germans would consider this an act of war against them. Germany quickly responded with an ultimatum that the Russians must halt their mobilization within twelve hours. When the Russians ignored it, Germany declared war on Russia on August 1.

At this stage of the conflict, German war plans determined whether France would become involved in the war. Under the guidance of General Alfred von Schlieffen (AHL-fret fun SHLEE-fun), chief of staff from 1891 to 1905, the German General Staff had devised a military plan based on the assumption of a two-front war with France and Russia because the two powers had formed a military alliance in 1894. The Schlieffen Plan called for a minimal troop deployment against Russia while most of the German army would make a rapid invasion of France before Russia could become effective in the east or before the British could cross the English Channel to help France. This meant invading France by advancing through neutral Belgium, with its level coastal plain on which the army could move faster than on the rougher terrain to the southeast. After the planned quick defeat of the French, the German army expected to redeploy to the east against Russia. Under the Schlieffen Plan, Germany could not mobilize its troops solely against Russia and therefore declared war on France on August 3 after issuing an ultimatum to Belgium on August 2 demanding the right of German troops to pass through Belgian territory. On August 4, Great Britain declared war on Germany, officially over this violation of Belgian neutrality but in fact over the British desire to maintain world power. As one British diplomat argued, if Germany and Austria were to win the war, "what would be the position of a friendless England?" By August 4, all the great powers of Europe were at war.

© Cengage Learning

The Schlieffen Plan

The Great War

FOCUS QUESTIONS: Why did the course of World War I turn out to be so different from what the belligerents had expected? How did World War I affect the belligerents' governmental and political institutions, economic affairs, and social life?

Before 1914, many political leaders had become convinced that war involved so many political and economic risks that it was not worth fighting. Others had believed that "rational" diplomats could control any situation and prevent the outbreak of war. At the beginning of August 1914, both of these prewar illusions were shattered, but the new illusions that replaced them soon proved to be equally foolish.

1914–1915: Illusions and Stalemate

Europeans went to war in 1914 with great enthusiasm (see the box on p. 600). Government propaganda had been successful in stirring up national antagonisms before the war. Now, in August 1914, the urgent pleas of governments for defense against aggressors found many receptive ears in every belligerent nation. A new set of illusions also fed the enthusiasm for war. In August 1914, almost everyone believed that the war would be over in a few weeks. People were reminded that the major battles in European wars since 1815 had ended in a matter of weeks. Both the soldiers who exuberantly boarded the trains for the war front in August 1914 and the jubilant citizens who bombarded them with flowers when they departed believed that the warriors would be home by Christmas.

German hopes for a quick end to the war rested on a military gamble. The Schlieffen Plan had called for the

The Excitement of War

POLITICS & GOVERNMENT

The incredible outpouring of patriotic enthusiasm that greeted the declaration of war at the beginning of August 1914 demonstrated the power that nationalistic feeling had attained at the beginning of the twentieth century. Many Europeans seemingly believed that the war had given them a higher purpose, a renewed dedication to the greatness of their nations. These selections are taken from three sources: the autobiography of Stefan Zweig (SHTE-fahn TSVYK), an Austrian writer; the memoirs of Robert Graves, a British writer; and a letter by a German soldier, Walter Limmer, to his parents.

Stefan Zweig, *The World of Yesterday*

The next morning I was in Austria. In every station placards had been put up announcing general mobilization. The trains were filled with fresh recruits, banners were flying, music sounded, and in Vienna I found the entire city in a tumult. . . . There were parades in the street, flags, ribbons, and music burst forth everywhere, young recruits were marching triumphantly, their faces lighting up at the cheering. . . .

And to be truthful, I must acknowledge that there was a majestic, rapturous, and even seductive something in this first outbreak of the people from which one could escape only with difficulty. And in spite of all my hatred and aversion for war, I should not like to have missed the memory of those days. As never before, thousands and hundreds of thousands felt what they should have felt in peace time, that they belonged together. A city of two million, a country of nearly fifty million, in that hour felt that they were participating in world history, in a moment which would never recur, and that each one was called upon to cast his infinitesimal self into the glowing mass, there to be purified of all selfishness. All differences of class, rank, and language were flooded over at that moment by the rushing feeling of fraternity. . . .

What did the great mass know of war in 1914, after nearly half a century of peace? They did not know war, they had hardly given it a thought. It had become legendary, and distance had made it seem romantic and heroic. They still saw it in the perspective of their school readers and of paintings in museums; brilliant cavalry attacks in glittering uniforms, the fatal shot always straight through the heart, the entire campaign a resounding march of victory—"We'll be home at Christmas," the recruits shouted laughingly to their mothers in August of 1914. . . . A rapid excursion into the romantic, a wild, manly adventure—that is how the war of 1914 was painted in the imagination of the simple man, and the younger people were honestly afraid that they might miss this most wonderful and exciting experience of their lives; that is why they hurried and thronged to the colors, and that is why they shouted and sang in the trains that carried them to the slaughter; wildly and feverishly the red wave of blood coursed through the veins of the entire nation.

Robert Graves, *Goodbye to All That*

I had just finished with Charterhouse and gone up to Harlech, when England declared war on Germany. A day or two later I decided to enlist. In the first place, though the papers predicted only a very short war—over by Christmas at the outside—I hoped that it might last long enough to delay my going to Oxford in October, which I dreaded. Nor did I work out the possibilities of getting actively engaged in the fighting, expecting garrison service at home, while the regular forces were away. In the second place, I was outraged to read of the Germans' cynical violation of Belgian neutrality. Though I discounted perhaps twenty percent of the atrocity details as wartime exaggeration, that was not, of course, sufficient.

Walter Limmer, Letter to His Parents

In any case I mean to go into this business. . . . That is the simple duty of every one of us. And this feeling is universal among the soldiers, especially since the night when England's declaration of war was announced in the barracks. We none of us got to sleep till three o'clock in the morning, we were so full of excitement, fury, and enthusiasm. It is a joy to go to the Front with such comrades. We are bound to be victorious! Nothing else is possible in the face of such determination to win.

What do these excerpts reveal about the motivations of people to join and support World War I? Do the passages reveal anything about the power of nationalism in Europe in the early twentieth century?

Source: From *The World of Yesterday* by Stefan Zweig, translated by Helmut Ripperger. Translation copyright 1943 by the Viking. Press, Inc.

German army to proceed through Belgium into northern France with a vast circling movement that would sweep around Paris and surround most of the French army. But the German advance was halted only 20 miles from Paris at the First Battle of the Marne (September 6–10). The war quickly turned into a stalemate as neither the Germans nor the French could dislodge each other from the trenches they had begun to dig for shelter (see Map 23.2).

In contrast to the Western Front, the war in the east was marked by much more mobility, although the cost in lives was equally enormous. At the beginning of the war, the Russian army moved into eastern Germany but was decisively defeated at the Battles of Tannenberg on August 30 and the Masurian Lakes on September 15. The Russians were no longer a threat to German territory.

The Austrians, Germany's allies, fared less well initially. They had been defeated by the Russians in Galicia (guh-LISH-ee-uh) and thrown out of Serbia as well. To make matters worse, the Italians betrayed the Germans and Austrians and entered the war on the Allied side by attacking Austria in May 1915. (France, Great Britain, and Russia were called the Allied Powers, or Allies.) By this time, the Germans had come to the aid of the Austrians. A German-Austrian army routed the Russian army in

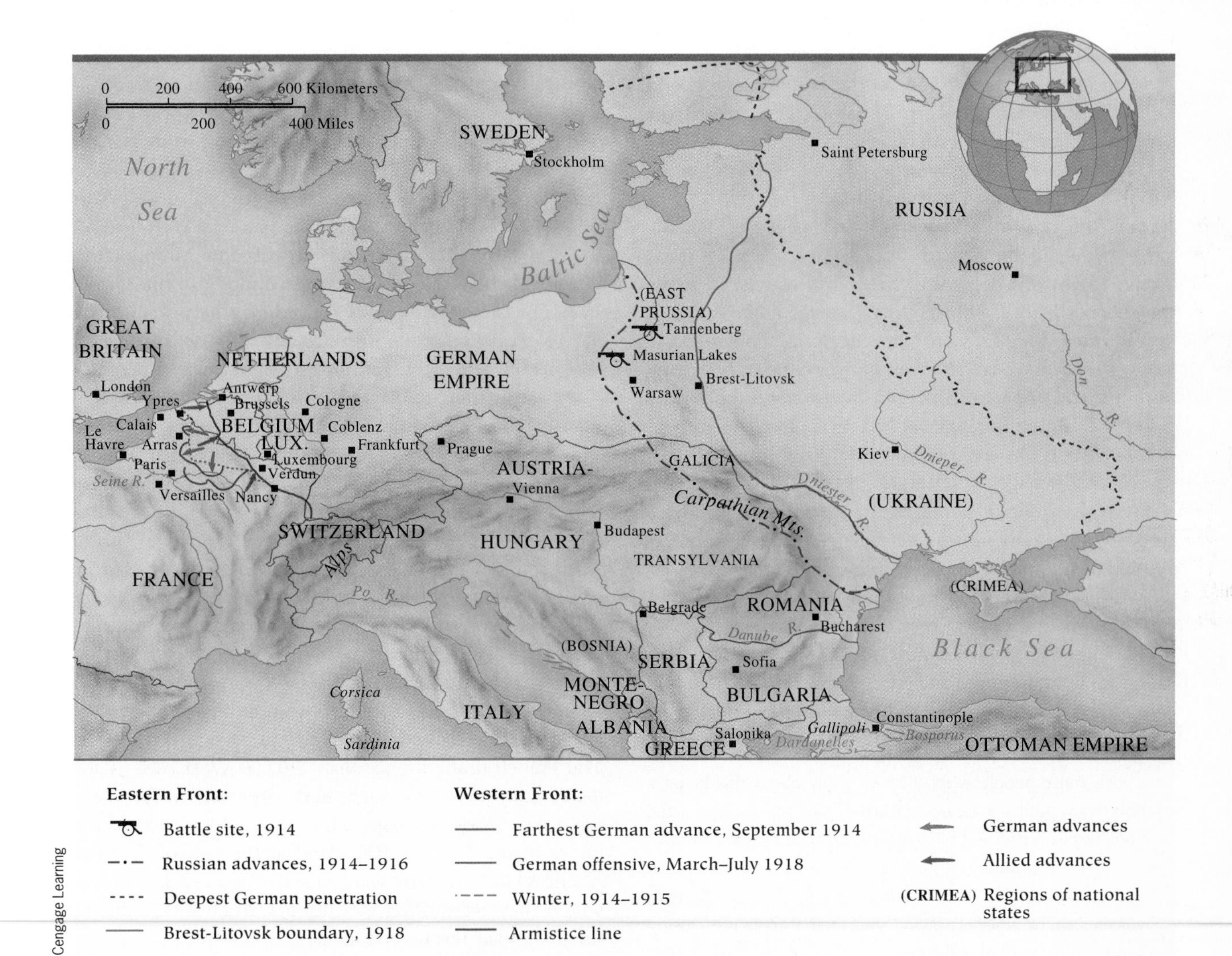

© Cengage Learning

MAP 23.2 World War I, 1914–1918. This map shows how greatly the Western and Eastern Fronts of World War I differed. After initial German gains in the west, the war became bogged down in trench warfare, with little change in the battle lines between 1914 and 1918. The Eastern Front was marked by considerable mobility, with battle lines shifting by hundreds of miles.

Q *How do you explain the difference in the two fronts?*

Galicia and pushed the Russians back 300 miles into their own territory. Russian casualties stood at 2.5 million killed, captured, or wounded; the Russians had almost been knocked out of the war. Buoyed by their success, the Germans and Austrians, joined by the Bulgarians in September 1915, attacked and eliminated Serbia from the war.

1916–1917: The Great Slaughter

The successes in the east enabled the Germans to move back to the offensive in the west. The early trenches dug in 1914, stretching from the English Channel to the frontiers of Switzerland, had by now become elaborate systems of defense. Both lines of trenches were protected by barbed-wire entanglements 3 to 5 feet high and 30 yards wide, concrete machine-gun nests, and mortar batteries, supported farther back by heavy artillery. Troops lived in holes in the ground, separated from each other by a "no-man's land."

The unexpected development of **trench warfare** on the Western Front baffled military leaders, who had been trained to fight wars of movement and maneuver. Periodically, the high command on either side would order an offensive that would begin with an artillery barrage to flatten the enemy's barbed wire and leave the enemy in a state of shock. After "softening up" the enemy in this fashion, a mass of soldiers would climb out of their trenches with fixed bayonets and hope to work their way toward the enemy trenches. The attacks rarely worked, as the machine gun put hordes of men advancing unprotected across open fields at a severe disadvantage. In 1916 and 1917, millions of young men were sacrificed in the search for the elusive breakthrough. In ten months at Verdun (ver-DUHN) in 1916, 700,000 men lost their lives over a few miles of terrain.

Warfare in the trenches of the Western Front produced unimaginable horrors (see the box on p. 603). Battlefields were hellish landscapes of barbed wire, shell holes, mud, and injured and dying men. The introduction of poison gas in 1915 produced new forms of injuries. As one British writer described them:

> I wish those people who write so glibly about this being a holy war could see a case of mustard gas . . . could see the poor things burnt and blistered all over with great mustard-coloured suppurating blisters with blind eyes all sticky . . . and stuck together, and always fighting for breath, with voices a mere whisper, saying that their throats are closing and they know they will choke.[3]

Soldiers in the trenches also lived with the persistent presence of death. Since combat went on for months, soldiers had to carry on in the midst of countless bodies of dead men or the remains of men dismembered by artillery barrages. Many soldiers remembered the stench of decomposing bodies and the swarms of rats that grew fat in the trenches.

The Widening of the War

As another response to the stalemate on the Western Front, both sides looked for new allies who might provide a winning advantage. The Ottoman Empire had already come into the war on Germany's side in August 1914. Russia, Great Britain, and France declared war on the Ottoman Empire in November. Although the Allies attempted to open a Balkan front by landing forces at Gallipoli (gah-LIP-poh-lee), southwest of Constantinople, in April 1915, the entry of Bulgaria into the war on the side of the Central Powers (as Germany, Austria-Hungary, and the Ottoman Empire were called) and a disastrous campaign at Gallipoli caused them to withdraw.

A GLOBAL CONFLICT Because the major European powers controlled colonial empires in other parts of the world, the war in Europe soon became a world conflict (see the comparative illustration on p. 604). In the Middle East, the British officer T. E. Lawrence (1888–1935), who came to be known as Lawrence of Arabia, incited Arab princes to revolt against their Ottoman overlords in 1917. In 1918, British forces from Egypt and Mesopotamia destroyed the rest of the Ottoman Empire in the Middle East. For their Middle East campaigns, the British mobilized forces from India, Australia, and New Zealand.

The Allies also took advantage of Germany's preoccupation in Europe and lack of naval strength to seize German colonies in Africa. The first British shots of World War I were actually fired in Africa when British African troops moved into the German colony of Togoland near the end of August 1914. But in East Africa, the German commander, Colonel Paul von Lettow-Vorbeck (POWL fun LEH-toh-FOR-bek), managed to keep his African troops fighting one campaign after another for four years; he did not surrender until two weeks after the armistice ended the war in Europe.

In the battles in Africa, Allied governments drew mainly on African soldiers, but some states, especially France, also recruited African troops to fight in Europe. The French drafted more than 170,000 West African soldiers, many of whom fought in the trenches on the Western Front. African troops were also used as occupation forces in the German Rhineland at the end of the war. About 80,000 Africans were killed or injured in Europe, where they were often at a distinct disadvantage due to the unfamiliar terrain and climate.

Hundreds of thousands of Africans were also used for labor, especially for carrying supplies and building roads and bridges. In East Africa, both sides drafted Africans as carriers for their armies. More than 100,000 of these workers died from disease and starvation resulting from neglect.

The immediate impact of World War I in Africa was the extension of colonial rule since Germany's African

The Reality of War: Trench Warfare

The romantic illusions about the excitement and adventure of war that filled the minds of so many young men as they marched off to battle quickly disintegrated after a short time in the trenches on the Western Front. This description of trench warfare is taken from the most famous novel that emerged from World War I, Erich Maria Remarque's *All Quiet on the Western Front*, published in 1929. Remarque had fought in the trenches in France.

Erich Maria Remarque, *All Quiet on the Western Front*

We wake up in the middle of the night. The earth booms. Heavy fire is falling on us. We crouch into corners. We distinguish shells of every calibre.

Each man lays hold of his things and looks again every minute to reassure himself that they are still there. The dugout heaves, the night roars and flashes. We look at each other in the momentary flashes of light, and with pale faces and pressed lips shake our heads.

Every man is aware of the heavy shells tearing down the parapet, rooting up the embankment and demolishing the upper layers of concrete. . . . Already by morning a few of the recruits are green and vomiting. They are too inexperienced. . . .

The bombardment does not diminish. It is falling in the rear too. As far as one can see it spouts fountains of mud and iron. A wide belt is being raked.

The attack does not come, but the bombardment continues. Slowly we become mute. Hardly a man speaks. We cannot make ourselves understood.

Our trench is almost gone. At many places it is only eighteen inches high; it is broken by holes, and craters, and mountains of earth. A shell lands square in front of our post. At once it is dark. We are buried and must dig ourselves out. . . .

Towards morning, while it is still dark, there is some excitement. Through the entrance rushes in a swarm of fleeing rats that try to storm the walls. Torches light up the confusion. Everyone yells and curses and slaughters. The madness and despair of many hours unloads itself in this outburst. Faces are distorted, arms strike out, the beasts scream; we just stop in time to avoid attacking one another. . . .

Suddenly it howls and flashes terrifically, the dugout cracks in all its joints under a direct hit, fortunately only a light one that the concrete blocks are able to withstand. It rings metallically; the walls reel; rifles, helmets, earth, mud, and dust fly everywhere. Sulfur fumes pour in. . . . The recruit starts to rave again and two others follow suit. One jumps up and rushes out, we have trouble with the other two. I start after the one who escapes and wonder whether to shoot him in the leg—then it shrieks again; I fling myself down and when I stand up the wall of the trench is plastered with smoking splinters, lumps of flesh, and bits of uniform. I scramble back.

The first recruit seems actually to have gone insane. He butts his head against the wall like a goat. We must try tonight to take him to the rear. Meanwhile we bind him, but so that in case of attack he can be released.

Suddenly the nearer explosions cease. The shelling continues but it has lifted and falls behind us; our trench is free. We seize the hand grenades, pitch them out in front of the dugout, and jump after them. The bombardment has stopped and a heavy barrage now falls behind us. The attack has come.

No one would believe that in this howling waste there could still be men; but steel helmets now appear on all sides out of the trench, and fifty yards from us a machine gun is already in position and barking.

The wire entanglements are torn to pieces. Yet they offer some obstacle. We see the storm troops coming. Our artillery opens fire. Machine guns rattle, rifles crack. The charge works its way across. Haie and Kropp begin with the hand grenades. They throw as fast as they can; others pass them, the handles with the strings already pulled. Haie throws seventy-five yards, Kropp sixty; it has been measured; the distance is important. The enemy as they run cannot do much before they are within forty yards.

We recognize the distorted faces, the smooth helmets: they are French. They have already suffered heavily when they reach the remnants of the barbed-wire entanglements. A whole line has gone down before our machine guns; then we have a lot of stoppages and they come nearer.

I see one of them, his face upturned, fall into a wire cradle. His body collapses, his hands remain suspended as though he were praying. Then his body drops clean away and only his hands with the stumps of his arms, shot off, now hang in the wire.

What is causing the "madness and despair" Remarque describes in the trenches? Why does the recruit in this scene apparently go insane?

Source: *All Quiet on the Western Front* by Erich Maria Remarque. "Im Westen Nichts Neues," copyright 1928 by Ullstein A.G.; copyright renewed © 1956 by Erich Maria Remarque. *All Quiet on the Western Front*, copyright 1929, 1930 by Little, Brown and Company; Copyright renewed © 1957, 1958 by Erich Maria Remarque. All Rights Reserved.

COMPARATIVE ILLUSTRATION

Soldiers from around the World. Although World War I began in Europe, it soon became a global conflict fought in different areas of the world and with soldiers from all parts of the globe. France, especially, recruited troops from its African colonies to fight in Europe. The photo at the top shows French African troops fighting in the trenches on the Western Front. About 80,000 Africans were killed or injured in Europe. The photo at the bottom shows a group of German soldiers in their machine-gun nest on the Western Front.

What do these photographs reveal about the nature of World War I and the role of African troops in the conflict?

© Bettmann/CORBIS

© General Photographic Agency/Getty Images

colonies were simply transferred to the winning powers, especially the British and the French. But the war also had unintended consequences for the Europeans. African soldiers who had gone to war for the Allies, especially those who left Africa and fought in Europe, became politically aware and began to advocate political and social equality. As one African who had fought for the French said, "We were not fighting for the French, we were fighting for ourselves [to become] French citizens."[4] Moreover, educated African elites, who had aided their colonial overlords in enlisting local peoples to fight, did so in the belief that they would be rewarded with citizenship and new political possibilities after the war. When their hopes were frustrated, they soon became involved in anticolonial movements (see Chapter 24).

In East Asia and the Pacific, Japan joined the Allies on August 23, 1914, primarily to seize control of German territories in Asia. As one Japanese statesman declared, the war in Europe was "divine aid . . . for the development of the destiny of Japan."[5] The Japanese took possession of German territories in China, as well as the German-occupied islands in the Pacific. New Zealand and Australia quickly joined the Japanese in conquering the German-held parts of New Guinea.

ENTRY OF THE UNITED STATES Most important to the Allied cause was the entry of the United States into the war. American involvement grew out of the naval conflict between Germany and Great Britain. Britain used its superior naval power to maximum effect by setting up a naval blockade of Germany. Germany retaliated by imposing a counterblockade enforced by the use of unrestricted submarine warfare. Strong American protests over the German sinking of passenger liners, especially the British ship *Lusitania* on May 7, 1915, when more than a hundred Americans lost their lives, forced the

German government to suspend unrestricted submarine warfare in September 1915.

In January 1917, however, eager to break the deadlock in the war, the Germans decided on another military gamble by returning to unrestricted submarine warfare. German naval officers convinced Emperor William II that the use of unrestricted submarine warfare could starve the British into submission within five months, certainly before the Americans could act. The return to unrestricted submarine warfare brought the United States into the war on April 6, 1917. Although U.S. troops did not arrive in Europe in large numbers until the following year, the entry of the United States into the war gave the Allied Powers a psychological boost when they needed it.

The year 1917 had not been a good year for them. Allied offensives on the Western Front were disastrously defeated. The Italian armies were smashed in October, and in November, the Bolshevik Revolution in Russia (see "The Russian Revolution" later in this chapter) led to Russia's withdrawal from the war and left Germany free to concentrate entirely on the Western Front. The cause of the Central Powers looked favorable, although war weariness in the Ottoman Empire, Bulgaria, Austria-Hungary, and Germany was beginning to take its toll. The home front was rapidly becoming a cause for as much concern as the war front.

The Home Front: The Impact of Total War

The prolongation of World War I made it a **total war** that affected the lives of all citizens, however remote they might be from the battlefields. The need to organize masses of men and matériel for years of combat (Germany alone had 5.5 million men in active units in 1916) led to increased centralization of government powers, economic regimentation, and manipulation of public opinion to keep the war effort going.

POLITICAL CENTRALIZATION AND ECONOMIC REGIMENTATION Because the war was expected to be short, little thought had been given to long-term wartime needs. Governments had to respond quickly, however, when the war machines failed to achieve their knockout blows and made ever greater demands for men and matériel. To meet these needs, governments expanded their powers. Countries drafted tens of millions of young men for that elusive breakthrough to victory.

Throughout Europe, wartime governments expanded their powers over their economies. Free market capitalistic systems were temporarily shelved as governments experimented with price, wage, and rent controls; rationed food supplies and materials; and nationalized transportation systems and industries. Under total war mobilization, the distinction between soldiers at war and civilians at home was narrowed. In the view of political leaders, all citizens constituted a national army.

CONTROL OF PUBLIC OPINION As the Great War dragged on and casualties mounted, the patriotic enthusiasm that had marked the early days of the conflict waned. By 1916, there were numerous signs that civilian morale was beginning to crack under the pressure of total war. Governments took strenuous measures to fight the growing opposition to the war. Even parliamentary regimes resorted to an expansion of police powers to stifle internal dissent. The British Parliament, for example, passed the Defence of the Realm Act (DORA), which allowed the public authorities to arrest dissenters and charge them as traitors. Newspapers were censored, and sometimes their publication was even suspended.

Wartime governments also made active use of propaganda to arouse enthusiasm for the war. At first, public

Musée des 2 Guerres Mondiales, Paris/© Gianni Dagli Orti/The Art Archive at Art Resource, NY

British Recruiting Poster. As the conflict persisted month after month, governments resorted to active propaganda campaigns to generate enthusiasm for the war. In this British recruiting poster, the government tried to pressure men into volunteering for military service. By 1916, the British were forced to adopt compulsory military service.

Women in the Factories

During World War I, women were called on to assume new job responsibilities, including factory work. In this selection, Naomi Loughnan, a young, upper-middle-class woman, describes the experiences in a munitions plant that considerably broadened her perspective on life.

Naomi Loughnan, "Munition Work"

We little thought when we first put on our overalls and caps and enlisted in the Munition Army how much more inspiring our life was to be than we had dared to hope. Though we munition workers sacrifice our ease, we gain a life worth living. Our long days are filled with interest, and with the zest of doing work for our country in the grand cause of Freedom. As we handle the weapons of war we are learning great lessons of life. In the busy, noisy workshops we come face to face with every kind of class, and each one of these classes has something to learn from the others. . . .

Engineering mankind is possessed of the unshakable opinion that no woman can have the mechanical sense. If one of us asks humbly why such and such an alteration is not made to prevent this or that drawback to a machine, she is told, with a superior smile, that a man has worked her machine before her for years, and that therefore if there were any improvement possible it would have been made. As long as we do exactly what we are told and do not attempt to use our brains, we give entire satisfaction, and are treated as nice, good children. Any swerving from the easy path prepared for us by our males arouses the most scathing contempt in their manly bosoms. . . . Women have, however, proved that their entry into the munition world has increased the output. Employers who forget things personal in their patriotic desire for large results are enthusiastic over the success of women in the shops. But their workmen have to be handled with the utmost tenderness and caution lest they should actually imagine it was being suggested that women could do their work equally well, given equal conditions of training—at least where muscle is not the driving force. . . .

The coming of the mixed classes of women into the factory is slowly but surely having an educative effect upon the men. "Language" is almost unconsciously becoming subdued. There are fiery exceptions, who make our hair stand up on end under our close-fitting caps, but a sharp rebuke or a look of horror will often straighten out the most savage. . . . It is grievous to hear the girls also swearing and using disgusting language. Shoulder to shoulder with the children of the slums, the upper classes are having their eyes opened at last to the awful conditions among which their sisters have dwelt. Foul language, immorality, and many other evils are but the natural outcome of overcrowding and bitter poverty. . . . Sometimes disgust will overcome us, but we are learning with painful clarity that the fault is not theirs whose actions disgust us, but must be placed to the discredit of those other classes who have allowed the continued existence of conditions which generate the things from which we shrink appalled.

What did Naomi Loughnan learn about men and lower-class women while working in the munitions factory? What did she learn about herself?

Source: From "Munition Work" by Naomi Loughnan in Gilbert Stone, ed., *Women War Workers* (London: George Harrap and Company, 1971), pp. 25, 35, 38.

officials needed to do little to achieve this goal. The British and French, for example, exaggerated German atrocities in Belgium and found that their citizens were only too willing to believe these accounts. But as the war dragged on and morale sagged, governments were forced to devise new techniques for stimulating declining enthusiasm.

WOMEN IN THE WAR EFFORT World War I also created new roles for women. With so many men off fighting at the front, women were called on to assume jobs and responsibilities that had not been open to them before, including jobs that had been considered beyond the "capacity of women." These included such occupations as chimney sweeps, truck drivers, farm laborers, and factory workers in heavy industry (see the box above). In Germany, 38 percent of the workers in the Krupp (KROOP) armaments works in 1918 were women. Nevertheless, despite the noticeable increase in women's wages that resulted from government regulations, women working at industrial jobs were still being paid less than men at the end of the war.

Even worse, women's place in the workforce was far from secure. Both men and women seemed to assume that many of the new jobs for women were only temporary, an expectation quite evident in the British poem "War Girls," written in 1916:

> *There's the girl who clips your ticket for the train,*
> *And the girl who speeds the lift from floor to floor,*
> *There's the girl who does a milk-round in the rain,*
> *And the girl who calls for orders at your door.*
> *Strong, sensible, and fit,*
> *They're out to show their grit,*
> *And tackle jobs with energy and knack.*
> *No longer caged and penned up,*
> *They're going to keep their end up*
> *Till the khaki soldier boys come marching back.*[6]

At the end of the war, governments moved quickly to remove women from the jobs they had encouraged them to take earlier, and wages for women who remained employed were lowered.

Nevertheless, in some countries, the role played by women in the wartime economies did have a positive impact on the women's movement for social and political emancipation. The most obvious gain was the right to vote, granted to women in Britain in January 1918 and in Germany and Austria immediately after the war. Contemporary media, however, tended to focus on the more noticeable yet in some ways more superficial social emancipation of upper- and middle-class women. In ever-larger numbers, these young women took jobs, had their own apartments, and showed their new independence by smoking in public, wearing shorter dresses, and adopting radical new hairstyles.

Crisis in Russia and the End of the War

FOCUS QUESTION: What were the causes of the Russian Revolution of 1917, and why did the Bolsheviks prevail in the civil war and gain control of Russia?

By 1917, total war was creating serious domestic turmoil in all of the European belligerent states. Only one, however, experienced the kind of complete collapse that others were predicting might happen throughout Europe. Out of Russia's collapse came the Russian Revolution.

The Russian Revolution

Tsar Nicholas II was an autocratic ruler who relied on the army and the bureaucracy to uphold his regime. But World War I magnified Russia's problems and severely challenged the tsarist government. Russian industry was unable to produce the weapons needed for the army. Ill-led and ill-armed, Russian armies suffered incredible losses. Between 1914 and 1916, 2 million soldiers were killed, and another 4 to 6 million were wounded or captured.

In the meantime, Tsar Nicholas II was increasingly insulated from events by his German-born wife, Alexandra, a well-educated woman who had fallen under the sway of Rasputin (rass-PYOO-tin), a Siberian peasant whom the tsarina regarded as a holy man because he alone seemed able to stop the bleeding of her hemophiliac son, Alexis. Rasputin's influence made him a power behind the throne, and he did not hesitate to interfere in government affairs. As the leadership at the top experienced a series of military and economic disasters, the middle class, aristocrats, peasants, soldiers, and workers grew more and more disenchanted with the tsarist regime. Even conservative aristocrats who supported the monarchy felt the need to do something to reverse the deteriorating situation. For a start, they assassinated Rasputin in December 1916. By then it was too late to save the monarchy, and its fall came quickly at the beginning of March 1917.

THE MARCH REVOLUTION In early 1917, a series of strikes led by working-class women broke out in the capital city of Petrograd (formerly Saint Petersburg). A few weeks earlier, the government had introduced bread rationing in the capital city after the price of bread had skyrocketed. Many of the women who stood in the lines waiting for bread were also factory workers who had put in twelve-hour days. The Russian government soon became aware of the volatile situation in the capital. One police report stated: "Mothers of families, exhausted by endless standing in line at stores, distraught over their half-starving and sick children, are today perhaps closer to revolution than [the liberal opposition leaders] and of course they are a great deal more dangerous because they are the combustible material for which only a single spark is needed to burst into flame."[7] On March 8, a day celebrated since 1910 as International Women's Day, about ten thousand Petrograd women marched in parts of the city demanding "peace and bread." Soon the women were joined by other workers, and together they called for a general strike that succeeded in shutting down all the factories in the city on March 10. Nicholas ordered his troops to disperse the crowds by shooting them if necessary, but large numbers of the soldiers soon joined the demonstrators. The Duma (DOO-muh), or legislative body, which the tsar had tried to dissolve, met anyway and on March 12 declared that it was assuming governmental responsibility. It established a provisional government on March 15; the tsar abdicated the same day.

The Provisional Government, which came to be led in July by Alexander Kerensky (kuh-REN-skee), decided to carry on the war to preserve Russia's honor—a major blunder because it satisfied neither the workers nor the peasants, who above all wanted an end to the war. The Provisional Government also faced another authority, the **soviets**, or councils of workers' and soldiers' deputies. The Petrograd soviet had been formed in March 1917; at the same time, soviets sprang up spontaneously in army units, factory towns, and rural areas. The soviets represented the more radical interests of the lower classes and were largely composed of socialists of various kinds. One group—the Bolsheviks (BOHL-shuh-viks)—came to play a crucial role.

LENIN AND THE BOLSHEVIK REVOLUTION The Bolsheviks were a small faction of Russian Social Democrats who had come under the leadership of Vladimir Ulianov (VLAD-ih-meer ool-YA-nuf), known to the world as Lenin (LEH-nin) (1870–1924). Under Lenin's direction, the Bolsheviks became a party dedicated to violent revolution. He believed that only a revolution could destroy the capitalist system and that a "vanguard" of activists must form a small party of well-disciplined professional revolutionaries to accomplish this task. Between 1900 and 1917, Lenin spent most of his time in exile in Switzerland. When the Provisional Government was set up in March 1917, he believed that an opportunity for the Bolsheviks to seize power had come. Just weeks later, with the connivance of the German High Command, which hoped to create disorder in Russia, Lenin was shipped to Russia in a "sealed train" by way of Finland.

Lenin believed that the Bolsheviks must work to gain control of the soviets of soldiers, workers, and peasants and then use them to overthrow the Provisional Government. At the same time, the Bolsheviks sought mass support through promises geared to the needs of the people: an end to the war, redistribution of all land to the peasants, the transfer of factories and industries from capitalists to committees of workers, and the relegation of government power from the Provisional Government to the soviets. Three simple slogans summed up the Bolshevik program: "Peace, Land, Bread," "Worker Control of Production," and "All Power to the Soviets."

By the end of October, the Bolsheviks had achieved a slight majority in the Petrograd and Moscow soviets. The number of party members had also grown from 50,000 to 240,000. With Leon Trotsky (TRAHT-skee) (1877–1940), a fervid revolutionary, as chairman of the Petrograd soviet, Lenin and the Bolsheviks were in a position to seize power in the name of the soviets. During the night of November 6, pro-soviet and pro-Bolshevik forces took control of Petrograd. The Provisional Government quickly collapsed, with little bloodshed. The following night, the All-Russian Congress of Soviets, representing local soviets from all over the country, affirmed the transfer of power. At the second session, on the night of November 8, Lenin announced the new Soviet government, the Council of People's Commissars, with himself as its head.

But the Bolsheviks, soon renamed the Communists, still had a long way to go. For one thing, Lenin had promised peace, and that, he realized, was not an easy task because of the humiliating losses of Russian territory that it would entail. There was no real choice, however. On March 3, 1918, Lenin signed the Treaty of Brest-Litovsk (BREST-li-TUFFSK) with Germany and gave up eastern Poland, Ukraine, and the Baltic provinces. He had promised peace to the Russian people, but real peace did not come, for the country soon sank into civil war.

CIVIL WAR There was great opposition to the new Communist regime, not only from groups loyal to the tsar but also from bourgeois and aristocratic liberals and anti-Leninist socialists. In addition, thousands of Allied troops were eventually sent to different parts of Russia in the hope of bringing Russia back into the war.

Between 1918 and 1921, the Communist (Red) Army was forced to fight on many fronts. The first serious threat to the Communists came from Siberia, where White (anti-Communist) forces attacked westward and advanced almost to the Volga River. Attacks also came from the Ukrainians in the southwest and from the Baltic regions. In mid-1919, White forces swept through Ukraine and advanced almost to Moscow before being pushed back. By 1920, the major White forces had been defeated, and Ukraine had been retaken. The next year, the Communist regime regained control over the independent nationalist governments in the Caucasus: Georgia, Russian Armenia, and Azerbaijan (az-ur-by-JAHN).

How had Lenin and the Bolsheviks triumphed over what seemed at one time to be overwhelming forces? For one thing, the Red Army became a well-disciplined fighting force, largely due to the organizational genius of Leon Trotsky. As commissar of war, Trotsky reinstated the draft and insisted on rigid discipline; soldiers who deserted or refused to obey orders were summarily executed.

The disunity of the anti-Communist forces seriously weakened their efforts. Political differences created distrust among the Whites and prevented them from cooperating effectively with each other. It was difficult

© Keystone/Getty Images

© Underwood & Underwood/CORBIS

Lenin and Trotsky. Vladimir Lenin and Leon Trotsky were important figures in the Bolsheviks' successful seizure of power in Russia. On the left, Lenin is seen addressing a rally in Moscow in 1917. On the right, Trotsky, who became commissar of war in the new regime, is shown haranguing his troops.

enough to achieve military cooperation; political differences made it virtually impossible. The lack of a common goal on the part of the Whites was in sharp contrast to the Communists' single-minded sense of purpose.

The Communists also succeeded in translating their revolutionary faith into practical instruments of power. A policy of **war communism**, for example, was used to ensure regular supplies for the Red Army. War communism included the nationalization of banks and most industries, the forcible requisition of grain from peasants, and the centralization of state power under Bolshevik control. Another Bolshevik instrument was "revolutionary terror." A new Red secret police, known as the Cheka (CHEK-uh), instituted the Red Terror, aimed at nothing less than the destruction of all who opposed the new regime.

Finally, the intervention of foreign armies enabled the Communists to appeal to the powerful force of Russian patriotism. Appalled by the takeover of power in Russia by the radical Communists, the Allied Powers intervened. At one point, more than 100,000 foreign troops—mostly Japanese, British, American, and French—were stationed on Russian soil. This intervention by the Allies enabled the Communist government to appeal to patriotic Russians to fight the attempts of foreigners to control their country.

By 1921, the Communists were in control of Russia. In the course of the civil war, the Communist regime had also transformed Russia into a bureaucratically centralized state dominated by a single party. It was also a state that was largely hostile to the Allied Powers that had sought to assist the Communists' enemies in the civil war.

The Last Year of the War

For Germany, the withdrawal of the Russians in March 1918 offered renewed hope for a favorable end to the war. The victory over Russia persuaded Erich von Ludendorff (LOO-dun-dorf) (1865–1937), who guided German military operations, and most German leaders to make one final military gamble—a grand offensive in the west to break the military stalemate. The German attack was launched in March and lasted into July, but an Allied counterattack, supported by the arrival of 140,000 fresh American troops, defeated the Germans at the Second Battle of the Marne on July 18. Ludendorff's gamble had failed.

On September 29, 1918, General Ludendorff informed German leaders that the war was lost and insisted that the government sue for peace at once. When German officials discovered, however, that the Allies were unwilling to make peace with the autocratic imperial

CHRONOLOGY World War I

	1914
Battle of Tannenberg	August 26–30
First Battle of the Marne	September 6–10
Battle of Masurian Lakes	September 15
	1915
Battle of Gallipoli begins	April 25
Italy declares war on Austria-Hungary	May 23
	1916
Battle of Verdun	February 21–December 18
	1917
United States enters the war	April 6
	1918
Last German offensive	March 21–July 18
Second Battle of the Marne	July 18
Allied counteroffensive	July 18–November 10
Armistice between Allies and Germany	November 11

government, reforms were instituted to create a liberal government. Meanwhile, popular demonstrations broke out throughout Germany. William II capitulated to public pressure and abdicated on November 9, and the Socialists under Friedrich Ebert (FREED-rikh AY-bert) (1871–1925) announced the establishment of a republic. Two days later, on November 11, 1918, the new German government agreed to an armistice. The war was over.

THE CASUALTIES OF THE WAR World War I devastated European civilization. Between 8 and 9 million soldiers died on the battlefields; another 22 million were wounded. Many of those who survived the war died later from war injuries or lived on without arms or legs or with other forms of mutilation. The birthrate in many European countries declined noticeably as a result of the death or maiming of so many young men. World War I also created a lost generation of war veterans who had become accustomed to violence and who would later band together in support of Mussolini and Hitler in their bids for power.

Nor did the killing affect only soldiers. Untold numbers of civilians died from war injuries or starvation. In 1915, using the excuse of a rebellion by the Armenian minority and their supposed collaboration with the Russians, the Turkish government began systematically to kill Armenian men and expel women and children. Within seven months, 600,000 Armenians had been killed, and 500,000 had been deported. Of the latter, 400,000 died while marching through the deserts and swamps of Syria and Mesopotamia. By September 1915, an estimated one million Armenians were dead, the victims of genocide.

The Peace Settlement

In January 1919, the delegations of twenty-seven victorious Allied nations gathered in Paris to conclude a final settlement of the Great War. Over a period of years, the reasons for fighting World War I had been transformed from selfish national interests to idealistic principles.

No one expressed these principles better than U.S. President Woodrow Wilson (1856–1924). Wilson's proposals for a truly just and lasting peace included "open covenants of peace, openly arrived at" instead of secret diplomacy; the reduction of national armaments to a "point consistent with domestic safety"; and the self-determination of people so that "all well-defined national aspirations shall be accorded the utmost satisfaction." As the spokesman for a new world order based on democracy and international cooperation, Wilson was enthusiastically cheered by many Europeans when he arrived in Europe for the peace conference, held at the palace of Versailles. Wilson's rhetoric on self-determination also inspired peoples in the colonial world, in Africa, Asia, and the Middle East, and was influential in developing anticolonial nationalist movements in these areas (see Chapter 24).

Wilson soon found, however, that more practical motives guided other states at the Paris Peace Conference. The secret treaties and agreements that had been made before the war could not be totally ignored, even if they did conflict with the principle of self-determination enunciated by Wilson. National interests also complicated the deliberations of the Paris Peace Conference. David Lloyd George (1863–1945), prime minister of Great Britain, had won a decisive electoral victory in December 1918 on a platform of making the Germans pay for this dreadful war.

France's approach to peace was primarily determined by considerations of national security. To Georges Clemenceau (ZHORZH kluh-mahn-SOH) (1841–1929), the feisty premier of France who had led his country to victory, the French people had borne the brunt of German aggression. They deserved revenge and security against future German aggression (see the box on p. 611).

The most important decisions at the Paris Peace Conference were made by Wilson, Clemenceau, and Lloyd George. In the end, only compromise made it possible to achieve a peace settlement. Wilson's wish that the creation of an international peacekeeping organization be the

OPPOSING ✂ VIEWPOINTS

Three Voices of Peacemaking

When the Allied powers met in Paris in January 1919, it soon became apparent that the victors had different opinions on the kind of peace they expected. The first selection is an excerpt from a speech by Woodrow Wilson in which the American president presented his idealistic goals for a peace based on justice and reconciliation.

The French leader Georges Clemenceau had a vision of peacemaking quite different from Wilson's. The French sought revenge and security. In this selection from his book *Grandeur and Misery of Victory*, Clemenceau revealed his fundamental dislike and distrust of Germany.

A third voice of peacemaking was heard in Paris in 1919, although not at the peace conference. W. E. B. Du Bois (doo-BOYZ), an African American writer and activist, had organized the Pan-African Congress to meet in Paris during the sessions of the Paris Peace Conference. The goal of the Pan-African Congress was to present a series of resolutions that promoted the cause of Africans and people of African descent. As can be seen in the selection presented here, the resolutions did not call for immediate independence for African nations.

Woodrow Wilson, Speech, May 26, 1917

We are fighting for the liberty, the self-government, and the undictated development of all peoples, and every feature of the settlement that concludes this war must be conceived and executed for that purpose. Wrongs must first be righted and then adequate safeguards must be created to prevent their being committed again. . . .

No people must be forced under sovereignty under which it does not wish to live. No territory must change hands except for the purpose of securing those who inhabit it a fair chance of life and liberty. No indemnities must be insisted on except those that constitute payment for manifest wrongs done. No readjustments of power must be made except such as will tend to secure the future peace of the world and the future welfare and happiness of its peoples.

And then the free peoples of the world must draw together in some common covenant, some genuine and practical cooperation that will in effect combine their force to secure peace and justice in the dealings of nations with one another.

Georges Clemenceau, *Grandeur and Misery of Victory*

War and peace, with their strong contrasts, alternate against a common background. For the catastrophe of 1914 the Germans are responsible. Only a professional liar would deny this. . . .

What after all is this war, prepared, undertaken, and waged by the German people, who flung aside every scruple of conscience to let it loose, hoping for a peace of enslavement under the yoke of a militarism, destructive of all human dignity? It is simply the continuance, the recrudescence, of those never-ending acts of violence by which the first savage tribes carried out their depredations with all the resources of barbarism. . . .

I have sometimes penetrated into the sacred cave of the Germanic cult, which is, as every one knows, the *Bierhaus* [beer hall]. A great aisle of massive humanity where there accumulate, amid the fumes of tobacco and beer, the popular rumblings of a nationalism upheld by the sonorous brasses blaring to the heavens the supreme voice of Germany, *Deutschland über alles! Germany above everything!* Men, women, and children, all petrified in reverence before the divine stoneware pot, brows furrowed with irrepressible power, eyes lost in a dream of infinity, mouths twisted by the intensity of willpower, drink in long draughts the celestial hope of vague expectations.

Pan-African Congress

Resolved

That the Allied and Associated Powers establish a code of law for the international protection of the natives of Africa. . . .

The Negroes of the world demand that hereafter the natives of Africa and the peoples of African descent be governed according to the following principles:

1. The Land: the land and its natural resources shall be held in trust for the natives and at all times they shall have effective ownership of as much land as they can profitably develop. . . .

(*Continued*)

(Opposing Viewpoints Continued)

3. Labor: slavery and corporal punishment shall be abolished and forced labor except in punishment for crime. . . .
5. The State: the natives of Africa must have the right to participate in the government as fast as their development permits, in conformity with the principle that the government exists for the natives, and not the natives for the government.

How did the peacemaking aims of Wilson and Clemenceau differ? How did their different views affect the deliberations of the Paris Peace Conference and the nature of the final peace settlement? How and why did the views of the Pan-African Congress differ from those of Wilson and Clemenceau?

Sources: Woodrow Wilson, Speech, May 26, 1917. Excerpts from *The Public Papers of Woodrow Wilson: War and Peace*, edited by Ray Stannard Baker. Copyright 1925, 1953 by Edith Bolling Wilson. Georges Clemenceau, *Grandeur and Misery of Victory*. From Georges Clemenceau, *Grandeur and Misery of Victory* (New York: Harcourt, 1930), pp. 105, 107, 280. Pan-African Congress. Excerpts from Resolution from the Pan-African Congress, Paris, 1919.

first order of business was granted, and already on January 25, 1919, the conference adopted the principle of the League of Nations. In return, Wilson agreed to make compromises on territorial arrangements to guarantee the establishment of the League, believing that a functioning League could later rectify bad arrangements.

THE TREATY OF VERSAILLES The final peace settlement consisted of five separate treaties with the defeated nations—Germany, Austria, Hungary, Bulgaria, and Turkey. The Treaty of Versailles with Germany, signed on June 28, 1919, was by far the most important one. The Germans considered it a harsh peace and were particularly unhappy with Article 231, the so-called **War Guilt Clause**, which declared Germany (and Austria) responsible for starting the war and ordered Germany to pay **reparations** for all the damage to which the Allied governments and their people were subjected as a result of the war.

The military and territorial provisions of the treaty also rankled Germans. Germany had to reduce its army to 100,000 men, cut back its navy, and eliminate its air force. German territorial losses included the return of Alsace and Lorraine to France and sections of Prussia to the new Polish state (see Map 23.3). German land west and as far as 30 miles east of the Rhine was established as a demilitarized zone and stripped of all armaments or fortifications to serve as a barrier to any future German military moves westward against France. Outraged by the "dictated peace," the new German government complained but accepted the treaty.

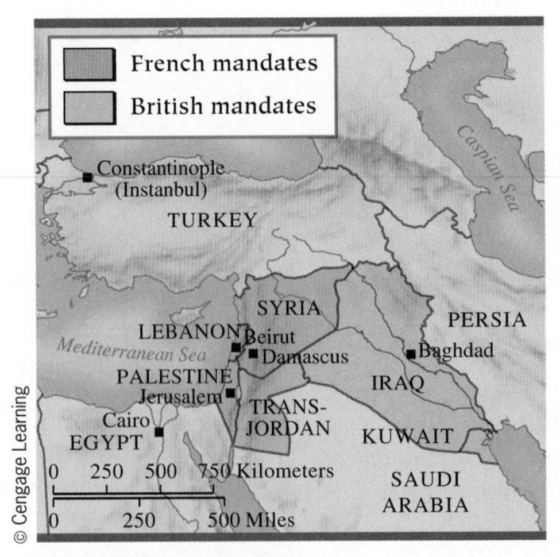

The Middle East in 1919

THE OTHER PEACE TREATIES The separate peace treaties made with the other Central Powers extensively redrew the map of eastern Europe. Many of these changes merely ratified what the war had already accomplished. Both the German and Russian Empires lost considerable territory in eastern Europe, and the Austro-Hungarian Empire disappeared altogether. New nation-states emerged from the lands of these three empires: Finland, Latvia, Estonia, Lithuania, Poland, Czechoslovakia, Austria, and Hungary. Territorial rearrangements were also made in the Balkans. Serbia formed the nucleus of a new southern Slavic state, called Yugoslavia, which combined Serbs, Croats, and Slovenes under a single monarch.

Although the Paris Peace Conference was supposedly guided by the principle of self-determination, the mixtures of peoples in eastern Europe made it impossible to draw boundaries along neat ethnic lines. As a result of compromises, virtually every eastern European state was left with a minorities problem that could lead to future conflicts. Germans in Poland; Hungarians, Poles, and Germans in Czechoslovakia; Hungarians in Romania; and the combination of Serbs, Croats, Slovenes, Macedonians, and Albanians in Yugoslavia all became sources of later conflict.

Yet another centuries-old empire, the Ottoman Empire, was dismembered by the peace settlement after the war. To gain Arab support against the Ottoman Turks during the war, the Western Allies had promised to recognize the independence of Arab states in the Middle Eastern lands of the Ottoman Empire. But the imperialist habits of Western nations died hard. After the war, France was given control of

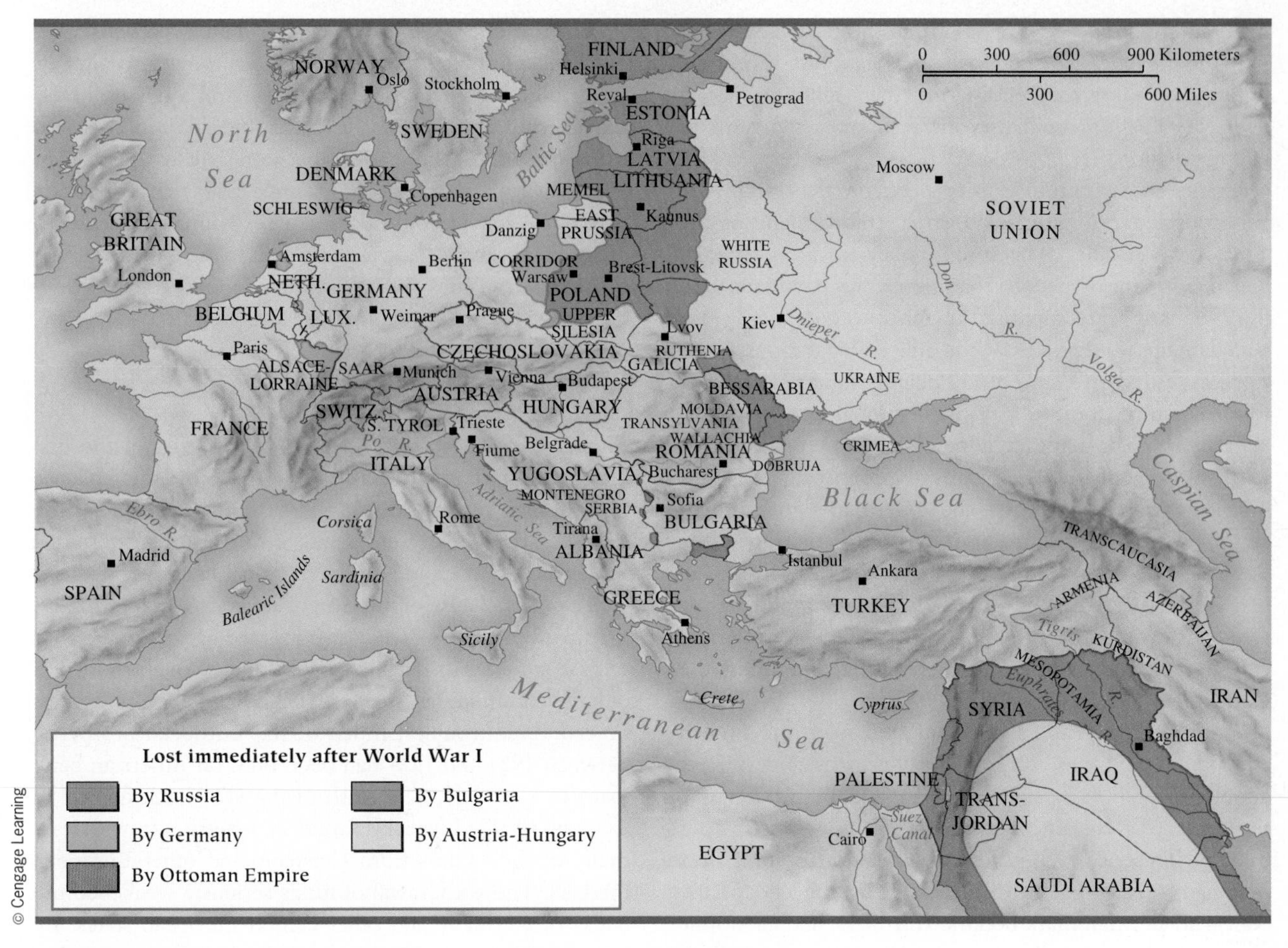

© Cengage Learning

MAP 23.3 Territorial Changes in Europe and the Middle East After World War I. The victorious Allies met in Paris to determine the shape and nature of postwar Europe. At the urging of U.S. President Woodrow Wilson, many nationalist aspirations of former imperial subjects were realized with the creation of several new countries from the prewar territory of Austria-Hungary, Germany, Russia, and the Ottoman Empire.

What new countries emerged in Europe and the Middle East?

Lebanon and Syria, while Britain received Iraq and Palestine (including Trans-Jordan). Officially, both acquisitions were called **mandates**, a system whereby a nation officially administered a territory on behalf of the League of Nations. The system of mandates could not hide the fact that the principle of national self-determination at the Paris Peace Conference was largely for Europeans.

An Uncertain Peace

FOCUS QUESTION: What problems did Europe and the United States face in the 1920s?

Four years of devastating war had left many Europeans with a profound sense of despair and disillusionment. The Great War indicated to many people that something was dreadfully wrong with Western values. In *The Decline of the West*, the German writer Oswald Spengler (1880–1936) reflected this disillusionment when he emphasized the decadence of Western civilization and posited its collapse.

The Search for Security

The peace settlement at the end of World War I had tried to fulfill the nineteenth-century dream of nationalism by creating new boundaries and new states. From its inception, however, this peace settlement had left nations unhappy and eager to revise it.

U.S. President Woodrow Wilson had recognized that the peace treaties contained unwise provisions that could serve as new causes for conflicts, and he had placed many of his hopes for the future in the League of Nations. The League, however, was not particularly effective in maintaining the peace. The failure of the United States to join the League in a backlash of isolationist sentiment undermined its effectiveness from the beginning. Moreover, the League could use only economic sanctions to halt aggression.

France's search for security between 1919 and 1924 was founded primarily on a strict enforcement of the Treaty of Versailles. This tough policy toward Germany began with the issue of reparations, the payments that the Germans were supposed to make to compensate for war damage. In April 1921, the Allied Reparations Commission settled on a sum of 132 billion marks ($33 billion) for German reparations, payable in annual installments of 2.5 billion (gold) marks. The new German republic made its first payment in 1921, but by the following year, facing financial problems, the German government announced that it was unable to pay more. Outraged, the French government sent troops to occupy the Ruhr valley, Germany's chief industrial and mining center. If the Germans would not pay reparations, the French would collect reparations in kind by operating and using the Ruhr mines and factories.

Both Germany and France suffered from the French occupation of the Ruhr. The German government adopted a policy of passive resistance to French occupation that was largely financed by printing more paper money. This only intensified the inflationary pressures that had already begun in Germany by the end of the war. The German mark became worthless, and economic disaster fueled political upheavals. All the nations, including France, were happy to cooperate with the American suggestion for a new conference of experts to reassess the reparations problem.

In August 1924, an international commission produced a new plan for reparations. The Dawes Plan, named after the American banker who chaired the commission, reduced the reparations and stabilized Germany's payments on the basis of its ability to pay. The Dawes Plan also granted an initial $200 million loan for German recovery, which opened the door to heavy American investments in Europe that helped create a new era of European prosperity between 1924 and 1929.

With prosperity came a new age of European diplomacy. A spirit of cooperation was fostered by the foreign ministers of Germany and France, Gustav Stresemann (GOOS-tahf SHTRAY-zuh-mahn) and Aristide Briand (ah-ruh-STEED bree-AHNH), who concluded the Treaty of Locarno (loh-KAHR-noh) in 1925. This guaranteed Germany's new western borders with France and Belgium. Although Germany's new eastern borders with Poland were conspicuously absent from the agreement, the Locarno pact was viewed by many as the beginning of a new era of European peace.

The spirit of Locarno was based on little real substance, however. Germany lacked the military power to alter its western borders even if it wanted to. And the issue of disarmament soon proved that even the spirit of Locarno could not bring nations to cut back on their weapons. Germany, of course, had been disarmed with the expectation that other states would do likewise. Numerous disarmament conferences, however, failed to achieve anything substantial as states were unwilling to trust their security to anyone but their own military forces.

The Great Depression

Almost as devastating as the two world wars in the first half of the twentieth century was the economic collapse that ravaged the world in the 1930s. Two events set the stage for the Great Depression: a downturn in domestic economic activities and an international financial crisis created by the collapse of the American stock market in 1929.

Already in the mid-1920s, prices for agricultural goods were beginning to decline rapidly due to overproduction of basic commodities, such as wheat. In addition to domestic economic troubles, much of the European prosperity between 1924 and 1929 had been built on American bank loans to Germany. The crash of the U.S. stock market in October 1929 led panicky American investors to withdraw many of their funds from Germany and other European markets. The withdrawal of funds seriously weakened the banks of Germany and other central European states. By 1931, trade was slowing down, industrialists were cutting back production, and unemployment was increasing as the ripple effects of international bank failures had a devastating impact on domestic economies.

Economic depression was by no means a new phenomenon in European history, but the depth of the economic downturn after 1929 fully justifies the Great Depression label. During 1932, the worst year of the depression, one British worker in four was unemployed; in Germany, 6 million people, or 40 percent of the labor force, were out of work. Unemployed and homeless people filled the streets of cities throughout the advanced industrial world.

Governments seemed powerless to deal with the crisis. The classic liberal remedy for depression was a deflationary policy of balanced budgets, which involved cutting costs by lowering wages and raising tariffs to exclude other countries' goods from home markets, but this policy only served to worsen the economic crisis and cause even greater mass discontent. This in turn led to serious political repercussions. Increased government activity in the economy was one reaction. Another effect was a renewed interest in Marxist doctrines. Hadn't Marx predicted that capitalism would destroy itself through overproduction? Communism took on new popularity,

© Harlingue/Roger Viollet/Getty Images

The Great Depression: Bread Lines in Paris. The Great Depression devastated the European economy and had serious political repercussions. Because of its more balanced economy, France did not feel the effects of the depression as quickly as other European countries. By 1931, however, even France was experiencing lines of unemployed people at free-food centers.

especially with workers and intellectuals. Finally, the Great Depression increased the attractiveness of simplistic dictatorial solutions, especially from a new movement known as fascism. Everywhere, democracy seemed on the defensive in the 1930s (see Chapter 25).

The Democratic States

After World War I, Great Britain went through a period of serious economic difficulties. During the war, Britain had lost many of the markets for its industrial products, especially to the United States and Japan. The postwar decline of such staple industries as coal, steel, and textiles led to a rise in unemployment, which reached the 2 million mark in 1921. But Britain soon rebounded and from 1925 to 1929 experienced an era of renewed prosperity.

By 1929, however, Britain faced the growing effects of the Great Depression. A national government (a coalition of Liberals and Conservatives) claimed credit for bringing Britain out of the worst stages of the depression, primarily by using the traditional policies of balanced budgets and protective tariffs. British politicians had largely ignored the new ideas of a Cambridge economist, John Maynard Keynes (KAYNZ) (1883–1946), who published his *General Theory of Employment, Interest and Money* in 1936. He condemned the traditional view that in a free economy, depressions should be left to work themselves out. Keynes argued that unemployment stemmed not from overproduction but from a decline in demand and maintained that demand could be increased by putting people back to work constructing highways and public buildings, even if governments had to go into debt to pay for these public works, a concept known as **deficit spending**.

After the defeat of Germany, France had become the strongest power on the European continent, but between 1921 and 1926, no French government seemed capable of solving the country's financial problems. Like other European countries, though, France did experience a period of relative prosperity between 1926 and 1929.

Because it had a more balanced economy than other nations, France did not begin to feel the full effects of the Great Depression until 1932. Then economic instability soon had political repercussions. During a nineteen-month period in 1932 and 1933, six different cabinets were formed as France faced political chaos. Finally, in June 1936, a coalition of leftist parties—Communists, Socialists, and Radicals—formed a new government, the Popular Front, but its policies failed to solve the problems of the depression. By 1938, the French were experiencing a serious decline of confidence in their political system.

After the imperial Germany of William II had come to an end in 1918 with Germany's defeat in World War I, a German democratic state known as the Weimar (VY-mar) Republic was established. From its beginnings, the Weimar Republic was plagued by a series of problems. The republic had no truly outstanding political leaders and faced serious economic difficulties. In 1922 and 1923, Germany experienced runaway inflation; widows, orphans, the retired elderly, army officers, teachers, civil servants, and others who lived on fixed incomes all watched their monthly stipends become worthless and their lifetime savings disappear. Their economic losses increasingly pushed the middle class to the rightist parties that were hostile to the republic. To make matters worse, after a period of prosperity from 1924 to 1929, Germany faced the Great Depression. Unemployment increased to 3 million in March 1930 and 4.4 million by December of the same year. The depression paved the way for the rise of extremist parties.

After Germany, no Western nation was more affected by the Great Depression than the United States. By 1932, U.S. industrial production fell to 50 percent of what it had been in 1929. By 1933, there were 15 million unemployed.

Under these circumstances, the Democrat Franklin Delano Roosevelt (1882–1945) was able to win a landslide electoral victory in 1932. He and his advisers pursued a policy of active government intervention in the economy that came to be known as the New Deal. Economic intervention included a stepped-up program of public works, such as the Works Progress Administration (WPA), which was established in 1935 and employed between 2 and 3 million people who worked at building bridges, roads, post offices, and airports. In 1935, the Social Security Act created a system of old-age pensions and unemployment insurance.

The New Deal provided some social reform measures, but it did not solve the unemployment problems of the Great Depression. In May 1937, during what was considered a period of full recovery, American unemployment still stood at 7 million.

Socialism in Soviet Russia

The civil war in Russia had taken an enormous toll of life. Lenin had pursued a policy of war communism, but once the war was over, peasants began to sabotage the program by hoarding food. Added to this problem was drought, which caused a great famine between 1920 and 1922 that claimed as many as 5 million lives. Industrial collapse paralleled the agricultural disaster. By 1921, industrial output was only 20 percent of its 1913 levels. Russia was exhausted. A peasant banner proclaimed, "Down with Lenin and horseflesh, Bring back the Tsar and pork." As Leon Trotsky said, "The country, and the government with it, were at the very edge of the abyss."[8]

In March 1921, Lenin pulled Russia back from the abyss by adopting his **New Economic Policy** (NEP), a modified version of the old capitalist system. Peasants were now allowed to sell their produce openly. Retail stores and small industries that employed fewer than twenty employees could now operate under private ownership, although heavy industry, banking, and mines remained in the hands of the government.

In 1922, Lenin and the Communists formally created a new state called the Union of Soviet Socialist Republics, known as the USSR by its initials or the Soviet Union by its shortened form. Already by that year, a revived market and a good harvest had brought the famine to an end; Soviet agricultural production climbed to 75 percent of its prewar level.

Lenin's death in 1924 inaugurated a struggle for power among the seven members of the Politburo (POL-it-byoor-oh), the institution that had become the leading organ of the party. The Politburo was severely divided over the future direction of the country. The Left, led by Leon Trotsky, wanted to end the NEP, launch Russia on the path of rapid industrialization, and spread the revolution abroad. Another group in the Politburo, called the Right, rejected the cause of world revolution and wanted instead to concentrate on constructing a socialist state. This group also favored a continuation of Lenin's NEP.

These ideological divisions were underscored by an intense personal rivalry between Leon Trotsky and Joseph Stalin (1879–1953). In 1924, Trotsky held the post of commissar of war and was the leading spokesman for the Left in the Politburo. Stalin was content to hold the dull bureaucratic job of party general secretary while other Politburo members held party positions that enabled them to display their brilliant oratorical abilities. Stalin was skillful at avoiding allegiance to either the Left or Right factions in the Politburo. He was also a good organizer (his fellow Bolsheviks called him "Comrade Index-Card") and used his post as party general secretary to gain complete control of the Communist Party. Trotsky was expelled from the party in 1927. By 1929, Stalin had succeeded in eliminating the Bolsheviks of the revolutionary era from the Politburo and establishing a dictatorship.

In Pursuit of a New Reality: Cultural and Intellectual Trends

FOCUS QUESTION: How did the cultural and intellectual trends of the post–World War I years reflect the crises of the time as well as the lingering effects of the war?

The enormous suffering and the deaths of almost 10 million people during the Great War had shaken society to its foundations. As they tried to rebuild their lives, Europeans wondered what had gone wrong with Western civilization. The Great Depression only added to the desolation left behind by the war.

Political and economic uncertainties were paralleled by social innovations. The Great War had served to break down many traditional middle-class attitudes, especially toward sexuality. In the 1920s, women's physical appearance changed dramatically. Short skirts, short hair, the use of cosmetics that were once thought to be the preserve of prostitutes, and the new practice of suntanning gave women a new image. This change in physical appearance, which stressed more exposure of a woman's body, was also accompanied by frank discussions of sexual matters. In 1926, the Dutch physician Theodor van de Velde (TAY-oh-dor vahn duh VEL-duh) published *Ideal Marriage: Its Physiology and Technique*, which became an international best-seller. Van de Velde described female and male anatomy, discussed birth control techniques, and glorified sexual pleasure in marriage.

COMPARATIVE ESSAY

A Revolution in the Arts

The period between 1880 and 1930 witnessed a revolution in the arts throughout Western civilization. Fueled in part by developments in physics and psychology, artists and writers rebelled against the traditional belief that the task of art was to represent "reality" and experimented with innovative new techniques in order to approach reality from a totally fresh perspective.

From Impressionism and Expressionism to Cubism, abstract art, Dadaism, and Surrealism, painters seemed intoxicated with the belief that their canvases would help reveal the radically changing world. Especially after the cataclysm of World War I, which shattered the image of a rational society, artists sought an absolute freedom of expression, confident that art could redefine humanity in the midst of chaos. Other arts soon followed their lead: James Joyce turned prose on its head by focusing on his characters' innermost thoughts, and Arnold Schönberg (AR-nawlt SHURN-bayrk) created atonal music by using a scale composed of twelve notes independent of any tonal key.

This revolutionary spirit had already been exemplified by Pablo Picasso's *Les Demoiselles d'Avignon*, painted in 1907 (see the illustration on p. 540). Picasso used geometrical designs to create a new reality and appropriated non-Western cultural resources, including African masks, in the desire to revitalize Western art.

Another example of the revolutionary approach to art was the decision by the French artist Marcel Duchamp (mar-SEL duh-SHAHN) to enter a porcelain urinal in a 1917 art exhibit held in New York City. By signing it and giving it the title *Fountain*, Duchamp proclaimed that he had transformed the urinal into a work of art. His "ready-mades" (as such art would henceforth be labeled) declared that art was whatever the artist proclaimed as art. The Dadaist Kurt Schwitters (KOORT SCHVIT-urz) brought together postage stamps, old handbills, streetcar tickets, newspaper scraps, and pieces of cardboard to form his works of art.

Such intentionally irreverent acts demystified the nearly sacred reverence that had traditionally been attached to works of art. Essentially, Duchamp and others claimed that anything under the sun could be selected as a work of art because the mental choice itself equaled the act of artistic creation. Therefore, art need not be a manual construct; it need only be a mental conceptualization. This liberating concept opened the floodgates of the art world, allowing the artists of the new century to swim in this free-flowing, exploratory torrent.

© 2012 Artists Rights Society (ARS), New York/VG Bild-Kunst, Bonn/Digital Image bpk, Berlin/Kupferstichkabinett (Jörg P. Anders)/Art Resource, NY

Kurt Schwitters, *Der Harz.* Kurt Schwitters became identified with the Dada movement when he began to create his collages. He wrote in 1928, "Fundamentally I cannot understand why one is not able to use in a picture, exactly in the same way as commercially made color . . . all the old junk which piles up in closets or the rubbish heaps."

How was the revolution in the arts between 1880 and 1930 related to the political, economic, and social developments of the same period?

Nightmares and New Visions

Uncertainty also pervaded the cultural and intellectual achievements of the postwar years. Artistic trends were largely a working out of the implications of prewar developments. Abstract painting, for example, became ever more popular (see the comparative essay "A Revolution in the Arts" above). In addition, prewar fascination with the absurd and the unconscious content of the mind seemed even more appropriate after the nightmare landscapes of World War I battlefronts. This gave rise to both the Dada movement and Surrealism.

Dadaism (DAH-duh-iz-um) attempted to enshrine the purposelessness of life; revolted by the insanity of life, the Dadaists tried to give it expression by creating "anti-art." The 1918 Berlin Dada Manifesto maintained that "Dada is the international expression of our times, the great rebellion of artistic movements." Many Dadaists assembled pieces of junk (wire, string, rags, scraps of newspaper, nails, washers) into collages, believing that they were transforming the refuse of their culture into art. In the hands of Hannah Höch (HURKH) (1889–1978), Dada became an instrument to comment on women's roles in the new mass culture.

Perhaps more important as an artistic movement was **Surrealism**, which sought a reality beyond the material, sensible world and found it in the world of the unconscious through the portrayal of fantasies, dreams, or nightmares. The Spaniard Salvador Dalí (sahl-vah-DOR dah-LEE) (1904–1989) became the high priest of Surrealism and in his mature phase became a master of representational Surrealism. Dalí portrayed recognizable objects entirely divorced from their normal context. By placing objects into unrecognizable relationships, Dalí created a disturbing world in which the irrational had become tangible.

Probing the Unconscious

The interest in the unconscious, evident in Surrealism, was also apparent in the development of new literary techniques that emerged in the 1920s. One of its most apparent manifestations was the "stream of consciousness" technique in which the writer presented an interior monologue or a report of the innermost thoughts of each character. One example of this genre was written by the Irish exile James Joyce (1882–1941). His *Ulysses*, published in 1922, told the story of one day in the life of ordinary people in Dublin by following the flow of their inner dialogue.

The German writer Hermann Hesse (hayr-MAHN HESS-uh) (1877–1962) dealt with the unconscious in a different fashion. His novels reflected the influence of new psychological theories and Eastern religions and focused on, among other things, the spiritual loneliness of modern human beings in a mechanized urban society. Hesse's novels made a large impact on German youth in the 1920s. He won the Nobel Prize for Literature in 1946.

For much of the Western world, the best way to find (or escape) reality was through mass entertainment. The 1930s represented the heyday of the Hollywood studio system, which in the single year of 1937 turned out nearly six hundred feature films. Supplementing the movies were cheap paperback books and radio, which brought sports, soap operas, and popular music to the masses.

The increased size of audiences and the ability of radio and cinema, unlike the printed word, to provide an immediate mass experience added new dimensions to mass culture. Favorite film actors and actresses became stars, whose lives then became subject to public adoration and scrutiny. Sensuous actresses such as Marlene Dietrich, whose appearance in the early sound film *The Blue Angel* catapulted her to fame, projected new images of women's sexuality.

© Salvador Dalí, Fundació Gala-Salvador Dalí/Artists Rights Society (ARS), New York 2012//
Digital image © The Museum of Modern Art/Licensed by Scala/Art Resource, NY

Salvador Dalí, *The Persistence of Memory*. Surrealism was an important artistic movement in the 1920s. Influenced by the theories of Freudian psychology, Surrealists sought to reveal the world of the unconscious, or the "greater reality" that they believed existed beyond the world of physical appearances. As is evident in this painting, Salvador Dalí sought to portray the world of dreams by painting recognizable objects in unrecognizable relationships.

CHAPTER SUMMARY

The assassination of Archduke Francis Ferdinand of Austria-Hungary in the summer of 1914 in the Bosnian capital of Sarajevo led within six weeks to a major war among the major powers of Europe. The Germans drove the Russians back in the east, but in the west a stalemate developed, with trenches defended by barbed wire and machine guns extending from the Swiss border to the English Channel. After German submarine attacks, the United States entered the war in 1917, but even from the beginning of the war, battles also took place in the African colonies of the European belligerents as well as in the East, making this a truly global war.

Unprepared for war, Russia soon faltered and collapsed, resulting in a revolution against the tsar. But the new provisional government in Russia also soon failed, enabling the revolutionary Bolsheviks of V. I. Lenin to seize power. Lenin established a dictatorship and made a costly peace with Germany. After American troops entered the war, the German government collapsed, leading to an armistice on November 11, 1918.

World War I was the defining event of the twentieth century. The incredible destruction and the deaths of almost 10 million people undermined the whole idea of progress. World War I was also a total war that required a mobilization of resources and populations and increased the centralization of government power. Civil liberties, such as freedom of the press, speech, and assembly, were circumscribed in the name of national security. Governments' need to plan the distribution of goods restricted economic freedom. World War I made the practice of strong central authority a way of life.

Finally, World War I ended the age of European hegemony over world affairs. In 1917, the Russian Revolution had laid the foundation for the creation of a new Eurasian power, the Soviet Union, and the United States had entered the war. The waning of the European age was not immediately evident to all, however, for it was clouded by American isolationism and the withdrawal of the Soviets from world affairs while they nurtured the growth of their own socialist system. These developments, though temporary, created a political vacuum in Europe that all too soon would be filled by the revival of German power.

Although World War I had destroyed the liberal optimism of the prewar era, many people in the 1920s still hoped that the progress of Western civilization could somehow be restored. These hopes proved largely unfounded. France, feeling vulnerable to another invasion, sought to weaken Germany. European recovery, largely the result of American loans and investments, ended with the onset of the Great Depression at the end of the 1920s. Democratic states, such as Great Britain, France, and the United States, spent much of the 1930s trying to recover from the depression. In the Soviet Union, Lenin's New Economic Policy helped to stabilize the economy, but on his death a struggle for power ensued that ended with the establishment of a dictatorship under Joseph Stalin.

CHAPTER TIMELINE

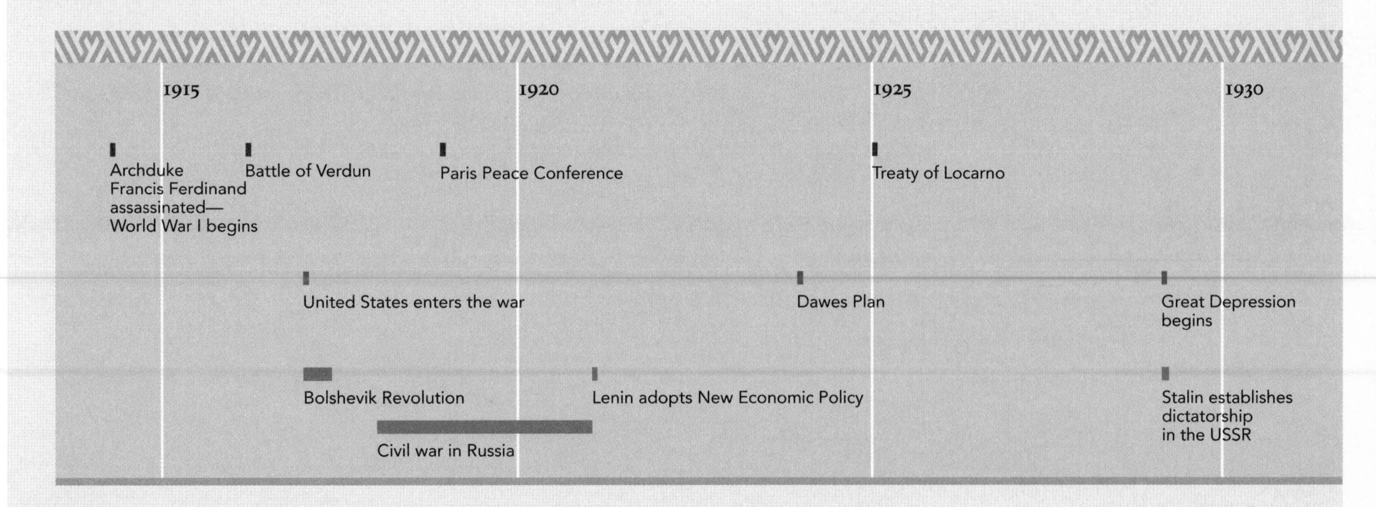

Upon Reflection

Q What nation, if any, was the most responsible for causing World War I? Why?

Q How did Lenin and the Bolsheviks manage to seize and hold power despite their small numbers?

Q What were the causes of the Great Depression, and how did European states respond to it?

Key Terms

conscription (p. 597)
militarism (p. 597)
trench warfare (p. 602)
total war (p. 605)
soviets (p. 608)
war communism (p. 609)
War Guilt Clause (p. 612)
reparations (p. 612)
mandates (p. 613)
deficit spending (p. 615)
New Economic Policy (p. 616)
Dadaism (p. 618)
Surrealism (p. 618)

Suggested Reading

GENERAL WORKS ON TWENTIETH-CENTURY EUROPE A number of general works on European history in the twentieth century provide a context for understanding both World War I and the Russian Revolution. Especially valuable is **N. Ferguson, *The War of the World: Twentieth-Century Conflict and the Descent of the West*** (New York, 2006). See also **R. Paxton, *Europe in the Twentieth Century,*** 4th ed. (New York, 2004).

CAUSES OF WORLD WAR I The historical literature on the causes of World War I is vast. Good starting points are the works by **J. Joll** and **G. Martel, *The Origins of the First World War,*** 3rd ed. (London, 2006), and **A. Mombauer, *The Origins of the First World War: Controversies and Consensus*** (London, 2002). On the events leading to war, see **D. Fromkin, *Europe's Last Summer: Who Started the Great War in 1914?*** (New York, 2004).

WORLD WAR I The best brief account of World War I is **H. Strachan, *The First World War*** (New York, 2004). On the global nature of World War I, see **M. S. Neiberg, *Fighting the Great War: A Global History*** (Cambridge, Mass., 2005), and **William S. Storey, *The First World War: A Concise Global History*** (New York, 2010). On the role of women in World War I, see **S. Grayzel, *Women and the First World War*** (London, 2002). On the Paris Peace Conference, see **M. MacMillan, *Paris, 1919: Six Months That Changed the World*** (New York, 2002).

THE RUSSIAN REVOLUTION A good introduction to the Russian Revolution can be found in **R. A. Wade, *The Russian Revolution, 1917,*** 2nd ed. (Cambridge, 2005), and **S. Fitzpatrick, *The Russian Revolution, 1917–1932,*** 2nd ed. (New York, 2001). On Lenin, see **R. Service, *Lenin: A Biography*** (Cambridge, Mass., 2000).

THE 1920s For a general introduction to the post–World War I period, see **M. Kitchen, *Europe Between the Wars,*** 2nd ed. (London, 2006). On European security issues after the Peace of Paris, see **S. Marks, *The Illusion of Peace: Europe's International Relations, 1918–1933,*** 2nd ed. (New York, 2003). On the Great Depression, see **C. P. Kindleberger, *The World in Depression, 1929–1939,*** rev. ed. (Berkeley, Calif., 1986).

CourseMate

Visit the CourseMate website at **www.cengagebrain.com** for additional study tools and review materials for this chapter.

CHAPTER

24

Nationalism, Revolution, and Dictatorship: Asia, the Middle East, and Latin America from 1919 to 1939

Bibliothèque Nationale, Paris//© Archives Charmet/The Bridgeman Art Library

Nguyen the Patriot at Tours

CHAPTER OUTLINE AND FOCUS QUESTIONS

The Rise of Nationalism

Q What were the various stages in the rise of nationalist movements in Asia and the Middle East, and what problems did they face?

Revolution in China

Q What problems did China encounter between the two world wars, and what solutions did the Nationalists and the Communists propose to solve them?

Japan Between the Wars

Q How did Japan address the problems of nation building in the first decades of the twentieth century, and why did democratic institutions not take hold more effectively?

Nationalism and Dictatorship in Latin America

Q What problems did the nations of Latin America face in the interwar years? To what degree were they a consequence of foreign influence?

CRITICAL THINKING

Q How did the societies discussed in this chapter deal with the political, economic, and social challenges that they faced after World War I, and how did these challenges differ from one region to another?

ON CHRISTMAS DAY IN 1920, a young Asian man in an ill-fitting rented suit stood up nervously to address the several hundred delegates of the French Socialist Party (FSP) who had gathered in the French city of Tours (TOOR). The speaker called himself Nguyen Ai Quoc (nuh-WEN EYE QUOHK), or Nguyen the Patriot, and was a Vietnamese subject of the French colony of Indochina.

The delegates had assembled to decide whether the FSP would follow the path of violent revolution recommended by the new Bolshevik regime in Soviet Russia. Among those voting in favor of the proposal was Nguyen Ai Quoc, who had decided that only the path of Karl Marx and Lenin could lead to national independence for his compatriots. Later he would become the founder of the Vietnamese Communist Party and become known to the world by the pseudonym Ho Chi Minh (HOH CHEE MIN).

The meeting in Tours was held at a time when resistance to colonial rule was on the rise, and the decision that Nguyen Ai Quoc faced of whether to opt for violent revolution was one that would be faced by colonial peoples throughout the world. As Europeans devastated their own civilization on the battlefields of Europe, the subject peoples of their vast colonial empires were quick to recognize the opportunity to shake free of foreign domination. In those areas, movements for national independence began to take shape. Some were inspired by the nationalist and liberal movements of the West, while others looked to the new Marxist model provided by the victory of the Communists in Soviet Russia, who soon worked to spread their revolutionary vision to African and Asian societies. In the Middle East, World War I ended the rule of the Ottoman Empire and led to the creation of new states, many of which were placed under Western domination.

The societies of Latin America were no longer under direct colonial rule and thus, for the most part, did not face the same types of challenges as their counterparts in Asia and Africa. Nevertheless, in some cases the economies of the Latin American countries were virtually controlled by foreign interests. A similar situation prevailed in China and Japan, which had managed with some difficulty to retain a degree of political independence, despite severe pressure from the West. But the political flux and economic disruption that characterized much of the world during the two decades following World War I had affected Latin America, China, and Japan as well, leading many in these regions to heed the siren call of fascist dictatorship or social revolution. For all the peoples of Asia, the Middle East, and Latin America, the end of the Great War had not created a world safe for democracy, as Woodrow Wilson had hoped, but an age of great peril and uncertainty.

The Rise of Nationalism

FOCUS QUESTION: What were the various stages in the rise of nationalist movements in Asia and the Middle East, and what problems did they face?

Although the West had emerged from World War I relatively intact, its political and social foundations and its self-confidence had been severely undermined. Within Europe, doubts about the viability of Western civilization were widespread, especially among the intellectual elite. These doubts were quick to reach perceptive observers in Asia and Africa and contributed to a rising tide of unrest against Western political domination throughout the colonial and semicolonial world. That unrest took various forms but was most evident in increasing worker activism, rural protests, and a rising national fervor among anticolonialist intellectuals. In areas of Asia, Africa, and Latin America where independent states had successfully resisted the Western onslaught, the discontent fostered by the war and later by the Great Depression led to a loss of confidence in democratic institutions and the rise of political dictatorships.

Modern Nationalism

The first stage of resistance to the West in Asia and Africa (see Chapters 21 and 22) had resulted in humiliation and failure and must have confirmed many Westerners' conviction that colonial peoples lacked the strength and the know-how to create modern states and govern their own destinies. In fact, the process was just beginning. The next phase—the rise of modern nationalism—began to take shape at the beginning of the twentieth century and was the product of the convergence of several factors. The most vocal source of anticolonialist sentiment was a new urban middle class of westernized intellectuals. In many cases, these merchants, petty functionaries, clerks, students, and professionals had been educated in Western-style schools. A few had spent time in the West. Many spoke Western languages, wore Western clothes, and worked in occupations connected with the colonial regime. Some even wrote in the languages of their colonial masters.

The results were paradoxical. On the one hand, this "new class" admired Western culture and sometimes harbored a deep sense of contempt for traditional ways. On the other hand, many strongly resented the foreigners and their arrogant contempt for colonial peoples. Though eager to introduce Western ideas and institutions into their own society, these intellectuals were dismayed at the gap between ideal and reality, theory and practice, in colonial policy. Although Western political thought exalted democracy, equality, and individual freedom, democratic institutions were primitive or nonexistent in the colonies.

Equality in economic opportunity and social life was also noticeably lacking. Normally, the middle classes did not suffer in the same manner as impoverished peasants or menial workers, but they, too, had complaints. They were usually relegated to low-level jobs in the government or business and paid less than Europeans in similar positions. The superiority of the Europeans was expressed in a variety of ways, including "whites only" clubs and the use of the familiar form of the language (normally used by adults to children) when addressing the locals.

Under these conditions, many of the new urban educated class were very ambivalent toward their colonial masters and the civilization that they represented. Out of this mixture of hope and resentment emerged the first stirrings of modern nationalism in Asia and Africa. During the first quarter of the century, in colonial and semicolonial societies from the Suez Canal to the Pacific Ocean, educated native peoples began to organize political parties and movements seeking reforms or the end of foreign rule and the restoration of independence.

RELIGION AND NATIONALISM At first, many of the leaders of these movements did not focus as much on nationhood as on the defense of indigenous religious beliefs or economic interests. In Burma, the first expression of modern nationalism came from students at the University of Rangoon, who protested against official persecution of the Buddhist religion and British lack of respect for local religious traditions (such as failing to remove footware when entering a Buddhist temple). The protesters adopted the name Thakin (TAHK-in), a polite term in the Burmese language meaning "lord" or "master," thus emphasizing their demand for the right to rule themselves. Only in the 1930s did the Thakins begin to focus specifically on national independence.

In the Dutch East Indies, Sarekat (SAR-eh-kaht) Islam (Islamic Association) began as a self-help society among Muslim merchants to fight against domination of the local economy by Chinese interests. Eventually, activist elements realized that the problem was not the Chinese merchants but the colonial presence, and in the 1920s, Sarekat Islam was transformed into the Nationalist Party of Indonesia (PNI), which focused on national independence. Like the Thakins in Burma, this party would lead the country to independence after World War II.

THE NATIONALIST QUANDARY: INDEPENDENCE OR MODERNIZATION? Building a new nation, however, requires more than a shared sense of grievances against the foreign invader. A host of other issues also had to be resolved. Soon patriots throughout the colonial world were debating such questions as whether independence or modernization should be their primary objective. The answer depended in part on how the colonial regime was perceived. If it was viewed as a source of needed reforms, a gradualist approach made sense. But if it was seen primarily as an impediment to change, the first priority, for many, was to bring it to an end. The vast majority of patriotic individuals were convinced that to survive, their societies must adopt much of the Western way of life; yet many were equally determined that the local culture would not, and should not, become a carbon copy of the West. What was the national identity, after all, if it did not incorporate some traditional elements?

Another reason for using traditional values was to provide ideological symbols that the common people could understand and would rally around. Though aware that they needed to enlist the mass of the population in the struggle, most urban intellectuals had difficulty communicating with the rural populations who did not understand such unfamiliar concepts as democracy and nationhood. As the Indonesian intellectual Sutan Sjahrir (SOO-tan syah-REER) lamented, many westernized intellectuals had more in common with their colonial rulers than with the people in the villages (see the box on p. 624). As one French colonial official remarked in some surprise to a French-educated Vietnamese reformist, "Why, Monsieur, you are more French than I am!"

Gandhi and the Indian National Congress

Nowhere in the colonial world were these issues debated more vigorously than in India. Before the Sepoy Rebellion (see Chapter 21), Indian consciousness had focused mainly on the question of religious identity. But in the latter half of the nineteenth century, a stronger sense of national consciousness began to arise, provoked by the conservative policies and racial arrogance of the British colonial authorities.

The first Indian nationalists were almost invariably upper class and educated. Many were from urban areas such as Bombay (now Mumbai), Madras (now Chennai), and Calcutta (now Kolkata). At first, many tended to prefer reform to revolution and believed that India needed modernization before taking on the problems of independence. Such reformists did have some effect. In the 1880s, the government allowed a measure of self-government, but all too often, such efforts were sabotaged by local British officials.

The slow pace of reform convinced many Indian nationalists that relying on British benevolence was futile. In 1885, a small group of Indians, with some British participation, met in Bombay to form the Indian National Congress (INC). They hoped to speak for all India, but most were high-class English-trained Hindus. Like their reformist predecessors, members of the INC did not demand immediate independence and accepted the need for reforms to end traditional abuses like child marriage and *sati*. At the same time, they called for an Indian share in the governing process and more spending on economic development and less on military campaigns along the frontier. The British responded with a few concessions, but change was glacially slow.

The INC also had difficulty reconciling religious differences within its ranks. Its stated goal was self-determination for all Indians regardless of class or religion, but many of its leaders were Hindu and inevitably reflected Hindu concerns. In the first decade of the twentieth

The Dilemma of the Intellectual

Sutan Sjahrir (1909–1966) was a prominent leader of the Indonesian nationalist movement who briefly served as prime minister of the Republic of Indonesia in the 1950s. Like many Western-educated Asian intellectuals, he was tortured by the realization that by education and outlook he was closer to his colonial masters—in his case, the Dutch—than to his own people. He wrote the following passage in a letter to his wife in 1935 and later included it in his book *Out of Exile*.

Sutan Sjahrir, *Out of Exile*

Am I perhaps estranged from my people? . . . Why are the things that contain beauty for them and arouse their gentler emotions only senseless and displeasing for me? In reality, the spiritual gap between my people and me is certainly no greater than that between an intellectual in Holland . . . and the undeveloped people of Holland. . . . The difference is rather . . . that the intellectual in Holland does not feel this gap because there is a portion—even a fairly large portion—of his own people on approximately the same intellectual level as himself. . . .

This is what we lack here. Not only is the number of intellectuals in this country smaller in proportion to the total population—in fact, very much smaller—but in addition, the few who are here do not constitute any single entity in spiritual outlook, or in any spiritual life or single culture whatsoever. . . . It is for them so much more difficult than for the intellectuals in Holland. In Holland they build—both consciously and unconsciously—on what is already there. . . . Even if they oppose it, they do so as a method of application or as a starting point.

In our country this is not the case. Here there has been no spiritual or cultural life, and no intellectual progress for centuries. There are the much-praised Eastern art forms but what are these except bare rudiments from a feudal culture that cannot possibly provide a dynamic fulcrum for people of the twentieth century? . . . Our spiritual needs are needs of the twentieth century; our problems and our views are of the twentieth century. . . .

We intellectuals here are much closer to Europe or America than we are to the Borobudur or Mahabharata or to the primitive Islamic culture of Java and Sumatra. . . .

So, it seems, the problem stands in principle. It is seldom put forth by us in this light, and instead most of us search unconsciously for a synthesis that will leave us internally tranquil. We want to have both Western science and Eastern philosophy, the Eastern "spirit," in the culture. But what is this Eastern spirit? It is, they say, the sense of the higher, of spirituality, of the eternal and religious, as opposed to the materialism of the West. I have heard this countless times, but it has never convinced me.

Why did Sutan Sjahrir feel estranged from his native culture? What was his answer to the challenges faced by his country in coming to terms with the modern world?

Source: From *The World of Southeast Asia: Selected Historical Readings*, Harry J. Benda and John A. Larkin, eds. Copyright © 1967 by Harper & Row, Publishers.

century, the separate Muslim League was created to represent the interests of the millions of Muslims in Indian society.

NONVIOLENT RESISTANCE In 1915, a young Hindu lawyer returned from South Africa to become active in the INC. He transformed the movement and galvanized India's struggle for independence and identity. Mohandas Gandhi (moh-HAHN-dus GAHN-dee) was born in 1869 in Gujarat (goo-juh-RAHT), in western India, the son of a government minister. After studying law in London, in 1893 he went to South Africa to work in a law firm serving Indian émigrés working as laborers there. He soon became aware of the racial prejudice and exploitation experienced by Indians living in the territory and tried to organize them to protect their interests.

On his return to India, Gandhi became active in the independence movement, setting up a movement based on nonviolent resistance—the Hindi term was ***satyagraha*** (SUHT-yuh-grah-hah), meaning "hold fast to the truth"—to try to force the British to improve the lot of the poor and grant independence to India. His goals were to convert the British to his views while simultaneously strengthening the unity and sense of self-respect of his compatriots. When the British attempted to suppress dissent, he called on his followers to refuse to obey British regulations. He began to manufacture his own clothes, dressing in a simple *dhoti* (DOH-tee) made of coarse homespun cotton, and adopted the spinning wheel as a symbol of Indian resistance to imports of British textiles.

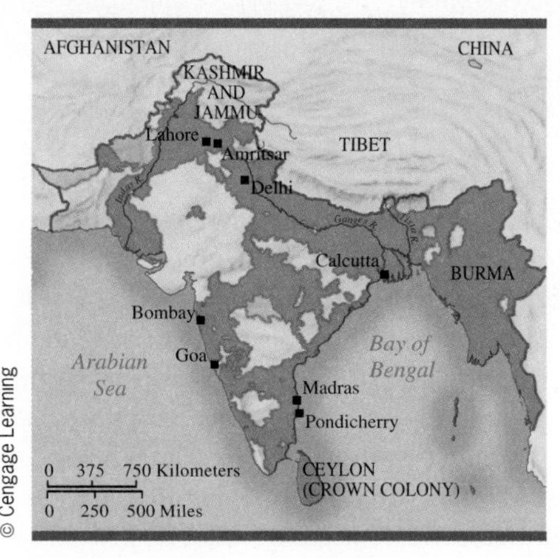

British India Between the Wars

Gandhi, now increasingly known as Mahatma (mah-HAHT-muh), India's "Great Soul," organized mass protests to achieve his aims, but in 1919, they got out of hand and led to violence and British reprisals. British troops killed hundreds of unarmed protesters in the city of Amritsar (am-RIT-sur) in northwestern India. Gandhi was horrified at the violence and briefly retreated from active politics. Nevertheless, he was arrested for his role in the protests and spent several years in prison.

Gandhi combined his anticolonial activities with an appeal to the spiritual instincts of all Indians. Though he had been born and raised a Hindu, his universalist approach to the idea of God transcended individual religion, although it was shaped by historical Hindu themes. In a speech in 1931, he described God as "an indefinable mysterious power that pervades everything . . . , an unseen power which makes itself felt and yet defies all proof."[1]

While Gandhi was in prison, the political situation continued to evolve. In 1921, the British passed the Government of India Act, transforming the heretofore advisory Legislative Council into a bicameral parliament, two-thirds of whose members would be elected. Similar bodies were created at the provincial level. In a stroke, 5 million Indians were enfranchised. But such reforms were no longer enough for many members of the INC, who wanted to push aggressively for full independence. The British exacerbated the situation by increasing the salt tax and prohibiting the Indian people from manufacturing or harvesting their own salt. Gandhi, now released from prison, returned to his earlier policy of **civil disobedience** by joining several dozen supporters in a 240-mile walk to the sea, where he picked up a lump of salt and urged Indians to ignore the law (see the Film & History feature on p. 626). Gandhi and many other members of the INC were arrested.

Organizations to promote women's rights in India had been established shortly after 1900, and Indian women now played an active role in the movement. Women accounted for about 20,000, or nearly 10 percent, of all those arrested for taking part in demonstrations during the interwar period. Women marched, picketed foreign shops, and promoted the spinning and wearing of homemade cloth. By the 1930s, women's associations were also actively promoting social reforms, including women's education, the introduction of birth control devices, the abolition of child marriage, and universal suffrage. In 1929, the Sarda Act raised the minimum age of marriage to fourteen.

NEW LEADERS AND NEW PROBLEMS In the 1930s, a new figure entered the movement in the person of Jawaharlal Nehru (juh-WAH-hur-lahl NAY-roo) (1889–1964), son of an earlier INC leader. Educated in the law in Great Britain and a *brahmin* by birth, Nehru personified the new Anglo-Indian politician: secular, rational, upper class, and intellectual. In fact, he appeared to be everything that Gandhi was not. With his emergence, the independence movement embarked on two paths, religious and secular, Indian and Western, traditional and modern. The dual character of the INC leadership may well have strengthened the movement by bringing together the two primary impulses behind the desire for independence: elite nationalism and the primal force of Indian traditionalism. But it portended trouble for the nation's new leadership in defining India's future path. In the meantime, Muslim discontent with Hindu dominance over the INC was increasing. In 1940, the Muslim League called for the creation of a separate Muslim state of Pakistan ("land of the pure") in the northwest. As strife between Hindus and Muslims increased, many Indians came to realize with sorrow (and some British colonialists with satisfaction) that British rule was all that stood between peace and civil war.

The Nationalist Revolt in the Middle East

In the Middle East, as in Europe, World War I hastened the collapse of old empires. The Ottoman Empire, which had dominated the eastern Mediterranean since the seizure of Constantinople in 1453, had been growing

FILM & HISTORY

Gandhi (1982)

To many of his contemporaries, Mohandas Gandhi was the conscience of India. Son of a senior Indian official from Gujarat and trained as a lawyer at University College in London, Gandhi first encountered racial discrimination when he provided legal assistance to Indian laborers living under the apartheid regime in South Africa. On his return to India, he rapidly emerged as a fierce critic of British colonial rule. His message of *satyagraha*—embodying the idea of steadfast but nonviolent resistance to the injustice and inhumanity inherent in the colonial enterprise—inspired his compatriots in their long struggle for national independence. It also earned the admiration and praise of sympathetic observers around the world. His death by assassination at the hands of a Hindu fanatic in 1948 shocked the world.

© Columbia Pictures/Courtesy The Everett Collection, Inc.

Jawaharlal Nehru (Roshan Seth), Mahatma Gandhi (Ben Kingsley), and Muhammad Ali Jinnah (Alyque Padamsee) confer before the partition of India into Hindu and Muslim states.

Time, however, has somewhat dimmed his message. Gandhi's vision of a future India was symbolized by the spinning wheel—he rejected the industrial age and material pursuits in favor of the simple life of the traditional Indian village. Since independence, however, India has followed the path of national wealth and power laid out by Jawaharlal Nehru, Gandhi's friend and colleague. Gandhi's appeal for religious tolerance and mutual respect at home rapidly gave way to a bloody conflict between Hindus and Muslims that has not yet been eradicated. His vision of world peace and brotherly love has been similarly ignored, first during the Cold War and more recently by the "clash of civilizations" between Western countries and the forces of militant Islam.

It was partly in an effort to revive Gandhi's message that the British filmmaker Richard Attenborough directed the film *Gandhi* (1982). Epic in length and scope, the film presents a faithful rendition of the life of its subject, from his introduction to apartheid in South Africa to his tragic death after World War II. Actor Ben Kingsley, son of an Indian father and an English mother, plays the title role with intensity and conviction. The film was widely praised and earned eight Academy Awards. Kingsley received an Oscar in the Best Actor category.

weaker since the end of the eighteenth century, troubled by government corruption, the declining effectiveness of the sultans, and the loss of considerable territory in the Balkans and southwestern Russia. In North Africa, Ottoman authority, tenuous at best, had disintegrated in the nineteenth century, enabling the French to seize Algeria and Tunisia and the British to establish a protectorate over the Nile River valley.

DECLINE OF THE OTTOMAN EMPIRE Reformist elements in Istanbul had tried from time to time to resist the trend, but military defeats continued: Greece declared its independence, and Ottoman power declined steadily in the Middle East. A rising sense of nationality among Serbs, Armenians, and other minority peoples threatened the stability and cohesion of the empire. In the 1870s, a new generation of reformers seized power in Istanbul and pushed through a constitution creating a legislative assembly representing all peoples in the state. But the sultan they placed on the throne suspended the new charter and attempted to rule by traditional authoritarian means.

By the end of the century, the defunct 1876 constitution had become a symbol of change for reformist elements, now grouped together under the name **Young Turks**. They found support in the army and administration and among Turks living in exile. In 1908, the Young Turks forced the sultan to restore the constitution, and he was removed from power the following year.

But the Young Turks had appeared at a moment of crisis for the empire. Internal rebellions, combined with Austrian annexations of Ottoman territories in the Balkans, undermined support for the new government and provoked the army to step in. With most minorities from the old empire now removed from Istanbul's authority, many ethnic Turks began to embrace a new concept of a Turkish state based on those of Turkish nationality.

The final blow to the old empire came in World War I, when the Ottoman government allied with Germany in the hope of driving the British from Egypt and restoring Ottoman rule over the Nile valley. In response, the British declared an official protectorate over Egypt and, aided by the efforts of the dashing if eccentric British adventurer T. E. Lawrence (popularly known as Lawrence of Arabia), sought to undermine Ottoman rule in the Arabian peninsula by encouraging Arab nationalists there. In 1916, the local governor of Mecca declared Arabia independent from Ottoman rule, while British troops, advancing from Egypt, seized Palestine (see the map on p. 631). In October 1918, having suffered more than 300,000 casualties during the war, the Ottoman Empire negotiated an armistice with the Allied Powers.

AP Images

Mustafa Kemal Atatürk. The war hero Mustafa Kemal took the initiative in creating the republic of Turkey. As president, Atatürk ("Father Turk") worked hard to transform Turkey into a modern secular state by restructuring the economy, adopting Western dress, and breaking the powerful hold of Islamic traditions. He is now reviled by Muslim fundamentalists for his opposition to an Islamic state. In this photograph, Atatürk, at the left in civilian clothes, hosts the shah of Persia during his visit to Turkey in 1934.

MUSTAFA KEMAL AND THE MODERNIZATION OF TURKEY During the next years, the tottering empire began to fall apart as the British and the French made plans to divide up Ottoman territories in the Middle East and the Greeks won Allied approval to seize the western parts of the Anatolian peninsula for their dream of re-creating the substance of the old Byzantine Empire. The impending collapse energized key elements in Turkey under the leadership of a war hero, Colonel Mustafa Kemal (moos-tah-FAH kuh-MAHL) (1881–1938), who had successfully defended the Dardanelles against the British during World War I. Now he resigned from the army and convoked a national congress that called for the creation of an elected government and the preservation of the empire's remaining territories in a new republic of Turkey. Establishing his capital at Ankara (AN-kuh-ruh), Kemal drove the Greeks from the Anatolian peninsula and persuaded the British to agree to a new treaty. In 1923, the last Ottoman sultan fled the country, which was now declared a Turkish republic. The Ottoman Empire had come to an end.

During the next few years, President Mustafa Kemal, now popularly known as Atatürk (ah-tah-TIRK), or "Father Turk," attempted to transform Turkey into a modern secular republic. The trappings of a democratic system were put in place, centered on an elected Grand National Assembly, but the president was relatively intolerant of opposition and harshly suppressed critics. Turkish nationalism was emphasized, and the Turkish language, now written in the Roman alphabet, was shorn of many of its Arabic elements. Popular education was emphasized, old aristocratic titles like *pasha* and *bey* were abolished, and all Turkish citizens were given family names in the European style.

Atatürk also took steps to modernize the economy. overseeing the establishment of a light industrial sector producing textiles, glass, paper, and cement and instituting a five-year plan on the Soviet model to provide for state direction over the economy. Atatürk was no admirer of Soviet communism, however, and the Turkish economy can be better described as a form of state capitalism. He also established training institutions and model farms in an effort to modernize the agricultural sector, but such reforms had little effect on the predominantly conservative peasantry.

Perhaps the most significant aspect of Atatürk's reform program was his attempt to break the power of the Islamic clerics and transform Turkey into a secular state. The caliphate was formally abolished in 1924 (see the box on p. 628), and *Shari'a* (Islamic law) was replaced

OPPOSING ≺ VIEWPOINTS

Islam in the Modern World: Two Views

As part of his plan to transform Turkey into a modern society, Mustafa Kemal Atatürk sought to eliminate what he considered to be outdated practices imposed by traditional beliefs. The first selection is from a speech in which he proposed an end to the caliphate, which had been in the hands of Ottoman sultans since the formation of the empire. But not all Muslims wished to move toward a more secular society. Mohammed Iqbal (ik-BAHL), a well-known Muslim poet in colonial India, was a prominent advocate of the creation of a separate state for Muslims in South Asia. The second selection is from an address he presented to the All-India Muslim League, explaining the rationale for his proposal.

Atatürk, Speech to the Assembly (October 1924)

The sovereign entitled Caliph was to maintain justice among the three hundred million Muslims on the terrestrial globe, to safeguard the rights of these peoples, to prevent any event that could encroach upon order and security, and confront every attack which the Muslims would be called upon to encounter from the side of other nations. It was to be part of his attributes to preserve by all means the welfare and spiritual development of Islam. . . .

If the Caliph and Caliphate, as they maintained, were to be invested with a dignity embracing the whole of Islam, ought they not to have realized in all justice that a crushing burden would be imposed on Turkey, on her existence; her entire resources and all her forces would be placed at the disposal of the Caliph? . . .

For centuries our nation was guided under the influence of these erroneous ideas. But what has been the result of it? Everywhere they have lost millions of men. "Do you know," I asked, "how many sons of Anatolia have perished in the scorching deserts of the Yemen? Do you know the losses we have suffered in holding Syria and Egypt and in maintaining our position in Africa? And do you see what has come out of it? Do you know?

"Those who favor the idea of placing the means at the disposal of the Caliph to brave the whole world and the power to administer the affairs of the whole of Islam must not appeal to the population of Anatolia alone but to the great Muslim agglomerations which are eight or ten times as rich in men.

"New Turkey, the people of New Turkey, have no reason to think of anything else but their own existence and their own welfare. She has nothing more to give away to others."

Mohammed Iqbal, Speech to the All-India Muslim League (1930)

It cannot be denied that Islam, regarded as an ethical ideal plus a certain kind of polity—by which expression I mean a social structure regulated by a legal system and animated by a specific ethical ideal—has been the chief formative factor in the life history of the Muslims of India. It has furnished those basic emotions and loyalties which gradually unify scattered individuals and groups and finally transform them into a well-defined people. Indeed it is no exaggeration to say that India is perhaps the only country in the world where Islam, as a people-building force, has worked at its best. In India, as elsewhere, the structure of Islam as a society is almost entirely due to the working of Islam as a culture inspired by a specific ethical ideal. What I mean to say is that Muslim society, with its remarkable homogeneity and inner unity, has grown to be what it is under the pressure of the laws and institutions associated with the culture of Islam.

Communalism in its higher aspect, then, is indispensable to the formation of a harmonious whole in a country like India. The units of Indian society are not territorial as in European countries. India is a continent of human groups belonging to different religions. Their behavior is not at all determined by a common race consciousness. Even the Hindus do not form a homogeneous group. The principle of European democracy cannot be applied to India without recognizing the fact of communal groups. The Muslim demand for the creation of a Muslim India within India is, therefore, perfectly justified. . . .

I therefore demand the formation of a consolidated Muslim State in the best interests of India and Islam. For India it means security and peace resulting from an

(Continued)

internal balance of power; for Islam an opportunity to rid itself of the stamp that Arabian imperialism was forced to give it, to mobilize its law, its education, its culture, and to bring them into closer contact with its own original spirit and with the spirit of modern times.

Why did Mustafa Kemal believe that the caliphate no longer met the needs of the Turkish people? Why did Mohammed Iqbal believe that a separate state for Muslims in India would be required? How did he attempt to persuade non-Muslims that this would be to their benefit as well?

Sources: Atatürk, Speech to the Assembly (October 1924). From *Ataturk's Speech to the Assembly*, pp. 432–433. A speech delivered by Ghazi Mustafa Kemal, President of the Turkish Republic, October 1927. Mohammed Iqbal, Speech to the All-India Muslim League (1930). Excerpt from *The Sources of Indian Tradition*, pp. 218–222 by Stephen Hay, ed. Copyright © 1988 by Columbia University Press, New York. Reprinted with permission of the publisher.

by a revised version of the Swiss law code. The fez (the brimless cap worn by Turkish Muslims) was abolished as a form of headdress, and women were discouraged from wearing the traditional Islamic veil. Women received the right to vote in 1934 and were legally equal to men in all aspects of marriage and inheritance. Education and the professions were now open to citizens of both genders, and some women even began to participate in politics. All citizens were given the right to convert to another religion at will.

The legacy of Mustafa Kemal Atatürk was enormous. Although not all of his reforms were widely accepted in practice, especially by devout Muslims, most of the changes he introduced were retained after his death in 1938. In virtually every respect, the Turkish republic was the product of his determined efforts to create a modern Turkish nation.

MODERNIZATION IN IRAN In the meantime, a similar process was under way in Persia. Under the Qajar (kuh-JAHR) dynasty (1794–1925), the country had not been very successful in resisting Russian advances in the Caucasus or resolving its domestic problems. To secure themselves from foreign influence, the Qajars moved the capital from Tabriz to Tehran (teh-RAHN), in a mountainous area south of the Caspian Sea. During the mid-nineteenth century, one modernizing shah attempted to introduce political and economic reforms but faced resistance from tribal and religious—predominantly Shi'ite—forces. Increasingly, the dynasty turned to Russia and Great Britain to protect itself from its own people.

Eventually, the growing foreign presence led to the rise of a Persian nationalist movement. Supported by Shi'ite religious leaders, opposition to the regime rose steadily among both peasants and merchants in the cities, and in 1906, popular pressure forced the shah to grant a constitution on the Western model.

As in the Ottoman Empire and Manchu China, however, the modernizers had moved too soon, before their power base was secure. With the support of the Russians and the British, the shah regained control, while the two foreign powers began to divide the country into separate spheres of influence. One reason for the foreign interest in Persia was the discovery of oil reserves there in 1908. Over the next years, oil exports increased rapidly, with the bulk of the profits going to British investors.

In 1921, Reza Khan (ree-ZAH KAHN) (1878–1944), an officer in the Persian army, seized power in Tehran. He had intended to establish a republic, but resistance from traditional forces impeded his efforts. In 1925, the new Pahlavi (PAH-luh-vee), dynasty with Reza Khan as shah, replaced the now defunct Qajar dynasty. During the next few years, Reza Khan attempted to follow the example of Atatürk in Turkey, introducing reforms to strengthen the central government, modernize the civilian and military bureaucracy, and establish a modern economic infrastructure. In 1935, he officially changed the name of the nation to Iran.

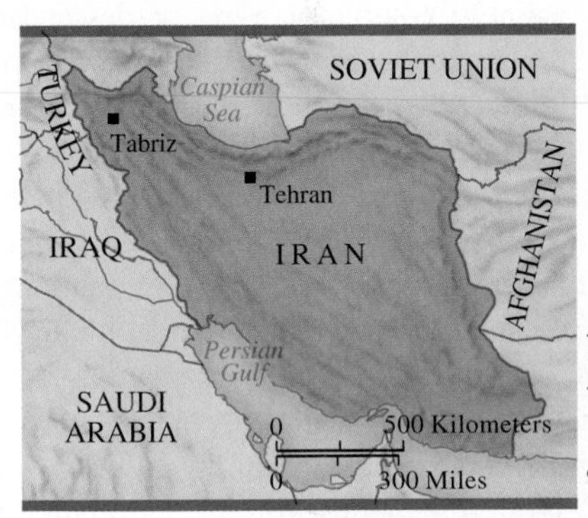

Iran Under the Pahlavi Dynasty

© Cengage Learning

Unlike Atatürk, Reza Khan did not attempt to destroy the power of Islamic beliefs, but he did encourage the establishment of a Western-style educational system and forbade women to wear the veil in public. Women continued to be exploited, however; the carpets produced by their intensive labor were a major export—second only to oil—in the interwar period. To strengthen Iranian nationalism and reduce the power of Islam, Reza Khan attempted to popularize the symbols and beliefs of pre-Islamic times. Like his Qajar predecessors, however, he was hindered by strong foreign influence. When the

Soviet Union and Great Britain decided to send troops into the country during World War II, he resigned in protest and died three years later.

NATION BUILDING IN IRAQ Another consequence of the collapse of the Ottoman Empire was the emergence of a new political entity along the Tigris and Euphrates Rivers, once the heartland of ancient empires. Lacking defensible borders and sharply divided along ethnic and religious lines—a Shi'ite majority in rural areas, a vocal Sunni minority in the cities, and a largely Kurdish population in the northern mountains—the region had been under Ottoman rule since the seventeenth century. During World War I, British forces occupied the area from Baghdad southward to the Persian Gulf to protect the oil-producing regions in neighboring Iran from a German takeover.

Although the British claimed to have arrived as liberators, in 1920 the League of Nations placed the country under British control as the mandate of Iraq. Civil unrest and growing anti-Western sentiment rapidly dispelled any plans for the emergence of an independent government, and in 1921, after the suppression of resistance forces, the country was placed under the titular authority of King Faisal (FY-suhl) of Syria, a descendant of the Prophet Muhammad. Faisal relied for support primarily on the politically more sophisticated urban Sunni population, although they represented less than a quarter of the population. The discovery of oil near Kirkuk (kir-KOOK) in 1927 increased the value of the area to the British, who granted formal independence to Iraq in 1932, although British advisers retained a strong influence over the fragile government.

THE RISE OF ARAB NATIONALISM As we have seen, the Arab uprising during World War I helped bring about the demise of the Ottoman Empire. There had been resistance to Ottoman rule in the Arabian peninsula since the eighteenth century, when the devoutly Muslim Wahhabi (wuh-HAH-bee) sect attempted to drive out outside influences and cleanse Islam of corrupt practices that had developed in past centuries. The revolt was eventually suppressed, but Wahhabi influence persisted.

CHRONOLOGY The Middle East Between the Wars	
Balfour Declaration on Palestine	1917
Reza Khan seizes power in Persia	1921
End of Ottoman Empire and establishment of a republic in Turkey	1923
Rule of Mustafa Kemal Atatürk in Turkey	1923–1938
Beginning of Pahlavi dynasty in Iran	1925
Establishment of kingdom of Saudi Arabia	1932

World War I offered an opportunity for the Arabs to throw off the shackles of Ottoman rule—but what would replace them? The Arabs were not a nation but an idea, a loose collection of peoples who often did not see eye to eye on matters that affected their community. Disagreement over what constitutes an Arab has plagued generations of political leaders who have sought unsuccessfully to knit together the disparate peoples of the region into a single Arab nation.

When the Arab leaders in Mecca declared their independence from Ottoman rule in 1916, they had hoped for British support, but they were to be sorely disappointed. At the close of the war, the British and French created a number of mandates in the area under the supervision of the League of Nations (see Chapter 23). Iraq was assigned to the British; Syria and Lebanon (the two areas were separated so that Christian peoples in Lebanon could be placed under Christian administration) were given to the French.

In the early 1920s, Ibn Saud (IB-un sah-OOD) (1880–1953), a Wahhabi leader and descendant of the family that had led the eighteenth-century revolt, united Arab tribes in the northern part of the Arabian peninsula and drove out the remnants of Ottoman rule. Devout and gifted, Ibn Saud won broad support among Arab tribal peoples and established the kingdom of Saudi Arabia throughout much of the peninsula in 1932.

At first, the new kingdom, consisting essentially of the vast desert wastes of central Arabia, was desperately poor and depended on the income from Muslim pilgrims visiting the holy sites in Mecca and Medina. But during the 1930s, American companies began to explore for oil, and in 1938, Standard Oil made a successful strike at Dhahran (dah-RAHN), on the Persian Gulf. Soon an Arabian-American oil conglomerate, popularly called Aramco, was established, and the isolated kingdom was suddenly inundated by Western oilmen and untold wealth.

THE ISSUE OF PALESTINE The land of Palestine—once the home of the Jews but now inhabited primarily by Muslim Arabs—was made a separate mandate and immediately became a thorny problem for the British. In 1897, the Austrian-born journalist Theodor Herzl (TAY-oh-dor HAYRT-sul) (1860–1904) had convened an international conference in Switzerland that led to the creation of the World Zionist Organization (WZO). Its aim was to create a homeland in Palestine for the Jewish people, who had long been dispersed throughout Europe, North Africa, and the Middle East.

Over the next decade, Jewish immigration into Palestine, then under Ottoman rule, increased with WZO support. By the outbreak of World War I, about 85,000 Jews lived in Palestine, representing about 15 percent of the total population. In 1917, responding to appeals from the

British chemist Chaim Weizmann (KY-im VYTS-mahn), British Foreign Secretary Lord Arthur Balfour (BAL-foor) issued a declaration saying Palestine was to be a national home for the Jews. The Balfour Declaration, which was later confirmed by the League of Nations, was ambiguous on the legal status of the territory and promised that the rights of non-Jewish peoples currently living in the area would not be undermined. But Arab nationalists were incensed. How could a national home for the Jewish people be established in a territory where the majority of the population was Muslim?

After World War I, more Jewish settlers began to arrive in Palestine in response to the promises made in the Balfour Declaration. As tensions between the new arrivals and existing Muslim residents began to escalate, the British tried to restrict Jewish immigration into the territory while Arab voices rejected the concept of a separate state. In a bid to relieve Arab sensitivities, Great Britain created the separate emirate of Trans-Jordan out of the eastern portion of Palestine. After World War II, it would become the independent kingdom of Jordan. The stage was set for the conflicts that would take place in the region after World War II.

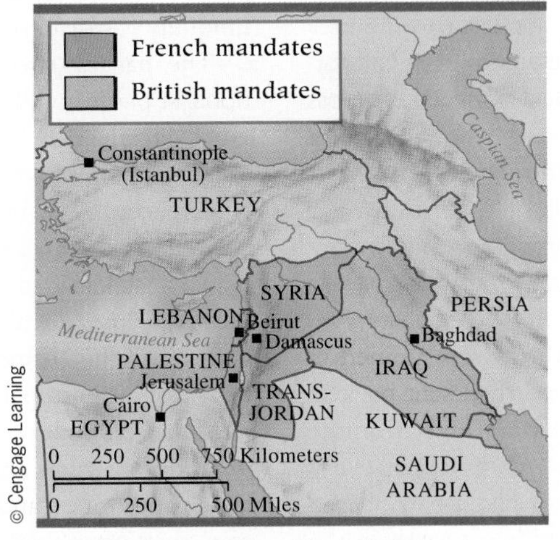

© Cengage Learning

The Middle East After World War I

THE BRITISH IN EGYPT Great Britain had maintained a loose protectorate over Egypt since the mid-nineteenth century, although the area remained nominally under Ottoman rule. London formalized its protectorate in 1914 to protect the Suez Canal and the Nile valley from possible seizure by the Central Powers. After the war, however, nationalist elements became restive and formed the Wafd (WAHFT) Party, a secular organization dedicated to the creation of an independent Egypt based on the principles of representative government. The Wafd received the support of many middle-class Egyptians who, like Atatürk in Turkey, hoped to meld Islamic practices with the secular tradition of the modern West. This modernist form of Islam did not have broad appeal outside the cosmopolitan centers, however, and in 1928 the Muslim cleric Hasan al-Bana (hah-SAHN al-BAN-ah) organized the Muslim Brotherhood, which demanded strict adherence to the teachings of the Prophet, as set forth in the Qur'an. The Brotherhood rejected Western ways and sought to create a new Egypt based firmly on the precepts of *Shari'a*. By the 1930s, the organization had as many as a million members.

Nationalism and Revolution

Before the Russian Revolution, to most intellectuals in Asia and Africa, "westernization" referred to the capitalist democratic civilization of western Europe and the United States, not the doctrine of social revolution developed by Karl Marx. Until 1917, Marxism was regarded as a utopian idea rather than a concrete system of government. Moreover, Marxism appeared to have little relevance to conditions in Asia and Africa. Marxist doctrine, after all, declared that a communist society would arise only from the ashes of an advanced capitalism that had already passed through an industrial revolution. From the perspective of Marxist historical analysis, most societies in Asia and Africa were still at the feudal stage of development; they lacked the economic conditions and political awareness to achieve a socialist revolution that would bring the working class to power. Finally, the Marxist view of nationalism and religion had little appeal in the non-Western world. Marx believed that nationhood and religion were false ideas that diverted the oppressed masses from the critical issues of class struggle. Instead, Marx stressed an "internationalist" outlook based on class consciousness and the eventual creation of a classless society with no artificial divisions based on culture, nation, or religion.

LENIN AND THE EAST The situation began to change after the Russian Revolution. Lenin's Bolsheviks had demonstrated that a revolutionary party espousing Marxist principles could overturn a corrupt, outdated system and launch a new experiment dedicated to ending human inequality and achieving a paradise on earth. In 1920, Lenin proposed a new revolutionary strategy designed to relate Marxist doctrine and practice to non-Western societies. His reasons were not entirely altruistic. Soviet Russia, surrounded by capitalist powers, desperately needed allies in its struggle to survive in a hostile world. To Lenin, the anticolonial movements emerging in North Africa, Asia, and the Middle East after World War I were natural allies of the beleaguered new regime in Moscow. Lenin was convinced that only the ability of the imperialist powers to find markets, raw materials, and sources of capital investment in the non-Western world kept capitalism alive. If the tentacles of capitalist influence in Asia and Africa could be severed, imperialism would weaken and collapse.

Establishing such an alliance was not easy, however. Most nationalist leaders in colonial countries belonged to the urban middle class, and many abhorred the idea of a comprehensive revolution to create a totally egalitarian society. In addition, many still adhered to traditional religious beliefs and were opposed to the atheistic principles of classic Marxism.

Since it was unrealistic to expect bourgeois nationalist support for social revolution, Lenin sought a compromise that would enable Communist parties to be organized among the working classes in the preindustrial societies of Asia and Africa. These parties would then forge informal alliances with existing middle-class parties to struggle against the traditional ruling class and Western imperialism. Such an alliance, of course, could not be permanent because many bourgeois nationalists in Asia and Africa would reject an egalitarian, classless society. Once the imperialists had been overthrown, therefore, the Communist parties would turn against their erstwhile nationalist partners to seize power on their own and carry out the socialist revolution.

Lenin's strategy became a major element in Soviet foreign policy in the 1920s. Soviet agents fanned out across the world to carry Marxism beyond the boundaries of industrial Europe. The primary instrument of this effort was the **Communist International**, or **Comintern** for short. Formed in 1919 at Lenin's prodding, the Comintern was a worldwide organization of Communist parties dedicated to world revolution. At its headquarters in Moscow, agents from around the world were trained in the precepts of world communism and then sent back to their countries to form Marxist parties and promote social revolution. By the end of the 1920s, almost every colonial or semicolonial society in Asia had a party based on Marxist principles. The Soviets had less success in the Middle East, where Marxism appealed mainly to minorities such as Jews and Armenians in the cities, and in black Africa, where Soviet strategists in any case felt that conditions were not sufficiently advanced for the creation of Communist organizations.

THE APPEAL OF COMMUNISM According to Marxist doctrine, Communist parties should be made up of urban factory workers alienated from capitalist society by inhuman working conditions. In practice, many of the leaders even in European Communist parties tended to be urban intellectuals or members of the lower middle class. That phenomenon was even more true in the non-Western world, where most early Marxists were rootless intellectuals. Some were probably drawn to the movement for patriotic reasons and saw Marxist doctrine as a new, more effective means of modernizing their societies and removing the colonial exploiters (see the box on p. 633). Others were attracted by the utopian dream of a classless society. For those who had lost their faith in traditional religion, communism often served as a new secular ideology that replaced the lost truth of traditional faiths.

Of course, the new doctrine's appeal was not the same in all non-Western societies. In Confucian societies such as China and Vietnam, where traditional belief systems had been badly discredited by their failure to counter the Western challenge, communism had an immediate impact and rapidly became a major factor in the anticolonial movement. In Buddhist and Muslim societies, where traditional religion remained strong and became a cohesive factor in the resistance movement, communism had less success. To maximize their appeal and minimize potential conflict with traditional ideas, Communist parties frequently attempted to adapt Marxist doctrine to indigenous values and institutions. In the Middle East, for example, the Ba'ath (BAHTH) Party in Syria adopted a hybrid socialism combining Marxism with Arab nationalism. In Africa, radical intellectuals talked vaguely of a uniquely "African road to socialism."

The parties' success in establishing alliances with nationalist parties while building support among the working classes also varied from place to place. In some instances, the Communists were briefly able to work with the bourgeois parties. The most famous example was the alliance between the Chinese Communist Party and Sun Yat-sen's Nationalist Party (discussed in the next section). In 1928, however, the Comintern, reacting to Chiang Kai-shek's betrayal of the alliance, gave up these efforts and declared that Communist parties should focus on recruiting the most revolutionary elements in society—notably, the urban intellectuals and the working class. Harassed by colonial authorities and saddled with directions from Moscow that often had little relevance to local conditions, Communist parties in most colonial societies had little success in the 1930s and failed to build a secure base of support among the mass of the population.

Revolution in China

FOCUS QUESTION: What problems did China encounter between the two world wars, and what solutions did the Nationalists and the Communists propose to solve them?

Overall, revolutionary Marxism had its greatest impact in China, where a group of young radicals founded the Chinese Communist Party (CCP) in 1921. The rise of the CCP was a consequence of the failed revolution of 1911. When political forces are too weak or too divided to consolidate their power during a period of instability, the military usually steps in to fill the vacuum. In China, Sun Yat-sen (SOON yaht-SEN) and his colleagues had accepted General Yuan Shikai (yoo-AHN shee-KY) as president of the new Chinese republic in 1911 because they lacked the

The Path of Liberation

In 1919, the Vietnamese revolutionary Ho Chi Minh (1890–1969) was living in exile in France, where he first became acquainted with the revolutionary experiment in Bolshevik Russia. Later he became a leader of the Vietnamese Communist movement. In the following passage, written in 1960, he reminisces about his reasons for becoming a Communist. The Second International, mentioned in the excerpt, was created in 1889 by moderate socialists who pursued their goal by parliamentary means. Lenin created the Third International, or Comintern, in 1919 to promote violent revolution.

Ho Chi Minh, "The Path Which Led Me to Leninism"

After World War I, I made my living in Paris, now as a retoucher at a photographer's, now as a painter of "Chinese antiquities" (made in France!). I would distribute leaflets denouncing the crimes committed by the French colonialists in Vietnam.

At that time, I supported the October Revolution [in Russia] only instinctively, not yet grasping all its historic importance. I loved and admired Lenin because he was a great patriot who liberated his compatriots; until then, I had read none of his books.

The reason for my joining the French Socialist Party was that these "ladies and gentlemen"—as I called my comrades at that moment—had shown their sympathy toward me, toward the struggle of the oppressed peoples. But I understood neither what was a party, a trade union, nor what was Socialism nor Communism.

Heated discussions were then taking place in the branches of the Socialist Party, about the question whether the Socialist Party should remain in the Second International, should a Second-and-a-Half International be founded, or should the Socialist Party join Lenin's Third International? I attended the meetings regularly, twice or three times a week, and attentively listened to the discussion. First, I could not understand thoroughly. Why were the discussions so heated? Either with the Second, Second-and-a-Half, or Third International, the revolution could be waged. What was the use of arguing then? As for the First International, what had become of it?

What I wanted most to know—and this precisely was not debated in the meetings—was: which International sides with the peoples of colonial countries?

I raised this question—the most important in my opinion—in a meeting. Some comrades answered: It is the Third, not the Second International. And a comrade gave me Lenin's "Thesis on the national and colonial questions," published by *l'Humanité*, to read.

There were political terms difficult to understand in this thesis. But by dint of reading it again and again, finally I could grasp the main part of it. What emotion, enthusiasm, clearsightedness, and confidence it instilled in me! I was overjoyed to tears. Though sitting alone in my room, I shouted aloud as if addressing large crowds: "Dear martyrs, compatriots! This is what we need, this is the path to our liberation!"

After that, I had entire confidence in Lenin, in the Third International.

Why did Ho Chi Minh believe that the Third International was the key to the liberation of the colonial peoples? What were the essential elements of Lenin's strategy for bringing that about?

Source: From *Vietnam: History, Documents, and Opinions on a Major World Crisis*, Marvin Gentleman, ed. (New York: Fawcett Publications, 1965), pp. 30–32.

military force to compete with his control over the army. But some had misgivings about Yuan's intentions. As one remarked in a letter to a friend, "We don't know whether he will be a George Washington or a Napoleon."

As it turned out, he was neither. Showing little comprehension of the new ideas sweeping into China from the West, Yuan ruled in a traditional manner, reviving Confucian rituals and institutions and eventually trying to found a new imperial dynasty. Yuan's dictatorial inclinations rapidly led to clashes with Sun's party, now renamed the Guomindang (gwoh-min-DAHNG) (Kuomintang), or Nationalist Party. When Yuan dissolved the new parliament, the Nationalists launched a rebellion. When it failed, Sun Yat-sen fled to Japan.

Yuan was strong enough to brush off the challenge from the revolutionary forces but not to turn back the clock of history. He died in 1916 and was succeeded by one of his military subordinates. For the next several years, China slipped into semianarchy as the power of the central government disintegrated and military warlords seized power in the provinces.

Mr. Science and Mr. Democracy: The New Culture Movement

In the meantime, discontent with existing conditions continued to rise. The most vocal protests came from radical intellectuals, who were now convinced that political change could not take place until the Chinese people were more familiar with trends in the outside world. Braving the displeasure of Yuan and his successors, intellectuals at Peking University launched the **New Culture Movement**, aimed at abolishing the remnants of the old system and introducing Western values and institutions. Through their classrooms and newly established progressive magazines and newspapers, the intellectuals introduced a host of new ideas, from the philosophy of Friedrich Nietzsche (FREED-rikh NEE-chuh) to the feminist plays of Henrik Ibsen. Soon educated Chinese youths were chanting "Down with Confucius and sons" and talking of a new era dominated by "Mr. Sai" (Mr. Science) and "Mr. De" (Mr. Democracy). No one was a greater defender of free thought and speech than the chancellor of Peking University, Cai Yuanpei (TSY yoo-wahn-PAY) (Ts'ai Yüan-p'ei): "Regardless of what school of thought a person may adhere to, so long as that person's ideas are justified and conform to reason and have not been passed by through the process of natural selection, although there may be controversy, such ideas have a right to be presented."[2] Not surprisingly, such views were not appreciated by conservative army officers, one of whom threatened to lob artillery shells into the university to destroy the poisonous new ideas.

Soon, however, the intellectuals' discontent was joined by a growing protest against Japan's efforts to expand its influence on the mainland. Early in the twentieth century, Japan had taken advantage of the Qing's decline to extend its domination over Manchuria and Korea (see Chapter 22). In 1915, the Japanese government insisted that Yuan Shikai accept twenty-one demands that would have given Japan a virtual protectorate over the Chinese government and economy. Yuan was able to fend off the most far-reaching demands by arousing popular outrage in China, but at the Paris Peace Conference four years later, Japan received Germany's sphere of influence in Shandong (SHAHN-doong) Province as a reward for its support of the Allied cause in World War I. On hearing that the Chinese government had accepted the decision, on May 4, 1919, patriotic students demonstrated in Beijing and other major cities. Although this May Fourth Movement did not lead to the restoration of Shandong to Chinese rule, it did alert the politically literate population to the threat to national survival and the incompetence of the warlord government.

The Nationalist-Communist Alliance

By 1920, central authority had almost ceased to exist in China. Two competing political forces now began to emerge from the chaos: Sun Yat-sen's Nationalist Party and the CCP. Following Lenin's strategy, Comintern agents advised the CCP to link up with the more experienced Nationalists. Sun Yat-sen needed the expertise and diplomatic support that Soviet Russia could provide because his anti-imperialist rhetoric had alienated many Western powers. In 1923, the two parties formed an alliance to oppose the warlords and drive the imperialist powers out of China.

For three years, the two parties submerged their mutual suspicions and mobilized a revolutionary army to march north and seize control over China. The so-called Northern Expedition began in the summer of 1926 (see Map 24.1). By the following spring, revolutionary forces were in control of all Chinese territory south of the Yangtze River, including the major river ports of Wuhan (WOO-HAHN) and Shanghai (SHANG-hy). But tensions between the two parties now surfaced. Sun Yat-sen had died in 1925 and was succeeded as head of the Nationalist Party by his military subordinate, Chiang Kai-shek (ZHANG ky-SHEK) (see the comparative illustration on p. 636). Chiang feigned support for the alliance with the Communists but actually planned to destroy them. In April 1927, he struck against the Communists in Shanghai, killing thousands. After the massacre, most of the Communist leaders went into hiding in the city, attempting to revive the movement in its traditional base among the urban working class. Some party members, however, led by the young Communist organizer Mao Zedong (mow zee-DOONG ["ow" as in "how"]) (Mao Tse-tung), fled to the hilly areas south of the Yangtze River.

Unlike most CCP leaders, Mao was convinced that the Chinese revolution must be based not on workers in the big cities but on the impoverished peasants in the countryside. The son of a prosperous farmer, Mao served as an agitator in villages in his native province of Hunan (HOO-NAHN) during the Northern Expedition in 1926. At that time, he wrote a report to the party leadership suggesting that the CCP support peasant demands for a

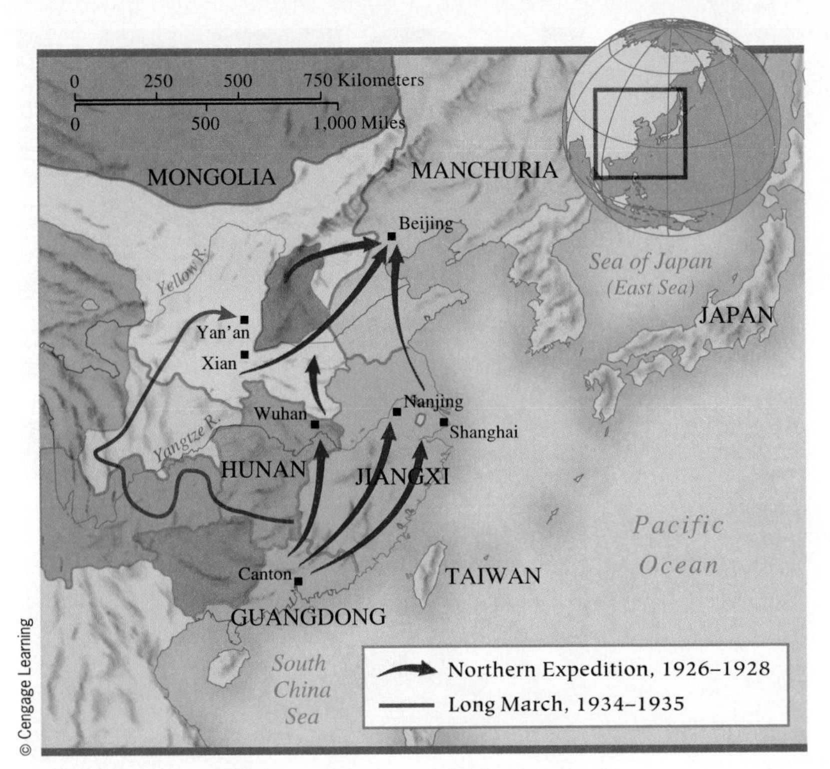

© Cengage Learning

MAP 24.1 The Northern Expedition and the Long March. This map shows the routes taken by the combined Nationalist-Communist forces during the Northern Expedition of 1926–1928. The blue arrow indicates the route taken by Communist units during the Long March led by Mao Zedong.

 *Where did Mao establish his new headquarters?*

land revolution (see the box on p. 637). But his superiors refused, fearing that such radical policies would destroy the alliance with the Nationalists.

The Nanjing Republic

In 1928, Chiang Kai-shek founded a new Chinese republic at Nanjing, and over the next three years, he sought to reunify China by a combination of military operations and inducements to various northern warlords to join his movement. He also attempted to put an end to the Communists, rooting them out of their urban base in Shanghai and their rural redoubt in the hills of Jiangxi (JAHNG-shee) (Kiangsi) Province. In 1931, he succeeded in forcing most party leaders to flee Shanghai for Mao's base in southern China. Three years later, Chiang's troops surrounded the Communist base in Jiangxi, causing Mao's People's Liberation Army (PLA) to embark on the famous Long March, an arduous journey of thousands of miles on foot to the provincial town of Yan'an (yuh-NAHN) (Yenan) in northern China (see Map 24.1).

Meanwhile, Chiang was trying to build a new nation. When the Nanjing Republic was established in 1928, Chiang publicly declared his commitment to Sun Yat-sen's Three People's Principles. In 1918, Sun had written about the all-important second stage of "political tutelage":

> China . . . needs a republican government just as a boy needs school. As a schoolboy must have good teachers and helpful friends, so the Chinese people, being for the first time under republican rule, must have a farsighted revolutionary government for their training. This calls for the period of political tutelage, which is a necessary transitional stage from monarchy to republicanism. Without this, disorder will be unavoidable.[3]

In keeping with Sun's program, Chiang announced a period of political indoctrination to prepare the Chinese people for constitutional government. In the meantime, the Nationalists would use their power to carry out a land reform program and modernize the industrial sector.

But it would take more than paper plans to create a new China. There were faint signs of an impending industrial revolution in the major urban centers, but most people in the countryside, drained by warlord exactions and civil strife, were still grindingly poor and overwhelmingly illiterate. A westernized urban middle class had begun to emerge and formed the natural constituency of the Nanjing government. But this new westernized elite, preoccupied with individual advancement and material accumulation, had few links with the peasants or the rickshaw drivers "running in this world of suffering," in the words of a Chinese poet. Some critics dismissed Chiang and his chief followers as "banana Chinese"—yellow on the outside, white on the inside.

THE BEST OF EAST AND WEST Aware of the difficulty of introducing exotic foreign ideas into a culturally conservative society, Chiang attempted to synthesize modern Western ideas with traditional Confucian values of hard work, obedience, and moral integrity. Through the New Life Movement, sponsored by his Wellesley-educated wife, Mei-ling Soong (may-LING SOONG), Chiang sought to propagate traditional Confucian social ethics such as propriety and righteousness, while rejecting what he considered the excessive individualism and material greed of Western capitalism.

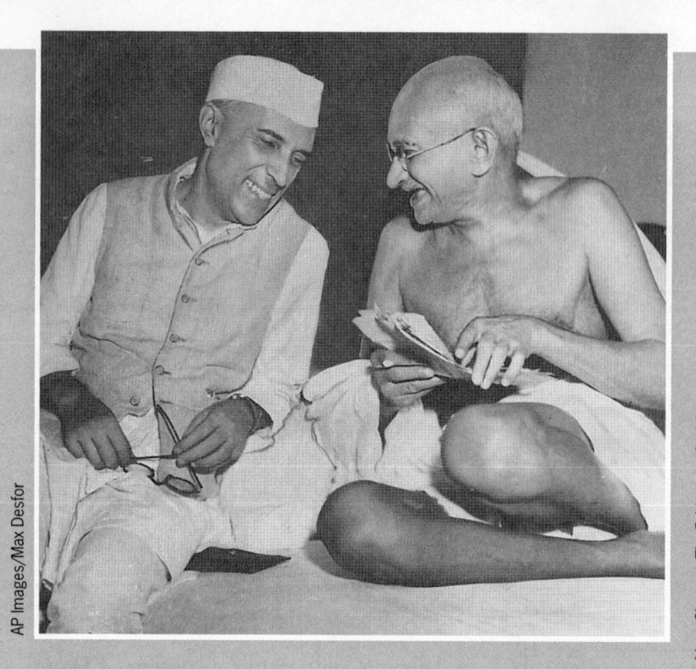

AP Images/Max Desfor

Private Collection//© Archives Charmet/The Bridgeman Art Library

COMPARATIVE ILLUSTRATION

Masters and Disciples. When the founders of nationalist movements passed leadership over to their successors, the result was often a change in the movement's strategy and tactics. When Jawaharlal Nehru (left photo, on the left) replaced Mahatma Gandhi (wearing a simple Indian *dhoti* rather than the Western dress favored by his colleagues) as leader of the Indian National Congress, the movement adopted a more secular posture. In China, Chiang Kai-shek (right photo, standing) took Sun Yat-sen's Nationalist Party in a more conservative direction after Sun's death in 1925.

How do these four leaders compare in terms of their roles in furthering political change in their respective countries?

Unfortunately for Chiang, Confucian ideas—at least in their institutional form—had been widely discredited by the failure of the traditional system to solve China's problems. With only a tenuous hold over the provinces, a growing Japanese threat in the north, and a world suffering from the Great Depression, Chiang made little progress. By repressing all opposition and censoring free expression, he alienated many intellectuals and moderates. A land reform program was enacted in 1930 but had little effect.

Chiang's government also made little progress in promoting industrial development. During the decade of precarious peace following the Northern Expedition, industrial growth averaged only about 1 percent annually. Much of the national wealth was in the hands of senior officials and close subordinates of the ruling elite. Military expenses consumed half the budget, and distressingly little was devoted to social and economic development.

The new government, then, had little success in dealing with China's deep-seated economic and social problems. The deadly combination of internal disintegration and foreign pressure now began to coincide with the virtual collapse of the global economic order during the Great Depression and the rise of militant political forces in Japan determined to extend Japanese influence and power in an unstable Asia. These forces and the turmoil they unleashed will be examined in the next chapter.

"Down with Confucius and Sons": Economic, Social, and Cultural Change in Republican China

The transformation of the old order that had begun at the end of the Qing era continued during the early Chinese republic. The industrial sector continued to grow, albeit slowly. Although about 75 percent of all industrial goods were still manually produced in the early 1930s, mechanization was beginning to replace manual labor in a number of traditional industries, notably in the manufacture of textile goods. Traditional Chinese exports, such as silk and tea, were hard-hit by the Great Depression, however, and manufacturing declined during the 1930s. In the countryside, farmers were often victimized by the

A Call for Revolt

In the fall of 1926, Nationalist and Communist forces moved north on their Northern Expedition to defeat the warlords. The young Communist Mao Zedong accompanied revolutionary troops to his home province of Hunan, where he submitted a report to the CCP Central Committee calling for a massive peasant revolt. The report shows his confidence that peasants could play an active role in the Chinese revolution despite the skepticism of many of his colleagues.

Mao Zedong, "The Peasant Movement in Hunan"

During my recent visit to Hunan I made a firsthand investigation of conditions. . . . In a very short time, . . . several hundred million peasants will rise like a mighty storm, . . . a force so swift and violent that no power, however great, will be able to hold it back. . . . They will sweep all the imperialists, warlords, corrupt officials, local tyrants, and evil gentry into their graves. Every revolutionary party and every revolutionary comrade will be put to the test, to be accepted or rejected as they decide. There are three alternatives. To march at their head and lead them? To trail behind them, gesticulating and criticizing? Or to stand in their way and oppose them? Every Chinese is free to choose, but events will force you to make the choice quickly.

The main targets of attack by the peasants are the local tyrants, the evil gentry and the lawless landlords, but in passing they also hit out against patriarchal ideas and institutions, against the corrupt officials in the cities and against bad practices and customs in the rural areas. . . . As a result, the privileges which the feudal landlords enjoyed for thousands of years are being shattered to pieces. . . . With the collapse of the power of the landlords, the peasant associations have now become the sole organs of authority, and the popular slogan "All power to the peasant associations" has become a reality.

The peasants' revolt disturbed the gentry's sweet dreams. When the news from the countryside reached the cities, it caused immediate uproar among the gentry. . . . From the middle social strata upwards to the Kuomintang right-wingers, there was not a single person who did not sum up the whole business in the phrase, "It's terrible!" . . . Even quite progressive people said, "Though terrible, it is inevitable in a revolution." In short, nobody could altogether deny the word "terrible." But . . . the fact is that the great peasant masses have risen to fulfill their historic mission. . . . What the peasants are doing is absolutely right; what they are doing is fine! "It's fine!" is the theory of the peasants and of all other revolutionaries. Every revolutionary comrade should know that the national revolution requires a great change in the countryside. The Revolution of 1911 did not bring about this change, hence its failure. This change is now taking place, and it is an important factor for the completion of the revolution. Every revolutionary comrade must support it, or he will be taking the stand of counterrevolution.

Why did Mao Zedong believe that the peasants could help bring about a social revolution in China? How does his vision compare with the reality of the Bolshevik Revolution in Russia?

Source: From *Selected Works of Mao Tse-Tung* (London: Lawrence and Wishart, Ltd., 1954), Vol. 1, pp. 21–23.

endemic conflict and the high taxes imposed by local warlords.

SOCIAL CHANGES Social changes followed shifts in the economy and the political culture. By 1915, the assault on the old system and values by educated youth was intense. The main focus of the attack was the Confucian concept of the family—in particular, filial piety and the subordination of women. Young people insisted on the right to choose their own mates and their own careers. Women began to demand rights and opportunities equal to those enjoyed by men (see the comparative essay "Out of the Doll's House" on p. 639). More broadly, progressives called for an end to the concept of duty to the community and praised the Western individualist ethos. The popular short story writer Lu Xun (loo SHUN) (Lu Hsun) criticized the Confucian concept of family as a "man-eating" system that degraded humanity. In a famous short story titled "Diary of a Madman," the protagonist remarks:

© Rene Burri/Magnum Photos

Mao Zedong on the Long March. In 1934, the Communist leader Mao Zedong led his bedraggled forces on the Long March from southern China to Yan'an, in the hills south of the Gobi Desert. The epic journey has ever since been celebrated as a symbol of the party's willingness to sacrifice for the revolutionary cause. In the photo shown here, Mao rides a white horse as he accompanies his followers on the march. Reportedly, he was the only participant allowed to ride a horse.

> I remember when I was four or five years old, sitting in the cool of the hall, my brother told me that if a man's parents were ill, he should cut off a piece of his flesh and boil it for them if he wanted to be considered a good son. I have only just realized that I have been living all these years in a place where for four thousand years they have been eating human flesh.[4]

Such criticisms did have some beneficial results. During the early republic, the tyranny of the old family system began to decline, at least in urban areas, under the impact of economic changes and the urgings of the New Culture intellectuals. Women began to escape their cloistered existence and seek education and employment. Free choice in marriage became commonplace among affluent families in the cities, where the teenage children of westernized elites aped the clothing, social habits, and even the musical tastes of their contemporaries in Europe and the United States.

But, as a rule, the new individualism and women's rights did not penetrate to the textile factories, where more than a million women worked in conditions resembling slave labor, or to the villages, where traditional attitudes and customs still held sway. Arranged marriages continued to be the rule rather than the exception, and concubinage remained common. According to a survey taken in the 1930s, well over two-thirds of the marriages even among urban couples had been arranged by their parents (see the box on p. 640).

CHRONOLOGY **Revolution in China**	
May Fourth demonstrations	1919
Formation of Chinese Communist Party	1921
Death of Sun Yat-sen	1925
Northern Expedition	1926–1928
Establishment of Nanjing Republic	1928
Long March	1934–1935

A NEW CULTURE Nowhere was the struggle between traditional and modern more visible than in the area of culture. Beginning in the New Culture era, radical reformists criticized traditional culture as the symbol and instrument of feudal oppression. During the 1920s and 1930s, Western literature and art became highly popular, especially among the urban middle class. Traditional culture continued to prevail among more conservative elements, however, and some intellectuals argued for a new art that would synthesize the best of Chinese and foreign culture. But the most creative artists were interested in imitating foreign trends, while traditionalists were more concerned with preservation.

Literature in particular was influenced by foreign ideas. Although most Chinese novels written after World War I dealt with Chinese subjects, they reflected the Western tendency toward social realism and often dealt with the new westernized middle class, as in *Midnight* by Mao Dun (mow DOON ["ow" as in "how"]), which describes the changing mores of Shanghai's urban elites. Another favorite theme was the disintegration of the traditional Confucian family—Ba Jin's novel *Family* is an example. Most of China's modern authors displayed a clear contempt for the past.

COMPARATIVE ESSAY

Out of the Doll's House

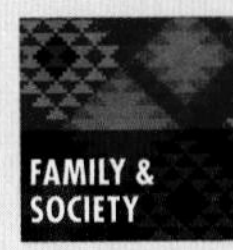

In Henrik Ibsen's play *A Doll's House* (1879), Nora Helmer informs her husband, Torvald, that she will no longer accept his control over her life and announces her intention to leave home to start her life anew (see the box on p. 531). When the outraged Torvald cites her sacred duties as wife and mother, Nora replies that she has other duties just as sacred, those to herself. "I can no longer be satisfied with what most people say," she declares. "I must think things out for myself."

To Ibsen's contemporaries, such remarks were revolutionary. In nineteenth-century Europe, the traditional characterization of the sexes, based on gender-defined social roles, had been elevated to a universal law. As the family wage earners, men went off to work, while women stayed home to care for home and family. Women were advised to accept their lot and play their role as effectively and gracefully as possible. In other parts of the world, women generally had even fewer rights. Often, as in traditional China, they were viewed as sex objects.

© Marc Charmet/CCI/The Art Archive at Art Resource, NY

The Chinese "Doll's House." A woman in traditional China binding her feet.

The ideal, however, did not always match the reality. With the advent of the Industrial Revolution, many women, especially those in the lower classes, were driven by the need for supplemental income to seek employment outside the home. Some women, inspired by the ideals of human dignity and freedom expressed during the Enlightenment and the French Revolution, began to protest against a tradition of female inferiority that had long kept them in a "doll's house" of male domination and to claim equal rights before the law.

The movement to liberate women first gained ground in English-speaking countries such as Great Britain and the United States, but it gradually spread to the European continent and then to colonies in Africa and Asia. By the early twentieth century, women's liberation movements were under way in parts of North Africa, the Middle East, and East Asia, calling for access to education, equal treatment before the law, and the right to vote. In China, a small minority of educated women began to agitate for equal rights with men.

Progress, however, was often agonizingly slow, especially in societies where traditional values had not been undermined by the Industrial Revolution. Colonialism had also been a double-edged sword, as the sexist bias of European officials combined with indigenous traditions of male superiority to marginalize women even further. As men moved to the cities to exploit opportunities provided by the colonial administration, women were left to cope with their traditional responsibilities in the villages, often without the safety net of male support that had sustained them during the precolonial era. With the advent of nationalist movements, the drive for women's rights in many colonial societies was subordinated to the goal of national independence. In some instances, too, women's liberation movements were led by educated elites who failed to take note of the concerns of working-class women.

To what extent, if at all, did women benefit from the policies applied by the Europeans in their colonies?

An Arranged Marriage

FAMILY & SOCIETY

Under Western influence, Chinese social customs changed dramatically for many urban elites in the interwar years. A vocal women's movement campaigned aggressively for universal suffrage and an end to sexual discrimination. Some progressives called for free choice in marriage and divorce and even for free love. By the 1930s, the government had taken some steps to free women from patriarchal marriage constraints. But life was generally unaffected in the villages, where traditional patterns held sway. This often created severe tensions between older and younger generations, as this passage from a novel by the popular twentieth-century writer Ba Jin (BAH JIN) shows.

Ba Jin, *Family*

Brought up with loving care, after studying with a private tutor for a number of years, Chueh-hsin entered middle school. One of the school's best students, he graduated four years later at the top of his class. He was very interested in physics and chemistry and hoped to study abroad, in Germany. . . .

In his fourth year at middle school, he lost his mother. . . . Chueh-hsin was aware of his loss, for he knew full well that nothing could replace the love of a mother. But her death left no irreparable wound in his heart; he was able to console himself with rosy dreams of his future. Moreover, he had someone who understood him and could comfort him—his pretty cousin Mei, "mei" for "plum blossom."

But then, one day, his dreams were shattered, cruelly and bitterly shattered. The evening he returned home carrying his diploma, the plaudits of his teachers and friends still ringing in his ears, his father called him into his room and said:

"Now that you've graduated, I want to arrange your marriage. Your grandfather is looking forward to having a great-grandson, and I, too, would like to be able to hold a grandson in my arms. You're old enough to be married; I won't feel easy until I fulfill my obligation to find you a wife. Although I didn't accumulate much money in my years away from home as an official, still I've put by enough for us to get along on. My health isn't what it used to be; I'm thinking of spending my time at home and having you help me run the household affairs. All the more reason you'll be needing a wife. I've already arranged a match with the Li family. The thirteenth of next month is a good day. We'll announce the engagement then. You can be married within the year. . . ."

Chueh-hsin did not utter a word of protest, nor did such a thought ever occur to him. He merely nodded to indicate his compliance with his father's wishes. But after he returned to his own room, and shut the door, he threw himself down on his bed, covered his head with the quilt and wept. He wept for his broken dreams.

He was deeply in love with Mei, but now his father had chosen another, a girl he had never seen, and said that he must marry within the year. What's more, his hopes of continuing his studies had burst like a bubble. It was a terrible shock to Chueh-hsin. His future was finished, his beautiful dreams shattered.

He cried his disappointment and bitterness. But the door was closed and Chueh-hsin's head was beneath the bedding. No one knew. He did not fight back, he never thought of resisting. He only bemoaned his fate. But he accepted it. He complied with his father's will without a trace of resentment. But in his heart he wept for himself, wept for the girl he adored—Mei, his "plum blossom."

Why does Chueh-hsin comply with the wishes of his father in the matter of his marriage? Why were arranged marriages so prevalent in traditional China?

Source: Excerpt from "Family" by Ba Jin. Copyright © 1964 Foreign Languages Press, 24 Baiwanzhuang Rd., Beijing 10037, P.R. China. Used with permission.

Japan Between the Wars

FOCUS QUESTION: How did Japan address the problems of nation building in the first decades of the twentieth century, and why did democratic institutions not take hold more effectively?

During the first two decades of the twentieth century, Japan made remarkable progress toward the creation of an advanced society on the Western model. The political system based on the Meiji Constitution of 1890 began to evolve along Western pluralistic lines, and a multiparty system took shape. The economic and social reforms launched during the Meiji era led to increasing prosperity and the development of a modern industrial and commercial sector.

Experiment in Democracy

During the first quarter of the twentieth century, Japanese political parties expanded their popular following and became increasingly competitive. Individual pressure groups began to appear, along with an independent press and a bill of rights. The influence of the old ruling oligarchy, the *genro*, had not yet been significantly challenged, however, nor had that of its ideological foundation, the *kokutai* (koh-kuh-TY).

These fragile democratic institutions were able to survive throughout the 1920s, often called the era of **Taisho** (TY-SHOH) **democracy**, from the reign title of the emperor. During this period, the military budget was reduced, and a suffrage bill enacted in 1925 granted the vote to all Japanese males. Although women were still disenfranchised, many women were active in the labor movement and in campaigning for social reforms.

But the era was also marked by growing social turmoil, and two opposing forces within the system were gearing up to challenge the prevailing wisdom. On the left, a Marxist labor movement began to take shape in the early 1920s. On the right, ultranationalist groups called for a rejection of Western models of development and a more militant approach to realizing national objectives.

This cultural conflict between old and new, indigenous and foreign, was reflected in literature. Japanese self-confidence had been restored after the victories over China and Russia and launched an age of cultural creativity in the early twentieth century. Fascination with Western literature gave birth to a striking new genre called the "I novel." Defying traditional Japanese reticence, some

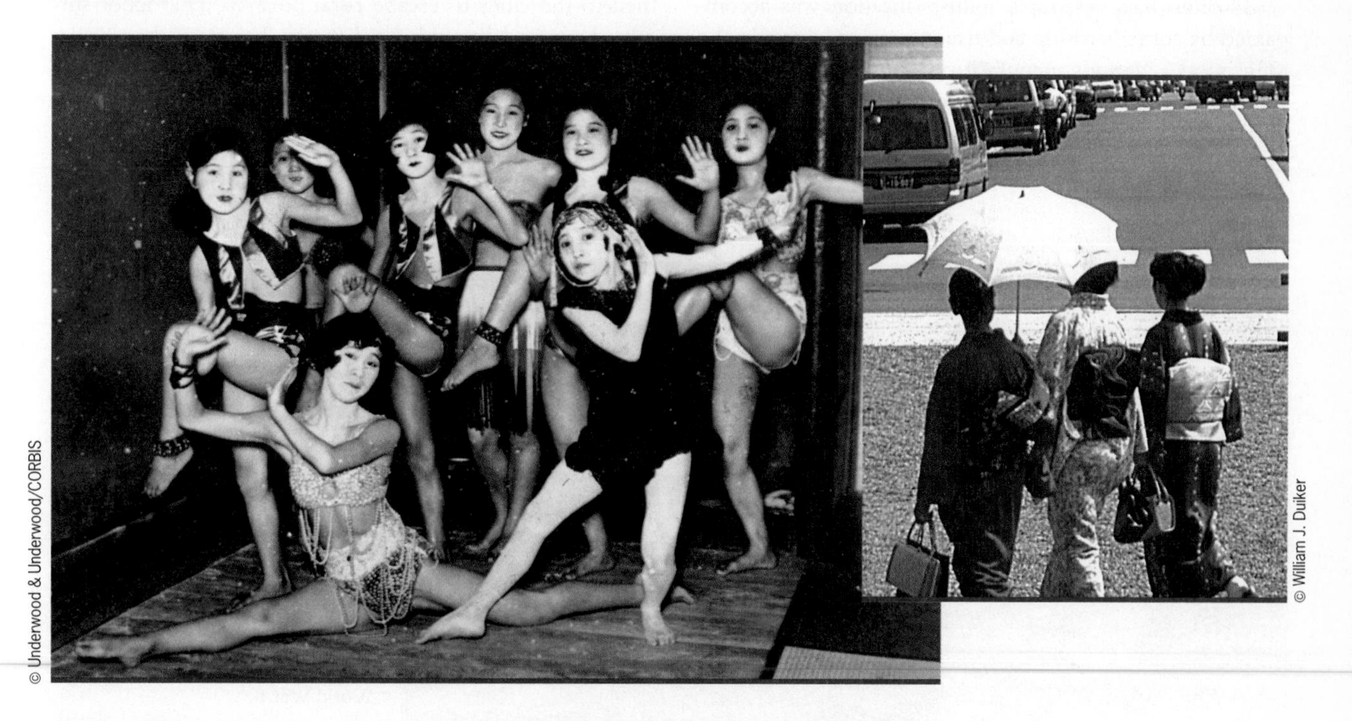

© Underwood & Underwood/CORBIS
© William J. Duiker

Geishas, Old and New. The geisha (GAY-shuh) ("accomplished person") was a symbol of old Japan. Dressed in traditional costumes, her body movements highly stylized, she served not only as an entertainer and an ornament but also as a beautiful purveyor of elite Japanese culture. That image was dramatically transformed in a new Japan that had been inundated by the influence of the modern West. In the photo on the left, geishas in early-twentieth-century Tokyo mimic Western fashions and dance positions. In the photo on the right, three young Japanese women in traditional costumes stroll in contemporary Kyoto.

authors reveled in self-exposure with confessions of their innermost thoughts. Others found release in the "proletarian literature" movement of the early 1920s. Inspired by Soviet literary examples, these authors wanted literature to serve socialist goals and improve the lives of the working class. Finally, some Japanese writers blended Western psychology with Japanese sensibility in exquisite novels reeking with nostalgia for the old Japan. One well-known example is *Some Prefer Nettles* (1929) by Junichiro Tanizaki (jun-ih-CHEE-roh tan-ih-ZAH-kee), which delicately juxtaposed the positive aspects of both traditional and modern Japan. By the 1930s, however, military censorship increasingly inhibited free literary expression.

A *Zaibatsu* Economy

Japan also continued to make impressive progress in economic development. Spurred by rising domestic demand and continued government investment in the economy, the production of raw materials tripled between 1900 and 1930, and industrial production increased more than twelvefold. Much of the increase went into exports, and Western manufacturers began to complain about competition from the Japanese.

As often happens, rapid industrialization was accompanied by some hardship and rising social tensions. In the Meiji model, various manufacturing processes were concentrated in a single enterprise, the ***zaibatsu*** (zy-BAHT-soo), or financial clique. Some of these firms were existing companies that had the capital and the foresight to move into new areas. Others were formed by enterprising samurai, who used their status and managerial experience to good account in a new environment. Whatever their origins, these firms, often with official encouragement, developed into large conglomerates that controlled major segments of the Japanese economy. By 1937, the four largest *zaibatsu*—Mitsui (MIT-swee), Mitsubishi (mit-soo-BEE-shee), Sumitomo (soo-mee-TOH-moh), and Yasuda (yah-SOO-duh)—controlled 21 percent of the banking industry, 26 percent of mining, 35 percent of shipbuilding, 38 percent of commercial shipping, and more than 60 percent of paper manufacturing and insurance.

This concentration of power and wealth in a few industrial combines created problems in Japanese society. In the first place, it resulted in the emergence of a dual economy: on the one hand, a modern industry characterized by up-to-date methods and massive government subsidies, and on the other, a traditional manufacturing sector characterized by conservative methods and small-scale production techniques.

Concentration of wealth also led to growing economic inequalities. As we have seen, economic growth had been achieved at the expense of the peasants, many of whom fled to the cities to escape rural poverty. That labor surplus benefited the industrial sector, but the urban proletariat was still poorly paid and ill-housed. A rapid increase in population (the total population of the Japanese islands increased from an estimated 43 million in 1900 to 73 million in 1940) led to food shortages and

© Topical Press Agency/Getty Images

The Great Tokyo Earthquake. On September 1, 1923, a massive earthquake struck the central Japanese island of Honshu, causing more than 130,000 deaths and virtually demolishing the capital city of Tokyo. Though the quake was a national tragedy, it also came to symbolize the ingenuity of the Japanese people, who rapidly reconstructed the city in a new and more modern style. That unity of national purpose would be demonstrated again a quarter of a century later in Japan's swift recovery from the devastation of World War II.

rising unemployment. In the meantime, those left on the farm continued to suffer. As late as the beginning of World War II, an estimated one-half of all Japanese farmers were tenants.

Shidehara Diplomacy

A final problem for Japanese leaders in the post-Meiji era was the familiar dilemma of finding sources of raw materials and foreign markets for the nation's manufactured goods. Until World War I, Japan had dealt with the problem by seizing territories such as Taiwan, Korea, and southern Manchuria and transforming them into colonies or protectorates. That policy had begun to arouse the concern and, in some cases, the hostility of the Western nations. China was also becoming apprehensive; as we have seen, Japanese demands for Shandong Province at the Paris Peace Conference in 1919 aroused massive protests in China.

The United States was especially concerned about Japanese aggressiveness. Although the United States had been less active than some European states in pursuing colonies in the Pacific, it had a strong interest in keeping the area open for U.S. commercial activities. In 1922, in Washington, D.C., the United States convened a major conference of nations with interests in the Pacific to discuss problems of regional security. The Washington Conference led to agreements on several issues, but the major accomplishment was a nine-power treaty recognizing the territorial integrity of China and the Open Door. The other participants induced Japan to accept these provisions by accepting its special position in Manchuria.

During the remainder of the 1920s, Japan attempted to play by the rules laid down at the Washington Conference. Known as Shidehara (shee-deh-HAH-rah) diplomacy, after the foreign minister (and later prime minister) who attempted to carry it out, this policy sought to achieve Japanese interests in Asia through diplomatic and economic means. But this approach came under severe pressure as Japanese industrialists began to move into new areas, such as chemicals, mining, and the manufacturing of appliances and automobiles. Because such industries needed resources not found in abundance locally, the Japanese government came under increasing pressure to find new sources abroad.

THE RISE OF MILITANT NATIONALISM In the early 1930s, with the onset of the Great Depression and growing tensions in the international arena, nationalist forces rose to dominance in the Japanese government. The changes that occurred in the 1930s, which we shall discuss in Chapter 25, were not in the constitution or the institutional structure, which remained essentially intact, but in the composition and attitudes of the ruling group. Party leaders during the 1920s had attempted to realize Tokyo's aspirations within the existing global political and economic framework. The military officers and ultranationalist politicians who dominated the government in the 1930s were convinced that the diplomacy of the 1920s had failed and advocated a more aggressive approach to protecting national interests in a brutal and competitive world.

TAISHO DEMOCRACY: AN ABERRATION? The dramatic shift in Japanese political culture that occurred in the early 1930s has caused some historians to question the breadth and depth of the trend toward democratic practices in the 1920s. Was Taisho democracy merely a fragile attempt at comparative liberalization in a framework dominated by the Meiji vision of empire and *kokutai*? Or was the militant nationalism of the 1930s an aberration brought on by the Great Depression, which caused the inexorable emergence of democracy in Japan to stall?

Clearly, there is some truth in both contentions. A process of democratization was taking place in Japan during the first decades of the twentieth century, but without shaking the essential core of the Meiji concept of the state. When the "liberal" approach of the 1920s failed to solve the problems of the day, the shallow roots of democracy in Japan were exposed, and the shift toward a more aggressive approach became inevitable.

Still, the course of Japanese history after World War II (see Chapter 30) suggests that the emergence of multiparty democracy in the 1920s was not an aberration but a natural consequence of evolutionary trends in Japanese society. The seeds of democracy nurtured during the Taisho era were nipped in the bud by the cataclysmic effects of the Great Depression, but in the more conducive climate after World War II, a democratic system—suitably adjusted to Japanese soil—reached full flower.

Nationalism and Dictatorship in Latin America

FOCUS QUESTIONS: What problems did the nations of Latin America face in the interwar years? To what degree were they a consequence of foreign influence?

Although the nations of Latin America played little role in World War I, that conflict nevertheless exerted an impact on the region, especially on its economy. By the end of the 1920s, the region was also strongly influenced by another event of global proportions—the Great Depression.

A Changing Economy

At the beginning of the twentieth century, virtually all of Latin America, except the three Guianas, British Honduras, and some of the Caribbean islands, had achieved independence (see Map 24.2). The economy of the region was based largely on the export of foodstuffs and raw materials. Some countries relied on exports of only one or two products. Argentina, for example, exported primarily beef and wheat; Chile, nitrates and copper; Brazil and the Caribbean nations, sugar; and the Central American states, bananas. A few reaped large profits from these exports, but for the majority of the population, the returns were meager.

THE ROLE OF THE YANKEE DOLLAR World War I led to a decline in European investment in Latin America and a rise in the U.S. role in the local economies. By the late 1920s, the United States had replaced Great Britain as the foremost source of investment in Latin America. Unlike the British, however, U.S. investors put their funds directly into production enterprises, causing large segments of the area's export industries to fall into American hands. A number of Central American states, for example, were popularly labeled "banana republics" because of the power and influence of the U.S.-owned United Fruit Company. American firms also dominated the copper mining industry in Chile and Peru and the oil industry in Mexico, Peru, and Bolivia.

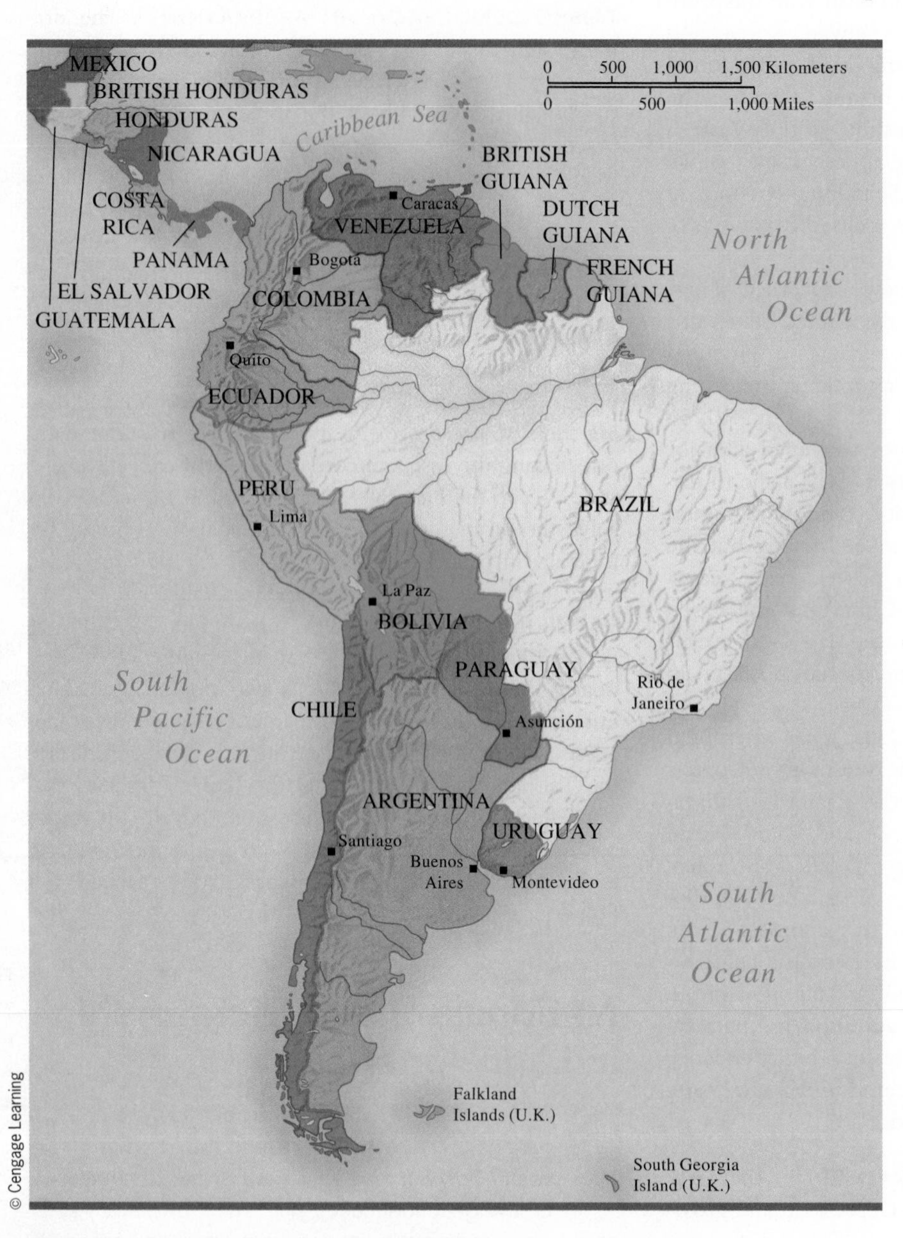

© Cengage Learning

MAP 24.2 Latin America in the First Half of the Twentieth Century. Shown here are the boundaries dividing the countries of Latin America after the independence movements of the nineteenth century.

Q *Which areas remained under European rule?*

The Effects of Dependency

During the late nineteenth century, most governments in Latin America had been increasingly dominated by landed or military elites, who controlled the mass of the population—mostly impoverished peasants—by the blatant use of military force. This trend toward authoritarianism increased during the 1930s as domestic instability caused by the effects of the Great Depression led to the creation of dictatorships throughout the region. This trend was especially evident in Argentina and Brazil and to a lesser degree in Mexico—three countries that together possessed more than half of the land and wealth of Latin America.

ARGENTINA The political domination of Argentina by an elite minority often had disastrous effects. The Argentine government, controlled by landowners who had benefited from the export of beef and wheat, was slow to recognize the importance of establishing a local industrial base. In 1916, Hipólito Irigoyen (ee-POH-lee-toh ee-ree-GOH-yen) (1852–1933), head of the Radical Party, was elected president on a program to improve conditions for the middle and lower classes. Little was achieved, however, as the party became increasingly corrupt and drew closer to the large landowners. In 1930, the army overthrew Irigoyen's government and reestablished the power of the landed class. But their efforts to return to the previous export economy and suppress the growing influence of the labor unions failed.

BRAZIL Brazil followed a similar path. In 1889, the army replaced the Brazilian monarchy with a republic, but it was controlled by landed elites, many of whom derived their wealth from vast rubber and coffee plantations. Exports of Brazilian rubber dominated the world market until just before World War I. When it proved easier to produce rubber in Southeast Asia, however, Brazilian exports suddenly collapsed, leaving the economy of the Amazon River basin in ruins.

The coffee industry also suffered problems. In 1900, three-quarters of the world's coffee was grown in Brazil. As in Argentina, the ruling oligarchy ignored the importance of establishing an urban industrial base. When the Great Depression ravaged profits from coffee exports, a wealthy rancher, Getúlio Vargas (zhi-TOO-lyoo VAHR-guhs) (1883–1954), seized power and ruled the country as president from 1930 to 1945. At first, Vargas sought to appease workers by instituting an eight-hour workday and a minimum wage, but influenced by the apparent success of fascist regimes in Europe, he ruled by increasingly autocratic means and relied on a police force that used torture to silence his opponents. His industrial policy was relatively enlightened, however, and by the end of World War II, Brazil had become Latin America's major industrial power. In 1945, the army, fearing that Vargas might prolong his power illegally after calling for new elections, forced him to resign.

MEXICO After the dictator Porfirio Díaz (por-FEER-yoh DEE-ahs) was ousted from power in 1910 (see Chapter 20), Mexico entered a state of turbulence that lasted for years. The ineffective leaders who followed Díaz were unable to solve the country's economic problems or bring an end to the civil strife. In southern Mexico, the landless peasants responded eagerly to Emiliano Zapata (ee-mee-LYAH-noh zup-PAH-tuh) (1879–1919), when he called for agrarian reform and began to seize the haciendas of wealthy landholders.

CHRONOLOGY Latin America Between the Wars	
Hipólito Irigoyen becomes president of Argentina	1916
Argentinian military overthrows Irigoyen	1930
Rule of Getúlio Vargas in Brazil	1930–1945
Beginning of Good Neighbor policy	1933
Presidency of Lázaro Cárdenas in Mexico	1934–1940

For the next several years, Zapata and rebel leader Pancho Villa (pahn-CHOH VEE-uh) (1878–1923), who operated in the northern state of Chihuahua (chih-WAH-wah), became an important political force by calling for measures to redress the grievances of the poor. But neither fully grasped the challenges facing the country, and power eventually gravitated to a more moderate group of reformists around the Constitutionalist Party. They were intent on breaking the power of the great landed families and U.S. corporations, but without engaging in radical land reform or the nationalization of property. After a bloody conflict that cost the lives of thousands, the moderates consolidated power, and in 1917, they promulgated a new constitution that established a strong presidency, initiated land reform, established limits on foreign investment, and set an agenda for social welfare programs.

In 1920, the Constitutionalist Party leader Alvaro Obregón (AHL-vah-roh oh-bree-GAHN) assumed the presidency and began to carry out his reform program. But real change did not take place until the presidency of General Lázaro Cárdenas (LAH-zah-roh KAHR-day-nahss) (1895–1970) in 1934. Cárdenas ordered the redistribution of 44 million acres of land controlled by landed elites and seized control of the oil industry, which had hitherto been dominated by major U.S. oil companies. In 1933, in a bid to improve relations with Latin American countries, U.S. President Franklin D. Roosevelt had announced the **Good Neighbor policy**, which renounced the use of U.S. military force in the region. Now Roosevelt refused to intervene, and eventually Mexico agreed to compensate U.S. oil companies for their lost property. It then set up PEMEX, a governmental organization, to run the oil industry.

Latin American Culture

The first half of the twentieth century witnessed a dramatic increase in literary activity in Latin America. Much of it reflected the region's ambivalent relationship with Europe and the United States. Many authors, while experimenting with imported modernist styles, also used native themes and social issues to express Latin America's unique identity. In *The Underdogs* (1915), for example,

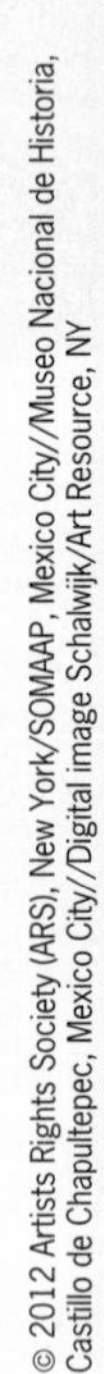
© 2012 Artists Rights Society (ARS), New York/SOMAAP, Mexico City//Museo Nacional de Historia, Castillo de Chapultepec, Mexico City//Digital image Schalwijk/Art Resource, NY

Struggle for the Banner. Like Diego Rivera, David Alfaro Siqueiros (dah-VEED al-FAHR-oh see-KAY-rohss) (1896–1974) decorated public buildings with large murals that celebrated the Mexican Revolution and the workers' and peasants' struggle for freedom. Beginning in the 1930s, Siqueiros expressed sympathy for the exploited and downtrodden peoples of Mexico in dramatic frescoes such as this one. He painted similar murals in Uruguay, Argentina, and Brazil and was once expelled from the United States, where his political art and views were considered too radical.

Mariano Azuela (mahr-YAHN-oh ah-SWAY-luh) (1873–1952) presented a sympathetic but not uncritical portrait of the Mexican Revolution.

Some writers extolled the region's vast virgin lands and the diversity of its peoples. In *Don Segundo Sombra* (1926), Ricardo Guiraldes (ree-KAHR-doh gwee-RAHL-dess) (1886–1927) celebrated the life of the gaucho (cowboy), defining Argentina's hope and strength as the enlightened management of its fertile earth. In *Dona Barbara* (1929), Romulo Gallegos (ROH-moo-loh gay-YAY-gohs) (1884–1969) wrote in a similar vein about his native Venezuela. Other authors pursued the theme of solitude and detachment, reflecting the region's physical separation from the rest of the world.

Latin American artists followed their literary counterparts in joining the Modernist movement in Europe, yet they too were eager to celebrate the emergence of a new regional and national essence. In Mexico, where the government provided financial support for painting murals on public buildings, the artist Diego Rivera (DYAY-goh rih-VAIR-uh) (1886–1957) began to produce a monumental style of mural art that served two purposes: to illustrate the national past by portraying Aztec legends and folk customs and to popularize a political message in favor of realizing the social goals of the Mexican Revolution. His wife, Frida Kahlo (FREE-duh KAH-loh) (1907–1954), incorporated Surrealist whimsy in her own paintings, many of which were portraits of herself and her family.

CHAPTER SUMMARY

The turmoil brought about by World War I not only resulted in the destruction of several major Western empires and a redrawing of the map of Europe but also opened the door to political and social upheavals elsewhere in the world. In the Middle East, the decline and fall of the Ottoman Empire led to the creation of the secular republic of Turkey. The state of Saudi Arabia emerged in the Arabian peninsula, and Palestine became a source of tension between newly arrived Jewish immigrants and longtime Muslim residents.

Other parts of Asia and Africa also witnessed the rise of movements for national independence. In many cases, these movements were spearheaded by local leaders who had been educated in Europe or the United States. In India, Mahatma Gandhi and his campaign of civil disobedience played a crucial role in his country's bid to be free of British rule. Communist movements also began to emerge in Asian societies as radical elements sought new methods of bringing about the overthrow of Western imperialism. Japan continued to follow its own path to modernization, which, although successful from an economic perspective, took a menacing turn during the 1930s.

Between 1919 and 1939, China experienced a dramatic struggle to establish a modern nation. Two dynamic political organizations—the Nationalists and the Communists—competed for legitimacy as the rightful heirs of the old order. At first, they formed an alliance in an effort to defeat their common adversaries, but cooperation ultimately turned to conflict. The Nationalists under Chiang Kai-shek emerged supreme, but Chiang found it difficult to control the remnants of the warlord regime in China, while the Great Depression undermined his efforts to build an industrial nation.

During the interwar years, the nations of Latin America faced severe economic problems because of their dependence on exports. Increasing U.S. investments in Latin America contributed to growing hostility toward the powerful neighbor to the north. The Great Depression forced the region to begin developing new industries, but it also led to the rise of authoritarian governments, some of them modeled after the fascist regimes of Italy and Germany.

By demolishing the remnants of their old civilization on the battlefields of World War I, Europeans had inadvertently encouraged the subject peoples of their vast colonial empires to begin their own movements for national independence. The process was by no means completed in the two decades following the Treaty of Versailles, but the bonds of imperial rule had been severely strained. Once Europeans began to weaken themselves in the even more destructive conflict of World War II, the hopes of African and Asian peoples for national independence and freedom could at last be realized. It is to that devastating world conflict that we must now turn.

CHAPTER TIMELINE

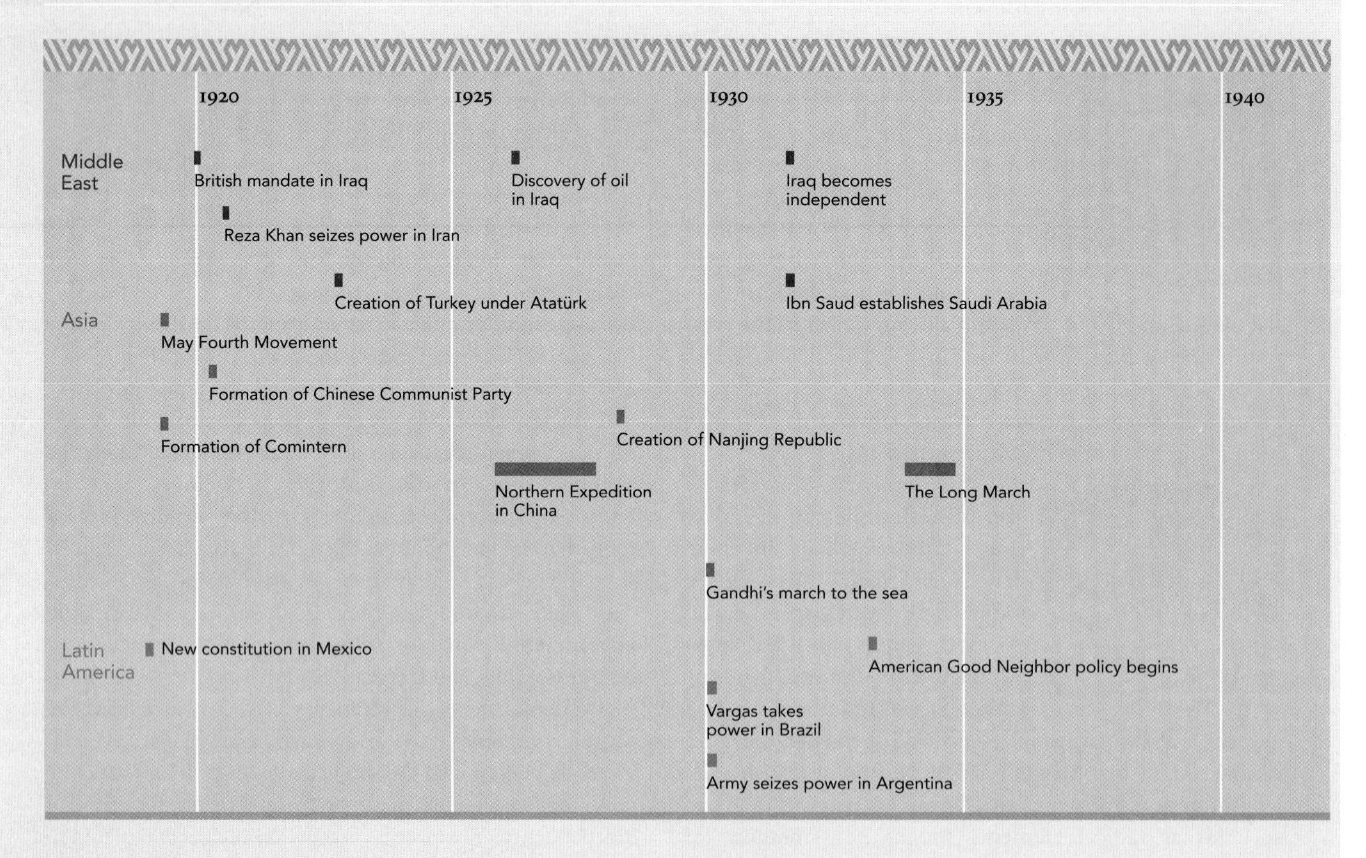

CHAPTER REVIEW

Upon Reflection

Q In what ways did Japan's political system and social structure in the interwar years combine modern and traditional elements? How successful was the attempt to create a modern political system while retaining indigenous traditions of civil obedience and loyalty to the emperor?

Q During the early twentieth century did conditions for women change for the better or for the worse in the countries discussed in this chapter? Why?

Q Communist parties were established in many Asian societies in the years immediately following the Bolshevik Revolution. How successful were these parties in winning popular support and achieving their goals?

Key Terms

satyagraha (p. 625)
civil disobedience (p. 625)
Young Turks (p. 627)
Communist International (Comintern) (p. 632)
New Culture Movement (p. 634)
Taisho democracy (p. 641)
zaibatsu (p. 642)
Good Neighbor policy (p. 645)

Suggested Reading

NATIONALISM The most up-to-date survey of modern nationalism is **E. Gellner, *Nations and Nationalism,*** 2nd ed. (Ithaca, N.Y., 2009), but it has little to say about the non-Western world. For a provocative study of the roots of nationalism in Asia, see **B. Anderson, *Imagined Communities: Reflections on the Origins and Spread of Nationalism*** (London, 1983).

INDIA There have been a number of studies of Mahatma Gandhi and his ideas. See, for example, **S. Wolpert, *Gandhi's Passion: The Life and Legacy of Mahatma Gandhi*** (Oxford, 1999), and **D. Dalton, *Mahatma Gandhi: Nonviolent Power in Action*** (New York, 1995). For a study of Nehru, see **J. M. Brown, *Nehru*** (New York, 2000).

MIDDLE EAST For a general survey of events in the Middle East in the interwar era, see **E. Bogle, *The***

Modern Middle East: From Imperialism to Freedom (Upper Saddle River, N.J., 1996). For more specialized studies, see **I. Gershoni et al.,** ***Egypt, Islam, and the Arabs: The Search for Egyptian Nationhood*** (Oxford, 1993), and **W. Laqueur,** ***A History of Zionism: From the French Revolution to the Establishment of the State of Israel*** (New York, 1996). The role of Atatürk is examined in **A. Mango,** ***Atatürk: The Biography of the Founder of Modern Turkey*** (New York, 2000). The Palestinian issue is dealt with in **B. Morris,** ***Righteous Victims: The Palestinian Conflict, 1880–2000*** (New York, 2001). On the founding of Iraq, see **S. Mackey,** ***The Reckoning: Iraq and the Legacy of Saddam Hussein*** (New York, 2002). For a penetrating account of the fall of the Ottoman Empire and its consequences for the postwar era, see **D. Fromkin,** ***A Peace to End All Peace: The Fall of the Ottoman Empire and the Creation of the Modern Middle East*** (New York, 2001).

CHINA AND JAPAN On the early Chinese republic, a good study is **J. Fitzgerald,** ***Awakening China: Politics, Culture, and Class in the Nationalist Revolution*** (Stanford, Calif., 1996). The rise of the Chinese Communist Party is charted in **A. Dirlik,** ***The Origins of Chinese Communism*** (Oxford, 1989). Also see **J. Taylor,** ***The Generalissimo: Chiang Kai-shek and the Struggle for Modern China*** (Cambridge, Mass., 2009). On Japan, see **J. McLain,** ***Japan: A Modern History*** (New York, 2001).

LATIN AMERICA For an overview of Latin American history during the interwar period, see **J. Chasteen,** ***Born in Blood and Fire: A Concise History of Latin America,*** 2nd ed. (New York, 2005). For documents, see **J. Wood** and **J. Chasteen, eds.,** ***Problems in Latin American History: Sources and Interpretations,*** 3rd ed. (New York, 2009).

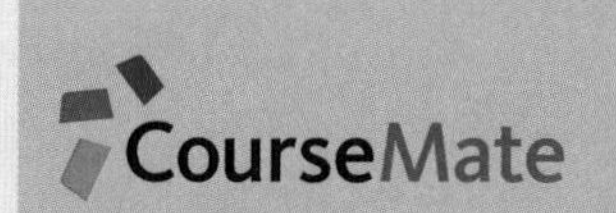

Visit the CourseMate website at **www.cengagebrain.com** for additional study tools and review materials for this chapter.

CHAPTER 25

The Crisis Deepens: World War II

© Hugo Jaeger/Time Life Pictures//Getty Images

Adolf Hitler salutes military leaders and soldiers during a military rally.

CHAPTER OUTLINE AND FOCUS QUESTIONS

Retreat from Democracy: Dictatorial Regimes

Q What are the characteristics of totalitarian states, and to what degree were these characteristics present in Fascist Italy, Nazi Germany, and Stalinist Russia? To what extent was Japan a totalitarian state?

The Path to War

Q What were the underlying causes of World War II, and what specific steps taken by Nazi Germany and Japan led to war?

World War II

Q What were the main events of World War II in Europe and Asia?

The New Order

Q What was the nature of the new orders that Germany and Japan attempted to establish in the territories they occupied?

The Home Front

Q What were conditions like on the home front for the major belligerents in World War II?

Aftermath of the War

Q What were the costs of World War II? How did World War II affect the European nations' colonial empires? How did the Allies' visions of the postwar differ, and how did these differences contribute to the emergence of the Cold War?

CRITICAL THINKING

Q What was the relationship between World War I and World War II, and how did the ways in which the wars were fought differ?

ON FEBRUARY 3, 1933, three days after he had been appointed chancellor of Germany, Adolf Hitler met secretly with Germany's leading generals. He revealed to them his desire to remove the "cancer of democracy," create a new authoritarian leadership, and forge a new domestic unity. All Germans would need to realize that "only a struggle can save us and that everything else must be subordinated to this idea." Since Germany's living space was too small for its people, Hitler said, Germany must rearm and prepare for "the conquest of new living space in the east and its ruthless Germanization." Even before he had consolidated his power, Adolf Hitler had a clear vision of his goals, and their implementation meant another war.

World War II in Europe was clearly Hitler's war. Although other countries may have helped make the war possible by not resisting Hitler earlier, it was Nazi Germany's actions that made World War II inevitable.

But World War II was more than just Hitler's war. It was in fact two separate and parallel conflicts, one provoked by the ambitions of Germany in Europe and the other by the ambitions of Japan in Asia. Around the same time that Hitler was consolidating his power in the early 1930s, the United States and major European nations raised the tariffs they imposed on Japanese imports in a desperate effort to protect local businesses and jobs. In response, militant groups in Tokyo began to argue that Japan must obtain by violent action what it could not secure by peaceful means. By 1941, when the United States became embroiled in both wars, the two had merged into a single global conflict.

Although World War I had been described as a total war, World War II was even more so and was fought on a scale unheard of in history. Almost everyone in the warring countries was involved in one way or another: as soldiers; as workers in wartime industries; as ordinary citizens subject to invading armies, military occupation, or bombing raids; as refugees; or as victims of mass extermination. The world had never witnessed such widespread human-induced death and destruction.

Retreat from Democracy: Dictatorial Regimes

FOCUS QUESTIONS: What are the characteristics of totalitarian states, and to what degree were these characteristics present in Fascist Italy, Nazi Germany, and Stalinist Russia? To what extent was Japan a totalitarian state?

The rise of dictatorial regimes in the 1930s had a great deal to do with the coming of World War II. By 1939, only two major states in Europe, France and Great Britain, remained democratic. Italy and Germany had succumbed to the political movement called **fascism**, and Soviet Russia under Stalin moved toward repressive totalitarianism. A host of other European states and Latin American countries adopted authoritarian structures of various kinds, while a militarist regime in Japan moved that country down the path to war.

The dictatorial regimes between the wars assumed both old and new forms. Dictatorship was not new, but the modern **totalitarian state** was. The totalitarian regimes, best exemplified by Stalinist Russia and Nazi Germany, greatly extended the functions and power of the central state. The new "total states" expected the active loyalty and commitment of citizens to the regime's goal, whether it be war, a socialist society, or a thousand-year Reich (RYKH) (empire). They used modern mass propaganda techniques and high-speed communications to conquer the minds and hearts of their subjects. The total state sought to control not only the economic, political, and social aspects of life but the intellectual and cultural aspects as well.

The modern totalitarian state was to be led by a single leader and a single party. It ruthlessly rejected the liberal ideal of limited government power and constitutional guarantees of individual freedoms. Indeed, individual freedom was to be subordinated to the collective will of the masses, organized and determined for them by the leader or leaders. Modern technology also gave total states unprecedented police controls to enforce their wishes on their subjects.

The Birth of Fascism

In the early 1920s, Benito Mussolini (buh-NEE-toh moos-suh-LEE-nee) (1883–1945) bestowed on Italy the first successful fascist movement in Europe. In 1919, Mussolini, a veteran of World War I, had established a new political group, the *Fascio di Combattimento* (FASH-ee-oh dee com-bat-ee-MEN-toh) (League of Combat), which won support from middle-class industrialists fearful of working-class agitation and large landowners who objected to strikes by farmers. The movement gained momentum as Mussolini's nationalist rhetoric and the middle-class fear of socialism, Communist revolution, and disorder made the Fascists seem more and more attractive. On October 29, 1922, after Mussolini and the Fascists threatened to march on Rome if they were not given power, King Victor Emmanuel (1900–1946) capitulated and made Mussolini prime minister of Italy.

By 1926, Mussolini had established the institutional framework for a Fascist dictatorship. The prime minister was made "head of government" with the power to legislate by decree. A law empowered the police to arrest and confine anybody for both nonpolitical and political crimes without pressing charges. The government was given the power to dissolve political and cultural associations. In 1926, all anti-Fascist parties were outlawed, and a secret police force was established. By the end of the year, Mussolini ruled Italy as *Il Duce* (eel DOO-chay), the leader.

Mussolini conceived of the Fascist state as totalitarian: "Fascism is totalitarian, and the Fascist State, the synthesis and unity of all values, interprets, develops and gives strength to the whole life of the people."[1] Mussolini did try to create a police state, but it was not very effective. Likewise, the Italian Fascists' attempt to exercise control over all forms of mass media, including newspapers, radio, and cinema, so that they could use propaganda as an instrument to integrate the masses into the state, was rarely effective. Most commonly, Fascist propaganda was disseminated through simple slogans, such as "Mussolini is always right," plastered on walls all over Italy.

The Fascists portrayed the family as the pillar of the state and women as the basic foundation of the family. "Woman into the home" became the Fascist slogan. Women were to be homemakers and baby producers, "their natural and fundamental mission in life," according to Mussolini, for population growth was viewed as an indicator of national strength. Employment outside the home might distract women from conception: "It forms an independence and consequent physical and moral habits contrary to child bearing."[2]

Despite the instruments of repression, the use of propaganda, and the creation of numerous Fascist organizations, Mussolini never achieved the degree of totalitarian control attained in Hitler's Germany or Stalin's Soviet Union. Mussolini and the Fascist Party never completely destroyed the old power structure, and they were soon overshadowed by a much more powerful fascist movement to the north.

Hitler and Nazi Germany

In 1923, a small rightist party led by an obscure Austrian rabble-rouser named Adolf Hitler (1889–1945) attempted to seize power in southern Germany in the notorious Beer Hall Putsch. Although the effort failed, the attempted putsch brought Hitler and the Nazis to national prominence.

HITLER'S RISE TO POWER, 1919–1933 At the end of World War I, after four years of service on the Western Front, Hitler went to Munich and decided to enter politics. In 1919, he joined the obscure German Workers' Party, one of a number of right-wing extreme nationalist parties in Munich. By the summer of 1921, Hitler had assumed control of the party, which he renamed the National Socialist German Workers' Party (NSDAP), or Nazi Party for short. In two years, membership reached 55,000, including 15,000 in the party militia known as the SA, the *Sturmabteilung* (SHTOORM-ap-ty-loonk) (Storm Troops).

Overconfident, Hitler staged an armed uprising against the government in Munich in November 1923. The so-called Beer Hall Putsch was quickly crushed, and Hitler was sentenced to prison. During his brief stay in jail, he wrote *Mein Kampf* (myn KAHMPF) (*My Struggle*), an autobiographical account of his movement and its underlying ideology. Extreme German nationalism, virulent anti-Semitism, and anticommunism are linked together by a social Darwinian theory of struggle that stresses the right of superior nations to *Lebensraum* (LAY-benz-rown) (living space) through expansion and the right of superior individuals to secure authoritarian leadership over the masses.

During his imprisonment, Hitler also came to the realization that the Nazis would have to come to power by constitutional means, not by overthrowing the Weimar (VY-mar) Republic. After his release from prison, Hitler reorganized the Nazi Party and competed for votes with the other political parties. By 1929, the Nazis had a national party organization.

Three years later, the Nazi Party had 800,000 members and had become the largest party in the Reichstag (RYKHSS-tahk). Germany's economic difficulties were a crucial factor in the Nazis' rise to power. Unemployment rose dramatically, from 4 million in 1931 to 6 million by the winter of 1932. Claiming to stand above all differences, Hitler promised that he would create a new Germany free of class differences and party infighting. His appeal to national pride, national honor, and traditional militarism struck receptive chords in his listeners. After attending one of Hitler's rallies, a schoolteacher in Hamburg said: "When the speech was over, there was roaring enthusiasm and applause. . . . Then he went—How many look up to him with touching faith as their savior, their deliverer from unbearable distress."[3]

Increasingly, the right-wing elites of Germany—the industrial magnates, landed aristocrats, military establishment, and higher bureaucrats—came to see Hitler as the man who had the mass support to establish a right-wing, authoritarian regime that would save Germany and their privileged positions from a Communist takeover. Under pressure, since the Nazi Party had the largest share of seats in the Reichstag, President Paul von Hindenburg agreed to allow Hitler to become chancellor (on January 30, 1933) and form a new government.

Within two months, Hitler had laid the foundations for the Nazis' complete control over Germany. The crowning step in Hitler's "legal seizure" of power came on March 23, when the Reichstag, by a two-thirds vote, passed the Enabling Act, which empowered the government to dispense with constitutional forms for four years while it issued laws to deal with the country's problems.

With their new source of power, the Nazis acted quickly to bring all institutions under Nazi control. The civil service was purged of Jews and democratic elements, concentration camps were established for opponents of the new regime, trade unions were dissolved, and all political parties except the Nazis were abolished. By the end of the summer of 1933, Hitler and the Nazis had established the foundations for a totalitarian state. When Hindenburg died on August 2, 1934, the office of Reich president was abolished, and Hitler became *der Führer* ((FYOOR-ur) (the leader)—sole ruler of Germany.

THE NAZI STATE, 1933–1939 Having smashed the parliamentary state, Hitler now felt the real task was at hand: to develop the "total state." Hitler's goal was the development of an Aryan racial state that would dominate Europe and possibly the world for generations to come. Hitler stated:

> We must develop organizations in which an individual's entire life can take place. Then every activity and every need of every individual will be regulated by the collectivity represented by the party. There is no longer any arbitrary will, there are no longer any free realms in which the individual belongs to himself. . . . The time of personal happiness is over.[4]

The Nazis pursued the realization of this totalitarian ideal in a variety of ways.

Mass demonstrations and spectacles were employed to integrate the German nation into a collective fellowship and to mobilize it as an instrument for Hitler's policies. These mass demonstrations, especially the party rallies that were held in Nuremberg every September, combined the symbolism of a religious service with the merriment of a popular amusement and usually evoked mass enthusiasm and excitement.

Despite the symbolism and Hitler's goal of establishing an all-powerful government that would maintain absolute control and order, in actuality, Nazi Germany was the scene of almost constant personal and institutional conflict, which resulted in administrative chaos. Struggle characterized relationships within the party, within the state, and between party and state. Hitler, of course, remained the ultimate decision maker and absolute ruler.

In the economic sphere, Hitler and the Nazis also worked to establish control. Although the regime used public works projects and "pump-priming" grants to private construction firms to foster employment and end the depression, there is little doubt that rearmament contributed far more to solving the unemployment problem. Unemployment, which had stood at 6 million in 1932, dropped to 2.6 million in 1934 and less than 500,000 in 1937. This was an important factor in convincing many Germans to accept the new regime, despite its excesses.

For Germans who needed coercion, the Nazi total state had its instruments of terror. Especially important were the *Schutzstaffel* (SHOOTS-shtah-fuhn) (guard squadrons), known simply as the SS. The SS, under the direction of Heinrich Himmler (1900–1945), came to control all of the regular and secret police forces. Himmler and the SS functioned on the basis of two principles: terror and ideology. Terror included the instruments of repression and murder: secret police, criminal police, concentration camps, and later execution squads and death camps for the extermination of the Jews. For Himmler, the primary goal of the SS was to further the Aryan "master race."

© Hugo Jaeger/Time Life Pictures//Getty Images

The Nazi Mass Spectacle. Hitler and the Nazis made clever use of mass spectacles to rally the German people behind the Nazi regime. These mass demonstrations evoked intense enthusiasm, as is evident in this photograph of Hitler arriving at the Bückeberg (BOOK-uh-bayrk) near Hamelin for the Harvest Festival in 1937. Almost one million people were present for the celebration.

The creation of the Nazi total state also had an impact on women. Women played a crucial role in the Aryan racial state as bearers of the children who would bring about the triumph of the Aryan race. To the Nazis, the differences between men and women were natural: men were destined to be warriors and political leaders; women were to be wives and mothers.

The Nazi total state was intended to be an Aryan racial state. From its beginning, the Nazi Party reflected the strong anti-Semitic beliefs of Adolf Hitler. Once in power, the Nazis translated anti-Semitic ideas into anti-Semitic policies. In September 1935, at the annual party rally in Nuremberg, the Nazis announced new racial laws, which excluded German Jews from German citizenship and forbade marriages and extramarital relations between Jews and German citizens.

A more violent phase of anti-Jewish activity took place in 1938 and 1939, initiated on November 9–10, 1938, by the infamous *Kristallnacht* (kri-STAHL-nahkht), or night of shattered glass. The assassination of a secretary in the German embassy in Paris became the excuse for a Nazi-led rampage against the Jews in which synagogues were burned, 7,000 Jewish businesses were destroyed, and at least one hundred Jews were killed. Jews were barred from all public buildings and prohibited from owning or working in any retail store.

The Stalinist Era in the Soviet Union

Joseph Stalin made a significant shift in economic policy in 1928 when he launched his first five-year plan. Its real goal was nothing less than the transformation of the agrarian Soviet Union into an industrial country virtually overnight. Instead of consumer goods, the first five-year plan emphasized maximum production of capital goods and armaments and succeeded in quadrupling the production of heavy machinery and doubling oil production. Between 1928 and 1937, during the first two five-year plans, steel production increased from 4 million to 18 million tons per year.

Rapid industrialization was accompanied by an equally rapid collectivization of agriculture. Its goal was to eliminate private farms and push people onto collective farms. Strong resistance to Stalin's plans from peasants who hoarded crops and killed livestock only caused him to step up the program. By 1934, Russia's 26 million family farms had been collectivized into 250,000 units, though at a tremendous cost, since the hoarding of food and the slaughter of livestock produced widespread famine. Perhaps 10 million peasants died in the artificially created famines of 1932 and 1933. The only concession Stalin made to the peasants was to allow each collective farm worker to have one tiny, privately owned garden plot.

To achieve his goals, Stalin strengthened the party bureaucracy under his control. Anyone who resisted was sent into forced labor camps in Siberia. Stalin's desire for sole control of decision making also led to purges of the Old Bolsheviks. Between 1936 and 1938, the most prominent Old Bolsheviks were put on trial and condemned to death. During this same time, Stalin undertook a purge of army officers, diplomats, union officials, party members, intellectuals, and numerous ordinary citizens. Estimates are that 8 million Russians were arrested; millions died in Siberian forced labor camps. This gave Stalin the distinction of being one of the greatest mass murderers in human history.

The Stalinist era also reversed much of the permissive social legislation of the early 1920s. Advocating complete equality of rights for women, the Communists had made divorce and abortion easy to obtain while also encouraging women to work outside the home and to set their own moral standards. After Stalin came to power, the family was praised as a miniature collective in which parents were responsible for inculcating values of duty, discipline, and hard work. Abortion was outlawed, and divorced fathers who failed to support their children were fined heavily.

The Rise of Militarism in Japan

The rise of militarism in Japan resulted not from a seizure of power by a new political party but from the growing influence of militant forces at the top of the political hierarchy. In the early 1930s, confrontations with China in Manchuria, combined with the onset of the Great Depression, brought an end to the fragile stability of the immediate postwar years.

The depression had a disastrous effect on Japan, as many European countries, along with the United States, raised stiff tariff walls against cheap Japanese imports in order to protect their struggling domestic industries. The ensuing economic slowdown imposed a heavy burden on the fragile democracy in Japan. Although civilian cabinets tried desperately to cope with the economic challenges presented by the world depression, the political parties were no longer able to stem the growing influence of militant nationalist elements. Extremist patriotic organizations began to terrorize Japanese society by assassinating businessmen and public figures identified with the policy of conciliation toward the outside world. Some argued that Western-style political institutions should be replaced by a new system that would return to traditional Japanese values and imperial authority. Their message of "Asia for the Asians" became increasingly popular as the Great Depression convinced many Japanese that capitalism was unsuitable for Japan.

During the mid-1930s, the influence of the military and extreme nationalists over the government steadily increased. National elections continued to take place, but cabinets were dominated by the military or advocates of Japanese expansionism. In February 1936, junior army officers led a coup, briefly occupying the Diet building and other key government installations in Tokyo and assassinating several members of the cabinet. The ringleaders were quickly tried and convicted of treason, but under conditions that further strengthened the influence of the military.

The Path to War

FOCUS QUESTION: What were the underlying causes of World War II, and what specific steps taken by Nazi Germany and Japan led to war?

Only twenty years after the "war to end war," the world plunged back into the nightmare. The efforts at collective security in the 1920s proved meaningless in view of the growth of Nazi Germany and the rise of militant Japan.

The Path to War in Europe

World War II in Europe had its beginnings in the ideas of Adolf Hitler, who believed that only so-called Aryans were capable of building a great civilization. To Hitler, Germany needed more land to support a larger population and be a great power. Already in the 1920s, in the second volume of *Mein Kampf*, Hitler had indicated that a National Socialist regime would find this land to the east—in Russia.

On March 9, 1935, in defiance of the Treaty of Versailles, Hitler announced the creation of an air force and one week later the introduction of a military draft that would expand Germany's army from 100,000 to 550,000 troops. Hitler's unilateral repudiation of the Versailles treaty brought a swift reaction as France, Great Britain, and Italy condemned Germany's action and warned against future aggressive steps. But nothing concrete was done.

Meanwhile, Hitler gained new allies. In October 1935, Benito Mussolini had committed Fascist Italy to imperial expansion by invading Ethiopia. Mussolini welcomed Hitler's support and began to draw closer to the German dictator. In October 1936, Hitler and Mussolini concluded an agreement that recognized their common interests, and one month later, Mussolini referred publicly to the new Rome-Berlin Axis. Also in November, Germany and Japan (the rising military power in the Far East) concluded the Anti-Comintern Pact and agreed to maintain a common front against communism.

By 1937, Germany was once more a "world power," as Hitler proclaimed. Hitler was convinced that neither the French nor the British would provide much opposition to his plans and decided in 1938 to move to achieve one of his longtime goals: union with Austria. By threatening Austria with invasion, Hitler coerced the Austrian chancellor into putting Austrian Nazis in charge of the government. The new government promptly invited German troops to enter Austria and assist in maintaining law and order. One day later, on March 13, 1938, after his triumphal return to his native land, Hitler formally annexed Austria to Germany.

Hitler's next objective was the destruction of Czechoslovakia, and he believed that France and Britain would not use force to defend that nation. He was right again. On September 15, 1938, Hitler demanded the cession of the Sudetenland (soo-DAY-tun-land) (an area in northwestern Czechoslovakia inhabited largely by ethnic Germans) to Germany and expressed his willingness to risk "world war" if he was refused. Instead of objecting, the British, French, Germans, and Italians—at a hastily arranged conference at Munich—reached an agreement that met all of Hitler's demands (see the box on p. 656). German troops were allowed to occupy the Sudetenland. Increasingly, Hitler was convinced of his own infallibility, and he had by no means been satisfied at Munich. In March 1939, Hitler occupied all the Czech lands (Bohemia and Moravia), while the Slovaks, with Hitler's encouragement, declared their independence of the Czechs and became a puppet state (Slovakia) of Nazi Germany. On the evening of March 15, 1939, Hitler triumphantly declared in Prague that he would be known as the greatest German of them all.

At last, the Western states reacted to Hitler's threat. When Hitler began to demand the return of Danzig (which had been made a free city by the Treaty of Versailles to serve as a seaport for Poland) to Germany, Britain offered to protect Poland in the event of war. At the same time, both France and Britain realized that only the Soviet Union was powerful enough to help contain Nazi aggression and began political and military negotiations with Stalin and the Soviets.

Meanwhile, Hitler pressed on. To preclude an alliance between the West and the Soviet Union, which would open the danger of a two-front war, Hitler negotiated his own nonaggression pact with Stalin and shocked the world with its announcement on August 23, 1939. The treaty with the Soviet Union gave Hitler the freedom to attack Poland. He told his generals: "Now Poland is in the position in which I wanted her. . . . I am only afraid that at the last moment some swine or other will yet submit to me a plan for mediation."[5] He need not have worried. On September 1, German forces invaded Poland; two days later, Britain and France declared war on Germany. Europe was again at war.

The Path to War in Asia

During the mid-1920s, Japan had maintained a strong military and economic presence in Manchuria, an area in northeastern China controlled by a Chinese warlord. Then, in September 1931, Japanese military officers stationed in the area launched a coup to bring about a complete Japanese takeover of the region. Despite worldwide protests from the League of Nations, which eventually

OPPOSING VIEWPOINTS

The Munich Conference

At the Munich Conference, the leaders of France and Great Britain capitulated to Hitler's demands on Czechoslovakia. Although the British prime minister, Neville Chamberlain, defended his actions at Munich as necessary for peace, another British statesman, Winston Churchill, characterized the settlement at Munich as "a disaster of the first magnitude."

Winston Churchill, Speech to the House of Commons, October 5, 1938

I will begin by saying what everybody would like to ignore or forget but which must nevertheless be stated, namely, that we have sustained a total and unmitigated defeat, and that France has suffered even more than we have. . . . The utmost my right honorable Friend the Prime Minister . . . has been able to gain for Czechoslovakia and in the matters which were in dispute has been that the German dictator, instead of snatching his victuals from the table, has been content to have them served to him course by course. . . . And I will say this, that I believe the Czechs, left to themselves and told they were going to get no help from the Western Powers, would have been able to make better terms than they have got. . . .

We are in the presence of a disaster of the first magnitude which has befallen Great Britain and France. Do not let us blind ourselves to that. . . .

And do not suppose that this is the end. This is only the beginning of the reckoning. This is only the first sip, the first foretaste of a bitter cup which will be proffered to us year by year unless by a supreme recovery of moral health and martial vigor, we arise again and take our stand for freedom as in the olden time.

Neville Chamberlain, Speech to the House of Commons, October 6, 1938

That is my answer to those who say that we should have told Germany weeks ago that, if her army crossed the border of Czechoslovakia, we should be at war with her. We had no treaty obligations and no legal obligations to Czechoslovakia. When we were convinced, as we became convinced, that nothing any longer would keep the Sudetenland within the Czechoslovakian State, we urged the Czech Government as strongly as we could to agree to the cession of territory, and to agree promptly. . . . It was a hard decision for anyone who loved his country to take, but to accuse us of having by that advice betrayed the Czechoslovakian State is simply preposterous. What we did was to save her from annihilation and give her a chance of new life as a new State, which involves the loss of territory and fortifications, but may perhaps enable her to enjoy in the future and develop a national existence under a neutrality and security comparable to that which we see in Switzerland today. Therefore, I think the Government deserve the approval of this House for their conduct of affairs in this recent crisis which has saved Czechoslovakia from destruction and Europe from Armageddon.

What were the opposing views of Churchill and Chamberlain on the Munich Conference? Why did they disagree so much? With whom do you agree? Why?

Sources: Winston Churchill, Speech to the House of Commons, October 5, 1938. From *Parliamentary Debates, House of Commons* (London: His Majesty's Stationery Office, 1938), vol. 339, pp. 361–369. Neville Chamberlain, Speech to the House of Commons, October 6, 1938. From Neville Chamberlain, *In Search of Peace* (New York: Putnam, 1939), pp. 215, 217.

condemned the seizure, Japan steadily strengthened its control over Manchuria, renaming it Manchukuo (man-CHOO-kwoh), and then began to expand into northern China.

For the moment, Chiang Kai-shek attempted to avoid a direct confrontation with Japan so that he could deal with the Communists, whom he he considered the greater threat. When clashes between Chinese and Japanese troops broke out, he sought to appease the Japanese by granting them the authority to administer areas in North China. But as the Japanese moved steadily southward, popular protests in Chinese cities against Japanese aggression intensified. In December 1936, Chiang ended his military efforts against the Communists in Yan'an and

© Keystone/Getty Images

A Japanese Victory in China. After consolidating their authority over Manchuria, the Japanese began to expand into northern China. Direct hostilities between Japanese and Chinese forces began in 1937. This photograph shows victorious Japanese forces riding under the arched Chungshan Gate in Nanjing in January 1938 after they had conquered the Chinese capital city. By 1939, Japan had conquered most of eastern China.

formed a new united front against the Japanese. When Chinese and Japanese forces clashed at the Marco Polo Bridge, south of Beijing, in July 1937, China refused to apologize, and hostilities spread.

Japan had not planned to declare war on China, but neither side would compromise, and the 1937 incident eventually turned into a major conflict. The Japanese advanced up the Yangtze River valley and seized the Chinese capital of Nanjing in December, but Chiang Kai-shek refused to capitulate and moved his government upriver to Hankou (HAHN-kow). When the Japanese seized that city, he retreated to Chongqing (chung-CHING), in remote Sichuan (suh-CHWAHN) province, and kept his capital there for the remainder of the war.

Japanese strategists had hoped to force Chiang to join a Japanese-dominated New Order in East Asia, comprising Japan, Manchuria, and China. This was part of a larger Japanese plan to seize Soviet Siberia, with its rich resources, and create a new "Monroe Doctrine for Asia," under which Japan would guide its Asian neighbors on the path to development and prosperity (see the box on p. 658). After all, who better to instruct Asian societies on modernization than the one Asian country that had already achieved it?

During the late 1930s, Japan began to cooperate with Nazi Germany on the assumption that the two countries would ultimately launch a joint attack on the Soviet Union and divide up its resources between them. But when Germany surprised the world by signing a nonaggression pact with the Soviets in August 1939, Japanese strategists were compelled to reevaluate their long-term objectives. The Japanese were not strong enough to defeat the Soviet Union alone and so began to shift their eyes southward, to the vast resources of Southeast Asia—the oil of the Dutch East Indies, the rubber and tin of Malaya, and the rice of Burma and Indochina.

A move southward, of course, would risk war with the European colonial powers and the United States. Japan's attack on China in the summer of 1937 had already aroused strong criticism abroad, particularly from the United States. When Japan demanded the right to occupy airfields and exploit economic resources in French Indochina in the summer of 1940, the United States warned the Japanese that it would cut off the sale of oil and scrap iron unless Japan withdrew from the area and returned to its borders of 1931.

The Japanese viewed the American threat of retaliation as an obstacle to their long-term objectives. Japan badly needed oil and scrap iron from the United States. Should they be cut off, Japan would have to find them elsewhere. The Japanese were thus caught in a vise. To obtain guaranteed access to natural resources that were necessary to fuel the Japanese military machine, Japan must risk being cut off from its current source of raw materials that would be needed in the event of a conflict. After much debate, Japan decided to launch a surprise attack on American and European colonies in Southeast Asia in the hope of a quick victory that would evict the United States from the region.

World War II

FOCUS QUESTION: What were the main events of World War II in Europe and Asia?

Unleashing an early form of **blitzkrieg** (BLITZ-kreeg), or "lightning war," Hitler stunned Europe with the speed and efficiency of the German attack. Armored columns

Japan's Justification for Expansion

POLITICS & GOVERNMENT

Advocates of Japanese expansion justified their proposals by claiming both economic necessity and moral imperatives. Note the familiar combination of motives in this passage written by an extremist military leader in the late 1930s.

Hashimoto Kingoro on the Need for Emigration and Expansion

We have already said that there are only three ways left to Japan to escape from the pressure of surplus population. We are like a great crowd of people packed into a small and narrow room, and there are only three doors through which we might escape, namely emigration, advance into world markets, and expansion of territory. The first door, emigration, has been barred to us by the anti-Japanese immigration policies of other countries. The second door, advance into world markets, is being pushed shut by tariff barriers and the abrogation of commercial treaties. What should Japan do when two of the three doors have been closed against her?

It is quite natural that Japan should rush upon the last remaining door.

It may sound dangerous when we speak of territorial expansion, but the territorial expansion of which we speak does not in any sense of the word involve the occupation of the possessions of other countries, the planting of the Japanese flag thereon, and the declaration of their annexation to Japan. It is just that since the Powers have suppressed the circulation of Japanese materials and merchandise abroad, we are looking for some place overseas where Japanese capital, Japanese skills and Japanese labor can have free play, free from the oppression of the white race.

We would be satisfied with just this much. What moral right do the world powers who have themselves closed to us the two doors of emigration and advance into world markets have to criticize Japan's attempt to rush out of the third and last door?

If they do not approve of this, they should open the doors which they have closed against us and permit the free movement overseas of Japanese emigrants and merchandise. . . .

At the time of the Manchurian incident, the entire world joined in criticism of Japan. They said that Japan was an untrustworthy nation. They said that she had recklessly brought cannon and machine guns into Manchuria, which was the territory of another country, flown airplanes over it, and finally occupied it. But the military action taken by Japan was not in the least a selfish one. Moreover, we do not recall ever having taken so much as an inch of territory belonging to another nation. The result of this incident was the establishment of the splendid new nation of Manchuria. The Powers are still discussing whether or not to recognize this new nation, but regardless of whether or not other nations recognize her, the Manchurian empire has already been established, and now, seven years after its creation, the empire is further consolidating its foundations with the aid of its friend, Japan.

And if it is still protested that our actions in Manchuria were excessively violent, we may wish to ask the white race just which country it was that sent warships and troops to India, South Africa, and Australia and slaughtered innocent natives, bound their hands and feet with iron chains, lashed their backs with iron whips, proclaimed these territories as their own, and still continues to hold them to this very day.

What arguments did Hashimoto Kingoro make in favor of Japanese territorial expansion? What was his reaction to the condemnation of Japan by Western nations?

Source: From *Sources of Japanese Tradition* by William Theodore de Bary. Copyright © 1958 by Columbia University Press.

or panzer divisions (a *panzer division* was a strike force of about three hundred tanks and accompanying forces and supplies) supported by airplanes broke quickly through Polish lines and encircled the bewildered Polish troops. Conventional infantry units then moved in to hold the newly conquered territory. Within four weeks, Poland had surrendered. On September 28, 1939, Germany and the Soviet Union officially divided Poland between them.

Europe at War

After a winter of waiting, Hitler resumed the war on April 9, 1940, with another blitzkrieg against Denmark and Norway (see Map 25.1). One month later, on May 10, the Germans launched their attack on the Netherlands, Belgium, and France. The main assault through Luxembourg and the Ardennes forest was completely unexpected by the French and British forces. German panzer divisions broke through the weak French defensive positions there and raced across northern France, splitting the Allied armies and trapping French troops and the entire British army on the beaches of Dunkirk. Only by heroic efforts did the British achieve a gigantic evacuation of 330,000 Allied troops. The French capitulated on June 22. German armies occupied about three-fifths of France while the French hero of World War I, Marshal Henri Petain (AHN-ree pay-TAHN), established an authoritarian regime—known as Vichy (VISH-ee) France—over the remainder. Germany was now in control of western and central Europe, but Britain still had not been defeated.

As Hitler realized, an amphibious invasion of Britain would be possible only if Germany gained control of the

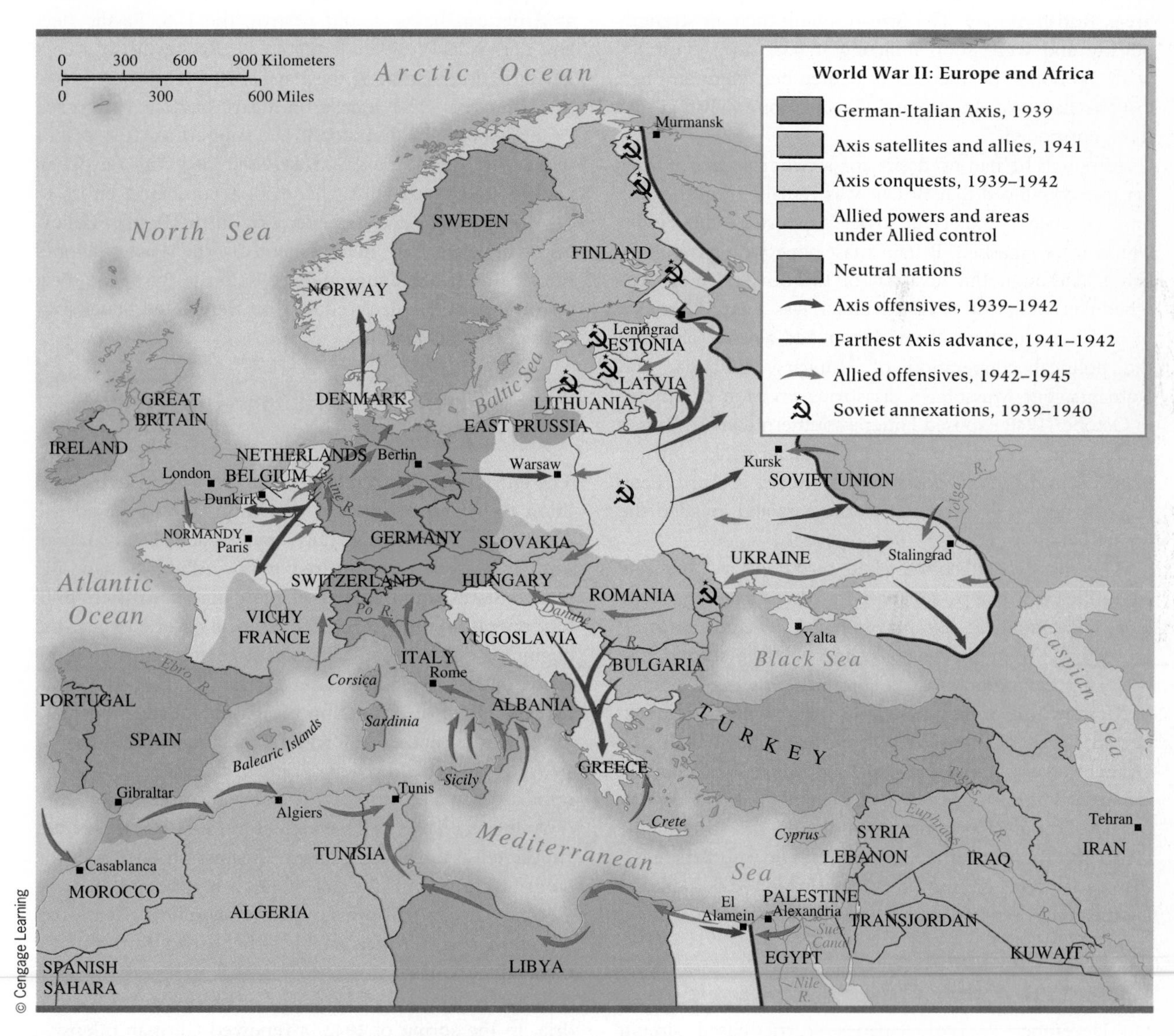

© Cengage Learning

MAP 25.1 World War II in Europe and North Africa. With its fast and effective military, Germany quickly overwhelmed much of western Europe. Hitler overestimated his country's capabilities, however, and underestimated those of his opponents. By late 1942, his invasion of the Soviet Union was failing, and the United States had become a major factor in the war. The Allies successfully invaded Italy in 1943 and France in 1944.

Q *Which countries were neutral, and how did geography help make their neutrality an option?*

air. At the beginning of August 1940, the German air force, or Luftwaffe (LOOFT-vahf-uh), launched a major offensive against British air and naval bases, harbors, communication centers, and war industries. The British fought back doggedly, supported by an effective radar system that gave them early warning of German attacks. Nevertheless, the British air force suffered critical losses by the end of August and was probably saved by a change in Hitler's strategy. In September, in retaliation for a British attack on Berlin, Hitler ordered a shift from military targets to massive bombing of British cities to break British morale. The British rebuilt their air strength quickly and were soon inflicting major losses on Luftwaffe bombers. By the end of September, Germany had lost the Battle of Britain, and the invasion of Britain had to be postponed.

Although he had no desire for a two-front war, Hitler became convinced that Britain was remaining in the war only because it expected Soviet support. If the Soviet Union were smashed, Britain's last hope would be eliminated. Although the invasion of the Soviet Union was scheduled for spring 1941, the attack was delayed because of problems in the Balkans. Hitler had already obtained the political cooperation of Hungary, Bulgaria, and Romania, but Mussolini's disastrous invasion of Greece in October 1940 exposed Hitler's southern flank to British air bases in Greece. To secure his Balkan flank, German troops seized both Yugoslavia and Greece in April. Feeling reassured, Hitler turned to the east and invaded the Soviet Union on June 22, 1941.

The massive attack stretched out along a 1,800-mile front. German troops advanced rapidly, capturing 2 million Soviet soldiers. By November, one German army group had swept through Ukraine, while a second was besieging Leningrad; a third approached within 25 miles of Moscow, the Soviet capital. An early winter and unexpected Soviet resistance, however, brought a halt to the German advance. For the first time in the war, German armies had been stopped. A Soviet counterattack in December 1941 came as an ominous ending to the year for the Germans. By that time, another of Hitler's decisions—the declaration of war on the United States—turned another European conflict into a global war.

Japan at War

On December 7, 1941, Japanese carrier-based aircraft attacked the U.S. naval base at Pearl Harbor in the Hawaiian Islands. The same day, other units launched assaults on the Philippines and began advancing toward the British colony of Malaya (see Map 25.2). Shortly thereafter, Japanese forces invaded the Dutch East Indies and occupied a number of islands in the Pacific Ocean. By the spring of 1942, almost all of Southeast Asia and much of the western Pacific had fallen into Japanese hands. Japan declared the establishment of the Greater East Asia Co-Prosperity Sphere, encompassing the entire region under Japanese tutelage, and announced its intention to liberate the colonial areas of Southeast Asia from Western colonial rule. For the moment, however, Japan needed the resources of the region for its war machine and placed the countries under its own rule on a wartime basis.

Japanese leaders had hoped that their lightning strike at American bases would destroy the U.S. Pacific fleet and persuade President Franklin D. Roosevelt to accept Japanese domination of the Pacific. But the Japanese had miscalculated. The attack on Pearl Harbor galvanized American opinion and won broad support for Roosevelt's war policy. The United States now joined with European nations and Nationalist China in a combined effort to defeat Japan and end its hegemony in the Pacific. Believing that American involvement in the Pacific would render the United States ineffective in the European theater of war, Hitler declared war on the United States four days after Pearl Harbor.

The Turning Point of the War, 1942–1943

The entry of the United States into the war created a coalition (the Grand Alliance) that ultimately defeated the Axis Powers (Germany, Italy, and Japan). To overcome mutual suspicions, the three major Allies, Britain, the United States, and the Soviet Union, agreed to stress military operations while ignoring political differences. At the beginning of 1943, the Allies also agreed to fight until the Axis Powers surrendered unconditionally, a decision that had the effect of cementing the Grand Alliance by making it nearly impossible for Hitler to divide his foes.

As 1942 began, however, defeat was far from Hitler's mind. As Japanese forces advanced into the Pacific after crippling the American naval fleet at Pearl Harbor, Hitler continued the war in Europe against Britain and the Soviet Union. Until the fall of 1942, it appeared that the Germans might still prevail on the battlefield. Reinforcements in North Africa enabled the Afrika Korps under General Erwin Rommel (RAHM-ul) to break through the British defenses in Egypt and advance toward Alexandria. In the spring of 1942, a renewed German offensive in the Soviet Union led to the capture of the entire Crimea. But by the fall of 1942, the war had turned against the Germans.

In North Africa, British forces had stopped Rommel's troops at El Alamein (ell ah-lah-MAYN) in the summer of 1942 and then forced them back across the desert. In

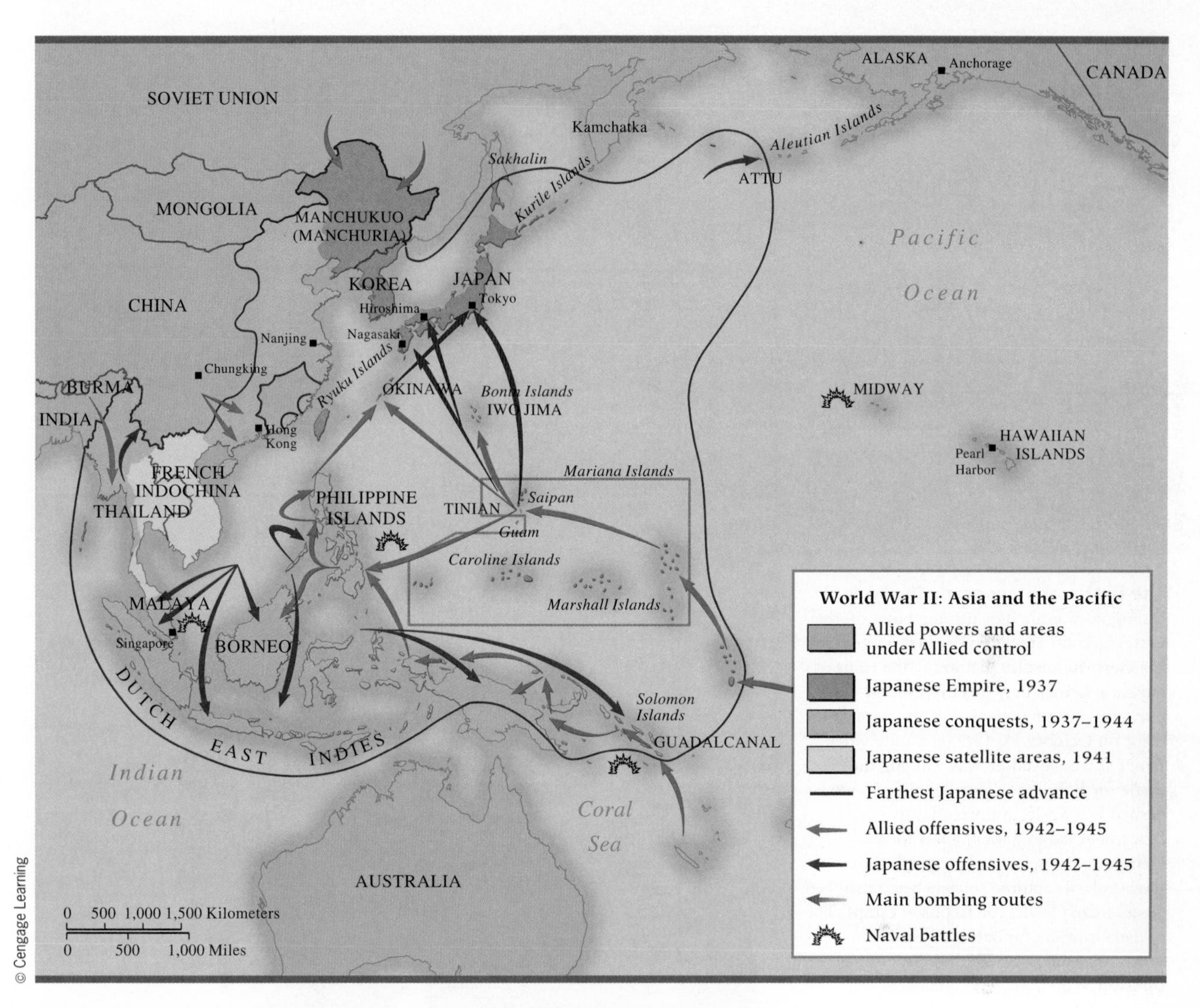

© Cengage Learning

MAP 25.2 World War II in Asia and the Pacific. In 1937, Japan invaded northern China, beginning its effort to create a "Great East Asia Co-Prosperity Sphere." Further Japanese expansion caused the United States to end iron and oil sales to Japan. Deciding that war with the United States was inevitable, Japan engineered a surprise attack on Pearl Harbor.

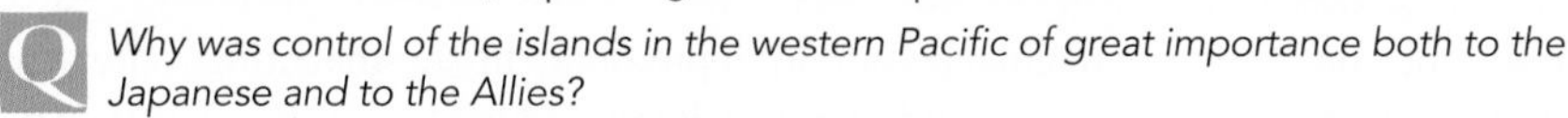
Why was control of the islands in the western Pacific of great importance both to the Japanese and to the Allies?

November 1942, British and American forces invaded French North Africa and forced the German and Italian troops to surrender in May 1943. On the Eastern Front, the turning point of the war occurred at Stalingrad. After the capture of the Crimea, Hitler decided that Stalingrad, a major industrial center on the Volga, should be taken next. Between November 1942 and February 1943, German troops were stopped, then encircled, and finally forced to surrender on February 2, 1943 (see the box on p. 663). The entire German Sixth Army of 300,000 men was lost. By February 1943, German forces in the Soviet Union were back to their positions of June 1942.

The tide of battle in the Far East also turned dramatically in 1942. In the Battle of the Coral Sea on May 7–8, 1942, American naval forces stopped the Japanese advance and temporarily relieved Australia of the threat of invasion. On June 4, at the Battle of Midway Island, American carrier planes destroyed all four of the attacking Japanese aircraft carriers and established American naval superiority in the Pacific. The victory came at a high cost; about two-fifths of the American planes were shot down in the encounter. By the fall of 1942, Allied forces were beginning to gather for offensive operations in three areas: from bases in north Burma and India into the

© AKG Images/The Image Works

© Dmitri Baltermants/The Dmitri Baltermants Collection/CORBIS

The Battle of Stalingrad. The Battle of Stalingrad was a major turning point on the Eastern Front. Shown in the first photograph is a German infantry platoon in the ruins of a tractor factory they had captured in the northern part of Stalingrad. This victory took place on October 15, 1942, at a time when Hitler still believed he was winning the battle for Stalingrad. That belief was soon dashed as a Soviet counteroffensive in November led to a total defeat for the Germans. The second photograph shows thousands of captured soldiers being marched across frozen Soviet soil to prison camps. The soldiers in white fur hats are Romanian. Fewer than 6,000 captured soldiers survived to go home; the remainder—almost 85,000 prisoners—died in captivity.

rest of Burma; in the Solomon Islands and on New Guinea, with forces under the direction of American general Douglas MacArthur moving toward the Philippines; and across the Pacific where combined U.S. Army, Marine, and Navy forces would mount attacks against Japanese held islands. After a series of bitter engagements in the waters of the Solomon Islands from August to November 1942, Japanese fortunes began to fade.

The Last Years of the War

By the beginning of 1943, the tide of battle had turned against Germany, Italy, and Japan. After the Axis forces had surrendered in Tunisia on May 13, 1943, the Allies crossed the Mediterranean and carried the war to Italy. After taking Sicily, Allied troops began the invasion of mainland Italy in September. In the meantime, after the ouster and arrest of Benito Mussolini, a new Italian government offered to surrender to Allied forces. But Mussolini was liberated by the Germans in a daring raid and then set up as the head of a puppet German state in northern Italy while German troops moved in and occupied much of Italy. The new defensive lines established by the Germans in the hills south of Rome were so effective that the Allied advance up the Italian peninsula was a painstaking affair accompanied by heavy casualties. Rome did not fall to the Allies until June 4, 1944. By that time, the Italian war had assumed a secondary role anyway as the Allies prepared to open their long-awaited "second front" in western Europe.

Under the direction of the American general Dwight D. Eisenhower (1890–1969), the Allies landed five assault

A German Soldier at Stalingrad

The Soviet victory at Stalingrad was a major turning point in World War II. This excerpt comes from the diary of a German soldier who fought and died in the Battle of Stalingrad. His dreams of victory and a return home with medals were soon dashed by the realities of Soviet resistance.

Diary of a German Soldier

Today, after we'd had a bath, the company commander told us that if our future operations are as successful, we'll soon reach the Volga, take Stalingrad, and then the war will inevitably soon be over. Perhaps we'll be home by Christmas.

July 29. The company commander says the Russian troops are completely broken, and cannot hold out any longer. To reach the Volga and take Stalingrad is not so difficult for us. The Führer knows where the Russians' weak point is. Victory is not far away. . . .

August 10. The Führer's orders were read out to us. He expects victory of us. We are all convinced that they can't stop us.

August 12. This morning outstanding soldiers were presented with decorations. Will I really go back to Elsa without a decoration? I believe that for Stalingrad the Führer will decorate even me. . . .

September 4. We are being sent northward along the front toward Stalingrad. We marched all night and by dawn had reached Voroponovo Station. We can already see the smoking town. It's a happy thought that the end of the war is getting nearer. That's what everyone is saying. . . .

September 8. Two days of nonstop fighting. The Russians are defending themselves with insane stubbornness. Our regiment has lost many men. . . .

September 16. Our battalion, plus tanks, is attacking the [grain storage] elevator, from which smoke is pouring—the grain in it is burning; the Russians seem to have set light to it themselves. Barbarism. The battalion is suffering heavy losses. . . .

October 10. The Russians are so close to us that our planes cannot bomb them. We are preparing for a decisive attack. The Führer has ordered the whole of Stalingrad to be taken as rapidly as possible. . . .

October 22. Our regiment has failed to break into the factory. We have lost many men; every time you move you have to jump over bodies. . . .

November 10. A letter from Elsa today. Everyone expects us home for Christmas. In Germany everyone believes we already hold Stalingrad. How wrong they are. If they could only see what Stalingrad has done to our army. . . .

November 21. The Russians have gone over to the offensive along the whole front. Fierce fighting is going on. So, there it is—the Volga, victory, and soon home to our families! We shall obviously be seeing them next in the other world.

November 29. We are encircled. It was announced this morning that the Führer has said: "The army can trust me to do everything necessary to ensure supplies and rapidly break the encirclement."

December 3. We are on hunger rations and waiting for the rescue that the Führer promised. . . .

December 14. Everybody is racked with hunger. Frozen potatoes are the best meal, but to get them out of the ice-covered ground under fire from Russian bullets is not so easy. . . .

December 26. The horses have already been eaten. I would eat a cat; they say its meat is also tasty. The soldiers look like corpses or lunatics, looking for something to put in their mouths. They no longer take cover from Russian shells; they haven't the strength to walk, run away, and hide. A curse on this war!

What did this soldier believe about the Führer? Why? What was the source of his information? Why is the battle for Stalingrad considered a major turning point in World War II?

Source: From Vasili Chuikov, *The Battle of Stalingrad* (Grafton Books).

divisions on the beaches of Normandy on June 6, 1944, in history's greatest naval invasion. An initially indecisive German response enabled the Allied forces to establish a beachhead. Within three months, they had landed 2 million men and a half-million vehicles that pushed inland and broke through German defensive lines.

After the breakout, Allied troops moved south and east and liberated Paris by the end of August. By March

1945, they had crossed the Rhine River and advanced farther into Germany. At the end of April 1945, Allied armies in northern Germany moved toward the Elbe River, where they finally linked up with the Soviets. The Soviets had come a long way since the Battle of Stalingrad in 1943. In the summer of 1943, they soundly defeated German forces at the Battle of Kursk (KOORSK) (July 5–12), the greatest tank battle of World War II. Soviet forces then began a relentless advance westward. The Soviets had reoccupied Ukraine by the end of 1943 and lifted the siege of Leningrad and moved into the Baltic states by the beginning of 1944. Advancing along a northern front, Soviet troops occupied Warsaw in January 1945 and entered Berlin in April. Meanwhile, Soviet troops along a southern front swept through Hungary, Romania, and Bulgaria.

In January 1945, Hitler had moved into a bunker 55 feet under Berlin to direct the final stages of the war. In his final political testament, Hitler, consistent to the end in his rabid anti-Semitism, blamed the Jews for the war. Hitler committed suicide on April 30, two days after Mussolini had been shot by partisan Italian forces. On May 7, German commanders surrendered. The war in Europe was over.

CHRONOLOGY The Course of World War II

Germany and the Soviet Union divide Poland	September 28, 1939
Blitzkrieg against Denmark and Norway	April 1940
Blitzkrieg against Belgium, Netherlands, and France	May 1940
France surrenders	June 22, 1940
Battle of Britain	Fall 1940
Nazi seizure of Yugoslavia and Greece	April 1941
Germany invades the Soviet Union	June 22, 1941
Japanese attack on Pearl Harbor	December 7, 1941
Battle of the Coral Sea	May 7–8, 1942
Battle of Midway Island	June 4, 1942
Allied invasion of North Africa	November 1942
German surrender at Stalingrad	February 2, 1943
Axis forces surrender in North Africa	May 1943
Battle of Kursk	July 5–12, 1943
Allied invasion of mainland Italy	September 1943
Allied invasion of France	June 6, 1944
Hitler commits suicide	April 30, 1945
Germany surrenders	May 7, 1945
Atomic bomb dropped on Hiroshima	August 6, 1945
Japan surrenders	August 14, 1945

DEFEAT OF JAPAN The war in Asia continued. Beginning in 1943, American forces had gone on the offensive and proceeded, slowly at times, across the Pacific. The Americans took an increasing toll of enemy resources, especially at sea and in the air. As Allied military power drew inexorably closer to the main Japanese islands in the first months of 1945 (see the Film & History feature on p. 665), President Harry Truman, who had succeeded to the presidency on the death of Franklin Roosevelt in April, had an excruciatingly difficult decision to make. Should he use atomic weapons (at the time, only two bombs had been developed, and their effectiveness had not been demonstrated) to bring the war to an end without the necessity of an Allied invasion of the Japanese homeland? As the world knows, Truman answered that question in the affirmative. The first bomb was dropped on the city of Hiroshima (hee-roh-SHEE-muh) on August 6. Three days later, a second bomb was dropped on Nagasaki (nah-gah-SAH-kee). Japan surrendered unconditionally on August 14. World War II was finally over.

The New Order

FOCUS QUESTION: What was the nature of the new orders that Germany and Japan attempted to establish in the territories they occupied?

The initial victories of the Germans and the Japanese had given them the opportunity to create new orders in Europe and Asia. Both followed policies of ruthless domination of their subject peoples.

The New Order in Europe

In 1942, the Nazi empire stretched across continental Europe from the English Channel in the west to the outskirts of Moscow in the east. Nazi-occupied Europe was largely organized in one of two ways. Some areas, such as western Poland, were directly annexed by Nazi Germany and made into German provinces. The rest of occupied Europe was administered by German military or civilian officials in combination with different degrees of indirect control from collaborationist regimes.

Because the conquered lands in the east contained the living space for German expansion and were populated in Nazi eyes by racially inferior Slavic peoples, Nazi administration there was considerably more ruthless than in the west. Soon after the conquest of Poland, Heinrich Himmler, a strong believer in Nazi racial ideology and the leader of the SS, was put in charge of German resettlement plans in the east. Himmler's task was to evacuate the inferior Slavic peoples and replace them with Germans, a policy first applied to the new German provinces

FILM & HISTORY

Letters from Iwo Jima (2006)

In February 1945, U.S. forces launched an attack on Iwo Jima, a 5-mile-long volcanic island, located about 650 miles southeast of Tokyo. With its three airstrips, Iwo Jima was an important element in the ring of defenses protecting Japan, and the Allies intended to use it as an air base from which to bomb the main Japanese islands.

The Battle of Iwo Jima is the subject of two films directed by Clint Eastwood and released in 2006: *Flag of Our Fathers* presented the battle from the American viewpoint, and *Letters from Iwo Jima* presented the Japanese perspective. The second film won numerous awards, including a nomination for Best Picture.

Letters from Iwo Jima is a realistic portrayal of the Japanese defense of the island. The plot focuses on two characters: the fictional Private Saigo (Kazunari Ninomiya), an ordinary soldier whose desire is to return home to his wife and daughter, and Lieutenant General Tadamichi Kuribayashi (Ken Watanabe), the actual commander of the Japanese forces on Iwo Jima. Kuribayashi is accurately portrayed as a man who shared the hardships of his men and had gained firsthand experience of the United States while spending three years there as a military attaché. Kuribayashi was largely responsible for the Japanese strategy of letting the U.S. Marines land on the beaches of Iwo Jima before attacking them with flanking fire from forces that were well protected in pillboxes and the miles of caves that permeated the island. The strategy proved very effective. The Japanese force of 22,000 men took a devastating toll on the Americans: out of the landing force of 110,000 men, 6,800 were killed and more than 17,000 were wounded. The assault that the U.S. military had expected to last only fourteen days dragged on instead for thirty-six.

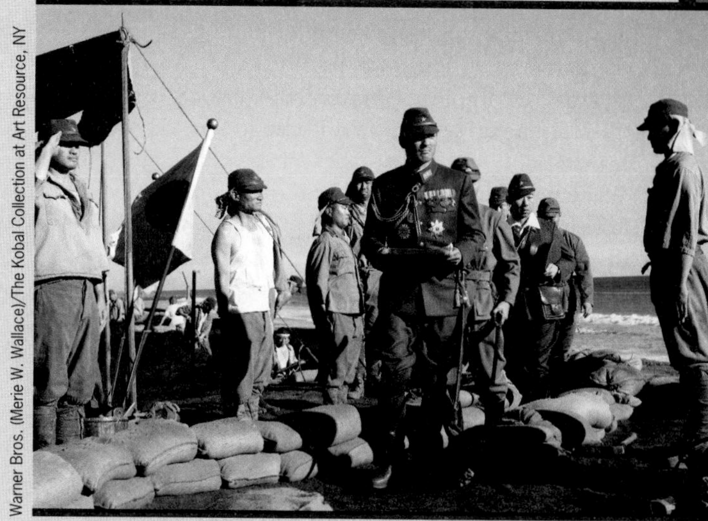

Warner Bros. (Merie W. Wallace)/The Kobal Collection at Art Resource, NY

General Tadamichi Kuribayashi (Ken Watanabe) prepares for the U.S. invasion of Iwo Jima.

The film also realistically portrays the code of *bushido* that motivated the Japanese forces. Based on an ideal of loyalty and service, the code emphasized the obligation to honor and defend emperor, country, and family, and to sacrifice one's life if one failed in this sacred mission. Before committing suicide, Captain Tanida (Takumi Bando) says to his men, "Men, we are honorable soldiers of the emperor. Don't ever forget that. The only way left for us is to die with honor." But the film also presents another, more human view of the Japanese soldiers that differs from the stereotype found in many American movies about World War II. For the most part, the Japanese and American soldiers are portrayed as being much the same: as men who were willing to kill and die, but who would prefer to simply go home and be with their families.

created from the lands of western Poland. One million Poles were uprooted and dumped in southern Poland. Hundreds of thousands of ethnic Germans (descendants of Germans who had migrated years earlier from Germany to different parts of southern and eastern Europe) were encouraged to colonize designated areas in Poland. By 1942, 2 million ethnic Germans had been settled in Poland.

Labor shortages in Germany led to a policy of ruthless mobilization of foreign labor for Germany. In 1942, a special office was created to recruit labor for German farms and industries. By the summer of 1944, 7 million foreign workers were laboring in Germany, constituting 20 percent of the labor force. At the same time, another 7 million workers were supplying forced labor in their own countries on farms, in industries, and even in military camps. The brutality of Germany's recruitment policies often led more and more people to resist the Nazi occupation forces.

The Holocaust

No aspect of the Nazi new order was more terrifying than the deliberate attempt to exterminate the Jews of Europe. Racial struggle was a key element in Hitler's ideology and meant to him a clearly defined conflict of opposites: the Aryans, creators of human cultural development, against the Jews, parasites who were trying to destroy the Aryans. Himmler and the SS organization closely shared Hitler's racial ideology. The SS was given responsibility for what the Nazis called their **Final Solution** to the "Jewish problem"—the annihilation of the Jewish people. After the defeat of Poland, the SS ordered the ***Einsatzgruppen*** (YN-zahtz-groop-un), or special strike forces, to round up all Polish Jews and concentrate them in ghettos established in a number of Polish cities.

In June 1941, the *Einsatzgruppen* were given new responsibilities as mobile killing units. These SS death squads followed the regular army's advance into Russia. Their job was to round up Jews in their villages and execute and bury them in mass graves, often giant pits dug by the victims themselves before they were shot. Such constant killing produced morale problems among the SS executioners. During a visit to Minsk in the Soviet Union, Himmler tried to build morale by pointing out that he "would not like it if Germans did such a thing gladly. But their conscience was in no way impaired, for they were soldiers who had to carry out every order unconditionally. He alone had responsibility before God and Hitler for everything that was happening."[6]

Although it has been estimated that as many as a million Jews were killed by the *Einsatzgruppen*, this approach to solving the Jewish problem was soon perceived as inadequate. So the Nazis opted for the systematic annihilation of the European Jewish population in death camps. Jews from countries occupied by Germany (or sympathetic to Germany) were rounded up, packed like cattle into freight trains, and shipped to Poland, where six extermination centers were built for this purpose. The largest and most famous was Auschwitz-Birkenau (OW-shvitz-BEER-kuh-now). Medical technicians chose Zyklon B (the commercial name for hydrogen cyanide) as the most effective gas for quickly killing large numbers of people in gas chambers designed to look like shower rooms to facilitate the cooperation of the victims.

The death camps were up and running by the spring of 1942; by the summer, Jews were also being shipped from France, Belgium, and the Netherlands. Even as the Allies were making significant advances in 1944, Jews were being shipped from Greece and Hungary. A harrowing experience awaited the Jews when they arrived at one of the six death camps. Rudolf Höss (HESS), commandant at Auschwitz-Birkenau, described it:

> We had two SS doctors on duty at Auschwitz to examine the incoming transports of prisoners. The prisoners would be marched by one of the doctors who would make spot decisions as they walked by. Those who were fit for work were sent into the camp. Others were sent immediately to the extermination plants. Children of tender years were invariably exterminated since by reason of their youth they were unable to work. . . . At Auschwitz we endeavored to fool the victims into thinking that they were to go through a delousing process. Of course, frequently they realized our true intentions and we sometimes had riots and difficulties due to that fact.[7]

About 30 percent of the arrivals at Auschwitz were sent to a labor camp; the remainder went to the gas chambers (see the box on p. 667). After they had been gassed, the bodies were burned in specially built crematoria. The victims' goods and even their bodies were used for economic gain. Women's hair was cut off, collected, and used to stuff mattresses or make cloth. Altogether, the Germans killed between 5 and 6 million Jews, more than 3 million of them in the death camps. About 90 percent of the Jewish populations of Poland, the Baltic countries, and Germany were exterminated. Overall, the Holocaust was responsible for the death of nearly two of every three Jews in Europe.

The Nazis were also responsible for another Holocaust, the death by shooting, starvation, or overwork of at least another 9 to 10 million people. Because the Nazis also considered the Gypsies of Europe (like the Jews) a race containing alien blood, they were systematically rounded up for extermination. About 40 percent of Europe's one million Gypsies were killed in the death camps. The leading elements of the "subhuman" Slavic peoples—the clergy, intelligentsia, civil leaders, judges, and lawyers—were arrested and deliberately killed. Probably an additional 4 million Poles, Ukrainians, and Byelorussians lost their lives as slave laborers for Nazi Germany, and 3 to 4 million Soviet prisoners of war were killed in captivity. The Nazis also singled out homosexuals for persecution, and thousands lost their lives in concentration camps.

The New Order in Asia

Once the takeover was completed, Japanese war policy in the occupied areas in Asia became essentially defensive, as Japan hoped to use its new possessions to meet its burgeoning needs for raw materials, such as tin, oil, and rubber, and also as an outlet for Japanese manufactured goods. To provide an organizational structure for the arrangement, Japanese leaders set up the Great East Asia Co-Prosperity Sphere, a self-sufficient economic community designed to provide mutual benefits to the occupied areas and the home country.

The Holocaust: The Camp Commandant and the Camp Victims

POLITICS & GOVERNMENT

The systematic annihilation of millions of men, women, and children in extermination camps makes the Holocaust one of the most horrifying events in history. The first document is taken from an account by Rudolf Höss, commandant of the extermination camp at Auschwitz-Birkenau. In the second document, a French doctor explains what happened at one of the crematoria described by Hoss.

Commandant Höss Describes the Equipment

The two large crematoria, Nos. I and II, were built during the winter of 1942–43. . . . Each . . . could cremate c. 2,000 corpses within twenty-four hours. . . . Crematoria I and II both had underground undressing and gassing rooms which could be completely ventilated. The corpses were brought up to the ovens on the floor above by lift. The gas chambers could hold c. 3,000 people.

The firm of Topf had calculated that the two smaller crematoria, III and IV, would each be able to cremate 1,500 corpses within twenty-four hours. However, owing to the wartime shortage of materials, the builders were obliged to economize, and so the undressing rooms and gassing rooms were built above ground and the ovens were of a less solid construction. But it soon became apparent that the flimsy construction of these two four-retort ovens was not up to the demands made on it. No. III ceased operating altogether after a short time and later was no longer used. No. IV had to be repeatedly shut down since after a short period in operation of 4–6 weeks, the ovens and chimneys had burnt out. The victims of the gassing were mainly burnt in pits behind crematorium IV.

The largest number of people gassed and cremated within twenty-four hours was somewhat over 9,000.

A French Doctor Describes the Victims

It is mid-day, when a long line of women, children, and old people enter the yard. The senior official in charge . . . climbs on a bench to tell them that they are going to have a bath and that afterward they will get a drink of hot coffee. They all undress in the yard. . . . The doors are opened and an indescribable jostling begins. The first people to enter the gas chamber begin to draw back. They sense the death which awaits them. The SS men put an end to this pushing and shoving with blows from their rifle butts beating the heads of the horrified women who are desperately hugging their children. The massive oak double doors are shut. For two endless minutes one can hear banging on the walls and screams which are no longer human. And then—not a sound. Five minutes later the doors are opened. The corpses, squashed together and distorted, fall out like a waterfall. . . . The bodies, which are still warm, pass through the hands of the hairdresser, who cuts their hair, and the dentist, who pulls out their gold teeth. . . . One more transport has just been processed through No. IV crematorium.

What "equipment" does Höss describe? What process does the French doctor describe? Is there any sympathy for the victims in either account? Why or why not? How could such a horrifying process have been allowed to occur?

Sources: Commandant Höss Describes the Equipment. From *Commandant of Auschwitz: The Autobiography of Rudolph Hoss*, Cleveland World Publishing Company. A French Doctor Describes the Victims. From *Nazism: A History in Documents and Eyewitness Accounts*, Vol. II by J. Noakes and G. Pridham. Copyright © 1988 by Department of History and Archaeology, University of Exeter.

The Japanese conquest of Southeast Asia had been accomplished under the slogan "Asia for the Asians." Japanese officials in the occupied territories quickly promised that independent governments would be established under Japanese tutelage. Such governments were eventually established in Burma, the Dutch East Indies, Vietnam, and the Philippines.

In fact, however, real power rested with the Japanese military authorities in each territory, and the local Japanese military command was directly subordinated to the army general staff in Tokyo. The economic resources of the colonies were exploited for the benefit of the Japanese war machine, while natives were recruited to serve in local military units or conscripted to work on public works projects. In some cases, the people living in the occupied areas were subjected to severe hardships. In Indochina, for example, forced requisitions of rice by the local Japanese authorities for shipment abroad created a food shortage that caused the starvation of more than a million Vietnamese in 1944 and 1945.

At first, many Southeast Asian nationalists took Japanese promises at face value and agreed to cooperate with their new masters. But as the exploitative nature of Japanese occupation policies became clear, sentiment turned against the new order. Japanese officials sometimes unwittingly provoked such attitudes by their arrogance and contempt for local customs.

Like German soldiers in occupied Europe, Japanese military forces often had little respect for the lives of their subject peoples. In their conquest of Nanjing, China, in 1937, Japanese soldiers had devoted several days to killing, raping, and looting. Almost 800,000 Koreans were sent overseas, most of them as forced laborers, to Japan. Tens of thousands of women from Korea and the Philippines were forced to be "comfort women" (prostitutes) for Japanese troops. The Japanese also made extensive use of both prisoners of war and local peoples as laborers on construction projects for the war effort. In building the Burma-Thailand railway in 1943, for example, the Japanese used 61,000 Australian, British, and Dutch prisoners of war and almost 300,000 workers from Burma, Malaya, Thailand, and the Dutch East Indies. By the time the railway was completed, 12,000 Allied prisoners of war and 90,000 local workers had died from the inadequate diet and appalling work conditions in an unhealthy climate.

The Home Front

FOCUS QUESTION: What were conditions like on the home front for the major belligerents in World War II?

World War II was even more of a total war than World War I. Fighting was much more widespread and covered most of the world. The number of civilians killed was also far higher.

Mobilizing the People: Three Examples

The initial defeats of the Soviet Union led to drastic emergency mobilization measures that affected the civilian population. Leningrad, for example, experienced nine hundred days of siege, during which its inhabitants became so desperate for food that they ate dogs, cats, and mice. As the German army made its rapid advance into Soviet territory, the factories in the western part of the Soviet Union were dismantled and shipped to the interior—to the Urals, western Siberia, and the Volga region. Machines were set down on the bare earth, and walls went up around them as workers began their work.

Stalin called the widespread military and industrial mobilization of the nation a "battle of machines," and the Soviets won, producing 78,000 tanks and 98,000 artillery pieces. In 1943, fully 55 percent of Soviet national income went for war matériel, compared to 15 percent in 1940 (see the comparative essay "Paths to Modernization" on p. 669).

Soviet women played a major role in the war effort. Women and girls were enlisted for work in industries, mines, and railroads. Overall the number of women working in industry increased almost 60 percent. Soviet women were also expected to dig antitank ditches and work as air raid wardens. In addition, the Soviet Union was the only country in World War II to use women as combatants. Soviet women functioned as snipers and as crews in bomber squadrons.

In August 1914, Germans had enthusiastically cheered their soldiers marching off to war; in September 1939, the streets were quiet. Many Germans were apathetic or, even worse for the Nazi regime, had a foreboding of disaster. Hitler was very aware of the importance of the home front. He believed that the collapse of the home front in World War I had caused Germany's defeat. To avoid a repetition of that experience, he adopted economic policies that may indeed have cost Germany the war.

To maintain the morale of the home front during the first two years of the war, Hitler refused to cut production of consumer goods or increase the production of armaments. After German defeats on the Russian front and the American entry into the war, however, the situation changed. Early in 1942, Hitler finally ordered a massive increase in armaments production and the size of the army. Hitler's architect, Albert Speer (AHL-bert SHPAYR), was made minister for armaments and munitions in 1942. By eliminating waste and rationalizing procedures, Speer was able to triple the production of armaments between 1942 and 1943, despite the intense Allied air raids. Speer's urgent plea for a total mobilization of resources for the war effort went unheeded, however. Hitler, fearful of civilian morale problems that would undermine the home front, refused any dramatic cuts in the production of consumer goods. A total mobilization of the economy was not implemented until 1944, but by that time, it was too late.

The war caused a reversal in Nazi attitudes toward women. Nazi resistance to female employment declined as the war progressed and more and more men were called up for military service. Nazi magazines now proclaimed, "We see the woman as the eternal mother of

COMPARATIVE ESSAY

Paths to Modernization

POLITICS & GOVERNMENT

To the casual observer, the most important feature of the first half of the twentieth century was the rise of a virulent form of competitive nationalism that began in Europe and ultimately descended into the cauldron of two destructive world wars. Behind the scenes, however, another competition was taking place over the most effective path to modernization.

The traditional approach, in which modernization was fostered by an independent urban merchant class, had been adopted by Great Britain, France, and the United States and led to the emergence of democratic societies on the capitalist model. In the second approach, adopted in the late nineteenth century by imperial Germany and Meiji Japan, modernization was carried out by traditional elites in the absence of a strong independent bourgeois class. Both Germany and Japan relied on strong government intervention to promote the growth of national wealth and power, and in both nations, modernization led ultimately to the formation of fascist and militarist regimes during the depression years of the early 1930s.

The third approach, selected by Vladimir Lenin after the Bolshevik Revolution in 1917, was designed to carry out an industrial revolution without going through an intermediate capitalist stage. Guided by the Communist Party in the almost total absence of an urban middle class, an advanced industrial society would be created by destroying the concept of private property. Although Lenin's plans called for the eventual "withering away of the state," the party adopted totalitarian methods to eliminate enemies of the revolution and carry out the changes needed to create a future classless utopia.

How did these various approaches contribute to the crises that afflicted the world during the first half of the twentieth century? The democratic-capitalist approach proved to be a considerable success in an economic sense, leading to advanced economies that could produce manufactured goods at a rate never seen before. Societies just beginning to undergo their own industrial revolutions tried to imitate the success of the capitalist nations by carrying out their own "revolutions from above," as in Germany and Japan. But the Great Depression and competition over resources and markets soon led to an intense rivalry between the established capitalist states and their ambitious late arrivals, a rivalry that ultimately erupted into global conflict.

© Bettmann/CORBIS

The Path to Modernization. One aspect of the Soviet effort to create an advanced industrial society was the collectivization of agriculture, which included the rapid mechanization of food production. In this photograph, peasants are watching a new tractor at work.

In the first decade of the twentieth century, imperial Russia appeared ready to launch its own bid to join the ranks of the industrialized nations. But that effort was derailed by its entry into World War I, and before that conflict had come to an end, the Bolsheviks were in power. Isolated from the capitalist marketplace by mutual consent, the Soviet Union was able to avoid being dragged into the Great Depression but, despite Stalin's efforts, was unsuccessful in staying out of the "battle of imperialists" that followed at the end of the 1930s. As World War II came to an end, the stage was set for a battle of the victors—the United States and the Soviet Union—over political and ideological supremacy.

What were the three major paths to modernization in the first half of the twentieth century, and why did they lead to conflict?

our people, but also as the working and fighting comrade of the man."[8] But the number of women working in industry, agriculture, commerce, and domestic service increased only slightly. In September 1944, 14.9 million women were employed, compared with 14.6 million in May 1939. Many women, especially those of the middle class, resisted regular employment, particularly in factories.

Wartime Japan was a highly mobilized society. To guarantee its control over all national resources, the government set up a planning board to control prices, wages, the utilization of labor, and the allocation of resources. Traditional habits of obedience and hierarchy, buttressed by the concept of imperial divinity, were emphasized to encourage citizens to sacrifice their resources, and sometimes their lives, for the national cause. The system culminated in the final years of the war, when young Japanese were encouraged to volunteer en masse to serve as pilots in the suicide missions—known as *kamikaze* (kah-mi-KAH-zee), or "divine wind"—against U.S. battleships.

Women's rights too were to be sacrificed to the greater national cause. Already by 1937, Japanese women were being exhorted to fulfill their patriotic duty by bearing more children and by espousing the slogans of the Greater Japanese Women's Association. Japan was extremely reluctant to mobilize women on behalf of the war effort, however. General Hideki Tojo (hee-DEK-ee TOH-joh), prime minister from 1941 to 1944, opposed female employment, arguing that "the weakening of the family system would be the weakening of the nation. . . . We are able to do our duties only because we have wives and mothers at home."[9] Female employment increased during the war, but only in areas where women traditionally worked, such as the textile industry and farming. Instead of using women to meet labor shortages, the Japanese government brought in Korean and Chinese laborers.

The Frontline Civilians: The Bombing of Cities

Bombing was used in World War II against nonhuman military targets, against enemy troops, and against civilian populations. The bombing of civilians made World War II as devastating for noncombatants as it was for frontline soldiers. A small number of bombing raids in the last year of World War I had given rise to the argument that public outcry over the bombing of civilian populations would be an effective way to coerce governments into making peace. Consequently, European air forces began to develop long-range bombers in the 1930s.

The first sustained use of civilian bombing failed to support the theory. Beginning in early September 1940, the German Luftwaffe subjected London and many other British cities and towns to nightly air raids, making the Blitz (as the British called the German air raids) a national experience. Londoners took the first heavy blows but kept up their morale, setting the standard for the rest of the British population (see the comparative illustration on p. 671).

The British failed to learn from their own experience, however. Prime Minister Winston Churchill and his advisers believed that destroying German communities would break civilian morale and bring victory. Major bombing raids began in 1942. On May 31, 1942, Cologne became the first German city to be subjected to an attack by a thousand bombers. Bombing raids added an element of terror to circumstances already made difficult by growing shortages of food, clothing, and fuel. Germans especially feared incendiary bombs, which ignited firestorms that swept destructive paths through the cities. The ferocious bombing of Dresden from February 13 to 15, 1945, created a firestorm that may have killed as many as 35,000 inhabitants and refugees.

Germany suffered enormously from the Allied bombing raids. Millions of buildings were destroyed, and possibly half a million civilians died from the raids. Nevertheless, it is highly unlikely that Allied bombing sapped the morale of the German people. Instead Germans, whether pro-Nazi or anti-Nazi, fought on stubbornly, often driven simply by a desire to live. Nor did the bombing destroy Germany's industrial capacity. The Allied strategic bombing survey revealed that the production of war matériel actually increased between 1942 and 1944.

In Japan, the bombing of civilians reached a horrendous new level with the use of the first atomic bomb. Attacks on Japanese cities by the new American B-29 Superfortresses, the biggest bombers of the war, had begun on November 24, 1944. By the summer of 1945, many of Japan's industries had been destroyed, along with one-fourth of its dwellings. After the Japanese government decreed the mobilization of all people between the ages of thirteen and sixty into the so-called People's Volunteer Corps, President Truman and his advisers decided that Japanese fanaticism might mean a million American casualties, and Truman decided to drop the newly developed atomic bomb on Hiroshima and Nagasaki. The destruction was incredible. Of 76,000 buildings near the hypocenter of the explosion in Hiroshima, 70,000 were flattened, and 140,000 of the city's 400,000 inhabitants had died by the end of 1945. Over the next five years, another 50,000 perished from the effects of radiation. The dropping of the atomic bomb on Hiroshima on August 6, 1945, announced the dawn of the nuclear age.

© J. R. Eyerman/Time Life Pictures//Getty Images

© Keystone/Getty Images

COMPARATIVE ILLUSTRATION

The Bombing of Civilians—East and West. World War II was the most destructive war in world history, not only for frontline soldiers but for civilians at home as well. The most devastating bombing of civilians came near the end of World War II when the United States dropped atomic bombs on the Japanese cities of Hiroshima and Nagasaki. At the left is a view of Hiroshima after the bombing that shows the incredible devastation produced by the atomic bomb. The picture at the right shows a street in Clydebank, near Glasgow in Scotland, the day after the city was bombed by the Germans in March 1941. Only 7 of the city's 12,000 houses were left undamaged; 35,000 of the 47,000 inhabitants became homeless overnight.

What was the rationale for bombing civilian populations? Did such bombing achieve its goal?

Aftermath of the War

FOCUS QUESTIONS: What were the costs of World War II? How did World War II affect the European nations' colonial empires? How did the Allies' visions of the postwar differ, and how did these differences contribute to the emergence of the Cold War?

World War II was the most destructive war in history. Much had been at stake. Nazi Germany followed a worldview based on racial extermination and the enslavement of millions in order to create an Aryan racial empire. The Japanese, fueled by extreme nationalist ideals, also pursued dreams of empire in Asia that led to mass murder and untold devastation. Fighting the Axis Powers in World War II required the mobilization of millions of ordinary men and women in the Allied countries who struggled to preserve a different way of life. As Winston Churchill once put it, "War is horrible, but slavery is worse."

The Costs of World War II

The costs of World War II were enormous. At least 21 million soldiers died. Civilian deaths were even greater and are now estimated at around 40 million, of whom more than 28 million were Russian and Chinese. The Soviet Union experienced the greatest losses: 10 million soldiers and 19 million civilians. In 1945, millions of people around the world faced starvation: in Europe, 100 million people depended on food relief of some kind.

Millions of people had also been uprooted by the war and became "displaced persons." Europe alone may have had 30 million displaced persons, many of whom found it hard to return home. In Asia, millions of Japanese were returned from the former Japanese empire to Japan, while thousands of Korean forced laborers returned to Korea.

Devastation was everywhere. Most areas of Europe had been damaged or demolished. China was in shambles after eight years of conflict, the Philippines had suffered heavy damage, and large sections of the major cities in Japan had been destroyed in air raids. The total monetary cost of the war has been estimated at $4 trillion. The economies of most belligerents, with the exception of the United States, were left drained and on the brink of disaster.

World War II and the European Colonies: Decolonization

As we saw in Chapter 24, movements for independence had begun in earnest in Africa and Asia in the years between World War I and World War II. After World War II, these movements grew even louder. The ongoing subjugation of peoples by colonial powers seemed at odds with the goals the Allies had pursued in overthrowing the repressive regimes of Germany, Italy, and Japan. Then, too, indigenous peoples everywhere took up the call for national self-determination and expressed their determination to fight for independence.

The ending of the European powers' colonial empires did not come easy, however. In 1941, Churchill had said, "I have not become His Majesty's Chief Minister in order to preside over the liquidation of the British Empire." Britain and France in particular seemed reluctant to let go of their colonies, but for a variety of reasons both eventually gave in the obvious—the days of empire were over.

During the war, the Japanese had already humiliated the Western states by overrunning their colonial empires. In addition, colonial soldiers who had fought on behalf of the Allies (India, for example, had contributed large numbers of troops to the British Indian Army) were well aware that Allied war aims included the principle of self-determination for the peoples of the world. Equally important to the process of **decolonization**, the power of the European states had been destroyed by the exhaustive struggles of World War II. The greatest empire builder, Great Britain, no longer had the energy or the wealth to maintain its empire. Given this combination of circumstances, a rush of decolonization swept the world after the war.

The Allied War Conferences

The total victory of the Allies in World War II was not followed by a real peace but by the emergence of a new conflict known as the **Cold War**, which dominated world politics until the end of the 1980s. The Cold War grew out of military, political, and ideological differences, especially between the Soviet Union and the United States, that became apparent at the Allied war conferences held in the last years of the war.

Stalin, Roosevelt, and Churchill, the leaders of the Big Three of the Grand Alliance, met at Tehran, the capital of Iran, in November 1943 to decide the future course of the war. Stalin and Roosevelt argued successfully for an American-British invasion of the Continent through France, which they scheduled for the spring of 1944. This meant that Soviet and British-American forces would meet in defeated Germany along a north-south dividing line and that Soviet forces would most likely liberate eastern Europe. The Allies also agreed to a partition of postwar Germany.

By the time of the conference at Yalta in southern Russia in February 1945, the defeat of Germany was a foregone conclusion. The Western powers now faced the reality of 11 million Red Army soldiers taking possession of eastern and central Europe. Stalin, deeply suspicious of the Western powers, desired a buffer to protect the Soviet Union from possible future Western aggression. At the same time, however, Stalin was eager to obtain economically important resources and strategic military positions. Roosevelt by this time was moving toward the idea of self-determination for Europe. The Grand Alliance approved a declaration on liberated Europe. This was a pledge to assist liberated European nations in the creation of "democratic institutions of their own choice." Liberated countries were to hold free elections to determine their political systems.

At Yalta, Roosevelt sought Russian military help against Japan. The atomic bomb was not yet assured, and American military planners feared the possibility of heavy losses in amphibious assaults on the Japanese home islands. Roosevelt therefore agreed to Stalin's price for military assistance against Japan: possession of Sakhalin and the Kurile Islands, as well as two warm-water ports and railroad rights in Manchuria.

The creation of the United Nations was a major American concern at Yalta. Roosevelt hoped to ensure the participation of the Big Three powers in a postwar international organization before difficult issues divided them into hostile camps. After a number of compromises, both Churchill and Stalin accepted Roosevelt's plans for a United Nations organization and set the first meeting for San Francisco in April 1945.

The issues of Germany and eastern Europe were treated less decisively. The Big Three reaffirmed that Germany must surrender unconditionally and created four occupation zones (see Map 25.3). A compromise was also worked out in regard to Poland. Stalin agreed to free elections in the future to determine a new government. But the issue of free elections in eastern Europe caused a serious rift between the Soviets and the Americans. In principle, eastern European governments were to be freely elected, but they were also supposed to be pro-Soviet. This attempt to reconcile two irreconcilable goals was doomed to failure, as soon became evident at the next conference of the Big Three.

The Potsdam conference of July 1945 began under a cloud of mistrust. Roosevelt had died on April 12 and

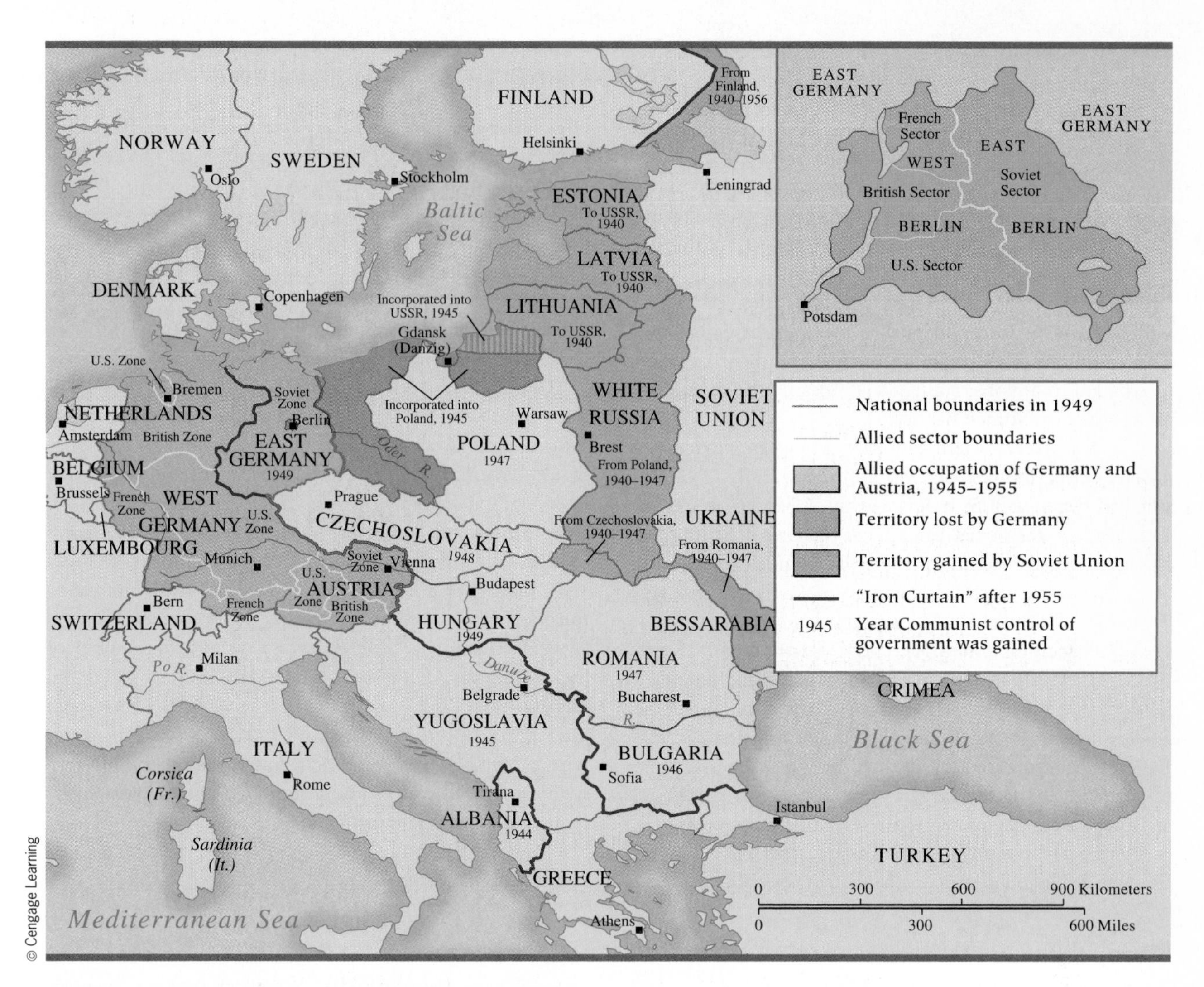

© Cengage Learning

MAP 25.3 Territorial Changes in Europe After World War II. In the last months of World War II, the Red Army occupied much of eastern Europe. Stalin sought pro-Soviet satellite states in the region as a buffer against future invasions from western Europe, whereas Britain and the United States wanted democratically elected governments. Soviet military control of the territory settled the question.

Q *Which country gained the greatest territory at the expense of Germany?*

had been succeeded as president by Harry Truman. At Potsdam, Truman demanded free elections throughout eastern Europe. Stalin responded, "A freely elected government in any of these East European countries would be anti-Soviet, and that we cannot allow."[10] After a bitterly fought and devastating war, Stalin sought absolute military security. To him, it could be gained only by the presence of Communist states in eastern Europe. Free elections might result in governments hostile to the Soviets. By the middle of 1945, only an invasion by Western forces could undo developments in eastern Europe, and few people favored such a policy.

As the war slowly receded into the past, the reality of conflicting ideologies had reappeared. Many in the West interpreted Soviet policy as part of a worldwide Communist conspiracy. The Soviets viewed Western, especially American, policy as nothing less than global capitalist expansionism or, in Leninist terms, economic imperialism. In March 1946, in a speech to an American audience, former British prime minister Winston Churchill declared that "an iron curtain" had "descended across the continent," dividing Germany and Europe into two hostile camps. Stalin branded Churchill's speech a "call to war with the Soviet Union." Only months after the world's most devastating conflict had ended, the world seemed once again to be bitterly divided in the Cold War.

CHAPTER SUMMARY

Between 1933 and 1939, Europeans watched as Adolf Hitler rebuilt Germany into a great military power. During that same period, Japan fell under the influence of military leaders who conspired with right-wing forces to push a program of expansion. The ambitions of Germany in Europe and those of Japan in Asia led to a global conflict that became the most devastating war in human history.

The Axis nations, Germany, Italy, and Japan, proved victorious during the first two years of the war. By 1942, the war had begun to turn in favor of the Allies, an alliance of Great Britain, the Soviet Union, and the United States. The Japanese advance was ended at the naval battles of the Coral Sea and Midway in 1942. In February 1943, the Soviets won the Battle of Stalingrad and began a push westward. By mid-1943, Germany and Italy had been driven out of North Africa; in June 1944, Rome fell to the Allies, and an Allied invasion force landed in Normandy in France. After the Soviets linked up with British and American forces in April 1945, Hitler committed suicide, and the war in Europe came to an end. After atomic bombs were dropped on Hiroshima and Nagasaki in August 1945, the war in Asia also ended.

During its domination of Europe, the Nazi empire brought death and destruction to many, especially Jews and others that the Nazis considered racially inferior. The Japanese New Order in Asia, while claiming to promote "Asia for the Asians" also brought exploitation, severe hardship, and often death for the peoples under Japanese control. All sides bombed civilian populations, making the war as devastating for civilians as for frontline soldiers.

If Hitler had been successful, the Nazi New Order, built on authoritarianism, racial extermination, and the brutal oppression of peoples, would have meant a triumph of barbarism and the end of freedom and equality, which, however imperfectly realized, had become important ideals in Western civilization.

The Nazis lost, but only after tremendous sacrifices and costs. Much of European civilization lay in ruins. Europeans now watched helplessly as the two new superpowers created by the two world wars took control of their destinies. Even before the last battles had been fought, the United States and the Soviet Union had arrived at different visions of the postwar European world. No sooner had the war ended than their differences gave rise to a new and potentially even more devastating conflict known as the Cold War.

CHAPTER TIMELINE

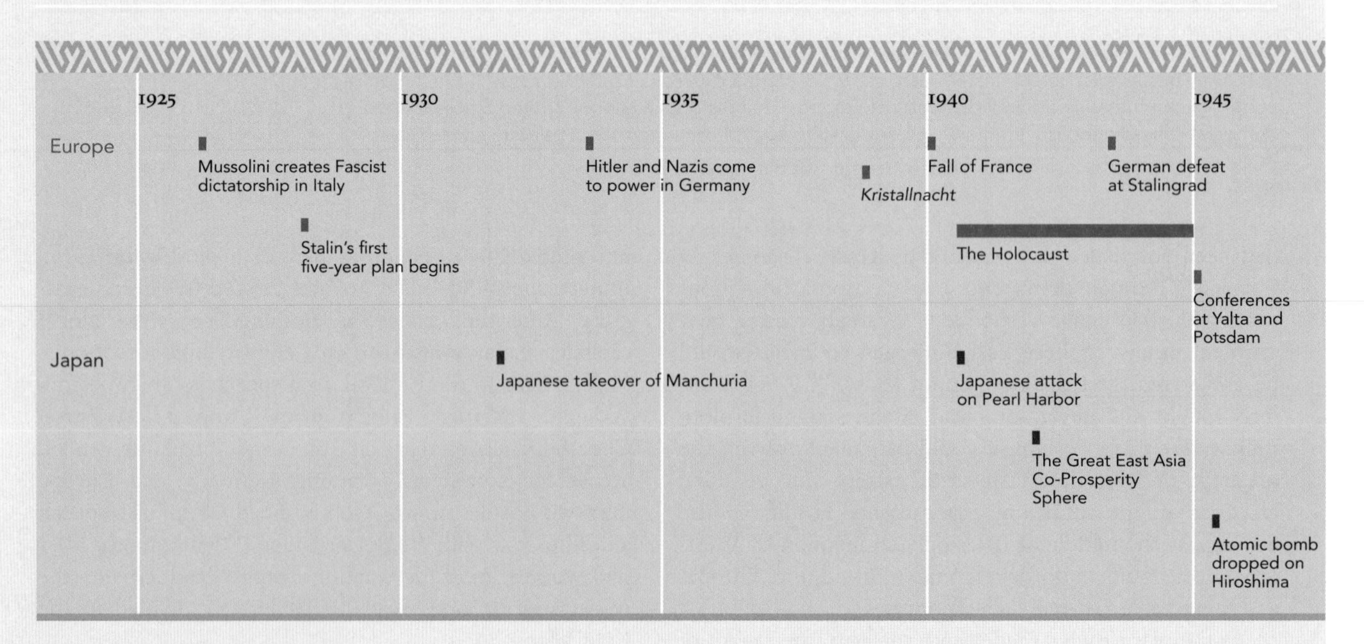

CHAPTER REVIEW

Upon Reflection

Q How do you account for the early successes of the Germans from 1939 to 1941?

Q How did the Nazis and the Japanese attempt to establish new orders in Europe and Asia after their military victories, and what were the results of their efforts?

Q How did the attempt to arrive at a peace settlement after World War II lead to the beginnings of a new conflict known as the Cold War?

Key Terms

fascism (p. 651)
totalitarian state (p. 651)
blitzkrieg (p. 657)
Final Solution (p. 666)
Einsatzgruppen (p. 666)
decolonization (p. 672)
Cold War (p. 672)

Suggested Reading

THE DICTATORIAL REGIMES The best biography of Mussolini is **R. J. B. Bosworth, *Mussolini*** (London, 2002). A brief but sound survey of Nazi Germany is **J. J. Spielvogel** and **D. Redles, *Hitler and Nazi Germany: A History,*** 6th ed. (Upper Saddle River, N.J., 2010). The best biography of Hitler is **I. Kershaw, *Hitler, 1889–1936: Hubris*** (New York, 1999), and ***Hitler: Nemesis*** (New York, 2000). On the Nazis in power, see **R. J. Evans, *The Third Reich in Power, 1933–1939*** (New York, 2005). The collectivization of agriculture in the Soviet Union is examined in **S. Fitzpatrick, *Stalin's Peasants: Resistance and Survival in the Russian Village After Collectivization*** (New York, 1995). On Stalin himself, see **R. Service, *Stalin: A Biography*** (Cambridge, Mass., 2006).

THE PATH TO WAR On the causes of World War II, see **A. J. Crozier, *Causes of the Second World War*** (Oxford, 1997). On the origins of the war in the Pacific, see **A. Iriye, *The Origins of the Second World War in Asia and the Pacific*** (London, 1987).

WORLD WAR II The best general work on World War II is **G. Weinberg, *A World at Arms: A Global History of World War II,*** 2nd ed. (Cambridge, 2005). A good military history of World War II can be found in **W. Murray** and **A. R. Millett, *A War to Be Won: Fighting the Second World War*** (Cambridge, Mass., 2000).

THE HOLOCAUST Excellent studies of the Holocaust include **S. Friedander, *The Years of Extermination: Nazi Germany and the Jews, 1939–1945*** (New York, 2007), and **L. Yahil, *The Holocaust*** (New York, 1990). For a brief study, see **D. Dwork** and **R. J. van Pelt, *Holocaust: A History*** (New York, 2002).

THE HOME FRONT On the home front in Germany, see **M. Kitchen, *Nazi Germany at War*** (New York, 1995). The Soviet Union during the war is examined in **M. Harrison, *Soviet Planning in Peace and War, 1938–1945*** (Cambridge, 1985). The Japanese home front is examined in **T. R. H. Havens, *The Valley of Darkness: The Japanese People and World War Two*** (New York, 1978). On the Allied bombing campaign against Germany, see **R. Hansen, *Fire and Fury: The Allied Bombing of Germany, 1942–1945*** (London, 2008).

Visit the CourseMate website at **www.cengagebrain.com** for additional study tools and review materials for this chapter.

PART V

Toward a Global Civilization? The World Since 1945

AS WORLD WAR II came to an end, the survivors of that bloody struggle could afford to face the future with a cautious optimism. There was reason to hope that the bitter rivalry that had marked relations among the Western powers would finally be put to an end and that the wartime alliance of the United States, Great Britain, and the Soviet Union could be maintained into the postwar era.

More than sixty years later, these hopes have been only partly realized. In the decades following the war, the Western capitalist nations managed to recover from the economic depression that had led into World War II. The bloody conflicts that had erupted among European nations during the first half of the twentieth century ended, and Germany and Japan were fully reintegrated into the world community.

At the same time, the prospects for a stable, peaceful world and an end to balance-of-power politics were hampered by the emergence of a grueling and sometimes tense ideological struggle between the socialist and capitalist camps, a competition headed by the only remaining great powers, the Soviet Union and the United States.

In the shadow of this rivalry, the Western European states made a remarkable economic recovery and reached untold levels of prosperity. In Eastern Europe, Soviet domination, both political and economic, seemed so complete that many people doubted it could ever be undone. But communism had never put down deep roots in Eastern Europe, and in the late 1980s, when Soviet leader Mikhail Gorbachev indicated that his government would no longer intervene militarily to keep the Eastern European states in line, they were quick to embrace their freedom and adopt new economic structures based on Western models.

The peoples of Africa and Asia had their own reasons for optimism as World War II came to a close. In the Atlantic Charter, Franklin Roosevelt and Winston Churchill had set forth a joint declaration of their peace aims calling for the self-determination of all peoples.

As it turned out, some colonial powers were reluctant to divest themselves of their colonies. Still, World War II had severely undermined the stability of the colonial order, and by the end of the 1940s, most colonies in Asia had received their independence. Africa followed a decade or two later.

Broadly speaking, the leaders of these newly liberated countries set forth three goals at the outset of independence. They wanted to throw off the shackles of Western economic domination and ensure material prosperity for all of their citizens. They wanted to introduce new political institutions that would enhance the right of self-determination of their peoples. And they wanted to develop a sense of common nationhood within the population and establish secure territorial boundaries. Most opted to follow a capitalist or a moderately socialist path toward economic development. In a few cases—most notably in China and Vietnam—revolutionary leaders opted for the communist mode of development.

Regardless of the path chosen, to many the results were often disappointing. Much of Africa and Asia remained economically dependent on the advanced industrial nations. Some societies faced severe problems of urban and rural poverty. Others were rent by bitter internal conflicts.

What had happened to tarnish the bright dream of economic affluence? During the late 1950s and early 1960s, the dominant school of thought among scholars and

Beijing//© Vittoriani Rastelli/CORBIS

government officials in the United States was modernization theory, which took the view that the problems faced by the newly independent countries were a consequence of the difficult transition from a traditional to a modern society. Modernization theorists were convinced that agrarian countries were destined to follow the West and create modern industrial societies but that they would need both time and substantial amounts of economic and technological assistance from the West to do so.

Eventually, modernization theory came under attack from a new generation of scholars, who argued that the responsibility for continued economic underdevelopment in the postcolonial world lay not with the countries themselves but with their continued domination by the former colonial powers. In this view, known as dependency theory, the countries of Asia, Africa, and Latin America were the victims of the international marketplace, in which high prices were charged for the manufactured goods of the West while low prices were paid to the preindustrial countries for their raw material exports. Efforts by such countries to build up their industrial sectors and move into the stage of self-sustaining growth were hampered by foreign control of many of their resources via European- and American-owned corporations. To end this "neocolonial" relationship, the dependency theory advocates argued, developing societies should reduce their economic ties with the West and institute a policy of economic self-reliance, thereby taking control over their own destinies.

Leaders of African and Asian countries also encountered problems creating new political cultures responsive to the needs of their citizens. At first, most accepted the concept of democracy as the defining theme of that culture. Within a decade, however, democratic systems throughout the developing world were replaced by military dictatorships or one-party governments that redefined the concept of democracy to fit their own preferences. It was clear that the difficulties in building democratic political institutions in developing societies had been underestimated.

The establishment of a common national identity has in some ways been the most daunting of all the challenges facing the new nations of Asia and Africa. Many of these new states were a composite of various ethnic, religious, and linguistic groups that found it difficult to agree on common symbols of nationalism or national values. The process of establishing an official language and delineating territorial boundaries left over from the colonial era created difficulties in many countries. Internal conflicts spawned by deep-rooted historical and ethnic hatreds have proliferated throughout the world, causing vast numbers of people to move across state boundaries in migrations as large as any since the great migrations of the thirteenth and fourteenth centuries.

The introduction of Western cultural values and customs has also had a destabilizing effect in many areas. Though welcomed by some groups, such ideas are firmly resisted by others. Where Western influence has the effect of undermining traditional customs and religious beliefs, it often provokes violent hostility and sparks tension and even conflict within individual societies. Much of the anger recently directed at the United States in Muslim countries has undoubtedly been generated by such feelings.

Nonetheless, social and political attitudes are changing rapidly in many Asian and African countries as new economic circumstances have led to a more secular worldview, a decline in traditional hierarchical relations, and a more open attitude toward sexual practices. In part, these changes are a consequence of the influence of Western music, movies, and television. But they are also a product of the growth of an affluent middle class in many societies of Asia and Africa.

Today, we live not only in a world economy but in a world society, where a revolution in the Middle East can cause a rise in the price of oil in the United States and a change in social behavior in Malaysia and Indonesia, where the collapse of an empire in Asia can send shock waves as far as Hanoi and Havana, and where a terrorist attack in New York City or London can disrupt financial markets around the world.

CHAPTER

26

East and West in the Grip of the Cold War

Imperial War Museum, London//© The Art Archive at Art Resource, NY

Churchill, Roosevelt, and Stalin at Yalta

CHAPTER OUTLINE AND FOCUS QUESTIONS

The Collapse of the Grand Alliance

Q Why were the United States and the Soviet Union suspicious of each other after World War II, and what events between 1945 and 1949 heightened the tensions between the two nations?

Cold War in Asia

Q How and why did Mao Zedong and the Communists come to power in China, and what were the Cold War implications of their triumph?

From Confrontation to Coexistence

Q What events led to the era of coexistence in the 1960s, and to what degree did each side contribute to the reduction in international tensions?

An Era of Equivalence

Q Why did the Cold War briefly flare up again in the 1980s, and why did it come to a definitive end at the end of the decade?

CRITICAL THINKING

Q How have historians answered the question of whether the United States or the Soviet Union bears the primary responsibility for the Cold War, and what evidence can be presented on each side of the issue?

"OUR MEETING HERE in the Crimea has reaffirmed our common determination to maintain and strengthen in the peace to come that unity of purpose and of action which has made victory possible and certain for the United Nations in this war. We believe that this is a sacred obligation which our Governments owe to our peoples and to all the peoples of the world."[1]

With these ringing words, drafted at the Yalta Conference in February 1945, U.S. President Franklin D. Roosevelt, Soviet leader Joseph Stalin, and British Prime Minister Winston Churchill affirmed their common hope that the Grand Alliance that had been victorious in World War II could be sustained into the postwar era. Only through continuing and growing cooperation and understanding among the three Allies, the statement asserted, could a secure and lasting peace be realized that, in the words of the Atlantic Charter, would "afford assurance that all the men in all the lands may live out their lives in freedom from fear and want."

Roosevelt hoped that the decisions reached at Yalta would provide the basis for a stable peace in the postwar era. Allied occupation forces—American, British, and French in the west and Soviet in the east—were to bring about the end of Axis administration and to organize the free election of democratic governments throughout Europe. To foster mutual trust and an end to the suspicions that had marked relations between the capitalist world and the Soviet Union prior to the war, Roosevelt tried to reassure Stalin that Moscow's legitimate territorial aspirations and genuine security needs would be adequately met in a durable peace settlement.

It was not to be. Within months after the German surrender, the mutual trust among the Allies—if it had ever truly existed—rapidly disintegrated, and the dream of a stable peace was replaced by the specter of a potential nuclear holocaust. The United Nations, envisioned by its founders as a mechanism for adjudicating international disputes, became mired in partisan bickering. As the Cold War between Moscow and Washington intensified, Europe was divided into two armed camps, while the two superpowers, glaring at each other across a deep ideological divide, held the survival of the entire world in their hands.

The Collapse of the Grand Alliance

FOCUS QUESTION: Why were the United States and the Soviet Union suspicious of each other after World War II, and what events between 1945 and 1949 heightened the tensions between the two nations?

The problems started in Europe. At the end of the war, Soviet military forces occupied all of Eastern Europe and the Balkans (except Greece, Albania, and Yugoslavia), while U.S. and other Allied forces secured the western part of the Continent. Roosevelt had assumed that free elections, administered promptly by "democratic and peace-loving forces," would lead to democratic governments responsive to the local population. But it soon became clear that the Soviet Union interpreted the Yalta agreement differently. When Soviet occupation authorities began forming a new Polish government, Stalin refused to accept the Polish government-in-exile—headquartered in London during the war and composed mostly of landed aristocrats who harbored a deep distrust of the Soviet Union—and instead set up a government composed of Communists who had spent the war in Moscow. Roosevelt complained to Stalin but eventually agreed to a compromise whereby two members of the London government were included in the new Communist regime. A week later, Roosevelt was dead of a cerebral hemorrhage, emboldening Stalin to do much as he pleased.

Soviet Domination of Eastern Europe

Similar developments took place in all of the states occupied by Soviet troops. Coalitions of all political parties (except fascist or right-wing parties) were formed to run the government, but within a year or two, the Communist Party in each coalition had assumed the lion's share of power. It was then a short step to the establishment of one-party Communist governments. Between 1945 and 1947, Communist governments became firmly entrenched in East Germany, Bulgaria, Romania, Poland, and Hungary. In Czechoslovakia, with its strong tradition of democratic institutions, the Communists did not achieve their goals until 1948. After the Czech elections of 1946, the Communist Party shared control of the government with the non-Communist parties. When the latter appeared likely to win new elections early in 1948, the Communists seized control of the government on February 25. All other parties were dissolved, and the Communist leader Klement Gottwald (KLEM-ent GUT-vald) (1896–1953) became the new president of Czechoslovakia.

Yugoslavia was a notable exception to the pattern of Soviet dominance in Eastern Europe. The Communist Party there had led resistance to the Nazis during the war and easily assumed power when the war ended. Josip Broz (yaw-SEEP BRAWZ), known as Tito (TEE-toh) (1892–1980), the leader of the Communist resistance movement, appeared to be a loyal Stalinist. After the war, however, he moved to establish an independent Communist state. Stalin hoped to take control of Yugoslavia, but Tito refused to capitulate to Stalin's demands and gained the support of the people (and some sympathy in the West) by portraying the struggle as one of Yugoslav national freedom. In 1958, the Yugoslav party congress asserted that Yugoslav Communists did not see themselves as deviating from communism, only from Stalinism. They considered their more decentralized system, in which workers managed themselves and local communes exercised some political power, closer to the Marxist-Leninist ideal.

To Stalin (who had once boasted, "I will shake my little finger, and there will be no more Tito"), the creation of pliant pro-Soviet regimes throughout Eastern Europe to serve as a buffer zone against the capitalist West may simply have represented his interpretation of the Yalta peace agreement and a reward for sacrifices suffered during the war. If the Soviet leader had any intention of promoting future Communist revolutions in Western Europe—and there is some indication that he did—such developments would have to await the appearance of a new capitalist crisis a decade or more into the future. As Stalin undoubtedly recalled, Lenin had always maintained that revolutions come in waves.

Descent of the Iron Curtain

To the United States, however, the Soviet takeover of Eastern Europe represented an ominous development that threatened Roosevelt's vision of a durable peace. Public suspicion of Soviet intentions grew rapidly, especially among the millions of Americans who still had relatives living in Eastern Europe. Winston Churchill was quick to put such fears into words. In a highly publicized speech at Westminster College in Fulton, Missouri, in March 1946, the former British prime minister declared that an "iron curtain" had "descended across the Continent," dividing Germany and Europe itself into two hostile camps. Stalin responded by branding Churchill's speech a "call to war with the Soviet Union." But he need not have worried. Although public opinion in the United States placed increasing pressure on Roosevelt's successor, Harry Truman (1884–1972), to devise an effective strategy to counter Soviet advances abroad, the American people were in no mood for another war.

Eastern Europe in 1948

The first threat of a U.S.-Soviet confrontation took place in the Middle East. During World War II, British and Soviet troops had been stationed in Iran to prevent Axis occupation of the rich oil fields in that country. Both nations had promised to withdraw their forces after the war, but at the end of 1945, there were ominous signs that Moscow might attempt to use its troops as a bargaining chip to annex Iran's northern territories—known as Azerbaijan (az-ur-by-JAHN)—into the Soviet Union. When the government of Iran, with strong U.S. support, threatened to take the issue to the United Nations, the Soviets backed down and removed their forces from that country in the spring of 1946.

The Truman Doctrine

A civil war in Greece created another potential arena for confrontation between the superpowers and an opportunity for the Truman administration to take a stand. Communist guerrilla forces supported by Tito's Yugoslavia had taken up arms against the pro-Western government in Athens. Great Britain had initially assumed primary responsibility for promoting postwar reconstruction in the eastern Mediterranean, but in 1947, continuing economic problems caused the British to withdraw from the active role they had been playing in both Greece and Turkey. President Truman, alarmed by British weakness and the possibility of Soviet expansion into the eastern Mediterranean, responded with the **Truman Doctrine**, which said in essence that the United States would provide financial aid to countries that claimed they were threatened by Communist expansion (see the box on p. 683). If the Soviets were not stopped in Greece, the Truman argument ran, then the United States would have to face the spread of communism throughout the free world. As Dean Acheson, the U.S. secretary of state, explained, "Like apples in a barrel infected by disease, the corruption of Greece would infect Iran and all the East . . . likewise Africa . . . Italy . . . France. . . . Not since Rome and Carthage has there been such a polarization of power on this earth."[2]

The somewhat apocalyptic tone of Acheson's statement was intentional. Not only were the American people in no mood for foreign adventures, but the administration's Republican opponents in Congress were in an isolationist frame of mind. Only the prospect of a dire threat from abroad, the president's advisers argued, could persuade the nation to take action. The tactic worked, and Congress voted to provide the aid Truman had requested.

The U.S. suspicion that Moscow was actively supporting the insurgent movement in Greece turned out to be unfounded, however. Stalin was apparently unhappy with Tito's role in the conflict, not only because he suspected that the latter was attempting to create his own sphere of influence in the Balkans but also because it risked provoking a direct confrontation between the United States and the Soviet Union. But the Truman Doctrine had its intended effect in the United States, as public concern about the future intentions of the Soviets rose to new heights.

The Marshall Plan

The proclamation of the Truman Doctrine was followed in June 1947 by the European Recovery Program, better known as the **Marshall Plan**, which provided $13 billion in U.S. assistance for the economic recovery of war-torn Europe. Underlying the program was the belief that Communist aggression fed off economic turmoil. General George C. Marshall had noted in a speech at Harvard University, "Our policy is not directed against any

The Truman Doctrine

In 1947, the battle lines in the Cold War had been clearly drawn. This excerpt is taken from a speech by President Harry Truman to the U.S. Congress in which he justified his request for aid to Greece and Turkey. Truman expressed the urgent need to contain the expansion of communism. Compare this statement with that of Soviet leader Leonid Brezhnev cited on p. 701.

Truman's Speech to Congress, March 12, 1947

The gravity of the situation which confronts the world today necessitates my appearance before a joint session of the Congress. The foreign policy and the national security of this country are involved.

One aspect of the present situation, which I wish to present to you at this time for your consideration and decision, concerns Greece and Turkey.

The United States has received from the Greek Government an urgent appeal for financial and economic assistance. Preliminary reports from the American Economic Mission now in Greece and reports from the American Ambassador in Greece corroborate the statement of the Greek Government that assistance is imperative if Greece is to survive as a free nation.

I do not believe that the American people and the Congress wish to turn a deaf ear to the appeal of the Greek Government.

Greece is not a rich country. Lack of sufficient natural resources has always forced the Greek people to work hard to make both ends meet. Since 1940, this industrious and peace loving country has suffered invasion, four years of cruel enemy occupation, and bitter internal strife. . . .

The peoples of a number of countries of the world have recently had totalitarian regimes forced upon them against their will. The Government of the United States has made frequent protests against coercion and intimidation, in violation of the Yalta agreement, in Poland, Rumania, and Bulgaria. I must also state that in a number of other countries there have been similar developments.

At the present moment in world history nearly every nation must choose between alternative ways of life. The choice is too often not a free one.

One way of life is based upon the will of the majority, and is distinguished by free institutions, representative government, free elections, guarantees of individual liberty, freedom of speech and religion, and freedom from political oppression.

The second way of life is based upon the will of a minority forcibly imposed upon the majority. It relies upon terror and oppression, a controlled press and radio; fixed elections, and the suppression of personal freedoms.

I believe that it must be the policy of the United States to support free peoples who are resisting attempted subjugation by armed minorities or by outside pressures.

I believe that we must assist free peoples to work out their own destinies in their own way.

I believe that our help should be primarily through economic and financial aid which is essential to economic stability and orderly political processes.

The world is not static, and the status quo is not sacred. But we cannot allow changes in the status quo in violation of the Charter of the United Nations by such methods as coercion, or by such subterfuges as political infiltration. In helping free and independent nations to maintain their freedom, the United States will be giving effect to the principles of the Charter of the United Nations.

It is necessary only to glance at a map to realize that the survival and integrity of the Greek nation are of grave importance in a much wider situation. If Greece should fall under the control of an armed minority, the effect upon its neighbor, Turkey, would be immediate and serious. Confusion and disorder might well spread throughout the entire Middle East.

Moreover, the disappearance of Greece as an independent state would have a profound effect upon those countries in Europe whose peoples are struggling against great difficulties to maintain their freedoms and their independence while they repair the damages of war.

It would be an unspeakable tragedy if these countries, which have struggled so long against overwhelming odds, should lose that victory for which they sacrificed so much. Collapse of free institutions and loss of independence would be disastrous not only for them but for the world. Discouragement and possibly failure would quickly be the lot of neighboring peoples striving to maintain their freedom and independence.

Should we fail to aid Greece and Turkey in this fateful hour, the effect will be far reaching to the West as well as to the East.

We must take immediate and resolute action. . . .

(Continued)

(Continued)

The assistance that I am recommending for Greece and Turkey amounts to little more than 1 tenth of 1 per cent of this investment. It is only common sense that we should safeguard this investment and make sure that it was not in vain.

The seeds of totalitarian regimes are nurtured by misery and want. They spread and grow in the evil soil of poverty and strife. They reach their full growth when the hope of a people for a better life has died. We must keep that hope alive.

The free peoples of the world look to us for support in maintaining their freedoms.

If we falter in our leadership, we may endanger the peace of the world—and we shall surely endanger the welfare of our own nation.

Great responsibilities have been placed upon us by the swift movement of events.

I am confident that the Congress will face these responsibilities squarely.

How did President Truman defend his request for aid to Greece and Turkey? What role did this decision play in intensifying the Cold War?

Source: U.S. Congress, *Congressional Record*, 80th Congress, 1st Session (Washington, D.C.: U.S. Government Printing Office, 1947), Vol. 93, p. 1981.

country or doctrine but against hunger, poverty, desperation, and chaos."[3]

From the Soviet perspective, the Marshall Plan was capitalist imperialism, a thinly veiled attempt to buy the support of the smaller European countries "in return for the relinquishing . . . of their economic and later also their political independence."[4] A Soviet spokesperson described the United States as the "main force in the imperialist camp," whose ultimate goal was "the strengthening of imperialism, preparation for a new imperialist war, a struggle against socialism and democracy, and the support of reactionary and antidemocratic, profascist regimes and movements." Although the Marshall Plan was open to the Soviet Union and its Eastern European satellite states, Soviet leaders viewed the offer as a devious capitalist ploy and refused to participate. Under heavy pressure from Moscow, Eastern European governments did so as well. The Soviets were in no position to compete financially with the United States, however, and could do little to counter the Marshall Plan except tighten their control in Eastern Europe.

Europe Divided

By 1947, the split in Europe between East and West had become a fact of life. At the end of World War II, the United States had favored a quick end to its commitments in Europe. But American fears of Soviet aims caused the United States to play an increasingly important role in European affairs. In an article in *Foreign Affairs* in July 1947, George Kennan, a well-known U.S. diplomat with much knowledge of Soviet affairs, advocated a policy of **containment** against further aggressive Soviet moves. Kennan favored the "adroit and vigilant application of counter-force at a series of constantly shifting geographical and political points, corresponding to the shifts and maneuvers of Soviet policy." When the Soviets blockaded Berlin in 1948, containment of the Soviet Union became formal U.S. policy.

THE BERLIN BLOCKADE The fate of Germany had become a source of heated contention between East and West. Aside from **denazification** (dee-naht-sih-fuh-KAY-shun) and the partitioning of Germany (and Berlin) into four occupied zones, the Allied powers had agreed on little with regard to the conquered nation. The Soviet Union, hardest hit by the war, took reparations from Germany by pillaging German industry. The technology-starved Soviets dismantled and removed to Russia 380 factories from the western zones of Berlin before transferring their control to the Western powers. By the summer of 1946, two hundred chemical, paper, and textile factories in the East German zone had likewise been shipped to the Soviet Union. At the same time, the German

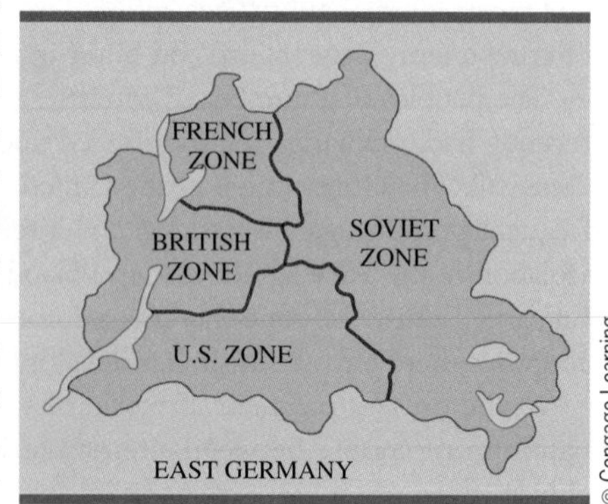

© Cengage Learning

Berlin at the Start of the Cold War

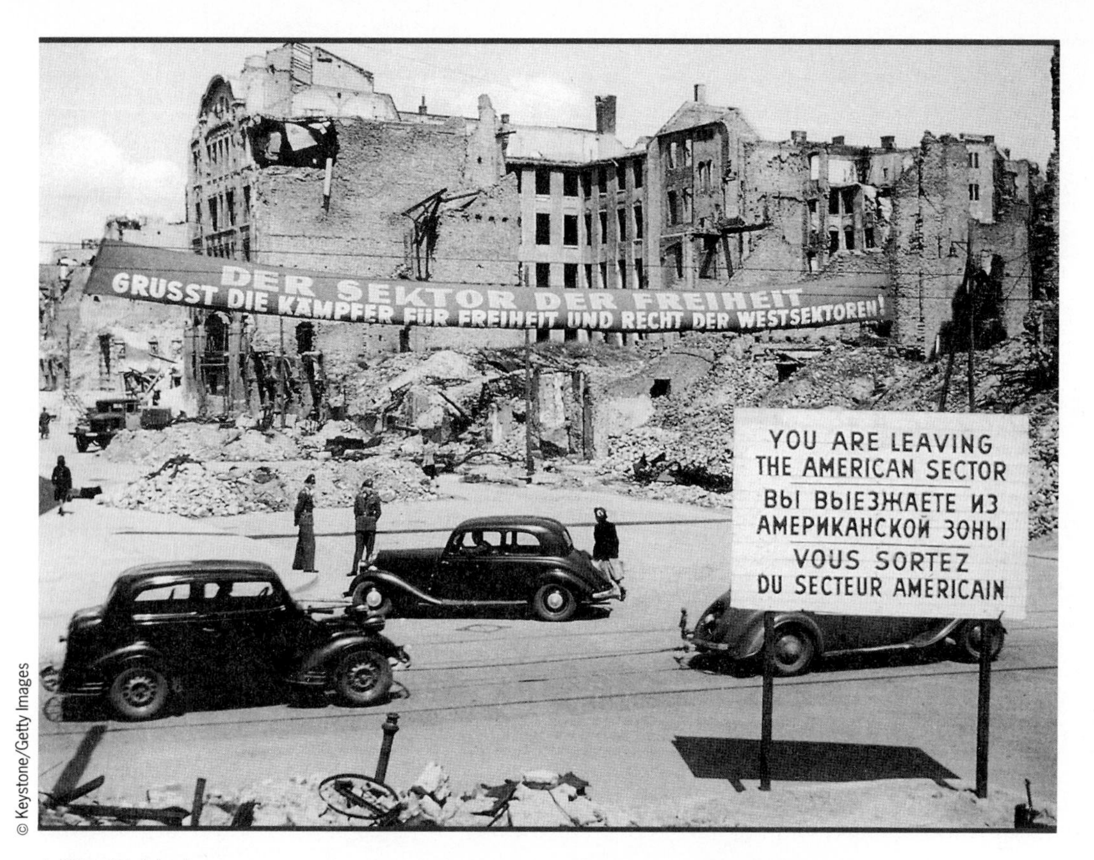

© Keystone/Getty Images

A City Divided. In 1948, U.S. planes airlifted supplies into Berlin to break the blockade that Soviet troops had imposed to isolate the city. Shown here is "Checkpoint Charlie," located at the boundary between the U.S. and Soviet zones of Berlin, just as Soviet roadblocks are about to be removed. The banner at the entrance to the Soviet sector reads, ironically, "The sector of freedom greets the fighters for freedom and right of the Western sectors."

Communist Party was reestablished, under the control of Walter Ulbricht (VAHL-tuh OOL-brikkt) (1893–1973), and was soon in charge of the political reconstruction of the Soviet zone in eastern Germany.

Although the foreign ministers of the four occupying powers kept meeting in an attempt to arrive at a final peace treaty with Germany, they moved further and further apart. At the same time, the British, French, and Americans gradually began to merge their zones economically and by February 1948 were making plans for unification of these sectors and the formation of a national government. In an effort to secure all of Berlin and to halt the creation of a West German government, the Soviet Union imposed a blockade of West Berlin that prevented all traffic from entering the city's western zones through Soviet-controlled territory in East Germany.

The Western powers faced a dilemma. Direct military confrontation seemed dangerous, and no one wished to risk World War III. Therefore, an attempt to break through the blockade with tanks and trucks was ruled out. The solution was to deliver supplies for the city's inhabitants by plane. At its peak, the Berlin Airlift flew 13,000 tons of supplies daily into Berlin. The Soviets, also not wanting war, did not interfere and finally lifted the blockade in May 1949. The blockade of Berlin had severely increased tensions between the United States and the Soviet Union and brought the separation of Germany into two states. The Federal Republic of Germany was formally created from the three Western zones in September 1949, and a month later, the separate German Democratic Republic (GDR) was established in East Germany. Berlin remained a divided city and the source of much contention between East and West.

NATO AND THE WARSAW PACT The search for security in the new world of the Cold War also led to the formation of military alliances. The North Atlantic Treaty Organization (NATO) was formed in April 1949 when Belgium, Denmark, France, Great Britain, Iceland, Italy, Luxembourg, the Netherlands, Norway, and Portugal signed a treaty with the United States and Canada. All the powers agreed to provide mutual assistance if any one of them was attacked. A few years later, Greece, Turkey, and West Germany joined NATO.

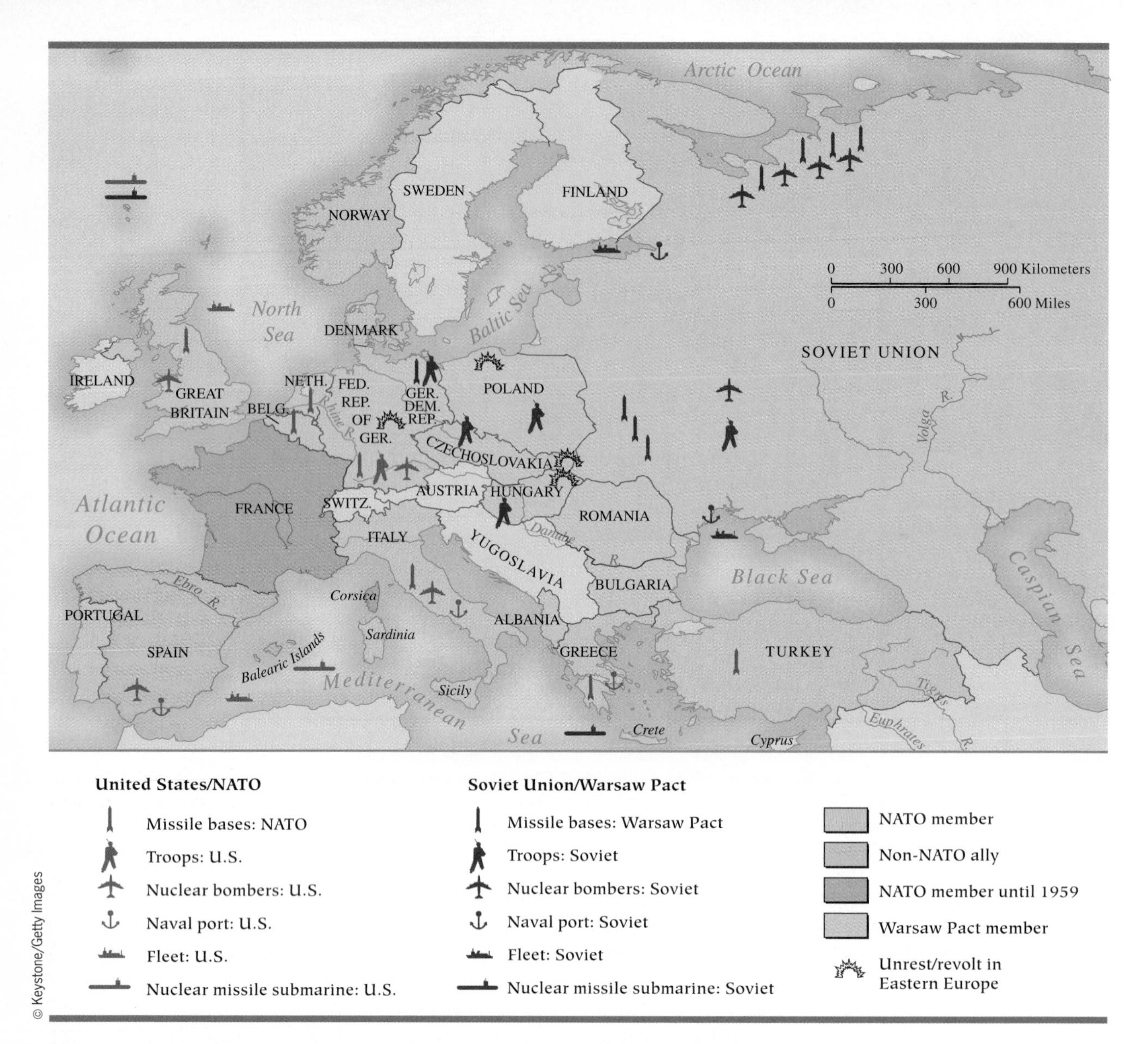

© Keystone/Getty Images

MAP 26.1 The New European Alliance Systems During the Cold War. This map shows postwar Europe as it was divided during the Cold War into two contending power blocs, the NATO alliance and the Warsaw Pact. Major military and naval bases are indicated by symbols on the map.

Where on the map was the "iron curtain"?

The Eastern European states soon followed suit. In 1949, they formed the Council for Mutual Economic Assistance (COMECON) for economic cooperation. Then, in 1955, Albania, Bulgaria, Czechoslovakia, East Germany, Hungary, Poland, Romania, and the Soviet Union organized a formal military alliance, the Warsaw Pact. Once again, Europe was tragically divided into hostile alliance systems (see Map 26.1).

WHO STARTED THE COLD WAR? There has been considerable historical debate over who bears responsibility for starting the Cold War. In the 1950s, most scholars in the West assumed that the bulk of the blame must fall on the shoulders of Stalin, whose determination to impose Soviet rule on Eastern Europe snuffed out hopes for freedom and self-determination there and aroused justifiable fears of Communist expansion in the West. During the next decade, however, revisionist historians—influenced in part by their hostility to aggressive U.S. policies in Southeast Asia—began to argue that the fault lay primarily in Washington, where Truman and his anti-Communist advisers abandoned the precepts of Yalta and sought to encircle the Soviet Union with a tier of pliant U.S. client states. More recently, many historians have adopted a more nuanced view, noting that both the United States and the Soviet Union took some unwise steps that contributed to rising tensions at the end of World War II.

In fact, both nations were working within a framework conditioned by the past. The rivalry between the two superpowers ultimately stemmed from their different historical perspectives and their irreconcilable political ambitions. Intense competition for political and military supremacy had long been a regular feature of Western civilization.

The United States and the Soviet Union were the heirs of that European tradition of power politics, and it should come as no surprise that two such different systems would seek to extend their way of life to the rest of the world. Because of its need to secure its western border, the Soviet Union was not prepared to give up the advantages it had gained in Eastern Europe from Germany's defeat. But neither were Western leaders prepared to accept without protest the establishment of a system of Soviet satellites that not only threatened the security of Western Europe but also deeply offended Western sensibilities because of its blatant disregard of the Western concept of human rights.

This does not necessarily mean that both sides bear equal responsibility for starting the Cold War. Some revisionist historians have claimed that the U.S. doctrine of containment was a provocative action that aroused Stalin's suspicions and drove him into a position of hostility toward the West. This charge lacks credibility. Although the Soviets were understandably concerned that the United States might use its monopoly of nuclear weapons to attempt to intimidate them, information now available from the Soviet archives and other sources makes it increasingly clear that Stalin's suspicions of the West were rooted in his Marxist-Leninist worldview and long predated Washington's enunciation of the doctrine of containment. As his foreign minister, Vyacheslav Molotov, once remarked, Soviet policy was inherently aggressive and would be triggered whenever the opportunity offered. Although Stalin apparently had no master plan to advance Soviet power into Western Europe, he was probably prepared to make every effort to do so once the next revolutionary wave arrived. Western leaders were fully justified in reacting to this possibility by strengthening their own lines of defense.

On the other hand, a case can be made that in deciding to respond to the Soviet challenge in a primarily military manner, Western leaders overreacted and virtually guaranteed that the Cold War would be transformed into an arms race that could conceivably result in a new and uniquely destructive war. George Kennan, the original architect of the doctrine of containment, had initially proposed a primarily political approach and eventually disavowed the means by which the containment strategy was carried out.

Cold War in Asia

FOCUS QUESTION: How and why did Mao Zedong and the Communists come to power in China, and what were the Cold War implications of their triumph?

The Cold War was somewhat slower to make its appearance in Asia. At Yalta, Stalin formally agreed to enter the Pacific War against Japan three months after the close of the conflict with Germany. As a reward for Soviet participation in the struggle against Japan, Roosevelt promised that Moscow would be granted "preeminent interests" in Manchuria (reminiscent of the interests possessed by imperial Russia prior to its defeat by Japan in 1904–1905) and be allowed to establish a Soviet naval base at Port Arthur. In return, Stalin promised to sign a treaty of alliance with the Republic of China, thus implicitly committing the Soviet Union not to aid the Chinese Communists in a possible future civil war. Although many observers would later question Stalin's sincerity in making such a commitment to the vocally anti-Communist Chiang Kai-shek, in Moscow the decision probably had a logic of its own. Stalin had no particular liking for the independent-minded Mao Zedong and indeed did not anticipate a Communist victory in any civil war in China. Only an agreement with Chiang could provide the Soviet Union with a strategically vital economic and political presence in northern China.

The Truman administration was equally reluctant to get embroiled in a confrontation with Moscow over the unfolding events in East Asia. Suspicion of Chiang Kai-shek ran high in Washington, and as we shall see, many key U.S. policymakers hoped to avoid a deeper involvement in China by brokering a compromise agreement between Chiang and his Communist rival, Mao.

Despite these commitments, the Allied agreements soon broke down, and East Asia was sucked into the vortex of the Cold War by the end of the 1940s. The root of the problem lay in the underlying weakness of Chiang's regime, which threatened to create a political vacuum in East Asia that both Moscow and Washington would be tempted to fill.

The Chinese Civil War

As World War II came to an end in the Pacific, relations between the government of Chiang Kai-shek in China and its powerful U.S. ally had become frayed. Although Roosevelt had hoped that republican China would be the keystone of his plan for peace and stability in Asia after the war, U.S. officials became disillusioned with the corruption of Chiang's government and his unwillingness to risk his forces against the Japanese (he hoped to save them for use against the Communists after the war in the Pacific ended), and China was no longer the object of Washington's close attention as the war came to a close. Nevertheless, U.S. military and economic aid to China had been substantial, and at the war's end, the new Truman administration still hoped that it could rely on Chiang to support U.S. postwar goals in the region.

While Chiang Kai-shek wrestled with Japanese aggression and problems of national development, the Communists were building up their strength in northern China. To enlarge their political base, they carried out a "mass line" policy (a term in Communist jargon that meant responding to the needs of the mass of the population), reducing land rents and confiscating the lands of wealthy landlords. By the end of World War II, 20 to 30 million Chinese were living under the administration of the Communists, and their People's Liberation Army (PLA) included nearly one million troops.

As the war came to an end, world attention began to focus on the prospects for renewed civil strife in China. Members of a U.S. liaison team stationed in Yan'an (yuh-NAHN) were impressed by the performance of the Communists, and some recommended that the United States should support them or at least remain neutral in a possible conflict between Communists and Nationalists for control of China. The Truman administration, though skeptical of Chiang's ability to forge a strong and prosperous country, was increasingly concerned about the spread of communism in Europe and tried to find a peaceful solution through the formation of a coalition government of all parties in China.

THE COMMUNIST TRIUMPH The effort failed. By 1946, full-scale war between the Nationalist government, now reinstalled in Nanjing, and the Communists resumed. Initially, most of the fighting took place in Manchuria, where newly arrived Communist units began to surround Nationalist forces occupying the major cities. Now Chiang Kai-shek's errors came home to roost. In the countryside, millions of peasants, attracted to the Communists by promises of land and social justice, flocked to serve in Mao Zedong's PLA. In the cities, middle-class Chinese, normally hostile to communism, were alienated by Chiang's brutal suppression of all dissent and his government's inability to slow the ruinous rate of inflation or solve the economic problems it caused. By the end of 1947, almost all of Manchuria was under Communist control.

The Truman administration reacted to the spread of Communist power in China with acute discomfort. Washington had no desire to see a Communist government on the mainland, but it had little confidence in Chiang Kai-shek's ability to realize Roosevelt's dream of a strong, united, and prosperous China. In December 1945, President Truman sent General George C. Marshall to China in a last-ditch effort to bring about a peaceful settlement, but anti-Communist elements in the Republic of China resisted U.S. pressure to create a coalition government with the Chinese Communist Party (CCP). During the next two years, the United States gave limited military support to Chiang's regime but refused to commit U.S. power to guarantee its survival. The administration's hands-off policy deeply angered many

© Jack Wilkes/Time Life Pictures//Getty Images

Mao Zedong and Chiang Kai-shek Exchange a Toast. After World War II, the United States sent General George C. Marshall to China in an effort to prevent civil war between Chiang Kai-shek's government and Mao Zedong's Communists. Marshall's initial success was symbolized by this toast between Mao (at the left) and Chiang. But suspicion ran too deep, and soon conflict ensued, leading to a Communist victory in 1949. Chiang's government retreated to the island of Taiwan.

members of Congress, who charged that the White House was "soft on communism" and called for increased military assistance to the Nationalist government.

With morale dropping in the cities, Chiang's troops began to defect to the Communists. Sometimes whole divisions, officers as well as ordinary soldiers, changed sides. By 1948, the PLA was advancing south out of Manchuria and had encircled Beijing. Communist troops took the old imperial capital, crossed the Yangtze the following spring, and occupied the commercial hub of Shanghai (see Map 26.2). During the next few months, Chiang's government and 2 million of his followers fled to Taiwan, which the Japanese had returned to Chinese control after World War II.

With the Communist victory in China, Asia became a major theater of the Cold War and an integral element in American politics. In a white paper issued by the State Department in the fall of 1949, the Truman administration placed most of the blame for the debacle on Chiang Kai-shek's regime (see the box on p. 688). Republicans in Congress, however, disagreed, arguing that Roosevelt had betrayed Chiang Kai-shek at Yalta by granting privileges in Manchuria to the Soviet Union. In their view, Soviet troops had hindered the dispatch of Nationalist forces to the area and provided the PLA with weapons to use against their rivals.

In later years, sources in Moscow and Beijing made clear that in actuality the Soviet Union gave little assistance to the CCP in its postwar struggle against the Nanjing regime. In fact, Stalin—likely concerned at the prospect of a military confrontation with the United States—advised Mao against undertaking the effort. Although Communist forces undoubtedly received some assistance from Soviet occupation troops in Manchuria, their victory ultimately stemmed from conditions inside China. Nevertheless, the White House responded to its critics. During the spring of 1950, under pressure from Congress and public opinion to define U.S. interests in Asia, the Truman administration adopted a new national security policy that implied that the United States would take whatever steps were necessary to stem the further expansion of communism in the region. Containment had come to East Asia.

The New China

Communist leaders in China, from their new capital of Beijing, probably hoped that their accession to power in 1949 would bring about an era of peace in the region and permit their new government to concentrate on domestic goals. But the desire for peace was tempered by their determination to erase a century of humiliation at the hands of imperialist powers and to restore the traditional outer frontiers of the empire. In addition to recovering territories that had been part of the Manchu Empire, such as Manchuria, Taiwan, and Tibet, the Chinese leaders also hoped to restore Chinese influence in former tributary areas such as Korea and Vietnam.

It soon became clear that these two goals were not always compatible. Negotiations between Mao and Stalin, held in Moscow in January 1950, led to Soviet recognition of Chinese sovereignty over Manchuria and Xinjiang (SHIN-jyahng)—the desolate lands north of Tibet that were known as Chinese Turkestan because many of the peoples in the area were of Turkic origin—although the Soviets retained a measure of economic influence in both areas. Chinese troops occupied Tibet in 1950 and brought it under Chinese administration for the first time in more than a century. But in Korea and Taiwan, China's efforts to re-create the imperial buffer zone provoked new conflicts with foreign powers.

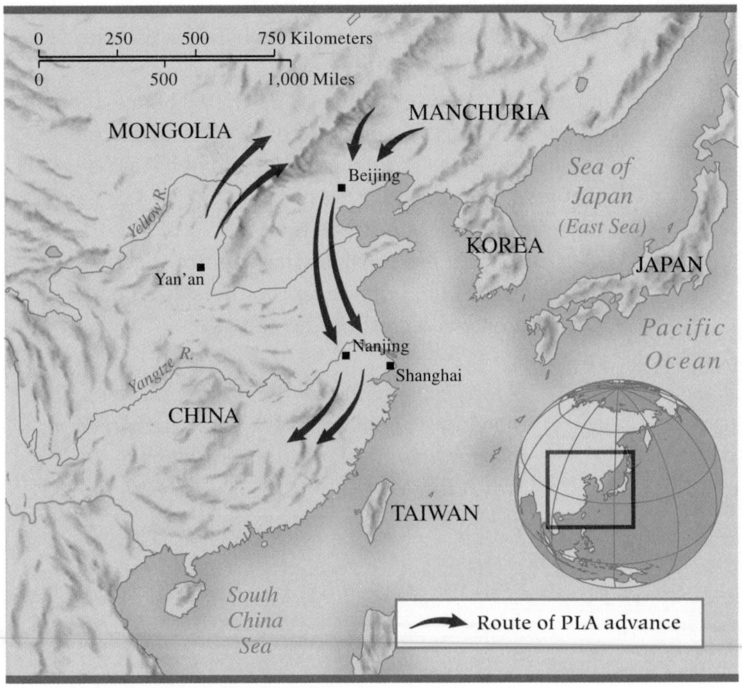

© Cengage Learning

MAP 26.2 The Chinese Civil War. After the close of the Pacific War in 1945, the Nationalist Chinese government and the Chinese Communists fought a bitter civil war that ended with a victory by the latter in 1949. The path of the Communist advance is shown on the map.

Q *Where did Chiang Kai-shek's government retreat to after its defeat?*

Who Lost China?

POLITICS & GOVERNMENT

In 1949, with China about to fall under the control of the Communists, President Truman instructed the State Department to prepare a "white paper" report explaining why the U.S. policy of seeking to avoid a Communist victory in China had failed. The authors of the paper concluded that responsibility lay at the door of Nationalist Chinese leader Chiang Kai-shek and that there was nothing the United States could have done to alter the result. Most China observers today would accept that assessment, but it did little at the time to deflect criticism of the administration for selling out the interests of our ally in China.

U.S. State Department White Paper on China, 1949

When peace came the United States was confronted with three possible alternatives in China: (1) it could have pulled out lock, stock, and barrel; (2) it could have intervened militarily on a major scale to assist the Nationalists to destroy the Communists; (3) it could, while assisting the Nationalists to assert their authority over as much of China as possible, endeavor to avoid a civil war by working for a compromise between the two sides.

The first alternative would, and I believe American public opinion at the time so felt, have represented an abandonment of our international responsibilities and of our traditional policy of friendship for China before we had made a determined effort to be of assistance. The second alternative policy, while it may look attractive theoretically, in retrospect, was wholly impracticable. The Nationalists had been unable to destroy the Communists during the ten years before the war. Now after the war the Nationalists were . . . weakened, demoralized, and unpopular. They had quickly dissipated their popular support and prestige in the areas liberated from the Japanese by the conduct of their civil and military officials. The Communists on the other hand were much stronger than they had ever been and were in control of most of North China. Because of the ineffectiveness of the Nationalist forces, which was later to be tragically demonstrated, the Communists probably could have been dislodged only by American arms. It is obvious that the American people would not have sanctioned such a colossal commitment of our armies in 1945 or later. We therefore came to the third alternative policy whereunder we faced the facts of the situation and attempted to assist in working out a modus vivendi which would avert civil war but nevertheless preserve and even increase the influence of the National Government. . . .

The distrust of the leaders of both the Nationalist and Communist Parties for each other proved too deep-seated to permit final agreement, notwithstanding temporary truces and apparently promising negotiations. The Nationalists, furthermore, embarked in 1946 on an overambitious military campaign in the face of warnings by General Marshall that it not only would fail but would plunge China into economic chaos and eventually destroy the National Government. . . .

The unfortunate but inescapable fact is that the ominous result of the civil war in China was beyond the control of the government of the United States. Nothing that this country did or could have done within the reasonable limits of its capabilities could have changed that result; nothing that was left undone by this country has contributed to it. It was the product of internal Chinese forces, forces which this country tried to influence but could not. A decision was arrived at within China, if only a decision by default.

How did the authors of the white paper explain the Communist victory in China? According to this argument, what actions might have prevented it?

Source: From *United States Relations with China* (Washington, D.C., Dept. of State, 1949), pp. iii–xvi.

The problem of Taiwan was a consequence of the Cold War. As the civil war in China came to an end, the Truman administration appeared determined to avoid entanglement in China's internal affairs and indicated that it would not seek to prevent a Communist takeover of the island, now occupied by Chiang Kai-shek's Republic of China. But as tensions between the United States and the new Chinese government escalated during the winter of 1949–1950, influential figures in the United States began to argue that Taiwan was crucial to U.S. defense strategy in the Pacific.

© Bibliothèque Nationale, Paris//Archives Charmet/The Bridgeman Art Library

A Pledge of Eternal Friendship. After the Communist victory in the Chinese civil war, Chairman Mao Zedong traveled to Moscow, where in 1950 he negotiated a treaty of friendship and cooperation with the Soviet Union. The poster shown here trumpets the results of the meeting: "Long live and strengthen the unbreakable friendship and cooperation of the Soviet and Chinese peoples!" The two leaders, however, did not get along. Mao reportedly complained to colleagues that obtaining assistance from Stalin was "like taking meat from a tiger's mouth."

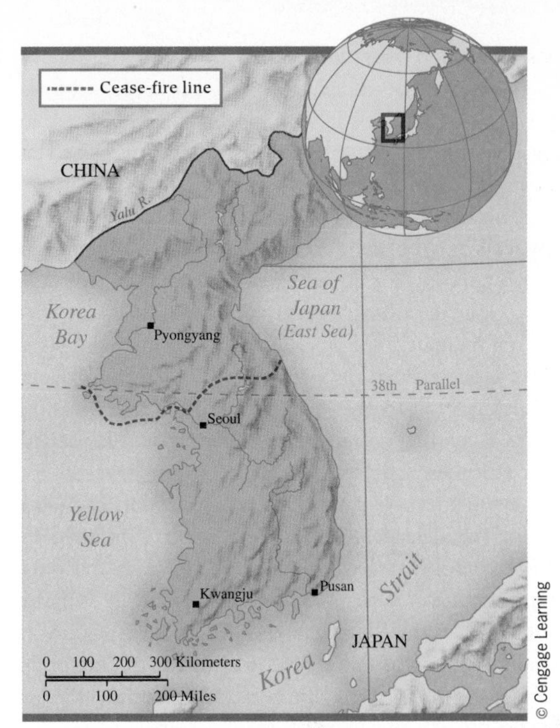

© Cengage Learning

MAP 26.3 The Korean Peninsula. In June 1950, North Korean forces crossed the 38th parallel in a sudden invasion of the south. Shown here is the cease-fire line that brought an end to the war in 1953.

What is the significance of the Yalu River?

The Korean War

The outbreak of war in Korea also helped bring the Cold War to East Asia. After the Sino-Japanese War in 1894–1895, Korea, long a Chinese tributary, had fallen increasingly under the rival influences of Japan and Russia. After the Japanese defeated the Russians in 1905, Korea became an integral part of the Japanese Empire and remained so until 1945. The removal of Korea from Japanese control had been one of the stated objectives of the Allies in World War II, and on the eve of the Japanese surrender in August 1945, the Soviet Union and the United States agreed to divide the country into two separate occupation zones at the 38th parallel. They originally planned to hold national elections after the restoration of peace to reunify Korea under an independent government. But as U.S.-Soviet relations deteriorated, two separate governments emerged in Korea, a Communist one in the north and an anti-Communist one in the south.

Tensions between the two governments ran high along the dividing line, and on June 25, 1950, with the apparent approval of Stalin, North Korean troops invaded the south. The Truman administration immediately ordered U.S. naval and air forces to support South Korea, and the United Nations Security Council (with the Soviet delegate absent to protest the UN's refusal to assign China's seat to the new government in Beijing) passed a resolution calling on member nations to jointly resist the invasion, in line with the security provisions of the United Nations Charter. By September, UN forces under the command of U.S. General Douglas MacArthur marched northward across the 38th parallel with the aim of unifying Korea under a single, non-Communist government.

President Truman worried that by approaching the Chinese border at the Yalu (YAH-loo) River, the UN troops could trigger Chinese intervention, but MacArthur assured him that China would not respond. In November, however, Chinese "volunteer" forces intervened in force on the side of North Korea and drove the UN troops southward in disarray. A static defense line was eventually established near the original dividing line at the 38th parallel (see Map 26.3), although the war continued.

To many Americans, the Chinese intervention in Korea was clear evidence that China intended to promote communism throughout Asia, and recent evidence suggests that Mao was convinced that a revolutionary wave was on the rise in Asia. In fact, however, China's decision to enter the war was probably motivated in large part by the fear that hostile U.S. forces might be stationed on the Chinese frontier and perhaps even launch an attack across the border. MacArthur intensified such fears by calling publicly for air attacks on Manchurian cities in preparation for an attack on Communist China.

In any case, the outbreak of the Korean War was particularly unfortunate for China. Immediately after the invasion, President Truman dispatched the U.S. Seventh Fleet to the Taiwan Strait to prevent a possible Chinese invasion of Taiwan. Even more unfortunate, the invasion hardened Western attitudes against the new Chinese government and led to China's isolation from the major capitalist powers for two decades. The United States continued to regard the Nationalist government in Taiwan as the only legal representative of the Chinese people and to support its retention of China's seat on the UN Security Council. As a result, China was cut off from all forms of economic and technological assistance and was forced to rely almost entirely on the Soviet Union, with which it had signed a pact of friendship and cooperation in early 1950.

Conflict in Indochina

During the mid-1950s, China sought to build contacts with the nonsocialist world. A cease-fire agreement brought the Korean War to an end in July 1953, and China signaled its desire to live in peaceful coexistence with other independent countries in the region. But a relatively minor conflict now began to intensify on China's southern flank, in French Indochina. The struggle had begun after World War II, when the Indochinese Communist Party led by Ho Chi Minh (HOH CHEE MIN) (1890–1969), at the head of a multiparty nationalist alliance called the Vietminh (vee-et-MIN) Front, seized power in northern and central Vietnam. After abortive negotiations between Ho's government and the returning French, war broke out in December 1946. French forces occupied the cities and the densely populated lowlands, while the Vietminh took refuge in the mountains.

For three years, the Vietminh waged a "people's war" of national liberation from colonial rule, gradually increasing in size and effectiveness. At the time, however, the conflict in Indochina attracted relatively little attention from world leaders, who viewed the events there as only one aspect of the transition to independence of colonial territories in postwar Asia. The Truman administration was uneasy about Ho's long-standing credentials as a Soviet agent but was equally reluctant to anger anticolonialist elements in the region by intervening on behalf of the French. Moscow had even less interest in the issue. Stalin—still hoping to see the Communist Party come to power in Paris—ignored Ho's request for recognition of his movement as the legitimate representative of the national interests of the Vietnamese people.

But what had begun as an anticolonial struggle by the Vietminh Front against the French became entangled in the Cold War after the CCP came to power in China. In early 1950, Beijing began to provide military assistance to the Vietminh to burnish its revolutionary credentials and protect its own borders from hostile forces. The Truman administration, increasingly concerned that a revolutionary "Red tide" was sweeping through the region, decided to provide financial and technical assistance to the French while pressuring them to prepare for an eventual transition to independent non-Communist governments in Vietnam, Laos, and Cambodia.

© AFP/Getty Images

Ho Chi Minh Plans an Attack on the French. Unlike many of the peoples of Southeast Asia, the Vietnamese had to fight for their independence after World War II. That fight was led by the talented Communist leader Ho Chi Minh. In this 1950 photograph taken at his secret base in the mountains of North Vietnam, Ho plans an attack on French positions. He changed the location of his headquarters on several occasions to evade capture by French forces.

Despite growing U.S. involvement in the war, Vietminh forces continued to gain strength, and in the spring of 1954, with Chinese assistance, they besieged a French military outpost at Dien Bien Phu (DEE-en bee-en FOO), not far from the border of Laos. The French sent reinforcements, and the decisive battle of the conflict was under way.

With casualties mounting and the French public tired of fighting the "dirty war" in Indochina, the French had agreed to hold peace talks with the Vietminh in May of 1954. On the day before the peace conference convened in Geneva, Switzerland, Vietminh forces overran the French bastion at Dien Bien Phu. The humiliating defeat weakened French resolve to maintain a presence in Indochina. In July, the two sides agreed to a settlement. Vietnam was temporarily divided into a Communist northern half, known as the Democratic Republic of Vietnam (DRV), and a non-Communist southern half based in Saigon (sy-GAHN) (now Ho Chi Minh City) that eventually came to be known as the Republic of Vietnam. A demilitarized zone separated the two at the 17th parallel. Elections were to be held in two years to create a unified government. Cambodia and Laos were both declared independent under neutral governments. French forces were withdrawn from all three countries.

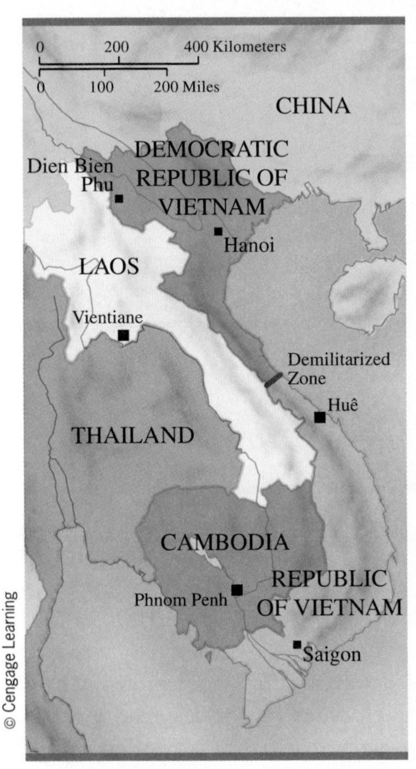

© Cengage Learning

Indochina After 1954

China had played an active role in bringing about the settlement and clearly hoped that it would reduce tensions in the area, but subsequent efforts to improve relations between China and the United States foundered on the issue of Taiwan. In the fall of 1954, the United States signed a mutual security treaty with the Republic of China guaranteeing U.S. military support in case of an invasion of Taiwan. When Beijing demanded U.S. withdrawal from Taiwan as the price for improved relations, diplomatic talks between the two countries collapsed.

From Confrontation to Coexistence

FOCUS QUESTION: What events led to the era of coexistence in the 1960s, and to what degree did each side contribute to the reduction in international tensions?

The decade of the 1950s opened with the world teetering on the edge of a nuclear holocaust. The Soviet Union had detonated its first nuclear device in 1949, and the two blocs—capitalist and socialist—viewed each other across an ideological divide that grew increasingly bitter with each passing year. Yet as the decade drew to a close, a measure of sanity crept into the Cold War, and the leaders of the major world powers began to seek ways to coexist in a peaceful and stable world (see Map 26.4).

The first clear sign of change occurred after Stalin's death in early 1953. His successor, Georgy Malenkov (gyee-OR-gyee muh-LEN-kawf) (1902–1988), openly hoped to improve relations with the Western powers in order to reduce defense expenditures and shift government spending to growing consumer needs. Nikita Khrushchev (nuh-KEE-tuh KHROOSH-chawf) (1894–1971), who replaced Malenkov in 1955, continued his predecessor's efforts to reduce tensions with the West and improve the living standards of the Soviet people.

In an adroit public relations touch, in 1956 Khrushchev promoted an appeal for a policy of **peaceful coexistence** with the West. In 1955, he had surprisingly agreed to negotiate an end to the postwar occupation of Austria by the victorious allies and allow the creation of a neutral country with strong cultural and economic ties with the West. He also called for a reduction in defense expenditures and reduced the size of the Soviet armed forces.

Ferment in Eastern Europe

At first, Western leaders were suspicious of Khrushchev's motives, especially in light of events that were taking place in Eastern Europe. The key to security along the western frontier of the Soviet Union was the string of Eastern European satellite states that had been assembled in the aftermath of World War II (see Map 26.1 on p. 684). Once Communist domination had been assured, a series of "little Stalins" put into power by Moscow instituted Soviet-type five-year plans that emphasized heavy industry rather than consumer goods, the collectivization of agriculture, and the nationalization of industry. They also appropriated the political tactics that Stalin had perfected in the Soviet Union, eliminating all non-Communist parties and establishing the classical institutions of

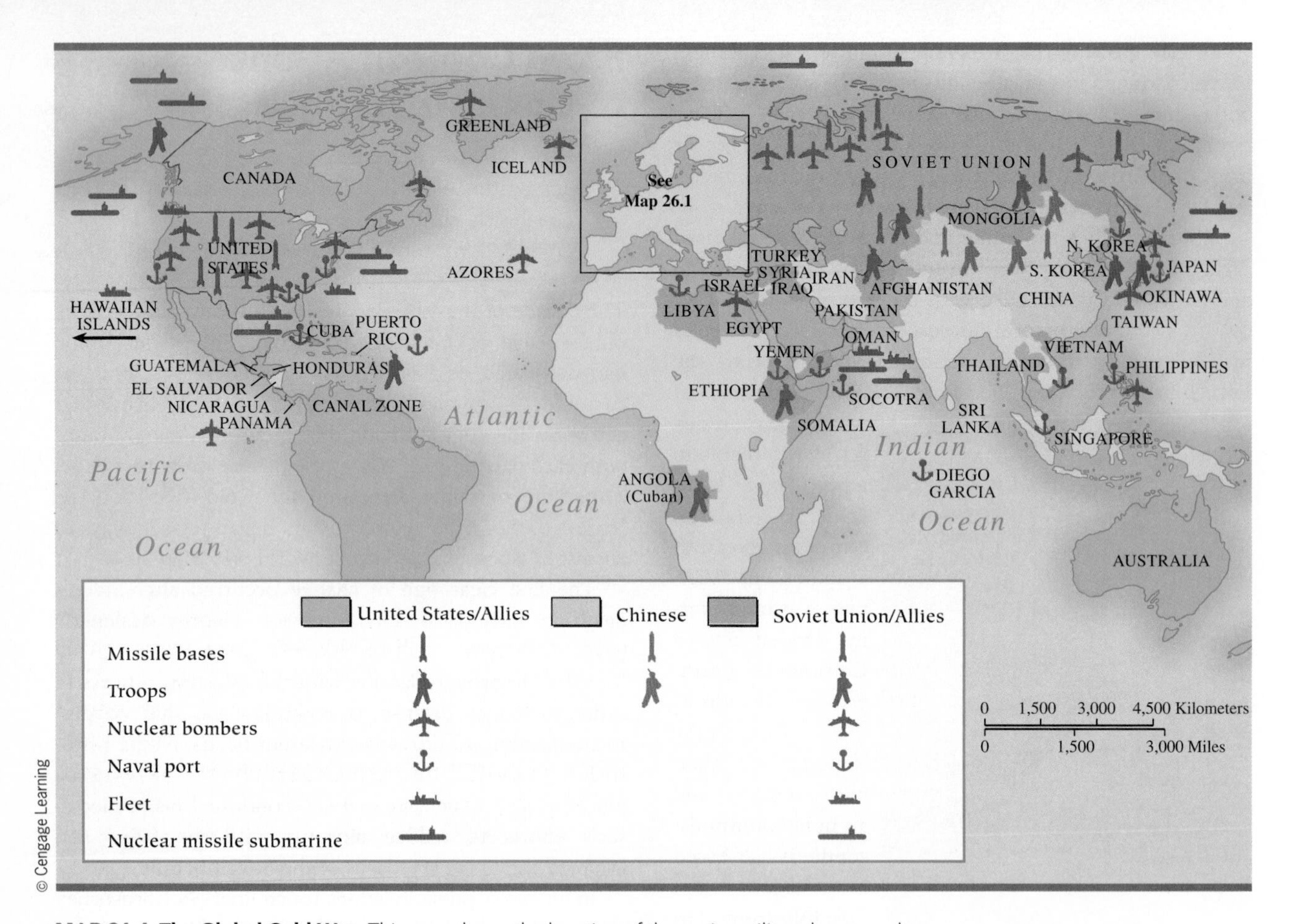

© Cengage Learning

MAP 26.4 The Global Cold War. This map shows the location of the major military bases and missile sites maintained by the three contending power blocs at the height of the Cold War.

Q *Which continents were the most heavily armed? Why?*

repression—the secret police and military forces. Dissidents were tracked down and thrown into prison, and "national Communists" who resisted total subservience to the Soviet Union were charged with treason in mass show trials and executed.

Despite these repressive efforts, discontent became increasingly evident in several Eastern European countries. Hungary, Poland, and Romania harbored bitter memories of past Russian domination and suspected that Stalin, under the guise of proletarian internationalism, was seeking to revive the empire of the tsars. For the vast majority of peoples in Eastern Europe, the imposition of so-called people's democracies (a term invented by Moscow to refer to societies in the early stage of socialist transition) resulted in economic hardship and severe threats to the most basic political liberties. The first indications of unrest appeared in East Berlin, where popular riots broke out against Communist rule in 1953. The riots eventually subsided, but the virus had spread to neighboring countries.

In Poland, public demonstrations against an increase in food prices in 1956 escalated into widespread protests against the regime's economic policies, restrictions on the freedom of Catholics to practice their religion, and the continued presence of Soviet troops (as called for by the Warsaw Pact) on Polish soil. In a desperate effort to defuse the unrest, the party leader stepped down and was replaced by Wladyslaw Gomulka (vlah-DIS-lahf goh-MOOL-kuh) (1905–1982), a popular figure who had previously been demoted for his "nationalist" tendencies. When Gomulka took steps to ease the crisis, Khrushchev flew to Warsaw to warn him against adopting policies that could undermine the political dominance of the party and weaken security links with the Soviet Union. After a tense confrontation, Poland agreed to remain in the Warsaw Pact and to maintain the sanctity of party rule; in return, Gomulka was authorized to adopt domestic reforms, such as easing restrictions on religious practice and ending the policy of forced collectivization in rural areas.

THE HUNGARIAN REVOLUTION The developments in Poland sent shock waves throughout the region. The impact was strongest in neighboring Hungary, where the methods of the local "little Stalin," Mátyás Rákosi (MAH-tyash RAH-koh-see) (1892–1971), were so brutal that he had been summoned to Moscow for a lecture. In late October 1956, student-led popular riots broke out in the capital of Budapest and soon spread to other towns and villages throughout the country. Rákosi was forced to resign and was replaced by Imre Nagy (IM-ray NAHJ) (1896–1958), a national Communist who attempted to satisfy popular demands without arousing the anger of Moscow. Unlike Gomulka, however, Nagy was unable to contain the zeal of leading members of the protest movement, who sought major political reforms and the withdrawal of Hungary from the Warsaw Pact. On November 1, Nagy promised free elections, which, given the mood of the country, would probably have brought an end to Communist rule. After a brief moment of uncertainty, Moscow decided on firm action. Soviet troops, recently withdrawn at Nagy's request, returned to Budapest and installed a new government under the more pliant party leader János Kádár (YAH-nush KAH-dahr) (1912–1989). While Kádár rescinded many of Nagy's measures, Nagy sought refuge in the Yugoslav embassy. A few weeks later, he left the embassy under the promise of safety but was quickly arrested, convicted of treason, and executed (see the box on p. 694).

DIFFERENT ROADS TO SOCIALISM The dramatic events in Poland and Hungary graphically demonstrated the vulnerability of the Soviet satellite system in Eastern Europe, and many observers throughout the world anticipated that the United States would intervene on behalf of the freedom fighters in Hungary. After all, the Eisenhower administration had promised that it would "roll back" communism, and radio broadcasts by the U.S.-sponsored Radio Liberty and Radio Free Europe had encouraged the peoples of Eastern Europe to rise up against Soviet domination. In reality, Washington was well aware that U.S. intervention could lead to nuclear war and limited itself to protests against Soviet brutality in crushing the uprising.

The year of discontent was not without consequences, however. Soviet leaders now recognized that Moscow could maintain control over its satellites in Eastern Europe only by granting them the leeway to adopt domestic policies appropriate to local conditions. Khrushchev had already embarked on this path in 1955 when he assured Tito that there were "different roads to socialism." Some Eastern European Communist leaders now took Khrushchev at his word and adopted reform programs to make socialism more palatable to their subject populations. Even Kádár, derisively labeled the "butcher of Budapest," managed to preserve many of Nagy's reforms to allow a measure of capitalist incentive and freedom of expression in Hungary.

CRISIS OVER BERLIN But in the late 1950s, a new crisis erupted over the status of Berlin. The Soviet Union had launched its first intercontinental ballistic missile (ICBM) in August 1957, arousing U.S. fears of a missile gap between the United States and the Soviet Union. Khrushchev attempted to take advantage of the U.S. frenzy over missiles to solve the problem of West Berlin, which had remained a "Western island" of prosperity inside the relatively poverty-stricken state of East Germany. Many East Germans sought to escape to West Germany by fleeing through West Berlin, a serious blot on the credibility of the GDR and a potential source of instability in East-West relations. In November 1958, Khrushchev announced that unless the West removed its forces from West Berlin within six months, he would turn over control of the access routes to the East Germans. Unwilling to accept an ultimatum that would have abandoned West Berlin to the Communists, U.S. President Dwight D. Eisenhower and the West stood firm, and Khrushchev eventually backed down.

Despite such periodic crises in East-West relations, there were tantalizing signs that an era of true peaceful coexistence between the two power blocs could be achieved. In the late 1950s, the United States and the Soviet Union initiated a cultural exchange program. While Leningrad's Kirov Ballet appeared at theaters in the United States, Benny Goodman and the film *West Side Story* played in Moscow. In 1958, Khrushchev visited the United States and had a brief but friendly encounter with President Eisenhower at the presidential retreat in northern Maryland.

Rivalry in the Third World

Yet Khrushchev could rarely avoid the temptation to gain an advantage over the United States in the competition for influence throughout the world, a posture that exacerbated the unstable relationship between the two global superpowers. Unlike Stalin, who had exhibited a profound distrust of all political figures who did not slavishly follow his lead, Khrushchev viewed the dismantling of colonial regimes in Asia, Africa, and Latin America as a potential advantage for the Soviet Union. When neutralist leaders like Nehru in India, Tito in Yugoslavia, and Sukarno (soo-KAHR-noh) in Indonesia founded the **Nonaligned Movement** in 1955 to provide an alternative to the two major power blocs, Khrushchev took every opportunity to promote Soviet interests in the Third

OPPOSING VIEWPOINTS

Soviet Repression in Eastern Europe: Hungary, 1956

Developments in Poland in 1956 inspired the Communist leaders of Hungary to begin to extricate their country from Soviet control. But there were limits to Khrushchev's tolerance, and he sent Soviet troops to crush Hungary's movement for independence. The first selection is a statement by the Soviet government justifying its use of troops, while the second is the brief and tragic final statement from Imre Nagy, the Hungarian leader.

Statement of the Soviet Government, October 30, 1956

The Soviet Government regards it as indispensable to make a statement in connection with the events in Hungary.

The course of the events has shown that the working people of Hungary, who have achieved great progress on the basis of their people's democratic order, correctly raise the question of the necessity of eliminating serious shortcomings in the field of economic building, the further raising of the material well-being of the population, and the struggle against bureaucratic excesses in the state apparatus.

However, this just and progressive movement of the working people was soon joined by forces of black reaction and counterrevolution, which are trying to take advantage of the discontent of part of the working people to undermine the foundations of the people's democratic order in Hungary and to restore the old landlord and capitalist order.

The Soviet Government and all the Soviet people deeply regret that the development of events in Hungary has led to bloodshed. On the request of the Hungarian People's Government the Soviet Government consented to the entry into Budapest of the Soviet Army units to assist the Hungarian People's Army and the Hungarian authorities to establish order in the town.

The Last Message of Imre Nagy, November 4, 1956

This fight is the fight for freedom by the Hungarian people against the Russian intervention, and it is possible that I shall only be able to stay at my post for one or two hours. The whole world will see how the Russian armed forces, contrary to all treaties and conventions, are crushing the resistance of the Hungarian people. They will also see how they are kidnapping the Prime Minister of a country which is a Member of the United Nations, taking him from the capital, and therefore it cannot be doubted at all that this is the most brutal form of intervention. I should like in these last moments to ask the leaders of the revolution, if they can, to leave the country. I ask that all that I have said in my broadcast, and what we have agreed on with the revolutionary leaders during meetings in Parliament, should be put in a memorandum, and the leaders should turn to all the peoples of the world for help and explain that today it is Hungary and tomorrow, or the day after tomorrow, it will be the turn of other countries because the imperialism of Moscow does not know borders, and is only trying to play for time.

How did the United States and its allies respond to the events in Hungary? Why did the United States decide not to intervene in support of the dissident forces?

Source: From *Department of State Bulletin*, Nov. 12,1956, pp. 746–747.

World (as the nonaligned countries of Asia, Africa, and Latin America were now popularly called). Khrushchev openly sought alliances with strategically important neutralist countries like India, Indonesia, and Egypt, while Washington's ability to influence events at the United Nations began to wane.

In January 1961, just as John F. Kennedy (1917–1963) assumed the U.S. presidency, Khrushchev unnerved the new president at an informal summit meeting in Vienna by declaring that the Soviet Union would provide active support to national liberation movements throughout the world. There were rising fears in Washington of Soviet meddling in such sensitive trouble spots as Southeast Asia, where insurgent activities in Indochina continued to simmer; in Central Africa, where the pro-Soviet tendencies of radical leader Patrice Lumumba (puh-TREES

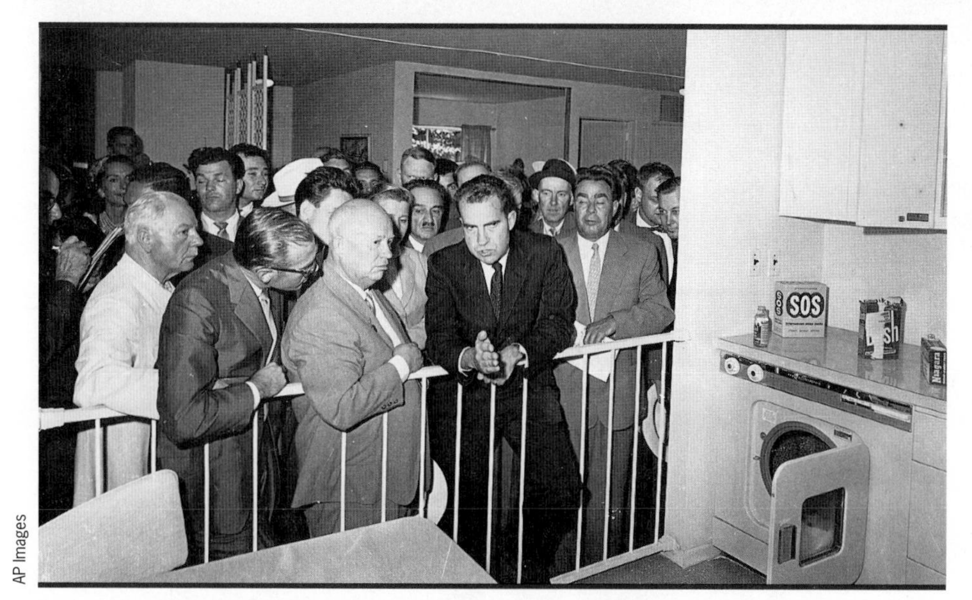

AP Images

The Kitchen Debate. During the late 1950s, the United States and the Soviet Union sought to defuse Cold War tensions by encouraging cultural exchanges between the two countries. On one occasion, U.S. Vice President Richard M. Nixon visited Moscow in conjunction with the arrival of an exhibit to introduce U.S. culture and society to the Soviet people. Here Nixon lectures Soviet Communist Party chief Nikita Khrushchev on the technology of the U.S. kitchen. On the other side of Nixon, at the far right, is future Soviet president Leonid Brezhnev.

loo-MOOM-buh) (1925–1961) aroused deep suspicion in Washington; and in the Caribbean, where a little-known Cuban revolutionary named Fidel Castro threatened to transform his country into an advanced base for Soviet expansion in the Americas.

The Cuban Missile Crisis and the Move Toward Détente

In 1959, a left-wing revolutionary named Fidel Castro (fee-DELL KASS-troh) (b. 1927) overthrew the Cuban dictator Fulgencio Batista (full-JEN-see-oh bah-TEES-tuh) and established a Soviet-supported totalitarian regime. As tensions increased between the new government in Havana and the United States, the Eisenhower administration broke relations with Cuba and drafted plans to overthrow Castro, who reacted by drawing closer to Moscow.

Soon after taking office in early 1961, Kennedy approved a plan to support an invasion of Cuba by anti-Castro exiles. But the attempted landing at the Bay of Pigs in southern Cuba was an utter failure. At Castro's invitation, the Soviet Union then began to station nuclear missiles in Cuba, within striking distance of the American mainland. (Khrushchev was quick to point out that the United States had placed nuclear weapons in Turkey within easy range of the Soviet Union.) When U.S. intelligence discovered that a Soviet fleet carrying more missiles was heading to Cuba, Kennedy decided to dispatch U.S. warships into the Atlantic to prevent the fleet from reaching its destination.

This approach to the problem was risky but had the benefit of delaying confrontation and giving the two sides time to find a peaceful solution. After a tense standoff during which the two countries came frighteningly close to a direct nuclear confrontation (the Soviet missiles already in Cuba were launch-ready), Khrushchev finally sent a conciliatory letter to Kennedy agreeing to turn back the fleet if Kennedy pledged not to invade Cuba. In a secret concession not revealed until many years later, the president also promised to dismantle U.S. missiles in Turkey. To the world, however (and to an angry Castro), it appeared that Kennedy had bested Khrushchev. "We were eyeball to eyeball," noted U.S. Secretary of State Dean Rusk, "and they blinked" (see the Film & History feature on p. 696).

The ghastly realization that the world might have faced annihilation in a matter of days had a profound effect on both sides. A communication hotline between Moscow and Washington was installed in 1963 to expedite rapid communication between the two superpowers in time of crisis. In the same year, the two powers agreed to ban nuclear tests in the atmosphere, a step that served to lessen the tensions between the two nations.

The Sino-Soviet Dispute

Nikita Khrushchev had launched his slogan of peaceful coexistence as a means of improving relations with the capitalist powers; ironically, one result of the campaign was to undermine Moscow's ties with its close ally China. During Stalin's lifetime, Beijing had accepted the Soviet Union as the acknowledged leader of the socialist camp. After Stalin's death, however, relations began to deteriorate. Part of the reason may have been Mao Zedong's contention that he, as the most experienced

FILM & HISTORY

The Missiles of October (1973)

Never has the world been closer to nuclear holocaust than in October 1962, when U.S. and Soviet leaders found themselves in direct confrontation over Nikita Khrushchev's decision to introduce Soviet missiles into Cuba, just 90 miles from the U.S. coast. When President John F. Kennedy announced that U.S. warships would intercept Soviet freighters destined for Cuban ports, the two countries teetered on the verge of war. Only after protracted and delicate negotiations was the threat defused. The confrontation sobered leaders on both sides and led to the signing of the first nuclear test ban treaty, as well as the opening of a hotline between Moscow and Washington.

The Missiles of October, a made-for-TV film produced in 1973, is a tense political drama that is all the more riveting because it is based on fact. Although less well known than the more recent *Thirteen Days* (2000), it is in many ways more persuasive, and the acting is demonstrably superior. The film stars William Devane as John F. Kennedy and Martin Sheen as his younger brother, Robert. Based in part on Robert Kennedy's book *Thirteen Days* (New York, 1969), the film traces the tense discussions that took place in the White House as the president's key advisers debated how to respond to the Soviet challenge. President Kennedy remains cool as he reins in his more bellicose advisers to bring about a compromise that successfully avoids a nuclear confrontation with Moscow.

Courtesy The Everett Collection, Inc.

John Kennedy (William Devane, seated) and Robert Kennedy (Martin Sheen) confer with advisers.

Because the film is based on the recollections of Robert Kennedy, it presents a favorable portrait of his brother's handling of the crisis, as might be expected, and the somewhat triumphalist attitude at the end is perhaps a bit exaggerated. But Khrushchev's colleagues in the Kremlin and his Cuban ally, Fidel Castro, viewed the U.S.-Soviet agreement as a humiliation for Moscow that nevertheless set the two superpowers on the road to a more durable and peaceful relationship. It was one Cold War story that had a happy ending.

Marxist leader, should now be acknowledged as the most authoritative voice within the socialist community. But another determining factor was that just as Soviet policies were moving toward moderation, China's were becoming more radical.

Several other issues were involved, including territorial disputes along the Sino-Soviet border and China's unhappiness with limited Soviet economic assistance. But the key sources of disagreement involved ideology and the Cold War. Chinese leaders were convinced that the successes of the Soviet space program confirmed that the socialists were now technologically superior to the capitalists (the East Wind, trumpeted the Chinese official press, had triumphed over the West Wind), and they urged Khrushchev to go on the offensive to promote world revolution. Specifically, China wanted Soviet assistance in retaking Taiwan from Chiang Kai-shek. But Khrushchev was trying to improve relations with the West and rejected Chinese demands for support against Taiwan.

By the end of the 1950s, the Soviet Union had begun to remove its advisers from China, and in 1961, the dispute broke into the open. Increasingly isolated, China voiced its hostility to what Mao described as the "urban industrialized countries" (which included the Soviet Union) and portrayed itself as the leader of the "rural underdeveloped countries" of Asia, Africa, and Latin America in a global struggle against imperialist oppression. In effect, China had applied Mao Zedong's concept of people's war in an international framework (see the box on p. 697).

OPPOSING ≺ VIEWPOINTS

Peaceful Coexistence or People's War?

INTERACTION & EXCHANGE

The Soviet leader Vladimir Lenin had contended that war between the socialist and imperialist camps was inevitable because the imperialists would never give up without a fight. That assumption had probably guided Joseph Stalin, who told colleagues shortly after World War II that a new war would break out in fifteen to twenty years. But Stalin's successor, Nikita Khrushchev, feared that a new world conflict could result in a nuclear holocaust and contended that the two sides must learn to coexist, although peaceful competition would continue. In this speech given in Beijing in 1959, Khrushchev attempted to persuade the Chinese to accept his views. But Chinese leaders argued that the "imperialist nature" of the United States would never change and countered that the crucial area of competition was in the Third World, where "people's wars" would bring down the structure of imperialism. That argument was presented in 1966 by Marshal Lin Biao (LIN BYOW) of China, at that time one of Mao Zedong's closest allies.

Khrushchev's Speech to the Chinese, 1959

Comrades! Socialism brings to the people peace—that greatest blessing. The greater the strength of the camp of socialism grows, the greater will be its possibilities for successfully defending the cause of peace on this earth. The forces of socialism are already so great that real possibilities are being created for excluding war as a means of solving international disputes. . . .

When I spoke with President Eisenhower—and I have just returned from the United States of America—I got the impression that the President of the U.S.A.—and not a few people support him—understands the need to relax international tension. . . .

There is only one way of preserving peace—that is the road of peaceful coexistence of states with different social systems. The question stands thus: either peaceful coexistence or war with its catastrophic consequences. Now, with the present relation of forces between socialism and capitalism being in favor of socialism, he who would continue the "cold war" is moving towards his own destruction. . . .

It is not at all because capitalism is still strong that the socialist countries speak out against war, and for peaceful coexistence. No, we have no need of war at all. If the people do not want it, even such a noble and progressive system as socialism cannot be imposed by force of arms. The socialist countries therefore, while carrying through a consistently peace-loving policy, concentrate their efforts on peaceful construction; they fire the hearts of men by the force of their example in building socialism, and thus lead them to follow in their footsteps. The question of when this or that country will take the path to socialism is decided by its own people. This, for us, is the holy of holies.

Lin Biao, "Long Live the Victory of People's War"

Many countries and peoples in Asia, Africa, and Latin America are now being subjected to aggression and enslavement on a serious scale by the imperialists headed by the United States and their lackeys. . . . As in China, the peasant question is extremely important in these regions. The peasants constitute the main force of the national-democratic revolution against the imperialists and their lackeys. In committing aggression against these countries, the imperialists usually begin by seizing the big cities and the main lines of communication. But they are unable to bring the vast countryside completely under their control. . . . The countryside, and the countryside alone, can provide the revolutionary basis from which the revolutionaries can go forward to final victory. Precisely for this reason, Mao Tse-tung's theory of establishing revolutionary base areas in the rural districts and encircling the cities from the countryside is attracting more and more attention among the people in these regions.

Taking the entire globe, if North America and Western Europe can be called "the cities of the world," then Asia, Africa, and Latin America constitute "the rural areas of the world." Since World War II, the proletarian revolutionary movement has for various reasons been temporarily held back in the North American and West European capitalist countries, while the people's revolutionary movement in Asia, Africa, and Latin America has been growing vigorously. In a sense, the contemporary world revolution also presents a picture of the encirclement of cities by the rural areas. In the final analysis, the whole cause of world revolution hinges on

(Continued)

the revolutionary struggles of the Asian, African, and Latin American peoples, who make up the overwhelming majority of the world's population. The socialist countries should regard it as their internationalist duty to support the people's revolutionary struggles in Asia, Africa, and Latin America. . . .

Ours is the epoch in which world capitalism and imperialism are heading for their doom and communism is marching to victory. Comrade Mao Tse-tung's theory of people's war is not only a product of the Chinese revolution, but has also the characteristic of our epoch. The new experience gained in the people's revolutionary struggles in various countries since World War II has provided continuous evidence that Mao Tse-tung's thought is a common asset of the revolutionary people of the whole world.

Why did Nikita Khrushchev feel that the conflict between the socialist and capitalist camps that Lenin had predicted was no longer inevitable? How did Lin Biao respond?

Sources: Khrushchev's Speech to the Chinese, 1959. From G. F. Hudson et al., eds. *The Sino-Soviet Dispute* (New York: Frederick Praeger, 1961), pp. 61–63, cited in *Peking Review*, No. 40, 1959. Lin Biao, "Long Live the Victory of People's War." From *Nationalism and Communism*, Norman Grabner, ed. Copyright © 1977 by D. C. Heath and Company.

The Second Indochina War

China's radicalism was intensified in the early 1960s by the renewed outbreak of war in Indochina. The Eisenhower administration had opposed the peace settlement at Geneva in 1954, which divided Vietnam temporarily into two separate regroupment zones, specifically because the provision for future national elections opened up the possibility that the entire country would come under Communist rule. But Eisenhower had been unwilling to send U.S. military forces to continue the conflict without the full support of the British and the French, who preferred to seek a negotiated settlement. In the end, Washington promised not to break the provisions of the agreement but refused to commit itself to the results.

During the next several months, the United States began to provide aid to the new government in South Vietnam. Under the leadership of the anti-Communist politician Ngo Dinh Diem (NGHOH din DEE-em), the government began to root out dissidents. With the tacit approval of the United States, Diem refused to hold the national elections called for by the Geneva Accords. It was widely anticipated, even in Washington, that the Communists would win such elections. In 1959, Ho Chi Minh, despairing of the peaceful unification of the country under Communist rule, decided to return to a policy of revolutionary war in the south.

Late the following year, a political organization that was designed to win the support of a wide spectrum of the population was founded in an isolated part of South Vietnam. Known as the National Liberation Front (NLF), it was under the secret but firm leadership of high-ranking Communists in North Vietnam (the Democratic Republic of Vietnam).

By 1963, South Vietnam was on the verge of collapse. Diem's autocratic methods and inattention to severe economic inequality had alienated much of the population, and revolutionary forces, popularly known as the Viet Cong (Vietnamese Communists) and supported by the Communist government in North Vietnam, expanded their influence throughout much of the country. In the fall of 1963, with the approval of the Kennedy administration, senior military officers overthrew the Diem regime. But factionalism kept the new military leadership from reinvigorating the struggle against the insurgent forces, and the situation in South Vietnam grew worse. By early 1965, the Viet Cong, their ranks now swelled by military units infiltrating from North Vietnam, were on the verge of seizing control of the entire country. In March, President Lyndon Johnson decided to send U.S. combat troops to South Vietnam to prevent the total defeat of the anti-Communist government in Saigon. Over the next three years, U.S. troop levels steadily increased as the White House counted on U.S. firepower to persuade Ho Chi Minh to abandon his quest to unify Vietnam under Communist leadership (see the comparative illustration on p. 699).

THE ROLE OF CHINA Chinese leaders observed the gradual escalation of the conflict in South Vietnam with mixed feelings. They were undoubtedly pleased to have a firm Communist ally—one that had in many ways followed the path of Mao Zedong—just beyond their southern frontier. Yet they were concerned that bloodshed in South Vietnam might enmesh China in a new conflict with the United States. Nor did they welcome the specter of a powerful and ambitious united Vietnam, which might wish to extend its influence throughout mainland Southeast Asia, an area that Beijing considered its own backyard.

Chinese leaders therefore tiptoed delicately through the minefield of the Indochina conflict. As the war escalated in 1964 and 1965, Beijing publicly announced that the Chinese people fully supported their comrades seeking

COMPARATIVE ILLUSTRATION

POLITICS & GOVERNMENT

War in the Rice Paddies. The first stage of the Vietnam War consisted primarily of guerrilla conflict, as Viet Cong insurgents relied on guerrilla tactics in their effort to bring down the U.S.-supported government in Saigon. In 1965, however, President Lyndon Johnson ordered U.S. combat troops into South Vietnam (top photo) in a desperate bid to prevent a Communist victory in that beleaguered country. The Communist government in North Vietnam responded in kind, sending its own regular forces down the Ho Chi Minh Trail to confront U.S. troops on the battlefield. In the photo on the bottom, North Vietnamese troops storm the U.S. Marine base at Khe Sanh (KAY SAHN), near the demilitarized zone, in 1968, the most violent year of the war. Although U.S. military commanders believed that helicopters would be a key factor in defeating the insurgent forces in Vietnam, this conflict was one instance when technological superiority did not produce a victory on the battlefield.

Q *How do you think helicopters were used to assist U.S. operations in South Vietnam? Why didn't their use result in a U.S. victory?*

AP Images

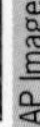

© Three Lions/Getty Images

national liberation but privately assured Washington that China would not directly enter the conflict unless U.S. forces threatened its southern border. Beijing also refused to cooperate fully with Moscow in shipping Soviet goods to North Vietnam through Chinese territory.

Despite its dismay at the lack of full support from China, the Communist government in North Vietnam responded to U.S. escalation by infiltrating more of its own regular troops into the South, and by 1968, the war had reached a stalemate. The Communists were not strong enough to overthrow the government in Saigon, whose weakness was shielded by the presence of half a million U.S. troops, but President Johnson was reluctant to engage in all-out war on North Vietnam for fear of provoking a global nuclear conflict. In the fall, after the Communist-led Tet offensive undermined claims of progress in Washington and aroused intense antiwar protests in the United States, peace negotiations began in Paris.

QUEST FOR PEACE Richard Nixon came into the White House in 1969 on a pledge to bring an honorable end to the Vietnam War. With U.S. public opinion sharply divided on the issue, he began to withdraw U.S. troops while continuing to hold peace talks in Paris. But the centerpiece of his strategy was to improve relations with China and thus undercut Chinese support for the North Vietnamese war effort. During the 1960s, relations between Moscow and Beijing had reached a point of extreme tension, and thousands of troops were stationed on both sides of their long common frontier. To intimidate their Communist rivals, Soviet sources hinted that they might launch a preemptive strike to destroy Chinese nuclear facilities in Xinjiang. Sensing an opportunity to split the two onetime allies, Nixon sent his emissary, Henry Kissinger, on a secret trip to China. Responding to assurances that the United States was determined to withdraw from Indochina and hoped to improve relations with the mainland regime, Chinese leaders invited President Nixon to visit China in early 1972. Nixon accepted, and the two sides agreed to set aside their differences over Taiwan to pursue a better mutual relationship.

THE FALL OF SAIGON Incensed at the apparent betrayal by their close allies, North Vietnamese leaders decided to seek a peaceful settlement of the war. In January 1973, a peace treaty was signed in Paris calling for the removal of all U.S. forces from South Vietnam. In return, the Communists agreed to halt military operations and to engage in negotiations to resolve their differences with the Saigon regime. But negotiations between north and south over the political settlement soon broke down, and in early 1975, the Communists resumed the offensive. At the end of April, under a massive assault by North Vietnamese military forces, the South Vietnamese government surrendered. A year later, the country was unified under Communist rule.

The Communist victory in Vietnam was a severe humiliation for the United States, but its strategic impact was limited because of the new relationship with China. During the next decade, Sino-American relations continued to improve. In 1979, diplomatic ties were established between the two countries under an arrangement whereby the United States renounced its mutual security treaty with the Republic of China in return for a pledge from China to seek reunification with Taiwan by peaceful means. By the end of the 1970s, China and the United States had forged a "strategic relationship" in which they would cooperate against the common threat of Soviet hegemony in Asia.

Why had the United States failed to achieve its objective of preventing a Communist victory in Vietnam? One leading member of the Johnson administration later commented that Washington had underestimated the determination of its adversary in Hanoi and overestimated the patience of the American people. Deeper reflection suggests, however, that another factor was equally important: the United States had overestimated the ability of its client state in South Vietnam to defend itself against a disciplined adversary. In subsequent years, it became a crucial lesson to the Americans on the perils of nation building.

An Era of Equivalence

FOCUS QUESTION: Why did the Cold War briefly flare up again in the 1980s, and why did it come to a definitive end at the end of the decade?

When the Johnson administration sent U.S. combat troops to South Vietnam in 1965, Washington's main concern was with Beijing, not Moscow. By the mid-1960s, U.S. officials viewed the Soviet Union as an essentially conservative power, more concerned with protecting its vast empire than with expanding its borders. In fact, U.S. policy makers periodically sought Soviet assistance in seeking a peaceful settlement of the Vietnam War. As long as Khrushchev was in power, they found a receptive ear in Moscow. Khrushchev was firmly dedicated to promoting peaceful coexistence (at least on his terms) and sternly advised the North Vietnamese against a resumption of revolutionary war in South Vietnam.

After October 1964, when Khrushchev was replaced by a new leadership headed by party chief Leonid Brezhnev (lee-oh-NYEET BREZH-neff) (1906–1982) and Prime Minister Alexei Kosygin (uh-LEK-say kuh-SEE-gun) (1904–1980), Soviet attitudes about Vietnam became more ambivalent. On the one hand, the new Soviet leaders had no desire to see the Vietnam conflict poison relations between the great powers. On the other hand, Moscow was eager to demonstrate its support for the North Vietnamese to deflect Chinese charges that the Soviet Union had betrayed the interests of the oppressed peoples of the world. As a result, Soviet officials publicly voiced sympathy for the U.S. predicament in Vietnam but put no pressure on their allies to bring an end to the war. Indeed, the Soviet Union became Hanoi's main supplier of advanced military equipment in the final years of the war.

The Brezhnev Doctrine

In the meantime, new Cold War tensions were brewing in Eastern Europe, where discontent with Stalinist policies began to emerge in Czechoslovakia. The latter had not shared in the thaw of the mid-1950s and remained under the rule of the hard-liner Antonín Novotný (AHN-toh-nyeen NOH-vaht-nee) (1904–1975), who had been installed in power by Stalin himself. By the late 1960s, however, Novotný's policies had led to widespread popular alienation, and in 1968, with the support of intellectuals and reformist party members, Alexander Dubček (DOOB-check) (1921–1992) was elected first secretary of the Communist Party. He immediately attempted to create what was popularly called "socialism with a human face," relaxing restrictions on freedom of speech and the press and the right to travel abroad. Economic reforms were announced, and party control over all aspects of society was reduced. A period of euphoria erupted that came to be known as the "Prague Spring."

It proved to be short-lived. Encouraged by Dubček's actions, some Czechs called for more far-reaching reforms, including neutrality and withdrawal from the Soviet bloc. To forestall the spread of this "spring fever," the Soviet Red Army, supported by troops from other

The Brezhnev Doctrine

POLITICS & GOVERNMENT

In the summer of 1968, when the new Communist Party leaders in Czechoslovakia were seriously considering proposals for reforming the totalitarian system there, the Warsaw Pact nations met under the leadership of Soviet party chief Leonid Brezhnev to assess the threat to the socialist camp. Soon afterward, military forces of several Soviet bloc nations entered Czechoslovakia and imposed a new government subservient to Moscow. The move was justified by the spirit of "proletarian internationalism" and was widely viewed as a warning to China and other socialist states not to stray too far from Marxist-Leninist orthodoxy, as interpreted by the Soviet Union. But Moscow's actions also raised tensions in the Cold War.

A Letter to the Central Committee of the Communist Party of Czechoslovakia

Dear comrades!

On behalf of the Central Committees of the Communist and Workers' Parties of Bulgaria, Hungary, the German Democratic Republic, Poland, and the Soviet Union, we address ourselves to you with this letter, prompted by a feeling of sincere friendship based on the principles of Marxism-Leninism and proletarian internationalism and by the concern of our common affairs for strengthening the positions of socialism and the security of the socialist community of nations.

The development of events in your country evokes in us deep anxiety. It is our firm conviction that the offensive of the reactionary forces, backed by imperialists, against your Party and the foundations of the social system in the Czechoslovak Socialist Republic, threatens to push your country off the road of socialism and that consequently it jeopardizes the interests of the entire socialist system. . . .

We neither had nor have any intention of interfering in such affairs as are strictly the internal business of your Party and your state, nor of violating the principles of respect, independence, and equality in the relations among the Communist Parties and socialist countries. . . .

At the same time we cannot agree to have hostile forces push your country from the road of socialism and create a threat of severing Czechoslovakia from the socialist community. . . . This is the common cause of our countries, which have joined in the Warsaw Treaty to ensure independence, peace, and security in Europe, and to set up an insurmountable barrier against the intrigues of the imperialist forces, against aggression and revenge. . . . We shall never agree to have imperialism, using peaceful or nonpeaceful methods, making a gap from the inside or from the outside in the socialist system, and changing in imperialism's favor the correlation of forces in Europe. . . .

That is why we believe that a decisive rebuff of the anti-Communist forces, and decisive efforts for the preservation of the socialist system in Czechoslovakia are not only your task but ours as well. . . .

We express the conviction that the Communist Party of Czechoslovakia, conscious of its responsibility, will take the necessary steps to block the path of reaction. In this struggle you can count on the solidarity and all-round assistance of the fraternal socialist countries.

Warsaw, July 15, 1968.

How did Leonid Brezhnev justify the Soviet decision to invade Czechoslovakia? To what degree do you find his arguments persuasive?

Source: From *Moscow News*, Supplement to No, 30 (917), 1968, pp. 3–6.

Warsaw Pact states, invaded Czechoslovakia in August 1968 and crushed the reform movement. Gustav Husák (goo-STAHV HOO-sahk) (1913–1991), a committed Stalinist, replaced Dubček and restored the old order, while Moscow attempted to justify its action by issuing the so-called **Brezhnev Doctrine** (see the box above).

In East Germany as well, Stalinist policies continued to hold sway. The ruling Communist government in East Germany, led by Walter Ulbricht, had consolidated its position in the early 1950s and became a faithful Soviet satellite. Industry was nationalized and agriculture collectivized. After the 1953 workers' revolt was crushed by Soviet tanks, a steady flight of East Germans to West Germany ensued, primarily through the city of Berlin. This exodus of mostly skilled laborers ("Soon only party chief Ulbricht will be left," remarked one Soviet observer sardonically) created economic problems and in 1961 led the East German government to erect a wall separating

East Berlin from West Berlin, as well as even more fearsome barriers along the entire border with West Germany. After building the Berlin Wall, East Germany succeeded in developing the strongest economy among the Soviet Union's Eastern European satellites. In 1971, Ulbricht was succeeded by Erich Honecker (AY-reekh HON-nek-uh) (1912–1994), a party hard-liner. Propaganda increased, and the use of the Stasi (SHTAH-see), the secret police, became a hallmark of Honecker's virtual dictatorship. Honecker ruled unchallenged for the next eighteen years.

An Era of Détente

Still, under Brezhnev and Kosygin, the Soviet Union continued to pursue peaceful coexistence with the West and adopted a generally cautious posture in foreign affairs. By the early 1970s, a new age in Soviet-American relations had emerged, often referred to as **détente** (day-TAHNT), a French term meaning a reduction of tensions between the two sides. One symbol of détente was the Anti-Ballistic Missile (ABM) Treaty, often called SALT I (for Strategic Arms Limitation Talks), signed in 1972, in which the two nations agreed to limit the size of their ABM systems.

Washington's objective in pursuing the treaty was to make it unlikely that either superpower could win a nuclear exchange by launching a preemptive strike against the other. U.S. officials believed that a policy of "equivalence," in which the two sides had roughly equal power, was the best way to avoid a nuclear confrontation. Détente was pursued in other ways as well. When President Nixon took office in 1969, he sought to increase trade and cultural contacts with the Soviet Union. His purpose was to set up a series of "linkages" in U.S.-Soviet relations that would persuade Moscow of the economic and social benefits of maintaining good relations with the West.

A symbol of that new relationship was the Helsinki Accords. Signed in 1975 by the United States, Canada, and all European nations on both sides of the iron curtain, these accords recognized all borders in Europe that had been established since the end of World War II, thereby formally acknowledging for the first time the Soviet sphere of influence in Eastern Europe. The Helsinki Accords also committed the signatories to recognize and protect the human rights of their citizens, a clear effort by the Western states to improve the performance of the Soviet Union and its allies in that arena.

CHRONOLOGY **The Cold War to 1980**	
Truman Doctrine	1947
Formation of NATO	1949
Soviet Union explodes first nuclear device	1949
Communists come to power in China	1949
Nationalist government retreats to Taiwan	1949
Korean War	1950–1953
Geneva Conference ends Indochina War	1954
Warsaw Pact created	1955
Khrushchev calls for peaceful coexistence	1956
Sino-Soviet dispute breaks into the open	1961
Cuban Missile Crisis	1962
SALT I treaty signed	1972
Nixon's visit to China	1972
Fall of South Vietnam	1975
Soviet invasion of Afghanistan	1979

Renewed Tensions in the Third World

Protection of human rights became one of the major foreign policy goals of the next U.S. president, Jimmy Carter (b. 1924). Ironically, just at the point when U.S. involvement in Vietnam came to an end and relations with China began to improve, U.S.-Soviet relations began to sour, for several reasons. Some Americans had become increasingly concerned about aggressive new tendencies in Soviet foreign policy. The first indication came in Africa. Soviet influence was on the rise in Somalia, across the Red Sea from South Yemen, and later in neighboring Ethiopia. In Angola, once a colony of Portugal, an insurgent movement supported by Cuban troops came to power. In 1979, Soviet troops were sent across the border into Afghanistan to protect a newly installed Marxist regime facing internal resistance from fundamentalist Muslims. Some observers suspected that the ultimate objective of the Soviet advance into hitherto neutral Afghanistan was to extend Soviet power into the oil fields of the Persian Gulf. To deter such a possibility, the White House promulgated the Carter Doctrine, which stated that the United States would use its military power, if necessary, to safeguard Western access to the oil reserves in the Middle East. In fact, sources in Moscow later disclosed that the Soviet advance had little to do with the oil of the Persian Gulf but was an effort to increase Soviet influence in a region increasingly beset by Islamic fervor. Soviet officials feared that Islamic activism could spread to the Muslim populations in the Soviet republics in Central Asia and were confident that the United States was too distracted by the so-called **Vietnam syndrome** (the public fear of U.S. involvement in another Vietnam-type conflict) to respond.

Another reason for the growing suspicion of the Soviet Union in the United States was that some U.S. defense analysts began to charge that the Soviet Union had rejected the policy of equivalence and was seeking strategic superiority in nuclear weapons. Accordingly, they argued for a substantial increase in U.S. defense spending. Such charges, combined with evidence of Soviet efforts in Africa and the Middle East and reports of the persecution of Jews and dissidents in the Soviet Union, helped undermine public support for détente in the United States. These changing attitudes were reflected in the failure of the Carter administration to obtain congressional approval of a new arms limitation agreement (SALT II), signed with the Soviet Union in 1979.

Countering the Evil Empire

The early years of the administration of President Ronald Reagan (1911–2004) witnessed a return to the harsh rhetoric, if not all of the harsh practices, of the Cold War. President Reagan's anti-Communist credentials were well known. In a speech given shortly after his election in 1980, he referred to the Soviet Union as an "evil empire" and frequently voiced his suspicion of Soviet motives in foreign affairs. In an effort to eliminate perceived Soviet advantages in strategic weaponry, the White House began a military buildup that stimulated a renewed arms race. In 1982, the Reagan administration introduced the nuclear-tipped cruise missile, whose ability to fly at low altitudes made it difficult to detect by enemy radar. Reagan also became an ardent exponent of the Strategic Defense Initiative (SDI), nicknamed **Star Wars**. The intent behind this proposed defense system was not only to create a space shield that could destroy incoming missiles but also to force Moscow into an arms race that it could not hope to win.

The Reagan administration also adopted a more activist, if not confrontational, stance in the Third World. That attitude was most directly demonstrated in Central America, where the revolutionary Sandinista (san-duh-NEES-tuh) regime had been established in Nicaragua after the overthrow of the Somoza dictatorship in 1979. Charging that the Sandinista regime was supporting a guerrilla insurgency movement in nearby El Salvador, the Reagan administration began to provide material aid to the government in El Salvador while simultaneously supporting an anti-Communist guerrilla movement (the **Contras**) in Nicaragua. Though the administration insisted that it was countering the spread of communism in the Western Hemisphere, its Central American policy aroused considerable controversy in Congress, where some members charged that growing U.S. involvement could lead to a repeat of the nation' s bitter experience in Vietnam.

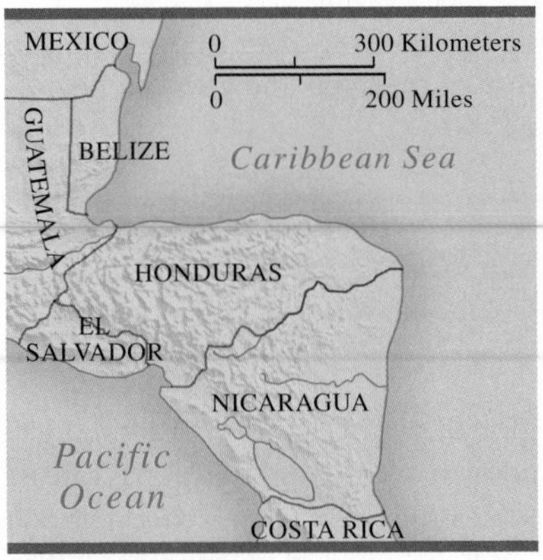

© Cengage Learning

Northern Central America

The Reagan administration also took the offensive in other areas. By providing military support to the anti-Soviet insurgents in Afghanistan, the White House helped maintain a Vietnam-like war in Afghanistan that entangled the Soviet Union in its own quagmire. Like the Vietnam War, the conflict in Afghanistan resulted in heavy casualties and demonstrated that the influence of a superpower was limited in the face of strong nationalist, guerrilla-type opposition.

Toward a New World Order

In 1985, Mikhail Gorbachev (meek-HAYL GOR-buh-chawf) (b. 1931) was elected secretary of the Communist Party of the Soviet Union. During Brezhnev's last years and the brief tenures of his two successors (see Chapter 27), the Soviet Union had entered an era of serious economic decline, and the dynamic new party chief was well aware that drastic changes would be needed to rekindle the dreams that had inspired the Bolshevik Revolution. During the next few years, he launched a program of restructuring, or *perestroika* (per-uh-STROI-kuh), to revitalize the Soviet system. As part of that program, he set out to improve relations with the United States and the rest of the capitalist world. When he met with President Reagan in Reykjavik (RAY-kyuh-vik), the capital of Iceland, the two leaders agreed to set aside their ideological differences.

Gorbachev's desperate effort to rescue the Soviet Union from collapse was too little and too late. In 1989, popular demonstrations against Communist rule broke out across Eastern Europe. The contagion soon spread eastward, and in 1991 the Soviet Union, so long an apparently permanent fixture on the global scene, suddenly disintegrated. In its place arose fifteen new nations. That same year, the string of Soviet satellites in Eastern Europe broke loose from Moscow's grip and declared their independence from Communist rule. The Cold War was over (see Chapter 27).

The end of the Cold War lulled many observers into the seductive vision of a new world order that would be characterized by peaceful cooperation and increasing prosperity. Sadly, such hopes have not been realized (see the comparative essay "Global Village or Clash of Civilizations?" on p. 704). A bitter civil war in the Balkans in the mid-1990s graphically demonstrated that old fault lines of national and ethnic hostility still divided the post–Cold War world. Elsewhere, bloody ethnic and religious disputes broke out in Africa and the Middle East. Then, on September 11, 2001, the world entered a dangerous new era when terrorists attacked the nerve centers of U.S. power in New York City and Washington, D.C.,

COMPARATIVE ESSAY

Global Village or Clash of Civilizations?

As the Cold War came to an end in 1991, policymakers, scholars, and political pundits began to forecast the emergence of a "new world order." One hypothesis, put forth by the political philosopher Francis Fukuyama, was that the decline of communism signaled that the industrial capitalist democracies of the West had triumphed in the world of ideas and were now poised to remake the rest of the world in their own image.

Not everyone agreed with this optimistic view of the world situation. In *The Clash of Civilizations and the Remaking of the World Order*, the historian Samuel P. Huntington suggested that the post–Cold War era, far from marking the triumph of Western ideals, would be characterized by increased global fragmentation and a "clash of civilizations" based on ethnic, cultural, or religious differences. According to Huntington, the twenty-first century would be dominated by disputatious cultural blocs in East Asia, Western Europe and the United States, Eurasia, and the Middle East. The dream of a universal order—a global village—dominated by Western values, he concluded, is a fantasy.

Recent events have lent some support to Huntington's hypothesis. The collapse of the Soviet Union led to the emergence of an atmosphere of conflict and tension all along the perimeter of the old Soviet empire. More recently, the terrorist attack on the United States in September 2001 set the advanced nations of the West and much of the Muslim world on a collision course. As for the new economic order—now enshrined as official policy in Western capitals—public anger at the impact of globalization has reached disturbing levels in many countries, leading to a growing demand for self-protection and group identity in an impersonal and rapidly changing world.

Are we then headed toward multiple power blocs divided by religion and culture as Huntington predicted? His thesis is indeed a useful corrective to the complacent tendency of many observers to view Western civilization as the zenith of human achievement. By dividing the world into competing cultural blocs, however, Huntington has underestimated the centrifugal forces at work in the various regions of the world. As the industrial and technological revolutions spread across the face of the earth, their impact is measurably stronger in some societies than in others, thereby intensifying historical rivalries in a given region while establishing links between individual societies and counterparts in other parts of the world. In recent years, for example, Japan has had more in common with the United States than with its traditional neighbors, China and Korea.

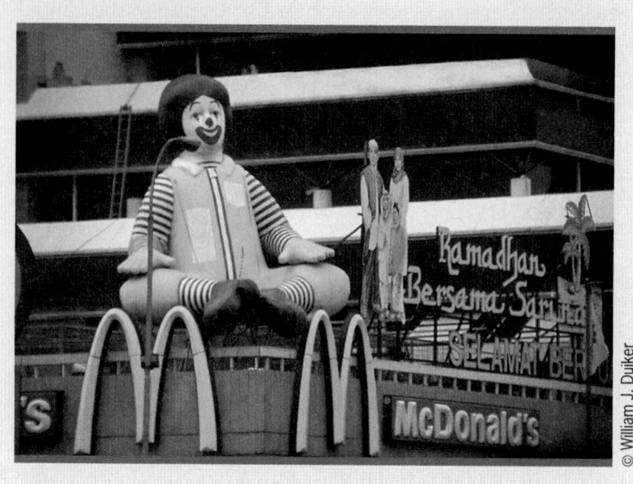

Ronald McDonald in Indonesia. This giant statue welcomes young Indonesians to a McDonald's restaurant in Jakarta, the capital city. McDonald's food chain symbolizes the globalization of today's world civilization.

The most likely scenario for the next few decades, then, is more complex than either the global village hypothesis or its rival, the clash of civilizations. The twenty-first century will be characterized by simultaneous trends toward globalization and fragmentation as the thrust of technology and information transforms societies and gives rise to counterreactions among societies seeking to preserve a group identity and sense of meaning and purpose in a confusing world.

How has the recent global economic recession affected the issues discussed in this essay?

inaugurating a new round of tension between the West and the forces of militant Islam. These events will be discussed in greater detail in the chapters that follow.

In the meantime, other issues beyond the headlines clamor for attention. Environmental problems and the threat of global warming, the growing gap between rich and poor nations, and tensions caused by migrations of peoples all present a growing threat to political stability and the pursuit of happiness. The recent financial crisis, which has severely undermined the overall health of the global economy, is an additional impediment. As the twenty-first century progresses, the task of guaranteeing the survival of the human race appears to be just as challenging, and even more complex, than it was during the Cold War.

CHAPTER SUMMARY

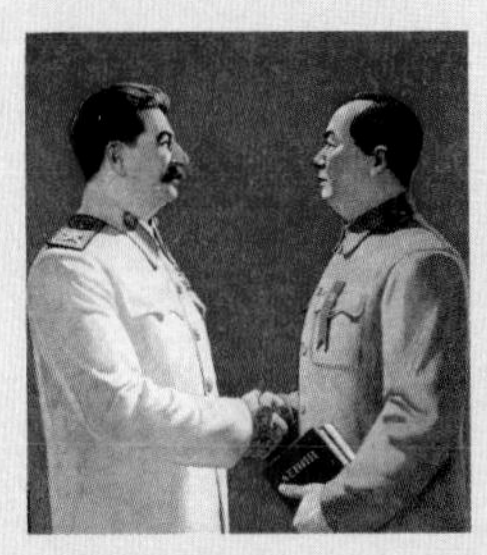

At the end of World War II, a new conflict arose as the two superpowers, the United States and the Soviet Union, began to compete for political domination. This ideological division soon spread throughout the world as the United States fought in Korea and Vietnam to prevent the spread of communism, promoted by the new Maoist government in China, while the Soviet Union used its influence to prop up pro-Soviet regimes in Asia, Africa, and Latin America.

What had begun, then, as a confrontation across the great divide of the "iron curtain" in Europe eventually took on global significance, much as the major European powers had jostled for position and advantage in Africa and eastern Asia prior to World War I. As a result, both Moscow and Washington became entangled in areas that in themselves had little importance in terms of real national security interests.

As the twentieth century wore on, however, there were tantalizing signs of a thaw in the Cold War. In 1979, China and the United States established mutual diplomatic relations, a consequence of Beijing's decision to focus on domestic reform and stop supporting wars of national liberation in Asia. Six years later, the ascent of Mikhail Gorbachev to leadership in the Soviet Union, which culminated in the dissolution of the Soviet Union in 1991, brought an end to almost half a century of bitter rivalry between the world's two superpowers.

The Cold War thus ended without the horrific vision of a mushroom cloud. Unlike the earlier rivalries that had resulted in two world wars, this time the antagonists had gradually come to realize that the struggle for supremacy could be carried out in the political and economic arena rather than on the battlefield. And in the final analysis, it was not military superiority, but political, economic, and cultural factors that brought about the triumph of Western civilization over the Marxist vision of a classless utopia. The world's policymakers could now shift their focus to other problems of mutual concern.

CHAPTER TIMELINE

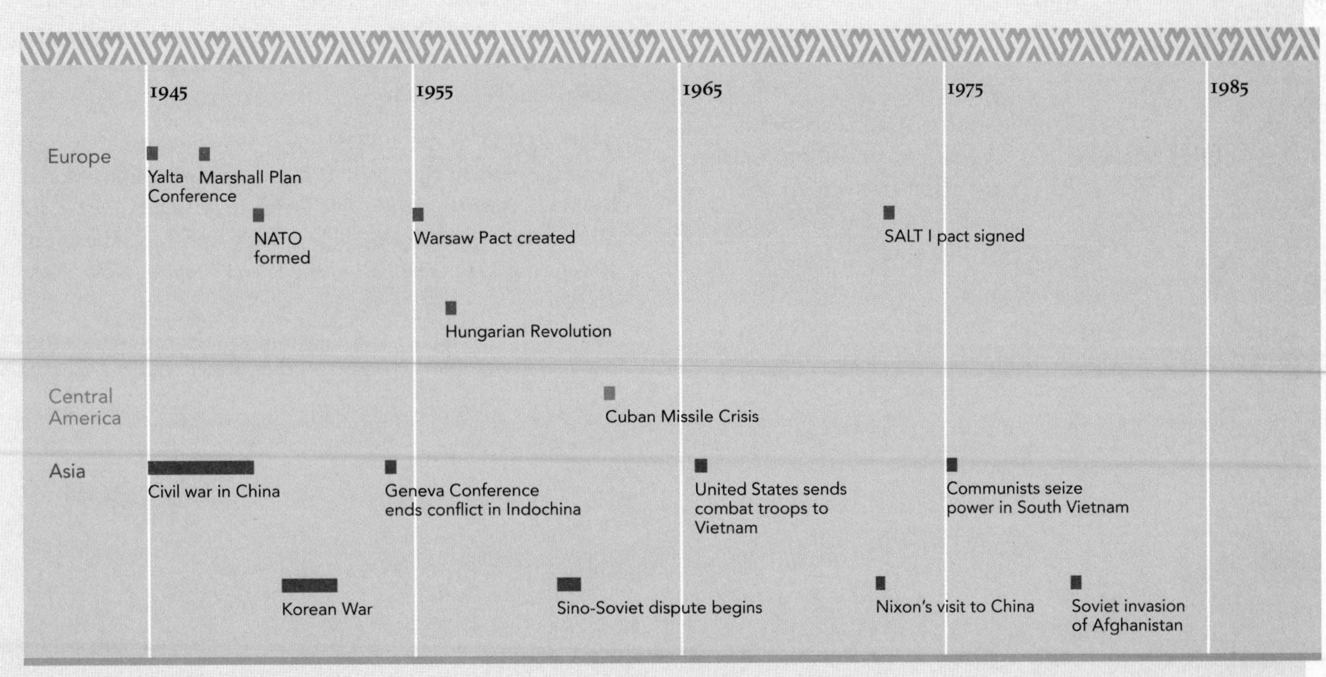

Upon Reflection

Q This chapter has described the outbreak of the Cold War as virtually inevitable, given the ambitions of the two superpowers and their ideological differences. Do you agree? How might the Cold War have been avoided?

Q What disagreements brought about an end to the Sino-Soviet alliance in 1961? Which factors appear to have been most important?

Q How did the wars in Korea and Vietnam relate to the Cold War and affect its course?

Key Terms

Truman Doctrine (p. 680)
Marshall Plan (p. 680)
containment (p. 682)
denazification (p. 682)
peaceful coexistence (p. 691)
Nonaligned Movement (p. 693)
Brezhnev Doctrine (p. 701)
détente (p. 702)
Vietnam syndrome (p. 702)
Star Wars (p. 703)
Contras (p. 703)

Suggested Reading

COLD WAR Literature on the Cold War is abundant. Revisionist studies have emphasized U.S. responsibility for the Cold War, especially its global aspects. See, for example, **W. La Feber, *America, Russia, and the Cold War, 1945–1966,*** 8th ed. (New York, 2002). For a highly competent retrospective analysis of the Cold War era, see **J. L. Gaddis, *We Now Know: Rethinking Cold War History*** (Oxford, 1997). Also see his more general work ***The Cold War: A New History*** (New York, 2005). For the perspective of a veteran journalist, see **M. Frankel, *High Noon in the Cold War: Kennedy, Khrushchev, and the Cuban Missile Crisis*** (New York, 2004).

A number of studies of the early stages of the Cold War are based on documents unavailable until the late 1980s or early 1990s. See, for example, **O. A. Westad, *Cold War and Revolution: Soviet-American Rivalry and the Origins of the Chinese Civil War*** (New York, 1993), and **Chen Jian, *China's Road to the Korean War: The Making of the Sino-American Confrontation*** (New York, 1994). **S. Goncharov, J. W. Lewis,** and **Xue Litai, *Uncertain Partners: Stalin, Mao, and the Korean War*** (Stanford, Calif., 1993), provides a fascinating view of the war from several perspectives. For a perspective that places much of the blame for the Korean War on the United States, see **B. Cumings, *The Korean War: A History*** (New York, 2010).

CHINA There are several informative surveys of Chinese foreign policy since the Communist rise to power. A particularly insightful account is **Chen Jian, *Mao's China and the Cold War*** (Chapel Hill, N.C., 2001). On Chinese policy in Korea, see **Shu Guang Zhang, *Mao's Military Romanticism: China and the Korean War*** (Lawrence, Kans., 2001), and **Xiaobing Li et al., *Mao's Generals Remember Korea*** (Lawrence, Kans., 2001). On Sino-Vietnamese relations, see **Ang Cheng Guan, *Vietnamese Communists' Relations with China and the Second Indochina Conflict*** (Jefferson, N.C., 1997).

THE COLD WAR ENDS Two recent works that deal with the end of the Cold War are the gripping account by **M. E. Sarotte, *1989: The Struggle to Create Post–Cold War Europe*** (Princeton, N.J., 2009), and **V. Sebestyen, *Revolution 1989: The Fall of the Soviet Empire*** (New York, 2008).

CourseMate

Visit the CourseMate website at **www.cengagebrain.com** for additional study tools and review materials for this chapter.

CHAPTER

27

Brave New World: Communism on Trial

© William J. Duiker

Shopping in Moscow

CHAPTER OUTLINE AND FOCUS QUESTIONS

The Postwar Soviet Union

Q How did Nikita Khrushchev change the system that the Soviet dictator Joseph Stalin had put in place before his death in 1953? To what degree did his successors adopt Khrushchev's policies?

The Disintegration of the Soviet Empire

Q What were the key components of *perestroika*, which Mikhail Gorbachev espoused during the 1980s? Why did it fail?

The East Is Red: China Under Communism

Q What were Mao Zedong's chief goals for China, and what policies did he institute to try to achieve them?

"Serve the People": Chinese Society Under Communism

Q What significant political, economic, and social changes have taken place in China since the death of Mao Zedong?

CRITICAL THINKING

Q Why has communism survived in China when it failed to survive in Eastern Europe and Russia? Are Chinese leaders justified in claiming that without party leadership, the country would fall into chaos?

ACCORDING TO KARL MARX, capitalism is a system that involves the exploitation of man by man; under socialism, it is the other way around. That wry joke was typical of popular humor in post–World War II Moscow, where the dreams of a future utopia had faded in the grim reality of life in the Soviet Union.

For the average Soviet citizen after World War II, few images better symbolized the shortcomings of the Soviet system than a long line of people queuing up outside an official state store selling consumer goods. Because the command economy was so inefficient, items of daily use were chronically in such short supply that when a particular item became available, people often lined up immediately to buy several for themselves and their friends. Sometimes, when people saw a line forming, they would automatically join the queue without even knowing what item was available for purchase!

Despite the evident weaknesses of the centralized Soviet economy, the Communist monopoly on power seemed secure, as did Moscow's hold over its client states in Eastern Europe. In fact, for three decades after the end of World War II, the Soviet empire appeared to be a permanent feature of the international landscape. But by the early 1980s, it was clear that there were cracks in the Kremlin wall. The Soviet economy was stagnant, the minority nationalities were restive, and Eastern European leaders were increasingly emboldened to test the waters of the global capitalist marketplace. In the United States, the newly elected president, Ronald Reagan, boldly predicted the imminent collapse of the "evil empire."

Within a period of less than three years (1989–1991), the Soviet Union ceased to exist as a nation. Russia and other former Soviet republics declared their separate independence, Communist regimes in Eastern Europe were toppled, and the long-standing division of postwar Europe came to an end. Although Communist parties survived the demise of the system and have showed signs of renewed vigor in some countries in the region, their monopoly is gone, and they must now compete with other parties for power.

The fate of communism in China has been quite different. Despite some turbulence, communism has survived in China, even as that nation takes giant strides toward becoming an economic superpower. Yet, as China's leaders struggle to bring the nation into the modern age, many of the essential principles of Marxist-Leninist dogma have been tacitly abandoned.

The Postwar Soviet Union

FOCUS QUESTIONS: How did Nikita Khrushchev change the system that the Soviet dictator Joseph Stalin had put in place before his death in 1953? To what degree did his successors adopt Khrushchev's policies?

At the end of World War II, the Soviet Union was one of the world's two superpowers, and its leader, Joseph Stalin, was in a position of strength. He and his Soviet colleagues were now in control of a vast empire that included Eastern Europe, much of the Balkans, and new territory gained from Japan in East Asia.

From Stalin to Khrushchev

At the same time, World War II had devastated the Soviet Union. Nearly 30 million citizens lost their lives, and cities such as Kiev (KEE-yev), Kharkov (KHAR-kawf), and Leningrad had suffered enormous physical destruction. As the lands that had been occupied by the German forces were liberated, the Soviet government turned its attention to restoring their economic structures. Nevertheless, in 1945, agricultural production was only 60 percent and steel output only 50 percent of prewar levels. The Soviet people faced incredibly difficult conditions: ill-housed and poorly clothed, they worked longer hours and ate less they than before the war.

STALINISM IN ACTION In the immediate postwar years, the Soviet Union removed goods and materials from occupied Germany and extorted valuable raw materials from its satellite states in Eastern Europe (see Map 27.1). More important, however, to create a new industrial base, Stalin returned to the method he had used in the 1930s—the extraction of development capital from Soviet labor. Working hard for little pay and for precious few consumer goods, Soviet laborers were expected to produce goods for export with little in return for themselves. The incoming capital from abroad could then be used to purchase machinery and Western technology. The loss of millions of men in the war meant that much of this tremendous workload fell upon Soviet women, who performed almost 40 percent of the heavy manual labor.

The pace of economic recovery in the years immediately after the war was impressive. By 1947, industrial production had returned to 1939 levels. New power plants, canals, and giant factories were built, and industrial enterprises and oil fields were established in Siberia and Soviet Central Asia.

Although Stalin's economic strategy was successful in promoting growth in heavy industry, primarily for the benefit of the military, consumer goods remained scarce as long-suffering Soviet citizens were still being asked to suffer for a better tomorrow. Heavy industry grew at a rate three times that of personal consumption. Moreover, the housing shortage was acute, with living conditions especially difficult in the overcrowded cities.

When World War II ended in 1945, Stalin had been in power for more than fifteen years. Political terror enforced by several hundred thousand secret police ensured that he would remain in power. By the late 1940s, an estimated 9 million Soviet citizens were in Siberian concentration camps.

Increasingly distrustful of potential competitors, Stalin exercised sole authority and pitted his subordinates against each other. His morbid suspicions extended to even his closest colleagues, causing them to become completely cowed. As he remarked mockingly on one occasion, "When I die, the imperialists will strangle all of you like a litter of kittens."[1]

THE RISE AND FALL OF KHRUSHCHEV Stalin died—presumably of natural causes—in 1953 and, after some bitter infighting within the party leadership, was

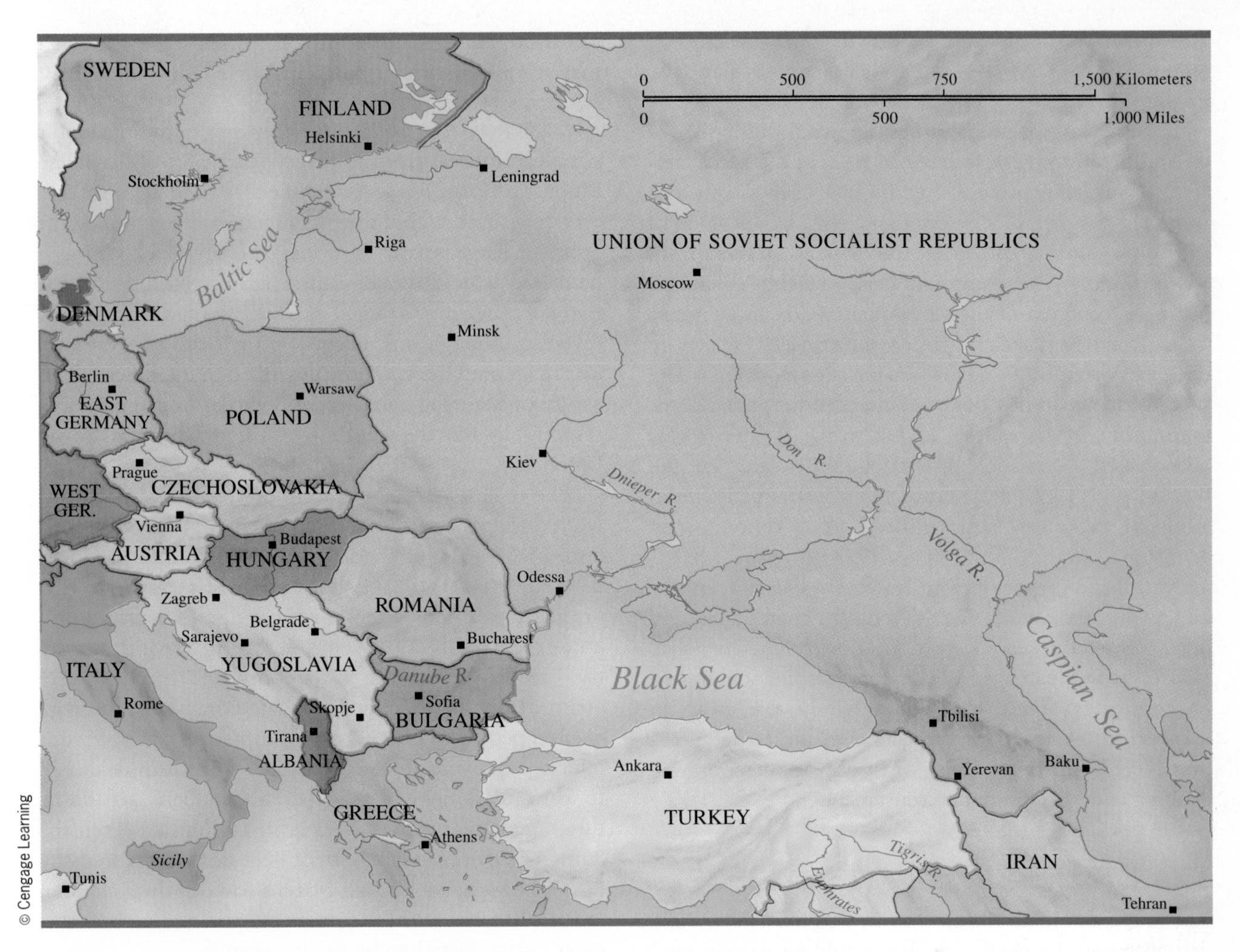

© Cengage Learning

MAP 27.1 Eastern Europe Under Soviet Rule. After World War II, the boundaries of Eastern Europe were redrawn as a result of Allied agreements reached at the Tehran and Yalta conferences. This map shows the new boundaries that were established throughout the region, placing Soviet power at the center of Europe.

How had the boundaries changed from the prewar era?

succeeded by Georgy Malenkov, a veteran administrator and ambitious member of the Politburo (POL-it-byoor-oh), the party's governing body. But Malenkov's reform goals did not necessarily appeal to key groups, including the army, the Communist Party, the managerial elite, and the security services (now known as the Committee on Government Security, or KGB). In 1953, Malenkov was removed from his position as party leader, and by 1955 power had shifted to his rival, the new party general secretary, Nikita Khrushchev.

Once in power, Khrushchev moved vigorously to boost the performance of the Soviet economy and revitalize Soviet society. In an attempt to release the national economy from the stranglehold of the central bureaucracy, he abolished dozens of government ministries and split up the party and government apparatus. Khrushchev also attempted to rejuvenate the stagnant agricultural sector. He attempted to spur production by increasing profit incentives and opened "virgin lands" in Soviet Kazakhstan (ka-zak-STAN *or* kuh-zahk-STAHN) to bring thousands of acres of new land under cultivation.

An innovator by nature, Khrushchev had to overcome the inherently conservative instincts of the Soviet bureaucracy, as well as those of the mass of the Soviet population. His plan to remove the "dead hand" of the state, however laudable in intent, alienated much of the Soviet official class, and his effort to split the party angered those who saw it as the central force in the Soviet system. Khrushchev's agricultural schemes inspired similar opposition. His effort to persuade Russians to eat more corn (an idea he had apparently picked up during a visit to the United States) earned him the mocking nickname

"Cornman." The industrial growth rate, which had soared in the early 1950s, now declined dramatically, from 13 percent in 1953 to 7.5 percent in 1964.

Khrushchev was probably best known for his policy of **de-Stalinization**. Khrushchev had risen in the party hierarchy as a Stalin protégé, but he had been deeply disturbed by his mentor's excesses and, once in a position of authority, moved to excise the Stalinist legacy from Soviet society The campaign began at the Twentieth National Congress of the Communist Party in February 1956, when Khrushchev gave a long speech in private criticizing some of Stalin's major shortcomings. The speech had apparently not been intended for public distribution, but it was quickly leaked to the Western press and created a sensation throughout the world (see the box on p. 711). Under Khrushchev's instructions, thousands of prisoners were released from concentration camps.

Khrushchev's personality, however, did not endear him to higher Soviet officials, who frowned at his tendency to crack jokes and play the clown. Foreign policy failures further damaged Khrushchev's reputation among his colleagues (see Chapter 26). While he was away on vacation in 1964, a special meeting of the Soviet Politburo voted him out of office (because of "deteriorating health") and forced him into retirement.

The Brezhnev Years (1964–1982)

The ouster of Nikita Khrushchev in October 1964 vividly demonstrated the challenges that would be encountered by any leader sufficiently bold to try to reform the Soviet system. Leonid Brezhnev (1906–1982), the new party chief, was undoubtedly aware of these realities of Soviet politics, and his long tenure in power was marked, above all, by the desire to avoid changes that might provoke instability, either at home or abroad. Brezhnev was himself a product of the Soviet system. He had entered the ranks of the party leadership under Stalin, and although he was not a particularly avid believer in party ideology, he was no partisan of reform.

Still, Brezhnev sought stability in the domestic arena. He and his prime minister, Alexei Kosygin (1904–1980), undertook what might be described as a program of "de-Khrushchevization," returning the responsibility for long-term planning to the central ministries and reuniting the Communist Party apparatus. Despite some cautious attempts to stimulate the stagnant agricultural sector, there was no effort to revise the basic system of collective farms. In the industrial sector, the regime launched a series of reforms designed to give factory managers (themselves employees of the state) more responsibility for setting prices, wages, and production quotas. These "Kosygin reforms" had little effect, however, because they were stubbornly resisted by the bureaucracy.

A CONTROLLED SOCIETY Brezhnev also initiated a significant retreat from Khrushchev's policy of de-Stalinization. Criticism of the "Great Leader" had angered conservatives both within the party hierarchy and among the public at large, many of whom still revered Stalin as a hero and a defender of Russia against Nazi Germany. Early in Brezhnev's reign, Stalin's reputation began to revive. Although his alleged shortcomings were not totally ignored, he was now described in the official press as "an outstanding party leader" who had been primarily responsible for the successes achieved by the Soviet Union.

The regime also adopted a more restrictive policy toward dissidents in Soviet society. Critics of the Soviet system, such as the physicist Andrei Sakharov (ahn-DRAY SAH-kuh-rawf) (1921–1989), were harassed and arrested or, like the famous writer Alexander Solzhenitsyn (sohl-zhuh-NEET-sin) (1918–2008), forced to leave the country. Free expression was also restricted. The media were controlled by the state and presented only what the state wanted people to hear. The government made strenuous efforts to prevent the Soviet people from being exposed to harmful foreign ideas, especially modern art, literature, and contemporary Western rock music. When the Summer Olympic Games were held in Moscow in 1980, Soviet newspapers advised citizens to keep their children indoors to prevent them from being polluted with "bourgeois" ideas passed on by foreign visitors.

For citizens of Western democracies, such a political atmosphere would seem highly oppressive, but for the Russian people, an emphasis on law and order was an accepted aspect of everyday life inherited from the tsarist period. It was firmly enshrined in the Soviet constitution, which subordinated individual freedom to the interests of the state (see the box on p. 712). Conformity was the rule in virtually every corner of Soviet society, from the educational system (characterized at all levels by rote memorization and political indoctrination) to child rearing (it was forbidden, for example, to be left-handed) and even to yearly vacations (most workers took their vacations at resorts run by their employer, where the daily schedule of activities was highly regimented). Young Americans studying in the Soviet Union reported that their Soviet friends were often shocked to hear U.S. citizens criticizing the U.S. president.

A STAGNANT ECONOMY Soviet leaders also failed to achieve their objective of revitalizing the national economy. Whereas growth rates during the early Khrushchev era had been impressive (prompting Khrushchev during

Khrushchev Denounces Stalin

POLITICS & GOVERNMENT

Three years after Stalin's death, the new Soviet premier, Nikita Khrushchev, addressed the Twentieth Congress of the Communist Party and denounced the former Soviet dictator for his crimes. This denunciation was the beginning of a policy of de-Stalinization.

Khrushchev Addresses the Twentieth Party Congress, February 1956

Comrades, . . . quite a lot has been said about the cult of the individual and about its harmful consequences. . . . The cult of the person of Stalin . . . became at a certain specific stage the source of a whole series of exceedingly serious and grave perversions of Party principles, of Party democracy, of revolutionary legality.

Stalin absolutely did not tolerate collegiality in leadership and in work and . . . practiced brutal violence, not only toward everything which opposed him, but also toward that which seemed to his capricious and despotic character, contrary to his concepts.

Stalin abandoned the method of ideological struggle for that of administrative violence, mass repressions and terror. . . . Arbitrary behavior by one person encouraged and permitted arbitrariness in others. Mass arrests and deportations of many thousands of people, execution without trial and without normal investigation created conditions of insecurity, fear, and even desperation.

Stalin showed in a whole series of cases his intolerance, his brutality, and his abuse of power. . . . He often chose the path of repression and annihilation, not only against actual enemies, but also against individuals who had not committed any crimes against the Party and the Soviet government. . . .

Many Party, Soviet, and economic activists who were branded in 1937–8 as "enemies" were actually never enemies, spies, wreckers, and so on, but were always honest communists; they were only so stigmatized, and often, no longer able to bear barbaric tortures, they charged themselves (at the order of the investigative judges-falsifiers) with all kinds of grave and unlikely crimes.

This was the result of the abuse of power by Stalin, who began to use mass terror against the Party cadres. . . . Stalin put the Party and the NKVD [the Soviet police agency] up to the use of mass terror when the exploiting classes had been liquidated in our country and when there were no serious reasons for the use of extraordinary mass terror. The terror was directed . . . against the honest workers of the Party and the Soviet state. . . .

Stalin was a very distrustful man, sickly, suspicious. . . . Everywhere and in everything he saw "enemies," "two-facers," and "spies." Possessing unlimited power, he indulged in great willfulness and choked a person morally and physically. A situation was created where one could not express one's own will. When Stalin said that one or another would be arrested, it was necessary to accept on faith that he was an "enemy of the people." What proofs were offered? The confession of the arrested. . . . How is it possible that a person confesses to crimes that he had not committed? Only in one way—because of application of physical methods of pressuring him, tortures, bringing him to a state of unconsciousness, deprivation of his judgment, taking away of his human dignity.

What were the key charges that Khrushchev made against Stalin? Can it be said that Khrushchev corrected these problems?

Source: From *Congressional Record*, 84th Congress, 2nd Session, Vol. 102, Part 7, pp. 9389–9402 (June 4, 1956).

a reception at the Kremlin in the 1950s to chortle to an American guest, "We will bury you," referring to the United States), under Brezhnev industrial growth declined to an annual rate of less than 4 percent in the early 1970s and less than 3 percent in the period from 1975 to 1980. Successes in the agricultural sector were equally meager.

One of the primary problems with the Soviet economy was the absence of incentives. Salary structures offered little reward for hard labor and extraordinary achievement. Pay differentials operated in a much narrower range than in most Western societies, and there was little danger of being dismissed. According to the Soviet constitution, every Soviet citizen was guaranteed an opportunity to work.

The Rights and Duties of Soviet Citizens

In the Soviet Union, and in other countries modeled on the Soviet system, the national constitution was viewed not as a timeless document, but as a reflection of conditions at the time it was framed. As Soviet society advanced from a state of "raw communism" to a fully socialist society, new constitutions were drafted to reflect the changes taking place in society as a whole. The first two constitutions of the Soviet Union, promulgated in 1924 and 1936, declared that the state was a "dictatorship of the proletariat" guided by the Communist Party, the vanguard organization of the working class in the Soviet Union. But the so-called Brezhnev constitution of 1977 described the Soviet Union as a "state of all the people," composed of workers, farmers, and "socialist intellectuals," although it confirmed the role of the Communist Party as the "leading force" in society. The provisions from the 1977 constitution presented here illustrate some of the freedoms and obligations of Soviet citizens. Especially noteworthy are Articles 39 and 62, which suggest that the interests and prestige of the state took precedence over individual liberties.

The Soviet Constitution of 1977

Chapter 1: The Political System

Article 6. The leading and guiding force of the Soviet society and the nucleus of its political system, of all state organizations and public organizations, is the Communist Party of the Soviet Union. The CPSU exists for the people and serves the people.

The Communist Party, armed with Marxism-Leninism, determines the general perspectives of the development of society and the course of the home and foreign policy of the USSR, directs the great constructive work of the Soviet people, and imparts a planned, systematic, and theoretically substantiated character to their struggle for the victory of communism.

Chapter 6: Equality of Citizens' Rights

Article 35. Women and men have equal rights in the USSR. Exercise of these rights is ensured by according women equal access with men to education and vocational and professional training, equal opportunities in employment, remuneration and promotion, and in social and political, and cultural activity, and by the special labor and health protection measures for women; by providing conditions enabling mothers to work; by legal protection, and material and moral support for mothers and children, including paid leaves and other benefits for expectant mothers and mothers, and gradual reduction of working time for mothers with small children.

Chapter 7: The Basic Rights, Freedoms, and Duties of Citizens of the USSR

Article 39. Citizens of the USSR enjoy in full the social, economic, political, and personal rights and freedoms proclaimed and guaranteed by the Constitution of the USSR and by Soviet laws. The socialist system ensures enlargement of the rights and freedoms of citizens and continuous improvement of their living standards as social, economic, and cultural development programs are fulfilled. Enjoyment by citizens of their rights and freedoms must not be to the detriment of the interests of society or the state, or infringe the rights of other citizens.

Article 62. Citizens of the USSR are obliged to safeguard the interests of the Soviet state, and to enhance its power and prestige. Defense of the Socialist Motherland is the sacred duty of every citizen of the USSR. Betrayal of the Motherland is the gravest of crimes against the people.

Which of these provisions would seem out of place if they were to appear in the U.S. Constitution?

Source: Excerpts from *The Soviet Constitution of 1977*. Novosti Press Agency Publishing House. Moscow, 1985.

There were, of course, some exceptions to the general rule. Athletic achievement was highly prized, and a gymnast of Olympic stature would receive great rewards in the form of prestige and lifestyle. Senior officials did not receive high salaries but were provided with countless perquisites, such as access to foreign goods, official automobiles with a chauffeur, and entry into prestigious institutions of higher learning for their children.

AN AGING LEADERSHIP Brezhnev died in November 1982 and was succeeded by Yuri Andropov (YOOR-ee ahn-DRAHP-awf) (1914–1984), a party veteran and head of the Soviet secret services. During his brief tenure as party chief, Andropov was a vocal advocate of reform, but when he died after only a few months in office, little had been done to change the system. He was succeeded, in turn, by a mediocre party stalwart, the elderly Konstantin Chernenko (kuhn-stuhn-TEEN chirn-YEN-koh) (1911–1985). With the Soviet system in crisis, Moscow seemed stuck in a time warp.

Cultural Expression in the Soviet Bloc

In his occasional musings about the future Communist utopia, Karl Marx had predicted that a new, classless society would replace the exploitative and hierarchical systems of feudalism and capitalism. In their free time, workers would produce a new, advanced culture, proletarian in character and egalitarian in content.

The reality in the post–World War II Soviet Union and Eastern Europe was somewhat different. Under Stalin, a series of government decrees made all forms of literary and scientific expression dependent on the state. All Soviet culture was expected to follow the party line. Historians, philosophers, and social scientists all grew accustomed to quoting Marx, Lenin, and, above all, Stalin as their chief authorities. Novels and plays, too, were supposed to portray Communist heroes and their efforts to create a better society. No criticism of existing social conditions was permitted. Some areas of intellectual activity were virtually abolished; the science of genetics disappeared, and few movies were made during Stalin's final years.

Stalin's death brought a modest respite from cultural repression. Writers and artists banned during the Stalin years were again allowed to publish. Still, Soviet authorities, including Khrushchev, were reluctant to allow cultural freedom to move far beyond official Soviet ideology.

These restrictions, however, did not prevent the emergence of some significant Soviet literature, although authors paid a heavy price if they alienated the Soviet authorities. Boris Pasternak (buh-REESS PASS-tur-nak) (1890–1960), who began his literary career as a poet, won the Nobel Prize in 1958 mainly for his celebrated novel *Doctor Zhivago*, written between 1945 and 1956 and published in Italy in 1957. But the Soviet government condemned Pasternak's anti-Soviet tendencies, banned the novel, and would not allow him to accept the prize. The author had alienated the authorities by describing a society scarred by the excesses of Bolshevik revolutionary zeal.

Alexander Solzhenitsyn created an even greater furor than Pasternak. Solzhenitsyn had spent eight years in forced labor camps for criticizing Stalin, and his *One Day in the Life of Ivan Denisovich*, one of the works that won him the Nobel Prize in 1970, was an account of life in those camps. Khrushchev allowed the book's publication as part of his de-Stalinization campaign. Solzhenitsyn then wrote *The Gulag Archipelago*, a detailed indictment of the whole system of Soviet oppression. Soviet authorities expelled Solzhenitsyn from the Soviet Union in 1973.

In the Eastern European satellites, cultural freedom varied considerably from country to country. In Poland, intellectuals had access to Western publications as well as greater freedom to travel to the West. Hungarian and Yugoslav Communists, too, tolerated a certain level of intellectual activity that was not liked but at least was not prohibited. Elsewhere, intellectuals were forced to conform to the regime's demands. After the Soviet invasion of Czechoslovakia in 1968, Czech Communists pursued a policy of strict cultural control.

© William J. Duiker

Stalinist Heroic: An Example of Socialist Realism. Under Stalin and his successors, art was assigned the task of indoctrinating the Soviet population on the public virtues, such as hard work, loyalty to the state, and patriotism. Grandiose statuary erected to commemorate the heroic efforts of the Red Army during World War II appeared in every Soviet city. Here is an example in Minsk, today the capital of Belarus.

Social Changes

According to Marxist doctrine, state control of industry and the elimination of private property were supposed to lead to a classless society. Although that ideal was never achieved, it did have important social consequences. The desire to create a classless society, for example, led to noticeable changes in education. In some countries, laws mandated quota systems based on class. As education became crucial for obtaining new jobs in the Communist system, enrollments rose in both secondary schools and universities.

The new managers of society, regardless of their class background, realized the importance of higher education and used their power to gain special privileges for their children. By 1971, 60 percent of the children of white-collar workers attended a university, but only 36 percent of the children of blue-collar families did so, although these families constituted 60 percent of the population.

Ideals of equality also did not include women. Men dominated the leadership positions of the Communist parties. Women did have greater opportunities in the workforce and even in the professions, however. In the Soviet Union, women comprised 51 percent of the labor force in 1980; by the mid-1980s, they constituted 50 percent of the engineers, 80 percent of the doctors, and 75 percent of the teachers and teachers' aides. But many of these were low-paying jobs; most female doctors, for example, worked in primary care and were paid less than skilled machinists. The chief administrators in hospitals and schools were still men.

Moreover, although women made up nearly half of the workforce, they were never freed from their traditional roles in the home. Most women had to work what came to be known as the "double shift." After working eight hours in their jobs, they came home to do the housework and care for the children. They might also spend two hours a day in long lines at a number of stores waiting to buy food and clothes. Because of the housing shortage, several families would share a kitchen, making even meal preparation a complicated task.

Nearly three-quarters of a century after the Bolshevik Revolution, then, the Marxist dream of an advanced, egalitarian society was as far away as ever. Although in some respects, conditions in the socialist camp were a distinct improvement over those before World War II, many problems and inequities were as intransigent as ever.

The Disintegration of the Soviet Empire

FOCUS QUESTIONS: What were the key components of *perestroika*, which Mikhail Gorbachev espoused during the 1980s? Why did it fail?

On the death of Konstantin Chernenko in 1985, party leaders selected the talented and vigorous Soviet official Mikhail Gorbachev to succeed him. The new Soviet leader had shown early signs of promise. Born into a peasant family in 1931, Gorbachev combined farmwork with school and received the Order of the Red Banner for his agricultural efforts. This award and his good school record enabled him to study law at the University of Moscow. After receiving his law degree in 1955, he returned to his native southern Russia, where he eventually became first secretary of the Communist Party in the city of Stavropol (STAH-vruh-puhl *or* stav-ROH-puhl). In 1978, he was made a member of the party's Central Committee in Moscow. Two years later, he became a full member of the ruling Politburo and secretary of the Central Committee.

During the early 1980s, Gorbachev began to realize the immensity of Soviet problems and the crucial need for massive reform to transform the system. During a visit to Canada in 1983, he discovered to his astonishment that Canadian farmers worked hard on their own initiative. "We'll never have this for fifty years," he reportedly remarked.[2] On his return to Moscow, he set in motion a series of committees to evaluate the situation and recommend measures to improve the system.

The Gorbachev Era

With his election as party general secretary in 1985, Gorbachev seemed intent on taking earlier reforms to their logical conclusions. The cornerstone of his program was ***perestroika*** (per-uh-STROI-kuh), or "restructuring." At first, it meant only a reordering of economic policy, as Gorbachev called for the beginning of a market economy with limited free enterprise and some private property (see the comparative illustration on p. 715). But Gorbachev soon perceived that in the Soviet system, the economic sphere was intimately tied to the social and political spheres. Any efforts to reform the economy without political or social reform would be doomed to failure. One of the most important instruments of *perestroika* was ***glasnost*** (GLAHZ-nohst), or "openness." Soviet citizens and officials were encouraged to openly discuss the strengths and weaknesses of the Soviet Union. The arts also benefited from the new policy as previously banned works were now published and motion pictures were allowed to depict negative aspects of Soviet life. Music based on Western styles, such as jazz and rock, could now be performed openly. Religious activities, long banned by the authorities, were once again tolerated.

Political reforms were equally revolutionary. In June 1987, the principle of two-candidate elections was introduced; previously, voters had been presented with only one candidate. At the Communist Party conference in 1988, Gorbachev called for the creation of a new Soviet

© William J. Duiker

© William J. Duiker

COMPARATIVE ILLUSTRATION

POLITICS & GOVERNMENT

Sideline Industries: Creeping Capitalism in a Socialist Paradise. In the late 1980s, Communist leaders in both the Soviet Union and China began to encourage their citizens to engage in private commercial activities as a means of reviving moribund economies. In the photo on the left, a Soviet farmworker displays fruits and vegetables for sale on a street corner in Odessa, a seaport on the Black Sea. On the right, a Chinese woman sells her dumplings to passersby in Shandong province. As her smile suggests, the Chinese took up the challenge of entrepreneurship with much greater success and enthusiasm than their Soviet counterparts did.

Why did Chinese citizens adopt capitalist reforms in the countryside more enthusiastically than their Soviet counterparts?

parliament, the Congress of People's Deputies, whose members were to be chosen in competitive elections. It convened in 1989, the first such meeting in the nation since 1918. Early in 1990, Gorbachev legalized the formation of other political parties and struck out Article 6 of the Soviet constitution, which guaranteed the "leading role" of the Communist Party. Hitherto, the position of first secretary of the party was the most important post in the Soviet Union, but as the Communist Party became less closely associated with the state, the powers of this office diminished. Gorbachev attempted to consolidate his power by creating a new state presidency, and in March 1990, he became the Soviet Union's first president.

THE BEGINNING OF THE END One of Gorbachev's most serious problems stemmed from the character of the Soviet Union. The Union of Soviet Socialist Republics was a truly multiethnic country, containing 92 nationalities and 112 recognized languages. Previously, the iron hand of the Communist Party, centered in Moscow, had kept a lid on the centuries-old ethnic tensions that had periodically erupted throughout the history of the region. As Gorbachev released this iron grip, ethnic groups throughout the Soviet Union began to call for sovereignty of the republics and independence from Russian-based rule centered in Moscow. Such movements sprang up first in Georgia in late 1988 and then in Latvia (LAT-vee-uh), Estonia (ES-toh-nee-uh), Moldova (mohl-DOH-vuh), Uzbekistan (ooz-BEK-ih-stan), Azerbaijan (az-ur-by-JAHN), and Lithuania (lih-thuh-WAY-nee-uh).

In December 1989, the Communist Party of Lithuania declared itself independent of the Communist Party of the Soviet Union. Despite pleas from Gorbachev, who supported self-determination but not secession, other Soviet republics eventually followed suit. Ukraine voted for independence on December 1, 1991. A week later, the leaders of Russia, Ukraine, and Belarus (bell-uh-ROOSS) announced that the Soviet Union had "ceased to exist" and would be replaced by a "commonwealth of independent states." Gorbachev resigned on December 25, 1991, and turned over his responsibilities as commander in chief to Boris Yeltsin (YELT-sun) (1931–2007),

CHRONOLOGY The Soviet Bloc and Its Demise	
Death of Joseph Stalin	1953
Rise of Nikita Khrushchev	1955
Khrushchev's de-Stalinization speech	1956
Removal of Khrushchev	1964
The Brezhnev era	1964–1982
Rule of Andropov and Chernenko	1982–1985
Gorbachev comes to power in Soviet Union	1985
Collapse of Communist governments in Eastern Europe	1989
Disintegration of Soviet Union	1991

the president of Russia. By the end of 1991, one of the largest empires in world history had come to an end, and a new era had begun in its lands (see Chapter 28).

Eastern Europe: From Satellites to Sovereign Nations

The disintegration of the Soviet Union had an immediate impact on its neighbors to the west. First to respond, as in 1956, was Poland, where popular protests at high food prices had erupted in the early 1980s, leading to the rise of an independent labor movement called Solidarity. Led by Lech Walesa (LEK vah-WENT-sah) (b. 1943), Solidarity rapidly became an influential force for change and a threat to the government's monopoly of power. In 1988, the Communist government bowed to the inevitable and permitted free national elections to take place, resulting in the election of Walesa as president of Poland in December 1990. When Moscow took no action to reverse the verdict in Warsaw, Poland entered the post-Communist era.

In Hungary, as in Poland, the process of transition had begun many years previously. After crushing the Hungarian revolution of 1956, the Communist government of János Kádár had tried to assuage popular opinion by enacting a series of far-reaching economic reforms (labeled "communism with a capitalist face-lift"). But as the 1980s progressed, the economy sagged, and in 1989, the regime permitted the formation of opposition political parties, leading eventually to the formation of a non-Communist coalition government in elections held in March 1990.

The transition in Czechoslovakia was more abrupt. After Soviet troops crushed the Prague Spring in 1968, hard-line Communists under Gustav Husák followed a policy of massive repression to maintain their power. In 1977, dissident intellectuals formed an organization called Charter 77 as a vehicle for protest against violations of human rights. Dissident activities increased during the 1980s, and when massive demonstrations broke out in several major cities in 1989, President Husák's government, lacking any real popular support, collapsed. At the end of December, he was replaced by Václav Havel (VAHT-slahf HAH-vul) (1936–2011), a dissident playwright who had been a leading figure in Charter 77.

But the most dramatic events took place in East Germany, where a persistent economic slump and the ongoing oppressiveness of the regime of Erich Honecker led to a flight of refugees and mass demonstrations against the regime in the summer and fall of 1989. Capitulating to popular pressure, the Communist government opened its entire border with the West. The Berlin Wall, the most tangible symbol of the Cold War, became the site of a massive celebration, and most of it was dismantled by joyful Germans from both sides of the border. In March 1990, free elections led to the formation of a non-Communist government that rapidly carried out a program of political and economic reunification with West Germany (see Chapter 28).

Why Did the Soviet Union Collapse?

What caused the sudden disintegration of the Soviet system? It is popular in some quarters in the United States to argue that the ambitious defense policies adopted by the Reagan administration forced Moscow into an arms race that it could not afford and that ultimately led to the collapse of the Soviet economy. This contention has some superficial plausibility as Soviet leaders did indeed react to Reagan's "Star Wars" program by increasing their own defense expenditures, which put a strain on the Soviet budget.

Most knowledgeable observers, however, believe that the fall of the Soviet Union was primarily a consequence of conditions inherent in the system, several of which have been pointed out in this chapter. For years, if not decades, leaders in the Kremlin had disguised or ignored the massive inefficiencies in the Soviet economy. In the 1980s, time began to run out. The perceptive Mikhail Gorbachev tried to stem the decline by instituting radical reforms, but by then it was too late.

An additional factor should also be considered. One of the most vulnerable aspects of the Soviet Union was its multiethnic character, with only a little more than half of the total population composed of ethnic Russians. Many of the minority nationalities were becoming increasingly restive and were demanding more autonomy or even independence for their regions. By the end of the 1980s, such demands brought about the final collapse of the system. The Soviet empire died at least partly from imperial overreach.

The East Is Red: China Under Communism

FOCUS QUESTION: What were Mao Zedong's chief goals for China, and what policies did he institute to try to achieve them?

"A revolution is not a dinner party, or writing an essay, or painting a picture, or doing embroidery; it cannot be so refined, so leisurely and gentle, so temperate and kind, courteous, restrained, and magnanimous. A revolution is an insurrection, an act of violence by which one class overthrows another."[3] With these words—written in 1926, at a time when the Communists, in cooperation with Chiang Kai-shek's Nationalist Party, were embarked on their Northern Expedition to defeat the warlords and reunify China—the young revolutionary Mao Zedong warned his colleagues that the road to victory in the struggle to build a Communist society would be arduous and would inevitably involve acts of violence against the class enemy.

In the fall of 1949, China was at peace for the first time in twelve years. The newly victorious Communist Party, under the leadership of its chairman, Mao Zedong, turned its attention to consolidating its power base and healing the wounds of war. Its long-term goal was to construct a socialist society, but its leaders realized that popular support for the revolution was based on the party's platform of honest government, land reform, social justice, and peace rather than on the utopian goal of a classless society. Accordingly, the new regime temporarily set aside Mao Zedong's stirring exhortation of 1926 and adopted a moderate program of political and economic recovery known as New Democracy.

New Democracy

With **New Democracy**—patterned roughly after Lenin's New Economic Policy in Soviet Russia in the 1920s (see Chapter 23)—the new Chinese leadership tacitly recognized that time and extensive indoctrination would be needed to convince the Chinese people of the superiority of socialism. In the meantime, the party would rely on capitalist profit incentives to spur productivity. Manufacturing and commercial firms were permitted to remain under private ownership, although with stringent government regulations. To win the support of the poorer peasants, who made up the majority of the population, a land redistribution program was adopted, but the collectivization of agriculture was postponed.

In a number of key respects, New Democracy was a success. About two-thirds of the peasant households in the country received land and thus had reason to be grateful to the new regime (see the box on p. 718). Spurred by official tolerance for capitalist activities and the end of internal conflict, the national economy began to rebound, although agricultural production still lagged behind both official targets and the growing population, which was increasing at an annual rate of more than 2 percent.

The Transition to Socialism

In 1953, party leaders launched the nation's first five-year plan (patterned after similar Soviet plans), which called for substantial increases in industrial output. Lenin had believed that mechanization would induce Russian peasants to join collective farms, which, because of their greater size and efficiency, could better afford to purchase expensive farm machinery. But the difficulty of providing tractors and reapers for millions of rural villages eventually convinced Mao that it would take years, if not decades, for China's infant industrial base to meet the needs of a modernizing agricultural sector. He therefore decided to begin collectivization immediately, in the hope that collective farms would increase food production and release land, labor, and capital for the industrial sector. Accordingly, beginning in 1955, virtually all private farmland was collectivized (although peasant families were allowed to retain small private plots), and most businesses and industries were nationalized.

Collectivization was achieved without provoking the massive peasant unrest that had taken place in the Soviet Union during the 1930s, but the hoped-for production increases did not materialize. In 1958, at Mao's insistent urging, party leaders approved a more radical program known as the **Great Leap Forward**. Existing rural collectives, normally the size of a traditional village, were combined into vast "people's communes," each containing more than 30,000 people. These communes were to be responsible for all administrative and economic tasks at the local level. The party's official slogan promised "Hard work for a few years, happiness for a thousand."[4]

The communes were a disaster. Administrative bottlenecks, bad weather, and peasant resistance to the new system (which, among other things, attempted to eliminate work incentives and destroy the traditional family as the basic unit of Chinese society) combined to drive food production downward, and over the next few years, as many as 15 million people may have died of starvation. In 1960, the experiment was essentially abandoned. Although the commune structure was retained, ownership and management were returned to the collective level. Mao was severely criticized by some of his more pragmatic colleagues.

Land Reform in Action

One of the great achievements of the new Communist regime in China was the land reform program, which resulted in the distribution of farmland to almost two-thirds of the rural population. The program consequently won the gratitude of millions of Chinese. But it also had a dark side as local land reform tribunals routinely convicted "wicked landlords" of crimes against the people and then put them to death. The following passage, written by a foreign observer, describes the process in one village.

Revolution in a Chinese Village

T'ien-ming [a Party cadre] called all the active young cadres and the militiamen of Long Bow [village] together and announced to them the policy of the county government, which was to confront all enemy collaborators and their backers at public meetings, expose their crimes, and turn them over to the county authorities for punishment. He proposed that they start with Kuo Te-yu, the puppet village head. Having moved the group to anger with a description of Te-yu's crimes, T'ien-ming reviewed the painful life led by the poor peasants during the occupation and recalled how hard they had all worked and how as soon as they harvested all the grain the puppet officials, backed by army bayonets, took what they wanted, turned over huge quantities to the Japanese devils, forced the peasants to haul it away, and flogged those who refused.

As the silent crowd contracted toward the spot where the accused man stood, T'ien-ming stepped forward. . . . "This is our chance. Remember how we were oppressed. The traitors seized our property. They beat us and kicked us. . . .

"Let us speak out the bitter memories. Let us see that the blood debt is repaid. . . ."

He paused for a moment. The peasants were listening to every word but gave no sign as to how they felt. . . .

"Come now, who has evidence against this man?"

Again there was silence.

Kuei-ts'ai, the new vice-chairman of the village, found it intolerable. He jumped up [and] struck Kuo Te-yu on the jaw with the back of his hand. "Tell the meeting how much you stole," he demanded.

The blow jarred the ragged crowd. It was as if an electric spark had tensed every muscle. Not in living memory had any peasant ever struck an official. . . .

The people in the square waited fascinated as if watching a play. They did not realize that in order for the plot to unfold they themselves had to mount the stage and speak out what was on their minds.

That evening T'ien-ming and Kuei-ts'ai called together the small groups of poor peasants from various parts of the village and sought to learn what it was that was really holding them back. They soon found the root of the trouble was fear of the old established political forces, and their military backers. The old reluctance to move against the power of the gentry, the fear of ultimate defeat and terrible reprisal that had been seared into the consciousness of so many generations, lay like a cloud over the peasants' minds and hearts.

Emboldened by T'ien-ming's words, other peasants began to speak out. They recalled what Te-yu had done to them personally. Several vowed to speak up and accuse him the next morning. After the meeting broke up, the passage of time worked its own leaven. In many a hovel and tumbledown house talk continued well past midnight. Some people were so excited they did not sleep at all. . . .

On the following day the meeting was livelier by far. It began with a sharp argument as to who would make the first accusation, and T'ien-ming found it difficult to keep order. Before Te-yu had a chance to reply to any questions, a crowd of young men, among whom were several militiamen, surged forward ready to beat him.

What was the Communist Party's purpose in carrying out land reform in China? How did the tactics employed here support that strategy?

Source: From Richard Solomon, *Mao's Revolution and the Chinese Political Culture*, pages 198–199. Copyright © 1971 Center for Chinese Studies, University of Michigan.

The Great Proletarian Cultural Revolution

But Mao was not yet ready to abandon either his power or his dream of a totally egalitarian society. In 1966, he returned to the attack, mobilizing discontented youth and disgruntled party members into revolutionary units soon to be known as Red Guards, who were urged to take to the streets to cleanse Chinese society—from local schools and factories to government ministries in Beijing—of impure elements who (in Mao's mind, at least) were guilty of "taking the capitalist road." Supported by his wife, Jiang Qing (jahng CHING), and other radical party figures, Mao launched China on a new forced march toward communism.

The so-called **Great Proletarian Cultural Revolution** lasted for ten years, from 1966 to 1976. Some Western observers interpreted it as a simple power struggle between Mao Zedong and some of his key rivals such as Liu Shaoqi (lyoo show-CHEE ["ow" as in "how"]) (Liu Shao-ch'i), Mao's designated successor, and Deng Xiaoping (DUHNG show-PING ["ow" as in "how"]) (Teng Hsiao-p'ing), the party's general secretary. Both were removed from their positions, and Liu later died, allegedly of torture, in a Chinese prison. But real policy disagreements were involved. Mao and his supporters feared that capitalist values and the remnants of "feudalist" Confucian ideas would undermine ideological fervor and betray the revolutionary cause. He was convinced that only an atmosphere of "**uninterrupted revolution**" could enable the Chinese to overcome the lethargy of the past and achieve the final stage of utopian communism.

Mao's opponents argued for a more pragmatic strategy that gave priority to nation building over the ultimate Communist goal of spiritual transformation (Deng Xiaoping reportedly once remarked, "Black cat, white cat, what does it matter so long as it catches the mice?"). But with Mao's supporters now in power, the party carried out vast economic and educational reforms that virtually eliminated any remaining profit incentives, established a new school system that emphasized "Mao Zedong thought," and stressed practical education at the elementary level at the expense of specialized training in

Punishing China's Enemies During the Cultural Revolution. The Cultural Revolution, which began in 1966, was a massive effort by Mao Zedong and his radical supporters to eliminate rival elements within the Chinese Communist Party and the government. Accused of being "capitalist roaders," such individuals were subjected to public criticism and removed from their positions. Some were imprisoned or executed. Here Red Guards parade a victim wearing a dunce cap through the streets of Beijing.

science and the humanities in the universities. School learning was discouraged as a legacy of capitalism, and Mao's famous Little Red Book (officially, *Quotations of Chairman Mao Zedong*, a slim volume of Maoist aphorisms to encourage good behavior and revolutionary zeal) was hailed as the most important source of knowledge in all areas.

The radicals' efforts to destroy all vestiges of traditional society were reminiscent of the Reign of Terror in revolutionary France, when the Jacobins sought to destroy organized religion and even created a new revolutionary calendar. Red Guards rampaged through the country, attempting to eradicate the "four olds" (old thought, old culture, old customs, and old habits). They destroyed temples and religious sculptures; they tore down street signs and replaced them with new ones carrying revolutionary names. At one point, the city of Shanghai even ordered that the significance of colors in stoplights be changed so that red (the revolutionary color) would indicate that traffic could move.

But a mood of revolutionary ferment and enthusiasm is difficult to sustain. Key groups, including bureaucrats, urban professionals, and many military officers, did not share Mao's belief in the benefits of "uninterrupted revolution" and constant turmoil. Inevitably, the sense of anarchy and uncertainty caused popular support for the movement to erode, and when the end came in 1976, the vast majority of the population may well have welcomed its demise.

From Mao to Deng

Mao Zedong died in September 1976 at the age of eighty-three. After a short but bitter succession struggle, the pragmatists led by Deng Xiaoping (1904–1997) seized power from the radicals and formally brought the Cultural Revolution to an end. The egalitarian policies of the previous decade were reversed, and a new program emphasizing economic modernization was introduced.

Under the leadership of Deng Xiaoping, who placed his supporters in key positions throughout the party and the government, attention focused on what were called the **Four Modernizations**: industry, agriculture, technology, and national defense. Many of the restrictions against private activities and profit incentives were eliminated, and people were encouraged to work hard to benefit themselves and Chinese society. The familiar slogan "Serve the people" was replaced by a new one repugnant to the tenets of Mao Zedong thought: "Create wealth for the people."

By adopting this pragmatic approach (in the Chinese aphorism, "cross the river by feeling the stones") in the years after 1976, China made great strides in ending its chronic problems of poverty and underdevelopment. Per capita income roughly doubled during the 1980s; housing, education, and sanitation improved; and both agricultural and industrial output skyrocketed.

Critics, both Chinese and foreign, complained that Deng Xiaoping's program had failed to achieve a "fifth modernization": democracy. In the late 1970s, ordinary citizens pasted "big character posters" criticizing the abuses of the past on the so-called Democracy Wall near Tiananmen (tee-AHN-ahn-muhn) Square in downtown Beijing. But it soon became clear that the new leaders would not tolerate any direct criticism of the Communist Party or of Marxist-Leninist ideology. Dissidents were suppressed, and some were sentenced to long prison terms.

Incident at Tiananmen Square

As long as economic conditions for the majority of Chinese were improving, the government was able to isolate dissidents from other elements in society. But in the late 1980s, an overheated economy led to rising inflation and growing discontent among salaried workers, especially in the cities. At the same time, corruption, nepotism, and favored treatment for senior officials and party members were provoking increasing criticism. In May 1989, student protesters carried placards demanding "Science and Democracy," an end to official corruption, and the resignation of China's aging party leadership. These demands received widespread support from the urban population (although notably less in rural areas) and led to massive demonstrations in Tiananmen Square (see the comparative illustration on p. 721).

The demonstrations divided the Chinese leaders. Reformist elements around party general secretary Zhao Ziyang (JOW dzee-YAHNG) were sympathetic to the protesters, but veteran leaders such as Deng Xiaoping saw the student demands for more democracy as a disguised call for an end to Chinese Communist Party (CCP) rule (see the box on p. 722). After some hesitation, the government sent tanks and troops into Tiananmen Square to crush the demonstrators. Dissidents were arrested, and the regime once again began to stress ideological purity and socialist values. Although the crackdown came under widespread criticism abroad, Chinese leaders insisted that economic reforms could take place only in conditions of party leadership and political stability.

Deng Xiaoping and other aging party leaders turned to the army to protect their base of power and suppress what they described as "counterrevolutionary elements." Deng was undoubtedly counting on the fact that many Chinese, particularly in rural areas, feared a recurrence of the disorder of the Cultural Revolution and craved economic prosperity more than political reform. In the months after troops and tanks rolled into Tiananmen Square to crush the demonstrations, the government

COMPARATIVE ILLUSTRATION

POLITICS & GOVERNMENT

Student Demonstrations in Beijing. On May 4, 1919, students gathered at the Gate of Heavenly Peace in Beijing to protest the Japanese takeover of the Shandong peninsula after World War I (top photo). The protests triggered the famous May Fourth Movement, which highlighted the demand by progressive forces in China for political and social reforms. Seventy years later, students and their supporters gathered in the same spot to demand democracy and an end to official corruption in China (bottom photo). The Heroes' Monument and Mao's mausoleum are in the background.

Compare and contrast the motives, participants, and consequences of the demonstrations that took place in 1919 and 1989.

© Topham/The Image Works

© William J. Duiker

issued new regulations requiring courses on Marxist-Leninist ideology in the schools, suppressed dissidents within the intellectual community, and made it clear that while economic reforms would continue, the CCP would not be allowed to lose its monopoly on power. Harsh punishments were imposed on those accused of undermining the Communist system and supporting its enemies abroad.

Back to Confucius?

In the 1990s, the government began to cultivate urban support by reducing the rate of inflation and guaranteeing the availability of consumer goods in great demand among the rising middle class. Under Deng Xiaoping's successor, Jiang Zemin (JAHNG zuh-MIN) (b. 1926), who occupied the positions of both party chief and president of China, the government promoted rapid economic growth while cracking down harshly on political dissent. That policy paid dividends in bringing about a perceptible decline in alienation among the urban populations. Industrial production continued to increase rapidly, leading to predictions that China would become one of the economic superpowers of the twenty-first century. But discontent in rural areas began to increase, as lagging farm incomes, high taxes, and official corruption sparked resentment in the countryside.

Partly out of fear that such developments could undermine the socialist system and the rule of the CCP, conservative leaders attempted to curb Western influence and restore faith in Marxism-Leninism. In what may have

OPPOSING VIEWPOINTS

Students Appeal for Democracy

POLITICS & GOVERNMENT

In the spring of 1989, thousands of students gathered in Tiananmen Square in downtown Beijing to provide moral support to their many compatriots who had gone on a hunger strike in an effort to compel the Chinese government to reduce the level of official corruption and enact democratic reforms, opening the political process to the Chinese people. The first selection is from an editorial published on April 26 by the official newspaper *People's Daily.* Fearing that the student demonstrations would get out of hand, as had happened during the Cultural Revolution, the editorial condemned the protests for being contrary to the Communist Party. The second selection is from a statement by Zhao Ziyang, the party general secretary, who argued that many of the students' demands were justified. On May 17, student leaders distributed flyers explaining the goals of the movement to participants and passersby, including the author of this chapter. The third selection is from one of these flyers.

People's Daily Editorial, April 26, 1989

This is a well-planned plot . . . to confuse the people and throw the country into turmoil. . . . Its real aim is to reject the Chinese Communist Party and the socialist system at the most fundamental level. . . . This is a most serious political struggle that concerns the whole Party and nation.

Statement by Party General Secretary Zhao Ziyang Before Party Colleagues, May 4, 1989

Let me tell you how I see all this. I think the student movement has two important characteristics. First, the students' slogans call for things like supporting the Constitution, promoting democracy, and fighting corruption. These demands all echo positions of the Party and the government. Second, a great many people from all parts of society are out there joining the demonstrations and backing the students. . . . This has grown into a nationwide protest. I think the best way to bring the thing to a quick end is to focus on the mainstream views of the majority.

"Why Do We Have to Undergo a Hunger Strike?"

By 2:00 P.M. today, the hunger strike carried out by the petition group in Tiananmen Square has been under way for 96 hours. By this morning, more than 600 participants have fainted. When these democracy fighters were lifted into the ambulances, no one who was present was not moved to tears.

Our petition group now undergoing the hunger strike demands that at a minimum the government agree to the following two points:

1. To engage on a sincere and equal basis in a dialogue with the "higher education dialogue group." In addition, to broadcast the actual dialogue in its entirety. We absolutely refuse to agree to a partial broadcast, to empty gestures, or to fabrications that dupe the people.
2. To evaluate in a fair and realistic way the patriotic democratic movement. Discard the label of "troublemaking" and redress the reputation of the patriotic democratic movement.

It is our view that the request for a dialogue between the people's government and the people is not an unreasonable one. Our party always follows the principle of seeking truths from actual facts. It is therefore only natural that the evaluation of this patriotic democratic movement should be done in accordance with the principle of seeking truths from actual facts.

Our classmates who are going through the hunger strike are the good sons and daughters of the people! One by one, they have fallen. In the meantime, our "public servants" are completely unmoved. Please, let us ask where your conscience is.

What were the key demands of the protesters in Tiananmen Square? Why were they rejected by the Chinese government?

Sources: *People's Daily* Editorial, April 26, 1989. From *People's Daily Editorial,* April 26, 1989. Statement by Party General Secretary Zhao Ziyang. Statement by Party Chairman Zhao Ziyang before Party colleagues, May 4, 1989. "Why Do We Have to Undergo a Hunger Strike?" Original flyer in possession of author.

been a tacit recognition that Marxist exhortations were no longer an effective means of enforcing social discipline, the party sought to make use of Confucianism. Ceremonies celebrating the birth of Confucius now received official sanction, and the virtues promoted by the Master, such as righteousness, propriety, and filial piety, were widely cited as an antidote to the tide of antisocial behavior. As a further indication of its willingness to employ traditional themes to further its national interest, the Chinese government has begun to sponsor the establishment of Confucian centers in countries around the world to promote its view that Confucian humanism is destined to replace traditional religious faiths in coming decades.

In effect, Chinese leaders have tacitly conceded that Marxism is increasingly irrelevant to today's China, which responds much more forcefully to the siren call of nationalism. In a striking departure from the precepts of Marxist internationalism, official sources in Beijing cite Confucian tradition to support their assertion that China is unique and will not follow the path of "peaceful evolution" (to use their term) toward a future democratic capitalist society.

That attitude is also reflected in foreign policy, as China is playing an increasingly active role in the region. To some of its neighbors, including Japan, India, and Russia, China's new posture is disquieting and raises suspicions that China is once again preparing to flex its muscle as it did in the imperial era. The first example of this new attitude took place as early as 1979, when Chinese forces briefly invaded Vietnam as punishment for the Vietnamese occupation of neighboring Cambodia. More recently, China has aroused concern in the region by claiming sole ownership over the Spratly (sprat-LEE) Islands in the South China Sea and over the Diaoyu (DYOW-you) Islands (also claimed by Japan, which calls them the Senkakus) near Taiwan (see Map 27.2).

To Chinese leaders, however, such actions represent legitimate efforts to resume China's rightful role in the affairs of the region. After a century of humiliation at the hands of the Western powers and neighboring Japan, the nation, in Mao's famous words of 1949, "has stood up" and no one will be permitted to humiliate it again. For the moment, at least, a fervent patriotism seems to be on the rise in China, actively promoted by the party as a means of holding the country together. The decision by the International Olympic Committee to award the 2008 Summer Games to Beijing led to widespread celebration throughout the country. The event served to symbolize China's emergence as a major national power on the world stage.

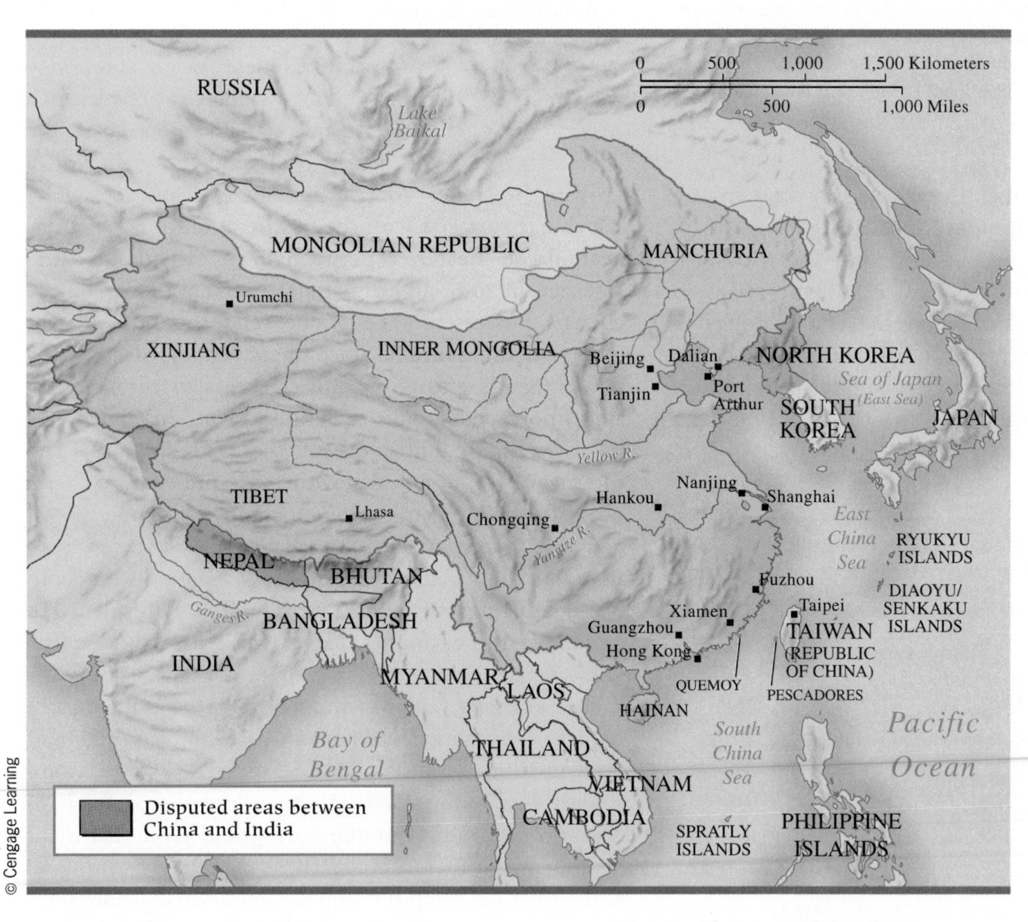

© Cengage Learning

MAP 27.2 The People's Republic of China. This map shows China's current boundaries. Major regions are indicated in capital letters.

Q *In which regions are there movements against Chinese rule?*

Pumping up the spirit of patriotism, however, is not the

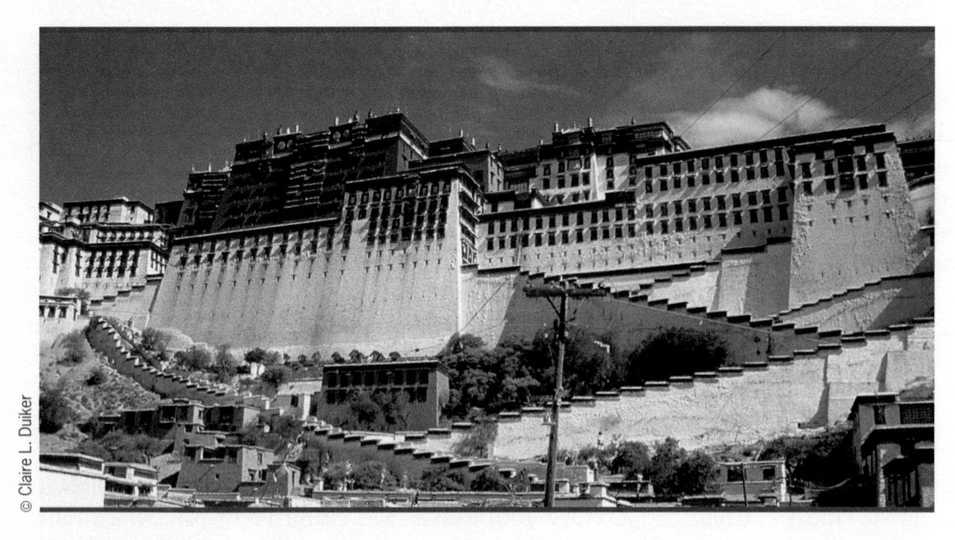

© Claire L. Duiker

The Potala Palace in Tibet. Tibet was a distant and reluctant appendage of the Chinese Empire during the Qing dynasty. Since the rise to power of the Communist Party in 1949, the regime in Beijing has consistently sought to integrate the region into the People's Republic of China. Resistance to Chinese rule, however, has been widespread. In recent years, the Dalai Lama, the leading religious figure in Tibetan Buddhism, has attempted without success to persuade Chinese leaders to allow a measure of autonomy for the Tibetan people. In 2008, massive riots by frustrated Tibetans took place in the capital city of Lhasa (LAH-suh) just before the opening of the Olympic Games in Beijing. The Potala Palace, symbol of Tibetan identity, was constructed in the seventeenth century in Lhasa and serves today as the foremost symbol of the national and cultural aspirations of the Tibetan people.

solution to all problems. Unrest is growing among China's national minorities: in Xinjiang (SHIN-jyahng), where restless Muslim peoples are observing with curiosity the emergence of independent Islamic states in Central Asia, and in Tibet, where the official policy of quelling separatist sentiment has led to the violent suppression of Tibetan culture and an influx of thousands of ethnic Chinese immigrants. In the meantime, the Falun Gong (FAH-loon GONG) religious movement, which the government has attempted to eliminate as a potentially serious threat to its authority, is an additional indication that with the disintegration of the old Maoist utopia, the Chinese people will need more than a pallid version of Marxism-Leninism or a revived Confucianism to fill the gap.

New leaders installed in 2002 and 2003 appeared aware of the magnitude of the problem. Hu Jintao (HOO jin-TOW ["ow" as in "how"]) (b. 1943), who replaced Jiang Zemin as CCP general secretary and head of state, called for further reforms to open up Chinese society and bridge the yawning gap between rich and poor. In recent years, the government has shown a growing tolerance for the public exchange of ideas, which has surfaced with the proliferation of bookstores, avant-garde theater, experimental art exhibits, and the Internet. In 2005, an estimated 27 percent of all Chinese citizens possessed a cellphone, and the number has increased dramatically since then. Today, despite the government's efforts to restrict access to certain websites, more people are "surfing the Net" in China than in any other country except the United States. The Internet is wildly popular with those under thirty, who use it for online games, downloading videos and music, and instant messaging. The challenges, however, continue to be daunting. At the CCP's Seventeenth National Congress, held in October 2007, President Hu emphasized the importance of adopting a "scientific view of development," a vague concept calling for social harmony, improved material prosperity, and a reduction in the growing income gap between rich and poor in Chinese society. But he insisted that the Communist Party must remain the sole political force in charge of carrying out the revolution. Ever fearful of chaos, party leaders are convinced that only a firm hand at the tiller can keep the ship of state from crashing onto the rocks.

CHRONOLOGY China Under Communist Rule

New Democracy	1949–1955
Era of collectivization	1955–1958
Great Leap Forward	1958–1960
Great Proletarian Cultural Revolution	1966–1976
Death of Mao Zedong	1976
Era of Deng Xiaoping	1978–1997
Tiananmen Square incident	1989
Presidency of Jiang Zemin	1993–2002
Hu Jintao becomes president	2002
Olympic Games held in Beijing	2008

"Serve the People": Chinese Society Under Communism

FOCUS QUESTION: What significant political, economic, and social changes have taken place in China since the death of Mao Zedong?

When the Communist Party came to power in 1949, Chinese leaders made it clear that their policies would differ from the Soviet model in one key respect. Whereas the Bolsheviks had relied almost exclusively on the use of force to achieve their objectives, the CCP carried out reforms aimed at winning support from the mass of the population. This "mass line" policy, as it was called, worked fairly well until the late 1950s, when Mao and his radical allies adopted policies such as the Great Leap Forward that began to alienate much of the population. Ideological purity was valued over expertise in building an advanced and prosperous society.

Economics in Command

When he came to power in the late 1970s, Deng Xiaoping recognized the need to restore credibility to a system on the verge of breakdown and hoped that rapid economic growth would satisfy the Chinese people and prevent them from demanding political reforms. The post-Mao leaders clearly emphasized economic performance over ideological purity. To stimulate the stagnant industrial sector, they reduced bureaucratic controls over state industries and allowed local managers to have more say over prices, salaries, and quality control. Productivity was encouraged by permitting bonuses for extra effort, a policy that had been discouraged during the Cultural Revolution. The regime also tolerated the emergence of a small private sector. The unemployed were encouraged to set up restaurants or small shops on their own initiative (see the comparative illustration on p. 715).

Finally, the regime opened up the country to foreign investment and technology. Special economic zones were established in urban centers near the coast (ironically, many were located in the old nineteenth-century treaty ports), where lucrative concessions were offered to encourage foreign firms to build factories. The tourist industry was encouraged, and students were sent abroad to study.

The new leaders especially stressed educational reform. The system adopted during the Cultural Revolution, emphasizing practical education and ideology at the expense of higher education and modern science, was rapidly abandoned (Mao's Little Red Book was even withdrawn from circulation), and a new system based generally on the Western model was instituted. Admission to higher education was based on success in merit examinations, and courses in science and mathematics received high priority.

AGRICULTURAL REFORM No economic reform program could succeed unless it included the countryside. Three decades of socialism had done little to increase food production or to lay the basis for a modern agricultural sector. China, with a population numbering one billion, could still barely feed itself. Peasants had little incentive to work and few opportunities to increase production through mechanization, the use of fertilizer, or better irrigation.

Under Deng Xiaoping, agricultural policy made a rapid about-face. Under the new **rural responsibility system**, collectives leased land to peasant families, who paid rent to the collective. Anything produced on the land above that payment could be sold on the private market or consumed. To soak up excess labor in the villages, the government encouraged the formation of so-called sideline industries, a modern equivalent of the traditional cottage industries in pre-modern China. Peasants raised fish, made consumer goods, and even assembled furniture and appliances for sale to their newly affluent compatriots.

The reform program had a striking effect on rural production. Grain production increased rapidly, and farm income doubled during the 1980s. Yet it also created problems. Income at the village level became more unequal as some enterprising farmers (known locally as "ten-thousand-dollar households") earned profits several times those realized by their less fortunate or less industrious neighbors. When some farmers discovered that they could earn more by growing cash crops they devoted less land to rice and other grain crops, thereby threatening the supply of China's most crucial staple. Finally, the agricultural policy threatened to undermine the government's population control program, which party leaders viewed as crucial to the success of the Four Modernizations.

Since a misguided period in the mid-1950s when Mao Zedong had argued that more labor would result in higher productivity, China had been attempting to limit its population growth. By 1970, the government had launched a stringent family planning program—including education, incentives, and penalties for noncompliance—to persuade the Chinese people to limit themselves to one child per family. The program has had some success, and population growth was reduced drastically in the early 1980s. The rural responsibility system, however, undermined the program because it encouraged farm families to pay the penalties for having additional children in the belief that their labor would increase family income and provide the parents with a form of social security for their old age. Today, China's population has surpassed 1.3 billion.

EVALUATING THE FOUR MODERNIZATIONS Still, the overall effects of the modernization program were impressive. The standard of living improved for the majority of the population. Whereas a decade earlier, the average Chinese had struggled to earn enough to buy a bicycle, by the late 1980s, many were beginning to purchase refrigerators and color television sets. Yet the rapid growth of the economy created its own problems: inflationary pressures, increased corruption, and—most dangerous of all for the regime—rising expectations. Young people in particular resented restrictions on employment (many are still required to accept the jobs that are offered to them by the government or school officials) and opportunities to study abroad. Disillusionment ran high, especially in the cities, where lavish living by officials and rising prices for goods aroused widespread alienation and cynicism. Such conditions undoubtedly contributed to the unrest that erupted during the spring of 1989.

During the 1990s, industrial growth rates continued to be high as domestic capital became increasingly available. The government finally recognized the need to close down inefficient state enterprises, and by the end of the decade, the private sector accounted for more than 10 percent of gross domestic product. A stock market opened, and with the country's entrance into the World Trade Organization (WTO) in 2001, China's prowess in the international marketplace improved dramatically. Today, China has the second-largest economy in the world and is the largest exporter of goods. Even the global economic crisis that struck the world in the fall of 2008 has not derailed the Chinese juggernaut, which quickly recovered from the drop in demand for Chinese goods in countries suffering from the economic downturn.

As a result of these developments, China now possesses a large and increasingly affluent middle class and a burgeoning domestic market for consumer goods. More than 80 percent of all urban Chinese now own a color television set, a refrigerator, and a washing machine. For the more affluent, a private automobile is increasingly a possibility, and in 2010, more vehicles were sold in China than in the United States.

But as Chinese leaders have discovered, rapid economic change never comes without cost. The closing of state-run factories led to the dismissal of millions of workers each year, and the private sector, although growing at more than 20 percent annually, initially struggled to absorb them. Poor working conditions and low salaries in Chinese factories have resulted in periodic outbreaks of labor unrest. Demographic conditions, however, are changing. The reduction in birthrates since the 1980s is creating a labor shortage, which is putting upward pressure on workers' salaries. As a result, China is facing inflation in the marketplace and increased competition from exports produced by factories located in lower-wage countries in South and Southeast Asia.

Discontent has also been increasing in the countryside, where farmers earn only about half as much as their urban counterparts. China's entry into the WTO was greeted with great optimism but has been of little benefit to farmers facing the challenges of cheap foreign imports. Taxes and local corruption add to their complaints. In desperation, millions of rural Chinese have left for the big cities, where many of them are unable to find steady employment and live in squalid conditions in crowded tenements or in the sprawling suburbs. Millions of others remain on their farms and attempt to augment their income by producing for the market or, despite the risk of stringent penalties, by increasing the size of their families. A land reform law passed in 2008 authorizes farmers to lease or transfer land use rights, although in principle all land in rural areas belongs to the local government.

Another factor hindering China's economic advance is the impact on the environment. With the rising population, fertile land is in increasingly short supply (China's population has doubled since 1950, but only two-thirds as much irrigable land is available). Soil erosion is a major problem, especially in the north, where the desert is encroaching on farmlands. Water is also a problem. An ambitious plan to transport water by canals from the Yangtze River to the more arid northern provinces has run into a number of roadblocks. Another massive project to construct dams on the Yangtze River has sparked protests from environmentalists, as well as from local peoples forced to migrate from the area. Air pollution is ten times the level in the United States. To add to the challenge, more than 700,000 new cars and trucks appear on the country's roads each year. To reduce congestion on roadways, China is constructing a network for high-speed bullet trains that will connect all the major regions in the country.

Social Problems

At the root of Marxist-Leninist ideology is the idea of building a new citizen free from the prejudices, ignorance, and superstition of the "feudal" era and the capitalist desire for self-gratification. This new citizen would be characterized not only by a sense of racial and sexual equality but also by the selfless desire to contribute his or her utmost for the good of all.

WOMEN AND THE FAMILY From the very start, the Chinese Communist government intended to bring an

AP Images/Xinhua Photo/Xia Lin

The Three Gorges Dam. The damming of the Yangtze River over the past two decades is one of the most massive and ambitious construction projects in human history. Designed to increase the amount of farmland in the Yangtze River valley and enable precious water resources to be redistributed to drought-prone regions of the country, the project has also caused considerable environmental damage throughout the Yangtze River valley and displaced several million Chinese from their ancestral homes. Shown here is the famous Three Gorges Dam at Yichang (EE-CHAHNG).

end to the Confucian legacy in modern China. Women were given the vote and encouraged to become active in the political process. At the local level, an increasing number of women became active in the CCP and in collective organizations. In 1950, a new marriage law guaranteed women equal rights with men. Most important, perhaps, it permitted women for the first time to initiate divorce proceedings against their husbands. Within a year, nearly one million divorces had been granted.

At first, the new government moved carefully on family issues to avoid unnecessarily alienating its supporters in the countryside. When collective farms were established in the mid-1950s, payment for hours worked in the form of ration coupons was made not to the individual but to the family head, thus maintaining the traditionally dominant position of the patriarch. When people's communes were established in the late 1950s, however, payments went to the individual.

During the Great Leap Forward, children were encouraged to report to the authorities any comments by their parents that criticized the system. Such practices continued during the Cultural Revolution, when children were expected to tell on their parents, students on their teachers, and employees on their superiors. Some have suggested that Mao encouraged such practices to bring an end to the traditional "politics of dependency." According to this theory, historically the famous "five relationships" forced individuals to swallow their anger and accept the hierarchical norms established by Confucian ethics (known in Chinese as "to eat bitterness"). By encouraging oppressed elements—the young, the female, and the poor—to voice their bitterness, Mao hoped to break the tradition of dependency. Such denunciations had been issued against landlords in the land reform tribunals of the late 1940s and early 1950s. Later, during the Cultural Revolution, they were applied to other authority figures.

LIFESTYLE CHANGES The post-Mao era brought a decisive shift away from revolutionary utopianism and back toward the pragmatic approach to nation building. For most people, this meant improved living conditions and a qualified return to family traditions. Young people whose parents had given them patriotic names such as Build the Country, Protect Mao Zedong, and Assist Korea began to choose more elegant and cosmopolitan names for their own children. Some names, such as Surplus Grain or Bring a Younger Brother, expressed hope for the future.

The new attitudes were also reflected in physical appearance. For a generation after the civil war, clothing had been restricted to the traditional baggy "Mao suit" in olive drab or dark blue, but by the 1980s, young people craved such fashionable Western items as designer jeans and trendy sneakers. Cosmetic surgery to create a more buxom figure or a more Western facial look became increasingly common among affluent young women in the cities. Many had the epicanthic fold over their eyelids removed or their noses enlarged—a curious decision in view of the tradition of referring derogatorily to foreigners as "big noses" (see the comparative essay "Family and Society in an Era of Change" on p. 729).

Religious practices and beliefs have also changed. As the government has become more tolerant, some Chinese have begun to return to the traditional Buddhist faith or to folk religions, and Buddhist and Taoist temples are crowded with worshipers. Despite official efforts to suppress its more evangelical forms, Christianity has become popular as well; like the "rice Christians" (persons who supposedly converted for economic reasons) of the past, many now view it as a symbol of success.

As with all social changes, China's reintegration into the outside world has had a price. Arranged marriages, nepotism, and mistreatment of females (for example, under the one-child rule, parents reportedly killed female infants to regain the possibility of having a son) have come back, although such behavior likely survived under the cloak of revolutionary purity for a generation (see the box on p. 730). Materialistic attitudes are prevalent among young people, along with a corresponding cynicism about politics and the CCP. Expensive weddings are now increasingly common, and bribery and favoritism are all too frequent. Crime of all types, including an apparently growing incidence of prostitution and sex crimes against women, appears to be on the rise. To discourage sexual abuse, the government now seeks to provide free legal services for women living in rural areas.

There is also a price to pay for the trend toward privatization. Under the Maoist system, the elderly and the sick were provided with retirement benefits and health care by the state or by the collective organizations. Under current conditions, with the latter no longer playing such a social role and more workers operating in the private sector, the safety net has been removed. The government recently attempted to fill the gap by enacting a social security law, but because of lack of funds, eligibility is limited primarily to individuals in the urban sector of the economy. Those living in the countryside—who still represent 60 percent of the population—are essentially unprotected, prompting legislation in 2010 to provide modest pensions and medical insurance to the poorest members of Chinese society. Yet much more needs to be done. As the population ages, the lack of a retirement system represents a potential time bomb.

China's Changing Culture

During the first half of the twentieth century, Chinese culture was strongly influenced by currents from the West (see Chapter 24). The rise to power of the Communists in 1949 added a new dimension to the debate over the future of culture in China. The new leaders rejected the Western attitude of "art for art's sake" and, like their Soviet counterparts, viewed culture as an important instrument of indoctrination. The standard would no longer be aesthetic quality or the personal preference of the artist but "art for life's sake," whereby culture would serve the interests of socialism.

CULTURE IN A REVOLUTIONARY ERA At first, the new emphasis on socialist realism did not entirely extinguish traditional culture. Mao and his colleagues tolerated—and even encouraged—efforts by artists to synthesize traditional ideas with socialist concepts. During the Cultural Revolution, however, all forms of traditional culture came to be viewed as reactionary. Socialist realism became the only acceptable standard. All forms of traditional expression were forbidden, and the deification of Mao and his central role in building a Communist paradise became virtually the only acceptable form of artistic expression.

Characteristic of the shifting cultural climate in China was the experience of author Ding Ling (DING LING). Born in 1904 and educated in a school for women set up by leftist intellectuals during the hectic years after the May Fourth Movement, she became involved in party activities in the early 1930s and settled in Yan'an, where she wrote her most famous novel, *The Sun Shines over the Sangan River,* which described the CCP's land reform program in favorable terms. It was awarded the Stalin Prize three years later.

During the early 1950s, Ding Ling was one of the most prominent literary lights of the new China, but in the more ideological climate at the end of the decade, she was attacked for her individualism and her previous criticism of the party. Although temporarily rehabilitated, she was sentenced to hard labor on a commune during the Cultural Revolution and was not released until the late 1970s after the death of Mao. Crippled and in poor health, she died in 1981. Ding Ling's fate mirrored the fate of thousands of progressive Chinese intellectuals who were not able to satisfy the constantly changing demands of a repressive regime.

ART AND MUSIC After Mao's death, Chinese culture was finally released from the shackles of socialist realism. In painting, where for a decade the only acceptable standard for excellence was praise for the party and its policies, the new permissiveness led to a revival of interest in both traditional and Western forms. Although some painters continued to blend Eastern and Western styles, others imitated trends from abroad, experimenting with a wide range of previously prohibited art styles, including Cubism and abstract painting.

In the late 1980s, two avant-garde art exhibits shocked the Chinese public and provoked the wrath of the party.

COMPARATIVE ESSAY

Family and Society in an Era of Change

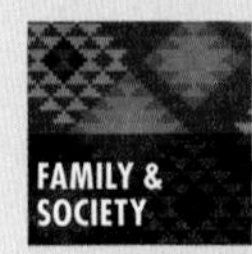

One of the paradoxes of the modern world is that at a time of political stability and economic prosperity for many people in the advanced capitalist societies, public cynicism about the system is increasingly widespread. Alienation and drug use are at dangerously high levels, and the crime rate in most areas remains much higher than in the immediate postwar era.

Although various reasons have been advanced to explain this paradox, many observers contend that the decline of the traditional family system is responsible for many contemporary social problems. There has been a steady rise in the percentage of illegitimate births and single-parent families in countries throughout the Western world. In the United States, approximately half of all marriages end in divorce. In many European countries, the birthrate has dropped to alarming levels.

Observers point to several factors as an explanation for these conditions: the growing emphasis on an individualistic lifestyle devoted to instant gratification; the rise of the feminist movement, which has not only freed women from the servitude imposed on their predecessors, but has also relieved them of full-time responsibility for the care of the next generation; and the increasing mobility of contemporary life, which disrupts traditional family ties and creates a sense of rootlessness.

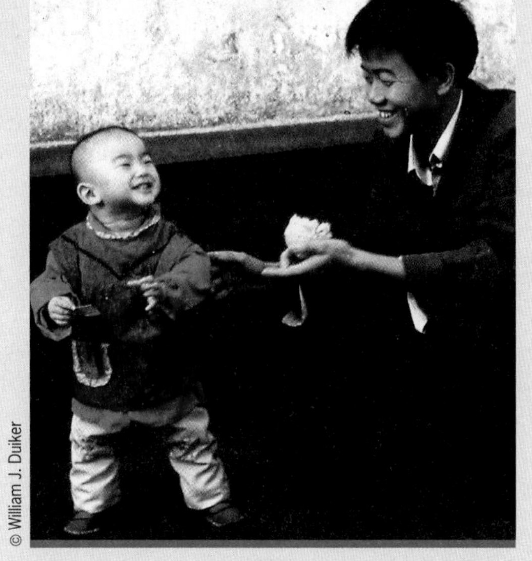

© William J. Duiker

China's "Little Emperors." To curtail population growth, Chinese leaders launched a massive family planning program that restricted urban families to a single child. Under these circumstances, in conformity with tradition, sons are especially prized, and some Chinese complain that many parents overindulge their children, turning them into spoiled "little emperors."

These trends are not unique to Western civilization. Even in East Asia, where the Confucian tradition of family solidarity has been endlessly touted as a major factor in the region's economic success, the incidence of divorce and illegitimate births is on the rise, as is the percentage of women in the workforce. Older citizens frequently complain that the Asian youth of today are too materialistic and steeped in the individualistic values of the West.

In societies less exposed to the individualist lifestyle portrayed in Western culture, traditional attitudes about the family continue to hold sway. In the Middle East, governmental and religious figures seek to prevent the Western media from undermining accepted mores. Success is sometimes elusive, however, as the situation in Iran demonstrates. Despite the zealous guardians of Islamic morality, many young Iranians are clamoring for the individual freedoms that have been denied to them since the Islamic Revolution (see Chapter 29).

To what degree and in what ways are young people in China becoming more like their counterparts in the West?

An exhibition of nude paintings, the first ever held in China, attracted many viewers but reportedly offended the modesty of many Chinese. The other exhibit, which presented various schools of modern and postmodern art, resulted in some expressions of public hostility. After a Communist critic lambasted the works as promiscuous and ideologically reactionary, the government declared that henceforth it would regulate all art exhibits. Since the 1990s, some Chinese artists, such as the world-famous Ai Weiwei (I WAY-WAY) (b. 1957), have aggressively challenged the government's authority. In response, the government razed Ai's art studio in Shanghai in 2011. He was subsequently taken into custody on charges related to tax evasion. Nonetheless, Chinese contemporary art has expanded exponentially and commands exorbitant prices on the world market.

Like the fine arts, Western classical music was suppressed during the Cultural Revolution. Significant changes have occurred in the post-Mao era, however, as the government has encouraged interest in classical

Love and Marriage in China

"What men can do, women can also do." So said Chairman Mao as he "liberated" and masculinized Chinese women to work alongside men. Women's individuality and sexuality were sacrificed for the collective good of his new socialist society. Marriage, which had traditionally been arranged by families for financial gain, was now dictated by duty to the state. The Western concept of romantic love did not enter into a Chinese marriage, as this interview of a schoolteacher by the reporter Zhang Xinxin (JANG SHEEN-SHEEN) in the mid-1980s illustrates. According to recent surveys, the same is true today.

Zhang Xinxin, *Chinese Lives*

My husband and I never did any courting—honestly! We registered our marriage a week after we'd met. He was just out of the forces and a worker in a building outfit. They'd been given a foreign-aid assignment in Zambia, and he was selected. He wanted to get his private life fixed up before he went, and someone introduced us. Seeing how he looked really honest, I accepted him.

No, you can't say I didn't know anything about him. The person who introduced us told me he was a Party member who'd been an organization commissar. Any comrade who's good enough to be an organization cadre is politically reliable. Nothing special about our standing of living—it's what we've earned. He's still a worker, but we live all right, don't we?

He went off with the army as soon as we'd registered our marriage and been given the wedding certificates. He was away three years. We didn't have the wedding itself before he went because we hadn't got a room yet.

Those three years were a test for us. The main problem was that my family was against it. They thought I was still only a kid and I'd picked the wrong man. What did they have against him? His family was too poor. Of course I won in the end—we'd registered and got our wedding certificates. We were legally married whether we had the family ceremony or not.

We had our wedding after he came back in the winter of 1973. His leaders and mine all came to congratulate us and give us presents. The usual presents those days were busts of Chairman Mao. I was twenty-six and he was twenty-nine. We've never had a row.

I never really wanted to take the college entrance exams. Then in 1978 the school leadership got us all to put our names forward. They said they weren't going to hold us back: the more of us who passed, the better it would be for the school. So I put my name forward, crammed for six weeks, and passed. I already had two kids then. . . .

I reckoned the chance for study was too good to miss. And my husband was looking after the kids all by himself. I usually only came back once a fortnight. So I couldn't let him down.

My instructors urged me to take the exams for graduate school, but I didn't. I was already thirty-four, so what was the point of more study? There was another reason too. I didn't want an even wider gap between us: he hadn't even finished junior middle school when he joined the army.

It's bad if the gap's too wide. For example, there's a definite difference in our tastes in music and art, I have to admit that. But what really matters? Now we've set up this family we have to preserve it. Besides, look at all the sacrifices he had to make to see me through college. Men comrades all like a game of cards and that, but he was stuck with looking after the kids. He still doesn't get any time for himself—it's all work for him.

We've got a duty to each other. Our differences? The less said about them the better. We've always treated each other with the greatest respect.

Of course some people have made suggestions, but my advice to him is to respect himself and respect me. I'm not going to be like those men who ditch their wives when they go up in the world.

I'm the head of our school now. With this change in my status I've got to show even more responsibility for the family. Besides, I know how much he's done to get me where I am today. I've also got some duties in the municipal Women's Federation and Political Consultative Conference. No, I'm not being modest. I haven't done anything worth talking about, only my duty.

We've got to do a lot more educating people. There have been two cases of divorce in our school this year.

Do you think the marriage described here is successful? Why or why not? What do you think this woman feels about her marriage?

Source: From *Chinese Lives: An Oral History of Contemporary China*, by Zhang Xinxin and Sang Ye, copyright © 1987 by W.J.F. Jenner and Delia Davin.

music by opening conservatories and building concert halls. China today is producing legions of musicians, who are filling orchestras in Western countries.

LITERATURE The limits of freedom of expression were most apparent in literature. During the early 1980s, party leaders encouraged Chinese writers to express their views on the mistakes of the past, and a new "literature of the wounded" began to describe the brutal and arbitrary character of the Cultural Revolution.

One of the most prominent writers was Bai Hua (by HWA) (b. 1930), whose film script *Bitter Love* described the life of a young Chinese painter who joined the revolutionary movement during the 1940s but whose work was condemned as counterrevolutionary during the Cultural Revolution. In describing the excesses of the Cultural Revolution, Bai Hua was only responding to Deng Xiaoping's appeal for intellectuals to speak out, but he was soon criticized for failing to point out the essentially beneficial role of the CCP in recent Chinese history. The film was withdrawn from circulation in 1981, and Bai Hua was compelled to recant his errors and to state that the great ideas of Mao Zedong on art and literature were "still of universal guiding significance today."[5] As the attack on Bai Hua illustrates, many party leaders remained suspicious of "decadent" bourgeois culture. The official press periodically warned that China should adopt only the "positive" aspects of Western culture (notably, its technology and its work ethic) and not the "negative" elements such as drug use, pornography, and hedonism.

Conservatives were especially incensed by the tendency of many writers to dwell on the shortcomings of the socialist system. One such writer is Mo Yan (muh YAHN) (b. 1956), whose novels *The Garlic Ballads* (1988) and *Life and Death Are Wearing Me Out* (2008), expose the rampant corruption of contemporary Chinese society, the roots of which he attributes to one-party rule. Yu Hua (yoo HWA) (b. 1960), another outstanding novelist, uses narratives marked by exaggerated and grotesque humor to criticize the cruelty of the Communist regime in *To Live* (2003).

Today, Chinese culture has been dramatically transformed by the nation's adoption of a market economy and the spread of the Internet. A new mass literature explores the aspirations and frustrations of a generation obsessed with material consumption and the right of individual expression. Lost in the din are the voices of China's rural poor.

Confucius and Marx: The Tenacity of Tradition

Why has communism survived in China, albeit in a substantially altered form, when it failed in Eastern Europe and the Soviet Union? One of the primary factors is probably cultural. Although the doctrine of Marxism-Leninism originated in Europe, many of its main precepts, such as the primacy of the community over the individual and the denial of the concept of private property, run counter to trends in Western civilization. This inherent conflict is especially evident in the societies of central Europe, which were strongly influenced by Enlightenment philosophy and the Industrial Revolution. These forces were weaker farther to the east, although they had begun to penetrate tsarist Russia by the end of the nineteenth century.

In contrast, Marxism-Leninism found a more receptive climate in China and other countries in the region influenced by Confucian tradition. In its political culture, the Communist system exhibits many of the same characteristics as traditional Confucianism—a single truth, an elite governing class, and an emphasis on obedience to the community and its governing representatives. Although a significant and influential minority of the Chinese population—primarily urban and educated—finds the idea of personal freedom against the power of the state appealing, such concepts have little meaning in rural villages, where the interests of the community have always been emphasized over the desires of the individual. It is no accident that Chinese leaders now seek to reintroduce the precepts of State Confucianism to bolster a fading belief in the existence of a future Communist paradise.

Party leaders today are banking on the hope that China can be governed as it has always been—by an elite class of highly trained professionals dedicated to pursing a predefined objective. In fact, however, real changes are taking place in China today. Although the youthful protesters in Tiananmen Square were comparable in some respects to the reformist elements of the early republic, the China of today is fundamentally different from that of the early twentieth century. Literacy rates and the standard of living are far higher, the pressures of outside powers are less threatening, and China has entered its own industrial and technological revolution. Many Chinese depend more on independent talk radio and the Internet for news and views than on the official media. Whereas Sun Yat-sen, Chiang Kai-shek, and even Mao Zedong broke their lances on the rocks of centuries of tradition, poverty, and ignorance, the present leaders rule a country much more aware of the world and China's place in it. Although the shift in popular expectations may be gradual, China today is embarked on a journey to a future for which the past no longer provides a roadmap.

CHAPTER SUMMARY

For four decades after the end of World War II, the two major Communist powers appeared to have become permanent features on the international landscape. Suddenly, though, in the late 1980s, the Soviet Union entered a period of internal crisis that shook the foundations of Soviet society. In 1991, the system collapsed, to be replaced by a series of independent states based primarily on ethnic and cultural differences that had existed long before the Bolshevik Revolution. China went through an even longer era of instability, beginning with the Cultural Revolution in 1966, but it managed to survive under a hybrid system that combines features of a Leninist command economy with capitalist practices adapted from the modern West.

Why were the outcomes so different? Although the cultural differences we have described were undoubtedly an important factor, the role of human action should not be ignored. Whereas Mikhail Gorbachev introduced the idea of *glasnost* to permit the emergence of a more pluralistic political system in the Soviet Union, Chinese leaders crushed the protest movement in the spring of 1989 and reasserted the authority of the Communist Party. Deng Xiaoping's gamble paid off, and today the party stands at the height of its power.

CHAPTER TIMELINE

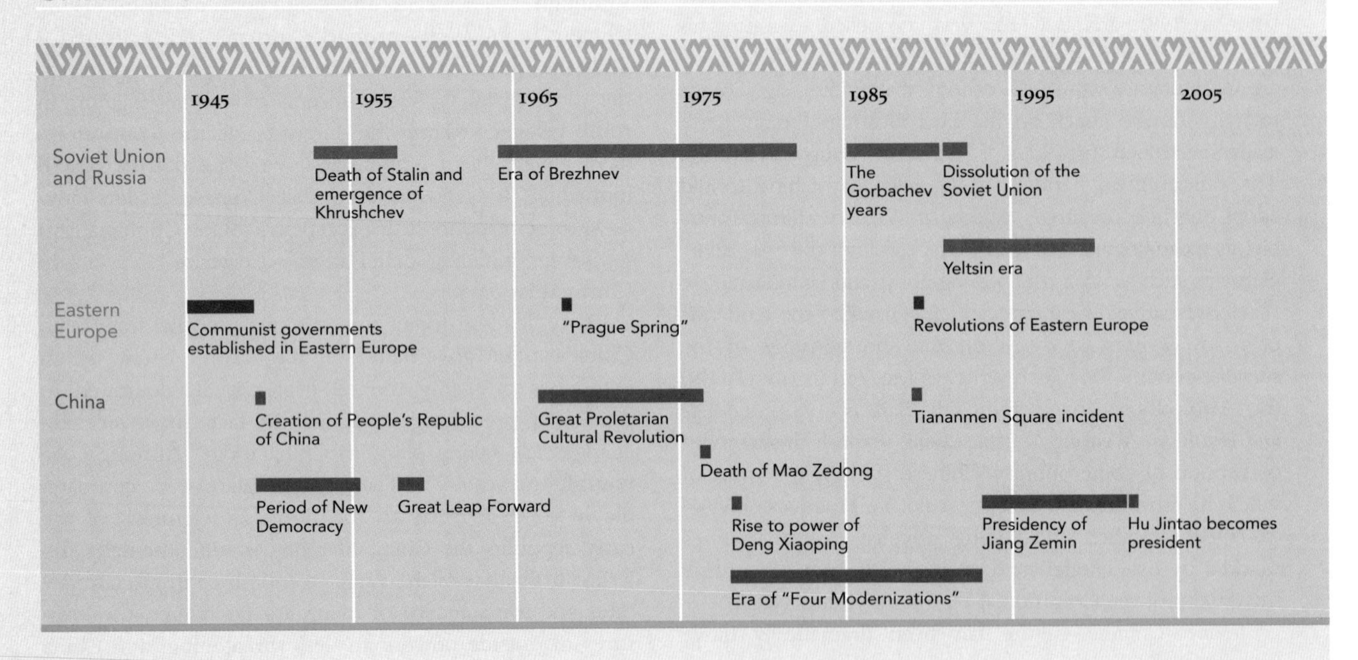

CHAPTER REVIEW

Upon Reflection

Q How have six decades of Communist rule affected the concept of the family in China? How does the current state of the family in China compare with the family in other parts of the world?

Q What strategies were used by the leaders of the Soviet Union and the People's Republic of China as they sought to build Communist societies in their countries? In what ways were the strategies different, and in what ways were they similar? To what degree were they successful?

Q How has the current generation of leadership in China made use of traditional values to solidify Communist control over the country? To what degree has this approach contradicted the theories of Karl Marx?

Key Terms

de-Stalinization (p. 710)
perestroika (p. 714)
glasnost (p. 714)
New Democracy (p. 717)
Great Leap Forward (p. 717)
Great Proletarian Cultural Revolution (p. 719)
uninterrupted revolution (p. 719)
Four Modernizations (p. 720)
rural responsibility system (p. 725)

Suggested Reading

RUSSIA AND THE SOVIET UNION For a general view of modern Russia, see **M. Malia, *Russia Under Western Eyes*** (Cambridge, Mass., 1999), and **M. T. Poe, *The Russian Moment in World History*** (Princeton, N.J., 2003). On the Khrushchev years, see **W. Taubman, *Khrushchev: The Man and His Era*** (New York, 2004). For an inquiry into the reasons for the Soviet collapse, see **R. Conquest, *Reflections on a Ravaged Century*** (New York, 1999), and **R. Strayer, *Why Did the Soviet Union Collapse? Understanding Historical Change*** (New York, 1998).

CHINA UNDER MAO ZEDONG A number of useful surveys deal with China after World War II. The most comprehensive treatment of the Communist period is **M. Meisner, *Mao's China and After: A History of the People's Republic*** (New York, 1999). Also see **R. Macfarquhar, ed., *The Politics of China: The Eras of Mao and Deng*** (Cambridge, 1997). A recent critical biography of China's "Great Helmsman" is **J. Chang** and **J. Halliday, *Mao: The Unknown Story*** (New York, 2005).

POST-MAO CHINA The 1989 demonstrations and their aftermath are described in an eyewitness account by **L. Feigon, *China Rising: The Meaning of Tiananmen*** (Chicago, 1990). Documentary materials relating to the events of 1989 are chronicled in **A. J. Nathan** and **P. Link, eds., *The Tiananmen Papers*** (New York, 2001). Subsequent events are analyzed in **J. Fewsmith, *China Since Tiananmen: The Politics of Transition*** (Cambridge, 2001). On China's challenge from the process of democratization, see **J. Gittings, *The Changing Face of China: From Mao to Market*** (Oxford, 2005). Also see **T. Saich, *Governance and Politics in China*** (New York, 2002). China's evolving role in the world is traced in **S. Shirk, *China: Fragile Superpower*** (Oxford, 2007).

CHINESE LITERATURE AND ART For a comprehensive introduction to twentieth-century Chinese literature, consult **E. Widmer** and **D. Der-Wei Wang, eds., *From May Fourth to June Fourth: Fiction and Film in Twentieth-Century China*** (Cambridge, Mass., 1993), and **J. Lau** and **H. Goldblatt, *The Columbia Anthology of Modern Chinese Literature*** (New York, 1995). For the most comprehensive analysis of twentieth-century Chinese art, consult **M. Sullivan, *Arts and Artists of Twentieth-Century China*** (Berkeley, Calif., 1996).

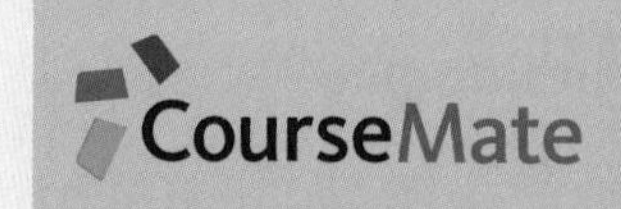

Visit the CourseMate website at **www.cengagebrain.com** for additional study tools and review materials for this chapter.

CHAPTER

28

Europe and the Western Hemisphere Since 1945

© Bettmann (Reginald Kenny)/CORBIS

Children play amid the ruins of Warsaw, Poland, at the end of World War II.

CHAPTER OUTLINE AND FOCUS QUESTIONS

Recovery and Renewal in Europe

Q What problems have the nations of Western Europe faced since 1945, and what steps have they taken to try to solve these problems? What problems have Eastern European nations faced since 1989?

Emergence of the Superpower: The United States

Q What political, social, and economic changes has the United States experienced since 1945?

The Development of Canada

Q What political, social, and economic developments has Canada experienced since 1945?

Latin America Since 1945

Q What problems have the nations of Latin America faced since 1945, and what role has Marxist ideology played in their efforts to solve these problems?

Society and Culture in the Western World

Q What major social, cultural, and intellectual developments have occurred in Western Europe and North America since 1945?

CRITICAL THINKING

Q What are the similarities and differences between the major political, economic, and social developments in the first half of the twentieth century and those in the second half of the century?

THE END OF WORLD WAR II in Europe had been met with great joy. A visitor in Moscow reported, "I looked out of the window [at 2 A.M.], almost everywhere there were lights in the windows—people were staying awake. Everyone embraced everyone else, someone sobbed aloud." But after the celebrations, Europeans awoke to a devastating realization: their civilization was in ruins. Almost 40 million people (soldiers and civilians) had been killed over the last six years. Air raids and artillery bombardments had reduced many of the cities of Europe to heaps of rubble. The Polish capital of Warsaw had been almost completely obliterated. An American general described Berlin: "Wherever we looked, we saw desolation. It was like a city of the dead. Suffering and shock were visible in every face. Dead bodies still remained in canals and lakes and were being dug out from under bomb debris." Millions of Europeans faced starvation as grain harvests were only half their 1939 levels. Millions were also homeless.

Yet by 1970, Western Europe had not only recovered from the effects of World War II but also experienced an economic resurgence that seemed nothing less than miraculous. Economic growth continued so long that the first postwar recession, in 1973, came as a shock. It was short-lived, however, and economic growth resumed. With this economic expansion came the creation of the welfare state—a prominent social development in postwar Europe. After the collapse of Communist governments in the revolutions of 1989, a number of Eastern European states sought to create market economies and join the military and economic unions first formed by Western European states.

The most significant factor after 1945 was the emergence of the United States as the world's richest and most powerful nation. American prosperity reached new heights in the first two decades after World War II, but the nation has nevertheless faced a series of social and economic problems—including racial division and staggering budget deficits—in the postwar era.

To the south of the United States, Latin America had its own unique heritage. Although some Latin Americans in the nineteenth century had looked to the United States as a model for their own development, in the twentieth century, many strongly criticized U.S. military and economic domination of Central and South America. At the same time, many Latin American countries struggled with economic and political instability.

Toward the end of the century, as the West adjusted from Cold War to post–Cold War realities, other changes were also shaping the Western outlook. The demographic face of European countries changed as massive numbers of immigrants created more ethnically diverse populations. New artistic and intellectual currents, the continued advance of science and technology, the effort to come to grips with environmental problems, and the women's liberation movement—all spoke of a vibrant, ever-changing world. At the same time, a devastating terrorist attack in the United States in 2001 made the Western world vividly aware of its vulnerability to international terrorism.

Recovery and Renewal in Europe

FOCUS QUESTIONS: What problems have the nations of Western Europe faced since 1945, and what steps have they taken to try to solve these problems? What problems have Eastern European nations faced since 1989?

All the nations of Europe faced similar problems at the end of World War II. First and foremost, they needed to rebuild their shattered economies. Remarkably, within a few years, an incredible economic revival brought renewed growth to Western Europe.

Western Europe: The Triumph of Democracy

With the economic aid of the Marshall Plan, the countries of Western Europe recovered relatively rapidly from the devastation of World War II. Between the early 1950s and late 1970s, industrial production surpassed all previous records, and Western Europe experienced virtually full employment.

FRANCE: FROM DE GAULLE TO NEW UNCERTAINTIES The history of France for nearly a quarter century after the war was dominated by one man—Charles de Gaulle (SHAHRL duh GOHL) (1890–1970). Initially, he had withdrawn from politics, but in 1958, frightened by the bitter divisions caused by the Algerian crisis (see Chapter 29), the leaders of the Fourth Republic offered to let de Gaulle take over the government and revise the constitution.

De Gaulle's constitution for the Fifth Republic greatly enhanced the office of the president, who now had the power to choose the prime minister, dissolve parliament, and supervise defense and foreign policy. As the new president, de Gaulle sought to return France to the status of a great power. With that goal in mind, he invested heavily in the nuclear arms race. France exploded its first nuclear bomb in 1960. Nevertheless, de Gaulle did not really achieve his ambitious goals; in truth, France was too small for such global ambitions.

Under de Gaulle, France became a major industrial producer and exporter, particularly in automobiles and armaments. But the expansion of traditional industries, such as coal, steel, and railroads, which had all been nationalized, led to large government deficits. The cost of living increased faster than in the rest of Europe. Growing dissatisfaction led to a series of student protests in May 1968, followed by a general strike by the labor unions. Although he restored order, de Gaulle resigned from office in April 1969 and died the next year.

The worsening of France's economic situation in the 1970s brought a shift to the left politically. By 1981, the Socialists had become the dominant party in the National Assembly, and the Socialist leader, François Mitterrand (frahnh-SWAH MEE-tayr-rahnh) (1916–1995), was elected president. Mitterrand passed a number of measures to aid workers: an increased minimum wage, expanded social benefits, a fifth week of paid vacation, and a thirty-nine-hour workweek. The Socialists also enacted some more radical reforms, nationalizing the major banks, the space and electronics industries, and important insurance firms.

The Socialist policies largely failed, however, and within three years, the Mitterrand government returned some of the economy to private enterprise. But France's economic decline continued, and in 1993, a coalition of conservative parties won 80 percent of the seats. The move to the right was strengthened when the conservative mayor of Paris, Jacques Chirac (ZHAHK shee-RAK) (b. 1932), was elected president in May 1995 and reelected in 2002. Resentment against foreign-born residents led to calls for restrictions on immigration. Chirac himself pursued a plan of sending illegal immigrants back to their home countries.

In the fall of 2005, however, antiforeign sentiment provoked a backlash, as young Muslims in the crowded suburbs of Paris rioted against dismal living conditions and the lack of employment opportunities. Tensions between the Muslim community and the remainder of the French population became a chronic source of unrest that Nicolas Sarkozy (nee-kohl-AH sar-koh-ZEE) (b. 1955), elected as president in 2007, promised to address, but without much success. In 2009, unemployment among those under twenty-five was almost 22 percent, but in the predominantly Muslim suburbs, youth joblessness exceeded 50 percent. In May 2012, Sarkozy lost his bid for a second term to the Socialist candidate, François Hollande (frahnh-SWAH oh-LAWND) (b. 1954), who promised to cancel tax cuts for the rich and raise the tax rate on those earning one million euros to 75 percent.

FROM WEST GERMANY TO GERMANY As noted in Chapter 26, the three western zones of Germany were unified as the Federal Republic of Germany in 1949. Konrad Adenauer (AD-uh-now-ur) (1876–1967), the leader of the Christian Democratic Union, served as chancellor from 1949 to 1963 and became the Federal Republic's "founding hero."

Adenauer's chancellorship is largely associated with the remarkable resurrection of the West German economy. Although West Germany had only 52 percent of the territory of prewar Germany, by 1955 the West German gross domestic product exceeded that of prewar Germany. Unemployment fell from 8 percent in 1950 to 0.4 percent in 1965.

After the Adenauer era, German voters moved politically from the center-right of the Christian Democrats to the center-left; in 1969, the Social Democrats became the leading party. The first Social Democratic chancellor was Willy Brandt (VIL-ee BRAHNT) (1913–1992). In 1971, Brandt negotiated a treaty with East Germany that led to greater cultural, personal, and economic contacts between West and East Germany. In 1972, he received the Nobel Peace Prize for this "opening toward the east"—known as *Ostpolitik* (OHST-poh-lee-teek).

In 1982, the Christian Democrat Helmut Kohl (HEL-moot KOHL) (b. 1930) formed a new center-right government. Kohl benefited from an economic boom in the mid-1980s and the 1989 revolution in East Germany, which led in 1990 to the reunification of the two Germanies, making the new restored Germany, with its 79 million people, the leading power in Europe. Soon, however, the realization set in that the revitalization of eastern Germany would cost far more than anticipated, and Kohl's government faced the politically unpopular prospect of raising taxes substantially. Moreover, the virtual collapse of the economy in eastern Germany led to extremely high unemployment. In 1998, voters responded by returning the Social Democrats to power with the election of Gerhard Schröder (GAYR-hahrt SHRUR-dur) (b. 1944). But Schröder failed to cure Germany's economic woes, and as a result of elections in 2005, Angela Merkel (AHNG-uh-luh MERK-uhl) (b. 1954), leader of the Christian Democrats, became Germany's first female chancellor. Merkel pursued health care reform and new energy policies at home while taking a leading role in the affairs of the European Union (EU). Elected to a second term in 2009, she led the EU effort that resulted in a bailout of Greece's deteriorating economy and a restructuring of its debt in 2012.

THE DECLINE OF GREAT BRITAIN The end of World War II left Britain with massive economic problems. In elections held immediately after the war, the Labour Party overwhelmingly defeated Winston Churchill's Conservatives. Labour's promise of far-reaching social welfare measures was quite appealing in a country with a tremendous shortage of consumer goods and housing. The new Labour government under Clement Attlee (1883–1967) proceeded to turn Britain into a modern **welfare state**.

The process began with the nationalization of the Bank of England, the coal and steel industries, public transportation, and public utilities, such as electricity and gas. In 1946, the new government established a comprehensive social security program and nationalized medical insurance. A health act established a system of socialized medicine that forced doctors and dentists to work with state hospitals, although private practice could be maintained. The British welfare state became the model for most European nations.

Continuing economic problems, however, brought the Conservatives back into power from 1951 to 1964. Although they favored private enterprise, the Conservatives accepted the welfare state. By now the British economy had recovered from the war, but its slow growth reflected a long-term economic decline. At the same time, Britain's ability to play the role of a world power had declined substantially. Between 1964 and 1979, Conservatives and Labour alternated in power, but neither party was able to deal with the ailing economy.

In 1979, the Conservatives returned to power under Margaret Thatcher (b. 1925), who became the first woman prime minister in British history (see the box on p. 738). The "Iron Lady," as she was called, broke the power of the labor unions, but she was not able to eliminate the basic components of the welfare state. Her economic policy, termed "Thatcherism," improved the economic situation, but at a price. The south of England, for example, prospered, but the old industrial areas of the Midlands and north declined and were beset by high unemployment, poverty and sporadic violence.

Thatcher dominated British politics in the 1980s. But in 1990, Labour's fortunes revived when Thatcher's government attempted to replace local property taxes with a flat-rate tax payable by every adult. Critics argued that this was effectively a poll tax that would allow the rich to pay the same rate as the poor. In 1990, Thatcher resigned, and later, in new elections in 1997, the Labour Party won a landslide victory. The new prime minister, Tony Blair (b. 1953), was a moderate whose youthful energy instilled new vigor on the political scene. Blair was one of the leaders in forming an international coalition against terrorism after the terrorist attack on the United States in 2001. Four years later, however, his support of the U.S. war in Iraq, when a majority of Britons opposed it, caused his popularity to plummet. In the summer of 2007, he stepped down and allowed the new Labour Party leader Gordon Brown (b. 1951) to become prime minister.

© Peter Turnley/CORBIS

Margaret Thatcher. Great Britain's first female prime minister, Margaret Thatcher was a strong leader who dominated British politics in the 1980s. This picture of Thatcher was taken during a meeting with French president François Mitterrand in 1986.

In 2010, in the wake of climbing unemployment and a global financial crisis, the Labour Party's thirteen-year rule ended when the Conservative Party candidate David Cameron (b. 1966) became prime minister on the basis of a coalition with the Liberal Democrats. Cameron promised to reduce the government debt by cutting government waste and social services and overhauling the health care system.

Eastern Europe After Communism

The fall of Communist governments in Eastern Europe during the revolutions of 1989 brought an end to a postwar European order that had been imposed on unwilling peoples by the victorious forces of the Soviet Union (see Chapter 26). In 1989 and 1990, new governments throughout Eastern Europe worked diligently to scrap the old system and introduce the democratic procedures and market systems they believed would revitalize their scarred lands. But this process proved to be neither simple nor easy. Nevertheless, by 2000, many of these states, especially Poland and the Czech Republic, were making a successful transition to free markets and democracy. In 1997, Poland, the Czech Republic, and Hungary joined the North Atlantic Treaty Organization (NATO).

In some states, the shift to non-Communist rule was complicated by old problems, especially ethnic issues. Although Czechs and Slovaks agreed to a peaceful division of Czechoslovakia into the Czech Republic and Slovakia, the situation was quite different in Yugoslavia.

THE DISINTEGRATION OF YUGOSLAVIA From its creation in 1919, Yugoslavia had been an artificial entity. Strong leaders—especially the dictatorial Marshal Tito after World War II—had managed to hold together the six disparate republics and two autonomous provinces that made up the country. After Tito's death in 1980, no strong leader emerged, and eventually Yugoslavia was caught up in the reform movements sweeping through Eastern Europe.

After negotiations among the six republics failed, Slovenia and Croatia declared their independence in June 1991. This action was opposed by Slobodan Milošević (sluh-BOH-dahn mih-LOH-suh-vich) (1941–2006), the leader of Serbia, who insisted that the republics adjust their borders to accommodate their Serb minorities who did not want to live outside the boundaries of Serbia. Serbian forces attacked both new states and, although

Muslim survivor from the town is eerily reminiscent of the activities of the Nazi *Einsatzgruppen* (see Chapter 25):

> When the truck stopped, they told us to get off in groups of five. We immediately heard shooting next to the trucks. . . . About ten Serbs with automatic rifles told us to lie down on the ground face first. As we were getting down, they started to shoot, and I fell into a pile of corpses. I felt hot liquid running down my face. I realized that I was only grazed. As they continued to shoot more groups, I kept on squeezing myself in between dead bodies.[1]

As the fighting spread, European nations and the United States began to intervene to stop the bloodshed, and in 1995, a fragile cease-fire agreement was reached. An international peacekeeping force was stationed in the area to prevent further hostilities.

Peace in Bosnia, however, did not bring peace to Yugoslavia. A new war erupted in 1999 over Kosovo (KAWSS-suh-voh), an autonomous province within the Serbian republic. Kosovo's inhabitants were mainly ethnic Albanians, but the province was also home to a Serbian minority. In 1994, groups of ethnic Albanians had founded the Kosovo Liberation Army (KLA) and begun a campaign against Serbian rule in Kosovo. When Serb forces began to massacre ethnic Albanians in an effort to crush the KLA, the United States and its NATO allies mounted a bombing campaign that forced Milošević to stop. In the elections of 2000, Milošević himself was ousted from power, and he was later put on trial by an international tribunal for war crimes against humanity for his ethnic cleansing policies. He died in prison in 2006 before his trial could be completed.

Peacekeeping forces still remain in Bosnia and Kosovo to maintain the uneasy peace. In 2004, Yugoslavia itself ceased to exist when the new national government

CHRONOLOGY Western Europe

Welfare state emerges in Great Britain	1946
Konrad Adenauer becomes chancellor of West Germany	1949
Charles de Gaulle reassumes power in France	1958
Student protests in France	1968
Willy Brandt becomes chancellor of West Germany	1969
Margaret Thatcher becomes prime minister of Great Britain	1979
François Mitterrand becomes president of France	1981
Helmut Kohl becomes chancellor of West Germany	1982
Reunification of Germany	1990
Conservative victory in France	1993
Election of Chirac	1995
Labour Party victory in Great Britain	1997
Social Democratic victory in Germany	1998
Angela Merkel becomes chancellor of Germany	2005
Nicolas Sarkozy becomes president of France	2007
David Cameron becomes prime minister of Great Britain	2010
Socialist victory in France	2012

AP Images/Rikard Larma

The War in Bosnia. By mid-1993, irregular Serb forces had overrun much of Bosnia and Herzegovina amid scenes of untold suffering. This photograph shows a woman running past the bodies of victims of a mortar attack on Sarajevo on August 21,1992. Three mortar rounds landed, killing at least three people.

officially renamed the truncated country Serbia and Montenegro. Two years later, Montenegrins voted in favor of independence. Thus, by 2006, all six republics cobbled together to form Yugoslavia in 1918 were once again independent nations. In 2008, Kosovo unilaterally proclaimed its independence from Serbia and was recognized by most other nations as the seventh sovereign state to emerge from the former Yugoslavia.

The New Russia

Soon after the disintegration of the Soviet Union in 1991, a new era began in Russia with the presidency of Boris Yeltsin. A new constitution created a two-chamber parliament and established a strong presidency. During the mid-1990s, Yeltsin was able to maintain a precarious grip on power while seeking to implement reforms that would lead to a pluralistic political system and a market economy. But the new post-Communist Russia remained as fragile as ever. Burgeoning economic inequality and rampant corruption shook the confidence of the Russian people in the superiority of the capitalist system over the Communist one. A nagging war in the Caucasus—where the people of Chechnya (CHECH-nee-uh) sought national independence from Russia—drained the government budget and exposed the decrepit state of the once vaunted Red Army. Yeltsin was reelected in 1996, but his precarious health raised serious questions about his ability to govern.

THE PUTIN ERA At the end of 1999, Yeltsin suddenly resigned and was replaced by Vladimir Putin (VLAD-ih-meer POO-tin) (b. 1952), a former member of the KGB. Putin vowed to bring an end to the rampant corruption and to strengthen the role of the central government. He also vowed to bring the breakaway state of Chechnya back under Russian authority and to assume a more assertive role in international affairs. The new president took advantage of growing public anger at Western plans to expand the NATO alliance into Eastern Europe to restore Russia's position as an influential force in the world.

Putin attempted to deal with Russia's chronic problems by centralizing his control over the system and by silencing critics—notably in the Russian media. Although these moves were criticized in the West, many Russians sympathized with Putin's attempts to restore a sense of pride and discipline. Putin's popularity among the Russian people was also strengthened by Russia's growing prosperity in the first years of the century. Putin made significant economic reforms while rising oil prices boosted the Russian economy, which grew dramatically until the 2008–2009 global economic crisis.

In 2008, Dmitry Medvedev (di-MEE-tree mehd-VYEH-dehf) (b. 1965) became president of Russia when Putin could not run for reelection under Russia's constitution. Instead, Putin became prime minister, and the two men shared power. In 2011, Putin's plans to run again for president sparked protests, but he was elected to a third term in March 2012.

The Unification of Europe

As we saw in Chapter 26, the divisions created by the Cold War led the nations of Western Europe to seek military security by forming NATO in 1949. The destructiveness of two world wars, however, caused many thoughtful Europeans to look for some additional form of unity.

In 1957, France, West Germany, the Benelux countries (Belgium, the Netherlands, and Luxembourg), and Italy signed the Treaty of Rome, which created the European Economic Community (EEC). The EEC eliminated customs barriers for the six member nations and created a large free-trade area protected by a common external tariff. All the member nations benefited economically. In 1973, Great Britain, Ireland, and Denmark joined what now was called the European Community (EC). Greece joined in 1981, followed by Spain and Portugal in 1986. In 1995, Austria, Finland, and Sweden also became members.

THE EUROPEAN UNION In the 1980s and 1990s, the EC moved toward even greater economic integration. The Treaty on European Union, which went into effect on January 1, 1994, turned the European Community into the European Union, a true economic and monetary union. By 2000, it contained 370 million people and constituted the world's largest single trading entity, transacting one-fourth of the world's commerce. One of its goals was achieved in 1999 with the introduction of a common currency, the euro. On January 1, 2002, the euro officially replaced twelve national currencies. By 2012, the euro had been adopted by seventeen countries and was serving approximately 327 million people.

A major crisis for the euro began in 2010, however, when Greece's burgeoning public debt threatened to cause the bankruptcy of that country as well as financial difficulties for many European banks. Other EU members, led by Germany, put together a financial rescue plan, but subsequently other nations, including Ireland, Portugal, and Spain, also faced serious financial problems.

In another step toward integration, the EU has established a common agricultural policy, which provides subsidies to farmers to enable them to compete on the world market. The end of national passports has given millions of Europeans greater flexibility in travel. The EU has been less successful in setting common foreign policy goals, primarily because individual nations still see foreign policy as a national priority and are reluctant to give up this power to a single overriding institution. In 2009, however, the EU ratified the Lisbon Treaty, which

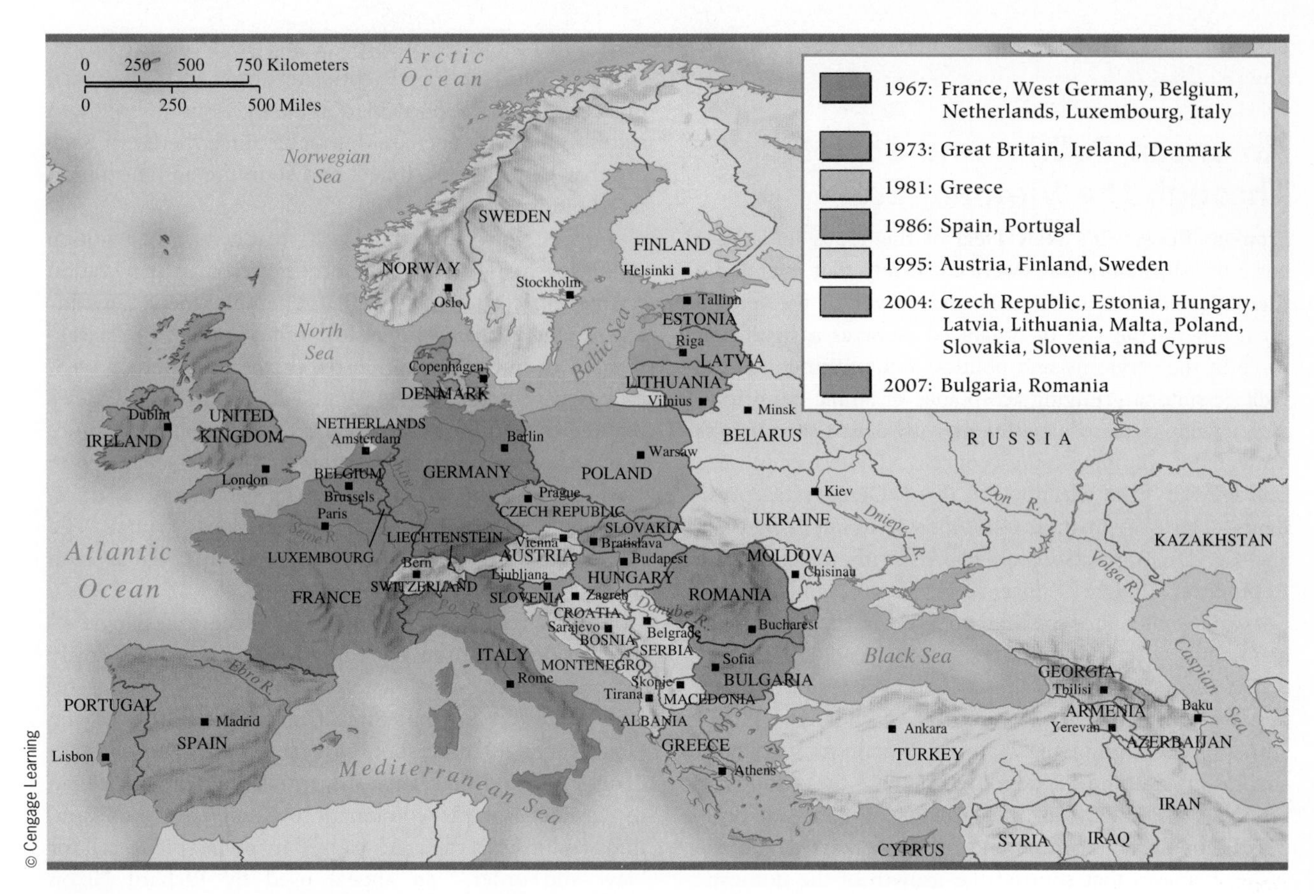

© Cengage Learning

MAP 28.1 European Union, 2007. Beginning in 1957 as the European Economic Community, or Common Market, the union of European states seeking to integrate their economies has gradually grown from six members to twenty-seven. By 2002, the European Union had achieved two major goals—the creation of a single internal market and a common currency—although it has been less successful at achieving common political and foreign policy goals.

 *What additional nations do you think will eventually join the European Union?*

created a full-time presidential post and a new voting system that reflects each country's population size. It also provided more power for the European Parliament in an effort to promote the EU's foreign policy goals.

TOWARD A UNITED EUROPE At the beginning of the twenty-first century, the EU established a new goal: to incorporate into the union the states of eastern and southeastern Europe, including the nations that had recently emerged from Communist rule. Many of these states were considerably poorer than the current members, which raised the possibility that adding these nations might weaken the EU itself. To lessen that danger, the EU required applicants to demonstrate their commitment both to market capitalism and to democracy, including respect for minorities and human rights. In 2004, the EU took the plunge and added ten new members: Cyprus, the Czech Republic, Estonia, Hungary, Latvia, Lithuania, Malta, Poland, Slovakia, and Slovenia, thereby enlarging the population of the EU to 455 million people. In 2007, the EU expanded again as Bulgaria and Romania joined the union (see Map 28.1).

Emergence of the Superpower: The United States

 FOCUS QUESTION: What political, social, and economic changes has the United States experienced since 1945?

At the end of World War II, the United States emerged as one of the world's two superpowers. As its Cold War confrontation with the Soviet Union intensified, the United States directed much of its energy toward combating the spread of communism. With the collapse of the Soviet Union at the beginning of the 1990s, the

United States became the world's foremost military power.

American Politics and Society Through the Vietnam Era

Franklin Roosevelt's New Deal of the 1930s initiated a basic transformation of American society that included a dramatic increase in the role and power of the federal government, the rise of organized labor as a significant force in the economy and politics, a commitment to the welfare state, a grudging acceptance of ethnic minorities, and a willingness to experiment with deficit spending as a means of stimulating the economy. These trends were bolstered by the election of three Democratic presidents—Harry Truman in 1948, John F. Kennedy in 1960, and Lyndon B. Johnson in 1964. Even the election of a Republican, Dwight D. Eisenhower, in 1952 and 1956 did not significantly alter the fundamental direction of American politics.

The economic boom after World War II fueled confidence in the American way of life. A shortage of consumer goods during the war left Americans with both surplus income and the desire to purchase these goods after the war. Then, too, the growing influence of organized labor enabled more and more workers to get the wage increases that spurred the growth of the domestic market. Between 1945 and 1973, real wages grew an average of 3 percent a year, the most prolonged advance in U.S. history.

Starting in the 1960s, however, problems that had been glossed over earlier came to the fore. The decade began on a youthful and optimistic note when John F. Kennedy (1917–1963), at age forty-three, became the youngest elected president in U.S. history and the first born in the twentieth century. His administration, cut short by an assassin's bullet on November 22, 1963, focused primarily on foreign affairs. Kennedy's successor, Lyndon B. Johnson (1908–1973), who won a new term as president in a landslide in 1964, used his mandate to expand the welfare state that had begun under the New Deal. Johnson's programs included health care for the elderly and the War on Poverty, to be fought with food stamps and the Job Corps.

Johnson's other domestic passion was achieving equal rights for black Americans. In August 1963, the eloquent Reverend Martin Luther King Jr. (1929–1968) led the March on Washington for Jobs and Freedom to dramatize blacks' desire for freedom. This march and King's impassioned plea for racial equality had an electrifying effect on the American people. At President Johnson's initiative, Congress enacted the Civil Rights Act of 1964, which created the machinery to end segregation and discrimination in the workplace and all public accommodations. The Voting Rights Act of 1965 eliminated obstacles to black participation in elections in southern states. But laws alone could not guarantee the Great Society that Johnson envisioned, and soon the administration faced bitter social unrest.

In the North and the West, blacks had had voting rights for many years, but local patterns of segregation resulted in considerably higher unemployment rates for blacks (and Hispanics) than for whites and left blacks segregated in huge urban ghettos. In the summer of 1965, race riots erupted in the Watts district of Los Angeles that led to thirty-four deaths and the destruction of more than a thousand buildings. After King was assassinated in 1968, riots erupted in more than one hundred cities, including Washington, D.C., the nation's capital. The riots led to a "white backlash" and a severe racial division of America.

Antiwar protests also divided the American people after President Johnson committed U.S. troops to a costly war in Vietnam (see Chapter 26). The killing of four student protesters at Kent State University in 1970 by the Ohio National Guard shocked both activists and ordinary Americans, and thereafter the antiwar movement began to subside. But the combination of antiwar demonstrations and riots in the cities caused many people to call for "law and order," an appeal used by Richard Nixon (1913–1994), the Republican presidential candidate in 1968. Nixon's election started a shift to the right in American politics.

The Shift Rightward After 1973

Nixon eventually ended American involvement in Vietnam by gradually withdrawing U.S. troops. Politically, he pursued a "southern strategy," calculating that "law and order" issues would appeal to southern whites. The Republican strategy, however, also won support among white Democrats in northern cities, where court-mandated busing to achieve racial integration had provoked a white backlash.

As president, Nixon was paranoid about conspiracies and resorted to subversive methods of gaining political intelligence on his opponents. Nixon's zeal led to the Watergate scandal—a botched attempt to bug the Democratic National Headquarters and the ensuing coverup. Although Nixon repeatedly denied involvement in the affair, secret tapes he made of his own conversations in the White House revealed otherwise. On August 9, 1974, Nixon resigned in disgrace, an act that saved him from almost certain impeachment and conviction.

After Watergate, American politics focused on economic issues. Gerald Ford (1913–2006) became president when Nixon resigned, only to lose in the 1976 election to Jimmy Carter (b. 1924). By 1980, the Carter administration faced two devastating problems. High inflation and a decline in average earnings were causing a perceptible drop in Americans' living standards. At the same time, a crisis abroad had erupted when fifty-three Americans were taken hostage by the Iranian government of Ayatollah Khomeini and held for nearly fifteen months (see Chapter 29). Carter's inability to gain the release of the hostages led to perceptions at home that he was a weak president. In the election of 1980, he suffered an overwhelming loss to Ronald Reagan (1911–2004), the chief exponent of right-wing Republican policies.

The Reagan Revolution, as it has been called, sent U.S. policy in new directions. Reagan cut back on the welfare state by decreasing spending on food stamps, school lunch programs, and job programs. At the same time, he fostered the largest peacetime military buildup in American history. Total federal spending rose from $631 billion in 1981 to more than $1 trillion by 1986. The administration's spending policies produced record government deficits, which loomed as an obstacle to long-term growth. In the 1970s, the total national debt was $420 billion; under Reagan it reached three times that level.

The inability of Reagan's successor, George H. W. Bush (b. 1924), to deal with the deficit problem, coupled with an economic downturn, led to the election of a Democrat, Bill Clinton (b. 1946), in 1992. The new president was a southerner who claimed to be a new Democrat—one who favored a number of the Republican policies of the 1980s. This was a clear indication that the Democratic victory had not ended the rightward drift in American politics.

Clinton's political fortunes were aided considerably by a lengthy economic revival. A steady reduction in the government's budget deficit strengthened confidence in the national economy. Much of Clinton's second term, however, was overshadowed by charges of misconduct stemming from the president's affair with a White House intern. After a bitter partisan struggle, the U.S. Senate acquitted the president on two articles of impeachment brought by the House of Representatives. But Clinton's problems helped the Republican candidate, George W Bush (b. 1946), to win the presidential election in 2000.

The first four years of Bush's administration were largely occupied with the war on terrorism and the U.S.-led war on Iraq (see Chapter 29). The Department of Homeland Security was established after the 2001 terrorist assaults to help protect the country from future terrorist acts. At the same time, Bush pushed tax cuts through Congress that favored the wealthy and helped produce record deficits reminiscent of the Reagan years. Environmentalists were disturbed by the administration's efforts to weaken environmental laws and regulations to benefit American corporations. During his second term, Bush's popularity plummeted as discontent grew over the Iraq War, financial corruption in the Republican Party, and the administration's poor handling of relief efforts after Hurricane Katrina devastated New Orleans in 2005.

The many failures of the Bush administration led to the lowest approval ratings for a modern president and opened the door for a dramatic change in American politics. The new and often inspiring voice of Barack Obama (b. 1961) who called for "change we can believe in" and ending the war in Iraq led to an overwhelming Democratic victory in the 2008 elections. The Democrats were aided by the financial crisis that began in the fall of 2008. In 2009, Obama moved quickly to deal with the economic recession that some called the worst since the Great Depression. At the same time, Obama emphasized the need to deal with the health care crisis, climate change, the decline in the educational system, and failed economic policies. The Obama administration succeeded in passing a health care reform bill and the Dodd-Frank Act on financial regulation, as well as establishing the Consumer Financial Protection Bureau.

The Development of Canada

FOCUS QUESTION: What political, social, and economic developments has Canada experienced since 1945?

For twenty-five years after World War II, Canada experienced extraordinary economic prosperity as it set out on a new path of development, including the electronic, aircraft, nuclear, and chemical engineering industries. Much of the Canadian growth, however, was financed by capital from the United States, which resulted in American ownership of Canadian businesses. While many Canadians welcomed the economic growth, others feared American economic domination of Canada.

After 1945, the Liberal Party continued to dominate Canadian politics. Under Lester Pearson (1897–1972), the Liberals created Canada's welfare state by enacting a national social security system (the Canada Pension Plan) and a national health insurance program. The most prominent Liberal government, however, was that of Pierre Trudeau (PYAYR troo-DOH) (1919–2000), who came to power in 1968.

Trudeau's government pushed a vigorous program of industrialization, but inflation and Trudeau's efforts to impose the will of the federal government on the powerful provincial governments alienated voters and weakened his government. Economic recession in the early 1980s brought Brian Mulroney (b. 1939), leader of the

Progressive Conservative Party, to power in 1984. Mulroney's government sought to privatize many of Canada's state-run corporations and negotiated a free-trade agreement with the United States. Bitterly resented by many Canadians, the agreement cost Mulroney's government much of its popularity. In 1993, the Conservatives were overwhelmingly defeated, and the Liberal leader, Jean Chrétien (ZHAHNH kray-TEN) (b. 1934), became prime minister. Chrétien's conservative fiscal policies, combined with strong economic growth, enabled his government to have a budgetary surplus by the late 1990s and led to another Liberal victory in the elections of 1997. Charges of widespread financial corruption in the government, however, led to a Conservative victory early in 2006, and Stephen Harper (b. 1959) became the new prime minister. Harper's government collapsed in March 2011, but elections held in May resulted in Harper remaining as prime minister.

Latin America Since 1945

FOCUS QUESTION: What problems have the nations of Latin America faced since 1945, and what role has Marxist ideology played in their efforts to solve these problems?

The Great Depression of the 1930s had led to political instability in many Latin American countries that resulted in military coups and militaristic regimes (see Chapter 24). But the depression also provided the impetus for Latin America to move from a traditional to a modern economic structure. Since the nineteenth century, Latin Americans had exported raw materials, especially minerals and foodstuffs, while buying the manufactured goods of the industrialized countries in Europe and the United States. As a result of the depression, however, exports were cut in half, and the revenues available to buy manufactured goods declined. This encouraged many Latin American countries to develop industries to produce goods that were formerly imported. Due to a shortage of capital in the private sector, governments often invested in the new industries, thus leading, for example, to government-run steel industries in Chile and Brazil and oil industries in Argentina and Mexico.

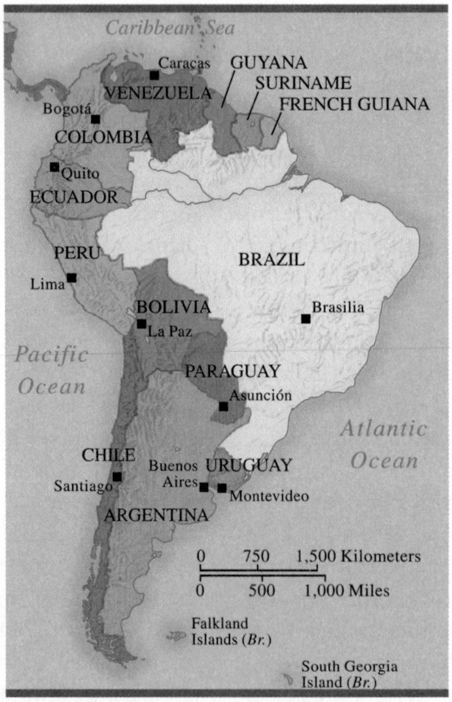

© Cengage Learning

South America

By the 1960s, however, Latin American countries were still dependent on the United States, Europe, and now Japan for the advanced technology needed for modern industries. Because of the great poverty in many Latin American countries, domestic markets were limited in size, and many countries failed to find markets abroad for their products. These failures led to instability and a new reliance on military regimes, especially to curb the power of the new industrial middle class and working classes, which had emerged as a result of industrialization. In the 1960s, repressive military regimes in Chile, Brazil, and Argentina abolished political parties and often returned to export-import economies financed by foreigners.

In the 1970s, Latin American regimes grew even more dependent on borrowing from abroad to maintain their failing economies. Between 1970 and 1982, debt to foreigners, mostly U.S. and European banks, increased from $27 billion to $315.3 billion. By 1982, several governments announced that they could no longer pay interest on their debts, and their economies began to crumble.

The debt crisis of the 1980s was accompanied by a move toward democracy. Many people realized that military power without popular consent was incapable of providing a strong state. By the 1980s and early 1990s, democratic regimes were in place everywhere except Cuba, some of the Central American states, Chile, and Paraguay. At the end of the twentieth century and beginning of the twenty-first, a noticeable political trend in Latin America has been the election of left-wing governments, evident in the election of Hugo Chávez (OO-goh CHAH-vez) (b. 1954) in Venezuela in 1998; Luiz Inácio Lula de Silva (LWEES ee-NAH-syoh LOO-luh duh SEEL-vuh) (b. 1945) in Brazil in 2002, followed by Dilma Rousseff (DIL-muh ROO-seff) (b. 1947) in 2010; Michelle Bachelet (mih-SHELL BAHSH-uh-let) (b. 1951) in Chile in 2006, followed by Sebastián Piñera (say-bahs-TYAHN peen-YAIR-uh) (b. 1949) in 2010, a center-right candidate who promised to uphold the Socialists' social and economic policies; and Daniel Ortega (dah-NYEL awr-TAY-guh) (b. 1945) in Nicaragua in 2007.

The United States has also played an important role in Latin America since 1945. Since the

1920s, the United States had been the foremost investor in Latin America. As a result, American companies had gained control of large segments of important Latin American industries including the copper and oil industries. This control by American investors reinforced a growing nationalist sentiment in Latin America against the United States as a neo-imperialist power.

But the United States also tried to pursue a new relationship with Latin America. In 1948, the nations of the Western Hemisphere formed the Organization of American States (OAS), which was intended to eliminate unilateral interference by one state in the internal or external affairs of any other state. But as the Cold War intensified, American policy makers grew anxious about the possibility of Communist regimes arising in Central America and the Caribbean and returned to a policy of unilateral action when they believed that Soviet agents were attempting to establish Communist governments. Especially after the success of Castro in Cuba (see the next section), the desire of the United States to prevent "another Cuba" largely determined American policy toward Latin America. Until the end of the Cold War in the early 1990s, the United States provided massive military aid to anti-Communist regimes, regardless of their nature.

The Threat of Marxist Revolutions: The Example of Cuba

A dictatorship, headed by Fulgencio Batista (1901–1973) and closely tied economically to American investors, had ruled Cuba since 1934. In the 1950s, Batista's government came under attack by a strong opposition movement, led by Fidel Castro. Castro maintained that only armed force could overthrow Batista, but when their initial assaults on Batista's regime met with little success, Castro's forces turned to guerrilla warfare (see the box on p. 746). Batista's regime responded with such brutality that he alienated his own supporters. The dictator fled in December 1958, and Castro's revolutionaries seized Havana on January 1, 1959.

Relations between Cuba and the United States quickly deteriorated early in 1960 when the Soviet Union agreed to buy Cuban sugar and provide $100 million in credits. In October 1960, the United States imposed a trade embargo on Cuba, which drove Castro closer to the Soviet Union. On January 3, 1961, the United States broke diplomatic relations with Cuba. The new American president, John F. Kennedy, supported a coup attempt against Castro's government, but the landing of 1,400 Cuban exiles with assistance from the Central Intelligence Agency (CIA) at the Bay of Pigs in Cuba on April 17, 1961, was a total military disaster. The Soviets now made an even greater commitment to Cuban independence by installing nuclear missiles in the country, an act that led to a showdown with the United States (see Chapter 26). As its part of the bargain to defuse the missile crisis, the United States agreed not to invade Cuba.

In Cuba, Castro's socialist revolution proceeded, with mixed results. The Cuban people obtained some social gains, especially in health care and education. The regime provided free medical services for all citizens, and the population's health improved noticeably. Illiteracy was wiped out by developing new schools and establishing teacher-training institutes that tripled the number of teachers within ten years.

Eschewing rapid industrialization, Castro encouraged agricultural diversification. But the Cuban economy continued to rely on the production of sugar. Economic problems forced the regime to depend on Soviet subsidies and the purchase of Cuban sugar by Soviet bloc countries. After the collapse of these Communist regimes in 1989, Cuba lost their support. Although economic conditions continued to decline, Fidel Castro remained in power until illness forced him to resign the presidency in 2008, when his brother, Raul Castro (b. 1931), succeeded him.

Nationalism and the Military: The Example of Argentina

The military became the power brokers of many twentieth-century Latin American nations. Fearful of the forces unleashed by industrialization, the military intervened in Argentine politics in 1930 and propped up the cattle and wheat oligarchy that had controlled the reins of power since the beginning of the century. In June 1943, a group of restless army officers overthrew the civilian oligarchy. One member of the new regime, Juan Perón (WAHN puh-ROHN) (1895–1974), used his position as labor secretary to curry favor with the workers. But as Perón grew more popular, other army officers grew fearful of his power and arrested him. An uprising by workers forced the officers to back down, and in 1946, Perón was elected president.

To please his chief supporters—labor and the urban middle class—Perón pursued a policy of increased industrialization. At the same time, he sought to free Argentina from foreign investors. The government bought the railways; took over the banking, insurance, shipping, and communications industries; and regulated imports and exports. But Perón's regime was also authoritarian. His wife, Eva Perón, founded women's organizations to support the government while Perón organized fascist gangs, modeled after Hitler's Brown Shirts, who used violence to intimidate his opponents. But growing corruption in Perón's government and the alienation of more and more people by the regime's excesses encouraged the military

Castro's Revolutionary Ideals

POLITICS & GOVERNMENT

On July 26, 1953, Fidel Castro and a small group of supporters launched an ill-fated attack on the Moncada Barracks in Santiago de Cuba. Castro was arrested and put on trial. This excerpt is taken from the speech he presented in his defense, in which he discussed the goals of the revolutionaries.

Fidel Castro, "History Will Absolve Me"

I stated that the second consideration on which we based our chances for success was one of social order because we were assured of the people's support. When we speak of the people we do not mean the comfortable ones, the conservative elements of the nation, who welcome any regime of oppression, any dictatorship, and despotism, prostrating themselves before the master of the moment until they grind their foreheads into the ground. When we speak of struggle, the people means the vast unredeemed masses, to whom all make promises and whom all deceive; we mean the people who yearn for a better, more dignified, and more just nation. . . .

In the brief of this cause there must be recorded the five revolutionary laws that would have been proclaimed immediately after the capture of the Moncada barracks. . . .

The First Revolutionary Law would have returned power to the people and proclaimed the Constitution of 1940 the supreme Law of the land, until such time as the people should decide to modify or change it. . . .

The Second Revolutionary Law would have granted property, not mortgageable and not transferable, to all planters, subplanters, lessees, partners, and squatters who hold parcels of five or less *caballerias* [about 33 acres] of land, and the state would indemnify the former owners on the basis of the rental which they would have received for these parcels over a period of ten years.

The Third Revolutionary Law would have granted workers and employees the right to share 30 percent of the profits of all the large industrial, mercantile, and mining enterprises, including the sugar mills. . . .

The Fourth Revolutionary Law would have granted all planters the right to share 55 percent of the sugar production and a minimum quota of forty thousand *arrobas* [25 pounds] for all small planters who have been established for three or more years.

The Fifth Revolutionary Law would have ordered the confiscation of all holdings and ill-gotten gains of those who had committed frauds during previous regimes, as well as the holdings and ill-gotten gains of all their legatees and heirs.

What did Fidel Castro intend to accomplish by his revolution in Cuba? On whose behalf did he fight this revolution?

Source: Excerpt *from Latin American Civilization* by Benjamin Keen, ed. (Boston: Houghton Mifflin, 1974), pp. 369–373.

to overthrow him in September 1955. Perón went into exile in Spain.

Overwhelmed by problems, however, the military leaders allowed Perón to return from exile. Reelected president in September 1973, Perón died one year later. In 1976, the military installed a new regime and used the occasion to kill more than six thousand leftists. But economic problems persisted, and the regime tried to divert people's attention by invading the Falkland Islands in April 1982. Great Britain, which had controlled the islands since the nineteenth century, decisively defeated the Argentine forces. The loss discredited the military and opened the door to civilian rule. In 1983, Raúl Alfonsín (rah-OOL al-fahn-SEEN) (1927–2009) was elected president and tried to reestablish democratic practices. In elections in 1989, the Perónist Carlos Saúl Menem (KAHR-lohs sah-OOL MEN-em) (b. 1930) won. This peaceful transfer of power gave hope that Argentina was moving on a democratic path. Despite problems of foreign debt and inflation, Argentina has witnessed economic growth since 2003, first under the government of President Nestor Kirchner (NAY-stor KEERCH-nehr) (b. 1950) and then under his wife, Cristina Fernández de Kirchner (kris-TEE-nuh fehr-NAHN-des day

© Bettmann/CORBIS

Juan and Eva Perón. Elected president of Argentina in 1946, Juan Perón soon established an authoritarian regime that nationalized some of Argentina's basic industries and organized fascist gangs to overwhelm its opponents. He is shown here with his wife, Eva, during the inauguration ceremonies initiating his second term as president in 1952.

KEERCH-nehr) (b. 1953), who in 2007 became the first elected female president of Argentina.

The Mexican Way

During the 1950s and 1960s, Mexico's ruling party—the Institutional Revolutionary Party, or PRI—focused on a balanced program of industrial policy. Fifteen years of steady economic growth combined with low inflation and real gains in wages made those years seem a golden age in Mexico's economic development. But at the end of the 1960s, students began to protest the one-party system. On October 2, 1968, police opened fire on a demonstration of university students in Mexico City, killing hundreds of the students. Leaders of the PRI became concerned about the need to change the system.

During the 1970s, the next two presidents, Luis Echeverría (loo-EES eh-cheh-vahr-REE-uh) (b. 1922) and José López Portillo (hoh-SAY LOH-pehz pohr-TEE-yoh) (1920–2004), introduced reforms. Rules for registering political parties were eased, making their growth more likely, and greater freedom of debate in the press and at universities was allowed. But economic problems continued. In the late 1970s, vast new reserves of oil were discovered, making the government even more dependent on oil revenues. When world oil prices dropped in the mid-1980s, Mexico was no longer able to make payments on its $80 billion of foreign debt. The debt crisis and rising unemployment increased dissatisfaction with the government, as was evident in the 1988 election, when the PRI's candidate, Carlos Salinas (KAHR-lohs sah-LEE-nahs) (b. 1948), won by only a 50.3 percent majority instead of the expected landslide. Growing dissatisfaction with the government's economic policies finally led to the unthinkable: in 2000, Vicente Fox (vee-SEN-tay FOKS) (b. 1942) defeated the PRI candidate for the presidency. Despite high hopes, Fox's administration failed to deal with police corruption and bureaucratic inefficiency in the government. His successor, Felipe Calderón (feh-LEE-pay kahl-duh-ROHN) (b. 1963), made immigration reform a priority, with little success. In 2012, the PRI returned to power when its candidate, Enrique Peña Nieto (en-REE-kay PAYN-yah nee-EH-toh) (b. 1966), was elected to the presidency.

Society and Culture in the Western World

FOCUS QUESTION: What major social, cultural, and intellectual developments have occurred in Western Europe and North America since 1945?

Socially, culturally, and intellectually, the Western world since 1945 has been marked by much diversity.

The Emergence of a New Society

During the postwar era, such products of new technologies as computers, television, jet planes, contraceptive devices, and new surgical techniques dramatically altered the nature of human life. The rapid changes in postwar society were fueled by scientific advances and economic growth. Called a *technocratic society* by some observers and the **consumer society** by others, postwar Western society was marked by a fluid social structure and new movements for change.

Especially noticeable in European society after 1945 were the changes in the middle class. Such traditional middle-class groups as businesspeople and professionals in law and medicine were greatly augmented by increasing numbers of white-collar supervisory and administrative personnel employed by large companies and government agencies.

Changes also occurred among the traditional lower classes. Especially notable was the shift of people from rural to urban areas. The number of people in agriculture declined drastically. But the size of the industrial working class did not expand. In West Germany, industrial workers made up 48 percent of the labor force throughout the 1950s and 1960s. Thereafter, the number of industrial workers began to dwindle as the number of white-collar service employees increased. At the same time, a substantial increase in real wages enabled the working classes to aspire to the consumption patterns of the middle class. Buying on the installment plan became widespread in the 1950s and enabled workers to purchase televisions, home appliances, and automobiles.

Rising incomes, combined with shorter working hours, also increased the market for mass leisure activities. Between 1900 and 1980, the workweek fell from sixty hours to around forty hours, and the number of paid holidays increased. All aspects of popular culture—music, sports, media—became commercialized and offered opportunities for leisure activities.

Social change was also evident in educational patterns. Before World War II, higher education had largely remained the preserve of the wealthier classes. After the war, European states began to foster greater equality of opportunity in higher education by eliminating fees, and universities experienced an influx of students from the middle and lower classes. Enrollments grew dramatically. In France, 4.5 percent of young people went to a university in 1950; by 1965, the figure had increased to 14.5 percent.

But there were problems. Overcrowded classrooms, professors who paid little attention to students, administrators who acted in an authoritarian fashion, and an education that many deemed irrelevant to the modern age led to an outburst of student revolts in the late 1960s. In part, these were an extension of the anti-Vietnam War protests in American universities in the mid-1960s. Perhaps the most famous student revolt occurred in France in 1968. It erupted at the University of Nanterre outside Paris but soon spread to the Sorbonne, the main campus of the University of Paris. French students demanded a greater voice in the university's administration, occupied buildings, and then expanded their protests by inviting workers to join them. Half of France's workforce went on strike. After the Gaullist government instituted a hefty wage hike, the workers returned to work, and the police repressed the remaining student protesters.

There were several reasons for the student radicalism. Some students were genuinely motivated by the desire to reform the university. Others were protesting the Vietnam War, which they viewed as a product of Western imperialism. They also attacked the materialism of Western society and expressed concern about becoming cogs in a large, impersonal bureaucratic machine. For many students, the calls for democratic decision making in the universities reflected their deeper concerns about the direction of Western society.

The Permissive Society

Some critics referred to the new society of postwar Europe as the **permissive society**. Sweden took the lead in the so-called sexual revolution of the 1960s, and the rest of Europe and the United States soon followed. Sex education in the schools and the decriminalization of homosexuality were but two aspects of Sweden's liberal approach. The introduction of the birth control pill, which was widely available by the mid-1960s, gave people more freedom. Meanwhile, sexually explicit movies, plays, and books broke new ground in the treatment of once-hidden subjects.

The new standards were evident in the breakdown of the traditional family. Divorce rates increased dramatically, especially in the 1960s, while premarital and extramarital sexual experiences also rose substantially. A survey in the Netherlands in 1968 revealed that 78 percent of men and 86 percent of women had engaged in extramarital sex.

The 1960s also saw the emergence of the drug culture. Marijuana, though illegal, was widely used by university students. For young people more interested in higher levels of consciousness, Timothy Leary, who had done research at Harvard on the psychedelic (perception-altering) effects of lysergic acid diethylamide (LSD), became the high priest of hallucinogenic experiences.

New attitudes toward sex and the use of drugs were only two manifestations of a growing youth movement that questioned authority and fostered rebellion against the older generation. Spurred on by opposition to the Vietnam War and a growing political consciousness, the youth rebellion became a youth protest movement by the second half of the 1960s (see the box on p. 750).

Women in the Postwar World

Despite their enormous contributions to the war effort, women were removed from the workforce at the end of World War II so that there would be jobs for the soldiers returning home. After the horrors of war, people seemed willing for a while to return to traditional family practices. Female participation in the workforce declined, and birthrates rose, creating a "baby boom." This increase in the birthrate did not last, however, and the size of

traditionally female jobs. Many women also still faced the double burden of earning income on the one hand and raising a family and maintaining the household on the other. Such inequalities led increasing numbers of women to rebel.

© Henry Diltz/CORBIS

The "Love-In." In the 1960s, outdoor public festivals for young people combined music, drugs, and sex. Flamboyant dress, face painting, free-form dancing, and drugs were vital ingredients in creating an atmosphere dedicated to "love and peace." Shown here are "hippies" dancing around a decorated bus at a "love-in" during 1967's Summer of Love.

families began to decline by the mid-1960s. Largely responsible for this decline was the widespread practice of birth control. The condom, invented in the nineteenth century, was already in wide use, but the development of birth control pills in the 1960s provided a convenient and reliable means of birth control that quickly spread to all Western countries.

The trend toward smaller families contributed to changes in women's employment in both Europe and the United States, primarily because women now needed to devote far fewer years to rearing children. That led to a large increase in the number of married women in the workforce. At the beginning of the twentieth century, even working-class wives tended to stay at home if they could afford to do so. In the postwar period, this was no longer the case. In the United States, for example, in 1900, married women made up about 15 percent of the female labor force; by 1970, their number had increased to 62 percent.

But the increased number of women in the workforce did not change some old patterns. Working-class women in particular still earned less than men for equal work. In the 1960s, women earned only 60 percent of men's wages in Britain, 50 percent in France, and 63 percent in West Germany. In addition, women still tended to enter

THE FEMINIST MOVEMENT: THE QUEST FOR LIBERATION The participation of women in World Wars I and II helped them achieve one of the major aims of the nineteenth-century feminist movement—the right to vote. After World War I, many governments acknowledged the contributions of women to the war effort by granting them suffrage. Sweden, Great Britain, Germany, Poland, Hungary, Austria, and Czechoslovakia did so in 1918, followed by the United States in 1920. Women in France and Italy did not obtain the right to vote until 1945. After World War II, little was heard of feminist concerns, but by the 1960s, women began to assert their rights again and speak as feminists. Along with the student upheavals of the late 1960s came renewed interest in feminism, or the **women's liberation movement**, as it was now called.

Of great importance to the emergence of the women's liberation movement was the work of Simone de Beauvoir (see-MUHN duh boh-VWAR) (1908–1986), who supported herself as a teacher and later as a writer. De Beauvoir believed that she lived a "liberated" life for a twentieth-century European woman, but she still came to perceive that as a woman, she faced limits that men did not. In her highly influential work *The Second Sex* (1949), she argued that as a result of male-dominated societies, women had been defined by their differences from men and consequently received second-class status: "What particularly signalizes the situation of woman is that she—a free autonomous being like all human creatures—nevertheless finds herself in a world where men compel her to assume the status of the Other."[2]

TRANSFORMATION IN WOMEN'S LIVES To ensure natural replacement of a country's population, women need to produce an average of 2.1 children each. Many

"The Times They Are a-Changin'": The Music of Youthful Protest

In the 1960s, the lyrics of rock music reflected the rebellious mood of many young people. Bob Dylan (b. 1941), a vastly influential performer and recording artist, expressed the feelings of the younger generation. His song "The Times They Are a-Changin'," released in 1964, has been called an "anthem for the protest movement."

Bob Dylan, "The Times They Are a-Changin'"

Come gather 'round people
Wherever you roam
And admit that the waters
Around you have grown
And accept it that soon
You'll be drenched to the bone
If your time to you
Is worth savin'
Then you better start swimmin'
Or you'll sink like a stone
For the times they are a-changin' . . .

Come senators, congressmen
Please heed the call
Don't stand in the doorway
Don't block up the hall
For he that gets hurt
Will be he who has stalled
There's a battle outside
And it is ragin'
It'll soon shake your windows
And rattle your walls
For the times they are a-changin'

Come mothers and fathers
Throughout the land
And don't criticize
What you can't understand
Your sons and your daughters
Are beyond your command
Your old road
Is rapidly agin'
Please get out of the new one
If you can't lend your hand
For the times they are a-changin'

The line it is drawn
The curse it is cast
The slow one now
Will later be fast
As the present now
Will later be past
The order is
Rapidly fadin'
And the first one now
Will later be last
For the times they are a-changin'

What caused the student campus revolts of the 1960s? What and whom does Dylan identify as the problem in this song?

Source: THE TIMES THEY ARE A-CHANGIN' Copyright © 1963 by Warner Bros. Inc. Copyright renewed 1991 by Special Rider Music. All rights reserved. International copyright secured. Reprinted by permission.

European countries fall far short of this mark; their populations stopped growing in the 1960s, and the trend has continued ever since. By the 1990s, in the nations of the European Union, the average number of children per mother was 1.4. At 1.31 in 2009, Spain's rate was among the lowest in the world.

At the same time, the number of women in the workforce has continued to rise. In Britain, for example, women accounted for 32 percent of the labor force in 1970 but 44 percent in 1990. Moreover, women have entered new employment areas. Greater access to universities and professional schools has enabled women to take jobs in law, medicine, government, business, and education. In the Soviet Union, for example, about 70 percent of doctors and teachers were women. Nevertheless, women still often are paid less than men for comparable work and receive fewer promotions to management positions.

Feminists in the women's liberation movement came to believe that women themselves must transform the fundamental conditions of their lives. In the 1960s and 1970s, hundreds of thousands of European women gained a measure of control over their own bodies by working to repeal laws that outlawed contraception and abortion. Even in Catholic countries, where the church opposed abortion, legislation allowing contraception and abortion was passed in the 1970s and 1980s.

As more women have become activists, they have also become involved in new issues. Some women have tried to affect the political environment by allying with the antinuclear movement. In 1981, a group of women protested American nuclear missiles in Britain by chaining themselves to the fence of a U.S. military base. Thousands more joined in creating a peace camp around the military compound. Enthusiasm ran high; one participant said, "I'll never forget that feeling; it'll live with me for ever. . . . As we walked round, and we clasped hands. . . . It was for women; it was for peace; it was for the world."[3]

Women in the West have also reached out to work with women from the rest of the world in changing the conditions of their lives. Between 1975 and 1995, the United Nations held a series of conferences on women's issues. These meetings made clear the differences between women from Western and non-Western countries. Whereas women from Western countries spoke about political, economic, cultural, and sexual rights, women from developing countries in Latin America, Africa, and Asia focused on bringing an end to the violence, hunger, and disease that haunt their lives.

The Growth of Terrorism

Acts of terror by individuals and groups opposed to governments have become a frightening aspect of modern Western society. During the late 1970s and early 1980s, small bands of terrorists used assassination, indiscriminate killing of civilians, the taking of hostages, and the hijacking of airplanes to draw attention to their demands or to destabilize governments in the hope of achieving their political goals.

Motivations for terrorist acts varied considerably. Left- and right-wing terrorist groups flourished in the late 1970s and early 1980s, but terrorist acts also stemmed from militant nationalists who wished to create separatist states. Most prominent was the Irish Republican Army (IRA), which resorted to vicious attacks against the ruling government and innocent civilians in Northern Ireland.

Although left- and right-wing terrorist activities declined in Europe in the 1980s, international terrorism continued. Angered by the loss of their territory to Israel, some militant Palestinians responded with terrorist attacks against Israel's supporters. Palestinian terrorists mounted attacks on both Europeans and American tourists in Europe, including attacks on vacationers at airports in Rome and Vienna in 1985. State-sponsored terrorism was often an integral part of international terrorism. Militant governments, especially in Iran, Libya, and Syria, assisted terrorist organizations that carried out attacks on Europeans and Americans. On December 21, 1988, Pan American flight 103 from Frankfurt to New York exploded over Lockerbie, Scotland, killing all 259 passengers and crew members. The bomb responsible for the explosion had been planted by two Libyan terrorists.

TERRORIST ATTACK ON THE UNITED STATES One of the most destructive acts of terrorism occurred on September 11, 2001, in the United States. Terrorists hijacked four commercial jet airplanes after takeoff from Boston, Newark, and Washington, D.C. The hijackers flew two of the airplanes into the towers of the World Trade Center in New York City, causing these buildings, as well as several surrounding buildings, to collapse. A third hijacked plane slammed into the Pentagon near Washington, D.C. The fourth plane, apparently headed for Washington, crashed in an isolated area of Pennsylvania. In total, more than three thousand people were killed.

These coordinated acts of terror were carried out by hijackers connected to the international terrorist organization known as al-Qaeda, run by Osama bin Laden (1957–2011). A native of Saudi Arabia of Yemeni extraction, bin Laden used an inherited fortune to set up terrorist training camps in Afghanistan, under the protection of that nation's militant fundamentalist Islamic rulers known as the Taliban.

U.S. president George W. Bush vowed to wage a war on terrorism and worked to create a coalition of nations to assist in ridding the world of al-Qaeda and other terrorist groups. Within weeks of the attack on America, U.S. and NATO air forces began bombing Taliban-controlled command centers and al-Qaeda hiding places in Afghanistan. On the ground, Afghan forces, assisted by U.S. special forces, pushed the Taliban out and gained control of the country by the end of 2001. A democratic multiethnic government was installed but continues to face problems from revived Taliban activity (see Chapter 29).

Guest Workers and Immigrants

As the economies of the Western European countries revived in the 1950s and 1960s, a severe labor shortage forced them to rely on foreign workers. Thousands of Turks and eastern and southern Europeans relocated to Germany, North Africans to France, and people from the Caribbean, India, and Pakistan to Great Britain. Overall, there were probably 15 million **guest workers** in Europe in the 1980s.

Although these workers were recruited for economic reasons, their presence has created social and political problems for their host countries. Not only has the influx of foreigners strained the social services of European countries, but high concentrations of guest workers, many of them nonwhite, in certain areas have led to tensions with the local native populations who oppose making their countries ethnically diverse. By 1998, English was not the first language of one-third of inner-city children in London. Foreign workers constitute almost one-fifth of the population in the German cities of Frankfurt, Munich, and Stuttgart. Antiforeign sentiment has increased with growing unemployment.

Even nations that have traditionally been open to immigrants are changing their policies. In the Netherlands, 19 percent of the people have a foreign background, representing almost 180 nationalities. In 2004, however, the Dutch government passed tough new immigration laws that required newcomers to pass a Dutch language and culture test before being admitted to the country. Sometimes these policies have been aimed at religious practices. In France, the growing number of Muslims has led to restrictions on the display of Islamic symbols. In 2004, France enacted a law prohibiting female students from wearing a headscarf (*hijib*) to school. Small religious symbols, such as small crosses or medallions, were not included. Critics argue that this law will exacerbate ethnic and religious tensions in France, while supporters maintain that it upholds the French tradition of secularism and equality for women (see the box on p. 753).

The Environment and the Green Movements

Environmentalism first became an important item on the European political agenda in the 1970s. By that time, serious ecological problems had become all too apparent. Air pollution, created by emissions from road vehicles, power plants, and industrial factories, was causing respiratory illnesses and having corrosive effects on buildings and monuments. Many rivers, lakes, and seas had become so polluted that they posed serious health risks. In 1986, a disastrous accident at the Soviet nuclear power plant at Chernobyl, Ukraine, made Europeans even more aware of potential environmental hazards. The opening of Eastern Europe after the revolutions of 1989 revealed the environmental destruction caused by unfettered industrial pollution in that region.

Growing ecological awareness gave rise to Green movements and Green parties throughout Europe beginning in the 1970s. Most visible was the Green Party in Germany, which was officially organized in 1979 and had elected forty-two delegates to the West German parliament by 1987. Green parties also competed successfully in Sweden, Austria, and Switzerland. As support for the Green movement grew, the major political parties began to advocate new environmental regulations, and 1987 was touted as the "year of the environment." By the 1990s, European governments were taking steps to safeguard the environment and clean up the worse sources of pollution.

By the early twenty-first century, European cities began to recognize the need for urban sustainability. Many cities have enacted laws that limit new construction, increase the quantity and quality of green spaces within the city, and foster the construction and use of public transportation systems, including rail, metro, bus, and bicycle (see the comparative illustration on p. 755).

Western Culture Since 1945

Intellectually and culturally, the Western world since World War II has been notable for innovation as well as diversity. Especially since 1970, new directions have led some observers to speak of a "Postmodern" cultural world.

POSTWAR LITERATURE A significant trend in postwar literature was the Theater of the Absurd. Its most famous proponent was the Irishman Samuel Beckett (1906–1990), who lived in France. In Beckett's *Waiting for Godot* (1952), the action on the stage is transparently unrealistic. Two men wait for someone, with whom they may or may not have an appointment. During the course of the play, nothing seems to be happening. The audience is never told if the action in front of them is real or imagined. Suspense is maintained not by having the audience wonder "What is going to happen next?" but simply "What is happening now?"

The Theater of the Absurd reflected its time. The postwar era was one of disillusionment with fixed ideological beliefs in politics and religion. The same disillusionment that underscored the bleak worldview of absurdist drama also inspired the **existentialism** of writers Albert Camus (ahl-BAYR ka-MOO) (1913–1960) and Jean-Paul Sartre (ZHAHNH-POHL SAR-truh) (1905–1980), with its sense of the world's meaninglessness. The beginning point of the existentialism of Sartre and Camus was the absence of God in the universe. Although the death of God was tragic, it also meant that humans had no preordained destiny and were utterly alone in the universe with no future and no hope. As Camus expressed it:

> A world that can be explained even with bad reasons is a familiar world. But, on the other hand, in a universe suddenly divested of illusions and lights, man feels an alien, a stranger. His exile is without remedy since he is deprived of

OPPOSING ✂ VIEWPOINTS

Islam and the West: Secularism in France

The ban on headscarves in French schools was preceded by a debate on the secular state in France. While recognizing the right to religious expression, French law dictates that religious expression must remain in the private sphere and cannot enter the public realm. Before the law banning headscarves was enacted, President Jacques Chirac set up a commission to interview school, religious, and political leaders on whether headscarves should be allowed in schools. The commission decided in favor of prohibiting all conspicuous religious symbols in schools. The first selection is taken from a speech by Chirac, who favored the ban. The second selection is taken from interviews with French Muslim women. Many of these women questioned how the law protects their individual rights and freedom of religious expression.

French President Jacques Chirac on Secularism in French Society

The debate on the principle of secularism goes to the very heart of our values. It concerns our national cohesion, our ability to live together, our ability to unite on what is essential. . . . Many young people of immigrant origin, whose first language is French, and who are in most cases of French nationality, succeed and feel at ease in society which is theirs. This kind of success must also be made possible by breaking the wall of silence and indifference which surrounds the reality of discrimination today. I know about the feeling of being misunderstood, of helplessness, sometimes even of revolt, among young French people of immigrant origin whose job applications are rejected because of the way their names sound, and who are too often confronted with discrimination in the fields of access to housing. . . . All of France's children, whatever their history, whatever their origin, whatever their beliefs, are the daughters and sons of the republic. They have to be recognized as such, in law but above all in reality. By ensuring respect for this requirement, by reforming our integration policy, by our ability to bring equal opportunities to life, we shall bring national cohestion to life again. We shall also do so by bringing to life the principle of secularism, which is a pillar of our constitution. . . . Secularism guarantees freedom of conscience. It protects the freedom to believe or not to believe. . . . We also need to reaffirm secularism in schools, because schools must be preserved absolutely. . . .

There is of course no question of turning schools into a place of uniformity, of anonymity, where religious life or belonging would be banned. . . . Until recently, as a result of a reasonable custom which was respected spontaneously, nobody ever doubted that pupils, who are naturally free to live their faith, should nevertheless not arrive in schools . . . in religious clothes. It is not a question of inventing new rules or of shifting the boundaries of secularism. It is a question of expressing, with respect but clearly and firmly, a rule which has been part of our customs and practices for a very long time. . . . I have examined the arguments put forward by . . . political parties, by religious authorities, by major representatives of major currents of thought. In all conscience, it is my view that the wearing of clothes or of symbols which conspicuously demonstrate religious affiliations must be banned in state schools.

North African Women in France Respond to the Headscarf Ban

Labiba (Thirty-Five-Year-Old Algerian)

I don't feel that they should interfere in the private life of people in the respect that we're in a secular country; France shouldn't take a position toward one religion to the detriment of another. . . . I think that in a secular school, we should all be secular, otherwise we need to have religious school and then everyone is free to wear what he wants.

Nour (Thirty-Four-Year-Old Algerian)

Honestly, you know the secular school, it doesn't miss celebrating Easter, and when they celebrate Easter, it doesn't bother me. My daughter comes home with painted Easter eggs and everything; it's pretty; it's cute. There are classes that are over 80 percent [Muslim] in the suburbs, and they celebrate Easter, they celebrate Christmas, you see? And that's not a problem for the secular school. And I don't find that fair.

I find that when it's Ramadan, they should talk about Ramadan. Honestly, me, it wouldn't be a problem. On the contrary, someone who comes into class . . . with a veil, that would pose a question actually, that we could

(Continued)

discuss in class, to know why this person wears the veil. So why punish them, amputate them from that part of their culture without discussing it? Why is it so upsetting to have someone in class who wears a veil, when we could make it a subject of discussion on all religions? Getting stuck on the veil hides the question. They make such a big deal out of it, the poor girls, they take them out of school. . . . In the end we turn them into people who have problems in their identities, in their culture and everything. . . . For a country that is home to so many cultures, there's no excuse.

Isma (Thirty-Six-Year-Old Algerian)

The girls who veil in France, especially in the high school and junior high students, it's first of all a question of identity, because these girls are born in France to foreign parents. . . . At a given time an adolescent wants to affirm himself, so he thinks, I'd say, he thinks that it's by his clothes that he shows that he comes from somewhere, that he's from someone. So then, I think you should let them do it, and afterwards, by themselves, people come back to who they really are.

What were the perspectives of the French president and the French Muslim women who were interviewed? How do they differ? Do you think there might be a way to reconcile the opposing positions? Why or why not?

Source: French President Jacques Chirac on Secularism in French Society. North African Women in France Respond to the Headscarf Ban. Caitlin Killian, *Gender and Society* Vol. 17, No. 4, pp. 567–590, copyright 2003 by SAGE Publications. Reprinted by permission of SAGE Publications.

> the memory of a lost home or the hope of a promised land. This divorce between man and his life, the actor and his setting, is properly the feeling of absurdity.[4]

According to Camus, then, the world was absurd and without meaning; humans, too, are without meaning and purpose. Reduced to despair and depression, humans have but one source of hope—themselves.

POSTMODERNISM The term *Postmodern* covers a variety of intellectual and artistic styles and ways of thinking that have been prominent since the 1970s. In the broadest sense, **Postmodernism** rejects the modern Western belief in an objective truth and instead focuses on the relative nature of reality and knowledge.

While existentialists wrestled with notions of meaning and existence, a group of French philosophers in the 1960s attempted to understand how meaning and knowledge operate through the study of language and signs. **Poststructuralism,** or **deconstruction**, formulated by Jacques Derrida (ZHAHK DEH-ree-duh) (1930–2004), holds that culture is created and can therefore be analyzed in a variety of ways, according to the manner in which people create their own meaning. Hence, there is no fixed truth or universal meaning.

Michel Foucault (mih-SHELL foo-KOH) (1926–1984) drew on Derrida to explore relationships of power. Believing that "power is exercised, rather than possessed," Foucault argued that the diffusion of power and oppression marks all relationships. For example, any act of teaching entails components of assertion and submission, as the student adopts the ideas of the person in power. Therefore, all norms are culturally produced and entail some degree of power struggle.

Postmodernism was also evident in literature. An example is the work of Milan Kundera (MEE-lahn koon-DAYR-uh) (b. 1929). Kundera blended fantasy with realism, using fantasy to examine moral issues while remaining optimistic about the human condition. In his novel *The Unbearable Lightness of Being* (1984), Kundera does not despair because of the political repression in his native Czechoslovakia that he so aptly describes but allows his characters to use love as a way to a better life. The human spirit can be lessened but not destroyed.

Trends in Art

After the war, the United States dominated the art world, much as it did the world of popular culture. New York City replaced Paris as the artistic center of the West. The Guggenheim Museum, the Museum of Modern Art, and the Whitney Museum of Modern Art, together with New York's numerous art galleries, promoted modern art and helped determine artistic tastes throughout much of the world. One of the styles that became synonymous with the emergence of the New York art scene was **Abstract Expressionism**.

Dubbed "action painting" by one critic, Abstract Expressionism was energetic and spontaneous, qualities evident in the enormous canvases of Jackson Pollock (1912–1956). In

© Jake Wyman/Getty Images

© Nightman1965/Dreamstime.com

COMPARATIVE ILLUSTRATION

Green Urbanism. One of the ways that many cities are combating carbon dioxide emissions and promoting urban sustainability is by encouraging the use of bicycles. In Beijing (shown on the left), almost 4 million cyclists use the bicycle as their main form of transportation. In Paris, a public bicycle program, called the *Velib*, short for "free bike," began in 2007, with 10,000 bicycles and 700 rental stations. Today, the program has 17,000 bikes and approximately 1,200 rental stations where visitors and citizens can rent a bike by the hour, as shown on the right.

How do you account for the success of the Velib program?

such works as *Lavender Mist* (1950), paint seems to explode, enveloping the viewer with emotion and movement. Pollock's swirling forms and seemingly chaotic patterns broke all conventions of form and structure. Inspired by Native American sand painters, Pollock painted with the canvas on the floor. He explained, "On the floor I am more at ease. I feel nearer, more a part of the painting, since this way I can walk around it, work from four sides and be literally in the painting. When I am in the painting, I am not aware of what I am doing. There is pure harmony."

Postmodernism's eclectic commingling of past tradition with Modernist innovation was especially evident in architecture. Robert Venturi argued that architects should look for inspiration as much to the Las Vegas Srip as to the historical styles of the past. The work of Charles Moore (1929–1993) provides an example. His *Piazza d'Italia* (1976–1980) in New Orleans is an outdoor plaza that combines Classical Roman columns with stainless steel and neon lights. This blending of modern-day materials with historical references distinguished the Postmodern architecture of the late 1970s and 1980s from the Modernist glass box.

Throughout the 1980s and 1990s, the art and music industries increasingly adopted the techniques of marketing and advertising. With large sums of money invested in painters and musicians, pressure mounted to achieve critical and commercial success. Negotiating the distinction between art and popular culture was essential since many equated merit with sales or economic value.

In the art world, Neo-Expressionism reached its zenith in the mid-1980s. Neo-Expressionist artists like Anselm Kiefer (AN-selm KEEF-uhr) (b. 1945) became increasingly popular. Born in Germany the year the war ended, Kiefer combines aspects of Abstract Expressionism, collage, and German Expressionism to create stark and haunting works. His *Departure from Egypt* (1984) is a meditation on Jewish history and its descent into the horrors of Nazism. Kiefer hoped that a portrayal of Germany's atrocities could free Germans from their past and bring some good out of evil.

The World of Science and Technology

Many of the scientific and technological achievements since World War II have revolutionized people's lives. During World War II, university scientists were recruited

Industrial Age to the Technological Age" on p. 757). One product of this alliance—the computer—may prove to be the most revolutionary of all the technological inventions of the twentieth century. Early computers were large and hot and took up considerable space. The transistor and then the silicon chip revolutionized computer design. With the invention of the microprocessor in 1971, the road was open for the development of the personal computer. By the 1990s, the personal computer had become a fixture in businesses, schools, and homes.

Despite the marvels produced by science and technology, some people have come to question the assumption that the ability to manipulate the environment that scientific knowledge provides is always beneficial. They maintain that some technological advances have far-reaching side effects that are damaging to the environment. Chemical fertilizers, for example, once touted for producing larger crops, have wreaked havoc with the ecological balance of streams, rivers, and woodlands.

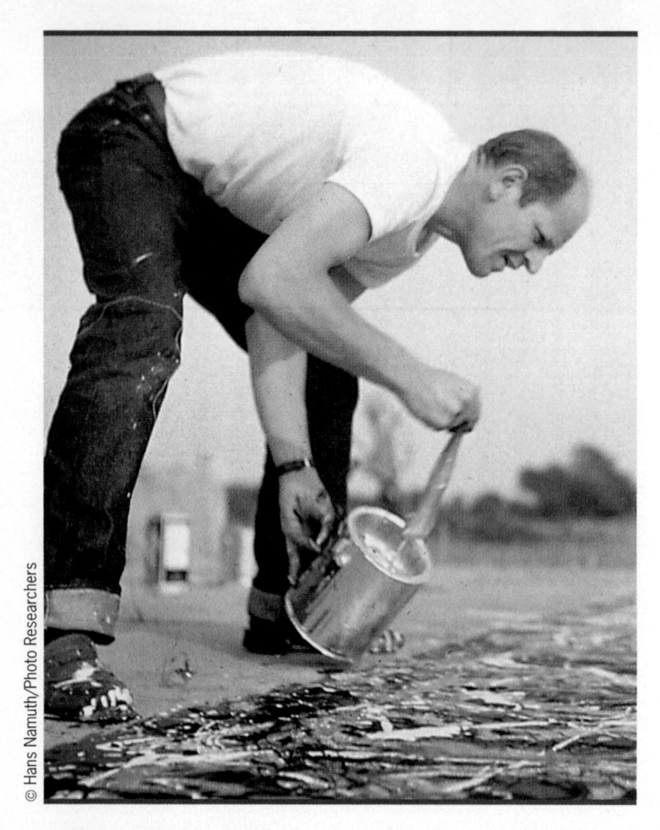

© Hans Namuth/Photo Researchers

Jackson Pollock at Work. After World War II, Abstract Expressionism moved to the center of the artistic mainstream. One of its best-known practitioners was Jackson Pollock, who achieved his ideal of total abstraction in his drip paintings. He is shown here at work at his Long Island studio. Pollock found it easier to cover his large canvases with exploding patterns of color when he put them on the floor.

to work for their governments and develop new weapons and practical instruments of war. British physicists played a crucial role in developing an improved radar system that helped defeat the German air force in the Battle of Britain in 1940. German scientists created self-propelled rockets as well as jet airplanes to keep Hitler's hopes alive for a miraculous turnaround in the war. The computer, too, was a wartime creation. The British mathematician Alan Turing designed a primitive computer to assist British intelligence in breaking the secret codes of German ciphering machines. The most famous product of wartime scientific research was the atomic bomb, created by a team of American and European scientists under the guidance of the physicist J. Robert Oppenheimer. Though created for destructive purposes, many wartime developments such as computers and nuclear energy were soon adapted for peacetime uses.

The postwar alliance of science and technology led to an accelerated rate of change that became a fact of life in Western society (see the comparative essay "From the

The Explosion of Popular Culture

Since 1900, and especially since World War II, popular culture has played an important role in helping Western people define themselves. It also reflects the economic system that supports it, for this system manufactures, distributes, and sells the images that people consume as popular culture. Thus, modern popular culture is inextricably tied to the mass consumer society in which it has emerged.

The United States has been the most influential force in shaping popular culture in the West and, to a lesser degree, the entire world. Through movies, music, advertising, and television, the United States has spread its particular form of consumerism and the American dream to millions around the world. In 1923, the *New York Morning Post* noted that "the film is to America what the flag was once to Britain. By its means Uncle Sam may hope some day . . . to Americanize the world."[5] That day has already come.

Motion pictures were the primary vehicle for the diffusion of American popular culture in the years immediately following World War I and continued to find ever wider markets as the century rolled on. Television, developed in the 1930s, did not become readily available until the late 1940s, but by 1954, there were 32 million sets in the United States as television became the centerpiece of middle-class life. In the 1960s, as television spread around the world, American networks unloaded their products on Europe and the Third World at extraordinarily low prices.

The United States has also dominated popular music since the end of World War II. Jazz, blues, rhythm and blues, rap, and rock and roll have been by far the most popular music forms in the Western world—and much of the non-Western world—during this time. All of them

COMPARATIVE ESSAY

From the Industrial Age to the Technological Age

As many observers have noted, the world economy is in transition to a "postindustrial age" that is both increasingly global and technology-intensive. Since World War II, an array of technological changes—especially in transportation, communications, medicine, and agriculture—have transformed the world. These changes have also raised new questions and concerns. Some scientists worry that genetic engineering might accidentally result in new strains of deadly bacteria. Some doctors warn that the overuse of antibiotics has created supergerms that are resistant to antibiotic treatment. Technological advances have also led to more deadly methods of destruction, including nuclear weapons.

The advent of the postindustrial world, which the futurologist Alvin Toffler has dubbed the Third Wave (the first two being the Agricultural and Industrial Revolutions), has led to difficulties for many people. They include blue-collar workers, whose jobs have disappeared as factories have moved abroad to use lower-cost labor; the poor and uneducated, who lack the technical skills to handle complex tasks; and even members of the middle class, who have lost their jobs as employers outsource jobs to compete in the global marketplace.

© Adastra/Getty Images

The Technological Age. A communication satellite is seen orbiting above the earth.

It is now increasingly clear that the Technological Revolution, like the Industrial Revolution that preceded it, will entail enormous consequences. The success of advanced capitalist states in the postwar era has been built on a consensus on the importance of two propositions: (1) the need for high levels of government investment in education, communications, and transportation and (2) the desirability of maintaining open markets for the free exchange of goods.

Today, these assumptions are increasingly under attack as citizens refuse to vote for the tax increases required to support education and oppose the formation of trading alliances to promote the free movement of goods and labor across national borders. The breakdown of the public consensus raises serious questions about whether the coming challenges of the Third Wave can be successfully met without a rise in political and social tension.

What is implied by the term Third Wave, *and what challenges does the Third Wave present to humanity?*

originated in the United States, and all are rooted in African American musical innovations. These forms later spread to the rest of the world, inspiring local artists, who then transformed the music in their own ways.

The introduction of the video music channel MTV in the early 1980s radically changed the music scene by making image as important as sound in the selling of records. Artists like Michael Jackson and Madonna became superstars by treating the music video as an art form. Rather than merely a recorded performance, many videos were short films with elaborate staging and special effects set to music.

In the postwar years, sports have become a major product of both popular culture and the leisure industry. Satellite television and various electronic breakthroughs have helped make sports a global phenomenon. Olympic Games can now be broadcast around the globe from anywhere in the world. In 2010, approximately 715 million people, or one out of every ten people in the world, watched the World Cup championship match. Sports have become a cheap form of entertainment, as fans do not have to leave their homes to enjoy athletic competitions. Many sports now receive the bulk of their yearly revenue from television contracts.

CHAPTER SUMMARY

Western Europe reinvented itself in the 1950s and 1960s as a remarkable economic recovery fostered a new optimism. Western European states embraced political democracy, and with the development of the European Community, many of them began to move toward economic unity. A new European society also emerged after World War II. White-collar workers increased in number, and installment plan buying helped create a consumer society. The welfare state provided both pensions and health care. Birth control led to smaller families, and more women joined the workforce.

Although many people were optimistic about a "new world order" after the collapse of communism, uncertainties still prevailed. Germany was successfully reunited, and the European Union adopted a common currency in the euro. Yugoslavia, however, disintegrated into warring states that eventually all became independent, and ethnic groups that had once been forced to live under distinct national banners began rebelling to form autonomous states. Although some were successful, others were brutally repressed.

In the Western Hemisphere, the United States and Canada built prosperous economies and relatively stable communities in the 1950s, but there, too, new problems, including ethnic, racial, and linguistic differences, along with economic difficulties, dampened the optimism of earlier decades. Although some Latin American nations shared in the economic growth of the 1950s and 1960s, it was not accompanied by political stability. Not until the 1980s did democratic governments begin with consistency to replace oppressive military regimes.

While the "new world order" was fitfully developing, other challenges emerged. The arrival of many foreigners, especially in Western Europe, not only strained the social services of European countries but also led to anti-foreign sentiment. Environmental abuses led to growing threats not only to Europeans but also to all humans. Terrorism, especially that perpetrated by some parts of the Muslim world, emerged as a threat to many Western states. Since the end of World War II, terrorism seems to have replaced communism as the number one enemy of the West. At the beginning of the twenty-first century, a major realization has been the recognition that the problems afflicting the Western world have become global problems.

CHAPTER TIMELINE

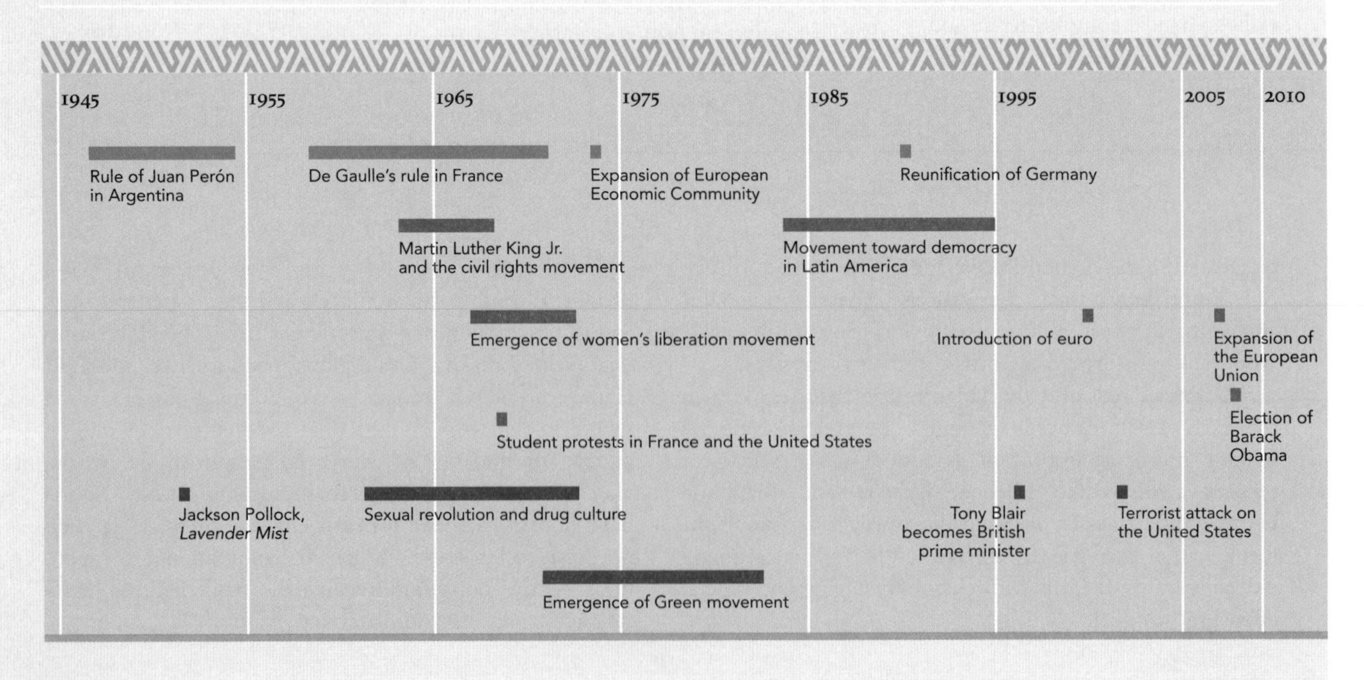

Upon Reflection

Q What were the major successes and failures of the Western European democracies between 1945 and 2010?

Q What directions did Eastern European nations take after they became free from Soviet control? Why did they react as they did?

Q What role did popular culture play in the Western world after 1945?

Key Terms

welfare state (p. 736)
ethnic cleansing (p. 738)
consumer society (p. 747)
permissive society (p. 748)
women's liberation movement (p. 749)
guest workers (p. 751)
existentialism (p. 752)
Postmodernism (p. 754)
Poststructuralism, or deconstruction (p. 754)
Abstract Expressionism (p. 754)

Suggested Reading

EUROPE SINCE 1945 For a well-written survey on Europe since 1945, see **T. Judt, *Postwar: A History of Europe Since 1945*** (New York, 2005). See also **W. I. Hitchcock, *The Struggle for Europe: The Turbulent History of a Divided Continent, 1945–2002*** (New York, 2002). On the building of common institutions in Western Europe, see **S. Henig, *The Uniting of Europe: From Discord to Concord*** (London, 1997). On Eastern Europe, see **P. Kenney, *The Burden of Freedom: Eastern Europe Since 1989*** (London, 2006).

THE UNITED STATES AND CANADA For a general survey of U.S. history since 1945, see **W. H. Chafe, *Unfinished Journey: America Since World War II*** (Oxford, 2006). More detailed accounts can be found in two volumes by **J. T. Patterson** in the Oxford History of the United States series: ***Grand Expectations: The United States, 1945–1974*** (Oxford, 1997) and ***Restless Giant: The United States from Watergate to Bush v. Gore*** (Oxford, 2005). Information on Canada can be found in **C. Brown, ed., *The Illustrated History of Canada,*** 4th ed. (Toronto, 2003).

LATIN AMERICA For general surveys of Latin American history, see **M. C. Eakin, *The History of Latin America: Collision of Cultures*** (New York, 2007), and **E. Bradford Burns** and **J. A. Charlip, *Latin America: An Interpretive History,*** 8th ed. (Upper Saddle River, N.J., 2007). The twentieth century is the focus of **T. E. Skidmore** and **P. H. Smith, *Modem Latin America,*** 6th ed. (Oxford, 2004).

SOCIETY IN THE WESTERN WORLD On the turbulent 1960s, see **A. Marwick, *The Sixties: Social and Cultural Transformation in Britain, France, Italy, and the United States*** (Oxford, 1999). On the sexual revolution of the 1960s, see **D. Allyn, *Make Love, Not War: The Sexual Revolution—An Unfettered History*** (New York, 2000).

The changing role of women is examined in **R. Rosen, *The World Split Open: How the Modern Women's Movement Changed America*** (New York, 2001). On terrorism, see **C. E. Simonsen** and **J. R. Spendlove, *Terrorism Today: The Past, the Players, the Future,*** 3rd ed. (Upper Saddle River, N.J., 2006). The problems of guest workers and immigrants are examined in **W. Laqueur, *The Last Days of Europe: Epitaph for an Old Continent*** (New York, 2007).

WESTERN CULTURE SINCE 1945 For a general view of postwar thought and culture, see **J. A. Winders, *European Culture Since 1848: From Modern to Postmodern and Beyond,*** rev. ed. (New York, 2001). On Postmodernism, see **C. Butler, *Postmodernism: A Very Short Introduction*** (Oxford, 2002). On the arts, see **A. Marwick, *Arts in the West Since 1945*** (Oxford, 2002).

Visit the CourseMate website at **www.cengagebrain.com** for additional study tools and review materials for this chapter.

Challenges of Nation Building in Africa and the Middle East

© Patrick Robert/Sygma/CORBIS

Answering the call of the muezzin

CHAPTER OUTLINE AND FOCUS QUESTIONS

Uhuru: The Struggle for Independence in Africa

Q What role did nationalist movements play in the transition to independence in Africa, and how did such movements differ from their counterparts elsewhere?

The Era of Independence

Q How have dreams clashed with realities in the independent nations of Africa, and how have African governments sought to meet these challenges?

Continuity and Change in Modern African Societies

Q How did the rise of independent states affect the lives and the role of women in African societies? How does that role compare with the role played by women in other parts of the contemporary world?

Crescent of Conflict

Q What problems have the nations of the Middle East faced since the end of World War II, and to what degree have they managed to resolve those problems?

Society and Culture in the Contemporary Middle East

Q How have religious issues affected economic, social, and cultural conditions in the Middle East in recent decades?

CRITICAL THINKING

Q What factors can be advanced to explain the chronic instability and internal conflict that have characterized conditions in Africa and the Middle East since World War II?

BY THE END OF World War II, many societies in Asia and Africa had endured more than half a century of colonial rule. Although Europeans complacently assumed that colonialism was a necessary step in the process of introducing civilization to "backward" peoples around the globe, many of their colonial subjects disagreed. Some even argued that the Western drive for political hegemony and economic profit, far from being a panacea for the world's ills, was a plague that threatened ultimately to destroy human civilization.

One of the aspects of Western civilization that some thoughtful Asians and Africans rejected was the concept of the nation-state as the natural unit of communal identity in the modern world. In their view, nationalism was at the root of many of the evils of the twentieth century and should be abandoned as a model for development in the postwar period. In Africa, some intellectuals pointed to the traditional village community as a unique symbol of the humanistic and spiritual qualities of the people; they felt that the village might serve as a common bond that would knit all the peoples of the continent into a cohesive African community. The nation-state was similarly repudiated by some observers in the Middle East, where many Muslims viewed Western materialist culture as a threat to the fundamental principles of Islam. To fend off the new threat from their old adversary, some leaders dreamed of resurrecting the concept of a global caliphate (see Chapter 7) to unify all Muslim peoples and allow them to pursue their common destiny throughout the Islamic world.

Time has not been kind to such dreams of transnational solidarity and cooperation in the postwar world. Although the peoples of Africa and the Middle East were gradually liberated from the formal trappings of European authority, most political elites in both regions adopted the model of the nation-state with enthusiasm. The results have been mixed, and sometimes costly. Political inexperience and continued European economic domination have frustrated efforts to achieve political stability. At the same time, arbitrary boundaries imposed by the colonial powers, in combination with ethnic and religious divisions, have led to bitter conflicts that undermine attempts to realize the dream of solidarity and cooperation. Today, these two regions, although blessed with enormous potential, are among the most volatile and conflict-ridden areas in the world.

Uhuru: The Struggle for Independence in Africa

FOCUS QUESTION: What role did nationalist movements play in the transition to independence in Africa, and how did such movements differ from their counterparts elsewhere?

In the three decades following the end of World War II, the peoples of Africa were gradually liberated from the formal trappings of European colonialism.

The Colonial Legacy

As in Asia, colonial rule had a mixed impact on the societies and peoples of Africa (see Chapter 21). The Western presence brought a number of short-term and long-term benefits to Africa, such as improved transportation and communication facilities, and in a few areas laid the foundation for a modern industrial and commercial sector. Improved sanitation and medical care increased life expectancy. Yet the benefits of colonialism were distributed very unequally, and the vast majority of Africans found their lives little improved, if at all. Most Africans continued to be subsistence farmers growing food for their own consumption. Only South Africa and French-held Algeria developed modern industrial sectors, extensive railroad networks, and modern communications systems. In both countries, European settlers were numerous, most investment capital for industrial ventures was European, and whites constituted almost the entire professional and managerial class. Members of the indigenous population were generally restricted to unskilled or semiskilled jobs at wages less than one-fifth those enjoyed by Europeans.

The Rise of Nationalism

Political organizations for African rights did not arise until after World War I, and then only in a few areas, such as British-ruled Kenya and the Gold Coast. After World War II, following the example of independence movements elsewhere, groups organized political parties with independence as their objective. In the Gold Coast, Kwame Nkrumah (KWAH-may en-KROO-muh) (1909–1972) led the Convention People's Party, the first formal political party in black Africa. In the late 1940s, Jomo Kenyatta (JOH-moh ken-YAHT-uh) (1894–1978) founded the Kenya African National Union (KANU), which focused on economic issues but had an implied political agenda as well.

For the most part, these political activities were basically nonviolent and were led by Western-educated African intellectuals. Their constituents were primarily urban professionals, merchants, and members of labor unions. But the demand for independence was not entirely restricted to the cities. In Kenya, for example, the widely publicized Mau Mau (MOW MOW ["ow" as in "how"]) movement among the Kikuyu (ki-KOO-yoo) people used guerrilla tactics as an essential element of its program to achieve ***uhuru*** (oo-HOO-roo) (Swahili for "freedom") from the British. Although most of the violence was directed against other Africans, the specter of a nationwide revolt alarmed the European population and convinced the British government in 1959 to promise eventual independence.

In areas such as South Africa and Algeria, where the political system was dominated by European settlers, the transition to independence was equally complicated. In South Africa, political activity by local Africans began with the formation of the African National Congress (ANC) in 1912. Initially, the ANC was dominated by

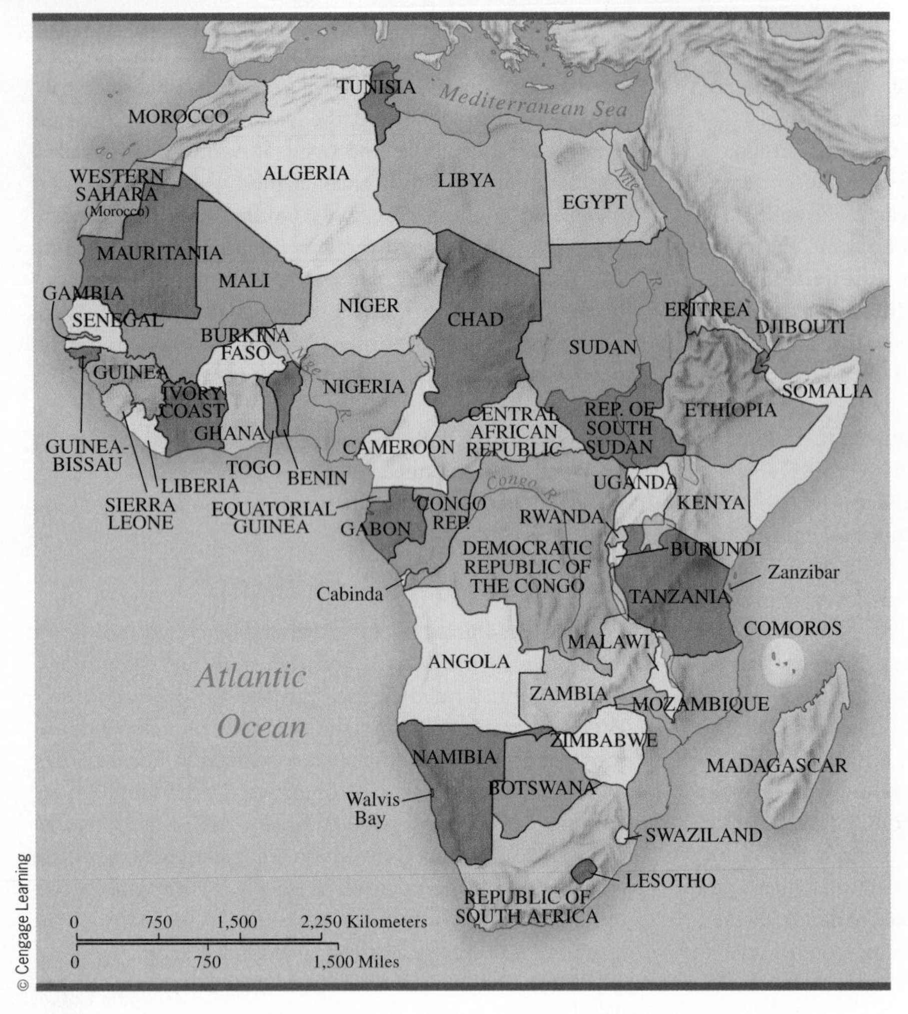

© Cengage Learning

MAP 29.1 Modern Africa. This map shows the independent states in Africa today.

Q *Why was unity so difficult to achieve in African regions?*

Western-oriented intellectuals and had limited mass support. Its goal was to achieve economic and political reforms, including full equality for educated Africans, within the framework of the existing system. But the ANC's efforts met with little success, while conservative white parties managed to stiffen the segregation laws and impose a policy of full legal segregation, called **apartheid** (uh-PAHRT-hyt), in 1948. In response, the ANC became increasingly radicalized, and by the 1950s, the prospects for a violent confrontation were growing.

In Algeria, resistance to French rule by Berbers and Arabs in rural areas had never ceased. After World War II, urban agitation intensified, leading to a widespread rebellion in the mid-1950s. At first, the French government tried to maintain its authority in Algeria. But when Charles de Gaulle became president in 1958, he reversed French policy, and Algeria became independent under President Ahmad Ben Bella (AH-muhd ben BELL-uh) (1918–2004) in 1962. The armed struggle in Algeria hastened the transition to statehood in its neighbors as well. Tunisia won its independence in 1956 after some urban agitation and rural unrest but retained close ties with Paris. The French attempted to suppress the nationalist movement in Morocco by sending Sultan Muhammad V into exile, but the effort failed; in 1956, he returned as the ruler of the independent state of Morocco.

Most black African nations achieved their independence in the late 1950s and 1960s, beginning with the Gold Coast, now renamed Ghana, in 1957 (see Map 29.1). It was soon followed by Nigeria; the Belgian Congo, renamed Zaire (zah-EER) and then the Democratic Republic of the Congo; Kenya; Tanganyika (tang-an-YEE-kuh), later joined with Zanzibar (ZAN-zi-bar) and renamed Tanzania (tan-zuh-NEE-uh); and several other countries. Most of the French colonies agreed to accept independence within the framework of de Gaulle's French Community. By the late 1960s, only parts of southern Africa and the Portuguese possessions of Mozambique and Angola remained under European rule.

The Era of Independence

FOCUS QUESTION: How have dreams clashed with realities in the independent nations of Africa, and how have African governments sought to meet these challenges?

The newly independent African states faced intimidating challenges. Although Western political institutions, values, and technology had been introduced, at least in the cities, the exposure to European civilization had been superficial at best for most Africans and tragic for many. At the outset of independence, most African societies were still primarily agrarian and traditional, and their modern sectors depended mainly on imports from the West.

The Destiny of Africa: Unity or Diversity?

Like their counterparts in South and Southeast Asia, most African leaders came from the urban middle class. They had studied in either Europe or the United States and spoke and read European languages. Although most were profoundly critical of colonial policies, they appeared to accept the relevance of the Western model to Africa and gave at least lip service to Western democratic values.

Their views on economics were somewhat more diverse. Some, like Jomo Kenyatta of Kenya and General Mobutu Sese Seko (moh-BOO-too SES-ay SEK-oh) (1930–1997) of Zaire, were advocates of Western-style capitalism. Others, like Julius Nyerere (ny-REHR-ee) (1922–1999) of Tanzania, Kwame Nkrumah of Ghana, and Sekou Touré (say-KOO too-RAY) (1922–1984) of Guinea, preferred an "African form of socialism," which bore slight resemblance to the Marxist-Leninist socialism practiced in the Soviet Union. According to its advocates, it was descended from traditional communal practices in precolonial Africa.

At first, most of the new African leaders accepted the national boundaries established during the colonial era. But as we have seen, these boundaries were artificial creations of the colonial powers. Virtually all of the new states included widely diverse ethnic, linguistic, and territorial groups. Zaire, for example, was composed of more than two hundred territorial groups speaking seventy-five different languages. Such conditions posed a severe challenge to the task of forming cohesive nation-states.

A number of leaders—including Nkrumah of Ghana, Touré of Guinea, and Nyerere of Tanganyika—were enticed by **pan-Africanism**, the concept of a continental unity that transcended national boundaries. Nkrumah in particular hoped that a pan-African union could be established that would unite all of the new countries of the continent in a broader community. His dream was not widely shared by other African political figures, however, who eventually settled on a more innocuous concept of regional cooperation on key issues. The concrete manifestation of this idea was the Organization of African Unity (OAU), founded in Addis Ababa (AH-diss AH-bah-buh) in 1963.

Dream and Reality: Political and Economic Conditions in Independent Africa

The program of the OAU called for an Africa based on freedom, equality, justice, and dignity and on the unity, solidarity, prosperity, and territorial integrity of African states. It did not take long for reality to set in. Vast disparities in education and wealth made it hard to establish material prosperity in much of Africa. Expectations that independence would lead to stable political structures based on "one person, one vote" were soon disappointed as the initial phase of pluralistic governments gave way to a series of military regimes and one-party states. Between 1957 and 1982, more than seventy leaders of African countries were overthrown by violence, and the pace has not abated in recent years.

THE PROBLEM OF NEOCOLONIALISM Part of the problem could be (and was) ascribed to the lingering effects of colonialism. Most new countries in Africa were dependent on the export of a single crop or natural resource. When prices fluctuated or dropped, these countries were at the mercy of the vagaries of the international market. In several cases, the resources were still controlled by foreigners, leading to the charge that colonialism had been succeeded by **neocolonialism**, in which Western domination was maintained primarily by economic rather than by political or military means. To make matters worse, most African states had to import technology and manufactured goods from the West, and the prices of those goods rose more rapidly than those of the export products.

The new states contributed to their own problems. Scarce national resources were squandered on military equipment or expensive consumer goods rather than used to create the infrastructure needed to provide the foundation for an industrial economy. Corruption, a painful reality throughout the modern world, became almost a way of life in Africa as bribery became necessary to obtain even the most basic services (see the box on p. 764).

AFRICA IN THE COLD WAR Many of the problems encountered by the new nations of Africa were also ascribed to the fact that independence did not bring an end to Western interference in Africa's political affairs. Many African leaders were angered when Western powers led by the United States conspired to overthrow the left-leaning politician Patrice Lumumba (put-TREES loo-MOOM-buh) (1925–1961) in the Congo in the early 1960s. Lumumba, who had been educated in the Soviet Union, aroused fears in Washington that he might promote Soviet influence in Central Africa (see Chapter 26). Eventually, he was assassinated under mysterious circumstances.

The episode was a major factor influencing African leaders to form the OAU as a means of reducing Western influence on the continent, but the strategy achieved few results. Although many African leaders agreed to adopt a neutral stance in the Cold War, competition between Moscow and Washington throughout the region was fierce, often undermining the efforts of fragile

Stealing the Nation's Riches

After 1965, African novelists transferred their anger from the foreign oppressor to their own national leaders, deploring their greed, corruption, and inhumanity. One of the most pessimistic expressions of this betrayal of newly independent Africa is found in *The Beautiful Ones Are Not Yet Born*, a novel published by the Ghanaian author Ayi Kwei Armah (AY-yee KWAY AR-mah) in 1968. The author decried the government of Kwame Nkrumah and was unimpressed with the rumors of a military coup, which, he predicted, would simply replace the regime with a new despot and his entourage of "fat men." Ghana today has made significant progress in reducing the level of corruption.

Ayi Kwei Armah, *The Beautiful Ones Are Not Yet Born*

The net had been made in the special Ghanaian way that allowed the really big corrupt people to pass through it. A net to catch only the small, dispensable fellows, trying in their anguished blindness to leap and to attain the gleam and the comfort the only way these things could be done. And the big ones floated free, like all the slogans. End bribery and corruption. Build Socialism. Equality. Shit. A man would just have to make up his mind that there was never going to be anything but despair, and there would be no way of escaping it. . . .

In the life of the nation itself, maybe nothing really new would happen. New men would take into their hands the power to steal the nation's riches and to use it for their own satisfaction. That, of course, was to be expected. New people would use the country's power to get rid of men and women who talked a language that did not flatter them. There would be nothing different in that. That would only be a continuation of the Ghanaian way of life. But here was the real change. The individual man of power now shivering, his head filled with the fear of the vengeance of those he had wronged. For him everything was going to change. And for those like him who had grown greasy and fat singing the praises of their chief, for those who had been getting themselves ready for the enjoyment of hoped-for favors, there would be long days of pain ahead. The flatterers with their new white Mercedes cars would have to find ways of burying old words. For those who had come directly against the old power, there would be much happiness. But for the nation itself there would only be a change of embezzlers and a change of the hunters and the hunted. A pitiful shrinking of the world from those days Teacher still looked back to, when the single mind was filled with the hopes of a whole people. A pitiful shrinking, to days when all the powerful could think of was to use the power of a whole people to fill their own paunches. Endless days, same days, stretching into the future with no end anywhere in sight.

According to Ayi Kwei Armah, who was to blame for conditions in his country? Could the OAU have dealt with situations such as this? Why or why not?

Source: From *The Beautiful Ones Are Not Yet Born* by Ayi Kwei Armah (Heinemann, 1989).

governments to build stable new nations. To make matters worse, African states had difficulty achieving a united position on many issues, and their disagreements left the region vulnerable to external influence and conflict. Border disputes festered in many areas of the continent, and in some cases—as with Morocco and a rebel movement in Western Sahara and between Kenya and Uganda—flared into outright war. In Central Africa, the ambition of Libyan president Muammar Qaddafi (moo-AHM-ahr guh-DAH-fee) (1942–2011) to create a greater Muslim nation in the Sahara led to conflict with neighboring Chad.

THE POPULATION BOMB Finally, rapid population growth crippled efforts to create modern economies. By the 1980s, annual population growth averaged nearly 3 percent throughout Africa, the highest rate of any continent. Drought conditions and the inexorable spread of the Sahara (usually known as *desertification*, caused partly by overcultivation of the land) led to widespread hunger and starvation, first in West African countries such as Niger and Mali and then in Ethiopia, Somalia, and Sudan.

Predictions are that the population of Africa will increase by at least 200 million over the next ten years, but that estimate does not take into account the prevalence of AIDS, which has reached epidemic proportions in Africa. According to a United Nations study, at least 5 percent of the entire population of sub-Saharan Africa is infected with the virus, including a high percentage of the urban middle class. More than 65 percent of the AIDS cases reported around the world are on the continent of Africa. Some observers estimate that without measures to curtail the effects of the disease, it will have a significant impact on several African countries by reducing population growth.

Poverty is widespread in Africa, particularly among the three-quarters of the population still living off the land. Urban areas have grown tremendously, but as in much of Asia, most are surrounded by massive squatter settlements of rural peoples who have fled to the cities in search of a better life. The expansion of the cities has overwhelmed fragile transportation and sanitation systems and led to rising pollution and perpetual traffic jams, while millions are forced to live without running water and electricity. Meanwhile, the fortunate few (all too often government officials on the take) live the high life and emulate the consumerism of the West (in a particularly expressive phrase, the rich in many East African countries are known as *wabenzi*, or "Mercedes-Benz people").

The Search for Solutions

While the problems of nation building described here have to one degree or another afflicted all of the emerging states of Africa, each has sought to deal with the challenge in its own way, sometimes with strikingly different consequences. Some African countries have made dramatic improvements in the past two decades, but others have encountered increasing difficulties. Despite all its shared problems, Africa today remains one of the most diverse regions of the globe.

TANZANIA: AN AFRICAN ROUTE TO SOCIALISM Concern over the dangers of economic inequality inspired a number of African leaders to restrict foreign investment and nationalize the major industries and utilities while promoting democratic ideals and values. Julius Nyerere of Tanzania was the most consistent, promoting the ideals of socialism and self-reliance through his Arusha (uh-ROO-shuh) Declaration of 1967, which set forth the principles for building a socialist society in Africa. Nyerere did not seek to establish a Leninist-style dictatorship of the proletariat in Tanzania, but neither was he a proponent of a multiparty democracy, which in his view would be divisive under the conditions prevailing in Africa:

> Where there is one party—provided it is identified with the nation as a whole—the foundations of democracy can be firmer, and the people can have more opportunity to exercise a real choice, than when you have two or more parties.

To import the Western parliamentary system into Africa, he argued, could lead to violence, since the opposition parties would be viewed as traitors by the majority of the population.[1]

Taking advantage of his powerful political influence, Nyerere placed limitations on income and established village collectives to avoid the corrosive effects of economic inequality and government corruption. Sympathetic foreign countries provided considerable economic aid to assist the experiment, and many observers noted that levels of corruption, political instability, and ethnic strife were lower in Tanzania than in many other African countries. Nyerere's vision was not shared by all of his compatriots, however. Political elements on the island of Zanzibar, citing the stagnation brought by two decades of socialism, agitated for autonomy or even total separation from the mainland. Tanzania also has poor soil, inadequate rainfall, and limited resources, all of which have contributed to its slow growth and continuing rural and urban poverty.

In 1985, Nyerere voluntarily retired from the presidency. In his farewell speech, he confessed that he had failed to achieve many of his ambitious goals to create a socialist society in Africa. But Nyerere insisted that many of his policies had succeeded in improving social and economic conditions, and he argued that the only real solution was to consolidate the multitude of small countries in the region into a larger East African Federation. Today, a quarter of a century later, Nyerere's Party of the Revolution continues to rule the country. The current president, Jakaya Kikwete (jah-KAH-yah kee-KWEH-tee) (b. 1950), was reelected in 2010 by a comfortable margin, although there were charges of electoral fraud.

KENYA: THE PERILS OF CAPITALISM The countries that opted for capitalism faced their own dilemmas. Neighboring Kenya, blessed with better soil in the highlands, a local tradition of aggressive commerce, and a residue of European settlers, welcomed foreign investment and profit incentives. The results have been mixed. Kenya has a strong current of indigenous African capitalism and a substantial middle class, mostly based in the capital, Nairobi (ny-ROH-bee). But landlessness, unemployment, and income inequities are high, even by African standards. The rate of population growth—about 2.5 percent annually—is one of the highest in the world. Almost 80 percent of the population remains rural, and 50 percent of the people live below the poverty line.

Kenya's problems have been exacerbated by chronic disputes between disparate ethnic groups and simmering tensions between farmers and pastoralists. For many years, the country maintained a fragile political stability under the dictatorial rule of President Daniel arap Moi (uh-RHAP moh-YEE) (b. 1924), one of the most authoritarian of African leaders. Plagued by charges of corruption, Moi finally agreed to retire in 2002, but under his successor, Mwai Kibaki (MWY kih-BAH-kee) (b. 1931), the twin problems of political instability and widespread poverty continue to afflict the country. When presidential elections held in 2008 led to a victory for Kibaki's party, opposition elements—angered by the government's perceived favoritism toward Kibaki's Kikuyu constituents—launched numerous protests, and violent riots occurred throughout the country. A fragile truce was eventually put in place, but popular anger at current conditions smolders just beneath the surface.

SOUTH AFRICA: AN END TO APARTHEID Perhaps Africa's greatest success story is South Africa. Under strong international pressure, the white government—which had long maintained a policy of racial segregation (apartheid) and restricted black sovereignty to a series of small "Bantustans" in relatively infertile areas of the country—finally accepted the inevitability of African involvement in the political process and the national economy. In 1990, the government of President Frederik W. de Klerk (b. 1936) released African National Congress leader Nelson Mandela (man-DELL-uh) (b. 1918) from prison, where he had been held since 1964. In 1993, the two leaders agreed to hold democratic national elections the following spring. In the meantime, ANC representatives agreed to take part in a transitional coalition government with de Klerk's National Party. Those elections resulted in a substantial majority for the ANC, and Mandela became president. In May 1996, a new constitution was approved, calling for a multiracial state.

In 1999, a major step toward political stability was taken when Mandela stepped down from the presidency, to be replaced by his long-time disciple Thabo Mbeki (TAH-boh uhm-BAY-kee) (b. 1942). The new president faced a number of intimidating problems, including rising unemployment, widespread lawlessness, chronic corruption, and an ominous flight of capital and professional personnel from the country. Mbeki's conservative economic policies earned the support of some white voters and the country's new black elite but were criticized by labor unions, which contended that the benefits of the new black leadership were not seeping down to the poor. The government's promises to carry out an extensive land reform program—aimed at providing farmland to the nation's 40 million black farmers—were not fulfilled, provoking some squatters to seize unused private lands near Johannesburg. In 2008, disgruntled ANC members forced Mbeki out of office. A year later, his onetime vice president and rival Jacob Zuma (ZOO-muh) (b. 1942) was elected president.

South Africa remains the wealthiest and most industrialized state in Africa and the best hope that a multiracial society can succeed on the continent. The country's black elite now number nearly one-quarter of its wealthiest households, compared with only 9 percent in 1991 (see the comparative illustration on p. 767).

NIGERIA: A NATION DIVIDED If the situation in South Africa provides grounds for modest optimism, the situation in Nigeria provides reason for serious concern. Africa's largest country in terms of population and one of its wealthiest because of substantial oil reserves, Nigeria was for many years in the grip of military strongmen. During his rule, General Sani Abacha (SAH-nee ah-BAH-chuh) (1943–1998) ruthlessly suppressed all opposition and in late 1995 ordered the execution of a writer despite widespread protests from human rights groups abroad. Ken Saro-Wiwa (SAH-roh WEE-wah) (1941–1995) had criticized environmental damage caused by foreign interests in southern Nigeria. When Abacha died in 1998 under mysterious circumstances, national elections led to the creation of a civilian government under Olusegun Obasanjo (ohl-OO-seh-goon oh-buh-SAHN-joh) (b. 1937).

Civilian leadership has not been a panacea for Nigeria's problems, however. Although Obasanjo promised reforms to bring an end to the corruption and favoritism that had long plagued Nigerian politics, the results were disappointing (the state power company—known as NEPA—was so inefficient that Nigerians joked that the initials stood for "never expect power again"). When presidential elections in 2007 led to the election of Umaru Yar'Adua (oo-MAHR-oo YAHR-ah-doo-uh) (b. 1951–2010), an obscure member of Obasanjo's ruling political party, opposition forces and neutral observers complained that the vote had been seriously flawed. After Yar'Adua died from an illness in 2010, he was succeeded by his vice president, Goodluck Jonathan (b. 1957), who was elected president in his own right in 2011.

One of the most critical problems facing the Nigerian government in recent years has its roots in religious disputes. In early 2000, riots between Christians and Muslims broke out in several northern cities as a result of the decision by Muslim provincial officials to apply *Shari'a* throughout their jurisdictions. The violence temporarily abated as local officials managed to craft compromise policies that limited the application of some of the harsher aspects of Muslim law, but periodic clashes between Christians and Muslims continue to threaten the fragile unity of Africa's most populous country.

TENSIONS IN THE DESERT The religious tensions that erupted in Nigeria have spilled over into neighboring states on the border of the Sahara. In the neighboring

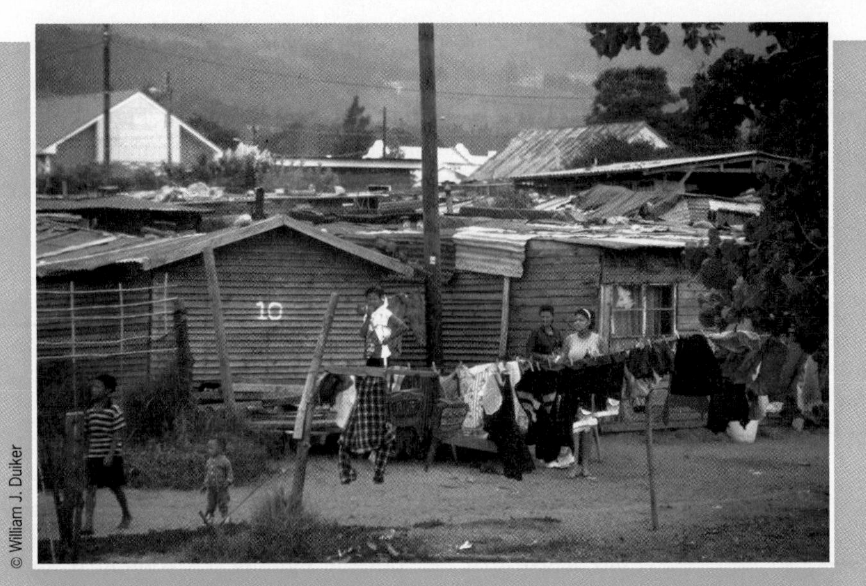

© William J. Duiker

© William J. Duiker

COMPARATIVE ILLUSTRATION

FAMILY & SOCIETY

New Housing for the Poor. Under apartheid, much of the black population in South Africa was confined to so-called townships, squalid slums located along the fringes of the country's major cities. The top photo shows a crowded township on the edge of Cape Town, one of the most modern cities on the continent of Africa. Today, the government is actively building new communities that provide better housing, running water, and electricity for their residents. The photo on the bottom shows a new township on the outskirts of the city of New London. The township has many modern facilities and even a new shopping mall with consumer goods for local residents.

How do the social and economic policies adopted by the current South African government compare with those practiced by the previous ruling class operating under the rule of apartheid?

state of Mali, a radical Islamic group has seized power in the northern part of the country, applying strict punishments on local residents for alleged infractions against *Shari'a* law and destroying Muslim shrines in the historic city of Timbuktu.

A similar rift has been at the root of the lengthy civil war that has been raging in Sudan. Conflict between Muslim pastoralists—supported by the central government in Khartoum—and predominantly Christian black farmers in the southern part of the country raged for years until the government finally agreed to permit a plebiscite in the south under the sponsorship of the United Nations to determine whether the local population there wished to secede from the country. In elections held in early 2011, voters overwhelmingly supported independence as the new nation of the Republic of South Sudan, but clashes along the disputed border continue to provoke tensions.

The dispute between Muslims and Christians throughout the southern Sahara is a contemporary African variant of the traditional tensions that have existed between farmers and pastoralists throughout recorded history. Muslim cattle herders, migrating southward to escape the increasing desiccation of the grasslands south of the Sahara, compete for precious land with primarily Christian farmers. As a result of the religious revival now under way throughout the continent, the confrontation often leads to outbreaks of violence with strong religious and ethnic overtones (see the comparative essay "Religion and Society" on p. 769).

CHRONOLOGY Modern Africa

Ghana gains independence from Great Britain	1957
Algeria gains independence from France	1962
Formation of the Organization of African Unity	1963
Arusha Declaration in Tanzania	1967
Nelson Mandela released from prison	1990
Nelson Mandela elected president of South Africa	1994
Genocide in Central Africa	1996–2000
Olusegun Obasanjo elected president of Nigeria	1999
Civil war in Sudan	2000s
Creation of the African Union	2001
Ethnic riots in Kenya	2008
Jacob Zuma elected president of South Africa	2009
Independence for the Republic of South Sudan	2011

CENTRAL AFRICA: CAULDRON OF CONFLICT The most tragic situation is in the Central African states of Rwanda and Burundi, where a chronic conflict between the minority Tutsis and the Hutu majority has led to a bitter civil war, with thousands of refugees fleeing to the neighboring Congo. The nomadic Tutsis, supported by the colonial Belgian government, had long dominated the sedentary Hutu population. It was the attempt of the Hutus to bring an end to Tutsi domination that initiated the most recent conflicts, marked by massacres on both sides. In the meantime, the presence of large numbers of foreign troops and refugees intensified centrifugal forces inside Zaire, where General Mobutu Sese Seko had long ruled with an iron hand. In 1997, military forces led by Mobutu's longtime opponent Laurent-Désiré Kabila (loh-RAHN-DAY-zee-ray kah-BEE-luh) (1939–2001) managed to topple the general's corrupt government. Once in power, Kabila renamed the country the Democratic Republic of the Congo and promised a return to democratic practices. The new government systematically suppressed political dissent, however, and in January 2001, Kabila was assassinated. He was succeeded by his son, Joseph Kabila (b. 1971). Peace talks to end the conflict began that fall, but the fighting has continued. In elections held in the fall of 2011, Kabila was returned to office after a campaign marked by widespread violence.

© Ruth Petzold

Morning in Timbuktu. The boundary between pastoral and agricultural peoples—the steppe and the sown—has been one of the crucial fault lines in human history. Nowhere is this more true today than in West Africa, where Muslim herders compete with Christian farmers for precious land and water resources. The dispute is at the root of the ethnic and religious conflicts that are now erupting throughout the region. In this photo, a pastoral family greets the new day just outside the historic city of Timbuktu, in the state of Mali.

Africa: A Continent in Flux

The brief survey of events in some of the more important African countries provided here illustrates the enormous difficulty that historians of Africa face in drawing any general conclusions about the pace and scope of change that has taken place in the continent in recent decades. Progress in some areas has been countered by growing problems elsewhere, and signs of hope in one region contrast with feelings of despair in another.

The shifting fortunes experienced throughout the continent are most prominently illustrated in the political arena. Over the past two decades, the collapse of one-party regimes has led to the emergence of fragile democracies in several countries. In other instances, however, democratic governments erupted in civil war or were replaced by authoritarian leaders. One prominent example of the latter is the Ivory Coast, long considered one of West Africa's most stable and prosperous countries. After the death of President Félix Houphouet-Boigny (fay-LEEKS oo-FWAY-

COMPARATIVE ESSAY

Religion and Society

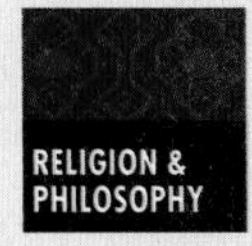

The nineteenth and twentieth centuries witnessed a steady trend toward secularization as people increasingly turned from religion to science for explanations of natural phenomena and for answers to the challenges of everyday life.

In recent years, however, the trend has reversed as religious faith in all its guises appears to be reviving in much of the world. Although the percentage of people regularly attending religious services or professing firm religious convictions has been dropping steadily in many countries, the intensity of religious belief appears to be growing among the faithful. This phenomenon has been widely publicized in the United States, where the evangelical movement has become a significant force in politics and an influential factor in defining many social issues. But it has also occurred in Latin America, where a drop in membership in the Roman Catholic Church has been offset by significant increases in the popularity of evangelical Protestant sects. In the Muslim world, the influence of traditional Islam has been steadily rising, not only in the Middle East but also in non-Arab countries such as Malaysia and Indonesia (see Chapter 30). In Africa, as we observe in this chapter, the appeal of both Christianity and Islam appears to be on the rise. Even in Russia and China, where half a century of Communist government sought to eradicate religion as the "opiate of the people," the popularity of religion is growing.

A major reason for the popularity of religion in contemporary life is the desire to counter the widespread sense of malaise brought on by the absence of any sense of meaning and purpose in life—a purpose that religious faith provides. For many evangelical Christians in the United States, for example, the adoption of a Christian lifestyle is seen as a necessary prerequisite for resolving problems of crime, drugs, and social alienation. It is likely that a similar phenomenon is present with other religions and in other parts of the world. Religious faith also provides a sense of community at a time when village and family ties are declining in many countries.

Historical evidence suggests, however, that although religious fervor may enhance the sense of community and commitment among believers, it can have a highly divisive impact on society as a whole, as the examples of Northern Ireland, Yugoslavia, Africa, and the Middle East vividly attest. Even if less dramatically, as in the United States and Latin America, religion divides as well as unites, and it will be a continuing task for religious leaders of all faiths to promote tolerance for peoples of other persuasions.

Another challenge for contemporary religion is to find ways to coexist with expanding scientific knowledge. Influential figures in the evangelical movement in the United States, for example, not only support a conservative social agenda but are also suspicious of the role of technology and science in the contemporary world. Similar views are often expressed by significant factions in other world religions. Although fear of the impact of science on contemporary life is widespread, efforts to turn the clock back to a mythical golden age are not likely to succeed in the face of powerful forces for change set in motion by advances in scientific knowledge.

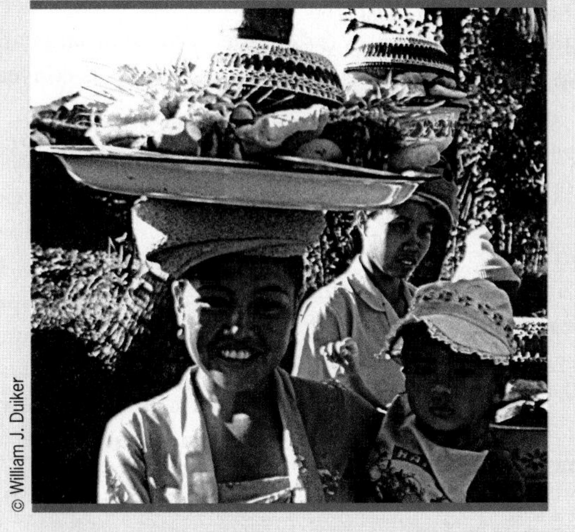

© William J. Duiker

Carrying Food to the Temple. Bali is the only island in Indonesia where the local population adheres to the Hindu faith. Here worshipers carry food to the local temple to be blessed before being consumed.

What are some of the reasons for the growing intensity of religious faith in many parts of the world today?

bwah-NYEE) in 1993, long-simmering resentment between Christians in the south and newly arrived Muslim immigrants in the north erupted into open conflict. National elections held in 2010 led to sporadic violence and a standoff between opposition forces and the sitting president, who was forced to resign the following year. By contrast, in Liberia, a bitter civil war recently gave way to the emergence of a stable democratic government under Ellen Johnson-Sirleaf (b. 1938), one of the continent's first female presidents.

The economic picture in Africa has also been mixed. Most African states are still poor and their populations illiterate. Moreover, African concerns continue to carry little weight in the international community. A recent agreement by the World Trade Organization (WTO) on the need to reduce agricultural subsidies in the advanced nations has been widely ignored. Some observers argue that external assistance cannot succeed unless the nations of Africa adopt measures to bring about good government and sound economic policies.

Despite the African continent's chronic economic problems, however, there are signs of hope. The overall rate of economic growth for the region as a whole is twice what it was during the 1980s and 1990s. African countries were also less affected by the recent economic downturn than was much of the rest of the world. Although poverty, AIDs, and a lack of education and infrastructure are still major impediments in much of the region, rising commodity prices—most notably, an increase in oil revenues—are enabling many countries to make additional investments and reduce their national debt.

THE AFRICAN UNION: A GLIMMER OF HOPE A significant part of the problem is that Africans must find better ways to cooperate with one another and to protect and promote their own interests. A first step in that direction was taken in 1991, when the OAU agreed to establish the African Economic Community (AEC). In 2001, the OAU was replaced by the **African Union**, which is intended to provide greater political and economic integration throughout the continent on the pattern of the European Union (see Chapter 28). The new organization has already sought to mediate several of the conflicts in the region. As Africa evolves, it is useful to remember that economic and political change is often an agonizingly slow and painful process. Introduced to industrialization and concepts of Western democracy only a century ago, African societies are still groping for ways to graft Western political institutions and economic practices onto a structure still significantly influenced by traditional values and attitudes.

Continuity and Change in Modern African Societies

FOCUS QUESTIONS: How did the rise of independent states affect the lives and the role of women in African societies? How does that role compare with the role played by women in other parts of the contemporary world?

In general, the impact of the West has been greater on urban and educated Africans and more limited on their rural and illiterate compatriots. After all, the colonial presence was first and most firmly established in the cities. Many cities, including Dakar, Lagos, Johannesburg, Cape Town, Brazzaville, and Nairobi, are direct products of the colonial experience. Most African cities today look like their counterparts elsewhere in the world. They have high-rise buildings, blocks of residential apartments, wide boulevards, neon lights, movie theaters, and traffic jams.

Education

Europeans introduced modern Western education into Africa in the nineteenth century. At first, the schools concentrated on vocational training, with some instruction in European languages and Western civilization. Eventually, pressure from Africans led to the introduction of professional training, and the first institutes of higher learning were established in the early twentieth century.

With independence, African countries established their own state-run schools. The emphasis was on the primary level, but high schools and universities were established in major cities. The basic objectives have been to introduce vocational training and improve literacy rates. Unfortunately, both funding and trained teachers are scarce in most countries, and few rural areas have schools. As a result, illiteracy remains high, estimated at about 70 percent of the population across the continent. There has been a perceptible shift toward education in the vernacular languages. In West Africa, only about one in four adults is conversant in a Western language.

Urban and Rural Life

The cities are where the African elites live and work. Affluent Africans, like their contemporaries in other developing countries, have been strongly attracted to the glittering material aspects of Western culture. They live in Western-style homes or apartments and eat Western foods stored in Western refrigerators, and those who can afford it drive Western cars. It has been said, not wholly in praise, that there are more Mercedes-Benz automobiles in Nigeria than in Germany, where they are manufactured.

Outside the major cities, where about three-quarters of the continent's inhabitants live, Western influence has had less impact. Millions of people throughout Africa live much as their ancestors did, in thatch huts without modern plumbing and electricity; they farm or hunt by traditional methods, practice time-honored family rituals, and believe in the traditional deities. Even here, however, change is taking place. Slavery has been eliminated, for the most part, although there have been persistent reports of raids by slave traders on defenseless villages in the southern Sudan. Economic need, though, has

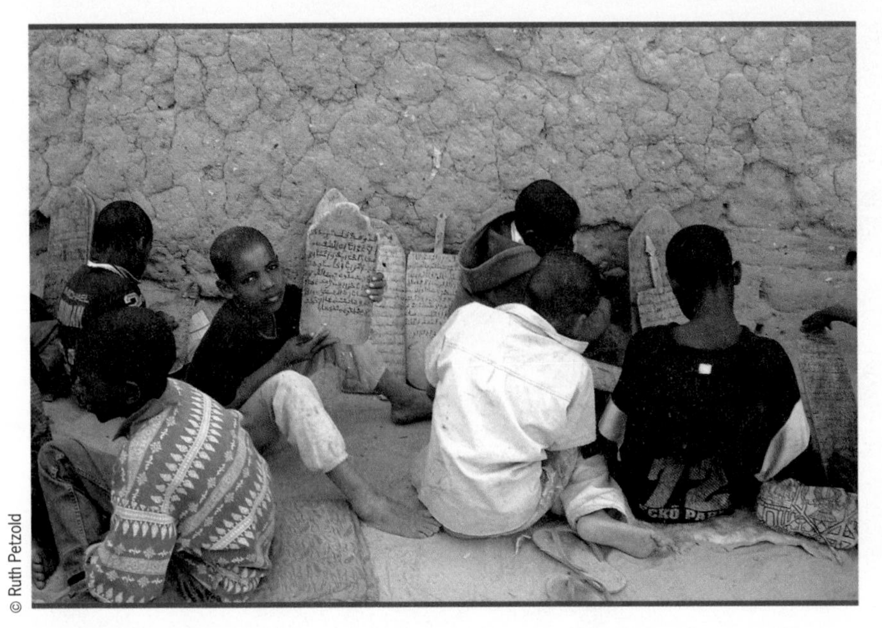

© Ruth Petzold

Learning the ABCs in Niger. Educating the young is one of the most crucial problems for many African societies today. Few governments are able to allocate the funds necessary to meet the challenge, so religious organizations—Muslim or Christian—often take up the slack. In this photo, students at a madrasa—a Muslim school designed to teach the Qur'an—are learning how to read Arabic, the language of Islam's holy scripture. Madrasas are one of the most prominent forms of schooling in Muslim societies in West Africa today.

brought about massive migrations as some leave to work on plantations, others move to the cities, and still others flee abroad or to refugee camps to escape starvation. Migration itself is a wrenching experience, disrupting familiar family and village ties and enforcing new social relationships.

African Women

As noted in Chapter 21, one of the consequences of colonialism in Africa was a change in the relationship between men and women. Some of these changes could be described as beneficial, but others were not. Women were often introduced to Western education and given legal rights denied to them in the precolonial era. But they also became a labor source and were sometime recruited or compelled to work on construction projects.

Independence has had a significant impact on gender roles in African society. Almost without exception, the new governments established the principle of sexual equality and permitted women to vote and run for political office. Yet as elsewhere, women continue to operate at a disability in a world dominated by males. Politics remains a male preserve, and although a few professions, such as teaching, child care, and clerical work, are dominated by women, most African women are employed in menial positions such as agricultural labor, factory work, and retail trade or as domestics. Education is open to all at the elementary level, but women comprise less than 20 percent of students at the upper levels in most African societies today.

URBAN WOMEN Not surprisingly, women have made the greatest strides in the cities. Most urban women, like men, now marry on the basis of personal choice, although a significant minority are still willing to accept their parents' choice. After marriage, African women appear to occupy a more equal position than their counterparts in most Asian countries. Each marriage partner tends to maintain a separate income, and women often have the right to possess property separate from their husbands. While many wives still defer to their husbands in the traditional manner, others are like the woman in Abioseh Nicol's story "A Truly Married Woman," who, after years of living as a common law wife with her husband, is finally able to provide the price and finalize the marriage. After the wedding, she declares, "For twelve years I have got up every morning at five to make tea for you and breakfast. Now I am a truly married woman [and] you must treat me with a little more respect. You are now my husband and not a lover. Get up and make yourself a cup of tea."[2]

WOMEN IN RURAL AREAS In rural areas, where traditional attitudes continue to exert a strong influence, individuals may still be subordinated to communalism. In some societies, female genital mutilation, the traditional rite of passage for a young girl's transit to womanhood, is still widely practiced. Polygamy is also not uncommon, and arranged marriages are still the rule rather than the exception. The dichotomy between rural and urban values can lead to acute tensions. Many African villagers regard the cities as the fount of evil, decadence, and corruption. Women in particular have suffered from the tension between the pull of the city and the village. As men are drawn to the cities in search of employment and excitement, their wives and girlfriends are left behind, both literally and figuratively, in the village.

African Culture

Inevitably, the tension between traditional and modern, indigenous and foreign, and individual and communal

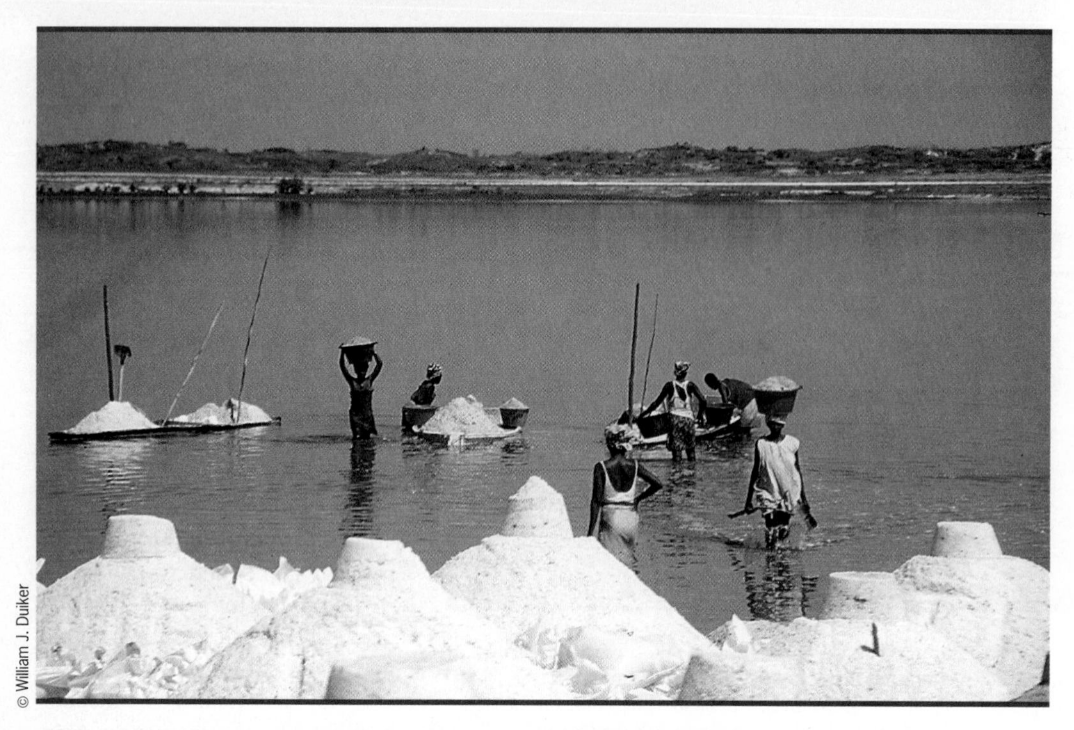

© William J. Duiker

Salt of the Earth. During the precolonial era, many West African societies were forced to import salt from Mediterranean countries in exchange for tropical products and gold. Today, the people of Senegal satisfy their domestic needs by mining salt deposits contained in lakes like this one in the interior of the country. These lakes are the remnants of vast seas that covered the region of the Sahara in prehistoric times. Note that women are doing much of the heavy labor while men hold the managerial positions.

that has permeated contemporary African society has spilled over into culture. In general, in the visual arts and music, utility and ritual have given way to pleasure and decoration. In the process, Africans have been affected to a certain extent by foreign influences but have retained their distinctive characteristics. Wood carving, metalwork, painting, and sculpture, for example, have preserved their traditional forms but are now increasingly adapted to serve the tourist industry and the export market.

LITERATURE Since independence, no area of African culture has been so strongly affected by political and social events as literature. Angry at the negative portrayal of Africa in Western literature, African authors initially wrote primarily for a European audience as a means of establishing black dignity and purpose. Many glorified the emotional and communal aspects of the traditional African experience (see the box on p. 773). The Nigerian Chinua Achebe (CHIN-wah ah-CHAY-bay) (b. 1930) is considered the first major African novelist to write in the English language. In his writings, he attempted to interpret African history from an African perspective and to forge a new sense of African identity. In his trailblazing novel *Things Fall Apart* (1958), he recounted the story of a Nigerian who refused to submit to the new British order and eventually committed suicide. Criticizing his contemporaries who accepted foreign rule, the protagonist lamented that the white man "has put a knife on the things that held us together and we have fallen apart."

In recent decades, the African novel has taken a dramatic turn, shifting its focus from the brutality of the foreign oppressor to the shortcomings of the the continent's indigenous leaders. Having reaped the benefits of independence, African politicians are portrayed as mimicking and even outdoing the injustices committed by their colonial predecessors. A prominent example of this genre is the work of the Kenyan Ngugi Wa Thiong'o (GOO-gee wah tee-AHNG-goh) (b. 1938). His first novel, *A Grain of Wheat*, takes place on the eve of *uhuru*, or independence. Although it mocks the racism, snobbishness, and superficiality of local British society, its chief interest lies in its unsentimental and even unflattering portrayal of ordinary Kenyans in their daily struggle for survival.

Many of Ngugi's contemporaries have followed his lead and focused their frustration on the failure of the continent's new leadership to carry out the goals of independence (see the box on p. 764). One of the most outstanding is the Nigerian Wole Soyinka (woh-LAY soh-YEENK-kuh) (b. 1934). His novel *The Interpreters* (1965) lambasted the corruption and hypocrisy of Nigerian

OPPOSING ≺ VIEWPOINTS

Africa: Dark Continent or Radiant Land?

Colonialism camouflaged its economic objectives under the cloak of a "civilizing mission," which in Africa was aimed at illuminating the so-called Dark Continent with Europe's brilliant civilization. In 1899, the Polish-born English author Joseph Conrad (1857–1924) fictionalized his harrowing journey up the Congo River in the novella *Heart of Darkness*. Conrad's protagonist, Marlow, travels upriver to locate a Belgian trader who has mysteriously disappeared. The novella describes Marlow's gradual recognition of the egregious excesses of colonial rule, as well as his realization that such evil lurks in everyone's heart. The story concludes with a cry: "The horror! The horror!" Voicing views that reflected his Victorian perspective, Conrad described an Africa that was incomprehensible, sensual, and primitive.

Over the years, Conrad's work has provoked much debate. Author Chinua Achebe, for one, lambasted *Heart of Darkness* as a radical diatribe. Since independence, many African writers have been prompted to counter Conrad's portrayal by reaffirming the dignity and purpose of the African people. One of the first to do so was the Guinean author Camara Laye (1928–1980), who in 1954 composed a brilliant novel, *The Radiance of the King,* which can be viewed as the mirror image of Conrad's *Heart of Darkness.* In Laye's work, Clarence, another European protagonist, undertakes a journey into the impenetrable heart of Africa. This time, however, he is enlightened by the process, thereby obtaining self-knowledge and ultimately salvation.

Joseph Conrad, *Heart of Darkness*

We penetrated deeper and deeper into the heart of darkness. It was very quiet there. At night sometimes the roll of drums behind the curtain of trees would run up the river and remain sustained faintly, as if hovering in the air high over our heads, till the first break of day. Whether it meant war, peace, or prayer we could not tell. . . . But suddenly, as we struggled round a bend, there would be a glimpse of rush walls, of peaked grass-roofs, a burst of yells, a whirl of black limbs, a mass of hands clapping, of feet stamping, of bodies swaying, of eyes rolling, under the droop of heavy and motionless foliage. The steamer toiled along slowly on the edge of a black and incomprehensible frenzy. The prehistoric man was cursing us, praying to us, welcoming us—who could tell? We were cut off from the comprehension of our surroundings; we glided past like phantoms, wondering and secretly appalled, as sane men would be before an enthusiastic outbreak in a madhouse.

Camara Laye, *The Radiance of the King*

At that very moment the king turned his head, turned it imperceptibly, and his glance fell upon Clarence. . . .

"Yes, no one is as base as I, as naked as I," he thought. "And you, lord, you are willing to rest your eyes upon me!" Or was it because of his very nakedness? . . . "Because of your very nakedness!" the look seemed to say. "That terrifying void that is within you and which opens to receive me; your hunger which calls to my hunger; your very baseness which did not exist until I gave it leave; and the great shame you feel. . . ."

When he had come before the king, when he stood in the great radiance of the king, still ravaged by the tongue of fire, but alive still, and living only through the touch of that fire, Clarence fell upon his knees, for it seemed to him that he was finally at the end of his seeking, and at the end of all seekings.

Compare the depictions of the continent of Africa in these two passages. Is Laye making a response to Conrad? If so, what is it?

Sources: Joseph Conrad, *Heart of Darkness*. From *Heart of Darkness* by Joseph Conrad. Penguin Books, 1991. Camara Laye, *The Radiance of the King*. From *The Radiance of the King* by Camara Laye, translated from the French by James Kirkup. New York: Vintage, 1989.

politics. Succeeding novels and plays have continued that tradition, resulting in a Nobel Prize for Literature in 1986.

A number of Africa's most prominent writers today are women. Traditionally, African women were valued for their talents as storytellers, but writing was strongly discouraged by both traditional and colonial authorities on the grounds that women should occupy themselves with their domestic obligations. In recent years, however, a number of women have emerged as prominent writers of African fiction. One example is Ama Ata Aidoo (b. 1942) of Ghana, who has focused on the identity of today's African women and the changing relations between men and women in society. In her novel *Changes: A Love Story* (1991), she chronicles the lives of three women, none presented as a victim but all caught up in the struggle for survival and happiness.

What Is the Future of Africa?

Nowhere in the developing world is the dilemma of continuity and change more agonizing than in Africa. Mesmerized by the spectacle of Western affluence yet repulsed by the bloody trail from slavery to World War II and the atomic bombs over Hiroshima and Nagasaki, African intellectuals have been torn between the dual images of Western materialism and African uniqueness. For the average African, of course, such intellectual dilemmas pale before the daily challenge of survival. But the fundamental gap between traditional and modern is perhaps wider in Africa than anywhere else in the world and may well be harder to bridge.

What is the future of Africa? It seems almost foolhardy to seek an answer to such a question, given the degree of ethnic, linguistic, and cultural diversity that exists throughout the vast continent. Not surprisingly, visions of the future are equally diverse. Some Africans still yearn for the dreams embodied in the program of the OAU. Novelist Ngugi Wa Thiong'o calls for "an internationalization of all the democratic and social struggles for human equality, justice, peace, and progress."[3] Others have discarded the democratic ideal and turned their attention to systems based on the subordination of the individual to the community as the guiding principle of national development. Like all peoples, Africans must ultimately find their own solutions within the context of their own traditions, not by seeking to imitate the example of others.

Crescent of Conflict

FOCUS QUESTION: What problems have the nations of the Middle East faced since the end of World War II, and to what degree have they managed to resolve those problems?

"We Muslims are of one family even though we live under different governments and in various regions."[4] So said Ayatollah Ruholla Khomeini (ah-yah-TUL-uh roo-HUL-uh khoh-MAY-nee), the Islamic religious figure and leader of the 1979 revolution that overthrew the shah in Iran. The ayatollah's remark was dismissed by some as just a pious wish by a religious mystic. In fact, however, it illustrates a crucial aspect of the political dynamics in the region.

If the concept of cultural uniqueness represents an alternative to the system of nation-states in Africa, the desire for Muslim unity has played a similar role in the Middle East. In both regions, a yearning for a sense of community beyond national borders tugs at the emotions and intellect of their inhabitants.

A dramatic example of the powerful force of pan-Islamic sentiment took place on September 11, 2001, when Muslim militants hijacked four U.S. airliners and turned them into missiles aimed at the center of world capitalism. The headquarters of the terrorist network that carried out the attack—known as al-Qaeda and led by Osama bin Laden (see Chapter 28)—was located in Afghanistan, but the militants themselves came from several different Muslim states. Although moderate Muslims throughout the world condemned the attack, it was clear that bin Laden and his cohorts had tapped into a wellspring of hostility and resentment directed at much of the Western world.

What were the sources of Muslim anger? In a speech released on videotape shortly after the attack, bin Laden declared that the attacks were a response to the "humiliation and disgrace" that have afflicted the Islamic world for more than eighty years, a period dating back to the end of World War I. For the Middle East, the period between the two world wars was an era of transition. With the fall of the Ottoman and Persian Empires, new modernizing regimes emerged in Turkey and Iran, and a more traditionalist but fiercely independent government was established in Saudi Arabia. Elsewhere, however, European influence was on the ascendant; the British and French had mandates in Syria, Lebanon, Jordan, and Palestine, and British influence persisted in Iraq, in southern Arabia, and throughout the Nile valley.

During World War II, the Middle East became the cockpit of European rivalries, as it had been during World War I. The region was more significant to the warring powers than previously because of the growing importance of oil and the Suez Canal's position as a vital sea route.

The Question of Palestine

The end of World War II led to the emergence of a number of independent states in the Middle East. Jordan, Lebanon, and Syria, all European mandates before the war, became independent. Egypt, Iran, and Iraq, though still under a degree of Western influence, became increasingly autonomous. Sympathy for the idea of Arab unity led to the formation of the Arab League in 1945, but different points of view among its members prevented it from achieving anything of substance.

The one issue on which all Muslim states in the area could agree was the question of Palestine. As tensions between Jews and Arabs in that mandate intensified during the 1930s, the British attempted to limit Jewish immigration into the area and firmly rejected proposals for independence, despite the promise made in the 1917 Balfour Declaration (see Chapter 24).

After World War II ended, the situation drifted rapidly toward crisis, as thousands of Jewish refugees, many of them from displaced persons camps in Europe, sought to migrate to Palestine despite British efforts to prevent their arrival. As violence between Muslims and Jews intensified in the fall of 1947, the issue was taken up in the United Nations General Assembly. After an intense debate, the assembly voted to approve the partition of Palestine into two separate states, one for the Jews and one for the Arabs. The city of Jerusalem was to be placed under international control. A UN commission was established to iron out the details and determine the future boundaries.

During the next several months, growing hostility between Jewish and Arab forces—the latter increasingly supported by neighboring Muslim states—caused the British to announce that they would withdraw their own peacekeeping forces by May 15, 1948. Shortly after the stroke of midnight, as the British mandate formally came to a close, the Zionist leader David Ben-Gurion (ben-GOOR-ee-uhn) (1886–1973) announced the independence of the state of Israel. Later that same day, the new state was formally recognized by the United States, while military forces from several neighboring Muslim states—all of which had vigorously opposed the formation of a Jewish state in the region—entered Israeli territory but were beaten back. Thousands of Arab residents of the new state fled. Internal dissonance among the Arabs, combined with the strength of Jewish resistance groups, contributed to the failure of the invasion, but the bitterness between the two sides did not subside. The Muslim states refused to recognize the new state of Israel, which became a member of the United Nations, legitimizing it in the eyes of the rest of the world. The stage for future conflict was set.

The exodus of thousands of Palestinian refugees into neighboring Muslim states had repercussions that are still felt today. Jordan, which had become an independent kingdom under its Hashemite (HASH-uh-myt) ruler, was flooded by the arrival of a million urban Palestinians, overwhelming its own half million people, most of whom were Bedouins. To the north, the state of Lebanon had been created to provide the local Christian community with a country of their own, but the arrival of the Palestinian refugees upset the delicate balance between Christians and Muslims. Moreover, the creation of Lebanon had angered the Syrians, who had lost that land as well as other territories to Turkey as a result of European decisions before and after the war.

Nasser and Pan-Arabism

The dispute over Palestine placed Egypt in an uncomfortable position. Technically, Egypt was not an Arab state. King Farouk (fuh-ROOK) (1920–1965), who had acceded to power in 1936, had frequently declared support for the Arab cause, but the Egyptian people were not Bedouins and shared little of the culture of the peoples across the Red Sea. In 1952, King Farouk, whose corrupt habits had severely eroded his early popularity, was overthrown by a military coup engineered by young military officers who abolished the monarchy and established a republic.

In 1954, one of those officers, Colonel Gamal Abdul Nasser (guh-MAHL AB-dool NAH-sur) (1918–1970), seized power in his own right and immediately instituted a land reform program. He also adopted a policy of neutrality in foreign affairs and expressed sympathy for the Arab cause. The British presence had rankled many Egyptians for years, for even after granting Egypt independence, Britain had retained control over the Suez Canal to protect its route to the Indian Ocean. In 1956, Nasser suddenly nationalized the Suez Canal Company, which had been under British and French administration. Seeing a threat to their route to the Indian Ocean, the British and the French launched a joint attack on Egypt to protect their investment. They were joined by Israel, whose leaders had grown exasperated at sporadic Arab commando raids on Israeli territory and now decided to strike back. But the Eisenhower administration in the United States, concerned that the attack smacked of a revival of colonialism, supported Nasser and brought about the withdrawal of foreign forces from Egypt and of Israeli troops from the Sinai peninsula.

THE UNITED ARAB REPUBLIC Nasser now turned to **pan-Arabism**. In 1958, Egypt united with Syria as the United Arab Republic (UAR). The union had been proposed by the Ba'ath (BAHTH) Party, which advocated the unity of all Arab states in a new socialist society. Nasser was named president of the new state.

Egypt and Syria hoped that the union would eventually include all Arab states, but other Arab leaders, including young King Hussein (1935–1999) of Jordan and the kings of Iraq and Saudi Arabia, were suspicious. The latter two in particular feared pan-Arabism on the reasonable assumption that they would be asked to share their vast oil revenues with the poorer states of the Middle East. Indeed, in Nasser's view, through Arab unity, this wealth could be used to improve the standard of living in the area.

In the end, Nasser's plans brought an end to the UAR. When the government announced the nationalization of a large number of industries and utilities in 1961, a military coup overthrew the Ba'ath leaders in Damascus, and the new authorities declared that Syria would end its relationship with Egypt.

The breakup of the UAR did not end the dream of pan-Arabism. During the mid-1960s, Egypt took the lead in promoting Arab unity against Israel. At a meeting of Arab leaders held in Jerusalem in 1964, the Palestine Liberation Organization (PLO) was set up under Egyptian sponsorship to represent the interests of the Palestinians. According to the charter of the PLO, only the Palestinian people (and thus not Jewish immigrants from abroad) had the right to form a state in the old British mandate. A guerrilla movement called al-Fatah (al-FAH-tuh), led by the dissident PLO figure Yasir Arafat (yah-SEER ah-ruh-FAHT) (1929–2004), began to launch terrorist attacks on Israeli territory.

The Arab-Israeli Dispute

Growing Arab hostility was a constant threat to the security of Israel, whose leaders dedicated themselves to creating a Jewish homeland. The government attempted to build a democratic and modern state that would be a magnet for Jews throughout the world and a symbol of Jewish achievement.

Ensuring the survival of the tiny state surrounded by antagonistic Arab neighbors was a considerable challenge, made more difficult by divisions within the Israeli population. Some were immigrants from Europe, while others came from other states in the Middle East. Some were secular and even socialist in their views, while others were politically and religiously conservative. The state was also home to Christians as well as Muslim Palestinians who had not fled to other countries. To balance these diverse interests, Israel established a parliament, called the Knesset (kuh-NESS-it), on the European model, with proportional representation based on the number of votes each party received in the general election. The parties were so numerous that none ever received a majority of votes, and all governments had to be formed from a coalition of several parties. As a result, moderate secular leaders such as longtime prime minister David Ben-Gurion had to cater to more marginal parties composed of conservative religious groups.

THE SIX-DAY WAR In the spring of 1967, Nasser attempted to improve his standing in the Arab world by imposing a blockade against Israeli commerce through the Gulf of Aqaba. Concerned that it might be isolated, and lacking firm support from Western powers (which had originally guaranteed Israel the freedom to use the Gulf of Aqaba), in June 1967, Israel suddenly launched air strikes against Egypt and several of its Arab neighbors. Israeli armies then broke the blockade at the head of the Gulf of Aqaba and occupied the Sinai peninsula. Other Israeli forces attacked Jordanian territory on the West Bank of the Jordan River (Jordan's King Hussein had recently signed an alliance with Egypt and placed his army under Egyptian command), occupied the whole of Jerusalem, and seized Syrian military positions in the Golan Heights, along the Israeli-Syrian border (see Map 29.2). Israel's brief, six-day war had tripled the size of its territory but aroused even more bitter hostility among the Arabs; one million Palestinians were added inside its borders, most of them on the West Bank of the Jordan River.

During the next few years, the focus of the Arab-Israeli dispute shifted as Arab states demanded the return of the territories lost in the 1967 war. Nasser died in 1970 and was succeeded by his vice president, ex-general Anwar al-Sadat (ahn-WAHR al-sah-DAHT) (1918–1981). Sadat attempted to renew Arab unity through a new confrontation with Israel. In 1973, on Yom Kippur (the Jewish Day of Atonement), an Israeli national holiday, Egyptian forces suddenly launched an air and artillery attack on Israeli positions in the Sinai just east of the Suez Canal. Syrian armies attacked Israeli positions in the Golan Heights. After early Arab successes, the Israelis managed to recoup some of their losses on both fronts. As a superpower confrontation between the United States and the Soviet Union loomed, a cease-fire was finally reached.

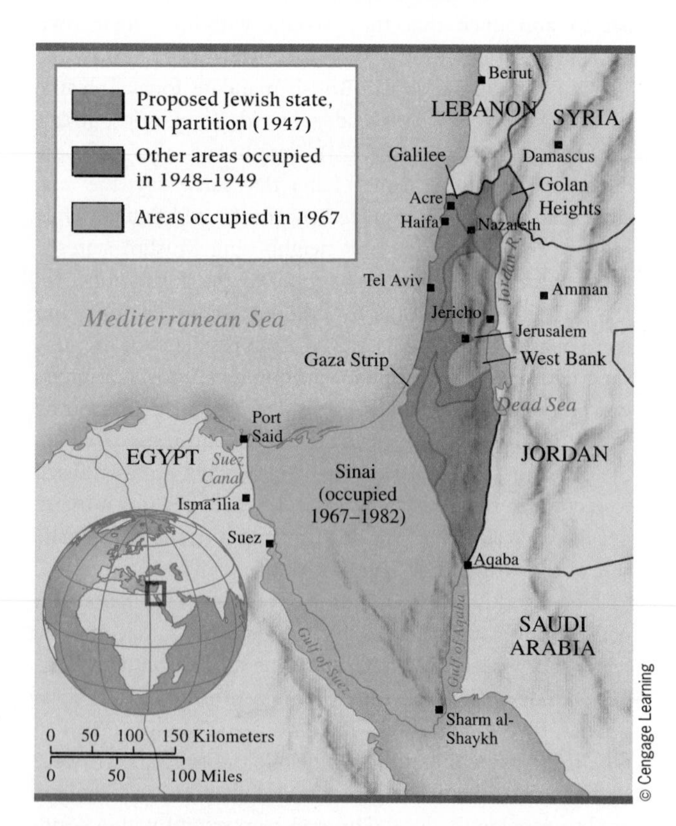

© Cengage Learning

MAP 29.2 Israel and Its Neighbors. This map shows the evolution of the state of Israel since its founding in 1948. Areas occupied by Israel after the Six-Day War in 1967 are indicated in green.

What is the significance of the West Bank?

THE CAMP DAVID AGREEMENT After his election as U.S. president in 1976, Jimmy Carter began to press for a compromise peace based on Israel's return of territories occupied during the 1967 war and Arab recognition of the state of Israel. In September 1978, Sadat and Israeli prime minister Menachem Begin (muh-NAH-kuhm BAY-gin) (1913–1992) met with Carter at Camp David, the presidential retreat in Maryland. In the first treaty signed with a Muslim state, Israel agreed to withdraw from the Sinai but not from other occupied territories unless other Muslim countries recognized Israel. The promise of the Camp David agreement however, was not fulfilled. One reason was the assassination of Sadat by Islamic militants in October 1981. But there were deeper causes, including the continued unwillingness of many Arab governments to recognize Israel and the Israeli government's encouragement of Jewish settlements on the occupied West Bank.

THE PLO AND THE *INTIFADA* During the 1980s, the militancy of the Palestinians increased, leading to rising unrest, popularly labeled the ***intifada*** (in-tuh-FAH-duh) (uprising), among PLO supporters living inside Israel. In response, U.S.-sponsored peace talks opened between Israel and a number of its neighbors, but progress was slow. Terrorist attacks by Palestinian militants resulted in heavy casualties and shook the confidence of many Jewish citizens that their security needs had been adequately protected. At the same time, Jewish residents of the West Bank resisted the extension of Palestinian authority in the area.

In 1999, a new Labour government under Prime Minister Ehud Barak (EH-hud bah-RAHK) (b. 1942) sought to revitalize the peace process. Negotiations resumed with the PLO and also got under way with Syria over a peace settlement in Lebanon and the possible return of the Golan Heights. But the talks broke down over the future of the city of Jerusalem, leading to massive riots by Palestinians and a dramatic increase in bloodshed on both sides. The death of Yasi Arafat in 2004 and his replacement by Palestinian moderate Mahmoud Abbas (mah-MOOD ah-BAHS) (b. 1935), as well as the withdrawal of Israeli settlers from Gaza in 2005, raised modest hopes for progress in peace talks, but a year later, radical Muslim forces operating in southern Lebanon launched massive attacks on Israeli cities. In response, Israeli troops crossed the border in an effort to wipe out the source of the assault. Two years later, militants in the Gaza Strip launched their own rocket attacks on sites in southern Israel. The latter responded forcefully, thereby raising the specter of a wider conflict. As attitudes hardened, national elections in early 2009 led to the return to office of former Israeli prime minister Benjamin Netanyahu (net-ahn-YAH-hoo) (b. 1949) and a virtual stalemate in the peace process.

CHRONOLOGY The Arab-Israeli Dispute

Formation of the state of Israel	1948
Founding of the Palestine Liberation Organization	1964
Six-Day War between Arab states and Israel	1967
Yom Kippur War between Arab states and Israel	1973
Camp David accords	1978
Peace talks between Israel and Syria begin	1999
Withdrawal of Israeli settlers from Gaza	2005
Resumption of hostilities in Gaza	2008
Netanyahu returns as Israeli prime minister	2009

© William J. Duiker

The Temple Mount at Jerusalem. The Temple Mount is one of the most sacred sites in the city of Jerusalem. Originally, it was the site of a temple built during the reign of Solomon, king of the Israelites, about 1000 B.C.E. The Western Wall of the temple is shown in the foreground. Beyond the wall is the Dome of the Rock complex, built on the place from which Muslims believe that Muhammad ascended to heaven. Sacred to both religions, the Temple Mount is now a major bone of contention between Muslims and Jews and a prime obstacle to a final settlement of the Arab-Israeli dispute.

Revolution in Iran

In the late 1970s, another trouble spot arose in Iran, one of the key oil-exporting countries in the region. Under the leadership of Shah Mohammad Reza Pahlavi (ree-ZAH PAH-luh-vee) (1919–1980), who had taken over from his father in 1941, Iran had become one of the richest countries in the Middle East. During the 1950s and 1960s, Iran became a prime U.S. ally in the Middle East. With encouragement from the United States, which hoped that Iran could become a force for stability in the Persian Gulf, the shah attempted to carry through a series of social and economic reforms to transform the country into the most advanced in the region. Per capita income increased dramatically, literacy rates improved, a modern communications infrastructure took shape, and an affluent middle class emerged in the capital of Tehran (teh-RAHN).

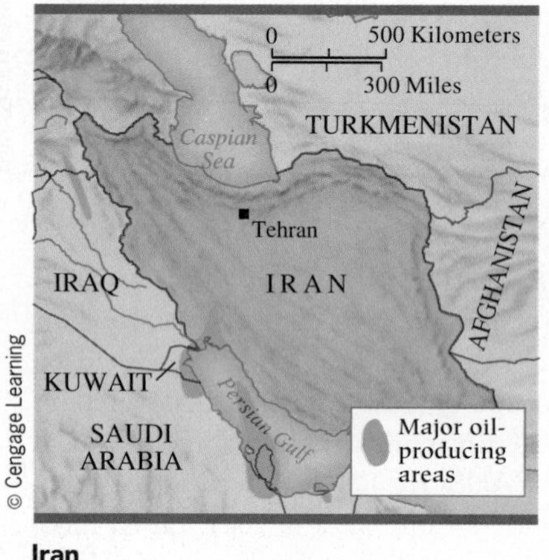

Iran

Under the surface, however, trouble was brewing. Despite an ambitious land reform program, many peasants were still landless, unemployment among intellectuals was dangerously high, and the urban middle class was squeezed by high inflation. Some of the unrest took the form of religious discontent as millions of devout Muslims looked with distaste at a new Iranian civilization based on greed, sexual license, and material accumulation.

THE FALL OF THE SHAH Leading the opposition was Ayatollah Ruholla Khomeini (1900–1989), an austere Shi'-ite cleric who had been exiled to Iraq and then to France because of his outspoken opposition to the shah's regime. From Paris, Khomeini continued his attacks in print, on television, and in radio broadcasts. By the late 1970s, large numbers of Iranians began to respond to Khomeini's diatribes against the "satanic regime," and demonstrations by his supporters were repressed with ferocity by the police. But workers' strikes grew in intensity. In 1979, the government collapsed and was replaced by a hastily formed Islamic republic. The new government, dominated by Shi'ite clergy under the guidance of Ayatollah Khomeini, immediately began to introduce traditional Islamic law (see the Film & History feature on p. 779). A new reign of terror ensued as supporters of the shah were rounded up and executed.

Though much of the outside world focused on the U.S. embassy in Tehran, where militants held a number of foreign hostages, the Iranian Revolution involved much more. In the eyes of the ayatollah and his followers, the United States was "the great Satan," the powerful protector of Israel, and the enemy of Muslim peoples everywhere. Furthermore, it was responsible for the corruption of Iranian society under the shah. With economic conditions in Iran rapidly deteriorating, the Islamic revolutionary government finally agreed to free the hostages in return for the release of Iranian assets in the United States.

During the late 1990s, the intensity of the Iranian Revolution moderated slightly as a new president, the moderate cleric Mohammad Khatami (KHAH-tah-mee) (b. 1941), displayed a modest tolerance for loosening clerical control over freedom of expression and social activities. But rising public criticism of rampant official corruption and a high rate of inflation sparked a new wave of government repression; newspapers were censored, the universities were purged of disloyal or "un-Islamic" elements, and religious militants raided private homes in search of blasphemous activities.

In 2004, presidential elections brought a new leader, Mahmoud Ahmadinejad (mah-MOOD ah-mah-dee-nee-ZHAHD) (b. 1956), to power in Tehran. He immediately inflamed the situation by calling publicly for the destruction of the state of Israel, while his government aroused unease throughout the world by indicating its determination to develop a nuclear energy program, ostensibly for peaceful purposes. Iran has also provided support for **Hezbollah** (hes-bah-LAH or HEZ-bull-lah), a militant Shi'ite organization based in Lebanon, and other terrorist groups in the region. Despite worsening conditions at home that eroded the government's popularity, Ahmadinejad was reelected in June 2009, although opponents claimed that numerous irregularities had occurred during the elections.

Crisis in the Persian Gulf

Although much of the Iranians' anger was directed against the United States during the early phases of the revolution, Iran had equally hated enemies closer to home. To the north, the immense power of the Soviet Union, driven by atheistic communism, was viewed as a modern version of the Russian threat of previous centuries. To the west was a militant and hostile Iraq, now under the leadership of the ambitious Saddam Hussein (suh-DAHM hoo-SAYN) (1937–2006). Iraq had just passed through a turbulent period. The monarchy had been overthrown by a military coup in 1958, but conflicts within the ruling military junta led to chronic instability, and in 1979 Colonel Saddam Hussein, a prominent member of the local Ba'athist Party, seized power on his own.

FILM & HISTORY

Persepolis (2007)

The Iranian author Marjane Satrapi (b. 1969) has re-created *Persepolis*, her autobiographical graphic novel, as an enthralling animated film of the same name. Using simple black-and-white animation, the movie recounts key stages in the turbulent history of modern Iran as seen through the eyes of a spirited young girl, also named Marjane. The dialogue is in French with English subtitles (a version dubbed in English is also available), and the voices of the characters are rendered beautifully by Danielle Darrieux, Catherine Deneuve, Chiara Mastroianni, and other European film stars.

In the film, Marjane is the daughter of middle-class left-wing intellectuals who abhor the dictatorship of the shah and actively participate in his overthrow in 1979. After the revolution, however, the severity of the ayatollah's Islamic rule arouses their secularist and democratic impulses. Encouraged by her loving grandmother, who reinforces her modernist and feminist instincts, Marjane resents having to wear a head scarf and the educational restrictions imposed by the puritanical new Islamic regime, but to little avail. Emotionally exhausted and fearful of political retribution from the authorities, her family finally sends her to study in Vienna.

Study abroad, however, is not a solution to Marjane's problems. She is distressed by the nihilism and emotional shallowness of her new Austrian school friends, who seem oblivious to the contrast between their privileged lives and her own experience of living under a tyrannical regime. Disillusioned by the loneliness of exile and several failed love affairs, she descends into a deep depression and then decides to return to Tehran. When she discovers that her family is still suffering from political persecution, however, she decides to leave the country permanently and settles in Paris.

Observing the events, first through the eyes of a child and then through the perceptions of an innocent schoolgirl, the viewer of the film is forced to fill in the blanks, as Marjane initially cannot comprehend the meaning of the adult conversations swirling around her. As Marjane passes through adolescence into adulthood, the folly of human intransigence and superstition becomes painfully clear, both to her and to the audience. Although animated films have long been a cinematic staple, thanks in part to Walt Disney, both the novel and the film *Persepolis* demonstrate how graphic design can depict a momentous event in history with clarity and compassion.

THE VISION OF SADDAM HUSSEIN Saddam Hussein was a fervent believer in the Ba'athist vision of a single Arab state in the Middle East and soon began to persecute non-Arab elements in Iraq, including Persians and Kurds. He then turned his sights to territorial expansion to the east.

Iraq and Iran had long had an uneasy relationship, fueled by religious differences (Iranian Islam is predominantly Shi'ite, while the ruling caste in Iraq was Sunni) and a perennial dispute over borderlands adjacent to the Persian Gulf, the vital waterway for the export of oil from both countries. Like several of its neighbors, Iraq had long dreamed of unifying the Arabs but had been hindered by internal factions and suspicion among its neighbors.

During the mid-1970s, Iran gave some support to a Kurdish rebellion in the mountains of Iraq. In 1975, the government of the shah agreed to stop aiding the rebels in return for territorial concessions at the head of the Gulf. Five years later, however, the Kurdish revolt had been suppressed.

Saddam Hussein now saw his opportunity; accusing Iran of violating the territorial agreement, he launched an attack on his neighbor in 1980. The war was a bloody one and lasted for nearly ten years. Poison gas was used against civilians, and children were employed to clear minefields. Finally, with both sides virtually exhausted, a cease-fire was arranged in the fall of 1988.

The bitter conflict with Iran had not slaked Saddam Hussein's appetite for territorial expansion. In early August 1990, Iraqi military forces suddenly moved across the border and occupied the small neighboring country of Kuwait at the head of the Gulf. The immediate pretext was the claim that Kuwait was pumping oil from fields inside Iraqi territory. Baghdad was also angry over the Kuwaiti government's demand for repayment of loans it had made to Iraq during the war with Iran. But the underlying reason was Iraq's contention that Kuwait was legally a part of Iraq. Kuwait had been part of the Ottoman Empire until the beginning of the twentieth century, when the local prince had agreed to place his patrimony under British protection. When Iraq became independent in 1932, it claimed the area on the grounds that the state of Kuwait had been created by British imperialism, but opposition from major Western powers and other countries in the region, which feared the consequences of a "greater Iraq," prevented an Iraqi takeover.

OPERATION DESERT STORM The Iraqi invasion of Kuwait in 1990 sparked an international outcry, and the United States assembled a multinational coalition that, under the name Operation Desert Storm, liberated the country and destroyed a substantial part of Iraq's armed forces. President George H. W. Bush had promised the American people that U.S. troops would not fight with one hand tied behind their backs (a clear reference to the Vietnam War), but the allied forces did not occupy Baghdad at the end of the war out of fear that doing so would cause a breakup of the country, an eventuality that would operate to the benefit of Iran. The allies hoped instead that Saddam's regime would be ousted by an internal revolt. In the meantime, harsh economic sanctions were imposed on the Iraqi government as the condition for peace. The anticipated overthrow of Saddam Hussein did not materialize, however, and his tireless efforts to evade the conditions of the cease-fire continued to bedevil the next U.S. president, Bill Clinton, and his successor, George W Bush.

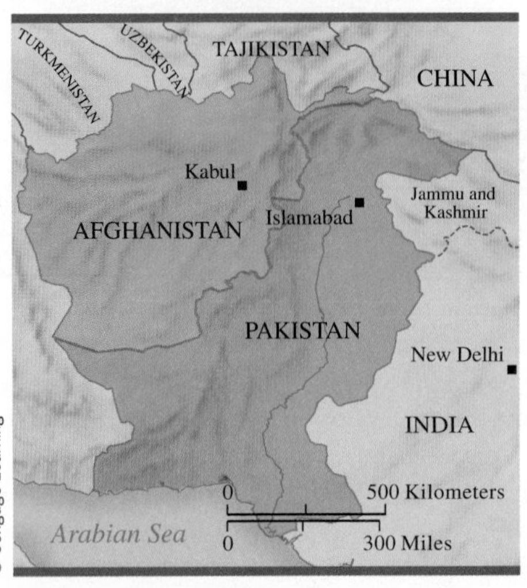

Afghanistan and Pakistan

CHRONOLOGY **The Modern Middle East**	
King Farouk overthrown in Egypt	1952
Egypt nationalizes the Suez Canal	1956
Formation of the United Arab Republic	1958
Iranian Revolution	1979
Iran-Iraq War begins	1980
Iraqi invasion of Kuwait	1990
Persian Gulf War (Operation Desert Storm)	1991
Al-Qaeda terrorist attack on the United States	2001
U.S.-led forces invade Iraq	2003
Ahmadinejad elected president of Iran	2005
Popular riots in the Middle East	2011–2012
Overthrow of Egyptian President Hosni Mubarak	2011

Conflicts in Afghanistan and Iraq

The terrorist attacks launched against U.S. cities in September 2001 added a new dimension to the Middle Eastern equation. After the failure of the Soviet Union to quell the rebellion in Afghanistan during the 1980s, a fundamentalist Muslim group known as the Taliban, supported covertly by the United States, seized power in Kabul and ruled the country with a fanaticism reminiscent of the Cultural Revolution in China. Backed by conservative religious forces in Pakistan, the Taliban provided a base of operations for Osama bin Laden's al-Qaeda terrorist network. After the attacks of September 11, a coalition of forces led by the United States overthrew the Taliban and attempted to build a new and moderate government in Afghanistan. But the country's history of bitter internecine warfare among tribal groups presented a severe challenge to those efforts, and Taliban forces have managed to regroup and continue to operate in the mountainous region adjacent to the Pakistani border. The terrorist threat from al-Qaeda, however, was dealt a major blow in May 2011, when Osama bin Laden was killed by U.S. special operations forces during a raid on his hideout in northern Pakistan.

After moving against the Taliban at the end of 2001, the administration of George W. Bush, charging that Iraqi dictator Saddam Hussein had not only provided support to bin Laden's terrorist organization but also stockpiled weapons of mass destruction for use against his enemies, threatened to invade Iraq and remove him from power. It was the president's hope that the overthrow of the Iraqi dictator would promote the spread of democracy throughout the region. The plan, widely debated in the media and opposed by many of the United States' traditional allies, disquieted Arab leaders and fanned anti-American sentiment throughout the Muslim world. Nevertheless, in March 2003, U.S.-led forces attacked Iraq and overthrew Saddam Hussein's regime. In the months that followed, occupation forces sought to restore stability to the country while setting out plans on which to build a democratic society. But although Saddam Hussein was captured by U.S. troops and later executed, armed resistance by militant Muslim elements continued.

When the Obama administration came into office in 2009, it focused its efforts on training an Iraqi military

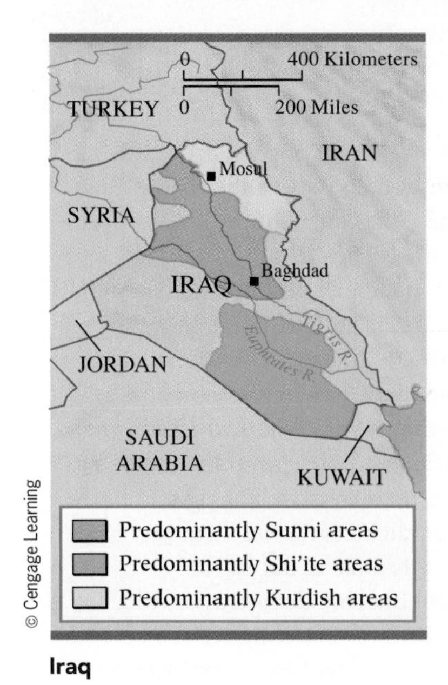

Iraq

force capable of defeating the remaining insurgents. In the meantime, a fragile government has been formed in Baghdad, the embryo of a possible pro-Western state that could serve as an emblem of democracy in the Middle East. Squabbling among Sunni, Shi'ite, and Kurdish elements within the country, however, continued as the last U.S. combat troops were removed in the fall of 2011.

Revolution in the Middle East

In the early months of 2011, popular protests against current conditions broke out in several countries in the Middle East. Beginning in Tunisia, the riots spread rapidly to Egypt—where they brought about the abrupt resignation of long-time president Hosni Mubarak (HAHS-nee moo-BAH-rahk) (b. 1929)—and then to other countries in the region, including Syria, Libya, and Yemen, where political leaders sought to quell the unrest, often by violent means. In Libya, the brutal regime of dictator Muammar Qaddafi was overthrown by a popular revolt with the assistance of NATO air strikes. The uprisings aroused hopes around the world that the seeds of democracy had been planted in a region long dominated by autocratic governments, but also provoked widespread concern that unstable conditions could lead to further violence and a rise in international terrorism. In the months following the outbreak of unrest, the prognosis for the future of the region was still unclear.

Society and Culture in the Contemporary Middle East

FOCUS QUESTION: How have religious issues affected economic, social, and cultural conditions in the Middle East in recent decades?

In the Middle East today, all aspects of society and culture—from political and economic issues to literature, art, and the role of the family—are intertwined with questions of religious faith.

Varieties of Government: The Politics of Islam

To many seasoned observers, the strategy applied by President George W. Bush in Iraq appeared unrealistic, since democratic values are not deeply rooted in the culture of the Middle East. In many countries, feudal rulers remain securely in power. The kings of Saudi Arabia, for example, continue to govern by traditional precepts and, citing the distinctive character of Muslim society, have been reluctant to establish representative political institutions.

To be sure, there have been variations in government throughout the region. In some societies, traditional authority has been replaced by charismatic one-party rule or military dictatorships. Nasser's Egypt was a single-party state where the leader won political power by the force of his presence or personality. The regimes of Ayatollah Khomeini in Iran, Muammar Qaddafi in Libya, and Saddam Hussein in Iraq could also trace much of their power to the personal appeal of the leader.

Other states have seen the emergence of modernizing bureaucratic regimes. Examples include the governments of Syria, Yemen, Turkey, and Egypt, where Anwar al-Sadat and his successor, Hosni Mubarak, focused on performance. Most of these regimes have remained highly autocratic in character, however, except in Turkey, where free elections and the sharing of power have become more prevalent in recent years.

A few Arab nations, such as Bahrain, Kuwait, and Jordan, have engaged in limited forms of democratic experimentation. Most of the region's recent leaders, however, have maintained that Western-style democracy is not appropriate for their societies. Bashar al Assad (bah-SHAHR al-ah-SAHD) (b. 1965), the president of Syria, once remarked that he would tolerate only "positive criticism" of his policies. President Mubarak of Egypt often insisted to foreign critics that only authoritarian rule could prevent the spread of Islamic radicalism throughout his country. Most world leaders have accepted the logic of these contentions, provoking some critics to charge that Western governments coddle Middle Eastern dictatorships as a means of maintaining stability in the region and preserving their access to the vast oil reserves located on the Arabian peninsula (see the box on p. 782).

The sudden outbreak of popular unrest that has erupted from North Africa to the Arabian peninsula since the spring of 2011 raises questions about the potential for democratic changes to emerge in the countries throughout the region. Are democratic institutions and the principles of human freedom truly antithetical to the culture of the Middle East and the principles of Islam? As we await the consequences of the current wave of popular unrest, the fate of the region hangs in the balance.

Islam and Democracy

RELIGION & PHILOSOPHY

One of George W. Bush's key objectives in launching the invasion of Iraq in 2003 was to promote the emergence of democratic states throughout the Middle East. According to U.S. officials, one of the ultimate causes of the formation of terrorist movements in Muslim societies is the prevalence in such countries of dictatorial governments that do not serve the interests of their citizens. According to the Pakistani author of this editorial, the problem lies as much with the actions of Western countries as it does with political attitudes in the Muslim world.

M. J. Akbar, "Linking Islam to Dictatorship"

Let us examine a central canard, that Islam and democracy are incompatible. This is an absurdity. There is nothing Islamic or un-Islamic about democracy. Democracy is the outcome of a political process, not a religious process.

It is glibly suggested that "every" Muslim country is a dictatorship, but the four largest Muslim populations of the world—in Indonesia, India, Bangladesh, and Turkey—vote to change governments. Pakistan could easily have been on this list.

Voting does not make these Muslims less or more religious. There are dictators among Muslims just as there are dictators among Christians, Buddhists, and Hindus (check out Nepal). . . . Christian Latin America has seen ugly forms of dictatorship, as has Christian Africa.

What is unique to the Muslim world is not the absence of democracy but the fact that in 1918, after the defeat of the Ottoman Empire, every single Muslim in the world lived under foreign subjugation.

Every single one, from Indonesia to Morocco via Turkey. The Turks threw out their invaders within a few years under the great leadership of Kemal Atatürk, but the transition to self-rule in other Muslim countries was slow, uncertain, and full of traps planted by the world's preeminent powers.

The West, in the shape of Britain, France, or America, was never interested in democracy when a helpful dictator or king would serve. When people got a chance to express their wish, it was only logical that they would ask for popular rule. It was the street that brought Mossadegh to power in Iran and drove the shah of Iran to tearful exile in Rome. Who brought the shah of Iran and autocracy back to Iran? The CIA.

If Iranian democracy had been permitted a chance in 1953, there would have been no uprising led by Ayatollah Khomeini in 1979. In other countries, where the struggle for independence was long and brutal, as in Algeria and Indonesia, the militias who had fought the war institutionalized army authority. In other instances, civilian heroes confused their own well-being with national health. They became regressive dictators. Once again, there was nothing Islamic about it.

Muslim countries will become democracies, too, because it is the finest form of modern governance. But it will be a process interrupted by bloody experience as the street wrenches power from usurpers.

Democracy has happened in Turkey. It has happened in Bangladesh. It is happening in Indonesia. It almost happened in Pakistan, and the opportunity will return. Democracy takes time in the most encouraging environments.

Democracy has become the latest rationale for the occupation of Iraq. . . . Granted, democracy is always preferable to tyranny no matter how it comes. But Iraqis are not dupes. They will take democracy and place it at the service of nationalism. A decade ago, America was careless about the definition of victory. Today it is careless about the definition of democracy.

There is uncertainty and apprehension across the Muslim nations: uncertainty about where they stand, and apprehension about both American power and the repugnant use of terrorism that in turn invites the exercise of American power. There is also anger that a legitimate cause like that of Palestine can get buried in the debris of confusion. Muslims do not see Palestinians as terrorists.

How does the author of this editorial answer the charge that democracy and Islam are incompatible? To what degree, in his view, is the West responsible for the problems of the Middle East?

Source: From M.J. Akbar, "Linking Islam to Dictatorship," in *World Press Review*, May 2004.

The Economics of the Middle East: Oil and Sand

Few areas exhibit a greater disparity of individual and national wealth than the Middle East. While millions live in abject poverty, a fortunate few rank among the wealthiest people in the world. The primary reason for this disparity is oil. Unfortunately for most of the peoples of the region, oil reserves are distributed unevenly and all too often are located in areas where the population density is low (see the spot map on p. 778). Egypt and Turkey, with more than 75 million inhabitants apiece, have almost no oil reserves. The combined population of oil-rich Kuwait, the United Arab Emirates, and Saudi Arabia is about 35 million people. This disparity in wealth inspired Nasser's quest for Arab unity but has also posed a major obstacle to that unity.

ECONOMICS AND ISLAM Not surprisingly, considering their different resources and political systems, the states of the Middle East have adopted diverse approaches to the problem of developing strong and stable economies. Some, like Nasser in Egypt and the leaders of the Ba'ath Party in Syria, briefly attempted to create a form of Arab socialism, favoring a high level of government involvement in the economy to relieve the inequities of the free enterprise system. Others turned to the Western capitalist model to maximize growth while using taxes or massive development projects to build a modern infrastructure, redistribute wealth, and maintain political stability and economic opportunity for all (see the comparative illustration on p. 784). Rapid population growth, widespread corruption, and the absence of adequate educational and technological skills, however, have all acted as a drag on economic growth throughout the region. Unfortunately, the Qur'an provides little guidance to Muslims searching for the proper road to economic prosperity.

AGRICULTURAL POLICIES Although the amount of arable land is relatively small, most countries in the Middle East rely on farming to supply food for their growing populations. Much of the fertile land was once owned by wealthy absentee landlords, but land reform programs in several countries have attempted to alleviate this problem.

The most comprehensive and probably the most successful land reform program was instituted in Egypt, where Nasser and his successors managed to reassign nearly a quarter of all cultivable lands by limiting the amount a single individual could hold. Similar programs in Iran, Iraq, Libya, and Syria generally had less effect. After the 1979 revolution in Iran, many farmers forcibly seized lands from the landlords, raising questions of ownership that the revolutionary government has tried to resolve with only minimal success

Agricultural productivity throughout the region has been plagued by a lack of water. With populations growing at more than 2 percent annually on average in the Middle East (more than 3 percent in some countries), several governments have tried to increase the amount of water available for irrigation. Many attempts have been sabotaged by government ineptitude, political disagreements, and territorial conflicts, however. For example, disputes between Israel and its neighbors over water rights and between Iraq and its neighbors over the exploitation of the Tigris and Euphrates Rivers have caused serious tensions in recent years. Today, the dearth of water in the region is reaching crisis proportions.

The Islamic Revival

In recent years, developments in the Middle East have often been described in terms of a resurgence of traditional values and customs in response to Western influence.

MODERNIST ISLAM Initially, many Muslim intellectuals responded to Western influence by trying to create a "modernized" set of Islamic beliefs and practices that would not clash with the demands of the twentieth century. This process took place to some degree in most Islamic societies, but it was especially prevalent in Turkey, Egypt, and Iran. Mustafa Kemal Atatürk embraced the strategy when he attempted to secularize the Islamic religion in the new Turkish republic. The Turkish model was followed by Shah Reza Khan and his son Mohammad Reza Pahlavi in Iran and then by Nasser in postwar Egypt, all of whom attempted to honor Islamic values while asserting the primacy of other issues such as political and economic development. Religion, in effect, had become the handmaiden of political power, national identity, and economic prosperity.

These secularizing trends were particularly noticeable among the political, intellectual, and economic elites in urban areas. They had less influence in the countryside, among the poor, and among devout elements within the clergy. Many of the clerics believed that Western influence in the cities had given birth to political and economic corruption, sexual promiscuity, hedonism, individualism, and the prevalence of alcohol, pornography, and drugs. Although such practices had long existed in the Middle East, they were now far more visible and socially acceptable.

RETURN TO TRADITION Reaction among conservatives against the modernist movement was quick to emerge in several countries and reached its zenith in the late 1970s with the return of the Ayatollah Khomeini to Iran. It is not surprising that Iran took the lead in light of its long tradition of ideological purity within the Shi'ite

© Scott E. Barbour/Getty Images

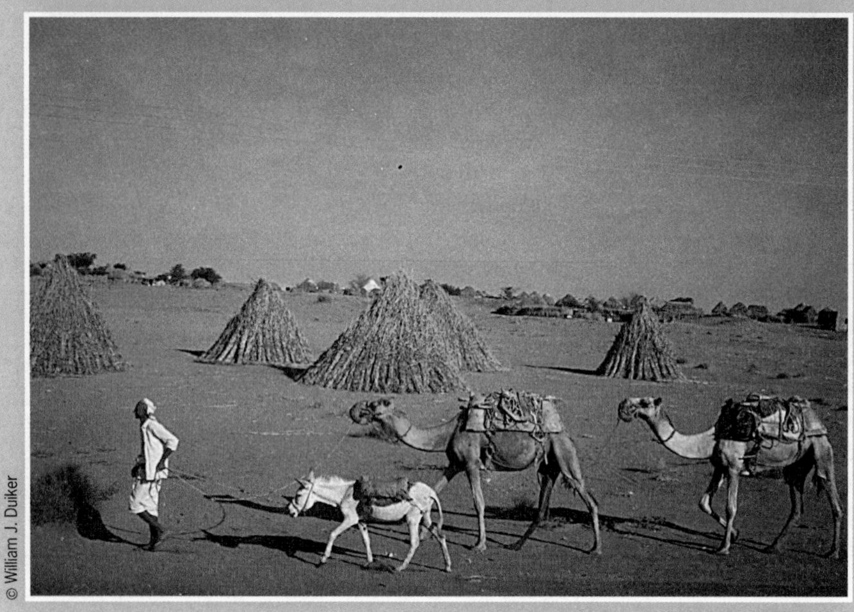

© William J. Duiker

COMPARATIVE ILLUSTRATION

POLITICS & GOVERNMENT

Wealth and Poverty in the Middle East. Although many of the countries in the Middle East are relatively poor by world standards, a favored few have amassed great wealth as a result of their fortunate geographic location. Such is the case with the United Arab Emirates, a small country situated strategically on the eastern edge of the Arabian peninsula and located directly over some of the most abundant oil reserves in the world. The modern city of Dubai (top photo), resplendent in its opulence, serves today as a playground for the rich and a vivid symbol of the wealth that has flowed into the region because of the world's thirst for energy. At the opposite extreme is Yemen, on the southern edge of the Arabian peninsula. Lacking valuable resources, the people of Yemen live by traditional pursuits, as shown in the photo at the bottom.

Which are the wealthiest states in the region? Which are the poorest?

sect as well as the uncompromisingly secular character of the shah's reforms in the postwar era. In Iran today, traditional Islamic beliefs are all-pervasive and extend into education, clothing styles, social practices, and the legal system. In recent years, for example, Iranian women have been heavily fined or even flogged for violating the Islamic dress code.

The cultural and social effects of the Iranian Revolution soon began to spread. In Algeria, the political influence of fundamentalist Islamic groups enabled them to win a stunning victory in the national elections in 1992. When the military stepped in to cancel the second round of elections and crack down on the militants, the latter responded with a campaign of terrorism against moderates that claimed thousands of lives.

A similar trend emerged in Egypt, where militant groups such as the Muslim Brotherhood, formed in 1928 as a means of promoting personal piety, engaged in terrorism, including the assassination of President Anwar al-Sadat and attacks on foreign tourists, who are considered carriers of corrupt Western influence. In recent years, the Brotherhood has adopted a more moderate public stance and received broad support in elections held after the overthrow of the Mubarak regime.

Even in Turkey, generally considered the most secular of Islamic societies, a Muslim political group took power in a coalition government formed in 1996. The new government adopted a pro-Arab stance in foreign affairs and threatened to reduce the country's economic and political ties to Europe. Worried moderates voiced their concern that the secular legacy of Kemal Atatürk was being eroded, and eventually the government resigned under heavy pressure from the military. But a new Islamist organization, known as the Justice and Development Party (the AK Party), won elections held in 2007 and has signaled its intention to guarantee the rights of devout Muslims to display their faith publicly. In elections held in June 2011, the AK Party won a clear victory with about 50 percent of the vote.

Throughout the Middle East, even individuals who do not support efforts to return to pure Islamic principles have adjusted their behavior and beliefs in subtle ways. In Egypt, for example, the authorities encourage television programs devoted to religion in preference to comedies and adventure shows imported from the West, and alcohol is discouraged or at least consumed more discreetly.

Women in the Middle East

Nowhere have the fault lines between tradition and modernity in Muslim societies in the Middle East been so sharp as in the ongoing debate over the role of women. At the beginning of the twentieth century, women's place in Middle Eastern society had changed little since the death of the prophet Muhammad. Women were secluded in their homes and had few legal, political, or social rights.

During the first decades of the twentieth century, advocates of modernist views began to contend that Islamic doctrine was not inherently opposed to women's rights. To modernists, Islamic traditions such as female seclusion, wearing the veil, and polygamy were actually pre-Islamic folk traditions that had been tolerated in the early Islamic era and continued to be practiced in later centuries. Such views had a considerable impact on a number of Middle Eastern societies, including Turkey and Iran. As we have seen, greater rights for women were a crucial element in the social revolution promoted by Kemal Atatürk in Turkey. In Iran, Shah Reza Khan and his son granted female suffrage and encouraged the education of women. In Egypt, a vocal feminist movement arose in educated women's circles in Cairo as early as the 1920s.

The same is true in Israel, where, except in Orthodox religious communities, women have achieved substantial equality with men and are active in politics, the professions, and even the armed forces. Golda Meir (may-EER) (1898–1978), prime minister of Israel from 1969 to 1974, became an international symbol of the ability of women to be world leaders.

In recent years, a more traditional view of women's role has tended to prevail in many Middle Eastern countries. Attacks by religious conservatives on the growing role of women contributed to the emotions underlying the Iranian Revolution of 1979. Iranian women were instructed to wear the veil and to dress modestly in public.

The most conservative nation by far remains Saudi Arabia, where following Wahhabi tradition, women are not only segregated and expected to wear the veil in public but also restricted in education and forbidden to drive automobiles (see the box on p. 786). Still, women's rights have been extended in a few countries. In 1999, women obtained the right to vote in Kuwait, and they have been granted an equal right with their husbands to seek a divorce in Egypt. Even in Iran, women have many freedoms that they lacked before the twentieth century; for example, they can receive military training, vote, practice birth control, and publish fiction. Most important, today nearly 60 percent of university entrants in Iran are women.

Literature and Art

As in other areas of Asia and Africa, the encounter with the West in the nineteenth and twentieth centuries stimulated a cultural renaissance in the Middle East. Muslim authors translated Western works into Arabic and Persian and began to experiment with new literary forms.

LITERATURE Iran has produced one of the most prominent national literatures in the contemporary Middle East. Since World War II, Iranian literature has been hampered somewhat by political considerations, since it has been expected to serve first the Pahlavi monarchy and then the Islamic republic. Nevertheless, Iranian writers are among the most prolific in the region and often write in prose, which has finally been accepted as the equal of poetry.

Despite the male-oriented character of Iranian society, many of the new writers have been women. Since the revolution, the veil and the *chador* (CHUH-der or CHAH-der), an all-enveloping cloak, have become the central metaphor in Iranian women's writing. Those who favor the veil and *chador* praise them as the last bastion of defense against Western cultural imperialism. Behind the veil, the Islamic woman can breathe freely, unpolluted by foreign exploitation and moral corruption. Other Iranian women, however, consider the *chador* a "mobile prison" or an oppressive anachronism from the Dark Ages. As one writer, Sousan Azadi, expressed it, "As I pulled the *chador* over me, I felt a heaviness descending over me. I was hidden and in hiding. There was nothing visible left of Sousan Azadi."[5] Whether or not they accept the veil and *chador*, women writers are a vital part of contemporary Iranian literature and are addressing all aspects of social issues.

Keeping the Camel out of the Tent

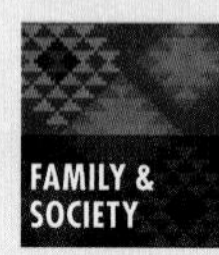

"Almighty God created sexual desire in ten parts; then he gave nine parts to women and one to men." So pronounced Ali, Muhammad's son-in-law, as he explained why women are held morally responsible as the instigators of sexual intercourse. Consequently, over the centuries, Islamic women have been secluded, veiled, and in many cases genitally mutilated in order to safeguard male virtue. Women are forbidden to look directly at, speak to, or touch a man prior to marriage. Even today, they are often sequestered at home or limited to strictly segregated areas away from all male contact. Women normally pray at home or in an enclosed antechamber of the mosque so that their physical presence will not disturb men's spiritual concentration.

Especially limiting today are the laws governing women's behavior in Saudi Arabia. Schooling for girls has never been compulsory because fathers believe that "educating women is like allowing the nose of the camel into the tent; eventually the beast will edge in and take up all the room inside." The country did not establish its first girls' school until 1956. The following description of Saudi women is from *Nine Parts Desire: The Hidden World of Islamic Women* by the journalist Geraldine Brooks.

Geraldine Brooks, *Nine Parts Desire*

Women were first admitted to university in Saudi Arabia in 1962, and all women's colleges remain strictly segregated. Lecture rooms come equipped with closed-circuit TVs and telephones, so women students can listen to a male professor and question him by phone, without having to contaminate themselves by being seen by him. When the first dozen women graduated from university in 1973, they were devastated to find that their names hadn't been printed on the commencement program. The old tradition, that it dishonors women to mention them, was depriving them of recognition they believed they'd earned. The women and their families protested, so a separate program was printed and a segregated graduation ceremony was held for the students' female relatives. . . .

But while the opening of women's universities widened access to higher learning for women, it also made the educational experience much shallower. Before 1962, many progressive Saudi families had sent their daughters abroad for education. They had returned to the kingdom not only with a degree but with experience of the outside world. . . . Now a whole generation of Saudi women have completed their education entirely within the country. . . .

Lack of opportunity for education abroad means that Saudi women are trapped in the confines of an education system that still lags men's. Subjects such as geology and petroleum engineering—tickets to influential jobs in Saudi Arabia's oil economy—remain closed to women. . . . Few women's colleges have their own libraries, and libraries shared with men's schools are either entirely off limits to women or open to them only one day per week. . . .

But women and men sit for the same degree examinations. Professors quietly acknowledge the women's scores routinely outstrip the men's. "It's no surprise," said one woman professor. "Look at their lives. The boys have their cars, they can spend the evenings cruising the streets with their friends, sitting in cafés, buying black-market alcohol and drinking all night. What do the girls have? Four walls and their books. For them, education is everything."

According to Geraldine Brooks, do women in Saudi Arabia have an opportunity to receive an education? To what degree do they take advantage of it?

Source: From *Nine Parts Desire: The Hidden World of Islamic Women*, by Geraldine Brooks (Doubleday, 1996).

Like Iran, Egypt in the twentieth century experienced a flowering of literature accelerated by the establishment of the Egyptian republic in the early 1950s. The most illustrious contemporary Egyptian writer was Naguib Mahfouz (nah-GEEB mah-FOOZ) (1911–2006), who won the Nobel Prize for Literature in 1988. His *Cairo Trilogy* (1952) chronicles three generations of a merchant family in Cairo during the tumultuous years between the world wars. Mahfouz was particularly adept at blending panoramic historical events with the intimate lives of ordinary human beings. Unlike many other modern writers, his message was essentially optimistic and reflected his hope that religion and science can work together for the overall betterment of humankind.

ART Like literature, the art of the modern Middle East has been profoundly influenced by its exposure to Western culture. At first, artists tended to imitate Western models, but later they began to experiment with national styles, returning to earlier forms for inspiration. Some emulated the writers in returning to the village to depict peasants and shepherds, but others followed international trends and attempted to express the alienation and disillusionment that characterize so much of modern life.

CHAPTER SUMMARY

The Middle East is one of the most unstable regions in the world today. In part, this turbulence is due to the continued interference of outsiders attracted by the massive oil reserves under the parched wastes of the Arabian peninsula and in the vicinity of the Persian Gulf. Oil is indeed both a blessing and a curse to the peoples of the region. The similarities with Africa are striking, as governments in both regions struggle to achieve regional cooperation among themselves while fending off the influence of powerful foreign states or multinational corporations.

Some would argue, however, that anger at Western meddling in the Middle East began generations or even centuries earlier. According to the historian Bernard Lewis, the roots of Muslim resentment emerged centuries ago, when Arab hegemony in the region was replaced by European domination. That sense of humiliation culminated in the early twentieth century, when much of the Middle East was occupied by Western colonial regimes. Today, the world is reaping the harvest of that long-cultivated bitterness, as recruits flock to terrorist movements like al-Qaeda in response to the call to eliminate all Western influence in the Arab world.

Another factor contributing to the volatility of the Middle East is the tug-of-war between the sense of ethnic identity in the form of nationalism and the intense longing to be part of a broader Islamic community, a dream that dates back to the time of the prophet Muhammad. Sometimes, the motive for seeking Arab unity may simply be self-aggrandizement—two such examples are Nasser and Saddam Hussein. But there are undoubtedly others who view restoration of the caliphate as a means of reversing the stain of moral decline that they see taking place throughout the region. Muslims, of course, are not alone in believing that a purer form of religious faith is the best antidote for such social evils as hedonism, sexual license, and political corruption. But it is hard to deny that the issue has been pursued with more anger and passion in the Middle East than in almost any other part of the world. The current wave of popular protest has been focused primarily on internal political and economic concerns in each country. But whatever the outcome, the role of Islam in society will be one of the foremost issues that will face new leaders in the region. The consequences of this struggle cannot yet be foreseen.

CHAPTER TIMELINE

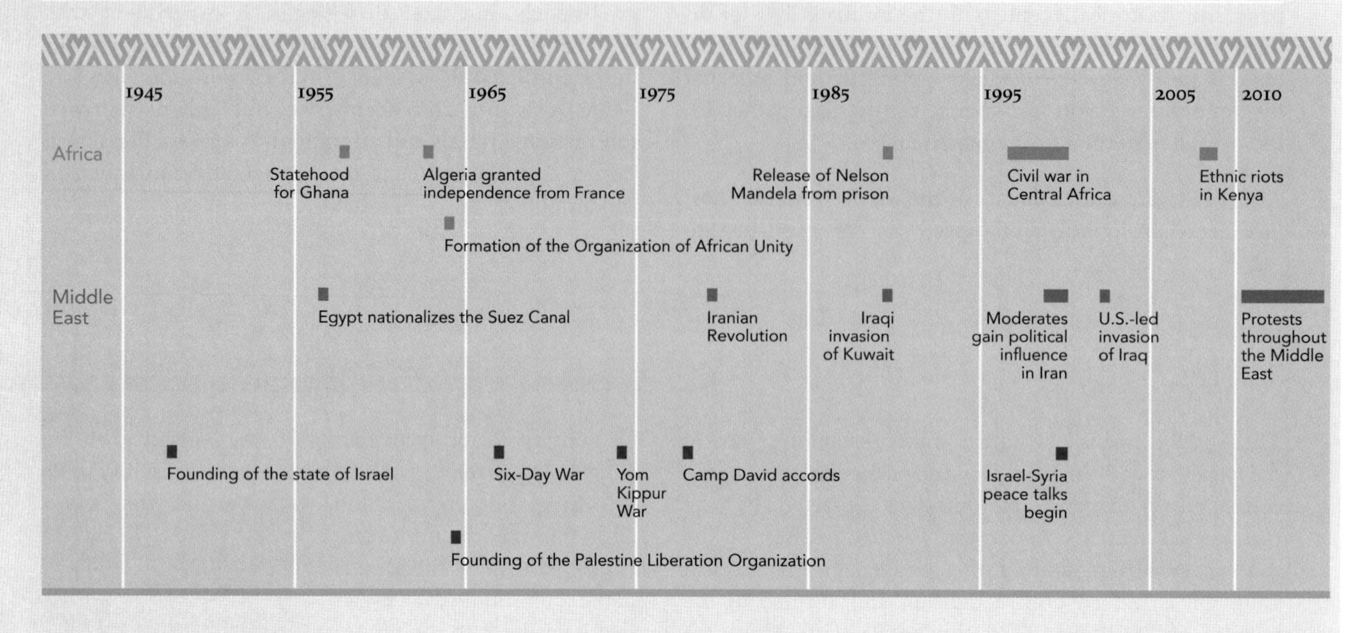

CHAPTER REVIEW

Upon Reflection

Q What are some of the key reasons advanced to explain why democratic institutions have been slow to take root in the Middle East?

Q Why do tensions between farmers and pastoral peoples appear to be on the rise in Africa today? In what parts of the continent is the problem most serious?

Q What are the main sources of discord in the Middle East today? How do they contribute to the popularity of radical terrorist organizations in the region?

Key Terms

uhuru (p. 761)
apartheid (p. 762)
pan-Africanism (p. 763)
neocolonialism (p. 763)
African Union (p. 770)
pan-Arabism (p. 775)
intifada (p. 777)
Hezbollah (p. 778)

Suggested Reading

AFRICA: GENERAL For general surveys of contemporary African history, see **P. Nugent, *Africa Since Independence*** (New York, 2004); **M. Meredith, *The Fate of Africa*** (New York, 2005); and **H. French, *A Continent for the Taking: The Tragedy and Hope of Africa*** (New York, 2004).

AFRICAN LITERATURE AND ART For a survey of African literature, see **A. Kalu, ed., *The Rienner Anthropology of African Literatures*** (London, 2007); **M. J. Hay, *African Novels in the Classroom*** (Boulder, Colo., 2000); and **M. J. Daymond et al., eds., *Women Writing Africa: The Southern Region*** (New York, 2003). On art, see **S. L. Kasfir, *Contemporary African Art*** (London, 1999).

WOMEN IN AFRICA For interesting analyses of women's issues in the Africa of this time frame, see **M. Kevane, *Women and Development in Africa: How Gender Works*** (Boulder, Colo., 2004).

RECENT EVENTS IN AFRICA For contrasting views on the reasons for Africa's current difficulties, see **J. Marah, *The African People in the Global Village: An Introduction to Pan-African Studies*** (Lanham, Md., 1998), and **G. Ayittey, *Africa in Chaos*** (New York, 1998).

THE MIDDLE EAST A good general survey of the modern Middle East is **A. Goldschmidt Jr., *A Concise History of the Middle East*** (Boulder, Colo., 2005).

ISRAEL AND PALESTINE On Israel and the Palestinian question, see **D. Ross, *The Missing Peace: The Inside Story of the Fight for Middle East Peace*** (New York, 2004). On Jerusalem, see **B. Wasserstein, *Divided Jerusalem: The Struggle for the Holy City*** (New Haven, Conn., 2000).

IRAN AND IRAQ On the Iranian Revolution, see **S. Bakash,** ***The Reign of the Ayatollahs*** (New York, 1984). Iran's role in Middle Eastern politics and diplomacy is analyzed in **T. Parsi,** ***Treacherous Alliance: The Secret Dealings of Israel, Iran, and the United States*** (New Haven, Conn., 2007). The Iran-Iraq War is discussed in **S. C. Pelletiere,** ***The Iran-Iraq War: Chaos in a Vacuum*** (New York, 1992). The issue of oil is examined in **D. Yergin et al.,** ***The Prize: The Epic Quest for Oil, Money, and Power*** (New York, 1993).

For historical perspective on the invasion of Iraq, see **J. Kendell,** ***Iraq's Unruly Century*** (New York, 2003). **R. Khalidi,** ***Resurrecting Empire: Western Footprints and America's Perilous Path in the Middle East*** (Boston, 2003), is a critical look at U.S. policy in the region.

For expert analysis on the current situation in the region, see **B. Lewis,** ***What Went Wrong? Western Impact and Middle Eastern Response*** (Oxford, 2001), and **P. L. Bergen,** ***Holy War, Inc.: Inside the Secret World of Osama bin Laden*** (New York, 2001). Also see **M. Afkhami** and **E. Friedl,** ***In the Eye of the Storm: Women in Post-Revolutionary Iran*** (Syracuse, N.Y., 1994).

MIDDLE EASTERN LITERATURE For a scholarly but accessible overview of Arabic literature, see **M. M. Badawi,** ***A Short History of Modern Arab Literature*** (Oxford, 1993).

Visit the CourseMate website at **www.cengagebrain.com** for additional study tools and review materials for this chapter.

Chapter 30

Toward the Pacific Century?

© Buena Vista Images/Getty Images

The Petronas Towers in Kuala Lumpur, Malaysia

CHAPTER OUTLINE AND FOCUS QUESTIONS

South Asia

Q How did Gandhi's and Nehru's goals for India differ, and what role did each leader's views play in shaping modern India?

Southeast Asia

Q What kinds of problems have the nations of Southeast Asia faced since 1945, and how have they attempted to solve these problems?

Japan: Asian Giant

Q How did the Allied occupation after World War II change Japan's political and economic institutions, and what remained unchanged?

The Little Tigers

Q What factors have contributed to the economic success achieved by the Little Tigers? To what degree have they applied the Japanese model in forging their developmental strategies?

CRITICAL THINKING

Q What differences and similarities do you see in the performances of the nations of South, Southeast, and East Asia since World War II? What do you think accounts for the differences?

FIRST-TIME VISITORS to the Malaysian capital of Kuala Lumpur (KWAH-luh loom-POOR) are astonished to observe a pair of twin towers thrusting up above the surrounding buildings into the clouds. The Petronas Towers rise 1,483 feet from ground level; they were the world's tallest buildings at the time of their completion in 1998. (They have since been surpassed by Taipei 101, in Taiwan; the Shanghai World Financial Center; and Burj Khalifa, in Dubai.)

Beyond their status as an architectural achievement, the Petronas Towers announced the emergence of Southeast Asia as a major player on the international scene. It is no accident that the foundations were laid on the site of the Selangor Cricket Club, symbol of British colonial hegemony in Southeast Asia. "These towers," commented one local official, "will do wonders for Asia's self-esteem and confidence, which I think is very important, and which I think at this moment are at the point of takeoff."[1]

The sky-piercing towers in Kuala Lumpur and Taipei (TY-PAY) are not alone in signaling Asia's new prominence on the world stage in the century now unfolding. Several other cities in the region, including Hong Kong, Singapore, Tokyo, and Shanghai, have become major capitals of finance and monuments of economic prowess, rivaling the traditional centers of New York, London, Berlin, and Paris.

That the nations of the Pacific Rim would become a driving force in global development was all but unimaginable after World War II, when the Communist triumph in China ushered in an era of intense competition between the capitalist and socialist camps. Bitter conflicts in Korea and Vietnam were visible manifestations of a region in turmoil. Yet today, many of the nations of eastern Asia have become models of successful nation building, characterized by economic prosperity and political stability. They have heralded the opening of what has been called the "Pacific Century."

South Asia

FOCUS QUESTION: How did Gandhi's and Nehru's goals for India differ, and what role did each leader's views play in shaping modern India?

In 1947, nearly two centuries of British colonial rule came to an end when two new independent nations, India and Pakistan, came into being.

The End of the British Raj

During the 1930s, the nationalist movement in India was severely shaken by factional disagreements between Hindus and Muslims. The outbreak of World War II subdued these sectarian clashes, but they erupted again after the war ended in 1945. Battles between Hindus and Muslims broke out in several cities, and Muhammad Ali Jinnah (muh-HAM-ad ah-LEE JIN-uh) (1876–1948), leader of the Muslim League, demanded the creation of a separate state for each. Meanwhile, the Labour Party, which had long been critical of the British colonial legacy on both moral and economic grounds, had come to power in Britain, and the new prime minister, Clement Attlee, announced that power would be transferred to "responsible Indian hands" by June 1948.

But the imminence of independence did not dampen communal strife. As riots escalated, the British reluctantly accepted the inevitability of partition and declared that on August 15, 1947, two independent nations—Hindu India and Muslim Pakistan—would be established. Pakistan would be divided between the main area of Muslim habitation in the Indus River valley in the west and a separate territory in east Bengal 2,000 miles to the east. Although Mahatma Gandhi warned that partition would provoke "an orgy of blood,"[2] he was increasingly regarded as a figure of the past, and his views were ignored.

The British instructed the rulers in the princely states to choose which state they would join by August 15, but problems arose in predominantly Hindu Hyderabad (HY-der-uh-bahd), where the nawab (viceroy) was a Muslim, and mountainous Kashmir (KAZH-meer), where a Hindu prince ruled over a Muslim population. After independence was declared, the flight of millions of Hindus and Muslims across the borders led to violence and the deaths of more than a million people. One of the casualties was Gandhi, who was assassinated on January 30, 1948, as he was going to morning prayer. The assassin, a Hindu militant, was apparently motivated by Gandhi's opposition to a Hindu India.

Independent India

With independence, the Indian National Congress, now renamed the Congress Party, moved from opposition to the responsibility of power under Jawaharlal Nehru (juh-WAH-hur-lahl NAY-roo), the new prime minister. The prospect must have been intimidating. The vast majority of India's 400 million people were poor and illiterate. The new nation encompassed a significant number of ethnic groups and fourteen major languages. Although Congress Party leaders spoke bravely of building a new nation, Indian society still bore the scars of past wars and divisions.

The government's first problem was to resolve disputes left over from the transition period. The rulers of Hyderabad and Kashmir had both followed their own preferences rather than the wishes of their subject populations. Nehru was determined to include both states within India. In 1948, Indian troops invaded Hyderabad and annexed the area. India was also able to seize most of Kashmir, but at the cost of creating an intractable problem that has poisoned relations with Pakistan to the present day.

AN EXPERIMENT IN DEMOCRATIC SOCIALISM Under Nehru's leadership, India adopted a political system on the British model, with a figurehead president and a parliamentary form of government. A number of political parties operated legally, but the Congress Party, with its enormous prestige and charismatic leadership, was dominant at both the central and the local levels.

Nehru had been influenced by British socialism and patterned his economic policy roughly after the program of the British Labour Party. The state took over ownership of the major industries and resources, transportation, and utilities, while private enterprise was permitted at the local and retail levels. Farmland remained in private hands, but rural cooperatives were officially encouraged.

OPPOSING ✂ VIEWPOINTS

Two Visions for India

Although Jawaharlal Nehru and Mohandas Gandhi agreed on their desire for an independent India, their visions of the future of their homeland were dramatically different. Nehru favored industrialization to build material prosperity, whereas Gandhi praised the simple virtues of manual labor. The first excerpt is from a speech by Nehru; the second is from a letter written by Gandhi to Nehru.

Nehru's Socialist Creed

I am convinced that the only key to the solution of the world's problems and of India's problems lies in socialism, and when I use this word I do so not in a vague humanitarian way but in the scientific economic sense. . . . I see no way of ending the poverty, the vast unemployment, the degradation and the subjection of the Indian people except through socialism. That involves vast and revolutionary changes in our political and social structure, the ending of vested interests in land and industry, as well as the feudal and autocratic Indian states system. That means the ending of private property, except in a restricted sense, and the replacement of the present profit system by a higher ideal of cooperative service. . . . In short, it means a new civilization, radically different from the present capitalist order. Some glimpse we can have of this new civilization in the territories of the U.S.S.R. Much has happened there which has pained me greatly and with which I disagree, but I look upon that great and fascinating unfolding of a new order and a new civilization as the most promising feature of our dismal age.

A Letter to Jawaharlal Nehru

I believe that if India, and through India the world, is to achieve real freedom, then sooner or later we shall have to go and live in the villages—in huts, not in palaces. Millions of people can never live in cities and palaces in comfort and peace. Nor can they do so by killing one another, that is, by resorting to violence and untruth. . . . We can have the vision of . . . truth and nonviolence only in the simplicity of the villages. That simplicity resides in the spinning wheel and what is implied by the spinning wheel. . . .

You will not be able to understand me if you think that I am talking about the villages of today. My ideal village still exists only in my imagination. . . . In this village of my dreams the villager will not be dull—he will be all awareness. He will not live like an animal in filth and darkness. Men and women will live in freedom, prepared to face the whole world. There will be no plague, no cholera, and no smallpox. Nobody will be allowed to be idle or to wallow in luxury. Everyone will have to do body labor. Granting all this, I can still envisage a number of things that will have to be organized on a large scale. Perhaps there will even be railways and also post and telegraph offices. I do not know what things there will be or will not be. Nor am I bothered about it. If I can make sure of the essential thing, other things will follow in due course. But if I give up the essential thing, I give up everything.

What are the key differences between these two views on the future of India? Why do you think Nehru's proposals triumphed over Gandhi's?

Sources: Nehru's Socialist Creed. From *Sources of Indian Tradition* by William Theodore De Bary. Copyright © 1988 by Columbia University Press, New York. A Letter to Jawaharlal Nehru. Excerpt from Gandhi "Letter to Jawaharlal Nehru" pp. 328–331 from *Gandhi In India: In His Own Words*, Martin Green, ed. Copyright © 1987 by Navajivan Trust. Lebanon, NH: University Press of New England.

In other respects, Nehru was a devotee of Western materialism. He was convinced that to succeed, India must industrialize. In advocating industrialization, Nehru departed sharply from Gandhi, who believed that materialism was morally corrupting and that only simplicity and nonviolence (as represented by the traditional Indian village and the symbolic spinning wheel) could save India, and the world itself, from self-destruction (see the box above).

The primary themes of Nehru's foreign policy were anticolonialism and antiracism. Under his guidance, India took a neutral stance in the Cold War and sought to provide leadership to all newly independent nations in Asia, Africa, and Latin America. India's neutrality put it at odds with the United States, which during the 1950s was trying to mobilize all nations against what it viewed as the menace of international communism.

Relations with Pakistan continued to be troubled. India refused to consider Pakistan's claim to Kashmir, even though the majority of the population there were Muslims. Tension between the two countries persisted, erupting into war in 1965. In 1971, when riots against the Pakistani government broke out in East Pakistan, India intervened on the side of East Pakistan, which declared its independence as the new nation of Bangladesh (see Map 30.1).

THE POST-NEHRU ERA Nehru's death in 1964 aroused concern that Indian democracy was dependent on the Nehru mystique. When his successor, a Congress Party veteran, died in 1966, party leaders selected Nehru's daughter, Indira Gandhi (in-DEER-uh GAHN-dee) (no relation to Mahatma Gandhi), as the new prime minister. Gandhi (1917–1984) was inexperienced in politics, but she quickly showed the steely determination of her father.

Like Nehru, Gandhi embraced democratic socialism and a policy of neutrality in foreign affairs, but she was more activist in promoting her objectives than her father. To combat rural poverty, she nationalized banks, provided loans to peasants on easy terms, built low-cost housing, distributed land to the landless, and introduced electoral reforms to enfranchise the poor.

Gandhi was especially worried by India's growing population and, in an effort to curb the growth rate, adopted a policy of forced sterilization. This policy proved unpopular, however, and, along with growing official corruption and Gandhi's authoritarian tactics, led to her defeat in the general election of 1975, the first time the Congress Party had failed to win a majority at the national level.

A minority government of procapitalist parties was formed, but within two years, Gandhi was back in power. She now faced a new challenge, however, in the rise of religious strife. The most dangerous situation was in the Punjab (pun-PAHB), where militant Sikhs (SEEKS *or* SEE-ikhz) were demanding autonomy or even independence from India. Gandhi did not shrink from a confrontation and attacked Sikh rebels hiding in their Golden Temple in the city of Amritsar (uhm-RIT-ser). The incident aroused widespread anger among the Sikh community, and in 1984, Sikh members of Gandhi's personal bodyguard assassinated her.

By now, Congress Party politicians were convinced that the party could not remain in power without a member of the Nehru family at the helm. Gandhi's son Rajiv Gandhi (rah-JEEV GAHN-dee) (1944–1991), a commercial airline pilot with little interest in politics, was persuaded to replace his mother as prime minister. Rajiv lacked the strong ideological and political convictions of his mother and grandfather and allowed a greater role for private enterprise. But his government was criticized for cronyism, inefficiency, and corruption.

Rajiv Gandhi also sought to play a role in regional affairs, mediating a dispute between the government in Sri Lanka and Tamil rebels (known as the Elam Tigers) who were ethnically related to the majority population in southern India. The decision cost him his life: while campaigning for reelection in 1991, he was assassinated by a member of the Tiger organization. India faced the future without a member of the Nehru family as prime minister.

During the early 1990s, the Congress Party remained the leading party, but the powerful hold it once had on the Indian electorate was gone. New parties, such as the militantly Hindu Bharatiya Janata (BAR-ruh-tee-uh JAH-nuh-tuh) Party (BJP), actively vied with the Congress Party for control of the central and state governments. Growing political instability at the center was accompanied by rising tensions between Hindus and Muslims.

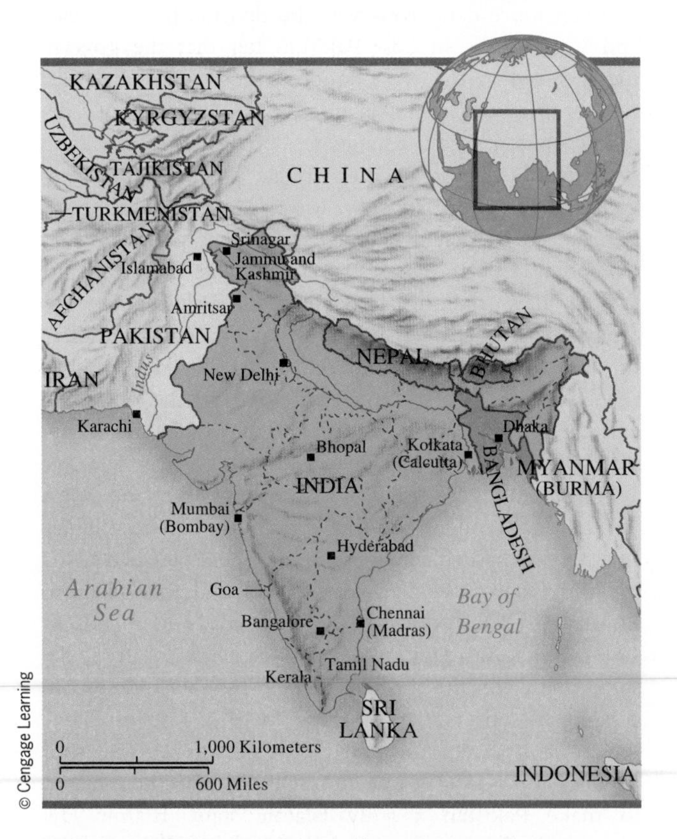

© Cengage Learning

MAP 30.1 Modern South Asia. This map shows the boundaries of all the states in contemporary South Asia.

 *Which of the countries on this map have a Muslim majority?*

CHRONOLOGY South Asia Since 1945	
India and Pakistan become independent	1947
Assassination of Mahatma Gandhi	1948
Death of Jawaharlal Nehru	1964
Indo-Pakistani War	1965
Indira Gandhi elected prime minister	1966
Bangladesh declares its independence	1971
Assassination of Indira Gandhi	1984
Assassination of Rajiv Gandhi	1991
Destruction of mosque at Ayodhya	1992
Benazir Bhutto removed from power in Pakistan	1997
Military coup overthrows civilian government in Pakistan	1999
U.S.-led forces oust Taliban in Afghanistan	2001
Congress Party returns to power in India	2004
Assassination of Benazir Bhutto	2007
Massive floods in the Indus River valley	2010
Osama bin Laden killed in Pakistan	2011

When a coalition government formed under Congress leadership collapsed, the BJP, under Prime Minister A. B. Vajpayee (VAHJ-py-ee) (b. 1924), ascended to power and played on Hindu sensibilities to build its political base. The new government based its success on an aggressive program of privatization in the industrial and commercial sectors and made a major effort to promote the nation's small but growing technological base. But BJP leaders had underestimated the discontent of India's less affluent citizens, and in the spring of 2004, a stunning defeat in national elections forced the Vajpayee government to resign. The Congress Party returned to power at the head of a coalition government based on a commitment to maintain economic growth while carrying out reforms in rural areas, including public works projects and hot lunch programs for all primary school children. The Congress Party remained in power after national elections held in the spring of 2009, but serious problems, including pervasive official corruption and sectarian strife between Hindus and Muslims, continue to bedevil the government.

The Land of the Pure: Pakistan Since Independence

When Pakistan achieved independence in August 1947, it was, unlike its neighbor India, in all respects a new nation, based on religious conviction rather than historical or ethnic tradition. The unique state consisted of two separate territories 2,000 miles apart. West Pakistan, including the Indus River basin and the West Punjab, was perennially short of water and was populated by dry crop farmers and peoples of the steppe. East Pakistan was made up of the marshy deltas of the Ganges and Brahmaputra Rivers. Densely populated with rice farmers, it was the home of the artistic and intellectual Bengalis (ben-GAH-leez).

The peoples of West Pakistan were especially diverse and included, among others, Pushtuns, Baluchis (buh-LOO-cheez), and Punjabis (pun-JAHB-eez). The Pushtuns are organized on a tribal basis and have kinship ties with the majority population across the border in neighboring Afghanistan. Many are nomadic and cross the border on a regular basis with their flocks. The Baluchis straddle the border with Iran, while the region of Punjab was divided between Pakistan and India at the moment of independence.

Even though the new state was an essentially Muslim society, its first years were marked by intense internal conflicts over religious, linguistic, and regional issues. Muhammad Ali Jinnah's vision of a democratic state that would assure freedom of religion and equal treatment for all was opposed by those who advocated a state based on Islamic principles.

Even more dangerous was the division between east and west. Many in East Pakistan felt that the government, based in the west, ignored their needs. In 1952, riots erupted in East Pakistan over the government's decision to adopt Urdu, a language derived from Hindi and used by Muslims in northern India, as the national language of the entire country. Most East Pakistanis spoke Bengali, an unrelated language. Tensions persisted, and in March 1971, East Pakistan declared its independence as the new nation of Bangladesh. Pakistani troops attempted to restore the central government's authority in the capital of Dhaka (DAK-uh *or* DAH-kuh), but rebel forces supported by India went on the offensive, and the government bowed to the inevitable and recognized independent Bangladesh.

The breakup of the union between East and West Pakistan undermined the fragile authority of the military regime that had ruled Pakistan since 1958 and led to its replacement by a civilian government under Zulfikar Ali Bhutto (ZOOL-fee-kahr ah-LEE BOO-toh) (1928–1979). But now religious tensions came to the fore, despite a new constitution that made a number of key concessions to conservative Muslims. In 1977, a new military government under General Zia Ul Ha'q (ZEE-ah ool HAHK) (1924–1988) came to power with a commitment to make Pakistan a truly Islamic state. Islamic law became the basis for social behavior as well as for the legal system. Laws governing the consumption of alcohol and the role of women were tightened in accordance with strict Muslim beliefs. But after Zia was killed in a plane crash, Pakistanis elected Benazir Bhutto (ben-uh-ZEER BOO-toh) (1953–2007), the daughter of Zulfikar Ali Bhutto and a supporter of secularism who had been educated in the United States. She too was removed from power by a military regime, in 1990, on charges of incompetence and corruption. Reelected in 1993, she attempted to crack down on opposition forces but was removed once again in 1997 amid renewed charges of official corruption. Her successor soon came under fire for the same reason and in 1999 was ousted by a military coup led by General Pervez Musharraf (pur-VEZ moo-SHAHR-uf) (b. 1943), who promised to restore political stability and honest government.

In September 2001, Pakistan became the focus of international attention when a coalition of forces arrived in neighboring Afghanistan to overthrow the Taliban regime and destroy the al-Qaeda terrorist network. Despite considerable support for the Taliban among the local population, President Musharraf pledged his help in bringing terrorists to justice. He also promised to return his country to the secular principles espoused by Muhammad Ali Jinnah. His situation was complicated by renewed tensions with India over Kashmir and a series of violent clashes between Muslims and Hindus in India. In 2003, however, relations began to improve as both sides promised to seek a peaceful solution to the Kashmir dispute.

By then, however, problems had begun to escalate on the domestic front. As Musharraf sought to fend off challenges from radical Muslim groups—some of them allied with Taliban forces in Afghanistan—secular opposition figures criticized the authoritarian nature of his regime. When Benazir Bhutto returned from exile to present herself as a candidate in presidential elections to be held early in 2008, she was assassinated, leading to widespread suspicions of official involvement. In September 2008, amid growing political turmoil, Benazir Bhutto's widower, Asif Ali Zardari (AH-seef ah-LEE zahr-DAR-ree) (b. 1955), was elected president of Pakistan.

The new civilian government, which is composed of an uneasy coalition of several political parties, faces a number of challenges in coping with the multitude of problems affecting the country today. Half of the entire population of 150 million live in poverty, and illiteracy is widespread. Massive flooding of the Indus River in 2010 killed nearly 2,000 people and left millions homeless.

In a nation where much of the rural population still professes loyalty to traditional tribal leaders, the sense of nationalism remains fragile, while military elites, who have long played a central role in Pakistani politics, continue to press their own agenda. The internal divisions within the country's ruling class became painfully apparent when the al-Qaeda leader Osama bin Laden was killed in a U.S. raid on his compound in the spring of 2011. The terrorist leader had been living secretly in Pakistan, in a villa in the military town of Abbottabad, within two hours' drive from the national capital of Islamabad. Many observers suspected that elements within Pakistan's military were aware of his presence, and the U.S. raid further exacerbated relations with its reputed ally.

Poverty and Pluralism in South Asia

The leaders of the new states that emerged in South Asia after World War II faced a number of problems. The peoples of South Asia were still overwhelmingly poor and illiterate, while the sectarian, ethnic, and cultural divisions that had plagued Indian society for centuries had not dissipated.

THE POLITICS OF COMMUNALISM Perhaps the most sincere effort to create democratic institutions was in India, where the new constitution called for social justice, liberty, equality of status and opportunity, and fraternity. All citizens were guaranteed protection from discrimination based on religious belief, race, caste, gender, or place of birth.

In theory, then, India became a full-fledged democracy on the British parliamentary model. In actuality, a number of distinctive characteristics made the system less than fully democratic in the Western sense but may also have enabled it to survive. As we have seen, India became in essence a one-party state. By leading the independence movement, the Congress Party had amassed massive public support, which enabled it to retain its preeminent position in Indian politics for three decades. After Nehru's death in 1964, however, problems emerged that had been disguised by his adept maneuvering. Part of the problem was the familiar one of a party too long in power. Party officials became complacent and all too easily fell prey to the temptations of corruption and pork-barrel politics.

Another problem was **communalism**. Beneath the surface unity of the new republic lay age-old ethnic, linguistic, and religious divisions. Because of India's vast size and complex history, no national language had ever emerged. Hindi was the most prevalent, but it was the native language of less than one-third of the population. During the colonial period, English had served as the official language of government, but it was spoken only by the educated elite and represented an affront to national pride. Eventually, India recognized fourteen official tongues, making the parliament sometimes sound like the Tower of Babel.

Divisiveness increased after Nehru's death, and under his successors, official corruption grew. Only the lack of appeal of its rivals and the Nehru family charisma carried on by his daughter Indira Gandhi kept the Congress Party in power. But she was unable to prevent the progressive disintegration of the party's power base at the state level, where regional or ideological parties won the allegiance of voters by exploiting ethnic or social revolutionary themes.

During the 1980s, religious tensions began to intensify. As we have seen, Gandhi's uncompromising approach to Sikh separatism led to her assassination in 1984. Under her son, Rajiv Gandhi, Hindu militants at Ayodhya (ah-YOHD-yuh), in northern India, demanded the destruction of a mosque built on the traditional site of King Rama's birthplace, where a Hindu temple had previously existed. In 1992, Hindu demonstrators destroyed the mosque and erected a temporary temple at the site, provoking clashes between Hindus and Muslims throughout the country. In protest, rioters in neighboring Pakistan destroyed a number of Hindu shrines in that country. In 2010, an Indian court ordered that the land that had contained the mosque be divided between the Hindu and Muslim plaintiffs.

In the early years of the new century, communal divisions intensified as militant Hindu groups demanded a state that would cater to the Hindu majority, now numbering more than 700 million people. In the eastern state of Orissa, pitched battles have broken out between Hindus and Christians over efforts by the latter to win converts to their faith. Manmohan Singh (MUHN-moh-hahn SING) (b. 1932), India's prime minister since 2004, has lamented what he calls an assault on India's "composite culture."[3]

THE ECONOMY Nehru's answer to the social and economic inequality that had long afflicted the subcontinent was socialism. He instituted a series of five-year plans, which led to the creation of a relatively large and reasonably efficient state-run industrial sector, centered on steel, vehicles, and textiles. Industrial production almost tripled between 1950 and 1965, and per capita income rose by 50 percent between 1950 and 1980, although it was still less than $300 (in U.S. dollars). By the 1970s, however, industrial growth had slowed. The lack of modern infrastructure was a problem, as was the rising price of oil, most of which had to be imported.

India's major economic weakness, however, was in agriculture. At independence, mechanization was almost unknown, fertilizer was rarely used, and most farms were small and uneconomical because of the Hindu tradition of dividing the land equally among all male children. As a result, the vast majority of the Indian people lived in conditions of abject poverty. Landless laborers outnumbered landowners by almost two to one. The government attempted to relieve the problem by redistributing land to the poor, limiting the size of landholdings, and encouraging farmers to form voluntary cooperatives. But all three programs ran into widespread opposition.

Another problem was overpopulation. Even before independence, the country had had difficulty supporting its people. In the 1950s and 1960s, the population grew by more than 2 percent annually, twice the nineteenth-century rate. Beginning in the 1960s, the Indian government sought to curb population growth. Indira Gandhi instituted a program combining monetary rewards and compulsory sterilization. Popular resistance undermined the program, however, and the goals were scaled back in the 1970s. Nevertheless, as a result of media popularization and better government programs, the trend today, even in poor rural villages, is toward smaller families. The average number of children a woman bears has declined from six in 1950 to three today. Still, India is on target to become the world's most populous nation, surpassing China by the year 2025.

After the death of Indira Gandhi in 1984, her son Rajiv proved more receptive to foreign investment and a greater role for the private sector in the economy. India began to export more manufactured goods, including computer software. The pace of change has accelerated under Rajiv Gandhi's successors, who have continued to transfer state-run industries to private hands. These policies have stimulated the growth of a prosperous new middle class, now estimated at more than 100 million. Consumerism has soared, and sales of television sets, DVD players, cell phones, and even automobiles have increased dramatically. Equally important, Western imports are being replaced by new products manufactured in India with Indian brand names, while large multinational corporations, such as the retail giant Walmart, have encountered difficulties in breaking into the Indian market (see the box on p. 797).

One consequence of India's entrance into the industrial age has been the emergence of a small but vibrant technological sector that provides many important services to the world's advanced nations. The city of Bengaluru (BEHNG-uh-luh-roo) (Bangalore) in South India has become an important technological center, benefiting from low wages and the presence of skilled labor with proficiency in the English language. It has also become a symbol of the "outsourcing" of jobs from the United States and Europe, a practice that has led to an increase in middle-class unemployment throughout the Western world.

As in the industrialized countries of the West, economic growth in India has been accompanied by environmental damage. Water and air pollution has led to illness

Say No to McDonald's and KFC!

One of the consequences of Rajiv Gandhi's decision to deregulate the Indian economy has been an increase in the presence of foreign corporations, including U.S. fast-food restaurant chains. Their arrival set off a storm of protest in India: from environmentalists concerned that raising grain for chickens is an inefficient use of land, from religious activists angry at the killing of animals for food, and from nationalists anxious to protect the domestic market from foreign competition. Fast-food restaurants now represent a growing niche in Indian society, but most cater to local tastes, avoiding beef products and offering many vegetarian dishes, such as the Veg Pizza McPuff. This piece, which appeared in the *Hindustan Times*, was written by Maneka Gandhi, a daughter-in-law of Indira Gandhi and a onetime minister of the environment who has emerged as a prominent rival of Congress Party president Sonia Gandhi.

Why India Doesn't Need Fast Food

India's decision to allow Pepsi Foods Ltd. to open 60 restaurants in India—30 each of Pizza Hut and Kentucky Fried Chicken—marks the first entry of multinational, meat-based junk-food chains into India. If this is allowed to happen, at least a dozen other similar chains will very quickly arrive, including the infamous McDonald's.

The implications of allowing junk-food chains into India are quite stark. As the name denotes, the foods served at Kentucky Fried Chicken (KFC) are chicken-based and fried. This is the worst combination possible for the body and can create a host of health problems, including obesity, high cholesterol, heart ailments, and many kinds of cancer. Pizza Hut products are a combination of white flour, cheese, and meat—again, a combination likely to cause disease. . . .

Then there is the issue of the environmental impact of junk-food chains. Modern meat production involves misuse of crops, water, energy, and grazing areas. In addition, animal agriculture produces surprisingly large amounts of air and water pollution.

KFC and Pizza Hut insist that their chickens be fed corn and soybeans. Consider the diversion of grain for this purpose. As the outlets of KFC and Pizza Hut increase in number, the poultry industry will buy up more and more corn to feed the chickens, which means that the corn will quickly disappear from the villages, and its increased price will place it out of reach for the common man. Turning corn into junk chicken is like turning gold into mud. . . .

It is already shameful that, in a country plagued by famine and flood, we divert 37 percent of our arable land to growing animal fodder. Were all of that grain to be consumed directly by humans, it would nourish five times as many people as it does after being converted into meat, milk, and eggs. . . .

Of course, it is not just the KFC and Pizza Hut chains of Pepsi Foods Ltd. that will cause all of this damage. Once we open India up by allowing these chains, dozens more will be eagerly waiting to come in. Each city in America has an average of 5,000 junk-food restaurants. Is that what we want for India?

Why does the author of this article oppose the introduction of fast-food restaurants in India? Do you think her complaints apply in the United States as well?

Source: From *World Press Review* (September 1995), p. 47.

and death for many people, and an environmental movement has emerged. Some critics, reflecting the traditional anti-imperialist attitude of Indian intellectuals, blame Western capitalist corporations for the problem, as in the highly publicized case of leakage from a foreign-owned chemical plant at Bhopal (boh-PAHL). Much of the problem, however, comes from state-owned factories erected with Soviet aid. And not all the environmental damage can be ascribed to industrialization. The Ganges River is so polluted by human overuse that it is risky for Hindu believers to bathe in it (see the comparative essay "One World, One Environment" on p. 798).

Moreover, many Indians have not benefited from the new prosperity. Nearly one-third of the population lives below the national poverty line. Millions continue to live in urban slums, such as the famous "City of Joy" in Kolkata (Calcutta), and most farm families remain desperately poor. Despite the socialist rhetoric of India's

COMPARATIVE ESSAY

One World, One Environment

A crucial factor affecting the evolution of society and the global economy in the early twenty-first century is the growing concern over the impact of industrialization on the earth's environment. Humans have always caused some harm to their natural surroundings, but never before has the danger of significant ecological damage been so extensive. The effects of chemicals introduced into the atmosphere or into rivers, lakes, and oceans are increasingly threatening the health and well-being of all living species.

For many years, environmental concern was focused on the developed countries of the West, where industrial effluents, automobile emissions, and the use of artificial fertilizers and insecticides led to urban smog, extensive damage to crops and wildlife, and a major reduction of the ozone layer in the upper atmosphere. In recent years, the problem has spread. China's headlong rush to industrialization has resulted in major ecological damage in that country. Industrial smog has created almost unlivable conditions in many cities in Asia, while hillsides denuded of their forests have led to severe erosion that has destroyed farmlands. Destruction of the rain forest is a growing problem in many parts of the world, notably in Brazil and Indonesia. With the forest cover across the earth rapidly disappearing, there is less plant life to perform the crucial process of reducing carbon dioxide levels in the atmosphere.

One positive note is that environmental concerns have taken on a truly global character. While the causes of global warming have not yet been definitively proved, though the release of carbon dioxide and other gases into the atmosphere as a result of industrialization apparently plays a part, it has become a source of sufficient concern to be the subject of an international conference in Kyoto, Japan, in December 1997. If, as many scientists predict, worldwide temperatures continue to increase, the rise in sea levels could pose a significant threat to low-lying islands and coastal areas throughout the world, while climatic change could lead to severe droughts or excessive rainfall in cultivated areas.

© Judyth Platt/Ecoscene/CORBIS

Destruction of the Environment. This stunted tree has been killed by acid rain, a combination of sulfuric and nitric acids mixed with moisture in the air. Entire forests of trees killed by acid rain are becoming common sights in Canada, the United States, and northern Europe.

It is one thing to recognize a problem, however, and another to solve it. So far, cooperative efforts among nations to alleviate environmental problems have all too often been hindered by economic forces or by political, ethnic, and religious disputes. The 1997 conference on global warming, for example, was marked by bitter disagreement over the degree to which developing countries should share the burden of cleaning up the environment. Few nations have been willing to take unilateral action that might pose an obstacle to economic development plans or lead to a rise in unemployment. In 2001, President George W. Bush refused to sign the Kyoto Agreement on the grounds that it discriminated against advanced Western countries. Subsequent conferences on global warming, including the 2009 conference in Copenhagen, Denmark, and the 2011 conference in Durban, South Africa, also have yielded few concrete results, despite a more active role by the United States.

What are the major reasons why progress in cleaning up the environment has been so difficult to achieve?

leaders, the inequality of wealth in India is as pronounced as it is in capitalist nations in the West. Indeed, India has been described as two nations: an educated urban India of 100 million people surrounded by more than nine times that many impoverished peasants in the countryside (see the comparative illustration on p. 799).

Such problems are even more serious in neighboring Pakistan and Bangladesh. The overwhelming majority of

COMPARATIVE ILLUSTRATION

EARTH & ENVIRONMENT

Two Indias. Contemporary India is a study in contrasts. In the photo at the top, middle-class students learn to use a computer, a symbol of their country's recent drive to join the global technological marketplace. Yet India today remains primarily a nation of villages. In the photo below, women in colorful saris fill their pails with water at the village well. As in many developing countries, the scarcity of water is one of India's most crucial problems.

Do such stark contrasts between wealth and poverty define conditions in all other countries in Asia?

© Indranil Mukherjee/AFP/Getty Images

© William J. Duiker

Pakistan's citizens are poor, and at least half are illiterate. The recent flooding along the Indus River has had a devastating effect on people living in the region and was described by a United Nations official as the worst humanitarian crisis in the sixty-five years of the UN's existence. Prospects for the future are not bright, for Pakistan lacks a modern technological sector to serve as a magnet for the emergence of a modern middle class.

CASTE, CLASS, AND GENDER The Indian constitution of 1950 guaranteed equal treatment and opportunity for all, regardless of caste, and prohibited discrimination based on untouchability. In recent years, the government has enacted a number of laws guaranteeing access to education and employment to all Indians, regardless of caste affiliation, and a number of individuals of low caste have attained high positions in Indian society. Nevertheless, prejudice is hard to eliminate, and the problem persists, particularly in rural villages, where *harijans* (HAR-ih-jans), now called ***dalits*** (DAH-lits), still perform menial tasks and are often denied fundamental rights.

Gender equality has also been difficult to establish. After independence, India's leaders also sought to equalize treatment of the sexes. The constitution expressly

© William J. Duiker

Young Hindu Bride in Gold Bangles. Awaiting the marriage ceremony, a young bride sits with her female relatives at the Meenakshi Hindu temple, one of the largest in southern India. Although child marriage is illegal, Indian girls are still married at a young age. With the marital union arranged by the parents, this young bride may not have met her groom. Bedecked in gold jewelry and rich silks—part of her dowry—she nervously waits the priest's blessing before she moves to her husband's home. There she will begin a life of servitude to her in-laws' family.

forbade discrimination based on gender and called for equal pay for equal work. Laws prohibited child marriage, *sati*, and the payment of a dowry by the bride's family. Women were encouraged to attend school and enter the labor market.

Such laws, along with the dynamics of economic and social change, have had a major impact on the lives of many Indian women. Middle-class women in urban areas are much more likely to seek employment outside the home, and many hold managerial and professional positions. Some Indian women, however, choose to play a dual role—a modern one in their work and in the marketplace and a more submissive, traditional one at home.

Like other aspects of life, the role of women has changed much less in rural areas. In the early 1960s, many villagers still practiced the institution of *purdah*. Female children are still much less likely to receive an education. The overall literacy rate in India today is about 60 percent, but it is less than 50 percent among women. Laws relating to dowry, child marriage, and inheritance are routinely ignored in the countryside. There have been a few highly publicized cases of *sati*, although undoubtedly more women die of mistreatment at the hands of their husband or of other members of his family.

South Asian Literature Since Independence

Recent decades have witnessed a prodigious outpouring of literature in India. Because of the vast quantity of works published (India is currently the third-largest publisher of English-language books in the world), only a few of the most prominent fiction writers can be mentioned here. Anita Desai (dess-SY) (b. 1937) was one of the first prominent female writers to emerge from contemporary India. Her writing focuses on the struggle of Indian women to achieve a degree of independence. In her first novel, *Cry, the Peacock*, the heroine finally seeks liberation by murdering her husband, preferring freedom at any cost to remaining a captive of traditional society.

The most controversial writer from India today is Salman Rushdie (b. 1947). In *Midnight's Children* (1980), he linked his protagonist, born on the night of independence, to the history of modern India, its achievements, and its frustrations. Rushdie's later novels have tackled such problems as religious intolerance, political tyranny, social injustice, and greed and corruption. His attack on Islamic fundamentalism in *The Satanic Verses* (1988) won plaudits from literary critics but provoked widespread criticism among Muslims, including a death sentence by Iran's Ayatollah Khomeini.

What Is the Future of India?

Indian society looks increasingly Western in form, if not in content. As in a number of other Asian and African societies, the distinction between traditional and modern, or indigenous and westernized, sometimes seems to be a simple dichotomy between rural and urban. The major cities appear modern and westernized, but the villages have changed little since precolonial days.

Yet traditional practices appear to be more resilient in India than in many other societies, and the result is often a synthesis rather than a clash between conflicting institutions and values. Clothing styles in the streets where the *sari* and *dhoti* continue to be popular, religious practices in the temples, and social relationships in the home all testify to the importance of tradition in India.

One disadvantage of the eclectic approach, which seeks to blend the old and the new rather than choosing one over the other, is that sometimes contrasting traditions cannot be reconciled. In his book *India: A Wounded Civilization*, V. S. Naipaul (NY-pahl) (b. 1932), a Trinidadian of Indian descent who received the Nobel Prize for Literature in 2001, charged that Mahatma Gandhi's glorification of poverty and the simple Indian village was an obstacle to efforts to overcome the poverty, ignorance, and degradation of India's past and build a prosperous modern society. Gandhi's vision of a spiritual India, Naipaul complained, was a balm for defeatism and an excuse for failure.

Yet the appeal of Gandhi's philosophy remains a major part of the country's heritage. As historian Martha Nussbaum points out in *The Clash Within: Democracy, Religious Violence, and India's Future*, much of India's rural population continues to hold traditional beliefs, such as the concept of *karma* and inherent caste distinctions, that are incompatible with the capitalist work ethic and the democratic belief in equality before the law. Yet these beliefs provide a measure of identity and solace often lacking in other societies where such traditional spiritual underpinnings have eroded.

India, like Pakistan, also faces a number of other serious challenges. As a democratic and pluralistic society, India is unable to launch major programs without popular consent and thus cannot move as quickly or often as effectively as an authoritarian system like China's. At the same time, India's institutions provide a mechanism to prevent the emergence of a despotic government elite interested only in its own survival. Nevertheless, whether India will be able to meet its challenges remains an open question.

Southeast Asia

FOCUS QUESTION: What kinds of problems have the nations of Southeast Asia faced since 1945, and how have they attempted to solve these problems?

As we have seen (see Chapter 25), Japanese wartime occupation had a great impact on attitudes among the peoples of Southeast Asia. It demonstrated the vulnerability of colonial rule in the region and showed that an Asian power could defeat Europeans. The Allied governments themselves also contributed—sometimes unwittingly—to rising aspirations for independence by promising self-determination for all peoples at the end of the war.

Some followed through on their promise. In July 1946, the United States granted total independence to the Philippines. The Americans maintained a military presence on the islands, however, and U.S. citizens retained economic and commercial interests in the new country.

The British, too, were willing to bring an end to a century of imperialism in the region. In 1948, the Union of Burma received its independence. Malaya's turn came in 1957, after a Communist guerrilla movement had been suppressed.

The French and the Dutch, however, both regarded their colonies in the region as economic necessities as well as symbols of national grandeur and refused to turn them over to nationalist movements at the end of the war. The Dutch attempted to suppress a rebellion in the East Indies led by Sukarno (soo-KAHR-noh) (1901–1970), leader of the Indonesian Nationalist Party. But the United States, which feared a Communist victory there, pressured the Dutch to grant independence to Sukarno and his non-Communist forces, and in 1950, the Dutch finally agreed to recognize the new Republic of Indonesia.

The situation was somewhat different in Vietnam, where the Communists seized power throughout most of the country. After the French refused to recognize the new government and reimposed their rule, war broke out in December 1946. At the time, it was only an anticolonial war, but it would soon become much more (see Chapter 26).

In the Shadow of the Cold War

Many of the leaders of the newly independent states in Southeast Asia (see Map 30.2 on p. 802) admired Western political institutions and hoped to adapt them to their own countries. New constitutions were patterned on Western democratic models, and multiparty political systems quickly sprang into operation.

THE SEARCH FOR A NEW POLITICAL CULTURE By the 1960s, most of these budding experiments in pluralist democracy had been abandoned or were under serious threat. Some had been replaced by military or one-party autocratic regimes. In Burma, a moderate government based on the British parliamentary system and dedicated to Buddhism and nonviolent Marxism had given way to a military dictatorship. In Thailand, too, the military now ruled. In the Philippines, President Ferdinand Marcos (MAHR-kohs) (1917–1989) discarded democratic restraints and established his own centralized control. In South Vietnam, under pressure from Communist-led insurgents, Ngo Dinh Diem and his successors paid lip

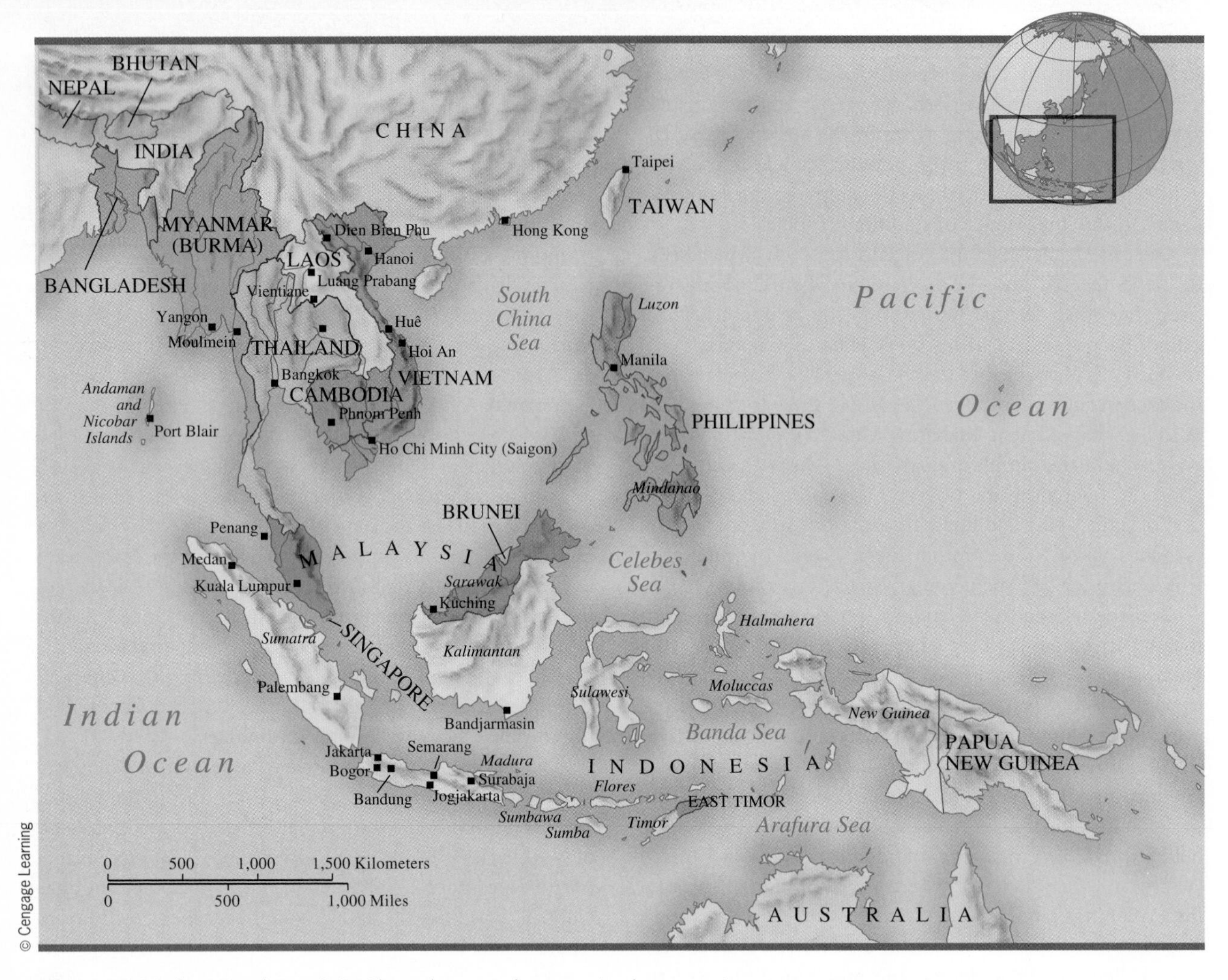

© Cengage Learning

MAP 30.2 Modern Southeast Asia. Shown here are the countries that comprise contemporary Southeast Asia. The names of major islands are indicated in italic type.

Which of the countries in Southeast Asia have democratic governments?

service to the Western democratic model but ruled by authoritarian means. The North, under the rule of Ho Chi Minh and his colleagues, became a Communist dictatorship.

One problem faced by most of these states was that independence had not brought material prosperity or ended economic inequality and the domination of the local economies by foreign interests. Most economies in the region were still characterized by tiny industrial sectors; they lacked technology, educational resources, and capital investment.

The presence of widespread ethnic, linguistic, cultural, and economic differences also made the transition to Western-style democracy difficult. In Malaya, for example, the majority Malays—most of whom were farmers—feared economic and political domination by the local Chinese minority, who were much more experienced in industry and commerce. In 1961, the Federation of Malaya, whose ruling party was dominated by Malays, integrated former British possessions on the island of Borneo into the new Union of Malaysia in a move to increase the non-Chinese proportion of the country's population.

The most prominent example of a failed experiment in democracy was in Indonesia. In 1950, the new leaders drew up a constitution creating a parliamentary system under a titular presidency. Sukarno was elected the first president. A spellbinding orator, Sukarno played a major role in creating a sense of national identity among the disparate peoples of the Indonesian archipelago (see the box on p. 803).

But Sukarno grew exasperated at the incessant maneuvering among devout Muslims, Communists, and the

The Golden Throat of President Sukarno

President Sukarno of Indonesia was a spellbinding speaker and a charismatic leader of his nation's struggle for independence. These two selections are from speeches in which Sukarno promoted two of his favorite projects: Indonesian nationalism and "guided democracy." The force that would guide Indonesia, of course, was to be Sukarno himself.

Sukarno on Indonesian Greatness

What was Indonesia in 1945? What was our nation then? It was only two things, only two things. A flag and a song. That is all. (Pause, finger held up as afterthought.) But no, I have omitted the main ingredient. I have missed the most important thing of all. I have left out the burning fire of freedom and independence in the breast and heart of every Indonesian. That is the most important thing—this is the vital chord—the spirit of our people, the spirit and determination to be free. This was our nation in 1945—the spirit of our people!

And what are we today? We are a great nation. We are bigger than Poland. We are bigger than Turkey. We have more people than Australia, than Canada, we are bigger in area and have more people than Japan. In population now we are the fifth-largest country in the world. In area, we are even bigger than the United States of America. The American Ambassador, who is here with us, admits this. Of course, he points out that we have a lot of water in between our thousands of islands. But I say to him—America has a lot of mountains and deserts, too!

Sukarno on Guided Democracy

Indonesia's democracy is not liberal democracy. Indonesian democracy is not the democracy of the world of Montaigne or Voltaire. Indonesia's democracy is not à la America, Indonesia's democracy is not the Soviet—NO! Indonesia's democracy is the democracy which is implanted in the breasts of the Indonesian people, and it is that which I have tried to dig up again, and have put forward as an offering to you. . . . If you, especially the undergraduates, are still clinging to and being borne along the democracy made in England, or democracy made in France, or democracy made in America, or democracy made in Russia, you will become a nation of copyists!

What are Sukarno's criticisms of Western democracy? Can you think of other instances in Asia or Africa where new leaders sought to adapt Western institutions to local realities?

Source: From Howard Jones, *Indonesia: The Possible Dream* (New York: Harcourt Brace Jovanovich, Hoover Institute, 1971), pp. 223, 237.

army, and in the late 1950s he dissolved the constitution and attempted to rule on his own through what he called guided democracy. As he described it, **guided democracy** was closer to Indonesian traditions and superior to the Western variety. Highly suspicious of the West, Sukarno nationalized foreign-owned enterprises and sought economic aid from China and the Soviet Union while relying for domestic support on the Indonesian Communist Party.

The army and many devout Muslims resented Sukarno's increasing reliance on the Communists, and Muslims were further upset by his refusal to consider a state based on Islamic principles. In 1965, military officers launched a coup d'état that provoked a mass popular uprising, which resulted in the slaughter of several hundred thousand suspected Communists, many of whom were overseas Chinese, long distrusted by the Muslim majority (see the Film & History feature on p. 804). In 1967, a military government under General Suharto (soo-HAHR-toh) (1921–2008) was installed.

The new government made no pretensions of reverting to democratic rule, but it did restore good relations with the West and sought foreign investment to repair the country's ravaged economy. But it also found it difficult to placate Muslim demands for an Islamic state.

On the Road to Political Reform

With the end of the Vietnam War and the gradual rapprochement between China and the United States in the late 1970s, the ferment and uncertainty that had marked the first three decades of independence in Southeast Asia

FILM & HISTORY

The Year of Living Dangerously (1982)

President Sukarno of Indonesia was one of the most prominent figures in Southeast Asia in the first two decades after World War II. A key figure in the nationalist movement while the country was under Dutch colonial rule, he was elected president of the new republic when it was granted formal independence in 1950. The charismatic Sukarno initially won broad popular support for his efforts to end colonial dependency and improve living conditions for the impoverished local population. But the government's economic achievements failed to match his fiery oratory, and when political unrest began to spread through Indonesian society in the early 1960s, Sukarno dismantled the parliamentary system that had been installed at independence and began to crack down on dissidents.

These conditions provide the setting for the Australian film *The Year of Living Dangerously* (1982). Based on a novel of the same name by Christian Koch, the movie takes place in the summer of 1965, when popular unrest against the dictatorial government had reached a crescendo and the country appeared about to descend into civil war. The newly arrived Australian reporter Guy Hamilton (Mel Gibson) is befriended by a diminutive Chinese-Indonesian journalist named Billy Kwan, effectively played by Linda Hunt, who won an Academy Award for her performance. Kwan, who has become increasingly disenchanted with Sukarno's failure to live up his promises, introduces Hamilton to the seamy underside of Indonesian society, as well as to radical elements connected to the Communist Party who are planning a coup to seize power in Jakarta.

The movie reaches a climax as Hamilton—a quintessentially ambitious reporter out to get a scoop on the big story—inadvertently becomes involved in the Communist plot and arouses the suspicions of

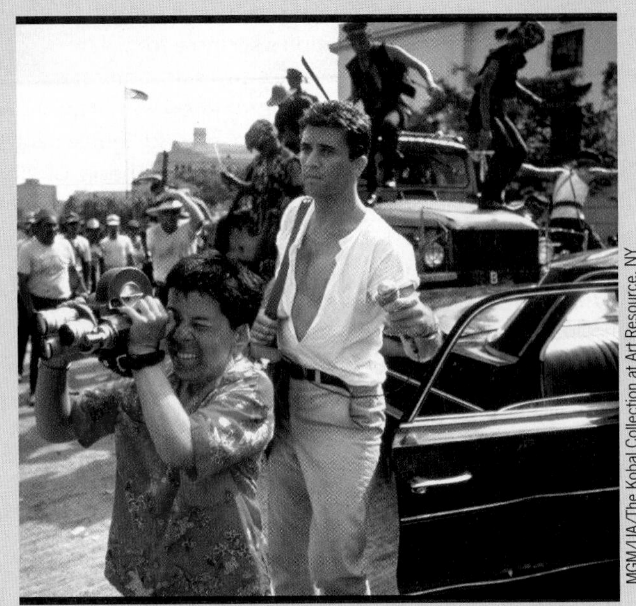

MGM/UA/The Kobal Collection at Art Resource, NY

Photographer Billy Kwan (Linda Hunt) and reporter Guy Hamilton (Mel Gibson) film a political protest.

government authorities. As Indonesia appears ready to descend into chaos, Hamilton finally recognizes the danger and manages to board the last plane from Jakarta. Others are not so fortunate, as Sukarno's security police crack down forcefully on critics of his regime.

The Year of Living Dangerously (the title comes from a remark made by Sukarno during his presidential address in August 1964) is an important if underrated film that dramatically portrays a crucial incident in a volatile region caught in the throes of the Cold War. The beautiful scenery (the movie was shot in the Philippines because the story was banned in Indonesia) and a haunting film score help create a mood of tension spreading through a tropical paradise.

gradually gave way to an era of greater political stability and material prosperity. In the Philippines, the dictatorial Marcos regime was overthrown by a massive public uprising in 1986 and replaced by a democratically elected government under President Corazon Aquino (KOR-uh-zahn ah-KEE-noh) (1933–2009), the widow of a popular politician assassinated a few years earlier. Aquino was unable to resolve many of the country's chronic economic and social difficulties, however, and political stability remains elusive. At the same time, Muslims on the southern island of Mindanao (min-duh-NAH-oh) have mounted a terrorist campaign in an effort to obtain autonomy or independence.

In other nations, the trends have been modestly favorable. Malaysia is a practicing democracy, although tensions persist between Malays and Chinese as well as between secular and orthodox Muslims who seek to create an Islamic state. In neighboring Thailand, the military has found it expedient to hold national elections for civilian governments, but the danger of a military takeover is never far beneath the surface. In the fall of 2008, massive protests against the existing government threatened to throw Thai society into a state of paralysis. Burma, now renamed Myanmar, continues to be ruled by a military junta, although the governement has recently shown tantalizing signs of willingness to moderate its policies to open doors to the outside world.

INDONESIA AFTER SUHARTO For years, a major exception to the trend toward political pluralism in the region was Indonesia, where Suharto ruled without restraints. But in 1997, protests against widespread official corruption and demands by Muslims for a larger role for Islam in Indonesian society led to violent street riots and calls for Suharto's resignation. Forced to step down in the spring of 1998, Suharto was replaced by his deputy B. J. Habibie (hab-BEEB-ee) (b. 1936), who called for the establishment of a national assembly to select a new government based on popular aspirations.

The new government faced internal challenges from dissident elements seeking autonomy or separation from the republic, as well as from religious forces seeking to transform the country into an Islamic state. Under pressure from the international community, Indonesia agreed to grant independence to the onetime Portuguese colony of East Timor, where the majority of the people are Roman Catholics. But violence provoked by pro-Indonesian militia units forced many refugees to flee the country. Religious tensions also erupted between Muslims and Christians elsewhere in the archipelago, and Muslim rebels in western Sumatra demanded a new state based on strict adherence to fundamentalist Islam. In the meantime, a terrorist attack directed at tourists on the island of Bali aroused fears that the Muslim nation had become a haven for terrorist elements throughout the region.

In direct presidential elections held in 2004, General Susilo Yudhyono (soo-SEE-loh yood-heh-YOH-noh) (b. 1949) defeated Megawati Sukarnoputri (meg-uh-WAH-tee soo-kahr-noh-POO-tree) (b. 1947), the incumbent president and Sukarno's daughter. The new chief executive promised a new era of political stability, honest government, and economic reform while ceding more authority to the country's thirty-three provinces. Pressure from traditional Muslims to abandon the nation's secular tradition and move toward the creation of an Islamic state continues, but the level of religious and ethnic tension has declined somewhat. In elections held in 2009, Yudhyono won a second term in office, while popular support for Islamic parties dropped from 38 percent to 26 percent. That the country was able to hold democratic elections in the midst of such tensions holds some promise for the future.

THE VIETNAMESE EXCEPTION As always, Vietnam is a special case. After achieving victory over South Vietnam with the fall of Saigon in the spring of 1975 (see Chapter 26), the Communist government in Hanoi pursued the rapid reunification of the two zones under Communist Party rule and laid plans to carry out a socialist transformation throughout the country, now renamed the Socialist Republic of Vietnam. The result was an economic disaster, and in 1986, party leaders followed the example of Mikhail Gorbachev in the Soviet Union and introduced their own version of *perestroika* in Vietnam (see Chapter 27). The trend in recent years has been toward a mixed capitalist-socialist economy along Chinese lines and a greater popular role in the governing process. Elections for the unicameral parliament are more open than in the past. The government remains suspicious of Western-style democracy, however, and represses any opposition to the Communist Party's guiding role over the state.

FINANCIAL CRISIS AND RECOVERY The trend toward more representative systems of government in the region has been due in part to increasing prosperity and the growth of an affluent and educated middle class. Although Indonesia, Burma, and the three Indochinese states are still overwhelmingly agrarian, Malaysia and Thailand have been undergoing relatively rapid economic development.

In the late summer of 1997, however, these economic gains were threatened and popular faith in the ultimate benefits of globalization was shaken as a financial crisis swept through the region. The crisis was triggered by a number of problems, including growing budget deficits caused by excessive government expenditures on ambitious development projects, irresponsible lending and investment practices by financial institutions, and an overvaluation of local currencies relative to the U.S. dollar. An underlying problem was the prevalence of backroom deals between politicians and business leaders that temporarily enriched both groups at the cost of eventual economic dislocation.

As local currencies plummeted in value, the International Monetary Fund agreed to provide assistance, but only on the condition that the governments concerned permit greater transparency in their economic systems and allow market forces to operate more freely, even at the price of bankruptcies and the loss of jobs. By the early 2000s, there were signs that the economies in the region had weathered the crisis and were beginning to recover. The massive tsunami that struck the region in

CHRONOLOGY **Southeast Asia Since 1945**	
Philippines becomes independent	1946
Beginning of Franco-Vietminh War	1946
Burma becomes independent	1948
Republic of Indonesia becomes independent	1950
Malaya becomes independent	1957
Beginning of Sukarno's "guided democracy" in Indonesia	1959
Military seizes power in Indonesia	1965
Founding of ASEAN	1967
Fall of Saigon to North Vietnamese forces	1975
Vietnamese invade Cambodia	1978
Corazon Aquino elected president in the Philippines	1986
Vietnamese withdraw from Cambodia	1991
Vietnam becomes a member of ASEAN	1996
Suharto steps down as president of Indonesia	1998
Tsunami causes widespread death and destruction throughout the region	2004
Antigovernment protests erupt in Thailand	2008
Reelection of President Yudhyono in Indonesia	2009

December 2004 was another setback to economic growth, as well as a human tragedy of enormous proportions, but as the decade wore on, progress resumed, and today the nations of Southeast Asia, with a few exceptions, are among the fastest growing in the world.

Regional Conflict and Cooperation: The Rise of ASEAN

Southeast Asian states have also been hampered by serious tensions among themselves. Some of these tensions were a consequence of historical rivalries and territorial disputes that had been submerged during the long era of colonial rule. Cambodia, for example, has bickered with both of its neighbors, Thailand and Vietnam, over mutual frontiers drawn up originally by the French for their own convenience.

After the fall of Saigon and the reunification of Vietnam under Communist rule in 1975, the lingering border dispute between Cambodia and Vietnam erupted again. In April 1975, a brutal revolutionary regime under the leadership of the Khmer Rouge (KMAIR ROOZH) dictator Pol Pot (POHL PAHT) (c. 1928–1998) came to power in Cambodia and proceeded to carry out the massacre of more than one million Cambodians. Then, claiming that vast territories in the Mekong delta had been seized from Cambodia by the Vietnamese in previous centuries, the Khmer Rouge regime launched attacks across the common border. In response, Vietnamese forces invaded Cambodia in December 1978 and installed a pro-Hanoi regime in Phnom Penh (puh-NAHM PEN). Fearful of Vietnam's increasing power in the region, China launched a brief attack on Vietnam to demonstrate its displeasure.

The outbreak of war among the erstwhile Communist allies aroused the concern of other countries in the neighborhood. In 1967, several non-Communist countries had

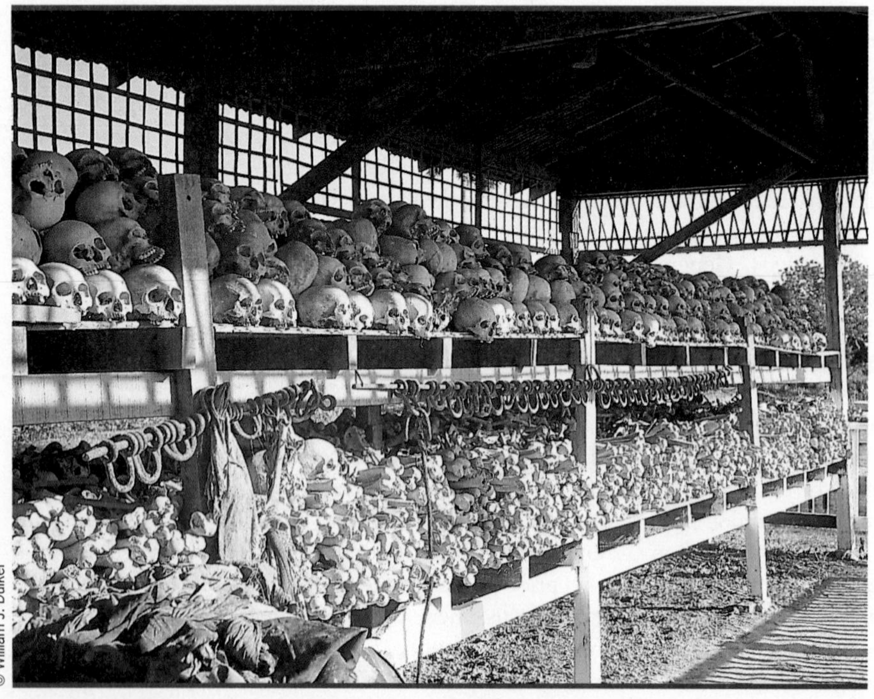
© William J. Duiker

Holocaust in Cambodia. When the Khmer Rouge seized power in Cambodia in April 1975, they immediately emptied the capital of Phnom Penh and systematically began to eliminate opposition elements throughout the country. Thousands were tortured in the infamous Tuol Sleng prison and then marched out to the countryside, where they were massacred. Their bodies were thrown into massive pits. The succeeding government disinterred the remains, which are now displayed at an outdoor museum on the site. Today, a measure of political and economic stability has begun to return to the country. In 2010, the commandant of the prison, Comrade Duch, was convicted of war crimes and crimes against humanity.

established the Association of Southeast Asian Nations, or **ASEAN**. Composed of Indonesia, Malaysia, Thailand, Singapore, and the Philippines, ASEAN at first concentrated on cooperative social and economic endeavors, but after the end of the Vietnam War, it cooperated with other states in an effort to force the Vietnamese to withdraw from Cambodia. In 1991, the Vietnamese finally withdrew, and a new government was formed in Phnom Penh.

The growth of ASEAN from a weak collection of diverse states into a stronger organization whose members cooperate militarily and politically has helped provide the nations of Southeast Asia with a more cohesive voice to represent their interests on the world stage. The admission of Vietnam into ASEAN in 1996 provided both Hanoi and its neighbors with greater leverage in dealing with China—their powerful neighbor to the north, whose claims of ownership over islands in the South China Sea have aroused widespread concern among its neighbors to the south.

Daily Life: Town and Country in Contemporary Southeast Asia

The urban-rural dichotomy observed in India also is found in Southeast Asia, where the cities resemble those in the West while the countryside often appears little changed from precolonial days. In cities such as Bangkok, Manila, and Jakarta, broad boulevards lined with skyscrapers alternate with muddy lanes passing through neighborhoods packed with wooden shacks topped by thatch or rusty tin roofs. Nevertheless, in recent decades, millions of Southeast Asians have fled to these urban slums. Although most available jobs are menial, the pay is better than in the villages.

TRADITIONAL CUSTOMS, MODERN VALUES The urban migrants change not only their physical surroundings but their attitudes and values as well. Sometimes the move leads to a decline in traditional beliefs. Nevertheless, Buddhist, Muslim, and Confucian beliefs remain strong, even in cosmopolitan cities such as Bangkok, Jakarta, and Singapore. This preference for the traditional also shows up in lifestyle. Native dress—or an eclectic blend of Asian and Western dress—is still common. Traditional music, art, theater, and dance remain popular, although Western rock music has become fashionable among the young, and Indonesian filmmakers complain that Western films are beginning to dominate the market.

CHANGING ROLES FOR WOMEN One of the most significant changes that has taken place in Southeast Asia in recent decades is in the role of women in society. In general, women in the region have historically faced fewer restrictions on their activities and enjoyed a higher status than women elsewhere in Asia. Nevertheless, they were not the equal of men in every respect. With independence, Southeast Asian women gained new rights. Virtually all of the constitutions adopted by the newly independent states granted women full legal and political rights, including the right to work. Today, women have increased opportunities for education and have entered careers previously reserved for men. Women have become more active in politics, and some have served as heads of state.

Yet women are not truly equal to men in any country in Southeast Asia. In Vietnam, women are legally equal to men, yet until recently no women had served in the Communist Party's ruling politburo. In Thailand, Malaysia, and Indonesia, women rarely hold senior positions in government service or in the boardrooms of major corporations.

A Region in Flux

Today, the Western image of a Southeast Asia mired in the Vietnam conflict and the tensions of the Cold War has become a memory. In ASEAN, the states in the region have created the framework for a regional organization that can serve their common political, economic, technological, and security interests. A few members of ASEAN are already on the road to advanced development.

To be sure, there are continuing signs of trouble. The financial crisis of the late 1990s aroused serious political unrest in Indonesia, and the region's economies, though recovering, still bear the scars of the crisis. Radical Islamic terrorist groups have established a presence in the region. Although there are tantalizing signs of change in Myanmar, the country remains mired in a state of chronic underdevelopment. The three states of Indochina remain potentially unstable and have not yet been fully integrated into the region as a whole. All things considered, however, the situation is more promising today than would have seemed possible a generation ago. Unlike the situation in Africa and the Middle East, the nations of Southeast Asia have put aside the bitter legacy of the colonial era to embrace the wave of globalization that has been sweeping the world in the post–World War II era.

Japan: Asian Giant

FOCUS QUESTION: How did the Allied occupation after World War II change Japan's political and economic institutions, and what remained unchanged?

In August 1945, Japan was in ruins, its cities destroyed, its vast Asian empire in ashes, its land occupied by a foreign army. Half a century later, Japan had emerged as the second-greatest industrial power in the world, democratic in form and content and a source of stability throughout the region. Japan's achievement spawned a number of Asian imitators.

The Transformation of Modern Japan

For five years after the end of the war in the Pacific, Japan was governed by an Allied administration under the command of U.S. General Douglas MacArthur. As commander of the occupation administration, MacArthur was responsible for demilitarizing Japanese society, destroying the Japanese war machine, trying Japanese civilian and military officials charged with war crimes, and laying the foundations of postwar Japanese society.

One of the sturdy pillars of Japanese militarism had been the giant business cartels, known as *zaibatsu* (see Chapter 24). Allied policy was designed to break up the *zaibatsu* into smaller units in the belief that corporate concentration not only hindered competition but was inherently undemocratic and conducive to political authoritarianism. Occupation planners also intended to promote the formation of independent labor unions in order to lessen the power of the state over the economy and provide a mouthpiece for downtrodden Japanese workers. Economic inequality in rural areas was to be reduced by a comprehensive land reform program that would turn the land over to those who farmed it. Finally, the educational system was to be remodeled along American lines so that it would turn out independent individuals rather than automatons subject to manipulation by the state.

The Allied program was an ambitious and even audacious plan to remake Japanese society and has been justly praised for its clear-sighted vision and altruistic motives. Parts of the program, such as the constitution, the land reforms, and the educational system, succeeded brilliantly. But as other concerns began to intervene, changes or compromises were made that were not always successful. In particular, with the rise of Cold War sentiment in the United States in the late 1940s, the goal of decentralizing the Japanese economy gave way to the desire to make Japan a key partner in the effort to defend East Asia against international communism. Convinced of the need to promote economic recovery in Japan, U.S. policy makers began to show more tolerance for the *zaibatsu*. Concerned about growing radicalism within the new labor movement, U.S. occupation authorities placed less emphasis on the independence of the labor unions.

The Cold War also affected U.S. foreign relations with Japan. On September 8, 1951, the United States and other former belligerent nations signed a peace treaty restoring Japanese independence. In turn, Japan renounced any claim to such former colonies or territories as Taiwan, Korea, and southern Sakhalin and the Kurile Islands (see Map 30.3). On the same day, Japan and the United States signed a defensive alliance and agreed that the latter could maintain military bases on the Japanese islands. Japan was now formally independent but in a new dependency relationship with the United States. A provision in the new constitution renounced war as an instrument of national policy and prohibited the raising of an army.

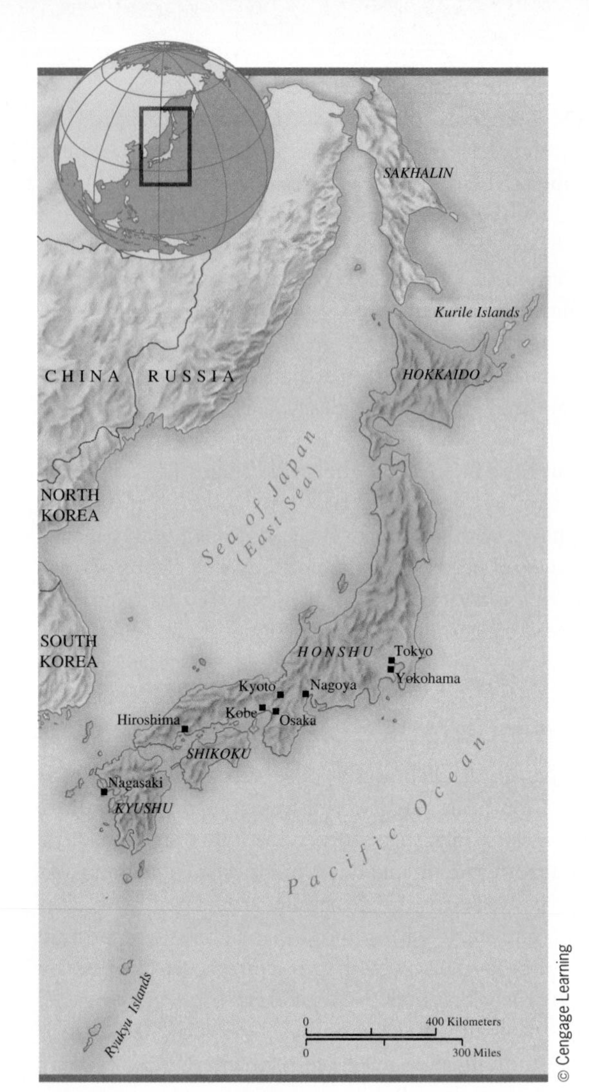

© Cengage Learning

MAP 30.3 Modern Japan. Shown here are the four main islands that comprise the contemporary state of Japan.

Q *Which island is the largest?*

POLITICS AND GOVERNMENT The Allied occupation administrators started with the conviction that Japanese expansionism was directly linked to the institutional and ideological foundations of the Meiji Constitution. Accordingly, they set out to change Japanese politics into something closer to the pluralistic model used in most Western nations. Yet a number of characteristics of the postwar Japanese political system reflected the tenacity of the traditional political culture. Although Japan had a multiparty system with two major parties, the Liberal Democrats and the Socialists, in practice there was a "government party" and a permanent opposition—the Liberal Democrats were not voted out of office for thirty years.

That tradition changed suddenly in 1993, when the ruling Liberal Democrats, shaken by persistent reports of corruption and cronyism between politicians and business interests, failed to win a majority of seats in parliamentary elections. The new coalition government, however, quickly split into feuding factions, and in 1995, the Liberal Democrats returned to power. Successive prime ministers proved unable to carry out promised reforms, and in 2001, Junichiro Koizumi (joo-nee-CHAY-roh koh-ee-ZOO-mee) (b. 1942), a former minister of health and welfare, was elected prime minister. His personal charisma raised expectations that he might be able to bring about significant changes, but bureaucratic resistance to reform and chronic factionalism within the Liberal Democratic Party thwarted his efforts. In 2009, three years after he left office, the Liberal Democrats were once again voted out of power. But subsequent governments have been criticized for the ineptitude of their recovery efforts after the massive earthquake and tsunami that struck the main island of Honshu in 2011.

JAPAN, INCORPORATED One of the problems plaguing the current system has been the centralizing tendencies that it inherited from the Meiji period. The government is organized on a unitary rather than a federal basis; the local administrative units, called prefectures, have few of the powers of states in the United States. Moreover, the central government plays an active and sometimes intrusive role in various aspects of the economy, mediating management-labor disputes, establishing price and wage policies, and subsidizing vital industries and enterprises producing goods for export. This government intervention in the economy has traditionally been widely accepted and is often cited as a key reason for the efficiency of Japanese industry and the emergence of the country as an industrial giant.

In recent years, though, the tradition of active government involvement in the economy has increasingly come under fire. Japanese businesses, which previously sought government protection from imports, now argue that deregulation is needed to enable Japanese firms to innovate in order to keep up with the competition. Such reforms, however, have been resisted by powerful government ministries in Tokyo, which are accustomed to playing an active role in national affairs.

A third problem is that the Liberal Democratic Party has long been divided into factions that seek to protect their own interests and often resist changes that might benefit society as a whole. This tradition of factionalism has tended to insulate political figures from popular scrutiny and encouraged susceptibility to secret dealing and official corruption. A number of senior politicians, including two recent prime ministers, have been forced to resign because of serious questions about improper financial dealings with business associates. Concern over political corruption was undoubtedly a major factor in the defeats suffered by the Liberal Democrats in 1993 and 2009, and the issue continues to plague the political scene.

ATONING FOR THE PAST Lingering social problems also need to be addressed. Minorities such as the *eta*, now known as the ***Burakumin*** (BOOR-uh-koo-min), and Korean residents in Japan continue to be subjected to legal and social discrimination. For years, official sources were reluctant to divulge growing evidence that thousands of Korean women were conscripted to serve as prostitutes (euphemistically called "comfort women") for Japanese soldiers during the war, and many Koreans living in Japan contend that such prejudicial attitudes continue to exist. Representatives of the "comfort women" have demanded both financial compensation and a formal letter of apology from the Japanese government for the treatment they received during the Pacific War. Negotiations over the issue have been under way for several years.

Japan's behavior during World War II has been an especially sensitive issue. During the early 1990s, critics at home and abroad charged that textbooks printed under the guidance of the Ministry of Education did not adequately discuss the atrocities committed by the Japanese armed forces during World War II. Other Asian governments were particularly incensed at Tokyo's failure to accept responsibility for such behavior and demanded a formal apology. The government expressed remorse, but only in the context of the aggressive actions of all colonial powers during the imperialist era.

The Economy

Nowhere are the changes in postwar Japan so visible as in the economic sector, where Japan developed into a major industrial and technological power in the space of a century, surpassing such advanced Western societies as Germany, France, and Great Britain. Although this "Japanese miracle" has often been described as beginning after the war as a result of the Allied reforms, rapid economic growth in fact began much earlier, with the Meiji reforms, which helped transform Japan from an autocratic society based on semifeudal institutions into an advanced capitalist democracy.

OCCUPATION REFORMS As noted earlier, the officials of the Allied occupation identified the Meiji economic system with centralized power and the rise of Japanese militarism. But with the rise of Cold War tensions, the policy of breaking up the *zaibatsu* was scaled back. Looser ties between companies were still allowed, and a new type of informal relationship, sometimes called the ***keiretsu*** (key-RET-soo), or "interlocking arrangement," began to take shape. Through such arrangements among suppliers, wholesalers, retailers, and financial institutions, the *zaibatsu* system was reconstituted under a new name.

The occupation administration had more success with its program to reform the agricultural system. Half of the population still lived on farms, and half of all farmers were still tenants. Under the land reform program, all lands owned by absentee landlords and all cultivated landholdings over an established maximum were sold on easy credit terms to the tenants. The program created a strong class of yeoman farmers, and tenants declined to about 10 percent of the rural population.

THE "JAPANESE MIRACLE"? During the next fifty years, Japan re-created the stunning results of the Meiji era. In 1950, the Japanese gross domestic product was about one-third that of Great Britain or France. Thirty years later, it was larger than both put together and well over half that of the United States. Japan is one of the greatest exporting nations in the world, and its per capita income equals or surpasses that of most advanced Western states.

In the last decades, however, the Japanese economy has run into serious difficulties, raising the question of whether the Japanese model is as appealing as many observers earlier declared. A rise in the value of the yen hurt exports and burst the bubble of investment by Japanese banks that had taken place under the umbrella of government protection. Lacking a domestic market equivalent in size to the United States, in the 1990s the Japanese economy slipped into a recession that has not yet entirely abated. Economic conditions worsened in 2008 and 2009 as Japanese exports declined significantly as a consequence of the global economic downturn.

These economic difficulties have placed heavy pressure on some of the vaunted features of the Japanese economy. The tradition of lifetime employment created a bloated white-collar workforce and has made downsizing difficult. Today, job security is on the decline as increasing numbers of workers are being laid off. A disproportionate burden has fallen on women, who lack seniority and continue to suffer from various forms of discrimination in the workplace.

A final change is that slowly but inexorably, the Japanese market is beginning to open up to international competition. Foreign automakers are winning a growing share of the domestic market, and the government—concerned at the prospect of food shortages—has committed itself to facilitating the importation of rice from abroad. Greater exposure to foreign competition may improve the performance of Japanese manufacturers. In recent years, Japanese consumers have become increasingly critical of the quality of some domestic products, causing one cabinet minister to complain about "sloppiness and complacency" among Japanese firms (even the Japanese automaker Toyota, whose vehicles consistently rank high in quality tests, has been faced with quality problems in its bestselling fleet of motor vehicles). The massive earthquake and tsunami that struck the coast of Japan in 2011 added to the nation's difficulties when they exposed the failure of the government to maintain proper safeguards for its nuclear plants in the vicinity. The costs of rebuilding after the disaster have posed a major challenge to Japanese leaders, who already face a crisis of confidence from their constituents.

A Society in Transition

During the occupation, Allied planners set out to change social characteristics that they believed had contributed to Japanese aggressiveness before and during World War II. The new educational system removed all references to filial piety, patriotism, and loyalty to the emperor while emphasizing the individualistic values of Western civilization. The new constitution and a revised civil code eliminated remaining legal restrictions on women's rights to obtain a divorce, hold a job, or change their domicile. Women were guaranteed the right to vote and were encouraged to enter politics.

Such efforts to remake Japanese behavior through legislation have had mixed success. During the past sixty years, Japan has unquestionably become a more individualistic and egalitarian society. At the same time, many of the distinctive characteristics of traditional Japanese society have persisted to the present day, although in somewhat altered form. The emphasis on loyalty to the group and community relationships, for example, is reflected in the strength of corporate loyalties in postwar Japan.

Emphasis on the work ethic also remains strong. The tradition of hard work is taught at a young age. The Japanese school year runs for 240 days a year, compared with 180 days in the United States, and work assignments outside class tend to be more extensive. The results are

Growing Up in Japan

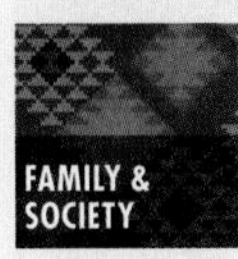

Japanese schoolchildren grow up in a much more regimented environment than U.S. children experience. Most Japanese schoolchildren, for example, wear black-and-white uniforms to school. These regulations are examples of rules adopted by middle school systems in various parts of Japan. The Ministry of Education in Tokyo concluded that these regulations were excessive, but they are probably typical.

School Regulations, Japanese Style

1. Boys' hair should not touch the eyebrows, the ears, or the top of the collar.
2. No one should have a permanent wave, or dye his or her hair. Girls should not wear ribbons or accessories in their hair. Hair dryers should not be used.
3. School uniform skirts should be _____ centimeters above the ground, no more and no less (differs by school and region).
4. Keep your uniform clean and pressed at all times. Girls' middy blouses should have two buttons on the back collar. Boys' pant cuffs should be of the prescribed width. No more than 12 eyelets should be on shoes. The number of buttons on a shirt and tucks in a shirt are also prescribed.
5. Wear your school badge at all times. It should be positioned exactly.
6. Going to school in the morning, wear your book bag strap on the right shoulder; in the afternoon on the way home, wear it on the left shoulder. Your book case thickness, filled and unfilled, is also prescribed.
7. Girls should wear only regulation white underpants of 100% cotton.
8. When you raise your hand to be called on, your arm should extend forward and up at the angle prescribed in your handbook.
9. Your own route to and from school is marked in your student rule handbook; carefully observe which side of each street you are to use on the way to and from school.
10. After school you are to go directly home, unless your parent has written a note permitting you to go to another location. Permission will not be granted by the school unless this other location is a suitable one. You must not go to coffee shops. You must be home by _____ o'clock.
11. It is not permitted to drive or ride a motorcycle, or to have a license to drive one.
12. Before and after school, no matter where you are, you represent our school, so you should behave in ways we can all be proud of.

What is the apparent purpose of these regulations? Why does Japan appear to place more restrictions on students' behavior than most Western countries do?

Source: From *The Material Child: Coming of Age in Japan and America* (New York: Free Press, 1993).

impressive: Japanese schoolchildren consistently earn higher scores on achievement tests than children in other advanced countries. At the same time, this devotion to success has often been accompanied by bullying by teachers and an emphasis on conformity (see the box above).

By all accounts, however, independent thinking is on the increase in Japan. In some cases, it leads to antisocial behavior, such as crime or membership in a teenage gang. Usually, it is expressed in more indirect ways, such as the recent fashion among young people of dyeing their hair brown (known in Japanese as "tea hair"). Because the practice is banned in many schools and generally frowned on by the older generation (one police chief dumped a pitcher of beer on a student with brown hair whom he noticed in a bar), many young Japanese dye their hair as a gesture of independence. When seeking employment or getting married, however, they often return their hair to its natural color.

WOMEN IN JAPANESE SOCIETY One of the most tenacious legacies of the past in Japanese society is sexual inequality. Although women are now legally protected against discrimination in employment, very few have reached senior levels in business, education, or politics.

© William J. Duiker
© Barry Cronin/Getty Images

From Conformity to Counterculture. Traditionally, schoolchildren in Japan have worn uniforms to promote conformity with the country's communitarian social mores. In the photo on the left, young students dressed in identical uniforms are on a field trip to Kyoto's Nijo Castle, built in 1603 by Tokugawa Ieyasu. Recently, however, a youth counterculture has emerged in Japan. On the right, fashion-conscious teenagers with "tea hair"—heirs of Japan's long era of affluence—revel in their expensive hip-hop outfits, platform shoes, and layered dresses. Such fashion choices symbolize the growing revolt against conformity in contemporary Japan.

Women now comprise nearly 50 percent of the workforce, but most are in retail or service occupations. Less than 10 percent of managerial workers in Japan are women, compared with nearly half in the United States. There is a feminist movement in Japan, but it has none of the vigor and mass support of its counterpart in the United States.

THE DEMOGRAPHIC CRISIS Many of Japan's current dilemmas stem from its growing demographic problems. Today, Japan has the highest proportion of people older than sixty-five of any industrialized country—almost 23 percent of the country's total population. By the year 2024, an estimated one-third of the Japanese population will be over the age of sixty-five, and the median age will be fifty, ten years older than the median in the United States. This demographic profile is due both to declining fertility and a low level of immigration. Immigrants make up only 1 percent of the total population of Japan. Together, the aging population and the absence of immigrants are creating the prospect of a dramatic labor shortage in coming years. Nevertheless, prejudice against foreigners persists in Japan, and the government remains reluctant to ease restrictions against immigrants from other countries in the region.

Japan's aging population has many implications for the future. Traditionally, it was the responsibility of the eldest child in a Japanese family to care for aging parents, but that system is beginning to break down because of limited housing space and the growing tendency of working-age women to seek jobs in the marketplace. The proportion of Japanese older than sixty-five years of age who live with their children has dropped from 80 percent in 1970 to about 50 percent today. At the same time, public and private pension plans are under increasing financial pressure, partly because of the low birthrate and the graying population.

RELIGION AND CULTURE As in the West, increasing urbanization has led to a decline in the practice of organized religion in Japan, although evangelical sects have proliferated in recent years. The largest and best-known sect is Soka Gakkai (SOH-kuh GAK-ky), a lay Buddhist organization that has attracted millions of followers and formed its own political party, the Komeito (koh-MAY-toh). Zen Buddhism retains its popularity, and some businesspeople seek to use Zen techniques to learn how to focus their willpower as a means of outwitting a competitor. Many Japanese also follow Shinto, no longer identified with reverence for the emperor and the state.

Western literature, art, and music have also had a major impact on Japanese society. After World War II, many of the writers who had been active before the war resurfaced, but now their writing reflected demoralization. Many were attracted to existentialism, and some turned to hedonism and nihilism. For these disillusioned authors, defeat was compounded by fear of the Americanization of postwar Japan. One of the best examples of this attitude was the novelist Yukio Mishima (yoo-KEE-oh mi-SHEE-muh) (1925–1970), who led a crusade to stem the tide of what he described as America's "universal and uniform 'Coca-Colonization'" of the world in general and Japan in particular.[4] Mishima's ritual suicide in 1970 was the subject of widespread speculation and transformed him into a cult figure.

One of Japan's most serious-minded contemporary authors is Kenzaburo Oe (ken-zuh-BOO-roh OH-ay) (b. 1935). His work, rewarded with a Nobel Prize for Literature in 1994, focuses on Japan's ongoing quest for modern identity and purpose. His characters reflect the spiritual anguish precipitated by the collapse of the imperial Japanese tradition and the subsequent adoption of Western culture—a trend that Oe contends has culminated in unabashed materialism, cultural decline, and a moral void. Yet unlike Mishima, Oe does not wish to reinstill the imperial traditions of the past but rather seeks to regain spiritual meaning by retrieving the sense of communality and innocence found in rural Japan.

Since the 1970s, increasing affluence and a high literacy rate have contributed to a massive quantity of publications, ranging from popular potboilers to first-rate fiction. Much of this new literature deals with the common concerns of all affluent industrialized nations, including the effects of urbanization, advanced technology, and mass consumption. A wildly popular genre is the "art-manga," or graphic novel. Some members of the youth counterculture have used manga to rebel against Japan's rigid educational and conformist pressures.

Other aspects of Japanese culture have also been influenced by Western ideas, although without the intense preoccupation with synthesis that is evident in literature. Western music is very popular in Japan, and scores of Japanese classical musicians have succeeded in the West. Even rap music has gained a foothold among Japanese youth, although without the association with sex, drugs, and violence that it has in the United States. Although some of the lyrics betray an attitude of modest revolt against the uptight world of Japanese society, most lack any such connotations.

The Japanese Difference

Whether the unique character of modern Japan will endure is unclear. Confidence in the Japanese "economic miracle" has been shaken by the long recession, and there are indications of a growing tendency toward hedonism and individualism among Japanese youth. Older Japanese frequently complain that the younger generation lacks their sense of loyalty and willingness to sacrifice. There are also signs that the concept of loyalty to one's employer may be beginning to erode among Japanese youth. Some observers have predicted that with increasing affluence Japan will become more like the industrialized societies in the West. Although Japan is unlikely to evolve into a photocopy of the United States, the vaunted image of millions of dedicated "salarymen" heading off to work with their briefcases and their pin-striped suits may no longer be an accurate portrayal of reality in contemporary Japan.

The Little Tigers

FOCUS QUESTIONS: What factors have contributed to the economic success achieved by the Little Tigers? To what degree have they applied the Japanese model in forging their developmental strategies?

The success of postwar Japan in meeting the challenge from the capitalist West soon caught the eye of other Asian nations. By the 1980s, several smaller states in the region—known collectively as the "Little Tigers"—had successively followed the Japanese example.

South Korea: A Peninsula Divided

In 1953, the Korean peninsula was exhausted from three years of bitter fraternal war, a conflict that took the lives of an estimated 4 million Koreans on both sides of the 38th parallel. Although a cease-fire was signed in July 1953, it was a fragile peace that left two heavily armed and mutually hostile countries facing each other suspiciously.

North of the truce line was the People's Republic of Korea (PRK), a police state under the dictatorial rule of the Communist leader Kim Il-Sung (KIM ILL SOONG) (1912–1994). To the south was the Republic of Korea, under the equally

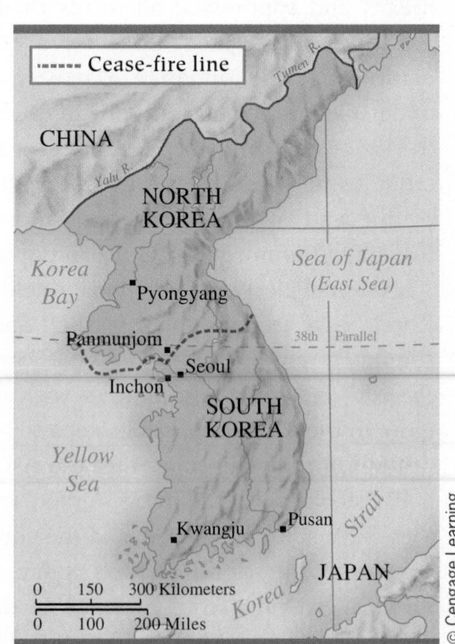

© Cengage Learning

The Korean Peninsula Since 1953

autocratic President Syngman Rhee (SING-muhn REE) (1875–1965), a fierce anti-Communist who had led the resistance to the northern invasion. After several years of harsh rule in the Republic of Korea, marked by government corruption, fraudulent elections, and police brutality, demonstrations broke out in the capital city of Seoul in the spring of 1960 and forced Rhee into retirement.

In 1961, a coup d'état in South Korea placed General Chung Hee Park (1917–1979) in power. The new regime promulgated a new constitution, and in 1963, Park was elected president of a civilian government. He set out to foster recovery of the economy from decades of foreign occupation and civil war. Because the private sector had been relatively weak under Japanese rule, the government played an active role in the process by instituting a series of five-year plans that targeted specific industries for development, promoted exports, and funded infrastructure development.

The program was a solid success. Benefiting from the Confucian principles of thrift, respect for education, and hard work, as well as from Japanese capital and technology, Korea gradually emerged as a major industrial power in East Asia. The largest corporations—including Samsung, Daewoo, and Hyundai—were transformed into massive conglomerates called ***chaebol*** (jay-BOHL *or* je-BUHL), the Korean equivalent of the *zaibatsu* of prewar Japan. Korean businesses began to compete actively with the Japanese for export markets in Asia and throughout the world.

But like many other countries in the region, South Korea was slow to develop democratic principles. Although his government functioned with the trappings of democracy, Park continued to rule by autocratic means and suppressed all forms of dissidence. In 1979, Park was assassinated. But after a brief interregnum of democratic rule, in 1980 a new military government under General Chun Doo Hwan (JUN DOH HWAHN) (b. 1931) seized power. The new regime was as authoritarian as its predecessors, but after student riots in 1987, by the end of the decade opposition to autocratic rule had spread to much of the urban population.

National elections were finally held in 1989, and South Korea reverted to civilian rule. Successive presidents sought to rein in corruption while cracking down on the *chaebols* and initiating contacts with the Communist regime in the PRK on possible steps toward eventual reunification of the peninsula. After the Asian financial crisis in 1997, economic conditions temporarily worsened, but they have since recovered, and the country is increasingly competitive in world markets today. Symbolic of South Korea's growing self-confidence is the nation's current president, Lee Myung-bak (LEE MYUNG-BAHK) (b. 1941), elected in 2007. An ex-mayor of Seoul, he is noted for his rigorous efforts to beautify the city and improve the quality of life of his compatriots, including the installation of a new five-day workweek. His most serious challenge, however, is to protect the national economy, which is heavily dependent on exports, from the ravages of the recent economic crisis.

In the meantime, relations with North Korea, now on the verge of becoming a nuclear power, remain tense. Multinational efforts to persuade the regime to suspend its nuclear program continue, although North Korea claimed to have successfully conducted a nuclear test in 2009. To add to the uncertainty, the regime faced a succession crisis, when Kim Jong-Il (1941–2011), the son and successor of founder Kim Il-Sung, died suddenly in 2011 and was replaced by his inexperienced son.

Taiwan: The Other China

After retreating to Taiwan following the defeat by the Communists, Chiang Kai-shek's government, which continued to refer to itself as the Republic of China (ROC), contended that it remained the legitimate representative of the Chinese people and would eventually return in triumph to the mainland.

In the relatively secure environment provided by a security treaty with the United States, signed in 1954, the ROC was able to concentrate on economic growth without worrying about a Communist invasion. The government moved rapidly to create a solid agricultural base. A land reform program led to the reduction of rents, and landholdings over 3 acres were purchased by the government and resold to the tenants at reasonable prices. At the same time, local manufacturing and commerce were strongly encouraged. By the 1970s, Taiwan had become one of the most dynamic industrial economies in East Asia.

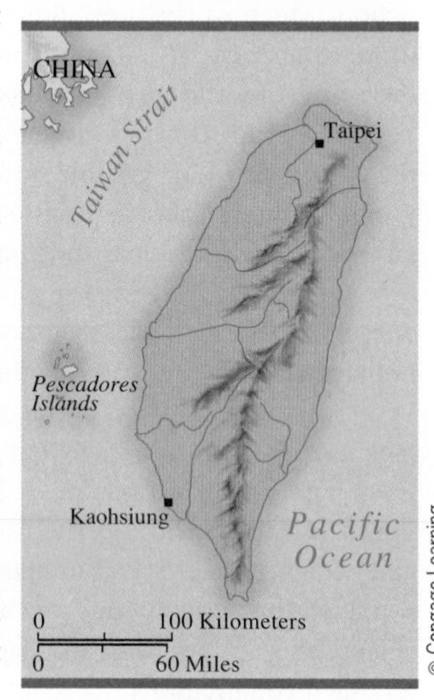

Modern Taiwan

In contrast to the Communist regime in the People's Republic of China (PRC), the ROC actively maintained Chinese tradition, promoting respect for Confucius and the ethical principles of the past, such as hard work, frugality, and filial piety. The overall standard of living increased substantially, health and sanitation improved, literacy rates were quite high, and an active family planning program reduced the rate of population growth.

After the death of Chiang Kai-shek in 1975, the ROC slowly began to move toward a more representative form of government, including elections and legal opposition parties. A national election in 1992 resulted in a bare majority for the Nationalists over strong opposition from the Democratic Progressive Party (DPP). But political liberalization had its dangers; some members of the DPP began to agitate for an independent Republic of Taiwan, a possibility that aroused concern within the Nationalist government in Taipei and frenzied hostility in the PRC. The election of DPP leader Chen Shui-bian (CHUHN SHWAY-BEE-ahn) (b. 1950) as ROC president in March 2000 angered Beijing, which threatened to invade Taiwan should the island continue to delay unification with the mainland. The return to power of the Nationalist Party in 2008 has at least for the time being eased relations with mainland China. As a result, economic and cultural contacts between Taiwan and the mainland are steadily increasing.

Singapore and Hong Kong: The Littlest Tigers

The smallest but by no means the least successful of the Little Tigers are Singapore and Hong Kong. Both contain large populations densely packed into small territories. Singapore, once a British colony and briefly a part of the state of Malaysia, is now an independent nation. Hong Kong was a British colony until it was returned to PRC control in 1997. In recent years, both have emerged as industrial powerhouses, with standards of living well above those of their neighbors.

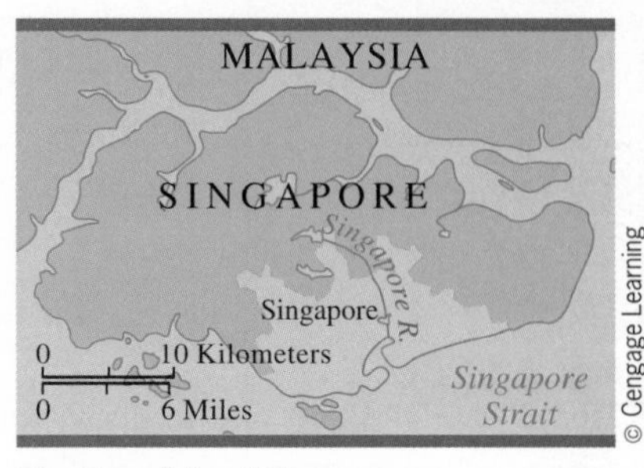

The Republic of Singapore

The success of Singapore must be ascribed in good measure to the will and energy of its political leaders. When it became independent in August 1965, Singapore's longtime position as an entrepôt for trade between the Indian Ocean and the South China Sea was on the wane.

Within a decade, Singapore's role and reputation had dramatically changed. Under the leadership of Prime Minister Lee Kuan-yew (LEE kwahn-YOO) (b. 1923), the government cultivated an attractive business climate while engaging in public works projects to feed, house, and educate its 2 million citizens. The major components of success have been shipbuilding, oil refineries, tourism, electronics, and finance—the city-state has become the banking hub of the entire region.

As in the other Little Tigers, an authoritarian political system has guaranteed a stable environment for economic growth. Until his retirement in 1990, Lee Kuan-yew and his People's Action Party dominated Singapore politics, and opposition elements were intimidated into silence or arrested. The prime minister openly declared that the Western model of pluralist democracy was not appropriate for Singapore. Confucian values of thrift, hard work, and obedience to authority were promoted as the ideology of the state.

But economic success has begun to undermine the authoritarian foundations of the system as a more sophisticated citizenry voices aspirations for more political freedoms and an end to

© William J. Duiker

The Taiwan Democracy Memorial in Taipei. While the Chinese government on the mainland attempted to destroy all vestiges of traditional culture, the Republic of China on Taiwan sought to preserve the cultural heritage as a link between past and present. This policy was graphically displayed in the mausoleum for Chiang Kai-shek that was erected in downtown Taipei. The mausoleum, with its massive entrance gate, was designed not only to glorify the nation's deceased president but also to recall the grandeur of old China. In 2007, the mausoleum was renamed the Taiwan Democracy Memorial Hall in a bid by the government to downplay the island's historical ties to the mainland.

CHRONOLOGY **Japan and the Little Tigers Since World War II**	
End of World War II in the Pacific	1945
Chiang Kai-shek retreats to Taiwan	1949
End of U.S. occupation of Japan	1951
End of Korean War	1953
United States–Republic of China security treaty	1954
Syngman Rhee overthrown in South Korea	1960
Rise to power of Chung Hee Park in South Korea	1961
Independence of Singapore	1965
Death of Chiang Kai-shek	1975
Chung Hee Park assassinated	1979
Lee Kuan-yew era ends in Singapore	1990
First free general elections on Taiwan	1992
Return of Hong Kong to Chinese control	1997
Financial crisis hits the region	1997
Chen Shui-bian elected president of Taiwan	2000
Junichiro Koizumi elected prime minister in Japan	2001
Lee Myung-bak elected president of South Korea	2007
Nationalist Party returns to power in Taiwan	2008
Massive tsunami strikes Japan	2011

government paternalism. In 2004, Lee Hsien-luong (LEE HAZ-ee-en-LAHNG) (b. 1952), the son of Lee Kuan-yew, became prime minister. Under his leadership, the government has relaxed its restrictions on freedom of speech and assembly, and elections held in 2011 resulted in growing support for members of opposition parties.

The future of Hong Kong is not so clear-cut. As in Singapore, sensible government policies and the hard work of its people have enabled Hong Kong to thrive. At first, the prosperity of the colony depended on a plentiful supply of cheap labor. Inundated with refugees from the mainland during the 1950s and 1960s, the population of Hong Kong burgeoned to more than 6 million. More recently, Hong Kong has benefited from increased tourism, manufacturing, and the growing economic prosperity of neighboring Guangdong province, the most prosperous region of the PRC.

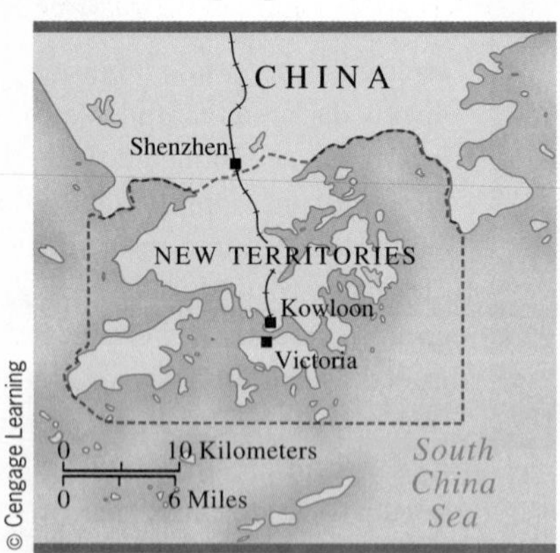

Hong Kong

Unlike the other societies discussed in this chapter, Hong Kong has relied on an unbridled free market system rather than active state intervention in the economy. At the same time, by allocating substantial funds for transportation, sanitation, education, and public housing, the government has created favorable conditions for economic development.

When Britain's ninety-nine-year lease on the New Territories, the foodbasket of the colony, expired on July 1, 1997, Hong Kong returned to mainland authority. Although the Chinese promised the British that for fifty years, the people of Hong Kong would live under a capitalist system and be essentially self-governing, recent statements by Chinese leaders have raised questions about the degree of autonomy Hong Kong will continue to receive under Chinese rule.

Explaining the East Asian Miracle

What explains the striking ability of Japan and the four Little Tigers to transform themselves into export-oriented societies capable of competing with the advanced nations of Europe and the Western Hemisphere? Some analysts point to the traditional character traits of Confucian societies, such as thrift, a work ethic, respect for education, and obedience to authority. In a recent poll of Asian executives, more than 80 percent expressed the belief that Asian values differ from those of the West, and most add that these values have contributed significantly to the region's recent success. Others place more emphasis on deliberate steps taken by government and economic leaders to meet the political, economic, and social challenges their societies face.

There seems no reason to doubt that cultural factors connected to East Asian social traditions have contributed to the economic success of these societies. Certainly, habits such as frugality, industriousness, and subordination of individual desires have all played a role in their governments' ability to concentrate on the collective interest. As this and preceding chapters have shown, however, without active encouragement by political elites, such traditions cannot be effectively harnessed for the good of society as a whole. The creative talents of the Chinese people, for example, were not efficiently utilized under Mao Zedong during the frenetic years of the Cultural Revolution. Only when Deng Xiaoping and other pragmatists took charge and began to place a high priority on economic development were the stunning advances of recent decades achieved. By the same token, political elites elsewhere in East Asia were aware of traditional values and willing to use them for national purposes. In effect, the rapid rise of East Asia in the postwar era was no miracle, but a fortuitous combination of favorable cultural factors and deliberate human action.

© William J. Duiker

The Hong Kong Skyline. Hong Kong reverted to Chinese sovereignty in 1997 after a century of British rule. To commemorate the occasion, the imposing Conference Center, shown here in the foreground, was built on reclaimed shore land in the Hong Kong harbor.

On the Margins of Asia: Postwar Australia and New Zealand

Technically, Australia and New Zealand are not part of Asia, and throughout their short history, both countries have identified culturally and politically with the West rather than with their Asian neighbors. Their political institutions and values are derived from Europe, and their economies resemble those of the advanced countries of the world rather than the preindustrial societies of much of Southeast Asia. Both are currently members of the British Commonwealth and of the U.S.-led ANZUS (Australia, New Zealand, and the United States) alliance.

Yet trends in recent years have been drawing both states, especially Australia, closer to Asia. In the first place, immigration from East and Southeast Asia has increased rapidly. More than one-half of current immigrants into Australia come from East Asia, and about 7 percent of the population of about 18 million people is now of Asian descent. In New Zealand, residents of Asian descent represent only about 3 percent of the population of 3.5 million, but about 12 percent of the population are Maoris, Polynesian peoples who settled on the islands about a thousand years ago. Second, trade relations with Asia are increasing rapidly. About 60 percent of Australia's export markets today are in East Asia, and the region is the source of about one-half of its imports. Asian trade with New Zealand is also on the increase. Concern about China's rising strength in the region is cause for concern, however, and was undoubtedly a factor in the agreement reached in 2011 to station 2,500 U.S. troops in Australia.

CHAPTER SUMMARY

In the years following the end of World War II, the peoples of Asia emerged from a century of imperial rule to face the challenge of building stable and prosperous independent states. Initially, progress was slow, as new political leaders were forced to deal with the legacy of colonialism and internal disagreements over their visions for the future. By the end of the century, however, most nations in the area were beginning to lay the foundations for the creation of advanced industrial societies. Today, major Asian states like China,

Japan, and India have become major competitors of the advanced Western nations in the international marketplace.

To some observers, these economic achievements have come at a high price, in the form of political authoritarianism and a lack of attention to human rights. Rapid economic development has also exacted an environmental price. Industrial pollution in China and India and the destruction of the forest cover in Southeast Asia increasingly threaten the fragile ecosystem and create friction among nations in the region. Unless they learn to cooperate effectively to deal with the challenge in future years, it will ultimately undermine the dramatic economic and social progress that has taken place.

Still, a look at the historical record suggests that, for the most part, the nations of southern and eastern Asia have made dramatic progress in coping with the multiple challenges of independence. Political pluralism is often a by-product of economic growth, while a rising standard of living should enable the peoples of the region to meet the social and environmental challenges that lie ahead.

CHAPTER TIMELINE

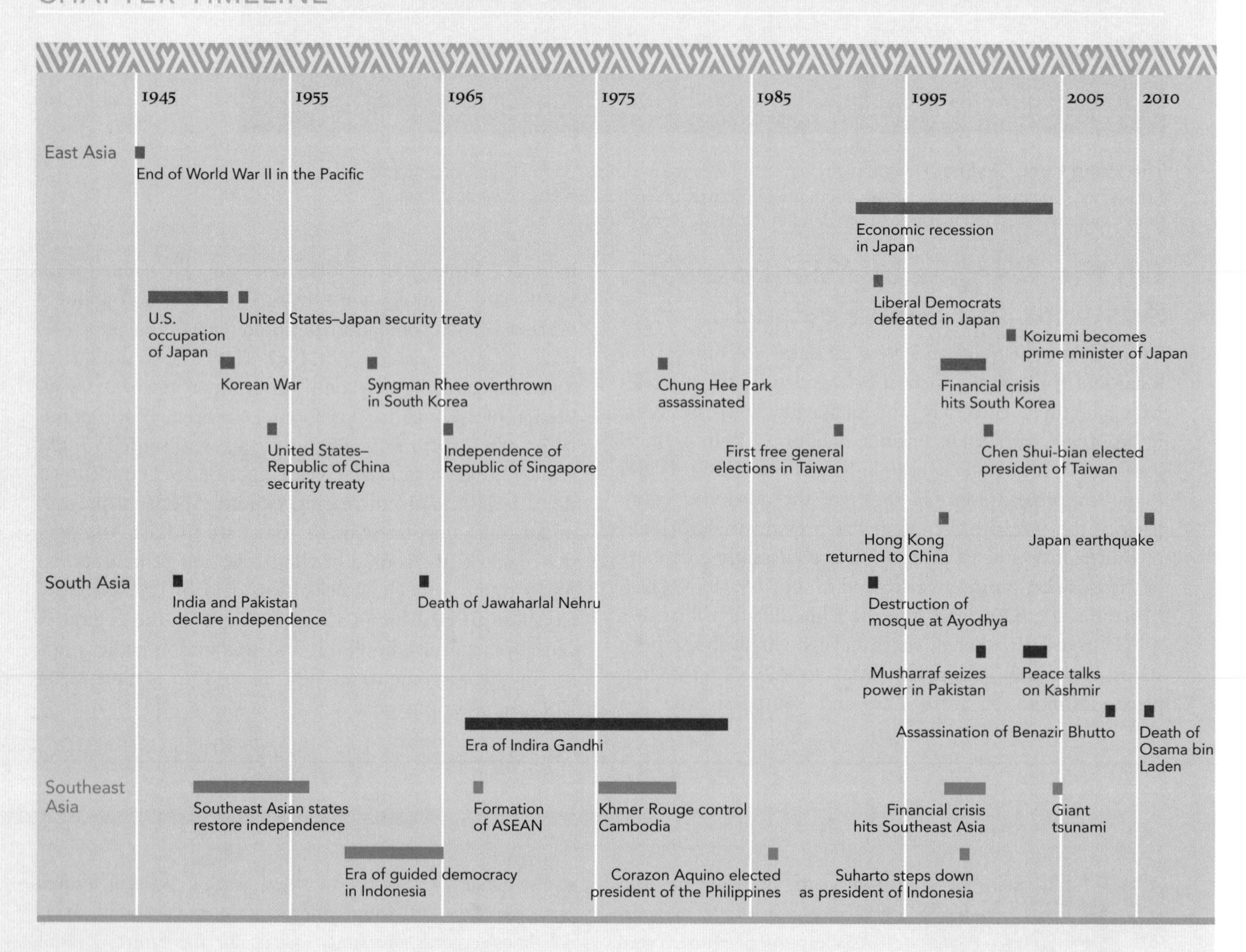

CHAPTER REVIEW

Upon Reflection

Q What kinds of environmental problems are currently being faced by the nations of southern and eastern Asia? How have the region's political leaders sought to deal with the problems?

Q How has independence affected the role of women in southern and eastern Asia? What factors are involved?

Q How have the nations in the region dealt with the challenge of integrating their ethnic and religious minorities into their political systems?

Key Terms

communalism (p. 795)
dalits (p. 799)
guided democracy (p. 803)
ASEAN (p. 807)
Burakumin (p. 809)
keiretsu (p. 810)
chaebol (p. 814)

Suggested Reading

THE INDIAN SUBCONTINENT SINCE 1945 For a survey of postwar Indian history, see **S. Tharoor, *India: From Midnight to the Millennium*** (New York, 1997). On India's founding father, see **J. Brown, *Nehru: A Political Life*** (New Haven, Conn., 2003). The life and career of Indira Gandhi have been well chronicled. See **K. Frank, *Indira: The Life of Indira Nehru Gandhi*** (New York, 2000). On Pakistan, see **O. B. Jones, *Pakistan: Eye of the Storm*** (New Haven, Conn., 2002). Also of interest is **C. Baxter, *Bangladesh: From a Nation to a State*** (Boulder, Colo., 1997).

SOUTHEAST ASIA SINCE 1945 There are a number of standard surveys of the history of modern Southeast Asia. One is **N. Tarling, *Southeast Asia: A Modern History*** (Oxford, 2002). For a more scholarly approach, see **N. Tarling, ed., *The Cambridge History of Southeast Asia,*** vol. 4 (Cambridge, 1999).

T. Friend, *Indonesian Destinies* (Cambridge, Mass., 2003), is a fine introduction to Indonesian society and culture. The rise of terrorism in the region is discussed in **Z. Abuza, *Militant Islam in Southeast Asia: Crucible of Terror*** (Boulder, Colo., 2003). For an overview of women's issues in contemporary South and Southeast Asia, consult **B. Ramusack** and **S. Sievers, *Women in Asia*** (Bloomington, Ind., 1999).

JAPAN SINCE 1945 For a balanced treatment of all issues relating to postwar Japan, see **J. McLain, *Japan: A Modern History*** (New York, 2001). **I. Buruma, *Inventing Japan*** (New York, 2002), offers a more journalistic approach that raises questions about the future of democracy in Japan.

THE LITTLE TIGERS On the four Little Tigers and their economic development, see **D. Oberdorfer, *The Two Koreas: A Contemporary History*** (Indianapolis, 1997); **Lee Kuan Yew, *From Third World to First: The Singapore Story, 1965–2000*** (New York, 2000); and **K. Rafferty, *City on the Rocks: Hong Kong's Uncertain Future*** (London, 1991). Also see **M. Rubinstein, *Taiwan: A New History*** (New York, 2001).

Visit the CourseMate website at **www.cengagebrain.com** for additional study tools and review materials for this chapter.

EPILOGUE: A GLOBAL CIVILIZATION

ON A VISIT TO NUREMBERG, Germany, with his family in 2000, Jackson Spielvogel, one of the authors of this textbook, was startled to find that the main railroad station, where he had once arrived as a Fulbright student, was now adorned with McDonald's Golden Arches. McDonald's was the brainstorm of two brothers who opened a cheap burger restaurant in California in 1940. When they expanded their operations to Arizona, they began to use two yellow arches to make their building visible from blocks away. After Ray Kroc, an enterprising businessman, bought the burgeoning business, McDonald's arches rapidly spread all over the United States. And they didn't stop there. The fast-food industry, which now relied on computers for the automated processing of its food, found an international market. McDonald's spread to Japan in 1971 and to Russia and China in 1990; by 1995, more than half of all McDonald's restaurants were located outside the United States. By 2000, McDonald's was serving 50 million people a day.

McDonald's is but one of numerous U.S. companies that use the latest technology and actively seek global markets. Indeed, sociologists have coined the term *McDonaldization* to refer to "the process whereby the principles of the fast-food restaurant are coming to dominate more and more sectors of American society as well as the rest of the world."[1] Multinational corporations like McDonald's have brought about a worldwide homogenization of societies and made us aware of the political, economic, and social interdependence of the world's nations and the global nature of our contemporary problems. An important part of this global awareness is the technological dimension. New technology has made possible levels of world communication that simply did not exist before. At the same time that Osama bin Laden and al-Qaeda were denouncing the forces of modernization, they were spreading their message through the use of recently developed telecommunication systems. The Technological Revolution has tied peoples and nations closely together and contributed to **globalization**, the term that is frequently used to describe the process by which peoples and nations have become more interdependent.

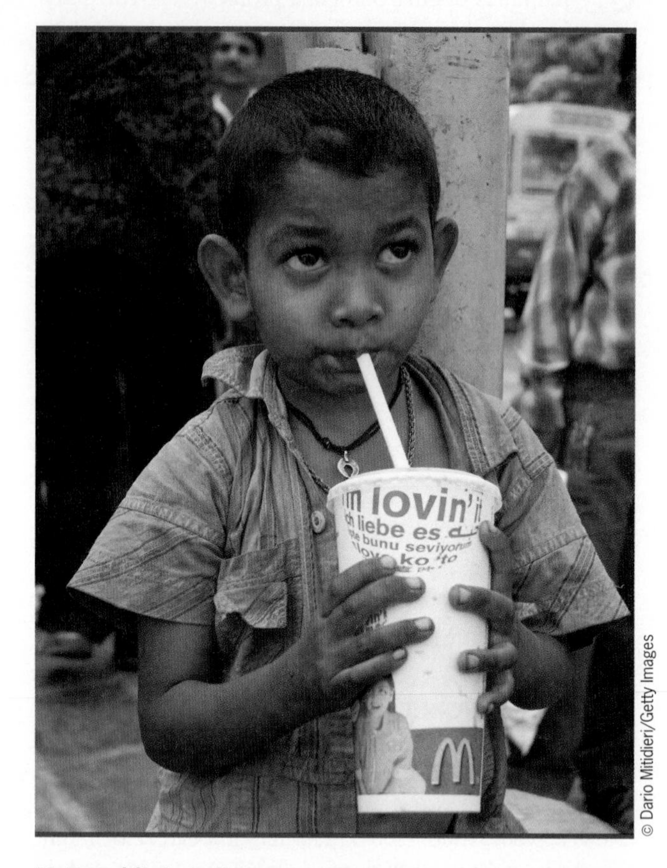
© Dario Mitidieri/Getty Images

McDonald's in India. McDonald's has become an important symbol of U.S. cultural influence throughout the world. Seen here is an Indian street child sipping a McDonald's soft drink at a McDonald's outside the Victoria Terminus Station in Mumbai.

The Global Economy

Especially since the 1970s, the world has developed a **global economy** in which the production, distribution, and sale of goods are accomplished on a worldwide scale. Several international institutions have contributed to the rise of the global economy. Soon after the end of World War II, the United States and other nations established the World Bank and the International Monetary Fund (IMF) as a means of expanding global markets and avoiding economic crises such as the Great Depression of the 1930s. The World Bank comprises five international organizations, largely controlled by developed countries, which provide grants, loans, and advice for economic development to developing countries. The IMF oversees the global financial system by supervising exchange rates and offering financial and technical assistance to developing nations. Today, 188 countries are members of the IMF. Critics have argued, however, that both the World Bank and the IMF sometimes push non-Western nations to adopt inappropriate Western economic practices that only aggravate the poverty and debt of developing nations.

Another reflection of the new global economic order is the **multinational** or **transnational corporation** (a company that has divisions in more than two countries). Prominent examples of multinational corporations include Siemens, Coca-Cola, ExxonMobil, Mitsubishi, and Sony. These companies are among the two hundred largest multinational corporations, which are responsible for more than half of the world's industrial production. In 2000, some 71 percent of these corporations were headquartered in just three countries—the United States, Japan, and Germany. These supercorporations have come to dominate much of the world's investment capital, technology, and markets. A recent comparison of corporate sales and national gross domestic product disclosed that only forty-nine of the world's hundred largest economic entities are nations; the remaining fifty-one are corporations. For this reason, some observers believe that economic globalization is more appropriately labeled "corporate globalization."

Another important component of economic globalization is free trade. In 1947, talks led to the creation of the General Agreement on Tariffs and Trade (GATT), a global trade organization that was replaced in 1995 by the World Trade Organization (WTO). With more than 150 member nations, the WTO arranges trade agreements and settles trade disputes. The WTO's goal is to open up world markets and maximize global production, but many critics charge that the WTO has ignored environmental and health concerns, harmed small and developing countries, and contributed to the growing gap between rich and poor nations.

While production, capital, and trade have increased as a result of globalization, the steps taken to increase trade have also led to an interconnected world of finance. The extent to which the financial markets are now globalized was evident in 2008 when a collapse of the largely unregulated financial markets in the United States quickly led to a worldwide recession. Manufacturing plunged, unemployment rose, and banks faltered as countries around the world faced new and daunting economic challenges. The IMF estimated that global output would fall by 1.3 percent in 2009, the first decline in sixty years. Although there were some signs of recovery by May of 2010, most economists believed that the worst global slump since the Great Depression of the 1930s was far from over.

Global Culture and the Digital Age

Since the invention of the microprocessor in 1971, the capabilities of computers have expanded by leaps and bounds, resulting in today's digital age. Beginning in the 1980s, companies like Apple and Microsoft competed to create more powerful computers and software. By the 1990s, the booming technology industry had made Microsoft founder Bill Gates the richest man in the world. Much of this success was due to several innovations that made computers indispensable for communication, information, and entertainment.

Global Communication

The advent of electronic mail, or e-mail, transformed communication in the mid-1990s. At the same time, the Internet, especially its World Wide Web, was becoming an information exchange for people around the world. As web capabilities have increased, new forms of communication have emerged including Twitter, Facebook, and YouTube, now used for international news broadcasts and for President Obama's weekly radio addresses.

Advances in telecommunications led first to cellular or mobile phones and later to smartphones. Though cellular phones existed in the 1970s and 1980s, it was not until the digital components of these devices were reduced in size in the 1990s that cellphones became truly portable. The ubiquity of cellphones and their ability to transfer data electronically have made text messaging a global form of communication. Text and instant messaging have revolutionized written language, as shorthand script has replaced complete sentences for relaying brief messages. Worldwide the number of people with access to a mobile phone increased from 12.4 million in 1990 to almost 4.6 billion in 2009. In 2012, more than a billion people worldwide were using smartphones.

A number of the innovations that have enhanced consumers' ability to share music, watch movies, and search the web were introduced by Apple, Inc., and subsequently imitated by other companies. The iPod, a portable digital music player, has revolutionized the music industry, as downloading music electronically from the Internet has largely replaced the purchasing of physical recordings. The iPhone enables users to connect to the Internet from their phone, allowing information to be instantly updated for various telecommunication sites, such as Twitter and Facebook. The iPad, a handheld tablet computer, is challenging computer sales worldwide, as almost 7.5 million iPads were sold in the first six months.

Reality in the Digital Age

Advances in communication and information during the digital age have led many people to suggest that world cultures are becoming increasingly interdependent and homogenized. Many contemporary artists have questioned the effects of the computer age on identity and material reality. According to some, the era of virtual reality has displaced cultural uniqueness and bodily presence.

THE BODY AND IDENTITY IN CONTEMPORARY ART By focusing on bodily experience and cultural norms, contemporary artists have attempted to restore what has been lost in the digital age. Kiki Smith (b. 1954), an American artist born in Germany, creates sculptures of the human body that often focus on anatomical processes. These works, commonly made of wax or plaster, question the politics surrounding the body, including AIDS and domestic abuse, while reconnecting to bodily experiences.

Contemporary artists also continue to explore the interaction between the Western and non-Western world, particularly the **multiculturalism** generated by global migrations. For example, the art of Yinka Shonibare (YEEN-kuh SHOH-nih-bar-eh) (b. 1962), who was born in London, raised in Nigeria, and now resides in England, investigates the notion of hybrid identity as he creates clothing and life-size figures that fuse European designs with African traditions.

Globalization and the Environmental Crisis

As many people take a global perspective in the twenty-first century, they are realizing that everywhere on the planet, human beings are interdependent in terms of the air they breathe, the water they drink, the food they consume, and the climate that affects their lives. At the same time, however, human activities are creating environmental challenges that threaten the very foundation of human existence on earth.

One problem is population growth. As of September 2012, the world population was estimated at more than 7 billion people, only twenty-four years after passing the 5 billion mark. At its current rate of growth, the world population could reach 12.8 billion by 2050, according to the United Nations' long-range population projections. The result has been an increased demand for food and other resources that has put great pressure on the earth's ecosystems. At the same time, the failure to grow enough food for more and more people, a problem exacerbated by drought conditions developing on several continents, has created a severe problem, as an estimated 1 billion people worldwide today suffer from hunger. Every year, more than 8 million people die of hunger, many of them young children.

Another problem is the pattern of consumption as the wealthy nations of the Northern Hemisphere consume vast quantities of the planet's natural resources. The United States, for example, which has 6 percent of the world's people, consumes 30 to 40 percent of its resources. The spread of these consumption patterns to other parts of the world raises serious questions about the ability of the planet to sustain itself and its population. As a result of the growing Chinese economy, for example, more automobiles are now sold annually in China than in the United States.

Yet another threat to the environment is **global climate change**, which has the potential to create a worldwide crisis. Virtually all of the world's scientists agree that the **greenhouse effect**, the warming of the earth because of the buildup of carbon dioxide in the atmosphere, is contributing to devastating droughts and storms, the melting of the polar ice caps, and rising sea levels that could inundate coastal regions in the second half of the twenty-first century. Also alarming is the potential loss of biodiversity. Seven out of ten biologists believe the planet is now experiencing an alarming extinction of both plant and animal species.

The Social Challenges of Globalization

Since 1945, tens of millions of people have migrated from one part of the world to another. These migrations have occurred for many reasons. Persecution for political reasons caused many people from Pakistan, Bangladesh, Sri Lanka, and eastern Europe to seek refuge in western European countries, while brutal civil wars in Asia, Africa, the Middle East, and Europe led millions of refugees to seek safety in neighboring countries. Most people who have migrated, however, have done so to find jobs. Latin Americans seeking a better life have migrated to the United States, while guest workers from Turkey, southern and eastern Europe, North Africa, India, and Pakistan have migrated to more prosperous western European countries. In 2005, nearly 200 million people, about 3 percent of the world's population, lived outside the country where they were born.

The migration of millions of people has also provoked a social backlash in many countries. Foreign workers often become scapegoats when countries face economic problems. Political parties in France and Norway, for example, have called for the removal of blacks, Muslims, and Arabs in order to protect the ethnic or cultural purity of their nations, while in Asian countries, there is animosity against other Asian ethnic groups.

Another challenge of globalization is the wide gap between rich and poor nations. The rich nations, or **developed nations**, are located mainly in the Northern Hemisphere. They include the United States, Canada, Germany, and Japan, which have well-organized industrial and agricultural systems, advanced technologies, and effective educational systems. The poor nations, or **developing nations**, include many nations in Africa,

Asia, and Latin America, which often have primarily agricultural economies with little technology. A serious problem in many developing nations is explosive population growth, which has led to severe food shortages often caused by poor soil but also by economic factors. Growing crops for export to developed countries, for example, may lead to enormous profits for large landowners but leaves many small farmers with little land on which to grow food.

Civil wars have also created food shortages. War not only disrupts normal farming operations, but warring groups try to limit access to food to weaken or kill their enemies. In Sudan, 1.3 million people starved when combatants of a civil war in the 1980s prevented food from reaching them. As unrest continued during the early 2000s in Sudan's Darfur region, families were forced to leave their farms. As a result, an estimated 70,000 people had starved by mid-2004.

Global Movements and New Hopes

As people have become aware that the problems humans face are not just national or regional but global in scope, they have responded to this challenge in different ways. One approach has been to develop grassroots social movements, including ones devoted to environmental concerns, women's and men's liberation, human potential, appropriate technology, and nonviolence. "Think globally, act locally" is frequently the slogan of these grassroots groups. Related to the emergence of these social movements is the growth of **nongovernmental organizations (NGOs)**. According to one analyst, NGOs are an important instrument in the cultivation of global perspectives: "Since NGOs by definition are identified with interests that transcend national boundaries, we expect all NGOs to define problems in global terms, to take account of human interests and needs as they are found in all parts of the planet."[2] NGOs are often represented at the United Nations and include professional, business, and cooperative organizations; foundations; religious, peace, and disarmament groups; youth and women's organizations; environmental and human rights groups; and research institutes. The number of international NGOs has increased from 176 in 1910 to 40,000 in 2007.

And yet hopes for global approaches to global problems have also been hindered by political, ethnic, and religious differences. Pollution of the Rhine River by factories along its banks provokes angry disputes among European nations, and the United States and Canada have argued about the effects of acid rain on Canadian forests. While droughts in Russia and China wreak havoc on the world's grain supply, floods in Pakistan challenge the stability of Asia. The collapse of the Soviet Union and its satellite system seemed to provide an enormous boost to the potential for international cooperation on global issues, but it has had almost the opposite effect. The bloody conflict in the former Yugoslavia indicates the dangers inherent in the rise of nationalist sentiment among various ethnic and religious groups in eastern Europe. The widening gap between wealthy nations and poor, developing nations threatens global economic stability. Many conflicts begin with regional issues and then develop into international concerns. International terrorist groups seek to wreak havoc around the world.

Thus, even as the world becomes more global in culture and interdependent in its mutual relations, centrifugal forces are still at work attempting to redefine the political, cultural, and ethnic ways in which the world is divided. Such efforts are often disruptive and can sometimes work against measures to enhance our human destiny. But they also represent an integral part of human character and human history and cannot be suppressed in the relentless drive to create a world society.

There are already initial signs that as the common dangers posed by environmental damage, overpopulation, and scarcity of resources become even more apparent, societies around the world will find ample reason to turn their attention from cultural differences to the demands of global interdependence. The greatest challenge of the twenty-first century may be to reconcile the drive for individual and group identity with the common needs of the human community.

Suggested Reading

Useful books on different facets of the new global civilization include **M. B. Steger, *Globalization: A Very Short Introduction*** (New York, 2003); **J. H. Mittelman, *The Globalization Syndrome*** (Princeton, N.J., 2000); **M. Waters, *Globalization***, 2nd ed. (London, 2001); **P. O'Meara et al., eds., *Globalization and the Challenges of the New Century*** (Bloomington, Ind., 2000); and **H. French, *Vanishing Borders*** (New York, 2000). For a comprehensive examination of the digital age, see **M. Castells, *The Information Age***, 3 vols. (Oxford, 1996–1998).

GLOSSARY

abbess the head of a convent or monastery for women.

abbot the head of a monastery.

absolutism a form of government where the sovereign power or ultimate authority rested in the hands of a monarch who claimed to rule by divine right and was therefore responsible only to God.

Abstract Expressionism a post–World War II artistic movement that broke with all conventions of form and structure in favor of total abstraction.

abstract painting an artistic movement that developed early in the twentieth century in which artists focused on color to avoid any references to visual reality

African Union the organization that replaced the Organization of African Unity in 2001; designed to bring about increased political and economic integration of African states.

Agricultural (Neolithic) Revolution *see* Neolithic Revolution.

agricultural revolution the application of new agricultural techniques that allowed for a large increase in productivity in the eighteenth century.

Amerindians earliest inhabitants of North and South America. Original theories suggested migration from Siberia across the Bering Land Bridge; more recent evidence suggests migration also occurred by sea from regions of the South Pacific to South America.

Analects the body of writing containing conversations between Confucius and his disciples that preserves his worldly wisdom and pragmatic philosophies.

ANC the African National Congress. Founded in 1912, it was the beginning of political activity by South African blacks. Banned by politically dominant European whites in 1960, it was not officially "unbanned" until 1990. It is now the official majority party of the South African government.

anti-Semitism hostility toward or discrimination against Jews.

apartheid the system of racial segregation practiced in the Republic of South Africa until the 1990s, which involved political, legal, and economic discrimination against nonwhites.

appeasement the policy, followed by the European nations in the 1930s, of accepting Hitler's annexation of Austria and Czechoslovakia in the belief that meeting his demands would assure peace and stability.

Aramaic a Semitic language dominant in the Middle East in the first century B.C.E.; still in use in small regions of the Middle East and southern Asia.

aristocracy a class of hereditary nobility in medieval Europe; a warrior class who shared a distinctive lifestyle based on the institution of knighthood, although there were social divisions within the group based on extremes of wealth.

Arthasastra an early Indian political treatise that sets forth many fundamental aspects of the relationship of rulers and their subjects. It has been compared to Machiavelli's *The Prince* and has provided principles upon which many aspects of social organization have developed in the region.

Aryans Indo-European-speaking nomads who entered India from the Central Asian steppes between 1500 and 1000 B.C.E. and greatly affected Indian society, notably by establishing the caste system. The term was later adopted by German Nazis to describe their racial ideal.

asceticism a lifestyle involving the denial of worldly pleasures. Predominantly associated with Hindu, Buddhist, or Christian religions, adherents perceive their practices as a path to greater spitiuality.

ASEAN the Association for the Southeast Asian Nations formed in 1967 to promote the prosperity and political stability of its member nations. Currently, Brunei, Cambodia, Indonesia, Laos, Malaysia, Myanmar, the Philippines, Singapore, Thailand, and Vietnam are members. Other countries in the region participate as "observer" members.

assimilation the concept, originating in France, that the colonial peoples should be assimilated into the parent French culture.

association the concept, developed by French colonial officials, that the colonial peoples should be permitted to retain their precolonial cultural traditions.

Atman in Brahmanism, the individual soul.

Ausgleich the "Compromise" of 1867 that created the dual monarchy of Austria-Hungary. Austria and Hungary each had its own capital, constitution, and legislative assembly, but were united under one monarch.

authoritarian state a state that has a dictatorial government and some other trappings of a totalitarian state, but does not demand that the masses be actively involved in the regime's goals as totalitarian states do.

bakufu the centralized government set up in Japan in the twelfth century. *See also* shogunate system.

Banners originally established in 1639 by the Qing dynasty, the Eight Banners were administrative divisions into which all Manchu families were placed. Banners quickly evolved into the basis of Manchu military organization with each required to raise and support a prescribed number of troops.

***Bao-jia* system** the Chinese practice, reportedly originated by the Qin dynasty in the third century B.C.E., of organizing families into groups of five or ten to exercise mutual control and surveillance and reduce loyalty to the family.

bard in Africa, a professional storyteller.

Baroque a style that dominated Western painting, sculpture, architecture, and music from about 1580 to 1730, generally characterized by elaborate ornamentation and dramatic effects. Important practitioners included Bernini, Rubens, Handel, and Bach.

Bedouins nomadic tribes originally from northern Arabia, who became important traders after the domestication of the camel during the first millennium B.C.E. Early converts to Islam, their values and practices deeply affected the religion of Islam.

Berbers an ethnic group indigenous to western North Africa.

bey a provincial governor in the Ottoman Empire.

bhakti in Hinduism, devotion as a means of religious observance open to all persons regardless of class.

Black Death the outbreak of plague (mostly bubonic) in the mid-fourteenth century that killed from 25 to 50 percent of Europe's population.

blitzkrieg "lightning war." A war conducted with great speed and force, as in Germany's advance at the beginning of World War II.

bodhi wisdom in India. Sometimes described as complete awareness of the true nature of the universe.

bodhisattvas in some schools of Buddhism, individuals who have achieved enlightenment but, because of their great compassion, have chosen to renounce Nirvana and to remain on earth in spirit form to help all human beings achieve release from reincarnation.

Boers the Afrikaans-speaking descendants of Dutch settlers in southern Africa who left the Cape Colony in the nineteenth century to settle in the Orange Free State and Transvaal; defeated by the British in the Boer War (1899–1902) and ultimately incorporated into the Union of South Africa.

Bolsheviks a small faction of the Russian Social Democratic Party who were led by Lenin and dedicated to violent revolution; seized power in Russia in 1917 and were subsequently renamed the Communists.

bonsai the cultivation of stunted trees and shrubs to create exquisite nature scenes in miniature; originated in China in the first millenium B.C.E. and imported to Japan between 700 and 900 C.E.

Brahman the Hindu word roughly equivalent to God; the Divine basis of all being; regarded as the source and sum of the cosmos.

Brahmanism the early religious beliefs of the Aryan people in India, which eventually gave rise to Hinduism.

brahmin a member of the Hindu priestly caste or class; literally "one who has realized or attempts to realize Brahman." Traditionally, duties of a *brahmin* include studying Hindu religious scriptures and transmitting them to others orally. The priests of Hindu temples are *brahmin*.

Brezhnev Doctrine the doctrine, enunciated by Leonid Brezhnev, that the Soviet Union had a right to intervene if socialism was threatened in another socialist state; used to justify the use of Soviet troops in Czechoslovakia in 1968.

Buddhism a religion and philosophy based on the teachings of Siddhartha Gautama in about 500 B.C.E. Principally practiced in China, India, and other parts of Asia, Buddhism has 360 million followers and is considered a major world releigion.

Burakumin a Japanese minority similar to *dalits* (untouchables) in Indian culture. Past and current discrimination has resulted in lower educational attainment and socioeconomic status for members of this group. Movements with objectives ranging from "liberation" to integration have tried over the years to change this situation.

Bushido the code of conduct observed by samurai warriors; comparable to the European concept of chivalry.

caliph the secular leader of the Islamic community.

calpulli in Aztec society, a kinship group, often of a thousand or more, which served as an intermediary with the central government, providing taxes and conscript labor to the state.

caravels mobile sailing ships with both lateen and square sails that began to be constructed in Europe in the sixteenth century.

caste system a system of rigid social hierarchcy in which all members of that society are assigned by birth to specific "ranks," and inherit specific roles and privileges.

Catholic Reformation a movement for the reform of the Catholic Church in the sixteenth century.

caudillos strong leaders in nineteenth-century Latin America, who were usually supported by the landed elites and ruled chiefly by military force, though some were popular; they included both modernizers and destructive dictators.

censorate one of the three primary Chinese ministries, originally established in the Qin dynasty, whose inspectors surveyed the efficiency of officials throughout the system.

centuriate assembly the chief popular assembly of the Roman Republic. It passed laws and elected the chief magistrates.

chaebol a South Korean business structure similar to the Japanese *keiretsu*.

Chan Buddhism a Chinese sect (Zen in Japanese) influenced by Daoist ideas, which called for mind training and a strict regimen as a means of seeking enlightenment.

chinampas in Mesoamerica, artificial islands crisscrossed by canals that provided water for crops and easy transportation to local markets.

chonmin in Korea, the lowest class in society consisting of slaves and workers in certain undesirable occupations such as butchers; literally, "base people."

Christian (northern) humanism an intellectual movement in northern Europe in the late fifteenth and early sixteenth centuries that combined the interest in the classics of the Italian Renaissance with an interest in the sources of early Christianity, including the New Testament and the writings of the church fathers.

chu nom an adaptation of Chinese written characters to provide a writing system for spoken Vietnamese; in use by the ninth century C.E.

civil disobedience the tactic of using illegal but nonviolent means of protest; designed by the Indian nationalist leader Mohandas Gandhi to resist British colonial rule.

civilization a complex culture in which large numbers of humans share a variety of common elements, including cities; religion; political, military, and social structures; writing; and significant artistic and intellectual activity.

civil service examination an elaborate Chinese system of selecting bureaucrats on merit, first introduced in 165 C.E., developed by the Tang dynasty in the seventh century C.E. and refined under the Song dynasty; later adopted in Vietnam and with less success in Japan and Korea. It contributed to efficient government, upward mobility, and cultural uniformity.

class struggle the basis of the Marxist analysis of history, which says that the owners of the means of production have always oppressed the workers and predicts an inevitable revolution. *See also* Marxism.

Cold War the ideological conflict between the Soviet Union and the United States after World War II.

Columbian Exchange the exchange of animals, plants, and culture, but also communicable diseases and human populations including slaves, between the Western and Eastern Hemispheres that occurred after Columbus's voyages to the Americas.

commercial capitalism beginning in the Middle Ages, an economic system in which people invested in trade and goods in order to make profits.

common law law common to the entire kingdom of England; imposed by the king's courts beginning in the twelfth century to replace the customary law used in county and feudal courts that varied from place to place.

communalism in South Asia, the tendency of people to band together in mutually antagonistic social subgroups; elsewhere used to describe unifying trends in the larger community.

Communist International (Comintern) a worldwide organization of Communist parties, founded by Lenin in 1919, dedicated to the advancement of world revolution; also known as the Third International.

Confucianism a system of thought based on the teachings of Confucius (551–479 B.C.E.) that developed into the ruling ideology of the Chinese state. *See also* Neo-Confucianism.

conquistadors "conquerors." Leaders in the Spanish conquests in the Americas, especially Mexico and Peru, in the sixteenth century.

conscription a military draft.
conservatism an ideology based on tradition and social stability that favored the maintenance of established institutions, organized religion, and obedience to authority and resisted change, especially abrupt change.
consuls the chief executive officers of the Roman Republic. Two were chosen annually to administer the government and lead the army in battle.
consumer society a term applied to Western society after World War II as the working classes adopted the consumption patterns of the middle class and installment plans, credit cards, and easy credit made consumer goods such as appliances and automobiles widely available.
containment a policy adopted by the United States in the Cold War. It called for the use of any means, but hopefully short of all-out war, to limit Soviet expansion.
Continental System Napoleon's effort to bar British goods from the Continent in the hope of weakening Britain's economy and destroying its capacity to wage war.
Contras in Nicaragua in the 1980s, an anti-Sandinista guerrilla movement supported by the U.S. Reagan administration.
Coptic a form of Christianity, originally Egyptian, that has thrived in Ethiopia since the fourth century C.E.
cottage industry a system of textile manufacturing in which spinners and weavers worked at home in their cottages using raw materials supplied to them by capitalist entrepreneurs.
council of the plebs in the Roman Republic, a council only for the plebeians. After 287 B.C.E., its resolutions were binding on all Romans.
creoles in Latin America, American-born descendants of Europeans.
Crusade in the Middle Ages, a military campaign in defense of Christendom.
Cubism an artistic style developed at the beginning of the twentieth century, especially by Pablo Picasso, that used geometric designs to re-create reality in the viewer's mind.
cuneiform "wedge-shaped." A system of writing developed by the Sumerians that consisted of wedge-shaped impressions made by a reed stylus on clay tablets.

Dadaism an artistic movement in the 1920s and 1930s by artists who were revolted by the senseless slaughter of World War I and used their "anti-art" to express contempt for the Western tradition.
daimyo prominent Japanese families who provided allegiance to the local shogun in exchange for protection; similar to vassals in Europe.
dalits commonly referred to as untouchables; the lowest level of Indian society, technically outside the caste system and considered less than human; named *harijans* ("children of God") by Gandhi, they remain the object of discrimination despite affirmative action programs.
Dao a Chinese philosophical concept, literally "the Way," central to both Confucianism and Daoism, that describes the behavior proper to each member of society; somewhat similar to the Indian concept of *dharma*.
Daoism a Chinese philosophy traditionally ascribed to the perhaps legendary Lao Tzu, which holds that acceptance and spontaneity are the keys to harmonious interaction with the universal order; an alternative to Confucianism.
decolonization the process of becoming free of colonial status and achieving statehood; occurred in most of the world's colonies between 1947 and 1962.
deficit spending the concept, developed by John Maynard Keynes in the 1930s, that in times of economic depression governments should stimulate demand by hiring people to do public works, such as building highways, even if this increases the public debt.
deism belief in God as the creator of the universe who, after setting it in motion, ceased to have any direct involvement in it and allowed it to run according to its own natural laws.
demesne the part of a manor retained under the direct control of the lord and worked by the serfs as part of their labor services.
denazification after World War II, the Allied policy of rooting out any traces of Nazism in German society by bringing prominent Nazis to trial for war crimes and purging any known Nazis from political office.
de-Stalinization the policy of denouncing and undoing the most repressive aspects of Stalin's regime; begun by Nikita Khrushchev in 1956.
détente the relaxation of tension between the Soviet Union and the United States that occurred in the 1970s.
devshirme in the Ottoman Empire, a system (literally, "collection") of training talented children to be administrators or members of the sultan's harem; originally meritocratic, by the seventeenth century, it degenerated into a hereditary caste.
dharma in Hinduism and Buddhism, the law that governs the universe, and specifically human behavior.
dictator in the Roman Republic, an official granted unlimited power to run the state for a short period of time, usually six months, during an emergency.
diffusion hypothesis the hypothesis that the Yellow River valley was the ancient heartland of Chinese civilization and that technological and cultural achievements radiated from there to other parts of East Asia. Recent discoveries of other early agricultural communities in China have led to some modification of the hypothesis to allow for other centers of civilization.
diocese the area under the jurisdiction of a Christian bishop; based originally on Roman administrative districts.
direct rule a concept devised by European colonial governments to rule their colonial subjects without the participation of local authorities. It was most often applied in colonial societies in Africa.
divination the practice of seeking to foretell future events by interpreting divine signs, which could appear in various forms, such as in entrails of animals, in patterns in smoke, or in dreams.
divine-right monarchy a monarchy based on the belief that monarchs receive their power directly from God and are responsible to no one except God.
dyarchy during the Qing dynasty in China, a system in which all important national and provincial admininstrative positions were shared equally by Chinese and Manchus, which helped to consolidate both Manchu rule and their assimilation.

economic imperialism the process in which banks and corporations from developed nations invest in underdeveloped regions and establish a major presence there in the hope of making high profits; not necessarily the same as colonial expansion in that businesses invest where they can make a profit, which may not be in their own nation's colonies.
Einsatzgruppen in Nazi Germany, special strike forces in the SS that played an important role in rounding up and killing Jews.
El Niño periodic changes in water temperature at the surface of the Pacific Ocean, which can lead to major environmental changes and may have led to the collapse of the Moche civilization in what is now Peru.
emir "commander" in Arabic; a title used by Muslim rulers in southern Spain and elsewhere.

encomienda a grant from the Spanish monarch to colonial conquistadors.

***encomienda* system** the system by which Spain first governed its American colonies. Holders of an *encomienda* were supposed to protect the Indians as well as using them as laborers and collecting tribute but in practice exploited them.

enlightened absolutism an absolute monarchy where the ruler follows the principles of the Enlightenment by introducing reforms for the improvement of society, allowing freedom of speech and the press, permitting religious toleration, expanding education, and ruling in accordance with the laws.

Enlightenment an eighteenth-century intellectual movement, led by the philosophes, that stressed the application of reason and the scientific method to all aspects of life.

Epicureanism a philosophy founded by Epicurus in the fourth century B.C.E. that taught that happiness (freedom from emotional turmoil) could be achieved through the pursuit of pleasure (intellectual rather than sensual pleasure).

eta in feudal Japan, a class of hereditary slaves who were responsible for what were considered degrading occupations, such as curing leather and burying the dead.

ethnic cleansing the policy of killing or forcibly removing people of another ethnic group; used by the Serbs against Bosnian Muslims in the 1990s.

Eucharist a Christian sacrament in which consecrated bread and wine are consumed in celebration of Jesus's Last Supper; also called the Lord's Supper or communion.

eunuch a man whose testicles have been removed; a standard feature of the Chinese imperial system, the Ottoman Empire, and the Mughal dynasty, among others.

existentialism a philosophical movement that arose after World War II that emphasized the meaninglessness of life, born of the desperation caused by two world wars.

fascism an ideology or movement that exalts the nation above the individual and calls for a centralized government with a dictatorial leader, economic and social regimentation, and forcible suppression of opposition; in particular, the ideology of Mussolini's Fascist regime in Italy.

feminism the belief in the social, political, and economic equality of the sexes; also, organized activity to advance women's rights.

fief a landed estate granted to a vassal in exchange for military services.

filial piety in traditional China, in particular, a hierarchical system in which every family member has his or her place, subordinate to a patriarch who has in turn reciprocal responsibilities.

Final Solution the physical extermination of the Jewish people by the Nazis during World War II.

Five Pillars of Islam the core requirements of the Muslim faith: belief in Allah and his Prophet Muhammad; prescribed prayers; observation of Ramadan; pilgrimage to Mecca; and giving alms to the poor.

five relationships in traditional China, the hierarchical interpersonal associations considered crucial to social order, within the family, between friends, and with the king.

foot binding an extremely painful process, common in China throughout the second millenium C.E., that compressed girls' feet to half their natural size, representing submissiveness and self-discipline, which were considered necessary attributes for an ideal wife.

Four Modernizations the slogan for radical reforms of Chinese industry, agriculture, technology, and national defense, instituted by Deng Xiaoping after his accession to power in the late 1970s.

genin landless laborers in feudal Japan, who were effectively slaves.

genro the ruling clique of aristocrats in Meiji Japan.

geocentric theory the idea that the earth is at the center of the universe and that the sun and other celestial objects revolve around the earth.

glasnost "openness." Mikhail Gorbachev's policy of encouraging Soviet citizens to openly discuss the strengths and weaknesses of the Soviet Union.

good emperors the five emperors who ruled from 96 to 180 (Nerva, Trajan, Hadrian, Antoninus Pius, and Marcus Aurelius), a period of peace and prosperity for the Roman Empire.

Good Neighbor policy a policy adopted by the administration of President Franklin D. Roosevelt to practice restraint in U.S. relations with Latin American nations.

Gothic a term used to describe the art and especially the architecture of Europe in the twelfth, thirteenth, and fourteenth centuries.

Gothic literature a form of literature used by Romantics to emphasize the bizarre and unusual, especially evident in horror stories.

Grand Council the top of the government hierarchy in the Song dynasty in China.

grand vizier the chief executive in the Ottoman Empire, under the sultan.

Great Leap Forward a short-lived, radical experiment in China, started in 1958, which created vast rural communes and attempted to replace the family as the fundamental social unit.

Great Proletarian Cultural Revolution an attempt to destroy all vestiges of tradition in China, in order to create a totally egalitarian society. Launched by Mao Zedong in 1966, it devolved into virtual anarchy and lasted only until Mao's death in 1976.

Great Schism the crisis in the late medieval church when there were first two and then three popes; ended by the Council of Constance (1414–1418).

guest workers foreign workers working temporarily in European countries.

guided democracy the name given by President Sukarno of Indonesia in the late 1950s to his style of government, which theoretically operated by consensus.

guild an association of people with common interests and concerns, especially people working in the same craft. In medieval Europe, guilds came to control much of the production process and to restrict entry into various trades.

guru teacher, especially in the Hindu, Buddhist and Sikh religious traditions, where it is an important honorific.

Hadith a collection of the sayings of the Prophet Muhammad, used to supplement the revelations contained in the Qur'an.

harem the private domain of a ruler such as the sultan in the Ottoman Empire or the caliph of Baghdad, generally large and mostly inhabited by the extended family.

Hegira the flight of Muhammad from Mecca to Medina in 622, which marks the first date on the official calendar of Islam.

heliocentric theory the idea that the sun (not the earth) is at the center of the universe.

Hellenistic literally, "to imitate the Greeks"; the era after the death of Alexander the Great when Greek culture spread into the Near East and blended with the culture of that region.

helots serfs in ancient Sparta, who were permanently bound to the land that they worked for their Spartan masters.

heresy the holding of religious doctrines different from the official teachings of the church.

Hezbollah a militant Shi'ite organization and political party based in modern Lebanon.

hieroglyphics a highly pictorial system of writing most often associated with ancient Egypt. Also used (with different "pictographs") by other ancient peoples such as the Maya.

high colonialism the more formal phase of European colonial policy in Africa after World War I when the colonial administrative network was extended to outlying areas and more emphasis was placed on improving social services and fostering economic development, especially the exploitation of natural resources, to enable the colonies to achieve self-sufficiency.

high culture the literary and artistic culture of the educated and wealthy ruling classes.

Hinayana the scornful name for Theravada Buddhism ("lesser vehicle") used by devotees of Mahayana Buddhism.

Hinduism the main religion in India. It emphasizes reincarnation, based on the results of the previous life, and the desirability of escaping this cycle. Its various forms feature both asceticism and the pleasures of ordinary life, and encompass a multitude of gods as different manifestations of one ultimate reality.

Holocaust the mass slaughter of European Jews by the Nazis during World War II.

Hopewell culture a Native American society that flourished from about 200 B.C.E. to 400 C.E., noted for large burial mounds and extensive manufacturing. Largely based in Ohio, its traders ranged as far as the Gulf of Mexico.

hoplites heavily armed infantry soldiers used in ancient Greece in a phalanx formation.

Hundred Schools schools of philosophy in China around the third century B.C.E. that engaged in a wide-ranging debate over the nature of human beings, society, and the universe; included Legalism and Daoism, as well as Confucianism.

hydraulic society a society organized around a large irrigation system to control the allocation of water.

iconoclasm an eighth-century Byzantine movement against the use of icons (pictures of sacred figures), which was condemned as idolatry.

imam an Islamic religious leader. Some traditions say there is only one per generation; others use the term more broadly.

imperialism the policy of extending one nation's power either by conquest or by establishing direct or indirect economic or cultural authority over another. Generally driven by economic self-interest, it can also be motivated by a sincere (if often misguided) sense of moral obligation.

Impressionism an artistic movement that originated in France in the 1870s. Impressionists sought to capture their impressions of the changing effects of light on objects in nature.

indirect rule a colonial policy of foreign rule in cooperation with local political elites. Though implemented in much of India and Malaya and in parts of Africa, it was not feasible where resistance was strong.

individualism emphasis on and interest in the unique traits of each person.

indulgence the remission of part or all of the temporal punishment in purgatory due to sin; granted for charitable contributions and other good deeds. Indulgences became a regular practice of the Christian church in the High Middle Ages, and their abuse was instrumental in sparking Luther's reform movement in the sixteenth century.

infanticide the practice of killing infants.

inflation a sustained rise in the price level.

informal empire the growing presence of Europeans in Africa during the first decades of the nineteenth century. During this period, most African states were nonetheless still able to maintain their independence.

interdict in the Catholic Church, a censure by which a region or country is deprived of receiving the sacraments.

intervention, principle of the idea, after the Congress of Vienna, that the great powers of Europe had the right to send armies into countries experiencing revolution to restore legitimate monarchs to their thrones.

intifada the "uprising" of Palestinians living under Israeli control, especially in the 1980s and 1990s.

Islam the religion derived from the revelations of Muhammad, the Prophet of Allah; literally, "submission" (to the will of Allah); also, the culture and civilization based on the faith.

Jainism an Indian religion, founded in the fifth century B.C.E. that stresses extreme simplicity.

Janissaries an elite core of eight thousand troops personally loyal to the sultan of the Ottoman Empire.

jati a kinship group, the basic social organization of traditional Indian society, to some extent specialized by occupation.

jihad in Islam, "striving in the way of the Lord." The term is ambiguous and has been subject to varying interpretations, from the practice of conducting raids against local neighbors to the conduct of "holy war" against unbelievers.

joint-stock company a company or association that raises capital by selling shares to individuals who receive dividends on their investment while a board of directors runs the company.

Jomon the earliest known Neolithic inhabitants of Japan, named for the cord pattern of their pottery.

justification by faith the primary doctrine of the Protestant Reformation; taught that humans are saved not through good works, but by the grace of God, bestowed freely through the sacrifice of Jesus.

Kabuki a form of Japanese theater that developed in the seventeenth century C.E. Originally disreputable, it became a highly stylized art form.

kami spirits worshiped in early Japan that resided in trees, rivers and streams. *See also* Shinto.

karma a fundamental concept in Hindu (and later Buddhist, Jain, and Sikh) philosophy, that rebirth in a future life is determined by actions in this or other lives. The word refers to the entire process, to the individual's actions, and also to the cumulative result of those actions, for instance, a store of good or bad *karma*.

keiretsu a type of powerful industrial or financial conglomerate that emerged in post–World War II Japan following the abolition of the *zaibatsu*.

khanates Mongol kingdoms, in particular the subdivisions of Genghis Khan's empire ruled by his heirs.

kokutai the core ideology of the Japanese state, particularly during the Meiji Restoration, stressing the uniqueness of the Japanese system and the supreme authority of the emperor.

kowtow the ritual of prostration and touching the forehead to the ground, demanded of all foreign ambassadors to the Chinese court as a symbol of submission.

kshatriya originally, the warrior class of Aryan society in India; ranked below (sometimes equal to) *brahmins*; in modern times, often government workers or soldiers.

laissez-faire "to let alone." An economic doctrine that holds that an economy is best served when the government does not interfere but allows the economy to self-regulate according to the forces of supply and demand.

latifundia large landed estates in the Roman Empire (singular: *latifundium*).

lay investiture the practice in which a layperson chose a bishop and invested him with the symbols of both his temporal office and his spiritual office; led to the Investiture Controversy, which was ended by compromise in the Concordat of Worms in 1122.

Legalism a Chinese philosophy that argued that human beings were by nature evil and would follow the correct path only if coerced by harsh laws and stiff punishments. Adopted as official ideology by the Qin dynasty, it was later rejected but remained influential.

legitimacy, principle of the idea that after the Napoleonic wars peace could best be reestablished in Europe by restoring legitimate monarchs who would preserve traditional institutions; guided Metternich at the Congress of Vienna.

liberal arts the seven areas of study that formed the basis of education in medieval and early modern Europe. Following Boethius and other late Roman authors, they consisted of grammar, rhetoric, and dialectic or logic (the *trivium*) and arithmetic, geometry, astronomy, and music (the *quadrivium*).

liberalism an ideology based on the belief that people should be as free from restraint as possible. Economic liberalism is the idea that the government should not interfere in the workings of the economy. Political liberalism is the idea that there should be restraints on the exercise of power so that people can enjoy basic civil rights in a constitutional state with a representative assembly.

limited (constitutional) monarchy a system of government in which the monarch is limited by a representative assembly and by the duty to rule in accordance with the laws of the land.

lineage group the descendants of a common ancestor; relatives, often as opposed to immediate family.

Longshan a Neolithic society from near the Yellow River in China, sometimes identified by its black pottery.

maharaja originally, a king in the Aryan society of early India (a great raja); later used more generally to denote an important ruler.

Mahayana a school of Buddhism that promotes the idea of universal salvation through the intercession of bodhisattvas; predominant in north Asia.

majlis a council of elders among the Bedouins of the Roman era.

Malayo-Polynesian a family of languages whose speakers originated on Taiwan or in southeastern China and spread from there to the Malay peninsula, the Indonesian archipelago, and many islands of the South Pacific.

mandate of Heaven the justification for the rule of the Zhou dynasty in China. The king was charged to maintain order as a representative of Heaven, which was viewed as an impersonal law of nature.

mandates a system established after World War I whereby a nation officially administered a territory (mandate) on behalf of the League of Nations. Thus, France administered Lebanon and Syria as mandates, and Britain administered Iraq and Palestine.

manor an agricultural estate operated by a lord and worked by peasants who performed labor services and paid various rents and fees to the lord in exchange for protection and sustenance.

mansa in the West African state of Mali, a chieftain who served as both religious and administrative leader and was responsible for forwarding tax revenues from the village to higher levels of government.

Marshall Plan the European Recovery Program, under which the United States provided financial aid to European countries to help them rebuild after World War II.

Marxism the political, economic, and social theories of Karl Marx, which included the idea that history is the story of class struggle and that ultimately the proletariat will overthrow the bourgeoisie and establish a dictatorship en route to a classless society.

mass education a state-run educational system, usually free and compulsory, that aims to ensure that all children in society have at least a basic education.

mass leisure forms of leisure that appeal to large numbers of people in a society including the working classes; emerged at the end of the nineteenth century to provide workers with amusements after work and on weekends; used during the twentieth century by totalitarian states to control their populations.

mass politics a political order characterized by mass political parties and universal male and (eventually) female suffrage.

mass society a society in which the concerns of the majority—the lower classes—play a prominent role; characterized by extension of voting rights, an improved standard of living for the lower classes, and mass education.

matrilinear passing through the female line, for example, from a father to his sister's son rather than his own, as practiced in some African societies; not necessarily, or even usually, combined with matriarchy, in which women rule.

megaliths large stones, widely used in Europe from around 4000 to 1500 B.C.E. to create monuments, including sophisticated astronomical observatories.

Meiji Restoration the period during the late nineteenth and early twentieth centuries in which fundamental economic and cultural changes occurred in Japan, tranforming it from a feudal and agrarian society to an industrial and technological society.

mercantilism an economic theory that held that a nation's prosperity depended on its supply of gold and silver and that the total volume of trade is unchangeable; therefore, advocated that the government play an active role in the economy by encouraging exports and discouraging imports, especially through the use of tariffs.

Mesoamerica the region stretching roughly from modern central Mexico to Honduras, in which the Olmec, Mayan, Aztec and other civilizations developed.

Mesolithic Age the period from 10,000 to 7000 B.C.E., characterized by a gradual transition from a food-gathering/hunting economy to a food-producing economy.

mestizos the offspring of intermarriage between Europeans, originally Spaniards, and native American Indians.

Middle Passage the journey of slaves from Africa to the Americas as the middle leg of the triangular trade.

Middle Path a central concept of Buddhism, which advocates avoiding extremes of both materialism and asceticism; also known as the Eightfold Way.

mihrab the niche in a mosque's wall that indicates the direction of Mecca, usually containing an ornately decorated panel representing Allah.

militarism a policy of aggressive military preparedness; in particular, the large armies based on mass conscription and complex, inflexible plans for mobilization that most European nations had before World War I.

millet an administrative unit in the Ottoman Empire used to organize religious groups.

ministerial responsibility a tenet of nineteenth-century liberalism that held that ministers of the monarch should be responsible to the legislative assembly rather than to the monarch.

Modernism the new artistic and literary styles that emerged in the decades before 1914 as artists rebelled against traditional efforts to portray reality as accurately as possible (leading to Impressionism and Cubism) and writers explored new forms.

monasticism a movement that began in early Christianity whose purpose was to create communities of men or women who practiced a communal life dedicated to God as a moral example to the world around them.

monk a man who chooses to live a communal life divorced from the world in order to dedicate himself totally to the will of God.

monotheistic/monotheism having only one god; the doctrine or belief that there is only one god.

muezzin the man who calls Muslims to prayer at the appointed times; nowadays often a tape-recorded message played over loudspeakers.

mulattoes the offspring of Africans and Europeans, particularly in Latin America.

mutual deterrence the belief that nuclear war could best be prevented if both the United States and the Soviet Union had sufficient nuclear weapons so that even if one nation launched a preemptive first strike, the other could respond and devastate the attacker.

mystery religions religions that involve initiation into secret rites that promise intense emotional involvement with spiritual forces and a greater chance of individual immortality.

nationalism a sense of national consciousness based on awareness of being part of a community—a "nation"—that has common institutions, traditions, language, and customs and that becomes the focus of the individual's primary political loyalty.

nationalization the process of converting a business or industry from private ownership to government control and ownership.

nation in arms the people's army raised by universal mobilization to repel the foreign enemies of the French Revolution.

nation-state a form of political organization in which a relatively homogeneous people inhabits a sovereign state, as opposed to a state containing people of several nationalities.

NATO the North Atlantic Treaty Organization; a military alliance formed in 1949 in which the signatories (Belgium, Canada, Denmark, France, Great Britain, Iceland, Italy, Luxembourg, the Netherlands, Norway, Portugal, and the United States) agreed to provide mutual assistance if any one of them was attacked; later expanded to include other nations, including former members of the Warsaw Pact—Poland, the Czech Republic, and Hungary.

natural law a body of laws or specific principles held to be derived from nature and binding upon all human society even in the absence of positive laws.

natural rights certain inalienable rights to which all people are entitled; include the right to life, liberty, and property, freedom of speech and religion, and equality before the law.

natural selection Darwin's idea that organisms that are most adaptable to their environment survive and pass on the variations that enabled them to survive, while other, less adaptable organisms become extinct; "survival of the fittest."

Nazi New Order the Nazis' plan for their conquered territories; included the extermination of Jews and others considered inferior, ruthless exploitation of resources, German colonization in the east, and the use of Poles, Russians, and Ukrainians as slave labor.

neocolonialism the use of economic rather than political or military means to maintain Western domination of developing nations.

Neo-Confucianism the dominant ideology of China during the second millennium C.E. It combined the metaphysical speculations of Buddhism and Daoism with the pragmatic Confucian approach to society, maintaining that the world is real, not illusory, and that fulfillment comes from participation, not withdrawal. It encouraged an intellectual environment that valued continuity over change and tradition over innovation.

Neolithic Revolution the shift from hunting animals and gathering plants for sustenance to producing food by systematic agriculture that occurred gradually between 10,000 and 4000 B.C.E. (the Neolithic or "New Stone" Age).

New Culture Movement a protest launched at Peking University after the failure of the 1911 revolution, aimed at abolishing the remnants of the old system and introducing Western values and institutions into China.

New Deal the reform program implemented by President Franklin Roosevelt in the 1930s, which included large public works projects and the introduction of Social Security.

New Democracy the initial program of the Chinese Communist government, from 1949 to 1955, focusing on honest government, land reform, social justice, and peace rather than on the utopian goal of a classless society.

New Economic Policy a modified version of the old capitalist system introduced in the Soviet Union by Lenin in 1921 to revive the economy after the ravages of the civil war and war communism.

new imperialism the revival of imperialism after 1880 in which European nations established colonies throughout much of Asia and Africa.

new monarchies the governments of France, England, and Spain at the end of the fifteenth century, where the rulers were successful in reestablishing or extending centralized royal authority, suppressing the nobility, controlling the church, and insisting upon the loyalty of all peoples living in their territories.

Nirvana in Buddhist thought, enlightenment, the ultimate transcendence from the illusion of the material world; release from the wheel of life.

Nok culture in northern Nigeria, one of the most active early ironworking societies in Africa, artifacts from which date back as far as 500 B.C.E.

Nonaligned Movement an organization of neutralist nations established in the 1950s to provide a counterpoise between the socialist bloc, headed by the Soviet Union, and the capitalist nations led by the United States. Chief sponsors of the movement were Jawaharlal Nehru of India, Gamal Abdul Nasser of Egypt, and Sukarno of Indonesia.

noncentralized societies societies characterized by autonomous villages organized by clans and ruled by a local chieftain or clan head; typical of the southern half of the African continent before the eleventh century C.E.

nuclear family a family group consisting only of father, mother, and children.

nun a woman who withdraws from the world and joins a religious community; the female equivalent of a monk.

old regime/old order the political and social system of France in the eighteenth century before the Revolution.

oligarchy rule by a few.

Open Door notes a series of letters sent in 1899 by U.S. Secretary of State John Hay to Great Britain, France, Germany, Italy, Japan, and Russia, calling for equal economic access to the China market for all states and for the maintenance of the territorial and administrative integrity of the Chinese Empire.

orders/estates the traditional tripartite division of European society based on heredity and quality rather than wealth or economic standing; first established in the Middle Ages and continuing into the eighteenth century; traditionally consisted of those who pray (the clergy), those who fight (the nobility), and those who work (all the rest).

organic evolution Darwin's principle that all plants and animals have evolved over a long period of time from earlier and simpler forms of life.

Organization of African Unity founded in Addis Ababa in 1963, it was intended to represent the interests of all the newly independent countries of Africa and provided a forum for the discussion of common problems; replaced by the African Union in 2001.

Oriental despotism a theory identified with the Sinologist Karl Wittfogel that traditional societies organized on the basis of large-scale irrigation networks—many of them in eastern Asia—often possessed tendencies to create autocratic political systems.

Paleolithic Age the period of human history when humans used simple stone tools (c. 2,500,000–10,000 B.C.E.).

pan-Africanism the concept of African continental unity and solidarity in which the common interests of African countries transcend regional boundaries.

pan-Arabism a movement promoted by Egyptian president Gamal Abdul Nasser and other Middle Eastern leaders to unify all Arab peoples in a single supra-national organization. After Nasser's death in 1971, the movement languished.

pantheism a doctrine that equates God with the universe and all that is in it.

pariahs members of the lowest level of traditional Indian society, technically outside the class system itself; also known as untouchables.

pasha an administrative official of the Ottoman Empire, responsible for collecting taxes and maintaining order in the provinces; later, some became hereditary rulers.

paterfamilias the dominant male in a Roman family whose powers over his wife and children were theoretically unlimited, though they were sometimes circumvented in practice.

patriarchal/patriarchy a society in which the father is supreme in the clan or family; more generally, a society dominated by men.

patricians great landowners who became the ruling class in the Roman Republic.

patrilinear passing through the male line, from father to son; often combined with patriarchy.

Pax Romana "Roman peace." A term used to refer to the stability and prosperity that Roman rule brought to the Mediterranean world and much of western Europe during the first and second centuries C.E.

peaceful coexistence the policy adopted by the Soviet Union under Khrushchev in 1955, and continued by his successors, that called for economic and ideological rivalry with the West rather than nuclear war.

perestroika "restructuring." A term applied to Mikhail Gorbachev's economic, political, and social reforms in the Soviet Union.

permissive society a term applied to Western society after World War II to reflect the new sexual freedom and the emergence of a drug culture.

Petrine supremacy the doctrine that the bishop of Rome—the pope—as the successor of Saint Peter (traditionally considered the first bishop of Rome) should hold a preeminent position in the church.

phalanx a rectangular formation of tightly massed infantry soldiers.

pharaoh the most common title used for ancient Egyptian kings. Pharaohs possessed absolute power and were seen as divine.

philosophes intellectuals of the eighteenth-century Enlightenment who believed in applying a spirit of rational criticism to all things, including religion and politics, and who focused on improving and enjoying this world, rather than on the afterlife.

plebeians the class of Roman citizens who included nonpatrician landowners, craftspeople, merchants, and small farmers in the Roman Republic. Their struggle for equal rights with the patricians dominated much of the Republic's history.

pluralism the practice in which one person holds several church offices simultaneously; a problem of the late medieval church.

pogroms organized massacres of Jews.

polis an ancient Greek city-state encompassing both an urban area and its surrounding countryside; a small but autonomous political unit where all major political and social activities were carried out in a central location.

polygyny the practice of having more than one wife at a time.

polytheistic/polytheism having many gods; belief in or the worship of more than one god.

popular culture as opposed to high culture, the unofficial, written and unwritten culture of the masses, much of which was passed down orally; centers on public and group activities such as festivals. In the twentieth and twenty-first centuries, the entertainment, recreation, and pleasures that people purchase as part of mass consumer society.

portolani charts of landmasses and coastlines made by navigators and mathematicians in the thirteenth and fourteenth centuries.

Post-Impressionism an artistic movement that began in France in the 1880s. Post-Impressionists sought to use color and line to express inner feelings and produce a personal statement of reality.

Postmodernism a term used to cover a variety of artistic and intellectual styles and ways of thinking prominent since the 1970s.

poststructuralism (deconstruction) a theory formulated by Jacques Derrida in the 1960s, holding that there is no fixed, universal truth because culture is created and can therefore be analyzed in various ways.

praetorian guard the military unit that served as the personal bodyguard of the Roman emperors.

praetors the two senior Roman judges, who had executive authority when the consuls were away from the city and could also lead armies.

Prakrit an ancient Indian language, a simplified form of Sanskrit.

predestination the belief, associated with Calvinism, that God, as a consequence of his foreknowledge of all events, has predetermined those who will be saved (the elect) and those who will be damned.

price revolution the dramatic rise in prices (inflation) that occurred throughout Europe in the sixteenth and early seventeenth centuries.

primogeniture an inheritance practice in which the eldest son receives all or the largest share of the parents' estate.

principate the form of government established by Augustus for the Roman Empire; continued the constitutional forms of the Republic and consisted of the *princeps* ("first citizen") and the senate, although the *princeps* was clearly the dominant partner.

proletariat the industrial working class; in Marxism, the class that will ultimately overthrow the bourgeoisie.

Protestant Reformation the western European religious reform movement in the sixteenth century that divided Christianity into Catholic and Protestant groups.

psychoanalysis a method developed by Sigmund Freud to resolve a patient's psychic conflict.

pueblo a three-story adobe communal house with a timbered roof. Pueblos were constructed by the Ancient Pueblo people in what is now the southwestern United States starting around the ninth century C.E.

Pueblo Bonito a large settlement built by the Ancient Pueblo people in what is now New Mexico in the ninth century C.E. It contained several hundred compounds housing several thousand residents.

puja in India, a popular tradition focused on personal worship that began to replace the Brahmanical emphasis on court sacrifice and ascetism during the early centuries of the first millennium C.E.; an aspect of the transition from Brahmanism to Hinduism.

purdah the Indian term for the practice among Muslims and some Hindus of isolating women and preventing them from associating with men outside the home.

Pure Land a Buddhist sect, originally Chinese but later popular in Japan, which taught that devotion alone could lead to enlightenment and release.

Puritans English Protestants inspired by Calvinist theology who wished to remove all traces of Catholicism from the Church of England.

quipu an Inka record-keeping system that used knotted strings rather than writing.

raj the British colonial regime in India.

raja originally, a chieftain in the Aryan society of early India, a representative of the gods; later used more generally to denote a ruler.

Ramadan the holy month of Islam, during which believers fast from dawn to sunset. Since the Islamic calendar is lunar, Ramadan migrates through the seasons.

rationalism a system of thought based on the belief that human reason and experience are the chief sources of knowledge.

Realism in the nineteenth century, a school of painting that emphasized the everyday life of ordinary people, depicted with photographic realism.

Realpolitik "politics of reality." Politics based on practical concerns rather than theory or ethics.

reincarnation the idea that the individual soul is reborn in a different form after death. In Hindu and Buddhist thought, release from this cycle is the objective of all living souls.

relativity theory Einstein's theory that holds, among other things, that (1) space and time are not absolute but are relative to the observer and interwoven into a four-dimensional space-time continuum and (2) matter is a form of energy ($E = mc^2$).

relics the bones of Christian saints or objects intimately associated with saints that were considered worthy of veneration.

Renaissance the "rebirth" of Classical culture that occurred in Italy between c. 1350 and c. 1550; also, the earlier revivals of Classical culture that occurred under Charlemagne and in the twelfth century.

Renaissance humanism an intellectual movement in Renaissance Italy based on the study of the Greek and Roman classics.

rentier a person who lives on income from property and is not personally involved in its operation.

reparations payments made by a defeated nation after a war to compensate another nation for damage sustained as a result of the war; required from Germany after World War I.

revisionism a socialist doctrine that rejected Marx's emphasis on class struggle and revolution and argued instead that workers should work through political parties to bring about gradual change.

revolution a fundamental change in the political and social organization of a state.

revolutionary socialism the socialist doctrine espoused by Georges Sorel who held that violent action was the only way to achieve the goals of socialism.

rhetoric the art of persuasive speaking; in the Middle Ages, one of the seven liberal arts.

Rococo a style, especially of decoration and architecture, that developed from the Baroque and spread throughout Europe by the 1730s. While still elaborate, it emphasized curves, lightness, and charm in the pursuit of pleasure, happiness, and love.

Romanticism a nineteenth-century intellectual and artistic movement that rejected the Enlightenment's emphasis on reason. Instead, Romantics stressed the importance of intuition, feeling, emotion, and imagination as sources of knowing.

ronin Japanese warriors made unemployed by developments in the early modern era, since samurai were forbidden by tradition to engage in commerce.

rural responsibility system post-Maoist land reform in China, under which collectives leased land to peasant families, who could consume or sell their surplus production and keep the profits.

sacraments rites considered imperative for a Christian's salvation. By the thirteenth century consisted of the Eucharist or Lord's Supper, baptism, marriage, penance, extreme unction, holy orders, and confirmation of children; Protestant reformers of the sixteenth century generally recognized only two—baptism and communion (the Lord's Supper).

sakoku during the Tokugawa shogunate in Japan, the policy of closing the country to trade with Europe and encouraging domestic production of goods that had previously been imported.

samurai literally "retainers"; similar to European knights. Usually in service to a particular shogun, these Japanese warriors lived by a strict code of ethics and duty.

sans-culottes the common people who did not wear the fine clothes of the upper classes (*sans-culottes* means "without breeches") and played an important role in the radical phase of the French Revolution.

Sanskrit an early Indo-European language, in which the Vedas were composed, beginning in the second millenium B.C.E. It survived as the language of literature and the bureaucracy in India for centuries after its decline as a spoken tongue.

sati the Hindu ritual requiring a wife to throw herself upon her deceased husband's funeral pyre.

satori enlightenment, in the Japanese, especially Zen, Buddhist tradition.

satrap/satrapy a governor with both civil and military duties in the ancient Persian Empire, which was divided into satrapies, or provinces, each administered by a satrap.

satyagraha the Hindi term for the practice of nonviolent resistance, as advocated by Mohandas Gandhi; literally, "hold fast to the truth."

scholar-gentry in Song dynasty China, candidates who passed the civil service examinations and whose families were nonaristocratic landowners; eventually, a majority of the bureaucracy.

scholasticism the philosophical and theological system of the medieval schools, which emphasized rigorous analysis of contradictory authorities; often used to try to reconcile faith and reason.

School of Mind a philosophy espoused by Wang Yangming during the mid-Ming era of China, which argued that mind and the universe were a single unit and knowledge was therefore obtained through internal self-searching rather than through investigation of the outside world; for a while, a significant but unofficial rival to Neo-Confucianism.

scientific method a method of seeking knowledge through inductive principles; uses experiments and observations to develop generalizations.

Scientific Revolution the transition from the medieval worldview to a largely secular, rational, and materialistic perspective; began in the seventeenth century and was popularized in the eighteenth.

secularization the process of becoming more concerned with material, worldly, temporal things and less with spiritual and religious things.

self-determination the doctrine that the people of a given territory or a particular nationality should have the right to determine their own government and political future.

self-strengthening a late-nineteenth-century Chinese policy, by which Western technology would be adopted while Confucian principles and institutions were maintained intact.

senate/senators the leading council of the Roman Republic; composed of about three hundred men (senators) who served for life and dominated much of the political life of the Republic.

separation of powers a doctrine enunciated by Montesquieu in the eighteenth century that separate executive, legislative, and judicial powers serve to limit and control each other.

sepoys native troops hired by the East India Company to protect British interests in south Asia; formed the basis of the British Indian Army.

serf a peasant who is bound to the land and obliged to provide labor services and pay various rents and fees to the lord; considered unfree but not a slave because serfs could not be bought and sold.

Shari'a a law code, originally drawn up by Muslim scholars shortly after the death of Muhammad, that provides believers with a set of prescriptions to regulate their daily lives.

sheikh originally, the ruler of a Bedouin tribe; later, also used as a more general honorific.

Shi'ite the second largest tradition of Islam, which split from the majority Sunni soon after the death of Muhammad, in a disagreement over the succession; especially significant in Iran and Iraq.

Shinto a kind of state religion in Japan, derived from beliefs in nature spirits and until recently linked with belief in the divinity of the emperor and the sacredness of the Japanese nation.

shogun a powerful Japanese leader, originally military, who ruled under the titular authority of the emperor.

shogunate system the system of government in Japan in which the emperor exercised only titular authority while the shogun (regional military dictators) exercised actual political power.

Sikhism a religion, founded in the early sixteenth century in the Punjab, which began as an attempt to reconcile the Hindu and Muslim traditions and developed into a significant alternative to both.

sipahis in the Ottoman Empire, local cavalry elites, who held fiefdoms and collected taxes.

social Darwinism the application of Darwin's principle of organic evolution to the social order; led to the belief that progress comes from the struggle for survival as the fittest advance and the weak decline.

socialism an ideology that calls for collective or government ownership of the means of production and the distribution of goods.

social security/social insurance government programs that provide social welfare measures such as old-age pensions and sickness, accident, and disability insurance.

Socratic method a form of teaching that uses a question-and-answer format to enable students to reach conclusions by using their own reasoning.

soviets councils of workers' and soldiers' deputies formed throughout Russia in 1917; played an important role in the Bolshevik Revolution.

sphere of influence a territory or region over which an outside nation exercises political or economic influence.

Star Wars nickname of the Strategic Defense Initiative, proposed by President Reagan, which was intended to provide a shield that would destroy any incoming missiles; named after a popular science-fiction movie.

State Confucianism the integration of Confucian doctrine with Legalist practice under the Han dynasty in China, which became the basis of Chinese political thought until the modern era.

stateless societies the pre-Columbian communities in much of the Americas that developed substantial cultures without formal states.

Stoicism a philosophy founded by Zeno in the fourth century B.C.E. that taught that happiness could be obtained by accepting one's lot and living in harmony with the will of God, thereby achieving inner peace.

stupa originally a stone tower holding relics of the Buddha; more generally a place for devotion, often architecturally impressive and surmounted with a spire.

Sublime Porte the office of the grand vizier in the Ottoman Empire.

sudras the classes that represented the great bulk of the Indian population from ancient times, mostly peasants, artisans or manual laborers; ranked below *brahmins*, *kshatriyas*, and *vaisyas*, but above the pariahs.

suffrage the right to vote.

suffragists those who advocate the extension of the right to vote (suffrage), especially to women.

Sufism a mystical school of Islam, noted for its music, dance, and poetry, which became prominent in about the thirteenth century.

sultan "holder of power," a title commonly used by Muslim rulers in the Ottoman Empire, Egypt, and elsewhere; still in use in parts of Asia, sometimes for regional authorities.

Sunni the largest tradition of Islam, from which the Shi'ites split soon after the death of Muhammad, in a disagreement over the succession.

Supreme Ultimate according to Neo-Confucianists, a transcendent world, distinct from the material world in which humans live, but to which humans may aspire; a set of abstract principles, roughly equivalent to the Dao.

Surrealism an artistic movement that arose between World War I and World War II. Surrealists portrayed recognizable objects in unrecognizable relationships in order to reveal the world of the unconscious.

Swahili a mixed African-Arabian culture that developed by the twelfth century along the east coast of Africa; also, the national language of Kenya and Tanzania.

syncretism the combining of different forms of belief or practice, as, for example, when two gods are regarded as different forms of the same underlying divine force and are fused together.

Taika reforms the seventh-century "great change" reforms that established the centralized Japanese state.

taille a French tax on land or property, developed by King Louis XI in the fifteenth century as the financial basis of the monarchy. It was largely paid by the peasantry; the nobility and the clergy were exempt.

Taisho democracy the era of the 1920s in Japan when universal (male) suffrage was instituted, political parties expanded, and other democratic institutions appeared to flourish. The process of democratization proved fragile, however, and failed to continue into the 1930s.

Tantrism a mystical Buddhist sect, which emphasized the importance of magical symbols and ritual in seeking a path to enlightenment.

tariffs duties (taxes) imposed on imported goods; usually imposed both to raise revenue and to discourage imports and protect domestic industries.

theocracy a government based on a divine authority.

Theravada a school of Buddhism that stresses personal behavior and the quest for understanding as a means of release from the wheel of life, rather than the intercession of bodhisattvas; predominant in Sri Lanka and Southeast Asia.

three-field system in medieval agriculture, the practice of dividing the arable land into three fields so that one could lie fallow while the others were planted in winter grains and spring crops.

three obediences the traditional duties of Japanese women, in permanent subservience: child to father, wife to husband, and widow to son.

three people's principles the three principles on which the program of Sun Yat-sen's Revolutionary Alliance (Tongmenghui) was based: nationalism (meaning primarily the elimination of Manchu rule over China), democracy, and people's livelihood.

tithe a tenth of one's harvest or income; paid by medieval peasants to the village church.

Tongmenghui the political organization—"Revolutionary Alliance"—formed by Sun Yat-sen in 1905, which united various revolutionary factions and ultimately toppled the Manchu dynasty.

totalitarian state a state characterized by government control over all aspects of economic, social, political, cultural, and intellectual life; the subordination of the individual to the state; and insistence that the masses be actively involved in the regime's goals.

total war warfare in which all of a nation's resources, including civilians at home as well as soldiers in the field, are mobilized for the war effort.

trade union an association of workers in the same trade, formed to help members secure better wages, benefits, and working conditions.

trench warfare warfare in which the opposing forces attack and counterattack from a relatively permanent system of trenches protected by barbed wire; characteristic of World War I.

tribunes of the plebs beginning in 494 B.C.E., Roman officials who were given the power to protect plebeians against arrest by patrician magistrates.

tribute system an important element of Chinese foreign policy, by which neighboring states paid for the privilege of access to Chinese markets, received legitimation and agreed not to harbor enemies of the Chinese Empire.

Truman Doctrine the doctrine, enunciated by Harry Truman in 1947, that the United States would provide economic aid to countries that were threatened by Communist expansion.

twice-born the males of the higher castes in traditional Indian society, who underwent an initiation ceremony at puberty.

tyrant/tyranny in an ancient Greek *polis* (or an Italian city-state during the Renaissance), a ruler who came to power in an unconstitutional way and ruled without being subject to the law.

uhuru "freedom" in Swahili; a key slogan in the African independence movements, especially in Kenya.

uji a clan in early Japanese tribal society.

ulama a convocation of leading Muslim scholars, the earliest of which shortly after the death of Muhammad drew up a law code, called the *Shari'a*, based largely on the Qur'an and the sayings of the Prophet, to provide believers with a set of prescriptions to regulate their daily lives.

umma the Muslim community, as a whole.

uninterrupted revolution the goal of the Great Proletarian Cultural Revolution launched by Mao Zedong in 1966.

vaisya the third-ranked class in traditional Indian society, usually merchants.

varna Indian classes, or castes. *See also* caste system.

vassal a person granted a fief, or landed estate, in exchange for providing military services to the lord and fulfilling certain other obligations such as appearing at the lord's court when summoned and making a payment on the knighting of the lord's eldest son.

veneration of ancestors the extension of filial piety to include care for the deceased, for instance, by burning replicas of useful objects to accompany them on their journey to the next world.

vernacular the everyday language of a region, as distinguished from a language used for special purposes. For example, in medieval Paris, French was the vernacular, but Latin was used for academic writing and for classes at the University of Paris.

viceroy the administrative head of the provinces of New Spain and Peru in the Americas.

vizier the prime minister in the Abbasid caliphate and elsewhere, a chief executive.

war communism Lenin's policy of nationalizing industrial and other facilities and requisitioning the peasants' produce during the civil war in Russia.

War Guilt Clause the clause in the Treaty of Versailles that declared that Germany (and Austria) were responsible for starting World War I and ordered Germany to pay reparations for the damage the Allies had suffered as a result of the war.

Warsaw Pact a military alliance, formed in 1955, in which Albania, Bulgaria, Czechoslovakia, East Germany, Hungary, Poland, Romania, and the Soviet Union agreed to provide mutual assistance. After it was dissolved in 1991, most former members eventually joined NATO.

welfare state a social/political system in which the government assumes the primary responsibility for the social welfare of its citizens by providing such things as social security, unemployment benefits, and health care.

well-field system the theoretical pattern of land ownership in early China, named for the appearance of the Chinese character for "well," in which farmland was divided into nine segments and a peasant family would cultivate one for their own use and cooperate with seven others to cultivate the ninth for the landlord.

wergeld "money for a man." In early Germanic law, a person's value in monetary terms, which was paid by a wrongdoer to the family of the person who had been injured or killed.

White Lotus a Chinese Buddhist sect, founded in 1133 C.E., that sought political reform; in 1796–1804, a Chinese peasant revolt.

women's liberation movement the struggle for equal rights for women, which has deep roots in history but achieved new prominence under this name in the 1960s, building on the work of, among others, Simone de Beauvoir and Betty Friedan.

world-machine Newton's conception of the universe as one huge, regulated, and uniform machine that operated according to natural laws in absolute time, space, and motion.

yangban the aristocratic class in Korea. During the Yi dynasty, entry into the bureaucracy was limited to members of this class.

Yangshao a Neolithic society from near the Yellow River in China, sometimes identified by its painted pottery.

yoga "union"; the practice of body training that evolved from the early ascetism and remains an important element of Hindu religious practice.

Young Turks a successful Turkish reformist group in the late nineteenth and early twentieth centuries.

zaibatsu powerful business cartels formed in Japan during the Meiji era and outlawed following World War II.

zamindars Indian tax collectors, who were assigned land, from which they kept part of the revenue. The British revived the system in a misguided attempt to create a landed gentry.

Zen Buddhism (in Chinese, Chan or Ch'an) a school of Buddhism particularly important in Japan, some of whose adherents stress that enlightenment (*satori*) can be achieved suddenly, though others emphasize lengthy meditation.

ziggurat a massive stepped tower upon which a temple dedicated to the chief god or goddess of a Sumerian city was built.

Zionism an international movement that called for the establishment of a Jewish state or a refuge for Jews in Palestine.

Zoroastrianism a religion founded by the Persian Zoroaster in the seventh century B.C.E.; characterized by worship of a supreme god Ahuramazda who represents the good against the evil spirit, identified as Ahriman.

DOCUMENTS

Continued from p. xvii

CHAPTER 23

CHAPTER 24

CHAPTER 25

CHAPTER 26

CHAPTER 27

CHAPTER 28

CHAPTER 29

CHAPTER 30

CHAPTER NOTES

CHAPTER 1

1. Quoted in A. Kuhrt, *The Ancient Near East, c. 3000–330 B.C.* (London, 1995), vol. 1, p. 68.
2. Quoted in M. Van de Mieroop, *A History of the Ancient Near East, ca. 3000–323 B.C.* (Oxford, 2004), p. 106.
3. Quoted in T. Jacobsen, "Mesopotamia," in H. Frankfort et al., *Before Philosophy* (Baltimore, 1949), p. 139.
4. Quoted in M. Covensky, *The Ancient Near Eastern Tradition* (New York, 1966), p. 51.
5. Ibid., p. 413.
6. Psalms 137:1, 4–6.
7. Psalms 145:8–9.
8. Exodus 20:13–15.
9. Isaiah 2:4.
10. Quoted in H. W. F. Saggs, *The Might That Was Assyria* (London, 1984), pp. 261–262.

CHAPTER 2

1. Quoted in R. Lannoy, *The Speaking Tree: A Study of Indian Culture and Society* (London, 1971), p. 318.
2. The quotation is from ibid., p. 319. Note also that the *Law of Manu* says that "punishment alone governs all created beings. . . . The whole world is kept in order by punishment, for a guiltless man is hard to find."
3. Strabo's *Geography*, bk. 15, quoted in M. Edwardes, *A History of India: From the Earliest Times to the Present Day* (London, 1961), p. 55.
4. Ibid., p. 54.
5. Ibid., p. 57.
6. From the *Law of Manu*, quoted in A. L. Basham, *The Wonder That Was India* (London, 1961), pp. 180–181.
7. According to historian of religion Karen Armstrong, a gradual shift of emphasis from sacrificial rites to ethics was characteristic of many early belief systems during the first millennium B.C.E. For a discussion, see her *The Great Transformation: The Beginning of Our Religious Traditions* (New York, 2006).
8. Quoted in A. K. Coomaraswamy, *Buddha and the Gospel of Buddhism* (New York, 1964), p. 34.

CHAPTER 3

1. *Book of Changes*, quoted in Chang Chi-yun, *Chinese History of Fifty Centuries*, vol. 1, *Ancient Times* (Taipei, 1962), pp. 15, 31, and 65.
2. Ibid., p. 381.
3. Quoted in E. N. Anderson, *The Food of China* (New Haven, Conn., 1988), p. 21.
4. According to Chinese tradition, the *Rites of Zhou* was written by the duke of Zhou himself near the time of the founding of the Zhou dynasty. Modern historians, however, believe that it was written much later, perhaps as late as the fourth century B.C.E.
5. From the *Book of Songs*, quoted in S. de Grazia, ed., *Masters of Chinese Political Thought: From the Beginnings to the Han Dynasty* (New York, 1973), pp. 40–41.
6. *Confucian Analects* (Lun Yu), ed. J. Legge (Taipei, 1963), 11:11 and 6:20. Author's translation.
7. Ibid., 15:23.
8. Ibid., 17:2.
9. *Book of Mencius* (Meng Zi), 4A:9, quoted in W. T. de Bary et al., eds., *Sources of Chinese Tradition* (New York, 1960), p. 107.
10. Quoted in de Bary, *Sources of Chinese Tradition*, p. 53.
11. M. Lewis, *The Early Chinese Empires: Qin and Han* (Cambridge, Mass., 2007), p. 31, citing Shiji 68, pp. 2230, 2232.
12. B. Watson, *Records of the Grand Historian of China* (New York, 1961), vol. 2, pp. 155, 160.
13. Ibid., pp. 32, 53.
14. C. Waltham, *Shu Ching: Book of History* (Chicago, 1971), p. 154.
15. Lewis, *Early Chinese Empires*, p. 85.
16. Quoted in H. A. Giles, *A History of Chinese Literature* (New York, 1923), p. 19.
17. A. Waley, ed., *Chinese Poems* (London, 1983), p. xx.
18. Chang Chi-yun, *Chinese History of Fifty Centuries*, vol. 1, p. 183.

CHAPTER 4

1. Xenophon, *Symposium*, trans. O. J. Todd (Harmondsworth, England, 1946), 3:5.
2. Quoted in T. R. Martin, *Ancient Greece* (New Haven, Conn., 1996), p. 62.
3. The words from Plutarch are quoted in E. Fantham et al., *Women in the Classsical World* (New York, 1994), p. 64.
4. Sophocles, *Oedipus the King*, trans. D. Grene (Chicago, 1959), pp. 68–69.
5. Sophocles, *Antigone*, trans. D. Taylor (London, 1986), p. 146.
6. Plato, *The Republic*, trans. F. M. Cornford (New York, 1945), pp. 178–179.
7. Quotations from Aristotle are in S. Blundell, *Women in Ancient Greece* (London, 1995), pp. 106, 186.

CHAPTER 5

1. Tacitus, *The Annals of Imperial Rome*, trans. M. Grant (Harmondsworth, England, 1964), p. 31.
2. Virgil, *The Aeneid*, trans. C. Day Lewis (Garden City, N.Y., 1952), p. 154.
3. Juvenal, *The Sixteen Satires*, trans. P. Green (New York, 1967), sat. 10, p. 207.
4. Quoted in C. Starr, *Past and Future in Ancient History* (Lanham, Md., 1987), pp. 38–39.
5. Matthew 7:12.
6. Mark 12:30–31.

CHAPTER 6

1. Quoted in S. Morley and G. W. Brainerd, *The Ancient Maya* (Stanford, Calif., 1983), p. 513.
2. B. Díaz, *The Conquest of New Spain* (Harmondsworth, England, 1975), p. 210.
3. Quoted in M. D. Coe, D. Snow, and E. P. Benson, *Atlas of Ancient America* (New York, 1988), p. 149.
4. G. de la Vega (El Inca), *Royal Commentaries of the Incas and General History of Peru*, pt. 1, trans. H. V. Livermore (Austin, Tex., 1966), p. 180.
5. J. Diamond, *Guns, Germs, and Steel: The Fates of Human Societies* (New York, 1997), pp. 187–188.

CHAPTER 7

1. M. M. Pickthall, trans., *The Meaning of the Glorious Koran* (New York, 1953), p. 89.
2. Quoted in T. W. Lippman, *Understanding Islam: An Introduction to the Moslem World* (New York, 1982), p. 118.
3. F. Hirth and W. W. Rockhill, trans., *Chau Ju-kua: His Work on the Chinese and Arab Trade in the Twelfth and Thirteenth Centuries, Entitled Chu-fan-chi* (New York, 1966), p. 115.
4. al-Mas'udi, *The Meadows of Gold: The Abbasids*, ed. P. Lunde and C. Stone (London, 1989), p. 151.
5. Quoted in G. Wiet, *Baghdad: Metropolis of the Abbasid Caliphate*, trans. S. Feiler (Norman, Okla., 1971), pp. 118–119.
6. L. Africanus, *The History and Description of Africa and of the Notable Things Therein Contained* (New York, n.d.), pp. 820–821.
7. E. Yarshater, ed., *Persian Literature* (Albany, N.Y., 1988), pp. 125–126.
8. Ibid., pp. 154–159.
9. E. Rehatsek, trans., *The Gulistan or Rose Garden of Sa'di* (New York, 1964), pp. 65, 67, 71.

CHAPTER 8

1. S. Hamdun and N. King, eds., *Ibn Battuta in Africa* (London, 1975), p. 19.
2. D. Barbosa, *The Book of Duarte Barbosa* (Nedeln, Liechtenstein, 1967), p. 28.
3. Herodotus, *The Histories*, trans. A. de Sélincourt (Baltimore, 1964), p. 307.
4. Quoted in M. Shinnie, *Ancient African Kingdoms* (London, 1965), p. 60.
5. C. R. Boxer, ed., *The Tragic History of the Sea, 1589–1622* (Cambridge, 1959), pp. 121–122.
6. Quoted in D. Nurse and T. Spear, *The Swahili: Reconstructing the History and Language of an African Society 800–1500* (Philadelphia, 1985), p. 84.
7. Hamdun and King, *Ibn Battuta in Africa*, p. 47.
8. Ibid., p. 28.
9. Ibid., pp. 28–30.

CHAPTER 9

1. Hiuen Tsiang, *Si-Yu-Ki: Buddhist Records of the Western World*, trans. S. Beal (London, 1982), pp. 89–90.
2. "Fo-Kwo-Ki" (Travels of Fa Xian), ch. 20, p. 43, in ibid.
3. E. C. Sachau, *Alberoni's India*, vol. 1 (London, 1914), p. 22.
4. Quoted in S. M. Ikram, *Muslim Civilization in India* (New York, 1964), p. 68.
5. Hiuen Tsiang, *Si-Yu-Ki*, pp. 73–74.
6. D. Barbosa, *The Book of Duarte Barbosa* (Nedeln, Liechtenstein, 1967), pp. 147–148.
7. From Hucker, Charles O., *China's Imperial Past*. Copyright © 1965 by the Board of Trustees of the Leland Stanford Junior University. With the permission of Stanford University Press, www.sup.org.
8. Quoted in S. Tharu and K. Lalita, *Women Writing in India*, vol. 1 (New York, 1991), p. 77.
9. Quoted in A. L. Basham, *The Wonder That Was India* (London, 1954), p. 426.
10. Quoted in S. Hughes and B. Hughes, *Women in World History*, vol. 1 (Armonk, N.Y., 1995), p. 217.

CHAPTER 10

1. *The Travels of Marco Polo* (New York, n.d.), pp. 128, 179.
2. Quoted in A. F. Wright, *Buddhism in Chinese History* (Stanford, Calif., 1959), p. 30.
3. Chu-yu, *P'ing-chow Table Talks*, quoted in R. Temple, *The Genius of China: 3,000 Years of Science, Discovery, and Invention* (New York, 1986), p. 150.
4. Quoted in E. H. Schafer, *The Golden Peaches of Samarkand: A Study of T'ang Exotics* (Berkeley, Calif., 1963), p. 43.
5. Quoted in J. K. Fairbank, E. O. Reischauer, and A. M. Craig, *East Asia: Tradition and Transformation* (Boston, 1973), p. 164.
6. A. M. Khazanov, *Nomads and the Outside World* (Cambridge, 1983), p. 241.
7. From C. Hucker, *China's Imperial Past* (Stanford, Calif., 1965).

CHAPTER 11

1. Cited in C. Holcombe, *The Genesis of East Asia, 221 B.C.–A.D. 907* (Honolulu, 2001), p. 41.
2. Quoted in D. J. Lu, *Sources of Japanese History*, vol. 1 (New York, 1974), p. 7.
3. From "The History of Wei," quoted in ibid., p. 10.
4. From "The Law of Households," quoted in ibid., p. 32.
5. From "On the Salvation of Women," quoted in ibid., p. 127.
6. Quoted in B. Ruch, "The Other Side of Culture in Medieval Japan," in K. Yamamura, ed., *The Cambridge History of Japan*, vol. 3, *Medieval Japan* (Cambridge, 1990), p. 506.
7. H. P. Varley, "A Sample of Linked Verse," in K. Yamamura, ed., *The Cambridge History of Japan*, vol. 3, *Medieval Japan* (Cambridge, 1990), p. 480.
8. K. W. Taylor, *The Birth of Vietnam* (Berkeley, Calif., 1983), p. 76.
9. Quoted in ibid., pp. 336–337.
10. Confucius, *Analects*, 17:2.

CHAPTER 12

1. N. F. Cantor, ed., *The Medieval World, 300–1300* (New York, 1963), p. 104.
2. A. Barbero, *Charlemagne: Father of a Continent*, trans. A. Cameron (Berkeley, Calif., 2004), p. 4.

3. Quoted in M. Perry, J. Peden, and T. Von Laue, *Sources of the Western Tradition*, vol. 1 (Boston, 1987), p. 218.
4. O. J. Thatcher and E. H. McNeal, eds., *A Source Book for Medieval History* (New York, 1905), p. 208.
5. Quoted in R. H. C. Davis, *A History of Medieval Europe from Constantine to Saint Louis*, 2nd ed. (New York, 1988), p. 252.
6. Quoted in H. E. Mayer, *The Crusades*, trans. J. Gillingham (New York, 1972), pp. 99–100.

CHAPTER 13

1. Quoted in P. Cesaretti, *Theodora: Empress of Byzantium*, trans. R. M. Frongia (New York, 2004), p. 197.
2. Quoted in J. Harris, *Constantinople: Capital of Byzantium* (New York, 2007), p. 40.
3. Procopius, *Buildings of Justinian* (London, 1897), pp. 9, 6–7.
4. Quoted in Harris, *Constantinople*, p. 118.
5. Quoted in C. S. Bartsocas, "Two Fourteenth-Century Descriptions of the 'Black Death,'" *Journal of the History of Medicine* (October 1966): 395.
6. Quoted in M. Dols, *The Black Death in the Middle East* (Princeton, N.J., 1977), p. 270.
7. G. Boccaccio, *The Decameron*, trans. F. Winwar (New York, 1955), p. xiii.
8. J. Froissart, *Chronicles*, ed. and trans. G. Brereton (Harmondsworth, England, 1968), p. 111.
9. Ibid., p. 89.
10. Quoted in J. Burckhardt, *The Civilization of the Renaissance in Italy*, trans. S. G. C. Middlemore (London, 1960), p. 81.

CHAPTER 14

1. From *A Journal of the First Voyage of Vasco da Gama* (London, 1898), cited in J. H. Parry, *The European Reconnaissance: Selected Documents* (New York, 1968), p. 82.
2. H. J. Benda and J. A. Larkin, eds., *The World of Southeast Asia: Selected Historical Readings* (New York, 1967), p. 13.
3. Parry, *European Reconnaissance*, quoting from A. Cortesão, *The Summa Oriental of Tomé Pires*, vol. 2 (London, 1944), pp. 283, 287.
4. Quoted in J. H. Parry, *The Age of Reconnaissance: Discovery, Exploration, and Settlement, 1450 to 1650* (New York, 1963), p. 33.
5. Quoted in R. B. Reed, "The Expansion of Europe," in R. DeMolen, ed., *The Meaning of the Renaissance and Reformation* (Boston, 1974), p. 308.
6. K. N. Chaudhuri, *Trade and Civilization in the Indian Ocean: An Economic History from the Rise of Islam to 1750* (Cambridge, 1985), p. 65.
7. Quoted in Parry, *Age of Reconnaissance*, pp. 176–177.
8. Quoted in M. Leon-Portilla, ed., *The Broken Spears: The Aztec Account of the Conquest of Mexico* (Boston, 1969), p. 51.
9. Quoted in B. Davidson, *Africa in History: Themes and Outlines* (London, 1968), p. 137.

CHAPTER 15

1. N. Machiavelli, *The Prince*, trans. D. Wootton (Indianapolis, Ind., 1995), p. 48.
2. Quoted in R. Bainton, *Here I Stand: A Life of Martin Luther* (New York, 1950), p. 144.
3. J. Calvin, *Institutes of the Christian Religion*, trans. J. Allen (Philadelphia, 1936), vol. 1, p. 228; vol. 2, p. 181.
4. Quoted in B. S. Anderson and J. P. Zinsser, *A History of Their Own: Women in Europe from Prehistory to the Present*, vol. 1 (New York, 1988), p. 259.
5. Quoted in J. O'Malley, *The First Jesuits* (Cambridge, Mass., 1993), p. 76.
6. Quoted in J. Klaits, *Servants of Satan: The Age of Witch Hunts* (Bloomington, Ind., 1985), p. 68.

CHAPTER 16

1. V. A. Smith, *The Oxford History of India* (Oxford, 1967), p. 341.
2. Quoted in M. Edwardes, *A History of India: From the Earliest Times to the Present Day* (London, 1961), p. 188.
3. Quoted in ibid., p. 220.
4. Quoted in R. C. Craven, *Indian Art: A Concise History* (New York, 1976), p. 205.

CHAPTER 17

1. From J. D. Spence, *Emperor of China: Self-Portrait of K'ang Hsi* (New York, 1974), pp. 143–144.
2. R. Strassberg, *The World of K'ang Shang-jen: A Man of Letters in Early Ch'ing China* (New York, 1983), p. 275.
3. L. Struve, *The Southern Ming, 1644–1662* (New Haven, Conn., 1984), p. 61.
4. J. L. Cranmer-Byng, *An Embassy to China: Lord Macartney's Journal, 1793–1794* (London, 1912), p. 340.
5. Quoted in D. J. Boorstin, *The Discoverers: A History of Man's Search to Know His World and Himself* (New York, 1983), p. 63.
6. C. R. Boxer, ed., *South China in the Sixteenth Century* (London, 1953), p. 265.
7. C. Nakane and S. Oishi, eds., *Tokugawa Japan* (Tokyo, 1990), p. 14.
8. Quoted in J. Elisonas, "Christianity and the Daimyo," in J. W. Hall, ed., *The Cambridge History of Japan*, vol. 4 (Cambridge, 1991), p. 360.
9. E. Kaempfer, *The History of Japan: Together with a Description of the Kingdom of Siam, 1690–1692*, vol. 2 (Glasgow, 1906), pp. 173–174.

CHAPTER 18

1. J. Locke, *An Essay Concerning Human Understanding* (New York, 1964), pp. 89–90.
2. Quoted in P. Burke, *Popular Culture in Early Modern Europe*, rev. ed. (New York, 1994), p. 186.
3. Quoted in W. Doyle, *The Oxford History of the French Revolution* (Oxford, 1989), p. 184.
4. Quoted in L. Gershoy, *The Era of the French Revolution* (Princeton, N.J., 1957), p. 157.
5. Quoted in Doyle, *The Oxford History of the French Revolution*, p. 254.

CHAPTER 19

1. Quoted in E. Royston Pike, *Human Documents of the Industrial Revolution in Britain* (London, 1966), p. 343.
2. Ibid., p. 315.

3. K. Marx and F. Engels, *The Communist Manifesto* (Harmondsworth, England, 1967), p. 80. Originally published in 1848.
4. Ibid., pp. 91, 94.
5. Quoted in L. L. Snyder, ed., *Documents of German History* (New Brunswick, N.J., 1958), p. 202.
6. Quoted in S. Galai, *The Liberation Movement in Russia, 1900–1905* (Cambridge, 1973), p. 26.

CHAPTER 20

1. Quoted in J. C. Chasteen, *Americanos: Latin America's Struggle for Independence* (Oxford, 2008), p. 122.
2. Quoted in P. Bakewell, *A History of Latin America* (Oxford, 1997), p. 367.
3. Quoted in M. C. Eakin, *The History of Latin America: Collision of Cultures* (New York, 2007), p. 188.
4. Quoted in E. B. Burns, *Latin America: A Concise Interpretive History*, 4th ed. (Englewood Cliffs, N.J., 1986), p. 116.
5. Quoted in N. Bullock and J. Read, *The Movement for Housing Reform in Germany and France, 1840–1914* (Cambridge, 1985), p. 42.
6. W. Wordsworth, "The Tables Turned," in *Poems of Wordsworth*, ed. M. Arnold (London, 1963), p. 138.
7. Quoted in A. E. E. McKenzie, *The Major Achievements of Science*, vol. 1 (New York, 1960), p. 310.
8. Quoted in A. Higonnet, *Berthe Morisot's Images of Women* (Cambridge, Mass., 1992), p. 19.

CHAPTER 21

1. Quoted in J. G. Lockhart and C. M. Wodehouse, *Rhodes* (London, 1963), pp. 69–70.
2. K. Pearson, *National Life from the Standpoint of Science* (London, 1905), p. 184.
3. Quoted in H. Braunschwig, *French Colonialism, 1871–1914* (London, 1961), p. 80.
4. Quoted in G. Garros, *Forceries Humaines* (Paris, 1926), p. 21.
5. Cited in B. Schwartz's review of D. Cannadine's *Ornamentalism: How the British Saw Their Empire*, in *The Atlantic*, November 2001, p. 135.
6. Quoted in R. Bartlett, ed., *The Record of American Diplomacy: Documents and Readings in the History of American Foreign Relations* (New York, 1952), p. 385.
7. Quoted in L. Roubaud, *Vietnam: La Tragédie Indochinoise* (Paris, 1926), p. 80.
8. Quoted in T. Pakenham, *The Scramble for Africa* (New York, 1991), p. 13.
9. Quoted in ibid., p. 182, citing a letter to Queen Victoria dated August 7, 1879.
10. Quoted in P. C. W. Gutkind and I. Wallerstein, eds., *The Political Economy of Contemporary Africa* (Beverly Hills, Calif., 1976), p. 14.

CHAPTER 22

1. H. B. Morse, *The International Relations of the Chinese Empire*, vol. 2 (London, 1910–1918), p. 622.
2. Quoted in S. Teng and J. K. Fairbank, eds., *China's Response to the West: A Documentary Survey, 1839–1923* (New York, 1970), p. 140.
3. Ibid., p. 167.
4. J. K. Fairbank, A. M. Craig, and E. O. Reischauer, *East Asia: Tradition and Transformation* (Boston, 1973), p. 514.
5. Quoted in J. W. Dower, ed., *The Origins of the Modern Japanese State: Selected Writings of E. H. Norman* (New York, 1975), p. 13.

CHAPTER 23

1. A. Toynbee, *Surviving the Future* (New York, 1971), pp. 106–107.
2. Quoted in J. Remak, "1914—The Third Balkan War: Origins Reconsidered," *Journal of Modern History* 43 (1971): 364–365.
3. Quoted in J. M. Winter, *The Experience of World War I* (New York, 1989), p. 142.
4. Quoted in H. Strachan, *The First World War* (New York, 2004), pp. 94–95.
5. Quoted in ibid., p. 72.
6. Quoted in C. W. Reilly, ed., *Scars upon My Heart: Women's Poetry and Verse of the First World War* (London, 1981), p. 90.
7. Quoted in W. M. Mandel, *Soviet Women* (Garden City, N.Y., 1975), p. 43.
8. Quoted in I. Howe, ed., *The Basic Writings of Trotsky* (London, 1963), p. 162.

CHAPTER 24

1. Speech by Mahatma Gandhi, delivered in London in September 1931 during his visit for the first Roundtable Conference.
2. Ts'ai Yuan-p'ei, "Ta Lin Ch'in-nan Han," in *Ts'ai Yuan-p'ei Hsien-sheng Ch'uan-chi* [Collected Works of Mr. Ts'ai Yuan-p'ei] (Taipei, 1968), pp. 1057–1058.
3. Quoted in W. T. de Bary et al., eds., *Sources of Chinese Tradition* (New York, 1963), p. 783.
4. Lu Xun, "Diary of a Madman," in *Selected Works of Lu Hsun*, vol. 1 (Peking, 1957), p. 20.

CHAPTER 25

1. B. Mussolini, "The Doctrine of Fascism," in A. Lyttleton, ed., *Italian Fascisms* (London, 1973), p. 42.
2. Quoted in A. De Grand, "Women Under Italian Fascism," *Historical Journal* 19 (1976): 958–959.
3. Quoted in J. J. Spielvogel, *Hitler and Nazi Germany: A History*, 5th ed. (Upper Saddle River, N.J., 2005), p. 60.
4. Quoted in J. Fest, *Hitler*, trans. R. Winston and C. Winston (New York, 1974), p. 418.
5. *Documents on German Foreign Policy*, ser. D, vol. 7 (London, 1956), p. 204.
6. Quoted in R. Hilberg, *The Destruction of the European Jews*, vol. 1, rev. ed. (New York, 1985), pp. 332–333.
7. *Nazi Conspiracy and Aggression*, vol. 6 (Washington, D.C., 1946), p. 789.
8. Quoted in C. Koonz, "Mothers in the Fatherland: Women in Nazi Germany," in R. Bridenthal and C. Koonz, eds., *Becoming Visible: Women in European History* (Boston, 1977), p. 466.

9. Quoted in J. Campbell, *The Experience of World War II* (New York, 1989), p. 143.
10. Quoted in N. Graebner, *Cold War Diplomacy, 1945–1960* (Princeton, N.J., 1962), p. 117.

CHAPTER 26

1. Quoted in *Department of State Bulletin*, February 11, 1945, pp. 213–216.
2. Quoted in J. M. Jones, *The Fifteen Weeks (February 21–June 5, 1947)*, 2nd ed. (New York, 1964), pp. 140–141.
3. Quoted in W. Laqueur, *Europe in Our Time* (New York, 1992), p. 111.
4. Quoted in W. Loth, *The Division of the World, 1941–1955* (New York, 1988), pp. 160–161.

CHAPTER 27

1. Quoted in V. Zubok and C. Pleshakov, *Inside the Kremlin's Cold War: From Stalin to Khrushchev* (Cambridge, Mass., 1996), p. 166.
2. Quoted in H. Smith, *The New Russians* (New York, 1990), p. 74.
3. "Report on an Investigation of the Peasant Movement in Hunan (March 1927)," in *Quotations from Mao Tse-tung* (Beijing, 1976), p. 12.
4. Quoted in S. Karnow, *Mao and China: Inside China's Cultural Revolution* (New York, 1972), p. 95.
5. Quoted in J. Spence, *Chinese Roundabout: Essays in History and Culture* (New York, 1992), p. 285.

CHAPTER 28

1. Quoted in W. I. Hitchcock, *The Struggle for Europe: The Turbulent History of a Divided Continent, 1945–2002* (New York, 2003), pp. 399–400.
2. S. de Beauvoir, *The Second Sex*, trans. H. M. Parshley (New York, 1961), p. xxviii.
3. Quoted in R. Bridenthal, "Women in the New Europe," in R. Bridenthal, S. Mosher Stuard, and M. E. Wiesner, eds., *Becoming Visible: Women in European History*, 3rd ed. (Boston, 1998), pp. 564–565.
4. Quoted in H. Grosshans, *The Search for Modern Europe* (Boston, 1970), p. 421.
5. Quoted in R. Maltby, ed., *Passing Parade: A History of Popular Culture in the Twentieth Century* (New York, 1989), p. 11.

CHAPTER 29

1. Cited in M. Meredith, *The Fate of Africa* (New York, 2005), p. 168.
2. A. Nicol, *A Truly Married Woman and Other Stories* (London, 1965), p. 12.
3. Ngugi Wa Thiong'o, *Decolonizing the Mind: The Politics of Language in African Literature* (Portsmouth, N.H., 1986), p. 103.
4. Quoted in R. R. Andersen, R. F. Seibert, and J. G. Wagner, *Politics and Change in the Middle East: Sources of Conflict and Accommodation*, 4th ed. (Englewood Cliffs, N.J., 1982), p. 51.
5. S. Azadi, with A. Ferrante, *Out of Iran* (London, 1987), p. 223.

CHAPTER 30

1. *New York Times*, May 2, 1996.
2. Quoted in L. Collins and D. Lapierre, *Freedom at Midnight* (New York, 1975), p. 252.
3. Quoted in S. Sengupta, "In World's Largest Democracy, Tolerance Is a Weak Pillar," *New York Times*, October 29, 2008.
4. Y. Mishima and G. Bownas, eds., *New Writing in Japan* (Harmondsworth, England, 1972), p. 16.

EPILOGUE

1. Quoted in J. N. Pieterse, *Globalization and Culture* (Lanham, Md., 2004), p. 49.
2. E. Boulding, *Women in the Twentieth Century World* (New York, 1977), pp. 187–188.

INDEX

Italicized page numbers show the locations of illustrations.